D1243854

UPGRADING AND REPAIRING LAPTOPS

Second Edition

Scott Mueller

Contents at a Glance

800 East 96th Street
Indianapolis, Indiana 46240

Upgrading and Repairing Laptops, 2nd Edition

Copyright © 2006 by Que Corporation

International Standard Book Number: 0-7897-3376-5

Library of Congress Catalog Card Number: 2005925004

Printed in the United States of America

First Printing: December 2005

08   07   06   05   4   3   2   1

Trademarks

Warning and Disclaimer

Bulk Sales

Que Publishing offers excellent discounts on this book when ordered in quantity for bulk purchases or special sales. For more information, please contact

U.S. Corporate and Government Sales
1-800-382-3419
corpsales@pearsontechgroup.com

For sales outside the United States, please contact

International Sales
international@pearsoned.com

Associate Publisher
Greg Wiegand

Acquisitions Editor
Todd Green

Development Editor
Todd Brakke

Managing Editor
Charlotte Clapp

Project Editor
Tonya Simpson

Copy Editor
Chuck Hutchinson

Indexer
Rebecca Salerno

Proofreader
Susan Eldridge

Technical Editors
Werner Heuser
David L. Prowse

Publishing Coordinator
Sharry Lee Gregory

Multimedia Developer
Dan Scherf

Book Designer
Anne Jones

Page Layout
Julie Parks

Contents

10 Removable Storage   405

11 Graphics and Sound   515

15 Software and Operating Systems 691

16 Problem Solving and Troubleshooting 725

17 Portable Resource Guide 765

To Lynn:

Your artistry, skill, tenacity, and intelligence still blow me away, even after all these years!

About the Author

Scott Mueller is president of Mueller Technical Research (MTR), an international research and corporate training firm. Since 1982, MTR has produced the industry's most in-depth, accurate, and effective seminars, books, articles, videos, and FAQs covering PC hardware and data recovery. MTR maintains a client list that includes Fortune 500 companies, the U.S. government and foreign governments, major software and hardware corporations, as well as PC enthusiasts and entrepreneurs. Scott's seminars have been presented to several thousands of PC support professionals throughout the world.

Scott personally teaches seminars nationwide covering all aspects of PC hardware (including troubleshooting, maintenance, repair, and upgrade), A+ Certification, and Data Recovery/Forensics. He has a knack for making technical topics not only understandable, but entertaining as well; his classes are never boring! If you have 10 or more people to train, Scott can design and present a custom seminar for your organization.

Although he has taught classes virtually nonstop since 1982, Scott is best known as the author of the longest running, most popular, and most comprehensive PC hardware book in the world, *Upgrading and Repairing PCs*, which has not only been produced in more than 15 editions, but has also become the core of an entire series of books.

Scott has authored many books over the past 20+ years, including *Upgrading and Repairing PCs*, 1st through 16th editions; *Upgrading and Repairing Microsoft Windows*; *Upgrading and Repairing PCs: A+ Certification Study Guide*, 1st and 2nd editions; *Upgrading and Repairing PCs Field Guide*; *Killer PC Utilities*; *The IBM PS/2 Handbook*; and *Que's Guide to Data Recovery*.

Scott has also produced videos over the years, including at least 2 hours of free video training included in each of the recent editions of *Upgrading and Repairing PCs*, and *Upgrading and Repairing Laptops*. Scott has always included unique video segments with his books, rather than using the same clips every year. Many people have collected each of the older editions just to get the unique video training segments included with them.

Contact MTR directly if you have a unique book, article, or video project in mind, or if you want Scott to conduct a custom PC troubleshooting, repair, maintenance, upgrade, or data-recovery seminar tailored for your organization:

> Mueller Technical Research
>
> 3700 Grayhawk Drive
>
> Algonquin, IL 60102
>
> 847-854-6794
>
> 847-854-6795 Fax
>
> Internet: scottmueller@compuserve.com
>
> Web: www.upgradingandrepairingpcs.com

Scott's premiere work, *Upgrading and Repairing PCs*, has sold well over 2 million copies, making it by far the most popular and longest-running PC hardware book on the market today. Scott has been featured in *Forbes* magazine and has written several articles for *Maximum PC* magazine, several newsletters, and the *Upgrading and Repairing PCs* website.

If you have suggestions for the next version of this book, any comments about the book in general, or new book or article topics you would like to see covered, send them to Scott via email at scottmueller@compuserve.com or visit www.upgradingandrepairingpcs.com and click the Ask Scott button.

When he is not working on PC-related books or on the road teaching seminars, Scott can usually be found in the garage working on several projects. He is currently working on a custom 1999 Harley-Davidson FLHRCI Road King Classic and a modified 1998 5.9L (360ci) Grand Cherokee—a hot rod 4×4.

Acknowledgments

Several people have helped me with both the research and production of this book. I would like to thank the following people: First, a very special thanks to my wife and partner, Lynn. Over the past few years she returned to school full time, in addition to helping to run our business. She recently graduated with full honors (congratulations!), receiving a degree in Multimedia and Web Design. I'm extremely proud of her, as well as all I've seen her accomplish in the past few years. The dedication she has shown to her schoolwork has been inspiring.

Thanks to Lisa Carlson of Mueller Technical Research for helping with product research and office management. She has fantastic organizational skills that have been a tremendous help in managing all the information that comes into and goes out of this office.

I'd like to thank Todd Brakke for doing the editing for this project. His excellent tips and suggestions really help to keep the material concise and up to date. I'd also like to thank Charlotte Clapp, Tonya Simpson, and Chuck Hutchinson, who also worked on the editing for this book, as well as all the illustrators, designers, and technicians at Que who worked so hard to complete the finished product and get this book out the door! The people at Que are a wonderful team that produces clearly the best computer books on the market. I am happy and proud to be closely associated with Que.

I would like to say thanks also to my publisher Greg Wiegand, who has stood behind all the *Upgrading and Repairing* book and video projects and is willing to take the risks in developing new versions, such as this *Laptop* and upcoming *Windows* and *Server* editions, as well as the (read expensive) video clips we are including.

Greg, Todd, and the rest all make me feel as if we are on the same team, and they are just as dedicated as I am to producing the best books possible.

Thanks to all the readers who have emailed me with suggestions; I welcome all your comments and even your criticisms. I take them seriously and apply them to the continuous improvement of my books. I especially enjoy answering the many questions you send me; your questions help me to understand areas that might need to be clarified, as well as to point out additional coverage that should be added.

Finally, I would like to thank the thousands of people who have attended my seminars; you might not realize how much I learn from each of you and all your questions!

Many of my all-night writing raves are fueled by a variety of possibly less-than-nutritious (but very tasty and loaded with energy) food and beverages. In particular, this edition was fueled by bags and bags of Starbucks coffee processed via a killer Capresso automatic coffee/espresso machine (utter nirvana for an addicted coffee drinker like me), many cases of Coke Classic (no Pepsi allowed—gotta have the burn!), Red Bull and AMP energy drinks, and cases of Trolli Brite Crawler Eggs and Pearson's Salted Nut Rolls. For special occasions when I really needed a boost, I enjoyed a couple bottles of Skeleteen's Brain Wash, the ultimate energy drink. Why, that covers the three major workaholic nerd/geek food groups right there: caffeine, sugar, and salt!

We Want to Hear from You!

As the reader of this book, *you* are our most important critic and commentator. We value your opinion and want to know what we're doing right, what we could do better, what areas you'd like to see us publish in, and any other words of wisdom you're willing to pass our way.

As an associate publisher for Que Publishing, I welcome your comments. You can email or write me directly to let me know what you did or didn't like about this book—as well as what we can do to make our books better.

Please note that I cannot help you with technical problems related to the topic of this book. We do have a User Services group, however, where I will forward specific technical questions related to the book.

When you write, please be sure to include this book's title and author as well as your name, email address, and phone number. I will carefully review your comments and share them with the author and editors who worked on the book.

Email: feedback@quepublishing.com

Mail: Greg Wiegand
           Associate Publisher
           Que Publishing
           800 East 96th Street
           Indianapolis, IN 46240 USA

For more information about this book or another Que title, visit our website at www.quepublishing.com. Type the ISBN (excluding hyphens) or the title of a book in the Search field to find the page you're looking for.

Introduction

Welcome to *Upgrading and Repairing Laptops*, the only book of its kind on the market!

Laptop computers are the largest growing part of the computer industry, with sales that continue to outpace desktop systems. For those in the industry, there has never been a better reason to get into upgrading and repairing laptops, because not only are they selling better than ever, but their higher prices allow you to charge more for services rendered.

But aren't laptops proprietary, which means they cannot easily be upgraded or repaired? Many people are familiar with the fact that desktop PCs normally use industry-standard components, which allow cost-effective upgrades and repairs to be performed. In fact, this philosophy is the basis for my best-selling book *Upgrading and Repairing PCs*, currently available in a 16th edition, with the 17th edition currently in the works. However, what many people don't know is that laptop and notebook computers have evolved from being mostly proprietary to using larger and larger numbers of industry-standard components. This means, in plain English, that laptop and notebook computers are more upgradeable and repairable than ever before. Being a long-time user of portable computers myself, I thought the time was finally right to explore this subject in more depth, resulting in this book.

In this book, you will learn about all the components that make up a modern laptop or notebook computer, which components are based on industry standards and which are proprietary, and which components can easily be upgraded or replaced. As most of you know, laptops are more expensive than desktops, so whereas desktop computers are becoming more and more of a commodity, laptops are still somewhat exclusive. They are more difficult to work on, and the components are smaller and more expensive. All of this contributes to upgrades and repairs that are more expensive overall.

You can look at this book two ways: From the perspective of a laptop user, knowing how to upgrade and repair your own system can save you a bundle of money! Using the information in this book, you can effectively troubleshoot a problem; isolate the defective component; obtain a replacement; and finally perform the physical interchange of parts, the actual upgrade, or repair. This capability is useful not only for older systems, where the cost of service might exceed the value of the system, but also with newer laptops, which can be easily upgraded with newer technology such as wireless networking, faster USB or FireWire ports, more memory, larger hard disks, and even faster processors.

From the perspective of a computer technician or support person working in the industry, knowing how to upgrade and repair laptop computers gives you a significant edge over others in the industry who are afraid to open laptop systems. They can be daunting. Many of the laptops on the market today are held together by upwards of 100 screws, often consisting of several different types! They also often include many intricately assembled plastic parts that can easily break or be damaged if you don't take them apart properly. The benefit is that as a repair technician, you can charge more for laptop service and repair, which gives you another edge over other technicians who can work only on commodity-level desktop systems.

Laptops or Notebooks?

I initially struggled with the terms *laptop* and *notebook* before even beginning work on this book, not only with how to use them in the content but especially with the title. Although it was not necessarily true in the beginning, in the current context of the industry, these terms are used interchangeably to describe systems. The truth is, there is no consistent industry-wide definition of what is a laptop computer and what is a notebook computer.

Originally, there was some unofficial size differentiation between what was considered a laptop versus what was considered a notebook (the term *notebook* was used to describe an arbitrarily smaller version of a laptop). However, more recently that distinction has completely disappeared. Standardization on screen technology, screen sizes, as well as keyboard/pointing device layout and size have all served to muddy and eventually dissolve any differences between what was once considered a laptop and what was considered a notebook. The fact that virtually all modern portables include 13-inch (diagonal) or larger screens (which is why innovations such as the ThinkPad 701 "butterfly" collapsible keyboard aren't used anymore) as well as industry-standard keyboard layouts, integrating a pointing device and palm rest, has served to greatly equalize the sizes of such systems. There are still differences in weight and thickness between various makes and models, but in general, modern laptop/notebook systems, from the least to the most powerful and expensive, come in very similar sizes.

So what do we call these systems now? Are they laptops or notebooks? Virtually all manufacturers now use the term *notebook* to describe all their portable systems, from huge desktop replacements down to ultra-slim or ultra-light models. Unfortunately, outside the advertising and marketing world, few people seem to use the term *notebook*. Perhaps that is because if you just say "notebook," it seems too generic and could refer to something other than a computer, and thus be easily misunderstood. You almost have to say "notebook computer" for it to become clear what you mean. On the other hand, if you say "laptop," most people immediately know that you mean "laptop computer," because the term is much more widely recognized.

I conducted some informal polls of my own. In the most telling of these, I showed people a picture of a modern portable computer system and asked them, "What do you call this type of computer?" Virtually everybody replied, "A laptop!" In other cases, I asked people what the word *notebook* means, and I received a variety of answers, not all having to do with computers. Then I asked them what the word *laptop* means, and almost everybody understood it as a type of portable computer. Maybe I've just been around too long, but I think you'll find as I did that *laptop* is simply a much more recognizable and familiar term than *notebook*, whether you actually ever use one on your lap or not.

So, in spite of the industry marketing preferences for the word *notebook*, and even though laptop computers and notebook computers are the same thing, I decided *not* to call this book *Upgrading and Repairing Notebooks* (it even sounds weird), but instead decided to use the more understandable and recognizable *Upgrading and Repairing Laptops* title instead.

Throughout this book, you'll find that just as is done in the industry, I use the terms interchangeably (that is, I say "laptop" or "notebook," or both), and in almost all cases they mean exactly the same thing.

Book Objectives

I wrote this book for people who want to upgrade, repair, maintain, and troubleshoot laptop computers, as well as for those enthusiasts who want to know more about laptops or portable PC hardware in general. This book covers the full gamut of laptop and portable PCs, from the oldest to the latest in high-end multi-gigahertz mobile workstations. If you need to know about everything from the original Compaq Portable PC to the latest in PC technology on the market today, this book and the accompanying information-packed DVD-ROM are definitely for you.

This book covers state-of-the-art mobile hardware and accessories that make modern mobile computers easier, faster, and more productive to use. Inside these pages you will find in-depth coverage of every mobile processor, from the original 386SL to the latest Mobile Pentium 4, Pentium M, and Mobile Athlon XP-M.

Upgrading and Repairing Laptops also doesn't ignore the less glamorous PC components. Every part of your mobile system plays a critical role in its stability and performance. Over the course of these pages, you'll find out exactly why your motherboard's chipset might just be the most important part of your laptop as well as what can go wrong when your processor runs too hot. You'll also find in-depth coverage of technologies such as DDR SDRAM, graphics, audio, AGP, Mini PCI, LCD displays, recordable CD and DVD drives, USB 2.0, FireWire, and high-capacity external or removable storage—it's all in here!

Chapter-by-Chapter Breakdown

This book is organized into chapters that cover the components of a portable or mobile PC, emphasizing modern laptop/notebook systems. A few chapters serve to introduce or expand in an area not specifically component related, but most parts in a laptop have a dedicated chapter or section, which will aid you in finding the information you want.

The first two chapters of this book serve primarily as an introduction. Chapter 1, "Portable Systems Background," begins with an introduction to the development of portable computers. This chapter incorporates some of the historical events that led to the development of modern portable PCs. Chapter 2, "Portable PC Overview: Types and Features," provides information about the various types of mobile or portable systems you will encounter and what separates one type of system from another.

Chapter 3, "System Maintenance and Assembly," is where I show you how to maintain and care for laptop systems. I provide a step-by-step process showing how to completely disassemble and reassemble a typical laptop. The drawings included in this chapter, as well as the video included on the DVD-ROM, will greatly aid you in understanding these procedures.

Chapter 4, "Processors," includes detailed coverage of Intel's mobile Pentium M (part of Centrino mobile technology), mobile Pentium 4 and Pentium 4-M, mobile Pentium III, mobile Pentium II, mobile Celeron, and earlier central processing unit (CPU) chips. There's also detailed coverage of AMD's line of high-performance mobile Athlon XP-M and Sempron processors as well as older mobile Athlon and mobile Duron processors. Because the processor is one of the most important parts of a laptop PC, this book features extensive mobile processor coverage, more than you'll find in any other book. All the unique form factors used in mobile processors are discussed, with diagrams, drawings, and examples. This information is invaluable in understanding how processors are implemented in portable systems and what upgrade options you may have at your disposal.

Chapter 5, "Motherboards," covers the motherboard, mobile chipsets, motherboard components, and primary system buses in detail. A chipset can either make a good processor better or choke the life out of an otherwise high-speed CPU. I cover the latest chipsets for current mobile processor families, including mobile chipsets from Intel, AMD, VIA, and more. This chapter also covers special bus architectures and devices, such as high-speed Peripheral Component Interconnect (PCI), including Mini PCI and PCI Express. Plug and Play (including Universal PnP) configuration of resources and ways to handle resource conflicts are also discussed.

Chapter 6, "Memory," provides a detailed discussion of laptop memory, including the latest memory specifications. After the processor and chipset, the system memory is one of the most important parts of a laptop or mobile computer. It's also one of the most difficult things to understand—it is somewhat intangible, and how it works is not always obvious. If you're confused about the difference between system memory and cache memory; SODIMMs and Micro-DIMMs; SDRAM versus DDR SDRAM; EDO versus PC133 versus PC3200, this is the chapter that can answer your questions.

Chapter 7, "Power," is a detailed investigation of laptop battery technology, as well as AC adapters and power-management schemes.

Chapter 8, "Expansion Card Buses," covers the ExpressCard, PC Card, and CardBus interfaces, otherwise sometimes called *PCMCIA slots*. Also covered are newer technologies such as USB 2.0 and FireWire (IEEE 1394/i.LINK), as well as older legacy serial and parallel ports. Due to the limited space in laptop computers, external USB 2.0 and FireWire devices offer a wide range of expansion capability.

Chapter 9, "Hard Disk Storage," covers the smaller 2.5-inch form factor drives used in laptop computers, and it even breaks down how data is stored to your drives and how it is retrieved when you double-click a file in Windows. Also covered is the ATA/IDE interface, including types and specifications, plus the Serial ATA interface.

Chapter 10, "Removable Storage," covers optical storage using CD and DVD technology, including CD recorders, rewritable CDs, and other optical technologies. There's even extensive coverage of DVD, with everything you need to know to understand the difference between the recordable DVD drives now available in laptops. Also covered are all the digital memory-storage devices, such as CompactFlash, SmartMedia, MultiMediaCard, SecureDigital, Memory Stick, xD-Picture Card, and USB "keychain" drives. Finally, this chapter covers magnetic removable storage, such as standard floppy and magnetic tape drives.

Chapter 11, "Graphics and Sound," covers everything there is to know about video chipsets and display technology, as well as the various interface standards for external displays. This chapter also covers sound and sound-related devices, including internal and external sound "boards" and speaker systems.

Chapter 12, "Communications," covers all aspects of connectivity, including everything from dial-up using modems, to both wired and wireless networking. An emphasis on wireless standards is designed to feature one of the best new technologies coming to mobile systems: 802.11a/b/g networking (otherwise known as Wi-Fi).

Chapter 13, "Keyboards and Pointing Devices," covers keyboards, pointing devices, and other input devices used to communicate with a laptop, including external wireless mice and keyboards.

Chapter 14, "Portable System Accessories," covers all the various accessories, gadgets, and gizmos that make using mobile computers easier and more productive.

Chapter 15, "Software and Operating Systems," covers the Windows versions used on laptops, including detail on the boot sequence, configuration options, as well as installation and configuration procedures.

Chapter 16, "Problem Solving and Troubleshooting," covers diagnostic and testing tools and procedures. This chapter includes information on general troubleshooting and problem determination. Here, I show you what prepared laptop technicians have in their toolkits, including a few tools you might have never seen or used before.

Finally, Chapter 17, "Portable Resource Guide," covers manufacturer, vendor, and alternative resources that are useful for upgrading, repairing, maintaining, and troubleshooting laptops. This information can be especially useful if you have a problem while on the road.

The *Upgrading and Repairing Laptops* DVD

I've included a DVD-ROM with the book that contains all-new, studio-quality, full-screen video, showing laptop construction, components, and disassembly! Also, on the disc you'll find a detailed vendor database. This custom database contains hundreds of entries of contact information for the industry's leading manufacturers and vendors. It's like having my Rolodex on your computer. This database is fully searchable and printable.

Scott's Website

Don't miss my book website at www.upgradingandrepairingpcs.com! Here, you'll find lots of helpful material to go along with the book you're holding. I've loaded this site with tons of material, from video clips to monthly book updates. I use this spot to keep you updated throughout the year on major changes in the PC hardware industry. Each month, I write new articles covering new technologies released after this book was printed. These articles are archived so you can refer to them anytime.

At the website, you can also sign up for the *Upgrading and Repairing PCs Newsletter*, which will bring you new articles, FAQs, special offers, and other goodies every month.

I also use this site to tell you about some of the other fantastic *Upgrading and Repairing* products, including these:

- *Upgrading and Repairing PCs, 16th Edition*
- *Upgrading and Repairing Networks, Fourth Edition*
- *Upgrading and Repairing Microsoft Windows*
- *Upgrading and Repairing Servers*

Don't miss out on this valuable resource!

A Personal Note

I believe this book is absolutely the best book of its kind on the market, and that is due in large part to the extensive feedback I have received from both my seminar attendees and book readers. I am so grateful to everyone who has helped me with all my books. I have had personal contact with many thousands of you via emails you have sent me, as well as through the seminars I have been teaching since 1982, and I enjoy your comments and even your criticisms. Using this book in a teaching environment has been a major factor in its development. Your comments, suggestions, and support have helped me to write the best PC hardware books on the market. I look forward to hearing your comments after you see this book.

—Scott

CHAPTER 1

Portable Systems Background

Defining the Portable Computer

Portables, like their desktop counterparts, have evolved a great deal since the days when the word *portable* could refer to a desktop-sized system with a handle on it. Today, much smaller portable systems can rival the performance of their desktop counterparts in nearly every way. Many portables are now being marketed as "desktop replacements," which are portable systems powerful enough to serve as a primary system. This chapter examines the phenomenon of portable computing, showing how it has evolved and why it is so popular.

Portables started out as suitcase-sized systems that differed from desktops mainly in that all the components, including a CRT-style monitor, were installed into a single case. In the early 1980s, a small Houston-based startup company named Compaq was among the first to market portable PCs such as these. Although their size, weight, and appearance are almost laughable when compared to today's laptop or notebook systems, they were cutting-edge technology for the time. In fact, unlike modern laptops, the components used by these bulky first generation portables were virtually identical to those used in the most powerful desktops of the day.

Most current portable systems are now approximately the size of the paper-based notebook they are often named for and are built using the clamshell design that has become an industry standard. Inside these systems, nearly every component has been developed specifically for use in mobile systems.

Portable PCs, however, are not the same as Personal Digital Assistants (PDAs), such as the Palm series, Handspring, and PocketPC. Portable computers differ from PDAs in that they use the same operating systems and application software as desktop computers and use memory, CPU, and drive technologies that are similar to desktop PCs as well. PDAs, on the other hand, use different operating systems, applications, and hardware compared to either desktop or portable PCs and thus fall outside the scope of this book. Instead, this book focuses primarily on laptops or notebook-style portable PCs. That said, in terms of technology, much of this book will also be applicable to a relatively new category of portables: Tablet PCs. Actually Tablet PCs have been around since the early '90s, but a lack of standardized software, combined with relatively low power and functionality, limited them to special applications rather than mainstream use. In many respects, modern Tablet PCs are identical to laptop/notebook computers except that they are equipped with a touch-sensitive display, lack the integrated removable storage (such as a CD/DVD-ROM drive), and include a special tablet-oriented version of Windows. While most include a keyboard and basically look like a standard notebook computer, a few Tablet PCs do not come with a keyboard at all. Those that don't include a keyboard generally offer one as an accessory or can use any standard external keyboard if desired.

Many people use portable systems as an adjunct or accessory to a primary desktop system in their principal working location. In those cases, the portable system may not need to have all the power of a desktop, since it will only be used when away from the main office. In my situation, the roles are reversed. All my professional life I have been teaching PC hardware and software, usually on the road. As such I have always needed a powerful computer I can take with me, and because the amount of time spent traveling is equal to or more than the amount of time spent at a home office, I have had to rely on portable PCs of one type or another as my primary system.

All my books on upgrading and repairing PCs, starting with my first self-published seminar workbooks in 1985, have been written on a portable system of one type or another. With the processing power of modern laptop/notebook systems evolving to the point where they are nearly equal to all but the most powerful desktop systems, I look forward to carrying even smaller, lighter, and more powerful laptops in the future.

Portable computers have settled into a number of distinct roles that now determine the size and capabilities of the systems available. Traveling users have specific requirements of portable computers, and the added weight and expense incurred by additional features make it less likely for a user to carry a system more powerful than is necessary. Others may not do much traveling, but simply like the flexibility and small footprint that a laptop provides.

Portable System Design Elements

Obviously, portable systems are designed to be smaller and lighter than desktops, and much of the development work that has been done on desktop components has certainly contributed to this end. Much of this development has been in simple miniaturization. For example, whereas 3.5-inch hard drives may be popular on desktops, most laptops would not have room for these devices. Instead, they normally use 2.5-inch hard drives, which are a direct result of the miniaturization that has occurred in hard-drive technology over the past few years. Some of the subnotebook and Tablet PC systems use even smaller 1.8-inch drives first made popular in portable music players.

In addition to miniaturization, however, advancements in three other areas have contributed greatly to the design of today's laptop computers: flat-panel displays, power systems, and thermal management.

Flat-Panel Displays

The sleek lines of flat-panel Liquid Crystal displays (LCDs) have caused them to be seen increasingly more often on desktops. It was not long ago, however, that these displays were almost exclusively in the domain of laptops.

A flat-panel display is one of the most visually apparent components of a laptop. They are also usually the component that has the greatest impact on the size, shape, and cost of a laptop. In the early days of portables, the only affordable portable display was the small CRT monitor, a device that was so power-hungry that it required AC power. These displays were also bulky, causing early portables to look like small suitcases. When gas-plasma displays became available, the size of portables diminished to that of a lunchbox or briefcase. Still, the power requirements of gas-plasma displays again mandated a nearby AC outlet. It was not until the development of large, low-power LCDs that the familiar clamshell-style, battery-powered laptop became a reality.

As the internal components of a laptop became increasingly small, the laptops gradually shrunk in size to the point where they were no larger than a paper notebook. Indeed, the category of notebook computers originally started out with a footprint no larger than 8.5×11 inches. In the past few years, however, as high-quality LCD screens became available in larger and larger sizes, the size of some notebooks also increased.

Low Power Consumption

Like the car that spends most of its time in a garage, or the pleasure boat that spends most of its time at the dock, portable computers spend most of their time in a decidedly non-mobile environment—on a desk connected to an AC power outlet. Take away a laptop's battery, however, and you have greatly diminished its value. In fact, one of the primary features of importance to a laptop buyer is the "battery life"—the length of time the system can run on a single battery charge.

Environmental concerns are leading to the development of more efficient power-management technologies, but, obviously, operating a computer from a battery imposes system limitations that designers of desktop systems never had to consider before the advent of battery-powered portable systems. What's more, the demand for additional features, such as DVD and CD-RW drives, larger displays, and ever faster processors, has enormously increased the power drain on the typical system. The problem of conserving power and increasing the system's battery life is typically addressed in three ways:

■ **Low-power components**—Nearly all the components in today's portable systems, from CPUs to memory to displays and drives, are specifically designed to use less power than their desktop counterparts.

- **Increased battery efficiency**—Newer battery technologies, such as lithium ion and lithium polymer, are enabling batteries and power supplies to be lighter and have greater capacities, allowing for longer battery life on a single charge.

- **Power management**—Operating systems and utilities that turn off specific system components, such as disk drives, when they are not in use can greatly increase battery life.

Thermal Management

Perhaps a more serious problem than battery life in portable systems is heat. All electrical components generate heat, of course, and in the confines of a laptop this heat can be a significant problem. Inside a laptop, a large number of components are packed in a relatively small space, creating an extremely high concentration of thermal energy. This energy must somehow be dissipated. In most desktop systems, this is accomplished by using fans that continuously ventilate the empty spaces inside the system. Because fans use up battery power, however, portable systems must be designed to run fan-free most of the time and therefore employ innovative systems for moving and dissipating heat.

The worst culprit, as far as heat is concerned, is the system processor. When they were first released, the amount of heat generated by Intel's 486 and Pentium processors became a problem even in desktop systems. Newer and faster processors consume more and more power. It became clear to processor manufacturers such as Intel and AMD that special processor designs would be necessary to reduce power consumption and thermal output in mobile systems. Modern mobile processors benefit from technology featuring lower voltages, smaller die sizes, larger integrated caches, and, in general, lower power consumption than their predecessors.

Because many portable systems are now being designed as replacements for desktops, they require the most powerful processors available. Even the newest and fastest processors designed for desktop systems are often adapted for use in mobile systems. Even with dedicated designs for mobile systems, these high-speed processors can generate surprisingly large quantities of heat.

To address this problem, Intel and AMD have created special methods for packaging mobile processors that are designed to keep heat output to a minimum. Mobile processors also reduce heat through the use of extra-low-voltage designs (multiple voltages in recent designs) and by integrating both the Level 1 and Level 2 memory cache directly on the processor die. These techniques, by the way, not only reduce heat but also lower power demands and thus increase battery endurance.

However, even the best mobile processor designs will still result in a substantial quantity of heat being generated in a small space. Usually this heat is more concentrated than that inside a desktop. To cope with this problem, many notebook components are designed not only to require little space and power but also to be able to withstand high temperatures.

The Popularity of Portables

Office staffers frequently have to take work home. Salespeople regularly crisscross the country, spending more time in their cars than at their desks. Construction engineers need computing power, but rarely sit inside a traditional office. It is no wonder that portable computers have had an almost continuous presence in the computer industry. In fact, not only do portable computers comprise a significant portion of total annual computer sales, that portion is continually growing, and is even exceeding that of desktop systems in some cases. For example, according to the research firm Current Analysis, laptops outsold desktop systems for the first time in the U.S. during the calendar month of May, 2005, accounting for 53 percent of the total market during that month, up from 46 percent during the same period in the previous year.

As further evidence of the popularity of laptops, Intel said that about 31 percent of its processors will end up in mobile computers in 2005, compared with only 17 percent in 1999. IBM reported in 2000 that they sold a total of 10 million ThinkPad laptops in the 8 years since their first appearance on the market in 1992. They doubled that figure to 20 million total ThinkPad laptops by 2003, only 3 years later. Not only are laptops growing in popularity as compared to desktops, but the total market for laptops has been increasing as well. According to DisplaySearch Inc., laptop sales for 2004 were expected to exceed 46 million units, an astonishing figure when you look at it.

Finally, according to Charles Smulders, vice president and chief analyst at Gartner Dataquest, "…the mobile segment has represented one of the few areas of sustained growth in an otherwise difficult PC market. Between 1998 and mid-2002, mobile PCs increased their unit share of the global PC market by over 50 percent. For every four PCs shipped, one is now a mobile, and this share is projected to rise further, approaching one in three by 2006."

Who's Selling Laptops?

Because of their popularity, laptop and notebook computers are available from a large number of vendors. Table 1.1 lists the major laptop/notebook vendors in the U.S., along with the brand names associated with those vendors.

Table 1.1   Major Laptop/Notebook Vendors in the United States

Vendor	Brand Names
Acer	TravelMate, Aspire, Ferrari
Alienware	Area-51m, Sentia
Amrel	Rocky
Ashton Digital	Excelente, Maximate, Passport
Asus	Asus
Casio	Cassiopeia FIVA MPC
Chem USA	ChemBook
Compaq	Evo, Presario
Cybernet	DeskBook
Dell	Inspiron, Latitude, Precision
Dolch	NotePAC
Electrovaya	Scribbler
FOSA	FOSA
Fujitsu PC	Celsius, LifeBook, Stylistic
Gateway	Solo
HP	OmniBook, Pavilion
Lenovo/IBM	ThinkPad
Itronix	GoBook
MicronPC, MPC	TransPort
NEC	Versa
Panasonic	ToughBook
Pelican	Executive, Rugged
Rugged Notebooks	Talon, Hawk, Rough Rider
Sager	NP

(continues)

Table 1.1   Continued

Vendor	Brand Names
Sceptre	Soundx, Mobility, N-Series
Sharp	Actius, Mebius
Sony	VAIO
Toshiba	Portege, Satellite, Satellite Pro, Tecra
Twinhead	Durabook, Stylebook
ViewSonic	ViewPad
WinBook	WinBook
Xplore Technologies	GeneSYS

Although there are many vendors of laptops, most vendors do not manufacture these devices themselves. In fact, 65% of all laptops are produced in Taiwan by one of several companies located there. These companies are not well known because the systems they manufacture are usually not labeled with their own name, but instead are privately labeled with the name of the vendor. Here's a list of the major manufacturers in Taiwan; while most of them sell systems under other names, a few of these companies also sell systems under their own labels as well:

Acer	Inventec
Anadem	MiTac
Arima	Quanta
Clevo	Sotec
CMC/Computex	Twinhead
Compal	Wistron

An increasing portion of notebooks is being produced in mainland China as well. The largest builder of notebooks in that country is Lenovo, who acquired IBM's Personal Computing Division (global desktop and notebook PC business) in 2005. This acquisition makes Lenovo/IBM the third-largest global PC leader, behind Dell and HP/Compaq.

Evolution of the Portable Computer

Except for a short time at the very beginning, the personal computer revolution has always been accompanied by an equally innovative portable computer revolution. Indeed, in many ways, the evolution of portables has been much more dramatic than that of desktops. Whereas standard desktop computers have not changed markedly in their overall size in more than 20 years, portables have shrunk from the size of a suitcase to the point where one can fit one into a shirt pocket.

Pre-PC Portables

Some people date the beginning of the personal computer revolution as August 1981, when the original IBM PC was introduced. This landmark system was preceded, however, by a number of important computers, some of which were portable.

Luggables

Most early portable systems started out as nothing more than desktop PCs with integrated CRT displays, keyboards, and of course a handle. These systems weighed between 25 and 50 pounds and were the size of sewing machines or small suitcases. At first, this category was simply labeled as *portable*.

But years later, when significantly smaller laptops appeared, these systems were branded as *transportables* or *luggables*.

It might be hard for current laptop users to believe this, but it was quite common in the 1980s to see businessmen lugging these 30 to 50-pound behemoths from one appointment to another. For obvious reasons, however, these giant computers were soon supplanted by a new generation of portables that were significantly easier to carry.

IBM 5100

In September 1975—just months after the original personal computer was introduced under the Altair name—IBM introduced its 5100 Portable Computer (see Figure 1.1). Although it was hardly something anyone would happily carry, weighing in at 50 pounds, the 5100 holds the distinction of being the first portable computer in history, and very nearly the first personal computer, period.

This device, which was larger than an IBM typewriter, was the result of a project called SCAMP, the goal of which was to create a small computer that could run IBM's APL programming language. The name SCAMP arose from "Special Computer, APL Machine Portable."

The IBM 5100 was available in 12 models, which varied in terms of memory size, from 16KB to 64KB. Data storage was supplied by a 1/4-inch tape drive that could store 204KB per tape cartridge. Prices ranged from $8,975 to an amazingly high $19,975. In March 1982, six months after the introduction of the IBM PC, the 5100 was discontinued.

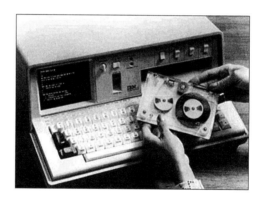

Figure 1.1   The IBM 5100. (Photo from *www.ibm.com*.)

The Osborne 1

Although the IBM 5100 holds the distinction of being one of the first portables, its stratospheric price tag kept it from being the first popular portable. That distinction would have to wait until April 1981, when the Osborne 1 was introduced. Like the 5100, the Osborne was much heavier than any of today's portables, but it was only half the weight of its predecessor from IBM.

One of the most important characteristics of the Osborne was that it was not compatible with the IBM PC. That is quite understandable, however, because the Osborne appeared no less than four months before the IBM PC was announced.

Like many pre-PC systems, the Osborne used an 8-bit Z80 processor and ran the CP/M (Control Program for Microprocessors) by Digital Research. Unlike other systems, the Osborne had an ingenious design. In its mobile configuration, it resembled a thick suitcase or a sewing machine. To use it, you would lay the system on its side and fold down its bottom panel, revealing a keyboard, two floppy drives, and an incredibly small CRT display (see Figure 1.2).

Figure 1.2　The Osborne 1, the first popular portable computer.

Aside from its portability, the Osborne 1 introduced another key feature for personal computers: bundled software. This system was probably the first to be bundled not only with an operating system, but also with word processing and spreadsheet software, as well as a number of utility programs. The list price of the Osborne, including software, was only $1,795, considerably less than most of the desktops of the time—a rare point in history when portables cost less than desktops.

The Osborne was not the easiest computer to use. Its display was so tiny—just 5 inches measured diagonally—that it could not display a full screen of 25 lines of 80 characters. To read a whole screen of text, users had to manipulate a small knob to scroll the small display around a large virtual display.

Despite the bulkiness of the Osborne and its quirky display, many of its users still to this day have fond memories of the device. And although the Osborne itself was soon discontinued, its general design carried on for several more years in products such as the Compaq Portable and the IBM Portable PC. A comparison of these luggable systems can be found later in the book, in Table 1.3.

The KayPro II

Yet another first for the Osborne was not so fortunate for its manufacturer. The design of the Osborne was so ingenious that it had the honor of being one of the first computers to spawn a clone. Not long after the appearance of the Osborne, a portable called the KayPro II debuted (see Figure 1.3).

Although similar in most respects to the original, the KayPro improved on the Osborne by having a larger display and a sturdy metallic case. And, unlike the Osborne 1, the KayPro's monitor could display a full line of 80 characters.

Laptops

The advent of non-CRT (cathode ray tube) flat panel displays allowed the development of the first "laptop" portable computers. Laptops can be characterized as portable systems with an integrated keyboard and flat-panel display in a clamshell design, where the display folds over the keyboard. Early flat-panel displays were smaller than they are today, so the early laptops had the display hinged near the middle of the system. As the display sizes grew, the display eventually became the same size as the keyboard and base of the system, resulting in the hinges being moved to the rear. Up until the mid-'90s, the size of a laptop was largely dictated by the keyboard and other components in the base. By 1995, screen sizes had grown such that the size of the system was then dictated by the display.

Figure 1.3   The KayPro II CP/M luggable. (Photo from *www.oldcomputers.net*.)

GRiD Compass 1100

Many people consider the GRiD Compass 1100, introduced in late 1982, to be the first laptop computer (see Figure 1.4). The GRiD Compass used a 16-bit 8086 processor combined with an innovative electroluminescent (EL) display, which displayed extremely bright yellow pixels on a black background. The display hinged near the middle of the system base, and folded down to cover the keyboard in what would become standard laptop design. The video circuitry driving the display could generate both textual and graphical images as well.

Figure 1.4   The GRiD Compass 1100 laptop.

The GRiD Compass introduced several other innovations as well, including 256KB of Intel bubble memory (a type of non-volatile RAM similar to flash memory today) that worked as a RAM disk. The case was made out of magnesium, which was utilized not only for strength but also to help dissipate the heat that the processor and display generated. Unlike modern laptops, the GRiD Compass ran only on AC power.

Unfortunately, all of this technology and performance was expensive, selling for $8,150 at the time. As you can imagine, with that price the Compass was not generally used as a mass-market system. In fact, the military and NASA (for use on the Space Shuttle) were the primary users of this system during the '80s.

Gavilan SC

A prototype of the Gavilan SC was first shown at the National Computer Conference show in May 1983, where it caused quite a stir. The Gavilan was another system that many people consider (along with the GRiD Compass) to be the first true laptop. Like the GRiD Compass, the Gavilan SC used a clamshell design with an 80x8 line text and graphics LCD that folds over the keyboard (see Figure 1.5). However, unlike the GRiD, the Gavilan also had built-in batteries complete with a charger and power management circuitry, the first touchpad (mounted at the base of the screen above the keyboard instead of below it as on modern laptops), a built-in floppy drive (with an optional snap-on second drive), a built-in 300bps modem, an optional snap-on printer, snap-in memory modules, and more.

Figure 1.5 The Gavilan SC laptop. (Photo from *www.oldcomputers.net*.)

The Gavilan was remarkably compact (11.4" square by 2.7" thick) for the time and weighed just nine pounds. The Gavilan included a 5MHz 8088 processor, 48KB ROM, and 64KB RAM, expandable with up to four 32KB plug-in capsules of blank memory or applications' ROM-based software packages.

Special power management circuits turned off power to various components when they were idle, allowing the built-in NiCad batteries to provide up to eight hours of operation. One of the most advanced features was the first touchpad integrated below the display, combined with a built-in graphical operating system that used a pointer along with pictorial representations of objects such as file drawers, file folders, documents, and a trash basket shown on the screen.

Unfortunately the Gavilan was being developed while the microfloppy drive standards were up in the air, and several different incompatible drives were being developed, including a 3" drive by Hitachi, a

3.25" drive by Tabor, a 3.5" drive by Sony, and a 4" drive by IBM. To sort all of these incompatible formats out, a consortium called the Microfloppy Industry Committee (MIC) was formed in May 1982 to create a standard microfloppy drive. They took the Sony 3.5" drive; modified the media format, casing, and shutter; and changed the interface to the same Shugart interface used on 5.25" drives. In January 1983, Sony and the MIC agreed on the format, and the 3.5" microfloppy as we know it today was established.

When the Gavilan was first developed it was to use the Hitachi 3" drive, but right as the prototype was being finished, it was clear the industry was going with the Sony/MIC 3.5" drive instead. In fact, Hitachi cancelled their 3" drive, forcing Gavilan to redesign the computer to accept the 3.5" format. This redesign combined with cash flow problems caused Gavilan to file for bankruptcy before the system could be introduced. After the floppy drive was changed, the Gavilan SC was finally released in June 1984 for $3,995, but by then the company was under Chapter 11 protection, from which they never fully recovered.

Notebooks

Notebook computers were originally described as being truly notebook sized, and generally used a fixed screen that did not fold over the keyboard like the clamshell design used for laptops. Later the notebook designation was used to describe a smaller, thinner, or lighter laptop (regardless of the actual size relation to a true paper notebook).

Today the definition of *notebook* is muddled to the point where the term is used interchangeably with the term *laptop*. In fact, pretty much all modern laptop computers are referred to as notebooks by their manufacturers, regardless of the actual size, thickness, or weight. Throughout the book, you'll see that I prefer the term laptop instead of notebook, since I find it more descriptive, and especially more intuitive for others to understand.

Epson HX-20

Epson introduced the HX-20 in November 1982, and advertised it as the world's first "notebook size" portable computer. The HX-20 is 8.5" by 11.4" and 1.7" thick, which is almost exactly the length and width of a standard sheet of notebook paper, thus making the notebook claim entirely true (see Figure 1.6). It also weighed only 4 lbs., much lighter than the typical laptop.

Figure 1.6 The Epson HX-20 notebook. (Photo from *www.oldcomputers.net*.)

The HX-20 uses two 6301 processors from Hitachi. The 6301 is an 8-bit CMOS (Complimentary Metal-Oxide Semiconductor) chip compatible with the Motorola 6800, running at a clock rate of 0.614MHz. The two processors each operate different areas of the system, and overall use very little power due to their CMOS design. This allowed the HX-20 to run for 50 hours using its built-in NiCad batteries, which is incredible by today's standards. The batteries required about eight hours to fully recharge.

The HX-20 included a full-sized keyboard and a tiny integrated 20 character by 4 line display that can also display graphics using 120x32 pixel resolution. The HX-20 also had a built-in speaker, four-octave sound generator, time and date clock, and a serial port. An optional micro-cassette drive for program or data storage fit into a special compartment to the right of the display.

The system came with 32KB of ROM (containing Microsoft BASIC as well as the operating system) and 16KB of RAM. An optional expansion unit that clips on the side of the case held an extra 16KB of RAM and/or 32KB of ROM. The HX-20 also included a built-in dot-matrix printer that prints graphics and text on plain paper rolls. The HX-20 sold for $795.

Although the HX-20 could be used as a general-purpose computer (it included a built-in word processor among other software), the small screen made it difficult to use. I did however see many HX-20s over the years being used by sales people as field sales estimators or behind the front desks of many hotels as room card-key managers.

The Radio Shack Model 100

In March 1983, Radio Shack introduced its TRS-80 Model 100, a $799 notebook computer similar to the Epson HX-20, but with a larger display. Although this computer was not PC compatible, it attracted a significant following owing to its portability and ease of use.

The Model 100 was the size of a sheet of paper and about 2 inches thick (see Figure 1.7). Half of its top panel was devoted to an LCD screen, the other half to a keyboard. Inside the system was an 8-bit processor along with 8–32MB of RAM. An additional 32MB of ROM was loaded with a rudimentary operating system and a simple word processing program. Power was supplied by a set of four large disposable batteries.

Figure 1.7 The Radio Shack TRS-80 Model 100, one of the first laptops.

By far the most impressive feature of the Model 100 was its weight of just 3 pounds. The system served as an adequately functional and highly portable word processing machine that became standard equipment for many journalists in the 1980s. Its keyboard lacked many of the keys found on the IBM PC, but the keys that the Model 100 did have were all full size and easy to use.

As useful as the Model 100 was, it had one glaring and increasingly important limitation. Yes, the notebook had proven to be a useful tool, but now that device had to be PC compatible.

Early PC Portables

In August 1981, the personal computer industry completely changed. The reason for this metamorphosis was the introduction of the IBM Personal Computer. As popular as the Osborne and other early portables were, their days were now numbered. It soon became clear that anything that was not compatible with the IBM PC would soon become obsolete. The only problem was that the IBM PC was not portable; however, other companies as well as IBM would rectify that by introducing many different portable systems fully compatible with the IBM PC.

PC Luggables

The first PC compatible portables were entire desktop PCs complete with a CRT and keyboard, stuffed into a suitcase or sewing machine sized chassis with a handle attached, and weighing between 30 and 50 lbs (13.6 to 22.6 kg). It seems almost laughable today, but many people (myself included) carried these systems around regularly. Although the size and weight were a drawback, these systems had all of the power of the desktop systems they were compatible with, since they essentially used the same desktop based components. The following section discusses the more notable of these machines.

The Compaq Portable

The first major milestone in PC portability practically defined the category single-handedly. Announced in November of 1982—just a little more than a year after the IBM PC—the Compaq was not only the first portable PC clone, it was the first PC clone *period*.

In general shape, the Compaq resembled the Osborne and KayPro luggables (see Figure 1.8). To use the system, you laid it on its side and unlatched the bottom panel, which was the keyboard. Removing the keyboard revealed the Compaq's green CRT display and a pair of full-height floppy disk drives.

Figure 1.8   The Compaq PC, the first PC-compatible portable.

Inside the Compaq was the same processor, memory, and expansion slots as in the original IBM PC. Unlike some other manufacturers of the time, Compaq was able to duplicate the PC's internal BIOS code without violating IBM's copyright. The result was a system that was one of the very few that could run all the software being developed for the IBM PC.

It is debatable whether the most important aspect of the Compaq was its portability or its compatibility. Needless to say, the combination of these two was very attractive and ended up propelling a tiny three-person startup company into what eventually became the largest personal computer company in the world.

The IBM Portable PC

In February 1984, almost 15 months after the Compaq Portable was announced, IBM introduced its own portable—in effect cloning the cloner. The IBM Portable Personal Computer 5155 Model 68 looked similar in size and shape to the Compaq system, being a small suitcase-sized system that weighed 30 pounds. Inside it had a built-in 9-inch, amber composite video monitor; one 5 1/4-inch, half-height floppy disk drive (with space for an optional second drive); an 83-key keyboard; two adapter cards; a floppy disk controller; and a CGA-style video adapter. The resolution of this adapter was only 640 by 200 with just two shades of gray. The unit also had a universal-voltage power supply capable of overseas operation on 220V power. The list price for the 30-pound computer was $4,225.00. Figure 1.9 shows the Portable PC exterior.

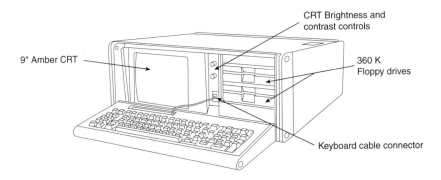

Figure 1.9 The IBM Portable PC.

The system board used in the IBM Portable PC was the same board used in the original IBM XT—the company's first PC equipped with a hard drive. The Portable PC lacked the hard drive, but did come with 256KB of memory. Because the XT motherboard was used, eight expansion slots were available for the connection of adapter boards, although only two slots could accept a full-length adapter card due to internal space restrictions. The power supply was basically the same as an XT's, with physical changes for portability and a small amount of power drawn to run the built-in monitor. In function and performance, the Portable PC system unit had identical characteristics to an equivalently configured IBM XT system unit. Figure 1.10 shows the Portable PC interior view.

IBM withdrew the Portable PC from the market on April 2, 1986, a date that coincides with the introduction of the IBM Convertible laptop PC, which is described later in this chapter. The Portable PC was not popular in the computer marketplace, although it compared to, and in many ways was better than, the highly successful Compaq Portable available at the time. The system was largely misunderstood by the trade press and user community. Most did not understand that the system was really a portable XT and had more to offer than the standard IBM PC. Maybe if IBM had called the system the Portable XT, it would have sold better!

Unfortunately, while Compaq introduced successive portable systems with hard disks and 286 and 386 processors, IBM never truly expanded on their original Portable PC concept.

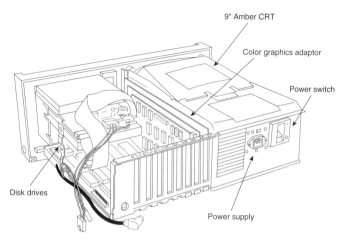

Figure 1.10   An interior view of the IBM Portable PC.

The Portable PC system unit had these major functional components:

- An Intel 8088 microprocessor
- 256KB of dynamic RAM
- A 9-inch, amber, composite video monitor
- Either one or two half-height 360KB floppy drives

The following is the complete technical data for the Portable PC system:

System Architecture

Microprocessor	Intel 8088
Clock speed	4.77MHz
Bus type	ISA (Industry Standard Architecture)
Bus width	8-bit

Memory

Standard on system board	256KB
Maximum on system board	256KB (640KB with a simple modification)
Maximum total memory	640KB
Memory speed (ns) and type	200ns dynamic RAM chips
System board memory-socket type	16-pin DIP
Number of memory-module sockets	36 (4 banks of 9)

Standard Features

ROM size	40KB
ROM shadowing	No
Optional math coprocessor	8087

Standard Features (continued)

Coprocessor speed	4.77MHz
Standard graphics	CGA adapter with built-in 9-inch amber CRT
RS232C serial ports	None standard
Pointing device (mouse) ports	None standard
Parallel printer ports	None standard
CMOS real-time clock (RTC)	No
CMOS RAM	None

Disk Storage

Internal disk/tape drive bays	2 half-height
Number of 3.5-/5.25-in. bays	0/2
Standard floppy drives	1 or 2×360KB

Expansion Slots

Total adapter slots	8
Number of long/short slots	2/6
Number of 8-/16-/32-bit slots	8/0/0
Available slots (with video)	6

Keyboard Specifications

101-key Enhanced keyboard	No
Fast keyboard speed setting	No
Keyboard cable length	6 feet

Physical Specifications

Footprint type	Desktop
Dimensions:	
Height	8.0 inches
Width	20.0 inches
Depth	17.0 inches
Weight	31 pounds

Environmental Specifications

Power-supply output	114 watts
Worldwide (110/60, 220/50)	Yes
Auto-sensing/switching	No

Table 1.2 shows the common part numbers for the configurable options available for the Portable PC.

Table 1.2   IBM Portable PC Model Configurations

Description	Part Number
256KB, one 360KB half-height drive	5155068
256KB, two 360KB half-height drives	5155076

The disk drive used in the Portable PC was a half-height drive, the same unit specified for use in the IBM PCjr, a short-lived consumer-oriented desktop. When the Portable PC was introduced, the PCjr was the only other IBM sold with the same half-height drive.

Table 1.3 lists and summarizes three luggable systems: the original Osborne CP/M luggable as well as the two most popular PC luggables.

Table 1.3   Luggable Systems

	Osborne 1	Compaq Portable	IBM Portable PC
Date Announced	April 1981	November 1982	February 1984
CPU	Zilog Z-80A	Intel 8088, 4.77MHz	Intel 8088, 4.77MHz
Memory	64KB RAM	256KB–640KB	256KB–640KB
Operating System	CP/M-80	Compaq DOS (MS-DOS)	PC DOS (MS-DOS)
Display Type	5-inch green monochrome CRT	9-inch green monochrome CRT	9-inch amber monochrome CRT
Display Resolution	52 characters by 24 lines, no graphics	80 characters by 25 lines, 640×200×2 shades of gray	80 characters by 25 lines, 640×200×2 shades of gray
Data Storage	Dual full-height 5.25-inch 100KB floppy drives	One or two full-height 360KB floppy disk drives	One to two half-height 360KB floppy disk drives
Expansion Slots	None	8-bit ISA	8-bit ISA
Weight	25 lbs.	31 lbs.	31 lbs.
List Price	$1,795	2,995	$2,995

PC Lunchbox/Briefcase Models

The next major category of portable computer was considerably smaller in size, but still large by today's standards. In size and shape, these computers resembled small briefcases or the lunchboxes that children once brought to school, ergo the category name.

The design of lunchbox computers was quite simple. One side of the lunchbox was taken up by a display. The keyboard module could be attached over the screen, protecting both it and the keyboard during travel.

To accomplish this relatively small size, lunchbox designers took advantage of a new technology that was just becoming available: flat-panel displays, such as high-contrast gas-plasma displays and electroluminescent panels. These panels were considerably smaller than the CRT displays on the luggable systems. They also had very high contrast. The downside, however, of these early flat-panel displays was their cost. Lunchbox computers equipped with these screens were incredibly expensive, in some cases carrying a price tag close to $20,000. That would be equivalent to at least $25,000–$30,000 in today's dollars.

Another cost of these early flat-panel displays was their power requirements. The electrical appetite of these screens was so great that few if any of these systems could survive on battery power alone. Instead, they required a nearby AC outlet. The development of an affordable battery-powered portable PC would have to wait until large, low-power, high-resolution LCD displays could be efficiently produced.

As limiting as the AC power cord was, the availability of this plentiful power coupled with the fairly large size of these systems had the benefit of making it easier for designers to incorporate the latest and most powerful computer components available. Instead of being required to wait for a low-power CMOS version of the Intel 80386 processor to become available, or for a super-thin hard drive to be ready, designers could use essentially the same components that were being incorporated into high-end desktops. The performance difference between desktops and lunchboxes was practically nil. It would be several years before a similar parity would occur between desktops and laptops.

The large size of the lunchbox computers provided one additional advantage that has never been fully realized in subsequent generations of advanced laptops and notebook computers. Like the luggable computers, the lunchboxes had a desktop-style expansion bus. Because of this, upgrading or customizing a lunchbox was almost as easy as it was on a desktop. If your application required a special AT-style expansion card, the lunchbox was your portable of choice. Laptop manufacturers try to emulate this capability by providing docking stations with one or more desktop-style expansion bus slots. But these docking stations are not portable at all.

IBM P70/P75

Two of the most notable of the lunchbox computers were the P70 and P75 from IBM. Both of these systems were portable variations of IBM's PS/2 Model 70 desktop introduced in 1987. Because good-quality LCD screens were not yet available, these portables used orange-and-black gas-plasma displays.

Both the P70 and P75 were quite large, being more like briefcases than lunchboxes. Inside, their high-power components were a match for any desktop. Table 1.4 contains a list of the specifications for both systems.

Table 1.4   Details on IBM's "Lunchbox" Portables: the P70 and P75

	IBM P70	IBM P75
Introduction Date	June 1988	November 1990
Processor	20MHz 386	33MHz 486
Bus Architecture	Two Micro Channel slots	Four Micro Channel slots
Memory	2MB–8MB	8MB–16MB
Video	VGA	XGA
Screen	10-inch gas plasma	10-inch gas plasma
Floppy Drive	3.5-inch	3.5-inch
Hard Drive (SCSI)	30MB; 60MB; 120MB	160MB; 400MB
Weight	20 lbs.	22 lbs.

A number of other companies, including Compaq, offered lunchbox computers for several years. As the much smaller laptops became more powerful, however, the need for lunchbox systems waned. Nevertheless, high-powered lunchbox/briefcase portables are still on the market from companies such as Dolch Computer Systems (www.dolch.com), and are prized for both their expansion capabilities and their ruggedness.

Dolch FlexPAC

One example of a modern lunchbox is the FlexPAC ruggedized portable from Dolch Computer Systems (see Figure 1.11).

Figure 1.11   The Dolch FlexPAC is an example of a powerful lunchbox computer that is still available. (Photo from *www.dolch.com*.)

This lunchbox weighs no less than 23 pounds and measures 16×11×9.8 inches in size. Inside there is room not only for a 14.1-inch screen, a Pentium 4 processor, one or two high capacity hard drives, a floppy drive, a CD-ROM/DVD drive, and up to 2GB of memory, but also for six desktop-style PCI slots, one of which doubles as an ISA slot.

PC Laptops

Luggable and lunchbox computers were certainly powerful, but anyone who has carried one of these devices has probably yearned for something considerably lighter. That something was the laptop—a PC-compatible laptop.

The IBM PC Convertible

The first true PC-compatible laptop as we know it appeared in the form of the IBM PC Convertible, which was introduced in April 1986 (see Figure 1.12). This system used a clamshell design, in which the screen folds over the keyboard when the system is being moved. That classic design is still used by almost all portables today.

In most other aspects, however, the Convertible was much different from current laptops. Its LCD display was not backlit and had a very flat aspect ratio. Data storage was supplied, not by a hard drive, but by dual 3.5-inch floppy drives. At this point, hard drives were still much too large and too power-hungry to fit into a battery-powered portable. The advent of the Convertible was, in fact, the first time IBM had used 3.5-inch floppies instead of the larger 5.25-inch versions on the older XT and AT desktops.

Inside the Convertible was an Intel 80C88 processor, a low-power CMOS version of the same processor used in the original IBM PC five years earlier. Its clock speed also was the same 4.77MHz as on that earlier system. Memory ranged from 256KB to 512KB, a typical amount for computers of that era. Perhaps the most surprising aspect of the Convertible was its weight. This prototype "laptop" tipped the scales at almost 13 pounds.

Figure 1.12   The IBM PC Convertible, the first PC-compatible clamshell-style laptop. (Photo from *www.ibm.com*.)

Of course, in the many years since the debut of the Convertible, laptops have undergone countless changes, becoming dramatically slimmer, lighter, faster, and less expensive. In fact, in its own time, the Convertible never gained respect in the marketplace. It is significant in two respects. The first is that the Convertible was the first IBM PC system supplied with 3.5-inch floppy drives. The second is that it marked IBM's entry into the laptop portable system market, a market where IBM now has tremendous success with its ThinkPad systems.

The PC Convertible was available in two models. The Model 2 had a CMOS 80C88 4.77MHz microprocessor, 64KB of ROM, 256KB of static RAM, an 80-column×25-line detachable liquid crystal display (LCD), two 3.5-inch floppy disk drives, a 78-key keyboard, an AC adapter, and a battery pack. Also included were software programs called Application Selector, SystemApps, Tools, Exploring the IBM PC Convertible, and Diagnostics. The Model 22 was the same basic computer as the Model 2 but with the diagnostics software only. You could expand either system to 512KB of RAM by using 128KB RAM memory cards, and you could include an internal 1200bps modem in the system unit. With aftermarket memory expansion, these computers could reach 640KB.

Although the unit was painfully slow at 4.77MHz, one notable feature was the use of static memory chips for the system's RAM. Static RAM does not require the refresh signal that normal dynamic RAM (DRAM) requires, which would normally require about 7% of the processor's time in a standard PC or XT system. This means that the Convertible was about 7% faster than an IBM PC or XT, even though they all operated at the same clock speed of 4.77MHz. Because of the increased reliability of the static RAM (compared to DRAM) used in the Convertible, as well as the desire to minimize power consumption, none of the RAM in the Convertible was parity checked. Of course, many users remarked that the best feature of static RAM was its instant-resume capability. Because this type of memory retains its contents even when the system is off, it does not need any time to restore its contents from a disk drive when the user turns the Convertible back on.

At the back of each system unit was an extendable bus interface. This 72-pin connector enabled you to attach the following options to the base unit: a printer, a serial or parallel adapter, and a CRT display adapter. Each feature was powered from the system unit. The CRT display adapter operated only when the system was powered from a standard AC adapter. An optional external CRT display or a television set attached through the CRT display adapter required a separate AC power source.

Each system unit included a detachable LCD. When the computer was being used on a desk, the LCD screen could be replaced by an external monitor. When the LCD was latched in the closed position, it formed a cover for the keyboard and floppy disk drives. Because the LCD was attached with a quick-disconnect connector, you could remove it easily to place the 5140 system unit below an optional IBM 5144 PC Convertible monochrome or IBM 5145 PC Convertible color monitor.

During the life of the Convertible, IBM offered three different LCD displays. The first display was a standard LCD, which suffered from problems with contrast and readability. Due to complaints, IBM then changed the LCD to a super-twisted-type LCD display, which had much greater contrast. Finally, in the third LCD, IBM added a fluorescent backlight to the super-twisted LCD display, which not only offered greater contrast but also made the unit usable in low-light situations.

Table 1.5 lists some technical specifications for the IBM 5140 PC Convertible system. The weights of the unit and options are listed because weight is an important consideration when you carry a laptop system.

Table 1.5   Details on IBM's PC Convertible Laptop

Dimensions	
Depth	14.17 in.; 14.72 in. including handle
Width	12.19 in.; 12.28 in. including handle
Height	2.64 in.; 2.68 in. including footpads
Weight	
Models 2 and 22 (including battery)	12.17 lbs.
128KB/256KB memory card	1.4 oz.
Printer	3.50 lbs.
Serial/parallel adapter	1.04 lbs.
CRT display adapter	1.40 lbs.
Internal modem	6 oz.
Printer cable	8 oz.
Battery charger	12 oz.
Automobile power adapter	4 oz.
5144 PC Convertible monochrome display	16 lbs.
5145 PC Convertible color display	37.04 lbs.

The PC Convertible required PC DOS version 3.2 or later. Previous DOS versions were not supported because they did not support the 3.5-inch 720KB floppy drive.

The following list cover the options and special features available for the PC Convertible. Several kinds of options were available, from additional memory to external display adapters, serial/parallel ports, modems, and even printers.

- **Memory Cards**—A 128KB or 256KB memory card could be used to expand the base memory in the system unit. You could add two of these cards, for a system-unit total of 640KB with one 256KB card and one 128KB card.

- **Optional Printer**—A special printer was available that attached to the back of the system unit or to an optional printer-attachment cable for adjacent printer operation (see Figure 1.13).

A special printer cable was available that was 22 inches (0.6 meters) long with a custom 72-pin connector attached to each end. With this cable, you could operate the Convertible printer when it was detached from the system unit and placed in a position offering better ease of use and visibility.

Figure 1.13   The IBM PC Convertible with optional portable printer attached. (Photo from *www.can.ibm.com*, IBM Canada.)

- **Serial/Parallel Adapter**—A serial/parallel adapter could be attached to the back of the system unit, the optional printer, or one of the other feature modules attached to the back of the system unit.

- **CRT Display Adapter**—The CRT display adapter was available for attachment to the back of the system unit, the printer, or another feature module attached to the back of the system unit. This adapter enabled you to connect a separate CRT display to the system.

- **Internal Modems**—IBM offered two different internal modems for the Convertible. Both ran Bell 212A (1200bps) and Bell 103A (300bps) protocols. The modems came as a complete assembly, consisting of two cards connected by a cable. The entire assembly was installed inside the system unit. The original first design of the modem was made for IBM by Novation, and it did not follow the Hayes standard for commands and protocols. This rendered the modem largely incompatible with popular software designed to use the Hayes command set. Later, IBM changed the modem to one that was fully Hayes compatible; this resolved the problems with software.

- **Battery Charger/Auto Power Adapter**—The battery charger was a 110-volt input device that charged the system's internal batteries. It did not provide sufficient power output, however, for the system to operate while the batteries were being charged. An available automobile power adapter plugged into the cigarette-lighter outlet in a vehicle with a 12-volt, negative-ground electrical system. You could use the system while the adapter also charged the Convertible's battery.

- **Optional Displays**—The 5144 PC Convertible monochrome display was an external 9-inch (measured diagonally) composite video CRT display that attached to the system unit through the CRT display adapter.

   The 5145 PC Convertible color display was a 13-inch external CRT color monitor that attached to the system unit through the CRT display adapter. It came with a display stand, an AC power cord, a signal cable that connected the 5145 to the CRT display adapter, and a speaker for external audio output. This monitor was a low-cost unit compatible with the standard IBM color CGA display for desktop PCs.

Table 1.6 shows the part numbers of the IBM Convertible system units.

Table 1.6   IBM PC Convertible Part Numbers

IBM 5140 PC Convertible System Units	Number
Two floppy drives, 256KB with system applications	5140002
Two floppy drives, 256KB without system applications	5140022

The Toshiba T1000

Just a year after the appearance of the IBM PC Convertible, another seminal laptop appeared, the Toshiba T1000 (see Figure 1.14). This new system was similar in many respects to the Convertible: it had the same processor, the same amount of memory, and the same floppy-based data-storage drives. But its one difference was a huge one: At approximately 6 pounds it was only half the weight of the Convertible. Because of the lighter weight and smaller design as compared to the clunky PC Convertible from IBM, many people regard the Toshiba T1000 as the first true PC compatible laptop computer.

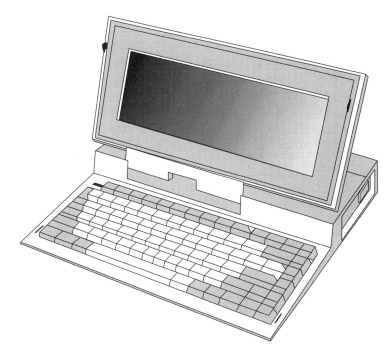

Figure 1.14 The Toshiba T1000.

Table 1.7 compares the core features of the three early laptops covered here. The Compaq SLT/286 is covered in the next section.

Table 1.7 Comparing the Early Laptops

	IBM Convertible PC	**Toshiba T1000**	**Compaq SLT/286**
Date Announced	April 1986	1987	1988
CPU	Intel 80C88, 4.77MHz	Intel 80C88, 4.77MHz	Intel 80C286, 12MHz
Memory	256KB–512KB CMOS SRAM, approx. 200ns, non-parity checked	512KB–1.2MB	640KB–12MB
Operating System	IBM PC-DOS (MS-DOS) 2.1	MS-DOS 2.11 in ROM	MS-DOS 3 or 4 or OS/2 v. 1.2

(continues)

Table 1.7 Continued

	IBM Convertible PC	**Toshiba T1000**	**Compaq SLT/286**
Display Type	Wide-aspect-ratio monochrome LCD, optional backlighting	Wide-aspect-ratio monochrome LCD, no backlighting	10-inch monochrome super-twist LCD, 7.8×5.9 inches, backlit
Display Resolution	80 characters by 25 lines; 640×200×2 shades of gray	80 characters by 25 lines, 640×200×2 shades of gray	80 characters by 25 lines, 640×480×8 shades of gray
Data Storage	Two 3.5-inch 720KB floppy drives	One 3.5-inch 720KB floppy drive	One 3.5-inch 1440KB floppy drive, 20MB or 40MB hard drive
Expansion Slots	One PCC 72-pin extendable bus connector	None	None
Footprint	12.2×14.7 in.	12.2×11.0 in.	13.5×8.5 in.
Thickness	2.6 in.	2.0 in.	4.1 in.
Weight	12.2 lbs.	6.4 lbs.	14 lbs.
List Price	Approx. $2,995	N/A	N/A

The Compaq SLT/286

Although IBM and Toshiba had already introduced groundbreaking laptops, the computer world was waiting for another shoe to drop. The leading manufacturer of portable computers was still Compaq. As late at 1988, it was still selling its large, bulky luggable and lunchbox computers. Everyone was waiting to see how Compaq would address the burgeoning laptop market. That same year the company satisfied this curiosity by introducing the Compaq SLT/286 (see Figure 1.15).

Figure 1.15 The Compaq SLT/286. (Photo from David Hales)

Compaq's entry into the laptop market was no lightweight system. It weighed 14 pounds. Even its AC adapter was heavy, weighing almost 2 pounds and often given the nickname *brick*. The SLT's depth (front to back) was only 8.5 inches, similar to many of the smallest notebooks of today's generation. But its width of 13.5 inches was quite large, and its thickness of over 4 inches was huge. A stack of four of today's thin notebooks would take up less space than this early laptop.

Although bulky and heavy by today's standards, the Compaq SLT/286 featured several innovations. Unlike previous laptops, it eschewed the dated Intel 8088 processor, which had been used seven years previously in the original IBM PC, and used instead the faster 80286 chip. Instead of two floppy drives, there was only one plus a 20MB hard drive (with 40MB available as an option).

This laptop also featured a new graphics adapter. It used VGA graphics (at a resolution of 640×480), which had been introduced on the IBM PS/2 desktops a year earlier. Along with the better graphics, the SLT had a better screen. Unlike the flattened screens of the PC Convertible and the Toshiba T1000, the Compaq screen had an aspect ratio that was more typical of desktop monitors. Its size was also notable, being all of 10 inches, measured diagonally.

Compaq's use of faster processors, hard drives, and better graphics has been imitated by generations of subsequent laptops. In fact, in its general design, the SLT was much closer in appearance to today's notebooks than any previous laptop (refer to Tables 1.8 and the following bulleted list).

One design feature of the Compaq SLT was very innovative, and was rarely copied (unfortunately). The SLT had a detachable keyboard, which meant that the relatively large unit could be left on a desk while only the lightweight keyboard was placed on your lap. Very few laptops today have removable keyboards, although Fujitsu has equipped some of their high performance Celsius mobile workstations with detachable keyboards. Rather than implement a cord, they use modern wireless technology such as Bluetooth to connect to the main system.

Table 1.8   Details of the Compaq SLT/286 Laptop

Compaq SLT/286 System Unit	
Power requirements:	
Operating voltage	12V DC
Average power	8.5W
Maximum power	11W
Peak power	17W
Keyboard	
Height	0.65 in. (1.65cm)
Depth	6.45 in. (16.38cm)
Width	13.50 in. (34.29cm)
Weight	1.38 lbs. (0.63kg)
Number of keys	82
Cable length	24 in. (60.96cm)
Display	
Size	10 in. (25.4cm)
Height	5.86 in. (14.88cm)
Width	7.81 in. (19.84cm)
Display type	Monochrome compensated super-twist LCD
Video modes supported	VGA, EGA, or CGA
Pixel resolution	640×480
Gray scale	8/16

There were two standard models of the Compaq SLT/286 available: the Model 20, with a 20MB hard drive, and the Model 40, with a 40MB hard drive. Both models had a number of standard features, including the following:

- 12MHz 80C286 microprocessor
- 640KB of memory
- 3.5-inch 1.44MB floppy drive
- VGA-resolution backlit monochrome LCD
- Removable keyboard
- Full-sized keys
- NiCad battery
- AC adapter
- Real-time clock/calendar
- External VGA connector
- Parallel connector
- Serial connector
- Keyboard connector
- External storage option connector
- One-year warranty

The following options were available for the Compaq SLT/286:

- 12MHz 80C287 coprocessor
- 1MB memory board
- 4MB memory board
- 40MB hard drive
- External storage module for use with:
  - 5.25-inch 1.2MB floppy drive
  - 5.25-inch 360KB floppy drive
  - 60MB tape drive with compression
- 2400-bps internal modem
- CD-ROM drive adapter
- Serial interface board

PC Notebooks

As indicated earlier, the term *notebook* was originally used to describe computers that had the same form-factor as an actual paper notebook, however this definition was eventually modified to describe smaller (as well as thinner or lighter) laptops, and eventually used interchangeably or to even replace the term laptop. Often the terms subnotebook or palmtop are used to describe very small laptops these days as well. Since there are no true standards for these terms, they are unfortunately not as descriptive as they could be. So while I will use the term here to describe any especially small laptop design, the industry now uses the notebook term to describe pretty much any laptop.

The NEC UltraLite

Around 1988, NEC introduced a groundbreaking computer called the UltraLite. This clamshell-style portable had no hard drive and not even any floppy drives. Instead, data was stored on a RAM drive.

Its greatest strength was its portability. It weighed no more than 4 pounds and its footprint was about the size of a piece of paper, 8.5 by 11 inches. Indeed, in its closed position, this computer was no larger than the thick computer magazines that published reviews of it. In fact, some people thought it looked remarkably like a paper notebook and christened it a notebook computer. Thus began the era of the notebook, a device that to this day still dominates the portable computer market—and, increasingly so, the entire personal computer industry.

Note that the dominance of the notebook computer did not come about overnight. The NEC designers had achieved the svelte profile of the UltraLite by jettisoning the hard drive, a compromise most users would not accept. Thus, until the sizes of hard drives diminished to the point where they could easily fit into the notebook form factor, laptops continued to enjoy a welcoming audience. For example, in 1990, two years after the introduction of the notebook computer, users continued to pay as much as $6,000 for laptops that were 3 inches thick and weighed 15 pounds. Eventually, however, when functional notebooks appeared with capacious hard drives and easy-to-read screens, the market for the larger laptops disappeared.

In addition to launching a new product category, the NEC UltraLite was notable for another reason. To provide storage options for this super-slim system, NEC designed a docking station, with a good assortment of storage device options and external connectors. Being the first with such a device, NEC trademarked the name *Docking Station*. In the years since, most other notebook manufacturers have offered docking stations for their notebooks, but never under that exact name.

GRiDCASE 1550sx

The GRiDCASE 1550sx was introduced in November 1989. This system was typical for GRiD in the use of a magnesium case and having a fairly high price, but what was really unique about it was the integrated pointing device. The GRiDCASE 1550sx began a revolution in portable pointing devices. Until then, most laptops didn't have an integrated pointing device at all, and those that did used a trackball which was mounted to either the right side of the keyboard or even on the base of the screen. GRiD broke that tradition by including the patented Isopoint pointing device designed by Craig Culver and built by Alps Electric.

The Isopoint was used on the GRiDCASE 1550sx portable, and was the first PC laptop pointing device mounted front and center of the keyboard, which made it possible for both right and left-hand users to operate (see Figure 1.16). Isopoint consisted of a cylindrical roller which was manipulated by the thumb. Rolling the cylinder up or down caused the pointer to move up and down, while sliding the roller left or right caused the pointer to move left and right. Buttons mounted on either side functioned as the mouse buttons.

The GRiDCASE 1550sx was touted as the first laptop PC designed for use with Windows by including a built-in ambidextrous pointing device. While the Isopoint did not catch on, by the end of the year after its introduction, virtually all laptops would include some sort of integral pointing device, and most of them would be mounted front and center where they could be reached easily by either hand.

The Apple PowerBook 100

It might seem out of place to mention an Apple laptop in a book about PC laptops, but Apple did have some influence on PC laptop design. Like IBM, Apple struggled with its early portable systems, introducing two mobile versions of its Macintosh—one a luggable model and the other a bulky laptop, both of which were poorly designed and which failed in the marketplace. Then, on its third attempt in late 1991, Apple finally got it right and introduced the PowerBook 100 (see Figure 1.17). Of course, this new laptop was by no means PC compatible, but as with many aspects of the Mac, it would have an influence on portable PCs to follow.

Figure 1.16 The GRiDCASE 1550sx Isopoint pointing device.

Figure 1.17 The Apple Macintosh PowerBook 100. (Photo from *www.apple-history.com*.)

The most striking aspect of the PowerBook was its solution to the pointing device problem. While others such as GRiD had figured out that the pointing device should be front and center, they were still somewhat difficult to use because there was no wrist-rest area. Apple's designers solved that problem by moving the keyboard back, thereby providing both a comfortable rest for the wrists of the user and a convenient place for a pointing device. Most laptops used a clumsy trackball in the beginning, but eventually the trackballs gave way to touchpads. Note that both trackballs and touchpads had been used by other manufacturers well before Apple, but until the PowerBook 100 nobody had built them into a generous wrist-rest area in front of the keyboard. This simple-but-brilliant concept of a pointing device in the center of a wrist-rest is now a standard feature of almost all laptops and note-books.

While built-in trackballs and touchpads meant that a laptop user could now work without plugging in an external mouse, they were still clumsy and inefficient. IBM would solve that problem with the ultimate laptop pointing device, the TrackPoint. IBM's legendary TrackPoint would not only be the most ergonomic, intuitive, and efficient solution, but also allow for the greatest productivity since the user's hands would never need to leave the home row on the keyboard.

The ThinkPad 700

IBM's first use of the ThinkPad name was for a pen-based tablet system that was demonstrated at the fall Comdex in 1991, and announced for trial use by corporate customers on April 16, 1992. The ThinkPad name was derived from IBM's original "THINK" slogan, which was created by Thomas Watson Sr. in 1914, and used on signs and other materials throughout the company from 1915 to the present. In 1991, a 30+ year veteran IBM employee named Denny Wainright had been assigned to come up with a name for the pen-based tablet system IBM was working on. The idea for the ThinkPad name came when Wainright noticed the small IBM notebook he had been carrying around in his shirt pocket for more than 30 years, which was a small black leather notebook with the word "THINK" embossed on the cover. The ThinkPad name seemed perfect for the new computer, which would essentially be an electronic notepad.

Unfortunately, delays in the PenPoint operating system from GO Corporation caused the system to be initially offered in a limited private trial release as the Model 2521 ThinkPad. By the time the system was officially released to the general public as the ThinkPad 700T on October 5th, 1992, other more powerful pen-based hardware and operating systems had been announced by competitors. Also the general public showed little interest in pen-based systems, which to this day remain a niche market.

So while IBM's first foray into pen-based computing wasn't very successful, one great thing came out of the project, and that is the ThinkPad brand name, which IBM would apply to the then-new line of laptop and notebook computers being developed at the same time as the tablet. Up to that point, IBM had made a number of forays into the portable market with mostly unsuccessful entries. That all was to change with the ThinkPad 700 (see Figure 1.18).

Figure 1.18   The IBM ThinkPad 700, the first of the ThinkPads.

On October 5th, 1992 IBM also introduced the first standard ThinkPad notebook computer, the model 700. The 700 featured a 25MHz 486SLC processor and 4MB of RAM standard. It was available in both monochrome and color (700C) versions. The ThinkPad 700C's color screen measures 10.4 inches on the diagonal and used active matrix thin-film transistor technology. It was the largest and best screen available at the time, and was the product of Display Technologies Inc., a joint venture between IBM and Toshiba formed exclusively to produce high-quality color displays.

The ThinkPad 700 was also an upgradeable system. The standard 25MHz 486SLC processor was upgradeable to 50MHz. The standard removable 120MB hard disk was upgradeable to 160MB, and the standard 4MB RAM was upgradeable to 16MB. The 700 used a NiMH battery that ran for 2 to 3.8 hours. The 700C weighed 7.6 pounds and cost $4,350. The monochrome model 700 used a smaller 9.5-inch screen and weighed 6.5 pounds. The ThinkPad 700 was available with an 80MB hard disk for $2,750, or with a 120MB drive for $2,950. All of this was packed in a sleek design with a charcoal black exterior, resulting in a system that would go on to eventually win more than 1,100 industry awards and accolades.. Table 1.9 lists the system's specifications.

Table 1.9   Details of the IBM ThinkPad 700 and 700C (from www.ibm.com)

Feature	Description
Processor (700, 700C)	486SLC 25MHz
Bus architecture	Micro Channel
Memory (standard)	4MB
Memory (maximum)	16MB, IC DRAM
CMOS RAM	8KB
Video	VGA
Floppy drive	3.5-inch
Hard drive options (all 2.5-inch)	80MB, 120MB, 160MB
Audio subsystem	Yes (standard)
PCMCIA slots	None

As with the PowerBook 100, one of the ThinkPad's most notable innovations had to do with its pointing device. But while Apple merely integrated the somewhat clumsy trackball pointing device technology that had previously existed, IBM instead developed an ingenious pointing stick called a TrackPoint that looked like a bright red pencil eraser stuck in the middle of the keyboard. As was the case with the trackball and touchpads, the TrackPoint pointing stick enabled users to move the system's mouse cursor without moving their hands from the keyboard. The TrackPoint, however, had distinct advantages over trackballs and touchpads: you could seamlessly move the pointer across the entire screen without moving your fingers off the home row, and without making multiple jerky finger movements. The TrackPoint was a boon to those who touch-type and allowed far greater pointing and typing speed and efficiency compared to any other integrated pointing device. Since the advent of the TrackPoint in the first ThinkPad 700, IBM has licensed the technology to several other vendors for use in their systems. Both IBM and others offer TrackPoint-equipped systems, most of which now include a touchpad as a backup for those who may not touch-type. Due to its superior design, the TrackPoint is the longest running pointing device in the industry, being available consistently for longer than any other single type of device except the mouse.

Figure 1.19 shows the internal design of the ThinkPad 700 in detail. See Table 1.10 for descriptions of the components.

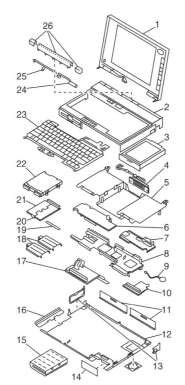

1. LCD (700); LCD (700C)
2. Frame, keyboard (700C)
3. Battery pack, Nickel Metal Hydride
4. Battery terminal assembly
5. Frame, stiffener
6. Voltage converter with suspend switch (700); voltage converter with suspend switch (700C)
7. Keyboard control card, 84-key (U.S.)
8. System board (700); system board (700C)
9. Backup battery, lithium
10. Processor card; 540MHz upgrade processor card (700, 700C)
11. I/O connectors cover group
12. Battery cover assembly (700); bottom cover assembly (700C)
13. Covers with spacers for LCD hinge (700); model 700C cover
14. Door, hard disk drive
15. Hard disk; 80MB. 120MB, 240MB
16. Cover, IC RAM card
17. Video card (700); video card (700C)
18. Tray
19. Guide, modem; modem Door (700); modem Door (700C)
20. Base memory card, 4MB
21. Slot holder, IC DRAM card
22. Floppy drive assembly
23. Keyboard
24. Standby battery
25. Indicator assembly (700); (700C)
26. Panel cover group (700); panel cover group (700C)

Figure 1.19   A diagram of the IBM ThinkPad 700. (Photo from *www.ibm.com*.)

Table 1.10   Internal Components of the IBM ThinkPad 700 and 700C. The Diagram Numbers Refer to the Diagram in Figure 1.14 (from *www.ibm.com*)

Diagram Number	Description	Part Number
1	LCD (700); LCD (700C)	44G3806; 48G8723
2	Frame, keyboard (700C)	48G8945
3	Battery pack, Nickel Metal Hydride	44G3811
4	Battery terminal assembly	44G3779
5	Frame, stiffener	44G3771
6	Voltage converter with suspend switch (700); voltage converter with suspend switch (700C)	44G3784; 48G8712
7	Keyboard control card, 84-key (U.S.)	44G3783
8	System board (700); system board (700C)	44G3780; 49G1975
9	Backup battery, lithium	44G3778
10	Processor card; 50MHz upgrade processor card (700,700C)	44G3781; 54G1045

(continues)

Table 1.10   Continued

Diagram Number	Description	Part Number
11	I/O connectors cover group	44G3769
12	Bottom cover assembly (700); bottom cover assembly (700C)	44G3800; 48G8719
13	Covers with spacers for LCD hinge (700); model 700C cover	53G7817; 48G8714
14	Door, hard disk drive	44G3777
15	Hard disk: 80MB, 120MB, 240MB	95F4743; 95F4744; 66G3200
16	Cover, IC DRAM card	49G1108
17	Video card (700); video card (700C)	44G3782; 35G4823
18	Tray	44G3773
19	Guide, modem; modem Door (700); modem Door (700C)	44G3774; 53G7815; 53G7817
20	Base memory card, 4MB	44G3785
21	Slot holder, IC DRAM card	44G3772
22	Floppy drive assembly	49G2198
23	Keyboard	Not available
24	Standby battery	44G3799
25	Indicator assembly (700); (700C)	44G3787; 48G8729
26	Panel cover group (700); panel cover group (700C)	44G3789; 48G8715

This innovative notebook helped IBM to establish ThinkPad as one of the most successful and well-recognized brands in the business, and a ThinkPad was even selected for the permanent collection of the Museum of Modern Art.

Subnotebooks

The smallest portable PCs are usually called *subnotebooks*, indicating that they are smaller than a notebook. The smallest of these are often called ultralights or ultraportables as well. These systems generally sacrifice performance and features in order to have the smallest possible size. As such they are an excellent alternative for those applications where small size and light weight are paramount. The following section details some of the important subnotebook, ultralight, and ultraportable systems that have been released over the years.

ThinkPad 701

IBM was always known for their high-quality keyboards, and to this day the ThinkPad keyboards are still among the best in the industry. But the ThinkPad 701 (codenamed "Butterfly" while under development) had a very special keyboard that became legendary for its innovative design.

The ThinkPad 701 was introduced in March 1995 as a 4.5-pound subnotebook system that was only 9.7" by 7.9" by 1.7" thick (smaller than a notebook), yet it included a full-sized keyboard that was 11.25" wide. How is it possible to design a system that is smaller than the built-in keyboard? The answer was an ingenious trick folding keyboard called the Butterfly.

When it was opened, two separate keyboard sections would automatically spread out, move over, and then interlock to form a full-sized 85-key keyboard that was almost two inches wider than the unit itself (see Figure 1.20). Of course the keyboard also featured the TrackPoint pointing device.

Figure 1.20 The ThinkPad 701 "Butterfly" subnotebook.

The innovative butterfly keyboard was invented by a team headed by John Karidis at IBM's Thomas J. Watson Research Center in Yorktown Heights, NY, and developed with another team at IBM's Research Triangle Park, NC facility.

The ThinkPad 701C also included a 50MHz 486DX2 or a 75MHz DX4 processor; a 10.4-inch diagonal active-matrix screen; a 360MB, 540MB, or 720MB hard drive; 4MB or 8MB of RAM (expandable to 40MB); an infrared port for wireless data transmission; built-in speakers; a microphone; and a 14.4 kbps data/fax modem. Battery life was between 2.5 to 7 hours, and prices were between $1,499 and $3,299 depending on the configuration.

Unfortunately, the Butterfly keyboard design was only used on one model, and remained on the market for just over a year before it was discontinued. It was doomed because having a thin system with a larger screen became more important than having such a small system. With larger screens, there was no need for the folding keyboard design, since a normal full-sized keyboard would fit as-is.

Still, for what became a niche product, it did fairly well. At the time of introduction, an IBM spokesman said that the company received more pre-production orders for the ThinkPad 701 than any other product in its history. And for its short time on the market, the ThinkPad 701 racked up an impressive 27 design awards and sold 215,000 units, making it the top-selling notebook PC of 1995 according to the market research firm International Data.

ThinkPad Firsts

The ThinkPad brand is easily the most successful single brand name in laptops and notebooks, with well over 20 million sold from its inception in October 1992 to 2003. By combining innovation, quality, performance, and style, IBM successfully established the ThinkPad brand as the Cadillac of laptops. ThinkPads replaced the GRiD systems originally used on the Space Shuttle, and have flown on every shuttle mission since Dec. 2, 1993. They are also used on the International Space Station.

ThinkPad's success is credited in part to its distinctive design, which has stayed roughly the same since its inception. Industrial designer Richard Sapper designed the ThinkPad's thin black case with beveled edges that give the illusion that the systems are smaller and thinner than they actually are.

Notable firsts from development of the ThinkPad line include

- A 10.4" color Thin Film Transistor (TFT) display: 700C (1992).
- The TrackPoint pointing device: ThinkPad 700C (1992).
- An integrated CD-ROM: ThinkPad 755CD (1994).
- An "ultraportable" notebook: ThinkPad 560 (1996).
- An integrated DVD-ROM: ThinkPad 770 (1997).
- A "thin and light" notebook: ThinkPad 600 (1998).
- A mini-notebook under three pounds; with standard ports and 95% of a full-size keyboard: ThinkPad 240 (1999).
- A keyboard floodlight: ThinkPad i-Series (1999).
- An integrated Wi-Fi Alliance certified wireless LAN: ThinkPad i-series (2000).
- An embedded security chip: ThinkPad T20 (2001).
- An extended battery life of up to 11 hours: ThinkPad X31 (March 2003).
- An Active Protection System for the hard drive: ThinkPad T41 (October 2003).

Since the ThinkPad brand was sold to Lenovo in 2005, one can hope that the tradition of quality, innovation, performance, and style IBM created with the ThinkPad will endure.

Ultralights/Ultraportables

The evolution of notebooks has followed an interesting path. As the internal components of notebooks continued to shrink in size, of course, so did the size of notebooks themselves.

Eventually, the sizes of certain notebooks shrunk to a weight of less than 3 pounds, and a new category was born—the subnotebook, also called an Ultralight. But a small size meant a small keyboard and screen, which further meant that the subnotebook could be difficult to use. Despite some initial excitement for these systems, they failed to attract a significant following, and the category was soon abandoned.

The question arose: At long last, had portable computers become so small that some of them were *too small*? The answer of course was "No." In the past few years, a number of new 3-pound notebooks have appeared. But, to avoid links with a previous failed category, they are no longer called *subnotebooks*. Now they are called *ultralights*.

The HP 95LX

In April 1991, HP introduced one of the first and probably the most popular handheld computer. The HP 95LX handheld computer was about the size of a videocassette, weighing just 11 oz. and measuring 6.3×3.4×1 inches. The screen could display only 16 lines of 40 characters each, about a third of a typical computer screen. Like many small systems, the screen was not backlit and was therefore hard to read in certain lighting conditions.

Inside the 95LX was the equivalent of the original IBM PC. The processor was an Intel 8088, complemented by 512KB of memory that was continually powered by the device's AA batteries. These batteries could power the device for several months. Included in the computer's ROM chips was the Lotus

1-2-3 spreadsheet and the MS-DOS 2.2 operating system. This computer may also have been the first to use infrared for communications with other devices. The list price was $699.

The HP 95LX was not alone on the market. It competed with the Poquet PC and the Atari Portfolio, both of which weighed more. The Poquet, for example, tipped the scales at 1 pound. The 95LX was quite popular and even spawned its own magazine. HP continued to sell the 95LX and its successors for a few years. But, as graphics-based operating systems such as Windows became increasingly popular, the need for a DOS-based portable declined.

The Toshiba Libretto

According to many industry observers, the best example of a handheld computer was the Toshiba Libretto, which was introduced in 1997. The Libretto weighed just under 2 pounds and had a form factor that was about the same as a VHS video cassette. Yet despite the small size, the Libretto was a full-function Windows-based notebook. It featured a built-in hard disk, TFT color screens ranging in size from 6.1 to 7.1 inches, and a tiny keyboard with an integral pointing stick. Although the position of the pointing stick (to the side of the screen) seemed unusual, it made more sense when you actually held the system in your hands and found that the pointing stick was right under one of your thumbs.

In external appearance, the Libretto was similar to many of the Windows CE handhelds available around the same time. But unlike the Windows CE handhelds, the Libretto ran a full version of Windows 95 and was compatible with thousands of programs designed for that operating system. Details on the specifications of the various Libretto systems can be found in Table 1.11.

Table 1.11 Details of Various Models of the Toshiba Libretto Handheld Computer (Data from _www.silverace.com/libretto_)

	Libretto Model 50	Libretto Model 70	Libretto Model 100
Introduction Date	January 1997	October 1997	February 1998
Model Numbers: Japan; U.S.	PA1237CA; PA1249U-T2A	PA1260CA; PA1260U-T2A	PA1254CA; PA1254U-T2A
Dimensions (in.)	8.3×4.5×1.3	8.3×4.5×1.3	8.3×5.2 ×1.4
Weight (lbs.)	1.9	1.9	2.1
Processor	75MHz Pentium	120MHz Pentium with MMX	166MHz Pentium with MMX
Bus Speed (MHz)	50	60	66
Memory (MB, Standard/Max)	16/32	16/32	32/64
ROM (KB)	256	256	512
Hard Drive	810MB	1.6GB	2.1GB
Screen Size (Diagonal)	6.1 in.	6.1 in.	7.1 in.
Screen Resolution	640×480	640×480	800×480
Graphics Memory	1MB	1MB	2MB
Keyboard (U.S.): Keys; Key Pitch	80; 15mm	80; 15mm	82; 15mm
PCMCIA Slots	1 Type II	1 Type II	2 Type II or 1 Type III, CardBus
Sound Chip	Yamaha OPL3 SA2	Yamaha OPL3 SA2	Yamaha OPL3 SA3
Battery Life (Hours)	1.5–2	2–3	1.5–2

Although a great achievement in miniaturization, the Libretto may have been too successful in its quest for compactness. Chief among complaints about the system was a concern about the tiny keys on the keyboard. For whatever reason, most handheld computers—whether based on Windows 95 or Windows CE—disappeared from the U.S. market a few years after their introduction.

Even though the Libretto was not available in the U.S. for several years, Toshiba still sold Librettos in Japan, including versions with English-language operating systems. One of the latest versions is the L5 (see Figure 1.21). This unit is approximately the same size as the original Libretto, but with enhanced components. For example, the L5 features a 10-inch screen with a wide-screen resolution of 1280×600. The screen is backed up by an ATI Mobility Radeon-M graphics accelerator with 8MB of video memory.

Figure 1.21 The Toshiba Libretto L5, the latest version of the Libretto handheld computer. (Photo from *www.toshiba.com*.)

More recently, Toshiba has reintroduced the Libretto in the U.S., but this time with a more-powerful Pentium M processor running at 1.2GHz, complemented with 512MB of DDR memory and a 60GB hard disk. Instead of a pointing stick being placed to the right of the screen, it is now in the middle of the wrist-rest area of the keyboard.

Personal Recollections of the Portable Revolution

Writing this chapter has brought back several memories. Because of their many advantages, I've used nothing but portables as my main systems since the early '80s. In fact, I have used portable systems even before there were PCs. In the pre-PC days, I used one of the original Osbornes (with its weird 52-character-wide display), as well as the KayPro II, 4, and 10 luggables. As mentioned earlier, these were sewing machine–sized portables that ran CP/M, the most popular operating system before Microsoft's MS-DOS existed.

My first DOS portable was the original Compaq sewing machine–sized portable. From there I graduated to an IBM Portable PC (also sewing machine sized). I very much enjoyed the IBM Portable, which was a fantastic machine, contrary to the press it received at the time. The great thing about the IBM Portable was that it used the same motherboard as the IBM XT, and it was very upgradeable. I installed a 100MB (CDC Wren III 5.25-inch half-height) SCSI hard drive in early 1987, along with a 12MHz 286 processor, a Token Ring network card, an AST SixPack multifunction card, and a number of other devices. I had that thing weighing up to 45 pounds and lugged it over half a million miles of air travel! I'm a sort of speed-walker and hate to slow down for anything. To maximize my through-put when cruising from one airport gate to another, I had perfected a method of "bowling" my brief-case and slinging the computer that allowed me to walk high-speed through an airport terminal. I'd start by carrying my 25-pound briefcase in one arm, and my 45-pound computer in the other. When the weight of the computer became too much for the one arm to bear, I had a system for transferring the briefcase and computer between arms without so much as breaking stride. I would start by sliding my briefcase along the floor about 10 feet in front of me in a bowling motion, then I would heave the 45-pound computer from one hand to the other, and finally snatch up the briefcase with the free hand as I caught up with it along the floor. All of this was done without missing a stride or even slowing down. As you might imagine, switching arms several times was necessary with a 45-pound computer and a long walk through the terminal. I still have two of the old IBM Portables, one of which my wife owned when we got married.

After the IBM Portable, I then moved on to a succession of briefcase- or lunchbox-sized portables. Even though laptops and some notebooks were then becoming available, I had to use these larger AC-powered systems because I needed a system with desktop power, performance, and especially storage. Two of these lunchbox systems were the IBM PS/2 P70 (running an Intel 80386) and P75 (equipped with a 486 CPU) in 1989 and 1991. Both of these systems used plasma screens. Into these systems I installed a 320MB SCSI hard drive and then a 1.2GB SCSI hard drive (the largest hard disks available at the time). A 486DX-33 processor was originally soldered into the motherboard of the P75. Nevertheless, in 1992 I removed it and soldered a 486DX2-66 in as an upgrade. That was quite a gamble at the time because a replacement motherboard (actually more of a CPU daughtercard) was $6,000! It is interesting to note that the P75 I used had an original list price of $18,890!—making it perhaps the most expensive PC ever sold.

When laptops appeared, I kept a close eye on them. I remember playing with the original GRiD Compass at a meeting of the Chicago Computer Society in 1983, and was amazed at the electro-luminescent display and use of internal "bubble" memory. Unfortunately it cost nearly $10,000 and was not PC compatible!

The first fully PC compatible laptop, the IBM PC Convertible, was nowhere near powerful enough to replace my suitcase sized Portable PC, nor was the dramatically improved Toshiba T1000 when it came out a year later. The Toshiba T3100 was one of the first 286 processor based laptops with a built-in hard drive, but due to the upgrades that were possible to the luggables, laptops were simply not a viable replacement for me at the time.

Because of my need for a portable system with desktop power and storage, the laptops of the 1980s and early 1990s simply couldn't do the job. In 1995, things finally changed. With the appearance of the mobile Pentium processor and the advent of truly high-capacity 2.5-inch drives, laptop and notebook systems finally reached parity with desktop systems in power and storage. Finally, I was able to graduate to a laptop as my primary working system, and I have been using them ever since.

I still have strong memories of carrying my 45-pound behemoth, so you can see why even a supposedly "heavy" 10-pound laptop doesn't even make me flinch!

Advantages of Laptops

If you are reading this book, you are probably already aware of at least some of the benefits of using a portable computer. Here is a list that possibly includes some benefits you had not considered before.

Multiple Uses

By their nature, portable computers are generally much more useful than desktops. Except for a mere handful of exceptions, portables can do anything that a desktop can, plus a range of other tasks that would be impossible for desktops.

The chief strength of the portable is its freedom from the desk. It can be used almost anywhere. Indeed, almost anywhere a human can go, so can a laptop.

Some uses for a laptop would not even make sense for a desktop. For example, an increasing number of notebook computers are being equipped with GPS antennas and mapping software. The same could be done with desktops, of course, but with much less interesting if not impractical results.

Ideal for People with Multiple Workplaces

For many people, the idea of working in a single workplace is no longer practical. Many workers have to travel as part of their job, whether across the country or around a metropolitan region. Even those workers who never travel may find it advantageous to bring work home, or to work while commuting. For all these workers, the notebook computer is ideal.

Instead of going through the expense of purchasing a desktop computer for each workplace, you can buy a single notebook. The notebook can be carried with you, from one workplace to another. If its battery is charged up, it can even be used while en route from one workplace to the other.

Flat-Panel Displays

Flat LCD panels were used in laptop systems long before they became popular for desktop systems. Laptops actually drove the development of LCDs, and desktop users (and television fans for that matter) can now enjoy the same benefits of these displays that laptop users have had many years earlier.

There are three main benefits of LCD flat-panel displays as compared to CRTs. The first is, of course, its flatness. Unlike most CRT screens, it does not bow out slightly in the middle. Instead, it is perfectly flat, just as a piece of paper. Many new CRT displays are emulating this flat-screen look to a remarkable degree. But even on these screens, the center of the display tends to bow out toward the user ever so slightly.

The second advantage is size. Actually, there are two benefits in this category. The first is plain truthfulness. The fact is that a 15-inch CRT monitor does not actually measure 15 inches diagonally. The usable display space is only about 14 inches in size. By convention, CRT manufacturers for some reason measure not just the usable display space on these monitors but the entire front surface of the tube. By contrast, with LCD screens, the manufacturers have been more honest. As you might expect, a 15-inch screen actually measures 15 inches.

The viewable surface is, of course, only one aspect of a screen's size. There is also the thickness to consider. Here, LCDs have a huge advantage. The traditional CRT monitor may be as thick as it is tall. The end result is that these monitors take up an extraordinary amount of desk space. By contrast, an LCD screen may be only 2 inches thick or less. But a laptop does an even better job of saving space: On these systems the LCD screen is usually less than a half-inch thick.

The third advantage of flat-panel screens is their sharpness. If you look at a CRT screen under high magnification, you will see that each pixel has indistinct borders and is slightly blurry. Sometimes the pixels exhibit microscopic jittery motions. Under the same magnification on an LCD screen, however, you'll see pixels with distinctly sharp edges and no jittery motion at all.

Laptop LCDs have had one special advantage over many desktop LCD panels, and that is that the laptops have always used a direct digital interface. After using laptops for many years and enjoying the advantages of the crisp LCD panels they used, I was excited to see LCD panels become widely available for desktop systems as well. However after seeing some of the available LCDs, I was extremely disappointed in their performance. They were visibly not near as crisp and accurate as what I was used to on my laptops.

The problem was that many low-end LCD panels were designed to use the analog VGA connection. If you use an LCD panel with a desktop system, and connect that panel to the system via a 15-pin VGA connector, then you are missing out on a great deal of quality. This is because the video signal is first generated in the video card as a digital signal, then converted to analog and sent to the display, where it is finally converted back to digital before being shown on the screen. This double conversion results in slightly fuzzy characters, colors that are not precise, and other undesirable artifacts such as moiré patterns. The only way to avoid such problems is to eliminate the analog conversion and send the digital signal directly from the video card to the display, which is exactly how it has always been done in laptops.

While this is not an issue for laptops due to their all-digital design, if you want the same quality display performance on a desktop LCD then I recommend using only LCD panels and video cards that incorporate a DVI (Digital Visual Interface) connector instead of the analog VGA connector. By using DVI to connect a video card in a desktop system to an LCD panel, you avoid the analog conversion entirely, and have the same crisp and clean image on the display as on a laptop display.

Low-Energy Consumption

In these days of energy consciousness, laptops have a tremendous advantage over desktops. Even an Energy Star–compliant desktop system uses up a fairly large amount of electricity. People who leave their systems powered up most of the day would be surprised to find out how much this adds to their monthly electrical bill. Notebook computers do not generally comply with the government's Energy Star conservation initiative. The simple reason is that they do not need to; they already use comparatively little electricity.

Built-in UPS

Power failures can be real calamities for computer users. When power is cut off to a system, everything in memory disappears. If the system was writing something to a disk, the write process may have been only partially completed, leading to a corrupted disk. In some cases whole files may be lost; in the worst case, a whole disk. To avoid this danger, many computer users have gone to considerable expense to purchase an uninterruptible power supply (UPS). This is a battery-powered device that will keep a system powered for a few minutes after a power failure so that it can be shut down properly. The cost of a UPS may be several hundred dollars.

Notebook computers are already equipped with a very good uninterruptible power supply. It is called the notebook's battery, and it will last not just for a few minutes, but for a few hours. If you work in an area where the local power company is not reliable, a notebook computer is a must.

Integrated Design

Notebook computers have a highly integrated design. All components are assembled by the manufacturer and tested prior to sale. By contrast, in the case of some small desktop vendors, components may be thrown together without sufficient testing, leading to all sorts of headaches for the user.

More Space Efficient

Even the largest notebook computers can be safely hidden inside a desk drawer. Indeed, some thin and light notebooks are so small that you might be able to stash several of these devices in a single drawer. On a small or cluttered desk, a notebook can easily find enough space for a home. In small offices, a notebook's ability to save space is highly appreciated. Ecologically oriented users will also be interested to know that at the end of the notebook's useful life, laptops are physically easier to recycle.

The Problems of Using Portables

One of the ever-present design consequences of laptop computers is compromise. For every element that you add to a laptop, there is another element that suffers as a result. For example, adding a larger screen lessens a laptop's portability. A brighter screen results in shorter battery endurance. Adding more internal drives or device bays means the system will have to be larger as well.

Because of these compromises, laptops are not perfect systems. While providing many benefits, they do have a few shortcomings.

More Expensive

There is, as they say, no free lunch. The extra versatility of the notebook computer comes at a price—in this case, a literal one (refer to Table 1.12). When desktop and notebook systems with similar performance and features are compared, the desktop is significantly less expensive. And even if you try to configure the systems equally, usually the desktop will have a performance advantage in several areas. The one price advantage of a notebook is that in many cases the purchase of a single notebook will avoid the need to purchase two desktops.

Table 1.12   Price Comparison: Desktop Versus Notebook

Feature	Desktop	Notebook
System	Dell Dimension 8400	Dell Inspiron 9300
Processor	Pentium 4 630, 3.0GHz/800MHz	Pentium M 760, 2.0GHz/533MHz
Memory	1GB	1GB
Hard drive	80GB	80GB
Display	20-inch 1680x1050 LCD	17-inch 1440x900 LCD
Video accelerator	256MB nVidia GeForce 6800	256MB nVidia GeForce 6800
Optical drives	16× DVD+/-RW, dual layer	8× DVD+/-RW, dual layer
Price	$2,185	$2,628
Difference (%)		20% higher

Although I tried to configure these systems as equally as possible, there are a few differences worth noting. First is that although the processor speeds seem radically different, they are actually very close in overall performance. This is because the higher clock speed Pentium 4 trades efficiency over the lower clock speed Pentium M. The 2GHz Pentium M actually performs very similarly to the 3GHz Pentium 4. The desktop system does have the advantage of a larger 20-inch display with 36% greater resolution, however the laptop display is usually much closer to the user so the overall object size will be similar. The main difference here isn't the size as much as the 36% greater resolution, which results in a Windows desktop with 36% greater real estate. Finally, the optical drive on the laptop suffers in comparison to the desktop. The DVD-burning speeds in both single and dual-layer modes will be about half as fast, which is perhaps the biggest single difference. The problem is that the very slim laptop optical drives simply aren't available at the same speeds as the fastest desktop optical drives. For any serious optical disc burning on a laptop, I always recommend connecting an external USB optical drive.

As you can see with this type of comparison, you get less performance for more money with a laptop/notebook system, which is a factor that must be considered.

Increased Risk of Loss

It is highly unlikely that some unfortunate person has lost a desktop computer because he or she simply left it on a train. But, that same regrettable mishap occurs every day in the laptop world. The simple fact is that because notebook computers are frequently taken out into the rough-and-tumble real world, they often fall victim to many more calamities than do the desktops in the well-sheltered office.

Perhaps the biggest risk for notebooks is physical damage caused by drops. Rare is the case where a desktop simply falls off a table, but it is all too common for someone to walk by a table and trip over a carelessly placed phone line, sending a poor notebook flying to the floor on the other side of the room. Other careless people have been known to leave notebooks on the roofs of their cars and then drive off. The real world is populated with laptop carrying cases whose shoulder straps never seem to break unless the user is walking on concrete. And what about liquid damage? Spilling a cup of coffee on a desktop keyboard means that a $50 component needs to be replaced. The same mishap on a laptop keyboard can lead to much greater damage.

In addition to notebooks being damaged, we must also consider their unfortunate tendency to disappear. Desktop theft is, of course, a serious problem, but it pales in comparison to notebook theft. Because notebooks are so easy to carry and so profitable in terms of price per pound, these devices are a frequent target for thieves. Often the monetary value of a notebook's hardware, however, is much less valuable than the information contained on its hard drive. Notebooks may be stolen not by thieves but by industrial spies.

Smaller Screens and Keyboards

Compared to models of only a few years ago, today's notebooks have sizable screens and comfortable keyboards. In comparison with desktops, however, these features tend to lose some of their brilliance. Although notebooks may have screens that measure 15 and even 16 inches, it is not uncommon to see desktop monitors in the 19- and 21-inch range. In the same way, most notebooks have the same 19mm key pitch as on desktop keyboards, but desktops offer much more space to provide such niceties as true numeric keypads and a handy inverted-T cursor key set.

Slower System Speed

Because of advances in system design, it has become harder to make a simple comparison of the performance of desktops with that of notebooks. A few years ago, you could get a fair estimate of system speed by examining the processor clock speed, the amount and type of memory, the size of the processor's memory caches, and the type of hard drive used. Now we need to examine all these areas plus two additional factors: the type of video accelerator used and the amount of video memory. Because most of today's most popular computer tasks require frequent screen updates, the speed of the video system is vitally important. This is particularly true in entertainment-related tasks such as DVD videos and electronic gaming.

Although the power of notebooks has increased substantially over time, there is still a slight lag in power between the average desktop and notebook. Most of the problem is due to the extra time needed by component manufacturers to design power-saving versions of the high-speed components used in desktops. For example, the low-power mobile version of a 2.4MHz processor will appear 6–12 months after the power-guzzling desktop version.

To avoid this delay, some notebook manufacturers in the past year or two have opted to sacrifice battery endurance to increase performance. They have begun incorporating desktop processor chips inside their systems. But, even in these cases, the slower speed of the surrounding components results in a system that is measurably slower than a top-of-the-line desktop.

If leading-edge performance is absolutely critical for your application—or if you need the fastest possible game-playing machine in order to master a certain online game tournament—a high-end desktop is still your best choice.

Upgrades Are More Difficult

If you have ever looked inside a laptop, you will wonder how the manufacturer was ever able to cram so many components into such a small space. Indeed, the miniaturization employed on an average notebook makes it very difficult to upgrade them to any substantial degree.

General Solutions to Laptop Problems

Although laptops are not perfect systems, they do offer tremendous advantages. Fortunately, what problems they do have can be ameliorated to a surprising degree. Table 1.13 summarizes the common problems and solutions covered in the following sections.

Table 1.13   Common Notebook Computer Shortcomings and Possible Solutions

Notebook Problem	Possible Solution
Expensive relative to an equivalent desktop	Actually, on a per-hour basis, a notebook may be more inexpensive.
Increased risk of damage, loss, and theft	Laptop insurance, extended warranties, frequent data backups, theft-deterrent locks, and encrypted hard disks.
Slower performance relative to high-end desktops	Buy a desktop as a notebook peripheral.
Difficult to upgrade and repair	No true solution. You must perform either limited upgrades or replace the notebook.

Possibly Cheaper Than Desktops

A simple comparison of price tags suggests that desktops are less expensive than laptops. A more intensive examination on a cost/benefit basis may suggest otherwise. Because a laptop may be used more often than a desktop, it could actually be less costly on a per-hour basis.

Laptop Insurance

Physical damage to laptops can be lessened by following two simple rules dictated by common sense. First, always transport your laptop in a well-cushioned bag specifically designed for that purpose. Second, never leave cables attached to your laptop in a place where someone can trip over them.

Even the most careful person, however, will occasionally subject the laptop to an environmental stress for which it was not designed. This could involve the system being dropped, dropped upon, run over, dunked, or a dozen other catastrophes. The only way to combat these mishaps is to be sure you're covered by either some form of insurance or an extended warranty that covers such disasters.

Protection from System Loss

Just as with desktops, frequent disk backups are a must. In fact, because the rougher environment that the laptop has to endure, backups are even more vital. Unfortunately, many people don't take backup seriously. Despite the difficulty, laptop users must make a habit of connecting to some type of storage device and backing up their data.

The increasing popularity of CD-RW and DVD+-RW disc drives on laptops may make this easier. It is a fairly simple task of popping in an inexpensive CD-R or DVD+R disc and copying the My Documents portion from one's hard drive to the optical disc. A good rule of thumb is to do this backup every time your antivirus software requires an update of its virus definitions. Other backup choices include copying data to flash memory drives and high capacity external USB hard drives.

People who have sensitive information on their laptops need some additional protection. Windows 2000 Professional and Windows XP Professional offer a decent encryption facility, along with secure password protection. Most laptops also offer secure passwords for both the system (booting) and for the hard drive contents as well. Using one or all of these features can protect your data should the system be lost or stolen.

Upgrades Are Indeed Possible

Because of their small size, laptops are more difficult to repair or upgrade than a desktop system. The components are often so small that you may need special tiny tools to access them. And, without the right guidance, you could really get into trouble. But despite the challenges involved, it is indeed possible to upgrade or repair a laptop —as long as you have the proper guidance. And that, of course, is what this book is all about.

CHAPTER 2

Portable PC Overview: Types and Features

Types and Classes of Portable Computers

As we saw in Chapter 1, "Portable Systems Background," over the years there have been several classes of portable computers, mainly defined by their form factor and/or size. This section examines the different classes and describes their distinctive features.

The evolution of portables over the past 20 years shows a continual trend in miniaturization. While the general appearance of desktop computers has not substantially changed much since 1985, the portable computer industry has spawned several new classes of computers. In general, each new class is smaller than the previous one. The end result is that computers with as much power as full-sized desktop systems can now fit into handheld or notebook-sized portables.

At least seven different categories of portable computers have appeared on the market. Today, while there are individual or niche market exceptions, only four main categories of PC-compatible portable computers remain popular:

- Laptops/notebooks
- Subnotebooks/ultraportables/ultralights
- Tablets
- Handhelds/palmtops

In general, as new, smaller classes appear, the older and larger classes become extinct. The laptop/notebook category, however, has not been replaced by a smaller category and instead has proved so powerful and useful that it continues to be the most popular class by far in the portable computer industry. The power of laptops has increased so much that many users are using them to replace their desktops. In fact, sales of laptops in the United States have exceeded that of desktops during some months.

Note that distinction between tablets and laptops/notebooks can be a fuzzy one. The options available on some systems cause particular models to ride the cusp of two categories. Specifically, a tablet computer with an optional keyboard could pass as a laptop. Likewise, a laptop with a flip-down touch-sensitive screen could be labeled a tablet.

Laptops Versus Notebooks

The dividing line between what we might call a *laptop* or *notebook* system was always somewhat poorly defined, and in fact today the terms are completely synonymous. While the marketing departments in the computer manufacturers have overwhelmingly decided to call all of their laptops *notebooks*, most people continue to use the more readily understood term *laptop* instead.

The definition of a laptop computer is fairly simple, a *laptop* is any portable computer featuring a clamshell design (where the screen and keyboard are hinged together), which is also small and light enough that it is capable of being used on one's lap. To that definition, most people would add the requirement that the system should be capable of running on internal batteries.

The definition of a notebook computer is unfortunately much less clear. Originally, notebook computers were just that, computers the size of a paper notebook. In other words, they had to be about 8.5 inches wide by 11 inches tall. They also had a fixed display, which means the system did not feature a hinged clamshell design like a laptop. Eventually, the marketing departments of the various computer companies began using the term *notebook* to apply to notebook-sized laptops, meaning systems that incorporated the hinged clamshell design. Eventually, they began using the term *notebook* on systems that were larger than a true notebook, but having a weight below some arbitrary figure like six pounds. Finally, all size and weight distinctions were dropped, and the marketers simply began to use the term *notebook* to describe all of their laptops. Perhaps they thought that calling them *notebooks* was sexier than *laptops* and somehow implied that the systems were smaller and lighter than they really were? I found it interesting to note that the engineers and system designers continued to use the more accurate and descriptive term *laptops* to describe the very same systems that the marketers had started calling *notebooks*. Similarly, I found that most people (myself included) also continue to refer to these systems generically as *laptops*.

In the end, remember that there are no official standards governing the use of these terms, and that they have now become completely interchangeable. For the sake of clarity and understanding, throughout this book I prefer to use the term *laptop* over *notebook*, even though the two terms have now become completely synonymous and interchangeable.

In any case, today's laptops have become high-end machines, offering features and performance comparable to a desktop system. Compare that to the original generation of laptop systems, which normally didn't even have a hard drive. Indeed, many high-performance laptops are now being issued to users as their sole computer, even if their only form of travel is to go from home to the office and back. Active-matrix displays as large as 17 inches, up to 2GB or more RAM, and hard drives of up to 160GB or more in size are all but ubiquitous, with virtually all systems now carrying fast DVD+/-RW or CD-RW drives, onboard speakers, and connectivity options that enable the use of an external display, high-speed storage, and a surround sound systems. Most models now include wireless Wi-Fi network capabilities as standard equipment as well.

Subnotebooks: The End of a Trend?

The evolution of laptops has followed an interesting path. As the internal components of laptops continued to shrink in size, of course, so did the size of laptops themselves.

Eventually, the sizes shrunk to a weight of less than 3 pounds, and thus a new category was born—the subnotebook. But a small size meant a small keyboard and screen, which further meant that the subnotebook could be difficult to use. Despite some initial excitement for these systems, they failed to attract a significant following, and the category was soon abandoned. At long last, portable computers had become so small that some of them were now *too small*.

Nevertheless, the idea of a highly portable laptop was too good to let die. As components continued to decrease in size, it soon became possible to design a laptop that was both lightweight and reasonably powerful. But instead of adopting the tainted name of *subnotebook*, these systems were now given the new name of *ultralight*, a category that will be discussed in more detail later in this chapter.

The Many Types of Laptops/Notebooks

As laptops and notebook computers became increasingly popular, manufacturers began to segment the market. As with most products, one of the primary ways to segment the market was by price. Most manufacturers thus began offering three lines of laptops according to price: high-end, medium, and bargain-basement or value.

Another way to segment the portable market was in terms of size and weight. In many cases, the smallest and lightest laptop was also the most expensive because it was using the latest components. But often users actually preferred heavier systems.

In the past few years, an interesting reverse evolution began to occur. While some laptops became smaller, others took a much different course. As LCD display screens grew in size from 10.5 inches to 12.1, 14.1, 15, and even 17 inches and beyond, a class of laptops had to grow in size to accommodate them. But while the footprint of the laptops increased, their profile has remained relatively thin—usually 1.5 inches or less. Most users don't seem to mind because a large, thin laptop is much easier to stuff into a briefcase than a small, thick one.

Today, most manufacturers segment the market into up to five classes: desktop replacement/gaming laptops, mainstream laptops, value laptops, thin & light laptops, and ultralight laptops. Some might combine the mainstream and value systems into a single category, or likewise combine the thin & light and ultralight into a single category as well. A small group of companies specialize in an additional class: ruggedized laptops. Table 2.1 compares the basic dimensions and costs associated with the most popular types of laptops.

Table 2.1 Typical Characteristics and Price Ranges for Various Types of Laptops

Laptop Type	Weight (lbs.)	Thickness (in.)	Display Size (in.)	Price Range
Desktop replacement	6.0–8.0	1.5–2.0	15–17	$1,000–$4,000
Mainstream	6.0–8.0	1.5–2.0	14–15	$1,000–$2,500
Value	6.0–8.0	1.5–2.0	14–15	$500–$1,500
Thin & light	4.5–5.5	1.0–1.5	12	$1,000–$3,000
Ultralight	3.0–4.0	0.8–1.2	7–10	$1,000–$3,000

Table 2.2 list the typical processors, maximum memory, and maximum hard drive capacities found in the various types of laptops.

Table 2.2 Typical Processors, Maximum Memory, and Maximum Hard Drive Capacities Available for the Different Laptop Types

Laptop Type	Typical Processors	Maximum Memory (GB)	Maximum Hard Drive Size (GB)
Desktop replacement	Pentium 4 Pentium M Athlon 64 Turion	4	160
Mainstream	Pentium 4 Pentium M Celeron M Athlon 64 Turion Sempron	2	120
Value	Pentium 4 Pentium M Celeron M Celeron Athlon 64 Turion Sempron	2	100
Thin & light	Pentium M Celeron M Turion Sempron	2	80
Ultralight	Pentium M Celeron M Turion Sempron	1	60

The various laptop form factors are described in more detail in the following sections. Note that these designations can be somewhat vague, and the marketing departments in most companies like to come up with their own terms for what they think a particular system might conform to.

Desktop Replacements

Desktop replacements are the heavy-weight division of the laptop family. Laptops of this class are very similar in size and weight to the original laptops. They typically weigh between 7 and 12 pounds or more and are usually large enough to accommodate the largest laptop displays available, now 15–17 inches measured diagonally.

As the name implies, the desktop-replacement system is designed to have most of the power and features of a typical desktop computer. This eliminates the need for a user to have both a desktop and portable, which saves quite a bit of money.

These laptops generally have two or three data-storage drives: A large hard drive and an optical drive of some type (usually a DVD drive or a combination DVD/CD-RW drive) are usually included as standard; plus in some cases an optional third drive bay might be available as well. Because all these drives employ rotating storage media, they are frequently referred to as *spindles*. Thus, most desktop replacement laptops have historically been referred to as two- or three-spindle systems. Note, however, that because of the decreasing use of floppy disks, many vendors are no longer bundling floppy drives as standard equipment and only offer them as $50 external USB attached options. This, combined with the emphasis on reducing size, weight, and power consumption, has also caused virtually all three-spindle designs to be discontinued. As such, most modern desktop-replacement laptops are now two-spindle designs, with the second drive contained in a swappable media bay with optional optical drives or hard drive carriers available to plug in.

Desktop-replacement laptops either come standard with top-of-the-line components or have them available as options. This means the fastest mobile processors, the largest amounts of memory and hard drive storage, and the best mobile video accelerators. Table 2.2 shows how the components in these laptops compare with those in other categories.

These systems generally de-emphasize battery life and power-conserving technology in favor of desktop type processors and video components, making them more suitable for gaming and multimedia applications. Many desktop replacements are being positioned in the market as gaming or multimedia systems suitable for delivering presentations on the road. Because of their greater weight, these laptops leave the desk only in the company of salespeople and other travelers who absolutely require the features they provide.

To use them as a desktop replacement, you can equip many laptops with a docking station (or a less expensive port replicator) that functions as the user's "home base," enabling connection to a network and the use of a full-size monitor and keyboard. For someone who travels frequently, this arrangement often works better than separate desktop and portable systems, on which data must continually be kept in sync.

All this power does not come cheap. The desktop-replacement laptops are typically among the most expensive laptops available. Prices now range from $1,000 to $4,000 or more. An equivalent desktop can often be purchased for half this amount, but keep in mind that desktop prices do not usually include a large flat-panel display.

Mainstream Laptops

People who buy large numbers of laptops are interested in the best combination of functionality and price. As with the thin & light laptops, the componentry of a mainstream laptop does not have to be of the latest and greatest vintage, but neither does the laptop have to be very light. The main goal is low price. The laptops have to be relatively powerful, but any component that is not absolutely essential is left out.

To cut costs, mainstream laptops use average-size displays (today, 14 or 15 inches in diagonal), lower capacity hard drives, and include an average amount of RAM. Floppy drives have universally been eliminated from virtually all modern laptops; however, most manufacturers enable users to attach (and optionally boot from) an external USB floppy drive if necessary.

Mainstream laptops are midway in size and weight between the thin & light and desktop-replacement laptops. Prices can range from $1,000 to $2,500 or more. Because they are two-spindle systems and do not need space for a large display, these laptops can be significantly smaller and lighter than the desktop-replacement systems.

Value Laptops

Value laptops are designed to appeal to people who require only a minimum level of performance. These laptops are designed to sell at low prices. To create their value line, some manufacturers simply take a variation of their existing mainstream laptops and configure them only with the most affordable components available. Some value laptops are stripped-down models with only the barest minimum of components. Value systems may be two generations behind the high-end laptops when it comes to performance and features. For example, it is quite common for value laptops to use Intel Celeron or AMD Sempron processors, which sacrifice performance for price when compared to higher powered CPUs. Nevertheless, the absolute decrease in functionality between successive generations of processors and other features is actually quite small. Although low-cost processors may have clock speeds only half that of the latest generation of CPUs, the actual performance difference may be substantially smaller. As the name implies, these laptops can represent a good value for the customer.

Value systems generally use chipsets with integrated graphics, which also shares some of the main memory for graphics use. Also, these laptops are invariably equipped with the smallest hard drives available—these days, 40GB, with larger drives as an optional upgrade. They also generally use the slowest 4200 rpm drives, which causes significantly longer boot and hibernation/resume times as well as slower operation reading and writing files in general. Some may include wireless networking as standard equipment, but the lowest cost models may offer wireless as an extra cost upgrade. Value systems generally include 14- or 15-inch displays, and prices range from $500 to $1,500 or more.

Thin & Light Laptops

Many users do not need to carry the equivalent of a desktop around with them. They especially do not want to carry around something that weighs close to 10 pounds. For these users, manufacturers have come up with the thin & light class of laptops, which attempts to combine an optimum amount of portability and functionality.

As the name suggests, this category of laptops keeps a low profile, generally about an inch in height. Likewise, its weight is relatively low, typically around 5 pounds.

Despite the low weight, these laptops can pack a considerable amount of power and incorporate numerous features. The processor is usually one generation removed from the fastest available, but this penalizes performance by only a small amount. The available memory and hard drive capacity are similarly reduced but still highly capable. Also, to fit into a 1-inch profile, these laptops require the thinnest available optical drives. Therefore, the latest and greatest combination rewritable drives may not be an option.

Note that portability is not cheap. Though the thin & light laptops do not use the fastest components, the highly compact components they do use are no bargain either. Expect to pay about

$1,500–$3,000, a bit less than for the desktop-replacement laptops. Displays for these systems are typically 12 inches diagonal.

Ultralights

Sometimes it seems you cannot keep a good idea down. The original lightweight laptops—called *subnotebooks*—never caught on with the public, and by the late 1990s most manufacturers had abandoned this segment. There was always, however, a group of highly mobile workers who needed the lightest functional laptop possible. Fortunately, by the turn of the century, mobile technology had caught up with them.

With the advent of tiny 1.8-inch hard disk drives, laptop designers could now design a highly functional laptop that weighed less than 3 or 4 pounds. Floppies were now completely unnecessary because most input and output was done via a network or USB connection. Even CD-ROM drives were less crucial. Large program or data files could be easily downloaded over a local network or USB connection. The only problem with this category of lightweight laptops was its name. The term *subnotebook* had negative connotations as an inferior technology. Thus was born the *ultralight* category.

The typical ultralight weighs no more than 3 or 4 pounds and is generally no larger than 8.5×11 inches in size. The most desirable characteristic—particularly among executives—is thinness. Laptop designers continually try to shave millimeters off the profile of these devices to get them as close as possible to measuring under an inch.

One weak point of ultralights is battery endurance. To keep the weight down, designers of these laptops employ the smallest possible batteries. This can offer significant weight savings because batteries are typically the heaviest component in the system. The smaller battery is partially offset by the decreased power requirements of the smaller components in these laptops, but in general ultralights are hampered with notably short battery lives, sometimes barely more than an hour.

Because the accent is on size and weight, the internal components are generally two generations behind the leading edge in terms of performance and capacity. Processor clock speeds are typically around 1.5GHz or less. Hard drives are generally no larger than about 60GB.

As with value laptops, the components may not be the latest and greatest but are generally good enough to handle most jobs. The most crucial compromises of these products, however, are not buried inside but plainly visible on the external surfaces. The keyboards are often shrunk by 90–95%. And screens are no larger than 12.1 inches—the smallest generally available for laptops. On the back panel, the lack of real estate often forces designers to jettison all but two or three of the most necessary connectors.

Some manufacturers achieve a good compromise with portability by combining the ultralight with a slab containing those components that are not needed very often. For example, the ThinkPad X-series uses a detachable module (or *slice*) that fits under the main system to carry CD-ROM or DVD drives and floppy drives.

In most types of products, devices become more inexpensive as they get smaller. But the situation is often the opposite in complex electronic gear, where prices often increase as the size gets smaller. Some ultralights are intended (and priced) as high-end executive jewelry, such as for the executive who uses the system for little else but email and scheduling but who wants a lightweight, elegant, and impressive-looking system. Ultralights range in price from under $1,000 to around $3,000, depending on features.

Ruggedized Laptops

Laptop computers are normally designed for relatively genteel environments: an office desk, an airline tray table, and maybe a hotel coffee table. Many workers, however, need computing power in the outside world, a place where even the most delicate electronic equipment may be caked with sand, rained on, and dropped repeatedly.

For that reason, a small number of manufacturers have specialized in creating ruggedized laptops. These devices are built to withstand varying degrees of stress. Almost all rugged laptops can handle drops well. Their delicate internal components, such as their hard drives, are shock-mounted to avoid damage. The outside case of the laptop may be reinforced by magnesium and have a rubber-like outside skin.

Rugged laptops vary in the degree to which they are waterproof. Most will withstand significant amounts of rainfall. Some are completely waterproof and can be safely dropped into a pool or even salt water.

Inside these computers, you can easily see that the emphasis has been placed on durability instead of performance. Most components are two generations old.

On the outside, ruggedness can sometimes interfere with usability. A waterproof keyboard is not as easy to use as a regular one. Note also that for true ruggedness, all the many connectors on a laptop must be securely covered with waterproof rubber plugs. Connecting and disconnecting these plugs can be tiresome.

Although rugged laptops use older, less powerful components, you would never know this by looking at the price. These units are typically the most expensive laptops on the market, often costing twice as much as a desktop-replacement system. Still, for many companies, the cost is well worth it. They would rather buy a single rugged laptop than a more delicate system that has to be replaced three times because of damage.

Tablets

In some applications, a keyboard is either unnecessary or a hindrance. For that reason, manufacturers have repeatedly offered tablet-style computers. These systems are like laptops without the keyboard. The top panel of the device consists solely of a large LCD panel. Except for a few buttons accompanying the screen, all input is accomplished via a stylus on a touch-sensitive panel that covers the tablet's screen.

A number of tablet systems appeared on the market with much fanfare in the early 1990s, but none of them caught on with the public. Nevertheless, a handful of companies, such as Fujitsu, have continued to quietly offer tablets in the intervening years.

In the fall of 2002, Microsoft launched a new initiative for tablets with a special version of its Windows operating system, dubbed Microsoft Windows XP Tablet PC Edition. This operating system differs from the regular version of Windows XP in that it enables users to manipulate the Windows interface with a stylus and to enter text using handwriting. Microsoft claimed that these new tablets would offer enhanced usability and would be better able to read the user's handwriting than previous attempts. Several companies, such as Acer, HP, and Gateway, are offering tablets that can use this operating system. Most of these devices are really hybrid notebook/tablets. The basic design looks like a notebook, except that the screen can be rotated and closed down on the keyboard, thus hiding it during tablet use.

A typical tablet is represented by the ThinkPad X-Series Tablet. At first the system looks like a small, 4-pound ultralight laptop with a 12.1-inch color display. Inside is a special low-voltage version of the Pentium M processor complemented with 512MB–1.5GB of DDR2 SDRAM and a 40–60GB hard drive.

The main difference between this system and a standard laptop is that this system includes a touch-sensitive display that can be twisted around and then folded back to cover the keyboard, at which time the included stylus can be used for input. The starting price is about $1,900.

Most Tablet PCs have the advantage that they can be used either as a tablet or an ultralight notebook. Other systems are permanently in tablet form, these are sometimes called *slates*. Despite having been on the market for a couple of years now, it is still too early to say how successful these devices will be. Their prices generally fall into the range of $1,000–$3,000, and they compete primarily with the thin & light laptops for market share.

Handhelds/Palmtops

The rarest category (at least outside of Japan these days) is the handheld or palmtop PC. Not to be confused with the PDAs (such as the Palm and Handspring series) or the PocketPC, these handheld mini-laptop computers are true PC compatibles even though they are hardly larger than a paperback book. The most famous handheld is the Toshiba Libretto. (For more information on the Libretto, see Chapter 1.)

Palmtops such as the Libretto offer a standard layout of keys, but with small keys spaced much more closely together than with a standard keyboard. As such, these systems are very difficult to use for extensive typing, but for simple field work, email, or Internet access—or anything that doesn't require a lot of data entry—they are incredibly useful.

PDAs

PDAs (Personal Digital Assistants) are another form of small computer often associated with PC compatible laptops. There are currently three main types of Personal Digital Assistants, differing primarily on the operating system on which they are based:

- Palm operating system
- Microsoft Windows Mobile (formerly known as Pocket PC or Windows CE)
- Linux/Java-based

While these systems can be used *with* PCs, none of them are PC compatible, and as such are not intended to be covered in this book.

Palm OS–based PDAs are meant to be used more as laptop accessories rather than laptop replacements. In their initial incarnation, Palm systems were designed only for simple management of personal information, data such as might be found in an address book or a daily calendar. The Palm's strongest feature was its easy communication with a laptop or desktop, allowing the user to quickly back up and update the data on the PDA. As the power of tiny PDA processors has increased and wireless communication has become more commonplace, the new generations of Palms are tackling more communications tasks, such as email and cellular voice communication.

Windows CE devices always had more ambitious designs. In their original form, they looked and acted like handheld computers, featuring a keyboard and simple computer-style applications such as word processing. For a short time, manufacturers even offered so-called "Jupiter" handhelds that were as large as ultralight laptops. Because they were not PC compatible, however, these tiny systems could not run the thousands of Windows programs on the market and had to wait for Windows CE applications to be developed. Because of this lack of software, Windows CE devices eventually evolved into a form factor that was similar to the Palm systems but could handle more applications. In 2003, Microsoft updated its PDA operating system and rechristened it Windows Mobile. These systems continue to have processors that are more powerful than Palm PDAs.

The Linux/Java-based PDAs are primarily embodied by the Sharp Zaurus models. They are sort of a combination of Palm and Windows Mobile devices, usually including a tiny keyboard, standard PDA software, as well as the ability to handle email, web browsing, and media playing.

In general, PDAs are viewed more as laptop accessories than laptop replacements. A small but growing number of people, however, are using PDAs as highly mobile email terminals, the advantage being that they can sometimes leave their heavier laptops home.

Major Features

No matter which type of laptop you have, you can be sure that it has a somewhat standard set of components. Later in this book we will discuss these components in more detail.

Processors

There has always been a range of processors available for laptops, but one rule has almost always applied: The fastest laptop is almost never as fast as the fastest desktop. The problem is one of power. Fast desktop processors run on AC power, of which there is a relatively limitless supply available. Portables in most cases at least occasionally must run on batteries, which have to be small enough so that the laptop can be lifted. Portable systems are also smaller than most desktops, and the tighter confines mean that the ability to run a high heat-producing processor is more limited. Therefore, a mobile processor in general has a more limited amount of electrical power available.

Intel has responded to the needs of mobile systems by offering low-power "M" versions of its most popular processors. Figure 2.1 shows the Pentium 4-M chip, the mobile version of the Pentium 4. These processors are generally similar to the desktop versions except they use lower voltages internally and can adjust their clock speeds depending on the user's requirements. By lowering their voltages and clock speeds, these chips can cut their power requirements and thus extend a notebook's battery endurance. Note also that the maximum clock speeds of these chips are almost always slower than those of desktop chips.

Table 2.3 shows a comparison of the clock speeds of various mobile processors from Intel.

Table 2.3   Clock Speeds (in GHz) Available for Intel's Mobile Processor Chips

Intel Mobile Processor	Clock Speeds (GHz)
Pentium M	1.0 to 2.26
Mobile Pentium 4	1.4 to 3.46
Celeron M	0.8 to 1.5
Mobile Celeron	0.65 to 2.8

In March of 2003, Intel introduced its Pentium M chip for laptops, a part of its Centrino platform. The Celeron M followed as a low-cost version of the Pentium M. Unlike previous mobile processors from Intel, these chips are not a variation on a desktop chip, but a Pentium-compatible processor built from the ground up for mobile applications. Intel claims that laptop designers can achieve 10–40% longer battery endurance if they use this chip.

In addition to the chips' energy conservation, Intel also claims that the Pentium M and Celeron M are faster than they may appear. Because they use a different internal architecture, they are able to squeeze out more effective work during each clock cycle. As a result, you cannot directly compare the clock speeds of Pentium M/Celeron M and other mobile Pentium chips. For example, Intel claims that a typical laptop running a 1.6GHz Pentium M chip will race through benchmark programs 15% faster than a Pentium 4-M running at 2.4GHz. Intel also claims that this same laptop's batteries last 78% longer on the Pentium M than on the Pentium 4-M.

Figure 2.1 The Pentium 4 Processor-M chip from Intel. (Photo courtesy of *www.intel.com*.)

Another processor specifically designed for portable applications is the Efficeon chip from Transmeta. This chip promises very low power consumption but at the expense of processing speed. The Efficeon has a different instruction set than Intel Pentium processors, requiring it to perform extra steps to translate the Pentium instructions into a form that the Efficeon can understand. Thus, although the Efficeon may have clock speeds comparable to Pentium M chips, its performance is considerably slower. Unfortunately, Transmeta has yet to capture much of the market and is concentrating more on licensing its power-saving technology rather than selling processors.

Some laptop manufacturers occasionally opt for the highest performance possible by using desktop processors. As can be expected, these power-hungry chips result in surprisingly short battery endurance. Note, however, that this quest for desktop performance is never completely successful. Overall system performance depends not merely on the processor but on several other components, and as a result these devices have yet to equal the performance of the fastest desktops.

You can find more information on mobile processors in Chapter 4.

Video Display Size and Resolution

Ever since the days of the luggables in the early 1980s, the design of portable computers has been highly dependent on the latest lightweight displays. When low-power LCDs became available, the development of the battery-powered laptop finally became possible. Today, the size of the display is the single most important determinant of the size of the laptop.

Currently, virtually all laptops use active-matrix color displays. These screens provide needle-sharp images of high contrast, in most cases better than the CRT displays that most desktops use. Indeed, many desktop users are now upgrading to flat panels. The prime impetus for this switch may be to save space, but the improved image quality is at least a partial factor.

There are, however, a few drawbacks to LCD displays. The first is that they have a fixed or native resolution. CRT displays can easily switch to higher or lower resolutions. When LCDs are moved above or below their native resolution, however, the image becomes decidedly blurry or even distorted.

The second drawback of LCDs is their limited field of view. These displays may present high-quality images, but only to viewers sitting directly in front of the screen. People who may be sitting a few feet to the right or left of that optimal position may see an image where the colors have been shifted and the contrast lowered. With the increasing popularity of LCD televisions, some LCD manufacturers are developing screens that are more suitable for wide-angle viewing. If you plan to use your laptop for informal presentations, you should take a look at laptops that advertise wide-angle capability. Of course, some people prefer a more limited viewing angle because it makes it harder for other people to read your screen when you are working in public.

One other downside of LCD screens is that they are considerably more expensive than CRTs. The good news here, however, is that the prices of LCDs have continually dropped over the years and will continue to do so. Indeed, the popularity of desktop LCD displays should lead to increased volumes and lower prices for both desktops and laptops.

Because the technologies used in today's LCDs are basically similar, the main differences among screens have to do with their sizes, their resolutions, and their aspect ratios. Chapter 11, "Graphics and Sound," includes more detailed information on displays.

Screen Size

Size is, of course, the most visually apparent property of an LCD screen. In general, as time progressed, screens became continually larger. There is, however, a size limit for laptops. As LCD screen sizes moved beyond 17 inches, measured diagonally, they became too large to be portable and were relegated to desktop use.

In today's laptops, screen sizes vary from 7.2 inches (measured diagonally) for the smallest systems to 17 inches for the largest. The most common size is now 14.1 inches, which represents a good compromise between size and portability.

In general, users are well advised to get the largest screen they can comfortably carry and afford. But note that for some screen sizes, there may be a choice of several different resolutions available. Choosing the wrong resolution may make the screen harder to read, or limit the amount of information that can be displayed.

Screen Resolution

The resolution of a screen depends somewhat on its size. As the size of the screen increases, it can comfortably accommodate more pixels, thus allowing for increased resolution.

For 14.1-inch screens—the most common variety—most laptop manufacturers offer two choices of resolution: XGA and SXGA+. A few vendors also offer SXGA, but the unique aspect ratio (5:4) makes that size and resolution somewhat rare. The increased resolution of SXGA+ over standard XGA enables users to display nearly 87% more onscreen information such as folders, documents, web pages, and so on, at the same time. Increased resolution also increases pixel density (the number of pixels per inch of screen size), which in turn increases the apparent sharpness of photographs and graphic images. Some people even maintain that increased pixel density increases the readability of text. On the downside, however, increased resolution also decreases the size of standard text and icons on the screen. As personal preference varies, users should personally examine several different size/resolution combinations to see which seems best to them.

Note that once you have chosen a resolution, it cannot be changed. A laptop's video circuitry can simulate a change in resolution, but the resulting image will be much less sharp than the image at the screen's original or native resolution.

Table 2.4 lists common LCD screen sizes and the resolution they support.

Table 2.4   Screen Size and Resolution: A Sampling of the Most Common Combinations Available for Laptops

Screen Size (in.)	Resolution Type	Resolution	Aspect Ratio	Pixel Density (Pixels/in.)
12.1	SVGA	800×600	4:3	83
12.1	XGA	1024×768	4:3	106
13.3	XGA	1024×768	4:3	96
14.1	XGA	1024×768	4:3	91
14.1	SXGA	1280×1024	5:4	116
14.1	SXGA+	1400×1050	4:3	124
15.0	XGA	1024×768	4:3	85
15.0	WXGA	1280×800	8:5	101
15.0	SXGA+	1400×1050	4:3	117
15.0	UXGA	1600×1200	4:3	133
15.4	WXGA	1280×800	8:5	98
15.4	SXGA	1280×1024	4:3	106
15.4	WSXGA+	1680×1050	8:5	129
15.4	WUXGA	1920×1200	8:5	147
17.0	WXGA+	1440×900	8:5	100
17.0	UXGA	1600×1200	4:3	118
17.0	WUXGA	1920×1200	8:5	133

Screen Aspect Ratio

The aspect ratio for most laptop displays is the same as that for desktops and televisions: 4:3 (that is, the height of the screen is 3/4 the width). In the distant past, some laptops, such as the IBM PC Convertible and the Toshiba T1000, used wider display screens because that was all that was available. When 4:3 LCD screens came out, the public quickly gravitated toward this standard shape.

Now, however, with the popularity of DVDs and high-definition TV, many manufacturers are installing widescreen displays on their systems (see Figure 2.2). These displays have a wider aspect ratio of 8:5 (16:10). Note that although this is much wider than the standard computer display, it is not quite as wide as the 16:9 proportions of HDTV, but is able to accommodate a full 16:9 HDTV picture within a 16:10 display with only a small upper and/or lower border (often used by the DVD player controls). Widescreen laptops are usually sold as multimedia or desktop replacement systems, due to their larger (and clumsier to carry) sizes. As more people use their laptops in home entertainment systems or as personal DVD players, expect this number to grow.

Figure 2.2 The Dell Inspiron XPS Gen 2, with its 17-inch WUXGA display. (Photo courtesy of Dell Inc.)

One interesting thing to note is that having a widescreen display doesn't necessarily mean you get more resolution or desktop screen real estate. For example, many so-called "widescreen" laptops have 15.4-inch WXGA (1280×800) displays. Personally, I would rather have a standard aspect ratio 15.1-inch SXGA+ (1400×1050) display because even though it doesn't have the "widescreen" aspect ratio, it actually offers an overall wider and deeper image in pixels than the so-called widescreen display. At the higher 1400×1050 pixel resolution, you'll actually be able to fit more open windows (web pages, applications, and so on) both in width *and* depth than you could on a WXGA screen. In fact, the SXGA+ screen has nearly 44% more overall resolution, meaning you can fit that much more content on the screen. The primary advantage of using a widescreen on a laptop is that human vision sees more peripherally than vertically, making wider screens better suited to what you actually see on them.

Video Accelerators

A crucial and sometimes overlooked aspect of computer performance is the speed of its video accelerator. This chip, shown in Figure 2.3, speeds up the process of moving pixels around the screen. Computer game players have been especially sensitive to the speed of their video processors because this can greatly influence the quality of their entertainment. But business users should also be aware that a video accelerator can impact tasks such as sales presentations.

Figure 2.3 Video accelerator chips from NVIDIA. (Photo courtesy of *www.nvidia.com*.)

Currently, the best laptop video accelerators are from ATI and NVIDIA. Note that as in the case of processors, laptop video accelerators are usually not quite as fast as those in desktop models. Typical video accelerators are listed in Table 2.5.

In addition to the type of video accelerator used, laptop users should also pay attention to the amount of video memory installed. The amount of video memory used for laptop graphics chipsets currently varies from 64MB to 256MB. In most cases the video memory is dedicated memory (separate from main RAM) used to hold information that will eventually be displayed on the screen. However, systems with video accelerators built into the motherboard chipset (such as the Intel Media Accelerator 900) use *shared memory*, which means that the video accelerator borrows main system RAM for video use. Since there is no dedicated video RAM, this results in a less expensive design (which also uses less power), but sacrifices performance when compared to dedicated video memory designs. The more video memory available, the more colors the laptop can display and the faster the video accelerator can operate. Large amounts of video memory are also useful for 3D graphics such as in games.

Table 2.5   Typical Video Components and the Best Optical Drives Available for Different Laptop Types

Laptop Type	Screen Size (in.)	Video Accelerator	Video Memory (MB)	Optical Drive
Desktop replacement	15.4/17	ATI Radeon X300/X600 NVIDIA GeForce Go 6800	128/256	DVD/CD-RW or DVD+/-RW
Mainstream	14.1/15	Intel Media Accelerator 900 ATI Radeon 9000 ATI Radeon X300/X600	64/128	DVD/CD-RW or DVD+/-RW
Value	14.1/15	Intel Media Accelerator 900	64/128	DVD/CD-RW
Thin & light	14.1	Intel Media Accelerator 900 ATI Radeon X300/X600	64/128	DVD/CD-RW
Ultralight	12.1	Intel Media Accelerator 900	64/128	None

Purchasers should be careful to note the type of video chipset and amount of video memory in a potential new notebook. Although there are a few select models with upgradeable graphics, in most cases the video accelerator components cannot be changed.

You'll find more detail about mobile video chipsets in Chapter 11.

Spindles (Storage)

The classic three-spindle laptop is disappearing. These systems generally had three forms of rotating memory: a hard drive, an optical drive, and a floppy drive. Now, because floppy disks are so rarely used, many laptop manufacturers have been leaving them off in order to save weight and lower costs. In some two-spindle systems, the floppy can be swapped into the storage bay normally occupied by the optical drive, but you can't run both simultaneously. In most cases, the floppy is relegated to being used as an external device that connects to the system via a USB cable. Since floppy drives aren't used much anymore, this doesn't seem to bother many people, which is one reason the three-spindle designs are fading. As average file sizes continue to grow well past the capacity of a floppy, this once familiar component may well disappear altogether. Currently, most vendors offer external USB floppy drives for laptops as a $50 option.

The most important drive in a laptop is its hard drive. Currently, drive sizes range from 20 to 160GB. Many experts suggest that users get as much hard drive storage space as they can afford. When users eventually purchase a digital camera or start storing audio and video on their hard drives, they will soon take advantage of all the storage space they have available. External USB drives can also be used to extend the storage of a laptop, and are actually quite excellent for backup, but when mobile, you generally have to rely on the drive that is installed internally in the system.

Some laptops have drives that rotate at higher speeds than other drives. The use of faster rotating drives will positively impact system performance by a significant amount. A faster-spinning drive enables the system to access information from the hard drive more quickly. Faster drives also have a major impact on startup (boot) times, as well as the time it takes to hibernate and resume from hibernation.

For some time there has been a variety of optical drives available for laptops. Most systems today include either a DVD-ROM drive, a combo DVD/CD-RW burner, or a DVD+/-RW drive, many of which can also handle DVD-RAM as well. In most cases these drives are not nearly as fast as their desktop counterparts, especially where DVD burning is concerned. In most cases if you plan on doing any significant DVD burning, I recommend attaching an external USB desktop DVD burner.

Chapters 9, "Hard Disk Storage," and 10, "Removable Storage," discuss storage options in more detail.

Expansion Options

Laptop components are so tightly crammed together that few expansion options are available. Often the only way to expand the capabilities of a laptop is to insert a PCMCIA (Personal Computer Memory Card International Association) card (see Figure 2.4). These cards, also known as *PC Cards* or *CardBus Cards*, were originally designed as memory cards but are now capable of providing a wealth of features. Almost any feature not provided on a laptop or not provided in sufficient quantity can be added via a PCMCIA card.

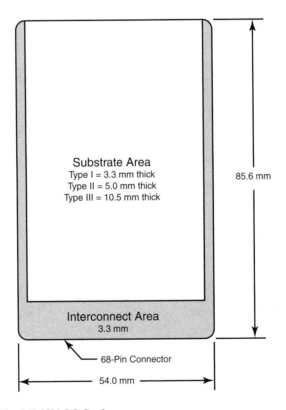

Figure 2.4   A diagram of the PCMCIA PC Card.

Note that there are two types of PCMCIA cards and three sizes. In addition to the older 16-bit PC Card, there is also a high-speed 32-bit CardBus Card that is required for high-speed wireless networking cards. The three sizes are Type I, Type II, and Type III, which mainly vary in thickness (see Figure 2.5).

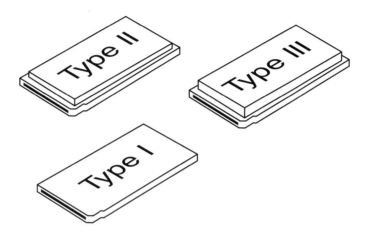

Figure 2.5   An illustration of the three sizes of PCMCIA PC Cards: Type I, II, and III.

Note that a Type III slot can accommodate a Type I or Type II card as well. Virtually all laptops have either a single Type III slot or two Type II slots stacked together so that they can also accommodate a single Type III card in the lower slot if necessary. Note that there are no Type I slots, and all laptops will take Type III cards in at least one slot. Because most of the capabilities formerly provided by these cards are now included as standard on the notebook's motherboard, many manufacturers have tried to save money by including only one Type III PCMCIA slot on their laptops. Although this does save a little on cost, it does limit the expansion capabilities of a laptop, in that you can install only a single Type I, II, or III card at any given time.

A sampling of the different kinds of PCMCIA expansion cards available includes:

- Encryption/Security
- Dual serial ports
- Data acquisition
- 10/100/1000 Ethernet
- USB/FireWire
- Flash card reader
- Hard disk card
- TV/FM tuner
- Video capture
- ATA/SATA interface
- SCSI interface

▶▶   See "PC Cards (PCMCIA)," p. 289.

See Chapter 8, "Expansion Card Buses," for more information on portable system expansion buses.

External Interfaces

A standard set of connectors for laptops includes a serial port and a parallel printer port. Because the devices that usually connect to these ports now are equipped with USB connectors, many laptop manufacturers are omitting these connectors.

It is quite common for laptops now to have several USB 2.0 connectors. They can connect to a variety of external devices, including a keyboard, mouse, printer, scanner, storage drive, and even a USB hub to allow connection to more than two devices.

A small number of laptops have IEEE 1394 (FireWire/i.LINK) connectors, RCA-style or S-Video connectors, and DVI interfaces. The IEEE 1394 connector, which is also known as *FireWire* or *i.LINK*, is mainly used to connect to digital camcorders. The RCA and S-Video connectors are used with TVs and VCRs. Most of the RCA, S-Video, or DVI connectors are video-out, but a few can also accept video input as well. The DVI interface is used with new display devices such as plasma TVs. Users who are interested in using their laptops for video applications should be sure that the necessary connectors are present. If they are not, they might be supplied via PC Cards.

One connector that should be on all laptops—large or small—is a standard analog VGA port. Without this, you will not be able to use your laptop with a video projector to make presentations.

Pointing Devices

Traditionally, there have been three types of pointing devices: trackballs, pointing sticks, and touchpads. If you do not like the device on your current notebook, you can always add an external mouse via a USB connector.

Chapter 13, "Keyboards and Pointing Devices," covers the various keyboard and pointing device options in detail.

Trackballs

Trackballs originally premiered on the Apple Macintosh Portable and soon appeared on several PC laptops. Because this type of pointing device takes up a relatively large amount of space, both in terms of its footprint and its height, it has been dropped from laptop designs.

TrackPoint (Pointing Sticks)

Pointing sticks originally premiered on the IBM ThinkPad but soon became a standard feature on many Toshiba, Dell, and other laptop systems. This device, which looks like a colored pencil eraser placed in the middle of the keyboard, can be accessed by the user without moving his hands from the keyboard (see Figure 2.6). IBM refers to it by the trademarked name *TrackPoint*.

Figure 2.6 The IBM TrackPoint, the original pointing stick. (Photo courtesy of IBM, *www.ibm.com*.)

Touchpads

Touchpads originally debuted on the short-lived Gavilan, one of the first laptops. Laptop designers particularly like them because they take up so little space. Beginners or casual users like them because they are easy to use; however, experienced laptop users do not find them nearly as fast or accurate as a TrackPoint.

Two manufacturers make most of the touchpads in use: Alps and Synaptic. Many reviewers prefer the Synaptic touchpad because its sensitivity can be adjusted. If the touchpad is too sensitive, you can activate it simply by floating your thumb a few millimeters above the surface, something that happens frequently during typing.

Combination Pointing Devices

Some laptops offer two pointing devices: a touchpad and a pointing stick. This is a great idea because many users have strong preferences for either one or the other device. The combination enables manufacturers to offer a single laptop that appeals to both groups of users.

Docking Options

All portable computers entail some type of compromise. One way to lessen that compromise is to purchase a docking station. Most laptops have available both a full-function docking station and less expensive port replicator. Laptop users can quickly snap their laptops into either of these devices and suddenly endow their systems with additional capabilities.

Unfortunately, port replicators and docking stations are not standardized in the industry; the connectors and physical formats are proprietary to the various manufacturers. This means that a port replicator or dock for one system will most likely not work with another, unless it is a compatible model from the same manufacturer. Most manufacturers that make port replicators and docking stations available try to make them work with multiple different models or even different product lines. For example, the same port replicators and docks work with several different series of ThinkPad laptops, so if I upgrade from an R40 to an R52 or even a T43, I can continue to use the same docking stations and port replicators that I currently own. In addition, I can use many of the same peripherals, such as AC adapters as well. This interchangeability makes upgrading to a new system less expensive overall and helps to maintain my loyalty to the ThinkPad brand.

Many bargain laptops do not have available port replicators or docking stations. Since I connect many devices to my laptop when I am working at my desk, I would personally never purchase a system that did not have at least a port replicator available because it would be far too inconvenient for my needs. On the other hand, if you rarely plug external devices into your laptop or never move it from a stationary location, then a port replicator or docking station might be something you could live without.

Docking Stations

Docking stations are designed by laptop manufacturers to provide laptops with many of the advantages of desktops. The exact features provided by a "dock" vary from one model to another. Some provide a wealth of storage options, such as extra hard drives and optical drives. A few will also provide desktop-style expansion slots. These slots can be used with a wide array of unusual expansion cards, such as signal-acquisition cards.

Port Replicators

Port replicators are designed to provide some of the benefits of docking stations at a low cost. One of the chief benefits of these devices is to make it easy to quickly connect a laptop to a number of external devices. For example, when many users take their laptop roaming, they need to disconnect and then later reconnect their external monitors, keyboards, mice, printers, network, and phone lines.

With port replicators, all they need to do is connect those devices to the port replicator a single time. Then they can simply dock and undock their laptop from the replicator as needed. Port replicators are a major convenience item, even if a laptop is used only at home. For example, I have no less than 14 external devices continuously connected to my laptop when it is at my desk, and with a single push of a button I can disconnect it from the port replicator and work wirelessly anywhere in the house, garage or yard. I would never consider purchasing a laptop that didn't have an available port replicator.

Note that there are generic USB-based port replicators available for laptops that don't have a port replicator option; however, they are often problematic, don't support many types of connections, and in general are a poor substitute for a true port replicator or dock.

Networking

In the laptop domain, networking components used to be relegated to PC Card add-ons, but as the need to attach a portable system to a network has increased, so have the networking options associated with portable systems.

Networking options for mobile systems are covered in Chapter 12, "Communications."

Wired Networking

Most recent laptops are equipped with internal LAN adapters that allow them to be connected quickly to any Ethernet network. This enables quick and easy connections to LANs in the office or cable and DSL modems at home. This connector is also useful in hotels where broadband connections are present. Most of the newest laptops include gigabit (1000Mbps) Ethernet support as well.

If a laptop is not equipped with an internal LAN adapter, users can still provide this capability by inserting a PC Card LAN adapter. Because of the high speeds required for 100Mbps or gigabit LAN connections, these cards will normally come in a 32-bit CardBus adapter.

Wireless Networking

At first an interesting novelty, wireless networking is quickly becoming an essential standard feature for laptops. For a slight investment in hardware, a wireless LAN (WLAN) offers the user the ability to have a high-speed connection to a local LAN or to the Internet while roaming anywhere in the office or at home.

On low-end systems where internal wireless network adapters are not standard, most laptop manufacturers are pre-installing wireless LAN antennas as standard equipment in their laptops. This allows the system to be wireless upgradeable via the installation of an internal Mini PCI either at purchase time or any time in the future.

Note that there are three different types of wireless LAN technologies: 802.11a, 802.11b, and 802.11g. Unfortunately, these standards are not all compatible with one another. To ensure greater compatibility, WLAN products can be certified by the Wireless Fidelity (Wi-Fi) Alliance.

802.11a

Despite its name, 802.11a was actually the *second* wireless LAN standard to appear. Being second, it also has the advantage of being faster (54Mbps) and of providing more channels for laptops to use. The disadvantage is that this equipment is more expensive than that of the more popular 802.11b technology. Because this standard supports more channels (and therefore more simultaneous users) and is less susceptible to interference from devices such as microwave ovens, it is the WLAN of choice for large office buildings.

802.11b

Originally, 802.11b was the most popular WLAN standard, available in many offices, homes, and even coffee shops. Unfortunately, it is also the slowest, with a nominal throughput rate of 11Mbps. Note that 802.11b is not compatible with 802.11a and that both require different types of antennas. Also note that 802.11b is vulnerable to interference from devices such as microwave ovens and wireless phones. Many laptops were equipped with 802.11b. For those laptops and notebooks not already equipped, an assortment of inexpensive 802.11b PC Cards is available.

802.11g

A newer variation of 802.11b, 802.11g is as fast as 802.11a yet is also backward compatible with the large installed base of 802.11b equipment. Because of this compatibility, 802.11g has replaced 802.11b in most new installations. Note, however, that because it uses the same spectrum as 802.11b, it is vulnerable to the same interference from microwave ovens and wireless phones. Therefore, many users in high-density areas might still opt for 802.11a.

802.11n

A new standard currently under development is 802.11n. This standard will offer up to 10 times the speed of 802.11g, operate over greater distances, and should be backward compatible with both 802.11g and 802.11b devices. The 802.11n standard uses a feature called multiple-input multiple-output (MIMO), meaning multiple transmitter and receiver antennas to allow for increased data throughput and range through multiplexing signals over several antennas at once. This standard is not expected to be completed until November of 2006, and it may be some time after that before certified products are available. Beware of products advertised as "MIMO" or "pre-n" only because they do not technically conform to this standard and may not be upgradeable to true 802.11n when the standard is finalized. Until Wi-Fi–certified 802.11n products are available, I recommend sticking with 802.11g for most uses.

Combinations

Not sure which standard will prevail? Would you like to cover all bases? Some cards offer the option of handling all three standards. These are called 802.11a/b/g dual-band/tri-mode cards. They are available both as internal Mini PCI cards as well as CardBus cards. Most laptops today include dual-mode 802.11b/g cards or tri-mode a/b/g cards.

▶▶   See "Wireless LANs," p. 601.

Wide Area Networking

The problem with all the 802.11 standards is that they have limited range, usually less than about 300 feet. If you want coverage over a greater area, in places such as a client's office or a parking lot, you can use directional antennas or range extenders to increase the range. Another option is to connect using a WAN (wide area network) via the cellular phone network. Users can easily connect to a WAN by purchasing a wireless modem PCMCIA card and setting up an account with a local cellular service. Some users may also be able to use their cellular phones as wireless modems through either a Bluetooth or USB connection.

Infrared (IrDA) is another type of wireless connection that is useful for slow-speed, short range, line-of-sight communications, especially for printing to IrDA-capable printers. However, be aware that not all laptops nor all printers have IrDA capabilities, so look for this feature in both laptops and printers if you feel it is something you might use.

▶▶   See "Wireless Modems," p. 597.

CHAPTER 3

System Maintenance and Assembly

Preventive Maintenance

Preventive maintenance is the key to obtaining years of trouble-free service from your computer. Laptop systems are especially prone to problems because they are portable and therefore exposed to potentially harsh environments, rougher handling, and more problems than desktop systems that remain in a single location. All it takes is an accident such as dropping the laptop onto a hard surface to turn thousands of dollars' worth of computer into so much junk. A little care combined with some simple preventive maintenance procedures can reduce problem behavior, data loss, and component failure as well as ensure a longer, trouble-free life for your system. In some cases, I have "repaired" ailing systems with nothing more than a preventive maintenance session. Preventive maintenance also can increase your system's resale value because it will look and run better.

Developing a preventive maintenance program is important to everyone who uses or manages laptops. The two main types of preventive maintenance procedures are passive and active.

Passive preventive maintenance includes precautionary steps you can take to protect a system from the environment, such as using power-protection devices; ensuring a clean, temperature-controlled environment; and preventing excessive vibration. In other words, passive preventive maintenance means treating your system well and with care.

An *active* preventive maintenance program includes performing procedures that promote a longer, trouble-free life for your laptop. This type of preventive maintenance primarily involves the periodic cleaning of the system and its components, as well as performing backups, antivirus and antispyware scans, and other software-related procedures. The following sections describe both passive and active preventive maintenance procedures.

Passive Preventive Maintenance Procedures

Passive preventive maintenance involves taking care of the system by providing the best possible environment—both physical and electrical—for the system. Physical concerns include conditions such as ambient temperature, thermal stress from power cycling, dust and smoke contamination, and disturbances such as shock and vibration. Electrical concerns include items such as static electricity, power-line noise (when the system is plugged into a wall outlet or other external power source), and radio-frequency interference. Each of these environmental concerns is discussed in the following subsections.

General System Care and Handling

Laptop computers are expensive machines built with significantly tighter tolerances than their desktop counterparts. Although most laptops are designed to function reliably in normal environments, it helps to use some common sense when transporting, operating, or otherwise handling a laptop system. If you treat the system as if it were a very expensive piece of precision electronic machinery (which it truly is!), you will greatly minimize the chances of problems occurring.

Instead of telling you what you *should* do to take care of your system, it is perhaps easier to tell you what you *shouldn't* do. I often observe people doing things to their laptop computers that make me cringe. While some of these are painfully obvious, here is a list of *bad* things you *should not* do to your laptop computer:

- Bump, jar, shake or physically punish the system, especially while it is running.
- Drop the system. Even if it is in a carrying case, many cases are not padded well enough for excessively rough treatment.
- Pack a laptop in luggage that will be checked at the airport, thus subjecting it to very rough handling.

- Place heavy cases or other objects on top of a laptop (such as in the overhead compartment on a plane), even if it is in a carrying case.
- Store the system where the temperature is below 41°F (5°C) or above 95°F (35° C).
- Operate the computer on a blanket or other soft surface where material might bunch up and cover the cooling vents on the sides or back, which will cause the system to overheat.
- Operate the computer while it is still half-inside a carrying case, which will block the cooling vents and cause overheating.
- Place the system closer than about 5 inches (13cm) from any electrical device that generates a strong magnetic field, such as electric motors, TVs, refrigerators, and large audio speakers.
- Operate two-way radio transmitters in close proximity to the system, which can induce currents and voltages causing lockups or failures.
- Spill liquids on the system, which may contaminate the internal components and/or cause a short circuit.
- Place heavy objects on the system with the lid closed or pack the system in a tightly compressed suitcase or bag, which may put excessive pressure on the LCD panel.
- Place an object between the display lid and keyboard, which may cause damage when the lid is closed.
- Pick up or hold the system by the LCD panel, which may damage the display and/or the hinges.
- Scratch, twist, or push on the surface of the LCD panel.
- Move the system or pull on the AC adapter cord while the adapter is plugged in, which may cause the plug to break off and/or damage the socket.
- Plug a modem cable into an Ethernet port (and vice versa), which may damage the connectors.
- Hard-mount the system in a vehicle or anywhere that it is subject to strong vibration.
- Crush, drop, or press on the cover of a disk drive while it is removed from the system.
- Insert a floppy disk into a floppy drive at an angle or upside down, which may cause it to jam in the drive.
- Place more than one label on a floppy disk, which might cause it to jam in the drive.
- Touch the lens on the CD-ROM tray when it is open, which may contaminate the lens and/or throw it out of alignment.
- Connect the internal modem in the system to a private branch exchange (PBX) or other digital telephone line that may subject the modem to improper voltages, thus causing permanent damage.
- Forget your passwords. If you forget a supervisor or hard disk password, there is no easy way to reset it, and you may have to replace the motherboard or hard disk.

Speaking from experience, I can tell you that the systems you use will last a lot longer if you avoid any of the aforementioned behavior.

The Operating Environment

Oddly enough, one of the most overlooked aspects of preventive maintenance is protecting the hardware—and the sizable financial investment it represents—from environmental abuse. Computers are relatively forgiving, and they are generally safe in an environment that is comfortable for people.

Portable computers, however, are often tossed around and treated with no more respect than a cheap calculator. The result of this type of abuse can be a variety of system crashes and failures.

Temperature, Humidity, and Altitude

All computers are designed to operate within specific ranges of temperature, humidity, and altitude. Exceeding the allowable ranges places stress on the system and can cause it to fail prematurely. Therefore, keeping an eye on the conditions where you both use and store your computer is important for the successful operation of the system.

Temperature, humidity, and altitude variations can lead to serious problems. If extreme temperature variations occur over a short period, expansion and contraction can cause signal traces on circuit boards to crack and separate, and solder joints can break. Extreme humidity can cause contacts in the system to undergo accelerated corrosion or condensation to form in the system and disk drives. Extremely dry conditions can cause problems with static electricity. Operating at high altitudes causes problems with cooling (lower density air renders the cooling system less effective) as well as the internal "air bearing" on which the heads float in the hard drive while operating.

To ensure that your system will be operated in the temperature, humidity, and altitude ranges for which it was designed, I recommend you consult your system specifications for the environmental range limits. Most manufacturers provide data about the correct operating temperature range for their systems in the owner's manual. Two sets of specifications are normally listed: one that applies to an operating system and the other for a system powered off. As an example, IBM indicates the following allowable environmental limits for most of its ThinkPad portable systems:

Maximum altitude without pressurization	10,000 ft. (3,048m)
Temperature range (not operating)	41°–110°F (5°–43°C)
Maximum temperature while operating	
Above 8,000 ft. (2,438m)	88°F (31°C)
Below 8,000 ft. (2,438m)	95°F (35°C)
Minimum temperature while operating	
Not using the floppy drive	41°F (5°C)
Using the floppy drive	50°F (10°C)
Minimum battery temperature when charging	50°F (10°C)
Relative humidity while operating	
Not using the floppy drive	8%–95%
Using the floppy drive	8%–80%

Note that the maximum allowable ambient temperature drops to only 88°F (31°C) at altitudes over 8,000 ft. (2,438m). This is due to the lower air density at high altitudes, which reduces the efficiency of the computer's cooling system. Also note the minimum operating and nonoperating temperature of 41°F (5°C). This means that for many areas of the country, it may not be wise to leave a laptop system in a car for more than a short period, or to ship a system using a mail or package carrier during the winter. As you can see from the preceding data, most environmental conditions that are comfortable for people are also good for laptop computer use.

Temperature Acclimation

In addition to the temperature limits just discussed, it is a good idea to avoid rapid changes in temperature as well. If a rapid rise in temperature occurs—for example, when a system is shipped during the winter and then brought indoors—you should allow the system (and the hard drive inside) to acclimate to normal room temperature before turning it on. In extreme cases, condensation can form on the internal electronics as well as on the platters inside the drive's head disk assembly (HDA), which is disastrous for the drive if you turn it on before the condensation has a chance to evaporate.

Most hard drives have a filtered port that bleeds air into and out of the head disk assembly (HDA) so that moisture can enter the drive; therefore, after some period of time, it must be assumed that the humidity inside any hard disk is similar to the humidity outside the drive. Humidity can become a serious problem if it is allowed to condense—and especially if you power up the drive while this condensation is present. Most hard disk manufacturers have specified procedures for acclimating a hard drive to a new environment with different temperature and humidity ranges, especially for bringing a drive into a warmer environment in which condensation can form. This situation should be of special concern to users of laptop and portable systems. If you leave a portable system in an automobile trunk during the winter, for example, it could be catastrophic to bring the machine inside and power it up without allowing it time to acclimate to the temperature indoors.

The following text, along with Table 3.1, are taken from the factory packaging that Control Data Corporation (later Imprimis, and eventually Seagate) used to ship with its hard drives:

> If you have just received or removed this unit from a climate with temperatures at or below 50°F (10°C), do not open this container until the following conditions are met; otherwise, condensation could occur and damage to the device and/or media may result. Place this package in the operating environment for the time duration according to the temperature chart.

Table 3.1   Hard Disk Drive Environmental Acclimation Table

Previous Climate Temperature	Acclimation Time	Previous Climate Temperature	Acclimation Time
+40°F (+4°C)	13 hours	0°F (–18°C)	18 hours
+30°F (–1°C)	15 hours	–10°F (–23°C)	20 hours
+20°F (–7°C)	16 hours	–20°F (–29°C)	22 hours
+10°F (–12°C)	17 hours	–30°F (–34°C) or less	27 hours

As you can see from Table 3.1, you must place a portable system with a hard drive that has been stored in a colder-than-normal environment into its normal operating environment for a specified amount of time to allow it to acclimate before you power it on. Manufacturers normally advise that you leave the system in its packing or carrying case until it is acclimated. Removing the system from a shipping carton when extremely cold increases the likelihood of condensation forming. Of course, condensation can also affect other parts of the computer, especially circuit boards and connectors, causing short circuits or corrosion that can negatively affect operation or even cause damage.

Static Electricity

Static electricity or electrostatic discharge (ESD) can cause numerous problems within a system. The problems usually appear during the winter months when humidity is low or in extremely dry climates where the humidity is low year-round. In these cases, you might need to take special precautions to ensure that your computer is not damaged. See the section "ESD Protection Tools," later in this chapter, for more information on ESD.

Static discharges outside a system-unit chassis are rarely a source of permanent problems within the system. Usually, the worst possible effect of a static discharge to the case, keyboard, or even a location near the computer is a system lockup, which can result in lost data. If you know you are carrying a charge, before touching the keyboard or system, you might try discharging yourself by touching some other metal object or device to bleed off some of the charge. Whenever you open a system unit or handle devices removed from the system, you must be more careful with static.

Radio-Frequency Interference

Radio-frequency interference (RFI) is easily overlooked as a problem factor. The interference is caused by any source of radio transmissions near a computer system. Living next door to a 50,000-watt commercial radio station is one sure way to get RFI problems, but less-powerful portable transmitters can cause problems, too. I know of many instances in which cordless telephones have caused sporadic random keystrokes to appear, as though an invisible entity were typing on the keyboard. I also have seen strong RFI from portable two-way radios cause a system to lock up. Solutions to RFI problems are more difficult to state because every case must be handled differently. Sometimes, simply moving the system eliminates the problem because radio signals can be directional in nature. If you have external devices attached to your laptop (such as an external keyboard, mouse, or display), sometimes you must invest in specially shielded cables for these devices. If the keyboard or mouse is wireless, then RFI can be especially problematic, and the only solution may be to try a different brand or model that operates on a different frequency.

One type of solution to an RFI noise problem with cables is to pass the cable through a toroidal iron core, a doughnut-shaped piece of iron placed around a cable to suppress both the reception and transmission of electromagnetic interference (EMI). You'll notice these cores on many of the laptop external data (USB, FireWire, and so on) and power cords. If you can isolate an RFI noise problem in a particular cable, you often can solve the problem by passing the cable through a toroidal core. Because the cable must pass through the center hole of the core, it often is difficult to add a toroid to a cable that already has end connectors installed.

RadioShack and other electronics supply stores sell special snap-together toroids designed specifically to be added to cables already in use. They look like a small cylinder that has been sliced in half. You simply lay the cable in the center of one of the halves and snap the two halves together over the cable. This type of construction makes adding the noise-suppression features of a toroid to virtually any existing cable easy.

Tip

For a comprehensive selection of electronics parts, tools and other supplies, I recommend the following sources:

Allied Electronics	www.alliedelec.com
Digi-Key	www.digi-key.com
Mouser Electronics	www.mouser.com
Newark InOne	www.newark.com
RadioShack	www.radioshack.com

For tools only, I also recommend:

Jensen Tools	www.jensentools.com

Most of these companies also have comprehensive paper catalogs, which can often make general browsing as well as finding what you need much easier.

The best, if not the easiest, way to eliminate an RFI problem is to correct it at the source. It is unlikely that you'll be able to convince the commercial radio station near your office to shut down, but if you are dealing with a small radio transmitter that is generating RFI, sometimes you can add a filter to the transmitter that suppresses spurious emissions. Unfortunately, problems sometimes persist until the transmitter is either switched off or moved some distance away from the affected computer.

Dust and Pollutants

It should be obvious that dirt, smoke, dust, and other pollutants are bad for your system. The cooling fan found in most modern laptop systems carries airborne particles through the system, where they can collect inside. I'm not saying that it is unsafe to use a laptop system outside or in an environment that isn't absolutely pristine, but I am saying that you should consider the working environment. If you take care of your system, it will serve you longer and with fewer problems.

If your system is going to be regularly used in an extreme working environment, you might want to investigate some of the specialized systems on the market specifically designed for use in harsh environments. Panasonic, for example, manufactures a complete line of systems called *Toughbooks*, which are specially designed to survive under harsh conditions. Durability features available in the Toughbook line include the following:

- Magnesium alloy case with handle
- Moisture- and dust-resistant LCD, keyboard, and touchpad
- Sealed port and connector covers
- Shock-mounted removable HDD in a stainless-steel case
- Vibration- and drop-shock-resistant design
- Rugged hinges

Unfortunately, in most cases, because rugged systems must be specially designed, and especially because they don't sell as well as the mainstream, nonrugged models, rugged systems are usually more limited in options, are not updated as frequently as mainstream models, and in general will offer much less performance than mainstream models. Still, if a mainstream model simply won't do for durability, you should consider one of the specially designed rugged models, such as the Panasonic Toughbooks. For more information on the Toughbook line of laptop systems, visit Panasonic at `www.panasonic.com/toughbook`.

Tips for Transporting Your System

When you are transporting a laptop computer, I recommend you consider the following guidelines in order to protect the system:

- Remove all floppy disk and/or CD/DVD disc media from the drives.
- Remove all PC Card/CardBus or ExpressCard adapters from their slots and place them in their protective covers. I often use small ziplock bags if they did not come with small cases or covers.
- Make sure the main battery is fully seated or possibly eject the battery for shipping if you suspect the handling will be rough. The battery is a relatively heavy component and your laptop could be seriously damaged if the battery isn't seated properly and the laptop (or bag containing your laptop) receives a sharp blow.
- Make sure the system is fully powered off (or optionally in Hibernate mode) and not in a Suspend or Standby mode.
- If the power switch is accessible with the lid closed, make sure the switch is locked or covered so that the system cannot be accidentally powered on while being transported.
- Make sure all access doors and covers are in position and closed.
- Use a carrying case that provides adequate shock protection (cushioning).

If your travel involves flying, you should be aware that FAA regulations now call for more rigorous screening of electronic devices, including laptop computers. The inspections normally require that you remove the system from its travel case and place the unprotected system on the conveyor belt that takes it through the X-ray machine. Make sure you don't put the system upside-down on the conveyor, because that can put pressure on the LCD, potentially causing damage.

In some cases you may be required to power-on the system after the trip through the X-ray machine in order to demonstrate computer functionality. In that situation, be sure you remember to power the system back off (or optionally place it in Hibernate mode) before returning it to its travel case. Note that X-rays do not harm either the computer or removable storage media. See "Airport X-Ray Machines and Metal Detectors" in Chapter 10, "Removable Storage," for more information.

If you ever need to ship the system via the mail or through a package carrier such as UPS or FedEx, it is extremely important that you properly pack the system to prevent damage. In general, it is hard to find a better shipping box and packing material than what the system was originally packed in when new. For that reason, I highly recommend you retain the original box and packing materials after purchasing a system. This will prove to be extremely useful in any case where you need to ship the system to a remote destination.

Following these guidelines for transporting or shipping the system will help to ensure the machine arrives in working order at the destination.

Active Preventive Maintenance Procedures

How often you should perform active preventive maintenance procedures depends on the environment in which you operate your system as well as the quality of the system's components. If your system is in a dirty environment, such as a machine shop floor or a gas station service area, you might need to clean your system every three months or less. For normal office environments, cleaning a system every few months to a year is usually fine. If you frequently use your system outdoors, it may require more frequent cleanings, depending on the amount of dirt and dust in the environment.

Other preventive maintenance procedures include making periodic backups of your data. Also, depending on what operating system and file system you use, you should defragment your hard disks at least once a month to maintain disk efficiency and speed, as well as to increase your ability to recover data should there be a more serious problem. See the section titled "Defragmenting Files" later in this chapter.

The following is a sample weekly disk-maintenance checklist:

- Back up any data or important files.
- Run a full system antivirus and antispyware scan. Before starting the scans, be sure to check for and install antivirus and antispyware software updates. Note that most of these programs have integrated update routines that automatically check for updates on a weekly or monthly basis, or at some other interval you may choose.
- Run the Windows Disk Cleanup tool, which searches the system for files you can safely delete, such as
  - Files in the Recycle Bin.
  - Temporary Internet files.
  - Windows temporary files.
  - Install programs for previously downloaded and installed programs.
  - System restore points except the most recent restore point.

- Optional Windows components that you are not using.
- Installed programs that you no longer use.

■ Finally, run a disk-defragmenting program.

About System Restore

System Restore is an automatic service in Windows Me, XP, and later versions that periodically creates *Restore Points*, which are snapshots of the Registry and certain other dynamic system files. These Restore Points do *not* include any user or application data and should therefore not be confused with or used in place of normal file or data backup procedures. The System Restore application (found in the Program menu under Accessories, System Tools) can be used to manually return a system to a previously created Restore Point, as well as to manually create a new Restore Point. Normally, you don't ever need to create Restore Points manually because they are automatically created

- Every time you install an application
- Every time an update is installed with Automatic Updates
- Every time an update is installed with Windows Update
- Every time you install an unsigned driver
- Every 24 hours if the system is turned on, or if it has been more than 24 hours since the last Restore Point was created

While it is generally not necessary to create Restore Points manually, I do recommend creating a manual Restore Point before editing the Windows Registry directly because that will essentially create a backup of the Registry you can restore if your edit causes problems.

The following are some monthly maintenance procedures you should perform:

■ Create an operating system startup disk or ensure you have access to a bootable OS installation CD for recovery purposes.

■ Check for and install any BIOS updates.

■ Check for and install any updated drivers for the video, sound, modem, and other devices.

■ Check for and install any operating system updates.

■ Clean the system, including the LCD screen, keyboard, and especially the cooling vents.

■ Check that the cooling fans are operating properly. Most laptops have only a single fan, but some have more than one.

Many people use a laptop as an accessory to a desktop system. In that case, you may have files that you work with while traveling that need to be synchronized with files on your desktop or on a server. You can use the Windows Briefcase or Synchronization Manager utility to accomplish this, but an easier-to-use and more effective solution is a simple file or directory synchronization tool like Good Sync (www.goodsync.com). Normally, you want to synchronize files every time you disconnect and reconnect to your desktop system or network.

System Backups

One of the most important preventive maintenance procedures is the performance of regular system backups. A sad reality in the computer-repair-and-servicing world is that hardware can always be repaired or replaced, but data cannot. Many hard disk troubleshooting and service procedures, for example, require that you repartition or reformat the disk, which overwrites all existing data.

The hard disk drive capacity in a typical laptop system has grown far beyond the point at which floppy disks are a viable backup solution. Backup solutions that employ floppy disk drives are insufficient and too costly due to the amount of media required. Table 3.2 shows the number of units of different types of media required to back up the 80GB drive in my current laptop system.

Table 3.2   Amounts and Costs of Different Media Required to Back Up a Full 80GB Drive

Media Type	Number Required	Unit Cost	Net Cost
1.44MB floppy disks	54,883	$0.15	$8,232
48× 80-minute/700MB CD-R discs	109	$0.25	$27
4× 4.7GB DVD+-R discs	18	$1.50	$27
DAT DDS-4 tapes (native)	4	$15.00	$60
DAT DDS-4 tapes (compressed)	2	$15.00	$30

Assuming the drive is full, it would take 54,883 1.44MB floppy disks, for example, to back up the 80GB hard disk in my current laptop system! That would cost more than $8,232 worth of floppy disks, not to mention the time involved. My laptop includes a CD-RW drive, as do many of the systems today, but as you can see, even using CD-R would be miserable, requiring 109 discs to back up the entire drive. DVD+-R, on the other hand, would require only 18 discs, which still wouldn't be much fun but is much more doable in a pinch. Tape really shines here, because only two DAT DDS-4 tapes are required to back up the entire drive, meaning I would have to switch tapes only once during the backup. Although the media cost is a little higher with the tape as compared to CD/DVD, the time-savings are enormous. Imagine trying to back up a full 300GB drive in a desktop system, which would require 64 DVD+-R discs, but only eight DAT DDS-4 tapes.

Of course, these examples are extreme; most people don't have a full 80GB worth of data to back up on their laptop. Of course, some may have more. Also, if you organize your system properly, keeping data files separated from program files, you can get away with backing up only the data, and not the programs. This works because in most cases, if there is a drive failure, you will have to reinstall your operating system and all your applications from their original discs. Once the OS and applications are installed, you would restore the data files from your backups.

The best form of backup has traditionally been magnetic tape. The two main standards are Travan and digital audio tape (DAT). Travan drives are generally slower and hold less than the newest DAT drives, but both are available in relatively competitive versions. The latest Travan tape drives store 20GB/40GB (raw/compressed) on a single tape, whereas fifth-generation DAT DDS drives store 36GB/72GB per tape. These tapes typically cost $15 or less. If you use larger drives, new versions of DAT and other technologies can be used to back up your drive.

Another alternative for backup is to use a second, external hard drive of equal (or larger) capacity and simply copy from one drive to the other. With the low cost of drives these days, and the ease of connecting an external drive via USB or IEEE-1394 (FireWire/i.LINK), this turns out to be a fast, efficient, and reasonably economical method. However, if a disaster occurs, such as theft or fire, you could still lose everything. Also, with only one backup, if your backup goes bad when you depend on it, you'll be without any other alternatives.

You can perform hard disk–based backups for more than one system with an external hard drive. External hard disks are available in capacities up to 500GB or more, and if the destination drive is as large as or larger than the source, the entire backup can be done in a single operation. Some external hard drive models even offer one-button automated backups. Hard drives have come down in price significantly over the years, as have the external USB and/or FireWire enclosures to contain them, making disk-to-disk backup a cheaper, easier, and significantly faster alternative to tape. Most laptops use 2.5-inch drives internally, which are more expensive than the 3.5-inch drives used in desktop systems or in most external enclosures. Because of this, you can purchase an external hard drive equal to or larger than the full capacity of the internal laptop drive for under $100 in most cases. As a minimum, I generally recommend purchasing one or two external drives equal to or larger than the internal drive in the laptop. By using two or more external drives, you can perform rotating backups of the entire laptop drive, moving one of the backups offsite for even greater protection from disaster.

Tip

No matter which backup solution you use, the entire exercise is pointless if you cannot restore your data from the storage medium. You should test your backup system by performing random file restores at regular intervals to ensure the viability of your data.

If your backup supports disaster recovery, be sure to test this feature as well by installing an empty drive and using the disaster-recovery feature to rebuild the operating system and restore the data.

Cleaning a System

One of the most important operations in a good preventive maintenance program is regular and thorough cleaning of the system inside and out. Unlike desktop systems, laptop systems don't have air flowing through all their parts, so they are more immune to dust internally and normally don't have to be disassembled for cleaning. Laptops do, however, usually have fans that draw air through cooling ducts with heatsinks mounted inside them. Dust buildup in these cooling passages can be a problem because the dust acts as a thermal insulator, which prevents proper cooling. Excessive heat shortens the life of components and adds to the thermal stresses caused by greater temperature changes between the system's full power and sleep/power-off states. Additionally, the dust can contain conductive elements that can cause partial short circuits in a system. Other elements in dust and dirt can accelerate corrosion of electrical contacts, resulting in improper connections. Regularly blowing out any dust and debris from the cooling passages (through the vents) will benefit that system in the long run.

Note that because laptop systems are much more difficult to disassemble, I normally don't recommend opening up or disassembling them just for cleaning. Of course, if you have the system open for some other reason, you should definitely take advantage of the opportunity and clean the interior components thoroughly. For most general preventive maintenance, cleaning the system externally or through any openings is sufficient. This means using either compressed air or a vacuum cleaner to clean dirt out of the keyboard, cooling vents, drive openings, data ports, or any other openings in the system.

Tip

Cigarette smoke contains chemicals that can conduct electricity and cause corrosion of computer parts. The smoke residue can infiltrate the entire system, causing corrosion and contamination of electrical contacts and sensitive components, such as floppy drive read/write heads and optical drive lens assemblies. You should avoid smoking near computer equipment and encourage your company to develop and enforce a similar policy.

Cleaning Tools

Properly cleaning the system requires certain supplies and tools. Here are some items used for cleaning:

- LCD/keyboard/case cleaning solution
- Canned air
- Contact cleaner/enhancer
- A small brush
- Lint-free foam cleaning swabs
- Antistatic wrist-grounding strap
- Computer vacuum cleaner

These simple cleaning tools and chemical solutions enable you to perform most common preventive maintenance tasks.

Chemicals

Chemicals can be used to help clean, troubleshoot, and even repair a system. You can use several types of cleaning solutions with computers and electronic assemblies. Most fall into the following categories:

- Standard cleaning solutions
- Contact cleaner/lubricants
- Dusters

Tip

The makeup of many of the chemicals used for cleaning electronic components has been changing because many of the chemicals originally used are now considered environmentally unsafe. They have been attributed to damaging the earth's ozone layer. Chlorine atoms from chlorofluorocarbons (CFCs) and chlorinated solvents attach themselves to ozone molecules and destroy them. Many of these chemicals are now strictly regulated by federal and international agencies in an effort to preserve the ozone layer. Most of the companies that produce chemicals used for system cleaning and maintenance have had to introduce environmentally safe replacements. The only drawback is that many of these safer chemicals cost more and usually do not work as well as those they've replaced.

Standard Cleaners

For the most basic function—cleaning exterior LCD screens, keyboards, and cases—various chemicals are available. I normally recommend one of the following:

- 50-50 mixture of isopropyl alcohol and water
- Nonammoniated glass cleaner
- Pure water (hot water works best)

Other solutions such as antistatic LCD cleaning cloths and Kimwipes are also acceptable alternatives.

Caution

Isopropyl alcohol is a flammable liquid. Do not use alcohol cleaner near an exposed flame or when the system is on.

The solutions should generally be in liquid form, not a spray. Sprays can be wasteful, and you should never spray the solution directly on the system anyway. Instead, lightly moisten a soft lint-free cloth, which is then used to wipe down the parts to be cleaned.

Contact Cleaner/Lubricants

Contact cleaners/lubricants are chemicals similar to the standard cleaners but are more pure and include a lubricating component. Although their cleaning applications are more limited when dealing with a laptop system, these chemicals do come in handy for cleaning connectors and internal or external cables. The lubricant eases the force required when plugging and unplugging cables and connectors, reducing strain on the devices. The lubricant coating also acts as a conductive protectant that insulates the contacts from corrosion. These chemicals can greatly prolong the life of a system by preventing intermittent contacts in the future.

A unique type of contact cleaner/enhancer and lubricant called Stabilant 22 is available. This chemical, which you apply to electrical contacts, enhances the connection and lubricates the contact point; it is much more effective than conventional contact cleaners or lubricants. Stabilant 22 is a liquid-polymer semiconductor; it behaves like liquid metal and conducts electricity in the presence of an electric current. The substance also fills the air gaps between the mating surfaces of two items that are in contact, making the surface area of the contact larger and also keeping out oxygen and other contaminants that can corrode the contact point.

This chemical is available in several forms. Stabilant 22 is the concentrated version, whereas Stabilant 22a is a version diluted with isopropyl alcohol in a 4:1 ratio. An even more diluted 8:1-ratio version is sold in many high-end stereo and audio shops under the name Tweek. Just 15ml of Stabilant 22a sells for about $40; a liter of the concentrate costs about $4,000!

As you can see, pure Stabilant 22 is fairly expensive, but only a little is required in any common application, and nothing else has been found to be quite as effective in preserving electrical contacts. NASA even uses this chemical on spacecraft electronics. An application of Stabilant can provide protection for up to 16 years, according to its manufacturer, D.W. Electrochemicals. In addition to enhancing the contact and preventing corrosion, an application of Stabilant lubricates the contact, making insertion and removal of the connector easier. See `www.stabilant.com` or check the Vendor List on this book's DVD for more information.

Compressed-Air Dusters

Compressed air (actually a gas such as carbon dioxide) is often used as an aid in system cleaning. You use the compressed-air can as a blower to remove dust and debris from a system or component. Originally, these dusters used chlorofluorocarbons (CFCs) such as Freon, whereas modern dusters use either hydrofluorocarbons (HFCs such as difluoroethane) or carbon dioxide, neither of which is known to damage the ozone layer. Be careful when you use these devices, because some of them can generate a static charge when the compressed gas leaves the nozzle of the can. Be sure you are using the type approved for cleaning or dusting off computer equipment and consider wearing a static grounding strap as a precaution. The type of compressed-air can used for cleaning camera equipment sometimes differs from the type used for cleaning static-sensitive computer components.

When using these compressed-air products, be sure you hold the can upright so that only gas is ejected from the nozzle. If you tip the can, the raw propellant will come out as a cold liquid, which not only is wasteful but can damage or discolor plastics. You should use compressed gas only on equipment that is powered off, to minimize any chance of damage through short circuits.

What I recommend with laptops is to turn them sideways or upside down (with the power off) and use the compressed air to blast any junk out of the keyboard as well as any openings on the front, sides, or rear, especially any cooling vents. If you have the system open for any reason, you should take advantage of the opportunity to use the compressed air to blow any dust or dirt out of the interior as well.

Vacuum Cleaners

Some people prefer to use a vacuum cleaner instead of canned gas dusters for cleaning a system. Canned air is usually better for cleaning in small areas as is usually the situation with a portable system. A vacuum cleaner is more useful when you are cleaning a larger desktop system loaded with dust and dirt. You can use the vacuum cleaner to suck out the dust and debris instead of simply blowing it around on the other components, which sometimes happens with canned air. Still, vacuum cleaners are especially useful for sucking dirt out of keyboards, whether on a laptop or desktop system. I also recommend vacuuming the cooling vents on laptops, which is an easy way to remove dust without having to open the unit.

For onsite servicing (when you are going to the location of the equipment instead of the equipment coming to you), canned air is easier to carry in a toolkit than a small vacuum cleaner. Tiny vacuum cleaners also are available for system cleaning. These small units are easy to carry and can serve as an alternative to compressed-air cans. Some special vacuum cleaners are specifically designed for use on and around electronic components; they are designed to minimize electrostatic discharge (ESD) while in use. If you are using a regular vacuum cleaner and not one specifically designed with ESD protection, you should take precautions, such as wearing a grounding wrist strap. Also, if the cleaner has a metal nozzle, be careful not to touch it to the circuit boards or components you are cleaning.

Brushes and Swabs

You can use a small makeup brush, photographic brush, or paintbrush to carefully loosen the accumulated dirt and dust inside a laptop PC before spraying it with canned air or using the vacuum cleaner. Be careful about generating static electricity, however. In most cases, you should not use a brush directly on any circuit boards, but only on the case interior and other parts, such as fan blades, air vents, and keyboards. Wear a grounded wrist strap if you are brushing on or near any circuit boards, and brush slowly and lightly to prevent static discharges from occurring.

Use cleaning swabs to wipe off electrical contacts and connectors, floppy or tape drive heads, and other sensitive areas. The swabs should be made of foam or synthetic chamois material that does not leave lint or dust residue. Unfortunately, proper foam or chamois cleaning swabs are more expensive than typical cotton swabs. Do not use cotton swabs because they leave cotton fibers on everything they touch. Cotton fibers are conductive in some situations and can remain on drive heads, which can scratch the disks. Foam or chamois swabs can be purchased at most electronics supply stores.

Caution

One item to avoid is an eraser for cleaning contacts. Many people (including me) have recommended using a soft pencil-type eraser for cleaning circuit-board or flex-cable contacts. Testing has proven this to be bad advice for several reasons. One reason is that any such abrasive wiping on electrical contacts generates friction and electrostatic discharge (ESD). This ESD can be damaging to boards and components, especially the newer low-voltage devices. These devices are especially static sensitive, and cleaning the contacts without a proper liquid solution is not recommended. Also, the eraser will wear off the gold coating on many contacts, exposing the tin contact underneath, which rapidly corrodes when exposed to air.

Some companies sell premoistened contact cleaning pads soaked in a proper contact cleaner and lubricant. These pads are safe to wipe on conductors and contacts with no likelihood of ESD damage or abrasion of the gold plating.

Lightweight Lubricants

You can use a lightweight lubricant such as WD-40 or silicone to lubricate the door mechanisms on disk drives and any other part of the system that might require clean, lightweight lubrication. Other items you can lubricate are the access doors for ports and PC Card/CardBus sockets, to provide smoother operation.

Using WD-40 or silicone instead of conventional oils is important because silicone does not gum up and collect dust and other debris. Always use the lubricant sparingly. Do not spray it anywhere near the equipment because it tends to migrate and will end up where it doesn't belong (such as on drive heads). Instead, apply a small amount to a toothpick or foam swab and dab the silicone lubricant on the components where needed.

Obtaining Tools and Accessories

You can obtain most of the cleaning chemicals and tools discussed in this chapter from an electronics supply house or even your local RadioShack. A company called Chemtronics specializes in chemicals for the computer and electronics industry. These and other companies that supply tools, chemicals, and other computer- and electronic-cleaning supplies are listed in the Vendor List on the DVD. With all these items on hand, you should be equipped for most preventive maintenance operations.

Cleaning Procedures

Before you clean your system, I recommend a partial disassembly. By *partial,* I mean taking out any items that can be easily removed without using tools. This would normally include the battery, any drives in removable bays, and any PC Cards. This may also include the hard drive in some systems as well. Finally, open the access doors on the sides, back, or base of the system as well. Because of the difficulty of opening the case on most laptops, I do not recommend a complete disassembly just for the purpose of cleaning. Once any easily accessible devices are removed and the access doors opened, use the canned air to blow out any dust from these areas.

Cleaning Connectors and Contacts

Cleaning the connectors and contacts in a system promotes reliable connections between devices. On a laptop system, the main connector you'll want to clean is that of the battery—both the contacts on the battery and the mating contacts in the system. If there is dirt or dust on the memory modules or sockets, you might want to remove the memory modules, clean the contacts, and then reinstall them. Also, if you disassemble the system and disconnect any flex-cables, it is recommended that you clean and treat the flex-cable contacts before reinserting them into their mating connectors.

To do this, first moisten the lint-free cleaning swabs in the cleaning solution. If you are using a spray, hold the swab away from the system and spray a small amount on the foam end until the solution starts to drip. Then use the swab to wipe the connectors and sockets. You might consider using Stabilant 22a contact enhancer on these terminals to prevent corrosion and ensure a good contact. Try to avoid touching any of the gold or tin contacts with your fingers, which will coat them with oils and debris that can cause problems later. Make sure the contacts are free of all finger oils and residue.

Cleaning the LCD and Case

To clean the exterior of your laptop system, use the following procedure:

Lightly moisten a soft lint-free cloth with either a 50-50 mixture of isopropyl alcohol and water, non-ammoniated glass cleaner, or pure water (hot water works best). Never spray liquid cleaner directly on the system, especially the display or keyboard.

Gently wipe the LCD panel with the moistened cloth and then follow with a dry cloth. Be sure the cloth is not wet enough to drip and that the LCD is completely dry when you're finished. Antistatic

LCD-cleaning cloths and Kimwipes are also acceptable alternatives. Do not use standard paper towels, which can scratch the LCD, or window cleaners with ammonia, which can damage or stain the LCD.

Note

Kimwipes are disposable 8.5- by 4.5-inch wipes, basically heavy-duty lint-free paper towels. They are a trademarked brand of Kimberly-Clark Corp., along with Kleenex, and are very popular in industrial, laboratory, and photographic use.

Cleaning the Keyboard

Keyboards are notorious for picking up dirt and garbage. If you ever look closely inside a used keyboard, you will be amazed at the junk you find in there! To keep the keyboard clean, I recommend periodically blowing out the dirt with a can of compressed air or sucking it out with a vacuum cleaner.

The best way to use the compressed air is to turn the system upside down and shoot the keyboard with a can of compressed air tilted back on an angle. This will blow out the dirt and debris that has accumulated inside the keyboard, allowing it to fall to the ground rather than into your system. If done regularly, this can prevent future problems with sticking keys or dirty keyswitches. If you are using a vacuum cleaner, you can leave the system in a normal orientation because the vacuum will suck the debris up and out without allowing it to fall deeper inside the system.

Once the dust and dirt are blown out of the keyboard, you can then clean any cosmetic dirt or stains from the keycaps. The best way to accomplish this is to wipe the keycaps with a soft cloth moistened in isopropyl alcohol cleaning solution and then follow with a dry cloth.

If a particular key is stuck or making intermittent contact, you'll want to soak or spray the faulty keyswitch with contact cleaner. This cannot be done with the keyboard mounted in the system because some of the cleaner may drip inside. To prevent that, before you attempt to clean the keyswitch, I recommend you remove the keyboard from the system. Consult your owner's manual (or maintenance manual if you have one) for the keyboard-removal procedure. Most laptops have keyboards that can be removed fairly easily. If you don't have a procedure for your system, use the sample procedure listed later in this chapter.

After the keyboard is removed, you can remove the keycap from the problem keyswitch and spray the cleaner into the switch. I usually do this over a sink so that the excess liquid doesn't drip onto the floor. Then replace the keycap, reinstall the keyboard, and test it to see whether the key works properly. If it doesn't, you may need to replace the keyboard with a new one. Normally, you cannot replace individual keyswitches. After that, periodic vacuuming or blowing out the keyboard with compressed air will go a long way toward preventing more serious problems with sticking keys and keyswitches.

Cleaning the TrackPoint or Touchpad

The TrackPoint or touchpad pointing devices used in laptops normally require very little or no maintenance. These devices are totally sealed and relatively immune to dirt or dust. Merely blow off the area around the TrackPoint with compressed air or wipe down the surface of the touchpad with a mild cleaning solution to remove oils and other deposits that have accumulated from handling them. If you have a TrackPoint and the cap is excessively stained or greasy, you can remove it and soak it in some cleaning solution. If the stain won't come out and/or the cap is excessively worn, it would be a good idea to simply replace the cap with a new one. Replacement TrackPoint caps are available in three different designs from a number of sources including Compu-Lock at www.compu-lock.com. Toshiba Accupoint caps can be obtained from any Toshiba Authorized Service Provider (ASP). To find the closest ASP, check with Toshiba at `http://pcsupport.toshiba.com`. Dell track stick caps can be ordered from Dell directly via its Customer Service department.

Hard Disk Maintenance

Certain preventive maintenance procedures protect your data and ensure that your hard disk works efficiently. Some of these procedures actually minimize wear and tear on your drive, which prolongs its life. Additionally, a higher level of data protection can be implemented by performing some simple commands periodically. These commands provide methods for backing up (and possibly later restoring) critical areas of the hard disk that, if damaged, would disable access to all your files.

Defragmenting Files

Over time, as you delete and save files to your hard disk, the files become fragmented. This means they are split into many noncontiguous areas on the disk. One of the best ways to protect both your hard disk and the data on it is to periodically defragment the files on the disk. This serves two purposes: One is that by ensuring that all the files are stored in contiguous sectors on the disk, head movement and drive "wear and tear" are minimized. This has the added benefit of improving the speed at which the drive retrieves files by reducing the head thrashing that occurs every time it accesses a fragmented file.

The second major benefit, and in my estimation the more important of the two, is that in the case of a disaster in which the file system is severely damaged, the data on the drive can usually be recovered much more easily if the files are contiguous. On the other hand, if the files are split up in many pieces across the drive, figuring out which pieces belong to which files is virtually impossible. For the purposes of data integrity and protection, I recommend defragmenting your hard disk drives on a monthly basis.

The three main functions in most defragmentation programs are as follows:

- File defragmentation
- File packing (free space consolidation)
- File sorting

Defragmentation is the basic function, but most other programs also add file packing. Packing the files is optional on some programs because it usually takes additional time to perform. This function packs the files at the beginning of the disk so that all free space is consolidated at the end of the disk. This feature minimizes future file fragmentation by eliminating any empty holes on the disk. Because all free space is consolidated into one large area, any new files written to the disk are capable of being written in a contiguous manner with no fragmentation.

The last function, file sorting (sometimes called *disk optimizing*), is not usually necessary and is performed as an option by many defragmenting programs. This function adds a tremendous amount of time to the operation and has little or no effect on the speed at which information is accessed later. It can be somewhat beneficial for disaster-recovery purposes because you will have an idea of which files came before or after other files if a disaster occurs. Not all defragmenting programs offer file sorting, and the extra time it takes is probably not worth any benefits you will receive. Other programs can sort the order in which files are listed in directories, which is a quick-and-easy operation compared to sorting the file listing (directory entries) on the disk.

Windows 9x/Me/2000/XP include a disk-defragmentation program with the operating system that you can use on any file system the OS supports. For older operating systems such as DOS, Windows 3.x, and some versions of NT, you must purchase a third-party defragmentation program.

The disk-defragmentation programs included with Windows are extremely slow and don't offer many options or features, so it is a good idea to purchase something better. Norton Utilities includes a disk defragmenter, as do many other utility packages. An excellent defrag program that works on all operating systems is VOPT by Golden Bow (www.vopt.com). It is one of the fastest and most efficient defragmenting programs on the market, and it is very inexpensive. See the Vendor List on the DVD for more information on these companies and their programs.

Windows Maintenance Wizard

Windows 98 and above include a Task Scheduler program that enables you to schedule programs for automatic execution at specified times. The Maintenance Wizard walks you through the steps of scheduling regular disk defragmentations, disk error scans, and deletions of unnecessary files. You can schedule these processes to execute during nonworking hours, so regular system activities are not disturbed.

Virus and Spyware Checking

Viruses and Sypware are a danger to any system, and making scans with antivirus and antispyware utilities a regular part of your preventive maintenance program is a good idea. Many aftermarket utility packages are available that scan for and remove viruses and sypware. No matter which of these programs you use, you should perform a scan periodically, especially before making hard-disk backups. This helps ensure that you catch any potential problem before it becomes a major catastrophe. In addition, selecting a product from a vendor that provides regular updates to the program's signatures is important. The signatures determine which viruses and sypware the software can detect and cure, and because new viruses and spyware are constantly being introduced, these updates are essential.

Tip

Because viruses and especially spyware are more dangerous and numerous than ever, it is a good idea to enable the automatic update feature found in most recent programs to keep your protection up to date. Even if you have a dial-up connection, it takes only a few minutes a day to get downloads. If you have a broadband connection, the latest protection is downloaded in just a few moments.

Maintenance Tools

To troubleshoot and repair laptop systems properly, you need a few basic tools. If you intend to troubleshoot and repair systems professionally, you may want to purchase many more specialized tools as well. These advanced tools enable you to more accurately diagnose problems and make jobs easier and faster. Here are the basic tools that should be in every troubleshooter's toolbox:

- Simple hand tools for basic disassembly and reassembly procedures, including a selection of flat-blade and Phillips screwdrivers (both medium and small sizes), tweezers, an IC extraction tool, and a parts grabber or hemostat. Most of these items are included in $10–$20 starter toolkits found at most computer stores. Although most of the same toolkits sold for conventional desktop systems will have these tools, for portable systems you may also need sets of smaller-sized flat-blade and Phillips screwdrivers and a set of small Torx drivers or Torx bits as well. For laptops, you may encounter Torx screws as small as T5, so consider purchasing a set including bits down to that size.

- Diagnostics software and hardware for testing components in a system.

- A multimeter that provides accurate measurements of voltage and resistance, as well as a continuity checker for testing cables and switches.

- Chemicals (such as contact cleaners), component freeze sprays, and compressed air for cleaning the system.
- Foam swabs, or lint-free cotton swabs if foam isn't available.
- Small nylon wire ties for "dressing" or organizing wires or small cables (such as internal Wi-Fi/Bluetooth antennas).

You may want to consider the following items, although they're not required for most work:

- Memory-testing machines (used to evaluate the operation of memory modules). Note these can be very expensive, on the order of $1,000 or more, but can be useful for professional shops or larger companies with a lot of systems to support.
- Serial and parallel loopback (or wrap) plugs to test serial and parallel ports.
- A network cable tester or scanner (many types with varying functionality are available, from simple loopback jacks to full-blown Time Domain Reflectometers).

These tools are discussed in more detail in the following sections.

Hand Tools

When you work with laptop PCs, the tools required for nearly all service operations are simple and inexpensive. You can carry most of the required tools in a small pouch. Even a top-of-the-line "master mechanics" set fits inside a briefcase-sized container. The cost of these toolkits ranges from about $20 for a small service kit to $500 for one of the briefcase-sized deluxe kits. Compare these costs with what might be necessary for an automotive technician. An automotive service technician normally has to spend $5,000–$10,000 or more for a complete set of tools. Not only are computer tools much less expensive, but I can tell you from experience that you don't get nearly as dirty working on computers as you do working on cars.

In this section, I'll cover the tools required to perform basic, board-level service on most systems. One of the best ways to start such a set of tools is to purchase a small kit sold especially for servicing computers and then augment this with a miniature screwdriver set. Note that the small screwdriver sets are often called "jeweler's" sets because they are commonly used in jewelry applications.

Figure 3.1 shows some of the basic tools you'll want to have at your disposal when working on laptop systems.

Note

Some tools aren't recommended as a separate purchase because they might be of limited use. However, they often come with these types of kits.

Most laptop systems use numerous small Phillips or Torx screws, so those drivers are the ones you'll be using most frequently. The screwdrivers that come in some standard tool sets may be too big, so you'll want to purchase a good set of miniature screwdrivers, or a set of miniature screwdriver bits and a handle. If slotted screws are used on a system you are working on, you need to be very careful because it is easy for the flat-blade screwdriver head to slip off and possibly damage the system.

Caution

When you're working in a cramped environment, such as the inside of a laptop, screwdrivers with magnetic tips can be a real convenience, especially for retrieving that screw you dropped into the case, as well as for holding a screw on the tip of the tool when inserting it into the threaded hole. However, although I have used these types of screwdrivers many times

(continues)

with no problems, you should be aware of the damage a magnetic field can cause to magnetic storage devices such as floppy disks. Laying the screwdriver on or near a floppy can damage the data on the disk. Fortunately, floppy disks aren't used that much anymore. Hard drives are shielded by a metal case; CD/DVD drives are not affected because they work optically; and memory and other chips are not affected by magnetic fields (unless they are magnitudes stronger than what you'll see in a hand tool).

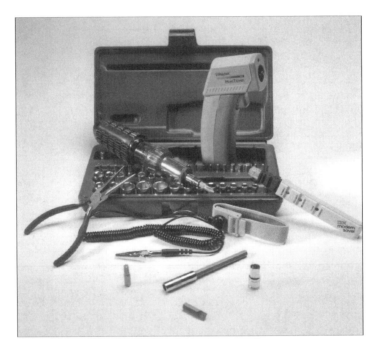

Figure 3.1   The basic tools you need to work on a laptop are shown here, although you might also need to obtain sets of smaller-sized flat-blade and Phillips screwdrivers and a set of small Torx drivers or Torx bits.

Chip-extraction tools, shown in Figure 3.2, are rarely needed to remove chips these days because memory chips are mounted on SIMMs or DIMMs, and processors use zero insertion force (ZIF) sockets (which are found in Pentium M and Pentium 4-M systems) or other user-friendly connectors; however, in some cases, they can be used as general-purpose prying or grabbing tools. The ZIF socket has a lever or screw lock that, when opened, releases the grip on the pins of the processor, enabling you to easily lift it out with your fingers.

That said, these tools can still be handy in current systems when used to pull out keyboard keys (even from integrated keyboards on a laptop system). In fact, for this role it works quite well. By placing the tool over a keycap on a keyboard and squeezing the tool so the hooks grab under the keycap on opposite sides, you can cleanly and effectively remove the keycap from the keyboard without damage. This technique works much better than trying to pry the caps off with a screwdriver, which often results in damaging them or sending them flying across the room.

Although I prefer magnetic tipped screwdrivers, the tweezers or parts grabber can be used to hold any small screws or jumper blocks that are difficult to hold in your hand. The parts grabber, shown in Figure 3.3, is especially useful when you're starting screws or when trying to retrieve one that has fallen into a nook or cranny inside the system. If you have dropped a screw inside and can't see it, you might try turning the system upside down and gently shaking it until the screw falls out.

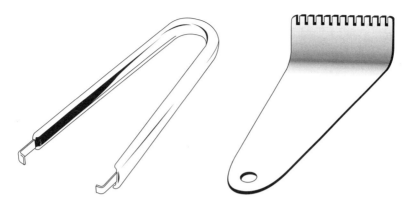

Figure 3.2   The chip extractor (left) was originally designed to remove individual RAM or ROM chips from a socket. An extractor such as the one on the right is used for extracting socketed processors—if the processor does not use a ZIF socket.

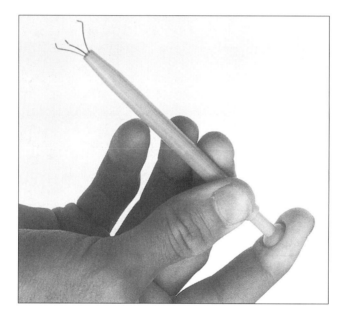

Figure 3.3   The parts grabber has three small metal prongs that can be extended to grab a part.

Finally, the Torx driver is a star-shaped driver that matches the special screws found in most systems (see Figure 3.4). Torx screws are vastly superior to other types of screws for computers because they offer greater grip, and the Torx driver is much less likely to slip. The most common cause of new circuit board failures is due to people using slotted screwdrivers and slipping off the screw head, scratching (and damaging) the motherboard. I never allow slotted screws or a standard flat-bladed screwdriver anywhere near the interior of my systems. You also can purchase tamperproof Torx drivers that can remove Torx screws with the tamper-resistant pin in the center of the screw. A tamperproof Torx driver has a hole drilled in it to allow clearance for the pin. Torx drivers come in a number of sizes, the most common being the T-10 and T-15. However, many laptops use smaller sizes from T-9 down through T-5. It is a good idea to have a set of miniature Torx drivers on hand when you're working on laptop systems.

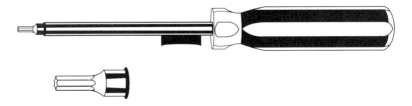

Figure 3.4 A Torx driver and bit.

Although a set of basic tools is useful, you should supplement your toolkit with some additional tools, such as the following:

- **Electrostatic discharge (ESD) protection kit, including wrist strap and mat (such as those from RadioShack or Jensen Tools)**—This kit prevents static damage to the components you are working on. The kit consists of a wrist strap with a ground wire and a specially conductive mat with its own ground wire. You also can get just the wrist strap or the antistatic mat separately. In areas where there is low humidity (or during certain seasons of the year), static charges are much more likely to build up as you move, increasing the need for ESD protection. A wrist strap is shown later in this chapter in Figure 3.5.

- **Needle-nose pliers and hemostats (curved and straight)**—These are great for gripping small items, setting jumpers, straightening bent pins, and so on.

- **Electric screwdriver, such as the Black & Decker VersaPak VP730 (www.blackanddecker.com)**—Combined with hex, Phillips, standard, and Torx bit sets, this tool really speeds up repetitive disassembly/assembly.

- **Flashlight**—Preferably a high-tech LED unit, such as those from www.longlight.com. This will allow you to see inside dark systems and will be easy on batteries.

- **Wire cutter or stripper**—This is useful for making or repairing cables or wiring. For example, you'd need these (along with a crimping tool) to make or repair 10BASE-T Ethernet cables using UTP cable and RJ-45 connectors.

- **Vise or clamp**—This is used to install connectors on cables, crimp cables to the shape you want, and hold parts during delicate operations. In addition to the vise, RadioShack sells a nifty "extra hands" device that has two movable arms with alligator clips on the end. This type of device is very useful for making cables or for other delicate operations during which an extra set of hands to hold something might be useful.

- **Markers, pens, and notepads**—These are for taking notes, marking cables, and so on.

- **Windows 98/98SE or Me startup floppy**—These disks have DOS 7.1 or 8.0 and real-mode CD-ROM/DVD drivers, which can be used to boot-test the system and possibly load other software.

- **Windows 2000/XP original (bootable) CD**—This disc can be used to boot-test the system from a CD-ROM/DVD drive, attempt system recovery, install the OS, or run other software. Microsoft also has a downloadable set of floppy disks (six disks for Windows XP) you can get from support.microsoft.com; however, most systems capable of running Windows 2000 or XP should be able to boot from the CD.

- **Diagnostics software**—This includes commercial, shareware, or freeware software for hardware verification and testing.

- **Nylon cable-ties**—These ties are used to help in routing and securing cables.

- **Digital pocket multimeter (such as those from RadioShack)**—This is used for checking power-supply voltages, connectors, and cables for continuity.

- **Cleaning swabs, canned air (dust blower), and contact cleaner chemicals, such as those from www.chemtronics.com, as well as contact enhancer chemicals, such as Stabilant 22a from www.stabilant.com**—These are used for cleaning, lubricating, and enhancing contacts on circuit boards and cable connections.

- **Data transfer cables and adapters**—These are used for quickly connecting two systems and transferring data from one system to another. This includes serial and parallel cables (often called Laplink, Interlink, or Direct Cable Connect cables), Ethernet crossover cables, as well as more specialized USB to Ethernet, USB to USB, or USB to parallel adapters.

- **2.5-inch ATA drive cables and adapters**—These are used for connecting 2.5-inch ATA drives to laptop or desktop systems for transferring or recovering data. This includes 44-pin (2.5-inch) ATA to 40-pin (3.5-inch) ATA ribbon cable/power adapters, 44-pin ATA to USB/FireWire adapters, or 2.5-inch USB/FireWire external drive enclosures.

- **External mouse, keyboard, and keyboard/mouse PS/2 "Y" adapter**—These are useful for operating a system where the internal keyboard or pointing device is defective or difficult to use. The "Y" adapter is required on most laptops to use an external PS/2 keyboard alone, or a PS/2 keyboard and mouse together.

- **USB-powered hub, USB/FireWire cable adapters**—This is useful for connecting external USB devices to a laptop, especially USB keyboards, mice, and external drives. The cable adapters and gender changers are recommended for connecting different types of USB and FireWire devices.

- **Spare screws, jumpers, standoffs, and so on**—These are used in case some go missing or are lost from the system you are working on.

- **Spare CR20xx lithium coin cell batteries**—These are used as the CMOS RAM battery in most laptop systems; therefore, it is a good idea to have a replacement or two on hand. While a number of different CR20xx models are available, most systems use the CR2032.

Safety

Before you begin working on a system, you should follow certain safety procedures. Some are to protect you; others are to protect the system you are working on. From a personal safety point of view, there really isn't that much danger in working on a laptop computer. Even if it is open with the power on, computers run on 20 volts or less internally, meaning there are no dangerous voltages present that are life threatening.

Before working on a laptop computer, you should unplug it from the wall. This is not really to protect you so much as it is to protect the system. Modern systems are always partially running—that is, as long as they are plugged in. Even if a system is off, standby voltages are still present. To prevent damage, it is recommended that the system be completely unplugged and the main power battery removed. If you accidentally turn the system all the way on, and plug in or remove a card or memory module, you can fry the card, module, or even the motherboard.

ESD Protection Tools

Electrostatic discharge (ESD) protection is another issue. While working on a PC, you should wear an ESD wrist strap, which is clipped to the chassis of the machine (see Figure 3.5). On a laptop, generally the best place to clip the cable is to one of the cable connector retention hex nuts adjacent to the external video connector on the system. This will ensure that you and the system remain at the same electrical potential and will prevent static electricity from damaging the system as you touch it. Some people feel that the system should be plugged in to provide an earth ground. Working on any system that is plugged in is not a good idea at all, as previously mentioned. No "earth" ground is necessary; all that is important is that you and the system remain at the same electrical potential, which is accomplished via the strap. Another issue for personal safety is to use a commercially available wrist strap rather than making your own. Commercially made wrist straps feature an internal 1 Meg ohm resistor designed to protect you. The resistor will ensure that you are not the best path to ground should you touch any "hot" wire.

When you remove components from the system, they should be placed on a special conductive anti-static mat, which is also a part of any good ESD protection kit. The mat will also be connected via a wire and clip to the system chassis. Any components removed from the system, especially items such as the processor, motherboard, adapter cards, and disk drives, should be placed on the mat. The connection between you, the mat, and the chassis will prevent any static discharges from damaging the components.

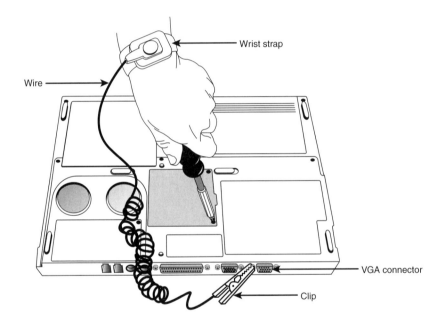

Figure 3.5   A typical ESD wrist strap; clip the end to a metallic surface in the chassis.

Note

It is possible (but not recommended) to work without an ESD protection kit if you're disciplined and careful about working on systems. If you don't have an ESD kit available, you can discharge yourself by touching any exposed metal on the chassis or case. In a laptop are exposed metal brackets and screws you could touch, and in most cases, even if the entire chassis is plastic, it will be coated with metallic paint on the inside, which acts as a shield for electromagnetic interference.

Again, also be sure that any system you are working on is unplugged. Laptop systems should also have the main battery removed. Many systems today continue to feed power to the motherboard through the motherboard power connection whenever the computer is plugged in, even when the power switch is turned off. Working inside a laptop that is still connected to a power source, or with a main battery installed, can be very dangerous.

The ESD kits, as well as all the other tools (and much more), are available from a variety of tool vendors. Specialized Products Company and Jensen Tools are two of the most popular vendors of computer and electronic tools and service equipment. Their catalogs show an extensive selection of very high quality tools. (These companies and several others are listed in the Vendor List on the CD.) With a simple set of hand tools, you will be equipped for nearly every computer repair or installation situation. The total cost of these tools should be less than $150, which is not much considering the capabilities they provide.

A Word About Hardware

This section discusses some problems you might encounter with the hardware (screws, nuts, bolts, and so on) used in assembling a system.

Types of Hardware

One of the biggest aggravations you encounter in dealing with various systems is the different hardware types and designs that hold the units together.

Laptop and portable systems are notorious for using many more screws than desktop systems in their assembly, and the screws are often of several different types. For example, a typical laptop is assembled with up to 85 or more screws of up to eight or more different types! Most systems use a variety of small Phillips, Torx, tamperproof Torx, and hex-head screws. A Torx screw has a star-shaped hole driven by the correct-size Torx driver. These drivers carry size designations from T-5 through T-40, although only sizes T-5 through T-10 are commonly used in laptops.

A variation on the Torx screw is the tamperproof Torx screw found in some systems. These screws are identical to the regular Torx screws, except that a pin sticks up from the middle of the star-shape hole in the screw. This pin prevents the standard Torx driver from entering the hole to grip the screw; a special tamperproof driver with a corresponding hole for the pin is required.

Many manufacturers also use the more standard slotted-head and Phillips-head screws. Slotted-head screws should almost *never* be used in a computer, because it is too easy for the screwdriver to slip, thus damaging a board. Using tools on these screws is relatively easy, but tools do not grip these fasteners as well as they do hexagonal head and Torx screws. In addition, the heads can be stripped more easily than the other types. Extremely cheap versions tend to lose bits of metal as they're turned with a driver, and the metal bits can fall onto the motherboard. Stay away from cheap fasteners whenever possible; the headaches of dealing with stripped screws aren't worth it.

English Versus Metric

Another area of aggravation with hardware is the fact that two types of thread systems exist: English and metric. Most laptop systems use metric fasteners.

Tip

Before you discard an obsolete computer, remove the screws and other reusable parts, such as cover plates, jumper blocks, and so on. Label the bag or container with the name and model of the computer to help you more easily determine where else you can use the parts later.

Caution

Some screws in a system can be length-critical, especially screws used to retain hard disk drives. You can destroy some hard disks by using a mounting screw that's too long; the screw can puncture or dent the sealed disk chamber when you install the drive and fully tighten the screw. When you install a new drive in a system, always make a trial fit of the hardware to see how far the screws can be inserted into the drive before they interfere with its internal components. When in doubt, the drive manufacturer's OEM documentation will tell you precisely which screws are required and how long they should be. Most drives sold at retail include correct-length mounting screws, but OEM drives usually don't include screws or other hardware.

Test Equipment

In some cases, you must use specialized devices to test a system board or component. This test equipment is not expensive or difficult to use, but it can add much to your troubleshooting abilities.

Electrical Testing Equipment

I consider a voltmeter to be required gear for proper system testing. A multimeter can serve many purposes, including checking for voltage signals at various points in a system, testing the output of the power supply, and checking for continuity in a circuit or cable. An outlet tester is an invaluable accessory that can check the electrical outlet for proper wiring. This capability is useful if you believe the problem lies outside the computer system.

Loopback Connectors (Wrap Plugs)

For diagnosing serial- and parallel-port problems, you need loopback connectors (also called *wrap plugs*), which are used to circulate, or *wrap*, signals (see Figure 3.6). The plugs enable the serial or parallel port to send data to itself for diagnostic purposes.

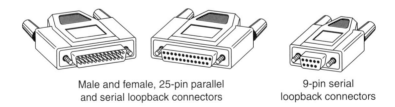

Male and female, 25-pin parallel   9-pin serial
and serial loopback connectors   loopback connectors

Figure 3.6   Typical wrap plugs, including 25-pin and 9-pin serial and 25-pin parallel versions.

Various types of loopback connectors are available. To accommodate all the ports you might encounter, you need one for the 9-pin serial port and one for the 25-pin parallel port. It is highly unlikely that a laptop will have a 25-pin serial port, although these ports are sometimes found on docking stations or port replicators. Many companies, including IBM, sell the plugs separately, but be aware that you also need diagnostic software that can use them. Some diagnostic software products, such as Micro 2000's Micro-Scope, include loopback connectors with the product, or you can purchase them as an option for about $30 a set. Note that there are some variations on how loopback connectors can be made, and not all versions work properly with all diagnostic software. It is best to use the loopback connectors recommended by the diagnostic software you will be using.

IBM sells a special combination plug that includes all three possible connector types in one compact unit. The device costs about the same as a normal set of wrap plugs. If you're handy, you can even make your own wrap plugs for testing. I include wiring diagrams for the three types of wrap plugs in

Chapter 8, "Expansion Card Buses." In that chapter, you also will find a detailed discussion of serial and parallel ports.

Besides simple loopback connectors, you also might want to have a breakout box for your toolkit. A breakout box is a DB25 connector device that enables you to make custom temporary cables or even to monitor signals on a cable. For most serial or parallel port troubleshooting uses, a "mini" breakout box works well and is inexpensive.

Meters

Some troubleshooting procedures require that you measure voltage and resistance. You take these measurements by using a handheld digital multimeter (DMM). The meter can be an analog device (using an actual meter) or a digital-readout device. The DMM has a pair of wires called *test leads* or *probes*. The test leads make the connections so that you can take readings. Depending on the meter's setting, the probes measure electrical resistance, direct current (DC) voltage, or alternating current (AC) voltage. Figure 3.7 shows a typical DMM being used to test the AC adapter on a typical laptop. In this particular example, I am testing an AC adapter that is rated for 15V output. As you can see, the DMM is reading 15.30V. The normal tolerance for voltage readings is plus or minus 5%, which in this case would be 14.25V through 15.75V. Therefore, the reading is well within that specification, meaning the adapter checks out as good.

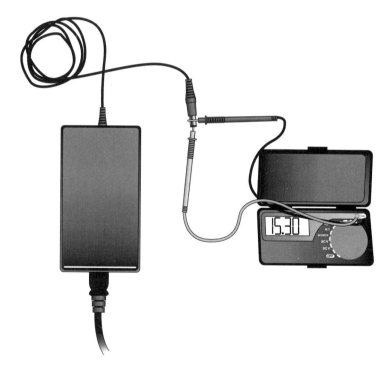

Figure 3.7   A typical digital multimeter tests a laptop AC adapter.

Most newer meters are autoranging, which means they automatically select the appropriate measurement range when you take a reading. All you have to do is set the meter properly to read DC volts or AC volts. All readings will normally be DC. The only time you'll measure AC voltage is when checking wall outlets.

In some meters, each measurement setting has several ranges of operation. DC voltage, for example, usually can be read in several scales, to a maximum of 200 millivolts (mV), 2V, 20V, 200V, and 1,000V. Because computers use +3.3V, +5V, and +12V for internal operations, and up to 20V for things like batteries and AC adapters, you should use the 20V scale for making your measurements. Making these measurements on the 200mV or 2V scale could "peg the meter" and possibly damage it because the voltage would be much higher than expected. Using the 200V or 1,000V scale works, but the readings at 5V and 12V are so small in proportion to the maximum that accuracy is low.

If you are taking a measurement and are unsure of the actual voltage, start at the highest scale and work your way down. Most of the better meters have an autoranging capability; the meter automatically selects the best range for any measurement. This type of meter is much easier to operate. You simply set the meter to the type of reading you want, such as DC volts, and attach the probes to the signal source. The meter selects the correct voltage range and displays the value. Because of their design, these types of meters always have a digital display rather than a meter needle.

Caution

Whenever you are using a multimeter to test any voltage that could potentially be 50V or above (such as AC wall socket voltage), always use one hand to do the testing, not two. Either clip one lead to one of the sources and probe with the other, or hold both leads in one hand.

If you hold a lead in each hand and accidentally slip, you can very easily become a circuit, allowing power to conduct or flow through you. When power flows from arm to arm, the path of the current is directly across the heart. The heart muscle tends to quit working when subjected to high voltages. It's funny that way.

I prefer the small digital meters. You can buy them for only slightly more than the analog style, and they're extremely accurate and much safer for digital circuits. Some of these meters are not much bigger than a cassette tape; they fit in a shirt pocket. RadioShack sells a good unit in the $25 price range; the meter (refer to Figure 3.7) is a half-inch thick, weighs 3 1/2 ounces, and is digital and autoranging, as well. This type of meter works well for most, if not all, computer troubleshooting and test uses.

Caution

You should be aware that many analog meters can be dangerous to digital circuits. Larger analog meters often use a 9V battery to power the meter for resistance measurements. If you use this type of meter to measure resistance on some digital circuits, you can damage the electronics because you essentially are injecting 9V into the circuit. The digital meters universally run on 3V–5V or less.

Logic Probes and Logic Pulsers

A logic probe can be useful for diagnosing problems in digital circuits (see Figure 3.8). In a digital circuit, a signal is represented as either high (+5V) or low (0V). Because these signals are present for only a short time (measured in millionths of a second) or oscillate (switch on and off) rapidly, a simple voltmeter is useless. A logic probe is designed to display these signal conditions easily.

Logic probes are especially useful for troubleshooting a dead system. By using the probe, you can determine whether the basic clock circuitry is operating and whether other signals necessary for system operation are present. In some cases, a probe can help you cross-check the signals at each pin on an integrated circuit chip. You can compare the signals present at each pin with the signals a known-good chip of the same type would show—a comparison that is helpful in isolating a failed component. Logic probes also can be useful for troubleshooting some disk drive problems by enabling you to test the signals present on the interface cable or drive-logic board.

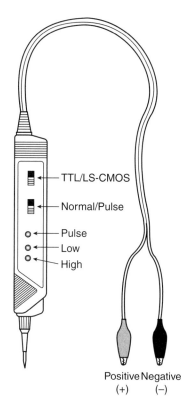

Figure 3.8   A typical logic probe.

A companion tool to the probe is the *logic pulser*, which is designed to test circuit reaction by delivering a logical high (+5V) pulse into a circuit, usually lasting from 1 1/2 to 10 millionths of a second. Compare the reaction with that of a known-functional circuit. This type of device normally is used much less frequently than a logic probe, but in some cases it can be helpful for testing a circuit.

Outlet (Receptacle) Testers

Outlet testers (also called receptacle testers) are very useful test tools. These simple, inexpensive devices, sold in hardware stores, test electrical outlets. You simply plug in the device, and three LEDs light up in various combinations, indicating whether the outlet is wired correctly (see Figure 3.9).

Although you might think that badly wired outlets would be a rare problem, I have seen a large number of installations in which the outlets were wired incorrectly. Most of the time, the problem is in the ground wire. An improperly wired outlet can result in unstable system operation, such as random parity checks and lockups. With an improper ground circuit, currents can begin flowing on the electrical ground circuits in the system. Because the system uses the voltage on the ground circuits as a comparative signal to determine whether bits are 0 or 1, a floating ground can cause data errors in the system.

Caution

Even if you use a surge protector, it will not protect your system from an improperly wired outlet. Therefore, you still should use an outlet tester to ensure your outlet is computer friendly.

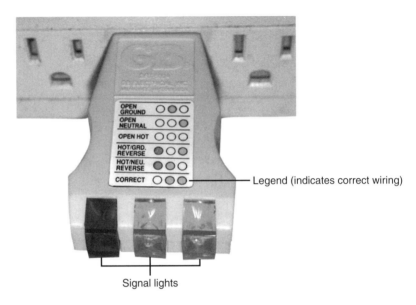

Figure 3.9   A typical outlet/receptacle tester.

Once, while running one of my PC troubleshooting seminars, I used a system that I literally could not approach without locking it up. Whenever I walked past the system, the electrostatic field generated by my body interfered with the system and the PC locked up, displaying a parity-check error message. The problem was that the hotel at which I was giving the seminar was very old and had no grounded outlets in the room. The only way I could prevent the system from locking up was to run the class in my stocking feet because my leather-soled shoes were generating the static charge.

Other symptoms of bad ground wiring in electrical outlets are continual electrical shocks when you touch the case or chassis of the system. These shocks indicate that voltages are flowing where they should not be. This problem also can be caused by bad or improper grounds within the system. By using the simple outlet tester, you can quickly determine whether the outlet is at fault.

If you just walk up to a system and receive an initial shock, it's probably only static electricity. Touch the chassis again without moving your feet. If you receive another shock, something is very wrong. In this case, the ground wire actually has voltage applied to it. You should check the outlet with an outlet/receptacle tester, and if it fails, have a professional electrician check the outlet immediately. If the outlet checks out okay, then the power supply inside the PC is probably failing (even though the system may seem to be otherwise running normally); it should be replaced.

Although I recommend using an outlet/receptacle tester, if you don't have one handy, it is possible to test an outlet using a multimeter. First, remember to hold both leads in one hand. Test from one blade hole to another. This should read between 110V and 125V, depending on the electrical service in the area. Then check from each blade to the ground (the round hole). One blade hole, the smaller one, should show a voltage almost identical to the one you got from the blade hole–to–blade hole test. The larger blade hole when measured to ground should show less than 0.5V.

Because ground and neutral are supposed to be tied together at the electrical panel, a large difference in these readings indicates that they are not tied together. However, small differences can be accounted for by current from other outlets down the line flowing on the neutral, when there isn't any on the ground.

If you don't get the results you expect, call an electrician to test the outlets for you. More weird computer problems are caused by improper grounding and other power problems than people like to believe.

Special Tools for the Enthusiast

All the tools described so far are commonly used by most technicians. However, a few additional tools do exist that a true computer enthusiast might want to have.

Electric Screwdriver

Perhaps the most useful tool I use is an electric screwdriver. It enables me to disassemble and reassemble a computer in record time and makes the job not only faster but easier as well. I like the type with a clutch you can use to set how tight it will make the screws before slipping; such a clutch makes it even faster to use. If you use the driver frequently, it makes sense to use the type with replaceable, rechargeable batteries, so when one battery dies, you can quickly replace it with a fresh one.

Caution

Note that using an electric screwdriver when installing circuit boards can be dangerous because the bit can easily slip off the screw and damage the board. A telltale series of swirling scratches near the screw holes on the board can be the result, for which most manufacturers rightfully deny a warranty claim. Be especially careful when using an electric screwdriver on Phillips-head screws because when the screw is either fully loose or fully tight, an electric screwdriver tip will continue rotating and tend to walk out of the screw. Torx-head or hex-head screws are less likely to allow this to happen, but care should be taken when using an electric screwdriver on them as well.

With the electric screwdriver, I recommend getting a complete set of English and metric nut driver tips as well as various sizes of Torx, flat-head, and Phillips-head screwdriver tips.

Tamperproof Torx Bits

As mentioned earlier, many laptop systems as well as devices such as power supplies and monitors are held together with tamperproof Torx screws. Tamperproof Torx driver sets are available from any good electronics tool supplier.

Temperature Probe

Determining the interior temperature of a laptop is often useful when diagnosing whether heat-related issues are causing problems. This requires some way of measuring the temperature inside the unit as well as the ambient temperature outside the system. The simplest and best tools I've found for the job are the digital thermometers sold at most auto parts stores for automobile use. They are designed to read the temperature inside and outside the car and normally come with an internal sensor, as well as one at the end of a length of wire.

With this type of probe, you can run the wired sensor inside the case (if it is metal, make sure it does not directly touch any exposed circuits where it might cause a short) with the wires slipped through a crack in the case or out one of the drive bays. Another option without opening the system is to clip the sensor to the exhaust vents to measure the air temperature exiting the system. Then, with the system running, you can take the internal temperature as well as read the room's ambient temperature. Many chips in the system can run at extremely high temperatures. For example, the Pentium 4-M is rated for a maximum die temperature of 100°C (212°F) and will automatically shut down if it reaches 135°C (275°F)! However the internal air temperature should be much less. Normally, internal air temperature should be 113°F (45°C) or less. If your system is running above that temperature, the chips will be running much hotter, and problems can be expected. Probing the temperature with a device such as this enables you to determine whether overheating might be the cause of lockups or other problems you may be having.

Infrared Thermometer

Another useful temperature tool is a noncontact infrared (IR) thermometer, which is a special type of sensor that can measure the temperature of an object without physically touching it (see Figure 3.10). You can take the temperature reading of an object in seconds by merely pointing the handheld device at the object you want to measure and pulling a trigger.

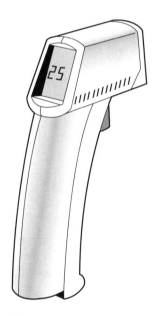

Figure 3.10   A noncontact infrared thermometer.

An IR thermometer works by capturing the infrared energy naturally emitted from all objects warmer than absolute zero (0° Kelvin or –459°F). Infrared energy is a part of the electromagnetic spectrum with a frequency below that of visible light, which means it is invisible to the human eye. Infrared wavelengths are between 0.7 microns and 1000 microns (millionths of a meter), although infrared thermometers typically measure radiation in the range 0.7–14 microns.

Because IR thermometers can measure the temperature of objects without touching them, they are ideal for measuring component temperatures directly—especially the temperature of the CPU heatsink. Unfortunately, most laptops are not designed to be powered on while partially disassembled, and in some cases the normal airflow will be disrupted enough to cause overheating problems. Still, you can use the IR thermometer to measure any hot spots on the surface of the system. By merely pointing the device at the place you wish to measure and pulling the trigger, you can get a very accurate measurement in about 1 second. To enable more accuracy in positioning, many IR thermometers incorporate a laser pointer, which is used to aim the device.

IR thermometers are designed to measure IR radiation from a device; they can't be used to measure air temperature. The sensors are specifically designed so that the air between the sensor and target does not affect the temperature measurement.

Although several IR thermometers are available on the market, I use and recommend the Raytek (www.raytek.com) MiniTemp series, which consists of the MT2 and MT4. Both units are identical, but the MT4 includes a laser pointer for aiming. The MT2 and MT4 are capable of measuring temperatures between 0° and 500°F (–18°–260°C) in one-half of a second with an accuracy of about plus or minus 3°F (2°C). They cost $80–$100 and are available from NAPA Auto Parts stores (these devices have many uses in automotive testing as well) and other tool outlets.

Upgrading and Repairing Laptops

From a technical standpoint, many of the components used in portable systems are similar to those in desktop computers. However, in many ways they are also different. Portable or laptop systems are in many ways less upgradeable or repairable than desktop systems, mainly because of the lack of standard form factors for cases/chassis, motherboards, keyboards, displays, and even batteries. They are also highly integrated, meaning functions that might be replaceable adapter cards in a desktop system (such as video, for example) are built in to the motherboard of a laptop system. However, despite these challenges, in some ways a laptop system can actually be *easier* to upgrade than a desktop because laptops often use modular bay storage devices that eliminate the need for ribbon cables, mounting rails, and separate electrical connections. Memory, hard disks, and Mini PCI slots are often accessible through easy-to-open access panels, making upgrades of these devices easy without disassembling the system. Therefore, common tasks such as adding memory, upgrading a hard drive, and upgrading an optical drive (on models with modular drive bays) can often be accomplished in seconds. Adding other interfaces, such as Ethernet, 802.11a/b/g Wi-Fi wireless, USB 2.0, and IEEE 1394 (FireWire/i.LINK), can be easily accomplished via plug-in PC Cards.

The problem with replacing other components in portables is that the hardware tends to be much less generic than it is in desktops. The exceptions are for PC Cards (which are interchangeable by definition), memory (on newer systems), and in some cases, hard drives. Purchasing a component that is not specifically intended for use in your exact system model can often be risky.

In some cases, these compatibility problems are a matter of simple logistics. Portable system manufacturers jam a great deal of machinery into a very small case, and sometimes a new device just will not fit in the space left by the old one. This is particularly true of devices that must be accessible from the outside of the case, such as CD-ROM and floppy drives. Keyboards and monitors, the most easily replaceable of desktop components, are so completely integrated into the case of a laptop system that they can normally be replaced only with specific parts from the original manufacturer.

In other cases, your upgrade path might be deliberately limited by the options available in the system BIOS. For example, depending on the BIOS date or revision, you might be limited in drive capacity, the same as desktop systems. Fortunately, most use a flash ROM BIOS that can easily be updated—that is, if the system manufacturer makes such updates available. When shopping for a portable system, you should check with the manufacturer to see whether it has a support website with BIOS updates, drivers, and any accessory or utility programs necessary to support and maintain the system. A lack of BIOS or driver updates can prevent you from moving to a newer operating system in the future, or at least make such a move difficult.

Most of the time, components for portable systems are sold by referencing the system model number, even when third parties are involved. If you look through a catalog for desktop memory, for example, you see parts listed generically by attributes such as chip speed, form factor, and parity/nonparity. The memory listings for portable systems, on the other hand, most likely consist of a series of systems manufacturers' names and model numbers, plus the amount of memory in the module. This has improved somewhat, with most modern laptops using industry-standard SODIMMs (small outline dual inline memory modules) instead of proprietary modules.

There are always exceptions to the rule, of course. However, purchasing compatible components that fit together properly is certainly more of a challenge for a portable system than it is for a desktop system. Table 3.3 explains which laptop system components can be upgraded.

Table 3.3   Upgradeable Laptop System Components

Component	Upgradeable	Notes
Motherboard	No	Nonstandard form factors prevent internal upgrades.
CPU	Yes	Installing a faster CPU of the same type and model is usually possible; however, there can be limitations due to voltage, thermal, and/or BIOS support issues, and clock speed increases will normally be small.
Memory	Yes	Normally, only one or two SIMM/DIMM sockets are available. You may need to remove lower-capacity existing modules to upgrade.
Video adapter/chipset	No	Video is integrated into a nonupgradeable motherboard.
Video display	No[1]	Nonstandard form factors and connections prevent internal upgrades.
Keyboard/pointing device	No[2]	Nonstandard form factors and connections prevent internal upgrades.
Hard disk	Yes	Older systems might not have BIOS support for drives larger than 8.4GB. Many systems are limited to 9.5mm- or 12.5mm-thick drives. Drive trays or caddies are often required for installation.
Removable-media drives (floppy, CD/DVD, CD-RW/DVD+-RW)	Yes	Install these internally via modular bays or use externall USB or IEEE 1394 (FireWire/i.LINK) drives.
USB, IEEE 1394 (FireWire/ i.LINK), serial (RS-232), parallel (IEEE 1284), SCSI, and so on	Yes	Install these via PC Card/CardBus or ExpressCard adapters.
10/100/1000Mbps Ethernet LAN	Yes	Install this via a PC Card or CardBus adapters.
Wireless 802.11a/b/g (Wi-Fi), Bluetooth	Yes	Install these via PC Card, CardBus, Mini PCI (internal) cards, or mobile daughter cards (MDCs). Internal cards may require preinstalled antennas.

1. *It is normally possible to connect an external display and use it in lieu of or in addition to the existing internal display.*

2. *It is normally possible to connect an external keyboard and/or pointing device to use in lieu of or in addition to the existing internal devices.*

System Disassembly

Most laptop systems are more difficult to disassemble than desktop systems. Laptop systems typically have many more screws than desktops, and the screws come in a number of different sizes and styles, and they are often hidden under stickers or covers. The chassis covers often feature thin plastic parts that interlock and can be tricky to separate without damage. Unlike desktop systems, which are substantially similar internally, laptop systems can vary greatly from manufacturer to manufacturer, and even from model to model. For this reason, it really helps to have specific documentation on disassembly/reassembly from the system manufacturer.

System Components

Figure 3.11 shows the components that make up a typical modern laptop system. Note that most modern manufacturers refer to all their laptop models as *notebooks*. The terms *laptop* and *notebook* mean the same thing with respect to portable computers, and these terms can be used interchangeably.

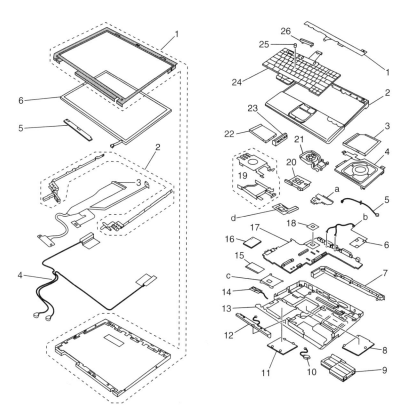

Figure 3.11 The components found in a typical laptop system; the ThinkPad R40 is used in this example.

LCD:

1	LCD bezel/rear cover
2	LCD hinge/bracket with antenna
3	LCD cable
4	Wi-Fi antenna
5	LCD inverter/LED card
6	LCD panel

System:

1	Keyboard bezel middle cover		16	802.11a/b Wi-Fi wireless card
2	Keyboard bezel upper case		17	Motherboard
3	Optical drive (UltraBay Plus CD/DVD)		18	CPU (Pentium M processor)
4	UltraBay Plus guide rail		19	Hard disk guide rails
5	Microphone cable		20	PC Card/CardBus slot
6	Communications daughter card (CDC) Bluetooth/modem		21	CPU heatsink/fan
7	I/O bracket		22	Hard disk drive with tray
8	Mini PCI access door		23	Hard disk drive access cover
9	Main battery (Li-ion)		24	Keyboard
10	Backup (CMOS) battery		25	TrackPoint cap
11	DIMM access door		26	Hinge cap
12	Speakers		a	Communications daughter card (CDC) plate
13	Lower case		b	Modem cable
14	Bluetooth antenna		c	Motherboard chipset heatsink
15	DDR SODIMM (double data rate small outline dual inline memory module)		d	Video chipset heatsink

Documentation is extremely important for laptop systems, due to their inherently proprietary nature. One reason I like the ThinkPad systems is that the hardware maintenance manuals, service and troubleshooting guides, and technical reference and user manuals for all ThinkPad systems are available on the ThinkPad website. These documents include complete disassembly and reassembly instructions and a complete parts list, including detailed exploded diagrams and part numbers. Lenovo (formerly IBM) offers unparalleled documentation for its systems, which makes working on them a relative pleasure. The detailed service manuals also provide the information needed to accomplish component replacements and upgrades, which would be daunting on other systems lacking this information.

Dell is another standout, providing detailed service manuals available for download from its website for all its laptop systems. In fact, the unfortunate reality is that currently the only laptop system manufacturers that do make service manuals available to end users are Lenovo (IBM) and Dell! That is perhaps one of the biggest reasons that those two manufacturers are among my favorites when it comes to laptops.

Toshiba used to make its service manuals available for purchase in printed form, but in the past few years Toshiba has changed its policy and its service manuals are now available to Toshiba-authorized dealers only. The good thing is that in most cases, if you purchase a repair or replacement part from one of the premier Toshiba Authorized Service Providers (ASPs), the ASP will include copies of the relevant pages from the service manual describing in detail the procedure for removing the old part and installing the new one in the system.

Most if not all other laptop system manufacturers do not provide service manuals for their systems, which I consider to be a major drawback. Virtually all of them do provide user manuals, which sometimes include simple troubleshooting or maintenance procedures, but these are not at the same level of a true service manual. Before you purchase a laptop system, I highly recommend you check to see what type of documentation is available. I normally make a point to avoid any systems for which I can't get detailed service or technical information from the manufacturer, because those manuals make future repairs and upgrades much easier.

In searching for documentation and spare parts for a system, I usually try to go direct to the manufacturer. This has led me to discover an interesting "secret" of the laptop business that isn't often discussed—the fact that most of the well-known laptop brands you may be familiar with are actually built by a handful of manufacturers located in Taiwan, including companies such as Quanta (www.quantatw.com), Compal (www.compal.com), Acer (global.acer.com), and others. These companies don't sell systems under their own names; instead, they design and manufacture them for other companies under contract. In fact, according to the Market Intelligence Center (MIC), Quanta and Compal were the number-one and number-two (respectively) laptop manufacturers in the world in 2002, followed by Toshiba and IBM. For me, that was a bit of a shock because Toshiba had been the largest laptop manufacturer every year since laptops were invented, until both Quanta and Compal out-sold Toshiba in 2001. Quanta makes laptops for Dell, HP, Compaq, eMachines, Best Buy, and Apple, among many other companies. Dell also purchases laptops from Compal and Acer (it isn't tied to one supplier). Now you know why Dell's different model lines look so different; they were designed and made by different companies. The contract manufacturing by companies such as Quanta and Compal is the main reason you see so many different brands of laptop systems that seem to look identical to each other. This stands to reason because they were actually made by the same company, one whose name can't be found on any of its systems. One potential drawback of this is that it is difficult for some companies to support the systems they sell, because in reality they didn't make them and may not have direct access to the parts and manufacturing.

Note

If you can figure out who really made your system and locate that company on the Web, in some cases you'll find more detailed information or can get newer drivers and BIOS updates direct from that manufacturer. If you don't know the actual manufacturer of your system and the vendor doesn't provide support, you may have difficulty tracking down repairs and spare parts for your system.

Recording Physical Configuration

While you are disassembling a laptop system, you should record the settings and configurations of each component, including any jumper and switch settings, ribbon or flex-cable orientations and placement, ground-wire locations, Wi-Fi/Bluetooth antenna locations, and even adapter board placement. Keep a notepad handy for recording these items. When it comes time to reassemble the system, these notes will prove valuable in helping you get everything back together correctly. It is also a good idea to use a digital camera to take close-up pictures of various parts of the system before you remove them. These pictures will be very helpful as a reference during reassembly.

You should mark or record what each cable was plugged into and its proper orientation. Ribbon and flex-cables usually have an odd-colored (red, green, blue, or black) wire at one end that indicates pin 1. There might also be a mark on the connector, such as a triangle or even the number 1. The devices the cables are plugged into are also marked in some way to indicate the orientation of pin 1. Often, a dot appears next to the pin-1 side of the connector, or a 1 or other mark might appear.

Although cable orientation and placement seem to be very simple, we rarely get through one of my computer troubleshooting seminars without at least some people having cable-connection problems. Fortunately, in most cases (except for power cables), plugging any of the ribbon or flex-cables inside the system backward rarely causes any permanent damage.

However, plugging in or installing the CMOS battery backward can damage the CMOS chip, which usually is soldered onto the motherboard; in such a case, the motherboard must be replaced.

System Disassembly

Although laptop systems aren't as standardized as most desktop systems with respect to motherboard form factors and such, there is still a lot of commonality among modern laptop systems. They are a bit trickier to disassemble, upgrade or repair, and then reassemble, but it's nothing you can't handle if you use some common sense, experience, and a little care. Of course, it helps to have a service or maintenance manual with detailed step-by-step procedures, but unfortunately, as mentioned earlier, that type of documentation is normally available for IBM and Dell systems, but not from most other manufacturers.

As an example of a typically constructed laptop system, I'm going to go through the steps required to disassemble a ThinkPad R40. This is a Pentium M processor system that optionally uses Intel's Centrino mobile technology. You've already seen an exploded diagram of the system showing all the components (refer to Figure 3.11); now you'll see how a system like this is assembled. We'll start with the removable devices first and then break out the tools for the harder-to-reach internal components.

Tip

As another point of reference, the video included with this book shows the disassembly of a system different from the one shown here. I recommend you review the steps shown here as well as in the video to get an idea of how different laptops are taken apart and reassembled. That way, even if you don't have a factory service manual for your own system, you should be able to see by example how it can be disassembled and reassembled.

Main Battery

Let's start with the main battery. To remove the battery, flip the system over, pull the battery latch away from the battery with your index finger, and lift the battery out (see Figure 3.12).

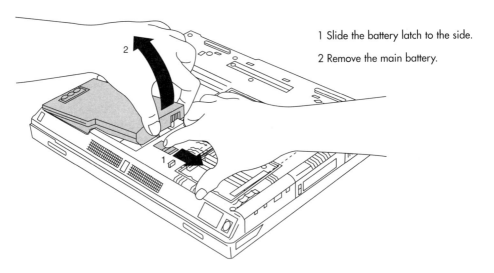

1 Slide the battery latch to the side.

2 Remove the main battery.

Figure 3.12 Removing the main battery.

UltraBay Plus Devices

Modular bays are used in many modern laptop systems. This system has what is called an *UltraBay Plus bay* on the right side. It allows for easy swapping in and out of many modular bay devices, including the following:

- CD-ROM
- DVD-ROM
- CD-RW/DVD-ROM combo
- DVD+-R/RW
- 1.44MB floppy
- Second HDD adapter
- Second battery
- Numeric keypad

All these devices are removed and installed in the same manner. To remove a modular bay device, slide the latch to the side, causing a lever to pop out. Grasp the lever and slide the device out of the bay (see Figure 3.13).

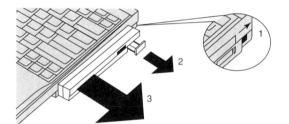

1 Release the modular bay latch.

2 Grasp the modular bay lever.

3 Pull out the modular bay device.

Figure 3.13   Removing a modular bay device.

Hard Disk

The hard disk in most modern laptop systems is a 2.5-inch form factor unit that is normally 9.5mm thick. To remove the drive, take out the drive cover retainer screw locking the drive cover, as shown in Figure 3.14.

Now grasp the cover and slide the drive and cover out of the system together. Then you can disengage the cover from the drive by bending the cover latches sideways and pulling the cover away from the drive (see Figure 3.15).

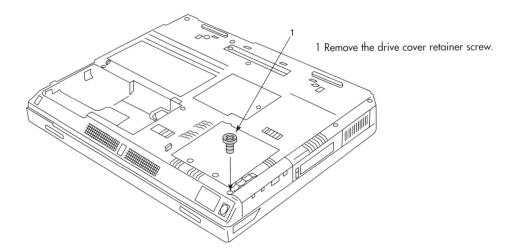

1 Remove the drive cover retainer screw.

Figure 3.14 Removing the hard disk drive cover retainer.

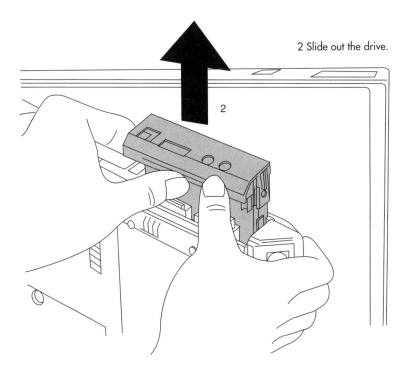

2 Slide out the drive.

Figure 3.15 Removing the hard disk drive.

Memory Modules (SODIMMs)

Most modern laptop systems use memory in 200-pin DDR SODIMM (double data rate small outline dual inline memory module) form. These are the equivalent of the larger 184-pin DDR DIMMs (dual inline memory modules) used in desktop systems. To remove the SODIMMs, merely take out the screws holding the memory-access door (on the bottom of the system) in place and then take off the door. Next, bend the latches holding the SODIMMs in place to the side and lift these modules up out of the system, as shown in Figure 3.16.

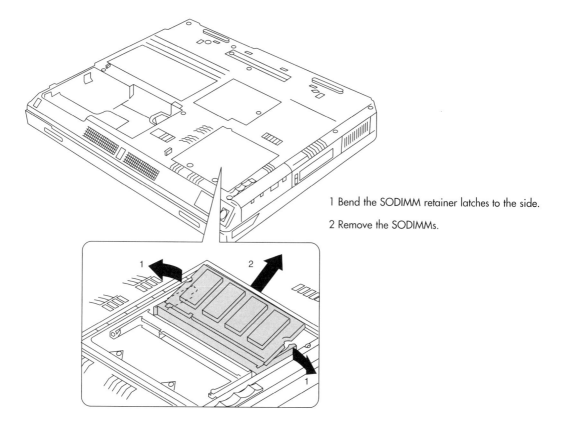

1 Bend the SODIMM retainer latches to the side.

2 Remove the SODIMMs.

Figure 3.16 Removing the memory modules.

Mini PCI Card

Laptop system manufacturers usually put wireless networking on Mini PCI cards so they can sell systems with and without this option. If you purchased a system that didn't come with built-in wireless networking, you may be able to install a Mini PCI 802.11a/b Wi-Fi card to add that capability to your system. To remove a Mini PCI card, first remove the screws holding the access door in place and then take out the door (see Figure 3.17).

When the card is exposed, carefully disconnect any antennas or other wires that may be attached to the card. Mini PCI cards are installed in exactly the same way as SODIMMs. To remove the card, bend the retainer latches to the side and then lift and pull the card up out of the slot (see Figure 3.18).

1a Phillips screw.

1b Tamperproof Torx screw.

2　Remove the Mini PCI access door.

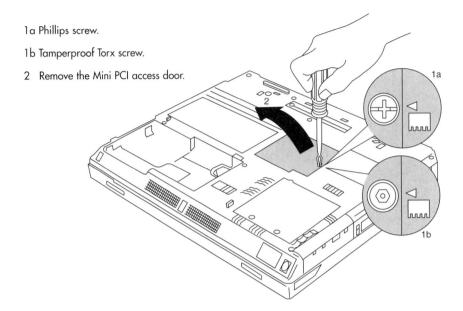

Figure 3.17　Removing the Mini PCI access door.

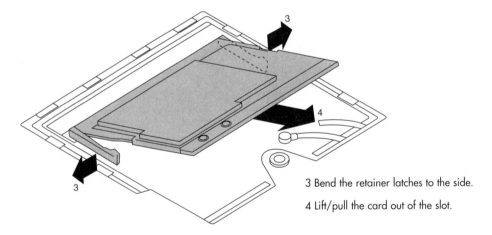

3 Bend the retainer latches to the side.

4 Lift/pull the card out of the slot.

Figure 3.18　Removing the Mini PCI card.

Keyboard

Keyboard removal and installation can be different from system to system. For this example, to remove the keyboard, you start by turning the system over and removing a couple screws, as shown in Figure 3.19.

Now turn the system over, reach under the front of the keyboard, lifting and pushing the keyboard toward the screen as you press the locking tab under the front to disengage it. Then lift the keyboard up and away from the system, disconnecting the cable that is underneath (see Figure 3.20).

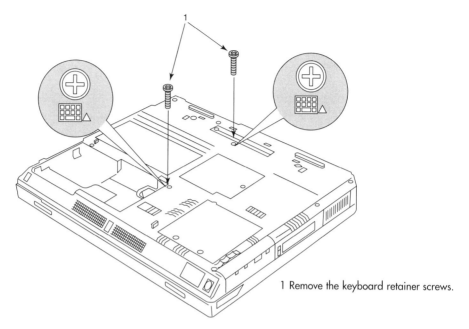

1 Remove the keyboard retainer screws.

Figure 3.19 Removing the keyboard retainer screws.

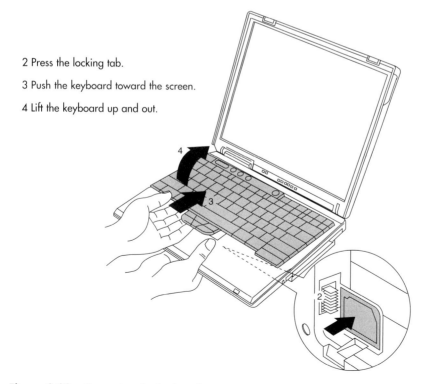

2 Press the locking tab.

3 Push the keyboard toward the screen.

4 Lift the keyboard up and out.

Figure 3.20 Removing the keyboard.

CMOS Battery

The CMOS battery powers the CMOS RAM and clock in the system. To remove it, simply unplug the cable and lift the battery out of the system, as shown in Figure 3.21.

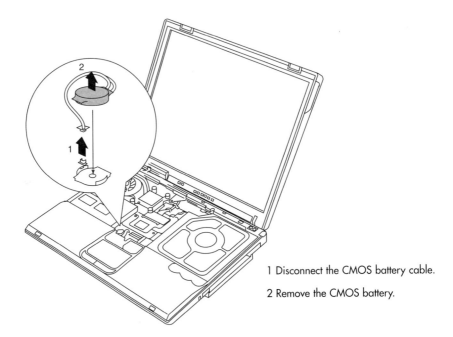

1 Disconnect the CMOS battery cable.

2 Remove the CMOS battery.

Figure 3.21 Removing the CMOS battery.

PC Card/CardBus Slot Assembly

The PC Card slots are removed as a complete assembly. Begin by turning the laptop over and removing the retainer screws from the bottom of the system. Note that some of them may be covered with small plastic stickers; if so, peel off the stickers to get to the necessary screws (see Figure 3.22).

Turn the system back right side up and then remove the PC Card slot assembly from the top (see Figure 3.23).

Communications Daughter Card (CDC)

Communications daughter cards (CDCs) are similar to Mini PCI cards in that they provide a way for modern laptop systems to offer expansion. CDCs are normally V.92 modem cards, but they are also available with Bluetooth wireless personal area networking as well. To remove the CDC, turn the system upside down and remove the retainer screws (see Figure 3.24).

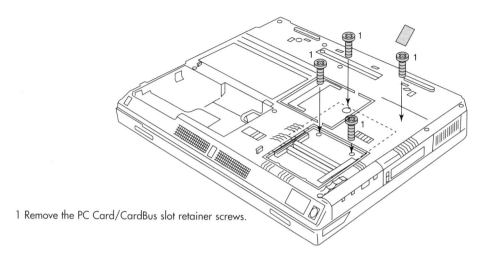

1 Remove the PC Card/CardBus slot retainer screws.

Figure 3.22 Removing PC Card/CardBus slot retainer screws.

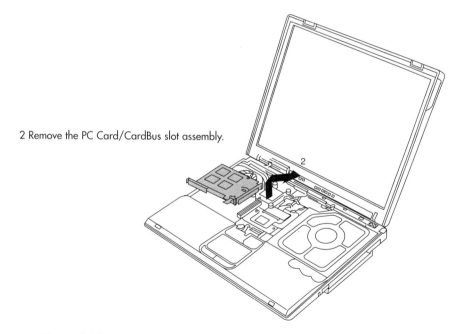

2 Remove the PC Card/CardBus slot assembly.

Figure 3.23 Removing the PC Card/CardBus slot assembly.

Now turn the system upright, locate the CDC, and then disconnect it and lift it out of the system. Note that there may be both modem and Bluetooth antenna connections, which will have to be unplugged (see Figure 3.25).

1 Remove the CDC retainer screws.

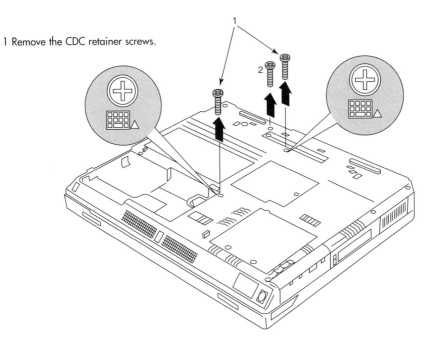

Figure 3.24 Removing communications daughter card (CDC) retainer screws.

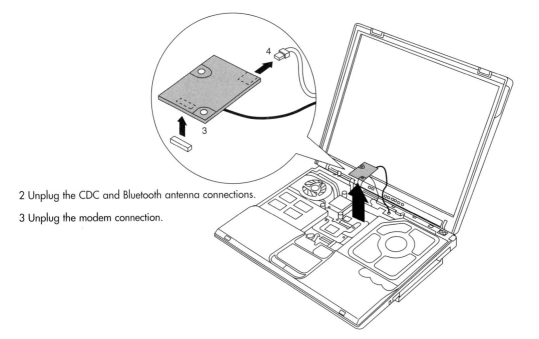

2 Unplug the CDC and Bluetooth antenna connections.

3 Unplug the modem connection.

Figure 3.25 Removing the communications daughter card (CDC).

CPU Heatsink/Fan

The CPU heatsink/fan assembly usually consists of a heat pipe assembly, with a fan at one end and a heavy metal plate that attaches to the CPU at the other. This device cools the processor and possibly the rest of the system as well. To remove it, take out the retainer screws and then lift the assembly up and out of the system, as shown in Figure 3.26.

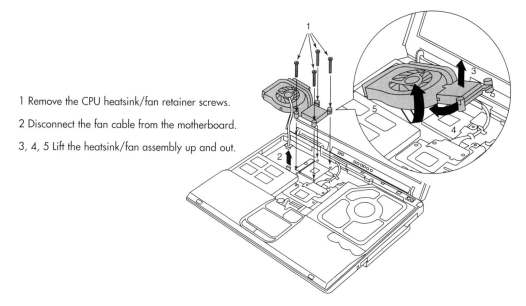

1 Remove the CPU heatsink/fan retainer screws.

2 Disconnect the fan cable from the motherboard.

3, 4, 5 Lift the heatsink/fan assembly up and out.

Figure 3.26   Removing CPU heatsink/fan assembly.

CPU (Pentium M Processor)

Most modern laptops utilize socketed desktop or mobile processors. They are normally installed in a zero insertion force (ZIF) socket that uses a locking mechanism to hold or release the chip. Instead of using a lever to actuate the socket, as on desktop systems, most laptops use a small screw. To unlock the ZIF socket, turn the screw counterclockwise. Then you can carefully lift the processor out of the socket (see Figure 3.27).

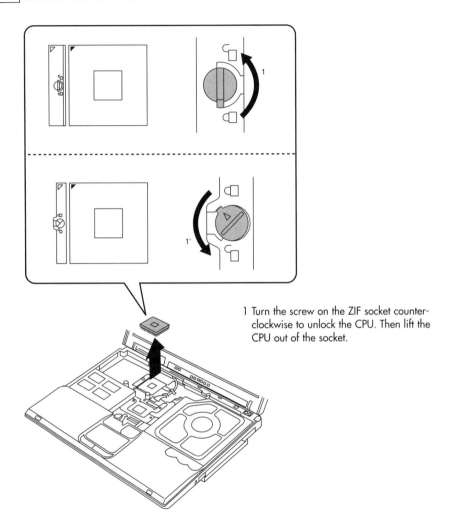

1 Turn the screw on the ZIF socket counter-clockwise to unlock the CPU. Then lift the CPU out of the socket.

Figure 3.27 Removing the CPU.

LCD Panel

To remove the LCD panel, first invert the system and remove the retaining screw from the bottom (see Figure 3.28).

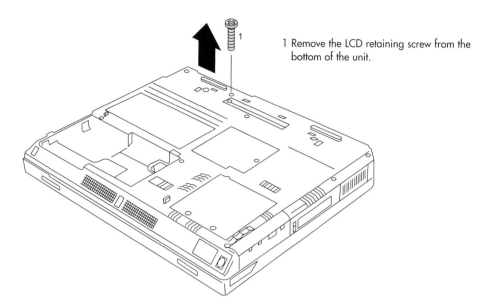

1 Remove the LCD retaining screw from the bottom of the unit.

Figure 3.28   Removing the LCD base retaining screw.

Now turn the system upright, remove the remaining screws holding the display hinges and the cable, and unplug the cable connections (see Figure 3.29).

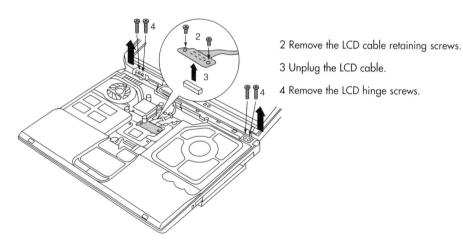

2 Remove the LCD cable retaining screws.

3 Unplug the LCD cable.

4 Remove the LCD hinge screws.

Figure 3.29   Removing the LCD hinge and cable retaining screws.

Next, you can lift the display hinges off the pegs or studs they are sitting on and then separate the display from the system, as shown in Figure 3.30.

Keyboard Bezel

To remove the keyboard bezel, turn the system upside down and remove the retaining screws. Note that many of these screws may be under cosmetic stickers, which you must remove in order to take out the screws (see Figure 3.31).

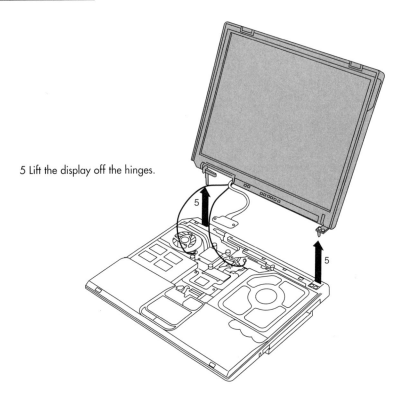

5 Lift the display off the hinges.

Figure 3.30 Removing the LCD.

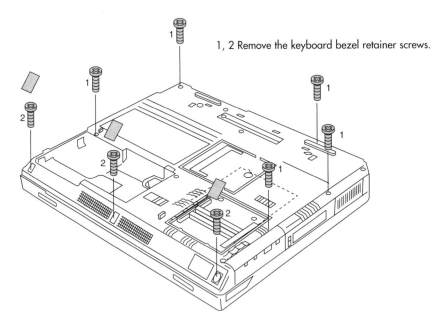

1, 2 Remove the keyboard bezel retainer screws.

Figure 3.31 Removing the keyboard bezel retaining screws.

Now turn the system upright and then lift the keyboard bezel up and off the chassis, as shown in Figure 3.32.

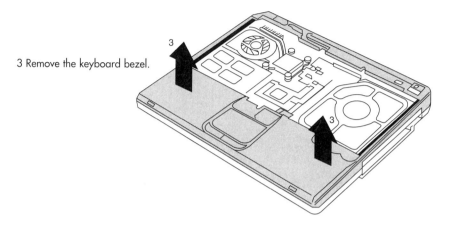

3 Remove the keyboard bezel.

Figure 3.32   Removing the keyboard bezel.

Motherboard

To remove the motherboard, begin by taking out the retaining screws, as shown in Figure 3.33.

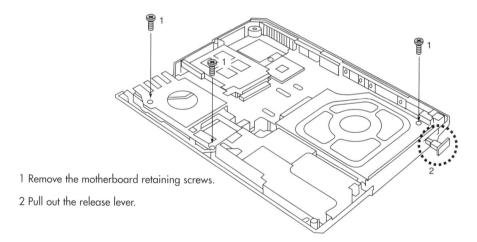

1 Remove the motherboard retaining screws.

2 Pull out the release lever.

Figure 3.33   Removing the motherboard retaining screws.

Now remove the board by pulling out the lever while lifting the board up and out of the system, as shown in Figure 3.34.

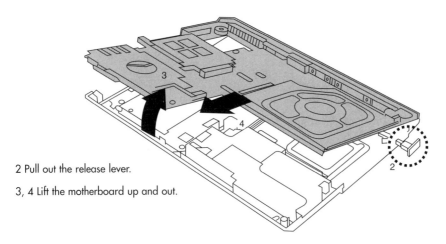

2 Pull out the release lever.

3, 4 Lift the motherboard up and out.

Figure 3.34 Removing the motherboard.

BIOS Setup

Most systems have the setup program built right in to the motherboard ROM BIOS. These built-in setup programs are activated by a key sequence usually entered during the Power On Self Test (POST). Most systems show a prompt on the screen during the POST indicating which key to press to enter the BIOS Setup.

The major vendors have standardized on the following keystrokes to enter the BIOS Setup:

- For AMI BIOS, press Del during POST.
- For Phoenix BIOS, press F2 during POST.
- For Award BIOS, press Del or Ctrl+Alt+Esc during POST.
- For Microid Research BIOS, press Esc during POST.

If your system does not respond to one of these common keystroke settings, you might have to contact the manufacturer or read the system documentation to find the correct keystrokes to enter Setup.

Here are some unique ones I have encountered:

- For IBM Aptiva/Valuepoint, press F1 during POST.
- For Older Phoenix BIOS, boot to a Safe Mode DOS command prompt and then press Ctrl+Alt+Esc or Ctrl+Alt+S.
- For Compaq, press F10 during POST.

After you're in the BIOS Setup main screen, you'll usually find a main menu allowing access to other menus and submenus offering various sections or screens. When you get the Setup program running, record all the settings. The easiest way to do this is to print it. If a printer is connected, press Shift+Print Screen; a copy of the screen display will be sent to the printer. Some setup programs have several pages of information, so you should record the information on each page.

Some setup programs allow for specialized control of the particular chipset used in the motherboard. These complicated settings can take up to several screens of information, which you may want to record. Most systems return these settings to a BIOS default if the CMOS battery is removed, and you lose any customized settings you might have changed.

Accessing BIOS Setup for Specific Makes and Models

This section shows some of the procedures required to enter BIOS Setup using keystrokes on specific popular laptop models.

ThinkPad

Table 3.4 shows the methods used to run the BIOS Setup routines on all ThinkPad systems.

Table 3.4 Entering BIOS Setup on IBM ThinkPads

Current ThinkPad Models	To Run BIOS Setup:
240 series 390 series 570 series i Series 1200 i Series 1300 i Series 1400 i Series 1500 i Series 172x A20, A21, A22, A30, A31 R30, R31, R32, S30, S31 T20, T21, T22, T23, T30 X20, X21, X22, X23, X24, X30, X31 TransNote	Power on. Press F1 when the ThinkPad logo is displayed during startup.
R40, R40e, R50, R51, R52, T40, T41, T42, T43	Power on. Press the blue Access IBM or black ThinkPad button during startup when the message "To interrupt normal startup..., press the blue Access IBM button" is displayed. Then select Start Setup Utility to run the BIOS Setup Utility.

Older ThinkPad Models	To Run BIOS Setup:
300 350 500, 510	Press Ctrl+Alt+F3 at an MS-DOS prompt. The system must be in MS-DOS mode and not in a DOS session under Windows.
310, 315 310E/ED 315ED	Power on. Press F2 while the ThinkPad logo is displayed during startup.
365C/CS 365CD/CSD 365E/ED	Press Ctrl+Alt+F11 at an MS-DOS prompt. The system must be in MS-DOS mode and not in a DOS session under Windows.
365X/XD	With the unit powered off, press and hold the F1 key while powering the unit on. Continue to hold down the F1 key until Setup appears.
360, 355 series 380, 385 series 560 series 600 series 701C/CS 75x series 76x series 770 series	With the unit powered off, press and hold the F1 key while powering the unit on. Continue to hold down the F1 key until Setup appears. On the TP 701, you can also access BIOS Setup by pressing the Fn+F1 keys at any time.

(continues)

Table 3.4   Continued

Older ThinkPad Models	To Run BIOS Setup:
700/C, 720/C	Power on. Press Ctrl+Alt+Ins when the cursor moves over to the upper right side of the screen, right after the memory count during startup.
710T, 730T	Press and hold the suspend/resume switch while powering on the computer.

Toshiba

The methods discussed first in this section are used to run the BIOS Setup routines on Toshiba laptop systems for the following Toshiba models:

All Libretto, all Portege, Satellite 100CS, 105CS, 105CT, 110CS, 110CT, 115CS, 115CT, 1555CDS, 200CDS, 205CDS, 2060CDS, 2065CDS, 2065CDT, 2100CDS, 2100CDT, 2105CDS, 2140XCDS, 2180CDT, 2210CDT, 2210XCDS, 2250CDT, 2250XCDS, 225CDS, 2500CDT, 2505CDS, 2505CDT, 2510CDS, 2515CDS, 2530CDS, 2535CDS, 2540CDS, 2545CDS, 2590CDT, 2595CDS, 2595CDT, 2595XDVD, 2615DVD, 2655XDVD, 2675DVD, 2715DVD, 2715XDVD, 2755DVD, 2775XDVD, 300CDS, 305CDS, 305CDT, 310CDS, 310CDT, 315CDS, 315CDT, 320CDS, 320CDT, 325CDS, 325CDT, 330CDS, 330CDT, 335CDS, 335CDT, 4000CDS, 4000CDT, 4005CDS, 4005CDT, 4010CDS, 4010CDT, 4015CDS, 1805-S177, 4015CDT, 4020CDT, 4025CDT, 4030CDT, 4060CDT, 4080CDT, 4080XCDT, 4085XCDT, 1415-S115, 1415-S105, 2410-S204, 1410-S174, 2410-S203, 1410-S173, 1415-S174, 1415-S173, 1405-S172, 1405-S171, 1400-S152, 2400-S252, 2400-S202, 2400-S251, 2400-S201, 1400-S151, 2405-S202, 1405-S152, 2405-S221, 2405-S201, 1405-S151, 4090XDVD, 4100XDVD, 2800-S201, 2805-S201, T2100, T2100CS, T2100CT, T2105CS, T2105CS, T2105CT, T2110CS, T2115CS, T2130CS, T2130CT, T2150CDS, T2150CDT, T2155CDS, 2800-S202, 2805-S301, 2805-S401, 2805-S202, 2805-S302, 2805-S402, 1805-S203, 1805-S253, 1800-S203, 1800-S253, 2805-S503, 2805-S603, 2590CDS, 2590XDVD, 2695DVD, 220CDS, 2545XCDT, 1805-S273, 1805-S204, 1805-S254, 1805-S274, 1800-S204, 1800-S254, 2060CDT, 1800-S206, 1800-S256, 1805-S255, 1805-S154, 1805-S207, 1800-S207, 1800-S274, 1805-S278, 1805-S208, all Satellite Pro, all TE-Series, and all Tecra

There are three ways to run the BIOS Setup on these models:

■ **From Windows, using the HWSetup program**—The HWSetup program comes preinstalled on these Toshiba models, and it is also contained in the Toshiba Utilities package for these models, which can be downloaded from the Toshiba support website. To run HWSetup, open the Control Panel and double-click the HWSetup program. If you change any settings, you may be required to restart the system.

■ **Starting with the system powered off (not in Sleep/Suspend or Hibernate mode)**—Start with the system powered off. Press the power button and then immediately press and hold the Esc key while the system runs the POST (Power On Self Test). When the POST finishes, a prompt will appear telling you to press the F1 key to enter BIOS Setup. At that time, press the F1 key to access the BIOS Setup program.

■ **From MS-DOS, running the TSETUP program**—TSETUP must be run under MS-DOS mode and not in a DOS session under Windows. The TSETUP utility will not work if a memory manager such as HIMEM.SYS, QEMM386, or equivalent is installed. TSETUP comes with the software provided with the system, or it can be downloaded from the Toshiba support website.

The next method discussed in this section is for the following Toshiba models:

Satellite 1605CDS, 1625CDT, 1675CDS, 1695CDT, 1715XCDS, 1735, 1755, 1730, 1750, 3005-S303, 3005-S403, 3000-S353, 3005-S304, 3000-S304, 3000-S307, 3005-S308, 1005-S157, 1000-S157, 1005-S158, 3005-S307, 3000-S309, 1905-S277, 1000-S158, 1200-S121, 1200-S122, 1905-S301, 1955-S801, 1955-S802, 1100-S101, 1905-S302, 1105, 1115-S103, 1905-S303, 1955-S803, 1905-S304, 1955-S804, 1110-S153, and 1115-S104

These models use a Phoenix BIOS. If you want to access the BIOS Setup on these systems, the system must be off, and not in Sleep/Suspend or Hibernate mode. Press the power button and then immediately press and hold down the F2 key. When the POST (Power On Self Test) finishes, the BIOS Setup screen will appear.

The final method discussed is for the following Toshiba models:

Satellite 5005-S504, 5005-S507, 5005-S508, 5105-S607, 5105-S608, 5105-S501, 5105-S701, 5105-S502, 5105-S702, 5105-S901, 5205-S503, 5205-S703, 5205-S504, and 5205-S704

These are "legacy-free" models, and they do not incorporate a BIOS Setup program in the motherboard ROM. The only way to run BIOS Setup is to use a Windows-based BIOS Setup utility called HWSetup. The HWSetup utility comes preinstalled on these Toshiba models, and it is also contained in the Toshiba Utilities package for these models, which can be downloaded from the Toshiba support website. To run HWSetup, open the Control Panel and double-click the HWSetup program. HWSetup provides a graphical front end for modifying BIOS settings. Note that if you change any settings, you may be required to restart the system.

Compaq

The following methods are used to run the BIOS Setup routines on Compaq laptop systems:

- For Presario models, power on the system and press F2 to enter BIOS Setup when the logo screen appears during startup.

- For Evo models, power on the system and press F10 while the "F10 = ROM Based Setup" message is displayed in the lower-left corner of the screen during startup.

- For Prosignia models, power on the system and press F10 when the blinking cursor appears in the upper-right corner of the display during startup.

Dell, Gateway, and Others

To run the BIOS Setup routines on Dell, Gateway, Sony, Acer, MPC, FOSA, and most other laptop systems, power on the system and then press F2 to enter BIOS Setup when the logo screen appears during startup.

Running the BIOS Setup Program (CMOS Setup)

After everything is reassembled, you can power up the system and run the BIOS Setup program. This enables you to configure the motherboard to access the installed devices and set the system date and time. The system also tests itself to determine whether any problems exist. Here are the steps to follow:

1. Power on the system. Observe the operation via the screen and listen for any beeps from the system speaker.

2. The system should automatically go through a Power On Self Test (POST) consisting of video BIOS checking, a RAM test, and usually an installed component report. If a fatal error occurs

during the POST, you might not see anything onscreen, and the system might beep several times, indicating a specific problem. Check the motherboard or the BIOS documentation to determine what the beep codes mean.

3. If there are no fatal errors, you should see the POST display onscreen. Depending on the type of motherboard BIOS, such as Phoenix, AMI, Award, or others, you must press a key or series of keys to interrupt the normal boot sequence and get to the Setup program screens that enable you to enter important system information. Normally, the system indicates via the onscreen display which key to press to activate the BIOS setup program during the POST, but if it doesn't, check the manual for the key(s) to press to enter the BIOS setup. Common keys used to enter BIOS Setup are F1, F2, F10, Esc, Ins, and Del.

4. After the Setup program is running, use the Setup program menus to enter the current date and time, your hard drive settings, floppy drive types, video cards, keyboard settings, and so on. Most newer BIOSes can autodetect the hard drive, so you should not have to manually enter any parameters for it.

5. Entering the hard drive information is the most critical when building a new system. Most modern BIOSes feature an autodetect or autotype setting for the drive; I recommend you choose that setting if it is available. This causes the BIOS to read the parameters directly from the drive, which eliminates a chance for errors—especially if the builder is less experienced. These parameters include cylinder head sector (CHS) specifications and transfer speed and translation settings. Most systems also let you set a *user-definable type*, which means that the cylinder, head, and sector counts for this type were entered manually and are not constant. If you set a user-definable type (not normally recommended unless you don't have "auto" as a choice), it is especially important that you write down the exact settings you use because this information might be very difficult to figure out if it is ever lost.

    Modern ATA drives also have additional configuration items that you should record. They include the translation mode and transfer speed setting. With drives larger than 528MB (504MiB), you should record the translation mode, which is expressed differently in different BIOS versions. Look for a setting such as CHS, ECHS (extended CHS), Large (which equals ECHS), or LBA (logical block addressing). Typically, you set LBA or Large for any drive over 528MB. Whatever you set, it should be recorded because changing this setting after the drive has been formatted can cause problems.

6. After you have checked over all the settings in the BIOS Setup, follow the instructions on the screen or in the motherboard manual to save the settings and exit the Setup menu.

Dealing with Passwords

Laptop systems have a level of integrated password security not found in most desktop systems. These passwords are separate and distinct from any passwords required by the operating system or other applications installed on the machine. This section examines the passwords specifically associated with laptop systems and their hard disks.

Password Types

Some laptop systems can have up to three passwords set on them. Two of these passwords are very secure, meaning that if they are lost, you have essentially no way to recover them, thus rendering the hard drive and/or motherboard completely nonfunctional.

Caution

The passwords described in this section are not benign passwords that can easily be circumvented or reset. If you lose these passwords, short of some very specialized and expensive services (for which you will have to provide proof of ownership), you will *not* be able to use the motherboard or access the data on the hard disk, even if you move the drive to another system! In fact, both the motherboard and the hard disk will have to be replaced, and all your data will be lost. Clearly, it is important to understand these passwords, because if you set them, the implications of losing or forgetting them are quite severe.

These three passwords are as follows:

- **Power-on password (POP)**—Protects the system from being powered on by an unauthorized user. The POP must be entered before an operating system will boot. The POP resides in the CMOS RAM on the motherboard. If it's lost, the POP can be cleared through a relatively simple procedure.

- **Hard disk password (HDP)**—Protects the information on your drive from access by an unauthorized user. If you set an HDP, others cannot access the data on your hard disk without knowing the password, even if the drive is installed in another system. The HDP resides on the hard disk, in an area inaccessible by the user and the system, and it cannot be accessed or reset if lost.

- **Supervisor password (SVP)**—Protects the information stored in the BIOS Setup. The SVP must be entered in order to get access to the BIOS Setup and make changes to configuration settings. The SVP is stored on the motherboard in a specialized type of memory and cannot be accessed or reset if lost.

If either the POP or HDP has been set, prompts for this password will appear on the screen whenever the system is powered on. The system will not continue until the respective password is entered. If only an SVP is set, it will also set the HDP to the same value, and yet no password prompt will appear during normal operation. Instead, the password prompt will appear only when the BIOS Setup is run.

Power-on Password (POP)

The power-on password is a feature available in many portable systems, and it's stored in the CMOS RAM. If it's lost, the POP can be erased in most systems by setting a password-clear jumper (located normally on the motherboard) or by removing the CMOS battery. You will normally find instructions for clearing the POP in the user manual or service manual for your specific system.

If a POP is set, you will be prompted (the prompt normally looks like an image of a padlock with a screen next to it) for the password at the following times:

- During the POST (Power On Self Test) each time the system is turned on.
- When the system returns to normal operation from Suspend mode.

To set a power-on password, follow these steps:

1. Run the BIOS Setup by pressing and holding the appropriate key while turning on the computer.

2. Select the Password icon and then the Power-On icon.

3. Type in your desired password and then press Enter. You can use any combination of up to seven alphanumeric characters (A–Z, 0–9). Letters are not case sensitive, meaning that upper- and lowercase letters are treated the same.

4. Type in the password again to verify it. Then press Enter.

5. Select Exit and then Restart.

To change a power-on password, follow these steps:

1. Turn off the system, wait at least 5 seconds, and then turn it back on.

2. When the POP prompt appears, type in the current password and then press the spacebar.

3. Type in the new password and then press the spacebar. Remember to use no more than seven characters.

4. Type in the new password again to verify it. Then press Enter.

To remove a power-on password, follow these steps:

1. Turn off the system, wait at least 5 seconds, and then turn it back on.

2. When the POP prompt appears, type in the current password, press the spacebar, and then press Enter.

To remove a power-on password that you have lost or forgotten, use one of the following two procedures.

First, if no supervisor password (SVP) has been set, follow these steps:

1. Turn off the system.

2. Remove the main battery.

3. Remove the backup (CMOS) battery. The CMOS battery is usually located under the keyboard or next to the memory modules in most systems. See the owner's or service manual to determine the exact location in a given system.

4. Turn the system on and wait until the POST ends. After the POST ends, no password prompt should appear, indicating that the POP has been removed.

5. Power the system off and then reinstall the backup (CMOS) and main batteries.

Second, if a supervisor password (SVP) has been set and is known, follow these steps:

1. Run the BIOS Setup by pressing and holding the F1 key while turning on the computer.

2. At the password prompt, type in the supervisor password and then press Enter. The BIOS Setup screen should appear.

3. Select the Password icon and then the Power-On icon.

4. Type in the supervisor password, press the spacebar, press Enter, and then press Enter again. This indicates you want to change the password, and sets and confirms a blank password.

5. Select Exit and then Restart.

Hard Disk Password (HDP)

A hard disk password provides a great deal of additional security for your data over the existing power-on password. Even if you set a POP, somebody could still remove the hard drive from your system and then install the drive into another system where he or she could access your data. However, if you set an HDP, nobody else will be able to access the data on the drive in any system without first knowing the password. Because the HDP is actually stored on the hard disk, it stays with the drive until you remove or change it. Doing that, however, requires that you know the password to begin with.

If a hard disk password is set, you will be prompted (the HDP prompt normally appears as an image of a padlock next to a disk cylinder) for the password at the following times and under the following circumstances:

- During the POST (Power On Self Test), each time the system is turned on.
- If you move the drive to another system, you will still be required to type in the HDP during the POST each time the system is turned on.
- If you have not set a supervisor password (SVP) in addition to the HDP, you will also be prompted to enter the HDP every time the system resumes from Suspend mode.

To set a hard disk password, follow these steps:

1. Run the BIOS Setup by pressing and holding the F1 key and then turning on the computer.
2. Select the Password icon and then the HDD-1 or HDD-2 icon, according to which drive you want to set.
3. Type in your desired password and then press Enter. You can use any combination of up to seven alphanumeric characters (A–Z, 0–9). Letters are not case sensitive, meaning that upper- and lowercase letters are treated the same.
4. Type in the password again to verify it. Then press Enter.
5. Select Exit and then Restart.

To change a hard disk password, follow these steps:

1. Turn off the system, wait at least 5 seconds, and then turn it back on.
2. When the HDP prompt appears, type in the current password and then press the spacebar.
3. Type in the new password and then press the spacebar. Remember to use no more than seven characters.
4. Type in the new password again to verify it. Then press Enter.

To remove a hard disk password, follow these steps:

1. Turn off the system, wait at least 5 seconds, and then turn it back on.
2. When the HDP prompt appears, type in the current password, press the spacebar, and then press Enter.

Most 2.5-inch laptop hard drives support the HDP feature, which can be set using the BIOS Setup in most laptop systems. The HDP can prevent any unauthorized user from ever accessing your hard disk, even if the drive is removed from the system. Make sure you keep a copy of the password in a safe place, because if you lose it, you have no way to ever access the drive again! Without the HDP, the drive and all your data will be forever locked up and inaccessible.

Supervisor Password (SVP)

The supervisor password provides a different level of security than the POP. The SVP protects the hardware configuration (BIOS Setup) from unauthorized modification.

If a supervisor password (SVP) is set on a system, you will normally be prompted (the SVP prompt normally appears as an image of a padlock next to a person) for the password only when the BIOS Setup is accessed.

The supervisor password is provided for a system administrator to control multiple systems. The SVP is set by the system administrator, and subsequently is not required by the users to use the system. In other words, the users can start their systems without knowing or providing the SVP. The SVP is required only to access the BIOS Setup, and it provides the following security features:

- Only a system administrator who knows the SVP can access the BIOS Setup. If a supervisor password is set, a password prompt appears whenever you try to run the BIOS Setup.

- A user can still set a different power-on password to protect his or her data from unauthorized use.

- The system administrator can use the SVP to access the computer even if the user has set a POP. The SVP overrides the POP.

- The SVP also functions in addition to the hard disk password. The hard disk is protected by both the SVP and the HDP if both are set. If no HDP is set, the SVP also sets the HDP to the same password value. If the HDP is lost, the SVP can be used to access the drive.

A system administrator can set the same SVP on multiple systems to make administration easier.

To set a supervisor password, follow these steps:

1. Run the BIOS Setup by pressing and holding the F1 key while turning on the computer.

2. Select the Password icon and then the Supervisor icon.

3. Type in your desired password and then press Enter. You can use any combination of up to seven alphanumeric characters (A–Z, 0–9). Letters are not case sensitive, meaning that upper- and lowercase letters are treated the same.

4. Type in the password again to verify it. Then press Enter.

5. Select Exit and then Restart.

To change a supervisor password, follow these steps:

1. Run the BIOS Setup by pressing and holding the F1 key while turning on the computer.

2. At the password prompt, type in the supervisor password and then press Enter. The BIOS Setup screen should then appear.

3. Select the Password icon and then the Supervisor icon.

4. Type in the current password and then press the spacebar.

5. Type in the new password and then press Enter.

6. Type in the new password again to verify it. Then press Enter twice.

7. Select Exit and then Restart.

To remove a supervisor password, follow these steps:

1. Run the BIOS Setup by pressing and holding the F1 key while turning on the computer.

2. At the password prompt, type in the supervisor password and press Enter. The BIOS Setup screen should then appear.

3. Select the Password icon and then the Supervisor icon.

4. Type in the current password and then press the spacebar.

5. Press Enter twice.

6. Select Exit and then Restart.

Note that when an SVP is set on a system, it automatically sets the HDP to the same value. The user will be unaware that any passwords are set, because in this situation when the system boots up, the BIOS will automatically provide both passwords and the system will appear to boot normally. However, as soon as an attempt is made to go into the BIOS Setup, or when the system hardware is upgraded or the hard disk is swapped into another system, it will refuse to boot unless the SVP (and HDP, which would be the same value) is provided.

Caution

If you are purchasing a used laptop system, be sure that all passwords, especially the supervisor password and hard disk password, are cleared from the system; otherwise, ensure that you know for certain what they are. A system with these passwords set and yet unknown is almost worthless, because without the SVP and HDP, you will not be able to use the system or access the hard disk and will instead have an expensive paperweight.

POP, HDP, and SVP Password Cracking?

If you lose the hard disk password and/or the supervisor password for a system, IBM and most other manufacturers will tell you straight out that pretty much all is lost. Here is a quote from IBM's documentation:

> If you forget your hard-disk-drive or supervisor password, there is *no way to reset your password or recover data from the hard disk.* You have to take your computer to an IBM reseller or an IBM marketing representative to have the hard disk or the system board replaced. Proof of purchase is required, and an additional charge might be required for the service. Neither an IBM reseller nor IBM marketing representative can make the hard disk drive usable.

Although this sounds pretty bleak, one company has broken the laptop hardware security, allowing recovery of both motherboards and hard drives with lost passwords. The company is called Nortek (www.nortek.on.ca), and it's the first company I know of to figure out a way around the hardware security. Unfortunately, the recovery services aren't cheap, because the security chip must be removed from the motherboard as well as the drive, and a new one soldered in—a fairly delicate operation. The fees for hard drive recovery are as follows:

- $85 for an HDP unlock only, with no data recovered and no testing or warranty on the drive
- $145 for an HDP unlock with a 30-day warranty on the drive (still no data though)
- $295 for an HDP unlock with all the data recovered as well

Considering that you can get a new 80GB or larger laptop hard drive for that price, you can see why you don't want to lose the HDP. Nortek can also recover a motherboard with a lost supervisor password for a flat fee of $95.

Because of the possibility of theft, I do recommend setting both the SVP and HDP on your laptop system. That way, if the system is ever stolen, the thief not only won't be able to get to the data on your drive, but he or she won't be able to use the laptop itself, because the motherboard will be locked up. If the thief then tries to send it to Nortek, he or she will run into a company policy that states:

Nortek Computers Ltd. realizes the significant responsibility that is associated with circumventing the security features of IBM ThinkPad laptop computers and their associated Travelstar hard disks. With our exclusive technology we provide hardware reclamation and data recovery services for only legitimate owners of these systems.

We will not knowingly recover lost passwords on equipment that has been unlawfully obtained. Nortek requires proof of ownership prior to performing any recovery procedures. Nortek retains the serial number from any system shipped to us for password removal. All systems received are thoroughly investigated to ensure the customer is the rightful owner; any suspicious units are dealt with promptly.

Nortek also has a link on its site to the Stolen Computer Registry at `www.stolencomputers.org`, which is a worldwide clearinghouse for information on stolen computers. If I had my system stolen, I would not hesitate to contact both the Stolen Computer Registry and Nortek to let them know the serial numbers of my system so they would be on the lookout for my system showing up for possible "recovery." That way, with the SVP and HDP both set, I can at least rest fairly assured that the thief will have a paperweight on his or her hands, with no access to my data.

Windows Passwords

The power-on password, hard disk password, and supervisor password are all based on the system hardware and have nothing to do with Windows or any other operating system. As such, these hardware-based passwords do not preclude the use of additional passwords that can be set and maintained through Windows or other operating systems. Refer to your operating system documentation for more information on passwords maintained by the operating system.

CHAPTER 4

Processors

Certainly, one of the most important parts in any computer is the central processing unit, or CPU. The CPU can also be referred to as a microprocessor, or just processor, for short. Several types of processors are used in portable systems from several different companies. Processors for portable systems can be the same as those used in desktop systems, but several processor companies also make special processors specifically optimized for use in portable systems. They are generally referred to as *mobile* processors. This chapter examines primarily the mobile processors used in laptop/notebook and other portable systems.

Currently, Intel and AMD both manufacture processors designed for either desktop or mobile use, and Transmeta makes a series of processors under the Crusoe and Efficeon names that are exclusively for mobile use. As with desktop systems, the majority of mobile systems use Intel processors, and creating chips designed specifically for mobile systems is a major part of Intel's development effort. Over the years, Intel has introduced many different processors for mobile use. Intel has focused on mobile processors since the 386SL came out October 1990 and since then has dramatically expanded mobile processor technology and features. Today the Pentium M processor and the Centrino mobile platform, which is composed of the Pentium M processor, motherboard chipset, and support for Wi-FI, have the largest market share in laptop computers and have gone through several revisions since their initial introduction in 2003. By comparison, AMD was late in catering specifically to the mobile processor market. AMD's first major mobile-only processors were mobile versions of the K6-2 and K6-III released in 1998. In May 2001, AMD announced a line of mobile Athlon 4 (Palomino) and Duron CPUs. The mobile Athlon XP came in April 2002, and the mobile XP-M processor was introduced in March 2003. In 2004 AMD migrated its Athlon 64 desktop processor to laptop computers and named it the Mobile Athlon 64 processor. Today, AMD has just introduced its Turion 64 mobile processor, which builds on the Mobile Athlon 64 processor and is designed to offer similar performance and battery efficiency as Intel's Centrino platform.

Transmeta has had some success in small form factor designs, but generally its processors have failed to keep pace with the mobile offerings from AMD and Intel. Transmeta's processors can, however, be found in subnotebooks, PDAs, and other portable devices. Intel more or less outclassed Transmeta's processors by introducing the Pentium M processor that had similar power consumption and battery efficiency as Transmeta's processors but offered vastly better performance. Transmeta's Efficeon processor succeeds the Crusoe and is, like the Crusoe processor before it, not actually an x86-based processor like Intel's or AMD's. Instead, it uses a different internal logic, Very Long Instruction Word (VLIW), and uses a software layer to convert data from x86-instructions into code the processor can understand.

Mobile Processor Features

As with most portable system components, the main concern with mobile processors is reducing their size, power usage, and heat generation. This allows them to function in the tight confines of a laptop system without overheating, while allowing the longest possible battery life. Mobile processors usually differ from desktop processors in packaging and power consumption, and they can have special features not found in desktop processors. Some of the special features first debuted in mobile processors are subsequently implemented in desktop processors as well. Features unique to mobile processors are discussed in the following sections.

SL Technology

SL technology and *SL architecture* are terms that Intel used to describe the first system level (SL) power-management improvements that were specially designed for mobile processors and later incorporated into all desktop processors. This technology was first introduced in the 386SL processor in October 1990 and was the first mobile-specific PC processor on the market. The 386SL was based on the 386SX core (16-bit data bus), with added power-management features that Intel then called SL technology.

In November 1992, the 386SL was followed by the 486SL processor, which was essentially a 486DX with the same SL technology included in the 386SL. At first, the 486SL was a unique model. However, starting in June 1993, SL technology was available in all desktop 486 processors and all Pentium processors from 75MHz and faster. Every Intel x86 processor introduced since then, from the Pentium II through the Pentium 4 and beyond, has incorporated SL technology.

SL technology consists of a number of processor features that operate at the system hardware level, independent of the operating system or application software. SL technology includes the following features:

- **System Management Mode**—This dedicated special-purpose interrupt and memory address space implements power management transparent to operating system and applications software.

- **I/O Restart**—An I/O instruction interrupted by a System Management Interrupt (SMI) can automatically be restarted following the execution of the Resume (RSM) instruction.

- **Stop Clock**—This control mechanism provides a fast–wake-up Stop Grant state and a slow–wake-up Stop Clock state, with the CPU operating at 0MHz.

- **AutoHALT powerdown**—After executing a HALT instruction, the processor issues a normal HALT bus cycle, and the clock input to the processor core is automatically stopped.

- **Auto Idle powerdown**—This allows the processor to reduce the core frequency to the bus frequency when both the core and the bus are idle.

The most important part of SL technology is System Management Mode (SMM), which can control and power up/down components without interfering with other system resources. SMM software executes in a dedicated memory space called System Management RAM (SMRAM), which is invisible to operating system and applications software. The CPU enters SMM upon receiving a System Management Interrupt (SMI), the highest-priority nonmaskable interrupt that the CPU can receive. When an event generates an SMI (for example, accessing a device that is currently powered down), the CPU responds by saving the state of the processor to SMRAM. The CPU then switches into SMM and executes the SMM code (also stored in the SMRAM). When the SMM task is complete (for example, powering on the device that was being accessed), the SMI handler executes a Resume (RSM) instruction, which restores the former state of the processor from the SMRAM.

I/O Restart is one of the SL technology functions used with System Management Mode. For example, if an application executes an I/O instruction that tries to access a disk drive that is powered down for battery savings, a System Management Interrupt occurs, powering up the drive and re-executing the I/O instruction automatically. This is transparent to the operating system and application program, allowing the software to run seamlessly.

SL technology also added special clock controls, including Stop Clock, AutoHALT, and Auto Idle. Stop Clock is an instruction that allows control over the CPU clock frequency. When Stop Clock is enabled, the internal frequency of the CPU can be throttled down as low as 0MHz, causing the CPU to consume only a few milliamps of power. This is also called sleep mode. For further power reductions, the external clock signal can be removed altogether, lowering power consumption to the microamp range. This is also called suspend mode.

AutoHALT is an enhancement to the existing HALT instruction and is related to Stop Clock. When a HALT instruction is executed (which stops the CPU from executing further instructions), the CPU automatically executes the Stop Clock instruction and enters sleep mode.

Auto Idle reduces the clock speed of the CPU from normal (clock multiplied) speed down to the CPU bus speed whenever the processor is idle during memory or I/O operations. For example, when the processor is executing an I/O instruction and waiting for the device to respond, the processor speed is automatically reduced to match the CPU bus speed, resulting in power savings without affecting overall performance.

Processor Performance Technology (SpeedStep/PowerNow!/LongRun)

Overall, power consumption is one of the biggest issues faced when designing mobile processors and systems. Most laptops are designed to run off battery power when disconnected from an AC power source. The less power required, the longer the system can run between recharges. In this case, battery life is not so much how many times you can discharge and recharge (expressed as the total number of cycles), but how long each cycle lasts. The less power the system requires, the greater the time you can run off an existing charge. Conserving power when connected to AC can also be useful for reducing component temperatures and heat generation in a laptop.

The Mobile Pentium III/Celeron, Pentium 4, Pentium M, AMD K6-2P, AMD K6-IIIP, AMD K6-III+, AMD Mobile Athlon 4, AMD Mobile Duron, AMD Mobile Athlon 64, AMD Mobile Sempron, and AMD Turion 64, as well as the Transmeta processors all feature processor performance-control technology to allow for longer battery life in mobile operation, as well as reduced thermal generation when under AC power. Intel calls this technology SpeedStep (originally code-named Geyserville), AMD calls it PowerNow!, and Transmeta calls it LongRun. This technology enables these processors to optionally reduce both speed and voltage when running on batteries. Earlier processors could reduce speed using SL technology, but by also reducing voltage, the overall power consumption (and heat production) is significantly reduced as well. More recent versions of this technology allow modes to be dynamically switched based on processor demand, not just by whether the system is running on battery or AC power.

Although processor performance-control technology is mainly designed to work when the laptop is running on battery power, it can also be used dynamically when under AC power to help reduce CPU temperature and energy consumption. When the laptop computer is connected to the AC outlet, CPU speed and voltage are normally at or near their maximum. When powered by a battery, the processor automatically drops to a lower frequency (by changing ratios, the bus frequency remains constant) and voltage, thus conserving battery life while still maintaining a relatively high level of performance. In most cases, the actual power consumption drops by half, which means about double the battery life as compared to full power, while reducing speed by only a small amount. For example, a 3.06GHz Mobile Pentium 4 consumes up to 101.4W at full power (3.06GHz and 1.55V), whereas in SpeedStep mode, the power consumption drops to only 40.9W (1.6GHz and 1.2V). This means that although power consumption drops by nearly 60%, the speed drops by only about 48%.

When the system is first powered up, the processor starts in the lower of its two speeds; that is, it starts in Battery Optimized mode. From there, BIOS, driver, or operating system instructions can rapidly switch the processor from mode to mode.

The requirements for this technology to work are as follows:

- A processor that supports SpeedStep/PowerNow!/LongRun technology
- A supporting motherboard (chipset, BIOS, and voltage regulator)
- A supporting operating system (Windows 9x/Me, Windows NT/2000/XP)
- SpeedStep/PowerNow!/LongRun driver (included with XP)

In general, all laptops that came with processors supporting performance-control technology included all of the other required support as well. Note that although it is possible to upgrade processors in many laptops, you generally cannot install a processor supporting SpeedStep/PowerNow!/LongRun technology into an older system that was originally equipped with a processor that did not support that technology.

Systems running Windows 9x/Me or NT/2000 require a special configuration utility or driver to control the processor performance settings. Because the driver must be configured to the specific laptop motherboard, it is available only from the manufacturer or vendor of a given system. Typically, the driver automatically switches processor performance modes when the power source changes from AC to battery power. Normally, the driver displays an indicator (usually a small flag) in the notification area or system tray of the Windows taskbar indicating in which mode the CPU is currently running. The driver also typically adds a processor performance-control tab to the Power Management tool in the Control Panel. By clicking on the indicator in the system tray, you can switch among Maximum Performance, Automatic (dynamically switchable), or Battery Optimized modes on demand. By using the Control tab added to the Power Management tool, you can select options allowing you to disable the processor performance-control technology, add or remove the icon from the taskbar, and enable or disable audio notification when performance changes.

Windows XP includes native support for processor performance-control technologies such as SpeedStep, PowerNow!, and LongRun, which means that manufacturer-supplied drivers are no longer necessary. This native support also includes an algorithm that dynamically balances system performance and power consumption, based on the current CPU workload and remaining battery life. Windows XP uses four specific *processor policies* (modes of operation) to control processor performance. The processor policies used by Windows XP are shown in Table 4.1 in order of power consumption from highest to lowest.

Table 4.1 Windows XP Processor Policies

Processor Policy	Description
None	The CPU always runs at the highest performance level.
Adaptive	The CPU performance level varies based on CPU demand.
Constant	The CPU always runs at the lowest performance level.
Degrade	The CPU starts at the lowest performance level and uses stop clock throttling to reduce power even further as the battery discharges.

These processor policies are directly tied into and selected via the various power schemes selected in the Power Options application in the Windows XP Control Panel. By setting a specific power scheme, you are also selecting the processor policies that will be used when under AC and battery power. Windows XP includes several standard power schemes with predefined processor policies. Your laptop might include a power-management accessory provided by the manufacturer, which allows you to select additional schemes provided or even to create your own custom schemes. Table 4.2 shows the standard power schemes and related processor policies that are provided with Windows XP, listed from highest to lowest power.

Table 4.2 Windows XP Standard Power Schemes and Related Processor Policies

Power Scheme	Processor Policy (AC Power)	Processor Policy (Battery Power)
Always On	None	None
Home/Office Desk	None	Adaptive

(continues)

Table 4.2   Continued

Power Scheme	Processor Policy (AC Power)	Processor Policy (Battery Power)
Minimal Power Management	Adaptive	Adaptive
Portable/Laptop	Adaptive	Adaptive
Presentation	Adaptive	Degrade
Max Battery	Adaptive	Degrade

Reducing processor speed and voltage conserves power and dramatically increases battery life, but it also significantly reduces processor performance. This means that applications that require extremely high performance could suffer when in a battery-optimized mode. Additionally, when the processor speed changes, access to memory is temporarily blocked. This can cause problems with applications that require streaming access to memory (such as video playback), resulting in glitches or dropouts in the display. If you want maximum performance when running under battery power, you can manually override or disable the performance control technology.

To disable processor performance-control technology and force the processor to run at maximum performance, if you are running Windows 9x/Me or NT/2000, you should use the application supplied by your laptop manufacturer to disable the technology. If you are using Windows XP, you should select the Always On power scheme, which can be accomplished using the following steps:

1. Select Start, Control Panel (make sure you're using the Control Panel classic view).
2. Double-click the Power Options tool and select the Power Schemes tab.
3. Under Power Schemes, select the Always On scheme.

As you can see from the previous tables, the Always On power scheme in Windows XP automatically selects processor policies of None for both AC and battery power, which means that the processor will be forced to run its highest performance level at all times.

Caution

If you use the Always On power scheme on a laptop, battery life will be greatly reduced, and the system might be prone to run extremely hot or even to overheat. If you find that the system is running too hot when using AC power, you can try selecting a power scheme such as Minimal Power Management or Portable/Laptop, which uses the Adaptive processor policy to reduce power under periods of lower demand. For minimum heat production and maximum battery life, you can try the Presentation or Max Battery schemes.

Mobile Processor Packaging

The heat that processors generate has been a concern since the first computer chips were released. In desktop systems, the heat problem is addressed to a great extent by computer case manufacturers. Multiple cooling fans and better internal layout designs can keep air flowing through the system to cool the processor, which is usually equipped with its own fan and heatsink.

For developers of portable systems, however, not as much can be accomplished with the case arrangement. So, it was up to the chip manufacturers to address the problem in the design and packaging of the chip. Although most portable systems use special mobile processors designed specifically for mobile use, some systems use desktop processors for lower cost, at the expense of battery life and heat generation.

Note

Some manufacturers of portable systems use standard desktop processors. Apart from a greatly diminished battery life, systems such as these can sometimes be too hot to touch comfortably. For this reason, before purchasing a portable system, you should determine whether it uses a mobile or desktop processor and understand the ramifications of each.

Most mobile processors include a built-in thermal diode that can be used to monitor CPU temperature. The laptop systems use this to control fan operation and also for processor performance control. Utilities are available that can use this sensor to display the processor temperature information onscreen.

Tape Carrier Packaging

An early solution to the size and heat problems for processors was the tape carrier package (TCP), a method of packaging processors for use in portable systems that reduces the size of the chip, its power consumed, and its heat generated. A Pentium mounted on a motherboard using TCP is much smaller and lighter than the standard staggered pin grid array (SPGA) that Pentiums used in desktop systems. The 49mm square of the SPGA is reduced to 29mm in the TCP processor, the thickness is reduced to approximately 1mm, and the weight is reduced from 55 grams to less than 1 gram.

Instead of using metal pins inserted into a socket on the motherboard, a TCP processor is essentially a raw die encased in an oversize piece of polyamide film. The film is similar to photographic film. The die is attached to the film using a process called tape automated bonding (TAB), the same process used to connect electrical connections to LCD panels. The film, called the tape, is laminated with copper foil that is etched to form the leads that connect the processor to the motherboard. This is similar to the way electrical connections are photographically etched onto a printed circuit board.

After the leads are formed, they are plated with gold to allow bonding to a gold bump on the silicon die and to guard against corrosion. Next, they are bonded to the processor chip itself, and then the whole package is coated with a protective polyamide siloxane resin and mounted on a filmstrip reel for machine assembly. To get a feel for the small size of this processor, look at Figure 4.1, where it is shown next to a standard-size push-pin for comparison.

Reels of TCP chips are loaded into special machines that stamp-solder them directly to the portable system's motherboard. As such, the installation is permanent; a TCP processor can never be removed from the board for repair or upgrade. Because no heatsink or physical container is directly attached to the processor, the motherboard itself becomes the conduit to a heatsink mounted underneath it, thus using the portable system's chassis to pull heat away. Some faster portable systems include thermostatically controlled fans to further aid in heat removal.

Mounting the TCP to the system circuit board requires specific tooling available from all major board assembly equipment vendors. A special tool cuts the tape containing the processor to the proper size and folds the ends containing the leads into a modified gull-wing shape that contacts the circuit board, leaving the processor suspended just above the board. Another tool dispenses a thermally conductive paste to the circuit board before the tape containing the processor is placed. This is done so that the heat can be dissipated through a sink on the underside of the motherboard while it is kept away from the soldered connections.

Finally, a hot bar soldering tool connects the leads on the tape to the circuit board. The completed TCP assembly forms an efficient thermal contact directly from the die to the motherboard, enabling the processor to run within its temperature limits even in such a raw state. Eliminating the package and essentially bonding the die directly to the motherboard save a significant amount of size and weight.

Figure 4.2 shows the pinout of a typical Pentium processor using TCP packaging.

Figure 4.1 Pentium MMX processor in TCP Mobile Package. (Photograph used by permission of Intel Corporation.)

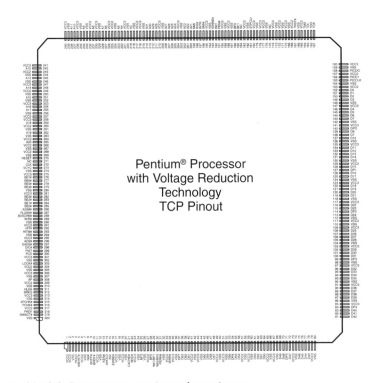

Figure 4.2 Intel Mobile Pentium tape carrier package pinout.

Mobile Module

Another form of processor packaging is called the Mobile Module, or MMO (see Figure 4.3).

The Mobile Module consists of a Pentium or Pentium II processor in its TCP form, mounted on a small daughterboard along with the power supply for the processor's unique voltage requirements, the system's Level 2 cache memory, and the North Bridge part of the motherboard chipset. This is the core logic that connects the processor to standard system buses containing the South Bridge part of the chipset, as shown in the block diagram in Figure 4.4. North Bridge and South Bridge describe what has come to be an accepted method for dividing the functionality of the chipset into halves that are mounted on separate modules. In a typical portable system design, the manufacturer purchases the Mobile Module (complete with the North Bridge) from Intel and uses a motherboard designed by another company that contains the South Bridge.

Figure 4.3   Mobile Pentium processors in Mobile Module versus tape carrier package form. (Photograph used by permission of Intel Corporation.)

A later version of the MMO is called the MMC, which stands for Mobile Module Connector and is available in MMC-1 and MMC-2 versions. The original Celeron and Pentium II were available in MMC-1 and MMC-2 versions, whereas the Pentium III was released in the MMC-2 version only. The Pentium II and III MMC-2 feature the Intel 440BX chipset's 82443BX host bridge, which connects to the PIIX4E/M PCI/ISA South Bridge built in to the portable computer's motherboard.

In many ways, the MMO/MMC is similar to the Pentium II Single Edge Cartridge (SEC) design, but with part of the motherboard included. The module interfaces electrically to its host system via a 3.3V PCI bus, a 3.3V memory bus, and Intel chipset control signals bridging the half of the chipset on the module to the other half of the chipset on the system motherboard. The Intel Mobile Module also incorporates a single thermal connection that carries all the module's thermal output to the mobile PC's main cooling mechanisms.

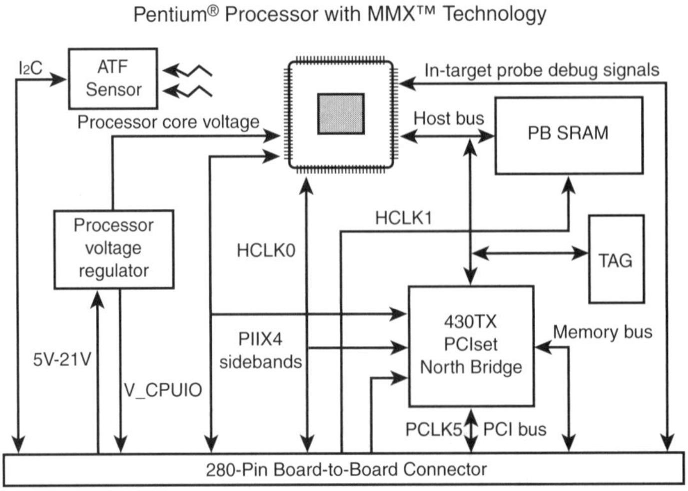

Pentium® Processor with MMX™ Technology

I2C — ATF Sensor

Processor core voltage

In-target probe debug signals

Host bus — PB SRAM

Processor voltage regulator

HCLK0

HCLK1

TAG

5V-21V

V_CPUIO

PIIX4 sidebands

430TX PCIset North Bridge — Memory bus

PCLK5 — PCI bus

280-Pin Board-to-Board Connector

Figure 4.4   Intel Pentium Mobile Module block diagram.

The MMO is mounted with screws and alignment guides to secure the module against the typical shock and vibration associated with mobile PC usage (see Figure 4.5). The MMO is 4 inches (101.6mm) long × 2.5 inches (63.5mm) wide × 0.315 inch (8mm) high (0.39 inch or 10mm high at the connector).

Figure 4.5   Intel Pentium MMX Mobile Module, including the processor, chipset, and L2 cache. (Photograph used by permission of Intel Corporation.)

The Mobile Module greatly simplifies the process of installing a Pentium III processor into a portable system, permits manufacturers to build more standardization into their portable computer designs, and eliminates the need for manufacturers to invest in the special tools needed to mount TCP processors on circuit boards themselves. The module also provides a viable processor upgrade path that was unavailable with a TCP processor permanently soldered to the motherboard. Portable systems that offer a range of processor options use Mobile Modules because it enables the vendor to use the same motherboard.

MMC-1

The Mobile Module Connector 1 (MMC-1) is an integrated assembly containing a Mobile Pentium II processor, 256KB or 512KB of L2 cache, a 443BX North Bridge, and a voltage regulator supporting input voltages from 5V to 21V. It is essentially most of a laptop motherboard in a single module (see Figure 4.6). The MMC-1 has a 66MHz bus speed and was available in versions running at speeds of up to 233, 266, 300, 333, 366, or 400MHz.

 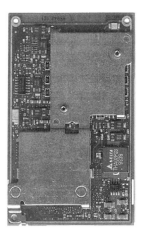

Figure 4.6   Intel Mobile Module Connector 1 (MMC-1), including the processor/L2 cache, North Bridge chip, and voltage regulator. (Photograph used by permission of Intel Corporation.)

The MMC-1 also includes a thermal transfer plate that is used for heatsink attachment, and it incorporates thermal sensors for internal and external temperature sensing with programmable trip points.

MMC-2

The Mobile Module Connector 2 (MMC-2) is an integrated assembly containing a Mobile Pentium II or III processor, 256KB or 512KB of L2 cache, a 443BX North Bridge, and a voltage regulator supporting input voltages from 5V to 21V. The MMC-2 has a 66MHz bus speed and was available in Pentium II versions running at speeds of up to 400MHz, or Pentium III versions up to 700MHz.

The MMC-2 also includes a thermal transfer plate that is used for heatsink attachment, and it incorporates thermal sensors for internal and external temperature sensing with programmable trip points (see Figure 4.7).

Because they include the voltage regulator module (VRM) and North Bridge components, the various Mobile Modules are more like minimotherboards than just processors. Although this made it easier for manufacturers to design a single base system that could accept a wider variety of processors, it was also an expensive design and essentially forced laptop manufacturers to purchase not only the processor from Intel, but essentially half the motherboard as well. All of the various Mobile Module formats were used starting with the Pentium systems through the Pentium II and early Pentium III systems.

Most of the later Pentium III systems and all of the Pentium 4 and Pentium M systems abandoned the Mobile Module designs and went back to the basic design of a separate processor in a socket.

Figure 4.7 Intel Mobile Module Connector 2 (MMC-2), including the processor/L2 cache, North Bridge chip, and voltage regulator. (Photograph used by permission of Intel Corporation.)

Minicartridge

Intel used another package called the minicartridge for the Pentium II. The minicartridge is designed especially for use in ultralight portable computers in which the height or bulk of the Mobile Module would interfere with the system design. It contains only the processor core and 256KB or 512KB of L2 cache memory in a stainless-steel case that exposes the connector and processor die (see Figure 4.8). This is the equivalent of the desktop Pentium II cartridge, but in a smaller mobile form factor.

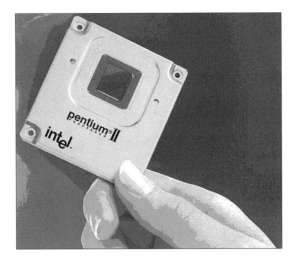

Figure 4.8 Pentium II minicartridge package. (Photograph used by permission of Intel Corporation.)

The minicartridge is approximately 51mm×47mm in size and 4.5mm in height. Overall, the package is about one-fourth the weight, is one-sixth the size, and consumes two-thirds of the power of a desktop Pentium II processor. To connect to the socket on the motherboard, the minicartridge has a 240-pin connector at one end of the bottom side, with the pins arranged in an 8×30 array.

BGA and PGA

The newest packaging for mobile processors is called micro-BGA (ball grid array) or micro-PGA (pin grid array). These packages are just processors, without any of the other circuits that were integrated into the previous Mobile Module designs. BGA packaging is unique in that it uses solder balls (instead of pins) on the bottom of the chip. The BGA design is mechanically stable (no pins to bend) and enables better heat transfer from the device to the board. The micro-PGA uses conventional pins instead of solder balls, allowing a standard socketed connection.

BGA chips can either be permanently soldered in or socketed, whereas PGA versions are almost always socketed. Both Intel and AMD use both BGA and PGA form factors for their newest mobile processors.

Micro-BGA2

The micro-BGA2 package consists of a die placed face down on an organic substrate, with an epoxy material surrounding the die and sealing it to the substrate. Instead of using pins, the packages use solder balls, which are either soldered directly to the motherboard or connected via a special socket.

Figure 4.9 shows a Pentium III processor in the micro-BGA2 package, which contains 495 balls.

Figure 4.9   Pentium III micro-BGA2 package. (Photograph used by permission of Intel Corporation.)

Micro-PGA2

The micro-PGA2 package consists of a BGA chip mounted to an interposer with small pins. The pins are 1.25mm long and 0.30mm in diameter.

Figure 4.10 shows a Pentium III processor in the micro-PGA2 package, which contains 495 pins.

Micro-FCBGA

The micro-FCBGA (flip chip ball grid array) package consists of a die placed face down on an organic substrate, with an epoxy material surrounding the die and sealing it to the substrate (see Figure 4.11). The package uses 479 balls, which are 0.78mm in diameter and normally soldered directly to the motherboard. Unlike micro-PGA, micro-FCBGA includes capacitors on the top side of the package.

Figure 4.10   Pentium III micro-PGA2 package. (Photograph used by permission of Intel Corporation.)

Figure 4.11   Pentium III micro-FCBGA package. (Photograph used by permission of Intel Corporation.)

Micro-FCPGA and FCPGA2

The micro-FCPGA (flip chip pin grid array) and micro-FCPGA2 packages consist of a die placed face down on an organic substrate, with an epoxy material surrounding the die and sealing it to the substrate. The micro-FCPGA2 version includes a heat spreader (metal cap) over the top of the die for additional mechanical strength and thermal management. Micro-FCPGA uses 478 pins, which are 2.03mm long and 0.32mm in diameter. Unlike micro-PGA2, micro-FCPGA and micro-FCPGA2 do not use an interposer board and include capacitors on the bottom side. Even though the package has 478 pins, the socket supports 479 pins.

Figure 4.12 shows a Pentium III processor in the micro-FCPGA package. Note that the mobile Celeron, Pentium 4, and Pentium M use the same packaging and look virtually identical.

Mobile versions of the Pentium III, Pentium 4, and Pentium M processor are all available in micro-FCPGA form. Although they plug into the same micro-479 pin socket (shown in Figure 4.13), the different processors are not pin-compatible or interchangeable. In other words, if your system has a Pentium III, you cannot install a Pentium 4 or Pentium M, even though they would physically fit into the same socket.

Figure 4.12   Pentium III micro-FCPGA package (mobile Celeron, Pentium 4, and Pentium M look similar). (Photograph used by permission of Intel Corporation.)

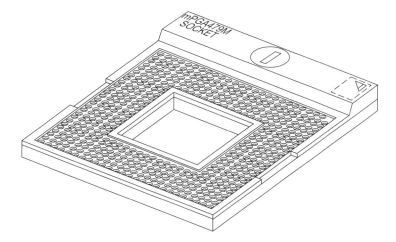

Figure 4.13   Micro-479 PGA socket for mobile Celeron, Pentium III, Pentium 4, and Pentium M processors in the micro-FCPGA (flip chip pin grid array) package. (Photograph used by permission of Intel Corporation.)

Virtually all of the more recent mobile processors have been introduced in micro-FCPGA and micro-FCBGA packages. The main reason is cost. These are "flip chip" packages, which means that the raw processor die sits face down on top of the substrate. It is connected directly to the substrate by very tiny solder balls around the perimeter. This is much less expensive than the old PGA form factors, in which the chip die was inserted into a cavity on the underside of the package and the contacts had to literally be stitched into place with a very expensive wire-bonding process using fine gold wires. The substrate also had to be ceramic, to withstand the tremendous heat that the processor put out, and a metal cap had to be installed on the bottom over the die to seal it. This involved many steps using many parts.

By comparison, a flip chip is much simpler, less expensive, easier to assemble, and easier to cool. The die is on the top, so the heat can be transferred directly into the heatsink without having to go through the substrate material. No wire bonding is needed because the tiny solder balls connect the die to the substrate. A fillet of epoxy seals the die to the substrate, eliminating the need for a metal seal. In short, all of the modern desktop and mobile processors from Intel and AMD have gone to the flip-chip design, mainly in the interest of lower manufacturing costs.

Processor Features

As new processors are introduced, new features are continually added to their architectures to help improve everything from performance in specific types of applications to the reliability of the CPU as a whole. The next few sections take a look at some of these technologies, including System Management Mode (SMM), Superscalar Execution, MMX, SSE, 3DNow!, and HT Technology.

SMM (Power Management)

Spurred on primarily by the goal of putting faster and more powerful processors in laptop computers, and yet maintaining reduced power consumption and decent battery life, Intel has created power-management circuitry. This circuitry enables processors to conserve energy use and lengthen battery life. This circuitry was introduced initially in the Intel 486SL processor, which is an enhanced version of the 486DX processor. Subsequently, the power-management features were universalized and incorporated into all Pentium and later processors. This feature set is called SMM, which stands for *System Management Mode*.

SMM circuitry is integrated into the physical chip but operates independently to control the processor's power use based on its activity level. It enables the user to specify time intervals after which the CPU will be partially or fully powered down. It also supports the Suspend/Resume feature that allows for instant power on and power off, used mostly with laptop PCs. These settings are typically controlled via system BIOS settings.

Superscalar Execution

The fifth-generation Pentium and newer processors feature multiple internal instruction-execution pipelines, which enable them to execute multiple instructions at the same time. The 486 and all preceding chips can perform only a single instruction at a time. Intel calls the capability to execute more than one instruction at a time *superscalar* technology. This technology provides additional performance compared with the 486.

Superscalar architecture usually is associated with high-output reduced instruction set computer (RISC) chips. A RISC chip has a less complicated instruction set with fewer and simpler instructions. Although each instruction accomplishes less, overall the clock speed can be higher, which can usually increase performance. The Pentium is one of the first complex instruction set computer (CISC) chips to be considered superscalar. A CISC chip uses a richer, fuller-featured instruction set, which has more complicated instructions. As an example, say that you wanted to instruct a robot to screw in a light bulb. Using CISC instructions, you would say this:

1. Pick up the bulb.

2. Insert it into the socket.

3. Rotate clockwise until tight.

Using RISC instructions, you would say something more along the lines of this:

1. Lower hand.

2. Grasp bulb.

3. Raise hand.

4. Insert bulb into socket.

5. Rotate clockwise one turn.

6. Is bulb tight? If not, repeat step 5.

7. End.

Overall, many more RISC instructions are required to do the job because each instruction is simpler (reduced) and does less. The advantage is that the robot (or processor) must deal with fewer overall commands and can execute the individual commands more quickly—and, thus, in many cases, execute the complete task (or program) more quickly as well. The debate goes on whether RISC or CISC is better, but, in reality, there is no such thing as a pure RISC or CISC chip; it is all just a matter of definition, and the lines are somewhat arbitrary.

Intel and compatible processors have generally been regarded as CISC chips, although the fifth- and sixth-generation versions have many RISC attributes and internally break down CISC instructions into RISC versions.

MMX Technology

Intel introduced MMX technology in January 1997 for both desktop and mobile Pentium processors. MMX was originally named for multimedia extensions or matrix math extensions, depending on whom you ask. Intel officially states that it is actually not an abbreviation and stands for nothing other than the letters MMX (not being an abbreviation was apparently required so that the letters could be trademarked); however, the internal origins are probably one of the preceding. MMX technology was introduced in the later fifth-generation Pentium processors as a kind of add-on that improves video compression/decompression, image manipulation, encryption, and I/O processing— all of which are used in a variety of today's software.

MMX consists of two main processor architectural improvements. The first is very basic: All MMX chips have a larger internal L1 cache than their non-MMX counterparts. This improves the performance of any and all software running on the chip, regardless of whether it actually uses the MMX-specific instructions. The other part of MMX is that it extends the processor instruction set with 57 new commands or instructions, as well as a new instruction capability called single instruction multiple data (SIMD).

Modern multimedia and communication applications often use repetitive loops that occupy 10% or less of the overall application code but can account for up to 90% of the execution time. SIMD enables one instruction to perform the same function on multiple pieces of data, similar to a teacher telling an entire class to sit down rather than addressing each student one at a time. SIMD enables the chip to reduce processor-intensive loops common with video, audio, graphics, and animation.

Intel also added 57 new instructions specifically designed to manipulate and process video, audio, and graphical data more efficiently. These instructions are oriented to the *highly parallel* and often repetitive sequences frequently found in multimedia operations. *Highly parallel* refers to the fact that the same processing is done on many data points, such as when modifying a graphic image. The main drawbacks to MMX were that it worked only on integer values and used the floating-point unit for processing, so time was lost when a shift to floating-point operations was necessary. These drawbacks were corrected in the additions to MMX from Intel and AMD.

Intel licensed the MMX capabilities to competitors such as AMD and Cyrix, which were then able to upgrade their own Intel-compatible processors with MMX technology.

SSE, SSE2, and SSE3

In February 1999, Intel introduced the Pentium III processor and included in that processor an update to MMX called Streaming SIMD Extensions (SSE). These extensions were also called Katmai New Instructions (KNI) until their debut because they were originally included on the Katmai processor, which was the code name for the Pentium III. The Celeron 533A and faster Celeron processors based on the Pentium III core also support SSE instructions. The earlier Pentium II and Celeron 533 and lower (based on the Pentium II core) do not support SSE.

SSE includes 70 new instructions for graphics and sound processing over what MMX provided. SSE is similar to MMX; in fact, besides being called KNI, SSE was also called MMX-2 by some before it was released. In addition to adding more MMX-style instructions, the SSE instructions allow for floating-point calculations and now use a separate unit within the processor instead of sharing the standard floating-point unit as MMX did.

When SSE2 was introduced in November 2000, along with the Pentium 4 processor, it added 144 additional SIMD instructions. SSE2 also included all the previous MMX and SSE instructions.

Streaming SIMD Extensions consist of several instructions, including SIMD floating-point, additional SIMD integer, and cacheability control instructions. Some of the technologies that benefit from the Streaming SIMD Extensions include advanced imaging, 3D video, streaming audio and video (DVD playback), and speech-recognition applications. The benefits of SSE include the following:

- Higher resolution and higher quality image viewing and manipulation for graphics software

- High-quality audio, MPEG-2 video, and simultaneous MPEG-2 encoding and decoding for multimedia applications

- Reduced CPU utilization for speech recognition, as well as higher accuracy and faster response times when running speech-recognition software

SSE3 debuted with the introduction of the 90nm Pentium processor previously known as Prescott in February 2004. It is the third iteration of the SIMD SSE instruction set for Intel's IA-32 architecture. AMD introduced SSE3 in the revision E of its Athlon 64 CPUs, released in April 2005.

SSE3 adds 13 new instructions to its predecessor, SSE2. The most notable addition is the capability to work horizontally in a register, as opposed to the more or less strictly vertical operation of all previous SSE instructions. This significantly speeds up often-used instructions in software such as MPEG-2, MP3, 3D graphics, and so on. Another new instruction converts floating-point values to integers without having to change the global rounding mode, thus avoiding costly pipeline stalls. Finally, another extension offers alternative integer vector handling, better suited for the Intel NetBurst architecture.

The SSE, SSE2, and SSE3 instructions are particularly useful with MPEG-2 decoding, which is the standard scheme used on DVD video discs. SSE-equipped processors should therefore be more capable of performing MPEG-2 decoding in software at full speed without requiring an additional hardware MPEG-2 decoder card. SSE-equipped processors are much better and faster than previous processors when it comes to speech recognition as well.

One of the main benefits of SSE over plain MMX is that it supports single-precision floating-point SIMD operations, which have posed a bottleneck in the 3D graphics processing. Just as with plain MMX, SIMD enables multiple operations to be performed per processor instruction. Specifically, SSE supports up to four floating-point operations per cycle; that is, a single instruction can operate on four pieces of data simultaneously. SSE floating-point instructions can be mixed with MMX instructions with no performance penalties. SSE also supports data *prefetching*, which is a mechanism for reading data into the cache before it is actually called for.

Note that for any of the SSE instructions to be beneficial, they must be encoded in the software you are using, so SSE-aware applications must be used to see the benefits. Most software companies writing graphics- and sound-related software today have updated those applications to be SSE aware and use the features of SSE. For example, high-powered graphics applications such as Adobe Photoshop support SSE instructions for higher performance on processors equipped with SSE. Microsoft includes support for SSE in its DirectX 6.1 and later video and sound drivers, which are included with Windows 98 Second Edition, Windows Me, Windows NT 4.0 (with Service Pack 5 or later), Windows 2000, and Windows XP.

SSE is an extension to MMX, and SSE2 is an extension to SSE, which subsequently makes SSE3 an extension of SSE2; therefore, processors that support SSE3 also support the SSE and SSE2 instructions as well as the original MMX instructions. This means that standard MMX-enabled applications run as they did on MMX-only processors.

3DNow!, Enhanced 3DNow!, and 3DNow! Professional

3DNow! technology was originally introduced as AMD's alternative to the SSE instructions in the Intel processors. Actually, 3DNow! was first introduced in the K6 series before Intel released SSE in the Pentium III and then AMD added Enhanced 3DNow! to the Athlon and Duron processors. The latest version, 3DNow! Professional, was introduced in the first Athlon XP processors. AMD licensed MMX from Intel, and all its K6 series, Athlon, Duron, and later processors include full MMX instruction support. Not wanting to additionally license the SSE instructions being developed by Intel, AMD first came up with a different set of extensions beyond MMX called 3DNow!. Introduced in May 1998 in the K6-2 processor and enhanced when the Athlon was introduced in June 1999, 3DNow! and Enhanced 3DNow! are sets of instructions that extend the multimedia capabilities of the AMD chips beyond MMX. This enables greater performance for 3D graphics, multimedia, and other floating-point–intensive PC applications.

3DNow! technology is a set of 21 instructions that use SIMD techniques to operate on arrays of data rather than single elements. Enhanced 3DNow! adds 24 more instructions (19 SSE and 5 DSP/communications instructions) to the original 21, for a total of 45 new instructions. Positioned as an extension to MMX technology, 3DNow! is similar to the SSE found in the Pentium III and Celeron processors from Intel. According to AMD, 3DNow! provides approximately the same level of improvement to MMX as did SSE, but in fewer instructions with less complexity. Although similar in capability, they are not compatible at the instruction level, so software specifically written to support SSE does not support 3DNow!, and vice versa. The latest version of 3DNow!, 3DNow! Professional, adds 51 SSE commands to 3DNow! Enhanced, meaning that 3DNow! Professional now supports all SSE commands; as a result, AMD chips now essentially have SSE capability. With the introduction of the AMD Athlon 64 processor (Clawhammer), AMD also started to support SSE2. Current AMD Athlon 64, Mobile Athlon 64, select AMD Sempron, and Mobile Sempron processors, as well as AMD Turion 64 processors all support both SSE2 and SSE3 and AMD's own 3DNow! instructions. Today AMD no longer specifically distinguishes between Enhanced 3DNow! and 3DNow! Professional since all current AMD processors feature the full set of both under the feature name 3DNow!.

Just as with SSE, 3DNow! supports single-precision floating-point SIMD operations and enables up to four floating-point operations per cycle. 3DNow! floating-point instructions can be mixed with MMX instructions with no performance penalties. 3DNow! also supports data prefetching.

Also like SSE, 3DNow! is well supported by software, including Windows 9x, Windows NT 4.0, and all newer Microsoft operating systems. 3DNow!–specific support is no longer a big issue if you are using an Athlon XP or Athlon 64 processor because they now fully support SSE through their support of 3DNow! Professional.

Dynamic Execution

First used in the P6 or sixth-generation processors (including the Pentium Pro, Pentium II/III, and Celeron processors based on the Pentium II and III designs), dynamic execution enables the processor to execute more instructions in parallel so that tasks are completed more quickly. This technology innovation is composed of three main elements:

- **Multiple branch prediction**—Predicts the flow of the program through several branches
- **Data flow analysis**—Schedules instructions to be executed when ready, independent of their order in the original program
- **Speculative execution**—Increases the rate of execution by looking ahead of the program counter and executing instructions that are likely to be necessary

Branch Prediction

Branch prediction is a feature formerly found only in high-end mainframe processors. It enables the processor to keep the instruction pipeline full while running at a high rate of speed. A special fetch/decode unit in the processor uses a highly optimized branch-prediction algorithm to predict the direction and outcome of the instructions being executed through multiple levels of branches, calls, and returns. It is similar to a chess player working out multiple strategies before game play by predicting the opponent's strategy several moves into the future. Because the instruction outcome is predicted in advance, the instructions can be executed with no waiting.

Data Flow Analysis

Data flow analysis studies the flow of data through the processor to detect any opportunities for out-of-order instruction execution. A special dispatch/execute unit in the processor monitors many instructions and can execute these instructions in an order that optimizes the use of the multiple superscalar execution units. The resulting out-of-order execution of instructions can keep the execution units busy even when cache misses and other data-dependent instructions might otherwise hold things up.

Speculative Execution

Speculative execution is the processor's capability to execute instructions in advance of the actual program counter. The processor's dispatch/execute unit uses data flow analysis to execute all available instructions in the instruction pool and store the results in temporary registers. A retirement unit then searches the instruction pool for completed instructions that are no longer data-dependent on other instructions to run or that have unresolved branch predictions. If any such completed instructions are found, the results are committed to memory by the retirement unit or the appropriate standard Intel architecture in the order they were originally issued. They are then retired from the pool.

Dynamic execution essentially removes the constraint and dependency on linear instruction sequencing. By promoting out-of-order instruction execution, it can keep the instruction units working rather than waiting for data from memory. Even though instructions can be predicted and executed out of order, the results are committed in the original order, to avoid disrupting or changing program flow. This enables the processors in the P6 generation to run existing Intel architecture software exactly as the Pentium (P5 generation) and previous processors did—just a whole lot more quickly!

Dual Independent Bus Architecture

The dual independent bus (DIB) architecture was another innovation that was first implemented in the sixth-generation processors from Intel and AMD. DIB was created to improve processor bus bandwidth and performance. Having two (dual) independent data I/O buses enables the processor to access data from either bus simultaneously and in parallel rather than in a singular sequential manner (as in a single-bus system). The main (often called front-side) processor bus is the interface between the processor and the motherboard or chipset. The second (back-side) bus in a processor with DIB is used for the L2 cache, enabling it to run at much greater speeds than if it shared the main processor bus.

Two buses make up the DIB architecture: the L2 cache bus and the main CPU bus, often called the front-side bus (FSB). The P6 class processors from the Pentium Pro to the Celeron, Pentium II/III/4, and Athlon/Duron processors can use both buses simultaneously, eliminating a bottleneck there. The dual-bus architecture enables the L2 cache of the newer processors to run at full speed inside the processor core on an independent bus, leaving the main CPU bus (FSB) to handle normal data flowing into and out of the chip. The two buses run at different speeds. The front-side bus or main CPU bus is coupled to the speed of the motherboard, whereas the back-side or L2 cache bus is coupled to the speed of the processor core. As the frequency of processors increases, so does the speed of the L2 cache.

The key to implementing DIB was to move the L2 cache memory off the motherboard and into the processor package. The L1 cache always has been a direct part of the processor die, but L2 was larger and originally had to be external. When the L2 cache was moved into the processor, the L2 cache could run at speeds more like the L1 cache, much faster than the motherboard or processor bus.

DIB also enables the system bus to perform multiple simultaneous transactions (instead of singular sequential transactions), accelerating the flow of information within the system and boosting performance. Overall, DIB architecture offers up to three times the bandwidth performance over a single-bus architecture processor.

Hyperthreading Technology

Computers with two or more physical processors have long had a performance advantage over single-processor computers when the operating system supports multiple processors, as is the case with Windows NT 4.0, 2000, XP Professional, and Linux. However, dual-processor motherboards and systems have always been more expensive than otherwise-comparable single-processor systems, and upgrading a dual-processor–capable system to dual-processor status can be difficult because of the need to match processor speeds and specifications. However, Intel's new hyperthreading (HT) technology allows a single processor to handle two independent sets of instructions at the same time. In essence, HT technology converts a single physical processor into two virtual processors.

Intel originally introduced HT technology in its line of Xeon processors for servers in March 2002. HT technology enables multiprocessor servers to act as if they had twice as many processors installed. HT technology was introduced on Xeon workstation-class processors with a 533MHz system bus and found its way into PC processors with the 3.06GHz Pentium 4 processor in November 2002. Since then, HT technology has appeared on desktop Pentium 4 processors from 2.4GHz through 3.6GHz, and mobile Pentium 4 processors from 2.66GHz through 3.46GHz, with the faster ones using the new Prescott core.

How Hyperthreading Works

Internally, an HT-enabled processor has two sets of general-purpose registers, control registers, and other architecture components, but both logical processors share the same cache, execution units, and buses. During operations, each logical processor handles a single thread (see Figure 4.14).

Although the sharing of some processor components means that the overall speed of an HT-enabled system isn't as high as a true dual-processor system would be, speed increases of 25% or more are possible when multiple applications or a single multithreaded application is being run.

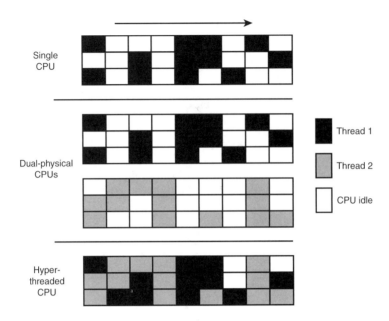

Figure 4.14 A processor with HT technology enabled can fill otherwise idle time with a second process, improving multitasking and performance of multithreading single applications.

Hyperthreading Requirements

The first HT-enabled PC processor is the Intel 3.06GHz Pentium 4. All faster Pentium 4 models also support HT technology, as do all processors 2.4GHz and faster that use the 800MHz bus. However, an HT-enabled Pentium 4 processor by itself can't bring the benefits of HT technology to your system. You also need the following:

- **A compatible motherboard (chipset)**—It might need a BIOS upgrade.

- **BIOS support to enable/disable HT technology**—If your operating system doesn't support HT technology, you should disable this feature.

- **A compatible operating system, such as Windows XP Home or Professional Editions**—When hyperthreading is enabled on these operating systems, the Device Manager shows two processors.

Although Windows NT 4.0 and Windows 2000 are designed to use multiple physical processors, HT technology requires specific operating system optimizations to work correctly. Linux distributions based on kernel 2.4.18 and higher also support HT technology.

Intel Mobile Processors

The following sections detail the specific mobile processors that Intel has introduced, starting with the SL Enhanced 486 processors, all the way up through the latest Mobile Pentium 4, Mobile Pentium 4-M, and Pentium M processors.

SL-Enhanced 486 Processors

The Intel486SL and SL-enhanced SX, DX2, and DX4 processors (with SL technology) were used in a number of laptop and other portable systems during the 1990s. The DX2 and DX4 versions are clock-doubled and -tripled versions, respectively, greatly adding to the speed and performance of the chip.

The following is a summary of features for the 486:

- 32-Bit RISC (reduced instruction set computer) integer core
- 8KB (SL/SX, DX2) or 16KB (DX4) on-die unified L1 cache
- Support for 4GB of physical memory
- Support for 64TB of virtual memory
- On-chip floating-point unit (math coprocessor)
- One cycle per instruction execution
- 33MHz 32-bit CPU bus (133MBps throughput)
- SL technology
- System Management Mode (SMM)
- 32-bit external data bus address range

The 486 uses a 32-bit wide (4-byte) processor data bus, which means that it moves 4 bytes per cycle on the processor bus. With a bus speed of 33MHz, that equates to 133MBps total throughput. The 486 also has a 32-bit address bus, which means that it can address 2^{32} bytes of memory, which is 4GB. However, most chipsets used with the 486 limit maximum memory to 64MB or less.

▶▶ See "SL Technology," p. 136.

Mobile Pentium

The main idea with most mobile processors is to shrink them as small as possible, which then lets them run at lower voltages; this saves power. The 200MHz and 233MHz Mobile Pentium processors with MMX technology (code-named Tillamook) were the first products manufactured using 0.25-micron process technology. Intel also made 300MHz, 266MHz, and 166MHz Mobile Pentium/MMX processors on the 0.25-micron process.

The 0.25-micron manufacturing process and Intel's voltage-reduction technology decreased the core voltage from 2.45V to 1.8V (2.0V for the 266MHz version), and the I/O interface from 3.3V to 2.5V, relative to previous-generation processors. The 0.25-micron manufacturing process increased chip speed up to 60%, while reducing power consumption (up to 53%) when compared to 166MHz Mobile Pentium processors with MMX technology on the 0.35-micron process. This reduction in voltages allows for higher speeds with less battery power use and less heat production. Typical power consumption can be reduced from 7.7W for 166MHz Mobile Pentium processors with MMX technology on the 0.35 process to 3.9W for the 233MHz processor. These improvements represent nearly a 50% decrease in power consumption.

Although Intel has largely replaced its Mobile Pentium processors with Mobile Pentium II/III/4/M and Mobile Celeron processors, the power and heat savings pioneered in the Mobile Pentium line live on in improved form in these newer processors for portable systems.

Intel also manufactured regular (non-MMX) Pentium chips at speeds of 75, 100, 120, 133, and 150MHz for use in low-end portable systems. These chips used voltage-reduction technology (VRT), which means that they draw the standard 3.3V from the motherboard, but internally they operate on only 2.9V (3.1V for the 150MHz model). Although this is not as dramatic of a reduction as that evidenced in the 0.25-micron process chips, VRT still reduces the overall power consumption and heat production of these processors. These processors are no longer being manufactured, but they will appear in older laptop computers that you might have or encounter.

Mobile Pentium II and III

In April 1998, Intel announced the first Mobile Pentium II processors. Running at 233MHz and 266MHz, these processors were also manufactured using the same 0.25-micron process used by the Mobile Pentium MMX. With a core voltage of 1.7V and an I/O buffer voltage of 1.8V, they run at even lower voltage levels than their Pentium MMX counterparts. Although at 8.6W, a 266MHz Pentium II consumes more power overall than a Pentium MMX running at the same speed, you must take into account that the Pentium II includes an integrated L2 cache, whereas the Pentium MMX, at 4.5W, does not.

To reduce power consumption and heat buildup while preserving speed, Intel redesigned the Mobile Pentium II in late 1998 to use a different method for accessing the L2 cache. The original Mobile Pentium II used a 512KB L2 cache running at half CPU speed, just like the desktop Pentium II processor, but the revised design changed to an integrated on-die L2 cache of just 256KB, but running at the same speed as the CPU. Because this cache is manufactured directly on the processor die, it runs at the same speed as the processor core and uses less power than slower external cache.

The Mobile Pentium III is an improved version of the Mobile Pentium II, also using an on-die 256KB L2 cache, but with several design improvements, including the use of the .18-micron architecture, core voltages ranging from 1.7V (for the 1GHz and 900MHz versions) to as low as 1.1V (for the 500MHz versions), and SpeedStep power-saving technology for the 600MHz and faster versions. To reduce size, most versions of the Mobile Pentium III use the BGA-2 and micro-PGA2 packaging. The Mobile Pentium III also supports seven clock states for a wider range of power-saving modes than on earlier mobile processors.

Table 4.3 lists the speed, manufacturing process, and voltage specifications for the Mobile Pentium II and III and Mobile Celeron CPUs manufactured by Intel.

Table 4.3   Intel Mobile Processor Specifications

Processor Voltage	Core Speed	Bus Speed	Manufacturing Process	Core Voltage	I/O Buffer
Pentium	75MHz	50MHz	0.35 micron	2.9V	3.3V
Pentium	100MHz	66MHz	0.35 micron	2.9V	3.3V
Pentium	120MHz	60MHz	0.35 micron	2.9V	3.3V
Pentium	133MHz	66MHz	0.35 micron	2.9V	3.3V
Pentium	150MHz	60MHz	0.35 micron	3.1V	3.3V
Pentium/MMX	120MHz	60MHz	0.35 micron	2.45V	3.3V
Pentium/MMX	133MHz	66MHz	0.35 micron	2.45V	3.3V
Pentium/MMX	150MHz	60MHz	0.35 micron	2.45V	3.3V
Pentium/MMX	166MHz	66MHz	0.35 micron	2.45V	3.3V
Pentium/MMX	166MHz	66MHz	0.25 micron	1.8V	2.5V
Pentium/MMX	200MHz	66MHz	0.25 micron	1.8V	2.5V
Pentium/MMX	233MHz	66MHz	0.25 micron	1.8V	2.5V
Pentium/MMX	266MHz	66MHz	0.25 micron	2.0V	2.5V
Pentium/MMX	300MHz	66MHz	0.25 micron	2.0V	2.5V
Pentium II	233MHz	66MHz	0.25 micron	1.7V	1.8V
Pentium II	266MHz	66MHz	0.25 micron	1.7V	1.8V

Table 4.3   Continued

Processor Voltage	Core Speed	Bus Speed	Manufacturing Process	Core Voltage	I/O Buffer
Pentium II	300MHz	66MHz	0.25 micron	1.6V	1.8V
Pentium II	333MHz	66MHz	0.25 micron	1.6V	1.8V
Pentium II	366MHz	66MHz	0.25 micron	1.6V	1.8V
Pentium II	400MHz	66MHz	0.25 micron	1.6V	1.8V
Celeron	266MHz-LV	66MHz	0.25 micron	1.5V	1.8V
Celeron	266MHz	66MHz	0.25 micron	1.6V	1.8V
Celeron	300MHz	66MHz	0.25 micron	1.6V	1.8V
Celeron	333MHz	66MHz	0.25 micron	1.6V	1.8V
Celeron	366MHz	66MHz	0.25 micron	1.6V	1.8V
Celeron	400MHz	66MHz	0.25 micron	1.6V	1.8V
Celeron	433MHz	66MHz	0.25 micron	1.9V	1.8V
Celeron	466MHz	66MHz	0.25 micron	1.9V	1.8V
Celeron	400MHz-LV	100MHz	0.18 micron	1.35V	1.5V
Celeron	450MHz	100MHz	0.18 micron	1.6V	1.5V
Celeron	500MHz-LV	100MHz	0.18 micron	1.35V	1.5V
Celeron	500MHz	100MHz	0.18 micron	1.6V	1.5V
Celeron	550MHz	100MHz	0.18 micron	1.6V	1.5V
Celeron	600MHz	100MHz	0.18 micron	1.6V	1.5V
Celeron	650MHz	100MHz	0.18 micron	1.6V	1.5V
Celeron	700MHz	100MHz	0.18 micron	1.6V	1.5V
Celeron	750MHz	100MHz	0.18 micron	1.6V	1.5V
Pentium III	400MHz	100MHz	0.18 micron	1.35V	1.5V
Pentium III	450MHz	100MHz	0.18 micron	1.6V	1.5V
Pentium III	500MHz	100MHz	0.18 micron	1.6V	1.5V
Pentium III	500MHz-ULV	100MHz	0.18 micron	1.1/0.975V[1]	1.5V
Pentium III	600MHz-LV	100MHz	0.18 micron	1.35/1.1V[1]	1.5V
Pentium III	600MHz	100MHz	0.18 micron	1.6/1.35V[1]	1.5V
Pentium III	650MHz	100MHz	0.18 micron	1.6/1.35V[1]	1.5V
Pentium III	700MHz	100MHz	0.18 micron	1.6/1.35V[1]	1.5V
Pentium III	700MHz-LV	100MHz	0.18 micron	1.35/1.1V[1]	1.5V
Pentium III	750MHz	100MHz	0.18 micron	1.6/1.35V[1]	1.5V
Pentium III	800MHz	100MHz	0.18 micron	1.6/1.35V[1]	1.5V
Pentium III	850MHz	100MHz	0.18 micron	1.6/1.35V[1]	1.5V
Pentium III	900MHz	100MHz	0.18 micron	1.7/1.35V[1]	1.5V
Pentium III	1GHz	100MHz	0.18 micron	1.7/1.35V[1]	1.5V

1. Uses Intel SpeedStep technology, optionally switching to lower speed and voltage to conserve battery life

LV = Low Voltage

ULV = Ultra Low Voltage

Mobile Pentium Processor Steppings

As with Intel's desktop processor, the chips of the mobile processor line undergo continual development and are modified in the form of steppings that incorporate corrections and refinements into the hardware-manufacturing process.

Note

The Mobile Pentium, Mobile Pentium MMX, and Mobile Pentium II processors are no longer being produced, but you might still encounter them in the field.

Tables 4.4 and 4.5 list various versions and steppings for the Mobile Pentium and Mobile Pentium MMX processors.

Table 4.4   Mobile Pentium Processor Versions and Steppings

Type	Family	Model	Stepping	Mfg. Stepping	Core/Bus	Spec. Number	Comments
0	5	2	1	B1	75/50	Q0601	TCP
0	5	2	2	B3	75/50	Q0606	TCP
0	5	2	2	B3	75/50	SX951	TCP
0/2	5	2	4	B5	75/50	Q0704	TCP
0	5	2	4	B5	75/50	SX975	TCP
0	5	2	5	C2	75/50	Q0725	TCP
0	5	2	5	C2	75/50	SK079	TCP
0	5	2	5	mA1	75/50	Q0686	VRT, TCP
0	5	2	5	mA1	75/50	Q0689	VRT
0	5	2	5	mA1	90/60	Q0694	VRT, TCP
0	5	2	5	mA1	90/60	Q0695	VRT
0	5	2	5	mA1	75/50	SK089	VRT, TCP
0	5	2	5	mA1	75/50	SK091	VRT
0	5	2	5	mA1	90/60	SK090	VRT, TCP
0	5	2	5	mA1	90/60	SK092	VRT
0	5	2	B	mcB1	100/66	Q0884	VRT, TCP
0	5	2	B	mcB1	120/60	Q0779	VRT, TCP
0	5	2	B	mcB1	120/60	Q0808	
0	5	2	B	mcB1	100/66	SY029	VRT, TCP
0	5	2	B	mcB1	120/60	SK113	VRT, TCP
0	5	2	B	mcB1	120/60	SK118	VRT, TCP
0	5	2	B	mcB1	120/60	SX999	
0	5	7	0	mA4	75/50	Q0848	VRT, TCP
0	5	7	0	mA4	75/50	Q0851	VRT
0	5	7	0	mA4	90/60	Q0849	VRT, TCP
0	5	7	0	mA4	90/60	Q0852	VRT
0	5	7	0	mA4	100/66	Q0850	VRT, TCP
0	5	7	0	mA4	100/66	Q0853	VRT

Table 4.4   Continued

Type	Family	Model	Stepping	Mfg. Stepping	Core/Bus	Spec. Number	Comments
0	5	7	0	mA4	75/50	SK119	VRT, TCP
0	5	7	0	mA4	75/50	SK122	VRT
0	5	7	0	mA4	90/60	SK120	VRT, TCP
0	5	7	0	mA4	90/60	SK123	VRT
0	5	7	0	mA4	100/66	SK121	VRT, TCP
0	5	7	0	mA4	100/66	SK124	VRT
0	5	2	C	mcC0	100/66	Q0887	VRT, TCP
0	5	2	C	mcC0	120/60	Q0879	VRT, TCP
0	5	2	C	mcC0	120/60	Q0880	3.1V
0	5	2	C	mcC0	133/66	Q0881	VRT, TCP
0	5	2	C	mcC0	133/66	Q0882	3.1V
0	5	2	C	mcC0	150/60	Q024	VRT, TCP
0	5	2	C	mcC0	150/60	Q0906	TCP, 3.1V
0	5	2	C	mcC0	150/60	Q040	VRT
0	5	2	C	mcC0	75/50	SY056	VRT/TCP
0	5	2	C	mcC0	100/66	SY020	VRT/TCP
0	5	2	C	mcC0	100/66	SY046	3.1V
0	5	2	C	mcC0	120/60	SY021	VRT, TCP
0	5	2	C	mcC0	120/60	SY027	3.1V
0	5	2	C	mcC0	120/60	SY030	
0	5	2	C	mcC0	133/66	SY019	VRT, TCP
0	5	2	C	mcC0	133/66	SY028	3.1V
0	5	2	C	mcC0	150/60	SY061	VRT, TCP
0	5	2	C	mcC0	150/60	SY043	TCP, 3.1V
0	5	2	C	mcC0	150/60	SY058	VRT
0	5	2	6	E0	75/50	Q0846	TCP
0	5	2	6	E0	75/50	SY009	TCP

Table 4.5   Mobile Pentium MMX Processor Versions and Steppings

Type	Family	Model	Stepping	Mfg. Stepping	Core/Bus	Spec. Number	Comments
0	5	4	4	mxA3	150/60	Q016	ES, TCP, 2.285V
0	5	4	4	mxA3	150/60	Q061	ES, PPGA, 2.285V
0	5	4	4	mxA3	166/66	Q017	ES, TCP, 2.285V
0	5	4	4	mxA3	166/66	Q062	ES, PPGA, 2.285V
0	5	4	4	mxA3	150/60	SL22G	TCP, 2.285V
0	5	4	4	mxA3	150/60	SL246	PPGA, 2.285V

(continues)

Table 4.5   Continued

Type	Family	Model	Stepping	Mfg. Stepping	Core/Bus	Spec. Number	Comments
0	5	4	4	mxA3	166/66	SL22F	TCP, 2.285V
0	5	4	4	mxA3	166/66	SL23Z	PPGA, 2.285V
0	5	4	3	mxB1	120/60	Q230	ES, TCP, 2.2V
0	5	4	3	mxB1	133/66	Q130	ES, TCP, 2.285V
0	5	4	3	mxB1	133/66	Q129	ES, PPGA, 2.285V
0	5	4	3	mxB1	150/60	Q116	ES, TCP, 2.285V
0	5	4	3	mxB1	150/60	Q128	ES, PPGA, 2.285V
0	5	4	3	mxB1	166/66	Q115	ES, TCP, 2.285V
0	5	4	3	mxB1	166/66	Q127	ES, PPGA, 2.285V
0	5	4	3	mxB1	133/66	SL27D	TCP, 2.285V
0	5	4	3	mxB1	133/66	SL27C	PPGA, 2.285V
0	5	4	3	mxB1	150/60	SL26U	TCP, 2.285V
0	5	4	3	mxB1	150/60	SL27B	PPGA, 2.285V
0	5	4	3	mxB1	166/66	SL26T	TCP, 2.285V
0	5	4	3	mxB1	166/66	SL27A	PPGA, 2.285V
0	5	8	1	myA0	166/66	Q255	TCP, 1.8V
0	5	8	1	myA0	200/66	Q146	TCP, 1.8V
0	5	8	1	myA0	233/66	Q147	TCP, 1.8V
0	5	8	1	myA0	200/66	SL28P	TCP, 1.8V
0	5	8	1	myA0	233/66	SL28Q	TCP, 1.8V
0	5	8	1	myA0	266/66	Q250	TCP, 2.0V

ES = Engineering Sample. These chips were not sold through normal channels but were designed for development and testing purposes.

STP = The cB1 stepping is logically equivalent to the C2 step but on a different manufacturing process. The mcB1 step is logically equivalent to the cB1 step (except that it does not support DP, APIC, or FRC). The mcB1, mA1, mA4, and mcC0 steps also use Intel's VRT (voltage-reduction technology) and are available in the TCP or SPGA package, primarily to support mobile applications. The mxA3 is logically equivalent to the xA3 stepping (except that it does not support DP or APIC).

TCP = tape carrier package

PPGA = Plastic PGA

VRT = voltage-reduction technology

2.285V = This is a Mobile Pentium processor with MMX technology with a core operating voltage of 2.285V–2.665V.

1.8V = This is a Mobile Pentium processor with MMX technology with a core operating voltage of 1.665V–1.935V and an I/O operating voltage of 2.375V–2.625V.

2.2V = This is a Mobile Pentium processor with MMX technology with a core operating voltage of 2.10V–2.34V.

2.0V = This is a Mobile Pentium processor with MMX technology with a core operating voltage of 1.850V–2.150V and an I/O operating voltage of 2.375V–2.625V.

Table 4.6 lists the steppings for Mobile Pentium II processors in the Mobile Module, mobile minicartridge, and other forms.

Table 4.6 Mobile Pentium II Processor Steppings

Family	Model	Core Stepping	L2 Cache Size (KB)	L2 Cache Speed	S-Spec	Core/Bus	Notes
6	5	mdA0	512	1/2 core	SL2KH	233/66	MC, 1.7V
6	5	mdA0	512	1/2 core	SL2KJ	266/66	MC, 1.7V
6	5	mmdA0	512	1/2 core	PMD233	233/66	MMO, 1.7V
6	5	mmdA0	512	1/2 core	PMD266	266/66	MMO, 1.7V
6	5	mdB0	512	1/2 core	SL2RS	300/66	MC, 1.6V1
6	5	mdB0	512	1/2 core	SL2RR	266/66	MC, 1.6V1
6	5	mdB0	512	1/2 core	SL2RQ	233/66	MC, 1.6V1
6	5	mdxA0	256	core	SL32M	266/66	MC, 1.6V1
6	5	mdxA0	256	core	SL32N	300/66	MC, 1.6V1
6	5	mdxA0	256	core	SL32P	333/66	MC, 1.6V1
6	5	mdxA0	256	core	SL36Z	366/66	MC, 1.6V1
6	5	mdbA0	256	core	SL32Q	266/66	BG, 1.6V2
6	5	mdbA0	256	core	SL32R	300/66	BG, 1.6V2
6	5	mdbA0	256	core	SL32S	333/66	BG, 1.6V2
6	5	mdbA0	256	core	SL3AG	366/66	BG, 1.6V2
6	5	mdbA0	256	core	SL3DR	266/66	BG, 1.5V
6	5	mdbA0	256	core	SL3HH	266/66	PG, 1.6V2
6	5	mdbA0	256	core	SL3HJ	300/66	PG, 1.6V2
6	5	mdbA0	256	core	SL3HK	333/66	PG, 1.6V2
6	5	mdbA0	256	core	SL3HL	366/66	PG, 1.6V2

1.7V = Core processor voltage is 1.7V for these Mobile Pentium processors.

1.6V1 = Core processor voltage is 1.6V +/– 120mV for these processors.

1.6V2 = Core processor voltage is 1.6V +/– 135mV for these processors.

1.5V = Core processor voltage is 1.6V +/– 135mV for this processor.

MC = Mobile Pentium II processor mounted in a minicartridge.

MMO = Mobile Pentium II processor mounted in a Mobile Module, including the 440BX North Bridge.

BG = Mobile Pentium II processor in BGA packaging for low-profile surface mounting.

PG = Mobile Pentium II processor in a micro-PGA1 package.

Mobile Pentium III Processors and Steppings

The Mobile Pentium III has also been available in a number of models and steppings, which can be distinguished by their specification numbers and other details (see Table 4.7).

Table 4.7 Mobile Pentium III Processor Models and Revisions

Speed (MHz)	Speed Step (MHz)	S-Spec	Stepping	CPUID	L2 Cache	Power (W)	Speed Step (W)	Voltage	Form Factor
400	—	SL3DU	BA2	0681	256K	10.1	—	1.35V	BGA2
400	—	SL43K	BB0	0683	256K	10.1	—	1.35V	BGA2

(continues)

Table 4.7 Continued

Speed (MHz)	Speed Step (MHz)	S-Spec	Step- ping	CPUID	L2 Cache	Power (W)	Speed Step (W)	Voltage	Form Factor
400	—	SL4JN	BC0	0686	256K	10.1	—	1.35V	BGA2
450	—	SL3KX	PA2	0681	256K	15.5	—	1.6V	BGA2
450	—	SL43L	BB0	0683	256K	15.5	—	1.6V	BGA2
450	—	SL4JA	BC0	0686	256K	15.5	—	1.6V	BGA2
450	—	SL4JQ	PC0	0686	256K	15.5	—	1.6V	PGA2
450	—	SL3RF	PA2	0681	256K	15.5	—	1.6V	PGA2
450	—	SL3LG	PA2	0681	256K	15.5	—	1.6V	PGA2
450	—	SL43N	PB0	0683	256K	15.5	—	1.6V	PGA2
450	—	PML45 00200 1AA	MA2	0681	256K	14.1	—	1.6/ 1.35V	MMC-2
450	—	PML45 00210 1AB	MB0	0683	256K	14.1	—	1.6/ 1.35V	MMC-2
450	—	PML45 00220 1AC	MC0	0686	256K	14.1	—	1.6V	MMC-2
500	—	SL3DT	BA2	0681	256K	16.8	—	1.6V	BGA2
500	—	SL43M	BB0	0683	256K	16.8	—	1.6V	BGA2
500	—	SL3PK	BA2	0681	256K	10.1	—	1.35V	BGA2
500	—	SL43Z	BB0	0683	256K	10.1	—	1.35V	BGA2
500	—	SL4JB	BC0	0686	256K	15.5	—	1.6V	BGA2
500	—	SL4JP	BC0	0686	256K	10.1	—	1.35V	BGA2
500	300	SL4ZH	BC0	0686	256K	8.1	4.5	1.1/ 0.975V	BGA2
500	—	SL4JR	PC0	0686	256K	16.8	—	1.6V	PGA2
500	—	SL3RG	PA2	0681	256K	16.8	—	1.6V	PGA2
500	—	SL3DW	PA2	0681	256K	16.8	—	1.6V	PGA2
500	—	SL43P	PB0	0683	256K	16.8	—	1.6V	PGA2
500	—	PML50 00200 1AA	MA2	0681	256K	15.0	—	1.6V	MMC-2
500	—	PML50 00210 1AB	MB0	0683	256K	15.0	—	1.6V	MMC-2
500	—	PML50 00220 1AC	MC0	0686	256K	15.0	—	1.6V	MMC-2
600	500	SL3PM	PA2	0681	256K	20.0	12.2	1.6/ 1.35V	BGA2

Table 4.7 Continued

Speed (MHz)	Speed Step (MHz)	S-Spec	Stepping	CPUID	L2 Cache	Power (W)	Speed Step (W)	Voltage	Form Factor
600	500	SL43Y	BA2	0683	256K	20.0	12.2	1.6/ 1.35V	BGA2
600	500	SL4GH	BB0	0683	256K	14.4	8.1	1.35/ 1.1V	BGA2
600	500	SL4JH	BC0	0686	256K	15.8	8.7	1.6/ 1.35V	BGA2
600	500	SL4JM	BC0	0686	256K	14.4	8.1	1.35/ 1.1V	BGA2
600	500	SL4JX	PC0	0686	256K	20.0	12.2	1.6/ 1.35V	PGA2
600	500	SL3TP	PA2	0681	256K	20.0	12.2	1.6/ 1.35V	PGA2
600	500	SL3PM	PA2	0681	256K	20.0	12.2	1.6/ 1.35V	PGA2
600	500	SL443	PB0	0683	256K	20.0	12.2	1.6/ 1.35V	PGA2
600	500	PML60 00200 1AA	MA2	0681	256K	16.6	12.2	1.6/ 1.35V	MMC-2
600	500	PML60 00210 1AB	MB0	0683	256K	16.6	12.2	1.6/ 1.35V	MMC-2
600	500	PMM60 00220 1AC	MC0	0686	256K	16.6	12.2	1.6/ 1.35V	MMC-2
650	500	SL3PG	BA2	0681	256K	21.5	12.2	1.6/ 1.35V	BGA2
650	500	SL43X	BB0	0683	256K	21.5	12.2	1.6/ 1.35V	BGA2
650	500	SL4JJ	BC0	0686	256K	21.5	12.2	1.6/ 1.35V	BGA2
650	500	SL4JY	PC0	0686	256K	21.5	12.2	1.6/ 1.35V	PGA2
650	500	SL3TQ	PA2	0681	256K	21.5	12.2	1.6/ 1.35V	PGA2
650	500	SL3PL	PA2	0681	256K	21.5	12.2	1.6/ 1.35V	PGA2
650	500	SL442	PB0	0683	256K	21.5	12.2	1.6/ 1.35V	PGA2

(continues)

Table 4.7   Continued

Speed (MHz)	Speed Step (MHz)	S-Spec	Step-ping	CPUID	L2 Cache	Power (W)	Speed Step (W)	Voltage	Form Factor
650	500	PML65 00200 1AA	MA2	0681	256K	17.8	12.2	1.6/ 1.35V	MMC-2
650	500	PMM65 00210 1AB	MB0	0683	256K	17.8	12.2	1.6/ 1.35V	MMC-2
650	500	PMM65 00210 1AC	MC0	0686	256K	17.8	12.2	1.6/ 1.35V	MMC-2
700	500	SL56R	BC0	0686	256K	16.1	8.1	1.35/ 1.1V	BGA2
700	550	SL3Z7	BB0	0683	256K	22.0	13.2	1.6/ 1.35V	BGA2
700	550	SL4JK	BC0	0686	256K	22.0	13.2	1.6/ 1.35V	BGA2
700	550	SL4JZ	PC0	0683	256K	22.0	13.2	1.6/ 1.35V	PGA2
700	550	SL4DL	PB0	0683	256K	22.0	13.4	1.6/ 1.35V	PGA2
700	550	SL3Z8	PB0	0683	256K	22.0	13.4	1.6/ 1.35V	PGA2
700	550	PMM70 00210 1AA	MB0	0683	256K	19.1	13.4	1.6/ 1.35V	MMC-2
700	550	PMM70 00220 1AB	MC0	0686	256K	19.1	13.4	1.6/ 1.35V	MMC-2
750	600	SL4JL	BC0	0686	256K	24.6	14.4	1.6/ 1.35V	BGA2
750	600	SL54A	BD0	068A	256K	24.6	14.4	1.6/ 1.35V	BGA2
750	600	SL4K2	PC0	0686	256K	24.6	14.4	1.6/ 1.35V	PGA2
750	600	SL53P	PD0	068A	256K	24.6	14.4	1.6/ 1.35V	PGA2
750	600	SL4DM	MB0	0683	256K	24.6	14.4	1.6/ 1.35V	PGA2
750	600	SL44T	MB0	0683	256K	24.6	14.4	1.6/ 1.35V	PGA2
750	600	SL4AS	MB0	0683	256K	24.6	14.4	1.6/ 1.35V	BGA2

Table 4.7   Continued

Speed (MHz)	Speed Step (MHz)	S-Spec	Step-ping	CPUID	L2 Cache	Power (W)	Speed Step (W)	Voltage	Form Factor
750	600	PMM75 00210 1AB	MB0	0683	256K	24.6	14.4	1.6/ 1.35V	MMC-2
750	600	PMM75 00210 1AA	MB0	0683	256K	24.6	14.4	1.6/ 1.35V	MMC-2
750	600	PMM75 00220 1AB	MC0	0686	256K	24.6	14.4	1.6/ 1.35V	MMC-2
800	650	SL4AK	BC0	0686	256K	25.9	15.1	1.6/ 1.35V	BGA2
800	650	SL548	BD0	068A	256K	25.9	15.1	1.6/ 1.35V	BGA2
800	650	SL4GT	PC0	0686	256K	25.9	15.1	1.6/ 1.35V	PGA2
800	650	SL53M	PD0	068A	256K	25.9	15.1	1.6/ 1.35V	PGA2
800	650	PMM80 00220 1AA	MC0	0686	256K	24.6	14.4	1.6/ 1.35V	MMC-2
850	700	SL4AG	BC0	0686	256K	27.5	16.1	1.6/ 1.35V	BGA2
850	700	SL547	BD0	068A	256K	27.5	16.1	1.6/ 1.35V	BGA2
850	700	SL4AH	PC0	0686	256K	27.5	16.1	1.6/ 1.35V	PGA2
850	700	SL53L	PD0	068A	256K	27.5	16.1	1.6/ 1.35V	PGA2
850	700	PMM85 00220 1AA	MC0	0686	256K	24.6	14.4	1.6/ 1.35V	MMC-2
900	700	SL59H	BC0	0686	256K	30.7	16.1	1.6/ 1.35V	BGA2
900	700	SL59J	PC0	0686	256K	30.7	16.1	1.7/ 1.35V	BGA2
1000	700	SL54F	BD0	068A	256K	34.0	16.1	1.7/ 1.35V	BGA2
1000	700	SL53S	PD0	068A	256K	34.0	16.1	1.7/ 1.35V	PGA2

PGA2 = 495-pin micro-PGA2 (pin grid array 2) form factor
BGA2 = 495-pin BGA2 (ball grid array 2) form factor
MMC-2 = Mobile Module Connector 2 form factor
SpeedStep = Technology that optionally runs the processor at a lower speed and voltage in a battery-optimized mode

Mobile Pentium 4 and Pentium 4-M Processors

The mobile Pentium 4-M, introduced in March 2002, represents a new generation in processors. If this one had a number instead of a name, it might be called the 786 because it represents a generation beyond the previous sixth-generation or 686-class processors. The Mobile Pentium 4-M utilizes a 478-pin, micro flip chip pin grid array (micro-FCPGA) package and plugs into a micro-479 PGA mobile (mPGA479M) socket (see Figure 4.15).

Figure 4.15   Mobile Pentium 4-M micro-FCPGA processor.

The main technical details for the Pentium 4-M include these:

- Speeds that range from 1.4GHz to 2.6GHz
- 55 million transistors, 0.13-micron process, 131mm² die (Northwood, see Figure 4.16) or 125 million transistors, 112mm² die, on the 0.09-micron process (Prescott)
- Software compatible with previous Intel 32-bit processors
- Processor (front-side) bus that runs at 400MHz
- Arithmetic logic units (ALUs) that run at twice the processor core frequency
- Hyperpipelined (up to 20-stage) technology
- Very deep out-of-order instruction execution
- Enhanced branch prediction
- 20KB L1 cache (12KB L1 execution trace cache plus 8KB L1 data cache)
- 512KB of on-die, full-core speed 128-bit L2 cache with eight-way associativity (Northwood) or 1MB on-die, full-core speed 128-bit L2 cache with eight-way associativity (Prescott)
- L2 cache that can handle up to 4GB RAM and that supports ECC
- SSE2—144 new SSE2 instructions for graphics and sound processing (Northwood)

■ SSE3—13 new SIMD instructions to supplement SSE2 (Prescott)

■ Enhanced floating-point unit

■ Multiple low-power states

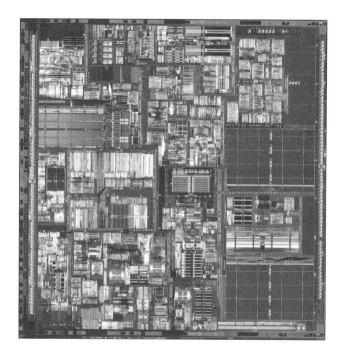

Figure 4.16   Pentium 4 Northwood die (0.13-micron process, 55 million transistors, 131mm²). (Photograph used by permission of Intel Corporation.)

Intel has abandoned Roman numerals for a standard Arabic numeral 4 designation. Internally, the Pentium 4-M introduces a new architecture that Intel calls *NetBurst microarchitecture*, which is a marketing term, not a technical term. Intel uses NetBurst to describe hyperpipelined technology, a rapid-execution engine, a high-speed (400MHz) system bus, and an execution trace cache. The hyperpipelined technology doubles the instruction pipeline depth as compared to the Pentium III, meaning that more and smaller steps are required to execute instructions. This might seem less efficient, but it enables much higher clock speeds to be more easily attained. The rapid-execution engine enables the two integer arithmetic logic units (ALUs) to run at twice the processor core frequency, which means that instructions can execute in half a clock cycle. The 400MHz system bus is a quad-pumped bus running off a 100MHz system clock transferring data four times per clock cycle. The execution trace cache is a high-performance Level 1 cache that stores approximately 12KB decoded micro-operations. This removes the instruction decoder from the main execution pipeline, increasing performance.

Of these, the high-speed processor bus is most notable. Technically, the processor bus is a 100MHz quad-pumped bus that transfers four times per cycle (4x), for a 400MHz effective rate. Because the bus is 64 bits (8 bytes) wide, this results in a throughput rate of 3200MBps.

In the new 20-stage pipelined internal architecture, individual instructions are broken down into many more substages, making this almost like a RISC processor. Unfortunately, this can add to the number of cycles taken to execute instructions if they are not optimized for this processor. Early benchmarks running existing software showed that existing Pentium III or AMD Athlon processors could easily keep pace with or even exceed the Pentium 4 in specific tasks; however, this is changing now that applications are being recompiled to work smoothly with the Pentium 4's deep pipelined architecture.

When used in conjunction with the requisite Intel SpeedStep technology driver, the Mobile Pentium 4-M supports Enhanced SpeedStep technology, which enables real-time dynamic switching of the voltage and frequency between two performance modes. This allows switching of the bus ratios, core operating voltage, and core processor speeds without resetting the system.

Table 4.8 lists the various models of the Pentium 4-M processors that Intel has released.

Table 4.8   Pentium 4-M Processor Models and Revisions

Speed	Bus Speed	S-Spec	Stepping	CPUID	L2-Cache	Thermal Design Power (W)
1.40GHz	400MHz	SL5ZX	PB0	0F24	512KB	25.8
1.50GHz	400MHz	SL5ZY	PB0	0F24	512KB	26.9
1.60GHz	400MHz	SL5ZY	PB0	0F24	512KB	30.0
	400MHz	SL5YU	PB0	0F24	512KB	30.0
1.70GHz	400MHz	SL5ZZ	PB0	0F24	512KB	30.0
	400MHz	SL5YT	PB0	0F24	512KB	30.0
1.80GHz	400MHz	SL69D	PB0	0F24	512KB	30.0
1.90GHz	400MHz	SL6DE	PB0	0F24	512KB	32.0
2.00GHz	400MHz	SL6DF	PB0	0F24	512KB	32.0
2.20GHz	400MHz	SL6LR	PC1	0F27	512KB	35.0
2.40GHz	400MHz	SL6K5	PC1	0F27	512KB	35.0
2.50GHz	400MHz	SL6P2	PC1/PD1	0F29	512KB	35.0
2.60GHz	400MHz	SL6WZ	PD1	0F29	512KB	35.0

In June 2003, Intel introduced the Mobile Pentium 4, which is different from the Mobile Pentium 4-M. The main differences between the Mobile Pentium 4 and the Mobile Pentium 4-M are shown Table 4.9.

Table 4.9   Mobile Pentium 4-M and Mobile Pentium 4 Processor Differences

Feature	Mobile Pentium 4-M	Mobile Pentium 4
Bus speed	400MHz	533MHz
CPU speed	Up to 2.6GHz	Up to 3.2GHz
SpeedStep	Yes	Yes
Hyperthreading	No	Optional
Voltage	1.3/1.2V	1.5/1.2V
Power	35W	70W

In essence, the Mobile Pentium 4 is based on the desktop Pentium 4 processor but is designed to run on a marginally lower voltage and with the addition of enhanced SpeedStep. This processor is designed for high-powered laptops that are used more as transportable desktop systems, in which battery life is not a big concern. Hence, this processor is meant for laptops used around the office that are more often plugged into the power socket than not, and not so much for use on the road.

Although the Pentium 4 is close to being a desktop chip, it still offers power-management and reduced voltage operation features that make it much more suitable for use in a laptop than the full desktop version of the Pentium 4. Table 4.10 shows the specifications for the Mobile Pentium 4 processors.

Table 4.10   Mobile Pentium 4 Processor Specifications

CPU Max Speed	CPU Min Speed	CPU Bus Speed	S-Spec	Power (Watts)
3.06GHz	1.6GHz	533MHz	SL726	70
2.80GHz	1.6GHz	533MHz	SL725	68.4
2.66GHz	1.6GHz	533MHz	SL724	66.1
2.40GHz	1.6GHz	533MHz	SL723	59.8

Pentium M

The Pentium M is the first Intel processor designed exclusively for mobile use. The Pentium M processor (code-named Banias) was officially introduced in March 2003 along with the 855 chipset family and the PRO/Wireless 2100 Mini PCI network adapter, which fall under what Intel calls the Centrino brand name when combined in a single system. Today, these components have been updated to offer either the Intel PRO/Wireless 2200BG or Intel PRO/Wireless 2915ABG network adapter, able to connect to 802.11b/g or 802.11a/ b/g wireless networks, respectively. The 855 chipset has been superseded by the Mobile Intel 915 PCI Express chipset, offering DDR2 SDRAM and PCI Express support. Figure 4.17 shows all of the components that make up the Centrino brand.

The core of Centrino is the Pentium M processor, which, in many ways, seems to be a combination of the best features of both the Pentium III and Pentium 4 processor cores, with a Pentium 4 bus and other major enhancements and features added. The major enhancements come in the form of several new internal architectural features, including the following:

- Micro-operation fusion. Micro-operations derived from the same instruction or macro-operation are fused together, resulting in greater throughput using less power.

- Extended Stack Pointer (ESP) Folding. High-level code often requires intensive stack manipulation. ESP Folding eliminates ESP-manipulation micro-operations in stack-related operations, enabling faster execution.

- 32KB L1 cache.

- Massive 1MB (Banias) or 2MB (Dothan) on-die L2 cache (twice as large as the Pentium 4 cache).

- Wider queues and translation lookaside buffers (TLBs).

- 128 entries in TLBs.

- Improved branch prediction.

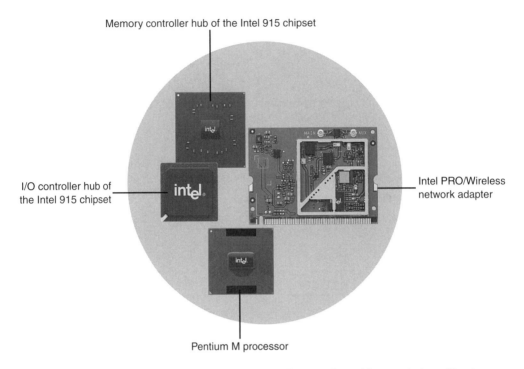

Figure 4.17 labels:
Memory controller hub of the Intel 915 chipset

I/O controller hub of the Intel 915 chipset

Intel PRO/Wireless network adapter

Pentium M processor

Figure 4.17 Pentium M and Centrino components. (Photograph used by permission of Intel Corporation.)

The Pentium M offers performance equal to or even greater than that of the Pentium 4, while consuming much less power and generating much less heat. Other features include these:

- 77 million transistors, 0.13-micron process, and 84mm² die (Banias, see Figure 4.18) or 140 million transistors, 0.09-micron process, 84mm² die (Dothan)
- Software compatible with previous Intel 32-bit processors
- Processor (front-side) bus that runs at 400MHz
- SSE2—144 new SSE2 instructions for graphics and sound processing (Banias)
- SSE3—13 new SIMD instructions to supplement SSE2 (Dothan)
- Enhanced floating-point unit
- Multiple low-power states, including the capability to power off portions of the processor and cache that aren't being used

The Pentium M processor with the Banias core contains 77 million transistors and is manufactured using 0.13-micron process technology. It is available in speeds ranging from 1.3GHz to 1.7GHz. A new version of the Pentium M, code-named Dothan, manufactured with a 0.09-micron process, was introduced in May 2004, offering higher clock speeds, 1.8GHz and up, as well as even lower power consumption and better performance. Dothan increased the transistor count to 140 million, largely due to the 2MB L2 cache that takes up about 56% of the die. Despite the higher transistor count and doubling in size of the cache, power consumption of the Dothan was lower, clock for clock, than the previous Pentium M. The Pentium M includes Enhanced SpeedStep technology with multiple voltage and frequency operating points to conserve power and Streaming SIMD Extensions 2 (SSE2), which is the latest version of MMX technology also included with the Pentium 4. The Pentium M die is shown in Figure 4.18.

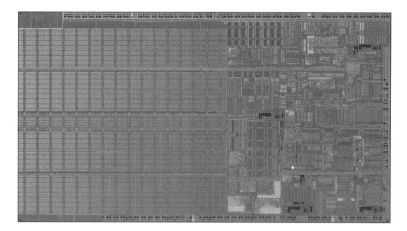

Figure 4.18   Pentium M Die, 0.09 micron Dothan core. (Photograph used by permission of Intel Corporation.)

Notice that the Pentium M die is dominated by the huge 1MB L2 cache, which takes up nearly half the space on the chip. The large cache is responsible for the high transistor count because, in general, it takes about six transistors for each bit of cache memory.

Table 4.11 lists the various models of the Pentium M processors that Intel has released.

Table 4.11   Pentium M Processor Models and Revisions

Processor Number	Speed	Bus Speed	Process	S-Spec	Stepping	CPUID	L2-Cache	Power (W)
N/A	1.30GHz	400MHz	0.13u	SL6N4	PB1	0695	1MB	22.0
N/A	1.40GHz	400MHz	0.13u	SL6F8	PB1	0695	1MB	22.0
N/A	1.50GHz	400MHz	0.13u	SL6F9	PB1	0695	1MB	24.5
N/A	1.60GHz	400MHz	0.13u	SL6FA	PB1	0695	1MB	24.5
N/A	1.70GHz	400MHz	0.13u	SL6N5	PB1	0695	1MB	24.5
715	1.50GHz	400MHz	0.09u	SL7GL	PB1	06D6	2MB	21.0
725	1.60GHz	400MHz	0.09u	SL7EG	PB1	06D6	2MB	21.0
730	1.60GHz	533MHz	0.09u	SL86G	PC0	06D8	2MB	27.0
735	1.70GHz	400MHz	0.09u	SL7EP	PB1	06D6	2MB	21.0
740	1.73GHz	533MHz	0.09u	SL7SA	PC0	06D8	2MB	27.0
745	1.80GHz	400MHz	0.09u	SL7EN	PB1	06D6	2MB	21.0
750	1.86GHz	533MHz	0.09u	SL7S9	PC0	06D8	2MB	27.0

(continues)

Table 4.11   Continued

Processor Number	Speed	Bus Speed	Process	S-Spec	Step-ping	CPUID	L2-Cache	Power (W)
755	2GHz	400MHz	0.09u	SL7EM	PB1	06D6	2MB	21.0
760	2GHz	533MHz	0.09u	SL7SM	PC0	06D8	2MB	27.0
765	2.1GHz	400MHz	0.09u	SL7V3	PB1	06D6	2MB	21.0
770	2.13GHz	533MHz	0.09u	SL7SL	PC0	06D8	2MB	27.0
780	2.26GHz	533MHz	0.09u	SL7VB	PC0	06D8	2MB	27.0

Mobile Celeron Processors

The mobile Celeron processor is available in several versions, including those based on Pentium III, Pentium 4, and Pentium M processors.

Currently, the 1.10GHz and faster versions of the Celeron processor are based on the Mobile Pentium 4-M design. They are essentially identical to Mobile Pentium 4-M processors, except that they include only half the amount of L2 cache and clock speed has been reduced slightly. Most of these processors, like the Mobile Pentium 4, utilize a 478-pin, micro-FCPGA package and plug into a micro-479 PGA mobile (mPGA479M) socket.

The Pentium 4-M–based Celeron is designed for low-cost, high-value portable systems. Features of the processor are the same as the Pentium 4, with the exception of cache size and, in some cases, bus speed.

Table 4.12 lists the various models of the Celeron processors that Intel has released.

Table 4.12   Celeron Processor Models and Revisions

Processor Number	Speed Thermal	Process	S-Spec	Stepping	CPUID	L2-Cache	Power (W)
N/A	1.10GHz	0.013u	SL5XR	cD0	068A	128KB	33.0
N/A	1.10A GHz	0.013u	SL5ZE	tA1	06B1	256KB	28.9
		0.013u	SL6JR	tB1	06B4	256KB	28.9
N/A	1.20GHz	0.013u	SL5Y5	tA1	06B1	256KB	29.9
		0.013u	SL68P	tA1	06B1	256KB	32.1
		0.013u	SL6JS	tB1	06B4	256KB	32.1
N/A	1.30GHz	0.013u	SL5ZJ	tA1	06B1	256KB	33.4
		0.013u	SL6JT	tB1	06B4	256KB	33.4
N/A	1.40GHz	0.013u	SL68G	tA1	06B1	256KB	38.8
		0.013u	SL6JU	tB1	06B4	256KB	38.8
N/A	1.70GHz	0.013u	SL69Z	E0	0F13	128KB	63.5
N/A	1.80GHz	0.013u	SL6A2	E0	0F13	128KB	66.1
N/A	1.80A GHz	0.013u	SL7RU	T0	0F29	128KB	59.1
N/A	2.00GHz	0.013u	SL6LC	C1	0F27	128KB	52.8

Table 4.12   Continued

Processor Number	Speed Thermal	Process	S-Spec	Stepping	CPUID	L2-Cache	Power (W)
N/A	2.10GHz	0.013u	SL6SY	B1	0F27	128KB	55.5
N/A	2.20GHz	0.013u	SL6SX	B1	0F27	128KB	57.1
N/A	2.30GHz	0.013u	SL6T5	C1	0F27	128KB	58.3
315	2.26GHz	0.09u	SL7XY	D0	0F34	256KB	73
320	2.40GHz	0.09u	SL7KX	D0	0F34	256KB	73
N/A	2.40GHz	0.013u	SL6XG	C1	0F27	128KB	59.8
N/A	2.50GHz	0.013u	SL72B	D1	0F29	128KB	61.0
325	2.53GHz	0.09u	SL7KY	D0	0F34	256KB	73
325J	2.53GHz	0.09u	SL7VR	E0	0F41	256KB	84
N/A	2.60GHz	0.13u	SL6W5	D1	0F29	128KB	62.6
330	2.66GHz	0.09u	SL7KZ	D0	0F34	256KB	73
330J	2.66GHz	0.09u	SL7VS	E0	0F41	256KB	84
N/A	2.70GHz	0.09u	SL77U	D1	0F29	128KB	66.8
335	2.80GHz	0.09u	SL7L2	D0	0F34	256KB	73
335J	2.80GHz	0.09u	SL7VT	E0	0F41	256KB	84
N/A	2.80GHz	0.013u	SL77V	D1	0F29	128KB	68.4
340	2.93GHz	0.09u	SL7RN	D0	0F34	256KB	73
340J	2.93GHz	0.09u	SL7VU	E0	0F41	256KB	84

Mobile Celeron processors from 450MHz through 1.2GHz are built on a 0.18-micron process, available in both 478-pin micro-FCPGA and 495-pin micro-PGA2 packages, and use the same core as the Mobile Pentium III. As with the Pentium III, these processors include Streaming SIMD instructions, an advanced transfer cache architecture, and a processor system bus speed of 100 or 133MHz. These features are offered in micro-FCPGA and micro-PGA2 packages.

Table 4.13 lists the various models of the mobile Celeron processors that Intel has released.

Table 4.13   Mobile Celeron Processor Models and Revisions

Speed	Bus Speed	S-Spec	Stepping	CPUID	L2-Cache	Power (W)	Package
450MHz	100MHz	SL3TM	PA2	0681	128KB	15.5	Micro-PGA2
	100MHz	SL46X	PB0	0683	128KB	15.5	Micro-PGA2
	100MHz	SL4PT	PC0	0686	128KB	15.5	Micro-PGA2
500MHz	100MHz	SL3TN	PA2	0681	128KB	16.8	Micro-PGA2
	100MHz	SL46Y	PB0	0683	128KB	16.8	Micro-PGA2
	100MHz	SL4PU	PC0	0686	128KB	16.8	Micro-PGA2

(continues)

Table 4.13   Continued

Speed	Bus Speed	S-Spec	Stepping	CPUID	L2-Cache	Power (W)	Package
550MHz	100MHz	SL4MT	PB0	0683	128KB	18.4	Micro-PGA2
	100MHz	SL4PV	PC0	0686	128KB	28.4	Micro-PGA2
600MHz	100MHz	SL4MU	PB0	0683	128KB	20.0	Micro-PGA2
	100MHz	SL4PW	PC0	0686	128KB	20.0	Micro-PGA2
650MHz	100MHz	SL4MV	PB0	0683	128KB	21.5	Micro-PGA2
	100MHz	SL4PX	PC0	0686	128KB	21.5	Micro-PGA2
	100MHz	SL68H	PD0	068A	128KB	21.5	Micro-PGA2
700MHz	100MHz	SL4PY	PC0	0686	128KB	23.0	Micro-PGA2
	100MHz	SL58J	PD0	068A	128KB	23.0	Micro-PGA2
733MHz	133MHz	SL5T4	FPD0	06B1	128KB	23.0	Micro-FCPGA
750MHz	100MHz	SL55Q	PC0	0686	128KB	24.6	Micro-PGA2
	100MHz	SL58K	PD0	068A	128KB	24.6	Micro-PGA2
800MHz	100MHz	SL5DC	PD0	068A	128KB	25.9	Micro-PGA2
800A MHz	133MHz	SL5T3	FPD0	06B1	128KB	27.4	Micro-FCPGA
866MHz	133MHz	SL5T2	FPD0	06B1	128KB	21.9	Micro-FCPGA
933MHz	133MHz	SL5SK	FPD0	06B1	128KB	22.7	Micro-FCPGA
1.06GHz	133MHz	SL64M	FPA1	06B1	256KB	23.2	Micro-FCPGA
1.13GHz	133MHz	SL64L	FPA1	06B1	256KB	23.8	Micro-FCPGA
1.2GHz	133MHz	SL64K	FPA1	06B1	256KB	24.4	Micro-FCPGA

The mobile Celeron M processor is based on the Pentium M processor and uses the 478-pin micro-FCPGA form factor. As with the Pentium M, these processors feature either a 400 or 533MHz front-side bus speed. Some Celeron M processors are based on the Pentium M Banias and are manufactured in 0.13-micron and offer 512KB of L2 cache. Other Celeron M processors are based on Pentium M Dothan and are manufactured in 0.09-micron and feature 1MB of L2 cache.

Table 4.14 lists the various models of the mobile Celeron M processors that Intel has released.

Table 4.14   Mobile Celeron M Processor Models and Revisions

Processor Number	Speed	Bus Speed	Process	S-Spec	Stepping	CPUID	L2-Cache	Power (W)
340	1.50GHz	400MHz	0.13u	SL7ME	PB1	0695	512KB	24.5
350	1.30GHz	400MHz	0.09u	SL7RA	PB1	06D6	1MB	21
350J	1.30GHz	400MHz	0.09u	SL86L	PC0	06D8	1MB	21
360	1.40GHz	400MHz	0.09u	SL7LS	PB1	06D6	1MB	21
360J	1.40GHz	400MHz	0.09u	SL86K	PC0	06D8	1MB	21
370	1.50GHz	400MHz	0.09u	SL86J	PC0	06D8	1MB	21

Table 4.14   Continued

Processor Number	Speed	Bus Speed	Process	S-Spec	Stepping	CPUID	L2-Cache	Power (W)
370	1.50GHz	400MHz	0.09u	SL8MM	PCO	06D8	1MB	21
380	1.60GHz	400MHz	0.09u	SL8MN	PCO	06D8	1MB	21

AMD Mobile Processors

AMD has had a series of mobile processors, including several mobile versions of the K6, as well as the Mobile Athlon 4, Mobile Duron, and Mobile Athlon XP-M. They are based on AMD's existing desktop processors, with added features such as PowerNow! (processor performance control), which allows for dynamically controlled speeds and voltage, as well as lower overall power consumption. Today, AMD offers mobile versions of its Athlon 64 and Sempron processors, as well as a new platform designed to compete with Intel's Centrino platform based on the AMD Turion 64 processor.

AMD K6-Series Mobile Processors

AMD's K6 series of processors has become popular among cost-conscious personal and corporate computer buyers. These processors have dominated the under–$1,000 computer market since the late 1990s. Starting in the fall of 1998, AMD began to develop this Socket 7–compatible series of processors for mobile use.

All mobile versions of the AMD K6 family share some common characteristics, including low-voltage operation, MMX technology, and a choice of either ceramic pin grid array (CPGA) or the more compact ceramic ball grid array (CBGA) packaging. Mobile K6 processors also have a large 64KB L1 memory cache, as their desktop siblings do.

Later versions of the Mobile K6 are called the K6-2+ and K6-III+. These new processors are both made on a 0.18-micron technology process, enabling reduced die size and voltage. They also both incorporate on-die L2 cache running at full processor speed and PowerNow! technology, which is AMD's version of Intel's SpeedStep technology. This allows for lower speed and voltage operation while on battery power to conserve battery life. The only difference between the K6-2+ and the K6-III+ is the size of their on-die L2 caches. They both incorporate 64KB of L1 on-die: The K6-2+ adds a further 128KB of on-die L2 cache, whereas the L2 size is increased to 256KB in the K6-3+.

AMD offers the Mobile K6 family processors shown in Table 4.15.

Table 4.15   Mobile AMD K6 Family Processors

CPU Model	Core Voltage	Clock Speeds	Notes
Mobile K6*	2.1V	233, 266	66
Mobile K6*	2.2V	300	66
Mobile K6-2*	1.7–1.9V	266, 300, 333, 350, 366, 380	100, 3DN
Mobile K6-2	2.0–2.2V 1.9–2.1V	450, 500, 475	100, 3DN 100, 3DN
Mobile K6-III*	2.2V	350, 366, 380	100, 256KL2, 3DN
Mobile K6-2P*	2.2V	400, 433, 450, 475	100, 3DN

(continues)

Table 4.15   Continued

CPU Model	Core Voltage	Clock Speeds	Notes
Mobile K6-III+#	1.9–2.1V	450, 475, 500	100, 256KL2, 3DN
Mobile K6-2+#	1.9–2.1V	450, 475, 500, 533, 550	100, 128KL2, 3DN

66 = Has a 66MHz bus speed

100 = Has a 100MHz bus speed

256KL2 = Contains a 256KB integrated L2 cache running at full processor speed and supports L3 cache on the motherboard

3DN = Supports 3DNow! multimedia enhancements

* = Built with the .25-micron process

 # = Built with the .18-micron process

AMD's Mobile Athlon and Athlon XP

Even though the K6 family of processors offers very good performance in its class, these processors are not fast enough to compete with the 600MHz and higher Mobile Pentium III and Mobile Celeron processors from Intel. In May 2001, AMD introduced its Mobile Athlon, known as the Athlon 4, and its Mobile Duron processors, which, similar to their desktop siblings, directly compete with the Intel Pentium III and Celeron processors.

The Athlon 4 features 256KB of on-die L2 cache and support for either PC-133 or DDR SDRAM. The Athlon 4 uses 1.4V of power at full speed and 1.2V in battery-saving mode.

The Mobile Duron features 64KB of on-die L2 cache and uses the standard 200MHz FSB introduced by the original Athlon CPU. The Mobile Duron uses 1.5V at full speed and 1.2V in battery-saving mode.

Both the Mobile Athlon 4 and the Mobile Duron use the 0.18-micron process, use a modified version of the 462-pin Socket A used by desktop Athlon and Duron processors, and feature 128KB of Level 1 cache and an improved version of AMD's PowerNow! battery-saving technology.

The mobile Athlon uses a 200MHz or 266MHz processor (front-side) bus called the EV6 to connect to the motherboard North Bridge chip as well as other processors. Licensed from Digital Equipment, the EV6 bus is the same as that used for the Alpha 21264 processor, now owned by Compaq. The EV6 bus uses a clock speed of 100MHz or 133MHz, but it double-clocks the data, transferring data twice per cycle, for a cycling speed of 200MHz or 266MHz. Because the bus is 8 bytes (64 bits) wide, this results in a throughput of 8 bytes × 200MHz/266MHz, which amounts to 1.6GBps or 2.1GBps. This bus is ideal for supporting PC1600 or PC2100 DDR memory, which also runs at those speeds. The AMD bus design eliminates a potential bottleneck between the chipset and the processor, and enables more efficient transfers compared to other processors. The use of the EV6 bus is one of the primary reasons that the Athlon and Duron chips perform so well.

The Athlon has a very large 128KB of L1 cache on the processor die, and 256KB or 512KB of full-core speed L2 cache in the latest Athlon XP models. The Athlon also has support for MMX and the Enhanced 3DNow! instructions, which are 45 new instructions designed to support graphics and sound processing. 3DNow! is very similar to Intel's SSE in design and intent, but the specific instructions are different and require software support. The Athlon XP adds the Intel SSE instructions, which it calls 3DNow! Professional. Fortunately, most companies producing graphics software have decided to support the 3DNow! instructions along with the Intel SSE instructions, with only a few exceptions.

Table 4.16 lists the AMD Mobile Duron and Mobile Athlon 4 processors initially offered by AMD.

Table 4.16   AMD Mobile Duron and Mobile Athlon 4 CPUs

CPU Type	Core Speed	L1 Cache	L2 Cache	Power Usage
Mobile Duron	800	128KB	64KB	1.2–1.5V
Mobile Duron	850	128KB	64KB	1.2–1.5V
Mobile Athlon 4	850	128KB	256KB	1.2–1.4V
Mobile Athlon 4	900	128KB	256KB	1.2–1.4V
Mobile Athlon 4	950	128KB	256KB	1.2–1.4V
Mobile Athlon 4	1000 (1.0GHz)	128KB	256KB	1.2–1.4V

AMD Mobile Duron

The AMD Duron processor (originally code-named Spitfire) is a derivative of the AMD Athlon processor in the same way that the Celeron was originally a derivative of the Pentium II and III (current Celerons are based on the Pentium 4). Basically, the Duron is an Athlon with less L2 cache; all other capabilities are essentially the same. It is designed to be a lower-cost version with less cache but only slightly less performance. In keeping with the low-cost theme, Duron contains 64KB on-die L2 cache and is designed for Socket A, a socket version of the Athlon Slot A. Except for the Duron markings, the Duron is almost identical externally to the Socket A versions of the original Athlon.

Essentially, the Duron was designed to compete against the Intel Celeron in the low-cost PC market, just as the Athlon was designed to compete in the higher-end Pentium III and Pentium 4 market. The Duron has since been discontinued, but most systems that use the Duron processor can use AMD Athlon or, in some cases, Athlon XP processors as an upgrade.

Because the Duron processor is derived from the Athlon core, it includes the Athlon 200MHz front-side system bus (interface to the chipset) as well as enhanced 3DNow! instructions in Model 3. Model 7 processors include 3DNow! Professional instructions (which include a full implementation of SSE instructions).

AMD Mobile Athlon XP-M

The newest mobile version of the Athlon is called the mobile Athlon XP (or XP-M) and was introduced in July 2002. This is basically an improved version of the previous Athlon, with improvements in the instruction set so that it can execute Intel SSE instructions and a new marketing scheme that directly competes with the Pentium 4. The latest Athlon XP models have also adopted a larger (512KB) full-speed on-die cache.

AMD uses the term *QuantiSpeed* (a marketing term, not a technical term) to refer to the architecture of the Athlon XP. AMD defines this as including the following:

- **A nine-issue superscalar, fully pipelined microarchitecture**—This provides more pathways for instructions to be sent into the execution sections of the CPU and includes three floating-point execution units, three integer units, and three address-calculation units.

- **A superscalar, fully pipelined floating-point calculation unit**—This provides faster operations per clock cycle and cures a long-time deficiency of AMD processors versus Intel processors.

- **A hardware data prefetch**—This gathers the data needed from system memory and places it in the processor's Level 1 cache, to save time.

■ **Improved translation lookaside buffers (TLBs)**—These enable the storage of data where the processor can access it more quickly without duplication or stalling for lack of fresh information.

These design improvements wring more work out of each clock cycle, enabling a "slower" Athlon XP to beat a "faster" Pentium 4 processor in doing actual work (and play).

The first models of the Athlon XP used the Palomino core, which is also shared by the original Athlon 4 mobile processor. Later models have used the Thoroughbred core, which was later revised to improve thermal characteristics. The different Thoroughbred cores are sometimes referred to as Thoroughbred-A and Thoroughbred-B. The latest Athlon XP processors use a new core with 512KB on-die full-speed L2 cache known as Barton. Additional features include these:

■ 3DNow! Professional multimedia instructions (adding compatibility with the 70 additional SSE instructions in the Pentium III but not the 144 additional SSE2 instructions in the Pentium 4)

■ 266MHz or 333MHz FSB

■ 128KB L1 and 256KB or 512KB on-die L2 memory caches running at full CPU speed

■ Copper (instead of aluminum) interconnects, for more electrical efficiency and less heat

Also new to the Athlon XP is the use of a thinner, lighter organic chip-packaging compound similar to that used by recent Intel processors. Figure 4.19 shows the latest Athlon XP processors that use the Barton core.

Figure 4.19   AMD Athlon XP 0.13-micron processor with 512KB of L2 cache for Socket A (PGA form factor). (Photo courtesy of Advanced Micro Devices, Inc.)

This packaging allows for a more efficient layout of electrical components. The latest versions of the Athlon XP are made using a new 0.13-micron die process that results in a chip with a smaller die that uses less power, generates less heat, and is capable of running faster as compared to the previous models. The newest 0.13-micron versions of the Athlon XP run at actual clock speeds exceeding 2GHz.

The Athlon XP-M is available in the following versions, designated by performance rating:

■ 2800+	■ 2200+	■ 1700+
■ 2600+	■ 2000+	■ 1600+
■ 2500+	■ 1900+	■ 1500+
■ 2400+	■ 1800+	■ 1400+

AMD Mobile Athlon 64 and Mobile Sempron

With AMD's introduction of the Athlon 64, the mobile version of that processor wasn't far off. Because it is equipped with the same space-saving integrated memory controller as the desktop version of the Athlon 64, the Mobile Athlon 64, shown in Figure 4.20, is ideally suited for use in the small confines of a notebook.

Figure 4.20   The AMD Mobile Athlon 64 processor. (Photo courtesy of AMD.)

The mobile Athlon 64 offers the same features as the desktop processor but uses a more stringent approach to power saving through implementation of its PowerNow! feature. Not long after the introduction of the budget desktop processor from AMD, the Sempron, which lacked 64-bit support and featured only half the L2 cache memory, it too was offered as a mobile processor: the mobile Sempron. Both the mobile Athlon 64 and the mobile Sempron use the lidless 754-pin micro-PGA socket that's derived from the 754-pin socket as used on the desktop for entry-level computers.

Table 4.17 lists the AMD Mobile Athlon 64 and Mobile Sempron processors offered by AMD.

Table 4.17   AMD Mobile Athlon 64 and Mobile Sempron CPUs

Name	Socket	Speed	Process	L2-Cache	64-bit	Codename
AMD Low Power Mobile Athlon 64 2700+	754	1.6GHz	0.09u	512KB	Yes	Oakville
AMD Low Power Mobile Athlon 64 2800+	754	1.8GHz	0.09u	512KB	Yes	Oakville
AMD Low Power Mobile Athlon 64 3000+	754	2.0GHz	0.09u	512KB	Yes	Oakville
AMD Mobile Athlon 64 2800+	754	1.6GHz	0.13u	1MB	Yes	Clawhammer

(continues)

Table 4.17 Continued

Name	Socket	Speed	Process	L2-Cache	64-bit	Codename
AMD Mobile Athlon 64 3000+	754	1.8GHz	0.09u	1MB	Yes	Newark
AMD Mobile Athlon 64 3000+	754	1.8GHz	0.13u	1MB	Yes	Clawhammer
AMD Mobile Athlon 64 3200+	754	2.0GHz	0.09u	1MB	Yes	Newark
AMD Mobile Athlon 64 3200+	754	2.0GHz	0.13u	1MB	Yes	Clawhammer
AMD Mobile Athlon 64 3400+	754	2.2GHz	0.09u	1MB	Yes	Newark
AMD Mobile Athlon 64 3400+	754	2.2GHz	0.13u	1MB	Yes	Clawhammer
AMD Mobile Athlon 64 3700+	754	2.4GHz	0.09u	1MB	Yes	Newark
AMD Mobile Athlon 64 4000+	754	2.6GHz	0.09u	1MB	Yes	Newark
AMD Mobile Sempron 2600+	754	1.6GHz	0.09u	128KB	No	Georgetown
AMD Mobile Sempron 2800+	754	1.6GHz	0.09u	256KB	No	Georgetown
AMD Mobile Sempron 3000+	754	1.8GHz	0.09u	128KB	No	Georgetown
AMD Mobile Sempron 3100+	754	1.8GHz	0.09u	256KB	No	Georgetown
AMD Mobile Sempron 3300+	754	2.0GHz	0.09u	128KB	No	Georgetown

AMD Turion 64

Unlike Intel does with its Centrino platform, AMD does not specifically define a whole platform with the Turion brand name. Rather, the AMD Turion 64 processor, shown in Figure 4.21, is optimized for use in mobile devices such as laptops, much like Intel's Pentium M processor. The AMD Turion 64 processor can be combined with a variety of different chipsets and wireless solutions from various third-party manufacturers that allow it to offer similar performance and battery life as compared to Intel's offering.

Figure 4.21 The AMD Turion 64 processor. (Photo courtesy of AMD.)

The AMD Turion 64 processor is based on the same 64-bit core that can be found in the AMD Athlon 64 and Sempron processors and also incorporates the same integrated memory controller. Like these other AMD processors, the Turion 64 offers compatibility with 32-bit and 64-bit operating systems and is able to address over 4GB of memory directly. The AMD Turion 64 offers 3DNow! technology and also supports SSE2 and SSE3. The AMD Turion 64 uses the same lidless 754-pin Micro-PGA socket as the mobile Athlon 64 and Sempron.

Table 4.18 lists the AMD Turion 64 processors offered by AMD.

Table 4.18   AMD Turion 64 Processors

Name	Socket	Speed	Process	L2-Cache	64-bit
AMD Turion 64 ML-28	754	1.6GHz	0.09u	512KB	Yes
AMD Turion 64 ML-30	754	1.6GHz	0.09u	1MB	Yes
AMD Turion 64 ML-32	754	1.8GHz	0.09u	512KB	Yes
AMD Turion 64 ML-34	754	1.8GHz	0.09u	1MB	Yes
AMD Turion 64 ML-37	754	2.0GHz	0.09u	1MB	Yes
AMD Turion 64 ML-40	754	2.2GHz	0.09u	1MB	Yes
AMD Turion 64 MT-28	754	1.6GHz	0.09u	512KB	Yes
AMD Turion 64 MT-30	754	1.6GHz	0.09u	1MB	Yes
AMD Turion 64 MT-32	754	1.8GHz	0.09u	512KB	Yes
AMD Turion 64 MT-34	754	1.8GHz	0.09u	1MB	Yes

CHAPTER 5

Motherboards

Form Factors

One of the drawbacks of laptop systems is that they use many nonstandard parts, including the motherboard. Unlike in desktop systems, there really aren't any industry-standard form factors for laptop motherboards. The mobile module versions of certain Intel Pentium through Pentium III processors included the processor and main chipset component and were somewhat of an attempt at laptop system motherboard standardization, but they have since been dropped because of the higher costs compared with using discrete chips.

Generally, this means that whatever motherboard came in the system will be the one it will keep for life. A motherboard can be replaced, but in most cases only with another example of the same board from the same manufacturer. This is suitable for a repair, but obviously not an upgrade. Although the motherboard cannot be replaced, most newer processors are socketed, making various types of processor upgrades possible even without changing the motherboard.

System Bus Types, Functions, and Features

The heart of any motherboard is the various signal pathways or buses that carry signals between the components. A *bus* is a common pathway across which data can travel within a computer. This pathway is used for communication and can be established between two or more computer elements.

The PC has a hierarchy of different buses. Most modern PCs have at least three main buses; some have four or more. They are hierarchical because each slower bus is connected to the faster one above it. Each device in the system is connected to one of the buses, and some devices (primarily the chipset) act as bridges between the various buses.

The main buses in a modern system are as follows:

- **Processor bus**—Also called the front-side bus (FSB), this is the highest-speed bus in the system and is at the core of the chipset and motherboard. This bus is used primarily by the processor to pass information to and from cache or main memory and the North Bridge of the chipset. The processor bus in a modern system runs at 66, 100, 133, 200, 266, 400, 533, or 800MHz and is normally 64 bits (8 bytes) wide.

- **AGP bus**—This is a high-speed 32-bit bus specifically for a video card. It runs at 66MHz (AGP 1x), 133MHz (AGP 2x), 266MHz (AGP 4x), or 533MHz (AGP 8x), which allows for a bandwidth of up to 2,133MBps. In laptop systems, the AGP interface is usually onboard, meaning that there is normally no slot; instead, it is a direct connection between the North Bridge or memory controller hub of the chipset and the video chipset. Some laptops do include nonstandard slots for video cards.

- **PCI Express bus**—This is a high-speed serial bus designed to replace PCI and AGP. It runs at 66MHz (AGP 1x), 133MHz (AGP 2x), 266MHz (AGP 4x), or 533MHz (AGP 8x), which allows for a bandwidth of up to 2,133MBps. The PCI Express interface to video is usually onboard, meaning that there is normally no slot; instead, it is a direct connection between the North Bridge or memory controller hub of the chipset and the video chipset. Some laptops do include nonstandard slots for video cards. The PCI Express interface is also available externally using ExpressCards via ExpressCard slots.

- **PCI bus**—This bus, as it originally appeared in newer 486 and all Pentium class systems, is usually a 33MHz 32-bit bus. This bus is generated by either the North Bridge chipset in North/South Bridge chipsets or the I/O controller hub in chipsets using hub architecture. Although this bus is manifested in a desktop system as a collection of 32-bit slots, normally white and numbering from four to six on most motherboards, laptops normally have a single Mini PCI slot. This Mini PCI slot is the same as the standard PCI, except for a different connector and smaller physical form factor. Additionally, the CardBus slots in most laptops are a specialized variation of PCI, which can accept credit card–size adapters. High-speed peripherals, such as SCSI adapters, network cards, video cards, and more, can be plugged into laptop Mini PCI or CardBus slots.

■ **LPC bus**—The low-pin-count bus is a 33MHz 4-bit bus that has a maximum bandwidth of 16.67MBps; it was designed as an economical onboard replacement for the obsolete ISA bus. In systems that use LPC, it typically is used to connect Super I/O chip or motherboard ROM BIOS components to the main chipset. LPC is faster than ISA and yet uses far fewer pins and enables ISA to be eliminated from the board entirely.

Some newer laptop motherboards feature a special mobile audio/modem daughter card (MDC) connector, which provides an interface for modem, audio, and networking solutions based on the AC'97 (audio coder/decoder) interface. Some laptop manufacturers refer to MDC cards and sockets as CDC (communications daughter card) cards and sockets, although they are the same thing. MDC connectors provide a low-cost, small form factor module suitable for mobile systems. They are dedicated connectors for cards that are specific to the system or motherboard design to offer communications and networking options. They are *not* designed to be general-purpose bus interfaces, and cards for these connectors are not sold on the open market. Usually, they're offered only as a preinstalled option with a given system. They are designed so that a system manufacturer can easily offer configurations with and without various communications options, without having to reserve space on the motherboard for optional chips.

For example, I recently purchased a laptop in which I wanted to integrate every type of wireless networking possible, including tri-mode 802.11a/b/g as well as Bluetooth. Unfortunately, the manufacturer did not offer a system that incorporated all of these devices, although various models included one or the other. Rather than add external CardBus devices, which would be unwieldy and use up the only available slot, I purchased an internal 802.11a/b/g Mini PCI card and a combination Modem/Bluetooth mobile daughter card and installed them myself. Because such cards are not normally sold retail, I merely ordered them as if they were repair parts for the various models that incorporated them and installed them myself. The particular laptop in question (an IBM R40) already had integrated WiFi antennas, so all I needed for the ultimate WiFi solution was the $99 Mini PCI 802.11a/b/g card. My particular system did not include an internal Bluetooth antenna, although one could be ordered and installed as a repair part. So, I ordered a Modem/Bluetooth MDC module for $37 and an internal Bluetooth antenna for $8, and installed them in a matter of minutes. Because of the standardization available with Mini PCI and MDC, it's possible to upgrade many other laptops in a similar manner. Now I have all of these communications devices internally mounted, and the CardBus socket remains free for other uses.

For the most part, modem, sound, and Bluetooth cards are implemented via MDC modules, while higher-speed WiFi wireless networking options are normally installed via Mini PCI cards. Mini PCI cards are available that support the 802.11a, 802.11b, or 802.11g standards individually, or in combo cards supporting 802.11a/b/g all in one.

The system chipset is the conductor that controls the orchestra of system components, enabling each to have its turn on its respective buses. Table 5.1 shows the widths, speeds, data cycles, and overall bandwidth of virtually all PC buses.

Table 5.1   Bandwidth (in MBps) and Detail Comparison of Most PC Buses and Interfaces

Bus Type	Bus Width (Bits)	Bus Speed (MHz)	Data Cycles per Clock	Bandwidth (MBps)
8-bit ISA (PC/XT)	8	4.77	1/2	2.39
8-bit ISA (AT)	8	8.33	1/2	4.17
LPC bus	4	33	1	16.67
16-bit ISA (AT-Bus)	16	8.33	1/2	8.33
DD Floppy Interface	1	0.25	1	0.03125
HD Floppy Interface	1	0.5	1	0.0625
ED Floppy Interface	1	1	1	0.125
EISA Bus	32	8.33	1	33
VL-Bus	32	33	1	133
MCA-16	16	5	1	10
MCA-32	32	5	1	20
MCA-16 Streaming	16	10	1	20
MCA-32 Streaming	32	10	1	40
MCA-64 Streaming	64	10	1	80
MCA-64 Streaming	64	20	1	160
PC Card (PCMCIA)	16	10	1	20
CardBus	32	33	1	133
PCI	32	33	1	133
PCI 66MHz	32	66	1	266
PCI 64-bit	64	33	1	266
PCI 66MHz/64-bit	64	66	1	533
PCI-X 66	64	66	1	533
PCI-X 133	64	133	1	1,066
PCI-X 266	64	266	1	2,133
PCI-X 533	64	533	1	4,266
PCI Express 1-lane	1	2,500	0.8	250
PCI Express 16-lanes	16	2,500	0.8	4,000
PCI Express 32-lanes	32	2,500	0.8	8,000
Intel Hub Interface 8-bit	8	66	4	266
Intel Hub Interface 16-bit	16	66	4	533
AMD HyperTransport 2×2	2	200	2	100
AMD HyperTransport 4×2	4	200	2	200
AMD HyperTransport 8×2	8	200	2	400

Table 5.1   Continued

Bus Type	Bus Width (Bits)	Bus Speed (MHz)	Data Cycles per Clock	Bandwidth (MBps)
AMD HyperTransport 16×2	16	200	2	800
AMD HyperTransport 32×2	32	200	2	1,600
AMD HyperTransport 2×4	2	400	2	200
AMD HyperTransport 4×4	4	400	2	400
AMD HyperTransport 8×4	8	400	2	800
AMD HyperTransport 16×4	16	400	2	1,600
AMD HyperTransport 32×4	32	400	2	3,200
AMD HyperTransport 2×8	2	800	2	400
AMD HyperTransport 4×8	4	800	2	800
AMD HyperTransport 8×8	8	800	2	1,600
AMD HyperTransport 16×8	16	800	2	3,200
AMD HyperTransport 32×8	32	800	2	6,400
ATI A-Link	16	66	2	266
SiS MuTIOL	16	133	2	533
SiS MuTIOL 1G	16	266	2	1,066
VIA V-Link 4x	8	66	4	266
VIA V-Link 8x	8	66	8	533
AGP	32	66	1	266
AGP 2x	32	66	2	533
AGP 4x	32	66	4	1,066
AGP 8x	32	66	8	2,133
RS-232 Serial	1	0.1152	1/10	0.01152
RS-232 Serial HS	1	0.2304	1/10	0.02304
IEEE 1284 Parallel	8	8.33	1/6	1.38
IEEE 1284 EPP/ECP	8	8.33	1/3	2.77
USB 1.1/2.0 low-speed	1	1.5	1	0.1875
USB 1.1/2.0 full-speed	1	12	1	1.5
USB 2.0 high-speed	1	480	1	60
IEEE 1394a S100	1	100	1	12.5
IEEE 1394a S200	1	200	1	25
IEEE 1394a S400	1	400	1	50
IEEE 1394b S800	1	800	1	100
IEEE 1394b S1600	1	1600	1	200

(continues)

Table 5.1   Continued

Bus Type	Bus Width (Bits)	Bus Speed (MHz)	Data Cycles per Clock	Bandwidth (MBps)
ATA PIO-4	16	8.33	1	16.67
ATA-UDMA/33	16	8.33	2	33
ATA-UDMA/66	16	16.67	2	66
ATA-UDMA/100	16	25	2	100
ATA-UDMA/133	16	33	2	133
SATA-150	1	750	2	150
SATA-300	1	1500	2	300
SATA-600	1	3000	2	600
SCSI	8	5	1	5
SCSI Wide	16	5	1	10
SCSI Fast	8	10	1	10
SCSI Fast/Wide	16	10	1	20
SCSI Ultra	8	20	1	20
SCSI Ultra/Wide	16	20	1	40
SCSI Ultra2	8	40	1	40
SCSI Ultra2/Wide	16	40	1	80
SCSI Ultra3 (Ultra160)	16	40	2	160
SCSI Ultra4 (Ultra320)	16	80	2	320
SCSI Ultra5 (Ultra640)	16	160	2	640
FPM DRAM	64	22	1	177
EDO DRAM	64	33	1	266
PC66 SDRAM DIMM	64	66	1	533
PC100 SDRAM DIMM	64	100	1	800
PC133 SDRAM DIMM	64	133	1	1,066
PC1600 DDR DIMM (DDR200)	64	100	2	1,600
PC2100 DDR DIMM (DDR266)	64	133	2	2,133
PC2700 DDR DIMM (DDR333)	64	167	2	2,666
PC3200 DDR DIMM (DDR400)	64	200	2	3,200
PC2-3200 DDR2 (DDR2-400)	64	200	2	3,200
PC2-4200 DDR2 (DDR2-533)	64	267	2	4,266
PC2-5300 DDR2 (DDR2-667)	64	333	2	5,333
PC2-6400 DDR2 (DDR2-800)	64	400	2	6,400

Table 5.1 Continued

Bus Type	Bus Width (Bits)	Bus Speed (MHz)	Data Cycles per Clock	Bandwidth (MBps)
RIMM1200 RDRAM (PC600)	16	300	2	1,200
RIMM1400 RDRAM (PC700)	16	350	2	1,400
RIMM1600 RDRAM (PC800)	16	400	2	1,600
RIMM2100 RDRAM (PC1066)	16	533	2	2,133
RIMM2400 RDRAM (PC1200)	16	600	2	2,400
RIMM3200 RDRAM (PC800)	32	400	2	3,200
RIMM4200 RDRAM (PC1066)	32	533	2	4,266
RIMM4800 RDRAM (PC1200)	32	600	2	4,800
33MHz 486 FSB	32	33	1	133
66MHz Pentium I/II/III FSB	64	66	1	533
100MHz Pentium I/II/III FSB	64	100	1	800
133MHz Pentium I/II/III FSB	64	133	1	1,066
200MHz Athlon FSB	64	100	2	1,600
266MHz Athlon FSB	64	133	2	2,133
333MHz Athlon FSB	64	167	2	2,666
400MHz Athlon FSB	64	200	2	3,200
533MHz Athlon FSB	64	267	2	4,266
400MHz Pentium 4 FSB	64	100	4	3,200
533MHz Pentium 4 FSB	64	133	4	4,266
800MHz Pentium 4 FSB	64	200	4	6,400
1066MHz Pentium 4 FSB	64	267	4	8,533
266MHz Itanium FSB	64	133	2	2,133
400MHz Itanium 2 FSB	128	100	4	6,400

Note: ISA, EISA, VL-Bus, and MCA are no longer used in current motherboard designs.

MBps = Megabytes per second

ISA = Industry Standard Architecture, also known as the PC/XT (8-bit) or AT-Bus (16-bit)

LPC = Low Pin Count bus

DD Floppy = Double Density (360/720KB) Floppy

HD Floppy = High Density (1.2/1.44MB) Floppy

ED Floppy = Extra-high Density (2.88MB) Floppy

EISA = Extended Industry Standard Architecture (32-bit ISA)

VL-Bus = VESA (Video Electronics Standards Association) Local Bus (ISA extension)

MCA = MicroChannel Architecture (IBM PS/2 systems)

PC-Card = 16-bit PCMCIA (Personal Computer Memory Card International Association) interface

CardBus = 32-bit PC-Card

Hub Interface = Intel 8xx chipset bus

HyperTransport = AMD chipset bus

V-Link = VIA Technologies chipset bus

MuTIOL = Silicon Integrated System chipset bus

PCI = Peripheral Component Interconnect

AGP = Accelerated Graphics Port

RS-232 = Standard Serial port, 115.2Kbps

RS-232 HS = High Speed Serial port, 230.4Kbps

IEEE-1284 Parallel = Standard Bidirectional Parallel Port

IEEE-1284 EPP/ECP = Enhanced Parallel Port/Extended Capabilities Port

USB = Universal serial bus

(continues)

IEEE-1394 = FireWire, also called i.Link

ATA PIO = AT Attachment (also known as IDE) Programmed I/O

ATA-UDMA = AT Attachment Ultra DMA

SCSI = Small computer system interface

FPM = Fast Page Mode, based on X-3-3-3 (1/3 max) burst mode timing on a 66MHz bus

EDO = Extended data out, based on X-2-2-2 (1/2 max) burst mode timing on a 66MHz bus

SDRAM = Synchronous dynamic RAM

RDRAM = Rambus dynamic RAM

DDR = Double data rate SDRAM

DDR2 = Next-generation DDR

CPU FSB = Processor front-side bus

Note that many of the buses use multiple data cycles (transfers) per clock cycle to achieve greater performance. Therefore, the data-transfer rate is higher than it would seem for a given clock rate, which provides an easy way to make an existing bus go faster in a backward-compatible way.

The following sections discuss the processor and other subset buses in the system and the main I/O buses mentioned in Table 5.1.

The Processor Bus (Front-Side Bus)

The processor bus (also called the front-side bus, or FSB) is the communication pathway between the CPU and motherboard chipset—more specifically, the North Bridge or memory controller hub. This bus runs at the full motherboard speed—typically between 66MHz and 533MHz in modern laptops, depending on the particular board and chipset design. Laptops that use desktop chipsets and processors may run even faster buses. This same bus also transfers data between the CPU and an external (L2) memory cache on older 386, 486, and Pentium systems.

Intel 800-series chipsets use what Intel calls hub architecture instead of the PCI connection used in the older North/South Bridge design. This moves the main connection between the chipset components to a separate 266MBps hub interface (which has twice the throughput of PCI) and enables PCI devices to use the full bandwidth of PCI without fighting for bandwidth with a South Bridge. In the 900 series chipsets, the connection between the North Bridge (memory controller hub) and South Bridge (I/O controller hub) is a new interface called Direct Media Interface (DMI), which is basically a modified PCI Express x4 interface supporting a throughput of 1GBps in each direction simultaneously.

The flash ROM BIOS chip is now referred to as a firmware hub and is connected to the system via the LPC bus instead of via the Super I/O chip, as in older North/South Bridge designs. Because the ISA bus is no longer used in most of these systems, the Super I/O is connected via the LPC bus instead of ISA. The Super I/O chip also can easily be eliminated in these designs. This is commonly referred to as a *legacy-free* system because the ports supplied by the Super I/O chip are now known as *legacy* ports. Devices that would have used legacy ports must then be connected to the system via USB instead, and such systems would feature two USB controllers, with up to four total ports (more can be added by attaching USB hubs).

AMD processor systems adopted a Socket A design, which is similar to Socket 370, except that it uses faster processor and memory buses. Although early versions retained the older North/South Bridge design, more recent versions use a design similar to Intel's hub architecture. Note that the high-speed CPU bus runs up to 333MHz (2,664MBps throughput), and DDR SDRAM SODIMM modules that support a matching bandwidth of 2,664MBps are used. It is always best for performance for the bandwidth of memory to match that of the processor. Finally, note that most of the South Bridge components include functions that are otherwise found in Super I/O chips; when these functions are included, the chip is called a Super South Bridge.

The Mobile Pentium 4 and Pentium 4-M use a Socket 478 design with the hub architecture. This design is most notable for including a 400 533, or 800MHz CPU bus with a bandwidth of 3,200,

4,266, or 6,400MBps. Many newer laptops use PC2100 (DDR266) or PC2700 (DDR333) DDR SDRAM. Although many desktop systems use dual-channel memory, which doubles the throughput of the modules by accessing two modules simultaneously, that is not common on laptop systems.

Because the purpose of the processor bus is to get information to and from the CPU at the fastest possible speed, this bus typically operates at a rate faster than any other bus in the system. The bus consists of electrical circuits for data, addresses (the address bus, which is discussed in the following section), and control purposes. Most processors since the original Pentium have a 64-bit data bus, so they transfer 64 bits (8 bytes) at a time over the CPU bus.

The processor bus operates at the same base clock rate as the CPU does externally. This can be misleading because most CPUs these days run at a higher clock rate internally than they do externally. For example, an AMD Athlon XP-M 2800+ system has a processor running at 2.13GHz internally but only 266MHz externally, whereas a Mobile Pentium 4 3.2GHz runs at 3.2GHz internally but only 533 or 800MHz externally. In these newer systems, the actual processor speed is some multiple (2×, 2.5×, 3×, and higher) of the processor bus. The processor bus is tied to the external processor pin connections and can transfer 1 bit of data per data line every cycle. Most modern processors transfer 64 bits (8 bytes) of data at a time.

To determine the transfer rate for the processor bus, you multiply the data width (64 bits or 8 bytes for a Celeron/Pentium III/4/M or Athlon/Duron/Athlon XP) by the clock speed of the bus (the same as the base or unmultiplied clock speed of the CPU).

For example, if you are using a Mobile Pentium 4 3.2GHz processor that runs on a 533MHz processor bus, you have a maximum instantaneous transfer rate of roughly 4,266MBps. You get this result by using the following formula:

533.33MHz × 8 bytes (64 bits) = 4,266MBps

With slower versions of the Mobile Pentium 4-M, you get this:

400MHz × 8 bytes (64 bits) = 3,200MBps

With Socket A (Athlon XP-M), you get:

266.66MHz × 8 bytes (64 bits) = 2,133MBps

or:

200MHz × 8 bytes (64 bits) = 1,600MBps

With Socket 370 (Pentium III), you get:

133.33MHz × 8 bytes (64 bits) = 1,066MBps

or:

100MHz × 8 bytes (64 bits) = 800MBps

This transfer rate, often called the *bandwidth* of the processor bus, represents the maximum speed at which data can move. Refer to Table 5.1 for a more complete list of various processor bus bandwidths.

The Memory Bus

The memory bus is used to transfer information between the CPU and main memory—the RAM in your system. This bus is connected to the motherboard chipset North Bridge or memory controller hub chip. Depending on the type of memory that your chipset (and, therefore, the motherboard) is designed to handle, the North Bridge runs the memory bus at various speeds. The best solution is for the memory bus to run at the same speed as the processor bus. Systems that use PC133 SDRAM have a memory bandwidth of 1,066MBps, which is the same as the 133MHz CPU bus. In another example, Athlon systems running a 266MHz processor bus also run PC2100 DDR SDRAM, which has a bandwidth of 2,133MBps—exactly the same as the processor bus in those systems.

Note

Notice that the main memory bus must normally transfer data in the same width as the processor bus. This defines the size of what is called a *bank* of memory. For most Pentium and newer mobile systems, a single small outline DIMM (SODIMM) is equal to a bank.

Types of I/O Buses

Since the introduction of the first PC, many I/O buses have been introduced. The reason is simple: Faster I/O speeds are necessary for better system performance. This need for higher performance involves three main areas:

■ Faster CPUs

■ Increasing software demands

■ Greater multimedia requirements

Each of these areas requires the I/O bus to be as fast as possible.

One of the primary reasons new I/O bus structures have been slow in coming is compatibility—that old catch-22 that anchors much of the PC industry to the past. One of the hallmarks of the PC's success is its standardization. This standardization spawned thousands of third-party I/O cards, each originally built for the early bus specifications of the PC. If a new high-performance bus system was introduced, it often had to be compatible with the older bus systems so that the older I/O cards would not be obsolete. Therefore, bus technologies seem to evolve rather than make quantum leaps forward.

The PCI Bus

In early 1992, Intel spearheaded the creation of another industry group. It was formed with the same goals as the VESA group in relation to the PC bus. Recognizing the need to overcome weaknesses in the ISA and EISA buses, the PCI Special Interest Group was formed.

The PCI bus specification was released in June 1992 as version 1.0 and since then has undergone several upgrades. Table 5.2 shows the various releases of PCI.

Table 5.2   PCI Specifications

PCI Specification	Released	Major Change
PCI 1.0	June 1992	Original 32-/64-bit specification.
PCI 2.0	April 1993	Defined connectors and expansion boards.
PCI 2.1	June 1995	66MHz operation, transaction ordering, latency changes.
PCI 2.2	January 1999	Power management, mechanical clarifications.
PCI-X 1.0	September 1999	133MHz operation, addendum to 2.2.
Mini PCI	November 1999	Small form factor boards, addendum to 2.2.

Table 5.2   Continued

PCI Specification	Released	Major Change
PCI 2.3	March 2002	3.3V signaling, low-profile add-in cards.
PCI-X 2.0	July 2002	266MHz and 533MHz operation, support for the subdivision of 64-bit data bus into 32-bit or 16-bit segments for use by multiple devices, 3.3V/1.5V signaling.
PCI Express 1.0	July 2002	2.5Gbps (gigabits per second) per lane per direction, using 0.8V signaling, resulting in 250MBps per lane. Designed to eventually replace PCI 2.x in PC systems.
PCI Express Mini Card	June 2003	Small form factor boards, addendum to PCI Express.

The PCI bus often is called a *mezzanine bus* because it adds another layer to the traditional bus configuration. Systems that integrate the PCI bus became available in mid-1993 and have since become a mainstay in the PC. In 1996, laptops adopted the CardBus standard, which is essentially a mobile hot-pluggable version of PCI. The Mini PCI standard became available in 1999, allowing laptops to accept internally replaceable PCI cards as well.

Information typically is transferred across the PCI bus at 33MHz 32 bits at a time. The bandwidth is 133MBps, as the following formula shows:

$$33.33\text{MHz} \times 4 \text{ bytes (32 bits)} = 133\text{MBps}$$

The PCI specification identifies three board configurations, each designed for a specific type of system with specific power requirements; each specification has a 32-bit version and a longer 64-bit version. The 5V specification is for stationary computer systems (using PCI 2.2 or earlier versions), the 3.3V specification is for portable systems (also supported by PCI 2.3), and the universal specification is for motherboards and cards that work in either type of system. The 64-bit versions of the 5V and universal PCI slots are found primarily on server motherboards. The PCI-X 2.0 specifications for 266 and 533 versions support 3.3V and 1.5V signaling; this corresponds to PCI version 2.3, which supports 3.3V signaling.

Another important feature of PCI is the fact that it was the model for the Intel PnP specification. Therefore, PCI cards do not have jumpers and switches, and are instead configured through software. True PnP systems are capable of automatically configuring the adapters, whereas non-PnP systems with ISA slots must configure the adapters through a program that is usually a part of the system CMOS configuration. Since late 1995, most PC-compatible systems have included a PnP BIOS that allows the automatic PnP configuration. Although laptops cannot accept normal PCI cards, most have a single internal Mini PCI card slot and one or two external CardBus slots.

PCI Express, a new version of PCI, was approved in July 2002, and a Mini Card version suitable for laptops called ExpressCard was approved in June 2003. PCI Express is a very fast serial bus design that is backward compatible with current PCI parallel bus software drivers and controls. This new bus specification was designed to initially augment and eventually replace the existing PCI bus. For more information on PCI Express, I recommend consulting the PCI-SIG website (`www.pcisig.org`).

Accelerated Graphics Port (AGP)

Intel created AGP as a new bus specifically designed for high-performance graphics and video support. AGP is based on PCI, but it contains several additions and enhancements and is physically, electrically, and logically independent of PCI. Unlike PCI, which is a true bus with multiple connectors (slots), AGP is more of a point-to-point high-performance connection designed specifically for a video card or processor in a system because only one AGP device is allowed.

Most laptops do not have a standard AGP slot as desktop systems do. Instead, they normally integrate the AGP video processor on the motherboard or as part of the motherboard chipset. Some, however, have specialized slots for proprietary video card devices. Even if the video is integrated, it acts exactly as would a card plugged into a standard AGP or PCI slot. For more information on possible graphics chipset upgrades for laptops, refer to Chapter 11, "Graphics and Sound."

▶▶ See "User-Upgradeable Laptop Graphics Modules," p. 558.

Intel originally released the AGP specification 1.0 in July 1996 and defined a 66MHz clock rate with 1x or 2x signaling using 3.3V. AGP version 2.0 was released in May 1998 and added 4x signaling as well as a lower 1.5V operating capability.

The latest revision for the AGP specification for PCs is AGP 8x, otherwise called AGP 3.0. AGP 8x defines a transfer speed of 2,133MBps, which is twice that of AGP 4x. The AGP 8x specification was first publicly announced in November 2000. Although AGP 8x has a maximum speed twice that of AGP 4x, the real-world differences between AGP 4x- and 8x-compatible devices with otherwise identical specifications are minimal. However, many 3D chipsets that support AGP 8x are also upgrading memory and 3D graphics core speeds and designs to better support the faster interface.

AGP is a high-speed connection and runs at a base frequency of 66MHz (actually 66.66MHz), which is double that of standard PCI. In the basic AGP mode, called 1x, a single transfer is done every cycle. Because the AGP bus is 32 bits (4 bytes) wide, at 66 million times per second, AGP 1x can transfer data at a rate of about 266MBps. The original AGP specification also defines 2x mode, in which transfers are performed twice every cycle, resulting in 533MBps. Using an analogy in which every cycle is equivalent to the back-and-forth swing of a pendulum, the 1x mode is thought of as transferring information at the start of each swing. In 2x mode, an additional transfer would occur every time the pendulum completed half a swing, thereby doubling performance while technically maintaining the same clock rate—or, in this case, the same number of swings per second. The AGP 2.0 specification added the capability for 4x transfers, in which data is transferred four times per cycle and equals a data-transfer rate of 1,066MBps. AGP 3.0 added 8x transfers (eight times per cycle), resulting in a transfer rate of 2,133MBps. Most newer AGP cards now have support for the 4x standard as a minimum, and the latest chipsets and graphics controllers support AGP 8x. Table 5.3 shows the differences in clock rates and data-transfer speeds (bandwidth) for the various AGP modes.

Table 5.3   AGP Modes Showing Clock Speeds and Bandwidth

AGP Type	Bus Width (Bytes)	Bus Speed (MHz)	Data Cycles per Clock (MBps)	Bandwidth
AGP 1x	4	66	1	266
AGP 2x	4	66	2	533
AGP 4x	4	66	4	1066
AGP 8x	4	66	8	2133

Because AGP is independent of PCI, processing graphics on the AGP video bus frees up the PCI bus for more traditional input and output, such as for SCSI, FireWire, or USB controllers; sound cards; network interface cards; and so on.

Besides faster video performance, one of the main reasons Intel designed AGP was to allow the video chipset to have a high-speed connection directly to the system RAM, which would enable a reasonably fast and powerful video solution to be integrated at a lower cost. AGP allows a video processor to have direct access to the system RAM, either enabling lower-cost video solutions to be directly built in to a motherboard without having to include additional video RAM or enabling an AGP video chip to share the main system memory. High-performance video processors will likely continue the trend of having more memory directly connected (even if it is integrated into the motherboard), which is especially important when running high-performance 3D video applications.

AGP allows the speed of the video processor to pace the requirements for high-speed 3D graphics rendering, as well as full-motion video on the PC.

PCI Express

During 2001, a group of companies called the Arapahoe Work Group (led primarily by Intel) developed a draft of a new high-speed bus specification code-named 3GIO (third-generation I/O). In August 2001, the PCI Special Interest Group (PCI-SIG) agreed to take over, manage, and promote the 3GIO architecture specification as the future generation of PCI. In April 2002, the 3GIO draft version 1.0 was completed, transferred to the PCI-SIG, and renamed PCI Express. Finally in July 2002, the PCI Express 1.0 specification was approved. The first chipsets, motherboards, and systems featuring PCI Express slots were released in June 2004.

The original 3GIO code name was derived from the fact that this new bus specification was designed to initially augment and eventually replace the previously existing ISA/AT-Bus (first-generation) and PCI (second-generation) bus architectures in PCs. Each of the first two generations of PC bus architectures was designed to have a 10- to 15-year useful life in PCs. In being adopted and approved by the PCI-SIG, PCI Express is now destined to be the dominant PC bus architecture designed to support the increasing bandwidth needs in PCs over the next 10–15 years.

The key features of PCI Express include

- Compatibility with existing PCI enumeration and software device drivers.
- Physical connection over copper, optical, or other physical media to allow for future encoding schemes.
- Maximum bandwidth per pin allows small form factors, reduced cost, simpler board designs and routing, and reduced signal integrity issues.
- Embedded clocking scheme enables easy frequency (speed) changes as compared to synchronous clocking.
- Bandwidth (throughput) increases easily with frequency and width (lane) increases.
- Low latency, which makes it suitable for applications that require isochronous (time-sensitive) data delivery, such as streaming video.
- Hot-plugging and hot-swapping capabilities.
- Power management capabilities.

PCI Express is another example of how the PC is moving from parallel to serial interfaces. Earlier generation bus architectures in the PC have been of a parallel design, in which multiple bits are sent simultaneously over several pins in parallel. The more bits sent at a time, the faster the bus throughput is. The timing of all the parallel signals must be the same, which becomes more and more difficult to do over faster and longer connections. Even though 32 bits can be transmitted simultaneously over a bus such as PCI or AGP, propagation delays and other problems cause them to arrive slightly skewed at the other end, resulting in a time difference between when the first and last of all the bits arrive.

A serial bus design is much simpler, sending 1 bit at a time over a single wire, at much higher rates of speed than a parallel bus would allow. Because this type of bus sends the bits serially, the timing of individual bits or the length of the bus becomes much less of a factor. And by combining multiple serial data paths, even faster throughputs can be realized that dramatically exceed the capabilities of traditional parallel buses.

PCI Express is a very fast serial bus design that is backward compatible with current PCI parallel bus software drivers and controls. In PCI Express, data is sent full duplex (simultaneously operating one-way paths) over two pairs of differentially signaled wires called a *lane*. Each lane allows for about 250MBps throughput in each direction, and the design allows for scaling from 1 to 2, 4, 8, 16, or 32 lanes. For example, a single lane connection uses two pairs of differential signal lines (4 wires total) allowing a throughput of 250MBps in each direction, while a high-bandwidth configuration with 16 lanes uses 32 differential signal pairs (64 wires) allowing a throughput of 4,000MBps in each direction. Future proposed increases in signaling speed could double the throughput over the current design.

Laptops featuring PCI Express implement an x16 connection to video internally on the motherboard and one or two x1 connectors in the form of ExpressCard sockets on the side of the system. ExpressCard sockets have only 26 pins and carry both x1 PCI Express (250MBps) signals as well as USB 2.0 (60MBps), and are significantly smaller and faster than PCI-based 68-pin CardBus (133MBps) sockets.

PCI Express uses an IBM-designed 8-bit–to–10-bit encoding scheme, which allows for self-clocked signals that allow future increases in frequency. The starting frequency is 2.5GHz, and will scale up to 10GHz in the future, which is about the limit of copper connections. By combining frequency increases with the capability to use up to 32 lanes, PCI Express is capable of supporting future bandwidths up to 32GBps.

In addition to replacing PCI, PCI Express is designed to augment and eventually replace many of the buses currently used in PCs, including the existing Intel hub architecture, HyperTransport, and similar high-speed interfaces between motherboard chipset components. Additionally, it will replace video interfaces such as AGP and act as a mezzanine bus to attach other interfaces, such as Serial ATA, USB 2.0, 1394b (FireWire or iLink), Gigabit Ethernet, and more.

Because PCI Express can be implemented over cables as well as onboard, it can be used to create systems constructed with remote "bricks" containing the bulk of the computing power. Imagine the motherboard, processor, and RAM in one small box hidden under a table, with the video, disk drives, and I/O ports in another box sitting out on a table within easy reach. This enables a variety of flexible PC form factors to be developed in the future without compromising performance.

Don't expect PCI Express to replace PCI or other interfaces overnight, however. System developers will most likely continue to integrate PCI, AGP, and other bus architectures into system designs for several more years. Just as with PCI and the ISA/AT-Bus before, there will likely be a long period of time during which both buses will be found on motherboards. Gradually, though, fewer PCI and more PCI Express connections will appear. Over time, PCI Express will eventually become the preferred general-purpose I/O interconnect over PCI. I expect the move to PCI Express will be similar to the transition from ISA/AT-Bus to PCI during the 1990s.

The first desktop PCs using PCI Express emerged in June 2004, timed with the introduction of the first PCI Express chipsets and motherboards from Intel. PCI Express first appeared in new laptop systems starting in January 2005, timed with the release of the first mobile PCI Express chipsets. Since then, PCI Express has been catching on rapidly, in that most new systems introduced since those dates incorporate PCI Express, but also still include PCI. This means that most new desktops can use both PCI Express and PCI cards, while most new laptops can use both ExpressCard and CardBus cards.

For more information on PCI Express, I recommend consulting the PCI-SIG website (`www.pcisig.org`).

Motherboard Components

A modern motherboard has several components built in, including various sockets, slots, connectors, chips, and so on. This section examines the components found on a typical motherboard.

Most modern laptop motherboards have at least the following major components on them:

- Processor socket/slot
- Chipset (North/South Bridge or memory and I/O controller hubs)
- Super I/O chip
- ROM BIOS (flash ROM/firmware hub)
- SODIMM (memory) sockets
- PC Card/CardBus chip and socket(s)
- Mini PCI slot
- Mobile daughter card (MDC) socket
- CPU voltage regulator
- Battery

Most laptop motherboards also include integrated video, audio, networking, or other optional interfaces, depending on the individual board. Most of these standard components are discussed in the following sections.

Processor Sockets/Slots

The CPU in a laptop system can be soldered directly into the motherboard, installed via a mobile module (a circuit board containing the CPU and other components), or plugged in via a socket similar to that of desktop systems. Most modern systems have the processor installed in a socket directly, allowing future replacement and even limited upgrades. Processors earlier than the Pentium III and Athlon were usually soldered in or installed via various mobile module designs, greatly limiting interchangeability. Table 5.4 shows the designations for the various processor sockets/slots used in laptop systems and lists the chips designed to plug into them.

Table 5.4   Mobile CPU Socket Specifications

Socket	Pins	Pin Layout	Voltage	Supported Processors
MMC-1	280	70×4	5V-21V*	Mobile Pentium/Celeron/Pentium II MMC-1
MMC-2	400	40×5	5V-21V*	Mobile Celeron/Pentium II/III MMC-2
MC	240	30×8	Auto VRM	Mobile Pentium II MC
Micro-PGA1	615	24×26 mPGA	Auto VRM	Mobile Celeron/Pentium II micro-PGA1
Micro-PGA2	495	21×24 mPGA	Auto VRM	Mobile Celeron/Pentium III micro-PGA2
Socket 478	478	26×26 mPGA	Auto VRM	Desktop Celeron/Pentium 4 FC-PGA2
mPGA479M	479	26×26 mPGA	Auto VRM	Mobile Celeron/Pentium III/4/M micro-FC-PGA

(continues)

Table 5.4   **Continued**

Socket	Pins	Pin Layout	Voltage	Supported Processors
Socket A (462)	462	37×37 SPGA	Auto VRM	Mobile/Desktop Duron/Athlon 4/Athlon XP-M
Socket 754	754	29×29 mPGA	Auto VRM	Mobile/Desktop Athlon 64

*Automatic voltage regulator module is built in to the MMC, allowing a wide range of voltage input

Auto VRM = Voltage regulator module with automatic voltage selection determined by processor VID pins

FC-PGA = Flip-chip pin grid array

PGA = Pin grid array

SPGA = Staggered pin grid array

mPGA = Micro-pin grid array

Note that some laptops use desktop processors, so they might use desktop processor sockets. Most, however, use specific processors and sockets designed for mobile use. Just because a processor fits into a particular socket does not mean that it will function. For example, versions of the Celeron, Pentium III, Pentium 4, and Pentium M all plug into an mPGA479M socket, but only the one that the system is designed for will work; in fact, plugging in the wrong one could cause damage. Despite having similar pin counts and physical arrangements, the actual pinouts vary among the different processors.

Chipsets

We can't talk about modern motherboards without discussing chipsets. The chipset *is* the motherboard; therefore, any two boards with the same chipsets are functionally identical. The chipset contains the processor bus interface (called the front-side bus, or FSB), memory controllers, bus controllers, I/O controllers, and more. All the circuits of the motherboard are contained within the chipset. If the processor in your PC is like the engine in your car, the chipset represents the chassis. It is the framework in which the engine rests and is its connection to the outside world. The chipset is the frame, suspension, steering, wheels and tires, transmission, driveshaft, differential, and brakes. The chassis in your car is what gets the power to the ground, allowing the vehicle to start, stop, and corner. In the PC, the chipset represents the connection between the processor and everything else. The processor can't talk to the memory, video processor, expansion cards, devices, and so on without going through the chipset. The chipset is the main hub and central nervous system of the PC. If you think of the processor as the brain, the chipset is the spine and the central nervous system.

Because the chipset controls the interface or connections between the processor and everything else, the chipset ends up dictating which type of processor you have; how fast it will run; how fast the buses will run; the speed, type, and amount of memory you can use; and more. In fact, the chipset might be the single most important component in your system, possibly even more important than the processor. I've seen systems with faster processors be outperformed by systems with slower processors but a better chipset, much like how a car with less power might win a race through better cornering and braking. When deciding on a system, I start by choosing the chipset because the chipset decision then dictates the processor, memory, I/O, and expansion capabilities.

Chipset Evolution

When IBM created the first PC motherboards, it used several discrete (separate) chips to complete the design. Besides the processor and optional math coprocessor, many other components were required to complete the system. These other components included items such as the clock generator, bus controller, system timer, interrupt and DMA controllers, CMOS RAM and clock, and keyboard controller. Additionally, many other simple logic chips were used to complete the entire motherboard circuit—plus, of course, things such as the actual processor, math coprocessor (floating-point unit), memory, and other parts. Table 5.5 lists all the primary chip components used on the original PC/XT and AT motherboards.

Table 5.5   Primary Chip Components on PC/XT and AT Motherboards

Chip Function	PC/XT Version	AT Version
Processor	8088	80286
Math coprocessor (floating-point unit)	8087	80287
Clock generator	8284	82284
Bus controller	8288	82288
System timer	8253	8254
Low-order interrupt controller	8259	8259
High-order interrupt controller	—	8259
Low-order DMA controller	8237	8237
High-order DMA controller	—	8237
CMOS RAM/real-time clock	—	MC146818
Keyboard controller	8255	8042

Although the specifications shown here are for PC/XT and AT systems, keep in mind that, in that day, portables were not really laptops. Instead, they mimicked desktop technology almost exactly. In essence, a portable was a desktop with a handle. By the time laptops really came around, chipsets were already invented and in use in desktops as well.

In addition to the processor/coprocessor, a six-chip set was used to implement the primary motherboard circuit in the original PC and XT systems. IBM later upgraded this to a nine-chip design in the AT and later systems, mainly by adding more interrupt and DMA controller chips and the nonvolatile CMOS RAM/real-time clock chip. All these motherboard chip components came from Intel or an Intel-licensed manufacturer, except the CMOS/clock chip, which came from Motorola. Building a clone or copy of one of these IBM systems required all these chips, plus many smaller discrete logic chips to glue the design together, totaling 100 or more individual chips. This kept the price of a motherboard high and left little room on the board to integrate other functions.

In 1986, a company called Chips and Technologies introduced a revolutionary component called the 82C206—the main part of the first PC motherboard chipset. This was a single chip that integrated into it all the functions of the main motherboard chips in an AT-compatible system. This chip included the functions of the 82284 clock generator, 82288 bus controller, 8254 system timer, dual 8259 interrupt controllers, dual 8237 DMA controllers, and even MC146818 CMOS/clock chip. Besides the processor, virtually all the major chip components on a PC motherboard could now be replaced by a single chip. Four other chips augmented the 82C206 acting as buffers and memory controllers, thus completing virtually the entire motherboard circuit with five total chips. Chips and Technologies called this first chipset the CS8220 chipset. Needless to say, this was a revolutionary concept in PC motherboard manufacturing. Not only did it greatly reduce the cost of building a PC motherboard, but it also made designing a motherboard much easier. The reduced component count meant that the boards had more room for integrating other items formerly found on expansion cards. Later, the four chips augmenting the 82C206 were replaced by a new set of only three chips, and the entire set was called the New Enhanced AT (NEAT) 82C836 Single Chip AT (SCAT) chipset, which finally condensed all the chips in the set to a single chip.

Since then, many chipset manufacturers have come and gone, and after a major shakeup in the chipset industry, only Intel, AMD, VIA Technologies, SiS, and ALi make motherboard chipsets. Intel has come to dominate the chipset market for systems using Intel processors, although other companies such as VIA Technologies, SiS, and ALi also make chipsets supporting Intel processors. AMD has developed its own chipsets for the K6 and Athlon family of processors, but it now emphasizes third-party chipset developers to support its products. Today VIA Technologies is the leading developer of AMD Athlon/Athlon XP/Duron chipsets. The popularity of AMD processors has also encouraged SiS, NVIDIA, and the ALi Corporation to develop chipsets for both Intel- and AMD-based systems.

It is interesting to note that the original PC chipset maker, Chips and Technologies, survived by changing course to design and manufacture video chips, and found a niche in that market specifically for laptop video chipsets. Chips and Technologies was subsequently bought out by Intel in 1998 as a part of Intel's video strategy.

Intel Chipsets

You can't talk about chipsets today without discussing Intel because it currently owns the vast majority of the chipset market, especially for Intel processor–equipped mobile systems.

Now as Intel develops new processors, it develops chipsets and motherboards simultaneously, which means that they can be announced and shipped in unison. This eliminates the delay between introducing new processors and waiting for motherboards and systems capable of using them, which was common in the industry's early days. For the consumer, this means no waiting for new systems. Since the original Pentium processor in 1993, you have been able to purchase ready-made systems on the same day a new processor is released.

Starting with the 486 in 1989, Intel began a pattern of numbering its chipsets as follows:

Chipset Number	Processor Family
420xx	P4 (486)
430xx	P5 (Pentium)
440xx	P6 (Pentium Pro/PII/PIII)
8xx	P6/P7 (PII/PIII/P4/PM) with hub architecture
9xx	P7 (P4/PM) with PCI Express
450xx	P6 server (Pentium Pro/PII/PIII Xeon)
E72xx	Xeon workstation with hub architecture
E75xx	Xeon server with hub architecture
460xx	Itanium processor
E88xx	Itanium 2 processor with hub architecture

The chipset numbers listed here are abbreviations of the actual chipset numbers stamped on the individual chips. For example, one of the popular laptop Pentium II/III chipsets was the Intel 440BX chipset, which consisted of two components: the 82443BX North Bridge and the 82371EX South Bridge. Likewise, the 845 chipset supports the Mobile Pentium 4 and consists of two main parts, including the 82845 memory controller hub (MCH, which replaces the North Bridge) and an 82801CAM I/O controller hub (ICH3-M, which replaces the South Bridge). By reading the logo (Intel or others) as well as the part number and letter combinations on the larger chips on your motherboard, you can quickly identify the chipset your motherboard uses.

Intel has used two distinct chipset architectures: a North/South Bridge architecture and a newer hub architecture. All its more recent 800 series chipsets use the hub architecture, while the newer 900 series use PCI Express. In the 900 series, the connection between the North Bridge (memory controller hub) and South Bridge (I/O controller hub) is a new interface called Direct Media Interface (DMI), which is basically a modified PCI Express x4 interface supporting a throughput of 1GBps in each direction simultaneously.

AMD Athlon/Duron Chipsets

AMD took a gamble—one that was ultimately successful—with its Athlon family of processors (Athlon, Athlon XP, Athlon MP, and the now-discontinued Duron). With these processors, AMD decided for the first time to create a chip that was Intel compatible with regard to software but not directly hardware or pin compatible. Whereas the K6 series would plug into the same Socket 7 that Intel designed for the Pentium processor line, the AMD Athlon and Duron would not be pin compatible with the Pentium II/III and Celeron chips. This also meant that AMD could not take advantage of the existing chipsets and motherboard designs when the Athlon and Duron were introduced; instead, AMD would have to either create its own chipsets and motherboards or find other companies that would.

Although it would take some time for AMD to put its processors and chipset designs into laptops systems, AMD took its first step into the world of chipsets when it bootstrapped the market by introducing its own chipset, referred to as the AMD-750 chipset (code-named Irongate). The AMD 750 chipset consists of the 751 system controller (North Bridge) and the 756 peripheral bus controller (South Bridge). More recently, AMD introduced the AMD-760 chipset for the Athlon/Duron processors, which is the first major chipset on the market that supports DDR SDRAM for memory. It consists of two chips: the AMD-761 system bus controller (North Bridge) and the AMD-766 peripheral bus controller (South Bridge). Although AMD no longer puts much emphasis on chipset sales, its pioneering efforts have inspired other companies, such as VIA Technologies, NVIDIA, and SiS, to develop chipsets specifically designed for the Slot A and current Socket A and Socket 754 processors from AMD. This has enabled the motherboard companies to make a variety of boards supporting these chips and the Athlon processors, taking a fair amount of market share away from Intel in the process.

North/South Bridge Architecture

Most older chipsets are broken into a multitiered architecture incorporating what are referred to as North and South Bridge components, as well as a Super I/O chip:

- **The North Bridge**—This component gets its name from its function as the connection between the high-speed processor bus (up to 800MHz) and the slower AGP (up to 533MHz) and PCI (33MHz) buses. The North Bridge component is what the chipset is named after, meaning that, for example, what we call the 440BX chipset is derived from the fact that the actual North Bridge chip part number for that set is 82443BX.

- **The South Bridge**—This component acts as a bridge between the 33MHz PCI bus (or CardBus in laptops) and the even slower ISA bus (or PC Card in laptops).

- **The Super I/O chip**—This separate chip is attached to the ISA bus, which is not really considered part of the chipset and often comes from a third party, such as National Semiconductor or Standard MicroSystems Corp. (SMSC). The Super I/O chip contains commonly used peripheral items all combined into a single chip. Note that many recent South Bridge chips now include Super I/O functions, in which case they no longer include a separate Super I/O chip.

The North Bridge is sometimes referred to as the PCI/AGP controller (PAC). It is essentially the main component of the motherboard and is the only motherboard circuit besides the processor that normally runs at full motherboard (processor bus) speed. Most modern chipsets use a single-chip North Bridge; however, some of the older ones actually consisted of up to three individual chips to make up the complete North Bridge circuit.

The South Bridge is the lower-speed component in the chipset and has always been a single individual chip. The South Bridge is a somewhat interchangeable component, in that different chipsets (North Bridge chips) often are designed to use the same South Bridge component. This modular design of the chipset allows for lower cost and greater flexibility for motherboard manufacturers. The South Bridge also typically contains dual ATA interfaces, several USB interfaces, and even the CMOS RAM and real-time clock functions. The South Bridge contains all the components that make up the ISA bus, including the interrupt and DMA controllers.

The third motherboard component, the Super I/O chip, is connected to the 8MHz ISA bus and contains all the standard peripherals that are built in to a motherboard. For example, most Super I/O chips contain the serial ports, parallel port, floppy controller, and keyboard/mouse interface.

Figure 5.1 shows a typical North/South Bridge architecture using the 440BX chipset. This was the most popular chipset and system architecture for late Pentium II or early Pentium III laptops.

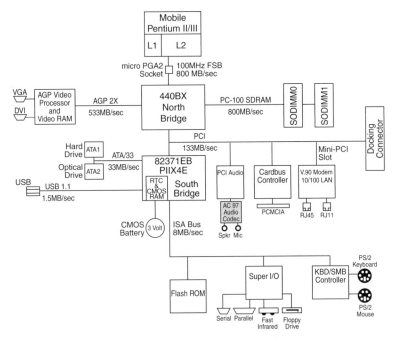

Figure 5.1   Typical 440BX chipset laptop motherboard block diagram.

More recent motherboards using North/South Bridge chipset designs often incorporate a Super South Bridge, which incorporates the South Bridge and Super I/O functions into a single chip.

Intel Hub Architecture

The newer 800-series chips from Intel use a hub architecture in which the former North Bridge chip is now called a memory controller hub (MCH) and the former South Bridge is called an I/O controller hub (ICH). Instead of being connected through the PCI bus as in a standard North/South Bridge design, they are connected via a dedicated hub interface that is twice as fast as PCI. The hub design offers several advantages over the conventional North/South Bridge design:

- **Better speed**—The hub interface is a 4× (quad-clocked) 66MHz 8-bit (4 × 66MHz × 1 byte = 266MBps) interface, which has twice the throughput of PCI (33MHz × 32 bits = 133MBps).

- **Reduced PCI loading**—The hub interface is independent of PCI and doesn't share or steal PCI bus bandwidth for chipset or Super I/O traffic. This improves performance of all other PCI bus–connected devices because the PCI bus is not involved in these transactions.

- **Reduced board wiring**—Although it is twice as fast as PCI, the hub interface is only 8 bits wide and requires only 15 signals to be routed on the motherboard. By comparison, PCI requires no fewer than 64 signals be routed on the board, causing increased electromagnetic interference (EMI) generation, greater susceptibility to signal degradation and noise, and increased board-manufacturing costs.

This hub interface design allows for a much greater throughput for PCI devices because no South Bridge chip (also carrying traffic from the Super I/O chip) is hogging the PCI bus. Because of bypassing PCI, hub architecture also enables greater throughput for devices directly connected to the I/O controller hub (formerly the South Bridge), such as the new higher-speed ATA-100/133, Serial ATA, and USB 2.0 interfaces.

The hub interface design is also very economical, at only 8 bits wide. Although this seems too narrow to be useful, there is a reason for the design. Because the interface is only 8 bits wide, it uses only 15 signals, compared to the 64 signals required by the 32-bit–wide PCI bus interface used by North/South Bridge chip designs. The lower pin count means that less circuit routing exists on the board, less signal noise and jitter occur, and the chips themselves have fewer pins, making them smaller and more economical to produce.

Although it transfers only 8 bits at a time, the hub interface executes four transfers per cycle and cycles at 66MHz. This gives it an effective throughput of 4 × 66MHz × 1 byte = 266MBps. This is twice the bandwidth of PCI, which is 32 bits wide but runs only one transfer per 33MHz cycles, for a total bandwidth of 133MBps. So, by virtue of a very narrow—but very fast—design, the hub interface achieves high performance with less cost and more signal integrity than with the previous North/South Bridge design.

The MCH interfaces between the high-speed processor bus (800/533/400/133/100/66MHz) and the hub interface (66MHz) and AGP bus (533/266/133/66MHz), whereas the ICH interfaces between the hub interface (66MHz) and the ATA(IDE) ports (66/100MHz) and PCI bus (33MHz).

The ICH also includes a new Low Pin Count (LPC) bus, consisting basically of a stripped 4-bit–wide version of PCI designed primarily to support the motherboard ROM BIOS and Super I/O chips. Because it uses the same 4 signals for data, address, and command functions, only 9 other signals are necessary to implement the bus, for a total of only 13 signals. This dramatically reduces the number of traces connecting the ROM BIOS chip and Super I/O chips in a system, compared to the 96 ISA bus signals necessary for older North/South Bridge chipsets that used ISA as the interface to those devices. The LPC bus has a maximum bandwidth of 16.67MBps, which is faster than ISA and more than enough to support devices such as ROM BIOS and Super I/O chips.

Figure 5.2 shows a typical hub interface architecture using the 855PM chipset. This is the most popular chipset and system architecture for Pentium M laptops, and it represents a modern state-of-the-art system design.

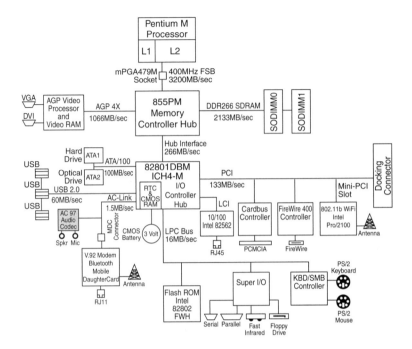

Figure 5.2   Typical 855PM chipset laptop motherboard block diagram.

Intel DMI Architecture

The 900 series chipsets from Intel have abandoned the hub interface in favor of a new interface called Direct Media Interface (DMI). DMI is basically a modified PCI Express x4 (4-lane) interface supporting a throughput of 1GBps in each direction simultaneously. Being a dedicated connection between the chips in the chipset, DMI incorporates all of the same advantages of the former hub interface, along with a significantly higher-speed interconnection. Figure 5.3 shows where DMI fits into the 915 chipset between the 915PM memory controller hub (MCH) and the ICH6-M I/O controller hub.

Note

Although other chipset makers typically use the North Bridge/South Bridge nomenclature for their chipsets, several have developed high-speed connections similar to Intel's hub architecture and DMI. For example, most of VIA's recent chipsets use the V-Link hub architecture, which provides a dedicated 266MHz bus between the North and South Bridge chips. The high-speed HyperTransport bus between the North and South Bridges originally developed by AMD has been licensed by chipset vendors such as NVIDIA, VIA, and ALi Corporation; SiS's MuTIOL Connect is used by recent SiS chipsets.

Other High-Speed North-South Bridge Connections

Intel is not alone in replacing the slow PCI bus connection between North and South Bridge–type chips with faster architectures that bypass the PCI bus. Other companies introducing high-speed chipset interconnects include these:

- **VIA**—It created the V-Link architecture to connect its North and South Bridge chips at speeds matching or exceeding those of the Intel hub architecture. V-Link uses a dedicated 8-bit data bus and is currently implemented in two versions: 4x V-Link and 8x V-Link. The 4x V-Link transfers data at 266MBps (4×66MHz), which is twice the speed of PCI and matches the speed of Intel's hub architecture. The 8x V-Link transfers data at 533MBps (4×133MHz), which is twice the speed of Intel's hub architecture. All VIA South Bridge chips in the VT82*xx* series support V-Link. The first chipsets to use V-Link were VIA's 266-series chipsets for the Pentium III, Pentium 4, and Athlon processor families. VIA's 333- and 400-series chipsets also use V-Link.

■ **SiS**—Its MuTIOL architecture provides performance comparable to that of VIA's 4x V-Link. Chipsets that support MuTIOL use separate address, DMA, input data, and output data buses for each I/O bus master. MuTIOL buffers and manages multiple upstream and downstream data transfers over a bidirectional 16-bit data bus. South Bridge chips in the SiS961 and 962 series support MuTIOL at a data-transfer rate of 533MBps (133MHz × 4), whereas the SiS963 series supports the faster MuTIOL 1G, which supports data-transfer rates exceeding 1GBps. The North Bridge chips that support MuTIOL are described in the sections listing SiS chipsets for Pentium 4 and Athlon-series processors.

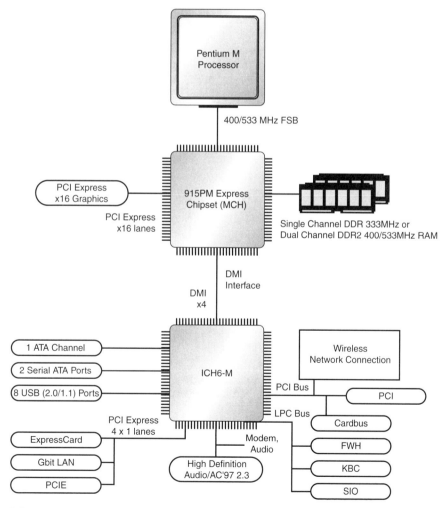

Figure 5.3 Typical 915PM chipset laptop motherboard block diagram.

- **ATI**—It uses a high-speed interconnect called A-Link in some of its IGP-integrated chipsets. A-Link runs at 266MBps, matching Intel's hub architecture and first-generation V-Link and MuTIOL designs. Its RS- and RX-series chipsets use the HyperTransport bus. HyperTransport, which is now developed and managed by the nonprofit HyperTransport Technology Consortium (www.hypertransport.org), uses a packetized point-to-point interconnect IP bus that uses low-voltage differential signaling. The 8×8 version of HyperTransport used by some ATI chipsets supports 800MHz clock speeds and a data-transfer rate of 1.6GBps.

- **NVIDIA**—Its nForce, nForce2, and nForce3 chipsets use the HyperTransport bus originally developed by AMD.

It's worth noting that although these chipsets were originally deployed in desktop systems, their appearance in laptop systems was simultaneous, in most cases.

Although the terms *North Bridge* and *South Bridge* continue to be used for chipsets using V-Link, MuTIOL, A-Link, or HyperTransport interconnects between these chipset components, these chipsets really use a hub-based architecture similar to that of Intel 8*xx*-series chipsets and receive corresponding boosts in performance as a consequence.

Chipset Profiles

To get the most out of any processor, you must use a high-performance chipset. As when shopping for a desktop system, you should be aware of what chipset is used in the portable computer you plan to buy and whether it fully supports the capabilities of the processor and the system's other components. The following sections describe the most popular chipsets found in portable systems using Pentium and newer processors.

Mobile Pentium Chipset

Intel had only a single mobile-specific chipset for Pentium systems. However, many laptops used desktop processors and chipsets, despite the drawbacks in power consumption.

Intel 430MX

Intel introduced the 430MX in October 1995, designed to support the Pentium and Pentium MMX processors. The 430MX mobile chipset was similar in architecture and performance to the then-popular 430FX desktop socket 7 chipset, although it is important to note that the processor was normally soldered in, not socketed in mobile designs of that time. Most Pentium-based laptop and portable systems used this chipset from the mid- to late-1990s.

The 82430MX consisted of four total chips, including a three-chip North Bridge: the 82437MX system controller and two 82438MX data path chips, and the 82371MX MPIIX (Mobile PCI I/O IDE Accelerator) South Bridge. These components are in Quad Flat Pack (QFP) and Thin Quad Flat Pack (TQFP) packaging, to allow thin and light designs. Notable features for the 430MX include these:

- Pentium processor bus speeds of 50, 60, and 66MHz
- Integrated L2 cache controller
- PCI 2.0 bus support for up to four PCI masters
- EDO (extended data out) RAM support
- Pipelined burst SRAM support for the L2 cache

To provide extended battery life for use in portable systems, the 430MX featured power-management functions not normally found in desktop chipsets:

- DRAM suspend with self-refresh
- Clock that can be throttled or stopped
- SRAM (cache) that can be powered down

The 430MX PCIset was originally priced at $32.50 (U.S.) in 10,000-unit quantities and was by far the most popular chipset used in Pentium- and Pentium MMX processor–based portables.

Pentium II/III Chipsets

Intel, VIA, and others offered several chipsets designed for mobile Pentium II and III processors and systems. Some, such as the 440BX, were originally designed for desktop use and then later were adapted for mobile processors. Others, such as the 440MX, were specifically designed for mobile use.

Intel 440BX

The Intel 440BX chipset was introduced in April 1998 and was the first chipset to run the processor host bus (often called the front-side bus, or FSB) at 100MHz. The 440BX was designed specifically to support the faster Pentium II/III processors at 350MHz and higher. This chipset was the first Pentium II/III chipset for laptop systems as well.

The main change from previous chipsets is that the 440BX chipset improves performance by increasing the bandwidth of the system bus from 66MHz to 100MHz. Because the chipset can run at either 66MHz or 100MHz, it allows one basic motherboard design to support all Pentium II/III processor speeds based on either the 66MHz or 100MHz processor bus.

Here are the Intel 440BX highlights:

- 100MHz or 66MHz Pentium II/III processor bus
- PC-100 SDRAM support
- 1GB maximum memory in up to four banks (four DIMMs)
- Support for ECC (error correcting code) memory
- Support for ACPI power management
- The first chipset to support the Mobile Intel Pentium II/III processors

The Intel 440BX consists of a single North Bridge chip called the 82443BX host bridge/controller, which is paired with an 82371EB PCI-ISA/IDE Xcelerator (PIIX4E) South Bridge chip. The South Bridge adds support for the advanced configuration and power interface (ACPI) specification version 1.0.

The 440BX is also used in mobile module versions of the Pentium II and III processors. In a mobile module design, the chipset's two halves, called the North Bridge and the South Bridge, are located on the mobile module and the motherboard, respectively.

The 440BX was the most popular chipset for portables of the late 1990s, which were based on the Pentium II and III and Celeron processors.

Intel 440MX

The 440MX chipset is essentially a 440BX North Bridge and PIIX4E South Bridge combined into a single chip. In addition to consolidating the two chips into one, the 440MX adds integrated AC'97 (audio codec 1997) audio and modem support, which provides a built-in sound card and modem comparable to those of PCI-based cards.

The 440MX is identical to the 440BX, except for the following features:

■ Combined North and South Bridge chips into a single 440MX component

■ No AGP support

■ Added AC'97 controller and AC-Link interface based on AC'97 2.1

■ X-bus (stripped down 8-bit ISA) interface (instead of standard ISA) for keyboard controller, Super I/O, and flash ROM

■ 256MB maximum RAM

■ PCI version 2.2

■ 2.1W (at 100MHz) and 1.6W (at 66MHz) typical power dissipation, with low-power features enabled

Intel 440ZX

The 440ZX-66M is a low-cost version of the 440BX designed specifically to support the low-end mobile Celeron processors based on Pentium II and III designs. The main difference from the 440BX is that the 440ZX is limited to a 66MHz processor front-side bus (FSB).

VIA PN133

The VIA PN133 is a Pentium III processor chipset combining an integrated Savage4 graphics core with 133MHz processor bus and 133MHz SDRAM support. The PN133 is ideally suited for thin and light or entry-level laptop systems. The main features of the PN133 include the following:

■ 66/100/133MHz Pentium III processor bus

■ Support for Mobile Intel Pentium III/Celeron and VIA C3 processors

■ Integrated S3 Savage4 AGP 4x graphics core

■ Shared memory architecture, with video that uses system RAM

■ Integrated 250MHz RAMDAC

■ Support for LVDS (low-voltage differential signaling), CRT, DVI, and TV display

■ Integrated AC'97 audio/modem

■ PC100/133 SDRAM support

■ 1.5GB maximum RAM

■ ATA-100 support

■ Four USB 1.1 ports

■ ACPI/OnNow power management

■ VT8603 North Bridge

■ VT8231 South Bridge

Built-in high performance 2D/3D graphics, flexible 66/100/133MHz system bus settings, support for PC100/133 SDRAM, and multiple power saving modes make the VIA ProSavage PN133 (code-named Twister) the ideal integrated SMA chipset for the Intel Pentium III, Intel Celeron, and VIA C3 processor laptops.

Intel 815EM

The 815EM chipset is a mainstream laptop Pentium III/Celeron chipset with an economical integrated AGP 2x video controller that shares system RAM.

Similar to the other 8*xx*-series chipsets from Intel, the 815EM (82815EM GMCH2-M) uses Intel's hub architecture, providing a 266MBps connection between the two main chipset components. This chipset does not share the PCI bus like the older North/South Bridge designs do.

The 815EM supports the following features:

- 100MHz Pentium II/III processor bus
- 266MBps hub interface
- ATA-100
- PC-100 SDRAM
- 512MB maximum RAM
- Intel SpeedStep technology support
- LAN connect interface (integrated LAN)
- Alert on LAN 2.0
- AC'97 controller (integrated sound)
- Low-power sleep modes
- Random number generator
- Two USB 1.1 controllers, four USB ports
- LPC bus for Super I/O and firmware hub (ROM BIOS)
- Elimination of ISA bus
- Integrated AGP 2x video controller (shares system RAM)
- Optional 4MB of dedicated video RAM
- DVI (Digital Visual Interface) for flat panel displays
- Software MPEG-2 DVD playback with hardware motion compensation

The 815EM uses the ICH2-M (82801BAM) I/O controller hub, which is most notable for providing ATA-100 support. Although few drives can really take advantage of this much throughput, in any case there won't be a bottleneck there. The other notable feature is having two USB 1.1 controllers and four total USB ports on board. This allows double the standard USB 1.1 performance by splitting up devices over the two ports, and can allow up to four connections before a hub is required.

A companion chip called the 82807AA video controller hub (VCH) connects directly to the digital video-out port on the GMCH2-M, enabling low-voltage differential signaling (LVDS) for LCD panel support with the 815EM integrated graphics.

Another important feature of the 815EM is the integration of a fast Ethernet controller directly into the chipset. The integrated LAN controller works with a physical-layer component that includes the following:

- Enhanced 10/100Mbps Ethernet with Alert on LAN technology
- Basic 10/100Mbps Ethernet

These physical-layer components can be placed directly on the motherboard (additional chips) or can be installed via an adapter that plugs into a Mini PCI slot. The 815EM chipset was a popular Pentium III–class chipset for the mainstream laptop market and was essentially designed to replace the venerable 440Bx chipset.

Intel 830M/MG/MP

The 830 chipset family is the last chipset Intel released for the Mobile Intel Pentium III and Celeron processor-based laptops. The 830 chipset increases the processor bus speed to 133MHz and also supports PC133 SDRAM.

The 830 chipset comes in three versions:

- **830MP**—AGP 4x interface for discrete video processors
- **830MG**—Integrated AGP 2x video processor
- **830M**—Integrated AGP 2x video processor and AGP 4x external interface

The 830 chipset family also supports the following:

- 133MHz Pentium III processor bus
- PC-133 SDRAM
- 1GB maximum RAM
- Three digital video output ports
- Hub architecture
- Six USB 1.1 ports
- AC'97 controller (integrated sound)
- LAN connect interface (integrated LAN)

Pentium 4 Chipsets

Intel introduced several chipsets for use with Mobile Pentium 4-M and Mobile Pentium 4 processors. Some, such as the 845MP/MZ, were simply mobile versions of desktop chipsets. Others, such as the 852 family, were specifically designed for mobile use.

Intel 845MP/MZ

The 845M chipset family is designed for low-end Mobile Pentium 4 systems. The 845M chipset family includes two versions, with the following differences:

- **845MP**—266MHz (PC-2100) DDR memory, maximum 1GB RAM
- **845MZ**—200MHz (PC-1600) DDR memory, maximum 512MB RAM

Both chips in the 845M chipset family (82845MP/MZ memory controller hub) support the following features:

- AGP 4x graphics
- 400MHz Pentium 4 processor bus
- Enhanced Intel SpeedStep technology
- Six USB 1.1 ports

- Hub architecture
- ICH3-M (82801CAM I/O controller hub)
- ACPI 2.0 power management
- ATA/100
- AC'97 controller (integrated sound)
- LAN connect interface (integrated LAN)

Intel 852PM/GM/GME

The 852 chipset family is a mainstream Mobile Pentium 4 chipset with advanced mobile power management, support for DDR SDRAM memory, and optional integrated graphics and/or AGP 4x support.

The most basic member of the family is the 852G, which supports a 400MHz processor bus, up to 1GB of DDR200/266 (PC1600/PC2100) memory, as well as an integrated Intel Extreme Graphics AGP 2x video processor with support for dual independent displays and integrated low-voltage differential signaling (LVDS) with up to SXGA+ (1400×1050) LCD resolution.

The 82852GM (MCH) includes the following:

- 400MHz Mobile Pentium 4-M processor bus
- DDR200/266 (PC1600/PC2100) support
- 1GB maximum RAM
- Integrated Intel Extreme Graphics AGP 2x video processor with support for dual independent displays and integrated LVDS with up to SXGA+ (1400×1050) LCD resolution
- High-speed USB 2.0 support, with up to six USB 2.0 ports
- Enhanced Intel SpeedStep (dynamic switching of CPU voltage and frequency) support
- Hub architecture
- 82801DBM (ICH4-M) I/O controller hub with Ultra ATA/100 support

The 852GME includes everything from the 852G and adds this:

- 533MHz Pentium 4 processor bus
- DDR266/333 (PC2100/PC2700) support
- 2GB maximum RAM
- Integrated Intel Extreme Graphics/2 AGP 2x video processor with support for dual independent displays and integrated LVDS, with up to UXGA+ (1600×1200) LCD resolution

The 852GME chipset is the same as the 852G, except that it supports the faster 533MHz Mobile Pentium 4 processor bus and up to 2GB of high-speed DDR266/333 (PC2100/PC2700) memory. The 852GME also includes an upgraded Intel Extreme Graphics/2 AGP 2x video processor with support for dual independent displays and integrated LVDS, with up to UXGA+ (1600×1200) LCD resolution.

The integrated video processors built in to the 852G and 852GME dynamically share the main system RAM (no separate video RAM is used). The integrated 2x video with shared RAM results in a less expensive system than one using a third-party AGP 4x video processor with discrete video RAM, but with lower video performance as well.

Most higher-performance laptops preferred to use a chipset without integrated video and instead build the equivalent of a video card on the motherboard, complete with a discrete video processor, video RAM, and video BIOS. In most laptops, the only difference between the built-in video and a separate video card (as in a desktop system) is that the built-in video card merely shares real estate with the rest of the motherboard.

The 852PM chipset is the same as the 852GME (faster 533MHz processor bus and up to 2GB of high-speed DDR266/333 [PC2100/PC2700] memory), but it lacks the integrated video. Instead, an AGP 4x interface is included for connecting to third-party video processors. This makes the 852PM the best choice for high-performance mobile Pentium 4 systems.

Pentium M Chipsets

Intel 855PM/GM

The Intel 855 chipset family is designed to support the 400MHz bus versions of the Pentium M and Celeron M mobile processors and is part of Intel's Centrino Mobile Technology platform when combined with an Intel wireless networking solution (see Figure 5.2). The combination of the 855 chipset and a Pentium M or Celeron M processor results in a powerful mobile system with low overall power consumption.

The 855PM is a standard memory controller hub with AGP 4x support for a discrete video processor and video RAM, while the 855GM version adds an integrated video processor that shares system RAM.

The 855PM includes the following features:

- 400MHz Pentium M processor bus
- 2GB maximum RAM
- DDR200/266 memory technology
- High-speed USB 2.0 support with up to six USB 2.0 ports
- AGP 4x interface
- Dynamic input/output buffer disabling for processor system bus and memory, which reduces chipset power consumption by activation or powerdown of the processor system bus or memory
- Hub interface
- 82801DBM (ICH4-M) I/O controller hub

The 855GM includes everything from the 855PM and also adds an Integrated Intel Extreme Graphics/2 AGP 2x video processor with support for dual independent displays and integrated low-voltage differential signaling (LVDS), with up to UXGA+ (1600×1200) LCD resolution.

Intel 915 Express Chipset Family

The Intel 915 mobile chipset family (code-named Alviso) was introduced in January 2005 and includes the 915PM/GM/GMS and 910GML. These chipsets are designed to support the Pentium M and Celeron M mobile processors in both 400MHz and 533MHz bus versions (dependent on the specific chipset), and are part of Intel's second generation Centrino Mobile Technology platform (code-named Sonoma) when combined with an internal Intel wireless networking solution. The combination of the 915 chipset and a Pentium M or Celeron M processor results in a powerful mobile system with low overall power consumption.

The 915 chipset supports up to 2GB of dual-channel DDR2 system memory, which allows for a significant increase in peak memory bandwidth and power benefits over the single-channel DDR that the 855 chipset supported. The 915 chipset also supports PCI Express bus architecture, which means that laptops using this chipset will have ExpressCard as well as CardBus sockets for expansion cards. Finally, the 915 chipset supports Intel High Definition Audio (HDA), which is an enhanced audio specification for high-quality surround-sound audio suitable for home theater.

The 915PM is a standard memory controller hub with PCI Express x16 support for a separate video processor and video RAM, while the 915GM version adds an integrated video processor that shares system RAM. The integrated video in the 915GM is the Intel Graphics Media Accelerator 900, which has about twice the graphics performance of the integrated video in the older 855GM chipset.

The 915 chipset family features include

- 400MHz/533MHz CPU bus support
- Support for dual-channel DDR2 400/533MHz memory
- PCI Express Bus Architecture for ExpressCard support
- PCI Express x16 graphics interface
- Integrated Intel Graphics Media Accelerator (GMA) 900
- Integrated TV output
- Serial ATA support (two ports)
- Direct Media Interface (DMI) chipset interconnect based on PCI Express x4 (1GBps)
- Integrated USB 2.0 (eight ports)
- Intel High Definition Audio support

There are four different chipsets in the family; the 915PM is the one that will be used in the highest-performance systems since it does not include built-in graphics but is instead designed to connect to a discrete PCI Express x16 graphics controller. The 915GM is the same chipset as the 915PM except that it does include the highest-performance version of Intel's GMA (Graphics Media Accelerator) integrated graphics technology. The 915GMS and 910GML are designed for smaller and lower-cost systems, and lack some of the features of the other chipsets in the family. Table 5.6 highlights the specific differences between all of the 915 family chipsets.

Table 5.6   Differences Between the 915 Family Chipsets

Feature	915PM	915GM	915GMS	910GML
Processor Supported	Pentium M, Pentium M LV, Pentium M ULV, Celeron M, Celeron M ULV	Pentium M, Pentium M LV, Pentium M ULV, Celeron M, Celeron M ULV	Pentium M LV, Pentium M ULV, Celeron M ULV	Celeron M, Celeron M ULV
CPU Bus Speed	400MHz/533MHz	400MHz/533MHz	400MHz	400MHz
Memory Type	DDR2 400/533, DDR 333	DDR2 400/533, DDR 333	DDR2 400	DDR2 400, DDR 333
Memory Channels	Dual-channel (DDR2 only) Single-channel	Dual-channel (DDR2 only) Single-channel	Single-channel	Dual-channel (DDR2 only) Single-channel

(continues)

Table 5.6   Continued

Feature	915PM	915GM	915GMS	910GML
Integrated Graphics	None	GMA 900 (200/222/ 333 MHz 1.5V), (190/200/213/ 222 MHz 1.05V)	GMA 900 (152/ 200 MHz 1.05V)	GMA 900 (200 MHz 1.05V)
Discrete Graphics	PCI Express x16	PCI Express x16	No	No
Integrated TV Out	Dependent on discrete graphics	Yes	Yes	Yes
Max Display Resolution	Dependent on discrete graphics	Digital: UXGA (1600x1200), Analog: QXGA (2048x1536)	Digital: SXGA (1400x1050), Analog: QXGA (2048x1536)	Digital: SXGA (1400x1050), Analog: QXGA (2048x1536)
Power Management	Enhanced SpeedStep, Deeper Sleep, ACPI	Enhanced SpeedStep, Deeper Sleep, ACPI	Enhanced SpeedStep, Deeper Sleep, ACPI	ACPI
Display Power Savings Technology	Dependent on discrete graphics	Yes	Yes	No

LV = Low Voltage

ULV = Ultra Low Voltage

USB = Universal serial bus

DDR2 = Next-generation DDR

DDR = Double data rate SDRAM

GMA = Graphics Media Accelerator

ACPI = Advanced Configuration and Power Interface

The 915 chipset includes either the 915PM/GM/GMS or 910GML memory controller hub (MCH) combined with the 82801FBM ICH6-M I/O controller hub (ICH).

AMD Processor Chipsets

Like most Intel chipsets, chipsets designed for use with AMD processors usually appeared in desktops first. Eventually (and often simultaneously), they were also implemented in laptop systems.

AMD-760

The AMD-760 chipset is a highly integrated system logic solution that delivers enhanced performance for the AMD Athlon processor and other AMD Athlon system bus-compatible processors. The AMD-760 chipset consists of the AMD-761 system controller in a 569-pin plastic ball-grid array (PBGA) package and the AMD-766 peripheral bus controller in a 272-pin PBGA package.

The AMD-761 system controller features the AMD Athlon system bus, DDR SDRAM system memory controller, accelerated graphics port (AGP 4X) controller, and Peripheral Component Interconnect (PCI) bus controller.

The AMD-766 peripheral bus controller features four primary blocks (PCI-to-ISA/LPC bridge, OHCI USB host controller, EIDE UDMA-33/66/100 controller, and system management logic), each with independent access to the PCI bus, a complete set of PCI interface signals and state machines, and the capability of working independently with separate devices.

VIA Apollo KN133

The VIA KN133 is designed to support the AMD Mobile Athlon and Mobile Duron processors, and includes integrated 2D/3D graphics, 200/266MHz processor bus settings, support for PC100/133 SDRAM and multiple power-saving modes. The main features of the KN133 include the following:

- 200/266MHz Athlon processor bus
- Integrated S3 Savage4 AGP 4x graphics core
- Shared memory architecture, with video that uses system RAM
- Integrated 250MHz RAMDAC
- Support for LVDS, CRT, DVI, and TV display
- Integrated AC'97 audio/modem
- PC100/133 SDRAM support
- 1.5GB maximum RAM
- ATA-100 support
- Four USB 1.1 ports
- ACPI/OnNow power management
- VT8363A North Bridge
- VT82C686B Super South Bridge

VIA KN266

The VIA KN266 chipset for AMD Athlon and Duron mobile processors includes an integrated S3 ProSavage8 2D/3D Graphics engine, plus support for up to 4GB of DDR266 (PC2100) memory. The integrated S3 ProSavage8 graphics incorporate AGP 8x bandwidth and DVD motion compensation, and are optimized for use with Windows XP. The integrated video uses shared memory architecture (SMA, also called unified memory architecture or UMA), which means that it shares the main system RAM instead of using discrete video RAM. The integrated graphics offer lower system power consumption and save motherboard real estate, thus enabling thinner and lighter form factors.

The KN266 uses VIA's V-Link hub architecture, which provides a dedicated 266MBps bus between the North and South Bridge (see Figure 5.4). This is similar to the hub architecture pioneered in the Intel 8*xx* chipsets. The KN266 also includes an integrated AC'97 audio/modem support for ATA-100 and up to six USB 1.1 ports. Other options include an integrated 3Com networking interface.

Features of the KN266 include these:

- 200MHz Athlon processor bus
- Integrated S3 ProSavage8 AGP 8x graphics core
- Shared memory architecture, with video that uses system RAM
- Integrated 250MHz RAMDAC
- Support for LVDS, CRT, DVI, and TV display
- DDR200/266 memory support
- 1.5GB maximum RAM
- 266MBps V-Link hub architecture
- Integrated AC'97 audio/modem

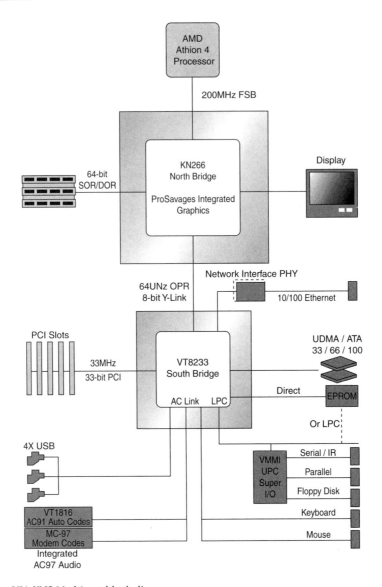

Figure 5.4   VIA KN266 chipset block diagram.

- Integrated 3Com 10/100Mb Ethernet Media Access Controller (VT8233C) or 10/100Mb Ethernet MAC
- Integrated KBC, PS/2 mouse interface, RTC
- ATA-100 support
- Four USB 1.1 ports
- ACPI/OnNow power management
- VT8372 North Bridge
- VT8233 family South Bridge

System Resources

System resources are the communication channels, addresses, and other signals that hardware devices use to communicate on the bus. At their lowest level, these resources typically include the following:

- IRQ (interrupt request) channels
- DMA (direct memory access) channels
- I/O port addresses

I have listed these roughly in the order you would experience problems with them.

IRQs cause more problems than DMAs because they are in much higher demand; virtually all cards use IRQ channels. Fewer problems exist with DMA channels because fewer cards use them, DMA channels are used only by the obsolete ISA standard, and there are usually more than enough channels to go around. I/O ports are used by all hardware devices on the bus, but there are technically 64KB of them, which means that there are plenty to go around. With all these resources, you must ensure that a unique card or hardware function uses each resource; in most cases, they cannot or should not be shared.

These resources are required and used by many components of your system. Adapter cards need these resources to communicate with your system and accomplish their purposes. Not all adapter cards have the same resource requirements. A serial communications port, for example, needs an IRQ channel and I/O port address, whereas a sound card needs these resources and at least one DMA channel. Most network cards use an IRQ channel and an I/O port address, and some also use a 16KB block of memory addresses.

As your system increases in complexity—and the more legacy devices you have, such as standard serial or parallel ports, infrared ports, conventional PC Cards (instead of CardBus cards), a non-USB floppy drive, and so on—the greater chance there is for resource conflicts. Some systems with several additional devices plugged in can really push the envelope and become a configuration nightmare for the uninitiated. Sometimes in these situations, the automatic configuration capability of Plug and Play (PnP) can get confused or fail to optimally configure resources so that everything will work. Most adapter cards enable you to modify resource assignments by using the Plug and Play software that comes with the card or the Device Manager in Windows 9x and later, so you can sometimes improve on a default configuration by making some changes. Even if the automatic configuration gets confused (which happens more often than it should), fortunately, in almost all cases, a logical way to configure the system exists—once you know the rules, that is.

Interrupts

Interrupt request channels, or hardware interrupts, are used by various hardware devices to signal the motherboard that a request must be fulfilled. This procedure is the same as a student raising his hand to indicate that he needs attention.

These interrupt channels are represented by wires on the motherboard and in the slot connectors. When a particular interrupt is invoked, a special routine takes over the system, which first saves all the CPU register contents in a stack and then directs the system to the interrupt vector table. This vector table contains a list of memory addresses that correspond to the interrupt channels. Depending on which interrupt was invoked, the program corresponding to that channel is run.

The pointers in the vector table point to the address of whatever software driver is used to service the card that generated the interrupt. For a network card, for example, the vector might point to the address of the network drivers that have been loaded to operate the card; for a hard disk controller, the vector might point to the BIOS code that operates the controller.

After the particular software routine finishes performing whatever function the card needed, the interrupt-control software returns the stack contents to the CPU registers, and the system resumes whatever it was doing before the interrupt occurred.

Through the use of interrupts, your system can respond to external events in a timely fashion. Each time a serial port presents a byte to your system, an interrupt is generated to ensure that the system reads that byte before another comes in. Keep in mind that, in some cases, a port device—in particular, a modem with a 16550 or higher UART chip—might incorporate a byte buffer that allows multiple characters to be stored before an interrupt is generated.

Hardware interrupts are generally prioritized by their numbers; with some exceptions, the highest-priority interrupts have the lowest numbers. Higher-priority interrupts take precedence over lower-priority interrupts by interrupting them. As a result, several interrupts can occur in your system concurrently, with each interrupt nesting within another.

If you overload the system—in this case, by running out of stack resources (too many interrupts were generated too quickly)—an internal stack overflow error occurs and your system halts. The message usually appears as `Internal stack overflow - system halted` at a DOS prompt. If you experience this type of system error and run DOS, you can compensate for it by using the `STACKS` parameter in your `CONFIG.SYS` file to increase the available stack resources. Most people will not see this error in Windows 9x/Me or Windows NT/2000/XP.

The ISA bus uses *edge-triggered* interrupt sensing, in which an interrupt is sensed by a changing signal sent on a particular wire located in the slot connector. A different wire corresponds to each possible hardware interrupt. Because the motherboard can't recognize which slot contains the card that used an interrupt line and, therefore, generated the interrupt, confusion results if more than one card is set to use a particular interrupt. Each interrupt, therefore, is usually designated for a single hardware device. Most of the time, interrupts can't be shared.

Originally, IBM developed ways to share interrupts on the ISA bus, but few devices followed the necessary rules to make this a reality. The PCI bus inherently allows interrupt sharing; in fact, virtually all PCI cards are set to PCI interrupt A and share that interrupt on the PCI bus. The real problem is that there are technically two sets of hardware interrupts in the system: PCI interrupts and ISA interrupts. Note that although laptops don't have ISA or PCI slots as you would see in a desktop system, the interfaces are there and are used by devices internally. For example, if your laptop has a serial port, parallel port, infrared port, floppy controller, keyboard and mouse controller, and PC Card slots, they are connected via an internal ISA (or ISA-like) bus. The same goes for CardBus, Mini PCI, USB, FireWire, Ethernet, Video, and other devices that are essentially connected to the system via PCI.

Additionally, for PCI cards to work in a PC using DOS or Windows 95a, the PCI interrupts are first mapped to ISA interrupts, which are then configured as nonshareable. Therefore, in many cases, you must assign a nonconflicting interrupt for each card, even PCI cards. The conflict between assigning ISA IRQs for PCI interrupts caused many configuration problems for early users of PCI motherboards and continued to cause problems even after the development of Windows 95 and its Plug and Play technology.

The solution to the interrupt-sharing problem for PCI cards was something called *PCI IRQ steering*, which is supported in the more recent operating systems (starting with Windows 95 OSR 2.x) and BIOSes. PCI IRQ steering allows a Plug and Play operating system such as Windows to dynamically map or "steer" PCI cards (which almost all use PCI INTA#) to standard PC interrupts and allows several PCI cards to be mapped to the same interrupt. You can find more information on PCI IRQ steering in the section "PCI Interrupts," later in this chapter.

Hardware interrupts are sometimes referred to as *maskable interrupts*, which means that the interrupts can be masked or turned off for a short time while the CPU is used for other critical operations. It is up to the system BIOS and programs to manage interrupts properly and efficiently for the best system performance.

Because interrupts usually can't be shared in an ISA bus system, you often run into conflicts and can even run out of interrupts when you are adding boards to a system. If two boards use the same IRQ to signal the system, the resulting conflict prevents either board from operating properly. The following sections discuss the IRQs that any standard devices use, as well as what might be free in your system.

16-Bit ISA, EISA, and MCA Bus Interrupts

The original 8-bit ISA architecture used in the first IBM PC allowed for only eight interrupts. The introduction of the AT, based on the 286 processor, was accompanied by an increase in the number of external hardware interrupts that the bus would support. The number of interrupts was doubled to 16 by using two Intel 8259 interrupt controllers, piping the interrupts generated by the second one through the unused IRQ2 in the first controller. This arrangement effectively makes only 15 IRQ assignments available, and IRQ2 effectively became inaccessible.

Because all the interrupts are routed from the second IRQ controller through IRQ2 on the first, all these new interrupts are assigned a nested priority level between IRQ1 and IRQ3. Thus, IRQ15 ends up having a higher priority than IRQ3. Figure 5.5 shows how the two 8259 chips were wired to create the cascade through IRQ2 on the first chip.

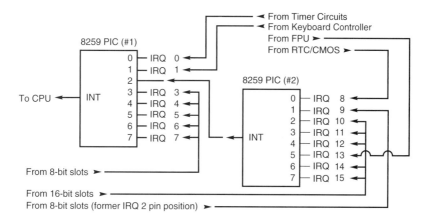

Figure 5.5 Interrupt controller cascade wiring.

To prevent problems with boards set to use IRQ2, the AT system designers routed one of the new interrupts (IRQ9) to fill the slot position left open after removing IRQ2. This means that any card you install in a modern system that claims to use IRQ2 is really using IRQ9 instead.

Table 5.7 shows the typical uses for interrupts in the 16-bit ISA and 32-bit PCI/AGP buses, and lists them in priority order from highest to lowest. The obsolete EISA and MCA buses used a similar IRQ map.

Table 5.7   16/32-Bit ISA/PCI/AGP Default Interrupt Assignments

IRQ	Standard Function	Bus Slot	Card Type	Recommended Use
0	System timer	No	—	—
1	Keyboard controller	No	—	—
2	Send IRQ controller cascade	No	—	—
8	Real-time clock	No	—	—
9	Available (as IRQ2 or network card IRQ9)	Yes	8/16-bit	
10	Available	Yes	16-bit	USB
11	Available	Yes	16-bit	SCSI Host adapter
12	Mouse port/available	Yes	16-bit	Mouse port
13	Math coprocessor	No	—	—
14	Primary ATA	Yes	16-bit	Primary ATA
15	Secondary ATA	Yes	16-bit	Secondary ATA
3	Serial 2 (COM2:)	Yes	8/16-bit	COM2:/internal modem
4	Serial 1 (COM1:)	Yes	8/16-bit	COM1:
5	Sound/parallel 2 (LPT2:)	Yes	8/16-bit	Sound card
6	Floppy controller	Yes	8/16-bit	Floppy controller
7	Parallel 1 (LPT1:)	Yes	8/16-bit	LPT1:

Notice that interrupts 0, 1, 2, 8, and 13 are not on the bus connectors and are not accessible to adapter cards. Interrupts 8, 10, 11, 12, 13, 14, and 15 are from the second interrupt controller and are accessible only by boards that use the 16-bit extension connector because this is where these wires are located. IRQ9 is rewired to the 8-bit slot connector in place of IRQ2, so IRQ9 replaces IRQ2 and, therefore, is available to 8-bit cards, which treat it as though it were IRQ2.

Note

Although the 16-bit ISA bus has twice as many interrupts as systems that have the 8-bit ISA bus, you still might run out of available interrupts because only 16-bit adapters can use most of the newly available interrupts. Any 32-bit PCI adapter can be mapped to any ISA IRQs.

The extra IRQ lines in a 16-bit ISA system are of little help unless the adapter boards that you plan to use enable you to configure them for one of the unused IRQs. Some devices are hard-wired so that they can use only a particular IRQ. If you have a device that already uses that IRQ, you must resolve the conflict before installing the second adapter. If neither adapter enables you to reconfigure its IRQ use, chances are good that you can't use the two devices in the same system.

PCI Interrupts

The PCI bus supports hardware interrupts (IRQs) that can be used by PCI devices to signal to the bus that they need attention. The four PCI interrupts are called INTA#, INTB#, INTC#, and INTD#. These INTx# interrupts are *level-sensitive*, which means that the electrical signaling enables them to be shared among PCI cards. In fact, all single-device or single-function PCI chips or cards that use only one interrupt must use INTA#. This is one of the rules in the PCI specification. If additional devices are within a chip or onboard a card, the additional devices can use INTB# through INTD#. Because there are very few multifunction PCI chips or boards, practically all the devices on a given PCI bus share INTA#.

For the PCI bus to function in a PC, the PCI interrupts must be mapped to ISA interrupts. Because ISA interrupts can't be shared, in most cases each PCI card using INTA# on the PCI bus must be mapped to a different nonshareable ISA interrupt. For example, you could have a system with four PCI slots and four PCI cards installed, each using PCI interrupt INTA#. These cards would each be mapped to a different available ISA interrupt request, such as IRQ9, IRQ10, IRQ11, or IRQ5, in most cases.

Finding unique IRQs for each device on both the ISA and PCI buses has always been a problem; there simply aren't enough free ones to go around. Setting two ISA devices to the same IRQ has never been possible, but on most newer systems, sharing IRQs among multiple PCI devices might be possible. Newer system BIOSes as well as Plug and Play operating systems, such as Windows 95B (OSR 2) or later, Windows 98, and Windows 2000/XP, all support a function known as PCI IRQ Steering. For this to work, both your system BIOS and operating system must support IRQ steering. Older system BIOSes and Windows 95 or 95A do not have support for PCI IRQ steering.

Generally, the BIOS assigns unique IRQs to PCI devices. If your system supports PCI IRQ steering and it is enabled, Windows assigns IRQs to PCI devices. Even when IRQ steering is enabled, the BIOS initially assigns IRQs to PCI devices. Although Windows has the capability to change these settings, it typically does not do so automatically, except where necessary to eliminate conflicts. If there are insufficient free IRQs to go around, IRQ steering allows Windows to assign multiple PCI devices to a single IRQ, thus enabling all the devices in the system to function properly. Without IRQ steering, Windows begins to disable devices after it runs out of free IRQs to assign.

To determine whether your Windows 9x/Me system is using IRQ steering, you can follow these steps:

1. Select Start, Settings, Control Panel. Then select the System tool and click the Device Manager tab.

2. Double-click the System Devices branch.

3. Double-click PCI Bus and then click the IRQ Steering tab (see Figure 5.6). There will be a check that displays IRQ steering as either enabled or disabled. If it is enabled, it also specifies where the IRQ table has been read from.

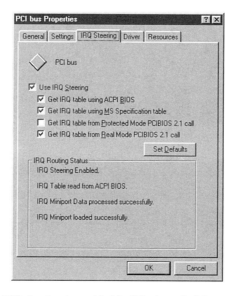

Figure 5.6 Ensuring that IRQ steering is enabled in Windows 9x/Me.

Note that with Windows 2000 and XP, you can't disable IRQ steering, and no IRQ Steering tab appears in the Device Manager.

IRQ steering is controlled by one of four routing tables that Windows attempts to read. Windows searches for the tables in order and uses the first one it finds. You can't control the order in which Windows searches for these tables, but by selecting or deselecting the Get IRQ Table Using check boxes, you can control which table Windows finds first by disabling the search for specific tables. Windows searches for the following tables:

- ACPI BIOS table
- MS specification table
- Protected mode PCIBIOS 2.1 table
- Real mode PCIBIOS 2.1 table

Windows first tries to use the ACPI BIOS table to program IRQ steering, followed by the MS specification table, the protected-mode PCIBIOS 2.1 table, and the real-mode PCIBIOS 2.1 table. Windows 95 OSR2 and later versions offer only a choice for selecting the PCIBIOS 2.1 tables via a single check box, which is disabled by default. Under Windows 98, all IRQ table choices are selected by default except the third one, which is the protected-mode PCIBIOS 2.1 table.

If you are having a problem with a PCI device related to IRQ settings under Windows 95, try selecting the PCIBIOS 2.1 table and restarting. Under Windows 98, try clearing the ACPI BIOS table selection and restarting. If the problem persists, try selecting the protected-mode PCIBIOS 2.1 table and restarting. You should select Get IRQ Table from Protected Mode PCIBIOS 2.1 Call only if a PCI device is not working properly.

If IRQ steering is shown as disabled in Device Manager, be sure that the Use IRQ Steering check box is selected. After you select this and restart, if IRQ steering is still showing as disabled, the IRQ routing table that the BIOS must provide to the operating system might be missing or might contain errors. Check your BIOS setup to ensure that PCI IRQ steering is enabled. If there is still no success, you might have to select the Get IRQ Table from Protected Mode PCIBIOS 2.1 Call check box, or your BIOS might not support PCI bus IRQ steering. Contact the manufacturer of your motherboard or BIOS to see whether your board or BIOS supports IRQ steering.

On systems that have support for IRQ steering, an IRQ holder for PCI steering might be displayed when you view the System Devices branch of Device Manager. This indicates that an IRQ has been mapped to PCI and is unavailable for ISA devices, even if no PCI devices are currently using the IRQ. To view IRQs programmed for PCI mode, follow these steps:

1. Select Start, Settings, Control Panel and then double-click System.
2. Click the Device Manager tab.
3. Double-click the System Devices branch.
4. Double-click the IRQ holder for PCI steering that you want to view and then click the Resources tab.

I have found this interrupt steering or mapping to be the source of a great deal of confusion. Even though PCI interrupts (INTx#) can be (and are, by default) shared, each card or device that might be sharing a PCI interrupt must be mapped or steered to a unique ISA IRQ, which, in turn, can't normally be shared. You can have several PCI devices mapped to the same ISA IRQ only under these circumstances:

- No ISA devices are using the IRQ.
- The BIOS and operating system support PCI IRQ steering.
- PCI IRQ steering is enabled.

Without PCI IRQ steering support, the sharing capabilities of the PCI interrupts are of little benefit because all PCI-to-ISA IRQ assignments must then be unique. Without PCI IRQ steering, you can easily run out of available ISA interrupts. If IRQ steering is supported and enabled, multiple PCI devices will be capable of sharing a single IRQ, allowing for more system expansion without running out of available IRQs. Better support for IRQ steering is one of the best reasons for upgrading to Windows 98 or newer versions, especially if you are using the original OSR1 release of 95.

Another source of confusion is that the interrupt listing shown in the Windows 9x Device Manager might show the PCI-to-ISA-interrupt mapping as multiple entries for a given ISA interrupt. One entry would be for the device actually mapped to the interrupt—for example, a built-in USB controller—whereas the other entry for the same IRQ would say IRQ Holder for PCI Steering. Despite claiming to use the same IRQ, this latter entry does not indicate a resource conflict; instead, it represents the chipset circuitry putting a reservation on that interrupt for mapping purposes. This is part of the Plug and Play capabilities of PCI and the modern motherboard chipsets. Windows 2000 and XP can also map multiple devices to the same IRQ, but they don't use the term *IRQ holder*, to avoid confusion.

Note that you can have internal devices on the PCI bus even though all the PCI slots are free. For example, most systems today have two IDE controllers and a USB controller as devices on the PCI bus. Normally, the PCI IDE controllers are mapped to ISA interrupts 14 (primary IDE) and 15 (secondary IDE), whereas the USB controller can be mapped to the available ISA interrupts 9, 10, 11, and 5.

PCI Bus Masters

The PCI bus enables two types of devices to exist, called *bus masters* (initiators) and *slaves* (targets). A bus master is a device that can take control of the bus and initiate a transfer. The target device is the intended destination of the transfer. Most PCI devices can act as both masters and targets; to be compliant with the PC 97 and newer system design guides, all PCI slots must support bus master cards.

The PCI bus is an arbitrated bus: A central arbiter (part of the PCI bus controller in the motherboard chipset) governs all bus transfers, giving fair and controlled access to all the devices on the bus. Before a master can use the bus, it must request control from the central arbiter; then it is granted control for only a specified maximum number of cycles. This arbitration allows equal and fair access to all the bus master devices, prevents a single device from hogging the bus, and also prevents deadlocks because of simultaneous multiple device access. In this manner, the PCI bus acts much like a local area network (LAN), albeit one that is contained entirely within the system and runs at a much higher speed than conventional external networks between PCs.

DMA Channels

Direct memory access (DMA) channels are used by communications devices that must send and receive information at high speeds. A serial or parallel port does not use a DMA channel, but a sound card or SCSI adapter often does. DMA channels sometimes can be shared if the devices are not the type that would need them simultaneously. Plug and Play systems automatically manage resources such as DMA, so it is rare to see any conflicts or problems.

Note

Several types of DMA exist in a modern PC. The DMA channels referred to in this section involve the ISA bus. Other buses, such as the ATA/IDE bus used by hard drives, have different DMA uses. The DMA channels explained here don't involve your ATA/IDE drives, even if they are set to use DMA or Ultra DMA transfers.

I/O Port Addresses

Your computer's I/O ports enable communication between devices and software in your system. They are equivalent to two-way radio channels. If you want to talk to your serial port, you need to know on which I/O port (radio channel) it is listening. Similarly, if you want to receive data from the serial port, you need to listen on the same channel on which it is transmitting.

Unlike IRQs and DMA channels, systems have an abundance of I/O ports. There are 65,535 ports, to be exact—numbered from 0000h to FFFFh—which is an artifact of the Intel processor design more than anything else. Even though most devices use up to eight ports for themselves, with that many to spare, you won't run out anytime soon. The biggest problem you have to worry about is setting two devices to use the same port. Most modern Plug and Play systems resolve any port conflicts and select alternative ports for one of the conflicting devices.

One confusing issue is that I/O ports are designated by hexadecimal addresses similar to memory addresses. They are not memory; they are ports. The difference is that when you send data to memory address 1000h, it gets stored in your SIMM or DIMM memory. If you send data to I/O port address 1000h, it gets sent out on the bus on that "channel," and anybody listening in can then "hear" it. If nobody is listening to that port address, the data reaches the end of the bus and is absorbed by the bus terminating resistors.

Driver programs are primarily what interact with devices at the various port addresses. The driver must know which ports the device is using to work with it, and vice versa. That is not usually a problem because the driver and the device come from the same company.

Motherboard and chipset devices usually are set to use I/O port addresses 0h–FFh, and all other devices use 100h–FFFFh. Table 5.8 shows the commonly used motherboard and chipset-based I/O port usage.

Table 5.8   Motherboard and Chipset-Based Device Port Addresses

Address (Hex)	Size	Description
0000–000F	16 bytes	Chipset—8237 DMA 1
0020–0021	2 bytes	Chipset—8259 interrupt controller 1
002E–002F	2 bytes	Super I/O controller configuration registers
0040–0043	4 bytes	Chipset—counter/timer 1
0048–004B	4 bytes	Chipset—counter/timer 2
0060	1 byte	Keyboard/mouse controller byte—reset IRQ
0061	1 byte	Chipset—NMI, speaker control
0064	1 byte	Keyboard/mouse controller, CMD/STAT byte
0070, bit 7	1 bit	Chipset—enable NMI
0070, bits 6:0	7 bits	MC146818—real-time clock, address

Table 5.8   Continued

Address (Hex)	Size	Description
0071	1 byte	MC146818—real-time clock, data
0078	1 byte	Reserved—board configuration
0079	1 byte	Reserved—board configuration
0080–008F	16 bytes	Chipset—DMA page registers
00A0–00A1	2 bytes	Chipset—8259 interrupt controller 2
00B2	1 byte	APM control port
00B3	1 byte	APM status port
00C0–00DE	31 bytes	Chipset—8237 DMA 2
00F0	1 byte	Math coprocessor reset numeric error

To find out exactly which port addresses are being used on your motherboard, consult the board documentation or look up these settings in the Windows Device Manager.

Bus-based devices typically use the addresses from 100h on up. Table 5.9 lists the commonly used bus-based device addresses and some common adapter cards and their settings.

Table 5.9   Bus-Based Device Port Addresses

Address (Hex)	Size	Description
0130–0133	4 bytes	Adaptec SCSI adapter (alternate)
0134–0137	4 bytes	Adaptec SCSI adapter (alternate)
0168–016F	8 bytes	Fourth IDE interface
0170–0177	8 bytes	Secondary IDE interface
01E8–01EF	8 bytes	Third IDE interface
01F0–01F7	8 bytes	Primary IDE/AT (16-bit) hard disk controller
0200–0207	8 bytes	Game port or joystick adapter
0210–0217	8 bytes	IBM XT expansion chassis
0220–0233	20 bytes	Creative Labs Sound Blaster 16 audio (default)
0230–0233	4 bytes	Adaptec SCSI adapter (alternate)
0234–0237	4 bytes	Adaptec SCSI adapter (alternate)
0238–023B	4 bytes	MS bus mouse (alternate)
023C–023F	4 bytes	MS bus mouse (default)
0240–024F	16 bytes	SMC Ethernet adapter (default)
0240–0253	20 bytes	Creative Labs Sound Blaster 16 audio (alternate)
0258–025F	8 bytes	Intel above board
0260–026F	16 bytes	SMC Ethernet adapter (alternate)
0260–0273	20 bytes	Creative Labs Sound Blaster 16 audio (alternate)
0270–0273	4 bytes	Plug and Play I/O read ports
0278–027F	8 bytes	Parallel port 2 (LPT2)
0280–028F	16 bytes	SMC Ethernet adapter (alternate)
0280–0293	20 bytes	Creative Labs Sound Blaster 16 audio (alternate)

Table 5.9   Continued

Address (Hex)	Size	Description
02A0–02AF	16 bytes	SMC Ethernet adapter (alternate)
02C0–02CF	16 bytes	SMC Ethernet adapter (alternate)
02E0–02EF	16 bytes	SMC Ethernet adapter (alternate)
02E8–02EF	8 bytes	Serial port 4 (COM4)
02EC–02EF	4 bytes	Video, 8514, or ATI standard ports
02F8–02FF	8 bytes	Serial port 2 (COM2)
0300–0301	2 bytes	MPU-401 MIDI port (secondary)
0300–030F	16 bytes	SMC Ethernet adapter (alternate)
0320–0323	4 bytes	XT (8-bit) hard disk controller
0320–032F	16 bytes	SMC Ethernet adapter (alternate)
0330–0331	2 bytes	MPU-401 MIDI port (default)
0330–0333	4 bytes	Adaptec SCSI adapter (default)
0334–0337	4 bytes	Adaptec SCSI adapter (alternate)
0340–034F	16 bytes	SMC Ethernet adapter (alternate)
0360–036F	16 bytes	SMC Ethernet adapter (alternate)
0366	1 byte	Fourth IDE command port
0367, bits 6:0	7 bits	Fourth IDE status port
0370–0375	6 bytes	Secondary floppy controller
0376	1 byte	Secondary IDE command port
0377, bit 7	1 bit	Secondary floppy controller disk change
0377, bits 6:0	7 bits	Secondary IDE status port
0378–037F	8 bytes	Parallel port 1 (LPT1)
0380–038F	16 bytes	SMC Ethernet adapter (alternate)
0388–038B	4 bytes	Audio—FM synthesizer
03B0–03BB	12 bytes	Video, mono/EGA/VGA standard ports
03BC–03BF	4 bytes	Parallel port 1 (LPT1) in some systems
03BC–03BF	4 bytes	Parallel port 3 (LPT3)
03C0–03CF	16 bytes	Video, EGA/VGA standard ports
03D0–03DF	16 bytes	Video, CGA/EGA/VGA standard ports
03E6	1 byte	Third IDE command port
03E7, bits 6:0	7 bits	Third IDE status port
03E8–03EF	8 bytes	Serial port 3 (COM3)
03F0–03F5	6 bytes	Primary floppy controller
03F6	1 byte	Primary IDE command port
03F7, bit 7	1 bit	Primary floppy controller disk change
03F7, bits 6:0	7 bits	Primary IDE status port
03F8–03FF	8 bytes	Serial port 1 (COM1)
04D0–04D1	2 bytes	Edge/level triggered PCI interrupt controller

Table 5.9   Continued

Address (Hex)	Size	Description
0530–0537	8 bytes	Windows sound system (default)
0604–060B	8 bytes	Windows sound system (alternate)
0678–067F	8 bytes	LPT2 in ECP mode
0778–077F	8 bytes	LPT1 in ECP mode
0A20–0A23	4 bytes	IBM Token Ring adapter (default)
0A24–0A27	4 bytes	IBM Token Ring adapter (alternate)
0CF8–0CFB	4 bytes	PCI configuration address registers
0CF9	1 byte	Turbo and reset control register
0CFC–0CFF	4 bytes	PCI configuration data registers
FF00–FF07	8 bytes	IDE bus master registers
FF80–FF9F	32 bytes	Universal serial bus
FFA0–FFA7	8 bytes	Primary bus master IDE registers
FFA8–FFAF	8 bytes	Secondary bus master IDE registers

To find out exactly what your devices are using, again I recommend consulting the documentation for the device or looking up the device in the Windows Device Manager. Note that the documentation for some devices might list only the starting address instead of the full range of I/O port addresses used.

Virtually all devices on the system buses use I/O port addresses. Most of these are fairly standardized, so conflicts or problems won't often occur with these settings.

Plug and Play

Plug and Play (PnP) represents a major revolution in interface technology. PnP first came on the market in 1995, and most systems since 1996 have taken advantage of it. Before that, PC users were forced to muddle through a nightmare of DIP switches and jumpers or proprietary configuration programs every time they wanted to add new devices to their systems. All too often, the results were system resource conflicts and nonfunctioning cards.

PnP was not an entirely new concept. It was a key design feature of MCA and EISA interfaces that preceded it by almost 10 years, but the limited appeal of MCA and EISA meant that they never became true de facto industry standards. Therefore, mainstream PC users still had to worry about I/O addresses, DMA channels, and IRQ settings. Early PCI-based systems also used a form of PnP configuration, but because there was no provision for managing conflicts between PCI and ISA cards, many users still had configuration problems. But now that PnP has become prevalent, worry-free hardware setup is the norm. PnP is especially important for hot-pluggable interfaces such as those found in most laptop systems, including PC Card/CardBus, USB, and FireWire.

For PnP to work, the following components are desired:

- PnP hardware
- PnP BIOS
- PnP operating system

Each of these components needs to be PnP-compatible, meaning that it complies with the PnP specifications.

The Hardware Component

The *hardware component* refers to both computer systems and adapter cards. However, the term does not mean that you can't use your older ISA adapter cards (referred to as *legacy cards*) in a PnP system. You can use these cards; in fact, your PnP BIOS automatically reassigns PnP-compatible cards around existing legacy components. Also, many late-model ISA cards can be switched into PnP-compatible mode.

PnP adapter cards communicate with the system BIOS and the operating system to convey information about which system resources are necessary. The BIOS and operating system, in turn, resolve conflicts (wherever possible) and inform the adapter card which specific resources it should use. The adapter card then can modify its configuration to use the specified resources.

The BIOS Component

The BIOS component means that most users of pre-1996 PCs need to update their BIOSes or purchase new machines that have PnP BIOSes. For a BIOS to be compatible, it must support 13 additional system function calls, which can be used by the OS component of a PnP system. The PnP BIOS specification was developed jointly by Compaq, Intel, and Phoenix Technologies.

The PnP features of the BIOS are implemented through an expanded POST. The BIOS is responsible for identification, isolation, and possible configuration of PnP adapter cards. The BIOS accomplishes these tasks by performing the following steps:

1. Disables any configurable devices on the motherboard or on adapter cards
2. Identifies any PnP PCI or ISA devices
3. Compiles an initial resource-allocation map for ports, IRQs, DMAs, and memory
4. Enables I/O devices
5. Scans the ROMs of ISA devices
6. Configures initial program-load (IPL) devices, which are used later to boot the system
7. Enables configurable devices by informing them which resources have been assigned to them
8. Starts the bootstrap loader
9. Transfers control to the operating system

The Operating System Component

The operating system component is found in most modern operating systems, such as Windows 9x/Me/2000/XP. In some cases, system manufacturers have provided extensions to the operating system for their specific hardware. This is especially true for laptop systems, for example. Be sure that you load these extensions if they are required by your system.

It is the responsibility of the operating system to inform users of conflicts that can't be resolved by the BIOS. Depending on the sophistication of the operating system, the user can configure the offending cards manually (onscreen) or turn off the system and set switches on the physical cards. When the system is restarted, the system is checked for remaining (or new) conflicts, any of which are brought to the user's attention. Through this repetitive process, all system conflicts are resolved.

Note

Because of revisions in some of the Plug and Play specifications, especially the ACPI specification, it can help to ensure that you are running the latest BIOS and drivers for your system. With the flash ROM used in most PnP systems, you can download the new BIOS image from the system vendor or manufacturer and run the supplied BIOS update program.

CHAPTER 6

Memory

Laptop systems generally use the same basic types of memory *chips* as desktop systems, but not the same types of *modules*. Instead of the standard single inline memory modules (SIMMs) or dual inline memory modules (DIMMs) that desktop systems use, laptops and other portable systems normally use different modules with smaller form factors, intended to better fit the more compact design of portable systems. This chapter examines the different types of memory chips and modules found in modern laptop and other portable systems, and it discusses how to upgrade memory in these systems as well.

Memory Standards

Older portables often used proprietary memory modules, meaning that they were custom designed by the system manufacturer and normally could be purchased only from that manufacturer. That meant not only that replacing or upgrading memory was expensive, but that memory was also harder to find, because in many cases the memory could be purchased only from the original manufacturer. Some of the first laptop systems in late '80s and early '90s used proprietary memory cartridges that looked like modern PC Cards but plugged into a dedicated Personal Computer Memory Card International Association (PCMCIA) memory socket inside the system. Gradually, most of the manufacturers shifted their designs to using industry-standard memory modules, which are interchangeable, much easier to find, and much less expensive overall. Most modern systems now use industry-standard memory modules that are specifically designed for smaller or portable systems. Most of these industry-standard memory chip and module designs are created by the Joint Electron Devices Engineering Council (JEDEC) Solid State Technology Association.

JEDEC

JEDEC (Joint Electron Devices Engineering Council) is the semiconductor engineering standardization body of the Electronic Industries Alliance (EIA), a trade association that represents all areas of the electronics industry. JEDEC, which was originally created in 1960, governs the standardization of all types of semiconductor devices, integrated circuits, and modules. JEDEC has about 300 member companies, including memory, chipset, and processor manufacturers as well as practically any company involved in manufacturing computer equipment using industry-standard components.

The idea behind JEDEC is simple: If one company were to create a proprietary memory technology, for example, then other companies that wanted to manufacture components compliant with that memory would have to pay license fees, assuming the company that owned it was interested in licensing at all! Parts would be more proprietary in nature, causing problems with interchangeability or sourcing reasonably priced replacements. In addition, those companies licensing the technology would have no control over future changes made by the owner company.

JEDEC helps to prevent that type of scenario for items such as memory, by getting all the memory manufacturers to work together creating shared industry standards covering memory chips and modules. JEDEC-approved standards for memory could then be freely shared by all the member companies, and no one single company would have control over a given standard, or any of the companies producing compliant components. FPM, SDRAM, DDR SDRAM, and DDR2 SDRAM are examples of JEDEC memory standards used in PCs, whereas EDO and RDRAM are proprietary examples. You can find out more about JEDEC standards for memory and other semiconductor technology at **www.jedec.org**.

Although there are various industry-standard types of memory and modules, most modern portables including laptops, notebooks, and Tablet PCs use one of several types of DIMMs called *small outline dual inline memory modules (SODIMMs)*. *SODIMMs* are physically smaller but similar electrically to the larger DIMMs used in desktop systems. SODIMMs typically are available in extended data out (EDO) or synchronous dynamic RAM (SDRAM) form, with various speeds and voltages available. An even smaller class of modules, called *micro dual inline memory modules* or *MicroDIMMs*, are used by subnotebook, palmtop, and handheld systems. They are available in several industry-standard JEDEC-approved designs as well.

In any case, be sure the memory you purchase works with your system or that you can get a refund or replacement if it doesn't. Even though industry standards exist and modules from many sources will often fit a given system, I normally recommend that you look for memory modules that the system manufacturer has approved for the system, in the configurations the manufacturer specified. Often you can find a list of approved modules or suppliers in the system documentation or on the system manufacturer's website.

How Much Memory?

The best philosophy to take when adding RAM to a notebook or laptop computer is "fill 'er up!" Because adding memory speeds up operations and can even extend battery life (up to a point, due to less use of the hard drive for virtual memory swapping), you should normally specify a minimum of 256MB, and preferably 512MB of RAM or more depending on the chipset and processor. If you are a power user or run memory-intensive applications such as photo- and video-editing applications, you might consider 1GB or even up to 2GB of RAM. Most older laptops won't accept nearly that much, so if you are upgrading an older system, the best tip may be to simply install as much memory as you can, with one caveat: I don't recommend installing more than 64MB in older Pentium or AMD 6x86 portable systems, because the chipsets in those systems do not support caching for any memory over 64MB, and installing any memory over that amount will dramatically slow down the system. On the other hand, Celeron, Pentium II/III/4, Athlon/Duron, Sempron/Turion, and Pentium M-based systems can generally cache up to 4GB, so in those systems you can install as much memory as will fit (or that you can afford).

Caution

If your portable computer uses Windows 9x or Windows Me, don't exceed 512MB of RAM because the VCACHE disk cache built in to these versions of Windows can't support the memory addresses needed for this amount of RAM along with the memory addresses required by AGP video. If you want to use more than 512MB of RAM, make sure you are running Windows 2000 or Windows XP.

The amount of memory you use can affect your battery life. Too little memory causes Windows to use the hard disk more often as virtual memory, which means increased disk activity and slower operation. In the end, this adds up to increased power consumption. Adding the right amount of memory to run your applications with a minimum of disk swapping (usually 256MB to 512MB in newer systems) improves performance and increases battery life. Unfortunately, going to extremes by adding up to 2GB of memory may reduce battery life, unless your applications really require that much. More memory often means more memory chips, and those chips need power to operate. If battery life is important, that should be a consideration. Additionally, doubling the amount of memory also doubles the amount of time it takes the system to hibernate as well as to resume from hibernation. The best recommendation is to consult the application program developers for their recommendations on memory. Of course, if battery life is not important to you (for example, you run your system from AC power most of the time and rarely use the hibernation feature), then the more memory the better!

When purchasing a new system, try to get it with all the memory you need right away. Many laptops have only one or two memory module sockets, and in many cases they will already be filled when the system is delivered. This means you will have to remove some of the existing memory in order to add more, which makes future upgrades more expensive.

Memory Speed

The speed and performance issue with memory is confusing to some people because of all the different ways to express the speeds of memory and processors. Memory speed was originally expressed in nanoseconds (ns), whereas the speeds of newer forms of memory are usually expressed in megahertz (MHz) and megabytes per second (MBps) instead. Processor speed was originally expressed in megahertz (MHz), whereas most current processor speeds are expressed in gigahertz (GHz). Although all these different speed units may seem confusing, fortunately, it is possible to translate from one to the other.

A *nanosecond* is defined as one billionth of a second—a very short piece of time indeed. To put some perspective on just how small a nanosecond really is, consider that the speed of light is 186,282 miles (299,792 kilometers) per second in a vacuum. In one billionth of a second (one nanosecond), a beam of light travels a mere 11.80 inches or 29.98 centimeters—slightly less than the length of a typical ruler!

Memory speeds have often been expressed in terms of their cycle times (or how long it takes for one cycle), whereas processor speeds have almost always been expressed in terms of their cycle speeds (number of cycles per second). Cycle time and cycle speed are really just different ways of saying the same thing; that is, you could quote chip speeds in cycles per second, or seconds per cycle, and mean the same thing.

As an analogy, you could express the speed of a bicycle using the same relative terms. For example, in the United States vehicle speeds are normally expressed in miles per hour. If you were riding a bicycle at 5 miles per hour (mph), it would take 0.2 hours per mile (hpm). At 10 mph, it would take 0.1 hpm. In other words, you could give the speed as either 0.2 hpm or 5 mph, and it would mean exactly the same thing.

Because it is confusing to speak in these different terms for chip speeds, I thought it would be interesting to see exactly how they compare. Table 6.1 shows the relationship between nanosecond (ns) cycle times and the megahertz (MHz) speeds they represent.

Table 6.1   The Relationship Between Memory Cycle Times in Nanoseconds (ns) and Clock Speeds in Megahertz (MHz)

Cycle Time (ns)	Clock Speed (MHz)
60.0	16.67
15.0	66.67
10.0	100.00
7.5	133.33
6.0	166.67
5.0	200.00
3.8	266.67
3.0	333.33
2.5	400.00
1.9	533.33
1.5	666.67

As you can see, as cycle time decreases, clock speed increases proportionately.

If you examine Table 6.1, you can clearly see that the 60ns DRAM memory used in older systems for many years is totally inadequate when compared to processor speeds of 2GHz and higher. Up until 1998, most DRAM memory used in PCs had been rated at an access time of 60ns, which works out to be 16.67MHz! The dominant standard in the year 2000 was to have 100MHz and even 133MHz memory, called PC100 and PC133, respectively. Starting in early 2001, double data rate (DDR) memory of 200MHz and 266MHz become popular. In 2002, we had 333MHz memory, and in 2003, 400MHz DDR memory became available. Note that these memory speed milestones are dated for desktop systems; laptops and notebooks are almost always somewhat behind the curve on memory speeds. For example, while desktop systems began using DDR2 memory in 2004, it wasn't until late 2005 that laptops began switching to DDR2 as well.

System memory timing is a little more involved than simply converting nanoseconds to megahertz. The transistors for each bit in a memory chip are most efficiently arranged in a grid, using a row and column scheme to access each transistor. All memory accesses involve selecting a row address and then a column address, and then transferring the data. The initial setup for a memory transfer where the row and column addresses are selected is a necessary overhead normally referred to as *latency*. The access time for memory is the cycle time plus latency for selecting the row and column addresses. For example, SDRAM memory rated at 133MHz (7.5ns) typically takes five cycles to set up and complete the first transfer ($5 \times 7.5ns = 37.5ns$) and then perform three additional transfers with no additional setup. Thus, four transfers take a total eight cycles, or an average of about two cycles per transfer.

Over the development life of the PC, memory has had a difficult time keeping up with the processor, requiring several levels of high-speed cache memory to intercept processor requests for the slower main memory. Table 6.2 shows the progress and relationship between system board (motherboard) speeds in PCs and the various types and speeds of main memory or RAM used and how these changes have affected total bandwidth.

Table 6.2   Portable System DRAM Memory Module and Bus Standards/Bandwidth (Past, Current, and Future)

Module Standard	Module Format	Chip Type	Clock Speed (MHz)	Cycles per Clock	Bus Speed (MTps)	Bus Width (Bytes)	Transfer Rate (MBps)
FPM	72/144-pin SO-DIMM	60ns	22	1	22	8	177
EDO	72/144-pin SO-DIMM	60ns	33	1	33	8	266
PC66	144-pin SO-DIMM	10ns	66	1	66	8	533
PC100	144-pin SO-DIMM	8ns	100	1	100	8	800
PC133	144-pin SO-DIMM	7/7.5ns	133	1	133	8	1,066
PC1600	200-pin SO-DIMM	DDR200	100	2	200	8	1,600
PC2100	200-pin SO-DIMM	DDR266	133	2	266	8	2,133
PC2700	200-pin SO-DIMM	DDR333	166	2	333	8	2,667
PC3200	200-pin SO-DIMM	DDR400	200	2	400	8	3,200
PC2100	200-pin SODIMM	DDR266	133	2	266	8	2,133
PC2700	200-pin SODIMM	DDR333	166	2	333	8	2,667
PC3200	200-pin SODIMM	DDR400	200	2	400	8	3,200

(continues)

Table 6.2   Continued

Module Standard	Module Format	Chip Type	Clock Speed (MHz)	Cycles per Clock	Bus Speed (MTps)	Bus Width (Bytes)	Transfer Rate (MBps)
PC2-3200	200-pin SODIMM	DDR400	200	2	400	8	3,200
PC2-4200	200-pin SODIMM	DDR533	266	2	533	8	4,266
PC2-5300	200-pin SODIMM	DDR667	333	2	667	8	5,333

*Some DDR standards listed here are proposed or future
   standards not yet available.*

MTps = megatransfers per second

MBps = megabytes per second

ns = nanoseconds (billionths of a second)

FPM = Fast Page Mode

EDO = extended data out

SODIMM = small outline dual inline memory module

DDR = double data rate

Generally, things work best when the throughput of the memory bus matches the throughput of the processor bus. Compare the memory bus transfer speeds (bandwidth) to the speeds of the processor bus as shown in Table 6.3, and you'll see that some of the memory bus rates match that of some of the processor bus rates. In most cases, the type of memory that matches the CPU bus transfer rate is the best type of memory for systems with that type of processor.

Table 6.3   Processor Bus Bandwidth

CPU Bus Type	Clock Speed (MHz)	Cycles per Clock	Bus Speed (MTps)	Bus Width (bytes)	Bandwidth (MBps)
33MHz 486 FSB	33	1	33	4	133
66MHz Pentium I/II/III FSB	66	1	66	8	533
100MHz Pentium I/II/III FSB	100	1	100	8	800
133MHz Pentium I/II/III FSB	133	1	133	8	1,066
200MHz Athlon FSB	100	2	200	8	1,600
266MHz Athlon FSB	133	2	266	8	2,133
333MHz Athlon FSB	166	2	333	8	2,667
400MHz Athlon FSB	200	2	400	8	3,200
400MHz Pentium 4/M FSB	100	4	400	8	3,200
533MHz Pentium 4/M FSB	133	4	533	8	4,266
800MHz Pentium 4/M FSB	200	4	800	8	6,400

FSB = front-side bus

MTps = megatransfers per second

MBps = megabytes per second

Because the L1 and L2 cache fairly well insulate the processor from directly dealing with main memory, memory performance has often lagged behind the performance of the processor bus. More recently, however, systems using SDRAM and DDR SDRAM have memory bus performance equaling that of the processor bus. When the speed of the memory bus equals the speed of the processor bus, memory performance is optimum for that system.

Memory Types

Over the years, the following main types of memory have been used in PCs:

- FPM (Fast Page Mode)
- EDO (extended data out)
- SDRAM (synchronous dynamic RAM)
- DDR SDRAM (double data rate SDRAM)
- DDR2 SDRAM (double data rate SDRAM)
- RDRAM (Rambus dynamic RAM)

All of these, except the RDRAM, have been used in laptops and other portable systems. The following sections discuss each of these memory types in more detail.

Fast Page Mode DRAM

Standard DRAM is accessed through a technique called *paging*. Normal memory access requires that a row and column address be selected, which takes time. Paging enables faster access to all the data within a given row of memory by keeping the row address the same and changing only the column. Memory that uses this technique is called *Page Mode* or *Fast Page Mode* memory. Other variations on Page Mode were called *Static Column* or *Nibble Mode* memory. Most Intel 486 as well as AMD or Cyrix 5x86-based laptops from the mid-1990s and earlier used FPM memory.

Paged memory is a simple scheme for improving memory performance that divides memory into pages ranging from 512 bytes to a few kilobytes long. The paging circuitry then enables memory locations in a page to be accessed with fewer wait states (idle or do-nothing cycles). If the desired memory location is outside the current page, one or more wait states are added while the system selects the new page.

To improve further on memory access speeds, systems have evolved to enable faster access to DRAM. One important change was the implementation of burst mode access in the 486 and later processors. Burst mode cycling takes advantage of the consecutive nature of most memory accesses. After setting up the row and column addresses for a given access, using burst mode, you can then access the next three adjacent addresses with no additional latency or wait states. A burst access usually is limited to four total accesses. To describe this, we often refer to the timing in the number of cycles for each access. A typical burst mode access of standard DRAM is expressed as *x-y-y-y*; *x* is the time for the first access (latency plus cycle time), and *y* represents the number of cycles required for each consecutive access.

Standard 60ns DRAM normally runs 5-3-3-3 burst mode timing. This means the first access takes a total of five cycles (on a 66MHz bus, this is about 75ns total or 5×15ns cycles), and the consecutive cycles take three cycles each (3×15ns = 45ns). As you can see, the actual system timing is somewhat less than the memory is technically rated for. Without the bursting technique, memory access would be 5-5-5-5 because the full latency is necessary for each memory transfer.

For laptop systems, FPM RAM generally came in 72-pin or 144-pin EDO SODIMM (small outline dual inline memory module) form. Figures 6.1 and 6.2 (later in this chapter) show the physical characteristics of these 72-pin and 144-pin SODIMMs. These modules normally operate on 3.3V, saving power as compared to their full-sized 5V counterparts for desktop systems.

Extended Data Out RAM

In 1995, a newer type of memory called *extended data out (EDO) RAM* became available for Pentium systems. EDO, a modified form of FPM memory, is sometimes referred to as *Hyper Page Mode*. EDO was invented and patented by Micron Technology, although Micron then licensed production to many other memory manufacturers. EDO memory consists of specially manufactured chips that allow a timing overlap between successive accesses. The name *extended data out* refers specifically to the fact that unlike FPM, the data output drivers on the chip are not turned off when the memory controller removes the column address to begin the next cycle. This enables the next cycle to overlap the previous one, saving approximately 10ns per cycle.

The effect of EDO is that cycle times are improved by enabling the memory controller to begin a new column address instruction while it is reading data at the current address. This is almost identical to what was achieved in older systems by interleaving banks of memory. Unlike interleaving, however, EDO doesn't require that you install two identical banks of memory in the system.

EDO RAM allows for burst mode cycling of 5-2-2-2, compared to the 5-3-3-3 of standard Fast Page Mode memory. To do four memory transfers, then, EDO would require 11 total system cycles, compared to 14 total cycles for FPM. This is a 22% improvement in overall cycling time, but in actual testing, EDO typically increases overall system benchmark speed by only about 5%. Even though the overall system improvement might seem small, the important thing about EDO was that it used the same basic DRAM chip design as FPM, meaning that there was practically no additional cost over FPM. In fact, in its heyday, EDO cost less than FPM and yet offered higher performance.

For laptop systems, EDO RAM generally came in 72-pin or 144-pin EDO SODIMM (small outline dual inline memory module) form. Figures 6.1 and 6.2 (later in this chapter) show the physical characteristics of these 72-pin and 144-pin SODIMMs. These modules normally operate on 3.3V, saving power as compared to their full-sized 5V counterparts for desktop systems.

To actually use EDO memory, your motherboard chipset must support it. Most laptop motherboard chipsets—starting in 1995 with the Intel 430MX (Mobile Triton) and through 1997 with the 430TX—offered support for EDO. Because EDO memory chips cost the same to manufacture as standard chips, combined with Intel's support of EDO in all its chipsets, the PC market jumped on the EDO bandwagon full force.

EDO RAM was ideal for systems with bus speeds of up to 66MHz, which fit perfectly with the PC market up through 1997 and into 1998. However, since 1998, the market for EDO rapidly declined as the newer and faster SDRAM architecture has become the standard for new PC and laptop system memory.

SDRAM

SDRAM is short for *synchronous dynamic RAM*, a type of DRAM that runs in synchronization with the memory bus. SDRAM delivers information in very high-speed bursts using a high-speed, clocked interface. SDRAM removes most of the latency involved in asynchronous DRAM because the signals are already in synchronization with the motherboard clock.

As with EDO RAM, your chipset must support this type of memory for it to be usable in your system. Starting in 1997 with the 430VX and 430TX (only the TX was used in mobile systems), most of Intel's chipsets began to support industry standard SDRAM, making it the most popular type of memory for new systems through 2000 and even into 2001.

SDRAM performance is a dramatic improvement over FPM and EDO RAM. Because SDRAM is still a type of DRAM, the initial latency is the same, but overall cycle times are much faster than with FPM or EDO. SDRAM timing for a burst access would be 5-1-1-1, meaning that four memory reads would complete in only 8 system bus cycles, compared to 11 cycles for EDO and 14 cycles for FPM. This makes SDRAM almost 20% faster than EDO.

Besides being capable of working in fewer cycles, SDRAM is also capable of supporting up to 133MHz (7.5ns) system bus cycling. As such, most new PC systems sold from 1998 to 2000 have included SDRAM memory.

For laptop and portable systems, SDRAM is sold in 144-pin SODIMM or MicroDIMM form. It is often rated by both megahertz speed and nanosecond cycling time, which can be kind of confusing. Figure 6.2 (later in this chapter) shows the physical characteristics of 144-pin SDRAM SODIMMs and 144-pin SDRAM MicroDIMMs. Like their full-sized DIMM desktop counterparts, the SODIMMs use 3.3V power.

To meet the stringent timing demands of its chipsets, Intel created specifications for SDRAM called PC66, PC100, and PC133. To meet the PC100 specification, 8ns chips usually are required. Normally, you would think 10ns would be considered the proper rating for 100MHz operation, but the PC100 specification calls for faster memory to ensure all timing parameters are met.

In May of 1999, JEDEC created a specification called PC133. It achieved this 33MHz speed increase by taking the PC100 specification and tightening up the timing and capacitance parameters. The faster PC133 quickly caught on as the most popular version of SDRAM for any systems running a 133MHz processor bus. The original chips used in PC133 modules were rated for exactly 7.5ns or 133MHz, whereas later ones were rated at 7.0ns or 143MHz. These faster chips were still used on PC133 modules, but they allowed for improvements in *CAS (column address strobe) Latency*, often abbreviated as *CL*, which improves overall memory cycling times somewhat.

Table 6.4 shows the timing, actual speed, and rated speed for various SDRAM DIMMs.

Table 6.4   SDRAM Timing, Actual Speed, and Rated Speed

Timing	Rated Chip Speed	Standard Module Speed
15ns	66MHz	PC66
10ns	100MHz	PC66
8ns	125MHz	PC100
7.5ns	133MHz	PC133
7.0ns	143MHz	PC133

DDR SDRAM

Double data rate (DDR) SDRAM memory is an evolutionary design of standard SDRAM in which data is transferred twice as quickly. Instead of doubling the actual clock rate, DDR memory achieves the doubling in performance by transferring data twice per transfer cycle: once at the leading (falling) edge and once at the trailing (rising) edge of the cycle. This is similar to the way RDRAM operates and effectively doubles the transfer rate, even though the same overall clock and timing signals are used.

DDR found most of its initial support in the graphics card market; since then it has become the mainstream PC memory standard for both desktop and portable systems.

DDR SDRAM came to market during 2000, but it didn't really catch on in the portable market until the advent of the Intel 845MP chipset in March 2002. For laptop and portable systems, DDR SDRAM uses either 200-pin SODIMMs or 172-pin MicroDIMMs. Figures 6.1 and 6.2 (later in this chapter) show both types of modules, respectively.

DDR SODIMMs come in various speed or throughput ratings and normally run on 2.5 volts, just like their full-sized desktop counterparts. They are basically an extension of the standard SDRAM SODIMMs redesigned to support double clocking, where data is sent on each clock transition (twice per cycle) rather than once per cycle, as with standard SDRAM. To eliminate confusion with DDR, regular SDRAM is often called *single data rate (SDR)*. Table 6.5 compares the different types of standard SDRAM and DDR SDRAM SODIMM modules available.

Table 6.5   SDRAM (SDR), DDR, and DDR2 Module Types and Bandwidth

Module Standard	Module Format	Chip Type	Clock Speed (MHz)	Cycles per Clock	Bus Speed (MTps)	Bus Width (Bytes)	Transfer Rate (MBps)
PC66	144-pin SO-DIMM	10ns	66	1	66	8	533
PC100	144-pin SO-DIMM	8ns	100	1	100	8	800
PC133	144-pin SO-DIMM	7/7.5ns	133	1	133	8	1,066
PC1600	200-pin SO-DIMM	DDR200	100	2	200	8	1,600
PC2100	200-pin SO-DIMM	DDR266	133	2	266	8	2,133
PC2700	200-pin SO-DIMM	DDR333	166	2	333	8	2,667
PC3200	200-pin SO-DIMM	DDR400	200	2	400	8	3,200
PC2-3200	200-pin SODIMM	DDR2-400	200	2	400	8	3,200
PC2-4200	200-pin SODIMM	DDR2-533	266	2	533	8	4,266
PC2-5300	200-pin SODIMM	DDR2-667	333	2	667	8	5,333

Some standards listed here are proposed or future standards not yet available.

MTps = megatransfers per second

MBps = megabytes per second

ns = nanoseconds (billionths of a second)

SODIMM = small outline dual inline memory module

DDR = double data rate

Note that several of these specifications either don't exist yet or could exist but haven't been developed into products. Currently the fastest standardized modules are PC3200. Faster modules don't exist yet, but faster modules are always being developed. Even faster technologies such as DDR are on the horizon.

DDR2 SDRAM

JEDEC and its members have been working on the DDR2 specification for several years now, and the specification has finally come to fruition. Although DDR2 chips and modules first appeared for desktop systems in 2004, they took a year longer to reach laptops and other portable systems. DDR2 SDRAM is simply a faster version of conventional DDR-SDRAM memory. It achieves higher throughput by using differential pairs of signal wires to allow faster signaling without noise and interference problems. The original DDR specification tops out at 400MHz for laptops, whereas DDR2 starts at 400MHz and will go up to 667MHz, 800MHz, and beyond.

In addition to providing greater speeds and bandwidth, DDR2 has other advantages. It uses lower voltage than conventional DDR (1.8V versus 2.5V), so power consumption and heat generation are reduced. Because of the greater number of pins required on DDR2 chips, the chips normally use fine-pitch ball grid array (FBGA) packaging rather than the thin small outline package (TSOP) chip packaging used by most DDR and conventional SDRAM chips. FBGA chips are connected to the substrate (meaning the memory module in most cases) via tightly spaced solder balls on the base of the chip.

RDRAM

Rambus dynamic RAM (RDRAM) is a fairly radical memory design found in high-end Pentium 4–based desktop PC systems starting in late 1999. Intel signed a contract with Rambus in 1996 ensuring it would support RDRAM into 2001. That period has elapsed, and Intel has abandoned RDRAM support for future chipsets beyond that date, even though RDRAM standards have been proposed that will support future processors. Because there never were any RDRAM supporting chipsets for laptop or notebook systems, you normally don't see RDRAM associated with portables. For more information on RDRAM, see the RDRAM section in the "Memory" chapter of my book *Upgrading and Repairing PCs*.

Memory Modules

Two main types of industry-standard memory modules are used in laptops and portable computers today: SODIMM (small outline dual inline memory module) and MicroDIMM (micro dual inline memory module). There are four main types of SODIMMs and two main types of MicroDIMMs, with different sizes, speeds, and configurations available in each type (see Table 6.6). The SODIMM and MicroDIMM form factors and pinouts are JEDEC standards, which means that they are industry standards, thus ensuring conformity, compatibility, and interchangeability among different systems and manufacturers.

Table 6.6   Laptop/Portable Memory Module Types

Number of Pins	Module Type	Data Width	Memory Type
72	SODIMM	32 bits	FPM/EDO
144	SODIMM	64 bits	FPM/EDO
144	SODIMM	64 bits	SDRAM
200	SODIMM	64 bits	DDR/DDR2 SDRAM
144	MicroDIMM	64 bits	SDRAM
172	MicroDIMM	64 bits	DDR SDRAM

SODIMMs are mainly used by laptop or notebook computers, whereas the smaller MicroDIMMs are used mainly by subnotebooks, PDAs, and palmtop computers.

SODIMMs

Most laptop and notebook computers use SODIMMs (small outline dual inline memory modules), which are basically smaller and more compact modules than the standard DIMMs used in desktop systems. Although they differ in form factor and pinout, as compared to standard DIMMs, SODIMMs perform the same function. They allow for easy, modular memory installations and upgrades. The modules are inserted into sockets in the system and can easily be installed or removed. As the name implies, SODIMMs have different pins on each side of the module, with the odd-numbered pins on the front and the even-numbered pins on the back. Special keying notches on either side allow the module to be inserted into the connector only in the proper orientation. The notches are normally offset in their space for voltage keying as well. Various SODIMMs are available for different system requirements. Because they are not all interchangeable, you must be sure to match the correct type for a given system.

72-pin SODIMM

The 72-pin SODIMM is an older type used primarily in older 486 class portables. The 72-pin SODIMM reads and writes data 32 bits (4 bytes) at a time, which is a perfect match for 32-bit 486 processors. These modules are largely obsolete and are not used in any new system designs. They are still available for upgrading older systems, but because the supply is dwindling, the prices are higher than for newer, more modern modules.

The 72-pin SODIMMs have the industry-standard form factor shown in the Figure 6.1.

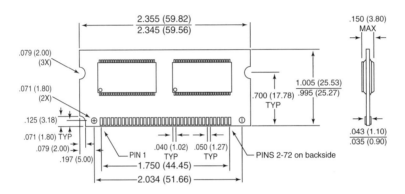

Figure 6.1   72-pin SODIMM.

The 72-pin SODIMMs are available in several versions, with capacities of up to 64MB. Most utilize FPM/EDO memory chips, which are rated 60ns for speed and run on 3.3 volts. The most common sizes, including the depths and widths of the modules, are shown in Table 6.7.

Table 6.7   72-pin SODIMM Module Capacities

Capacity	(Depth × Width)
4MB	(1M × 32b)
8MB	(2M × 32b)
16MB	(4M × 32b)
32MB	(8M × 32b)
64MB	(16M × 32b)

The 72-pin modules have a 32-bit-wide data bus, which is equal to 4 bytes. For example, a 64MB 72-pin SODIMM is arranged internally as 16 million rows, with 32 bits (4 bytes) in each row, for a total of 64 million (16 million × 4) bytes.

The JEDEC standard pinout for 72-pin SODIMMs is listed in Tables 6.8 and 6.9.

Table 6.8   72-pin SO-DIMM Pinout (Front)

Pin	Signal	Pin	Signal	Pin	Signal	Pin	Signal
1	VSS	19	A10	37	DQ16	55	NC
3	DQ1	21	DQ8	39	VSS	57	DQ25
5	DQ3	23	DQ10	41	CAS2#	59	DQ28
7	DQ5	25	DQ12	43	CAS1#	61	VDD
9	DQ7	27	DQ14	45	RAS1#	63	DQ30
11	PRD1	29	A11	47	WE#	65	NC
13	A1	31	A8	49	DQ18	67	PRD3
15	A3	33	RAS3#	51	DQ20	69	PRD5
17	A5	35	DQ15	53	DQ22	71	PRD7

Table 6.9   72-pin SO-DIMM Pinout (Back)

Pin	Signal	Pin	Signal	Pin	Signal	Pin	Signal
2	DQ0	20	NC	38	DQ17	56	DQ24
4	DQ2	22	DQ9	40	CAS0#	58	DQ26
6	DQ4	24	DQ11	42	CAS3#	60	DQ27
8	DQ6	26	DQ13	44	RAS0#	62	DQ29
10	VDD	28	A7	46	A12	64	DQ31
12	A0	30	VDD	48	A13	66	PRD2
14	A2	32	A9	50	DQ19	68	PRD4
16	A4	34	RAS2#	52	DQ21	70	PRD6
18	A6	36	NC	54	DQ23	72	VSS

All SODIMM contacts are normally gold plated and should match the plating on the mating connector for reliable operation. You should avoid modules with tin-plated contacts because tin will react with the gold plating on the connector contacts, causing corrosion and eventual memory failures.

144-pin SODIMM

The 144-pin SODIMMs are very popular in Pentium or Athlon class and newer laptop and notebook computers. They can read or write data 64 bits at a time, which makes them a perfect match for 64-bit processors such as the Pentium and newer chips. The 144-pin SODIMMs are available in several different memory chip types, including EDO, 66MHz SDRAM, PC100 SDRAM, and PC133 SDRAM versions. The 144-pin SODIMMs are not available in versions supporting error correcting code (ECC).

When installing these modules, you must ensure that the type you are using matches the requirements of the system. In most cases, you can put a faster module in place of a slower one, but only if it is the same basic memory type. For example, you can usually install PC133 memory even if the system requires only PC100 or even 66MHz SDRAM, but you cannot use SDRAM modules in systems that require EDO, or vice versa. Also, you should not install modules that are slower than the system requires, even if they are the correct memory type.

The speeds of 144-pin SODIMMs are rated as shown in Table 6.10.

Table 6.10   144-pin SDRAM SODIMM Speeds

Module Type	Cycle Time	Module Frequency	Module Width	Module Bandwidth
PC66	10.0ns	66MHz	8 bytes	533MBps
PC100	8.0ns	100MHz	8 bytes	800MBps
PC133	7.5ns	133MHz	8 bytes	1,066MBps

The throughput or bandwidth is simply the frequency multiplied by the width, which gives the rate at which data can be read from or written to the module.

Another specification to consider that is related to speed is the *CAS (column address strobe) Latency*, often abbreviated as *CL*. This is also sometimes called *read latency*, and it's the number of clock cycles occurring between the registration of the CAS signal and the resultant output data, with lower numbers of cycles indicating faster (better) performance. Typically, you find SDRAM modules rated CL 2 or CL 3. If possible, choose modules with a lower CL figure, because the motherboard chipset will read that specification out of the serial presence detect (SPD) ROM on the module and switch to slightly faster cycling rates.

The 144-pin SODIMMs have the industry-standard form factor shown in Figure 6.2.

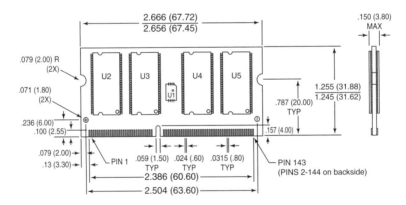

Figure 6.2   144-pin SODIMM.

All 144-pin SODIMMs have the odd-numbered pins (1–143) on the front and even-numbered pins (2–144) on the back and are 2.66" (67.6mm) long. The number of actual chips on the modules can vary, as can the physical height of the module. The modules are normally either 1" (25.4mm) or 1.25" (31.75mm) high, although the heights may vary slightly.

The 144-pin SODIMMs use an SPD ROM (read-only memory) onboard, which the motherboard reads to determine the exact specifications of the modules installed. The ROM is normally a small chip on the module and can be seen as component "U1" in Figure 6.2.

The modules are keyed via a small notch in the connector area on the bottom (seen between pins 59 and 61 on the front), which prevents them from being installed backward and provides voltage keying as well. The voltage keying is shown Figure 6.3.

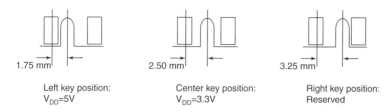

Left key position:
V_{DD}=5V

Center key position:
V_{DD}=3.3V

Right key position:
Reserved

Figure 6.3   144-pin SODIMM voltage keying.

Although the standard allowed for 5V modules, currently all 144-pin SODIMMs have the notch in the center position, indicating 3.3V operation. All the systems I am aware of will accept only 3.3V 144-pin modules, which draw less power and generate less heat.

The 144-pin SODIMMs are available in several versions, with capacities of up to 512MB. They can utilize either EDO (extended data out) memory chips or SDRAM (synchronous dynamic RAM) at several different rated speeds. The most common sizes are shown in Table 6.11.

Table 6.11   144-pin SODIMM Module Capacities

Capacity	(Depth × Width)
32MB	(4M × 64b)
64MB	(8M × 64b)
128MB	(16M × 64b)
256MB	(32M × 64b)
512MB	(64M × 64b)

The capacity can be determined by multiplying the depth by the width. The 144-pin modules have a 64-bit-wide data bus, which is equal to 8 bytes. For example, a 512MB 144-pin SODIMM is arranged internally as 64 million rows, with 64 bits (8 bytes) in each row, for a total of 512 million (64 million × 8) bytes.

The JEDEC standard pinout for 144-pin SODIMMs using FPM or EDO RAM is listed in Tables 6.12 and 6.13.

Table 6.12   144-pin EDO/FPM SODIMM Pinout (Front)

Pin	Signal	Pin	Signal	Pin	Signal	Pin	Signal
1	VSS	37	DQ8	73	OE#	109	A9
3	DQ0	39	DQ9	75	VSS	111	A10
5	DQ1	41	DQ10	77	NC	113	VDD
7	DQ2	43	DQ11	79	NC	115	CAS2#
9	DQ3	45	VDD	81	VDD	117	CAS3#
11	VDD	47	DQ12	83	DQ16	119	VSS
13	DQ4	49	DQ13	85	DQ17	121	DQ24
15	DQ5	51	DQ14	87	DQ18	123	DQ25

(continues)

Table 6.12 Continued

Pin	Signal	Pin	Signal	Pin	Signal	Pin	Signal
17	DQ6	53	DQ15	89	DQ19	125	DQ26
19	DQ7	55	VSS	91	VSS	127	DQ27
21	VSS	57	NC	93	DQ20	129	VDD
23	CAS0#	59	NC	95	DQ21	131	DQ28
25	CAS1#	61	NC	97	DQ22	133	DQ29
27	VDD	63	VDD	99	DQ23	135	DQ30
29	A0	65	NC	101	VDD	137	DQ31
31	A1	67	WE#	103	A6	139	VSS
33	A2	69	RAS0#	105	A8	141	SDA
35	VSS	71	NC	107	VSS	143	VDD

Table 6.13 144-pin EDO/FPM SODIMM Pinout (Back)

Pin	Signal	Pin	Signal	Pin	Signal	Pin	Signal
2	VSS	38	DQ40	74	NC	110	A12
4	DQ32	40	DQ41	76	VSS	112	A13
6	DQ33	42	DQ42	78	NC	114	VDD
8	DQ34	44	DQ43	80	NC	116	CAS6#
10	DQ35	46	VDD	82	VDD	118	CAS7#
12	VDD	48	DQ44	84	DQ48	120	VSS
14	DQ36	50	DQ45	86	DQ49	122	DQ56
16	DQ37	52	DQ46	88	DQ50	124	DQ57
18	DQ38	54	DQ47	90	DQ51	126	DQ58
20	DQ39	56	VSS	92	VSS	128	DQ59
22	VSS	58	NC	94	DQ52	130	VDD
24	CAS4#	60	NC	96	DQ53	132	DQ60
26	CAS5#	62	NC	98	DQ54	134	DQ61
28	VDD	64	VDD	100	DQ55	136	DQ62
30	A3	66	NC	102	VDD	138	DQ63
32	A4	68	NC	104	A7	140	VSS
34	A5	70	NC	106	A11	142	SCL
36	VSS	72	NC	108	VSS	144	VDD

The JEDEC standard pinout for 144-pin SODIMMs using SDRAM is listed in Tables 6.14 and 6.15.

Table 6.14   144-pin SDRAM SODIMM Pinout (Front)

Pin	Signal	Pin	Signal	Pin	Signal	Pin	Signal
1	VSS	37	DQ8	73	NC	109	A9
3	DQ0	39	DQ9	75	VSS	111	A10
5	DQ1	41	DQ10	77	NC	113	VDD
7	DQ2	43	DQ11	79	NC	115	DQMB2
9	DQ3	45	VDD	81	VDD	117	DQMB3
11	VDD	47	DQ12	83	DQ16	119	VSS
13	DQ4	49	DQ13	85	DQ17	121	DQ24
15	DQ5	51	DQ14	87	DQ18	123	DQ25
17	DQ6	53	DQ15	89	DQ19	125	DQ26
19	DQ7	55	VSS	91	VSS	127	DQ27
21	VSS	57	NC	93	DQ20	129	VDD
23	DQMB0	59	NC	95	DQ21	131	DQ28
25	DQMB1	61	CK0	97	DQ22	133	DQ29
27	VDD	63	VDD	99	DQ23	135	DQ30
29	A0	65	RAS#	101	VDD	137	DQ31
31	A1	67	WE#	103	A6	139	VSS
33	A2	69	S0#	105	A8	141	SDA
35	VSS	71	S1#	107	VSS	143	VDD

Table 6.15   144-pin SDRAM SODIMM Pinout (Back)

Pin	Signal	Pin	Signal	Pin	Signal	Pin	Signal
2	VSS	38	DQ40	74	CK1	110	BA1
4	DQ32	40	DQ41	76	VSS	112	A11
6	DQ33	42	DQ42	78	NC	114	VDD
8	DQ34	44	DQ43	80	NC	116	DQMB6
10	DQ35	46	VDD	82	VDD	118	DQMB7
12	VDD	48	DQ44	84	DQ48	120	VSS
14	DQ36	50	DQ45	86	DQ49	122	DQ56
16	DQ37	52	DQ46	88	DQ50	124	DQ57
18	DQ38	54	DQ47	90	DQ51	126	DQ58
20	DQ39	56	VSS	92	VSS	128	DQ59
22	VSS	58	NC	94	DQ52	130	VDD
24	DQMB4	60	NC	96	DQ53	132	DQ60
26	DQMB5	62	CKE0	98	DQ54	134	DQ61
28	VDD	64	VDD	100	DQ55	136	DQ62
30	A3	66	CAS#	102	VDD	138	DQ63
32	A4	68	CKE1	104	A7	140	VSS

(continues)

Table 6.15   Continued

Pin	Signal	Pin	Signal	Pin	Signal	Pin	Signal
34	A5	70	A12	106	BA0	142	SCL
36	VSS	72	NC	108	VSS	144	VDD

All DIMM contacts are normally gold plated and should match the plating on the mating connector for reliable operation.

200-pin SODIMM

The 200-pin SODIMMs are used to provide DDR (double data rate) and DDR2 SDRAM (synchronous dynamic RAM) memory for laptop computers. DDR2 SDRAM is the type of memory most recent high-performance laptops use. DDR modules run on 2.5 volts, whereas DDR2 modules use only 1.8V, making the DDR2 modules even more efficient for longer battery life. Each 200-pin SODIMM incorporates a 64-bit data path, which is ideal because these SODIMMs can be installed individually in 64-bit (Pentium and newer) systems. The 200-pin SODIMMs are available in PC1600 (200MHz), PC2100 (266MHz), PC2700 (333MHz), and PC3200 (400MHz) DDR SDRAM versions, as well as PC2-3200 (400MHz), PC2-4200 (533MHz), and PC2-5300 (667MHz) DDR2 versions. They are also available in versions supporting ECC (error correcting code), which offers 1-bit error detection and correction for greater integrity. Note, however, that ECC requires support from the chipset and motherboard, and very few laptops support this feature.

When installing these modules, you must ensure the type you are using matches the requirements of the system. In most cases, you can put a faster module in place of a slower one, but only if it is the same basic memory type. Although both DDR and DDR2 modules have 200 pins and are the exact same size, they have slightly different pinouts and run on different voltages. To prevent installing the improper module type, the key notch is placed according to voltage. The notch is positioned to the left (facing the front of the module) for DDR modules (2.5V) and to the right for DDR2 modules (1.8V). The different notch positions make it impossible to fit the wrong module type into the socket.

One thing the notch will not prevent, however, is installing a module that doesn't support the required speed. It is generally okay to install a module that is faster than the system requires, but you should not install a slower module than required by the motherboard. For example, you can usually install PC2700 memory even if the system requires only PC2100 or even PC1600, but if the system requires PC2700, you should not install the slower PC2100 or PC1600 modules.

The speeds of 200-pin SODIMMs are rated as shown in Table 6.16.

Table 6.16   200-pin DDR2/DDR SDRAM SODIMM Speeds

Module Type	Module Speed	Cycle Time	Frequency SDR/DDR	Module Width	Module Bandwidth
DDR2	PC2-5300	3.0ns	333/667MHz	8 bytes	5,333MBps
DDR2	PC2-4200	3.8ns	266/533MHz	8 bytes	4,266MBps
DDR2	PC2-3200	5.0ns	200/400MHz	8 bytes	3,200MBps
DDR	PC3200	5.0ns	200/400MHz	8 bytes	3,200MBps
DDR	PC2700	6.0ns	166/333MHz	8 bytes	2,667MBps
DDR	PC2100	7.5ns	133/266MHz	8 bytes	2,133MBps
DDR	PC1600	10.0ns	100/200MHz	8 bytes	1,600MBps

The cycle time in nanoseconds (billionths of a second) matches the single data rate (SDR) clock speed, but double data rate (DDR) modules transfer twice per cycle, so the DDR frequency is always equal to double the SDR frequency. The throughput or bandwidth is simply the DDR frequency times the width, which gives the rate at which data can be read from or written to the module.

Another specification to consider that is related to speed is the *CAS (column address strobe) Latency*, often abbreviated as *CL*. This is also sometimes called *read latency*, and it's the number of clock cycles occurring between the registration of the CAS signal and the resultant output data, with lower numbers of cycles indicating faster (better) performance. Typically, you can find DDR SDRAM modules rated CL 2 or CL 2.5. If possible, choose modules with a lower CL figure, because the motherboard chipset will read that specification out of the SPD (serial presence detect) ROM on the module and switch to slightly faster cycling rates.

The 200-pin SODIMMs have the JEDEC industry-standard form factor shown in Figures 6.4 (DDR) and 6.5 (DDR2).

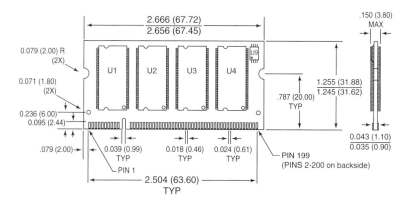

Figure 6.4   200-pin DDR SDRAM SODIMM.

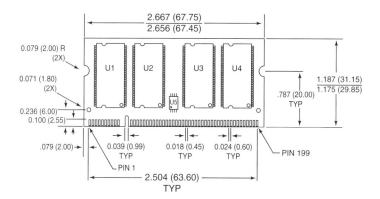

Figure 6.5   200-pin DDR2 SDRAM SODIMM.

Note that the physical form factors for DDR and DDR2 are the same, except for the location of the key notch in the module. This prevents DDR modules from being installed in place of DDR2 modules and vice-versa.

All 200-pin SODIMMs have the odd-numbered pins (1–199) on the front and even-numbered pins (2–200) on the back and are 2.66" (67.6mm) long. The number of actual chips on the module can vary, as can the physical height of the module. The modules are normally either 1" (25.4mm) or 1.25" (31.75mm) high, although some versions can be up to 1.5" (38.1mm) high (the heights may vary slightly). The taller modules may not fit in all systems, so be sure to check before ordering.

Although the 200-pin modules are the same physical size as 144-pin modules, the pin spacing is tighter and the notch is offset much farther to the left, preventing the installation of 200-pin modules in 144-pin sockets, and vice versa.

The 200-pin SODIMMs use an SPD ROM (read-only memory) onboard, which the motherboard reads to determine the exact specifications of the modules installed. The ROM is normally a small chip on the module, much smaller than the memory chips, and may be mounted on the front or back side. The SPD chip can be seen as component "U9" in Figure 6.4.

The modules are keyed via a small notch in the connector area on the bottom (seen between pins 39 and 41 on the front), which prevents them from being installed backward and provides voltage keying as well. The voltage keying is shown in Figure 6.6.

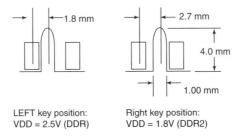

LEFT key position:
VDD = 2.5V (DDR)

Right key position:
VDD = 1.8V (DDR2)

Figure 6.6   200-pin SODIMM DDR and DDR2 voltage keying.

DDR modules are 2.5V, whereas DDR2 modules are 1.8V. The notch prevents plugging in modules of the improper voltage and type into a given system.

The 200-pin SODIMMs are available in several versions, with capacities of up to 1GB. They utilize DDR or DDR2 SDRAM at several different rated speeds. The most common capacities are shown in Table 6.17.

Table 6.17   200-pin DDR/DDR2 SODIMM Module Capacities

Capacity	(Depth × Width)
32MB	(4M × 64b)
64MB	(8M × 64b)
128MB	(16M × 64b)
256MB	(32M × 64b)
512MB	(64M × 64b)
1GB	(128M × 64b)

The capacity can be determined by multiplying the depth by the width. The 200-pin modules have a 64-bit-wide data bus, which is equal to 8 bytes. For example, a 1GB 200-pin SODIMM is arranged internally as 128 million rows, with 64 bits (8 bytes) in each row. If you multiply 128 million by 8, you get 1,024 million bytes, or 1GB.

The JEDEC standard pinout for 200-pin SODIMMs is listed in Tables 6.18 and 6.19.

Table 6.18   200-pin DDR SDRAM SODIMM Pinout (Front)

Pin	Signal	Pin	Signal	Pin	Signal	Pin	Signal
1	VREF	51	VSS	101	A9	151	DQ42
3	VSS	53	DQ19	103	VSS	153	DQ43
5	DQ0	55	DQ24	105	A7	155	VDD
7	DQ1	57	VDD	107	A5	157	VDD
9	VDD	59	DQ25	109	A3	159	VSS
11	DQS0	61	DQS3	111	A1	161	VSS
13	DQ2	63	VSS	113	VDD	163	DQ48
15	VSS	65	DQ26	115	A10	165	DQ49
17	DQ3	67	DQ27	117	BA0	167	VDD
19	DQ8	69	VDD	119	WE#	169	DQS6
21	VDD	71	CB0	121	S0#	171	DQ50
23	DQ9	73	CB1	123	A13	173	VSS
25	DQS1	75	VSS	125	VSS	175	DQ51
27	VSS	77	DQS8	127	DQ32	177	DQ56
29	DQ10	79	CB2	129	DQ33	179	VDD
31	DQ11	81	VDD	131	VDD	181	DQ57
33	VDD	83	CB3	133	DQS4	183	DQS7
35	CK0	85	NC	135	DQ34	185	VSS
37	CK0#	87	VSS	137	VSS	187	DQ58
39	VSS	89	CK2	139	DQ35	189	DQ59
41	DQ16	91	CK2#	141	DQ40	191	VDD
43	DQ17	93	VDD	143	VDD	193	SDA
45	VDD	95	CKE1	145	DQ41	195	SCL
47	DQS2	97	NC	147	DQS5	197	VDDSPD
49	DQ18	99	A12	149	VSS	199	VDDID

See Table 6.20 for pin descriptions.

Table 6.19   200-pin DDR SDRAM SODIMM Pinout (Back)

Pin	Signal	Pin	Signal	Pin	Signal	Pin	Signal
2	VREF	52	VSS	102	A8	152	DQ46
4	VSS	54	DQ23	104	VSS	154	DQ47
6	DQ4	56	DQ28	106	A6	156	VDD
8	DQ5	58	VDD	108	A4	158	CK1#
10	VDD	60	DQ29	110	A2	160	CK1
12	DM0	62	DM3	112	A0	162	VSS

(continues)

Table 6.19   Continued

Pin	Signal	Pin	Signal	Pin	Signal	Pin	Signal
14	DQ6	64	VSS	114	VDD	164	DQ52
16	VSS	66	DQ30	116	BA1	166	DQ53
18	DQ7	68	DQ31	118	RAS#	168	VDD
20	DQ12	70	VDD	120	CAS#	170	DM6
22	VDD	72	CB4	122	S1#	172	DQ54
24	DQ13	74	CB5	124	NC	174	VSS
26	DM1	76	VSS	126	VSS	176	DQ55
28	VSS	78	DM8	128	DQ36	178	DQ60
30	DQ14	80	CB6	130	DQ37	180	VDD
32	DQ15	82	VDD	132	VDD	182	DQ61
34	VDD	84	CB7	134	DM4	184	DM7
36	VDD	86	NC	136	DQ38	186	VSS
38	VSS	88	VSS	138	VSS	188	DQ62
40	VSS	90	VSS	140	DQ39	190	DQ63
42	DQ20	92	VDD	142	DQ44	192	VDD
44	DQ21	94	VDD	144	VDD	194	SA0
46	VDD	96	CKE0	146	DQ45	196	SA1
48	DM2	98	NC	148	DM5	198	SA2
50	DQ22	100	A11	150	VSS	200	NC

See Table 6.20 for pin descriptions.

All DIMM contacts are normally gold plated and should match the plating on the mating connector for reliable operation.

Table 6.20 describes the pin functions.

Table 6.20   200-pin DDR SDRAM SODIMM Pin Descriptions

Signal	Description	Number of pins
A(0:9,11:13)	Address Inputs	13
A10/AP	Address Input/AutoPrecharge	1
BA(0:1)	SDRAM Bank Address	2
CAS#	Column Address Strobe (Active Low)	1
CB(7:0)	Data Check Bits Input/Output	8
CK(0:2)	Clock Inputs, Positive Line	3
CK(0:2)#	Clock Inputs, Negative Line	3
CKE(0:1)	Clock Enables	2
DM(0:8)	Data Masks	9
DQ(0:63)	Data Input/Output	64
DQS(0:8)	Data Strobes	9
NC	Not Connected (Reserved)	6

Table 6.20   Continued

Signal	Description	Number of pins
RAS#	Row Address Strobe (Active Low)	1
S(0:1)#	Chip Selects (Active Low)	2
SA(0:2)	SPD Address	3
SCL	SPD Clock Input	1
SDA	SPD Data Input/Output	1
VDD	Core and I/O Power	33
VDDID	VDD, VDDQ Level Detection	1
VDDSPD	Serial Presence Detect (SPD) Power	1
VREF	Input/Output Reference	2
VSS	Ground	33
WE#	Write Enable (Active Low)	1

MicroDIMMs

MicroDIMMs (micro dual inline memory modules) are a newer and smaller type of memory module used mainly in subnotebooks, PDAs, and palmtop computers. As with all DIMMs, they have pins on both sides that perform different functions. The two main types of MicroDIMMs are 144-pin and 172-pin. The 144-pin versions contain SDRAM (synchronous dynamic RAM) and are similar to 144-pin SODIMMs, whereas the 172-pin versions contain DDR (double data rate) SDRAM and are similar to 200-pin SODIMMs. The MicroDIMMs are about half the size of the SODIMMs and yet offer similar capacities and performance.

144-pin SDRAM MicroDIMM

The 144-pin SDRAM MicroDIMMs are similar to the 144-pin SDRAM SODIMMs, but they're made to about half the physical size so as to fit the very tight form factors of smaller systems. Other than size, they have the same specifications as the 144-pin SDRAM SODIMMs, including the following features:

- JEDEC-standard form factor and pinout
- 64-bit (8-byte) data bus
- Single data rate SDRAM
- PC100 (100MHz) and PC133 (133MHz) operation
- 3.3V power
- Serial presence detect (SPD)

The 144-pin SDRAM MicroDIMMs are only 1.5" (38mm) long and 1.18" (30mm) high, which is about half the size of an equivalent SODIMM. Unlike SODIMMs, MicroDIMMs do not have any notches in the connector pin area; however, a notch is used on the left side to ensure proper insertion. They also have a unique size that is not interchangeable with other modules.

The 144-pin SDRAM MicroDIMMs are available in PC100 and PC133 speeds. You can generally use PC133 modules in place of PC100 modules, but not the other way around. The speeds of 144-pin MicroDIMMs are rated as shown in Table 6.21.

Table 6.21   144-pin SDRAM MicroDIMM Speeds

Module Type	Cycle Time	Module Frequency	Module Width	Module Bandwidth
PC100	8.0ns	100MHz	8 bytes	800MBps
PC133	7.5ns	133MHz	8 bytes	1,066MBps

The throughput or bandwidth is simply the frequency times the width, which gives the rate at which data can be read from or written to the module.

As with SDRAM SODIMMs, another performance specification to consider that is related to speed is the *CAS (column address strobe) Latency*, often abbreviated as *CL*. Typically, you find SDRAM modules rated CL 2 or CL 3. If possible, choose modules with a lower CL figure, because the motherboard chipset will read that specification out of the SPD ROM on the module and switch to slightly faster cycling rates.

The 144-pin SDRAM MicroDIMMs have the industry-standard form factor shown in Figure 6.7.

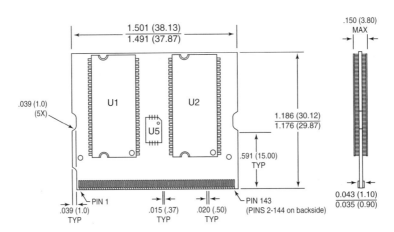

Figure 6.7   144-pin SDRAM MicroDIMM.

All 144-pin MicroDIMMs have the odd-numbered pins (1–143) on the front and even-numbered pins (2–144) on the back and are 1.5" (38mm) long and 1.18" (30mm) high. The number of actual chips on the modules can vary.

The 144-pin MicroDIMMs use an SPD ROM onboard, which the motherboard reads to determine the exact specifications of the modules installed. The ROM is normally a small chip on the module and can be seen as the smaller component "U5" in Figure 6.7. The modules are keyed via a small notch on the left side of the connector area, which prevents them from being installed backward.

The 144-pin MicroDIMMs are available in several versions, with capacities of up to 256MB. The most common sizes are shown Table 6.22.

Table 6.22   144-pin SDRAM MicroDIMM Module Capacities

Capacity	(Depth × Width)
64MB	(8M × 64b)
128MB	(16M × 64b)
256MB	(32M × 64b)

The capacity can be determined by multiplying the depth by the width. The 144-pin modules have a 64-bit-wide data bus, which is equal to 8 bytes. For example, a 256MB MicroDIMM is arranged internally as 32 million rows, with 64 bits (8 bytes) in each row, for a total of 256 million (32 million × 8) bytes.

The JEDEC standard pinout for 144-pin SDRAM MicroDIMMs is listed in Tables 6.23 and 6.24.

Table 6.23   144-pin SDRAM MicroDIMM Pinout (Front)

Pin	Signal	Pin	Signal	Pin	Signal	Pin	Signal
1	VSS	37	DQ8	73	NC	109	A9
3	DQ0	39	DQ9	75	VSS	111	A10
5	DQ1	41	DQ10	77	NC	113	VDD
7	DQ2	43	DQ11	79	NC	115	DQM2
9	DQ3	45	VDD	81	VDD	117	DQM3
11	VDD	47	DQ12	83	DQ16	119	VSS
13	DQ4	49	DQ13	85	DQ17	121	DQ24
15	DQ5	51	DQ14	87	DQ18	123	DQ25
17	DQ6	53	DQ15	89	DQ19	125	DQ26
19	DQ7	55	VSS	91	VSS	127	DQ27
21	VSS	57	NC	93	DQ20	129	VDD
23	DQM0	59	NC	95	DQ21	131	DQ28
25	DQM1	61	CK0	97	DQ22	133	DQ29
27	VDD	63	VDD	99	DQ23	135	DQ30
29	A0	65	RAS#	101	VDD	137	DQ31
31	A1	67	WE#	103	A6	139	VSS
33	A2	69	S0#	105	A8	141	SDA
35	VSS	71	NC	107	VSS	143	VDD

Table 6.24   144-pin SDRAM MicroDIMM Pinout (Back)

Pin	Signal	Pin	Signal	Pin	Signal	Pin	Signal
2	VSS	38	DQ40	74	NC	110	BA1
4	DQ32	40	DQ41	76	VSS	112	A11
6	DQ33	42	DQ42	78	NC	114	VDD
8	DQ34	44	DQ43	80	NC	116	DQM6

(continues)

Table 6.24   Continued

Pin	Signal	Pin	Signal	Pin	Signal	Pin	Signal
10	DQ35	46	VDD	82	VDD	118	DQM7
12	VDD	48	DQ44	84	DQ48	120	VSS
14	DQ36	50	DQ45	86	DQ49	122	DQ56
16	DQ37	52	DQ46	88	DQ50	124	DQ57
18	DQ38	54	DQ47	90	DQ51	126	DQ58
20	DQ39	56	VSS	92	VSS	128	DQ59
22	VSS	58	NC	94	DQ52	130	VDD
24	DQM4	60	NC	96	DQ53	132	DQ60
26	DQM5	62	CKE0	98	DQ54	134	DQ61
28	VDD	64	VDD	100	DQ55	136	DQ62
30	A3	66	CAS#	102	VDD	138	DQ63
32	A4	68	NC	104	A7	140	VSS
34	A5	70	A12	106	BA0	142	SCL
36	VSS	72	NC	108	VSS	144	VDD

All DIMM contacts are normally gold plated and should match the plating on the mating connector for reliable operation.

172-pin DDR SDRAM MicroDIMM

The 172-pin DDR SDRAM MicroDIMMs are similar to the 200-pin DDR SDRAM SODIMMs, but they're about half the physical size so as to fit the very tight form factors of smaller systems. Other than that, they have the same specifications as the 200-pin DDR SDRAM SODIMMs, including the following features:

- JEDEC-standard form factor and pinout
- 64-bit (8-byte) data bus
- DDR (double data rate) SDRAM
- PC1600 (200MHz), PC2100 (266MHz), and PC2700 (333MHz) operation
- 2.5V power
- Serial presence detect (SPD)

The 172-pin DDR SDRAM MicroDIMMs are only 1.8" (45.5mm) long and 1.18" (30mm) high, which is about half the size of an equivalent SODIMM. Unlike SODIMMs, MicroDIMMs do not have any notches in the connector pin area; however, a notch is used on the left side to ensure proper insertion. They also have a unique size that is not interchangeable with other modules. Unlike the DDR SODIMMs, DDR MicroDIMMs do not support ECC (error correcting code) functions.

The 144-pin SDRAM MicroDIMMs are available in PC1600, PC2100, and PC2700 speeds. You can generally use faster modules in place of slower modules, but not the other way around. The speeds of 172-pin DDR SDRAM MicroDIMMs are rated as shown in Table 6.25.

Table 6.25   172-pin DDR SDRAM MicroDIMM Speeds

Module Type	Cycle Time	Frequency SDR/DDR	Module Width	Module Bandwidth
PC2700	6.0ns	166/333MHz	8 bytes	2,666MBps
PC2100	7.5ns	133/266MHz	8 bytes	2,133MBps
PC1600	10.0ns	100/200MHz	8 bytes	1,600MBps

The cycle time in nanoseconds (billionths of a second) matches the single data rate (SDR) clock speed, but double data rate (DDR) modules transfer twice per cycle, so the DDR frequency is always double the SDR frequency. The throughput or bandwidth is simply the DDR frequency times the width, which gives the rate at which data can be read from or written to the module.

As with DDR SDRAM SODIMMs, another performance specification to consider that is related to speed is the *CAS (column address strobe) Latency*, often abbreviated as *CL*. Typically, you find SDRAM modules rated CL 2 or CL 2.5. If possible, choose modules with a lower CL figure, because the motherboard chipset will read that specification out of the SPD ROM on the module and switch to slightly faster cycling rates.

The 172-pin SDRAM MicroDIMMs have the industry-standard form factor shown in Figure 6.8.

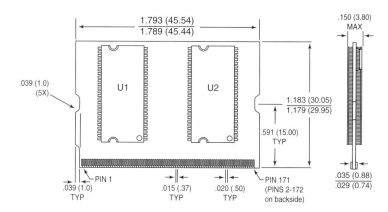

Figure 6.8   172-pin DDR SDRAM MicroDIMM.

All 172-pin DDR SDRAM MicroDIMMs have the odd-numbered pins (1–171) on the front and even-numbered pins (2–172) on the back and are 1.8" (45.5mm) long and 1.18" (30mm) high. The number of actual chips on the modules can vary.

The 172-pin DDR SDRAM MicroDIMMs use an SPD ROM onboard, which the motherboard reads to determine the exact specifications of the modules installed. The ROM is normally a small chip on the module. The modules are keyed via a small notch on the left side of the connector area, which prevents them from being installed backward.

The 172-pin DDR SDRAM MicroDIMMs are available in several versions, with capacities of up to 256MB. The most common sizes are shown in Table 6.26.

Table 6.26   172-pin DDR SDRAM MicroDIMM Module Capacities

Capacity	(Depth × Width)
64MB	(8M × 64b)
128MB	(16M × 64b)
256MB	(32M × 64b)

The capacity can be determined by multiplying the depth by the width. The 172-pin modules have a 64-bit-wide data bus, which is equal to 8 bytes. For example, a 256MB MicroDIMM is arranged internally as 32 million rows, with 64 bits (8 bytes) in each row, for a total of 256 million (32 million × 8) bytes.

The JEDEC standard pinout for 172-pin SDRAM MicroDIMMs is listed in Tables 6.27 and 6.28.

Table 6.27   172-pin DDR SDRAM MicroDIMM Pinout (Front)

Pin	Signal	Pin	Signal	Pin	Signal	Pin	Signal
2	VREF	46	VDD	88	BA1	132	CK1#
4	VSS	48	DM2	90	VDD	134	CK1
6	DQ4	50	DQ22	92	RAS#	136	VSS
8	DQ5	52	VSS	94	CAS#	138	DQ52
10	VDD	54	DQ23	96	NC	140	DQ53
12	DM0	56	DQ28	98	NC	142	VDD
14	DQ6	58	VDD	100	VSS	144	DM6
16	VSS	60	DQ29	102	DQ36	146	DQ54
18	DQ7	62	DM3	104	DQ37	148	VSS
20	DQ12	64	VSS	106	VDD	150	DQ55
22	VDD	66	DQ30	108	DM4	152	DQ60
24	DQ13	68	DQ31	110	DQ38	154	VDD
26	DM1	70	VDD	112	VSS	156	DQ61
28	VSS	72	CKE0	114	DQ39	158	DM7
30	DQ14	74	A11	116	DQ44	160	VSS
32	DQ15	76	A8	118	VDD	162	DQ62
34	VDD	78	A6	120	DQ45	164	DQ63
36	VDD	80	VSS	122	DM5	166	VDD
38	VSS	82	A4	124	VSS	168	SA0
40	VSS	84	A2	126	DQ46	170	SA1
42	DQ20	86	A0	128	DQ47	172	SA2
44	DQ21			130	VDD		

Table 6.28   172-pin DDR SDRAM MicroDIMM Pinout (Back)

Pin	Signal	Pin	Signal	Pin	Signal	Pin	Signal
1	VREF	45	VDD	87	A10/AP	131	VDD
3	VSS	47	DQS2	89	VDD	133	VSS
5	DQ0	49	DQ18	91	BA0	135	VSS
7	DQ1	51	VSS	93	WE#	137	DQ48
9	VDD	53	DQ19	95	S0#	139	DQ49
11	DQS0	55	DQ24	97	NC	141	VDD
13	DQ2	57	VDD	99	VSS	143	DQS6
15	VSS	59	DQ25	101	DQ32	145	DQ50
17	DQ3	61	DQS3	103	DQ33	147	VSS
19	DQ8	63	VSS	105	VDD	149	DQ51
21	VDD	65	DQ26	107	DQS4	151	DQ56
23	DQ9	67	DQ27	109	DQ34	153	VDD
25	DQS1	69	VDD	111	VSS	155	DQ57
27	VSS	71	NC	113	DQ35	157	DQS7
29	DQ10	73	A12	115	DQ40	159	VSS
31	DQ11	75	A9	117	VDD	161	DQ58
33	VDD	77	A7	119	DQ41	163	DQ59
35	CK0	79	VSS	121	DQS5	165	VDD
37	CK0#	81	A5	123	VSS	167	SDA
39	VSS	83	A3	125	DQ42	169	SCL
41	DQ16	85	A1	127	DQ43	171	VDDSPD
43	DQ17			129	VDD		

All DIMM contacts are normally gold plated and should match the plating on the mating connector for reliable operation.

Memory Upgrades

Adding more memory is one of the most common upgrades performed on computers, and portables are no exception. Perhaps the biggest problem with laptop system upgrades is that most have only one or two sockets for additional modules, and often one or both are filled when the system is new. If both are filled, you will have to remove one of the modules when adding another.

For example, many of the higher-powered laptop systems today will accept 2GB to 4GB of RAM and can be ordered with 512MB when new. These same systems normally have only two or four 200-pin DDR or DDR2 SDRAM SODIMM sockets on the motherboard. Unfortunately, because it costs less to purchase two 512MB modules than a single 1GB module, most of the time the system will be delivered with two 512MB modules to make up the 1GB, leaving no other sockets available for expansion in some systems. If you wanted to upgrade that system to 2GB, you would have to literally remove and discard *both* 512MB modules currently in the system and replace them with two 1GB modules, for a total of 2GB. Obviously, throwing all your existing memory away and starting over is not a cheap way to upgrade. If you are ordering a new system, try to ensure that the initial amount of memory you order is supplied on a single module, leaving at least one free socket open for future expansion. Some manufacturers allow you to specify your system that way, but you may have to pay for the service.

Removing or installing memory in most laptop computers is very simple. Most have an access panel on the bottom of the unit that can be removed with one or two screws, as shown in Figure 6.9.

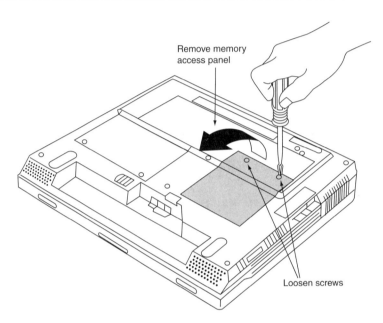

Remove memory
access panel

Loosen screws

Figure 6.9   Removing memory access panel.

If your system is different, you should consult the manual that came with the system for the location of the memory and the methods for gaining access. Once you remove the memory access panel, it is a simple matter to remove or install the DIMMs. Remove the DIMMs by bending the retainers on each side away from the module and then pivoting the module up and out of the socket (see Figure 6.10).

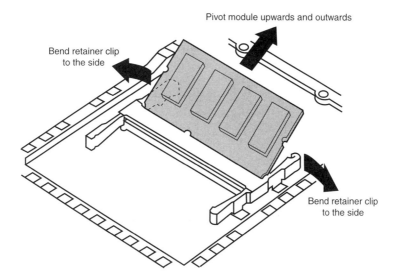

Pivot module upwards and outwards

Bend retainer clip
to the side

Bend retainer clip
to the side

Figure 6.10 Removing a DIMM.

The installation process is just the opposite: Merely slide the connector end of module into the socket (look at the key notch for proper orientation) and then pivot the DIMM downward and allow the retainers to click into place.

CHAPTER 7

Power

This chapter covers power for portable systems. Normally, laptop or portable systems have options for several sources of power, including AC (alternating current; found in the wall sockets of most buildings), power sockets in automobiles and airplanes, and several types of batteries. This chapter examines all the power sources found in a modern portable system and also focuses on power management for portables.

AC/DC Power Supplies

All portable systems at one time or another must depend on an external power source either for operation, to recharge their batteries, or both. The most commonly used external power sources are

- 120V 60Hz AC wall current (USA)
- 240V 50Hz AC wall current (Europe)
- 12V DC current (auto/airplane)

Note that these are nominal values; the tolerances in some areas may allow variations. For example, 120V may actually be anywhere between 100V to 127V, and 240V may actually be from 220V to 240V. Power adapters for laptops and other portable computers are designed with these tolerances in mind and will work within the acceptable ranges. For more information on the specific standards for voltage/frequency as well as the types of plugs used in a given country, see "Electricity around the world" at http://users.pandora.be/worldstandards/electricity.htm.

The internal electronics on most portable systems run on DC (direct current) power of voltages from 2V to 24V, depending on the system and battery design. Some systems can accept several different types of batteries, and some may even supply different voltages. The actual voltage used by the motherboard and processor is normally much less than what the batteries actually supply. The reason is that battery voltage drops as the batteries discharge, and the system electronics require an absolutely steady voltage to operate. To facilitate this, a higher battery voltage is used, which is regulated down to the lower level that the motherboard, processor, and other components need. Also note that the voltage that the external power adapter provides is different from the internal batteries as well. The reason is that modern batteries require the charge voltage and current to be varied during the recharging process, and the external power adapter must simultaneously power the system under a full load during the recharging process as well.

Because the battery-charging circuits require different voltage levels than either the wall outlet or vehicle power systems will supply, some type of external power adapter is required. When designed to convert the 120/240V wall current, these are normally called *AC adapters*, because in addition to transforming the voltage they also convert or rectify AC (alternating current) to DC (direct current), which is then input to the system. Those that run on 12V DC are normally called *DC* or *auto/air adapters*, because 12V DC is the power provided in most automobiles and airplanes. Sometimes these AC or DC adapters are called *power bricks*, because they can easily weigh up to a half pound or more and be the size of a small brick. A very few laptop or portable models incorporate the AC/DC adapter internally within the unit, meaning only a power cord is required to plug them into the wall. This means that all the circuitry normally associated with the adapter is now built in to the system, adding considerably to the size, weight, and heat load of the system. Some laptops don't even have internal batteries and use only an external power source instead. These systems can be operated only when plugged into either a wall or auto/air outlet and are normally sold as portable desktop-replacement systems.

Note

AC (alternating current) is the type of power supplied by wall outlets. AC is so named because it reverses direction at regular intervals, normally 60 times per second (60Hz) in the United States, and 50 times per second (50Hz) in other countries. DC (direct current) is the type of power supplied by batteries, and it maintains a constant direction. Vehicles such as automobiles and aircraft run on DC power, and a portable computer's built-in batteries also supply DC power. Power adapters are used to convert AC to DC as well as to convert DC to the proper voltage level required by each particular system.

When an AC or DC adapter is used, it converts the 120/240V AC or 12V DC to the proper DC input voltage for the system. The problem here is that the actual voltage required can vary from 2V to 24V for different systems (although most are 15V or 16V), and many different types of physical plugs and connectors can be used. Sometimes even the same type of plug can be used on different systems but have the opposite polarity! The fact that different voltages and even polarities can be used on similar plugs means that it is possible in some cases to actually damage a portable system by plugging in the wrong type of power adapter, even though the connector might physically fit. As you can see, it is important to keep the proper adapter with the system for which it is designed. If you lose the adapter or it fails, ordering a new one from the original system vendor or manufacturer is one way to ensure you will get the right one. Normally, most system manufacturers make AC adapters available, and some also offer DC (auto/air) adapters as well.

You have four main issues to consider when plugging an external power adapter into a device:

- **Voltage output**—All portable systems I know of require DC input from 2V through 24V, with most using either 15V or 16V. If you supply the wrong voltage, it may or may not cause damage to the unit, depending on the design of the internal regulators and battery charging circuits.

- **Current**—Most devices (such as portable computers) require DC power input; however, some devices use AC current. Plugging an adapter with AC output into a device requiring DC power (or vice versa) will likely cause damage to the unit.

- **Tip size and shape**—Obviously, the correct size and shape tip is required for the tip to fit into the receptacle and make good contact.

- **Tip polarity (DC only)**—A power tip will normally have an inner and an outer conductor. The inner conductor may be positive or negative (most use a positive inner conductor). If you get this one wrong, it will most likely do permanent damage to the device.

If you study the small writing on the adapter, it normally tells you the voltage output, current capacity and type, and tip polarity (via a small diagram). Unfortunately, although most adapters carry all this information, they don't usually identify what device they came with, and the devices themselves are usually not as well marked for power requirements as the adapters. This means that if you get several adapters mixed up, it can be difficult to determine which adapter goes with which device. For that reason, I recommend labeling each adapter so that you know exactly which device it is intended to power. I also recommend labeling the device as well. Merely affix a small piece of tape to the device and label it with the power output specifications from the adapter, as well as the adapter make and model.

If you mix up or lose adapters, and are unsure of which adapter goes with a specific device, you may need the manual or documentation for the device to determine the power requirements. In some cases the documentation is inadequate. As an example, I was recently trying to use an external FireWire drive that required an external power adapter. The original adapter was lost, and the manual indicated only that the unit required 9V of DC power, but nothing about the tip polarity. I purchased a universal adapter that came with multiple tips and the ability to set different voltages. I determined which tip was required by testing each one, and I set the voltage properly to 9V. However, I didn't know for sure what the tip polarity should be because it was not marked on the unit or in the documentation. Because most devices use a positive inner conductor, I set up the universal adapter that way and plugged it in. After only a few seconds, visible smoke began coming from the drive, and it was destroyed! Obviously, the tip polarity was incorrect, but it was too late to change. All this could have been averted had I properly labeled both the adapter and device when I first unpacked them.

Although it is usually best to use the original power adapters that come with the computer or other device, several companies make universal replacement AC (wall current) or DC (auto/air) power adapters that feature interchangeable tips and voltage settings (see Figure 7.1). Perhaps the best of these is the ChargeSource adapter created by Comarco and distributed exclusively by Targus.

Figure 7.1   ChargeSource universal AC adapter with interchangeable tips.

The ChargeSource adapters incorporate a patented design with interchangeable tips (called PowerTips) that automatically selects the correct voltage and polarity for the intended unit. Interchangeable wall socket plugs allow the unit to operate on any type of wall socket, either in the United States or overseas. A DC (auto/air) version is also available that will plug into any standard 12V automobile or airplane socket (see Figure 7.2).

The ChargeSource power adapters are only a half inch (12.7mm) thick and weigh 8.5 ounces (241 grams) including the cables and will work with almost any laptop, PDA, or cell phone on the market. They are rated at 70 watts of output power, which is enough for most laptops. Note that some laptop models require up to 120 watts of power, and using more power than the adapter is designed to supply may cause it to overheat. Some versions are sold with specific tips, whereas other less commonly used tips are available separately to cover most of the systems on the market. With the right tip, this type of universal adapter can even power cell phones, PDAs, digital cameras, portable printers, and more. The PowerTips are also interchangeable between the universal AC adapter and the universal auto/air adapter, allowing operation from either the wall current or the 12V DC in an automobile or airplane. Both of these adapters are distributed by Targus and are sold by many vendors.

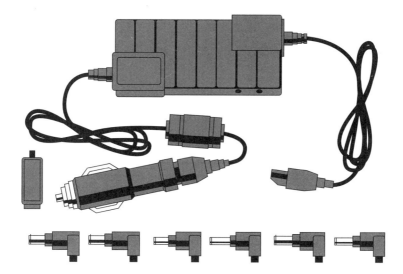

Figure 7.2   ChargeSource universal DC (auto/air) adapter with interchangeable tips.

For more information on the ChargeSource adapters, you can visit these sites:

- `www.comarco.com`
- `www.chargesource.com`
- `www.targus.com`

I recommend having at least one spare power adapter because, as with most power supplies, they take a lot of stress and can potentially fail, leaving you without the ability to run your system or recharge your batteries. I like to take two with me when I travel, and I leave a third behind in my office along with a port replicator. This way, when I return from a trip, I can merely connect the unit to the port replicator, and everything else is already connected.

Batteries

One of the best features of using a laptop computer is that it can run on batteries. Even if you don't normally run your laptop computer on battery power, the fact that the battery is there and can take over instantly whenever necessary is like having an uninterruptible power supply (UPS) built in to the system. A UPS capable of running a full-function PC, including a monitor, normally costs upward of $1,000, and you'll have to spend even more than that if you want one that can run the system for more than just a few minutes. The built-in UPS capability of the modern laptop has saved me from losing my work on several occasions when unexpected power outages have interrupted operation. While desktop users would be down for the count (often losing any unsaved work in the process), laptop users with a fully charged battery can continue working for up to 4 hours or more during a power outage. Although the typical laptop computer costs up to twice as much (or more) as a desktop system of similar speed and power, you should factor in that you are also getting a built-in UPS worth easily $1,000 or more with the deal.

Many people are not aware that laptop computers can have up to three different batteries:

- Main battery (or batteries)
- Suspend/standby battery
- CMOS/clock battery

The first two battery types are rechargeable, whereas the CMOS/clock battery is not. Many systems don't incorporate a suspend/standby battery, instead using only the main battery for power when in Suspend or Standby mode. Most people are aware of the main battery, and many know that like desktop systems, laptops also have a CMOS/clock battery. The other battery found in some laptop models is the suspend/standby battery, which powers the RAM when the system is in Suspend or Standby mode. This battery is rechargeable, just like the main battery, and will power the memory for a limited time when the system is in Suspend or Standby mode. I recommend always saving any work before you use Suspend or Standby mode, because when the main or suspend/standby battery discharges, you will lose everything currently in RAM. If present, the suspend/standby battery normally lasts the life of the system and recharges automatically any time the system is powered on. Not all laptop systems use a suspend/standby battery, and instead draw a small amount of power from the main battery. Unfortunately, if the main battery fully discharges, the suspend will fail and all unsaved information will be lost.

Most systems have an additional "Hibernate" mode, which copies the RAM to the hard disk and then shuts off the system. When the notebook is in Hibernate mode, no power is used, so the system can be left that way and restarted later without losing data. Still, it is possible for the system to lose track of whether it was in Hibernate mode, so I highly recommend saving your work before using this mode.

CMOS/Clock Battery

Portable systems normally incorporate a chip that combines a real-time clock (RTC) with at least 64 bytes (including 14 bytes of clock data) of nonvolatile RAM (NVRAM) memory. This is officially called the *RTC/NVRAM chip*, but it is often referred to as the *CMOS* or *CMOS RAM chip* because the chip is produced using a CMOS (complementary metal-oxide semiconductor) process. CMOS design chips are known for very low power consumption, and the RTC/NVRAM chip is designed to run off a battery for several years. The RTC/NVRAM chip is built in to the motherboard chipset South Bridge or I/O Controller Hub (ICH) component in most modern systems.

The function of the real-time clock should be obvious: The clock enables software to read the date and time and preserves the date and time data even when the system is powered off or unplugged. The NVRAM portion of the chip has another function. It is designed to store the basic system configuration, including the amount of memory installed, types of disk drives installed, Plug and Play device configuration, power-on passwords, and other information. Most chipsets incorporate 256 bytes of NVRAM, of which the clock uses 14 bytes. The system reads this information every time you power it on.

The RTC/NVRAM is powered by a battery while the system is off. This battery preserves the information in the NVRAM and powers the clock. Most systems use a lithium coin cell battery because it has a very long life, especially at the low power draw from the typical RTC/NVRAM chip. Typical batteries include the 20xx series (20mm diameter, varying thicknesses), available in two slightly different battery chemistries. Figure 7.3 shows a cutaway view of a CR20xx lithium coin cell battery.

Table 7.1 lists the specifications of 20xx lithium coin cell batteries.

Table 7.1   20xx Lithium Coin Cell Specifications

Type	Voltage (V)	Capacity (mAh)	Diameter (mm)	Height (mm)
------	-------	--------	--------	------
BR2016	3.00	75	20.00	1.60
BR2020	3.00	100	20.00	2.00
BR2032	3.00	190	20.00	3.20

Table 7.1   Continued

Type	Voltage (V)	Capacity (mAh)	Diameter (mm)	Height (mm)
------	-------	--------	--------	------
CR2012	3.00	55	20.00	1.20
CR2016	3.00	90	20.00	1.60
CR2025	3.00	165	20.00	2.50
CR2032	3.00	220	20.00	3.20

BR = Carbon monoflouride
CR = Manganese dioxide

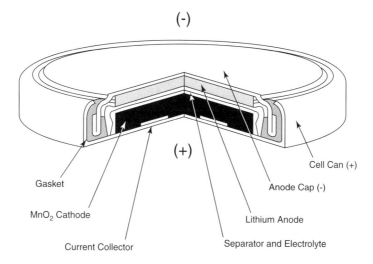

Figure 7.3   CR20xx lithium coin cell construction.

The BR and CR series are normally interchangeable because they have only slight differences in chemistry and performance. The CR types are more plentiful (easier to get) and offer slightly higher capacity. The BR types are useful for higher temperature operation (above 60°C or 140°F).

Battery life can be calculated by dividing the battery capacity by the average current required. For example, a typical CR2032 battery is rated 220 mAh (milli-amp hours), and the RTC/NVRAM circuit in the Intel 855 chipset (for Pentium M mobile processor systems) draws 5 µA (micro-amps) with the power off. In a Pentium M–based laptop using a CR2032 battery and the Intel 855 chipset, battery life can be calculated as follows:

> 220,000 µAh / 5 µA = 44,000 hours = 5 years

If a smaller capacity battery such as the CR2025 is used, battery life becomes this:

> 165,000 µAh / 5 µA = 33,000 hours = 3.7 years

Battery life starts when the system is first assembled, which can be several months or more before you purchase the system, even if it is new. Also, it is possible that the battery may be partially discharged before it is installed in the system, and higher temperatures both in storage and in the system can contribute to shorter battery life. All these reasons and more may cause battery life to be less than might be indicated by calculation.

As the battery drains, output voltage will drop somewhat, and lower battery voltage can impair the accuracy of the RTC (real-time clock). Most lithium coin cell batteries are rated at 3.0V; however, actual readings on a new battery are usually higher. If your system clock seems inaccurate (runs slow, for example), check the voltage on the CMOS battery. The highest accuracy will be obtained if the battery voltage is maintained at 3.0V or higher. Lithium batteries normally maintain a fairly steady voltage until they are nearly fully discharged, whereupon the voltage drops quickly. If you check the battery voltage and find it is below 3.0V, you might consider replacing the battery, even if it is before the intended replacement time.

Main Battery

Relatively limited battery life is one of the biggest complaints users have about portable systems. A great deal has been done to improve the power-management capabilities and efficiency of today's portable computers, and better battery technologies, such as lithium-ion, have also been adopted on many systems. However, the larger power requirements of faster CPUs, more RAM, larger drives, and near-universal adoption of active-matrix displays have left the battery life of a typical portable system approximately the same as it was several years ago.

The goal sought by many mobile users has been the same for many years: a full-featured portable system that can run on a single battery for the entire duration of a transcontinental U.S. airplane flight. Some airlines are now providing 12V automotive-type power connectors under the seat for use with automotive power adapters; in this case, battery life on a plane is no longer an issue. For those who are relegated to using batteries, you still typically must carry two or more battery packs for a 6-hour flight. Although mobile power technologies are improving, the demands of today's systems have also increased. However, although typical battery life has remained in the 2- to 4-hour range for most reputable manufacturers, the new notebooks have the advantage of larger hard drives, bigger and brighter screens, more RAM, faster processors, integrated speakers, and CD-ROM drives. System manufacturers have been able to better manage system power use by selectively turning off or shutting down components that are not being used, which is referred to as *power management*. Through better and better power-management techniques implemented in the latest processors, chipsets, and systems, overall power use has been maintained, even though consumption of individual components (when on) has risen. Such power management is the cornerstone of more recent designs, such as the Intel Centrino, which includes a processor, chipset, and wireless LAN component.

Based on the increasing popularity of these notebook systems, the buying consumer has clearly voiced that a more powerful notebook with continuing average battery life is more important and useful than a system that would run for 6–10 hours but sacrifice features she has grown used to using. For users who simply must have a system that can run for 6–10 hours, check for airlines that are adding at-seat power connections designed for notebook computers.

Battery Types

Battery technology also plays a major role in the portable power issue. Most portable systems today use one of four battery types for their main power batteries:

- Nickel cadmium (NiCd)
- Nickel metal-hydride (NiMH)
- Lithium-ion (Li-ion)
- Lithium-ion polymer (LIP or Li-Poly)

Table 7.2 shows a comparison between the different types of rechargeable batteries used in portable computers.

Table 7.2 Rechargeable Battery Types and Specifications

Specification	NiCd	NiMH	Li-ion	Li-Poly
Energy density (Wh/kg)	60	90	140	120
Avg. cycle life	1500	400	400	400
Cell voltage (nominal)	1.2	1.2	3.6V	3.6V
Memory effect	Yes	Yes	No	No
Relative cost	1	1.2	2	2
Fast charge time (hours)	1	3	3	3
Overcharge danger	Moderate	High	Very High	High
Self-discharge (per month)	20%	30%	10%	10%
First used (year)	1950	1990	1991	1999

The following sections analyze the features and benefits of each of these types of batteries.

Nickel Cadmium (NiCd)

As the oldest of the four technologies, nickel cadmium (NiCd, often called *Ni-Cad*) batteries are rarely used for main power in today's portable systems (although some use NiCd for standby batteries). They have a high current capacity but store less energy than other technologies, resulting in shorter laptop battery runtimes. Overall, NiCd is a very durable technology, offering greater cycle life (discharge/recharge cycles) with less degradation than other types, if properly maintained.

The battery runtime from a NiCd battery's charge can be shortened by as much as 40% if the battery is not periodically fully discharged, or if it is frequently overcharged. For NiCd batteries, permanent damage to the cells can be prevented by periodically discharging them to 1 volt or less, say once every month or so. Despite this so-called "memory" effect, NiCd batteries do hold a charge well when not in use, losing only about 20% of their charge per month. The memory effect is actually due to changes in the crystalline structures inside the battery. Normally, the cadmium material is contained in very tiny crystal structures. When repeated shallow discharges and recharges occur, these crystal structures grow in size, reducing the surface area and thus the total battery capacity. Periodic deep discharges can actually rejuvenate a battery by breaking up the larger crystals, thus restoring the battery capacity to normal levels.

NiCd batteries can be recharged 1,500 times or more, which combined with their high current output, makes them ideal for portable two-way radios or other applications in which high demands are made for short periods of time. NiCd cells are rated at a nominal 1.2V per cell, and in laptop systems were normally combined in packs with 6 or 7 cells combined to produce 8.4V to 9.6V. Despite their durability, their lower energy density (resulting in lower battery runtimes) has caused them to fall out of favor in laptop and portable computers, such that virtually no new systems use NiCd batteries today. The cadmium in NiCd batteries is also considered a toxic metal, and recycling is highly recommended if not required.

Nickel Metal-Hydride (NiMH)

Nickel metal-hydride (NiMH) batteries have become a near universal replacement for nickel cadmium (NiCd) batteries in portable computers. They have the same cell voltage (1.2V), come in the same physical form factors, and use the same charging equipment. Although they cost about 20% more, NiMH batteries have approximately a 40% higher energy density than NiCd batteries, resulting in longer battery runtimes for portable computers. They are less sensitive to the memory effect caused by improper charging and discharging, and they do not use the environmentally dangerous cadmium found in NiCd batteries.

In addition to their slightly higher cost, the main drawback of NiMH batteries is that they can withstand far fewer cycles (discharge/recharge) than NiCd batteries. In other words, while they support 40% longer battery runtimes, they have overall a much shorter life, generally lasting about 400 cycles before they lose their capacity to hold a charge. They also have a recommended discharge current that is lower than that of a NiCd battery (one-fifth to one-half of their rated capacity) and a higher self-discharge rate. NiMH batteries also require more than twice as long to recharge as NiCd batteries. Although they are still used in many portable systems, NiMH batteries are now found mostly in computers at the lower end of the price range, having been replaced by lithium-ion batteries at the midrange and high end.

Lithium-Ion (Li-ion)

As the current industry standard, lithium-ion batteries support longer battery runtimes than NiCd and NiMH technologies, can't be overcharged (due to the special charging equipment required), and hold a charge well when not in use. Li-ion batteries have an extremely high energy density; that is, they store more energy than other types for a given size and weight. This is primarily because lithium is one of the lightest of all metals.

Lithium-ion batteries in laptop systems are really battery packs normally constructed of several individual cells. Each cell puts out between 2.5V (discharged) to 4.2V (fully charged) and is normally rated about 3.6V nominal. The cells are combined in battery packs of normally between 2 to 12 cells, arranged in serial and parallel connections resulting in 7.2V, 10.8V, or 14.4V (nominal) voltage ratings. Capacity ratings generally go from 2000 mAh (milli-amp hours) to 6600 mAh or more. The higher the capacity rating, the longer the battery lasts in a given application.

Lithium is an unstable substance, and when first released, rechargeable lithium batteries had problems. After a number of discharge/recharge cycles, it was found that metallic lithium plating would occur on the lithium electrode, causing a potential thermal runaway condition resulting in a violent reaction. A vent in the battery would prevent an outright explosion; however, extremely hot gases or flames would be released under these conditions, causing damage to the surrounding equipment or even burns to individuals nearby. Several incidents of batteries overheating and venting flames resulted in a number of recalls and redesigns in the early 1990s.

Subsequent models were manufactured using built-in protection circuits that limit the peak voltage of each cell during charge (usually to 4.3V or less), prevent the cell voltage from dropping too low (usually below 2.5V) on discharge, limit the maximum charge and discharge currents, and monitor the cell temperatures. With these electronic precautions, the possibility of thermal runaway and violent reactions has been virtually eliminated. But also because of the careful design requirements for Li-ion batteries, raw cells are not sold to individuals and instead are sold only in assembled battery packs, with the protection circuitry built in.

Various types of Li-ion batteries use different active materials for their positive and negative electrodes. For the positive electrode, higher-output versions use cobalt, whereas lower-output versions use manganese. Negative electrodes use either coke or graphite, each with slightly different discharge profiles.

The main advantages of Li-ion batteries are their high energy density, resulting in the longest battery runtimes in portable computers. They also have a lower self-discharge rate than other types, meaning they will hold a charge longer during nonuse or storage. Finally, they require no maintenance; that is, they do not need periodic deep discharges, as with NiCd and NiMH types. In fact, in Li-on batteries, unlike NiCd and NiMH batteries, periodic deep discharges only serve to use up the fewer remaining charge cycles available.

Li-ion batteries do have a few disadvantages, starting with their higher cost and the need for built-in protection circuitry in order to maintain safe operation. Similar to NiMH batteries, Li-ion types are normally limited to 300 total cycles (some may have higher limits), after which the internal protection circuits will refuse to accept a charge. By about 200 cycles, the full capacity of the battery is normally cut in half, which means that on a full charge it will power the system for only about half the time it would when it was new. But perhaps the biggest drawback is uncontrollable aging. What this means is that there will be a noticeable loss in capacity after the battery ages one year, whether the battery is actually used or not. This continues such that over two or three years the battery will fail to hold a charge, even if it has never been used. Because of this aging characteristic, you should avoid purchasing used Li-ion batteries, and if you keep a laptop or notebook system for more than two years, you will most likely be forced to replace the expensive main battery, no matter how much (or little) the battery was actually used.

Finally, unlike NiCd and NiMH batteries, which can be used in the same system without modification to the circuitry, Li-ion batteries can be used only in systems specifically designed for them. Because of the special charging techniques required, merely inserting a Li-ion battery into a system designed for a NiCd or NiMH can result in the protection circuitry shutting the battery down (permanently in some cases).

Although lithium-ion batteries are the most expensive and finicky of the four technologies, they have come to be used in all but the very low end of the portable system market.

Lithium-Ion Polymer (LIP or Li-Poly)

Lithium-ion polymer is a fourth battery type that has been in development for several years, but has only recently appeared on the market, and has yet to achieve popularity in portable computer usage. Lithium-ion polymer batteries are manufactured using a lithium-ion and cobalt oxide cell with a proprietary polymer electrolyte and can be formed into flat sheets as small as 1mm thick and of almost any size. This allows a very thin battery shape, resulting in designs that can fit in places not previously thought possible (such as behind an LCD panel). Lithium-ion polymer batteries provide an energy density that is somewhat lower than standard Li-ion types, giving up capacity for their thinner and smaller size and weight. Besides allowing thinner designs with less weight and a slightly lower energy density, Li-Poly batteries are similar to standard Li-ion batteries in most other respects and share most of the same characteristics.

Lithium-ion polymer batteries are finding most use in cell phones, PDAs, or other extremely small devices, but their lower energy density as compared to standard Li-ion types has prevented them from achieving widespread use in laptop and notebook systems.

Battery Maintenance

NiCd and NiMH batteries function best when they are completely discharged before being recharged. In fact, NiCd or NiMH batteries that have gone unused for several months should be reconditioned by putting them through two or three full discharge/recharge cycles. You can do this by leaving the system on until it automatically suspends or shuts down; alternatively, battery-conditioning utilities are available that can manage this process for you.

Although lithium-ion batteries do not need such conditioning (in fact, it would unnecessarily use up available charge cycles), there is a situation in which a full discharge and recharge cycle may be beneficial. All modern laptop batteries are intelligent designs, containing special circuits used to indicate the state of charge to the system. These circuits can lose track of the actual state of charge if the battery remains topped off for a period of time. Then the battery gauge indicator becomes inaccurate, resulting in what seems to be shorter runtimes before the gauge drops to zero. Performing a full discharge and recharge cycle allows the intelligent battery "gas gauge" circuits to reset, placing them back in synchronization with the actual state of charge.

Another indication that you need to discharge-cycle your batteries is if charging stops before the charge indicator reaches 100%. Cycling the battery a few times usually corrects this situation and allows for proper charge indication. Lithium-ion batteries are affected the least by incomplete discharging and have a higher discharge cut-off point (2.5V–3V versus 1V for NiCd batteries), but due to the gas gauge circuits, the effect on the apparent life is still noticeable.

Unfortunately, buying a portable computer with a more efficient battery does not necessarily mean that you will realize longer runtimes. Power consumption depends on the components installed in the system, the power-management capabilities provided by the system software, and the size of the battery itself. Some manufacturers, for example, when moving from NiMH to Li-ion batteries, see this as an opportunity to save some space inside the computer. They decide that because they are using a more efficient power-storage technology, they can make the battery smaller and still deliver the same performance.

Battery technology trails behind nearly all the other subsystems found in a portable computer as far as the development of new innovations is concerned. Because of the continuing trend of adding more features and components to mobile computers, their power consumption has risen enormously in recent years, and power systems have barely been capable of keeping up. On a high-end laptop system, a battery life of three hours is very good, even with all the system's power-management features activated.

Using Multiple Batteries

Carrying several batteries can give you the ability to work for longer periods of time while unplugged or away from an AC power outlet. The standard method would be to carry a spare main battery that is fully charged. Then, when the main battery is low, you can swap the main battery with your fully charged spare and continue working on a fresh charge. In addition to carrying a spare main battery, systems that have swappable bays usually have bay batteries available as well. There are some important issues to consider when using spare main batteries as well as bay batteries.

I almost always recommend purchasing a spare main battery immediately when purchasing a new laptop. You can use it to effectively double the amount of time you can operate the system while unplugged, and the fact is, most lithium-ion batteries have a fixed life of about 300 cycles, and by about 200 cycles they will power the system for only half the time as when they were new. By alternating between two batteries, you effectively double the life of both of them by limiting the total number of cycles each one will see. Another often overlooked benefit is that batteries can be problematic devices, and if you are having problems with your main battery, having a known-good spare to swap in for testing purposes is very useful. For example, if the battery refuses to take a charge or the system will not run on battery power, you can swap in the known-good spare to determine if the problem is in the battery or perhaps the laptop or AC adapter instead.

You cannot swap a main battery with the system operating normally, even if it is plugged in. Before removing the battery, you have to either shut down the system completely or put the system into Standby or Hibernate mode. In addition, Standby mode can be used during a main battery swap only if the system actually has a separate Standby battery to power the RAM. Most laptops no longer include a separate Standby battery, which means that if you do put the system into Standby mode and remove the main battery, the state of the system that had been saved in RAM will be lost, including all unsaved work. When you restart the system, it will not resume from Standby, but will reboot from scratch instead, possibly with an error message indicating an improper shutdown. Unless you are sure your system has a Standby battery, the only safe way to replace the main battery is to either put the system into Hibernate mode or to shut it down completely.

Setting Your Laptop to Hibernate

If you are using Windows XP and want to set your laptop to Hibernate, note that you will normally see only Stand By, Turn Off, and Restart buttons as available options when selecting the Turn Off Computer option. To select Hibernate, press and hold the Shift key on the keyboard, which changes the Stand By button to Hibernate.

If the Hibernate option does not appear or if Hibernate is missing as an option in other Windows versions, check to see that hibernation is enabled via the Power Options or Power Management tool in the Control Panel.

To do this, open the Power Options or Power Management tool in the Control Panel, select the Hibernate tab, and check the Enable Hibernation box. If there is no Hibernate tab under Power Options or Power Management, your system may not support Hibernation. Check with your system manufacturer to see if there are any special power management drivers you may need to download and install.

One other way manufacturers are addressing the battery life problem is by designing systems capable of carrying two batteries internally. The inclusion of multipurpose swappable device bays within the system's case on some laptops enables users to replace the CD/DVD, second hard drive, or floppy drive with a second battery pack, effectively doubling the computer's battery life.

Most laptops that include one or more swappable device bays usually have a special device bay battery as an available accessory. These are usually different from the main battery; however, for a few rare models they might be the same. Because they normally have a different form factor, they are not physically interchangeable with the main battery. In other words, the main battery will not work in the device bay, and the bay battery will not work in the main battery compartment. Swappable bay batteries usually have about the same or slightly less overall power capacity (measured in milli-amp hours or watt-hours) as the main battery, which means that using a bay battery can virtually double your battery running time.

Swappable bay batteries have one major advantage over carrying a spare main battery, and that is they are seamless in operation. This means that the system automatically and seamlessly switches from one battery to the other when one of them runs down, with no interruption at all in operation. Conversely, when the system is connected to an AC adapter, charging is automatic as well. Once the main battery is charged, the system will automatically switch to charging the bay battery as well. The overall net effect with both a main and bay battery installed is just as if you have a main battery with twice the capacity.

Another advantage of a bay battery is that it can be hot-swapped under most operating systems. This means you can install or remove the battery from the system while it is operating normally, without the need to hibernate or power off the system. For example, say you are operating under battery power and currently have a DVD drive in the swappable bay, and have a fully charged bay battery carried separately. If the main battery power is running dangerously low, you can simply remove the DVD drive from the bay and insert the bay battery while the system is operating. Unlike when changing a main battery, when inserting or removing a bay battery, you do not need to put the system into Standby mode, Hibernate mode, or power it off.

One problem with having a spare main battery and/or swappable bay battery is that they can normally be recharged only when installed in the system. If you have several spares, this can be somewhat inconvenient as it may mean juggling several batteries around in and out of the system order to get them all charged. To alleviate this problem, most of the premium laptop manufacturers such as Lenovo (formerly IBM) and Toshiba have optional external battery chargers that can charge two batteries simultaneously. If you have several extra batteries and want an easy way to keep them all fully charged and ready to go, an external battery charger is a great option.

Finally, another option for extended runtime is to use an external battery like the N-Charge by Valence Technology (www.valence.com). This external battery uses interchangeable power tips to plug into your laptop just like your AC adapter. When the N-Charge is plugged in, your laptop thinks it is on AC power, and not only will the external battery run the system that way, it will also charge your laptop's internal batteries as well. These devices are normally rated for about 120 watt-hours of power, which is about twice the power capability of most internal laptop batteries. That means that if your internal battery would run your system for 4 hours, using one of these external batteries could add up to 8 hours of additional use, for a total of 12 hours of runtime.

Fuel Cells

Fuel cells are a promising source of power that may be used in future laptops and other portable devices. Fuel cells can be used to either replace or augment battery operation.

A fuel cell is a power-generating device that converts chemical energy into electrical energy. Batteries store electrical energy as chemical energy (during the recharging process), and later convert the stored chemical energy back into electrical energy (while discharging). Fuel cells are like batteries in that they convert chemical energy into electrical energy; however, unlike a battery, a fuel cell is "recharged" by refueling. Therefore, instead of taking hours to recharge, a fuel cell can be refueled in seconds, and can consequently supply power almost continuously.

Fuel cells typically combine a fuel (usually hydrogen) with oxygen to produce electricity. The byproduct of this reaction is pure water, heat, and electrical energy. Fuel cells operate by creating an electrolytic charge between a positively charged anode and a negatively charged cathode separated by an electrolyte. When hydrogen is used as the basic fuel, this reaction yields only water and heat as byproducts while converting chemical energy into electricity, as shown in Figure 7.4.

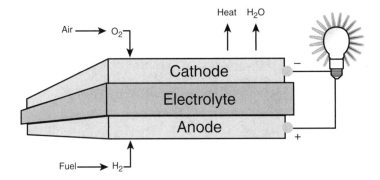

Figure 7.4   Fuel cell operation.

There are actually several different types of fuel cells using different fuels and electrolytes. Many require dangerous fuels or operate at extremely high temperatures, making them unsuitable for personal use. The type of fuel cell being designed for laptop computers and other portable devices is called a direct methanol fuel cell, or DMFC. Compared to other fuel cell technologies, a DMFC works at lower operating temperatures and uses methanol as a fuel, which has a high hydrogen content and is easy to store.

Current fuel cell technology compares favorably to rechargeable battery technology such as lithium-ion in both energy output and power density, and future fuel cells are expected to improve dramatically (see Table 7.3).

Table 7.3   Fuel Cells Versus Li-ion Batteries

Feature	Li-ion Battery Technology	Current Fuel Cell Technology	Fuel Cell Technology in 2010
Specific Power	50 Watt/kg	30 Watt/kg	100 Watt/kg
Power Density	60 Watt/liter	30 Watt/liter	100 Watt/liter
Energy Density	150 Watt*hr/liter	500 Watt*hr/liter	1,000 Watt*hr/liter
Cost	$3/Watt	$5/W	$3/Watt
Lifetime	300–500 cycles	1,000 hours	5,000 hours

Fuel cells have the advantage that they produce energy as long as fuel is continuously supplied, whereas batteries have to be periodically recharged. Fuel cells also do not self-discharge when not in use, and are more environmentally friendly than batteries when it comes to both manufacturing and disposal.

While it may be a few years before fuel cells replace rechargeable batteries in laptops, companies like Toshiba and NEC have been working on fuel cell technology for several years now and have introduced several prototypes. NEC demonstrated the first working notebook PC with a prototype external fuel cell in February 2003, and Toshiba followed with its first external fuel cell prototype in March (see Figure 7.5).

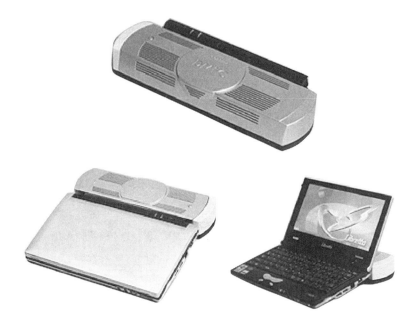

Figure 7.5   The laptop fuel cell prototype shown by Toshiba in March 2003.

These early external fuel cells had an average output of 12W, a maximum output of 20W, and could run about five hours on a replaceable methanol fuel cartridge. Just a few months later in June 2003, NEC unveiled the first prototype laptop with an internal fuel cell (see Figure 7.6).

Figure 7.6   The first prototype laptop with an internal fuel cell shown by NEC in June 2003.

Later on October 19, 2004, NEC announced development of a laptop that included a separate fuel cell unit (see Figure 7.7). This allowed the laptop to dock with the fuel cell as well as to run on internal batteries. This fuel cell had a higher energy density and output compared to the previous models.

Figure 7.7   Protoype laptop with a separate fuel cell shown by NEC in October 2004.

As fuel cell technology has evolved, smaller and smaller cells have become possible. On February 28, 2005, Toshiba announced that Guinness World Records had officially certified its highly compact direct methanol fuel cell (DMFC) as the world's smallest DMFC, with dimensions of only 22×56×4.5mm (9.1mm with fuel tank), which is just about as long and wide as an average thumb (see Figure 7.8).

Figure 7.8   The world's smallest fuel cell shown by Toshiba in February 2005.

This tiny fuel cell is designed to power personal electronics devices such as PDAs (Personal Digital Assistants), cell phones, or MP3 players for as long as 20 hours on a single 2cc charge of highly concentrated methanol.

Fuel cells look to be an excellent future source of energy for laptops, since they can be "recharged" in seconds by merely inserting a new fuel cartridge. While there has been a lot of exciting development occurring in fuel cells over the past few years, it will likely be several more years before fuel cells become commercially viable. Besides cost issues, several technological and safety hurdles must be overcome. For example, since these fuel cells are powered by methanol (a flammable liquid), they may not be allowed on aircraft until the FAA regulations regarding such materials are modified or changed. Once the technological, cost, safety and regulatory problems are solved, fuel cells should be an excellent auxiliary or even main power source for future laptops and other portable computing devices.

Power Management

Power management is defined as the capability of the system to automatically enter power-conserving modes during periods of inactivity. Two main classes of power management exist. The original standard was called *Advanced Power Management (APM)* and has been supported by most systems since Intel first released the 386 and 486 processors. More recently, a new type of power management called *Advanced Configuration and Power Interface (ACPI)* was developed and began appearing in systems in 1998. Most systems sold in 1998 or later support the more advanced ACPI type of power management. In APM, the hardware does the actual power management, and the operating system or other software has little control. With ACPI, the operating system and BIOS now handle the power management instead of the hardware. This makes the control more centralized and easier to access, and it enables applications to work with power-management functions.

Various components in a computer do not need to run continuously while the system is turned on. Mobile systems often conserve battery power by shutting down these components based on the activities of the user. If, for example, you open a text file in an editor and the entire file is read into memory, there is no need for the hard drive to spin while you are working on the file.

After a certain period of inactivity, a power-management system can park the hard drive heads and stop the platters from spinning until you save the file to disk or issue any other command that requires drive access. Other components, such as floppy and CD-ROM drives and PC Cards, can also be powered down when not in use, resulting in a significant reduction of the power needed to run the system.

Most portables also have systemic power-saver modes that suspend the operation of the entire system when it is not in use. The names assigned to these modes can differ, but there are usually two system states. They differ in that one continues to power the system's RAM, whereas the other does not. Typically, a "Suspend" mode shuts down virtually the entire system (except for the memory) after a preset period of inactivity. This requires only a small amount of power and allows the system to be reawakened in a few seconds, rather than having to go through the complete boot process. When in this "Standby" mode, the memory is maintained by the main battery, or the standby battery if the main battery is dead or you are changing the main battery. The standby battery usually powers the RAM for a few minutes to a few hours or more in some models. For this reason, it is important that you save any work before suspending the system.

Portable systems usually have a "Hibernate" mode as well, which writes the current contents of the system's memory to a special file on the hard disk and then shuts down the system, erasing memory in the process. The Hibernate mode does not require any power from either the main or standby batteries, so a system can theoretically hibernate indefinitely. When the computer is reactivated (powered up), it reads the contents of the hibernation file back into memory, restoring the system to exactly the condition it was in when hibernation started, and then work can continue. The reactivation process takes a bit longer than a normal resume from Suspend mode, but the system conserves more power by shutting down the memory array. Either mode is much faster than cold-booting the system.

Note

The memory swap file used for Hibernate mode might, in some machines, be located in a special partition on the hard drive dedicated to this purpose. If you inadvertently destroy this partition, you might need a special utility from the system manufacturer to re-create the file. Newer operating systems such as Windows Me, 2000, and XP create their own hibernation file, normally called *hiberfil.sys* and stored in the root directory of the system drive.

In most cases, these functions are defined by the APM standard, a document developed jointly by Intel and Microsoft that defines an interface between an operating system's power-management policy driver and the hardware-specific software that addresses devices with power-management capabilities. This interface is usually implemented in the system BIOS.

Advanced Power Management

Advanced Power Management (APM) is a specification jointly developed by Intel and Microsoft that defines a series of interfaces between power-management–capable hardware and a computer's operating system. When it is fully activated, APM can automatically switch a computer between five states, depending on the system's current activity. Each state represents a further reduction in power use, accomplished by placing unused components into a low-power mode. The five system states are as follows:

- **Full On**—The system is completely operational, with no power management occurring.
- **APM Enabled**—The system is operational, with some devices being power-managed. Unused devices can be powered down and the CPU clock slowed or stopped.
- **APM Standby**—The system is not operational, with most devices in a low-power state. The CPU clock can be slowed or stopped, but operational parameters are retained in memory. When triggered by a specific user or system activity, the system can return to the APM Enabled state almost instantaneously.
- **APM Suspend**—The system is not operational, with most devices unpowered. The CPU clock is stopped and operational parameters are saved to disk for later restoration. When triggered by a wakeup event, the system returns to the APM Enabled state relatively slowly.
- **Off**—The system is not operational. The power supply is off.

APM requires support from both hardware and software to function. Newer systems incorporate software-controlled power-on and power-off capability built in to the hardware. Manufacturers are also integrating the same sort of control features into other system components, such as motherboards, monitors, and disk drives.

Operating systems that support APM trigger power-management events by monitoring the activities performed by both the computer user and the applications running on the system. However, the OS does not directly address the power-management capabilities of the hardware. All versions of Windows from 3.1 up include APM support.

A system can have many hardware devices and many software functions participating in APM functions, which makes communication difficult. To address this problem, both the operating system and the hardware have an abstraction layer that facilitates communication between the various elements of the APM architecture.

The operating system runs an APM driver that communicates with the various applications and software functions that trigger power-management activities, while the system's APM-capable hardware devices all communicate with the system BIOS. The APM driver and the BIOS communicate directly, completing the link between the OS and the hardware.

Therefore, for APM to function, support for the standard must be built in to the system's individual hardware devices, the system BIOS, and the operating system (which includes the APM driver). Without all these components, APM activities cannot occur.

Advanced Configuration and Power Interface

As power-management techniques continue to develop, maintaining the complex information states necessary to implement more advanced functions becomes increasingly difficult for the BIOS. Therefore, another standard was developed by Intel, Microsoft, and Toshiba. Called *Advanced Configuration and Power Interface (ACPI)*, this standard was designed to implement power-management functions in the operating system. Microsoft Windows 98, Me, 2000, and XP automatically use ACPI if ACPI functions are found in the system BIOS when these operating systems are first installed. The need to update system BIOSes for ACPI support is one reason many computer vendors have recommended performing a BIOS update before installing Windows 98, Me, 2000, or XP.

If your BIOS and operating system support ACPI, full power-management control is now done by the operating system rather than by the BIOS. ACPI is intended to offer a single place for power-management and system-configuration control; in the past, with APM you would often be able to configure power-management settings in the BIOS setup as well as the operating system. This has often resulted in settings that overlap or conflict with each other. ACPI is supported in newer systems in lieu of APM.

Tip

If, for any reason, you find that power-management activities cause problems on your system, such as operating system freeze-ups or hardware malfunctions, the easiest way to disable APM is through the system BIOS. Most BIOSes that support APM include an option to disable it. This breaks the chain of communication between the operating system and the hardware, causing all power-management activities to cease. Although you also can achieve the same end by removing the APM driver from the operating system, Windows 9x's Plug and Play (PnP) feature detects the system's APM capabilities whenever you restart the computer, and attempts to reinstall the APM driver.

If you have a newer system with ACPI, you can disable the power-management settings via the Power Management icon in the Windows control panel.

Placing power management under the control of the OS enables a greater interaction with applications. For example, a program can indicate to the operating system which of its activities are crucial, forcing an immediate activation of the hard drive, and which can be delayed until the next time the drive is activated for some other reason. For example, a word processor may be set to automatically save files in the background, which an OS using ACPI can then delay until the drive is activated for some other reason, resulting in fewer random spin-ups of the drive.

ACPI goes far beyond the previous standard, Advanced Power Management (APM), which consisted mainly of processor, hard disk, and display control. ACPI controls not only power but also all the Plug and Play hardware configuration throughout the system. With ACPI, system configuration (Plug and Play) and power-management configuration are no longer controlled via the BIOS setup; they are instead controlled entirely within the operating system.

ACPI enables the system to automatically turn internal peripherals on and off (such as CD-ROM drives, network cards, hard disk drives, and modems) as well as external devices such as printers, monitors, or any devices connected to serial, parallel, USB, video, or other ports in the system. ACPI technology also enables peripherals to turn on or wake up the system. For example, a telephone answering machine application can request that it be able to respond to answer the telephone within one second. Not only is this possible, but if the user subsequently presses the power or sleep button, the system will only go into the deepest sleep state that is consistent with the ability to meet the telephone answering application's request.

ACPI enables system designers to implement a range of power-management features that are compatible with various hardware designs while using the same operating system driver. ACPI also uses the Plug and Play BIOS data structures and takes control over the Plug and Play interface, providing an operating system–independent interface for configuration and control.

ACPI defines several system states and substates. There are four Global System states labeled from G0 through G3, with G0 being the fully operational state and G3 being mechanically turned off. Global System states are immediately obvious to the user of the system and apply to the entire system as a whole. Within the G0 state, there are four CPU Power states (C0–C3) and four Device Power states (D0–D3) for each device. Within the C0 CPU Power state there are up to 16 CPU Performance states (P0–P15).

Device power states are states for individual devices when the system is in the G0 (Working) state. The device states may or may not be visible to the user. For example, it may be obvious when a hard disk has stopped or when the monitor is off; however, it may not be obvious that a modem or other device has been shut down. The device power states are somewhat generic; many devices do not have all four power states defined.

Within the G1 Global Sleep state, there are four Sleep states (S1–S4). The G2 Global Soft Off state is also known as the *S5 Sleep state*, in which case the system is powered off but still has standby power. Finally, G3 is the Mechanical Off state, where all power is disconnected from the system.

The following list shows the definitions and nested relationship of the various Global, CPU/Device Power, and Sleep states:

- **G0 Working**—This is the normal working state in which the system is running and fully operational. Within this state, the Processor and Device Power states apply. The Device Power states are defined as follows:

  - **G0/D0 Fully-On**—The device is fully active.

  - **G0/D1**—Depends on the device; uses less power than D0.

  - **G0/D2**—Depends on the device; uses less power than D1.

  - **G0/D3 Off**—The device is powered off (except for wake-up logic).

The Processor Power states are defined as follows:

- **G0/C0 CPU On**—Normal processor operation.
- **G0/C1 CPU Halted**—The processor is halted.
- **G0/C2 CPU Stopped**—The clock has been stopped.
- **G0/C3 CPU/Cache Stopped**—The clock has been stopped and cache snoops are ignored.

■ **G1 Sleeping**—The system appears to be off but is actually in one of four Sleep states—up to full hibernation. How quickly the system can return to G0 depends on which of the Sleep states the system has selected. In any of these Sleep states, system context and status are saved such that they can be fully restored. The Sleep states available in the Global G1 state are defined as follows:

- **G1/S1 Halt**—A low-latency idle state. The CPU is halted; however, system context and status are fully retained.
- **G1/S2 Halt-Reset**—Similar to the S1 sleeping state except that the CPU and cache context is lost, and the CPU is reset upon wakeup.
- **G1/S3 Suspend to RAM**—All system context is lost except memory. The hardware maintains memory context. The CPU is reset and restores some CPU and L2 context upon wakeup.
- **G1/S4 Suspend to Disk (Hibernation)**—The system context and status (RAM contents) have been saved to nonvolatile storage—usually the hard disk. This is also known as *Hibernation*. To return to G0 (working) state, you must press the power button, and the system will restart, loading the saved context and status from where they were previously saved (normally the hard disk). Returning from G2/S5 to G0 requires a considerable amount of latency (time).

■ **G2/S5 Soft Off**—This is the normal power-off state that occurs after you select Shutdown or press the power button to turn the system off. The system and all devices are essentially powered off; however, the system is still plugged in and standby power is coming from the power supply to the motherboard, allowing the system to wake up (power on) if commanded by an external device. No hardware context or status is saved. The system must be fully rebooted to return to the G0 (working) state.

■ **G3 Mechanical Off**—Power is completely removed from the system. In most cases this means the system must be unplugged or the power turned off via a power strip. This is the only state in which it is save to disassemble the system. Except for the CMOS/clock circuitry, power consumption is completely zero.

Figure 7.9 shows the relationships between the various ACPI Global, Device/CPU, and Sleep states.

In normal use, a system alternates between the G0 (Working) and G1 (Sleeping) states. In the G1 (Working) state, individual devices and processors can be power-managed via the Device Power (D1–D3) and Processor Power (C1–C3) states. Any device that is selectively turned off can be quickly powered on in a short amount of time, from virtually instantaneous to only a few seconds (such as a hard disk spinning up).

When the system is idle (no keyboard or mouse input) for a preset period of time, the system enters the Global G1 (Sleeping) state, which means also selecting one of the S1–S4 sleep states. In these states the system appears to be off, but all system context and status are saved, enabling the system to return to exactly where it left off, with varying amounts of latency. For example, returning to the G0 (Working) state from the G1/S4 (Hibernation) state requires more time than when returning from the G1/S3 (Suspend) state.

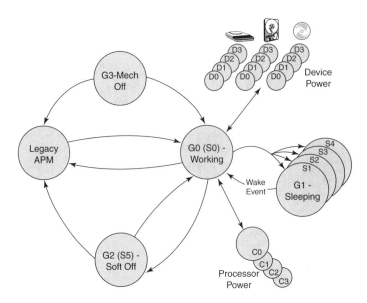

Figure 7.9   ACPI Global, Device/CPU, and Sleep states.

When the user presses the power button to turn the system off, or if she selects Shutdown via the operating system, the system enters the G2/S5 (Soft Off) state. In this state no context is saved, and the system is completely off except for standby power. Fully disconnecting AC or battery power causes the system to be in the Global G3 (Mechanical Off) state, which is the only state in which the system should be disassembled.

During the system setup and boot process, ACPI performs a series of checks and tests to see whether the system hardware and BIOS support ACPI. If support is not detected or is found to be faulty, the system typically reverts to standard Advanced Power Management control, which is referred to as *legacy power management* under ACPI. If problems with power management are detected during bootup, the system may lock up with either a red or blue screen showing an ACPI error code.

A red screen indicates that the problem is probably related to hardware or the BIOS. A blue screen indicates that the problem is probably related to software or is an obscure problem. The ACPI error codes are described in Table 7.4.

Table 7.4   ACPI Error Codes

Error Code	Description
1xxx -	Indicates an error during the initialization phase of the ACPI driver and usually means the driver can't read one or more of the ACPI tables
2xxx -	Indicates an ACPI machine language (AML) interpreter error
3xxx -	Indicates an error within the ACPI driver event handler
4xxx -	Indicates thermal-management errors
5xxx -	Indicates device power-management errors

Virtually all these errors are the result of partial or incomplete ACPI implementations or incompatibilities in either the BIOS or device drivers. If you encounter any of these errors, contact your motherboard manufacturer for an updated BIOS or the device manufacturers for updated drivers.

APM BIOS Power Management Menu

Most of the BIOS Setup settings related to power management are for APM mode, which will be used only if you run legacy operating systems that are not ACPI aware. In APM mode, BIOS reduces power consumption by spinning down hard drives and reducing power to or turning off monitors that comply with Video Electronics Standards Association (VESA) and Display Power-Management Signaling (DPMS). While in Standby mode, the system can still respond to external interrupts, such as those from keyboards, mice, fax/modems, and network adapters. For example, any keyboard or mouse activity brings the system out of Standby mode and immediately restores power to the monitor.

If both the motherboard BIOS and operating system support ACPI, the operating system uses ACPI to take over the power management, even overriding the APM BIOS settings.

Some systems feature a number of different power-management settings in their BIOSes, which are especially important if you are not using an ACPI-aware operating system. Some of the more common settings are shown in Table 7.5.

Table 7.5   Typical Power-Management Settings

ACPI Function	Select Enabled only if your operating system supports the ACPI specification. Windows 98 and all later versions support ACPI.
Power Management	This option enables you to select the type (or degree) of power saving for Doze, Standby, and Suspend modes. The following are the individual mode settings: **Max Saving**—Maximum power savings. Inactivity period is 1 minute in each mode. **User Define**—Set each mode individually. Select timeout periods in the section for each mode. **Min Saving**—Minimum power savings. Inactivity period is 1 hour in each mode (except the hard drive).
PM Control by APM	If Advanced Power Management (APM) is installed on your system, selecting Yes gives better power savings.
Video Off Method	Determines the manner in which the screen is turned blank.
V/H SYNC+Blank	The system turns off vertical and horizontal synchronization ports and writes blanks to the video buffer.
DPMS Support	Select this option if your monitor supports the DPMS standard of VESA. Use the software supplied for your video subsystem to select video power-management values.
Blank Screen	The system writes only blanks to the video buffer.
Video Off After	As the system moves from lesser to greater power-saving modes, select the mode in which you want the screen to turn blank.
MODEM Use IRQ	Name the IRQ line assigned to the modem (if any) on your system. Activity of the selected IRQ always awakens the system.
Doze Mode	After the selected period of system inactivity, the CPU clock throttles to a small percentage of its duty cycle: between 10% and 25% for most chipsets. All other devices still operate at full speed.
Standby Mode	After the selected period of system inactivity, the CPU clock stops, the hard drive enters an idle state, and the L2 cache enters a power-save mode. All other devices still operate at full speed.
Suspend Mode	After the selected period of system inactivity, the chipset enters a hardware-suspend mode, stopping the CPU clock and possibly causing other system devices to enter power management modes.

(continues)

Table 7.5   Continued

HDD Power Down	After the selected period of drive inactivity, any system IDE devices compatible with the ATA-2 specification or later power-manage themselves, putting themselves into an idle state after the specified timeout and then waking themselves up when accessed.
Throttle Duty Cycle	When the system enters Doze mode, the CPU clock runs only part of the time. You can select the percentage of time the clock runs.
VGA Active Monitor	When this setting is enabled, any video activity restarts the global timer for Standby mode.
Soft Off by PWR-BTTN	When you select Instant Off or Delay 4 Sec., turning off the system with the On/Off button places the system in a very low power-usage state, either immediately or after 4 seconds, with only enough circuitry receiving power to detect power button activity or Resume by Ring activity.
CPUFAN Off in Suspend	When this setting is enabled, the CPU fan turns off during Suspend mode.
Resume by Ring	When this setting is enabled, an input signal on the serial Ring Indicator (RI) line (in other words, an incoming call on the modem) awakens the system from a soft off state.
Resume by Alarm	When this setting is enabled, you can set the date and time at which the real-time clock (RTC) alarm awakens the system from Suspend mode.
Date (of Month) Alarm	Select a date in the month when you want the alarm to go off.
Time (hh:mm:ss) Alarm	Set the time you want the alarm to go off.
Wake Up On LAN	When this setting is enabled, an input signal from a local area network (LAN) awakens the system from a soft off state.
IRQ8 Break [Event From]	You can select Enabled or SuspendDisabled for monitoring of IRQ8 (the real-time clock) so that it does not awaken the system from Suspend mode.
Reload Global Timer Events	When this setting is enabled, an event occurring on eachdevice listed restarts the global timer for Standby mode: IRQ3-7, 9-15, NMI Secondary IDE 1 Primary IDE 0 Floppy Disk Primary IDE 1 Serial Port Secondary IDE 0 Parallel Port

Using the power-management settings in the BIOS Setup is especially helpful if you are using an older operating system or one that is not ACPI aware, such as Windows 95, DOS, or Linux. If you are using an ACPI-aware operating system such as Windows 98/Me, 2000, or XP, it is better to control the power-management settings through the OS. Many laptop systems also include their own custom supplemental utility software for power management or control, which can add to the operating system ACPI control.

CHAPTER 8

Expansion Card Buses

In an effort to give notebook computers the kind of expandability users have grown used to in desktop systems, the Personal Computer Memory Card International Association (PCMCIA) established several standards for credit card–size (and smaller) expansion boards that fit into small slots found in laptop and other portable computers such as Tablet PCs. These slots are designed to be externally accessible so that the cards can be quickly inserted and removed without opening up the system. They are also designed to be hot-puggable, meaning they can be inserted or removed with the system running.

PCMCIA was founded in 1989 as a non-profit trade association to establish technical standards for PC Card technology. Originally, the PCMCIA also worked with Japan Electronic Industry Development Association (JEIDA) on some of the earlier standards, and currently PCMCIA has more than 200 member companies worldwide. The development and evolution of the PCMCIA's PC Card and new ExpressCard standards have proven to be successful in a market notorious for proprietary designs.

The words "Memory Card" in the PCMCIA name allude to the original 1.0 specification it released in September 1990, which was for memory cards only. The 2.0 release that came in September 1991 added support for input/output (I/O) cards as well. Subsequent releases have enhanced the standard further, adding higher performance modes, lower power consumption, and greater compatibility. While the original PCMCIA standard was based on the 16-bit AT-bus (also called ISA for Industry Standard Architecture), the latest ExpressCard standard is based on the high-speed PCI Express serial bus found in the latest desktop systems, as well as USB 2.0. Over the years from PCMCIA cards to PC Cards (CardBus) and ExpressCards, expansion cards for laptops have grown well beyond their simple memory card origins. Table 8.1 shows the history of PCMCIA, PC Card, and ExpressCard standards and revisions.

Table 8.1   PCMCIA, PC Card, and ExpressCard Revisions

Standard	Date Released	Major Features/Changes
PCMCIA 1.0 (JEIDA 4.0)	June 1990	Based on 16-bit AT-bus (ISA) 68-pin memory-only interface Type I/II form factors Card Information Structure (CIS) defined
PCMCIA 2.0 (JEIDA 4.1)	September 1991	PC Card name adopted I/O interface added Dual-voltage memory card support Environmental requirements Socket Services API specification Enhanced Metaformat (geometry and interleaving tuples added) XIP (eXecute In Place) spec. added
PCMCIA 2.01	November 1992	PC Card ATA specification Type III form factor Auto-Indexing Mass Storage (AIMS) specification Card Services API specification Enhanced Socket Services support Enhanced Metaformat
PCMCIA 2.1 (JEIDA 4.2)	July 1993	Card and Socket Services enhanced Electrical and physical spec. enhanced Enhanced Metaformat
PC Card 5.0	February 1995	32-bit CardBus added, based on PCI CIS (Card Information Structure) required Low voltage (3.3V) only operation

Table 8.1   Continued

Standard	Date Released	Major Features/Changes
		Hardware DMA support Advanced Power Management (APM) added Multi-function cards Guidelines document added
PC Card 5.01	March 1995	General editorial changes
PC Card 5.02	May 1995	Electrical spec. editorial changes
PC Card 5.03	November 1995	Support for custom interfaces added
PC Card 5.04	March 1996	Zoomed Video support added Flash Translation Layer (FTL)
PC Card 6.0	March 1997	Thermal ratings system ISDN, Security, and Instrumentation Card Tuples Hot Dock/Undock support Streamlined configuration
PC Card 6.1	April 1998	PCI power management Small PC Card form factor Win32 Socket Services bindings
PC Card 7.0	February 1999	PC Card memory paging Digital Video Broadcast (DVB) interface WinNT 4.0 Kernel mode Socket Services bindings
PC Card 7.1	March 2000	OpenCable POD interface support
PC Card 7.2	November 2000	Removal of DMA support Zoomed Video port register model Updated PC Card ATA spec. Limited host guidelines
PC Card 8.0	April 2001	CardBay USB interface Vcore supplemental voltage added
PC Card 8.1	2003	Dedicated LPC (Low Pin Count) interfaces
ExpressCard 1.0	September 2003	PCI Express and USB 2.0 combined ExpressCard/34 and 54 form factors

Note: A tuple gives a set of things that participate in a relation between those things. For example, John and Jane can be linked by the marriage relation and classified as the tuple (John, Jane).

The following sections discuss these expansion card buses in further detail.

PC Cards (PCMCIA)

Although they were originally called *PCMCIA Cards*, after the second release of the specification in 1991, these cards are more accurately (and officially) called *PC Cards* instead. However, to this day many people (including myself) still call them PCMCIA Cards, even though that is no longer technically correct.

Modern PC Cards support a variety of applications; the functionality that can be added to a system through PC Card technology is enormous. Virtually any type of interface or adapter that can be added to a desktop system via ISA (Industry Standard Architecture) or PCI (Peripheral Component Interconnect) bus cards can also be added to a laptop or notebook system via PC Cards.

The PC Card slots found in laptop and notebook systems enable you to add USB ports, FireWire ports, serial (RS-232) ports, parallel ports, fax/modems, cellular modems, Parallel or Serial ATA ports, SCSI adapters, wireless or wired network interface adapters, 1.8-inch hard drives, TV tuners, sound cards, GPS (global positioning satellite) receivers, and many other types of devices to your system. If your computer has PC Card slots that conform to the standards developed by the PCMCIA, you can insert any type of PC Card (built to the same standard) into your machine and expect it to be recognized and usable.

Although the original PC Card specification was only for memory cards, in fact that has turned out to be the least popular use, and almost nobody uses PCMCIA memory cards today (often called linear memory, to distinguish them from modern flash memory cards). The memory card function was designed at a time when the systems ran much slower, and it was thought that opening up a laptop to add chip-based memory would be too difficult. The idea was that you could insert a memory card into the system, thereby upgrading the memory in an extremely easy fashion. Compared to a standard SIMM (single inline memory module) or DIMM (dual inline memory module), the original PCMCIA memory cards were very expensive. They were also much slower. The original PC Card bus was based on the slow ISA bus and ran at only 10MHz, which was fast enough for systems back in 1990, but not fast enough for systems that followed. Most laptop manufacturers opted to use smaller and faster SODIMMs (small outline DIMMs) for adding memory to laptop systems instead. The SODIMMs were normally installed in sockets under a cover plate, and ran at the full speed of the memory bus in the system.

PC Card Bus Types

PC Cards evolved into a method for adding the same level of expansion to portable systems that was already available on desktop systems. There are two bus standards for PC Cards: PC Card-16 (16-bit) and CardBus (32-bit). PC Card-16 runs at 10MHz and does 16-bit transfers, for a maximum throughput of 20MBps. It can be thought of as the mobile equivalent of the ancient ISA bus. CardBus runs at 33MHz and does 32-bit transfers, for a maximum throughput of 133MBps (same as PCI). It's essentially mobile PCI. Table 8.2 summarizes the differences between PC Card-16 and CardBus.

Table 8.2   PC Card Bus Types

Feature	PC Card-16	CardBus
Voltage	5V/3.3V	3.3V
Design	ISA	PCI
Interrupts	Non-Shareable	Shareable
Speed	10MHz	33MHz
Data width	8/16-bit	32-bit
Transfer rate	20MBps	133MBps

Although both PC Card-16 and CardBus cards use the same basic 68-pin connectors, they are actually slightly different in keying, such that a PC Card-16 card plugs into a CardBus slot, but a CardBus card does not plug into an older PC Card-16 slot. All CardBus slots are required to support PC Card-16 cards as well as CardBus cards. Virtually all 486 processor and most early Pentium processor–based notebooks include only PC Card-16 slots, whereas most systems based on mid-1996 and later Pentium or higher processors include CardBus slots. If a system has two slots, in some cases only one of them is CardBus capable.

If you are unsure about what type of PC Card slots your laptop includes, check the specifications. If the specifications indicate that the slots support PCMCIA 2.x, then they support only PC Card-16 cards because CardBus is included in the 5.x and later standards only. Normally, the specifications state that the slots are CardBus slots if they have that capability. CardBus cards include a metal shield with raised bumps around the 68-pin connector. The bumps are part of the keying that prevents them from being inserted into older PC Card 2.x slots.

Because CardBus cards are based on PCI, they can share interrupts using PCI bus IRQ steering, unlike ISA-based PC Card-16 cards, which cannot share interrupts. PCI bus IRQ steering gives the operating system the flexibility to reprogram and share PCI IRQs when it rebalances Plug and Play resources. When PC Card-16 cards are used without shareable interrupts, the operating system may not be able to find enough free interrupts for all devices to work, and some may end up being disabled by the device manager.

Most newer and faster PC Cards use the CardBus interface, which virtually all newer laptops support. Still, you should check to be sure your laptop does have CardBus support before purchasing CardBus cards. Depending on the card you purchase, you should look for CardBus-type cards as well. Cards supporting slower interfaces (such as modems, for example) are usually available in PC Card versions because they don't have a need for greater than 20MBps throughput. Still, because CardBus cards support PCI IRQ sharing, they have benefits beyond their higher throughput.

For example, Adaptec makes two PC Card SCSI adapters, called the APA-1460 (PC Card-16) and the APA-1480 (CardBus). The 1460 is a Fast-SCSI adapter, whereas the 1480 is an Ultra-SCSI adapter with twice the speed of the 1460. The 1460 has only one advantage, and it will work in *any* system with a PC Card slot. The 1480 will work in CardBus slots, which would be found in most systems dating from mid-1996 to the present. Switching to the faster 1480 CardBus adapter cut my tape backup times in half, and it allows my SCSI CD-ROM drive to work at full speed. For most situations in which you have a choice between a PC Card-16 and CardBus version of a card, you're best off going with the CardBus version.

PC Card Physical Types

The PC Card standard also defines three physical types for PC Cards, which apply to either those using the PC Card-16 or CardBus interface. The three physical designs are shown in Table 8.3.

Table 8.3   PC Card Physical Types

PC Card Sizes	Length	Width	Thickness	Volume
Type I	54.0mm (2.13in)	85.6mm (3.37in)	3.3mm (0.13in)	15.25cc (0.93ci)
Type II	54.0mm (2.13in)	85.6mm (3.37in)	5.0mm (0.20in)	23.11cc (1.41ci)
Type II	54.0mm (2.13in)	85.6mm (3.37in)	10.5mm (0.41in)	48.54cc (2.96ci)

As you can see from the table, all the PC Cards have the same length and width; only the thickness varies. All the cards are physically backward compatible, which means that if a slot will fit a Type III card, then a Type II or Type I will fit as well. Slots that accept Type II cards will fit Type I cards, but not Type III cards. On rare occasions, you will see a Type I–only slot, which accommodates only Type I cards.

Most systems incorporate two PC Card slots in a stacked arrangement. The upper slot can accommodate Type I or II cards, whereas the bottom slot can accommodate Type I, II, or III cards. Unfortunately, if a Type III card is used in the lower slot, it will physically encroach on the space for the upper slot, and it will not be possible to use the upper slot at all. Many newer laptops include only a single PC Card slot, which accommodates Type I, II, or III cards. Some multifunction network/modem cards have an extended portion with full-sized connectors, such that even though the card is technically a Type I or II card, the connector portion may preclude using the upper slot.

Note

A Type IV PC Card, thicker still than the Type III, was proposed by Toshiba for higher-capacity PC Card–based hard drives. This card type was never recognized by the PCMCIA, however, and has rarely been implemented in actual systems or devices.

A PC Card usually has a sturdy metal case and is sealed, except for the interface to the PCMCIA adapter in the computer at one end, which consists of 68 tiny pinholes. The other end of the card might contain a connector for a cable leading to a telephone line, a network, or some other external device. Type I, Type II, and Type III PC Cards are compared to each other in Figure 8.1.

The pinouts for the PC Card interfaces are shown in Table 8.4.

Table 8.4   PC Card-16 and CardBus Pinouts

Pin	PC Card-16	CardBus	Pin	PC Card-16	CardBus
1	GND	GND	35	GND	GND
2	D3	CAD0	36	-CD1	-CCD1
3	D4	CAD1	37	D11	CAD2
4	D5	CAD3	38	D12	CAD4
5	D6	CAD5	39	D13	CAD6
6	D7	CAD7	40	D14	RFU
7	-CE1	CC/-BE0	41	D15	CAD8
8	A10	CAD9	42	-CE2	CAD10
9	-OE	CAD11	43	-VS1	CVS1
10	A11	CAD12	44	-IORD/RFU	CAD13
11	A9	CAD14	45	-IOWR/RFU	CAD15
12	A8	CC/-BE1	46	A17	CAD16
13	A13	CPAR	47	A18	RFU
14	A14	-CPERR	48	A19	-CBLOCK
15	-WE	-CGNT	49	A20	-CSTOP
16	READY/-IREQ	-CINT	50	A21	-CDEVSEL
17	Vcc	Vcc	51	Vcc	Vcc
18	Vpp/Vcore	Vpp/Vcore	52	Vpp/Vcore	Vpp/Vcore
19	A16	CCLK	53	A22	-CTRDY
20	A15	-CIRDY	54	A23	-CFRAME
21	A12	CC/-BE2	55	A24	CAD17
22	A7	CAD18	56	A25	CAD19
23	A6	CAD20	57	-VS2	CVS2
24	A5	CAD21	58	RESET	-CRST
25	A4	CAD22	59	-WAIT	-CSERR
26	A3	CAD23	60	-INPACK/RFU	-CREQ
27	A2	CAD24	61	-REG	CC/-BE3
28	A1	CAD25	62	BVD2(-SPKR)	CAUDIO

Table 8.4   Continued

Pin	PC Card-16	CardBus	Pin	PC Card-16	CardBus
29	A0	CAD26	63	BVD1(-STSCHG/-RI)	CSTSCHG
30	D0	CAD27	64	D8	CAD28
31	D1	CAD29	65	D9	CAD30
32	D2	RFU	66	D10	CAD31
33	WP(-IOIS16)	-CCLKRUN	67	-CD2	-CCD2
34	GND	GND	68	GND	GND

The later versions of the standard include many features designed to increase the speed and efficiency of the interface, including the following:

- **5V or 3.3V operation**—PC Card-16 cards can operate at 3.3V or 5V, depending on the card. Cards that run on the lower voltage use less power and save battery life. All CardBus cards use 3.3V.

- **Support for the ACPI (Advanced Configuration and Power Interface) and APM (Advanced Power Management) power-saving protocols**—This support allows cards to be moved into various power-conserving states, as well as powered off.

- **Plug and Play (PnP) support**—PnP allows the operating system to configure the cards, thus eliminating conflicts with other devices.

- **PC Card ATA standard**—This standard allows manufacturers to use the AT Attachment protocols to implement PC Card hard disk drives or flash memory–based solid-state drives.

- **Support for multiple functions on a single card**—This support allows multiple devices to coexist, such as a modem and a network adapter.

- **Zoomed video (ZV)**—This is a direct video bus connection between the PC Card adapter and the system's graphics controller. It allows high-speed video displays for videoconferencing applications, TV tuners, and MPEG decoders.

- **Thermal ratings system**—This system allows software to detect excessive heat conditions, which can be used to warn users.

PC Card Software Support

PC Cards are by definition *hot-swappable*, meaning that with the proper software support you can remove a card from a slot and replace it with a different one without having to reboot the system. If your PC Card devices and operating system conform to the Plug and Play standard, inserting a new card into the slot causes the appropriate drivers for the device to be loaded and configured automatically.

To make this possible, two separate software layers are needed on the computer that provide the interface between the PCMCIA adapter (which controls the card slots) and the applications that use the services of the PC Card devices (see Figure 8.2). These two layers are called *Socket Services* and *Card Services*. A third module, called an *enabler*, actually configures the settings of the PC Cards.

Socket Services is a BIOS-level software layer that isolates PC Card software from the system hardware and detects the insertion and removal of PC Cards. Card Services manages the automatic allocation of system resources, such as memory and interrupts, after Socket Services detects that a card has been inserted.

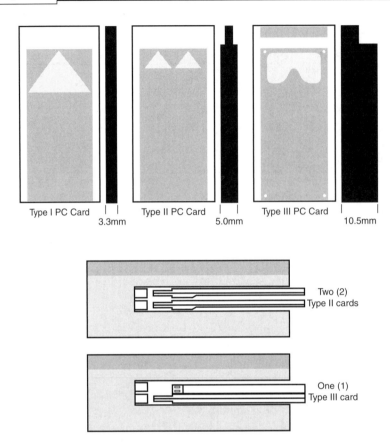

Figure 8.1   PC Card Physical Types. One or two Type I or Type II PC Cards (upper center) can be inserted into most notebook computers (center), but only one Type III PC Card (upper right) can be used at a time (lower center).

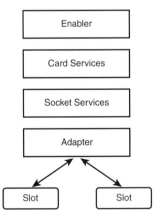

Figure 8.2   Card and Socket Services enable an operating system to recognize the PC Card inserted into a slot and configure the appropriate system hardware resources for the device.

Socket Services

The PCMCIA chipset that provides the interface between the card slots and the rest of the computer is one of the only parts of the PCMCIA architecture not fully standardized. Many different chipsets are available to portable systems manufacturers; as a result, an application or operating system can't address the slot hardware directly, as it can a parallel or serial port. Most laptop systems include PC Card interface chipsets from Texas Instruments.

Instead, a software layer called Socket Services is designed to address a specific make of PCMCIA adapter hardware. The Socket Services software layer isolates the proprietary aspects of the adapter from all the software operating above it. The communications between the driver and the adapter might be unique, but the other interface, between the Socket Services driver and the Card Services software, is defined by the PCMCIA standard.

Socket Services can take the form of a device driver, a TSR (terminate-and-stay-resident) program run from the DOS prompt (or the AUTOEXEC.BAT file), or a service running on an operating system such as Windows 9x/Me or Windows NT/2000/XP. The services provided in Windows support the most common PC Card chipsets, including those from Texas Instruments. A computer can have PC Card slots with different adapters, as in the case of a docking station that provides extra slots in addition to those in the portable computer itself. In this case, the computer can run multiple Socket Services drivers, which all communicate with the same Card Services program.

Card Services

The Card Services software communicates with Socket Services and is responsible for assigning the appropriate hardware resources to PC Cards. PC Cards are no different from other types of bus expansion cards, in that they require access to specific hardware resources to communicate with the computer's processor and memory subsystems.

The PCMCIA standard requires that the computer be capable of assigning hardware resources to different devices as they are inserted into a slot. Card Services addresses this problem by maintaining a collection of various hardware resources that it allots to devices as necessary and reclaims as the devices are removed.

If, for example, you have a system with two PC Card slots, the Card Services software might be configured to use two hardware interrupts, two I/O ports, and two memory addresses, regardless of whether any cards are in the slots at boot time. No other devices in the computer can use those interrupts. When cards are inserted, Card Services assigns configuration values for the settings requested by the devices, ensuring that the settings allotted to each card are unique.

Card Services is not the equivalent of Plug and Play, although the two might seem similar. In fact, in Windows 9x/Me/2000/XP, Card Services obtains the hardware resources it assigns to PC Cards using Plug and Play. For other operating systems, the resources can be allotted to the Card Services program using a text file or command-line switches. In a non–Plug and Play system, you must configure the hardware resources assigned to Card Services with the same care you would configure an ISA board. Although Card Services won't allow two PC Cards to be assigned the same interrupt, nothing in the PCMCIA architecture prevents conflicts between the resources assigned to Card Services and those of other devices in the system.

You can have multiple Socket Services drivers loaded on one system, but there can be only one Card Services program. Socket Services must always be loaded before Card Services. Normally, both Socket and Card Services are built in to Windows.

Enablers

In spite of their other capabilities, neither Socket Services nor Card Services is capable of actually configuring the hardware settings of PC Cards. This job is left to a software module called an *enabler*. The enabler receives the configuration settings assigned by Card Services and actually communicates with the PC Card hardware itself to set the appropriate values. This software is also included in Windows versions that support Plug and Play.

Note

Windows 9x/Me or Windows 2000/XP are the preferred operating systems for running PC Card devices. The combination of their advanced memory management, Plug and Play capabilities, and integration of the Card and Socket Services into the operating system makes the process of installing a PC Card (usually) as easy as inserting it into the slot.

With Windows NT 4.0, for example, you must shut down the system and reboot to change the PC Card in a slot. What's more, it can be difficult to find Windows NT drivers for many of the PC Cards on the market. DOS has similar limitations and requires that specialized device drivers be loaded via the **CONFIG.SYS** and **AUTOEXEC.BAT** startup files.

If you are going to run PC Cards under DOS, you have to load the Socket Services, Card Services, and Enabler software separately. They are normally supplied by your laptop or notebook system manufacturer in a single package for supporting PC Cards under DOS. After those files are installed, you still have to install the DOS-level driver for the cards you are using, which normally comes with the card or from the card manufacturer.

ExpressCards

The original PCMCIA PC Card standards have been in use for over 15 years now and through enhancements have evolved from about 20MBps to 133MBps in throughput. Unfortunately, the PC Card specification has evolved to the point where further improvements in performance and functionality are almost impossible.

Recognizing that a new type of small expansion card standard was needed for modern laptops and other portable computing devices, on February 19, 2003, the PCMCIA announced that it was developing a new interface card specification, codenamed NEWCARD, that was designed to replace existing PC Cards for portable systems.

On September 16, 2003, the ExpressCard 1.0 interface standard was officially announced by the PCMCIA at the Fall Intel Developer's Forum. After several years of chipset and motherboard development, laptops with ExpressCard slots finally began appearing on the market in April 2005, along with a variety of ExpressCard devices, such as Gigabit Ethernet, Bluetooth, and others (see Figure 8.3). As systems with ExpressCard slots become predominant, the number of ExpressCards on the market will also increase.

Figure 8.3 PCI Express for Laptops: ExpressCard/34 and ExpressCard/54 cards.

Note

The official ExpressCard standard can be ordered from the PCMCIA via the official ExpressCard website at `www.expresscard.org`.

Although the PCMCIA is leading the ExpressCard specification development effort, the Peripheral Component Interconnect-Special Interest Group (PCI-SIG), the USB Implementers Forum (USB-IF), and the PC Quality/Ease of Use Roundtable (an industry group that focuses on reducing end-user issues) are also collaborating on the project. Intel and Microsoft are among those supporting development of the new standard, as are several other major players in the PC industry.

While it is possible to use PC Cards in desktop systems with an appropriate adapter, ExpressCards were designed with more emphasis on the ability to be used in both mobile and desktop PCs, potentially allowing the same devices to be shared between mobile and desktop systems. ExpressCard offers several advantages over existing PC Cards:

- **Speed**—ExpressCard is based on a 250MBps single-lane PCI Express serial bus combined with 60MBps USB 2.0, which is both simpler and faster than the 133MBps PCI parallel bus technology used by CardBus PC Cards.

- **Size**—ExpressCard/34 cards are roughly half the size of existing CardBus PC Cards, and they are lighter as well.

- **Cost**—ExpressCard is based on existing serial bus technology natively supported by the motherboard chipset, requiring fewer components, fewer pins and signals, and lower cost connectors.

- **Power**—ExpressCards require less power than current PC Cards and generate less heat. While it doesn't save enough to be billed as a feature, it does offer a minor, but measurable, improvement in battery life when these cards are installed (as compared to PC Cards).

- **Ease of use**—ExpressCards use existing operating systems and drivers, allowing for easy installation and configuration.

ExpressCards will be available in two sizes: ExpressCard/34 (34mm wide) and ExpressCard/54 (54mm wide). Both feature a standard 75mm length and a thickness of 5mm. They are differentiated only by the overall width and shape of the card. Figure 8.4 shows a comparison between the dimensions of a CardBus PC Card, ExpressCard/54, and ExpressCard/34.

ExpressCard slots are also available in two sizes: 34mm wide and 54mm wide. The 34mm wide slots support only ExpressCard/34 modules, while 54mm wide slots support either type of module. Most laptops will have one or two 54mm wide slots, allowing use of either size card. Figure 8.5 shows how ExpressCard/54 or ExpressCard/34 cards can fit into a 54mm slot.

Because ExpressCard is based on existing PCI Express and USB serial interfaces, the ExpressCard interface contains only 26 pins and is much simpler than the older 68-pin CardBus interface, which was based on the parallel PCI bus. In addition to being simpler in design and componentry, ExpressCard is also less costly since CardBus normally requires an extra CardBus controller chip to act as an interface between PCI and CardBus, while ExpressCard merely uses the existing native PCI Express and USB 2.0 interfaces, which are already built in to the motherboard chipset. This allows ExpressCard support to be easily implemented in desktop systems as well.

Unlike PC Cards, ExpressCards don't require a complicated mechanical card ejection mechanism. Instead, to further reduce costs, ExpressCards are designed with a simple finger grip ridge on the outside edge, while the slot has a recessed area to allow you to easily grab the card and pull it out.

The pinout for the ExpressCard interface is shown in Table 8.5.

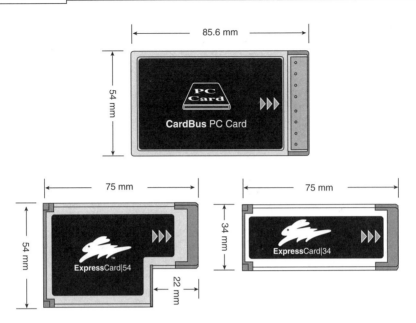

Figure 8.4   Relative size comparison between a CardBus PC Card, an ExpressCard/54, and an ExpressCard/34.

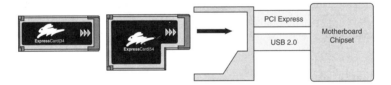

Figure 8.5   A single 54mm wide ExpressCard slot can accommodate either an ExpressCard/54 or ExpressCard/34 module.

Table 8.5   ExpressCard Pinout

Pin	Signal	Description	Pin	Signal	Description
1	GROUND	Return current path	14	+3.3V	Primary voltage source
2	USBD-	USB data interface	15	+3.3V	Primary voltage source
3	USBD+	USB data interface	16	CLKREQ#	Request REFCLK be enabled
4	CPUSB#	USB presence detect	17	CPPE#	PCI Express presence detect
5	RESERVED	-	18	REFCLK-	PCI Express reference clock
6	RESERVED	-	19	REFCLK+	PCI Express reference clock
7	RESERVED	-	20	GROUND	Return current path
8	SMB_CLK	System Management Bus	21	PERn0	PCI Express receive differential pair
9	SMB_DATA	System Management Bus	22	PERp0	PCI Express receive differential pair
10	+1.5V	Secondary voltage source	23	GROUND	Return current path

Table 8.5 Continued

Pin	Signal	Description	Pin	Signal	Description
11	WAKE#	Request host attention	24	PETn0	PCI Express transmit differential pair
12	+3.3VAUX	Auxiliary voltage source	25	PETp0	PCI Express transmit differential pair
13	PERST#	PCI Express reset	26	GROUND	Return current path

A single ExpressCard can be designed to connect to the system via the PCI Express or USB interfaces (but not both). Higher speed cards like Gigabit Ethernet cards will use the faster integrated PCI Express interface, while lower speed cards such as Bluetooth or flash memory cards will connect via the integrated USB 2.0 interface. Both types of cards have access to the common power and System Management Bus (SMBus) pins as well. The SMBus is part of the Advanced Configuration and Power Interface (ACPI) standard and is a low-speed bus primarily used by "smart" batteries, chargers, and other power management devices to communicate status information.

ExpressCards are designed to use very little power, and consequently generate little heat. Each type of ExpressCard is limited to the following maximum thermal power dissipation according to the specification:

ExpressCard/34 = 1.3W thermal

ExpressCard/54 = 2.1W thermal

The specification also dictates the maximum power that can be supplied via an ExpressCard slot. Table 8.6 shows the average and maximum power rating limits for an ExpressCard slot.

Table 8.6 ExpressCard Slot Power Rating Limits

Supply	Average Limit	Max. Limit
+3.3V	1000mA	1300mA
+3.3VAUX	250mA	325mA
+1.5V	500mA	650mA

The sum of +3.3V & +3.3VAUX averages may not exceed 1000mA.
Maximum current combined across all power rails is 1750mA.

Because ExpressCard is based on PCI Express, the availability of ExpressCard slots in laptop systems depended on the availability of laptop motherboard chipsets supporting PCI Express as well. The first desktop motherboard chipsets with PCI Express support were the Intel 910, 915, and 925 Express chipsets (codenamed Grantsdale) ,which were introduced on June 21, 2004 (915/925), and September 22, 2004 (910). The first mobile chipsets for laptops supporting PCI Express were the Mobile Intel 915GM/PM/GMS and 910GML Express chipsets, which were introduced on January 19, 2005. The first laptop systems using these chipsets and incorporating ExpressCard slots became available a few months later in the spring of 2005. Most new laptops introduced since then will include ExpressCard slots.

Although your next laptop should include at least one ExpressCard slot, it should still include at least one PC Card slot for backward compatibility. Nobody expects the transition from PC Cards to ExpressCards to happen overnight; in fact, it will most likely take several years, just as newer desktop PC motherboards contain both PCI Express and regular PCI slots. I fully expect that over time ExpressCards will slowly replace CardBus PC Cards as the predominant type of mobile expansion card.

High-Speed External Connections

The two most popular high-speed serial-bus architectures for desktop and portable PCs are universal serial bus (USB) and IEEE 1394 (IEEE stands for the Institute of Electrical and Electronic Engineers), which is also called *i.LINK* or *FireWire*. Each interface type is available in two versions: USB 1.1 and USB 2.0; IEEE 1394a and IEEE 1394b (also called FireWire 800). The USB and IEEE 1394 port families are high-speed communications ports that far outstrip the capabilities of older standard serial and parallel ports. In addition to performance, these ports offer I/O device consolidation, which means that all types of external peripherals can be designed to connect to these ports.

Serial Versus Parallel

The current trend in high-performance peripheral bus design is to use a serial architecture, in which 1 bit at a time is sent down a wire. Because parallel architecture uses 8, 16, or more wires to send bits simultaneously, the parallel bus is actually much faster at the same clock speed. However, increasing the clock speed of a serial connection is much easier than increasing that of a parallel connection.

Parallel connections in general suffer from several problems, the biggest being signal skew and jitter. Skew and jitter are the reasons high-speed parallel buses such as SCSI (small computer systems interface) are limited to short distances of 3 meters or less. The problem is that, although the 8 or 16 bits of data are fired from the transmitter at the same time, by the time they reach the receiver, propagation delays have conspired to allow some bits to arrive before the others. The longer the cable, the longer the time between the arrival of the first and last bits at the other end! This *signal skew*, as it is called, prevents you from running a high-speed transfer rate or a longer cable—or both. *Jitter* is the tendency for the signal to reach its target voltage and float above and below for a short period of time.

With a serial bus, the data is sent 1 bit at a time. Because there is no worry about when each bit will arrive, the clocking rate can be increased dramatically. For example, the top transfer rate possible with EPP/ECP parallel ports is 2.77MBps, whereas IEEE 1394a ports (which use high-speed serial technology) support transfer rates as high as 400Mbps (about 50MBps)—25 times faster than parallel ports. USB 2.0 supports transfer rates of 480Mbps (about 60MBps), which is about 30 times faster than parallel ports, and the IEEE 1394b (FireWire 800) ports reach transfer rates as high as 800Mbps (or about 100MBps), which is about 50 times faster than the venerable parallel printer port!

At high clock rates, parallel signals tend to interfere with each other. Serial, again, has an advantage because, with only one or two signal wires, crosstalk and interference between the wires in the cable are negligible.

In general, parallel cabling is more expensive than serial cabling. In addition to the many extra wires needed to carry the multiple bits in parallel, the cable also must be specially constructed to prevent crosstalk and interference between adjacent data lines. This is one reason external SCSI cables are so expensive. Serial cabling, by comparison, is very inexpensive. For one thing, it has significantly fewer wires. Furthermore, the shielding requirements are far simpler, even at very high speeds. Because of this, transmitting serial data reliably over longer distances is also easier, which is why parallel interfaces have shorter recommended cable lengths than do serial interfaces.

For these reasons—in addition to the need for new Plug and Play external peripheral interfaces and the elimination of the physical port crowding on portable computers—these high-performance serial buses were developed. USB is a standard feature on virtually all PCs today and is used for most general-purpose high-speed external interfacing, and it's the most compatible, widely available, and fastest general-purpose external interface. In addition, IEEE 1394 (more commonly known as *FireWire* or *i.LINK*), although mainly used in certain niche markets—such as connecting DV (digital video) camcorders—is also spreading into other high-bandwidth uses, such as high-resolution scanners and external hard drives.

Universal Serial Bus (USB)

Universal serial bus (USB) is an external peripheral bus standard designed to bring Plug and Play capability for attaching peripherals externally to the PC. USB eliminates the need for special-purpose ports, reduces the need to use special-purpose I/O cards or PC Cards (thus reducing the need to reconfigure the system with each new device added), and saves important system resources such as interrupts (IRQs). Regardless of the number of devices attached to a system's USB ports, only one IRQ is required. PCs equipped with USB enable peripherals to be automatically recognized and configured as soon as they are physically attached, without the need to reboot or run a setup program. USB allows up to 127 devices to run simultaneously on a single bus, with some peripherals such as monitors and keyboards acting as additional plug-in sites, or *hubs*.

Intel has been the primary proponent of USB, and all its PC chipsets starting with the PIIX3 South Bridge chipset component (introduced in February 1996) have included USB support as standard. Other chipset vendors have followed suit, making USB as standard a feature of today's desktop and notebook PCs as the serial and parallel ports once were. Although most desktop systems started incorporating USB back in mid-1996, most laptops did not begin including USB ports until 1998. The reason was mainly that it wasn't until Windows 98 was released that the Windows operating system provided full support for USB.

Six other companies initially worked with Intel in co-developing the USB, including Compaq, Digital, IBM, Microsoft, NEC, and Northern Telecom. Together, these companies established the USB Implementers Forum (USB-IF) to develop, support, and promote USB architecture.

The USB-IF formally released USB 1.0 in January of 1996, USB 1.1 in September of 1998, and USB 2.0 in April of 2000. The 1.1 revision was mostly a clarification of some issues related to hubs and other areas of the specification. Most devices and hubs should be 1.1 compliant, even if they were manufactured before the release of the 1.1 specification. The biggest change came with the introduction of USB 2.0, which was 40 times faster than the original USB and yet fully backward compatible. USB ports can be retrofitted to older computers that lack built-in USB connectors through the use of either an add-on PCI card (for desktop computers) or a PC Card on CardBus-compatible notebook computers. By mid-2002, virtually all desktop motherboards included four to six (or more) USB 2.0 ports as standard. Notebook computers were a little slower to catch on to the USB 2.0 bandwagon; it wasn't until early 2003 that most notebook and laptop computers included USB 2.0 ports as standard. Currently most laptops include between two and four USB 2.0 ports as standard, and with hubs or port replicators, many more can easily be added.

USB Technical Details

USB 1.1 runs at 12Mbps (1.5MBps) over a simple four-wire connection. The bus supports up to 127 devices connected to a single root hub and uses a tiered-star topology, built on expansion hubs that can reside in the PC, any USB peripheral, or even standalone hub boxes. Note that although the standard allows you to attach up to 127 devices, they all must share the 1.5MBps bandwidth, meaning that for every active device you add, the bus will slow down some. In practical reality, few people will have more than eight devices attached at any one time.

For low-speed peripherals, such as pointing devices and keyboards, the USB also has a slower 1.5Mbps subchannel.

USB employs what is called non-return to zero inverted (NRZI) data encoding. NRZI is a method of encoding serial data in which 1s and 0s are represented by opposite and alternating high and low voltages where there is no return to a zero (or reference) voltage between the encoded bits. In NRZI encoding, a 1 is represented by no change in signal level, and a 0 is represented by a change in level. A string of 0s causes the NRZI data to toggle signal levels for each bit. A string of 1s causes long periods with no transitions in the data. This is an efficient transfer encoding scheme because it eliminates the need for additional clock pulses that would otherwise waste time and bandwidth.

USB devices are considered either *hubs* or *functions*, or both. Functions are the individual devices that attach to the USB, such as a keyboard, mouse, camera, printer, telephone, and so on. Hubs provide additional attachment points to the USB, enabling the attachment of additional hubs or functions. The initial ports in the system unit are called the *root hub*, and they are the starting point for the USB. Most motherboards have two, three, or four USB ports, any of which can be connected to functions or additional hubs. Some systems place one or two of the USB ports in the sides of the computer, which is very convenient for devices you use only occasionally, such as digital cameras or flash memory card readers.

Hubs are essentially wiring concentrators, and through a star-type topology they allow the attachment of multiple devices. Each attachment point is referred to as a *port*. Most hubs have either four or eight ports, but more are possible. For more expandability, you can connect additional hubs to the ports on an existing hub. The hub controls both the connection and distribution of power to each of the connected functions. A typical hub is shown in Figure 8.6.

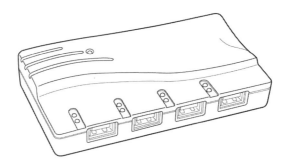

Figure 8.6 A typical USB hub with four ports.

Besides providing additional sockets for connecting USB peripherals, a hub can provide power to any attached peripherals. A hub recognizes the dynamic attachment of a peripheral and provides at least 0.5W of power per peripheral during initialization. Under control of the host driver software, the hub can provide more device power, up to a maximum of 2.5W, for peripheral operation.

Tip

For the most reliable operation, I recommend that you use self-powered hubs, which plug into an AC adapter. Bus-powered hubs pull power from the PC's USB root hub connector and aren't always capable of providing adequate power for power-hungry devices, such as optical mice.

A newly attached hub is assigned a unique address, and hubs can be cascaded up to five levels deep (see Figure 8.7). A hub operates as a bidirectional repeater and repeats USB signals as required both upstream (toward the PC) and downstream (toward the device). A hub also monitors these signals and handles transactions addressed to itself. All other transactions are repeated to attached devices. A USB 1.1 hub supports both 12Mbps (full-speed) and 1.5Mbps (low-speed) peripherals.

Maximum cable length between two full-speed (12Mbps) devices or a device and a hub is 5 meters using twisted-pair shielded cable with 20-gauge wire. Maximum cable length for low speed (1.5Mbps) devices using non-twisted-pair wire is 3 meters. These distance limits are shorter if smaller gauge wire is used (see Table 8.7).

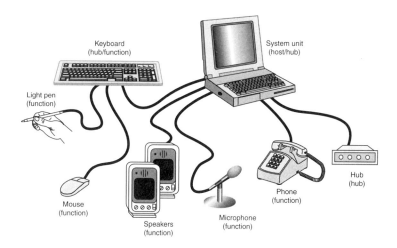

Figure 8.7 A typical laptop with USB devices can use multiple USB hubs to support a variety of peripherals, connected to whichever hub is most convenient.

Table 8.7 Maximum Cable Lengths Versus Wire Gauge

Gauge	Resistance (in Ohms/Meter Ω/m)	Length (Max. in Meters)
28	0.232 Ω/m	0.81m
26	0.145 Ω/m	1.31m
24	0.091 Ω/m	2.08m
22	0.057 Ω/m	3.33m
20	0.036 Ω/m	5.00m

Although USB 1.1 is not as fast at data transfer as FireWire or SCSI, it is still more than adequate for the types of peripherals for which it is designed. USB 2.0 operates a surprising 40 times faster than USB 1.1 and allows transfer speeds of 480Mbps, or 60MBps. Because it is fully backward compatible and will support older 1.1 devices, I recommend purchasing only laptops or notebooks that conform to the faster USB 2.0 (high-speed USB) standard. One of the additional benefits of USB 2.0 is the capability to handle concurrent transfers, which enables your USB 1.1 devices to transfer data at the same time without tying up the USB bus.

USB 2.0 drivers were not provided with the initial launch of Windows XP but are available through system update downloads or service packs. Merely use the Windows Update feature to connect to the Microsoft site and download any updates as needed. Add-on USB 2.0 cards may include their own drivers, which should be installed.

USB Connectors

Four main styles of connectors are specified for USB, called Series A, Series B, Mini-A, and Mini-B connectors. The A connectors are used for upstream connections between a device and the host or a hub. The USB ports on notebooks and hubs are normally Series A connectors. Series B connectors are designed for the downstream connection to a device that has detachable cables. In all cases the Mini connectors are simply smaller versions of the larger ones, in a physically smaller form factor for smaller devices.

The physical USB plugs are small (especially the Mini plugs) and, unlike a typical serial or parallel cable, the plug is not attached by screws or thumbscrews. There are no pins to bend or break, making USB devices very user friendly to install and remove. The USB plugs shown in Figure 8.8 slide into place on the USB connector.

Note that a Mini-A/B socket is a dual-purpose socket that can accept either Mini-A or Mini-B plugs. The newer Mini plugs and sockets have plastic portions inside the connectors, which are required to be color coded as shown in Table 8.8. The mini plugs and sockets were designed for extremely small systems, such as PDAs and cell phones, and are not normally used on laptop or even notebook-sized systems.

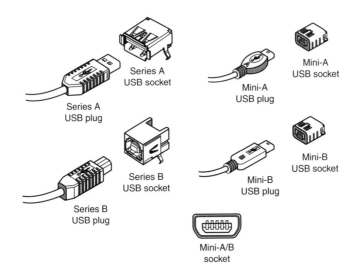

Figure 8.8   USB Standard and Mini Series A and Series B plugs and receptacles.

Table 8.8   Color Coding for USB Mini Plugs and Sockets

Connector	Color
Mini-A socket	White
Mini-A plug	White
Mini-B socket	Black
Mini-B plug	Black
Mini-AB socket	Gray

Tables 8.9 and 8.10 show the pinouts for the USB connectors and cables. Most notebooks with USB connectors feature one or two Series A connectors on the rear or sides of the system.

Table 8.9   USB Connector Pinouts for Series A/B Connectors

Pin	Signal Name	Wire Color	Comment
1	Vbus	Red	Bus power
2	- Data	White	Data transfer
3	+ Data	Green	Data transfer
4	Ground	Black	Cable ground
Shell	Shield	—	Drain wire

Table 8.10   USB Connector Pinouts for Mini-A/B Connectors

Pin	Signal Name	Wire Color	Comment
1	Vbus	Red	Bus power
2	- Data	White	Data transfer
3	+ Data	Green	Data transfer
4	ID	—	A/B identification*
5	Ground	Black	Cable ground
Shell	Shield	—	Drain wire

* Used to identify a Mini-A from a Mini-B connector to the device. ID is connected to Ground in a Mini-A plug and is not connected (open) in a Mini-B plug.

USB conforms to Intel's PnP specification, including *hot-plugging*, which means that devices can be plugged in dynamically without powering down or rebooting the system. Simply plug in the device, and the USB controller in the PC detects the device and automatically determines and allocates the required resources and drivers. To prevent data loss with USB drives and storage devices, when disconnecting them via hot-plugging, you need to use the Eject Hardware or Safely Remove Hardware feature in the Windows system tray. Click the device, select Stop, click OK, and wait for the system to indicate that the device has been stopped before you remove it.

Microsoft has developed USB drivers and included them automatically in Windows 98 and later. Windows 95B and 95C have very limited support for USB 1.1; the necessary drivers are not present in the original Windows 95 or 95A. With Windows 95B, the USB drivers are not automatically included; they are provided separately, although a late release of Windows 95—Windows 95C—includes USB support. Many USB devices will not work with any Windows 95 releases, including those that supposedly have the USB support files included.

Windows 98 and later include USB 1.1 support built in; however, additional drivers are required for high-speed USB 2.0 or later. In most cases these drivers can be downloaded from Microsoft using the Windows Update feature.

USB support is also required in the BIOS for devices such as keyboards and mice. This is included in all newer systems with USB ports built in. Aftermarket PC Cards also are available for adding USB to laptops and notebooks that don't include it as standard. USB peripherals include printers, optical drives, modems, scanners, telephones, joysticks, keyboards, and pointing devices such as mice and trackballs.

A free utility called *USBready* is available from the www.usb.org site that examines your system's hardware and software and informs you of your system's USB capabilities. Most laptop systems built in 1997 or earlier don't support USB. During 1998, most laptops began supporting USB, and if your system dates from 1999 or later, built-in USB support is almost a certainty. One interesting feature of USB is that with certain limitations, attached devices can be powered by the USB bus. The PnP aspects of USB enable the system to query the attached peripherals as to their power requirements and issue a warning if available power levels are being exceeded. This is important for USB when it is used in portable systems because the battery power allocated to run the external peripherals might be limited.

Another of the benefits of the USB specification is the self-identifying peripheral, a feature that greatly eases installation because you don't have to set unique IDs or identifiers for each peripheral—the USB handles that automatically.

One of the biggest advantages of an interface such as USB is that it requires only a single interrupt (IRQ) from the system. Therefore, you can connect up to 127 devices, and they will not use separate interrupts as they might if each were connected over a separate interface. This is a major benefit of the USB interface.

USB 2.0

USB 2.0 is a backward-compatible extension of the USB 1.1 specification that uses the same cables, connectors, and software interfaces but that runs 40 times faster than the original 1.0 and 1.1 versions. The higher speed enables higher-performance peripherals, such as higher-resolution web/video-conferencing cameras, scanners, and faster printers, to be connected externally with the same easy Plug and Play installation of current USB peripherals. From the end-user point of view, USB 2.0 works exactly the same as 1.1—only faster and with more interesting, higher-performance devices available. All existing USB 1.1 devices work in a USB 2.0 bus because USB 2.0 supports all the slower-speed connections. USB data rates are shown in Table 8.11.

Table 8.11   USB Data Rates

Interface	Speed Terminology	Megabits per Second	Megabytes per Second
USB 1.1	Low speed	1.5Mbps	0.1875MBps
USB 1.1	Full speed	12Mbps	1.5MBps
USB 2.0	High speed	480Mbps	60MBps

Note the terminology, which can be confusing. *Full speed* designates the 1.5MBps throughput of USB 1.1, while *high speed* designates the 60MBps throughput of USB 2.0. Because any USB 1.1 device will work on a 2.0 bus (at the slower 1.1 speeds), many devices or components have been advertised as "USB 2.0 Compatible" when they do not actually support high-speed operation. The key to finding true USB 2.0 (high-speed) devices is to look for the device to state that it is "USB 2.0 Compliant" or "USB 2.0 Certified."

The support of higher-speed USB 2.0 peripherals requires using a USB 2.0–compliant hub. You can still use older USB 1.1 hubs on a 2.0 bus, but any peripherals or additional hubs connected downstream from a 1.1 hub will operate at the slower 1.5MBps USB 1.1 maximum speed. Devices connected to USB 2.0 hubs will operate at the maximum speed of the device, up to the full USB 2.0 speed of 60MBps. The higher transmission speeds through a 2.0 hub are negotiated on a device-by-device basis, and if the higher speed is not supported by a peripheral, the link operates at a lower USB 1.1 speed.

As such, a USB 2.0 hub accepts high-speed transactions at the faster USB 2.0 frame rate and must deliver them to high-speed USB 2.0 peripherals as well as USB 1.1 peripherals. This data rate–matching responsibility requires increased complexity and buffering of the incoming high-speed data. When communicating with an attached USB 2.0 peripheral, the 2.0 hub simply repeats the high-speed signals; however, when communicating with USB 1.1 peripherals, a USB 2.0 hub will buffer and manage the transition from the high speed of the USB 2.0 host controller (in the system) to the lower speed of a USB 1.1 device. This feature of USB 2.0 hubs means that USB 1.1 devices can operate along with USB 2.0 devices and not consume any additional bandwidth. USB 2.0 devices and root hubs are not yet widely available, but they are slowly being introduced by manufacturers. USB 2.0 devices, unlike USB 1.1 devices, might be located inside your system. Some manufacturers of add-on USB 2.0 cards are equipping the cards with both external and internal USB 2.0 ports.

How can you tell at a glance which devices are designed to support USB 1.1 versus the faster USB 2.0 standard? The USB Implementer's Forum (USB-IF), which owns and controls the USB standard, introduced new logos in late 2000 for products that have passed its certification tests. The new logos are shown in Figure 8.9.

Figure 8.9 The USB Basic Speed (1.1–compliant) logos (left) compared to the new USB Hi-Speed (USB 2.0–compliant) logos (right). The lower left and right logos indicate USB On-The-Go compliance.

As you can see from Figure 8.9, USB 1.1 is called simply "USB," and USB 2.0 is now called "Hi-Speed USB."

USB cables, connectors, hubs, and peripherals can also be identified by icons, as shown in Figure 8.10. The "plus" symbol added to the upper icon indicates that port or device would support USB 2.0 (Hi-Speed USB) in addition to the standard 1.1 support.

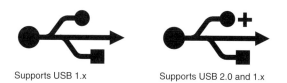

Supports USB 1.x   Supports USB 2.0 and 1.x

Figure 8.10 These icons identify USB cables, connectors, hubs, and peripherals.

Note that these icon guidelines do not apply to USB cables or connectors because the cable and connector design did not change from USB 1.1 to 2.0. Cables are supposed to use the standard icon (without the "plus" symbol), and all cables that support USB 1.1 also support 2.0.

USB On-The-Go

In December 2001, the USB-IF released a supplement to the USB 2.0 standard called *USB On-The-Go*. This was designed to address the one major shortcoming of USB—that a PC was required to transfer data between two devices. In other words, you could not connect two cameras together and transfer pictures between them without a notebook orchestrating the transfer. With USB On-The-Go, devices that conform to the specification will still work normally when they are connected to a notebook, but they will also have additional capabilities when connected to other devices supporting the standard.

Although this capability can also work with notebook peripherals, it was mainly added to address issues using USB devices in the consumer electronics area, where a notebook might not be available. Using this standard, devices such as digital video recorders can connect to other recorders to transfer recorded movies or shows, items such as personal organizers can transfer data to other organizers, and so on. The addition of the "On-The-Go" supplement to USB 2.0 greatly enhances the usage and capabilities of USB, both in the notebook PC and in the consumer electronics markets.

Wireless USB

Wireless USB (WUSB) is just what the name denotes, USB without wires. WUSB is based on ultrawideband (UWB) radio technology, which the military originally developed in 1962 for secure radio communications and radar use. Recognizing the usefulness of this radio technology for the public, in 2002 the Federal Communications Commission released frequencies from 3.1GHz to 10.6GHz for general-purpose UWB use.

In June 2003, a group called the Multiband OFDM (orthagonal frequency division multiplexing) Alliance Special Interest Group (MBOA-SIG) formed to develop an ultrawideband physical layer interface standard. The MBOA-SIG completed its UWB physical layer 1.0 specification in November 2004 and subsequently merged with another group called the WiMedia Alliance in March 2005. The WiMedia Alliance had originally formed in 2002 to promote the standardization and adoption of UWB wireless standards.

Then, in February 2004, several companies, including Agere, HP, Intel, Microsoft, NEC, Philips, and Samsung, together announced the formation of the Wireless USB Promoter Group and began working on the wireless USB specification, which would use the common WiMedia MB-OFDM (multiband orthagonal frequency division multiplexing) Ultrawideband radio platform for the physical connection layer. The Wireless USB Promoter Group subsequently developed and released the Wireless USB 1.0 specification on May 12, 2005.

Wireless USB devices are now certified to conform to the standard by the USB Implementers Forum and enable high-speed wireless connectivity by adapting USB protocols to the MB-OFDM Ultrawideband radio platform as developed by the WiMedia Alliance. Certified Wireless USB devices carry the official Wireless USB logo. as shown in Figure 8.11.

Wireless USB uses a portion of the UWB radio spectrum, including three 528MHz-wide channels from 3168MHz (3.1GHz) to 4753MHz (4.8GHz). These wideband channels allow for very high bandwidths up to 480Mbps (60MBps), which exactly matches the wired USB 2.0 specification in maximum throughput.

Wireless USB is designed for very low power consumption, short-range, high-speed connections, with performance of 480Mbps (60MBps) at 3 meters (approximately 10 feet), dropping to 110Mbps (13.75MBps) at 10 meters (approximately 33 feet). This is similar in range to Bluetooth, but at significantly higher transfer speeds. The radio frequencies used for Wireless USB (3.1 to 4.8GHz) are also designed so as not to overlap or interfere with the popular 2.4GHz 802.11b/g WiFi and Bluetooth or 5GHz 802.11a WiFi radios, as well as common cordless phones and microwave ovens.

Figure 8.11   The Wireless USB logo carried by devices certified to comply with the Wireless USB specification.

The uses for Wireless USB are almost endless; basically anything that can be connected via a wired USB connection will be able to be connected wirelessly as well. Imagine being able to merely place a wireless USB hard drive near a PC and have it be automatically recognized and usable as a high-speed storage or backup device. A wireless USB camera could be placed near a PC, and you could transfer images or movies quickly with no cables. Existing wired USB devices can even be connected wirelessly by attaching a special wireless USB adapter called a Host Wire Adapter (HWA) on the PC side and a Device Wire Adapter (DWA) on the peripheral side. Figure 8.12 shows one possible configuration for connecting wired devices that way.

Note that the Host Wire Adapter doesn't necessarily have to be an external device; it can also be installed in the form of an internal PCI or PCI Express card for desktop systems, as well as a Mini PCI, PC-Card, or ExpressCard for use in laptops. Future desktop and laptop systems may even come with wireless USB built in. Future WiFi network adapters may include Wireless USB functionality as well. Wireless USB adapters and peripherals first appeared on the market in 2006.

USB Adapters

If you still have a variety of older peripherals and yet you want to take advantage of the USB connector on your motherboard, a number of signal converters or adapters are available. Companies such as Belkin and others currently have adapters in the following types:

- USB to parallel (printer)
- USB to serial
- USB to SCSI
- USB to Ethernet
- USB to keyboard/mouse
- USB to TV/video

These adapters normally look just like a cable, with a USB connector at one end (which you plug into your USB port) and various other interface connectors at the other end. There is more to these devices than just a cable: Active electronics are hidden in a module along the cable or are sometimes packed into one of the cable ends. The electronics are powered by the USB bus and convert the signals to the appropriate other interface. Some drawbacks do exist for these adapters. One is cost—they normally cost $50–$100 or more. It can be tough to spend $70 on a USB-to-parallel adapter to drive a printer that barely cost twice that amount. In addition, other limitations might apply. For example, USB-to-parallel converters work only with printers and not other parallel-connected devices, such as scanners, cameras, external drives, and so on. Before purchasing one of these adapters, ensure that it will work with the device or devices you have in mind. If you need to use more than one non-USB device with your system, consider special USB hubs that also contain various combinations of other port types. These special hubs are more expensive than USB-only hubs but are less expensive than the combined cost of a comparable USB hub and two or more USB adapters.

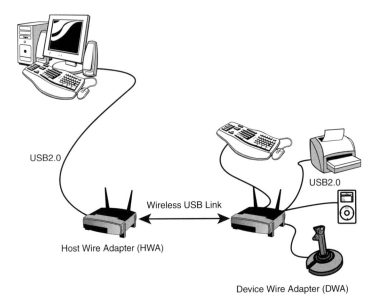

Figure 8.12 Using a Host Wire Adapter and Device Wire Adapter to wirelessly connect traditional wired USB devices to a system.

Another type of adapter available is a direct-connect bridge cable, which enables you to connect two USB-equipped PCs directly together using USB as a network. These are popular for people playing two-player games, with each player on his own system. Another use is for transferring files, because this connection usually works as well or better than the direct parallel connection that otherwise might be used. Also available are USB switchboxes that enable one peripheral to be shared among two or more USB buses. Note that both the direct-connect cables and USB switchboxes are technically not allowed as a part of the USB specification, although they do exist.

Legacy-Free PCs

USB will find more use in the future as more and more legacy-free systems are shipped. A *legacy-free PC* is one that lacks any components that were connected to or part of the traditional ISA bus. This especially includes the otherwise standard Super I/O chip, which integrated serial, parallel, keyboard, mouse, floppy, and other connections. A legacy-free system will therefore lack the standard serial, parallel, and keyboard/mouse connectors on the back, and also will not include an integrated floppy controller. The devices previously connected to those ports must instead be connected via USB, ATA/IDE, PCI, and other interfaces.

Legacy-free systems are becoming more and more popular, especially in the laptop/notebook systems. Most are abandoning traditional serial and parallel ports as well as external keyboard/mouse ports for USB and/or IEEE 1394 (FireWire) instead. To compensate for the loss of the other external interfaces, most legacy-free motherboards will feature up to four or more integrated USB connectors on one or two buses.

IEEE 1394 (FireWire or i.LINK)

The Institute of Electrical and Electronic Engineers Standards Board introduced IEEE 1394 (or just 1394 for short) in late 1995. The number comes from the fact that this happened to be the 1,394th standard the board published. It is the result of the large data-moving demands of today's audio and video multimedia devices. The key advantage of 1394 is that it's extremely fast; the current standard supports data-transfer rates up to 400Mbps (1394a) or 800Mbps (early 1394b implementations).

1394 Standards

The most popular version of the 1394 standard is actually referred to as 1394a, or sometimes as 1394a-2000 (for the year this version was adopted). The 1394a standard was introduced to solve interoperability and compatibility issues in the original 1394 standard; it uses the same connectors and supports the same speeds as the original 1394 standard.

The faster 1394b standard was introduced in early 2003. Initially, 1394b supports 800Mbps transfer rates, but future versions of the standard might reach speeds of up to 3,200Mbps. 1394b is capable of reaching much higher speeds than the current 1394/1394a standard because it can also support network technologies such as glass and plastic fiber-optic cable and Category 5 UTP cable, increased distances when Category 5 cabling is used between devices, and improvements in signaling. 1394b is fully backward compatible with 1394a devices. 1394 is also known by two other common names: i.LINK and FireWire. *i.LINK* is an IEEE 1394 designation initiated by Sony in an effort to put a more user-friendly name on IEEE 1394 technology. Most companies that produce 1394 products for PCs have endorsed this new name initiative. Originally, the term *FireWire* was an Apple-specific trademark that Apple licensed to vendors on a fee basis. However, in May 2002, Apple and the 1394 Trade Association announced an agreement to allow the trade association to provide no-fee licenses for the FireWire trademark on 1394-compliant products that pass the trade association's tests. Apple continues to use *FireWire* as its marketing term for IEEE 1394 devices. FireWire 400 refers to Apple's IEEE 1394a–compliant products, whereas FireWire 800 refers to Apple's IEEE 1394b–compliant products. Intel has always licensed USB on a royalty-free basis.

1394a Technical Details

The IEEE 1394a standard currently exists with three signaling rates: 100Mbps, 200Mbps, and 400Mbps (12.5MBps, 25MBps, and 50MBps). A maximum of 63 devices can be connected to a single IEEE 1394 adapter card by way of daisy-chaining or branching. Unlike USB devices, 1394 devices can be used in a daisy-chain without using a hub, although hubs are recommended for devices that will be hot-swapped. Cables for IEEE 1394a devices use Nintendo GameBoy–derived connectors and consist of six conductors: Four wires transmit data, and two wires conduct power. Connection with the motherboard is made either by a dedicated IEEE 1394a interface or by a PC Card adapter card. Figure 8.13 shows the 1394a cable, socket, and connector.

The 1394 bus was derived from the FireWire bus originally developed by Apple and Texas Instruments. 1394a uses a simple six-wire cable with two differential pairs of clock and data lines, plus two power lines; the four-wire cable shown in Figure 8.13 is used with self-powered devices, such as DV camcorders. Just as with USB, 1394 is fully PnP, including the capability for hot-plugging (insertion and removal of components without powering down). Unlike the much more complicated parallel SCSI bus, 1394 does not require complicated termination, and devices connected to the bus can draw up to 1.5 amps of electrical power. 1394a offers equal or greater performance compared to ultra-wide SCSI, with a much less expensive and less complicated connection.

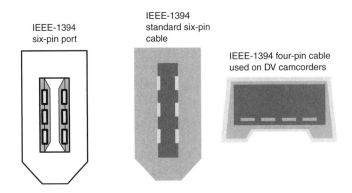

IEEE-1394
six-pin port

IEEE-1394
standard six-pin
cable

IEEE-1394 four-pin cable
used on DV camcorders

Figure 8.13   IEEE 1394a port, 6-pin cable connector, and 4-pin cable connector.

Built on a daisy-chained and branched topology, 1394 allows up to 63 nodes, with a chain of up to 16 devices on each node. If this is not enough, the standard also calls for up to 1,023 bridged buses, which can interconnect more than 64,000 nodes! Additionally, as with SCSI, 1394 can support devices with various data rates on the same bus. Most 1394 adapters have three nodes, each of which can support 16 devices in a daisy-chain arrangement. Some 1394 adapters also support internal 1394 devices.

The types of devices that can be connected to the PC via 1394 include mainly video cameras and editing equipment, as well as all forms of disk drives, including hard disk, optical, and floppy drives. Also, digital cameras, tape drives, high-resolution scanners, and many other high-speed peripherals that feature 1394 have interfaces built in. The 1394 bus appears in some desktop and portable computers as a replacement or supplement for other external high-speed buses, such as USB or SCSI.

Chipsets enabling PC Card/CardBus and ExpressCard adapters for the 1394 bus are available from a number of manufacturers, including some models that support both 1394 and other port types in a single slot. Microsoft has developed drivers to support 1394 in Windows 9x and later, including Windows XP. The most popular devices that conform to the IEEE 1394 standard primarily are camcorders and digital video recorders. Sony was among the first to release such devices under the i.LINK name. In typical Sony fashion, however, its products have a unique four-wire connector that requires a 6-pin-to-4-pin adapter cord to be used with some IEEE 1394 PC Cards, and Sony doesn't even call it IEEE 1394 or FireWire; it has created its own designation (i.LINK) instead. Just remember that whether it is called IEEE 1394, FireWire, or i.LINK, it is all basically the same thing. DV products using 1394 also are available from Panasonic, Sharp, Matsushita, and others. Non-computer IEEE 1394 applications include DV conferencing devices, satellite audio and video data streams, audio synthesizers, DVD, and other high-speed disc drives.

Because of the current DV emphasis for IEEE 1394 peripherals, many FireWire PC Cards currently offered are bundled with DV capturing and editing software. With a DV camera or recording equipment, these items provide substantial video-editing and dubbing capabilities on your system. Of course, you need IEEE 1394 I/O connectivity, which is a growing but still somewhat rare feature on current motherboards.

IEEE 1394b Technical Details

IEEE 1394b is the second generation of the 1394 standard, with the first products (high-performance external hard drives) introduced in January 2003. IEEE 1394b uses one of two new 9-pin cables and connectors to support speeds of 800Mbps–3,200Mbps with copper or fiber-optic cabling. In addition to supporting faster transfer rates, 1394b has other new features, including the following:

- Self-healing loops. If you improperly connect 1394b devices together to create a logical loop, the interface corrects the problem instead of failing, as with 1394a.

- Continuous dual simplex. Of the two wire pairs used, each pair transmits data to the other device so that speed remains constant.

- Support for fiber-optic and CAT5 network cable as well as standard 1394a and 1394b copper cable.

- Improved arbitration of signals to support faster performance and longer cable distances.

- Support for CAT5 cable, even though it uses pairs on pins 1 and 2 and 7 and 8 only for greater reliability. It also doesn't require crossover cables.

The initial implementations of IEEE 1394b use a new nine-wire interface with two pairs of signaling wires. However, to enable a 1394b port to connect to 1394a-compatible devices, two different versions of the 1394b port are used:

- Beta
- Bilingual

Beta connectors support only 1394b devices, whereas bilingual connectors can support both 1394b and 1394a devices. As Figure 8.14 shows, the connectors and cables have the same pinout but are keyed differently.

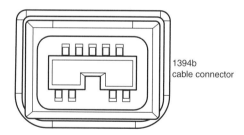

1394b cable connector

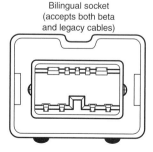
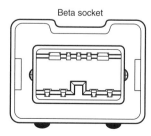

Bilingual socket (accepts both beta and legacy cables)

Beta socket

Figure 8.14 Bilingual and beta 1394b connectors and cables. Many 1394b implementations use both types of connectors.

Note that bilingual sockets and cables have a narrower notch than beta sockets and cables. This prevents cables designed for 1394a devices from being connected to the beta socket. Figure 8.15 compares a beta-to-beta 1394b cable to bilingual-to-1394a cables.

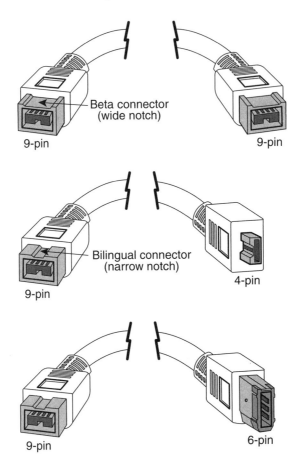

Beta connector
(wide notch)

9-pin

9-pin

Bilingual connector
(narrow notch)

4-pin

9-pin

9-pin

6-pin

Figure 8.15 A beta-to-beta cable (top) compared to bilingual–to–4-pin (middle) and bilingual–to–6-pin 1394a devices (bottom).

Comparing IEEE 1394a and USB 1.1/2.0

Because of the similarity in both the form and function of USB and 1394, there has been some confusion about the two. Table 8.12 summarizes the differences between the two technologies.

Table 8.12 IEEE 1394a and USB Comparison

	IEEE 1394a[1]	IEEE 1394b[2]	USB 1.1	USB 2.0
PC host required	No	No	Yes	Yes/No[3]
Maximum number of devices	63	63	127	127

Table 8.12   Continued

	IEEE 1394a[1]	IEEE 1394b[2]	USB 1.1	USB 2.0
Hot-swappable	Yes	Yes	Yes	Yes
Maximum cable length between devices	4.5 meters	4.5 meters[4]	5 meters	5 meters
Transfer rate	400Mbps (50MBps)	800Mbps (100MBps)	12Mbps (1.5MBps)	480Mbps (60MBps)
Typical devices	DV camcorders; digital cameras; HDTV; set-top boxes; hard disk drives; scanners; musical instruments	All 1394a devices	Keyboards; mice; joysticks; digital cameras; hard disk drives; modems; printers; scanners	All USB 1.1 devices; DV camcorders; HDTV; set-top boxes; musical instruments

1. *IEEE 1394a is also called FireWire 400 or i.LINK.*
2. *IEEE 1394b is also called FireWire 800.*
3. *No with USB On-The-Go.*
4. *9-pin copper; 100 meters with fiber optic.*

Because the overall performance and physical specifications are similar, the main difference between USB and 1394 would be popularity. The bottom line is that USB is by far the most popular external interface for PCs, eclipsing all others by comparison. The reason primarily is that Intel developed most of USB and has placed built-in USB support in all its motherboard chipsets since 1996. There are virtually no motherboard chipsets that integrate 1394; in most cases it has to be added as an extra-cost chip to the motherboard. The cost of the additional 1394 circuitry, the Apple royalties, and the fact that all motherboards already have USB have conspired to greatly limit the popularity of 1394 (FireWire) in the notebook PC marketplace.

Many people like to bring any comparison of USB and 1394 down to speed, but that is a constantly changing parameter. 1394a offers a data transfer rate more than 33 times faster than that of USB 1.1, but is only about 83% as fast as USB 2.0. However, 1394b is about 66% faster than USB 2.0.

Because both USB 2.0 and 1394a (FireWire) offer relatively close to the same overall capabilities and performance, you make your choice based on which devices you intend to connect. If the digital video camera you want to connect has only a 1394 (FireWire/i.LINK) connection, you will need to add a 1394 FireWire card to your system, if such a connection isn't already present on your motherboard. Most general-purpose PC storage, I/O, and other devices are USB, whereas only video devices usually have 1394 connections. However, many devices now offer both USB 2.0 and 1394 interfaces to enable use with the widest range of computers.

Between the popularity and capabilities of USB, I recommend seeking out only USB peripherals over their 1394 (FireWire) counterparts, where possible. Because the only real use for FireWire over USB is for transferring and editing video from DV (digital video) camcorders, most people won't need a FireWire port.

Low-Speed External Connections

Traditionally, the most basic communication ports in any PC system have been the serial and parallel ports; however, these ports are quickly disappearing from newer laptop/notebook systems in favor of USB.

Serial ports (also known as *communication* or *COM* ports) were originally used for devices that had to communicate bidirectionally with the system. Such devices include modems, mice, scanners, digitizers, and any other devices that "talk to" and receive information from the notebook PC. Newer parallel port standards now allow the parallel port to perform high-speed bidirectional communications.

Several companies manufacture communications programs that perform high-speed transfers between notebook PC systems using serial or parallel ports. Versions of these file-transfer programs have been included with DOS 6.0 and higher (Interlink) and with Windows 95 and newer versions (DCC—Direct Cable Connection). Numerous products have made nontraditional use of the parallel port. For example, over the years there have been network adapters, high-capacity floppy disk drives, CD-ROM drives, scanners, and tape backup units that attach to the parallel port. The tasks traditionally performed by both serial and parallel ports are increasingly being performed by newer port types, such as USB and IEEE 1394, but, for some time to come, both legacy and newer port types will continue to be important I/O interface types.

Serial Ports

The asynchronous serial interface was designed as a system-to-system communications port. *Asynchronous* means that no synchronization or clocking signal is present, so characters can be sent with any arbitrary time spacing.

Each character that is sent over a serial connection is framed by a standard start-and-stop signal. A single 0 bit, called the *start bit*, precedes each character to tell the receiving system that the next eight bits constitute a byte of data. One or two stop bits follow the character to signal that the character has been sent. At the receiving end of the communication, characters are recognized by the start-and-stop signals instead of by the timing of their arrival. The asynchronous interface is character oriented and has about a 20% overhead for the extra information that is needed to identify each character.

Serial refers to data that is sent over a single wire, with each bit lining up in a series as the bits are sent. This type of communication is used over the phone system because it provides one wire for data in each direction.

Typical Locations for Serial Ports

Typical laptop systems include one serial port, with the connector located normally at the rear of the system. Built-in serial ports are controlled by either a Super I/O chip on the motherboard or a highly integrated South Bridge chip in the latest motherboard designs.

If you need more serial ports than your system has as standard, or if your notebook did not include a serial port at all, you can purchase single-port or multiport serial port PC Cards. Note that PC Card–based modems also incorporate a built-in serial port on the card as part of the modem circuitry. Figure 8.16 shows the standard 9-pin DB-9 connector used with most modern external serial ports. Figure 8.17 shows the original standard 25-pin version.

Serial ports can connect to a variety of devices, such as modems, plotters, printers, other computers, bar code readers, scales, and device control circuits. The official specification recommends a maximum cable length of 50 feet. The limiting factor is the total load capacitance of cable and input circuits of the interface. The maximum capacitance is specified as 2,500pF (picofarads). Special low-capacitance cables can effectively increase the maximum cable length greatly, to as much as 500 feet or more. Also available are line drivers (amplifier/repeaters) that can extend cable length even further.

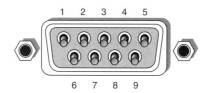

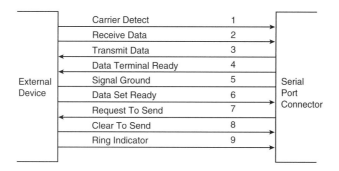

Figure 8.16　Modern (AT-style) 9-pin serial port connector specifications.

Tables 8.13, 8.14, and 8.15 show the pinouts of the 9-pin serial connector, the 25-pin serial connector, and the 9-pin-to-25-pin serial adapter, respectively.

Table 8.13　9-Pin Serial Port Connector

Pin	Signal	Description	I/O
1	CD	Carrier detect	In
2	RD	Receive data	In
3	TD	Transmit data	Out
4	DTR	Data terminal ready	Out
5	SG	Signal ground	—
6	DSR	Data set ready	In
7	RTS	Request to send	Out
8	CTS	Clear to send	In
9	RI	Ring indicator	In

Table 8.14　25-Pin Serial Port Connector

Pin	Signal	Description	I/O
1	—	Chassis ground	—
2	TD	Transmit data	Out
3	RD	Received data	In
4	RTS	Request to send	Out

(continues)

Table 8.14   Continued

Pin	Signal	Description	I/O
5	CTS	Clear to send	In
6	DSR	Data set ready	In
7	SG	Signal ground	—
8	CD	Received line signal detector	In
9	—	+Transmit current loop data	Out
11	—	-Transmit current loop data	Out
18	—	+Receive current loop data	In
20	DTR	Data terminal ready	Out
22	RI	Ring indicator	In
25	—	-Receive current loop return	In

Table 8.15   9-Pin-to-25-Pin Serial Adapter Connections

9-Pin	25-Pin	Signal	Description
1	8	CD	Carrier detect
2	3	RD	Receive data
3	2	TD	Transmit data
4	20	DTR	Data terminal ready
5	7	SG	Signal ground
6	6	DSR	Data set ready
7	4	RTS	Request to send
8	5	CTS	Clear to send
9	22	RI	Ring indicator

UARTs

The heart of any serial port is the Universal Asynchronous Receiver/Transmitter (UART) chip. This chip completely controls the process of breaking the native parallel data within the PC into serial format and later converting serial data back into the parallel format.

Several types of UART chips have been available on the market. The 16550 UART includes a 16-byte buffer that aids in faster communications. This is sometimes referred to as a *FIFO (first in, first out)* buffer.

Even though virtually all Pentium-class and newer systems have 16550-equivalent UART functionality in their serial ports, any search for a socketed 16550 chip on most of these systems would be done in vain. Instead, the functionality of the 16550, parallel port, and other ports is included as part of the Super I/O chip or, on the newest systems, the South Bridge chip.

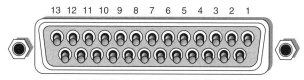

Description	Pin
NC	1
Transmitted Data	2
Received Data	3
Request to Send	4
Clear to Send	5
Data Set Ready	6
Signal Ground	7
Received Line Signal Detector	8
+ Transmit Current Loop Data	9
NC	10
- Transmit Current Loop Data	11
NC	12
NC	13
NC	14
NC	15
NC	16
NC	17
+ Receive Current Loop Data	18
NC	19
Data Terminal Ready	20
NC	21
Ring Indicator	22
NC	23
NC	24
- Receive Current Loop Return	25

External Device

Serial Port Connector

Figure 8.17 Original 25-pin serial port connector specifications.

Note

Another way to tell whether you have a 16550 UART in Windows is to click the Start menu and then select Settings, Control Panel. Next, double-click Modems and then click the Diagnostics tab. The Diagnostics tab shows a list of all COM ports in the system, even if they don't have a modem attached to them. Select the port you want to check in the list and click More Info. Windows communicates with the port to determine the UART type, and that information is listed in the Port Information portion of the More Info box. If a modem is attached, additional information about the modem is displayed.

Onboard Serial Ports

Starting with late-model 486-based systems in the mid-1990s, a component on the motherboard called a *Super I/O* chip began to replace separate UART chips. This normally has two serial port UARTs as well as a multimode parallel port, floppy controller, keyboard controller, and sometimes the CMOS memory, all built in to a single tiny chip. Still, this chip acts as if all these separate devices were installed: That is, from a software point of view, both the operating system and applications still act as if separate UART chips were installed on serial port adapter cards. The most recent systems integrate the functions of a Super I/O chip into the South Bridge chip. As with the Super I/O chip, South Bridge chips with integrated I/O are transparent to software. Many of the newer systems have become *legacy free*, which means they don't include a Super I/O chip or any of the functions found on them, such as serial ports.

Serial Port Configuration

Each time a serial port receives a character, it has to get the attention of the computer by raising an interrupt request line (IRQ). Eight-bit ISA bus systems have eight of these lines, and systems with a 16-bit ISA bus have 16 lines. The 8259 interrupt controller chip or equivalent usually handles these requests for attention. In a standard configuration, COM1 uses IRQ4, and COM2 uses IRQ3. Even on the latest systems, the default COM port assignments remain the same for compatibility with older software and hardware.

When a serial port is installed in a system, it must be configured to use specific I/O addresses (called *ports*) and interrupts (called *IRQs*). The best plan is to follow the existing standards for how these devices are to be set up. For configuring serial ports, use the addresses and interrupts indicated in Table 8.16.

Table 8.16 Standard Serial I/O Port Addresses and Interrupts

COM	I/O Ports	IRQ
COM1	3F8-3FFh	IRQ4
COM2	2F8-2FFh	IRQ3
COM3	3E8-3EFh	IRQ4*
COM4	2E8-2EFh	IRQ3*

* Note that although many serial ports can be set up to share IRQ3 and IRQ4 with COM1 and COM2, this is not recommended. The best recommendation is setting COM3 to IRQ10 and COM4 to IRQ11 (if available).

If you are adding more than the standard COM1 and COM2 serial ports, be sure they use unique and nonconflicting interrupts. If you purchase a serial port adapter card and intend to use it to supply ports beyond the standard COM1 and COM2, be sure it can use interrupts other than IRQ3 and IRQ4; the latest CardBus-based serial port cards take advantage of IRQ-sharing features to allow COM3 and above to use a single IRQ without conflicts.

Note that BIOS manufacturers never built support for COM3 and COM4 into the BIOS. Therefore, DOS cannot work with serial ports above COM2 because DOS gets its I/O information from the BIOS. The BIOS finds out what is installed in your system, and where it is installed, during the Power On Self Test (POST). The POST checks only for the first two installed ports. This is not a problem under Windows because Windows 95 and later have built-in support for up to 128 ports.

Testing Serial Ports

You can perform several tests on serial and parallel ports. The two most common types of tests are those that involve software only and those that involve both hardware and software. The software-only tests are done with diagnostic programs, such as Microsoft's MSD or the modem diagnostics built in to Windows, whereas the hardware and software tests involve using a wrap plug to perform loopback testing.

▶▶ See "Testing Parallel Ports," p. 331.

▶▶ See "Advanced Diagnostics Using Loopback Testing," p. 322.

Microsoft Diagnostics

Microsoft Diagnostics (MSD) is a diagnostic program supplied with MS-DOS 6.x, Windows 3.x, and Windows 9x/Me/2000. Note that with Windows 95, this program can be found on the CD-ROM in the \other\msd directory. In Windows 98/Me/2000, you can find it on the CD-ROM in the \tools\oldmsdos directory. MSD is not automatically installed when you install the operating system. To use it, you must run it from the CD-ROM directly or copy the program from the CD-ROM to your hard disk.

For the most accurate results, many diagnostics programs, such as MSD, are best run in a DOS-only environment. Because of this, you need to restart the machine in DOS mode before using them. Then, to use MSD, switch to the directory in which it is located. This is not necessary, of course, if the directory that contains the program is in your search path—which is often the case with the DOS 6.x or Windows-provided versions of MSD. Then, simply type **MSD** at the DOS prompt and press Enter. Soon you see the MSD screen.

Select the Serial Ports option. Notice that you are given information about which type of serial chip you have in your system, as well as information about which ports are available. If any of the ports are in use (with a mouse, for example), that information is provided as well. MSD is helpful in at least determining whether your serial ports are responding. If MSD cannot determine the existence of a port, it does not provide the report which indicates that the port exists. This sort of "look-and-see" test is the first action I usually take to determine why a port is not responding.

Troubleshooting Ports in Windows

Windows 9x/Me can tell you whether your ports are functioning. First, you must verify that the required communications files are present to support the serial ports in your system:

1. Verify the file sizes and dates of both COMM.DRV (16-bit serial driver) and SERIAL.VXD (32-bit serial driver) in the SYSTEM directory, compared to the original versions of these files from the Windows 9x/Me CD-ROM.

2. Confirm that the following lines are present in SYSTEM.INI:

   ```
   [boot]
   comm.drv=comm.drv
   [386enh]
   device=*vcd
   ```

The SERIAL.VXD driver is not loaded in SYSTEM.INI; instead, it is loaded through the Registry. Windows 2000 and XP use the SERIAL.SYS and SERENUM.SYS drivers for handling RS-232 devices. You can compare the file sizes and dates for these files to those on the Windows 2000 CD-ROM. If both drivers are present and accounted for, you can determine whether a particular serial port's I/O address and IRQ settings are properly defined by following these steps for Windows 9x/Me/2000:

1. Right-click the My Computer icon on the desktop and select Properties, or double-click the System icon in the Control Panel. Click the Device Manager tab, click Ports, and then select a specific port (such as COM1).

2. Click the Properties button and then click the Resources tab to display the current resource settings (IRQ, I/O) for that port.

3. Check the Conflicting Devices List to see whether the port is using resources that conflict with other devices. If the port is in conflict with other devices, click the Change Setting button and then select a configuration that does not cause resource conflicts. You might need to experiment with these settings until you find the correct one.

4. If the resource settings cannot be changed, most likely they must be changed via the BIOS Setup. Shut down and restart the system, enter the BIOS setup, and change the port configurations there.

A common problem with non–Plug and Play modems can occur when people try to use a modem on COM3 with a serial mouse or other device on COM1. Normally, COM1 and COM3 ports use the same IRQ, meaning that they cannot be used simultaneously. The COM2 and COM4 ports have the same problem sharing IRQs. If possible, change the COM3 or COM4 port to an IRQ setting that is not in conflict with COM1 or COM2. Note also that some video adapters have an automatic address conflict with COM4.

Advanced Diagnostics Using Loopback Testing

One of the most useful types of diagnostic tests is the loopback test, which can be used to ensure the correct function of the serial port and any attached cables. Loopback tests are basically internal (digital) or external (analog). You can run internal tests by simply unplugging any cables from the port and executing the test via a diagnostics program.

The external loopback test is more effective. This test requires that a special loopback connector or wrap plug be attached to the port in question. When the test is run, the port is used to send data out to the loopback plug, which simply routes the data back into the port's receive pins so the port is transmitting and receiving at the same time. A loopback or wrap plug is nothing more than a cable that is doubled back on itself. Most diagnostics programs that run this type of test include the loopback plug. If not, these types of plugs easily can be purchased or even built.

Following is a list of the wiring needed to construct your own serial port loopback or wrap plugs:

■ Standard IBM-type 25-pin serial (female DB25S) loopback connector (wrap plug). Connect the following pins:

    1 to 7

    2 to 3

    4 to 5 to 8

    6 to 11 to 20 to 22

    15 to 17 to 23

    18 to 25

■ Norton Utilities (Symantec) 25-pin serial (female DB25S) loopback connector (wrap plug). Connect the following pins:

2 to 3

4 to 5

6 to 8 to 20 to 22

- Standard IBM-type 9-pin serial (female DB9S) loopback connector (wrap plug). Connect the following pins:

1 to 7 to 8

2 to 3

4 to 6 to 9

- Norton Utilities (Symantec) 9-pin serial (female DB9S) loopback connector (wrap plug). Connect the following pins:

2 to 3

7 to 8

1 to 4 to 6 to 9

▶▶   See "Serial Ports," p. xxx (this chapter).

To make these loopback plugs, you need a connector shell with the required pins installed. Then wire-wrap or solder the wires, interconnecting the appropriate pins inside the connector shell as specified in the preceding list.

In most cases, purchasing a set of loopback connectors that are premade is less expensive than making them yourself. Most companies that sell diagnostics software can also sell you a set of loopback plugs. Some hardware diagnostic programs include loopback plugs with the software. One advantage of using loopback connectors is that you can plug them into the ends of a cable that is included in the test. This can verify that both the cable and the port are working properly.

Parallel Ports

Parallel ports normally are used for connecting printers to a notebook PC. Even though that was their sole original purpose, parallel ports have become much more useful over the years as a more general-purpose, relatively high-speed interface between devices (when compared to serial ports). Today, USB ports are faster, and are even replacing parallel ports on newer laptops. Originally, parallel ports were "one way" only; however, modern parallel ports can send and receive data when properly configured.

Parallel ports are so named because they have eight lines for sending all the bits that comprise 1 byte of data simultaneously across eight wires. This interface is fast and traditionally has been used for printers. However, programs that transfer data between systems always have used the parallel port as an option for transmitting data because it can do so 4 bits at a time rather than 1 bit at a time, as with a serial interface.

The following section looks at how these programs transfer data between parallel ports. The only problem with parallel ports is that their cables cannot be extended for any great length without amplifying the signal; otherwise, errors occur in the data. Table 8.17 shows the pinout for a standard notebook or desktop PC parallel port.

Table 8.17   25-Pin PC-Compatible Parallel Port Connector

Pin	Description	I/O
1	-Strobe	Out
2	+Data Bit 0	Out
3	+Data Bit 1	Out
4	+Data Bit 2	Out
5	+Data Bit 3	Out
6	+Data Bit 4	Out
7	+Data Bit 5	Out
8	+Data Bit 6	Out
9	+Data Bit 7	Out
10	-Acknowledge	In
11	+Busy	In
12	+Paper End	In
13	+Select	In
14	-Auto Feed	Out
15	-Error	In
16	-Initialize Printer	Out
17	-Select Input	Out
18	-Data Bit 0 Return (GND)	In
19	-Data Bit 1 Return (GND)	In
20	-Data Bit 2 Return (GND)	In
21	-Data Bit 3 Return (GND)	In
22	-Data Bit 4 Return (GND)	In
23	-Data Bit 5 Return (GND)	In
24	-Data Bit 6 Return (GND)	In
25	-Data Bit 7 Return (GND)	In

IEEE 1284 Parallel Port Standard

The IEEE 1284 standard, called *Standard Signaling Method for a Bidirectional Parallel Peripheral Interface for Personal Computers*, was approved for final release in March 1994. This standard defines the physical characteristics of the parallel port, including data-transfer modes and physical and electrical specifications. IEEE 1284 defines the electrical signaling behavior external to the notebook or desktop PC for a multimodal parallel port that can support 4-bit modes of operation. Not all modes are required by the 1284 specification, and the standard makes some provision for additional modes.

The IEEE 1284 specification is targeted at standardizing the behavior between a notebook or desktop PC and an attached device, specifically attached printers. However, the specification is of interest to vendors of parallel port peripherals (removable-media drives, scanners, and so on). IEEE 1284 pertains only to hardware and line control and does not define how software is to talk to the port. An offshoot of the original 1284 standard has been created to define the software interface. The IEEE 1284.3 committee was formed to develop a standard for software that is used with IEEE 1284–compliant hardware. This standard, designed to address the disparity among providers of parallel port chips, contains a specification for supporting EPP (Enhanced Parallel Port) mode via the notebook or desktop PC's system BIOS.

IEEE 1284 ports and cables enable higher throughput (as compared to noncompliant hardware) in a connection between a computer and a printer or between two computers. The result is that the printer cable is no longer the standard printer cable. The IEEE 1284 printer cable uses twisted-pair technology, which results in a much more reliable and error-free connection.

The IEEE 1284 standard also defines the parallel port connectors, including the two preexisting types (Type A and Type B), as well as an additional high-density Type C connector. Type A refers to the standard DB25 connector used on most PC systems for parallel port connections, whereas Type B refers to the standard 36-pin Centronics-style connector found on most printers. Type C is a more recent high-density 36-pin connector that can be found on some printers on the market, such as those from HP. The three connectors are shown in Figure 8.18.

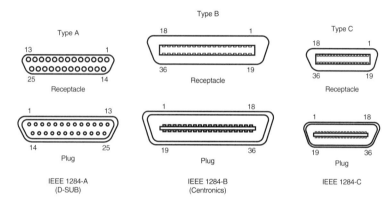

Figure 8.18   The three different types of IEEE 1284 parallel port connectors.

Most parallel ports use the standard Type A receptacle, as shown in Figure 8.19.

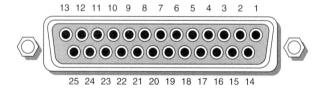

Figure 8.19   Standard Type A parallel port connector.

The IEEE 1284 parallel port standard defines five port-operating modes, emphasizing the higher-speed EPP and ECP modes. Some of the modes are input only, whereas others are output only. These five modes combine to create four types of ports, as shown in Table 8.18.

Table 8.18   Types of IEEE 1284 Ports

Parallel Port Type	Input Mode	Output Mode	Comments
SPP (Standard Parallel Port)	Nibble	Compatible	4-bit input, 8-bit output
Bidirectional	Byte	Compatible	8-bit I/O
EPP (Enhanced Parallel Port)	EPP	EPP	8-bit I/O
ECP (Enhanced Capabilities Port)	ECP	ECP	8-bit I/O, uses DMA

The 1284-defined parallel port modes are shown in Table 8.19, which also shows the approximate transfer speeds.

Table 8.19   IEEE 1284 Parallel Port Modes

Parallel Port Mode	Direction	Transfer Rate
Nibble (4-bit)	Input only	50KBps
Byte (8-bit)	Input only	150KBps
Compatible	Output only	150KBps
EPP (Enhanced Parallel Port)	Input/Output	500KBps–2.77MBps
ECP (Enhanced Capabilities Port)	Input/Output	500KBps–2.77MBps

Each of the port types and modes is discussed in the following sections.

Standard Parallel Ports

Older systems did not have different types of parallel ports available. The only available port was the parallel port that was used to send information from the computer to a device such as a printer. The unidirectional nature of the original PC parallel port is consistent with its primary use—that is, sending data to a printer. There were times, however, when it was desirable to have a bidirectional port—for example, when it was necessary to receive feedback from a printer, which was common with PostScript printers. This could not be done easily with the original unidirectional ports.

Although it was never intended to be used for input, a clever scheme was devised in which four of the signal lines can be used as a 4-bit input connection. Thus, these ports can do 8-bit (byte) output (called *compatible mode*) and 4-bit input (called *nibble mode*). This is still very common on low-end desktop systems. Systems built after 1993 are likely to have more capable parallel ports, such as bidirectional, EPP, or ECP. Standard parallel ports are capable of effective transfer rates of about 150KBps output and about 50KBps input.

Bidirectional (8-Bit) Parallel Ports

With the introduction of the PS/2 series of machines in 1987, IBM introduced the bidirectional parallel port. These ports are commonly found in PC-compatible systems today and can be designated "bidirectional," "PS/2 type," or "extended" parallel ports. This port design opened the way for true communication between the computer and the peripheral across the parallel port. This was done by defining a few of the previously unused pins in the parallel connector, and by defining a status bit to indicate in which direction information was traveling across the channel. This allows for true 8-bit (called *byte mode*) input.

These ports can do both 8-bit input and output using the standard eight data lines and are considerably faster than the 4-bit ports when used with external devices. Bidirectional ports are capable of approximately 150KBps transfer rates on both output and input. Some newer systems use this as their "standard" mode.

Enhanced Parallel Port

EPP is a newer specification, sometimes referred to as the *Fast Mode* parallel port. Intel, Xircom, and Zenith Data Systems developed and announced, in October 1991, the EPP. The first products to offer EPP were Zenith Data Systems laptops, Xircom Pocket LAN adapters, and the Intel 82360 SL I/O chip. Currently, almost all systems include a multimode parallel port, usually built in to the Super I/O chip on the motherboard, that supports EPP mode.

EPP operates at almost ISA bus speed and offers a tenfold increase in the raw throughput capability over a conventional parallel port. EPP is especially designed for parallel port peripherals, such as LAN adapters, disk drives, and tape backups. EPP has been included in the new IEEE 1284 Parallel Port standard. Transfer rates of up to 2.77MBps are possible with EPP.

Since the original Intel 82360 SL I/O chip in 1992, other major chip vendors (such as National Semiconductor, SMC, Western Digital, and VLSI) have also produced I/O chipsets that offer some form of EPP capability. One problem is that the procedure for enabling EPP across the various chips differs widely from vendor to vendor, and many vendors offer more than one I/O chip.

EPP version 1.7 (March 1992) identifies the first popular version of the hardware specification. With minor changes, this has since been abandoned and folded into the IEEE 1284 standard. Some technical reference materials have erroneously made reference to "EPP specification version 1.9," causing confusion about the EPP standard. Note that "EPP version 1.9" technically does not exist, and any EPP specification after the original (version 1.7) is more accurately referred to as a part of the IEEE 1284 specification.

Unfortunately, this has resulted in two somewhat incompatible standards for EPP parallel ports: the original EPP Standards Committee version 1.7 standard and the IEEE 1284 Committee standard, normally called *EPP version 1.9*. The two standards are similar enough that new peripherals can be designed to support both, but older EPP 1.7 peripherals might not operate with EPP 1284 (EPP 1.9) ports. For this reason, many multimode ports allow configuration in either EPP 1.7 or 1.9 mode, normally selected via the BIOS Setup.

EPP ports are now supported in virtually all Super I/O chips that are used on modern motherboards and in South Bridge chips that integrate I/O functions. Because the EPP port is defined in the IEEE 1284 standard, it also has gained software and driver support, including support in Windows NT.

Enhanced Capabilities Port

In 1992, Microsoft and Hewlett-Packard announced another type of high-speed parallel port: the Enhanced Capabilities Port (ECP). Similar to EPP, ECP offers improved performance for the parallel port and requires special hardware logic.

Since the original announcement, ECP is included in IEEE 1284—just like EPP. Unlike EPP, however, ECP is not tailored to support portable PCs' parallel port peripherals; its purpose is to support an inexpensive attachment to a very high-performance printer or scanner. Furthermore, ECP mode requires the use of a DMA channel, which EPP did not define and which can cause troublesome conflicts with other devices that use DMA. Most PCs with newer Super I/O chips can support either EPP or ECP mode.

Most new systems are being delivered with ECP ports that support high-throughput communications. In most cases, the ECP ports can be turned into EPPs or standard parallel ports via BIOS. However, it's recommended that the port be placed in ECP mode for the best throughput.

Depending on the motherboard, the DMA channel assignment used for ECP mode on a built-in parallel port might be performed through the BIOS Setup program or through moving a jumper block on the motherboard itself.

Virtually every new or recent system today supports both the EPP and ECP modes of the IEEE 1284 Parallel Port standard. If you want to test the parallel ports in a system, especially to determine which type they are, I highly recommend a utility called Parallel. This handy parallel port information utility examines your system's parallel ports and reports the port type, I/O address, IRQ level, BIOS name, and an assortment of informative notes and warnings in a compact and easy-to-read display. The output can be redirected to a file for tech support purposes. Parallel uses very sophisticated techniques for port and IRQ detection, and it is aware of a broad range of quirky port features. You can get it from Parallel Technologies (www.1pt.com).

High-speed parallel ports such as EPP and ECP often are used for supporting external peripherals, such as Zip drives, CD-ROM drives, scanners, tape drives, and even hard disks. Most of these devices attach to the parallel port using a pass-through connection. This means that your local printer can still work through the port, along with the device. The device will have its own drivers that mediate both the communications with the device and the printer pass-through. Using EPP or ECP mode, communications speeds as high as 2.77MBps can be achieved. This can enable a relatively high-speed device to function almost as if it were connected to the system bus internally.

Parallel Port Configuration

The configuration of parallel ports is not as complicated as it is for serial ports. Even the original IBM PC had BIOS support for three LPT ports. Table 8.20 shows the standard I/O address and interrupt settings for parallel port use.

Table 8.20   Parallel Interface I/O Port Addresses and Interrupts

Standard LPTx	Alternate LPTx	I/O Ports	IRQ
LPT1	—	3BC-3BFh	IRQ7
LPT1	LPT2	378-37Ah	IRQ5
LPT2	LPT3	278h-27Ah	IRQ5

Because the BIOS and DOS have always provided three definitions for parallel ports, problems with older systems are infrequent. Problems can arise, however, from the lack of available interrupt-driven ports for ISA/PCI bus systems. Normally, an interrupt-driven port is not absolutely required for printing operations; in fact, many programs do not use the interrupt-driven capability. However, some programs do use the interrupt, such as network print programs and other types of background or spooler-type printer programs.

Also, high-speed laser-printer utility programs often use the interrupt capabilities to enable printing. If you use these types of applications on a port that is not interrupt driven, you see the printing slow to a crawl—if it works at all. The only solution is to use an interrupt-driven port. Windows supports up to 128 parallel ports.

To configure parallel ports, you normally use the BIOS Setup program for ports that are built in to the motherboard, or you might need to set jumpers and switches or use a setup program for adapter card–based ports inserted into laptop docking stations. Because each board on the market is different, you always should consult the OEM manual for that particular card if you need to know how the card should be configured.

Linking Systems with Serial or Parallel Ports

It is possible to connect two systems locally using their serial or parallel ports along with specially wired cables. This form of connection has been used over the years to set up a quick and easy mini-LAN that allows for the transfer of data between two systems. This connection can be especially useful when you are migrating your data from an older system that does not include a network adapter.

Note that although using serial or parallel ports to connect two systems in order to migrate data can be useful, a much better way to connect two systems would be to use Ethernet cards and what is commonly called a *crossover cable*. Using this type of connection, you can establish a LAN link between the two systems and transfer data at the full speed of the Ethernet network, which is either 10, 100, or 1,000Mbps (1.25, 12.5, or 125MBps). Using serial or parallel ports to transfer data between two systems was more prevalent when most systems did not include some form of network interface card (NIC).

A number of free and commercial programs can support serial or parallel port file transfers. MS-DOS 6.0 and later include a program called Interlink, whereas Windows 95 and later include software called either Direct Cable Connection or Direct Parallel Connection. Other commercially available software includes Laplink.com's LapLink, SmithMicro's CheckIt Fast Move, and Symantec's PC Anywhere, among others.

Serial Port Transfers

Serial ports have always been used for communications between systems, but normally the ports would be connected to modems that convert the data to be transmitted over telephone lines, enabling long-distance connections. If the systems were in the same room, you could connect the serial ports directly without the use of modems by using instead what is commonly referred to as a *null modem cable*. The name comes from the fact that there really aren't any modems present; the cable effectively replaces the modems that would be used at either end. The only drawback is that because serial ports evolved to support relatively low-speed modem communications, even using a null modem cable the connection would be slow because most ports can transmit at 115.2Kbps (14.4KBps).

With a null modem cable, serial ports can be used to transfer data between systems, although the performance will be much lower than if parallel ports are used. A serial null modem cable will have either a 9-pin or a 25-pin female connector on both ends. The cable should be wired as shown in Table 8.21.

Table 8.21 Serial Null Modem Cable Wiring (9-Pin or 25-Pin Connectors)

9 Pin	25 Pin	Signal	<-to->	Signal	25 Pin	9 Pin
Pin 5	Pin 7	Ground	<->	Ground	Pin 7	Pin 5
Pin 3	Pin 2	Transmit	<->	Receive	Pin 3	Pin 2
Pin 7	Pin 4	RTS	<->	CTS	Pin 5	Pin 8
Pin 6	Pin 6	DSR	<->	DTR	Pin 20	Pin 4
Pin 2	Pin 3	Receive	<->	Transmit	Pin 2	Pin 3
Pin 8	Pin 5	CTS	<->	RTS	Pin 4	Pin 7
Pin 4	Pin 20	DTR	<->	DSR	Pin 6	Pin 6

If both systems feature infrared serial ports, you can connect the two systems together via an infrared connection that uses no cable at all. This type of connection is subject to the limitations of the infrared ports, which will allow only very short (a few feet at most) distances with fairly slow data rates.

Because they work so slowly, normally I would recommend using serial ports only as a last resort to transfer data between two systems. If possible, you should try to use Ethernet cards and a crossover cable, or parallel ports with an interlink cable, for faster connections.

Parallel Port Transfers

Although the original intention for the parallel port was to be used to connect a printer, later implementations allowed for bidirectional data transfer. Bidirectional parallel ports can be used to quickly and easily transfer data between one system and another. If both systems use an EPP/ECP port, you can actually communicate at rates of up to 2.77MBps, which is far faster than the speeds achievable with serial port or infrared (IR) data transfers.

Connecting two computers with parallel ports requires a special cable known as either a *Direct Cable Connection (DCC)*, *Interlink*, *Laplink*, *parallel crossover*, or *parallel null modem* cable. Many of the commercial file-transfer programs provide these cables with their software, or you can purchase them separately from most computer stores or companies that sell cables. However, if you need to make one for yourself, Table 8.22 provides the wiring diagram you need.

Table 8.22   Direct Cable Connection (DCC)/Interlink, LapLink, or Parallel Null Modem Cable Wiring (25-Pin Connectors)

25 Pin	Signal Description	<-to->	Signal Description	25 Pin
Pin 2	Data Bit 0	<->	-Error	Pin 15
Pin 3	Data Bit 1	<->	Select	Pin 13
Pin 4	Data Bit 2	<->	Paper End	Pin 12
Pin 5	Data Bit 3	<->	-Acknowledge	Pin 10
Pin 6	Data Bit 4	<->	Busy	Pin 11
Pin 15	-Error	<->	Data Bit 0	Pin 2
Pin 13	Select	<->	Data Bit 1	Pin 3
Pin 12	Paper End	<->	Data Bit 2	Pin 4
Pin 10	-Acknowledge	<->	Data Bit 3	Pin 5
Pin 11	Busy	<->	Data Bit 4	Pin 6
Pin 25	Ground	<->	Ground	Pin 25

Tip

Even though cables usually are provided with data-transfer programs, notebook users might want to look for an adapter that makes the appropriate changes to a standard parallel printer cable. This can make traveling lighter by preventing the need for additional cables.

Although the prebuilt parallel cables referred to in the preceding tip work for connecting two machines with ECP/EPP ports, they can't take advantage of the advanced transfer rates of these ports. Special cables are needed to communicate between ECP/EPP ports. Parallel Technologies is a company that sells ECP/EPP cables for connecting to other ECP/EPP computers, as well as a universal cable for connecting any two parallel ports to use the highest speed.

Windows 95 and later versions include a special program called *Direct Cable Connection (DCC)* or *Direct Parallel Connection*, which enables two systems to be networked together via a parallel transfer cable. Consult the Windows documentation for information on how to establish a DCC/Direct Parallel connection. Parallel Technologies has been contracted by Microsoft to supply the special DCC cables used to connect the systems, including a special type of cable that uses active electronics to ensure a reliable high-speed interconnection.

Testing Parallel Ports

The procedures for testing parallel ports are effectively the same as those used for serial ports, except that when you use the diagnostics software, you obviously select choices for parallel ports rather than serial ports. Even though the software tests are similar, the hardware tests require the proper plugs for the loopback tests on the parallel port. Several loopback plugs are required, depending on what software you are using. Most use the IBM-style loopback, but some use the style that originated in the Norton Utilities diagnostics.

You can purchase loopback plugs or build them yourself. The following wiring is needed to construct your own parallel loopback or wrap plugs to test a parallel port:

- IBM 25-pin parallel (male DB25P) loopback connector (wrap plug). Connect the following pins:

    1 to 13

    2 to 15

    10 to 16

    11 to 17

    12 to 14

- Norton Utilities 25-pin parallel (male DB25P) loopback connector (wrap plug). Connect the following pins:

    2 to 15

    3 to 13

    4 to 12

    5 to 10

    6 to 11

CHAPTER 9

Hard Disk
Storage

Over the years, hard drives have been available in a number of physical formats, called *form factors*. These are normally based on the size of the platter used in the drive. Whereas desktop systems continue to use 3.5-inch drives, virtually all laptop/notebook systems use 2.5-inch drives, which were first introduced in 1988. There are also smaller form factors—all the way down to the 1-inch MicroDrive originally introduced in 1999. Except for the size of the disks and their packaging, the technology used in the 2.5-inch and smaller drives is the same as for the larger 3.5-inch models. This chapter covers hard drives, focusing primarily on the 2.5-inch and smaller drives that are used primarily in laptop/notebook or other portable systems.

Hard Drive History and Advancements

In 1957, Cyril Northcote Parkinson published his famous compilation of essays titled *Parkinson's Law*, which starts off with the statement, "Work expands so as to fill the time available for its completion." A corollary of Parkinson's most famous "law" can be applied to hard drives: Data expands so as to fill the space available for its storage. This, of course, means that no matter how big a drive you get, you *will* find a way to fill it. I have lived by that dictum since purchasing my first hard disk drive over 20 years ago.

Although I am well aware of the exponential growth of everything associated with computers, I am still amazed at how large and fast modern drives have become. The first hard drive I purchased in 1983 was a 10MB (that's 10 megabytes, *not* gigabytes). The Miniscribe model 2012 was a 5.25-inch (platter) drive that was about 8"×5.75"×3.25" (203mm×146mm×83mm) in overall size and weighed 5.5 lb. (2.5kg). That's heavier than some of today's laptop computers! By comparison, one of the biggest drives available to date, the 500GB Hitachi 7K500 SATA drive uses smaller 3.5-inch platters, is about 5.75"×4"×1" (146mm×102mm×25mm) in overall size, weighs only 1.54 lb. (0.70kg), and stores a whopping 500GB, which is 50,000 times more storage in a package that is about one-sixth the size and one-fourth the weight of my old Miniscribe. By another comparison, a 160GB 2.5-inch Seagate Momentus 5400.3 160 drive uses even smaller 2.5-inch platters, is about 3.94"×2.76"×0.37" (100mm×70mm×9.5mm) in overall size, weighs only 0.22 lb. (99g), and stores 160GB, which is 16,000 times more storage in a package that is about 37 times smaller and 1/25th the weight of my first drive.

Obviously the large storage capacities found on modern drives are useless unless you can also transfer the data to and from the disk quickly. The hard disk as found in the original IBM XT in 1983 had a constant data transfer rate from the media of about 100KBps. Today, most commonly used drives feature the Serial Ata interface offering variable media data transfer rates of up to 66MBps (average rates are lower, up to about 50MBps). Much like the increase in drive capacity the speed of the interface has also come a long way since the MFM and RLL interfaces that were commonplace in the '80s. As always, the interfaces are much faster than the actual drives. The Parallel ATA, Serial ATA, and SCSI interfaces are commonplace nowadays offer data transfer rates of up to 133MBps for Parallel ATA, 150 and 300MBps for Serial ATA and 320MBps bandwidth for Ultra-320 SCSI. All of these interfaces are much faster than the drives they support, meaning that the true transfer rate you will see is almost entirely limited by the drive and not the interface you choose. The modern interfaces have bandwidth to spare for future developments and advances in hard disk technology.

In summary, it is clear that these are pretty large steps in just over 20 years time!

Note

The book *Parkinson's Law* (ISBN 1568490151) is still in print and is considered one of the essential tomes of business or management study today.

To give you an idea of how far hard drives have come in the past 20 years, I've outlined some of the more profound changes in hard disk storage:

- Maximum storage capacities have increased from the 5MB and 10MB 5.25-inch full-height drives available in 1982 to 500GB in 2005 for 3.5-inch half-height drives (Hitachi 7K500, 500GB SATA), 160GB for notebook system with 2.5-inch drives (Seagate Momentus 5400.3 160), and 60GB for 1.8-inch drives (Toshiba MK-6006GAH, 60GB). Hard drives smaller than 40GB are rare in desktop or even laptop systems.

- Data-transfer rates to and from the media (sustained transfer rates) have increased from about 100KBps for the original IBM XT in 1983 to an average of 50MBps for some of the fastest drives today (Western Digital Raptor WD74GD) or more than 80MBps for the fastest SCSI drive (Seagate Cheetah 15K.4).

- Average seek times (how long it takes to move the heads to a particular cylinder) have decreased from more than 85ms (milliseconds) for the 10MB drives used by IBM in the 1983 vintage PC-XT to 3.3ms for some of the fastest drives today (Seagate Cheetah 15K.4).

- In 1982 and 1983, a 10MB drive and controller cost more than $2,000 ($200 per megabyte), which would be more than double that in today's dollars. Today, the cost of desktop hard drives (with integrated controllers) has dropped to 0.05 cent per megabyte or less, or about 100GB for $50. Laptop drives have fallen to 0.1 cents per megabyte or less, or about 100GB for $100!

Areal Density

Areal density is often used as a technology growth-rate indicator for the hard disk drive industry. *Areal density* is defined as the product of the linear bits per inch (bpi), measured along the length of the tracks around the disk, multiplied by the number of tracks per inch (tpi), measured radially on the disk (see Figure 9.1). The results are expressed in units of megabits or gigabits per square inch (Mbit/sq. in. or Gbit/sq. in.) and are used as a measure of efficiency in drive-recording technology. Current high-end 2.5-inch drives record at areal densities over 100Gbit/sq. in. This density will allow for 3.5-inch drives with capacities of 1000GB or 1TB in the next few years.

Drives record data in tracks, which are circular bands of data on the disk. Each track is divided into sectors. Figure 9.2 shows an actual floppy disk sprayed with magnetic developer (powdered iron) such that an image of the actual tracks and sectors can be clearly seen. The disk shown is a 5.25-inch 360KB floppy, which has 40 tracks per side, and each track is divided into nine sectors. Note that each sector is delineated by gaps in the recording, which precede and follow the track and sector headers (where ID and address information resides). You can clearly see the triple gap preceding the first sector, which includes the track and sector headers. Then, following in a counterclockwise direction, you see each subsequent sector, preceded by gaps delineating the header for that sector. Data is written in the area between the headers.

Notice that sector 9 is longer than the rest; this is to enable rotational speed differences between drives so that all the data can be written before running into the start of the track. Also notice that a good portion of the disk surface isn't used because it is simply impractical to have the heads travel in and out that far, and the difference in length between the sectors on the inner and outer tracks becomes more of a problem.

Areal density has been rising steadily since the first magnetic storage drive (IBM RAMAC) was introduced in 1956, initially at a growth rate of about 25% per year (doubling every four years), and since the early 1990s at a growth rate of about 60% per year (doubling every 1.5 years). The development and introduction of magneto-resistive heads in 1991 and giant magneto-resistive heads in 1997 propelled the increase in the areal density growth rate. In the 47+ years since the RAMAC drive was introduced, the areal density of magnetic storage has increased more than five million fold.

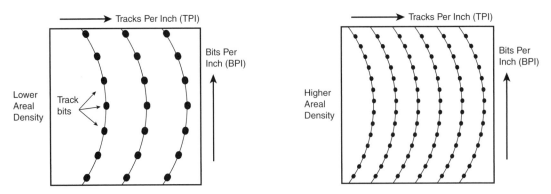

Figure 9.1 Areal density, combining tracks per inch and bits per inch.

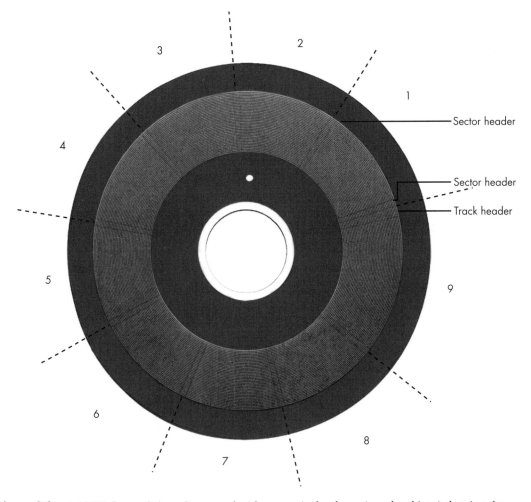

Figure 9.2 A 360KB floppy disk media sprayed with magnetic developer (powdered iron) showing the actual track and sector images.

Currently, drive manufacturers have achieved areal densities greater than 100Gbit/sq. in., which is considered near the point at which the superparamagnetic effect takes place. This is an effect in which the magnetic domains become so small that they are intrinsically unstable at room temperature. Techniques such as extremely high coercivity media and perpendicular (vertical polarity) recording are projected to enable magnetic storage densities of 200Gbit/sq. in. or more. Vertical polarity recording, or perpendicular recording as it is often called, aligns the bits vertically, perpendicular to the disk, which allows additional room on a disk to pack more data, thus enabling higher recording densities.

Several drive manufacturers have already announced 2.5- and 3.5-inch drives based on this technology. This technology will see its debut in 2.5-inch drives for laptops and 1-inch drives for portable electronics, such as digital cameras and PDAs first, before finding its way into 3.5-inch drives for desktop PCs and servers.

Figure 9.3 shows how areal density has increased from when magnetic storage was first developed (1956 RAMAC) through the present time.

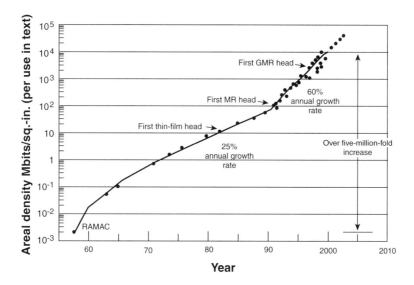

Figure 9.3   Evolution of areal density in magnetic disk storage.

To increase areal density while maintaining the same external drive form factors, drive manufacturers have developed media and head technologies to support these higher areal densities, such as ceramic/glass platters, giant magneto-resistive (GMR) heads, pseudo-contact recording, and partial response maximum likelihood (PRML) electronics. The primary challenge in achieving higher densities is manufacturing drive heads and disks to operate at closer tolerances. Improvements in tolerances and the use of more platters in a given form factor continue to fuel improvements in drive capacity, but drive makers continue to seek even greater capacity increases, both by improving current technologies and by developing new ones.

To fit more data on a platter of a given size, the tracks must be placed closer together, and the heads must be capable of achieving greater precision in their placements over the tracks. This also means that as hard disk capacities increase, heads must float ever closer to the disk surface during operation. The gap between the head and disk is as close as 10 nanometers (0.01 microns) in some drives, which is approximately the thickness of a cell membrane. By comparison, a human hair is typically 80 microns in diameter, which is 8,000 times thicker than the gap between the head and disk in some drives. The prospect of actual contact or near contact recording is being considered for future drives to further increase density.

Form Factors

The cornerstone of the PC industry has always been *standardization*. With disk drives, this is evident in the physical and electrical form factors that comprise modern drives. By using industry-standard form factors, you can purchase a system or chassis from one manufacturer and yet physically and electrically install a drive from a different manufacturer. Form factor standards ensure that available drives will fit in the bay, the screw holes will line up, and the standard cables and connections will plug in. Without industry standards for form factors, there would be no compatibility between different chassis, motherboards, cables, and drives.

You might wonder how these form factors are established. In some cases, it is simply that one manufacturer makes a popular product of a particular shape and connection protocol, and others simply copy or clone those parameters, making other products that are physically and/or electrically compatible. In other cases, various committees or groups that dictate certain industry standards have been formed. Then it is up to the companies that make applicable products to create them to conform to these standards.

Over the years, disk drives have been introduced in several industry-standard form factors, normally identified by the approximate size of the platters contained inside the drive. Table 9.1 lists the different disk drive form factors that have been used in PCs and portables.

Table 9.1   Hard Disk Form Factors

5.25-inch Drives:			5.25-inch Half-Height Drives:		
Height	3.25 in.	82.6mm	Height	1.63 in.	41.3mm
Width	5.75 in.	146.0mm	Width	5.75 in.	146.0mm
Depth	8.00 in.	203.2mm	Depth	8.00 in.	203.2mm
Volume	149.5 ci	2449.9 cc	Volume	74.8 ci	1224.9 cc
3.5-inch Half-Height Drives:			**3.5-inch 1/3-Height Drives:**		
Height	1.63 in.	41.3mm	Height	1.00 in.	25.4mm
Width	4.00 in.	101.6mm	Width	4.00 in.	101.6mm
Depth	5.75 in.	146.0mm	Depth	5.75 in.	146.0mm
Volume	37.4 ci	612.5 cc	Volume	23.0 ci	376.9 cc
2.5-inch Drives:					
Height1	19.0mm	0.75 in.			
Height2	17.0mm	0.67 in.			
Height3	12.7mm	0.50 in.			

Table 9.1   Continued

2.5-inch Drives:

Height4	12.5mm	0.49 in.
Height5	9.5mm	0.37 in.
Height6	8.5mm	0.33 in.
Width	70.0mm	2.76 in.
Depth	100.0mm	3.94 in.
Vol1	133.0 cc	8.1 ci
Vol2	119.0 cc	7.3 ci
Vol3	88.9 cc	5.4 ci
Vol4	87.5 cc	5.3 ci
Vol5	66.5 cc	4.1 ci
Vol6	59.5 cc	3.6 ci

1.8-inch Drives: 1.8-inch PC Card Drives:

Height1	9.5mm	0.37 in.	Height1	8.0mm	0.31 in.
Height2	7.0mm	0.28 in.	Height2	5.0mm	0.20 in.
Width	70.0mm	2.76 in.	Width	54.0mm	2.13 in.
Depth	60.0mm	2.36 in.	Depth	78.5mm	3.09 in.
Vol1	39.9 cc	2.4 ci	Vol1	33.9 cc	2.1 ci
Vol2	29.4 cc	1.8 ci	Vol2	21.2 cc	1.3 ci

1-inch MicroDrives:

Height	5.0mm	0.20 in.
Width	42.8mm	1.69 in.
Depth	36.4mm	1.43 in.
Volume	7.8 cc	0.5 ci

Note that the first figure listed for each dimension is the dimension on which the standard is based, the second one is derived through a conversion. Some standards are based on SAE (English) measurements, while others were based on SI (metric) measurements.

Currently, 3.5-inch drives are the most popular for desktop whereas the 2.5-inch and smaller drives are popular in laptops and other portable devices. Parallel ATA 3.5-inch drives are quickly being phased out to be replaced by Serial ATA drives, which are now the most commonplace drive interface in new desktop systems, while notebooks are just beginning to transition towards 2.5-inch drives featuring the Serial ATA interface. Part of the reason most laptop systems continue to support Parallel ATA is that until recently the motherboard chipsets only supported Parallel ATA natively, and adding an extra chip for SATA support was cost, space, and power prohibitive. Not to mention that there were originally no SATA 2.5-inch drives on the market as well. But that is changing. The 900 series chipsets from Intel found in newer systems include native SATA support, and SATA 2.5-inch drives are now available as well.

5.25-Inch Drive

Shugart Associates first introduced the 5.25-inch form factor along with the first 5.25-inch floppy drive back in 1976. The story goes that Founder Al Shugart then left that company and founded Seagate Technologies, which introduced the first 5.25-inch (Model ST-506, 5MB capacity) hard disk in 1980, predating the IBM PC. IBM later used the Seagate ST-412 (10MB) drive in some of its PC-XT models, which were among the very first PCs to be sold with hard drives built in. The physical format of the 5.25-inch hard disk back then was the same as the 5.25-inch full-height floppy drive, so both would fit the same size bay in a chassis. For example, the original IBM PC and XT models had two 5.25-inch full-height bays that could accept these drives. The first portable systems (such as the original Compaq Portable) used these drives as well. Later, the 5.25-inch form factor was reduced in height by one-half when the appropriately named 5.25-inch half-height floppy drives and hard drives were introduced. This allowed two drives to fit in a bay originally designed for one. The 5.25-inch half-height form factor is still used as the form factor for modern desktop CD-ROM and DVD drives, and is the standard form factor for the larger drive bays in all modern desktop PC chassis. Early portable PCs (such as the IBM Portable PC) used this form factor as well.

3.5-Inch Drive

Sony introduced the first 3.5-inch floppy drive in 1981, which used a smaller width and depth but the same height as the half-height 5.25-inch form factor. These were called *3.5-inch half-height drives*, even though there was no such thing as a "full-height" 3.5-inch drive. Rodime followed with the first 3.5-inch half-height hard disk in 1983. Later 3.5-inch floppy and hard drives would be reduced in height to only 1 inch, which was just under one-third of the original 5.25-inch full-height form factor (these were sometimes called *1/3-height drives*). Today, the 1-inch-high version has become the modern industry standard 3.5-inch form factor.

2.5-Inch Drive

PrairieTek introduced the 2.5-inch form factor in 1988, which proved to be ideal for laptop/notebook computers. As laptop sales grew, so did sales of the 2.5-inch drives. Although PrairieTek was the first with that form factor, other drive manufacturers quickly capitalized on the market by also introducing 2.5-inch drives. Finally, in 1994 Conner Peripherals Inc. paid $18 million for PrairieTek's 2.5-inch disk drive technology, and PrairieTek went out of business. Since the 2.5-inch drives first appeared, virtually all laptop/notebook systems used them. Although 2.5-inch drives can also be used in desktop systems, the 3.5-inch drive continues to dominate the desktop market due to greater capacity and speed along with lower cost.

The 2.5-inch drives have been manufactured in various thicknesses (or heights), and many notebook or laptop systems are restricted as to how thick a drive they will support. Here are the common thicknesses that have been available:

- 8.5mm
- 9.5mm
- 12.5mm
- 12.7mm
- 17.0mm
- 19.0mm

By far the popular sizes are 9.5mm and 12.5mm, which are the sizes used by most laptop/notebook systems. Currently, most drive manufacturers are concentrating on the 9.5mm form factor. A thinner drive can almost always be installed in place of a thicker one; however, most systems will not have the room to accept a thicker drive than they were originally designed to use.

1.8-Inch Drive

The 1.8-inch drive was first introduced by Integral Peripherals in 1991 and has had problems gaining acceptance in the marketplace ever since. This size was initially created because it fit perfectly in the PC Card (PCMCIA) form factor, making it ideal as add-on removable storage for laptop/notebook systems. Unfortunately, the 1.8-inch drive market has been slow to take shape, and in 1998 an investment group called Mobile Storage bought Integral Peripherals 1.8-inch drive technology for $5.5 million, and Integral Peripherals went out of business. Several other companies have introduced 1.8-inch drives over the years, most notably HP, Calluna, Toshiba, and Hitachi. Of those, only Toshiba and Hitachi continue to manufacture drives in that format. HP exited the disk drive market completely in 1996, and Calluna finally ceased operation in 2001. Toshiba introduced its 1.8-inch drives (available in the physical format of a Type II PC-Card) in 2000, and Hitachi entered the 1.8-inch drive market in 2003. The 1.8-inch drives are available in capacities of up to 60GB or more, and depending on the model can be used anywhere a standard PC Card can be plugged in.

1-Inch Drives

During 1998, IBM introduced a 1-inch drive called the MicroDrive, incorporating a single platter about the size of a quarter! Current versions of the MicroDrive can store up to 4GB or more. These drives are in the physical and electrical format of a Type II Compact Flash (CF) card, which means they can be used in almost any device that takes CF cards, including digital cameras, Personal Digital Assistants (PDAs), MP3 players, and anywhere else Compact Flash memory cards can be used. IBM's disk drive division was sold to Hitachi in 2003 and combined with Hitachi's storage technology business as Hitachi Global Storage Technologies.

Note

HP introduced a 20MB 1.3-inch disk drive called the *KittyHawk* in 1992, originally intended for the handheld computer market. In 1994 HP followed with a 40MB model. These small drives were expensive and proved to be too far ahead of their time, as were the handheld computers they were intended for. After two years of low sales, HP discontinued the KittyHawk family in 1994.

Other Form Factor Issues

Laptop manufacturers have various ways of mounting hard drives in the system, which can cause installation or upgrade compatibility problems. Most systems use a caddy or some type of special bracketry to hold the drive and possibly to make the electrical connections to the system.

This type of mount makes the physical part of an upgrade as easy as inserting a new drive into the caddy and then mounting it in the system. You can purchase the drive with the caddy already installed, you can get a bare drive and swap it into your existing caddy, or you can get a bare drive and a new caddy separately. Usually, it is much less expensive to get the bare drive—whether you also add the caddy or not—than it is to get one with the caddy preinstalled.

If you purchase a drive as a repair part from the system manufacturer, it will normally include the caddy or bracket with the drive (see Figure 9.4). However, you will usually pay more than double the price of a bare drive alone. If you purchase a bare drive from a third-party manufacturer, it will not include the caddy or bracket, unless you ask for this separately. Depending on the model, a caddy alone can sell for $50 or more. If you are merely swapping the new drive for the one that is in the system, you won't need an extra caddy and instead can simply swap the caddy or bracket from the old drive to the new one.

Figure 9.4   Hard drive caddy used in ThinkPad 770 laptops.

Using a caddy can make swapping drives very easy. In many midrange and high-end portables, replacing a hard drive is much simpler than in a desktop system. Quite a few manufacturers now design their portable systems with external bays that let you easily swap out hard drives without opening the case, as long as the drives are preinstalled in the appropriate caddies. Multiple users can share a single machine by snapping in their own hard drives, or you can use the same technique to load different operating systems on the same computer.

For example, in the ThinkPad 770 series, you can remove the existing hard drive and install a different one in less than 10 seconds! To remove the drive, you merely move a slide switch to release the cover plate, grab the pull tab on the drive caddy, and slide the caddy (with the drive inside) out of the chassis. To install a new drive, you slide the caddy (with the drive inside) into the bay, attach the cover plate, and slide a switch to lock it into place.

Unfortunately, not all systems are designed in this manner, and if you purchase a bare drive that did not come with the correct caddy for your system, it will take time to remove and reinstall the drive from the existing caddy. Note that the caddies and brackets are not very interchangeable; that is, they are normally unique to the make and model (or series) of system they are designed for.

If you wish to have several drives that can be quickly installed in a system, then having extra caddies or brackets can be convenient. Usually, it takes several minutes to install or remove a drive from a caddy, but once a drive is installed into a caddy, it can be removed from or installed into the system in seconds.

One important aspect of laptop hard drive installation or upgrades that you must be aware of is the drive support provided by the system's BIOS. The BIOS in some systems, and particularly older ones, might offer limited hard drive size options. In some cases, Flash BIOS upgrades, which provide support for additional drives, might be available for your system.

After BIOS support, you need to be concerned about the physical mounting. Whether you are going to use your existing caddy or get a new one (if required), you must be concerned about the height of the drive. The 2.5-inch drives have been manufactured in various thicknesses over the years, and many notebook or laptop systems are restricted as to how thick a drive they will support. Normally, you can always install a thinner drive in place of a thicker one.

Hard Disk Drive Operation

The basic physical construction of a hard disk drive consists of spinning disks with heads that move over the disks and store data in tracks and sectors. The heads read and write data in concentric rings called *tracks*. These tracks are divided into segments called *sectors*, which normally store 512 bytes each (see Figure 9.5).

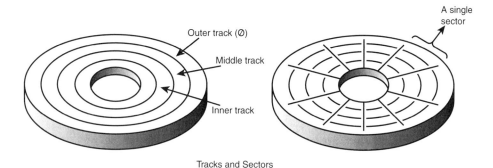

Tracks and Sectors

Figure 9.5   *The tracks and sectors on a disk.*

Hard disk drives usually have multiple disks, called *platters*, that are stacked on top of each other and spin in unison, each with two sides on which the drive stores data. Most drives have one, two, or three platters, resulting in two, four, or six sides. The identically aligned tracks on each side of every platter together make up a cylinder (see Figure 9.6). A hard disk drive normally has one head per platter side, with all the heads mounted on a common carrier device or rack. The heads move radially across the disk in unison; they cannot move independently because they are mounted on the same carrier or rack, called an *actuator*.

Originally, most hard disks spun at 3,600rpm—approximately 10 times faster than a floppy disk drive. For many years, 3,600rpm was pretty much a constant among hard drives. Now, however, most drives spin even faster. Although speeds can vary, modern drives normally spin the platters at either 4,200, 5,400, 7,200, 10,000, or 15,000rpm. Most standard-issue drives found in portable systems spin at the slower 4,200 or 5,400rpm speeds, with a few high performance models now available that spin at 7,200rpm. The 10,000 or 15,000rpm drives are normally found only in very high performance desktop-based workstations or servers, where their higher prices, heat generation, and noise can be more easily dealt with. High rotational speeds combined with a fast head-positioning mechanism and more sectors per track are what make one hard disk overall faster than another.

The heads in most hard disk drives do not (and should not!) touch the platters during normal operation. However, on most drives, the heads do rest on the platters when the drive is powered off. In most drives, when the drive is powered off, the heads move to the innermost cylinder, where they land on the platter surface. This is referred to as contact start stop (CSS) design. When the drive is powered on, the heads slide on the platter surface as they spin up, until a very thin cushion of air builds up between the heads and platter surface, which causes the heads to lift off and remain suspended a short distance above or below the platter. If the air cushion is disturbed by a particle of dust or a shock, the head can come into contact with the platter while it is spinning at full speed. When contact with the spinning platters is forceful enough to do damage, the event is called a *head crash*. The result of a head crash can be anything from a few lost bytes of data to a completely ruined drive. Most drives have special lubricants on the platters and hardened surfaces that can withstand the daily "takeoffs" and "landings" as well as more severe abuse.

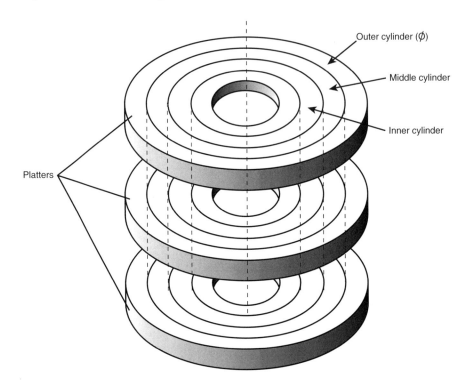

Figure 9.6   Hard disk cylinders.

Some newer drives do not use CSS design and instead use a load/unload mechanism, which does not allow the heads to contact the platters, even when the drive is powered off. First used in the 2.5-inch form factor notebook or laptop drives, where resistance to mechanical shock is more important, load/unload mechanisms use a ramp positioned just off the outer part of the platter surface. When the drive is powered off or in a power-saving mode, the heads ride up on the ramp. When powered on, the platters are allowed to come up to full speed before the heads are released down the ramp, allowing the airflow (air bearing) to prevent any head/platter contact.

Because the platter assemblies are sealed and nonremovable, the track densities on the disk can be very high. Hard drives today have up to 96,000 or more tracks per inch (tpi) recorded on the media (for example, Hitachi Travelstar 80GN). Head disk assemblies (HDAs), which contain the platters, are assembled and sealed in clean rooms under absolutely sanitary conditions. Because few companies repair HDAs, repair or replacement of the parts inside a sealed HDA can be expensive. Every hard disk ever made eventually fails. The only questions are when the failure will occur and whether your data is backed up.

Caution

It is strongly recommended that you do not even attempt to open a hard disk drive's HDA unless you have the equipment and the expertise to make repairs inside. Most manufacturers deliberately make the HDA difficult to open, to discourage the intrepid do-it-yourselfer. Opening the HDA voids the drive's warranty.

Tracks and Sectors

A *track* is a single ring of data on one side of a disk. A disk track is too large to manage data effectively as a single storage unit. Many disk tracks can store 100,000 or more bytes of data, which would be very inefficient for storing small files. For that reason, tracks are divided into several numbered divisions known as *sectors*. These sectors represent arc-shaped pieces of the track.

Various types of disk drives split their disk tracks into different numbers of sectors, depending on the density of the tracks. For example, floppy disk formats use 8–36 sectors per track, although hard disks usually store data at a higher density and today can have 900 or more sectors per track physically. The sectors created by the standard formatting procedure have a capacity of 512 bytes, which has been one constant throughout the history of the PC. In order to be compatible with most older BIOS and drivers, drives will usually perform an internal translation so that they pretend to have 63 sectors per track when addressed in CHS (cylinder, head, sector) mode.

The sectors on a track are numbered starting with 1, unlike the heads or cylinders that are numbered starting with 0. For example, a 1.44MB floppy disk contains 80 cylinders, numbered 0–79, and two heads, numbered 0 and 1, whereas each track on each cylinder has 18 sectors numbered 1–18.

When a disk is formatted, the formatting program creates ID areas before and after each sector's data that the disk controller uses for sector numbering and for identifying the start and end of each sector. These areas precede and follow each sector's data area and consume some of the disk's total storage capacity. This accounts for the difference between a disk's unformatted and formatted capacities. Note that most modern hard drives are sold preformatted and advertise only the formatted capacity. The unformatted capacity is usually not mentioned anymore. Another interesting development is that many new drives use what is called *No-ID sector formatting*, which means that the sectors are recorded without ID marks before and after each sector. This means that more of the disk can be used for actual data.

Each sector on a disk normally has a prefix portion, or *header*, that identifies the start of the sector and contains the sector number, as well as a suffix portion, or *trailer*, that contains a checksum (which helps ensure the integrity of the data contents). Many newer drives omit this header and have what is called a *No-ID recording*, allowing more space for actual data. With a No-ID recording, the start and end of each sector are located via predetermined clock timing.

Each sector contains 512 bytes of data. The low-level formatting process normally fills the data bytes with some specific value, such as F6h (hex) or some other repeating test pattern used by the drive manufacturer. Some patterns are more difficult for the electronics on the drive to encode/decode, so these patterns normally are used when the manufacturer is testing the drive during initial formatting. A special test pattern might cause errors to surface that a normal data pattern would not show. This way, the manufacturer can more accurately identify marginal sectors during testing.

Note

The type of disk formatting discussed here is a physical or low-level format, not the high-level format you perform when you use Windows Explorer or the DOS **FORMAT** program on a disk. See the section "Disk Formatting" later in this chapter to learn about the difference between these two types of formatting.

The sector headers and trailers are independent of the operating system, the file system, and the files stored on the drive. In addition to the headers and trailers, gaps exist within the sectors, between the sectors on each track, and also between tracks, but none of these gaps contain usable data space. The gaps are created during the low-level format process when the recording is turned off momentarily. They serve the same function as having gaps of silence between the songs recorded on a cassette tape. The prefix, suffix, and gaps account for the lost space between the unformatted capacity of a disk and the formatted capacity. For example, a 2MB (unformatted) floppy has a formatted capacity of 1.44MB, and an older 20GB unformatted capacity hard disk (for instance, a Quantum Fireball LCT20) has a capacity of only 18.3GB when it is formatted. Because the ATA and SCSI hard drives you purchase today are low-level formatted at the factory, the manufacturers now advertise only the formatted capacity. Even so, nearly all drives use some reserved space for managing the data that will be stored on the drive.

Disk Formatting

Two formatting procedures are required before you can write user data to a disk:

■ Physical (low-level) formatting

■ Logical (high-level) formatting

When you format a blank floppy disk, Windows Explorer or the DOS FORMAT command performs both types of formats simultaneously. If the floppy was already formatted, DOS and Windows will default to doing only a high-level format.

A hard disk, however, requires two separate formatting operations. Moreover, a hard disk requires a third step, between the two formatting procedures, to write the partitioning information to the disk. Partitioning is required because a hard disk is designed to be used with more than one operating system. Using multiple operating systems on one hard drive is possible by separating the physical formatting in a procedure that is always the same, regardless of the operating system used and the high-level format (which is different for each operating system). Partitioning enables a single hard disk drive to run more than one type of operating system, or it can enable a single operating system to use the disk as several volumes or logical drives. A *volume* or *logical drive* is any section of the disk to which the operating system assigns a drive letter or name.

Consequently, preparing a hard disk drive for data storage involves three steps:

1. Low-level formatting (LLF)

2. Partitioning

3. High-level formatting (HLF)

Low-level Formatting

During a low-level format, the formatting program divides the disk's tracks into a specific number of sectors, creating the intersector and intertrack gaps and recording the sector header and trailer information. The program also fills each sector's data area with a dummy byte value or a pattern of test values. For floppy disks, the number of sectors recorded on each track depends on the type of disk and drive. For hard disks, the number of sectors per track depends on the drive and the controller interface.

Originally, PC hard disk drives used a separate controller that took the form of an expansion card or was integrated into the motherboard. Because the controller could be used with various disk drives and might even have been made by a different manufacturer, some uniformity had to exist in the communications between the controller and the drive. For this reason, the number of sectors written to a track tended to be relatively consistent.

The original ST-506/412 MFM controllers always placed 17 sectors per track on a disk, although ST-506/412 controllers with RLL encoding increased the number of sectors to 25 or 26 per track; ESDI drives had 32 or more sectors per track. The drives found in portable PCs can have anywhere from 17 to 900 or more sectors per track, and the upper figure continues to rise in newer models.

Virtually all PATA, SATA, and SCSI drives use a technique called *zoned-bit recording (ZBR),* sometimes shortened to *zoned recording,* which writes a variable number of sectors per track. Without zoned recording, the number of sectors, and therefore bits, on each track is a constant. This means the actual number of bits per inch will vary. More bits per inch will exist on the inner tracks, and fewer will exist on the outer. The data rate and rotational speed will remain constant, as will the number of bits per track. Figure 9.7 shows a drive recorded with the same number of sectors per track.

A standard recording wastes capacity on the outer tracks because they are longer and yet hold the same amount of data (more loosely spaced) as the inner tracks. One way to increase the capacity of a hard drive during the low-level format is to create more sectors on the disks' outer cylinders than on the inner ones. Because they have a larger circumference, the outer cylinders can hold more data. Drives without zoned recording store the same amount of data on every cylinder, even though the tracks of the outer cylinders might be twice as long as those of the inner cylinders. The result is wasted storage capacity, because the disk medium must be capable of storing data reliably at the same density as on the inner cylinders. When the number of sectors per track is fixed, as in older controllers, the drive capacity is limited by the density of the innermost (shortest) track.

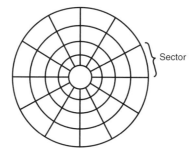

Figure 9.7 Standard recording, where the same number of sectors comprise every track.

Drives that use zoned recording split the cylinders into groups called *zones,* with each successive zone having more sectors per track as you move outward from the center of the disk. All the cylinders in a particular zone have the same number of sectors per track. The number of zones varies with specific drives, but most drives have 10 or more zones. Figure 9.8 shows a drive with zoned-bit recording.

Another effect of zoned recording is that transfer speeds vary depending on which zone the heads are in. A drive with zoned recording still spins at a constant speed; because more sectors exist per track in the outer zones, however, data transfer is fastest there. Consequently, data transfer is slowest when reading or writing to the inner zones. That is why virtually all drives today report minimum and maximum sustained transfer rates, which depend on where on the drive you are reading from or writing to.

As an example, Table 9.2 shows the zones defined for a Hitachi Travelstar 7K60 2.5-inch notebook drive, the sectors per track for each zone, and the resulting data transfer rate.

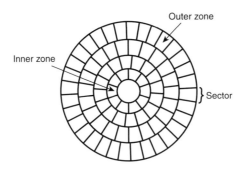

Figure 9.8   Zoned recording, where the number of sectors per track increases within each zone, moving out from the center.

Table 9.2   Zoned Recording Information for the Hitachi Travelstar 7K60 60GB 2.5-inch Hard Disk Drive

Zone	Sectors per Track	Data Transfer Rate (MBps)
0	720	44.24
1	704	43.25
2	696	42.76
3	672	41.29
4	640	39.32
5	614	37.72
6	592	36.37
7	556	34.16
8	528	32.44
9	480	29.49
10	480	29.49
11	456	28.02
12	432	26.54
13	416	25.56
14	384	23.59
15	360	22.12

512 bytes per sector, 7,200 rpm

This drive has a total of 54,288 tracks on each platter surface and, as you can see, the tracks are divided into 16 zones. It is not essential for all the zones to be the same size; this is up to the drive engineers. Zone 0 consists of the outermost tracks, which are the longest and contain the most sectors: 720. In most cases the inner zone has half the number of sectors per track as the outer zone, although this may vary slightly as well. Because each sector is 512 bytes, each track in this zone can therefore provide about 368,640 bytes of user data storage, although the 360 sector tracks in zone 15 can hold only 184,320 bytes.

Thus, with zoned recording, this drive has an average of about 545 sectors per track. Without zoned recording, the number of sectors per track would be limited to 360 over the entire surface of each platter. Using a zoned recording provides a 51% increase in the storage capacity of this particular drive.

Notice also the difference in the data transfer rates for each of the zones. The tracks in the outermost zone (0) yield a transfer rate of 44.24MBps, which is 100% faster than the 22.12MBps of the innermost zone (15). This is one reason you might notice large discrepancies in the results produced by disk drive benchmark programs. A test that reads or writes files on the outer tracks of the disk naturally yields far better results than one conducted on the inner tracks. It might appear as though your drive is running more slowly, when the problem is actually that the test results you are comparing stem from disk activity on different zones.

Another thing to note is that this drive conforms to the ATA-6 specification and is capable of running in Ultra-DMA mode 5 (also called Ultra-ATA/100 or UDMA-100), which results in a transfer speed of 100MBps. As you can see, that is entirely theoretical because the true *media transfer speed* of this drive varies between about 22MBps and 44MBps, averaging about 33MBps overall. The interface transfer rate is just that: what the interface is capable of. It has little bearing on the actual capabilities of the drive. Drives with separate controllers used in the past could not handle zoned recording because no standard way existed to communicate information about the zones from the drive to the controller.

With SCSI, ATA, and SATA disks, however, formatting individual tracks with different numbers of sectors became possible because these drives have the disk controller built in. The built-in controllers on these drives are fully aware of the zoning algorithm and can translate the physical cylinder, head, and sector numbers to logical cylinder, head, and sector numbers so that the drive appears to have the same number of sectors on each track. Because the PC BIOS is designed to handle only a single number of sectors per track throughout the entire drive, a zoned drive must run by using a sector-translation scheme.

The use of zoned recording enables drive manufacturers to increase the capacity of their hard drives by 20%–50% compared with a fixed sector-per-track arrangement. All modern hard disk drives today use zoned recording.

Partitioning

Creating a partition on a hard disk drive enables it to support separate file systems, each in its own partition.

Each file system can then use its own method to allocate file space in logical units called *clusters* or *allocation units*. Every hard disk drive must have at least one partition on it and can have up to four partitions, each of which can support the same or different type file systems. Three common file systems are used today:

- **File Allocation Table (FAT)**—This is the standard file system supported by DOS and Windows 9x/Me. FAT partitions support filenames of 11 characters maximum (eight characters plus a three-character extension) under DOS, and 255 characters under Windows 9x (or later). The standard FAT file system uses 12- or 16-bit numbers to identify clusters, resulting in a maximum volume size of 2GB.

  Using FDISK, you can create only two physical FAT partitions on a hard disk drive—primary and extended—but you can subdivide the extended partition into as many as 25 logical volumes. Alternative partitioning programs, such as Partition Magic, can create up to four primary partitions or three primary and one extended.

- **File Allocation Table, 32 bit (FAT32)**—An optional file system supported by Windows 95 OSR2 (OEM Service Release 2), Windows 98, Windows Me, and Windows 2000/XP. FAT32 uses 32-bit numbers to identify clusters, resulting in a maximum single volume size of 2TB or 2,048GB.

- **Windows NT File System (NTFS)**—The native file system for Windows NT/2000/XP that supports filenames up to 256 characters long and partitions up to (a theoretical) 16 exabytes. NTFS also provides extended attributes and file system security features that do not exist in the FAT file system.

Until the release of XP, FAT32 was by far the most popular file system. Because NTFS is native to XP, NTFS is now becoming more popular in newer systems. Still, the FAT file system is accessible by nearly every operating system, which makes it the most compatible in a mixed OS environment. FAT32 and NTFS provide additional features but are not universally accessible by other operating systems.

Partitioning normally is accomplished by running the disk-partitioning program that comes with your operating system. The name and exact operation of the disk partitioning program varies with the operating system. For example, FDISK is used by DOS and Windows 9x/Me for this task, whereas the DISKPART command or the Disk Management snap-in component of the Computer Management service is used with Windows XP. FDISK, DISKPART, and other disk-partitioning tools enable you to select the amount of space on the drive to use for a partition, from a single megabyte or 1% of the drive up to the entire capacity of the drive, or as much as the particular file system will allow. Normally, it is recommended to have as few partitions as possible, and many people (myself included) try to stick with only one or two at the most. This was more difficult before FAT32 because the maximum partition size for a FAT16 partition was only 2GB. With FAT32, the maximum partition size can be up to 2,048GB. Note that Windows 2000 and XP refuse to format a FAT32 volume over 32GB, even though they will recognize existing FAT32 volumes up to the 2,048GB limit.

Caution

FDISK, DISKPART, and other disk-partitioning tools included in operating systems cannot be used to change the size of a partition; all they can do is remove or create partitions. The act of removing or creating a partition destroys and/or loses access to data that was contained in the partition or was on that part of the disk. To manipulate partitions without destroying data, you can use third-party utility programs, such as Partition Magic from Symantec or Partition Commander from V-Communications.

After a drive is partitioned, each partition must then be high-level formatted by the operating system that will use it.

High-Level Formatting

During the high-level format, the operating system writes the structures necessary for managing files and data on the disk. For example, FAT partitions have a Volume Boot Sector (VBS), two copies of a file allocation table (FAT), and a root directory on each formatted logical drive. These data structures enable the operating system to manage the space on the disk, keep track of files, and even manage defective areas so they do not cause problems.

High-level formatting is not really a physical formatting of the drive but rather the creation of a table of contents for the disk. In low-level formatting, which is the real physical formatting process, tracks and sectors are written on the disk. As mentioned, the DOS and Windows FORMAT command can perform both low-level and high-level format operations on a floppy disk, but it performs only the high-level format for a hard disk. Low-level formats of ATA and SCSI hard disk drives are performed by the manufacturer and should almost never be performed by the end user. The only time I do a low-level format of an ATA or SCSI drive is when I am attempting to repair a format that has become damaged (parts of the disk become unreadable), or in some cases when I want to wipe away all data on the drive.

Basic Hard Disk Drive Components

Many types of hard disk drives are on the market, but nearly all share the same basic physical components. Some differences might exist in the quality of these components (and in the quality of the materials used to make them), but the operational characteristics of most drives are similar. The basic components of a typical hard disk drive are as follows:

- Disk platters
- Read/write heads
- Head actuator mechanism
- Spindle motor (inside platter hub)
- Logic board (controller or printed circuit board)
- Cables and connectors
- Configuration items (such as jumpers or switches)

You can see each of these components in Figure 9.9.

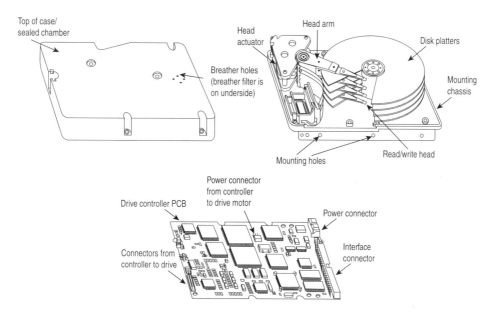

Figure 9.9   Typical hard disk drive components.

The platters, spindle motor, heads, and head actuator mechanisms usually are contained in a sealed chamber called the *head disk assembly (HDA)*. The HDA is usually treated as a single component; it is rarely opened. Other parts external to the drive's HDA, such as the logic boards, bezel, and other configuration or mounting hardware, can be disassembled from the drive.

Hard Disk Platters (Disks)

A hard disk drive has one or more platters, or *disks*. Table 9.3 lists the hard disk drive form factors, the associated platter sizes that have been used in PC hard disk drives, and year they were first introduced:

Table 9.3   Hard Disk Form Factors vs. Actual Platter Sizes

Hard Disk Form Factor	Actual Platter Dia. (mm)	Actual Platter Dia.(in)	Year Introduced
5.25-inch	130 mm	5.12 in	1980
3.5-inch	95 mm	3.74 in	1983
2.5-inch	65 mm	2.56 in	1988
1.8-inch	48 mm	1.89 in	1991
1-inch	34 mm	1.33 in	1999

As you can see from the table, the dimensions used in describing the form factors are approximations; the actual platter diameters are usually somewhat different. Earlier in the chapter, I listed the exterior dimensions of drives using these various form factors.

Most hard disk drives have two or more platters, although some of the smaller drives used in portable systems have only one. The number of platters a drive can have is limited by the drive's vertical physical size. The maximum number of platters I have seen in any 3.5-inch drive is 12; however, most drives have six or fewer.

Platters have traditionally been made from an aluminum/magnesium alloy, which provides both strength and light weight. However, manufacturers' desire for higher and higher densities and smaller drives has led to the use of platters made of glass (or, more technically, a glass-ceramic composite). One such material, produced by the Dow Corning Corporation, is called *MemCor*. MemCor is made of a glass-ceramic composite that resists cracking better than pure glass. Glass platters offer greater rigidity than metal (because metal can be bent and glass cannot) and can therefore be machined to one-half the thickness of conventional aluminum disks—sometimes less. Glass platters are also much more thermally stable than aluminum platters, which means they do not expand or contract very much with changes in temperature. Several hard disk drives made by companies such as IBM, Western Digital, Seagate, Toshiba, and Maxtor currently use glass or glass-ceramic platters. In fact, Hitachi Global Storage Technologies (Hitachi and IBM's joint hard disk venture) is designing all new drives with only glass platters. For most other manufacturers as well, glass disks will probably replace the standard aluminum/magnesium substrate over the next few years.

Recording Media

No matter which substrate is used, the platters are covered with a thin layer of a magnetically retentive substance, called the *medium*, on which magnetic information is stored. Three popular types of magnetic media are used on hard disk platters:

- Oxide media
- Thin-film media
- AFC (antiferromagnetically coupled) media

Oxide Media

The oxide medium is made of various compounds, containing iron oxide as the active ingredient. The magnetic layer is created on the disk by coating the aluminum platter with a syrup containing iron-oxide particles. This syrup is spread across the disk by spinning the platters at a high speed; centrifugal force causes the material to flow from the center of the platter to the outside, creating an even coating of the material on the platter. The surface is then cured and polished. Finally, a layer of material that protects and lubricates the surface is added and burnished smooth. The oxide coating is normally about 30 millionths of an inch thick. If you could peer into a drive with oxide-coated platters, you would see that the platters are brownish or amber.

As drive density increases, the magnetic medium needs to be thinner and more perfectly formed. The capabilities of oxide coatings have been exceeded by most higher-capacity drives. Because the oxide medium is very soft, disks that use it are subject to head-crash damage if the drive is jolted during operation. Most older drives, especially those sold as low-end models, use oxide media on the drive platters. Oxide media, which have been used since 1955, remained popular because of their relatively low cost and ease of application. Today, however, very few drives use oxide media.

Thin-Film Media

The thin-film medium is thinner, harder, and more perfectly formed than the oxide medium. Thin film was developed as a high-performance medium that enabled a new generation of drives to have lower head-floating heights, which in turn made increases in drive density possible. Originally, thin-film media were used only in higher-capacity or higher-quality drive systems, but today, virtually all drives use thin-film media.

The thin-film medium is aptly named. The coating is much thinner than can be achieved by the oxide-coating method. Thin-film media are also known as *plated* or *sputtered* media because of the various processes used to deposit the thin film on the platters.

Thin-film-plated media are manufactured by depositing the magnetic medium on the disk with an electroplating mechanism, in much the same way that chrome plating is deposited on the bumper of a car. The aluminum/magnesium or glass platter is immersed in a series of chemical baths that coat the platter with several layers of metallic film. The magnetic medium layer itself is a cobalt alloy about 1 μ-inch thick.

Thin-film sputtered media are created by first coating the aluminum platters with a layer of nickel phosphorus and then applying the cobalt-alloy magnetic material in a continuous vacuum-deposition process called *sputtering*. This process deposits magnetic layers as thin as 1 μ-inch or less on the disk, in a fashion similar to the way that silicon wafers are coated with metallic films in the semiconductor industry. The same sputtering technique is then used again to lay down an extremely hard, 1 μ-inch protective carbon coating. The need for a near-perfect vacuum makes sputtering the most expensive of the processes described here.

The surface of a sputtered platter contains magnetic layers as thin as 1 μ-inch. Because this surface also is very smooth, the head can float more closely to the disk surface than was possible previously. Floating heights as small as 10nm (nanometers, or about 0.4 μ-inch) above the surface are possible. When the head is closer to the platter, the density of the magnetic flux transitions can be increased to provide greater storage capacity. Additionally, the increased intensity of the magnetic field during a closer-proximity read provides the higher signal amplitudes needed for good signal-to-noise performance.

Both the sputtering and plating processes result in a very thin, hard film of magnetic medium on the platters. Because the thin-film medium is so hard, it has a better chance of surviving contact with the heads at high speed. In fact, modern thin-film media are virtually uncrashable. If you could open a drive to peek at the platters, you would see that platters coated with the thin-film medium look like mirrors.

AFC Media

The latest advancement in drive media is called *antiferromagnetically coupled (AFC) media*, which is designed to allow densities to be pushed beyond previous limits. Any time density is increased, the magnetic layer on the platters must be made thinner and thinner. Areal density (tracks per inch times bits per inch) has increased in hard drives to the point where the grains in the magnetic layer used to store data are becoming so small that they become unstable over time, causing data storage to become unreliable. This is referred to as the *superparamagnetic limit*, which has been determined to be between 30 and 50Gbit/sq. in. Drives today have already reached 35Gbit/sq. in., which means the superparamagnetic limit is now becoming a factor in drive designs.

AFC media consist of two magnetic layers separated by a very thin 3-atom (6 angstrom) film layer of the element ruthenium. IBM has coined the term "pixie dust" to refer to this ultra-thin ruthenium layer. This sandwich produces an antiferromagnetic coupling of the top and bottom magnetic layers, which causes the apparent magnetic thickness of the entire structure to be the difference between the top and bottom magnetic layers. This allows the use of physically thicker magnetic layers with more stable, larger grains to function as if they were really a single layer that was much thinner overall.

IBM has introduced AFC media into several drives, starting with the 2.5-inch Travelstar 30GN series of notebook drives introduced in 2001, the first drives on the market to use AFC media. In addition, IBM has introduced AFC media in desktop 3.5-inch drives starting with the Deskstar 160 GXP. I expect other manufacturers to introduce AFC media into their drives as well. The use of AFC media is expected to allow areal densities to be extended to 100Gbit/sq. in. and beyond. Being a form of thin-film media, these platters would also look like mirrors if you could see them.

Read/Write Heads

A hard disk drive usually has one read/write head for each platter surface (meaning that each platter has two sets of read/write heads—one for the top side and one for the bottom side). These heads are connected, or *ganged*, on a single movement mechanism. The heads, therefore, move across the platters in unison.

Mechanically, read/write heads are simple. Each head is on an actuator arm that is spring-loaded to force the head into contact with a platter. Few people realize that each platter actually is "squeezed" by the heads above and below it. If you could open a drive safely and lift the top head with your finger, the head would snap back down into the platter when you released it. If you could pull down on one of the heads below a platter, the spring tension would cause it to snap back up into the platter when you released it. Figure 9.10 shows a typical hard disk head-actuator assembly from a voice coil drive.

When the drive is at rest, the heads are forced into direct contact with the platters by spring tension, but when the drive is spinning at full speed, air pressure develops below the heads and lifts them off the surface of the platter. On a drive spinning at full speed, the distance between the heads and the platter can be anywhere from 0.5 to 5 µ-inch or more in a modern drive.

In the early 1960s, hard disk drive recording heads operated at floating heights as large as 200–300 µ-inch; today's drive heads are designed to float as low as 10nm (nanometers) or 0.4 µ-inch above the surface of the disk. To support higher densities in future drives, the physical separation between the head and disk is expected to drop even further, such that on some drives there will even be contact with the platter surface. New media and head designs will be required to make full or partial contact recording possible.

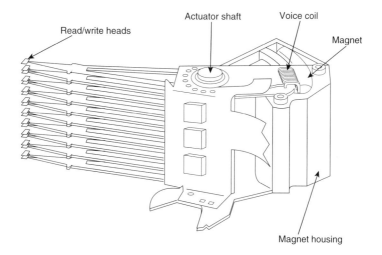

Figure 9.10   Read/write heads and rotary voice coil actuator assembly.

Caution

The small size of the gap between the platters and the heads is why you should never open the disk drive's HDA except in a clean-room environment. Any particle of dust or dirt that gets into this mechanism could cause the heads to read improperly or possibly even to strike the platters while the drive is running at full speed. The latter event could scratch the platter or the head, causing permanent damage.

To ensure the cleanliness of the interior of the drive, the HDA is assembled in a class-100 or better clean room. This specification means that a cubic foot of air cannot contain more than 100 particles that measure up to 0.5 microns (19.7 µ-inch). A single person breathing while standing motionless spews out 500 such particles in a single minute! These rooms contain special air-filtration systems that continuously evacuate and refresh the air. A drive's HDA should not be opened unless it is inside such a room.

Although maintaining a clean-room environment might seem to be expensive, many companies manufacture tabletop or bench-size clean rooms that sell for only a few thousand dollars. Some of these devices operate like a glove box: The operator first inserts the drive and any tools required and then closes the box and turns on the filtration system. Inside the box, a clean-room environment is maintained, and a technician can use the built-in gloves to work on the drive.

In other clean-room variations, the operator stands at a bench where a forced-air curtain maintains a clean environment on the bench top. The technician can walk in and out of the clean-room field by walking through the air curtain. This air curtain is very similar to the curtain of air used in some stores and warehouses to prevent heat from escaping in the winter while leaving a passage wide open. Because the clean environment is expensive to produce, few companies, except those that manufacture the drives, are properly equipped to service hard disk drives.

As disk drive technology has evolved, so has the design of the read/write head. The earliest heads were simple iron cores with coil windings (electromagnets). By today's standards, the original head designs were enormous in physical size and operated at very low recording densities. Over the years, head designs have evolved from the first simple ferrite core designs into the magneto-resistive and giant magneto-resistive types available today.

Head Actuator Mechanisms

Possibly more important than the heads themselves is the mechanical system that moves them: the head actuator. This mechanism moves the heads across the disk and positions them accurately above the desired cylinder.

The voice coil actuators used in hard disk drives made today use a feedback signal from the drive to accurately determine the head positions and adjust them, if necessary. This arrangement provides significantly greater performance, accuracy, and reliability than traditional stepper motor actuator designs.

A voice coil actuator works by pure electromagnetic force. The construction of the mechanism is similar to that of a typical audio speaker, from which the term *voice coil* is derived. An audio speaker uses a stationary magnet surrounded by a voice coil, which is connected to the speaker's paper cone. Energizing the coil causes it to move relative to the stationary magnet, which produces sound from the cone. In a typical hard disk drive's voice coil system, the electromagnetic coil is attached to the end of the head rack and placed near a stationary magnet. No physical contact occurs between the coil and the magnet; instead, the coil moves by pure magnetic force. As the electromagnetic coils are energized, they attract or repulse the stationary magnet and move the head rack. Systems such as these are extremely quick and efficient and usually much quieter than systems driven by stepper motors.

Voice coil actuators use a guidance mechanism called a *servo* to tell the actuator where the heads are in relation to the cylinders and to place the heads accurately at the desired positions. This positioning system often is called a *closed-loop feedback mechanism*. It works by sending the index (or servo) signal to the positioning electronics, which return a feedback signal that is used to position the heads accurately. The system also is called *servo controlled*, which refers to the index or servo information that is used to dictate or control head-positioning accuracy.

A voice coil actuator with servo control is not affected by temperature changes, as a stepper motor is. When temperature changes cause the disk platters to expand or contract, the voice coil system compensates automatically because it never positions the heads in predetermined track positions. Rather, the voice coil system searches for the specific track, guided by the prewritten servo information, and then positions the head rack precisely above the desired track, wherever it happens to be. Because of the continuous feedback of servo information, the heads adjust to the current position of the track at all times. For example, as a drive warms up and the platters expand, the servo information enables the heads to "follow" the track. As a result, a voice coil actuator is sometimes called a *track-following system*.

Automatic Head Parking

When you power off a hard disk drive using a CSS (contact start stop) design, the spring tension in each head arm pulls the heads into contact with the platters. The drive is designed to sustain thousands of takeoffs and landings, but it is wise to ensure that the landings occur at a spot on the platter that contains no data. Older drives required manual head parking; you had to run a program that positioned the drive heads to a landing zone, usually the innermost cylinder, before turning the system off. Modern drives automatically park the heads, so park programs are no longer necessary.

Some amount of abrasion occurs during the landing and takeoff process, removing just a "micro puff" from the magnetic medium—but if the drive is jarred during the landing or takeoff process, real damage can occur. Newer drives that use load/unload designs incorporate a ramp positioned outside the outer surface of the platters to prevent any contact between the heads and platters, even if the drive is powered off. Load/unload drives automatically park the heads on the ramp when the drive is powered off.

One benefit of using a voice coil actuator is automatic head parking. In a drive that has a voice coil actuator, the heads are positioned and held by magnetic force. When the power to the drive is removed, the magnetic field that holds the heads stationary over a particular cylinder dissipates, enabling the head rack to skitter across the drive surface and potentially cause damage. In the voice coil design, the head rack is attached to a weak spring at one end and a head stop at the other end. When the system is powered on, the spring is overcome by the magnetic force of the positioner. When the drive is powered off, however, the spring gently drags the head rack to a park-and-lock position before the drive slows down and the heads land. On some drives, you could actually hear the "ting...ting...ting...ting" sound as the heads literally bounce-park themselves, driven by this spring.

On a drive with a voice coil actuator, you activate the parking mechanism by turning off the computer; you do not need to run a program to park or retract the heads. In the event of a power outage, the heads park themselves automatically. (The drives unpark automatically when the system is powered on.)

Air Filters

Nearly all hard disk drives have two air filters. One is called the *recirculating filter*, and the other is called either a *barometric* or *breather filter*. These filters are permanently sealed inside the drive and are designed never to be changed for the life of the drive, unlike many older mainframe hard disks that had changeable filters.

Although it is vented, a hard disk does not actively circulate air from inside to outside the HDA or vice versa. The recirculating filter permanently installed inside the HDA is designed to filter only the small particles scraped off the platters during head takeoffs and landings (and possibly any other small particles dislodged inside the drive). Because hard disk drives are permanently sealed and do not circulate outside air, they can run in extremely dirty environments (see Figure 9.11).

The HDA in a hard disk drive is sealed but not airtight. The HDA is vented through a barometric or breather filter element that enables pressure equalization (breathing) between the inside and outside of the drive. For this reason, most hard drives are rated by the drive's manufacturer to run in a specific range of altitudes, usually from 1,000 feet below to 10,000 feet above sea level. In fact, some hard drives are not rated to exceed 7,000 feet while operating because the air pressure would be too low inside the drive to float the heads properly. As the environmental air pressure changes, air bleeds into or out of the drive, so internal and external pressures are identical. Although air does bleed through a vent, contamination usually is not a concern because the barometric filter on this vent is designed to filter out all particles larger than 0.3 microns (about 12 μ-inch) to meet the specifications for cleanliness inside the drive. You can see the vent holes on most drives, which are covered internally by this breather filter. Some drives use even finer-grade filter elements to keep out even smaller particles.

I conducted a seminar in Hawaii several years ago, and several of the students were from one of the astronomical observatories atop Mauna Kea. They indicated that virtually all the hard disk drives they had tried to use at the observatory site had failed very quickly, if they worked at all. This was no surprise because the observatories are at the 13,796-foot peak of the mountain, and at that altitude, even people don't function very well! At the time, they had to resort to solid-state (RAM) disks, tape drives, or even floppy disk drives as their primary storage medium. Since then, IBM's Adstar division (which produces all IBM hard drives) has introduced a line of rugged 3.5-inch drives that are hermetically sealed (airtight), although they do have air inside the HDA. Because they carry their own internal air under pressure, these drives can operate at any altitude and can also withstand extremes of shock and temperature. The drives are designed for military and industrial applications, such as systems used aboard aircraft and in extremely harsh environments. They are, of course, more expensive than typical hard drives that operate under ambient air pressure.

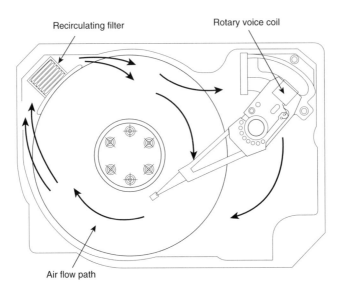

Figure 9.11 Air circulation in a hard disk.

Hard Disk Temperature Acclimation

Because hard drives have a filtered port to bleed air into or out of the HDA, moisture can enter the drive, and after some period of time, it must be assumed that the humidity inside any hard disk is similar to that outside the drive. Humidity can become a serious problem if it is allowed to condense—and especially if you power up the drive while this condensation is present. Most hard disk manufacturers have specified procedures for acclimating a hard drive to a new environment with different temperature and humidity ranges, and especially for bringing a drive into a warmer environment in which condensation can form. This situation should be of special concern to users of laptop or portable systems. If you leave a portable system in an automobile trunk during the winter, for example, it could be catastrophic to bring the machine inside and power it up without allowing it to acclimate to the temperature indoors.

The following text and Table 9.4 are taken from the factory packaging that Control Data Corporation (later Imprimis and eventually Seagate) used to ship with its hard drives:

> If you have just received or removed this unit from a climate with temperatures at or below 50°F (10°C), do not open this container until the following conditions are met; otherwise, condensation could occur and damage to the device and/or media may result. Place this package in the operating environment for the time duration according to the temperature chart.

Table 9.4   Hard Disk Drive Environmental Acclimation Table

Previous Climate Temperature	Acclimation Time	Previous Climate Temperature	Acclimation Time
+40°F (+4°C)	13 hours	−10°F (−23°C)	20 hours
+30°F (−1°C)	15 hours	−20°F (−29°C)	22 hours
+20°F (−7°C)	16 hours	−30°F (−34°C) or less	27 hours
+10°F (−12°C)	17 hours		
0°F (−18°C)	18 hours		

As you can see from this table, you must place a hard disk drive that has been stored in a colder-than-normal environment into its normal operating environment for a specified amount of time to allow it to acclimate before you power it on.

Spindle Motors

The motor that spins the platters is called the *spindle motor* because it is connected to the spindle around which the platters revolve. Spindle motors in hard disk drives are always connected directly; no belts or gears are involved. The motor must be free of noise and vibration; otherwise, it can transmit a rumble to the platters, which can disrupt reading and writing operations.

The spindle motor also must be precisely controlled for speed. The platters in hard disk drives revolve at speeds ranging from 3,600rpm to 15,000rpm (60–250 revolutions per second) or more, and the motor has a control circuit with a feedback loop to monitor and control this speed precisely. Because the speed control must be automatic, hard drives do not have a motor-speed adjustment. Some diagnostics programs claim to measure hard drive rotation speed, but all these programs do is estimate the rotational speed by the timing at which sectors pass under the heads.

There is actually no way for a program to measure the hard disk drive's rotational speed; this measurement can be made only with sophisticated test equipment. Don't be alarmed if some diagnostics program tells you that your drive is spinning at an incorrect speed; most likely, the program is wrong, not the drive. Platter rotation and timing information is not provided through the hard disk controller interface. In the past, software could give approximate rotational speed estimates by performing multiple sector read requests and timing them, but this was valid only when all drives had the same number of sectors per track and spun at the same speed. Zoned-bit recording—combined with the many various rotational speeds used by modern drives, not to mention built-in buffers and caches—means that these calculation estimates cannot be performed accurately by software.

On most drives, the spindle motor is on the bottom of the drive, just below the sealed HDA. Many drives today, however, have the spindle motor directly built in to the platter hub inside the HDA. By using an internal hub spindle motor, the manufacturer can stack more platters in the drive because the spindle motor takes up no vertical space.

Note

Spindle motors, particularly on the larger form-factor drives, can consume a great deal of 12-volt power. Most drives require two to three times the normal operating power when the motor first spins the platters. This heavy draw lasts only a few seconds or until the drive platters reach operating speed. If you have more than one drive, you should try to sequence the start of the spindle motors so the power supply does not have to provide such a large load to all the drives at the same time. Most SCSI and some ATA drives have a delayed spindle-motor start feature.

Fluid Dynamic Bearings

Traditionally, spindle motors have used ball bearings in their design, but limitations in their performance have now caused drive manufacturers to look for alternatives. The main problem with ball bearings is that they have approximately 0.1 micro-inch (millionths of an inch) of runout, which is lateral side-to-side play in the bearings. Although that may seem small, with the ever-increasing density of modern drives it has become a problem. This runout allows the platters to move randomly that distance from side to side, which causes the tracks to wobble under the heads. Additionally, the runout plus the metal-to-metal contact nature of ball bearings allows an excessive amount of mechanical noise and vibration to be generated, and that is becoming a problem for drives that spin at higher speeds.

The solution to this problem came in the form of *fluid dynamic bearings*, which use a highly viscous lubricating fluid between the spindle and sleeve in the motor. This fluid serves to dampen vibrations and movement, allowing runout to be reduced to 0.01 micro-inches or less. Fluid dynamic bearings also allow for better shock resistance, improved speed control, and reduced noise generation. Today, the majority of hard drives use fluid dynamic bearings, especially the drives that have very high storage capacities of 160GB and up and/or high spindle speeds. The traditional ball bearings are, however, still used in low-cost entry-level drives, but even these will likely be phased out completely in the next few years.

Logic Boards

All hard disk drives have one or more logic boards mounted on them. The logic boards contain the electronics that control the drive's spindle and head actuator systems and present data to the controller in some agreed-upon form. On ATA drives, the boards include the controller itself, whereas SCSI drives include the controller and the SCSI bus adapter circuit.

Many disk drive failures occur in the logic board, not in the mechanical assembly. (This statement does not seem logical, but it is true.) Therefore, you sometimes can repair a failed drive by replacing the logic board rather than the entire drive. Replacing the logic board, moreover, enables you to regain access to the data on the drive—something that replacing the entire drive does not provide. Unfortunately, none of the drive manufacturers sell logic boards separately. The only way to obtain a replacement logic board for a given drive would be to purchase a functioning identical drive and then cannibalize it for parts. Of course, it doesn't make sense to purchase an entire new drive just to repair an existing one, except in the case where data recovery from the old drive is necessary.

If you have an existing drive that contains important data, and the logic board fails, you will be unable to retrieve the data from the drive unless the board is replaced. Because the value of the data in most cases will far exceed the cost of the drive, a new drive that is identical to the failed drive can be purchased and cannibalized for parts such as the logic board, which can be swapped onto the failed drive. This method is common among companies that offer data-recovery services. They will stock a large number of popular drives that they can use for parts to allow data recovery from the defective customer drives they receive.

Most of the time the boards are fairly easy to change with nothing more than a screwdriver. Merely removing and reinstalling a few screws as well as unplugging and reconnecting a cable or two are all that is required to remove and replace a typical logic board.

Cables and Connectors

The 2.5-inch and smaller drives used in laptop systems normally use a single unified connector with a single cable or connection.

Configuration Items

The 2.5-inch and smaller drives normally don't use any jumpers because only a single drive is connected at a time, and no jumpers are required for a master setting. However, if you wish to set a drive to slave, or cable select, then jumpers may be required.

Hard Disk Features

To make the best decision in purchasing a hard disk for your system or to understand what distinguishes one brand of hard disk from another, you must consider many features. This section examines some of the issues you should consider when you evaluate drives:

- Capacity
- Performance
- Reliability
- Cost

Capacity

As stated earlier, a corollary of Parkinson's famous "law" can be applied to hard drives: Data expands so as to fill the space available for its storage. This, of course, means that no matter how big a drive you get, you *will* find a way to fill it.

If you've exhausted the space on your current hard disk, you might be wondering, "How much storage space is enough?" Because it is much more likely that you will run out of space rather than have too much, generally it is best to aim high and go for the largest drive that will fit within your budget. Modern systems are used to store many space-hungry file types, including digital photos, music, video, newer operating systems, applications, and games. As an example, according to hard drive manufacturer Western Digital, storing 600 high-res photos (500KB each), 12 hours of digital music, five games, 20 applications, and just 90 minutes of digital video would require an estimated 43GB of space.

Running out of space causes numerous problems in a modern system, mainly due to the fact that Windows (as well as many newer applications) uses a large amount of drive space for temporary files and virtual memory. When Windows runs out of room, system instability, crashes, and data loss are inevitable.

Capacity Limitations

How big a hard drive you can use depends somewhat on the interface you choose. Although the ATA interface is by far the most popular interface for hard drives, SCSI interface drives are also available. Each has different limitations, but those of ATA have always been lower than those of SCSI.

When ATA was first created in 1986, it had a maximum capacity limitation of 137GB (65,536×16×255 sectors). BIOS issues further limited capacity to 8.4GB in systems earlier than 1998, and 528MB in systems earlier than 1994. Even after the BIOS problems were resolved, however, the 137GB limit of ATA remained. Fortunately, this was broken in the ATA-6 specification drafted in 2001. ATA-6 augments the addressing scheme used by ATA to allow drive capacity to grow to 144PB (petabytes, or quadrillion bytes), which is 2^{48} sectors. This has opened the door for ATA drives over 137GB to be released. Obviously, any drives larger than 137GB would by nature conform to ATA-6; however, if you are installing a drive larger than that, you should ensure that your motherboard BIOS has ATA-6 support as well. With the introduction of ATA-7, the speed of the interface has been increased from 100MBps for ATA-6 to 133MBps, but the 144PB limit remains.

BIOS Limitations

Motherboard ROM BIOSes have been updated throughout the years to support larger and larger drives. The following shows the most important relative dates when drive capacity limits were changed:

BIOS Date	Capacity Limit
August 1994	528MB
January 1998	8.4GB
September 2002	137GB

These dates are when the limits were broken, such that BIOSes older than August 1994 will generally be limited to drives of up to 528MB, whereas BIOSes older than January 1998 will generally be limited to 8.4GB. Most BIOSes dated 1998 or newer will support drives up to 137GB, and those dated September 2002 or newer should support drives larger than 137GB. These are only general guidelines. To accurately determine this for a specific system, you should check with your motherboard manufacturer. You can also use the BIOS Wizard utility from www.unicore.com/ bioswiz/index2.html. It will tell you the BIOS date from your system and specifically whether your system supports the "Enhanced Hard Disk Drive" specification, which means drives over 8.4GB.

If your BIOS does not support EDD (drives over 8.4GB), you have two possible solutions:

- ■ Update your motherboard BIOS upgrade to a 1998 or newer version that supports more than 8.4GB.
- ■ Install a software patch to add support for more than 8.4GB.

Of these, the first one is the most desirable because it is normally free and works more seamlessly in the system. Visit your motherboard manufacturer's website to see whether it has any newer BIOS available for your motherboard that will support large drives. I almost never recommend the software patch solution because it merely installs a program in the boot sector area of the hard drive, which can result in numerous problems when booting from different drives, installing new drives, or recovering data.

If your current hard drive is 8GB or smaller, your system might not be able to handle a larger drive without a BIOS upgrade, because many older (pre-1998) BIOSes can't handle drives above the 8.4GB limit, and others (pre-2002) have other limits, such as 137GB. Although most ATA hard drives ship with a setup disk containing a software BIOS substitute such as OnTrack's Disk Manager or Phoenix Technologies' EZ-Drive (Phoenix purchased EZ-Drive creator StorageSoft in January 2002), I don't recommend using a software BIOS replacement. EZ-Drive, Disk Manager, and their OEM offshoots (Drive Guide, MAXBlast, Data Lifeguard, and others) can cause problems if you need to boot from floppy or CD media or if you need to repair the nonstandard master boot record these products use.

If your motherboard ROM BIOS dates before 1998 and is limited to 8.4GB, or dates before 2002 and is limited to 137GB, and you wish to install a larger drive, I recommend you first contact your motherboard (or system) manufacturer to see if an update is available. Virtually all motherboards incorporate a Flash ROM, which allows for easy updates via a utility program.

Operating System Limitations

Newer operating systems such as Windows XP as well as Windows 2000 and Me fortunately don't have any problems with larger drives; however, older operating systems may have limitations when it comes to using large drives.

DOS will generally not recognize drives larger than 8.4GB because those drives are accessed using logical block addressing (LBA), and DOS versions 6.x and lower only use cylinder, head, sector (CHS) addressing.

Windows 95 has a 32GB hard disk capacity limit, and there is no way around it other than upgrading to Windows 98 or a newer version. Additionally, the retail or upgrade versions of Windows 95 (also called Windows 95 OSR 1 or Windows 95a) are further limited to using only the FAT16 (16-bit file allocation table) file system, which carries a maximum partition size limitation of 2GB. This means if you had a 30GB drive, you would be forced to divide it into 15 2GB partitions, each appearing as a separate drive letter (drives C: through Q: in this example). Windows 95B and 95C can use the FAT32 file system, which allows partition sizes up to 2TB (terabytes). Note that due to internal limitations, no version of FDISK can create partitions larger than 512MB.

Windows 98 supports large drives, but a bug in the FDISK program included with Windows 98 reduces the reported drive capacity by 64GB for drives over that capacity. The solution is an updated version of FDISK that you can download from Microsoft. Another bug appears in the FORMAT command with Windows 98. If you run FORMAT from a command prompt on a partition over 64GB, the size isn't reported correctly, although the entire partition will be formatted.

Performance

When you select a hard disk drive, one of the important features you should consider is the performance (speed) of the drive. Hard drives can have a wide range of performance capabilities. As is true of many things, one of the best indicators of a drive's relative performance is its price. An old saying from the automobile-racing industry is appropriate here: "Speed costs money. How fast do you want to go?"

Normally, the speed of a disk drive is measured in several ways:

- Interface (external) transfer rate
- Media (internal) transfer rates
- Average access time

Transfer Rates

The transfer rate is probably more important to overall system performance than any other statistic, but it is also one of the most misunderstood specifications. The problem stems from the fact that several transfer rates can be specified for a given drive; however, the most important of these is usually overlooked.

A great deal of confusion arises from the fact that drive manufacturers can report up to seven different transfer rates for a given drive. Perhaps the least important of these (but the one people seem to focus on the most) is the raw interface transfer rate, which for the 2.5-inch ATA drives used in portable systems is 100MBps. Unfortunately, few people seem to realize that the drives actually read and write data much slower than that. The most important transfer rate specifications are the media (or internal) transfer rates, which express how fast a drive can actually read or write data. Media transfer rates can be expressed as a raw maximum, raw minimum, formatted maximum, formatted minimum, or averages of any of these. Few report the averages, but they can be easily calculated.

The media transfer rate is far more important than the interface transfer rate because it is the true rate at which data can be read from (or written to) the disk. In other words, it tells how fast data can be moved to and from the drive platters (media). It is the rate that any sustained transfer can hope to achieve. This rate will normally be reported as a minimum and maximum figure, although many drive manufacturers report the maximum only.

Media transfer rates have minimum and maximum figures because drives today use zoned recording with fewer sectors per track on the inner cylinders than the outer cylinders. Typically, a drive is divided into 16 or more zones, with the inner zone having about half the sectors per track (and therefore about half the transfer rate) of the outer zone. Because the drive spins at a constant rate, data can be read twice as fast from the outer cylinders than from the inner cylinders.

Two primary factors contribute to transfer rate performance: rotational speed and the linear recording density or sector-per-track figures. When two drives with the same number of sectors per track are being compared, the drive that spins more quickly will transfer data more quickly. Likewise, when two drives with identical rotational speeds are being compared, the drive with the higher recording density (more sectors per track) will be faster. A higher-density drive can be faster than one that spins faster—both factors have to be taken into account to know the true score.

To find the transfer specifications for a given drive, look in the data sheet or preferably the documentation or manual for the drive. You usually can download them from the drive manufacturer's website. This documentation will often report the maximum and minimum sector-per-track specifications, which—combined with the rotational speed—can be used to calculate true formatted media performance. Note that you would be looking for the true number of physical sectors per track for the outer and inner zones. Be aware that many drives (especially zoned-bit recording drives) are configured with sector translation, so the number of sectors per track reported by the BIOS has little to do with the actual physical characteristics of the drive. You must know the drive's true physical parameters rather than the values the BIOS uses.

When you know the true sector per track (SPT) and rotational speed figures, you can use the following formula to determine the true media data transfer rate in millions of bytes per second (MBps):

$$\text{Media Transfer Rate (MBps)} = \text{SPT} \times 512 \text{ bytes} \times \text{rpm}/60 \text{ seconds}/1,000,000$$

For example, the Hitachi/IBM Travelstar 7K60 drive spins at 7,200rpm and has an average of 540 sectors per track. The average media transfer rate for this drive is figured as follows:

$$540 \times 512 \times (7,200/60)/1,000,000 = 33.18 \text{ MBps}$$

Some drive manufacturers don't give the sector per track values for the outer and inner zones, instead offering only the raw unformatted transfer rates in Mbps (megabits per second). To convert raw megabits per second to formatted megabytes per second in a modern drive, divide the figure by 11. For example, Toshiba reports transfer rates of 373Mbps maximum and 203Mbps minimum for its MK6022GAX 60GB drive. This is an average of 288Mbps, which equates to an average formatted transfer rate of about 26MBps.

Using these formulas (or slight variations thereof), you can calculate the media transfer rate of any drive. Table 9.5 shows the transfer rate specifications of the biggest and fastest 2.5-inch drives, listed in order from fastest to slowest.

Table 9.5   60GB+ 2.5-inch Hard Disk Transfer Rates

Drive	Size	Interface Transfer Rate (MBps)	Cache	Outer Zone (SPT)	Inner Zone (SPT)	Speed (rpm)	Max. Media Rate (MBps)	Min. Media Rate (MBps)	Avg. Transfer Rate (MBps)
Hitachi TS 7K60	60GB	100	8MB	720	360	7200	44.24	22.12	33.18
Hitachi TS 5K80	80GB	100	8MB	885	440	5400	40.78	20.28	30.53

Table 9.5   Continued

Drive	Size	Interface Transfer Rate (MBps)	Cache	Outer Zone (SPT)	Inner Zone (SPT)	Speed (rpm)	Max. Media Rate (MBps)	Min. Media Rate (MBps)	Avg. Transfer Rate (MBps)
Toshiba MK6022GAX	60GB	100	16MB	736	400	5400	33.91	18.43	26.17
Hitachi TS 80GN	80GB	100	8MB	868	448	4200	31.11	16.06	23.58
Toshiba MK8025GAS	80GB	100	8MB	866	443	4200	31.04	15.88	23.46
Toshiba MK6021GAS	60GB	100	2MB	755	391	4200	27.06	14.01	20.54
Hitachi TS 60GH	60GB	100	2MB	556	307	5400	25.62	14.15	19.88

As you can see from the table, even though all these drives have a theoretical interface transfer rate of 100MBps, the fastest 2.5-inch drive has an average true media transfer rate of just over 33MBps. As an analogy, think of the drive as a tiny water faucet, and the ATA interface as a huge firehouse connected to the faucet that is being used to fill a swimming pool. No matter how much water can theoretically flow through the hose, you will be able to fill the pool only at the rate the faucet can flow water.

The cache in a drive allows for burst transfers at the full interface rate. In our analogy, the cache is like a bucket that, once filled, can be dumped at full speed into the pool. The only problem is that the bucket is also filled by the faucet, so any data transfer larger than the size of the bucket can proceed only at the rate that the faucet can flow water.

When you study drive specifications, it is true that larger caches and faster interface transfer rates are nice, but in the end, they are limited by the true transfer rate, which is the rate at which data can be read from or written to the actual drive media. In general, the *media* (also called *internal* or *true*) transfer rate is the most important specification for a drive.

Note

There is a price to pay for portability, both in actual cost and performance. In general, the smaller a drive, the more expensive it is, and the slower the transfer rate performance. For example, a 2.5-inch notebook drive generally costs twice as much as the same capacity 3.5-inch desktop drive. Also, it will be slower. The fastest of the larger 3.5-inch drives normally used in desktop systems has an average transfer rate of between 44MBps and 50MBps, which is significantly faster than the 20MBps to 33MBps average rates of the fastest 2.5-inch notebook drives. Very small drives such as the Hitachi MicroDrive cost even more. A 1GB MicroDrive costs more than an 80GB 2.5-inch drive or a 250GB 3.5-inch drive, and it transfers at an average of just under 5MBps, significantly slower than any other drive.

Average Seek Time

Average seek time, normally measured in milliseconds (ms), is the average amount of time it takes to move the heads from one cylinder to another a random distance away. One way to measure this specification is to run many random track-seek operations and then divide the timed results by the number of seeks performed. This method provides an average time for a single seek.

The standard method used by many drive manufacturers when reporting average seek times is to measure the time it takes the heads to move across one-third of the total cylinders. Average seek time depends only on the drive itself; the type of interface or controller has little effect on this specification. The average seek rating is primarily a gauge of the capabilities of the head actuator mechanism.

Note

Be wary of benchmarks that claim to measure drive seek performance. Most ATA and SCSI drives use a scheme called *sector translation*, so any commands the drive receives to move the heads to a specific cylinder might not actually result in the intended physical movement. This situation renders some benchmarks meaningless for those types of drives. SCSI drives also require an additional step because the commands first must be sent to the drive over the SCSI bus. These drives might seem to have the fastest access times because the command overhead is not factored in by most benchmarks. However, when this overhead is factored in by benchmark programs, these drives receive poor performance figures.

Latency

Latency is the average time (in milliseconds) it takes for a sector to be available after the heads have reached a track. On average, this figure is half the time it takes for the disk to rotate once. A drive that spins twice as fast would have half the latency.

Latency is a factor in disk read and write performance. Decreasing the latency increases the speed of access to data or files and is accomplished only by spinning the drive platters more quickly. Latency figures for the most popular drive rotational speeds are shown in Table 9.6.

Table 9.6   Hard Disk Rotation Speeds and Their Latencies

Revs/Minute	Revs/Second	Latency
3,600	60	8.33
4,200	70	7.14
5,400	90	5.56
7,200	160	4.17
10,000	167	3.00
15,000	250	2.00

Many 3.5-inch drives today spin at 7,200rpm, resulting in a latency time of only 4.17ms, whereas others spin at 10,000rpm and even 15,000rpm, resulting in incredible 3.00ms and 2.00ms latency figures. Most 2.5-inch drives spin at either 4,200 or 5,400rpm. However, several high-performance 7,200rpm 2.5-inch drives are now on the market. In addition to increasing performance where real-world access to data is concerned, spinning the platters more quickly also increases the data transfer rate after the heads arrive at the desired sectors.

Average Access Time

A measurement of a drive's average access time is the sum of its *average seek time* plus *latency*. The average access time is normally expressed in milliseconds (ms), which are thousandths of a second. A measurement of a drive's average access time (average seek time plus latency) provides the average total amount of time required for the drive to access a randomly requested sector.

Cache Programs and Caching Controllers

At the software level, disk cache programs, such as SMARTDRV (DOS) and VCACHE (Windows), can have a major effect on disk drive performance. These cache programs hook into the BIOS hard drive and interrupt and intercept the read and write calls to the disk BIOS from application programs and device drivers.

When an application program wants to read data from a hard drive, the cache program intercepts the read request, passes the read request to the hard drive controller in the usual way, saves the data read from the disk in its cache memory buffer, and then passes the data back to the application program. Depending on the size of the cache buffer, data from numerous sectors can be read into and saved in the buffer.

When the application wants to read more data, the cache program again intercepts the request and examines its buffers to see whether the requested data is still in the cache. If so, the program passes the data back from the cache to the application immediately, without another hard drive operation. Because the cached data is stored in memory, this method speeds access tremendously and can greatly affect disk drive performance measurements.

Most controllers now have some form of built-in hardware buffer or cache that doesn't intercept or use any BIOS interrupts. Instead, the drive caches data at the hardware level, which is invisible to normal performance-measurement software. Manufacturers originally included track read-ahead buffers in controllers to permit 1:1 interleave performance. Some manufacturers now increase the size of these read-ahead buffers in the controller, whereas others add intelligence by using a cache instead of a simple buffer.

Most PATA, SATA, and SCSI drives have cache memory directly built in to the drive's onboard controller. Most newer ATA drives have between 2MB through 16MB of built-in cache, whereas many SCSI drives have 16MB or more. I remember the days when 1 or 2MB of RAM was a lot of memory for an entire system. Nowadays, some 2.5-inch hard disk drives can have up to 16MB of cache memory built right in!

Although software and hardware caches can make a drive faster for routine or repetitive data transfer operations, a cache will not affect the true maximum transfer rate the drive can sustain.

SMART

SMART (Self-Monitoring Analysis and Reporting Technology) is an industry standard providing failure prediction for disk drives. When SMART is enabled for a given drive, the drive monitors predetermined attributes that are susceptible to or indicative of drive degradation. Based on changes in the monitored attributes, a failure prediction can be made. If a failure is deemed likely to occur, SMART makes a status report available so the system BIOS or driver software can notify the user of the impending problems, perhaps enabling the user to back up the data on the drive before any real problems occur.

Predictable failures are the types of failures SMART attempts to detect. These failures result from the gradual degradation of the drive's performance. According to Seagate, 60% of drive failures are mechanical, which is exactly the type of failures SMART is designed to predict.

Of course, not all failures are predictable, and SMART cannot help with unpredictable failures that occur without any advance warning. These can be caused by static electricity, improper handling or sudden shock, or circuit failure, such as thermal-related solder problems or component failure.

SMART originated in technology that was created by IBM in 1992. That year IBM began shipping 3.5-inch hard disk drives equipped with Predictive Failure Analysis (PFA), an IBM-developed technology that periodically measures selected drive attributes and sends a warning message when a predefined threshold is exceeded. IBM turned this technology over to the ANSI organization, and it subsequently became the ANSI-standard SMART protocol for SCSI drives, as defined in the ANSI-SCSI Informational Exception Control (IEC) document X3T10/94-190.

Interest in extending this technology to ATA drives led to the creation of the SMART Working Group in 1995. Besides IBM, other companies represented in the original group were Seagate Technology, Conner Peripherals (now a part of Seagate), Fujitsu, Hewlett-Packard, Maxtor, Quantum, and Western Digital. The SMART specification produced by this group and placed in the public domain covers both ATA and SCSI hard disk drives and can be found in most of the more recently produced drives on the market. The SMART design of attributes and thresholds is similar in ATA and SCSI environments, but the reporting of information differs.

In an ATA environment, driver software on the system interprets the alarm signal from the drive generated by the SMART "report status" command. The driver polls the drive on a regular basis to check the status of this command and, if it signals imminent failure, sends an alarm to the operating system, where it will be passed on via an error message to the end user. This structure also enables future enhancements, which might allow reporting of information other than drive failure conditions. The system can read and evaluate the attributes and alarms reported in addition to the basic "report status" command.

SCSI drives with SMART communicate a reliability condition only as either good or failing. In a SCSI environment, the failure decision occurs at the disk drive, and the host notifies the user for action. The SCSI specification provides for a sense bit to be flagged if the drive determines that a reliability issue exists. The system then alerts the end user via a message.

The basic requirements for SMART to function in a system are simple. All you need are a SMART-capable hard disk drive and a SMART-aware BIOS or hard disk driver for your particular operating system. If your BIOS does not support SMART, utility programs are available that can support SMART on a given system. They include Norton Disk Doctor from Symantec, EZ-Drive from StorageSoft, and Data Advisor from Ontrack Data International.

Note that traditional disk diagnostics, such as Scandisk and Norton Disk Doctor, work only on the data sectors of the disk surface and do not monitor all the drive functions that are monitored by SMART. Most modern disk drives keep spare sectors available to use as substitutes for sectors that have errors. When one of these spares is reallocated, the drive reports the activity to the SMART counter but still looks completely "defect free" to a surface analysis utility, such as Scandisk.

Drives with SMART monitor a variety of attributes that vary from one manufacturer to another. Attributes are selected by the device manufacturer based on their capability to contribute to the prediction of degrading or fault conditions for that particular drive. Most drive manufacturers consider the specific set of attributes being used and the identity of those attributes as vendor specific and proprietary.

Some drives monitor the floating height of the head above the magnetic media. If this height changes from a nominal figure, the drive could fail. Other drives can monitor different attributes, such as error correcting code (ECC) circuitry that indicates whether soft errors are occurring when reading or writing data. Some of the attributes monitored on various drives include the following:

- Head floating height
- Data throughput performance
- Spin-up time
- Reallocated (spared) sector count

- Seek error rate
- Seek time performance
- Drive spin-up retry count
- Drive calibration retry count

Each attribute has a threshold limit that is used to determine the existence of a degrading or fault condition. These thresholds are set by the drive manufacturer, can vary among manufacturers and models, and cannot be changed.

Any drives reporting a SMART failure should be considered likely to fail at any time. Of course, you should back up the data on such a drive immediately, and you might consider replacing the drive before any actual data loss occurs. When sufficient changes occur in the monitored attributes to trigger a SMART alert, the drive sends an alert message via an ATA or a SCSI command (depending on the type of hard disk drive you have) to the hard disk driver in the system BIOS, which then forwards the message to the operating system. The operating system then displays a warning message as follows:

Immediately back up your data and replace your hard disk drive. A failure may be imminent.

The message might contain additional information, such as which physical device initiated the alert; a list of the logical drives (partitions) that correspond to the physical device; and even the type, manufacturer, and serial number of the device.

The first thing to do when you receive such an alert is to heed the warning and back up all the data on the drive. It also is wise to back up to new media and not overwrite any previous good backups you might have, just in case the drive fails before the backup is complete.

After you back up your data, what should you do? SMART warnings can be caused by an external source and might not actually indicate that the drive itself is going to fail. For example, environmental changes, such as high or low ambient temperatures, can trigger a SMART alert, as can excessive vibration in the drive caused by an external source. Additionally, electrical interference from motors or other devices on the same circuit as your PC can induce these alerts.

If the alert was not caused by an external source, a drive replacement might be indicated. If the drive is under warranty, contact the vendor and ask whether they will replace it. If no further alerts occur, the problem might have been an anomaly, and you might not need to replace the drive. If you receive further alerts, replacing the drive is recommended. If you can connect both the new and existing (failing) drive to the same system, you might be able to copy the entire contents of the existing drive to the new one, saving you from having to install or reload all the applications and data from your backup. Because standard copy commands or drag and drop methods won't copy system files, hidden files, or files that are open, to copy an entire drive successfully and have the destination copy remain bootable, you will need a special application like Symantec Norton Ghost or Acronis Drive Image.

Cost

The cost of hard disk storage is continually falling. You can now purchase a 2.5-inch 80GB ATA drive for around $80, which is 0.1 cent (one tenth of a cent) per megabyte. A drive I bought in 1983 had a maximum capacity of 10MB and cost me $1,800 at the time. At current 2.5-inch drive pricing (0.1 cent per megabyte or less), that drive is worth about 1 cent!

Of course, the cost of drives continues to fall, and eventually, even 0.1 cents per megabyte will seem expensive. Because of the low costs of disk storage today, not many 2.5-inch drives with capacities of less than 40GB are even being manufactured.

The ATA (IDE) Interface

The interface used to connect a hard disk drive to a modern PC is typically called *IDE (Integrated Drive Electronics)*. However, the true name of the interface is *ATA (AT Attachment)*. ATA refers to the fact that this interface originally was designed to connect a combined drive and controller directly to the bus of the 1984 vintage IBM AT (Advanced Technology) computer, otherwise known as the *ISA (Industry Standard Architecture)* or *AT bus*. *IDE* is a term originated by the marketing departments of some drive manufacturers to describe the drive/controller combination used in drives with the ATA interface. *Integrated Drive Electronics* refers to the fact that the interface electronics or controller is built in to the drive and is not a separate board, as with earlier drive interfaces.

Today, ATA is used to connect not only hard disks but also CD and DVD drives, high-capacity SuperDisk floppy drives, and tape drives. Even so, ATA is still thought of primarily as a hard disk interface, and it evolved directly from the separate controller and hard drive interfaces that were used prior to ATA. This chapter covers the ATA interface in detail, as well as the original interfaces from which ATA evolved. Because the ATA interface is directly integrated into virtually all motherboard chipsets, ATA is the primary storage interface used by most PCs, including both desktops and portables.

ATA is a 16-bit parallel interface, meaning that 16 bits are transmitted simultaneously down the interface cable. A new interface, called *Serial ATA*, was officially introduced in late 2000 and was adopted in desktop systems starting in 2003, and in laptops starting in late 2005. Serial ATA (SATA) sends 1 bit down the cable at a time, enabling thinner and smaller cables to be used, as well as providing higher performance due to the higher cycling speeds allowed. SATA is a completely new and updated physical interface design, while remaining compatible on the software level with Parallel ATA. Throughout this book, *ATA* refers to the parallel version, whereas Serial ATA is explicitly referenced as *SATA*.

Note

Many people who use systems with ATA connectors on the motherboard believe that a hard disk controller is built in to their motherboards, but in a technical sense the controller is actually in the drive. Although the integrated ATA ports on a motherboard often are referred to as *controllers*, they are more accurately called *host adapters* (although you'll rarely hear this term). A host adapter can be thought of as a device that connects a controller to a bus.

The primary advantage of ATA drives over the older, separate controller–based interfaces and newer host bus interface alternatives, such as SCSI and IEEE 1394 (i.LINK or FireWire), is cost. Because the separate controller or host adapter is eliminated and the cable connections are simplified, ATA drives cost much less than a standard controller and drive combination.

ATA Standards

Today what we call the ATA interface is controlled by an independent group of representatives from major PC, drive, and component manufacturers. This group is called *Technical Committee T13* (www.t13.org) and is responsible for all interface standards relating to the parallel AT Attachment storage interface. T13 is a part of the International Committee on Information Technology Standards (INCITS), which operates under rules approved by the American National Standards Institute (ANSI), a governing body that sets rules that control nonproprietary standards in the computer industry as well as many other industries. A second group, called the *Serial ATA Working Group* (www.serialata.org), has formed to create the Serial ATA standards that will also come under ANSI control. Although these are different groups, many of the same people are in both of them. It seems as if little further development will be done on Parallel ATA past the ATA-7 (ATA/133) specification. The further evolution of ATA will be in the Serial ATA form (discussed later in this chapter).

The rules these committees operate under are designed to ensure that voluntary industry standards are developed by the consensus of people and organizations in the affected industry. INCITS specifically develops Information Processing System standards, whereas ANSI approves the process under which they are developed and then publishes them. Because T13 is essentially a public organization, all the working drafts, discussions, and meetings of T13 are open for all to see.

The Parallel ATA interface has evolved into several successive standard versions, introduced as follows:

- ATA-1 (1986–1994)
- ATA-2 (1995; also called Fast-ATA, Fast-ATA-2, or EIDE)
- ATA-3 (1996)
- ATA-4 (1997; also called Ultra-ATA/33)
- ATA-5 (1998–present; also called Ultra-ATA/66)
- ATA-6 (2000–present; also called Ultra-ATA/100)
- ATA-7 (2001–present; also called Ultra-ATA/133)

Each version of ATA is backward compatible with the previous versions. In other words, older ATA-1 or ATA-2 devices work fine on ATA-6 and ATA-7 interfaces. In cases in which the device version and interface version don't match, they work together at the capabilities of the lesser of the two. Newer versions of ATA are built on older versions and with few exceptions can be thought of as extensions of the previous versions. This means that ATA-7, for example, is generally considered equal to ATA-6 with the addition of some features.

Table 9.7 breaks down the various ATA standards. The following sections describe all the ATA versions in more detail.

Table 9.7   ATA Standards

Standard	Timeframe	PIO	DMA Modes	UDMA Modes	Speed[1] Modes	Features
ATA-1	1986–1994	0–2	0	—	8.33	Drives support up to 136.9GB. BIOS issues not addressed.
ATA-2	1995–1996	0–4	0–2	—	16.67	Faster PIO modes. CHS/LBA BIOS translation defined up to 8.4GB. PC Card.
ATA-3	1996–1997	0–4	0–2	—	16.67	SMART. Improved signal integrity. LBA support mandatory. Eliminated single-word DMA modes.
ATA-4	1997–1998	0–4	0–2	0–2	33.33	Ultra-DMA modes. BIOS support up to 136.9GB.
ATA-5	1998–2000	0–4	0–2	0–4	66.67	Faster UDMA modes. 80-pin cable with auto-detection.
ATA-6	2000–2002	0–4	0–2	0–5	100.00	100MBps UDMA mode. Extended drive and BIOS support up to 144PB.
ATA-7	2002–present	0-4	0–2	0–6	133.00	133MBps UDMA mode.

1. *Speed is megabytes per second*
SMART = Self-Monitoring Analysis and Reporting Technology
MB = megabyte (million bytes)
GB = gigabyte (billion bytes)
PB = petabyte (quadrillion bytes)

CHS = cylinder, head, sector
LBA = logical block address
PIO = programmed I/O
DMA = direct memory access
UDMA = Ultra-DMA (direct memory access)

ATA-1

Although ATA-1 had been used since 1986 before being published as a standard, and although it was first published in 1988 in draft form, ATA-1 wasn't officially approved as a standard until 1994 (committees often work slowly). ATA-1 defined the original AT Attachment interface, which was an integrated bus interface between disk drives and host systems based on the ISA (AT) bus. Here are the major features introduced and documented in the ATA-1 specification:

- 40/44-pin connectors and cabling
- Master/slave or cable select drive configuration options
- Signal timing for basic programmed I/O (PIO) and direct memory access (DMA) modes
- CHS (cylinder, head, sector) and LBA (logical block address) drive parameter translations supporting drive capacities up to 2^{28}–2^{20} (267,386,880) sectors, or 136.9GB

ATA-1 was officially published as "ANSI X3.221-1994, AT Attachment Interface for Disk Drives," and was officially withdrawn on August 6, 1999. ATA-2 and later are considered backward-compatible replacements.

Although ATA-1 supported theoretical drive capacities up to 136.9GB (2^{28}–2^{20} = 267,386,880 sectors), it did not address BIOS limitations that stopped at 528MB (1,024×16×63 = 1,032,192 sectors). The BIOS limitations would be addressed in subsequent ATA versions because, at the time, no drives larger than 528MB had existed.

ATA-2

Approved in 1996, ATA-2 was a major upgrade to the original ATA standard. Perhaps the biggest change was almost a philosophical one. ATA-2 was updated to define an interface between host systems and storage devices in general and not only disk drives. The major features added to ATA-2 as compared to the original ATA standard include the following:

- Faster PIO and DMA transfer modes.
- Support for power management.
- Support for removable devices.
- PCMCIA (PC card) device support.
- More information reported from the Identify Drive command.
- Defined standard CHS/LBA translation methods for drives up to 8.4GB in capacity.

The most important additions in ATA-2 were the support for faster PIO and DMA modes as well as the methods to enable BIOS support up to 8.4GB. The BIOS support was necessary because, although even ATA-1 was designed to support drives of up to 136.9GB in capacity, the PC BIOS could originally only handle drives of up to 528MB. Adding parameter-translation capability now allowed the BIOS to handle drives up to 8.4GB. This is discussed in more detail later in this chapter.

ATA-2 also featured improvements in the Identify Drive command, which enabled a drive to tell the software exactly what its characteristics are. This is essential for both Plug and Play (PnP) and compatibility with future revisions of the standard.

ATA-2 was also known by unofficial marketing terms, such as fast-ATA or fast-ATA-2 (Seagate/Quantum) and EIDE (Enhanced IDE, Western Digital). ATA-2 was officially published as "ANSI X3.279-1996 AT Attachment Interface with Extensions."

ATA-3

First published in 1997, ATA-3 was a comparatively minor revision to the ATA-2 standard that preceded it. It consisted of a general cleanup of the specification and had mostly minor clarifications and revisions. The most major changes included the following:

■ Eliminated single-word (8-bit) DMA transfer protocols.

■ Added SMART (Self-Monitoring Analysis and Reporting Technology) support for the prediction of device performance degradation.

■ LBA mode support was made mandatory (previously it had been optional).

■ Added security mode, allowing password protection for device access.

■ Made recommendations for source and receiver bus termination to solve noise issues at higher transfer speeds.

ATA-3 has been officially published as "ANSI X3.298-1997, AT Attachment 3 Interface."

ATA-3, which builds on ATA-2, adds improved reliability, especially of the faster PIO Mode 4 transfers; however, ATA-3 does not define any faster modes. ATA-3 also adds a simple password-based security scheme, more sophisticated power management, and SMART. This enables a drive to keep track of problems that might result in a failure and thus avoid data loss. SMART is a reliability prediction technology that was initially developed by IBM.

ATA/ATAPI-4

First published in 1998, ATA-4 included several important additions to the standard. It included the Packet Command feature, known as the *AT Attachment Packet Interface (ATAPI)*, which allowed devices such as CD-ROM and CD-RW drives, LS-120 SuperDisk floppy drives, tape drives, and other types of storage devices to be attached through a common interface. Until ATA-4 came out, ATAPI was a separately published standard. ATA-4 also added the 33MBps transfer mode known as *Ultra-DMA* or *Ultra-ATA*. ATA-4 is backward compatible with ATA-3 and earlier definitions of the ATAPI. The major revisions added in ATA-4 were as follows:

■ Ultra-DMA (UDMA) transfer modes up to Mode 2, which is 33MBps (called UDMA/33 or Ultra-ATA/33).

■ Integral ATAPI support.

■ Advanced power-management support.

■ Defined an optional 80-conductor, 40-pin cable for improved noise resistance.

■ Compact Flash Adapter (CFA) support.

■ Introduced enhanced BIOS support for drives over 9.4ZB (zettabytes, or trillion gigabytes) in size (even though ATA was still limited to 136.9GB).

ATA-4 was published as "ANSI NCITS 317-1998, ATA-4 with Packet Interface Extension."

The speed and level of ATA support in your system is mainly dictated by your motherboard chipset. Most motherboard chipsets come with a component called either a *South Bridge* or an *I/O controller hub* that provides the ATA interface (as well as other functions) in the system. Check the specifications for your motherboard or chipset to see whether yours supports the faster ATA/33, ATA/66, ATA/100, or ATA/133 mode.

ATA-4 made ATAPI support a full part of the ATA standard; therefore, ATAPI was no longer an auxiliary interface to ATA but rather was merged completely within. This promoted ATA for use as an interface for many other types of devices. ATA-4 also added support for new Ultra-DMA modes (also called *Ultra-ATA*) for even faster data transfer. The highest-performance mode, called *UDMA/33*, had 33MBps bandwidth—twice that of the fastest programmed I/O mode or DMA mode previously supported. In addition to the higher transfer rate, because UDMA modes relieve the load on the processor, further performance gains were realized.

An optional 80-conductor cable (with cable select) is defined for UDMA/33 transfers. Although this cable was originally defined as optional, it would later be required for the faster ATA/66, ATA/100, and ATA/133 modes in ATA-5 and later.

Also included was support for queuing commands, similar to that provided in SCSI-2. This enabled better multitasking as multiple programs make requests for ATA transfers.

ATA/ATAPI-5

The ATA-5 version of the ATA standard was approved in early 2000 and builds on ATA-4. The major additions in the standard include the following:

- Ultra-DMA (UDMA) transfer modes up to Mode 4, which is 66MBps (called UDMA/66 or Ultra-ATA/66).
- 80-conductor cable now mandatory for UDMA/66 operation.
- Added automatic detection of 40- or 80-conductor cables.
- UDMA modes faster than UDMA/33 are enabled only if an 80-conductor cable is detected.

ATA-5 includes Ultra-ATA/66 (also called *Ultra-DMA* or *UDMA/66*), which doubles the Ultra-ATA burst transfer rate by reducing setup times and increasing the clock rate. The faster clock rate increases interference, which causes problems with the standard 40-pin cable used by ATA and Ultra-ATA. To eliminate noise and interference, the new 40-pin, 80-conductor cable has now been made mandatory for drives running in UDMA/66 or faster modes. This cable was first announced in ATA-4 but is now mandatory in ATA-5 to support the Ultra-ATA/66 mode. This cable adds 40 additional ground lines between each of the original 40 ground and signal lines, which help shield the signals from interference. Note that this cable works with older non-Ultra-ATA devices as well because it still has the same 40-pin connectors.

For reliability, Ultra-DMA modes incorporate an error-detection mechanism known as *cyclic redundancy checking (CRC)*. CRC is an algorithm that calculates a checksum used to detect errors in a stream of data. Both the host (controller) and the drive calculate a CRC value for each Ultra-DMA transfer. After the data is sent, the drive calculates a CRC value, and this is compared to the original host CRC value. If a difference is reported, the host might be required to select a slower transfer mode and retry the original request for data.

ATA/ATAPI-6

ATA-6 began development during 2000 and was officially published as a standard early in 2002. The major changes or additions in the standard include the following:

- Ultra-DMA (UDMA) Mode 5 added, which allows 100MBps transfers (called UDMA/100, Ultra-ATA/100, or just ATA/100).
- Sector count per command increased from 8 bits (256 sectors or 131KB) to 16 bits (65,536 sectors or 33.5MB), allowing larger files to be transferred more efficiently.
- LBA addressing extended from 2^{28} to 2^{48} (281,474,976,710,656) sectors, supporting drives up to 144.12PB (petabyte = quadrillion bytes).
- CHS addressing made obsolete. Drives must use 28-bit or 48-bit LBA addressing only.

ATA-6 includes Ultra-ATA/100 (also called *Ultra-DMA* or *UDMA/100*), which increases the Ultra-ATA burst transfer rate by reducing setup times and increasing the clock rate. As with ATA-5, the faster modes require the improved 80-conductor cable. Using the ATA/100 mode requires both a drive and motherboard interface that supports that mode.

Besides adding the 100MBps UDMA Mode 5 transfer rate, ATA-6 also extended drive capacity greatly, and just in time. ATA-5 and earlier standards supported drives of up to only 137GB in capacity, which was becoming a limitation as larger drives became available. Commercially available 3.5-inch drives exceeding 137GB were introduced during 2001 but originally were available only in SCSI versions because SCSI doesn't share the same limitations as ATA. With ATA-6, the sector addressing limit has been extended from (2^{28}) sectors to (2^{48}) sectors. What this means is that LBA addressing previously could use only 28-bit numbers, but with ATA-6 LBA addressing can use larger, 48-bit numbers if necessary. With 512 bytes per sector, this raises the maximum supported drive capacity to 144.12PB. That is equal to more than 144.12 quadrillion bytes! Note that the 48-bit addressing is optional and necessary only for drives larger than 137GB. Drives 137GB or less can use either 28-bit or 48-bit addressing.

ATA/ATAPI-7

Work on ATA-7, which began late in 2001, was completed in 2003. As with the previous ATA standards, ATA-7 is built on the previous standard (ATA-6), with some additions.

The primary additions to ATA-7 include the following:

- Ultra-DMA (UDMA) Mode 6 added, which allows for 133MBps transfers (called UDMA/133, Ultra-ATA/133, or just ATA/133). As with UDMA Mode 5 (100MBps) and UDMA Mode 4 (66MBps), the use of an 80-conductor cable is required.

- Added support for long physical sectors, which allows a device to be formatted so that there are multiple logical sectors per physical sector. Each physical sector stores an ECC field, so long physical sectors allow increased format efficiency with fewer ECC bytes used overall.

- Added support for long logical sectors, which allows additional data bytes to be used per sector (520 or 528 bytes instead of 512 bytes) for server applications. Devices using long logical sectors are not backward compatible with devices or applications that use 512-byte sectors, meaning standard desktop and laptop systems.

- Incorporated Serial ATA as part of the ATA-7 standard.

- Split the ATA-7 document into three volumes: Volume 1 covers the command set and logical registers, Volume 2 covers the parallel transport protocols and interconnects, and Volume 3 covers the serial transport protocols and interconnects.

The ATA/133 transfer mode was actually proposed by Maxtor, and so far it is the only drive manufacturer to adopt this mode. Other drive manufacturers have not adopted the 133MBps interface transfer rate because most drives have actual media transfer rates that are significantly slower than that. VIA, ALi, and SiS have added ATA/133 support to their latest chipsets, but Intel has decided to skip ATA/133 in lieu of adding Serial ATA (150MBps) instead. This means that even if a drive can transfer at 133MBps from the circuit board on the drive to the motherboard, data from the drive media (platters) through the heads to the circuit board on the drive moves at less than half that rate. For that reason, running a drive capable of UDMA Mode 6 (133MBps) on a motherboard capable of only UDMA Mode 5 (100MBps) really won't slow things down much, if at all. Likewise, upgrading your ATA host adapter from one that does 100MBps to one that can do 133MBps won't help much if your drive can only read data off the disk platters at half that speed. Always remember that the media transfer rate is far more important than the interface transfer rate when selecting a drive, because the media transfer rate is the limiting factor.

ATA Features

The ATA standards have gone a long way toward eliminating incompatibilities and problems with drive interfacing. The ATA specifications define the signals on the 40- or 44-pin connector, the functions and timings of these signals, cable specifications, and so on. This section lists some of the elements and functions defined by the ATA specification.

ATA I/O Connector

The ATA interface connector is normally a 40-pin (for 3.5-inch drives) or 44-pin (for 2.5-inch or smaller drives) header-type connector with pins spaced 0.1 inches (2.54mm) apart and generally is keyed to prevent installing it upside down (see Figures 9.12 and 9.13). To create a keyed connector, the manufacturer generally removes pin 20 from the male connector and blocks pin 20 on the female cable connector, which prevents the user from installing the cable backward. Some cables also incorporate a protrusion on the top of the female cable connector that fits into a notch in the shroud surrounding the mating male connector on the device. The use of keyed connectors and cables is highly recommended; plugging in an ATA cable backward normally won't cause any permanent damage. However, it can lock up the system and prevent it from running at all.

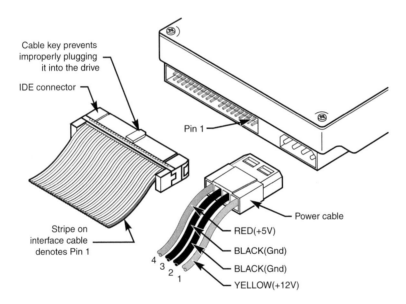

Figure 9.12   Typical ATA hard drive connectors.

Table 9.8 shows the standard 40-pin ATA interface connector pinout.

Table 9.8   40-Pin ATA Connector

Signal Name	Pin	Pin	Signal Name
-RESET	1	2	GROUND
Data Bit 7	3	4	Data Bit 8
Data Bit 6	5	6	Data Bit 9
Data Bit 5	7	8	Data Bit 10

Table 9.8   Continued

Signal Name	Pin	Pin	Signal Name
Data Bit 4	9	10	Data Bit 11
Data Bit 3	11	12	Data Bit 12
Data Bit 2	13	14	Data Bit 13
Data Bit 1	15	16	Data Bit 14
Data Bit 0	17	18	Data Bit 15
GROUND	19	20	KEY (pin missing)
DRQ 3	21	22	GROUND
-IOW	23	24	GROUND
-IOR	25	26	GROUND
I/O CH RDY	27	28	CSEL:SPSYNC[1]
-DACK 3	29	30	GROUND
IRQ 14	31	32	Reserved[2]
Address Bit 1	33	34	-PDIAG
Address Bit 0	35	36	Address Bit 2
-CS1FX	37	38	-CS3FX
-DA/SP	39	40	GROUND
+5V (Logic)	41	42	+5V (Motor)
GROUND	43	44	Reserved

1. *Pin 28 is normally cable select, but some older drives could use it for spindle synchronization between multiple drives.*

2. *Pin 32 was defined as -IOCS16 in ATA-2 but is no longer used.*

Note that "-" preceding a signal name (such as with -RESET) indicates the signal is "active low."

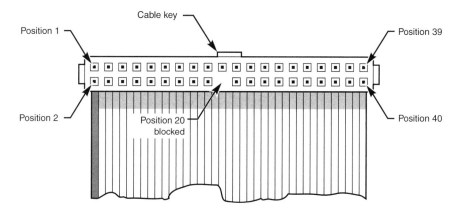

Figure 9.13   ATA 40-pin interface connector detail.

The 2.5-inch drives found in notebook/laptop-size computers normally use a smaller unitized 50-pin header connector with pins spaced only 2.0mm (0.079 inches) apart.

The main 40-pin part of the connector is the same as the standard ATA connector (except for the physical pin spacing), but there are added pins for power and jumpers. Normally, the cable that plugs into this connector has 44 pins, carrying power as well as the standard ATA signals. The jumper pins normally have a jumper on them (the jumper position controls cable select, master, or slave settings). Figure 9.14 shows the unitized 50-pin connector used on 2.5-inch ATA drives normally found in laptop or notebook computers.

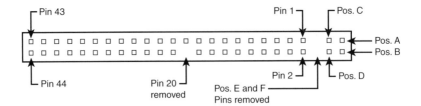

Figure 9.14   50-pin unitized ATA connector detail (used on 2.5-inch notebook/laptop ATA drives with a 44-pin cable).

Note the jumper pins at positions A–D and that the pins at positions E and F are removed. A jumper usually is placed between positions B and D to set the drive for cable select operation. On this connector, pin 41 provides +5V power to the drive logic (circuit board), pin 42 provides +5V power to the motor (2.5-inch drives use 5V motors, unlike larger drives, which normally use 12V motors), and pin 43 provides a power ground. The last pin (44) is reserved and not used.

Table 9.9 shows the 50-pin unitized ATA interface connector pinout as used on most 2.5-inch (laptop or notebook computer) drives.

Table 9.9   50-Pin Unitized ATA 2.5-Inch (Notebook/Laptop Drive) Connector Pinout

Signal Name	Pin	Pin	Signal Name
Jumper pin	A	B	Jumper pin
Jumper pin	C	D	Jumper pin
KEY (pin missing)	E	F	KEY (pin missing)
-RESET	1	2	GROUND
Data Bit 7	3	4	Data Bit 8
Data Bit 6	5	6	Data Bit 9
Data Bit 5	7	8	Data Bit 10
Data Bit 4	9	10	Data Bit 11
Data Bit 3	11	12	Data Bit 12
Data Bit 2	13	14	Data Bit 13
Data Bit 1	15	16	Data Bit 14
Data Bit 0	17	18	Data Bit 15
GROUND	19	20	KEY (pin missing)
DRQ 3	21	22	GROUND
-IOW	23	24	GROUND
-IOR	25	26	GROUND
I/O CH RDY	27	28	CSEL

Table 9.9   Continued

Signal Name	Pin	Pin	Signal Name
-DACK 3	29	30	GROUND
IRQ 14	31	32	Reserved
Address Bit 1	33	34	-PDIAG
Address Bit 0	35	36	Address Bit 2
-CS1FX	37	38	-CS3FX
-DA/SP	39	40	GROUND
+5V (Logic)	41	42	+5V (Motor)
GROUND	43	44	Reserved

Not All Cables and Connectors Are Keyed

Note that many lower-cost board and cable manufacturers leave out the keying. Cheaper motherboards often won't have pin 20 removed on their ATA connectors, and consequently they won't supply a cable with pin 20 blocked. If they don't use a shrouded connector with a notch and a corresponding protrusion on the cable connector, no keying exists and the cables can be inserted backward. Fortunately, the only consequence of this in most cases is that the device won't work until the cable is attached with the correct orientation.

In rare situations in which you are mixing and matching items, you might encounter a cable with pin 20 blocked (as it should be) and a board with pin 20 still present. In that case, you can break off pin 20 from the board, or for the more squeamish, remove the block from the cable. Some cables have the block permanently installed as a part of the connector housing, in which case you must break off pin 20 on the board or device end or use a different cable.

The simple rule of thumb is that pin 1 should be oriented toward the power connector on the device, which normally corresponds to the stripe on the cable.

ATA I/O Cable

A 40-conductor ribbon cable is specified to carry signals between the bus adapter circuits and the drive (controller). To maximize signal integrity and eliminate potential timing and noise problems, the cable should not be longer than 18 inches (0.46 meters).

Note that ATA drives supporting the higher-speed transfer modes, such as PIO Mode 4 or any of the Ultra-DMA (UDMA) modes, are especially susceptible to cable integrity problems and cables that are too long. If the cable is too long, you can experience data corruption and other errors that can be maddening. This will be manifested in any type of problem reading from or writing to the drive. In addition, any drive using UDMA Mode 4 (66MBps transfer rate), Mode 5 (100MBps transfer rate), or Mode 6 (133MBps transfer rate) must use a special higher-quality 80-conductor cable (the extra conductors are grounds to reduce noise). I also recommend this type of cable if your drive is running at UDMA Mode 2 (33MBps) or slower because it can't hurt and can only help. Although cable length is not a problem inside portable systems, finding replacement cables that fit can be difficult. Many portables use special cables, called *flex-cables*, that are constructed like a filmstrip with the "wires" printed on much like on a circuit board. Because of their custom construction, you normally can't replace the cables inside a laptop with different ones than supplied by the manufacturer. Figure 9.15 shows the typical desktop ATA cable layout and dimensions. Unlike standard ATA ribbon cables, which allow for two drives to be connected, the flex-cables in a laptop will normally support only a single drive at a time.

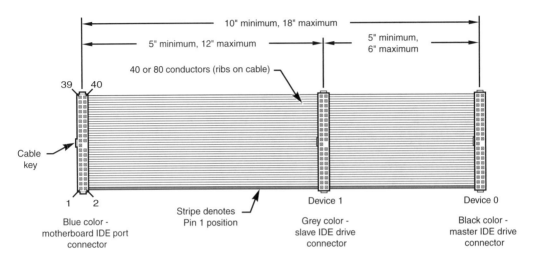

Figure 9.15 An ATA cable with 40-pin connectors and either 40- or 80-conductor cables (additional wires are grounded in 80-conductor versions).

Note

Most 40-conductor cables do not color-code the connectors, whereas all 80-conductor cables do color-code the connectors.

Two primary variations of ATA cables are used today: one with 40 conductors and the other with 80 conductors. Both use 40-pin connectors, and the additional wires in the 80-conductor version are simply wired to ground. The additional conductors are designed to reduce noise and interference and are required when setting the interface to run at 66MBps (ATA/66) or faster. The drive and host adapter are designed to disable the higher-speed ATA/66, ATA/100, and ATA/133 modes if an 80-conductor cable is not detected. The 80-conductor cable can also be used at lower speeds; although this is unnecessary, it improves the signal integrity. Therefore, it is the recommended version no matter which drive you use. Note the keying on the cable, which is designed to prevent backward installation.

Dual-Drive Configurations

Dual-drive ATA installations can be problematic because each drive has its own controller, and both controllers must function while being connected to the same bus. There has to be a way to ensure that only one of the two controllers will respond to a command at a time.

The ATA standard provides the option of operating on the AT bus with two drives in a daisy-chained configuration. The primary drive (drive 0) is called the *master*, and the secondary drive (drive 1) is called the *slave*. You designate a drive as being master or slave by setting a jumper or switch on the drive or by using a special line in the interface called the *cable select pin* and setting the CS jumper on the drive.

When only one drive is installed, the controller responds to all commands from the system. When two drives (and, therefore, two controllers) are installed, both controllers receive all commands from the system. Each controller then must be set up to respond only to commands for itself. In this situation, one controller must be designated as the master and the other as the slave. When the system sends a command for a specific drive, the controller on the other drive must remain silent while the selected controller and drive are functioning. Setting the jumper to master or slave enables discrimination between the two controllers by setting a special bit (the DRV bit) in the Drive/Head Register of a command block.

Configuring ATA drives can be simple, as is the case with most single-drive installations, or troublesome, especially when it comes to mixing two older drives from different manufacturers on a single cable.

Most ATA drives can be configured with four possible settings:

- Master (single drive)
- Master (dual drive)
- Slave (dual drive)
- Cable select

Many drives simplify this to three settings: master, slave, and cable select. Because each ATA drive has its own controller, you must specifically tell one drive to be the master and the other to be the slave. No functional difference exists between the two, except that the drive that's specified as the slave will assert a signal called DASP (drive active/slave present) after a system reset informs the master that a slave drive is present in the system. The master drive then pays attention to the drive select line, which it otherwise ignores. Telling a drive that it's the slave also causes it to delay its spin-up for several seconds to allow the master to get going and thus lessens the load on the system's power supply.

Until the official ATA specifications were developed, no common implementation for IDE drive configuration was in use. Some drive companies even used different master/slave methods for different models of drives. Because of these incompatibilities, some drives work together only in a specific master/slave or slave/master order. This situation mostly affects older drives introduced before the ATA specification was officially adopted.

Most drives that fully follow the ATA specification now need only one jumper (master/slave) for configuration. A few also need a slave present jumper. Table 9.10 shows the jumper settings required by most 3.5-inch ATA drives.

Table 9.10   Jumper Settings for Most 3.5-inch ATA Drives on Standard (Non–Cable Select) Cables

Jumper Name	Single-Drive	Dual-Drive Master	Dual-Drive Slave
Master (M/S)	On	On	Off
Slave present (SP)	Off	On	Off
Cable select (CS)	Off	Off	Off

Note

If a cable select cable is used, the CS jumper should be set to On and all others should be Off. The cable connector then determines which drive will be master or slave.

Figure 9.16 shows the jumpers on a typical 3.5-inch ATA drive.

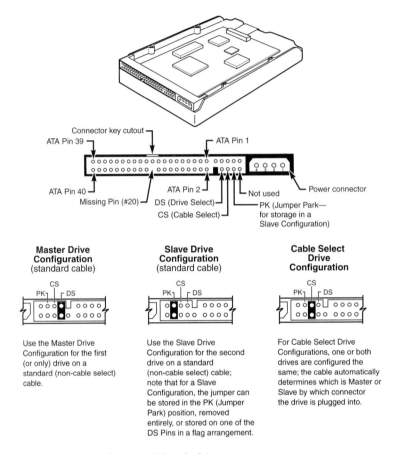

Figure 9.16 ATA drive jumpers for most 3.5-inch drives.

The master jumper indicates that the drive is a master or a slave. Some drives also require a slave present jumper, which is used only in a dual-drive setup and then installed only on the master drive—which is somewhat confusing. This jumper tells the master that a slave drive is attached. With many ATA drives, the master jumper is optional and can be left off. Installing this jumper doesn't hurt in these cases and can eliminate confusion; I recommend that you install the jumpers listed here.

Note

Some drives have these jumpers on the drive circuit board, and as such they might not be visible on the rear.

The 2.5-inch drives used internally in most portables have a different jumper arrangement. The four jumper pins, labeled A, B, C, and D, are shown in Figure 9.17.

Because most 2.5-inch drives are installed as the only drive on the cable, you normally don't install any jumper, which results in a default master setting. Installing a jumper connecting the A-B pins results in a slave setting, and jumpering B-D is for cable select. Other jumper settings are not used.

To eliminate confusion over master/slave settings, most newer systems with cables supporting dual drives now use the cable select option. This involves two things. The first is having a special ATA cable that has all the wires except pin 28 running from the motherboard connector to both drive connectors. Pin 28 is used for cable select and is connected to one of the drive connectors (labeled master) and not to the other (labeled slave). Both drives are then configured in cable select mode via the CS jumper on each drive.

With cable select, the drive that receives signals on pin 28 automatically becomes the master, and the other becomes the slave. Most cables implement this by removing the metal insulation displacement bit from the pin-28 hole, which can be difficult to see at a glance. Other cables have a section of pin 28 visibly cut from the cable somewhere along the ribbon. Because this is such a minor modification to the cable and can be difficult to see, cable select cables normally have the connectors labeled master, slave, and system, indicating that the cable controls these options rather than the drive. All 80-conductor Ultra-ATA cables are designed to use cable select.

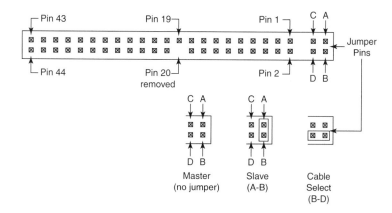

Figure 9.17 ATA drive jumpers for most 2.5-inch drives.

With cable select, you simply set the CS jumper on all drives and then plug the drive you want to be the master into the connector labeled master on the cable and the drive you want to be the slave into the connector labeled slave.

The only downside I see to using cable select is that it may restrict how the cable is routed or where you mount the drive that is to be the master versus the slave, because they must be plugged into specific cable connector positions.

ATA Commands

One of the best features of the ATA interface is the enhanced command set. The ATA interface was modeled after the WD1003 controller IBM used in the original AT system. All ATA drives must support the original WD command set (eight commands) with no exceptions, which is why ATA drives are so easy to install in systems today. All IBM-compatible systems have built-in ROM BIOS support for the WD1003, so they essentially support ATA as well.

In addition to supporting all the WD1003 commands, the ATA specification added numerous other commands to enhance performance and capabilities. These commands are an optional part of the ATA interface, but several of them are used in most drives available today and are very important to the performance and use of ATA drives in general.

Perhaps the most important is the Identify Drive command. This command causes the drive to transmit a 512-byte block of data that provides all details about the drive. Through this command, any program (including the system BIOS) can find out exactly which type of drive is connected, including the drive manufacturer, model number, operating parameters, and even the serial number of the drive. Many modern BIOSes use this information to automatically receive and enter the drive's parameters into CMOS memory, eliminating the need for the user to enter these parameters manually during system configuration. This arrangement helps prevent mistakes that can later lead to data loss when the user no longer remembers what parameters he used during setup.

The Identify Drive data can tell you many things about your drive, including the following:

- Number of logical block addresses available using LBA mode
- Number of physical cylinders, heads, and sectors available in P-CHS mode
- Number of logical cylinders, heads, and sectors in the current translation L-CHS mode
- Transfer modes (and speeds) supported
- Manufacturer and model number
- Internal firmware revision
- Serial number
- Buffer type/size, indicating sector buffering or caching capabilities

Several public-domain programs can execute this command to the drive and report the information onscreen. For more up-to-date information, use IDEDIAG, which is available from www.penguin.cz/~mhi/idediag, or HWINFO, which is available from www.hwinfo.com. I find these programs especially useful when I am trying to install ATA drives on a system that has a user-defined drive type but doesn't support auto-detection, and I need to know the correct parameters for a user-definable BIOS type. These programs get the information directly from the drive.

Two other important commands are the Read Multiple and Write Multiple commands. These commands permit multiple-sector data transfers and, when combined with block-mode PIO capabilities in the system, can result in incredible data transfer rates, many times faster than single-sector PIO transfers.

Many other enhanced commands are available, including room for a given drive manufacturer to implement what are called vendor-unique commands. Certain vendors often use these commands for features unique to each vendor. Often, vendor-unique commands control features such as low-level formatting and defect management. This is why low-level format (LLF) programs can be so specific to a particular manufacturer's ATA drives and why many manufacturers make their own LLF programs available.

Drive Capacity Limitations

ATA interface versions up through ATA-5 suffered from a drive capacity limitation of about 137GB (billion bytes). Depending on the BIOS used, this limitation can be further reduced to 8.4GB, or even as low as 528MB (million bytes). This is due to limitations in both the BIOS and the ATA interface, which when combined create even further limitations. To understand these limits, you have to look at the BIOS (software) and ATA (hardware) interfaces together.

The limitations when dealing with ATA drives are those of the ATA interface itself as well as the BIOS interface used to talk to the drive. A summary of the limitations is provided in Table 9.11.

Prefixes for Decimal and Binary Multiples

Many readers will be unfamiliar with the MiB (mebibyte), GiB (gibibyte), PiB (pebibyte), and ZiB (zebibyte) designations I am using in this section and throughout the book. These are part of a standard designed to eliminate confusion between decimal- and binary-based multiples, especially in computer systems. Standard SI (system international or metric system) units are based on multiples of 10. This works well for most things, but not for computers, which operate in a binary world where most numbers are based on powers of 2. This resulted in different meanings being assigned to the same prefix—for example, 1MB (megabyte) could mean either 1 million bytes (106) or 1,048,576 bytes (220).

To eliminate confusion, in December 1998 the International Electrotechnical Commission (IEC) approved as an international standard the prefix names and symbols for binary multiples used in data processing and transmission. Some of these prefixes are shown in Table 9.12.

Under this standard terminology, an MB (megabyte) would be 1,000,000 bytes, whereas an MiB (mebibyte) would be 1,048,576 bytes.

Note

For more information on these industry-standard decimal and binary prefixes, check out the National Institute for Standards and Technology (NIST) website at `physics.nist.gov/cuu/Units/prefixes.html`.

Note that even though these designations are official, they have yet to be widely adopted and in many cases confusion still reigns. *MB* is still often used to indicate both decimal *millions of bytes* and binary *megabytes*. Similarly, *GB* is often used to refer to decimal *billions of bytes* and binary *gigabytes*. In general, memory values are expressed by using the binary values, although disk capacities can go either way. This often leads to confusion in reporting disk capacities because many manufacturers tend to use whichever value makes their products look better. For example, drive capacities are often rated in decimal billions (G or giga), whereas most BIOS chips and operating system utilities, such as Windows FDISK, rate the same drive in binary gigabytes (Gi or gibi). Note also that when bits and bytes are used as part of some other measurement, the difference between bits and bytes is often distinguished by the use of a lower- or uppercase B. For example, the "bits" part of megabits is typically abbreviated with a lowercase *b*, resulting in the abbreviation *Mbps* for *megabits per second*, whereas *MBps* indicates *megabytes per second*.

CHS Versus LBA

There are two primary methods to address (or number) sectors on an ATA drive. The first method is called *CHS (cylinder, head, sector)* after the three respective coordinate numbers used to address each sector of the drive. The second method is called *LBA (logical block address)*, which uses a single number to address each sector on a drive. CHS was derived from the physical way drives were constructed (and is how they work internally), whereas LBA evolved as a simpler and more logical way to number the sectors regardless of the internal physical construction.

When reading a drive sequentially in CHS mode, we start with cylinder 0, head 0, and sector 1, which is the first sector on the disk. Then all the remaining sectors on that first track are read, then the next head is selected, and all the sectors on that track are read, and so on until all the heads on the first cylinder are read. Then the next cylinder is selected, and the sequence starts over. Think of CHS as an odometer of sorts: The sector numbers must roll over before the head number can change, and the head numbers must roll over before the cylinder number can change.

When reading a drive sequentially in LBA mode, we start with sector 0, then read 1, then 2, and so on. The first sector on the drive in CHS mode would be 0,0,1; the same sector in LBA mode would be 0.

As an example, imagine a drive with one platter, two heads (both sides of the platter are used), two tracks on each platter (cylinders), and two sectors on each track. We would say the drive has two cylinders (tracks per side), two heads (sides), and two sectors per track. This would result in a total

Table 9.11 ATA Capacity Limitations for Various Sector-Addressing Methods

Sector- Addressing Method	Total Sectors Calculation	Max. Total Sectors
CHS: BIOS w/o TL	1024×16×63	1,032,192
CHS: BIOS w/ bit-shift TL	1024×240×63	15,482,880
CHS: BIOS w/ LBA-assist TL	1024×255×63	16,450,560
CHS: BIOS INT13h	1024×256×63	16,515,072
CHS: ATA-1/ATA-5	65536×16×255	267,386,880
LBA: ATA-1/ATA-5	2^{28}	268,435,456
LBA: ATA-6+	2^{48}	281,474,976,710,655
LBA: EDD BIOS	2^{64}	18,446,744,073,709,551,600

BIOS = Basic Input Output System
ATA = AT Attachment (IDE)
CHS = cylinder, head, sector
LBA = logical block (sector) address
w/ = with

w/o = without
TL = translation
INT13h = interrupt 13 hex
EDD = Enhanced Disk Drive specification (Phoenix/ATA)

Table 9.12 Standard Prefix Names and Symbols for Binary Multiples

Decimal Prefixes:			
Factor	Symbol	Name	Value
10^3	k	Kilo	1,000
10^6	M	Mega	1,000,000
10^9	G	Giga	1,000,000,000
10^{12}	T	Tera	1,000,000,000,000
10^{15}	P	Peta	1,000,000,000,000,000
10^{18}	E	Exa	1,000,000,000,000,000,000
10^{21}	Z	Zetta	1,000,000,000,000,000,000,000

Note that the symbol for kilo (k) is in lowercase (which is technically correct according to the SI standard), whereas all other decimal prefixes are uppercase.

capacity of eight (2×2×2) sectors. Noting that cylinders and heads begin numbering from 0, while physical sectors on a track number from 1, using CHS addressing we would say the first sector on the drive is cylinder 0, head 0, sector 1 (0,0,1), the second sector is 0,0,2, the third sector is 0,1,1, the fourth sector is 0,1,2, and so on until we get to the last sector, which would be 1,1,2.

Now imagine that we could take the eight sectors and rather than refer directly to the physical cylinder, head, and sector, we number the sectors in order from 0 through 7. Therefore, if we wanted to address the fourth sector on the drive, we could reference it as sector 0,1,2 in CHS mode, or as sector 3 in LBA mode. Table 9.13 shows the correspondence between CHS and LBA sector numbers for this eight-sector imaginary drive.

Max. Capacity (Bytes)	Capacity (Decimal)	Capacity (Binary)
528,482,304	528.48MB	504.00MiB
7,927,234,560	7.93GB	7.38GiB
8,422,686,720	8.42GB	7.84GiB
8,455,716,864	8.46GB	7.88GiB
136,902,082,560	136.90GB	127.50GiB
137,438,953,472	137.44GB	128.00GiB
144,115,188,075,855,360	144.12PB	128.00PiB
9,444,732,965,739,290,430,000	9.44ZB	8.00ZiB

MB = megabyte (million bytes)
MiB = mebibyte
GB = gigabyte (billion bytes)
GiB = gibibyte

PB = petabyte (quadrillion bytes)
PiB = pebibyte
ZB = zettabyte (sextillion bytes)
ZiB = zebibyte

Binary Prefixes:

Factor	Symbol	Name	Derivation	Value
2^{10}	Ki	Kibi	Kilobinary	1,024
2^{20}	Mi	Mebi	Megabinary	1,048,576
2^{30}	Gi	Gibi	Gigabinary	1,073,741,824
2^{40}	Ti	Tebi	Terabinary	1,099,511,627,776
2^{50}	Pi	Pebi	Petabinary	1,125,899,906,842,624
2^{60}	Ei	Exbi	Exabinary	1,152,921,504,606,846,980
2^{70}	Zi	Zebi	Zettabinary	1,180,591,620,717,411,300,000

Table 9.13   CHS and LBA Sector Numbers for an Imaginary Drive with Two Cylinders, Two Heads, and Two Sectors per Track (Eight Sectors Total)

Mode	Equivalent Sector Numbers							
CHS:	0,0,1	0,0,2	0,1,1	0,1,2	1,0,1	1,0,2	1,1,1	1,1,2
LBA:	0	1	2	3	4	5	6	7

As you can see from the example, using LBA numbers is simpler and generally easier to handle. However, when the PC was first developed, all BIOS and ATA drive-level addressing was done using CHS addressing.

CHS/LBA and LBA/CHS conversions

It is possible to address the same sectors in either CHS or LBA mode. The conversion from CHS to LBA is always consistent in that for a given drive, a particular CHS address will always convert to a given LBA address, and vice versa. The ATA-1 document specifies a simple formula that can be used to convert CHS parameters to LBA:

$$LBA = (((C * HPC) + H) * SPT) + S - 1$$

By reversing this formula, you can convert the other way (that is, from LBA back to CHS):

$$C = int (LBA / SPT / HPC)$$

$$H = int ((LBA / SPT) \bmod HPC)$$

$$S = (LBA \bmod SPT) + 1$$

For these formulae

- LBA = logical block address
- C = cylinder
- H = head
- S = sector
- HPC = heads per cylinder (total number of heads)
- SPT = sectors per track
- int X = integer portion of X
- X mod Y = modulus (remainder) of X/Y

Using these formulae, you can calculate the LBA for any given CHS address, and vice versa. Given a drive of 16,383 cylinders, 16 heads, and 63 sectors per track, Table 9.14 shows the equivalent CHS and LBA addresses.

Table 9.14   Equivalent CHS and LBA Sector Numbers for a Drive with 16,383 Cylinders, 16 Heads, and 63 Sectors per Track (16,514,064 Sectors Total)

Cylinders	Heads	Sectors	LBA
0	0	1	0
0	0	63	62
1	1	1	63
999	15	63	1,007,999
1,000	0	1	1,008,000
9,999	15	63	10,079,999
10,000	0	1	10,080,000
16,382	15	63	16,514,063

BIOS Commands Versus ATA Commands

In addition to the two methods of sector addressing (CHS and LBA), there are two levels of interfaces where sector addressing occurs. One interface is where the operating system talks to the BIOS (using BIOS commands); the other is where the BIOS talks to the drive (using ATA commands). The specific commands at these levels are different, but both support CHS and LBA modes. Figure 9.18 illustrates the two interface levels.

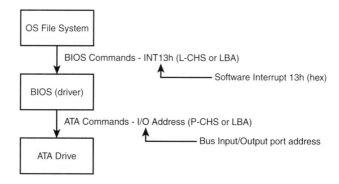

Figure 9.18 Typical ATA hard drive connectors. (In this figure, L-CHS stands for Logical CHS, and P-CHS stands for Physical CHS.)

When the operating system talks to the BIOS to read or write sectors, it issues commands via software INT13h, which is how the BIOS subroutines for disk access are called. Various INT13h subfunctions allow sectors to be read or written using either CHS or LBA addressing. The BIOS routines then convert the BIOS commands into ATA hardware-level commands, which are sent over the bus I/O ports to the drive controller. Commands at the ATA hardware level can also use either CHS or LBA addressing, although the limitations are different. Whether your BIOS and drive use CHS or LBA addressing depends on the drive capacity, the age of the BIOS and drive, as well as the BIOS Setup settings and operating system used.

CHS Limitations (The 528MB Barrier)

The original BIOS-based driver for hard disks is accessed via software interrupt 13h (13 hex) and offers functions for reading and writing drives at the sector level. Standard INT13h functions require that a particular sector be addressed by its cylinder, head, and sector location, otherwise known as *CHS addressing*. This interface is used by the operating system and low-level disk utilities to access the drive. IBM originally wrote the INT13h interface for the BIOS on the PC XT hard disk controller in 1983. In 1984, IBM incorporated it into the AT motherboard BIOS. This interface used numbers to define the particular cylinder, head, and sector being addressed. Table 9.15, which shows the standard INT13h BIOS CHS parameter limits, includes the maximum values for these numbers.

Table 9.15   INT13h BIOS CHS Parameter Limits

Field	Field Size	Maximum Value	Range	Total Usable
Cylinder	10 bits	1024	0–1023	1024
Head	8 bits	256	0–255	256
Sector	6 bits	64	1–63	63

The concept of a maximum value given a number of digits is simple: If you had, for example, a hotel with two-digit decimal room numbers, you could have only 100 (10^2) rooms, numbered 0–99. The CHS numbers used by the standard BIOS INT13h interface are binary, and with a 10-bit number being used to count cylinders, you can have only 1,024 (2^{10}) maximum, numbered 0–1,023. Because the head is identified by an 8-bit number, the maximum number of heads is 256 (2^8), numbered 0–255. Finally, with sectors per track, there is a minor difference. Sectors on a track are identified by a 6-bit number, which would normally allow a maximum of 64 (2^6) sectors; however, because sectors are numbered starting with 1 (instead of 0), the range is limited to 1–63, which means a total of 63 sectors per track is the maximum the BIOS can handle.

These BIOS limitations are true for all BIOS versions or programs that rely on CHS addressing. Using the maximum numbers possible for CHS at the BIOS level, addressing a drive with 1,024 cylinders, 256 heads, and 63 sectors per track is possible. Because each sector is 512 bytes, the math works out as follows:

```
                       Max. Values
       - - - - - - - - - - - - - - - - - - - - - - - - -
         Cylinders          1,024
            Heads             256
      Sectors/Track            63
      ===============================
      Total Sectors      16,515,072
      - - - - - - - - - - - - - - - - - - - - - - - - -
      Total Bytes    8,455,716,864
      Megabytes (MB)         8,456
      Mebibytes (MiB)        8,064
      Gigabytes (GB)           8.4
      Gibibytes (GiB)          7.8
```

From these calculations, you can see that the maximum capacity drive addressable via the standard BIOS INT13h interface is about 8.4GB (where GB equals roughly one billion bytes), or 7.8GiB (where GiB means *gigabinary bytes*).

Unfortunately, the BIOS INT13h limits are not the only limitations that apply. Limits also exist in the ATA interface itself. The ATA CHS limits are shown in Table 9.16.

Table 9.16   Standard ATA CHS Parameter Limitations

Field	Field Size	Maximum Value	Range	Total Usable
Cylinder	16 bits	65536	0–65535	65536
Head	4 bits	16	0–15	16
Sector	8 bits	256	1–255	255

As you can see, the ATA interface uses different sized fields to store CHS values. Note that the ATA limits are higher than the BIOS limits for cylinders and sectors but lower than the BIOS limit for heads. The CHS limits for capacity according to the ATA-1 through ATA-5 specifications are as follows:

```
                       Max. Values
       - - - - - - - - - - - - - - - - - - - - - - - - -
         Cylinders         65,536
            Heads             16
      Sectors/Track          255
      ===============================
      Total Sectors    267,386,880
      - - - - - - - - - - - - - - - - - - - - - - - - -
```

```
Total Bytes    136,902,082,560
Megabytes (MB)         136,902
Mebibytes (MiB)        130,560
Gigabytes (GB)           136.9
Gibibytes (GiB)          127.5
```

When you combine the limitations of the BIOS and ATA CHS parameters, you end up with the situation shown in Table 9.17.

Table 9.17   Combined BIOS and ATA CHS Parameter Limits

Field	BIOS CHS Parameter Limits	ATA CHS Parameter Limits	Combined CHS Parameter Limits
Cylinder	1,024	65,536	1,024
Head	256	16	16
Sector	63	255	63
Total sectors	16,515,072	267,386,880	1,032,192
Maximum capacity	8.4GB	136.9GB	528MB

As you can see, the lowest common denominator of the combined CHS limits results in maximum usable parameters of 1,024 cylinders, 16 heads, and 63 sectors, which results in a maximum drive capacity of 528MB. This became known as the *528MB barrier*, and it affects virtually all PCs built in 1993 or earlier.

CHS Translation: Breaking the 528MB Barrier

Having a barrier that limits drive capacity to 528MB wasn't a problem when the largest drives available were smaller than that. But by 1994, drive technology had developed such that it was possible to make drives larger than what the combined BIOS and ATA limitations could address. Clearly, a fix for the problem was needed.

Starting in 1993, the BIOS developer Phoenix Technologies had begun working on BIOS extensions to work around the combined CHS limits. In January of 1994 it released the "BIOS Enhanced Disk Drive (EDD) Specification," which was later republished by the T13 committee (also responsible for ATA) as "BIOS Enhanced Disk Drive Services." The EDD documents detail several methods for circumventing the limitations of previous BIOSes without causing compatibility problems with existing software. These include

- BIOS INT13h extensions supporting 64-bit LBA
- Bit-shift geometric CHS translation
- LBA-assist geometric CHS translation

The method for dealing with the CHS problem was called *translation*, because it allowed for additional subroutines in the BIOS to translate CHS parameters from ATA maximums to BIOS maximums (and vice versa). In an effort to make its methods standard among the entire PC industry, Phoenix released the EDD document publicly and allowed the technology to be used free of charge, even among its competitors, such as AMI and Award. The T13 committee in charge of ATA subsequently adopted the EDD standard and incorporated it into official ATA documents.

Starting in 1994, most BIOSes began implementing the Phoenix-designed CHS translation methods, which enabled drives up to the BIOS limit of 8.4GB to be supported. The fix involved what is termed *parameter translation* at the BIOS level, which adapted or translated the cylinder, head, and sector numbers to fit within the allowable BIOS parameters. There are two types of translation: One works via a technique called *CHS bit-shift* (usually called *Large* or *Extended CHS* in the BIOS Setup), whereas the other uses a technique called *LBA-assist* (usually called just *LBA* in the BIOS Setup). They refer to the different mathematical methods of doing essentially the same thing—that is, converting one set of CHS numbers to another.

Virtually all PC BIOSes since 1994 have translation capability in the BIOS Setup, and virtually all offer both translation modes as well as an option to disable translation entirely. If both CHS bit-shift ("Large" or "ECHS") and LBA-assist ("LBA") translation modes are offered, you should probably choose the LBA method of translation because it is the more efficient and flexible of the two. LBA-assist translation also gets around the 4.2GB operating system bug because it is designed to allow a maximum of 255 logical heads no matter what.

You usually can tell whether your BIOS supports translation by the capability to specify more than 1,024 cylinders in the BIOS Setup, although this can be misleading. The best clue is to look for the translation setting parameters in the drive setup page in the BIOS Setup. See Chapter 5, "Motherboards," for more information on how to enter the BIOS Setup on your system. If you see drive-related settings, such as LBA or ECHS (sometimes called Large or Extended), these are telltale signs of a BIOS with translation support. Most BIOSes with a date of 1994 or later include this capability. If your system currently does not support parameter translation, you might be able to get an upgrade from your motherboard manufacturer.

Table 9.18 summarizes the four ways today's BIOSes can handle addressing sectors on the drive: Standard CHS (no translation), Extended CHS translation, LBA translation, and pure LBA addressing.

Table 9.18   Drive Sector Addressing Methods

BIOS Mode	OS to BIOS	BIOS to Drive
Standard (Normal; no translation)	P-CHS	P-CHS
CHS bit-shift (ECHS) translation	L-CHS	P-CHS
LBA-assist (LBA) translation	L-CHS	LBA
Pure LBA (EDD BIOS)	LBA	LBA

In Standard CHS, there is only one possible translation step internal to the drive. The drive's actual physical geometry is completely invisible from the outside with all zone-recorded ATA drives today. The cylinders, heads, and sectors printed on the label for use in the BIOS Setup are purely logical geometry and do not represent the actual physical parameters. Standard CHS addressing is limited to 16 heads and 1,024 cylinders, which provides a limit of 504MB.

This is often called "Normal" in the BIOS Setup and causes the BIOS to behave like an old-fashioned one without translation. Use this setting if your drive has fewer than 1,024 cylinders or if you want to use the drive with a non-DOS operating system that doesn't understand translation.

"ECHS" or "Large" in the BIOS Setup is CHS bit-shift, and most from 1997 and later use the revised method (240 logical heads maximum). "LBA" as selected in the BIOS Setup indicates LBA-assist translation, not pure LBA mode. This allows software to operate using L-CHS parameters while the BIOS talks to the drive in LBA mode.

The only way to select a pure LBA mode, from the OS to the BIOS as well as from the BIOS to the drive, is with a drive that is over 8.4GB. All drives over 137GB must be addressed via LBA at both the BIOS and drive level, and most PC BIOSes will automatically address any drive over 8.4GB in that manner as well. In this case, no special BIOS Setup settings are needed other than setting the type to auto or auto-detect.

Caution

A word of warning with these BIOS translation settings: If you have a drive 8.4GB or less in capacity and switch between Standard CHS, ECHS, or LBA, the BIOS can change the (translated) geometry. The same thing can happen if you transfer a disk that has been formatted on an old, non-LBA computer to a new one that uses LBA. This causes the logical CHS geometry seen by the operating system to change and the data to appear in the wrong locations from where it actually is! This can cause you to lose access to your data if you are not careful. I always recommend recording the CMOS Setup screens associated with the hard disk configuration so you can properly match the setup of a drive and the settings to which it was originally set. This does not affect drives over 8.4GB because in that case pure LBA is automatically selected.

The 8.4GB Barrier

Although CHS translation breaks the 528MB barrier, it runs into another barrier at 8.4GB. Supporting drives larger than 8.4GB requires that we leave CHS behind and change from CHS to LBA addressing at the BIOS level. The ATA interface had always supported LBA addressing, even in the original ATA-1 specification. One problem was that originally LBA support at the ATA level was optional, but the main problem was that there was no LBA support at the BIOS interface level. You could set LBA-assist translation in the BIOS Setup, but all that did was convert the drive LBA numbers to CHS numbers at the BIOS interface level.

Phoenix Technologies recognized that the BIOS interface needed to move from CHS to LBA early on and, beginning in 1994, published the "BIOS Enhanced Disk Drive (EDD) Specification," which addressed this problem with new extended INT13h BIOS services that worked with LBA rather than CHS addresses.

To ensure industry-wide support and compatibility for these new BIOS functions, in 1996 Phoenix turned this document over to the National Committee on Information Technology Standards (NCITS) T13 technical committee for further enhancement and certification as a standard called the "BIOS Enhanced Disk Drive (EDD) Specification." Starting in 1998, most of the other BIOS manufacturers began installing EDD support in their BIOSes, enabling BIOS-level LBA mode support for ATA drives larger than 8.4GB. Coincidentally (or not), this support arrived just in time because ATA drives of that size and larger became available that same year.

The EDD document describes new extended INT13h BIOS commands that allow LBA addressing up to 2^{64} sectors, which results in a theoretical maximum capacity of more than 9.44ZB (zettabytes, or quadrillion bytes). That is the same as saying 9.44 trillion gigabytes (9.44×10^{21} bytes or, to be more precise, 9,444,732,965,739,290,430,000 bytes)! I say "theoretical capacity" because even though by 1998 the BIOS could handle up to 2^{64} sectors, ATA drives were still using only 28-bit addressing (2^{28} sectors) at the ATA interface level. This limited an ATA drive to 268,435,456 sectors, which was a capacity of 137,438,953,472 bytes or 137.44GB. Thus, the 8.4GB barrier had been broken, but another barrier remained at 137GB due to the 28-bit LBA addressing used in the ATA interface. The numbers work out as follows:

```
                        Max. Values
- - - - - - - - - - - - - - - - - - - - - - - - - - - - -
Total Sectors           268,435,456
- - - - - - - - - - - - - - - - - - - - - - - - - - - - -
Total Bytes         137,438,953,472
Megabytes (MB)              137,439
Mebibytes (MiB)            131,072
Gigabytes (GB)              137.44
Gibibytes (GiB)             128.00
```

Through use of the new extended INT13h 64-bit LBA mode commands at the BIOS level, as well as the existing 28-bit LBA mode commands at the ATA level, no translation would be required, and the LBA numbers would be passed unchanged. The combination of LBA at the BIOS level and the ATA interface level meant that the clumsy CHS addressing could finally die. This also means that when you install an ATA drive larger than 8.4GB in a PC that has an EDD-capable BIOS (1998 or newer), both the BIOS and the drive are automatically set to use LBA mode.

An interesting quirk is that to allow backward compatibility in case you boot an older operating system that doesn't support LBA mode addressing (DOS or the original release of Windows 95 for example), most drives larger than 8.4GB will report 16,383 cylinders, 16 heads, and 63 sectors per track, which is 8.4GB. This allows a 160GB drive, for example, to be seen by older BIOSes or older operating systems as an 8.4GB drive. That sounds strange, but I guess having a 160GB drive being recognized as an 8.4GB drive is better than not having it work at all. If you do want to install a drive larger than 8.4GB into a system dated before 1998, then either a motherboard BIOS upgrade or an add-on BIOS card with EDD support (available from MicroFirmware, for example) is recommended.

The 137GB Barrier and Beyond

By 2001 the 137GB barrier had become a problem because 3.5-inch hard drives were poised to breach that capacity level. The solution came in the form of ATA-6, which was being developed during that year. To allow for addressing drives of greater capacity, ATA-6 upgraded the LBA functions from using 28-bit numbers to using larger, 48-bit numbers instead.

The ATA-6 specification extends the LBA interface such that it can use 48-bit sector addressing. This means that maximum capacity is increased to 2^{48} (281,474,976,710,656) total sectors. Because each sector stores 512 bytes, this results in the following maximum drive capacity:

```
                          Max. Values
- - - - - - - - - - - - - - - - - - - - - - - - - - - - - - - -
Total Sectors         281,474,976,710,656
- - - - - - - - - - - - - - - - - - - - - - - - - - - - - - - -
Total Bytes       144,115,188,075,855,888
Megabytes (MB)        144,115,188,076
Mebibytes (MiB)       137,438,953,472
Gigabytes (GB)           144,115,188
Gibibytes (GiB)          134,217,728
Terabytes (TB)               144,115
Tebibytes (TiB)              131,072
Petabytes (PB)               144.12
Pebibytes (PiB)              128.00
```

As you can see, the 48-bit LBA in ATA-6 allows a capacity of just over 144PB (petabytes = quadrillion bytes)!

Because the EDD BIOS functions use a 64-bit LBA number, they have a much larger limit:

```
                              Max. Values
        -------------------------------------------------
        Total Sectors        18,446,744,073,709,551,600
        -------------------------------------------------
        Total Bytes       9,444,732,965,739,290,430,000
        Megabytes (MB)        9,444,732,965,739,291
        Mebibytes (MiB)       9,007,199,254,740,993
        Gigabytes (GB)            9,444,732,965,739
        Gibibytes (GiB)           8,796,093,022,208
        Terabytes (TB)                9,444,732,966
        Tebibytes (TiB)               8,589,934,592
        Petabytes (PB)                    9,444,733
        Pebibytes (PiB)                   8,388,608
        Exabytes (EB)                         9,445
        Exbibytes (EiB)                       8,192
        Zettabytes (ZB)                        9.44
        Zebibytes (ZiB)                        8.00
```

Although the BIOS services use 64-bit LBA (allowing up to 2^{64} sectors) for even greater capacity, the 144PB ATA-6 limitation will be the lower of the two that will apply. Still, that should hold us for some time to come.

Given that hard disk drives have been doubling in capacity every 1.5–2 years (Moore's Law), and considering that 160GB ATA drives were available in late 2001, I estimate that it will take us until between the years 2031 to 2041 before we reach the 144PB barrier (assuming hard disk technology hasn't been completely replaced by this point). Similarly, I estimate the 9.44ZB EDD BIOS barrier won't be reached until between the years 2055 to 2073! Phoenix originally claimed that the EDD specification would hold us until 2020; it seems Phoenix was being quite conservative.

The 137GB barrier has proven a bit more complicated than previous barriers—not only are there BIOS issues but also operating system and chipset-based ATA host adapter driver issues as well. Drives larger than 137GB are accessed using 48-bit LBA (logical block address) numbers, which require BIOS support, chipset driver support, and operating systems support. Generally, you will need the following:

- A BIOS with 48-bit LBA support (normally dated September 2002 or newer)
- The latest chipset driver, such as the Intel Application Accelerator (for motherboards using Intel chipsets; go to www.intel.com/support/chipsets/iaa)
- Windows XP with Service Pack 1 (or later) installed

If you have a system without the BIOS support, check with your motherboard manufacturer for an update, or optionally you can use a card with onboard BIOS, such as the Ultra ATA 133 PCI card from Maxtor. If your motherboard uses an Intel chipset, you can download the latest chipset driver (Intel calls it the Intel Application Accelerator) from www.intel.com/support/chipsets/iaa. If your motherboard uses a non-Intel chipset, check with the motherboard or chipset manufacturer for driver updates to enable 48-bit LBA support.

Finally, note that the original version of XP, as well as Windows 2000/NT and Windows 95/98/Me, does not currently provide native support for ATA hard drives larger than 137GB. You will need to use Windows XP and ensure you have Service Pack 1 or later installed.

Operating System and Other Software Limitations

Note that if you use older software, including utilities, applications, or even operating systems that rely exclusively on CHS parameters, they will see all drives over 8.4GB as 8.4GB only. You will need not only a newer BIOS but also newer software designed to handle the direct LBA addressing to work with drives over 8.4GB.

Operating systems limitations with respect to drives over 8.4GB are shown in Table 9.19.

Table 9.19   Operating Systems Limitations

Operating System	Limitations for Hard Drive Size
DOS/Windows 3x	DOS 6.22 or lower cannot support drives greater than 8.4GB. DOS 7.0 or higher (included with Windows 95 or later) is required to recognize a drive over 8.4GB.
Windows 9X/Me	Windows 95a (original version) does support the INT13h extensions, which means it does support drives over 8.4GB; however, due to limitations of the FAT16 file system, the maximum individual partition size is limited to 2GB. Windows 95B/OSR2 or later (including Windows 98/Me) supports the INT13h extensions, which allows drives over 8.4GB, and also supports FAT32, which allows partition sizes up to the maximum capacity of the drive. However, Windows 95 doesn't support hard drives larger than 32GB because of limitations in its design. Windows 98 requires an update to FDISK to partition drives larger than 64GB.
Windows NT	Windows NT 3.5x does not support drives greater than 8.4GB. Windows NT 4.0 does support drivers greater than 8.4GB, however. When a drive larger than 8.4GB is being used as the primary bootable device, Windows NT will not recognize more than 8.4GB. Microsoft has released Service Pack 4, which corrects this problem.
Windows 2000/XP	Windows 2000/XP supports drives greater than 8.4GB.
OS/2 Warp	Some versions of OS/2 are limited to a boot partition size of 3.1GB or 4.3GB. IBM has a Device Driver Pack upgrade that enables the boot partition to be as large as 8.4GB. The HPFS file system in OS/2 will support drives up to 64GB.
Novell	NetWare 5.0 or later supports drives greater than 8.4GB.

In the case of operating systems that support drives over 8.4GB, the maximum drive size limitations are dependent on the BIOS and the hard drive interface standard, not the OS. Instead, other limitations come into play for the volumes (partitions) and files that can be created and managed by the various operating systems. These limitations are dependent not only on the operating system involved but also the file system that is used for the volume. Table 9.20 shows the minimum and maximum volume (partition) size and file size limitations of the various Windows operating systems. You must use Windows 98/Me or a Windows NT–type operating system (NT, 2000, or XP) if you want to use a drive larger than 137GB. Note that the original version of XP, as well as Windows 2000/NT and Windows 95/98/Me, does not currently provide native support for ATA hard drives larger than 137GB. You will need to use Windows XP and ensure you have Service Pack 1 or later installed to use an ATA drive over 137GB. This does not affect drives interfaced via USB, FireWire, SCSI, or other interfaces.

Table 9.20   Operating Systems Volume/File Size Limitations by File System

OS Limitations by File System	FAT16	FAT32	NTFS
Min. Volume Size (9x/Me)	2.092MB	33.554MB	—
Min. Volume Size (NT/2000/XP)	2.092MB	33.554MB	1.000MB
Max. Volume Size (9x)	2.147GB	136.902GB	—
Max. Volume Size (Me)	2.147GB	8.796TB	—
Max. Volume Size (NT/2000/XP)	4.294GB	8.796GB	281.475TB
Max. File Size (all)	4.294GB	4.294GB	16.384TB

— = not applicable   *GB = gigabyte = 1,000,000,000 bytes*
MB = megabyte = 1,000,000 bytes   *TB = terabyte = 1,000,000,000,000 bytes*

ATA Transfer Modes

ATA-2 and ATA-3 defined the first of several higher-performance modes for transferring data to and from the drive. These faster modes were the main part of the newer specifications and were the main reason they were initially developed. The following subsections discuss these modes.

PIO Mode

The PIO (Programmed I/O) mode determines how fast data is transferred to and from the drive using PIO transfers. In the slowest possible mode—PIO mode 0—the data cycle time cannot exceed 600 nanoseconds (ns). In a single cycle, 16 bits are transferred into or out of the drive, making the theoretical transfer rate of PIO Mode 0 (600ns cycle time) 3.3MBps, whereas PIO Mode 4 (120ns cycle time) achieves a 16.6MBps transfer rate.

Table 9.21 shows the PIO modes, with their respective transfer rates.

Table 9.21   PIO (Programmed I/O) Modes and Transfer Rates

PIO Mode	Bus Width (bits)	Cycle Speed (ns)	Bus Speed (MHz)	Cycles per Clock	Transfer Rate (MBps)	ATA Specification
0	16	600	1.67	1	3.33	ATA-1
1	16	383	2.61	1	5.22	ATA-1
2	16	240	4.17	1	8.33	ATA-1
3	16	180	5.56	1	11.11	ATA-2
4	16	120	8.33	1	16.67	ATA-2

ATA-2 was also referred to as EIDE (Enhanced IDE) or Fast-ATA

ns = nanoseconds (billionths of a second)

MB = million bytes

Most motherboards with ATA-2 or greater support have dual ATA connectors on the motherboard. Most of the motherboard chipsets include the ATA interface in their South Bridge components, which in most systems is tied into the PCI bus.

Older 486 and some early Pentium boards have only the primary connector running through the system's PCI local bus. The secondary connector on those boards usually runs through the ISA bus and therefore supports up to Mode 2 operation only.

When interrogated with an Identify Drive command, a hard disk returns, among other things, information about the PIO and DMA modes it is capable of using. Most enhanced BIOSes automatically set the correct mode to match the capabilities of the drive. If you set a mode faster than the drive can handle, data corruption results.

ATA-2 and newer drives also perform Block Mode PIO, which means they use the Read/Write Multiple commands that greatly reduce the number of interrupts sent to the host processor. This lowers the overhead, and the resulting transfers are even faster.

DMA Transfer Modes

ATA drives also support *direct memory access (DMA)* transfers. DMA means that the data is transferred directly between drive and memory without using the CPU as an intermediary, as opposed to PIO. This has the effect of offloading much of the work of transferring data from the processor, in effect allowing the processor to do other things while the transfer is taking place.

There are two distinct types of direct memory access: singleword (8-bit) and multiword (16-bit) DMA. Singleword DMA modes were removed from the ATA-3 and later specifications and are obsolete. DMA modes are also sometimes called *busmaster ATA modes* because they use a host adapter that supports busmastering. Ordinary DMA relies on the legacy DMA controller on the motherboard to perform the complex task of arbitration, grabbing the system bus and transferring the data. In the case of busmastering DMA, all this is done by a higher-speed logic chip in the host adapter interface (which is also on the motherboard).

Systems using the Intel PIIX (PCI IDE ISA eXcelerator) or mobile PIIX and later South Bridge chips (or equivalent) have the capability of supporting busmaster ATA. The singleword and doubleword busmaster ATA modes and transfer rates are shown in Tables 9.22 and 9.23.

Table 9.22   Singleword (8-bit) DMA Modes and Transfer Rates

8-bit DMA Mode	Bus Width (bits)	Cycle Speed (ns)	Bus Speed (MHz)	Cycles per Clock	Transfer Rate (MBps)	ATA Specification
0	16	960	1.04	1	2.08	ATA-1[1]
1	16	480	2.08	1	4.17	ATA-1[1]
2	16	240	4.17	1	8.33	ATA-1[1]

1. Singleword (8-bit) DMA modes were removed from the ATA-3 and later specifications.

Table 9.23   Multiword (16-bit) DMA Modes and Transfer Rates

16-bit DMA Mode	Bus Width (bits)	Cycle Speed (ns)	Bus Speed (MHz)	Cycles per Clock	Transfer Rate (MBps)	ATA Specification
0	16	480	2.08	1	4.17	ATA-1
1	16	150	6.67	1	13.33	ATA-2
2	16	120	8.33	1	16.67	ATA-2

ATA-2 was also referred to as EIDE (Enhanced IDE) or Fast-ATA.

Note that doubleword DMA modes are also called *busmaster DMA modes* by some manufacturers. Unfortunately, even the fastest mode (doubleword DMA Mode 2) results in the same 16.67MBps transfer speed as PIO Mode 4. However, even though the transfer speed is the same as PIO, because DMA offloads much of the work from the processor, overall system performance would be higher. Even so, multiword DMA modes were never very popular and have been superseded by the newer Ultra-DMA modes supported in ATA-4 through ATA-7 compatible devices.

Table 9.24 shows the Ultra-DMA modes now supported in the ATA-4 through ATA-7 specifications.

Table 9.24   Ultra-DMA Support in ATA-4 Through ATA-7

Ultra-DMA Mode	Bus Width (bits)	Cycle Speed (ns)	Bus Speed (MHz)	Cycles per Clock	Transfer Rate (MBps)	ATA Specification
0	16	240	4.17	2	16.67	ATA-4
1	16	160	6.25	2	25.00	ATA-4
2	16	120	8.33	2	33.33	ATA-4

Table 9.24   Ultra-DMA Support in ATA-4 Through ATA-7

Ultra-DMA Mode	Bus Width (bits)	Cycle Speed (ns)	Bus Speed (MHz)	Cycles per Clock	Transfer Rate (MBps)	ATA Specification
3	16	90	11.11	2	44.44	ATA-5
4	16	60	16.67	2	66.67	ATA-5
5	16	40	25.00	2	100.00	ATA-6
6	16	30	33.00	2	133.00	ATA-7

ATA-4 UDMA Mode 2 is sometimes called Ultra-ATA/33 or ATA-33.
ATA-5 UDMA Mode 4 is sometimes called Ultra-ATA/66 or ATA-66.
ATA-6 UDMA Mode 5 is sometimes called Ultra-ATA/100 or ATA-100.
ATA-7 UDMA Mode 6 is sometimes called Ultra-ATA/133 or ATA-133.

ATAPI (ATA Packet Interface)

ATAPI (or the ATA Packet Interface) is a standard designed to provide the commands needed for devices such as CD-ROMs, DVD-ROMs and tape drives that plug into an ordinary ATA connector. The principal advantage of ATAPI hardware is that it's cheap and works on your current adapter. For CD-ROMs and DVD-ROMs, it has a somewhat lower CPU usage compared to proprietary adapters, but there's no performance gain otherwise. For tape drives, ATAPI has potential for superior performance and reliability compared to the popular floppy controller–attached tape devices. ATAPI is also used to run other removable storage devices, such as the LS-120 SuperDisk drives and internal Iomega Zip and Jaz drives as well as CDRW and DVD+-RW drives.

Although ATAPI CD-ROMs use the hard disk interface, this does not mean they look like ordinary hard disks; to the contrary, from a software point of view, they are a completely different kind of animal. They closely resemble a SCSI device. All modern ATA CD-ROMs support the ATAPI protocols, and generally the terms are synonymous. In other words, an ATAPI CD-ROM is an ATA CD-ROM, and vice versa.

Caution

ATAPI support other than for booting is not found directly in the BIOS of many systems. Systems without ATAPI support in the BIOS cannot boot from an ATAPI CD-ROM, so you still must load a driver to use ATAPI under DOS or Windows. Windows 95 and later (including 98 and Me) and Windows NT (including Windows 2000 and XP) have native ATAPI support. Newer systems with ATAPI-aware BIOSes are now available, which allow booting from an ATAPI CD-ROM. However, ATAPI drivers still need to be loaded by the OS for access after booting. Some versions of the Windows 98, NT, 2000, and XP CD-ROMs are directly bootable on those systems, greatly easing installation.

I normally recommend keeping different types of ATA devices on separate channels because ATA does not normally support overlapping access. When one drive is being accessed, the other cannot. By keeping the CD-ROM and hard disk on separate channels, you can more effectively overlap accessing between them.

Serial ATA

With the introduction of ATA-7, it seems that the Parallel ATA standard that has been in use for more than 10 years is running out of steam. Sending data at rates faster than 133MBps down a parallel ribbon cable is fraught with all kinds of problems because of signal timing, electromagnetic interference

(EMI), and other integrity problems. The solution is in a new ATA interface called *Serial ATA (SATA)*, which is an evolutionary backward-compatible replacement for the Parallel ATA physical storage interface. Serial ATA is backward compatible in that it is compatible with existing software, which will run on the new architecture without any changes. In other words, the existing BIOS, operating systems, and utilities that work on Parallel ATA will also work on Serial ATA. This means Serial ATA supports all existing ATA and ATAPI devices, including CD-ROM and CD-RW drives, DVD drives, tape devices, SuperDisk drives, and any other storage device currently supported by Parallel ATA.

Of course, they do differ physically; that is, you won't be able to plug Parallel ATA drives into Serial ATA host adapters, and vice versa. The physical changes are all for the better because Serial ATA uses much thinner cables with only seven pins that are easier to route inside the PC and easier to plug in with smaller redesigned cable connectors. The interface chip designs also are improved with fewer pins and lower voltages. These improvements are all designed to eliminate the design problems inherent in Parallel ATA.

Serial ATA won't be integrated into systems overnight; however, it is clear to me that it will eventually replace Parallel ATA as the de facto standard internal storage device interface found in both desktop and portable systems. The transition from ATA to SATA is a gradual one, and during this transition Parallel ATA capabilities will continue to be available. I would also expect that with more than a 10-year history, Parallel ATA devices will continue to be available even after most PCs have gone to SATA.

Development for Serial ATA started when the Serial ATA Working Group effort was announced at the Intel Developer Forum in February 2000. The initial members of the Serial ATA Working Group included APT Technologies, Dell, IBM, Intel, Maxtor, Quantum, and Seagate. The first Serial ATA 1.0 draft specification was released in November 2000 and officially published as a final specification in August 2001. The Serial ATA II extensions to this specification, which make Serial ATA suitable for network storage, were released in October 2002. Both can be downloaded from the Serial ATA Working Group website at www.serialata.org. Since forming, the group has added more than 100 Contributor and Adopter companies to the membership from all areas of industry. Systems using Serial ATA were first released in late 2002.

The performance of SATA is impressive, although current hard drive designs can't fully take advantage of its bandwidth. Three proposed variations of the standard all use the same cables and connectors; they differ only in transfer rate performance. Initially, only the first version will be available, but the roadmap to doubling and quadrupling performance from there has been clearly established. Table 9.25 shows the specifications for the current and future proposed SATA versions; the next-generation 300MBps version was just introduced in 2005, whereas the 600MBps version is not expected until 2007.

Table 9.25 SATA Standards Specifications

Serial ATA Type	Bus Width (Bits)	Bus Speed (MHz)	Data Cycles per Clock	(MBps)	Bandwidth
SATA-150	1	1500	1	150	
SATA-300	1	3000	1	300	
SATA-600	1	6000	1	600	

From the table, you can see that Serial ATA sends data only a single bit at a time. The cable used has only seven wires and is a very thin design, with keyed connectors only 14mm (0.55 inches) wide on each end. This eliminates problems with airflow around the wider, Parallel ATA ribbon cables. Each cable has connectors only at each end and connects the device directly to the host adapter (normally on the motherboard). There are no master/slave settings because each cable supports only a single device. The cable ends are interchangeable: The connector on the motherboard is the same as on the device, and both cable ends are identical. Maximum SATA cable length is 1 meter (39.37 inches), which is considerably longer than the 18-inch maximum for Parallel ATA. Even with this thinner, longer, and less expensive cable, transfer rates initially of 150MBps (nearly 13% greater than Parallel ATA/133), and 300MBps (25% greater than Parallel ATA/133), and even 600MBps, are possible.

Serial ATA uses a special encoding scheme called *8B/10B* to encode and decode data sent along the cable. The 8B/10B transmission code originally was developed (and patented) by IBM in the early 1980s for use in high-speed data communications. This encoding scheme is now used by many high-speed data-transmission standards, including Gigabit Ethernet, Fibre Channel, FireWire, and others. The main purpose of the 8B/10B encoding scheme is to guarantee that there are never more than four 0s (or 1s) transmitted consecutively. This is a form of run length limited (RLL) encoding (called RLL 0,4) in which the 0 represents the minimum and the 4 represents the maximum number of consecutive 0s in each encoded character.

The 8B/10B encoding also ensures that there are never more than six or fewer than four 0s (or 1s) in a single encoded 10-bit character. Because 1s and 0s are sent as voltage changes on a wire, this ensures that the spacing between the voltage transitions sent by the transmitter will be fairly balanced, with a more regular and steady stream of pulses. This presents a more steady load on the circuits, increasing reliability. The conversion from 8-bit data to 10-bit encoded characters for transmission leaves a number of 10-bit patterns unused. Several of these additional patterns are used to provide flow control, delimit packets of data, perform error checking, or perform other special needs.

The physical transmission scheme for SATA uses what is called *differential NRZ (Non Return to Zero)*. This uses a balanced pair of wires, each carrying plus or minus 0.25V (one-quarter volt). The signals are sent differentially: If one wire in the pair is carrying +0.25V, the other wire is carrying—0.25V, where the differential voltage between the two wires is always 0.5V (a half volt). This means that for a given voltage waveform, the opposite voltage waveform is sent along the adjacent wire. Differential transmission minimizes electromagnetic radiation and makes the signals easier to read on the receiving end.

A 15-pin power cable and power connector are optional with SATA, providing 3.3V power in addition to the 5V and 12V provided via the industry-standard 4-pin device power connectors. Although it has 15 pins, this new power connector design is only 24mm (0.945 inches). With three pins designated for each of the 3.3V, 5V, and 12V power levels, enough capacity exists for up to 4.5 amps of current at each voltage, which is ample for even the most power-hungry drives. For compatibility with existing power supplies, SATA drives can be made with either the original, standard 4-pin device power connector or the new 15-pin SATA power connector, or both. If the drive doesn't have the type of connector you needed, adapters are available to convert from one type to the other.

Figure 9.19 shows what the new SATA signal and power connectors look like. The pinouts for the Serial ATA data and optional power connectors are shown in Tables 9.26 and 9.27.

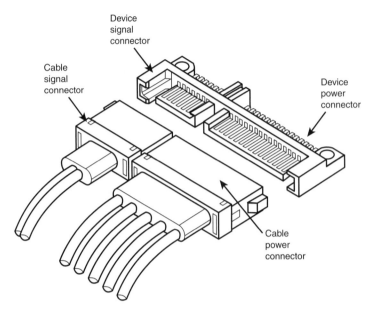

Figure 9.19   SATA (Serial ATA) signal and power connectors.

Table 9.26   Serial ATA (SATA) Data Connector Pinout

Signal Pin	Signal	Description
S1	Gnd	First mate
S2	A+	Host Transmit +
S3	A–	Host Transmit –
S4	Gnd	First mate
S5	B–	Host Receive –
S6	B+	Host Receive +
S7	Gnd	First mate

All pins are in a single row spaced 1.27mm (.050") apart.

All ground pins are longer so they will make contact before the signal/power pins to allow hot plugging.

Table 9.27   Serial ATA (SATA) Optional Power Connector Pinout

Power Pin	Signal	Description
P1	+3.3V	3.3V power
P2	+3.3V	3.3V power
P3	+3.3V	3.3V power
P4	Gnd	First mate
P5	Gnd	First mate
P6	Gnd	First mate

Table 9.27   Continued

Power Pin	Signal	Description
P7	+5V	5V power
P8	+5V	5V power
P9	+5V	5V power
P10	Gnd	First mate
P11	Gnd	First mate
P12	Gnd	First mate
P13	+12V	12V power
P14	+12V	12V power
P15	+12V	12V power

All pins are in a single row spaced 1.27mm (.050") apart.

All ground pins are longer so they will make contact before the signal/power pins to allow hot plugging.

Three power pins are used to carry 4.5 A maximum current for each voltage.

The configuration of Serial ATA devices is also much simpler because the master/slave or cable select jumper settings used with Parallel ATA are no longer necessary.

Serial ATA is ideal for laptop and notebook systems, and it will eventually replace Parallel ATA in those systems as well. In late 2002, Fujitsu demonstrated a prototype 2.5-inch SATA drive. Most 2.5-inch hard drive manufacturers were waiting for mobile chipsets supporting SATA to be delivered before officially introducing mobile SATA drives. Both the chipsets and the drives began arriving in 2005, and by late 2005 the first laptops were available with SATA drives. Even if your laptop system does not support SATA internally, you can add an SATA interface externally via a PC Card, such as the Addonics CardBus Serial ATA adapter. This card adds two high-speed Serial ATA ports to any laptop or notebook computer via a PC Card slot. This enables you to connect drives with 2.5 times the data transfer rate of USB 2.0. The card plus an external cable sells for under $100.

Figure 9.20 shows the Addonics CardBus Serial ATA adapter.

Figure 9.20   Addonics CardBus Serial ATA adapter.

Although SATA is not normally designed to be used as an external interface, Addonics has available external drive enclosures as well as a special cable that pulls power from a spare USB port. Using a special cable that's provided, you can connect external hard drives or even CD-ROM/DVD drives via a high-speed SATA connection. Figure 9.21 shows the special Addonics cable, which allows a variety of external SATA devices to be connected to any portable system.

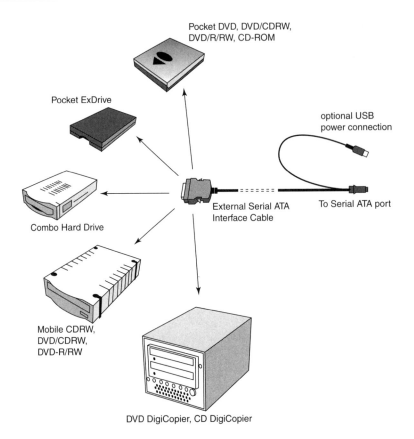

Pocket DVD, DVD/CDRW, DVD/R/RW, CD-ROM

Pocket ExDrive

optional USB power connection

External Serial ATA Interface Cable

To Serial ATA port

Combo Hard Drive

Mobile CDRW, DVD/CDRW, DVD-R/RW

DVD DigiCopier, CD DigiCopier

Figure 9.21 Addonics Serial ATA devices for Laptops.

Like Parallel ATA, Serial ATA was designed to be the primary storage interface used inside a PC and was not designed to be used as an external interface. As such, SATA is not designed to compete with high-speed external device interfaces, such as SCSI, USB 2.0, or IEEE 1394 (FireWire).

CHAPTER 10

Removable Storage

Removable Media

Since the mid-1980s, the primary storage device used by computers has been the hard disk drive. However, for software loading, data backup, data transport between computers, and temporary storage, removable-media storage devices such as optical drives, magneto-optical drives, magnetic disk drives, tape drives, and flash memory devices are useful supplements to primary storage. These types of drives can be used as a supplement to hard disk storage as well as for primary storage.

The options for purchasing removable devices vary. Some removable-media drives use media as small as a quarter of your index finger, whereas others use larger media, up to 5 1/4". Most popular removable storage drives today have capacities that range from as little as 32MB to as much as 500GB or more. These drives offer fairly speedy performance and the capability to store anything from a few data files or less frequently used programs to complete hard disk images on a removable disk or tape.

Three main types of technology are available for removable storage on laptop PCs (or desktops):

- Magnetic disk
- Optical disc
- Flash (ROM)

Magnetic disks include floppy drives, Zip drives, LS-120/240 SuperDisk drives, and external hard drives. Optical discs include CD/DVD-ROM, CD-RW, and DVD+-RW. Flash memory includes CompactFlash, SecureDigital, MultiMediaCard, Smart Media, USB thumb and keychain flashdisks, and more. This chapter examines these three main classes of removable storage.

Apart from hard disk drives, laptop systems can use many other types of storage media that can provide access to larger amounts of data. CD-ROM drives have been standard in laptop systems for many years now, with most of the newer systems offering combo DVD/CD-RW drives or even dual-layer DVD+-RW drives. As accessories, some systems also offer removable high-capacity floppy or cartridge drives, such as the LS-120, LS-240, or Iomega's Zip drive. This has been made possible by the enhanced IDE specifications that let other types of devices share the same interface as the hard drive.

Another important issue is the floppy drive. Many systems now omit the floppy drive to save space, either offering an external drive connected via USB or one that can work in a drive bay interchangeably with other devices, such as optical drives. Depending on the type of user, the lack of a floppy drive might or might not be an acceptable inconvenience. Many users of portables, especially those who frequently connect to networks, have little use for a floppy drive. This is now true even for the installation of applications because virtually all software now ships on CD-ROMs.

One feature becoming increasingly common in laptop systems is modular drive bays that are capable of supporting several types of interchangeable components. Most systems with modular bays offer multiple devices for these bays, including a floppy drive, several types of optical drives, hard drives, and secondary batteries. This arrangement lets you customize the configuration of your system to suit your immediate needs. For example, when traveling, you might remove the DVD/CD-RW drive and replace it with an extra battery or a second hard drive.

Laptop vendors and magazine reviews might refer to the number of spindles when discussing the number of drives a laptop can have installed simultaneously. Nearly all laptop systems can be classified as one-, two-, or three-spindle systems. One-spindle systems are the smallest and lightest, incorporating only a single internal hard disk, and no other internal drives. Other drives, such as floppy or CD/DVD drives, must be connected externally (via USB in most cases) or via some type of docking station. The ThinkPad X series from IBM is an example of a one-spindle system.

Most laptops are two-spindle systems. If a system has two spindles, the most common configuration is an internal hard drive along with a modular bay supporting several interchangeable devices including a floppy drive, several types of CD or DVD drives, a battery, a second hard drive, and possibly other items as well.

A three-spindle system normally includes an internal hard drive, a floppy drive, and a single modular bay, or possibly an internal hard drive and two modular bays. They are sometimes called *all-in-one systems*, referring to the fact that a floppy, hard disk, and optical drive can be mounted in the system simultaneously. With the elimination of the floppy drive from newer laptops, three-spindle systems are becoming rare. When evaluating your laptop needs and hardware, be sure to determine which devices included with a model can be used simultaneously and which require removing another device.

Tip

If a particular laptop is described as a *one-spindle* or *two-spindle* system, you should determine which drive(s) has been omitted and decide whether it's acceptable to use an external drive as a substitute. Many two-spindle systems use an internal hard disk and one modular bay drive. This means that if you want to use a floppy drive, you'll have to either carry an external USB floppy drive or swap a modular bay floppy drive for the optical drive, which means the floppy and optical drives cannot be used simultaneously.

If lightweight travel is a concern, determine which parts you don't need for travel that can be swapped out. Modular bays can sometimes be equipped with a "weight-saving module," which is a dummy drive for the open bay to prevent dirt and foreign objects from entering when the bay is empty. If a particular system doesn't include a dummy drive, one may be available as an option.

If you aren't satisfied with the removable modular bay drives your current laptop offers, the PC Card slots and USB or FireWire connectors are your gateway to virtually unlimited choices in external drives. All the popular desktop choices, such as CD-RW drives, DVD+-RW drives, high-capacity hard drives, tape backup drives, floppy drives, and Zip or LS-120 SuperDisk drives, can be attached via USB, FireWire, or SCSI interfaces. If these interfaces are not built in (most systems have USB, many also have FireWire, but few if any have SCSI), they can be added via PC Card or CardBus adapters.

In most cases, external drives should be interfaced via high-speed USB 2.0 or FireWire, because those are among the highest performance and most popular interfaces. In the past, external drives were available in parallel port versions. Although parallel port drives were popular at one time, most newer laptops lack legacy serial and parallel ports, and you'll normally suffer a big speed drop for large file transfers, especially if you don't use the high-speed EPP/ECP IEEE 1284 LPT port modes. Instead of the parallel port, you should consider using your system's USB or FireWire ports.

You can transfer files between two systems by directly connecting them together via their Ethernet ports, parallel ports, or even USB ports. Note that special cables are required for these connections. LPT.com, the originator of the Direct Cable Connection program provided with Windows, is a popular source for these cables and setup help.

Interfaces for Removable-Media Drives

In addition to choosing a type of device, you need to choose which type of interface is ideally suited for connecting it to your system. Several connection options are available for the leading removable drives. The most common interface for internally mounted drives is the same ATA (AT Attachment) interface used for most hard drives. SCSI interfacing is as fast or even faster for use with external drives; however, SCSI devices are expensive and require the addition of a PC Card that provides a SCSI interface. It should be noted that high-end tape backups like DAT often require a SCSI interface.

FireWire (IEEE 1394/i.LINK) is commonly used for connecting video cameras and high-capacity external hard drives.

The most commonly used external interface, however, is now the USB port, which is replacing legacy ports such as the venerable parallel port for printing as well as interfacing external drives and other types of I/O devices. The USB port is available on all recent PCs (both desktop and laptop models); it can be hot-swapped, and it's supported by Windows 98 and later versions, including Windows Me, Windows 2000, and Windows XP. Older interfaces, such as the parallel port and PC Card (for laptop computers), are still used on some devices but have limited performance. These are recommended only for systems that don't support USB 2.0 High-Speed operation (such as those with USB 1.1 ports or those still running Windows 95 or Windows NT). Some external removable-media drives allow you to interchange interfaces to enable a single drive to work with a variety of systems.

Note

Although late versions of Windows 95 (Win95C or OSR2.1 and above) also have USB drivers, many developers of USB devices do not support their use with Windows 95. For reliable results and manufacturer support, use Windows 98SE (second edition), Windows Me, Windows 2000, or Windows XP.

As you will see in the following sections, most removable-media drives are available in two or more of these interface types, allowing you to choose the best interface option for your needs.

Note

Connecting or installing removable-media drives is similar to connecting and installing other internal and external peripherals. The external USB, FireWire (IEEE 1394/i.LINK), and parallel port drives are the simplest of the available interfaces, requiring only a special cable that comes with the drive and the installation of special software drivers. See the instructions that come with each drive type for the specifics of its installation.

See Chapter 8, "Expansion Card Buses," and Chapter 9, "Hard Disk Storage," for details on how these interfaces operate.

Removable Magnetic Disk and Optical Disc Storage

Computers have basically two types of disk/disc storage: magnetic and optical. *Magnetic* storage is represented by the standard floppy and hard disks that are installed in most systems, where the data is recorded magnetically on rotating disks. *Optical* disc storage is similar to magnetic disk storage in basic operation, but it reads and records using light (optically) instead of magnetism. Although most magnetic disk storage is fully read and write capable many times over, many optical storage media are either read-only or write-once. Note the convention in which we refer to magnetic as *disk* and optical as *disc*. This is not a law or rule, but it seems to be followed by most in the industry.

Some media combine magnetic and optical techniques, using either an optical guidance system (called a *laser servo*) to position a magnetic read/write head (as in the LS-120 or SuperDisk floppy drive) or a laser to heat the disk so it can be written to magnetically, thus polarizing areas of the track, which can then be read by a lower-powered laser, as in magneto-optical (MO) drives.

At one time, it was thought that optical storage would replace magnetic as the primary online storage medium. However, optical storage has proven to be much slower and far less dense than magnetic storage and is much more adaptable to removable-media designs. As such, optical storage is more often used for backup or archival storage purposes and as a mechanism by which programs or data can be loaded onto magnetic drives. Magnetic storage, being significantly faster and capable of holding much more information than optical media in the same amount of space, is more suited for direct online storage and most likely won't be replaced in that role by optical storage anytime soon.

The most promising development in the optical area is that in the near future CD-RW (compact disc-rewritable) or DVD+RW (DVD+rewritable) drives with EasyWrite (Mount Rainier) support are starting to replace the venerable floppy disk as the de facto standard interchangeable, transportable drive and media of choice. In fact, some would say that has already happened. Most new systems today include a CD-RW drive as a minimum, and many systems no longer include a floppy drive. Even if a floppy drive is included, it is rarely used except for updating the system's firmware, running tests or diagnostics, or doing basic system maintenance, disk formatting, preparation for OS installation, or configuration.

The next series of sections in this chapter investigate the popular and standard forms of removable storage used with modern laptop systems.

Backing Up Your Data

Any computer book worth reading warns repeatedly that you should back up your system regularly. Backups are necessary because at any time a major problem, or even some minor ones, can corrupt the important information and programs stored on your computer's hard disk drive, rendering this information useless. A wide range of problems can cause a loss of the data on your hard drive. Here is a list of some of these data-damaging problems:

- Sudden fluctuations (power spikes) in the electricity that powers your computer, resulting in data damage or corruption.

- Overwriting a file by mistake.

- Mistakenly formatting your hard disk when you meant to format a floppy or other type of removable media.

- Hard drive failure resulting in loss of data that has not been backed up. Not only do you have to install a new drive, but, because you have no backup, you also must reinstall all your software.

- Catastrophic damage or complete loss of your computer (storm, flood, lightning strike, fire, theft, and so on). A single lightning strike near your office or home can destroy the circuitry of your computer, including your hard drive. Theft of your computer, of course, is equally devastating, and especially problematic for laptop systems because they are so easily moved. A recent, complete backup greatly simplifies the process of setting up a replacement computer.

- Loss of valuable data due to a computer-related virus. One single download or floppy disk can contain a virus that can damage valuable files and even your entire hard disk. With several hundred new viruses appearing each month, no antivirus software program can keep you entirely safe. A recent backup of uninfected, critical files can help repair even the worst damage.

Backups are also the cure for such common headaches as a full hard drive and the need to transfer data between computers. By backing up data you rarely use and deleting the original data from your hard drive, you free up space once occupied by that data. If you later need a particular data file, you can retrieve that file from your backup. You also can more easily share large amounts of data between computers—when you send data from one city to another, for example—by backing up the data to a tape, CD-R(W), DVD+-R(W), or other media and then sending the media.

Regardless of how important regular backups are, many people avoid making them. A major reason for this lapse is that for many people, backing up their systems is tedious work when they have to use floppy disks or other low-capacity media. When you use these media, you might have to insert and remove many disks to back up all the important programs and data.

Optical storage, high-capacity magnetic media, and tapes are all useful devices for making backups. Historically, tape backups have been regarded as the most powerful of these technologies because they are among the few backup devices capable of recording the contents of today's multigigabyte drives to a single cartridge for restoration.

Optical Disc and Drive Technology

Optical technology standards for computers can be divided into two major types:

- CD (CD-ROM, CD-R, CD-RW)

- DVD (DVD-ROM, DVD-RAM, DVD+/-R, DVD+/-RW, DVD+/-RW DL)

Both CD and DVD storage devices are descended from popular entertainment standards; CD-based devices can also play music CDs, and DVD-based devices can play the same DVD videos you can purchase or rent. However, computer drives that can use these types of media also offer many additional features. In the following sections, you will learn how CD and DVD drives and media are similar, how they differ from each other, and how they can be used to enhance your storage and playback options.

CD-Based Optical Technology

The first type of optical storage that became a widespread computing standard is the CD-ROM. CD-ROM, or *compact disc read-only memory*, is an optical read-only storage medium based on the original CD-DA (digital audio) format first developed for audio CDs. Other formats, such as CD-R (CD-recordable) and CD-RW (CD-rewritable), are expanding the compact disc's capabilities by making it writable. As you will see later in this chapter, technologies such as DVD (digital versatile disc) enable you to store more data than ever on the same size disc.

CD-ROM drives have been considered standard equipment on most laptops for many years now. The primary exceptions to this rule are *ultralight* laptops, which are too small to include an optical drive.

CD-ROM discs are capable of holding up to 74 or 80 minutes of high-fidelity audio (depending on the disc used). If used for data, the traditional 74-minute disc can hold up to 650MiB (or 682MB), whereas the 80-minute disc can hold up to 700MiB (or 737MB). A combination of music and data can be stored on one side (only the bottom is used) of a 120mm (4.72") diameter, 1.2mm (0.047") thick plastic disc.

CD-ROM has exactly the same form factor (physical shape and layout) of the familiar CD-DA audio compact disc and can, in fact, be inserted in a normal audio player. It usually isn't playable, though, because the player reads the subcode information for the track, which indicates that it is data and not audio. If it could be played, the result would be noise—unless audio tracks precede the data on the CD-ROM (see the entry in Table 10.9, "Blue Book—CD EXTRA," later in this chapter). Accessing data from a CD-ROM using a computer is quite a bit faster than from a floppy disk but slower than a modern hard drive. The term *CD-ROM* refers to both the discs themselves and the drive that reads them.

Although only a few dozen CD-ROM discs, or titles, were published by 1988, currently hundreds of thousands of individual titles exist, containing data and programs ranging from worldwide agricultural statistics to preschool learning games. Individual businesses, local and federal government offices, and large corporations also publish thousands of their own limited-use titles. As one example, the storage space and expense that so many business offices once dedicated to the maintenance of a telephone book library can now be replaced by two discs containing the telephone listings for the entire United States.

CDs: A Brief History

In 1979, the Philips and Sony corporations joined forces to co-produce the CD-DA (compact disc-digital audio) standard. Philips had already developed commercial laserdisc players, and Sony had a decade of digital recording research under its belt. The two companies were poised for a battle—the introduction of potentially incompatible audio laserdisc formats—when instead they came to terms on an agreement to formulate a single industry-standard digital audio technology.

Philips contributed most of the physical design, which was similar to the laserdisc format it had previously created with regard to using pits and lands on the disc that are read by a laser. Sony contributed the digital-to-analog circuitry, and especially the digital encoding and error correcting code designs.

In 1980, the companies announced the CD-DA standard, which has since been referred to as the *Red Book format* (so named because the cover of the published document was red). The Red Book included the specifications for recording, sampling, and—above all—the 120mm (4.72-inch) diameter physical format you live with today. This size was chosen, legend has it, because it could contain all of Beethoven's approximately 70-minute *Ninth Symphony* without interruption.

After the specification was set, both manufacturers were in a race to introduce the first commercially available CD audio drive. Because of its greater experience with digital electronics, Sony won that race and beat Philips to market by one month, when on October 1, 1982, Sony introduced the CDP-101 player and the world's first commercial CD recording—Billy Joel's *52nd Street* album. The player was first introduced in Japan and then Europe; it wasn't available in the U.S. until early 1983. In 1984, Sony also introduced the first automobile and portable CD players.

Sony and Philips continued to collaborate on CD standards throughout the decade, and in 1984 they jointly released the Yellow Book CD-ROM standard. It turned the CD from a digital audio storage medium to one that could now store read-only data for use with a computer. The Yellow Book used the same physical format as audio CDs but modified the decoding electronics to allow data to be stored reliably. In fact, all subsequent CD standards (usually referred to by their colored book binders) have referred back to the original Red Book standard for the physical parameters of the disc. With the advent of the Yellow Book standard (CD-ROM), what originally was designed to hold a symphony could now be used to hold practically any type of information or software.

For more information on the other CD "Book" formats, see the section "Compact Disc and Drive Formats" later in this chapter.

CD-ROM Construction and Technology

Although identical in appearance to CD-DAs, CD-ROMs store data instead of (or in addition to) audio. The CD-ROM drives in computers that read the data discs are almost identical to audio CD players, with the main changes in the circuitry to provide additional error detection and correction. This is to ensure data is read without errors, because what would be a minor—if not unnoticeable—glitch in a song would be unacceptable as missing data in a file.

A CD is made of a polycarbonate wafer, 120mm in diameter and 1.2mm thick, with a 15mm hole in the center. This wafer base is stamped or molded with a single physical track in a spiral configuration starting from the inside of the disc and spiraling outward. The track has a pitch, or spiral separation, of 1.6 microns (millionths of a meter, or thousandths of a millimeter). By comparison, an LP record has a physical track pitch of about 125 microns. When viewed from the reading side (the bottom), the disc rotates counterclockwise. If you examined the spiral track of a CD under a microscope, you would see that along the track are raised bumps, called *pits*, and flat areas between the pits, called *lands*. It seems strange to call a raised bump a *pit*, but that term is used because when the discs are pressed, the stamper works from the top side. So, from that perspective, the pits are actually depressions made in the plastic.

The laser used to read the disc would pass right through the clear plastic, so the stamped surface is coated with a layer of metal—usually aluminum—to make it reflective. Then, the aluminum is coated with a thin, protective layer of acrylic lacquer, and finally a label or printing is added.

Caution

CD-ROM media should be handled with the same care as a photographic negative. The CD-ROM is an optical device and degrades as its optical surface becomes dirty or scratched. Also, it is important to note that although discs are read from the bottom, the layer containing the track is actually much closer to the top of the disc. The reason is that the protective lacquer overcoat is only 6 to 7 microns (about one quarter of a thousandth of an inch) thick. Writing on the top surface of a disc with a ballpoint pen, for example, will easily damage the recording underneath. You need to be careful even when using a marker to write on the disc. The inks and solvents used in some markers can damage the print and lacquer overcoat on the top of the disc, and subsequently the information layer right below. Use only markers designed for writing on CDs. The important thing is to treat both sides of the disc carefully, especially the top (label) side.

Mass-producing CD-ROMs

Commercial mass-produced CDs are stamped or pressed and not burned by a laser, as many people believe (see Figure 10.1). Although a laser is used to etch data onto a glass master disc that has been coated with a photosensitive material, using a laser to directly burn discs would be impractical for the reproduction of hundreds or thousands of copies.

The steps in manufacturing CDs are as follows (use Figure 10.1 as a visual):

- **Photoresist coating**—A circular 240mm-diameter piece of polished glass 6mm thick is spin-coated with a photoresist layer about 150 microns thick and then hardened by baking at 80°C (176°F) for 30 minutes.

- **Laser recording**—A laser beam recorder (LBR) fires pulses of blue/violet laser light to expose and soften portions of the photoresist layer on the glass master.

- **Master development**—A sodium hydroxide solution is spun over the exposed glass master, which then dissolves the areas exposed to the laser, thus etching pits in the photoresist.

- **Electroforming**—The developed master is then coated with a layer of nickel alloy through a process called *electroforming*. This creates a metal master called a *father*.

- **Master separation**—The metal master father is then separated from the glass master. The father is a metal master that can be used to stamp discs, and for short runs, it may in fact be used that way. However, because the glass master is damaged when the father is separated, and because a stamper can produce only a limited number of discs before it wears out, the father often is electroformed to create several reverse-image mothers. These mothers are then subsequently electroformed to create the actual stampers. This enables many more discs to be stamped without ever having to go through the glass-mastering process again.

- **Disc-stamping operation**—A metal stamper is used in an injection molding machine to press the data image (pits and lands) into approximately 18 grams of molten (350°C or 662°F) polycarbonate plastic with a force of about 20,000psi. Normally, one disc can be pressed every 2 to 3 seconds in a modern stamping machine.

- **Metalization**—The clear stamped disc base is then sputter-coated with a thin (0.05–0.1 micron) layer of aluminum to make the surface reflective.

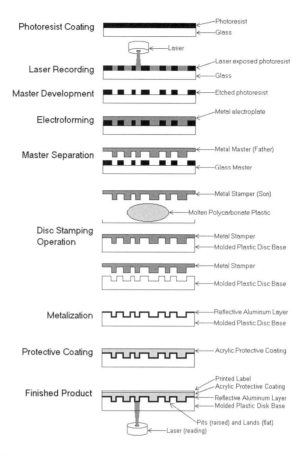

Photoresist Coating — Photoresist / Glass

Laser Recording — Laser / Laser exposed photoresist / Glass

Master Development — Etched photoresist

Electroforming — Metal electroplate

Master Separation — Metal Master (Father) / Glass Master

Disc Stamping Operation — Metal Stamper (Son) / Molten Polycarbonate Plastic / Metal Stamper / Molded Plastic Disc Base / Metal Stamper / Molded Plastic Disc Base

Metalization — Reflective Aluminum Layer / Molded Plastic Disc Base

Protective Coating — Acrylic Protective Coating

Finished Product — Printed Label / Acrylic Protective Coating / Reflective Aluminum Layer / Molded Plastic Disk Base / Pits (raised) and Lands (flat) / Laser (reading)

Figure 10.1 The CD-manufacturing process.

- **Protective coating**—The metalized disc is then spin-coated with a thin (6–7 micron) layer of acrylic lacquer, which is then cured with ultraviolet (UV) light. This protects the aluminum from oxidation.

- **Finished product**—Finally, a label is affixed or screen-printed on the disc and also cured with UV light.

This manufacturing process is identical for both data CD-ROMs and audio CDs.

Pits and Lands

Reading the information back from a disc is a matter of bouncing a low-powered laser beam off the reflective layer in the disc. The laser shines a focused beam on the underside of the disc, and a photo-sensitive receptor detects when the light is reflected back. When the light hits a land (flat spot) on the track, the light is reflected back; however, when the light hits a pit (raised bump), no light is reflected back.

As the disc rotates over the laser and receptor, the laser shines continuously while the receptor sees what is essentially a pattern of flashing light as the laser passes over pits and lands. Each time the laser passes over the edge of a pit, the light seen by the receptor changes in state from being reflected to not reflected, or vice versa. Each change in state of reflection caused by crossing the edge of a pit is translated into a 1 bit digitally. Microprocessors in the drive translate the light/dark and dark/light (pit edge) transitions into 1 bits, translate areas with no transitions into 0 bits, and then translate the bit patterns into actual data or sound.

The individual pits on a CD are 0.125 microns deep and 0.6 microns wide (1 micron equals one-millionth of a meter). Both the pits and lands vary in length from about 0.9 microns at their shortest to about 3.3 microns at their longest. The track is a spiral with 1.6 microns between adjacent turns (see Figure 10.2).

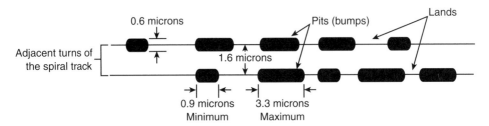

Figure 10.2   Pit, land, and track geometry on a CD.

The height of the pits above the land is especially critical as it relates to the wavelength of the laser light used when reading the disc. The pit (bump) height is exactly 1/4 of the wavelength of the laser light used to read the disc. Therefore, the light striking a land travels 1/2 of a wavelength of light further than light striking the top of a pit (1/4 + 1/4 = 1/2). This means the light reflected from a pit is 1/2 wavelength out of phase with the rest of the light being reflected from the disc. The out-of-phase waves cancel each other out, dramatically reducing the light that is reflected back and making the pit appear dark even though it is coated with the same reflective aluminum as the lands.

The read laser in a CD drive is a 780nm (nanometer) wavelength laser of about 1 milliwatt in power. The polycarbonate plastic used in the disc has a refractive index of 1.55, so light travels through the plastic 1.55 times more slowly than through the air around it. Because the frequency of the light passing through the plastic remains the same, this has the effect of shortening the wavelength inside the plastic by the same factor. Therefore, the 780nm light waves are now compressed to 780nm / 1.55, which equals 500nm. One quarter of 500nm is 125nm, which is 0.125 microns—the specified height of the pit.

Drive Mechanical Operation

A CD-ROM drive operates by using a laser to reflect light off the bottom of the disc. The reflected light is then read by a photo detector. The overall operation of a CD-ROM drive is as follows (see Figure 10.3):

1. The laser diode emits a low-energy infrared beam toward a reflecting mirror.

2. The servo motor, on command from the microprocessor, positions the beam onto the correct track on the CD-ROM by moving the reflecting mirror.

3. When the beam hits the disc, its refracted light is gathered and focused through the first lens beneath the platter, bounced off the mirror, and sent toward the beam splitter.

4. The beam splitter directs the returning laser light toward another focusing lens.

5. The last lens directs the light beam to a photo detector that converts the light into electric impulses.

6. These incoming impulses are decoded by the microprocessor and sent along to the host computer as data.

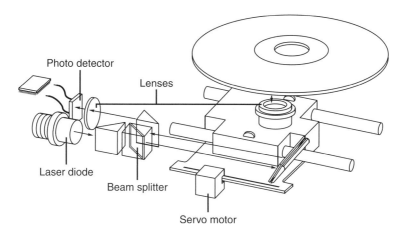

Figure 10.3   Typical components inside a CD-ROM drive.

When first introduced, CD-ROM drives were too expensive for widespread adoption. In addition, drive manufacturers were slow in adopting standards, causing a lag time for the production of CD-ROM titles. Without a wide base of software to drive the industry, acceptance was slow.

Although Philips introduced the first CD-ROM drive in 1985, most other drive manufacturers didn't introduce CD-ROM drives until 1987, when Microsoft introduced Bookshelf, its first CD-ROM software title. In 1988, Microsoft and many other companies started releasing their larger applications on CD-ROMs, which made installation much easier and quicker than with floppies. It was during that time frame that CD-ROM drives first started appearing on desktop systems.

Unfortunately, the large physical size, heavy weight, and high power consumption of the early CD-ROM drives prevented their installation in laptops, although in some cases they could be connected externally. In fact, the first laptop with an internal CD-ROM drive was the IBM ThinkPad 755CD, introduced in 1994. The first laptop with a DVD-ROM drive was the IBM ThinkPad 770, introduced in 1997.

With many systems no longer including floppy drives, virtually all software today is supplied on CD- or DVD-ROM, even if the disc doesn't contain data representing a tenth of its potential capacity. For large programs, the advantage is obvious. The Windows XP operating system, for example, would require more than 400 floppy disks, an amount certainly nobody would want to deal with.

Track and Sectors

The pits are stamped into a single spiral track with a spacing of 1.6 microns between turns, corresponding to a track density of 625 turns per millimeter, or 15,875 turns per inch. This equates to a total of 22,188 turns for a normal 74-minute (650MiB) disc. The disc is divided into six main areas (discussed here and shown in Figure 10.4):

- **Hub clamp area**—The hub clamp area is just that: a part of the disc where the hub mechanism in the drive can grip the disc. No data or information is stored in that area.

- **Power calibration area (PCA)**—This area is found only on writable (CD-R/RW) discs and is used only by recordable drives to determine the laser power necessary to perform an optimum burn. A single CD-R or CD-RW disc can be tested this way up to 99 times.

- **Program memory area (PMA)**—This area is found only on writable (CD-R/RW) discs and is the place where the TOC (table of contents) is temporarily written until a recording session is closed. After the session is closed, the TOC information is written to the lead-in area.

- **Lead-in**—The lead-in area contains the disc (or session) TOC in the Q subcode channel. The TOC contains the start addresses and lengths of all tracks (songs or data), the total length of the program (data) area, and information about the individual recorded sessions. A single lead-in area exists on a disc recorded all at once (Disc At Once or DAO mode), or a lead-in area starts each session on a multisession disc. The lead-in takes up 4,500 sectors on the disc (1 minute if measured in time, or about 9.2MB worth of data). The lead-in also indicates whether the disc is multisession and what the next writable address on the disc is (if the disc isn't closed).

- **Program (data) area**—This area of the disc starts at a radius of 25mm from the center.

- **Lead-out**—The lead-out marks the end of the program (data) area or the end of the recording session on a multisession disc. No actual data is written in the lead-out; it is simply a marker. The first lead-out on a disc (or the only one if it is a single session or Disk At Once recording) is 6,750 sectors long (1.5 minutes if measured in time, or about 13.8MB worth of data). If the disc is a multisession disc, any subsequent lead-outs are 2,250 sectors long (0.5 minutes in time, or about 4.6MB worth of data).

The hub clamp, lead-in, program, and lead-out areas are found on all CDs, whereas only recordable CDs (such as CD-Rs and CD-RWs) have the additional power calibration area and program memory area at the start of the disc.

Figure 10.4 shows these areas in actual relative scale as they appear on a disc.

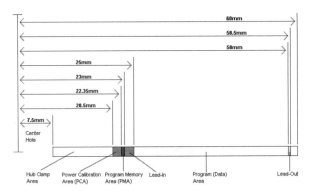

Figure 10.4   Areas on a CD (side view).

Officially, the spiral track of a standard CD-DA or CD-ROM disc starts with the lead-in area and ends at the finish of the lead-out area, which is 58.5mm from the center of the disc, or 1.5mm from the outer edge. This single spiral track is about 5.77 kilometers or 3.59 miles long. An interesting fact is that in a 56× constant angular velocity (CAV) drive, when reading the outer part of the track, the data moves at an actual speed of 162.8 miles per hour (262km/h) past the laser. What is more amazing is that even when the data is traveling at that speed, the laser pickup can accurately read bits (pit/land transitions) spaced as little as only 0.9 microns or 35.4 millionths of an inch apart!

Table 10.1 shows some of the basic information about the two main CD capacities (74 and 80 minutes). The CD standard originally was created around the 74-minute disc; the 80-minute versions were added later and basically stretch the standard by tightening up the track spacing within the limitations of the original specification. It is possible that a poorly performing or worn-out drive may have trouble reading the 80-minute discs.

Table 10.1   CD-ROM Technical Parameters

Advertised CD length (minutes)	74	80
Advertised CD capacity (MiB)	650	700
1× read speed (m/sec)	1.3	1.3
Laser wavelength (nm)	780	780
Numerical aperture (lens)	0.45	0.45
Media refractive index	1.55	1.55
Track (turn) spacing (microns)	1.6	1.48
Turns per mm	625	676
Turns per inch	15,875	17,162
Total track length (m)	5,772	6,240
Total track length (feet)	18,937	20,472
Total track length (miles)	3.59	3.88
Pit width (microns)	0.6	0.6
Pit depth (microns)	0.125	0.125
Min. nominal pit length (microns)	0.90	0.90
Max. nominal pit length (microns)	3.31	3.31
Lead-in inner radius (mm)	23	23
Data zone inner radius (mm)	25	25
Data zone outer radius (mm)	58	58
Lead-out outer radius (mm)	58.5	58.5
Data zone width (mm)	33	33
Total track area width (mm)	35.5	35.5
Max. rotating speed 1× CLV (rpm)	540	540
Min. rotating speed 1× CLV (rpm)	212	212
Track revolutions (data zone)	20,625	22,297
Track revolutions (total)	22,188	23,986

B = byte (8 bits)
CLV = constant linear velocity
KB = kilobyte (1,000 bytes)
KiB = kibibyte (1,024 bytes, or 1 kilobinary-byte)
MB = megabyte (1,000,000 bytes)
MiB = mebibyte (1,048,576 bytes, or 1 megabinary-byte)

m = meters
mm = millimeters (thousandths of a meter)
nm = nanometers (billionths of a meter)
microns = micrometers (millionths of a meter)
rpm = revolutions per minute

The spiral track is divided into sectors that are stored at the rate of 75 per second. On a disc that can hold a total of 74 minutes of information, that results in a maximum of 333,000 sectors. Each sector is then divided into 98 individual frames of information. Each frame contains 33 bytes, of which 24 bytes are audio data, 1 byte contains subcode information, and 8 bytes are used for parity/ECC (error correcting code) information. Table 10.2 shows the sector, frame, and audio data calculations.

Table 10.2   CD-ROM Sector, Frame, and Audio Data Information

Advertised CD length (minutes)	74	80
Sectors/second	75	75
Frames/sector	98	98
Number of sectors	333,000	360,000
Sector length (mm)	17.33	17.33
Byte length (microns)	5.36	5.36
Bit length (microns)	0.67	0.67
Each Frame		
Subcode bytes	1	1
Data bytes	24	24
Q+P parity bytes	8	8
Total bytes/frame	33	33
Audio Data		
Audio sampling rate (Hz)	44,100	44,100
Samples per Hz (stereo)	2	2
Sample size (bytes)	2	2
Audio bytes per second	176,400	176,400
Sectors per second	75	75
Audio bytes per sector	2,352	2,352
Each Audio Sector (98 Frames)		
Q+P parity bytes	784	784
Subcode bytes	98	98
Audio data bytes	2,352	2,352
Bytes/sector RAW (unencoded)	3,234	3,234

Hz = hertz (cycles per second)
mm = millimeters (thousandths of a meter)
microns = micrometers (millionths of a meter)

Sampling

When music is recorded on a CD, it is sampled at a rate of 44,100 times per second (Hz). Each music sample has a separate left and right channel (stereo) component, and each channel component is digitally converted into a 16-bit number. This allows for a resolution of 65,536 possible values, which represents the amplitude of the sound wave for that channel at that moment.

The sampling rate determines the range of audio frequencies that can be represented in the digital recording. The more samples of a wave that are taken per second, the closer the sampled result will be to the original. The Nyquist theorem (originally published by American physicist Harry Nyquist in 1928) states that the sampling rate must be at least twice the highest frequency present in the sample to reconstruct the original signal accurately. That explains why Philips and Sony intentionally chose the 44,100Hz sampling rate when developing the CD; that rate could be used to accurately reproduce sounds of up to 20,000Hz, which is the upper limit of human hearing.

Today with the arrival of the DVD-audio and Super Audio CD standard, this sampling frequency has been raised significantly to enable more accurate reproduction of the actual recording. DVD-audio defines up to six channels, with 24-bit resolution per channel and a 96,000Hz sample rate. Super Audio CD (SACD) also uses up to six channels but has a different sampling scheme; here, a 1-bit resolution is used at a 2,800,000Hz, or 2.8MHz, sampling rate.

But getting back to the data as stored on the CD you can see that audio sectors combine 98 frames of 33 bytes each, which results in a total of 3,234 bytes per sector, of which only 2,352 bytes are actual audio data. Besides the 98 subcode bytes per frame, the other 784 bytes are used for parity and error correction.

Subcodes

Subcode bytes enable the drive to find songs (which are confusingly also called *tracks*) along the spiral track and also contain or convey additional information about the disc in general. The subcode bytes are stored as 1 byte per frame, which gives 98 subcode bytes for each sector. Two of these bytes are used as start block and end block markers, leaving 96 bytes of subcode information. These are then divided into eight 12-byte subcode blocks, each of which is assigned a letter designation P–W. Each subcode channel can hold about 31.97MB of data across the disc, which is about 4% of the capacity of an audio disc. The interesting thing about the subcodes is that the data is woven continuously throughout the disc; in other words, subcode data is contained piecemeal in every sector on the disc.

The P and Q subcode blocks are used on all discs, and the R–W subcodes are used only on CD+G (graphics) or CD TEXT–type discs.

The P subcode is used to identify the start of the tracks on the CD. The Q subcode contains a multitude of information, including the following:

- **Whether the sector data is audio (CD-DA) or data (CD-ROM)**—This prevents most players from trying to "play" CD-ROM data discs, which might damage speakers due to the resulting noise that would occur.

- **Whether the audio data is two or four channel**—Four channel is rarely, if ever, used.

- **Whether digital copying is permitted**—PC-based CD-R and CD-RW drives ignore this; it was instituted to prevent copying to DAT (digital audio tape) or home audio CD-R/RW drives.

- **Whether the music is recorded with preemphasis**—This is a hiss- or noise-reduction technique.

- **The track (song) layout on the disc.**

- **The track (song) number.**

- The minutes, seconds, and frame number from the start of the track (song).
- A countdown during an intertrack (intersong) pause.
- The minutes, seconds, and frames from the start of the first track (song).
- The barcode of the CD.
- The International Standard Recording Code (ISRC)—This is unique to each track (song) on the disc.

The R–W subcodes are used on CD+G (graphics) discs to contain graphics and text. This enables a limited amount of graphics and text to be displayed while the music is being played. These same subcodes are used on CD TEXT discs to store disc- and track-related information that is added to standard audio CDs for playback on compatible CD audio players. The CD TEXT information is stored as ASCII characters in the R–W channels in the lead-in and program areas of a CD. On a CD TEXT disc, the lead-in area subcodes contain text information about the entire disc, such as the album, track (song) titles, and artist names. The program area subcodes, on the other hand, contain text information for the current track (song), including track title, composer, performers, and so on. The CD TEXT data is repeated throughout each track to reduce the delay in retrieving the data.

CD TEXT–compatible players typically have a text display to show this information, ranging from a simple one- or two-line, 20-character display—such as on many newer radio broadcast data system (RBDS) automobile radio/CD players—up to 21 lines of 40-color, alphanumeric or graphics characters on home or computer-based players. The specification also allows for future additional data, such as Joint Photographics Expert Group (JPEG) images. Interactive menus also can be used for the selection of text for display.

Handling Read Errors

Handling errors when reading a disc was a big part of the original Red Book CD standard. CDs use parity and interleaving techniques called *cross-interleave Reed-Solomon code (CIRC)* to minimize the effects of errors on the disk. This works at the frame level. When being stored, the 24 data bytes in each frame are first run through a Reed-Solomon encoder to produce a 4-byte parity code called "Q" parity, which then is added to the 24 data bytes. The resulting 28 bytes are then run though another encoder that uses a different scheme to produce an additional 4-byte parity value called "P" parity. These are added to the 28 bytes from the previous encoding, resulting in 32 bytes (24 of the original data, plus the Q and P parity bytes). An additional byte of subcode (tracking) information is then added, resulting in 33 bytes total for each frame. Note that the P and Q parity bytes are not related to the P and Q subcodes mentioned earlier.

To minimize the effects of a scratch or physical defect that would damage adjacent frames, several interleaves are added before the frames are actually written. Parts of 109 frames are cross-interleaved (stored in different frames and sectors) using delay lines. This scrambling decreases the likelihood of a scratch or defect affecting adjacent data because the data is actually written out of sequence.

With audio CDs and CD-ROMs, the CIRC scheme can correct errors up to 3,874 bits long (which would be 2.6mm in track length). In addition, for audio CDs, only the CIRC can also conceal (through interpolation) errors up to 13,282 bits long (8.9mm in track length). *Interpolation* is the process in which the data is estimated or averaged to restore what is missing. That would, of course, be unacceptable on a CD-ROM data disc, so this applies only to audio discs. The Red Book CD standard defines the *block error rate (BLER)* as the number of frames (98 per sector) per second that have any bad bits (averaged over 10 seconds) and requires that this be less than 220. This allows a maximum of up to about 3% of the frames to have errors, and yet the disc will still be functional.

An additional layer of error detection and correction circuitry is the key difference between audio CD players and CD-ROM drives. Audio CDs convert the digital information stored on the disc into analog signals for a stereo amplifier to process. In this scheme, some imprecision is acceptable because it would be virtually impossible to hear in the music. CD-ROMs, however, can't tolerate any imprecision. Each bit of data must be read accurately. For this reason, CD-ROM discs have a great deal of additional ECC (error correcting code) information written to them, along with the actual stored information. The ECC can detect and correct most minor errors, improving the reliability and precision to levels that are acceptable for data storage.

In the case of an audio CD, missing data can be interpolated; that is, the information follows a predictable pattern that enables the drive to guess the missing values. For example, if three values are stored on an audio disc, say 10, 13, and 20 appearing in a series, and the middle value is missing— because of damage or dirt on the CD's surface—you could interpolate a middle value of 15, which is midway between 10 and 20. Although this might not be exactly correct, in the case of audio recording, it will probably not be noticeable to the listener. If those same three values appear on a CD-ROM in an executable program, there is no way to guess at the correct value for the middle sample. Interpolation can't work because executable program instructions or data must be exact; otherwise, the program will crash or improperly read data needed for a calculation. Using the previous example with a CD-ROM running an executable program, to guess 15 is not merely slightly off, it is completely wrong.

In a CD-ROM on which data is stored instead of audio information, additional information is added to each sector to detect and correct errors as well as to identify the location of data sectors more accurately. To accomplish this, 304 bytes are taken from the 2,352 that originally were used for audio data and are instead used for sync (synchronizing bits), ID (identification bits), ECC, and EDC information. This leaves 2,048 bytes for actual user data in each sector. Just as when reading an audio CD, on a 1× (standard speed) CD-ROM, sectors are read at a constant speed of 75 per second. This results in a standard CD-ROM transfer rate of 2,048 bytes × 75, or 153,600 bytes per second, which is expressed as either 153.6KBps or 150KiBps.

Note

Some of the copy-protection schemes used on audio CDs intentionally interfere with the audio data and CIRC information in such a way as to make the disc appear to play correctly, but copies of the audio files or of the entire disc will be filled with noise. Copy protection for both audio and data CDs is discussed in more detail later in this chapter, including how you can find software that can circumvent it.

CD Capacity

Because a typical disc can hold a maximum of 74 minutes of data, and each second contains 75 blocks of 2,048 bytes each, you can calculate the absolute maximum storage capacity of a CD-ROM at 681,984,000 bytes—rounded as 682MB (megabytes) or 650MiB (mebibytes). Table 10.3 shows the structure and layout of each sector on a CD-ROM on which data is stored.

Table 10.3   CD-ROM Sector Information and Capacity

Each Data Sector (Mode 1)	74 Minute	80 Minute
Q+P parity bytes	784	784
Subcode bytes	98	98
Sync bytes	12	12
Header bytes	8	8
ECC/EDC bytes	284	284
Data bytes	2,048	2,048
Bytes/sector RAW (unencoded)	3,234	3,234
Actual CD-ROM Data Capacity		
B	681,984,000	737,280,000
KiB	666,000	720,000
KB	681,984	737,280
MiB	650.39	703.13
MB	681.98	737.28

B = byte (8 bits)
KB = kilobyte (1,000 bytes)
KiB = kibibyte (1,024 bytes)
MB = megabyte (1,000,000 bytes)
MiB = mebibyte (1,048,576 bytes)
ECC = error correcting code
EDC = error detection code

This information assumes the data is stored in Mode 1 format, which is used on virtually all data discs. You can learn more about the Mode 1/Mode 2 formats in the section on the Yellow Book and XA standards later in this chapter.

With data sectors, you can see that out of 3,234 actual bytes per sector, only 2,048 are actual CD-ROM user data. Most of the 1,186 other bytes are used for the intensive error detection and correction schemes to ensure error-free performance.

Data Encoding on the Disc

The final part of how data is actually written to the CD is very interesting. After all 98 frames are composed for a sector (whether audio or data), the information is then run through a final encoding process called EFM (8 to 14 modulation). This scheme takes each byte (8 bits) and converts it into a 14-bit value for storage. The 14-bit conversion codes are designed so that there are never fewer than two or more than ten adjacent 0 bits. This is a form of run length limited (RLL) encoding called *RLL 2,10* (RLL *x,y*, where *x* equals the minimum and *y* equals the maximum run of 0s). This is designed to prevent long strings of 0s, which could more easily be misread, as well as to limit the minimum and maximum frequency of transitions actually placed on the recording media. With as few as two or as many as ten 0 bits separating 1 bits in the recording, the minimum distance between 1s is three bit time intervals (usually referred to as *3T*), and the maximum spacing between 1s is 11 time intervals (*11T*).

Because some of the EFM codes start and end with a 1 or more than five 0s, three additional bits called *merge bits* are added between each 14-bit EFM value written to the disc. The merge bits usually are 0s but might contain a 1 if necessary to break a long string of adjacent 0s formed by the adjacent 14-bit EFM values. In addition to the now 17 bits created for each byte (EFM plus merge bits), a 24-bit sync word (plus three more merge bits) is added to the beginning of each frame. This results in a total of 588 bits (73.5 bytes) actually being stored on the disc for each frame. Multiply this for 98 frames per sector, and you have 7,203 bytes actually being stored on the disc to represent each sector. A 74-minute disc, therefore, really has something like 2.4GB of actual data being written, which after being fully decoded and stripped of error correcting codes and other information, results in about 682MB (650MiB) of actual user data.

The calculations for EFM-encoded frames and sectors are shown in Table 10.4.

Table 10.4   EFM-Encoded Data Calculations

EFM-Encoded Frames	74 Minute	80 Minute
Sync word bits	24	24
Subcode bits	14	14
Data bits	336	336
Q+P parity bits	112	112
Merge bits	102	102
EFM bits per frame	588	588
EFM-Encoded Sectors		
EFM bits per sector	57,624	57,624
EFM bytes per sector	7,203	7,203
Total EFM data on disc (MB)	2,399	2,593

B = byte (8 bits)
KB = kilobyte (1,000 bytes)
KiB = kibibyte (1,024 bytes)
MB = megabyte (1,000,000 bytes)
MiB = mebibyte (1,048,576 bytes)
EFM = 8 to 14 modulation

To put this into perspective, see Table 10.5 for an example of how familiar data would actually be encoded when written to a CD. As an example, I'll use the letters *N* and *O* as they would be written on the disk. The table shows the digitally encoded representations of these letters.

Table 10.5 EFM Data Encoding on a CD

Character	N	O
ASCII decimal code	78	79
ASCII hexadecimal code	4E	4F
ASCII binary code	01001110	01001111
EFM code	00010001000100	00100001000100

ASCII = American Standard Code for Information Interchange
EFM = 8 to 14 modulation

Figure 10.5 shows how the encoded data would actually appear as pits and lands stamped into a CD.

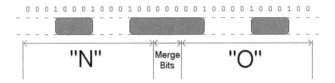

Figure 10.5 EFM data physically represented as pits and lands on a CD.

The edges of the pits are translated into the binary 1 bits. As you can see, each 14-bit grouping is used to represent a byte of actual EFM-encoded data on the disc, and each 14-bit EFM code is separated by three merge bits (all 0s in this example). The three pits produced by this example are 4T (four transitions), 8T, and 4T long. The string of 1s and 0s on the top of the figure represents how the actual data would be read; note that a 1 is read wherever a pit-to-land transition occurs. It is interesting to note that this drawing is actually to scale, meaning the pits (raised bumps) would be about that long and wide relative to each other. If you could use a microscope to view the disc, this is what the word *NO* would look like as actually recorded.

DVD Technology

DVD stands for *digital versatile disc* and in simplest terms is a high-capacity CD. In fact, every DVD-ROM drive *is* a CD-ROM drive; that is, it can read CDs as well as DVDs (many standalone DVD players can't read CD-R or CD-RW discs, however). DVD uses the same optical technology as CD, with the main difference being higher density. The DVD standard dramatically increases the storage capacity of, and therefore the useful applications for, CD-ROM-sized discs. A CD-ROM can hold a maximum of about 737MB (80-minute disc) of data, which might sound like a lot but is simply not enough for many up-and-coming applications, especially where the use of video is concerned. DVDs, on the other hand, can hold up to 4.7GB (single layer) or 8.5GB (dual layer) on a single side of the disc, which is more than 11 1/2 times greater than a CD. Double-sided DVDs can hold up to twice that amount, but are a rarity, partly because it is cumbersome to manually flip the disc over to read the other side, especially when this DVD holds a movie that you are watching.

Up to two layers of information can be recorded to DVDs, with an initial storage capacity of 4.7GB of digital information on a single-sided, single-layer disc—a disk that is the same overall diameter and thickness of a current CD-ROM. With Moving Picture Experts Group–standard 2 (MPEG-2) compression, that's enough to contain approximately 133 minutes of video, which is enough for a full-length, full-screen, full-motion feature film—including three channels of CD-quality audio and four channels of subtitles. Using both layers, a single-sided disc could easily hold 240 minutes of video or more. This initial capacity is no coincidence; the creation of DVD was driven by the film industry, which has long sought a storage medium cheaper and more durable than videotape.

Note

It is important to know the difference between the DVD-Video and DVD-ROM standards. DVD-Video discs contain only video programs and are intended to be played in a DVD player connected to a television and possibly an audio system. DVD-ROM is a data storage medium intended for use by PCs and other types of computers. The distinction is similar to that between an audio CD and a CD-ROM. Computers might be capable of playing audio CDs as well as CD-ROMs, but dedicated audio CD players can't use a CD-ROM's data tracks. Likewise, computer DVD drives can play DVD-Video discs (with MPEG-2 decoding in either hardware or software), but DVD video players can't access data on a DVD-ROM. This is the reason you must select the type of DVD you are trying to create when you make a writable or rewritable DVD.

The initial application for DVDs was as an upgrade for CDs as well as a replacement for prerecorded videotapes. DVDs can be rented or purchased like prerecorded VCR tapes, but they offer much higher resolution and quality with greater content. As with CDs, which initially were designed only for music, DVDs have since developed into a wider range of uses, including computer data storage and high-quality audio.

DVD History

DVD had a somewhat rocky start. During 1995, two competing standards for high-capacity CD-ROM drives were being developed to compete with each other for future market share. One standard, called Multimedia CD, was introduced and backed by Philips and Sony, whereas a competing standard, called the Super Density (SD) disc, was introduced and backed by Toshiba, Time Warner, and several other companies. If both standards had hit the market as is, consumers as well as entertainment and software producers would have been in a quandary over which one to choose.

Fearing a repeat of the Beta/VHS situation that occurred in the videotape market, several organizations, including the Hollywood Video Disc Advisory Group and the Computer Industry Technical Working Group, banded together to form a consortium to develop and control the DVD standard. The consortium insisted on a single format for the industry and refused to endorse either competing proposal. With this incentive, both groups worked out an agreement on a single, new, high-capacity CD-type disc in September of 1995. The new standard combined elements of both previously proposed standards and was called *DVD*, which originally stood for *digital video disc*, but has since been changed to *digital versatile disc*. The single DVD standard has avoided a confusing replay of the VHS versus Beta tape fiasco for movie fans and has given the software, hardware, and movie industries a single, unified standard to support.

After agreeing on copy protection and other items, the DVD-ROM and DVD-Video standards were officially announced in late 1996. Players, drives, and discs were announced in January 1997 at the Consumer Electronics Show (CES) in Las Vegas, and the players and discs became available in March of 1997. The initial players were about $1,000 each. Only 36 movies were released in the first wave, and they were available only in seven cities nationwide (Chicago, Dallas, Los Angeles, New York, San Francisco, Seattle, and Washington, D.C.) until August 1997 when the full release began. After a somewhat rocky start (much had to do with agreements on copy protection to get the movie companies to go along, and there was a lack of titles available in the beginning), DVD has become an incredible success. The relatively recent proliferation of rewritable DVD drives and media has also helped drive the growth of DVDs.

The first laptop with an internal DVD-ROM drive was the IBM ThinkPad 770, released in October 1997. Although it was one of the fastest laptops available at the time, the 200MHz or 233MHz Pentium processor used in the system was far too slow to handle software-based DVD video decoding. To play DVD videos, the system required an expensive optional hardware MPEG-2 decoder (which IBM called the "DVD and Enhanced Video Adapter") in order to actually play DVD movies. Desktop systems slower than 400MHz required similar hardware-based decoders as well. It wasn't until processors ran faster than about 400MHz that software decoding became possible, at which point adding an expensive hardware MPEG-2 decoder became unnecessary.

The organization that controls the DVD video standard is called the DVD Forum and was founded by 10 companies, including Hitachi, Matsushita, Mitsubishi, Victor, Pioneer, Sony, Toshiba, Philips, Thomson, and Time Warner. Since its founding in April 1997, more than 230 companies have joined the forum. Because it is a public forum, anybody can join and attend the meetings; the site for the DVD Forum is www.dvdforum.org. Because the DVD Forum was unable to agree on a universal record-able format, its members who are primarily responsible for CD and DVD technology (Philips, Sony, and others) split off to form the DVD+RW Alliance in June 2000; their site is www.dvdrw.com. They have since introduced the DVD+RW format, which is the fastest, most flexible, and backward-compatible recordable DVD format. DVD+-RW drives first became available for laptops in 2003, and they are rapidly replacing combo DVD/CD-RW drives as the preferred type of internal optical storage.

DVD Construction and Technology

DVD technology is similar to CD technology. Both use the same size (120mm diameter, 1.2mm thick, with a 15mm hole in the center) discs with pits and lands stamped in a polycarbonate base. Unlike a CD, though, DVDs can have two layers of recordings on one side—a dual-layer DVD—or can be double-sided, with both sides containing a recording layer. Each layer is separately stamped, and they are all bonded together to make the final 1.2mm-thick disc. The manufacturing process is largely the same, with the exception that each layer on each side is stamped from a separate piece of polycarbonate plastic and then both sides are bonded together to form the completed disc. The main difference between CD and DVD is that DVD is a higher-density recording read by a laser with a shorter wavelength, focused more closely to the disc, which enables more information to be stored.

As with CDs, each layer is stamped or molded with a single physical track in a spiral configuration starting from the inside of the disc and spiraling outward. The disc rotates counterclockwise (as viewed from the bottom), and each spiral track contains pits (bumps) and lands (flat portions), just as on a CD. Each recorded layer is coated with a thin film of metal to reflect the laser light. The outer layer has a thinner coating to allow the light to pass through to read the inner layer. If the disc is single-sided, a label can be placed on top; otherwise, if it's double-sided, only a small ring near the center provides room for labeling.

Just as with a CD, reading the information back on a DVD is a matter of bouncing a low-powered laser beam off one of the reflective layers in the disc. The laser shines a focused beam on the underside of the disc, and a photosensitive receptor detects when the light is reflected back. When the light hits a land (flat spot) on the track, it is reflected back; when the light hits a pit (raised bump), the phase differential between the projected and reflected light causes the waves to cancel, and no light is reflected back.

The individual pits on a DVD are 0.105 microns deep and 0.4 microns wide. Both the pits and lands vary in length from about 0.4 microns at their shortest to about 1.9 microns at their longest (on single-layer discs). See the section "CD-ROM Construction and Technology" earlier in this chapter for more information on how the pits and lands are read and converted into actual data, as well as how the drives physically and mechanically work.

DVDs use the same optical laser-read pit and land storage that CDs do. The greater capacity is made possible by several factors, including the following:

- A 2.25 times smaller pit length (0.9–0.4 microns)
- A 2.16 times reduced track pitch (1.6–0.74 microns)
- A slightly larger data area on the disc (8,605–8,759 square millimeters)
- About 1.06 times more efficient channel bit modulation
- About 1.32 times more efficient error correcting code
- About 1.06 times less sector overhead (2,048/2,352–2,048/2,064 bytes)

The DVD disc's pits and lands are much smaller and closer together than those on a CD, allowing the same physical-sized platter to hold much more information. Figure 10.6 shows how the grooved tracks with pits and lands are just over four times as dense on a DVD as compared to a CD.

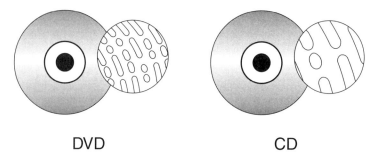

DVD   CD

Figure 10.6 DVD data markings (pits and lands) versus those of a standard CD.

DVD drives use a shorter wavelength laser to read these smaller pits and lands. A DVD can have nearly double the initial capacity by using two separate layers on one side of a disc and double it again by using both sides of the disc. The second data layer is written to a separate substrate below the first layer, which is then made semireflective to enable the laser to penetrate to the substrate beneath it. By focusing the laser on one of the two layers, the drive can read roughly twice the amount of data from the same surface area.

DVD Tracks and Sectors

The pits are stamped into a single spiral track (per layer) with a spacing of 0.74 microns between turns, corresponding to a track density of 1,351 turns per millimeter or 34,324 turns per inch. This equates to a total of 49,324 turns and a total track length of 11.8km or 7.35 miles in length. The track is composed of sectors, with each sector containing 2,048 bytes of data. The disc is divided into four main areas:

- **Hub clamp area**—The hub clamp area is just that, a part of the disc where the hub mechanism in the drive can grip the disc. No data or information is stored in this area.
- **Lead-in zone**—The lead-in zone contains buffer zones, reference code, and mainly a control data zone with information about the disc. The control data zone consists of 16 sectors of information repeated 192 times for a total of 3,072 sectors. Contained in the 16 (repeated) sectors is information about the disc, including disc category and version number, disc size and maximum transfer rate, disc structure, recording density, and data zone allocation. The entire lead-in

zone takes up to 196,607 (2FFFFh) sectors on the disc. Unlike CDs, the basic structure of all sectors on a DVD is the same. The buffer zone sectors in the lead-in zone have all 00h (zero hex) recorded for data.

■ **Data zone**—The data zone contains the video, audio, or other data on the disc and starts at sector number 196,608 (30000h). The total number of sectors in the data zone can be up to 2,292,897 per layer for single-layer discs.

■ **Lead-out (or middle) zone**—The lead-out zone marks the end of the data zone. The sectors in the lead-out zone all contain zero (00h) for data. This is called the *middle zone* if the disc is dual layer and is recorded in opposite track path (OPT) mode, in which the second layer starts from the outside of the disc and is read in the opposite direction from the first layer.

The center hole in a DVD is 15mm in diameter, so it has a radius of 7.5mm from the center of the disc. From the edge of the center hole to a point at a radius of 16.5mm is the hub clamp area. The lead-in zone starts at a radius of 22mm from the center of the disc. The data zone starts at a radius of 24mm from the center and is followed by the lead-out (or middle) zone at 58mm. The disc track officially ends at 58.5mm, which is followed by a 1.5mm blank area to the edge of the disc. Figure 10.7 shows these zones in actual relative scale as they appear on a DVD.

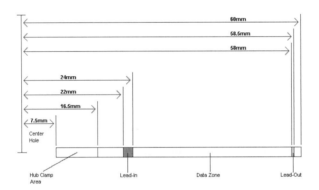

Figure 10.7   Areas on a DVD (side view).

Officially, the spiral track of a standard DVD starts with the lead-in zone and ends at the finish of the lead-out zone. This single spiral track is about 11.84 kilometers or 7.35 miles long. An interesting fact is that in a 20× CAV drive, when the outer part of the track is being read, the data moves at an actual speed of 156 miles per hour (251km/h) past the laser. What is more amazing is that even when the data is traveling at that speed, the laser pickup can accurately read bits (pit/land transitions) spaced as little as only 0.4 microns or 15.75 millionths of an inch apart!

DVDs come in both single- and dual-layer as well as single- and double-sided versions. The double-sided discs are essentially the same as two single-sided discs glued together back to back, but subtle differences do exist between the single- and dual-layer discs. Table 10.6 shows some of the basic information about DVD technology, including single- and dual-layer DVDs. The dual-layer versions are recorded with slightly longer pits, resulting in slightly less information being stored in each layer.

Table 10.6   DVD Technical Parameters

DVD Type	Single Layer	Dual Layer
1× read speed (m/sec)	3.49	3.84
Laser wavelength (nm)	650	650
Numerical aperture (lens)	0.60	0.60
Media refractive index	1.55	1.55
Track (turn) spacing (microns)	0.74	0.74
Turns per mm	1,351	1,351
Turns per inch	34,324	34,324
Total track length (m)	11,836	11,836
Total track length (feet)	38,832	38,832
Total track length (miles)	7.35	7.35
Media bit cell length (nm)	133.3	146.7
Media byte length (microns)	1.07	1.17
Media sector length (mm)	5.16	5.68
Pit width (microns)	0.40	0.40
Pit depth (microns)	0.105	0.105
Min. nominal pit length (microns)	0.40	0.44
Max. nominal pit length (microns)	1.87	2.05
Lead-in inner radius (mm)	22	22
Data zone inner radius (mm)	24	24
Data zone outer radius (mm)	58	58
Lead-out outer radius (mm)	58.5	58.5
Data zone width (mm)	34	34
Data zone area (mm2)	8,759	8,759
Total track area width (mm)	36.5	36.5
Max. rotating speed 1× CLV (rpm)	1,515	1,667
Min. rotating speed 1× CLV (rpm)	570	627
Track revolutions (data zone)	45,946	45,946
Track revolutions (total)	49,324	49,324
Data zone sectors per layer per side	2,292,897	2,083,909
Sectors per second	676	676
Media data rate (Mbps)	26.15625	26.15625

(continues)

Table 10.6   Continued

DVD Type	Single Layer	Dual Layer
Media bits per sector	38,688	38,688
Media bytes per sector	4,836	4,836
Interface data rate (Mbps)	11.08	11.08
Interface data bits per sector	16,384	16,384
Interface data bytes per sector	2,048	2,048
Track time per layer (minutes)	56.52	51.37
Track time per side (minutes)	56.52	102.74
MPEG-2 video per layer (minutes)	133	121
MPEG-2 video per side (minutes)	133	242

B = byte (8 bits)

KB = kilobyte (1,000 bytes)

KiB = kibibyte (1,024 bytes)

MB = megabyte (1,000,000 bytes)

MiB = mebibyte (1,048,576 bytes)

GB = gigabyte (1,000,000,000 bytes)

GiB = gibibyte (1,073,741,824 bytes)

m = meters

mm = millimeters (thousandths of a meter)

mm2 = square millimeters

microns = micrometers (millionths of a meter)

nm = nanometers (billionths of a meter)

rpm = revolutions per minute

ECC = error correcting code

EDC = error detection code

CLV = constant linear velocity

CAV = constant angular velocity

As you can see from the information in Table 10.6, the spiral track is divided into sectors that are stored at the rate of 676 per second. Each sector contains 2,048 bytes of data.

When being written, the sectors are first formatted into data frames of 2,064 bytes, of which 2,048 are data, 4 bytes contain ID information, 2 bytes contain ID error detection (IED) codes, 6 bytes contain copyright information, and 4 bytes contain EDC for the frame.

The data frames then have ECC information added to convert them into ECC frames. Each ECC frame contains the 2,064-byte data frame plus 182 parity outer (PO) bytes and 120 parity inner (PI) bytes, for a total of 2,366 bytes for each ECC frame.

Finally, the ECC frames are converted into physical sectors on the disc. This is done by taking 91 bytes at a time from the ECC frame and converting them into recorded bits via 8 to 16 modulation. In this process, each byte (8 bits) is converted into a special 16-bit value, which is selected from a table. These values are designed using an RLL 2,10 scheme, which is designed so that the encoded information never has a run of fewer than two or more than ten 0 bits in a row. After each group of 91 bytes is converted via the 8 to 16 modulation, 320 bits (4 bytes) of synchronization information are added. After the entire ECC frame is converted into a physical sector, 4,836 total bytes are stored.

Table 10.7 shows the sector, frame, and audio data calculations.

Table 10.7   DVD Data Frame, ECC Frame, and Physical Sector Layout and Information

DVD Data Frame

Identification data (ID) bytes	4
ID error detection code (IED) bytes	2
Copyright info (CI) bytes	6
Data bytes	2,048
Error detection code (EDC)	4
Data frame total bytes	2,064

DVD ECC Frame

Data frame total bytes	2,064
Parity outer (PO) bytes	182
Parity inner (PI) bytes	120
ECC frame total bytes	2,366

DVD Media Physical Sectors

ECC frame bytes	2,366
8 to 16 modulation bits	37,856
Synchronization bits	832
Total encoded media bits/sector	38,688
Total encoded media bytes/sector	4,836
Original data bits/sector	16,384
Original data bytes/sector	2,048
Ratio of original to media data	2.36

Unlike CDs, DVDs do not use subcodes and instead use the ID bytes in each data frame to store the sector number and information about the sectors.

Handling Errors

DVDs use more powerful error correcting codes than were first devised for CDs. Unlike CDs, which have different levels of error correction depending on whether audio/video or data is being stored, DVDs treat all information equally and apply the full error correction to all sectors.

The main error correction in DVDs takes place in the ECC frame. Parity outer (column) and parity inner (row) bits are added to detect and correct errors. The scheme is simple and yet very effective. The information from the data frames is first broken up into 192 rows of 172 bytes each. Then, a polynomial equation is used to calculate and add 10 PI (parity inner) bytes to each row, making the rows now 182 bytes each. Finally, another polynomial equation is used to calculate 16 PO (parity outer) bytes for each column, resulting in 16 bytes (rows) being added to each column. What started out as 192 rows of 172 bytes becomes 208 rows of 182 bytes with the PI and PO information added.

The function of the PI and PO bytes can be explained with a simple example using simple parity. In this example, 2 bytes are stored (01001110 = N, 01001111 = O). To add the error correcting information, they are organized in rows, as shown here:

```
              Data bits
              1 2 3 4 5 6 7 8
       ----------------------------------
       Byte 1    0 1 0 0 1 1 1 0
       Byte 2    0 1 0 0 1 1 1 1
       ----------------------------------
```

Then, 1 PI bit is added for each row, using odd parity. This means you count up the 1 bits: In the first row there are 4 bits, so the parity bit is created as a 1, making the sum an odd number. In the second row, the parity bit is a 0 because the sum of the 1s was already an odd number. The result is as follows:

```
              Data bits
              1 2 3 4 5 6 7 8       PI
       -------------------------------+-------------------------
       Byte 1    0 1 0 0 1 1 1 0      1
       Byte 2    0 1 0 0 1 1 1 1      0
       -------------------------------+-------------------------
```

Next, the parity bits for each column are added and calculated the same as before. In other words, the parity bit will be such that the sum of the 1s in each column is an odd number. The result is as follows:

```
              Data bits
              1 2 3 4 5 6 7 8       PI
       ---------------------------+------
       Byte 1    0 1 0 0 1 1 1 0   |  1
       Byte 2    0 1 0 0 1 1 1 1   |  0
       ---------------------------+------
       PO    1 1 1 1 1 1 1 0       |  1
```

Now the code is complete, and the extra bits are stored along with the data. So, instead of just the 2 bytes being stored, 11 addition bits are stored for error correction. When the data is read back, the error correction bit calculations are repeated and they're checked to see whether they are the same as before. To see how it works, let's change one of the data bits (due to a read error) and recalculate the error correcting bits, as follows:

```
              Data bits
              1 2 3 4 5 6 7 8          PI
       -------------------------------+-------
       Byte 1    0 1 0 0 1 0 1 0       |  0
       Byte 2    0 1 0 0 1 1 1 1       |  0
       -------------------------------+-------
       PO    1 1 1 1 1 0 1 0           |  1
```

Now, when you compare the PI and PO bits you calculated after reading the data to what was originally stored, you see a change in the PI bit for byte (row) 1 and in the PO bit for bit (column) 6. This identifies the precise row and column where the error was, which is at byte 1 (row 1), bit 6 (column 6). That bit was read as a 0, and you now know it is wrong, so it must have been a 1. The error correcting circuitry then simply changes it back to a 1 before passing it back to the system. As you can see, with some extra information added to each row and column, error correcting codes can indeed detect and correct errors on the fly.

Besides the ECC frames, DVDs also scramble the data in the frames using a bit-shift technique and also interleave parts of the ECC frames when they are actually recorded on the disc. These schemes serve to store the data somewhat out of sequence, preventing a scratch from corrupting consecutive pieces of data.

DVD Capacity (Sides and Layers)

Four main types of DVD discs are available, categorized by whether they are single- or double-sided, and single- or dual-layered. They are designated as follows:

- **DVD-5: 4.7GB, single side, single layer**—A DVD-5 is constructed from two substrates bonded together with adhesive. One is stamped with a recorded layer (called Layer 0), and the other is blank. An aluminum coating typically is applied to the single recorded layer.

- **DVD-9: 8.5GB, single side, dual layer**—A DVD-9 is constructed of two stamped substrates bonded together to form two recorded layers for one side of the disc, along with a blank substrate for the other side. The outer stamped layer (0) is coated with a semitransparent gold coating to both reflect light if the laser is focused on it and pass light if the laser is focused on the layer below. A single laser is used to read both layers; only the focus of the laser is changed.

- **DVD-10: 9.4GB, double side, single layer**—A DVD-10 is constructed of two stamped substrates bonded together back to back. The recorded layer (Layer 0 on each side) usually is coated with aluminum. Note that these discs are double-sided; however, drives have a read laser on the bottom only, which means the disc must be removed and flipped for the other side to be read.

- **DVD-18: 17.1GB, double side, dual layer**—A DVD-18 combines both double layers and double sides. Two stamped layers form each side, and the substrate pairs are bonded back to back. The outer layers (Layer 0 on each side) are coated with semitransparent gold, whereas the inner layers (Layer 1 on each side) are coated with aluminum. The reflectivity of a single-layer disc is 45%–85%, and for a dual-layer disc the reflectivity is 18%–30%. The automatic gain control (AGC) circuitry in the drive compensates for the different reflective properties.

Figure 10.8 shows the construction of each of the DVD disc types. Note that although Figure 10.8 shows two lasers reading the bottom of the dual-layer discs, in actual practice only one laser is used. Only the focus is changed to read the different layers.

Dual-layer discs can have the layers recorded in two ways: either opposite track path (OTP) or parallel track path (PTP). OTP minimizes the time needed to switch from one layer to the other when reading the disc. When reaching the inside of the disc (end of Layer 0), the laser pickup remains in the same location; it merely moves toward the disc slightly to focus on Layer 1. When the disc is written in OTP mode, the lead-out zone toward the outer part of the disc is called the *middle zone* instead.

Discs written in PTP have both spiral layers written (and read) from the inside out. When changing from Layer 0 to Layer 1, PTP discs require the laser pickup to move from the outside (end of the first layer) back to the inside (start of the second layer), as well as for the focus of the laser to change. Virtually all discs are written in OTP mode to make the layer change quicker.

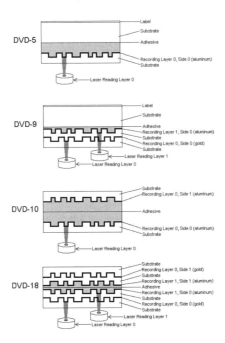

Figure 10.8 DVD disc types and construction.

To allow the layers to be read more easily even though they are on top of one another, discs written in PTP mode have the spiral direction changed from one layer to the other. Layer 0 has a spiral winding clockwise (which is read counterclockwise), whereas Layer 1 has a spiral winding counterclockwise. This typically requires that the drive spin the disc in the opposite direction to read that layer, but with OTP the spiral is read from the outside in on the second layer. Therefore, Layer 0 spirals from the inside out, and Layer 1 spirals from the outside in.

Figure 10.9 shows the differences between PTP and OTP on a DVD.

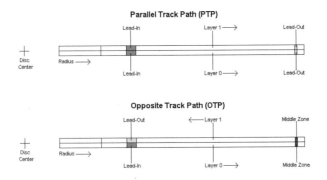

Figure 10.9 PTP versus OTP.

DVDs store 4.7GB up to 17.1GB, depending on the type. Table 10.8 shows the precise capacities of the various types of DVDs.

Table 10.8 DVD Capacity

	Single Layer	Dual Layer
DVD Designation	DVD-5	DVD-9
B	4,695,853,056	8,535,691,264
KiB	4,585,794	8,335,636
KB	4,695,853	8,535,691
MiB	4,586	8,336
MB	4,696	8,536
GiB	4.6	8.3
GB	4.7	8.5
MPEG-2 video (approx. minutes)	133	242
MPEG-2 video (hours:minutes)	2:13	4:02

	Single Layer Double Sided	Dual Layer Double Sided
DVD Designation	DVD-10	DVD-18
B	9,391,706,112	17,071,382,528
KiB	9,171,588	16,671,272
KB	9,391,706	17,071,383
MiB	9,172	16,671
MB	9,392	17,071
GiB	9.2	16.7
GB	9.4	17.1
MPEG-2 video (approx. minutes)	266	484
MPEG-2 video (hours:minutes)	4:26	8:04

B = byte (8 bits)
KB = kilobyte (1,000 bytes)
KiB = kibibyte (1,024 bytes)
MB = megabyte (1,000,000 bytes)
MiB = mebibyte (1,048,576 bytes)
GB = gigabyte (1,000,000,000 bytes)
GiB = gibibyte (1,073,741,824 bytes)

As you might notice, the capacity of dual-layer discs is slightly less than twice that of single-layer discs, even though the layers take up the same space on the discs (the spiral tracks are the same length). This was done intentionally to improve the readability of both layers in a dual-layer configuration. To do this, the bit cell spacing was slightly increased, which increases the length of each pit and land. When reading a dual-layer disc, the drive spins slightly faster to compensate, resulting in the same data rate. However, because the distance on the track is covered more quickly, less overall data can be stored.

Besides the standard four capacities listed here, a double-sided disc with one layer on one side and two layers on the other can also be produced. This would be called a DVD-14 and have a capacity of 13.2GB, or about 6 hours and 15 minutes of MPEG-2 video. Additionally, 80mm discs, which store less data in each configuration than the standard 120mm discs, can be produced.

Because of the manufacturing difficulties and the extra expense of double-sided discs—and the fact that they must be ejected and flipped to play both sides—most DVDs are configured as either a DVD-5 (single-sided, single-layer) or a DVD-9 (single-sided, dual-layer), which allows up to 8.5GB of data or 242 minutes of uninterrupted MPEG-2 video to be played. The 133-minute capacity of DVD-5 video discs accommodates 95% or more of the movies ever made.

Data Encoding on the Disc

As with CDs, the pits and lands themselves do not determine the bits; instead, the transitions (changes in reflectivity) from pit to land and from land to pit are what determine the actual bits on the disc. The disc track is divided into bit cells or time intervals (T), and a pit or land used to represent data is required to be a minimum of 3T or a maximum of 11T intervals (cells) long. A 3T-long pit or land represents a 1001, and a 11T-long pit or land represents a 100000000001.

Data is stored using 8 to 16 modulation, which is a modified version of the 8 to 14 modulation (EFM) used on CDs. Because of this, 8 to 16 modulation is sometimes called EFM+. This modulation takes each byte (8 bits) and converts it into a 16-bit value for storage. The 16-bit conversion codes are designed so that there are never fewer than 2 or more than 10 adjacent 0 bits (resulting in no fewer than 3 or no more than 11 time intervals between 1s). EFM+ is a form of RLL encoding called RLL 2,10 (RLL x,y, where x equals the minimum and y equals the maximum run of 0s). This is designed to prevent long strings of 0s, which could more easily be misread due to clocks becoming out of sync, as well as to limit the minimum and maximum frequency of transitions actually placed on the recording media. Unlike CDs, no merge bits exist between codes. The 16-bit modulation codes are designed so that they will not violate the RLL 2,10 form without needing merge bits. Because the EFM used on CDs really requires more than 17 bits for each byte (because of the added merge and sync bits), EFM+ is slightly more efficient because only slightly more than 16 bits are generated for each byte encoded.

Note that although no more than 10 0s are allowed in the modulation generated by EFM+, the sync bits added when physical sectors are written can have up to 13 0s, meaning a time period of up to 14T between 1s written on the disc, and pits or lands up to 14T intervals or bit cells in length.

Optical Disc Formats

CD and DVD drives can use many types of disc formats and standards. The following sections discuss the formats and file systems used by CD and DVD drives, so you can make sure you can use media recorded in a particular format with your drive.

Compact Disc and Drive Formats

After Philips and Sony had created the Red Book CD-DA format discussed earlier in the chapter, they began work on other format standards that would allow CDs to store computer files, data, and even video and photos. These standards control how the data is formatted so that the drive can read it, and additional file format standards can then control how the software and drivers on your system can be designed to understand and interpret the data properly. Note that the physical format and storage of data on the disc as defined in the Red Book was adopted by all subsequent CD standards. This refers to the encoding and basic levels of error correction provided by CD-DA discs. What the other "books" specify is primarily how the 2,352 bytes in each sector are to be handled, what type of data can be stored, how it should be formatted, and more.

All the official CD standard books and related documents can be purchased from Philips for $100–$150 each. See the Philips licensing site at www.licensing.philips.com for more information.

Table 10.9 describes the various standard CD formats.

Table 10.9   Compact Disc Formats

Format	Name	Introduced	Notes
Red Book	CD-DA (compact disc-digital audio)	In 1980 by Philips and Sony	This is the original CD audio standard on which all subsequent CD standards are based.
Yellow Book	CD-ROM (compact disc-read-only memory)	In 1983 by Philips and Sony	Specifies additional ECC and EDC for data in several sector formats, including Mode 1 and Mode 2.
Green Book	CD-i (compact disc-interactive)	In 1986 by Philips and Sony	Specifies an interactive audio/video standard for non–PC-dedicated player hardware (now mostly obsolete) and discs used for interactive presentations. Also defines the Mode 2, Form 1 and the Mode 2, Form 2 sector formats, along with interleaved MPEG-1video and ADPCM audio.
CD-ROM XA	CD-ROM XA (extended architecture)	In 1989 by Philips, Sony, and Microsoft	Combines Yellow Book and CD-i to bring CD-i audio and video capabilities to PCs.
Orange Book	CD-R (recordable) and CD-RW (rewritable)	In 1989 by Philips and Sony (Part I/II); in 1996 by Philips and Sony (Part III)	Defines single session, multisession, and packet writing on recordable discs. • **Part I**—CD-MO (magneto-optical; withdrawn). • **Part II**—CD-R (recordable). • **Part III**—CD-RW (rewritable).
Photo-CD	CD-P	In 1990 by Philips and Kodak	Combines CD-ROM XA with CD-R multisession capability in a standard for photo storage on CD-R discs.
White Book	Video CD	In 1993 by Philips, JVC, Matsushita, and Sony	Based on CD-i and CD-ROM XA. It stores up to 74 minutes of MPEG-1 video and ADPCM digital audio data.
Blue Book	CD EXTRA (formerly CD-Plus or enhanced music)	In 1995 by Philips and Sony	Multisession format for stamped discs; used by musical artists to incorporate videos, liner notes, and other information on audio CDs.

Multisession Recording

Before the Orange Book specification, CDs had to be written as a single session. A *session* is defined as a lead-in, followed by one or more tracks of data (or audio), followed by a lead-out. The lead-in takes up 4,500 sectors on the disc (1 minute if measured in time or about 9.2MB worth of data). The lead-in also indicates whether the disc is multisession and what the next writable address on the disc is (if the disc isn't closed). The first lead-out on a disc (or the only one if it is a single session or Disk At Once recording) is 6,750 sectors long (1.5 minutes if measured in time or about 13.8MB worth of data). If the disc is a multisession disc, any subsequent lead-outs are 2,250 sectors long (0.5 minutes in time or about 4.6MB worth of data).

A multisession CD has multiple sessions, with each individual session complete from lead-in to lead-out. The mandatory lead-in and lead-out for each session does waste space on the disc. In fact, 48 sessions would literally use up all of a 74-minute disc, even with no data recorded in each session! Therefore, the practical limit for the number of sessions you can record on a disc would be much less than that.

CD-DA and older CD-ROM drives couldn't read more than one session on a disc, so that is the way most pressed CDs are recorded. The Orange Book allows multiple sessions on a single disc. To allow this, the Orange Book defines three main methods or modes of recording:

- Disk At Once (DAO)
- Track At Once (TAO)
- Packet writing

Disc At Once

Disc At Once means pretty much what it says: It is a single-session method of writing CDs in which the lead-in, data tracks, and lead-out are written in a single operation without ever turning off the writing laser, and the disc is closed. A disc is considered closed when the last (or only) lead-in is fully written and the next usable address on the disc is not recorded in that lead-in. In that case, the CD recorder is incapable of writing any further data on the disc. Note that you do not need to close a disc to read it in a normal CD-ROM drive, although if you were submitting a disc to a CD-duplicating company for replication, most require that it be closed.

Track At Once

Multisession discs can be recorded in either Track At Once (TAO) or packet-writing mode. In Track At Once recording, each track can be individually written (laser turned on and off) within a session, until the session is closed. Closing a session is the act of writing the lead-out for that session, which means no more tracks can be added to that session. If the disc is closed at the same time, no further sessions can be added either.

The tracks recorded in TAO mode are divided by gaps of normally 2 seconds. Each track written has 150 sectors of overhead for run-in, run-out, pre-gap, and linking. A CD-R/RW drive can read the tracks even if the session is not closed, but to read them in a CD-DA or CD-ROM drive, the session must be closed. If you intend to write more sessions to the disc, you can close the session and not close the disc. At that point, you could start another session of recording to add more tracks to the disc. The main thing to remember is that each session must be closed (lead-out written) before another session can be written or before a normal CD-DA or CD-ROM drive can read the tracks in the session.

Packet Writing

Packet writing is a method whereby multiple writes are allowed within a track, thus reducing the overhead and wasted space on a disc. Each packet uses four sectors for run-in, two for run-out, and one for linking. Packets can be of fixed or variable length, but most drives and packet-writing software use a fixed length because it is much easier and more efficient to deal with file systems that way.

With packet writing, you normally use the Universal Disk Format (UDF) version 1.5 or later file system, which enables the CD to be treated essentially like a big floppy drive. That is, you can literally drag and drop files to it, use the `copy` command to copy files onto the disc, and so on. The packet-writing software and UDF file system manage everything. If the disc you are using for packet writing is a CD-R, every time a file is overwritten or deleted, the file seems to disappear, but you don't get the space back on the disc. Instead, the file system simply forgets about the file. If the disc is a CD-RW, the space is indeed reclaimed and the disc won't be full until you literally have more than the limit of active files stored there.

Unfortunately, Windows versions up through Windows XP don't support packet writing or the UDF file system directly, so drivers must be loaded to read packet-written discs, and a packet-writing application must be used to write them. Fortunately, though, these drivers and applications typically are included with CD-RW drives. One of the most popular packet-writing programs is Drag-to-Disc (originally called DirectCD) from Roxio, which is included as part of the Easy Media Creator packages it sells. To read packet-written UDF discs on other machines, you can download a free universal UDF volume reader application from Roxio, which will allow you to read UDF 1.5 (packet-written) discs on virtually any CD-ROM or CD-RW drive. This reader also enables some MultiRead CD-ROM drives to read UDF-formatted CD-RW discs (such as those written with DirectCD or Drag-to-Disc) under Windows 98 and 98 SE, Windows Me, and Windows 2000/XP. You can download the reader free from Roxio at `http://www.roxio.com/en/support/software_updates.jhtml`.

Note

Windows XP also has limited CD-RW support in the form of the Image Mastering Application Programming Interface (IMAPI), which allows data to be temporarily stored on the hard drive (staged) before being written to the CD in one session. Additional sessions can be written to the same disc, but there is a 50MB overhead for each session. This gives some of the appearance of packet writing, but it is not really the same thing. To read packet-written discs in the UDF 1.5 or later format, you must install a UDF reader just as with previous versions of Windows. Instead of using IMAPI, I recommend installing a third-party CD-mastering program that also includes packet-writing UDF support, such as Roxio's Easy Media Creator with Drag-to-Disc or Ahead's Nero Burning ROM with InCD.

When you remove a packet-written disc from the drive, the packet-writing software first asks whether you want the files to be visible to normal CD-ROM drives. If you do, the session must be closed. Even if the session is closed, you can still write more to the disc later, but there is an overhead of wasted space every time you close a session. If you are going to read the disc in a CD-RW drive, you don't have to close the session because the drive will be capable of reading the files even if the session isn't closed.

A newer standard called *Mount Rainier* (or EasyWrite) adds even more capability to packet writing and is one of the most important developments in CD and DVD drives. With Mount Rainier, packet writing can become an official part of the operating system, and the drives can support the defect management needed to make them usable as removable storage in the real world. For more information on Mount Rainier, see the section later in this chapter.

Note

Microsoft has released updates for Windows XP that add native support for the Mount Rainier standard, which supports full drag-and-drop packet writing through CD-MRW drives as well as DVD+MRW drives.

CD-ROM File Systems

Manufacturers of early CD-ROM discs required their own custom software to read the discs. The reason is that the Yellow Book specification for CD-ROM details only how data sectors—rather than audio sectors—can be stored on a disc, and it did not cover the file systems or deal with how data should be stored in files and how they should be formatted for use by systems with different operating systems. Obviously, noninterchangeable file formats presented an obstacle to the industrywide compatibility for CD-ROM applications.

In 1985–1986, several companies got together and published the High Sierra file format specification, which finally enabled CD-ROMs to be universally readable. That was the first industry-standard CD-ROM file system that made CD-ROMs universally usable in PCs. This wasn't so much an issue for computer users at the time because the first software on CD-ROM didn't appear until 1987, after the High Sierra format had been published. Most desktop PCs didn't begin incorporating CD-ROM drives until 1987 or later, and the first laptop with an internal CD-ROM drive didn't appear until October 1994. Today, several file systems are used on CDs, including the following:

- High Sierra
- ISO 9660 (based on High Sierra)
- Joliet
- UDF (Universal Disk Format)
- Mac HFS (Hierarchical File System)
- Rock Ridge
- Mount Rainier

Not all CD-ROM file system formats can be read by all operating systems. Table 10.10 shows the primary file systems used and which operating systems support them.

Table 10.10 CD-ROM File System Formats

CD File System	DOS/ Windows 3.x	Windows 9x/Me	Windows NT/2000/XP	Mac OS
High Sierra	Yes	Yes	Yes	Yes
ISO 9660	Yes	Yes	Yes	Yes
Joliet	Yes[1]	Yes	Yes	Yes[1]
UDF	No	Yes[2]	Yes[2]	Yes[2]
Mac HFS	No	No	No	Yes
Rock Ridge	Yes[1]	Yes[1]	Yes[1]	Yes[1]
Mount Rainier	No	Yes[3]	Yes[3]	Yes[3]

1. A short name, such as (SHORTN~1.TXT), will be shown in place of long filenames.
2. Only if a third-party UDF reader is installed.
3. Requires Mount Rainier (also called EasyWrite) hardware and driver software (Win98 or above) or a third-party reader program.

Note

The Mac HFS and UNIX Rock Ridge file systems are not supported by PC operating systems such as DOS and Windows and therefore are not covered in depth here.

High Sierra

To make CD-ROM discs readable on all systems without having to develop custom file systems and drivers, it was in the best interests of all PC hardware and software manufacturers to resolve the CD-ROM file format standardization issue. In 1985, representatives from TMS, DEC, Microsoft, Hitachi, LaserData, Sony, Apple, Philips, 3M, Video Tools, Reference Technology, and Xebec met at what was then called the High Sierra Hotel and Casino in Lake Tahoe, Nevada, to create a common logical format and file structure for CD-ROMs. In 1986, they jointly published this standard as the "Working Paper for Information Processing: Volume and File Structure of CD-ROM Optical Discs for Information Exchange (1986)." This standard was subsequently referred to as the High Sierra format.

This agreement enabled all drives using the appropriate driver (such as MSCDEX.EXE supplied by Microsoft with DOS) to read all High Sierra–formatted discs, opening the way for the mass production and acceptance of CD-ROM software publishing. Adoption of this standard also enabled disc publishers to provide cross-platform support for their software, easily manufacturing discs for DOS, UNIX, and other operating system formats. Without this agreement, the maturation of the CD-ROM marketplace would have taken years longer, and the production of CD-ROM-based information would have been stifled.

The High Sierra format was submitted to the International Standards Organization (ISO). Two years later (in 1988) with several enhancements and changes, it was republished as the ISO 9660 standard. ISO 9660 was not exactly the same as High Sierra, but all drivers that could read High Sierra–formatted discs were quickly updated to handle both ISO 9660 and the original High Sierra format upon which it was based.

For example, Microsoft wrote the MSCDEX.EXE (Microsoft CD-ROM Extensions) driver in 1988 and licensed it to CD-ROM hardware and software vendors to include with their products. It wasn't until 1993 when MS-DOS 6.0 was released that MSCDEX was included with DOS as a standard feature. MSCDEX enables DOS to read ISO 9660–formatted (and High Sierra–formatted) discs. This driver works with the AT Attachment Packet Interface (ATAPI) or Advanced SCSI Programming Interface (ASPI) hardware-level device driver that comes with the drive. Microsoft built ISO 9660 and Joliet file system support directly into Windows 95 and later, with no additional drivers necessary.

ISO 9660

The ISO 9660 standard enabled full cross-compatibility among different computers and operating systems. ISO 9660 was released in 1988 and was based on the work done by the High Sierra group. Although based on High Sierra, ISO 9660 does have some differences and refinements. ISO 9660 has three levels of interchange that dictate the features that can be used to ensure compatibility with different systems.

ISO 9660 Level 1 is the lowest common denominator of all CD file systems and is capable of being read by almost every computer platform, including UNIX and Macintosh. The downside of this file system is that it is very limited with respect to filenames and directories. Level 1 interchange restrictions include the following:

- Only uppercase characters A–Z, numbers 0–9, and the underscore (_) character are allowed in filenames.

- Eight characters for the filename and three characters for the extension are the maximum (based on the DOS 8.3 format limitation).
- Directory names are eight characters maximum (no extension allowed).
- Directories are limited to eight levels deep.
- Files must be contiguous.

Level 2 interchange rules have the same limitations as Level 1, except that the filename and extension can be up to 30 characters long (both added together, not including the . separator). Finally, Level 3 interchange rules are the same as Level 2 except that files don't have to be contiguous.

Note that Windows 95 and later versions enable you to use file and folder names up to 255 characters long, which can include spaces as well lowercase and many other characters not allowed in ISO 9660. To maintain backward compatibility with DOS, Windows 95 and later associate a short 8.3 format filename as an alias for each file that has a longer name. These alias short names are created automatically by Windows. You can view them in the properties for each file or by using the DIR command at a command prompt. To create these alias names, Windows truncates the name to six (or fewer) characters followed by a tilde (~) and a number starting with 1 and truncates the extension to three characters. Other numbers are used in the first part if other files that would have the same alias when truncated already exist. For example, the filename This is a.test gets THISIS~1.TES as an alias.

This filename alias creation is independent of your CD-ROM drive, but it is important to know that if you create or write to a CD using the ISO 9660 format using Level 1 restrictions, the alias short names are used when the files are recorded to the disc, meaning any long filenames will be lost in the process. In fact, even the alias short name will be modified because ISO 9660 Level 1 restrictions don't allow a tilde; that character is converted to an underscore in the names written to the CD.

The ISO 9660 data starts at 2 seconds and 16 sectors into the disc, which is also known as *logical sector 16 of track one*. For a multisession disc, the ISO 9660 data is present in the first data track of each session containing CD-ROM tracks. This data identifies the location of the volume area—where the actual data is stored. The system area also lists the directories in this volume as the volume table of contents (VTOC), with pointers or addresses to various named areas, as illustrated in Figure 10.10. A significant difference between the CD directory structure and that of a normal hard disk is that the CD's system area also contains direct addresses of the files within the subdirectories, allowing the CD to seek specific sector locations on the spiral data track. Because the CD data is all on one long spiral track, when speaking of tracks in the context of a CD, we're actually talking about sectors or segments of data along that spiral.

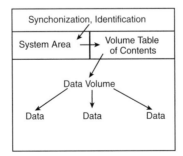

Figure 10.10 A diagram of the basic ISO 9660 file organizational format.

To put the ISO 9660 format in perspective, the disc layout is roughly analogous to that of a floppy disk. A floppy disk has a system track that not only identifies itself as a floppy disk and reveals its density and operating system, but also tells the computer how it's organized—into directories, which are made up of files.

Joliet

Joliet is an extension of the ISO 9660 standard, which Microsoft developed for use with Windows 95 and later. Joliet enables CDs to be recorded using filenames up to 64 characters long, including spaces and other characters from the Unicode international character set. Joliet also preserves an 8.3 alias for those programs that can't use the longer filenames.

In general, Joliet features the following specifications:

- File or directory names can be up to 64 Unicode characters (128 bytes) in length.
- Directory names can have extensions.
- Directories can be deeper than eight levels.
- Multisession recording is inherently supported.

Tip

Because Joliet supports a shorter path than Windows 9x and newer versions, you might have difficulties mastering a Joliet-format CD that contains extremely long pathnames. I recommend that you shorten the folder names in the file structure you create with the CD-mastering software to avoid problems. Unfortunately, many CD-mastering programs don't warn you about a pathname that is too long until after the burning process starts.

Due to backward-compatibility provisions, systems that don't support the Joliet extensions (such as older DOS systems) should still be capable of reading the disc. However, it will be interpreted as an ISO 9660 format using the short names instead.

Note

A bit of trivia: Chicago was the code name Microsoft used for Windows 95. Joliet is the town outside of Chicago where Jake was locked up in the movie *The Blues Brothers*.

Universal Disk Format

The Universal Disk Format (UDF) is a relatively new file system created by the Optical Storage Technology Association (OSTA) as an industry-standard format for use on optical media such as CD-ROMs and DVDs. UDF has several advantages over the ISO 9660 file system used by standard CD-ROMs but is most noted because it is designed to work with packet writing, a technique for writing small amounts of data to a CD-R/RW disc, treating it much like a standard magnetic drive.

The UDF file system allows long filenames up to 255 characters per name. There have been several versions of UDF, with most packet-writing software using UDF 1.5 or later. Packet-writing software such as Drag-to-Disc from Roxio writes in the UDF file system. Standard CD-ROM drives, drivers, or operating systems such as DOS can't read UDF-formatted discs. Recordable drives can read them, but regular CD-ROM drives must conform to one of the MultiRead specifications (see the section "MultiRead Specifications," later in this chapter) to be capable of reading UDF discs.

After you are sure that your drive can read UDF, you must check the OS. Most operating systems can't read UDF natively; the support has to be added via a driver. DOS can't read UDF at all; however, with

Windows 95 and later, UDF-formatted discs can be read by installing a UDF driver. Normally, such a driver is included with the software that is included with most CD-RW drives. If you don't have a UDF driver, you can download one free from Roxio at `http://www.roxio.com/en/support/software_updates.jhtml`. After the UDF driver is installed, you do not need to take any special steps to read a UDF-formatted disc. The driver will be in the background waiting for you to insert a UDF-formatted disc.

You can close a packet-written disc to make it readable in a normal CD-ROM drive, which converts the filenames to Joliet format, causing them to be truncated to 64 characters. You can download the latest version of the Universal Disk Format from the OSTA website at `www.osta.org/specs`.

Macintosh HFS

HFS (Hierarchical File System) is the file system used by the Macintosh OS. HFS can also be used on CD-ROMs; however, if that is done, they will not be readable on a PC. A hybrid disc can be produced with both Joliet and HFS or ISO 9660 and HFS file systems, and the disc would then be readable on both PCs and Macs. In that case, the system will see only the part of the disc that is compatible, which is ISO 9660 or Joliet in the case of PCs.

Rock Ridge

The Rock Ridge Interchange Protocol (RRIP) was developed by an industry consortium called the Rock Ridge Group. It was officially released in 1994 by the IEEE CD-ROM File System Format Working Group and specifies an extension to the ISO 9660 standard for CD-ROM that enables the recording of additional information to support UNIX/POSIX file system features. Neither DOS nor Windows includes support for the Rock Ridge extensions. However, because it is based on ISO 9660, the files are still readable on a PC and the RRIP extensions are simply ignored.

Note

Another interesting bit of trivia: The Rock Ridge name was taken from the fictional Western town in the movie *Blazing Saddles*.

Mount Rainier

Mount Rainier is a standard promoted by Philips, Sony, Microsoft, and Compaq. Also called *EasyWrite* (see Figure 10.11), Mount Rainier enables native operating system support for data storage on CD-RW and DVD+RW. This makes the technology much easier to use (no special drivers or packet-writing software is necessary) and enables CD-RW and DVD+RW drives to become fully integrated storage solutions.

Figure 10.11   The EasyWrite logo is used on CD-RW and DVD+R/RW drives manufactured in 2003 and beyond that support the Mount Rainier standard.

The main features of Mount Rainier are as follows:

- **Integral defect management**—Standard drives rely on driver software to manage defects.

- **Direct addressing at the 2KB sector level to minimize wasted space**—Standard CD-RW media use a block size of 64KB.

- **Background formatting so that new media can be used in seconds after first insertion**—Standard CD-RW formatting can take up to 45 minutes depending on drive speed.

- **Standardized command set**—Standard software cannot work with new drives until revised command files are available.

- **Standardized physical layout**—Differences in standard UDF software can make reading media written by another program difficult.

To use Mount Rainier, you must have a drive that supports the standard. These are sometimes called *CD-MRW* or *DVD+MRW drives* and might instead bear either the Mount Rainier or EasyWrite logo. You can update some existing CD-RW drives to MRW status by reflashing the firmware in the drive; however, you will need to replace most older drives instead.

▶▶ See "Updating the Firmware in a CD-RW or Rewritable DVD Drive," p. 491.

Also required is software support directly in the operating system (such as with Windows XP or later), or software support can be added via a third-party add-on application for older operating systems. Software Architects (www.softarch.com) produces WriteCD-RW Pro! Software, which enables interchange between Mount Rainier and conventional UDF media, as well as between UDF media written with different programs and to different standards.

The first Mount Rainier drive (Philips RWDV1610B) for desktop systems was released in April 2002, and since then, many more have followed. Mount Rainier drives are common today for desktops and laptops. Because only minor changes are required in the drive circuitry and firmware to enable Mount Rainier support, most drives include Mount Rainier capability. Check the drive vendor's website or manual to determine compatibility. In addition, the DVD+RW standard was designed with Mount Rainier compatibility in mind; defect management was included inherently from the beginning. (DVD-RW drives don't support defect management, so they are not compatible with Mount Rainier.) The first DVD+RW drives with Mount Rainier/EasyWrite compatibility began shipping in early 2003.

Because Mount Rainier essentially makes CD-MRW and DVD+MRW drives function as high-capacity replacements for floppy, Zip, and SuperDisk drives, it won't be long before those are but a distant memory.

The latest version of the Mount Rainier specification, version 1.1, includes DVD+RW as well as CD-RW drives. You can order it from the Philips Intellectual Property and Standards website (www.licensing.philips.com). For more information, go to the Mount Rainier website at www.mt-rainier.org.

DVD Formats and Standards

As with the CD standards, the DVD standards are published in reference books produced mainly by the DVD forum, but also by other companies.

The DVD-Video and DVD-ROM standards are pretty well established, and recordable DVD technology is not expected to go beyond DVD+R DL, due to new formats such as HD-DVD and Blu-ray that will have significantly higher storage capabilities. The standards situation for recordable DVD has been confusing in the past, with two incompatible formats DVD-R and DVD+R and two camps of manufacturers developing DVD recordable drives. Today, however, DVD+-RW drives are multistandard; hence, they can record to and read back from either the -R or +R format.

The current standard DVD formats are shown in Table 10.11.

Table 10.11 Standard DVD Formats and Capacities

Format	Disc Size	Sides	Layers	Data Capacity	MPEG-2 Video Capacity
DVD-ROM Formats and Capacities					
DVD-5	120mm	Single	Single	4.7GB	2.2 hours
DVD-9	120mm	Single	Double	8.5GB	4.0 hours
DVD-10	120mm	Double	Single	9.4GB	4.4 hours
DVD-14	120mm	Double	Both	13.2GB	6.3 hours
DVD-18	120mm	Double	Double	17.1GB	8.1 hours
DVD-1	80mm	Single	Single	1.5GB	0.7 hour
DVD-2	80mm	Single	Double	2.7GB	1.3 hours
DVD-3	80mm	Double	Single	2.9GB	1.4 hours
DVD-4	80mm	Double	Double	5.3GB	2.5 hours
Recordable DVD Formats and Capacities					
DVD-R 1.0	120mm	Single	Single	3.95GB	1.9 hours
DVD-R 2.0	120mm	Single	Single	4.7GB	2.2 hours
DVD-RAM 1.0	120mm	Single	Single	2.58GB	N/A
DVD-RAM 1.0	120mm	Double	Single	5.16GB	N/A
DVD-RAM 2.0	120mm	Single	Single	4.7GB	N/A
DVD-RAM 2.0	120mm	Double	Single	9.4GB	N/A
DVD-RAM 2.0	80mm	Single	Single	1.46GB	N/A
DVD-RAM 2.0	80mm	Double	Single	2.65GB	N/A
DVD-RW 2.0	120mm	Single	Single	4.7GB	N/A
DVD+RW 2.0	120mm	Single	Single	4.7GB	2.2 hours
DVD+RW 2.0	120mm	Double	Single	9.4GB	4.4 hours
DVD+R 1.0	120mm	Single	Single	4.7GB	2.2 hours
CD-ROM Formats and Capacities (for comparison)					
CD-ROM/R/RW	120mm	Single	Single	0.737GB	N/A
CD-ROM/R/RW	80mm	Single	Single	0.194GB	N/A

With advancements made in blue-light lasers, this capacity will be increased several-fold by the upcoming HD-DVD and Blu-ray formats that can store up to 50GB per disc.

DVD drives are fully backward compatible and, as such, are capable of playing today's CD-ROMs as well as audio CDs. When they are playing existing CDs, the performance of current models is equivalent to a 40× or faster CD-ROM drive. As such, users who currently own slower CD-ROM drives might want to consider a DVD drive instead of upgrading to a faster CD-ROM drive. Several manufacturers have announced plans to phase out their CD-ROM drive products in favor of DVD. DVD is rapidly making CD-ROMs obsolete, in the same way that audio CDs displaced vinyl records in the 1980s. The only thing keeping the CD-ROM format alive is the battle between competing DVD recordable standards and the fact that CD-R and CD-RW are rapidly becoming the de facto replacements for floppy drives.

The current crop of DVD drives feature several improvements over the first-generation models of 1997. Those units were expensive, slow, and incompatible with either CD-R or CD-RW media. Many early units asked your overworked video card to try to double as an MPEG decoder to display DVD movies, with mediocre results in speed and image quality. As is often the case with "leading-edge" devices, their deficiencies make them eminently avoidable.

Many laptop vendors have integrated DVD/CD-RW or even DVD+-RW drives into their new high-end computers, usually as an option. Some of those (including models from Panasonic) also support reading and writing DVD-RAM discs as well. Originally, most of these installations included an MPEG-2 decoder board for processing the compressed video on DVD discs. This offloads the intensive MPEG calculations from the system processor and enables the display of full-screen, full-motion video on a PC. After processors crossed 400MHz in speed, performing MPEG-2 decoding reliably in software became possible, so any system faster than that usually doesn't include a hardware decoder card.

DVD Drive Compatibility

When DVD drives first appeared on the market, they were touted to be fully backward compatible with CD-ROM drives. Although that might be the case when reading commercially pressed CD-ROM discs, that was not necessarily true when reading CD-R or CD-RW media. Fortunately, the industry has responded with standards that let you know in advance how compatible your DVD drive will be. These standards are called *MultiRead* for computer-based drives and *MultiPlay* for consumer standalone devices, such as DVD-Video and CD-DA players. See the section "MultiRead Specifications," later in this chapter.

Playing DVD Movies on a Laptop

In order to play DVDs, you need an MPEG-2 decoder. This can take the form of hardware, either custom made or in the form of a PC Card, or software, included in your DVD player application. Almost all modern laptops with DVD-ROM, DVD/CD-RW, or DVD+-RW drives include a DVD playback program such as WinDVD, MyDVD, or SoftDVD, which includes a software-based MPEG-2 decoder. These programs enable you to play DVD movies the same way you would if it were being played through a set-top DVD player connected to a television.

If your laptop is slower than 400MHz, however, it simply won't have enough horsepower to perform the software-based MPEG-2 decoding, and the result will be movies that stutter, drop frames, and in general will be difficult to watch. To rectify this, some of the early DVD-equipped laptops included optional hardware-based MPEG-2 decoders. These decoders could be custom made for a specific laptop model, such as the hardware MPEG-2 decoder IBM offered for its ThinkPad 770 series, or they could be more universal, in the form of a PC Card such as the DVD-to-Go card from Margi Systems.

In systems running slower than 400MHz, using a hardware-based decoder was essential if you wanted to successfully play DVD movies. Unfortunately, the hardware-based MPEG-2 decoders for older laptops are generally not available any longer (most have been discontinued) because after they crossed 400MHz in speed, laptops could perform software-based MPEG-2 decoding. Essentially, this means if you install a DVD drive in a laptop that is slower than 400MHz, you may not be able to play DVD movies, unless you can locate a hardware MPEG-2 decoder.

DVD Copy Protection

DVD video discs employ several levels of protection, which are mainly controlled by the DVD Copy Control Association (DVD CCA) and a third-party company called Macrovision. This protection typically applies only to DVD-Video discs, not DVD-ROM software. So, for example, copy protection might affect your ability to make backup copies of *The Matrix*, but it won't affect a DVD encyclopedia or other software application distributed on DVD-ROM discs.

Note that every one of these protection systems has been broken, which means that with a little extra expense or the correct software, the protection can be defeated and you can make copies of your DVDs either to other digital media (hard drive, DVD+RW, CD-R/RW, and so on) or to analog media (such as VHS or other tape format).

Lots of time and money are wasted on these protection schemes, which can't really foil the professional bootleggers willing to spend the time and money to work around them. But they can make it difficult for the average person to legitimately back up his or her expensive media.

Here are the three main protection systems used with DVD-Video discs:

- Regional Playback Control (RPC)
- Content Scrambling System (CSS)
- Analog Protection System (APS)

Caution

The Digital Millennium Copyright Act (DCMA) signed into law in 1998 prohibits the breaking of copy-protection schemes or the distribution of information (such as tools, website links, and so forth) on how to break these schemes.

Regional Playback Control

Regional playback was designed to allow discs sold in specific geographical regions of the world to play only on players sold in those same regions. The idea was to allow a movie to be released at different times in different parts of the world, and to prevent people from ordering discs from regions in which the movie had not been released yet.

Nine regions are defined in the RPC standard. Discs (and players) usually are identified by a small logo or label showing the region number superimposed on a world globe. Multiregion discs are possible, as are discs that are not region locked. If a disc plays in more than one region, it will have more than one number on the globe. The regions are as follows:

- **Region Code 0**—Region code free; plays on all DVD-Video players
- **Region Code 1**—United States, Canada, U.S. Territories
- **Region Code 2**—Japan, Europe, South Africa, and the Middle East
- **Region Code 3**—Southeast Asia and East Asia
- **Region Code 4**—Australia, New Zealand, Pacific Islands, Central America, Mexico, South America, and the Caribbean
- **Region Code 5**—Eastern Europe (east of Poland and the Balkans), Indian subcontinent, Africa, North Korea, and Mongolia
- **Region Code 6**—China and Tibet
- **Region Code 7**—Reserved for future use
- **Region Code 8**—Special international or mobile venues, such as airplanes, cruise ships, and so on

The region code is embedded in the hardware of DVD-Video players. Most players are preset for a specific region and can't be changed. Some companies who sell the players modify them to play discs from all regions; these are called *region-free* or *code-free* players. Some newer discs have an added region code enhancement (RCE) function that checks to see whether the player is configured for multiple or all regions and then, if it is, refuses to play. Most newer region-free modified players know how to query the disc first to circumvent this check as well.

DVD-ROM drives used in PCs originally did not have RPC in the hardware, placing that responsibility instead on the software used to play DVD-Video discs on the PC. The player software would normally lock the region code to the first disc that was played and then from that point on play only discs from that region. Reinstalling the software enabled the region code to be reset, and numerous patches were posted on websites to enable resetting the region code even without reinstalling the software. Because of the relative ease of defeating the region-coding restrictions with DVD-ROM drives, starting on January 1, 2000, all DVD-ROM drives were required to have RPC-2, which embeds the region coding directly into the drive.

RPC-2 (or RPC-II) places the region lock in the drive, and not in the playing or MPEG-2 decoding software. You can set the region code in RPC-2 drives up to five times total, which basically means you can change it up to four times after the initial setting. Usually, you can make the change using the player software you are using, or you can download region-changing software from the drive manufacturer. After you make the fourth change (which is the fifth setting), the drive is locked on the last region set.

Content Scrambling System

The Content Scrambling System (CSS) provides the main protection for DVD-Video discs. It wasn't until this protection was implemented that the Motion Picture Association of America (MPAA) would agree to release movies in the DVD format, which is the main reason the rollout of DVD had been significantly delayed.

CSS originally was developed by Matsushita (Panasonic) and is used to digitally scramble and encrypt the audio and video data on a DVD-Video disc. Descrambling requires a pair of 40-bit (5-byte) keys (numeric codes). One of the keys is unique to the disc, whereas the other is unique to the video title set (VTS file) being descrambled. The disc and title keys are stored in the lead-in area of the disc in an encrypted form. The CSS scrambling and key writing are carried out during the glass mastering procedure, which is part of the disc-manufacturing process.

You can see this encryption in action if you put a DVD disc into the DVD-ROM drive on your PC, copy the files to your hard drive, and then try to view the files. The files are usually called VTS_*xx_yy*.VOB (video object), where the *xx* represents the title number and the *yy* represents the section number. Usually, all the files for a given movie have the same title number, and the movie is spread out among several 1GB or smaller files with different section numbers. These VOB files contain both the encrypted video and audio streams for the movie interleaved together. Other files, with an .IFO extension, contain information used by the DVD player to decode the video and audio streams in the VOB files. If you copy the VOB and IFO files onto your hard drive and try to click or play the VOB files directly, you either see and hear scrambled video and audio or receive an error message about playing copy-protected files.

This encryption is not a problem if you use a CSS-licensed player (either hardware or software) and play the files directly from the DVD disc. All DVD players, whether they are consumer standalone units or software players on your computer, have their own unique CSS unlock key assigned to them. Every DVD-Video disc has 400 of these 5-byte keys stamped onto the disc in the lead-in area (which is not usually accessible by programs) on the DVD in encrypted form. The decryption routine in the player uses its unique code to retrieve and unencrypt the disc key, which is then used to retrieve and unencrypt the title keys. CSS is essentially a three-level encryption that originally was thought to be very secure, but has proven otherwise.

In October 1999, a 16-year-old Norwegian programmer was able to extract the first key from one of the commercial PC-based players, which allowed him to very easily decrypt disc and title keys. A now-famous program called DeCSS was then written that can break the CSS protection on any DVD-Video title and save unencrypted VOB files to a hard disk that can be played by any MPEG-2 decoder program. Needless to say, this utility (and others based on it) has been the cause of much concern in the movie industry and has caused many legal battles over the distribution and even links to this code on the Web. Do a search on DeCSS for some interesting legal reading.

As if that wasn't enough, in March 2001, two MIT students published an incredibly short (only seven lines long!) and simple program that can unscramble CSS so quickly that a movie can essentially be unscrambled in real time while it is playing. They wrote and demonstrated the code as part of a two-day seminar they conducted on the controversial Digital Millennium Copyright Act, illustrating how trivial the CSS protection really is.

Because of the failure of CSS, the DVD Forum is now actively looking into other means of protection, especially including digital watermarks. This type of protection consists essentially of digital noise buried into the data stream, which is supposed to be invisible to normal viewing. Unfortunately, when similar technology was applied to DIVX (the discontinued proprietary DVD standard), these watermarks caused slight impairment of the image; a raindrop or bullet-hole effect could be seen by some in the picture. Watermarks also might require new equipment to play the discs.

Analog Protection System

APS (also called *CopyGuard* by Macrovision) is an analog protection system developed by Macrovision and is designed to prevent making VCR tapes of DVD-Video discs. APS requires codes to be added to the disc, as well as special modifications in the player. APS starts with the creation or mastering of a DVD, where APS is enabled by setting predefined control codes in the recording. During playback in an APS-enabled (Macrovision-enabled) player, the digital-to-analog converter (DAC) chip inside the player adds the APS signals to the analog output signal being sent to the screen. These additions to the signal are designed so that they are invisible when viewed on a television or monitor but cause copies made on most VCRs to appear distorted. Unfortunately, some TVs or other displays can react to the distortions added to create a less-than-optimum picture.

APS uses two signal modifications called automatic gain control and colorstripe. The automatic gain control process consists of pulses placed in the vertical scan interval of the video signal, which TVs can't detect but which cause dim and noisy pictures, loss of color, loss of video, tearing, and so forth on a VCR. This process has been used since 1985 on many prerecorded video tapes to prevent copying. The colorstripe process modifies colorburst information that is also transparent on television displays but produces lines across the picture when recorded on a VCR.

Note that many older players don't have the licensed Macrovision circuits and simply ignore the code to turn on the APS signal modifications. Also, various image stabilizer, enhancer, and copyguard decoder units are available that can plug in between the player and VCR to remove the APS copyguard signal and allow a perfect recording to be made.

Caring for Optical Media

Some people believe that optical discs and drives are indestructible when compared to their magnetic counterparts. Actually, modern optical drives are far less reliable than modern hard disk drives. Reliability is the bane of any removable media, and CD-ROMs and DVD-ROMs are no exceptions.

By far the most common causes of problems with optical discs and drives are scratches, dirt, and other contamination. Small scratches or fingerprints on the bottom of the disc should not affect performance because the laser focuses on a point inside the actual disc, but dirt or deep scratches can interfere with reading a disc.

To remedy this type of problem, you can clean the bottom surface of the CD with a soft cloth, but be careful not to scratch the surface in the process. The best technique is to wipe the disc in a radial fashion, using strokes that start from the center of the disc and emanate toward the outer edge. This way, any scratches will be perpendicular to the tracks rather than parallel to them, minimizing the interference they might cause. You can use any type of solution on the cloth to clean the disc, as long as it will not damage plastic. Most window cleaners are excellent at removing fingerprints and other dirt from the disc and don't damage the plastic surface.

If your disc has deep scratches, they can often be buffed or polished out. A commercial plastic cleaner such as that sold in auto parts stores for cleaning plastic instrument cluster and tail-lamp lenses is very good for removing these types of scratches. This type of plastic polish or cleaner has a very mild abrasive that polishes scratches out of a plastic surface. Products labeled as cleaners usually are designed for more serious scratches, whereas those labeled as polishes are usually milder and work well as a final buff after using the cleaner. Polishes can be used alone if the surface is not scratched very deeply. The Skip Doctor device made by Digital Innovations (`www.skipdoctor.com`) can be used to make the polishing job easier.

Most people are careful about the bottom of the disc because that is where the laser reads, but the top is actually more fragile! The reason is that the lacquer coating on top of the disc is very thin, normally only 6–7 microns (0.24–0.28 thousandths of an inch). If you write on a disc with a ball point pen, for example, you will press through the lacquer layer and damage the reflective layer underneath, ruining the disc. Also, certain types of markers have solvents that can eat through the lacquer and damage the disc as well. You should write on discs only with felt tip pens that have compatible inks, such as the Sharpie or Staedtler Lumocolor brand, or other markers specifically sold for writing on CDs. In any case, remember that scratches or dents on the top of the disc are more fatal than those on the bottom.

Read errors can also occur when dust accumulates on the read lens of your CD-ROM drive. You can try to clean out the drive and lens with a blast of "canned air" or by using a drive cleaner (which you can purchase at most stores that sell audio CDs).

If your discs and your drive are clean, but you still can't read a particular disc, your trouble might be due to disc capacity. Many older CD-ROM drives are unreliable when they try to read the outermost tracks of newer discs where the last bits of data are stored. You're more likely to run into this problem with a CD that has lots of data—including some multimedia titles. If you have this problem, you might be able to solve it with a firmware or driver upgrade for your CD-ROM drive, but the only solution might be to replace the drive.

▶▶ See "Updating the Firmware in a CD-RW or Rewritable DVD Drive," p. 491.

Sometimes too little data on the disc can be problematic as well. Some older CD-ROM drives use an arbitrary point on the disc's surface to calibrate their read mechanism, and if there happens to be no data at that point on the disc, the drive will have problems calibrating successfully. Fortunately, this problem usually can be corrected by a firmware or driver upgrade for your drive.

Many older drives have had problems working under Windows 9x. If you are having problems, contact your drive manufacturer to see whether a firmware or software-driver upgrade is available that might take care of your problem. With new high-speed drives available for well under $100, it might not make sense to spend any time messing with an older drive that is having problems. It might be more cost-effective to upgrade to a new drive (which won't have these problems and will likely be much faster) instead.

If you have problems reading a particular brand or type of disk in some drives but not others, you might have a poor drive/media match. Use the media types and brands recommended by the drive vendor.

If you are having problems with only one particular disc and not the drive in general, you might find that your difficulties are in fact caused by a defective disc. See whether you can exchange the disc for another to determine whether that is indeed the cause.

CD/DVD Read-Only Drives and Specifications

When evaluating a CD or DVD drive in a laptop computer, you should consider the following criteria:

- The drive's performance specifications
- The interface the drive requires for connection to your system

These criteria will affect how fast the drive operates, how it is connected to your system, and how convenient (or inconvenient) it may be to use.

Performance Specifications

Many factors in a drive can affect performance, and several specifications are involved. Typical performance figures published by manufacturers are the data-transfer rate, the access time, the internal cache or buffers (if any), and the interface the drive uses. The following sections will examine these specifications.

Data-Transfer Rate

The data-transfer rate tells you how quickly the drive can read from the disc and transfer to the host computer. Normally, transfer rates indicate the drive's capability for reading large, sequential streams of data.

Transfer speed is measured two ways. The one most commonly quoted with CD/DVD drives is the "×" speed, which is defined as a multiple of the particular standard base rate. For example, CD-ROM drives transfer at 153.6KBps according to the original standard. Drives that transfer twice that are 2×, 40 times that are 40×, and so on. DVD drives transfer at 1,385KBps at the base rate, whereas drives that are 20 times faster than that are listed as 20×. Note that because almost all faster drives feature CAV, the "×" speed usually indicated is a maximum that is seen only when data is read near the outside (end) of a disc. The speed near the beginning of the disc might be as little as half that, and, of course, average speeds are somewhere in the middle.

With recordable CD drives, the speed is reported for various modes. CD-R drives have two speeds listed (one for writing, the other for reading), CD-RW drives have three, and CD-RW/DVD-ROM drives have four. On a CD-RW drive, the speeds are in the form *A/B/C*, where *A* is the speed when writing CD-Rs, *B* is the speed when writing CD-RWs, and *C* is the speed when reading CDs. The first CD-RW drives on the market were 2/2/6, with versions up to 24/10/24 available for laptops today. CD-RW/DVD-ROM drives use the format *A/B/C-D*, where the fourth number represents the DVD-ROM reading speed. Some of the fastest CD-RW/DVD-ROM drives today report 24/10/24-8.

See the next sections in this chapter, "CD Drive Speed" and "DVD Drive Speed," for more information about speeds and transfer rates.

CD Drive Speed

When a drive seeks out a specific data sector or musical track on the disc, it looks up the address of the data from a table of contents contained in the lead-in area and positions itself near the beginning of this data across the spiral, waiting for the right string of bits to flow past the laser beam.

Because CDs originally were designed to record audio, the speed at which the drive reads the data had to be constant. To maintain this constant flow, CD-ROM data is recorded using a technique called *constant linear velocity (CLV)*. This means that the track (and thus the data) is always moving past the read laser at the same speed, which originally was defined as 1.3 meters per second. Because the track is a spiral that is wound more tightly near the center of the disc, the disc must spin at various rates to maintain the same track linear speed. In other words, to maintain a CLV, the disk must spin more quickly when the inner track area is read than when the outer track area is read. The speed of rotation in a 1× drive (1.3 meters per second is considered 1× speed) varies from 540rpm when reading the start (inner part) of the track, down to 212rpm when reading the end (outer part) of the track.

In the quest for greater performance, drive manufacturers began increasing the speeds of their drives by making them spin more quickly. A drive that spins twice as fast was called a 2× drive, one that spins four times faster was called 4×, and so on. This was fine until about the 12× point, where drives were spinning discs at rates from 2,568rpm to 5,959rpm to maintain a constant data rate. At higher speeds than this, it became difficult to build motors that could change speeds (spin up or down) as quickly as necessary when data was read from different parts of the disc. Because of this, most drives rated faster than 12× spin the disc at a fixed rotational rather than linear speed. This is termed *constant angular velocity (CAV)* because the angular velocity (or rotational speed) is what remains a constant.

CAV drives are also generally quieter than CLV drives because the motors don't have to try to accelerate or decelerate as quickly. A drive (such as most rewritables) that combines CLV and CAV technologies is referred to as *Partial-CAV* or *P-CAV*. Most writable drives, for example, function in CLV mode when burning the disc and in CAV mode when reading the disc. Table 10.12 compares CLV and CAV.

Table 10.12   CLV Versus CAV Technology Quick Reference

	CLV (Constant Linear Velocity)	CAV (Constant Angular Velocity)
Speed of CD rotation	Varies with data	Constant position on the CD—faster on inner tracks than on outer tracks
Data transfer rate	Constant	Varies with data position on the CD—faster on outer tracks than on inner tracks
Average noise level	Higher	Lower

CD-ROM drives have been available in speeds from 1× up to 56× and beyond. Most nonrewritable drives up to 12× are CLV; most drives from 16× and up are CAV. With CAV drives, the disc spins at a constant speed, which means that track data moves past the read laser at various speeds, depending on where the data is physically located on the CD (near the inner or outer part of the track). This also means that CAV drives read the data at the outer edge (end) of the disk more quickly than data near the center (beginning). This allows for some misleading advertising. For example, a 12× CLV drive reads data at 1.84MBps, no matter where that data is on the disc. On the other hand, a 16× CAV drive reads data at speeds up to 16× (2.46MBps) on the outer part of the disc, but it also reads at a much lower speed of only 6.9× (1.06MBps) on the inner part of the disc (that is the part they don't tell you). On average, this would be only 11.5×, or about 1.76MBps. In fact, the average is actually overly optimistic because discs are read from the inside (slower part) out, and an average would relate only to reading completely full discs. The real-world average could be much less than that.

What this all means is that on average the 12× CLV drive would be noticeably faster than the 16× drive, and faster than even a 20× drive! Remember that all advertised speeds on CAV drives are only the maximum transfer speed the drive can achieve, and it can achieve that only when reading the very outer (end) part of the disc.

Table 10.13 contains data showing CD-ROM drive speeds along with transfer rates and other interesting data.

Table 10.13   **CD-ROM Drive Speeds and Transfer Rates**

Column 1	Column 2	Column 3	Column 4	Column 5	Column 6
Advertised CD-ROM Speed (Max. if CAV)	Time to Read 74-Minute CD if CLV	Time to Read 80-Minute CD if CLV	Transfer Rate (Bytes/sec) (Max. if CAV)	Actual CD-ROM Speed (Min. if CAV)	Min. Transfer Rate if CAV (Bytes/sec)
1×	74.0	80.0	153,600	0.4×	61,440
2×	37.0	40.0	307,200	0.9×	138,240
4×	18.5	20.0	614,400	1.7×	261,120
6×	12.3	13.3	921,600	2.6×	399,360
8×	9.3	10.0	1,228,800	3.4×	522,240
10×	7.4	8.0	1,536,000	4.3×	660,480
12×	6.2	6.7	1,843,200	5.2×	798,720
16×	4.6	5.0	2,457,600	6.9×	1,059,840
20×	3.7	4.0	3,072,000	8.6×	1,320,960
24×	3.1	3.3	3,686,400	10.3×	1,582,080
32×	2.3	2.5	4,915,200	13.8×	2,119,680
40×	1.9	2.0	6,144,000	17.2×	2,641,920
48×	1.5	1.7	7,372,800	20.7×	3,179,520
50×	1.5	1.6	7,680,000	21.6×	3,317,760
52×	1.4	1.5	7,987,200	22.4×	3,440,640
56×	1.3	1.4	8,601,600	24.1×	3,701,760

Each of the columns in Table 10.13 are explained here:

Column 1. *Indicates the advertised drive speed. This is a constant speed if the drive is CLV (most 12× and lower) or a maximum speed only if CAV.*

Columns 2–4. *Indicate how long it would take to read a full disc if the drive is CLV. For CAV drives, those figures would be longer because the average read speed is less than the advertised speed. The fourth column indicates the data-transfer rate, which for CAV drives would be a maximum figure only when reading the end of a disc.*

Columns 5–6. *Indicate the actual minimum "×" speed for CAV drives, along with the minimum transfer speed (when reading the start of any disc) and an optimistic average speed (true only when reading a full disc; otherwise, it would be even lower) in both "×" and byte-per-second formats.*

Vibration problems can cause high-speed drives to drop to lower speeds to enable reliable reading of CD-ROMs. Your CD-ROM can become unbalanced, for example, if you apply a small paper label to its surface to identify the CD or affix its serial number or code for easy reinstallation. For this reason, many of the faster CD and DVD drives come with autobalancing or vibration-control mechanisms to overcome these problems. The only drawback is that if they detect a vibration, they slow down the disc, thereby reducing the transfer rate performance.

DVD Drive Speed

As with CDs, DVDs rotate counterclockwise (as viewed from the reading laser) and typically are recorded at a constant data rate called *constant linear velocity (CLV)*. This means that the track (and thus the data) is always moving past the read laser at the same speed, which originally was defined as

Column 7	Column 8	Column 9	Column 10	Column 11	Column 12
Average CD-ROM Speed if CAV	Average Transfer Rate if CAV (Bytes/sec)	Max. Linear Speed (m/sec)	Max. Linear Speed (mph)	Rotational Speed (Min. if CLV; Max. if CAV) (rpm)	Rotational Speed (Max. if CLV) (rpm)
0.7×	107,520	1.3	2.9	214	497
1.5×	222,720	2.6	5.8	428	993
2.9×	437,760	5.2	11.6	856	1,986
4.3×	660,480	7.8	17.4	1,284	2,979
5.7×	875,520	10.4	23.3	1,712	3,973
7.2×	1,098,240	13.0	29.1	2,140	4,966
8.6×	1,320,960	15.6	34.9	2,568	5,959
11.5×	1,758,720	20.8	46.5	3,425	7,945
14.3×	2,196,480	26.0	58.2	4,281	9,931
17.2×	2,634,240	31.2	69.8	5,137	11,918
22.9×	3,517,440	41.6	93.1	6,849	15,890
28.6×	4,392,960	52.0	116.3	8,561	19,863
34.4×	5,276,160	62.4	139.6	10,274	23,835
35.8×	5,498,880	65.0	145.4	10,702	24,828
37.2×	5,713,920	67.6	151.2	11,130	25,821
40.1×	6,151,680	72.8	162.8	11,986	27,808

Columns 7–8. Indicate the maximum linear speeds the drive will attain, in both meters per second and miles per hour. CLV drives maintain those speeds everywhere on the disc, whereas CAV drives reach those speeds only on the outer part of the disc.

Columns 9–12. Indicate the rotational speeds of a drive. The first of these columns shows how fast the disc spins when the start of the disc is being read; this would apply to either CAV or CLV drives. For CAV drives, that figure is constant no matter where on the disc the drive is reading. The last column shows the maximum rotational speed if the drive were a CLV type. Because most drives over 12× are CAV, these figures are mostly theoretical for the 16× and faster drives.

3.49 meters per second (or 3.84m/sec on dual-layer discs). Because the track is a spiral that is wound more tightly near the center of the disc, the disc must spin at varying rates to maintain the same track linear speed. In other words, to maintain a CLV, the disk must spin more quickly when the inner track area is read and more slowly when the outer track area is read. The speed of rotation in a 1× drive (3.49 meters per second is considered 1× speed) varies from 1,515rpm when reading the start (inner part) of the track down to 570rpm when reading the end (outer part) of the track.

Single-speed (1×) DVD-ROM drives provide a data-transfer rate of 1.385MBps, which means the data-transfer rate from a DVD-ROM at 1× speed is roughly equivalent to a 9× CD-ROM (the 1× CD-ROM data-transfer rate is 153.6KBps, or 0.1536MBps). This does not mean, however, that a 1× DVD drive can read CDs at 9× rates: DVD drives actually spin at a rate that is just under three times faster than a CD-ROM drive of the same speed. So, a 1× DVD drive spins at about the same rotational speed as a

Table 10.14   DVD Speeds and Transfer Rates

Column 1	Column 2	Column 3	Column 4	Column 5	Column 6	Column 7
Advertised DVD-ROM Speed (Max. if CAV)	Time to Read Single Layer DVD if CLV	Time to Read Dual-Layer DVD if CLV	Transfer Rate (Bytes/sec) (Max. if CAV)	Actual DVD Speed (Minimum if CAV)	Minimum Transfer Rate if CAV (Bytes/sec)	Average DVD Speed if CAV
1×	56.5	51.4	1,384,615	0.4×	553,846	0.7×
2×	28.3	25.7	2,769,231	0.8×	1,107,692	1.4×
4×	14.1	12.8	5,538,462	1.7×	2,353,846	2.9×
6×	9.4	8.6	8,307,692	2.5×	3,461,538	4.3×
8×	7.1	6.4	11,076,923	3.3×	4,569,231	5.7×
10×	5.7	5.1	13,846,154	4.1×	5,676,923	7.1×
12×	4.7	4.3	16,615,385	5.0×	6,923,077	8.5×
16×	3.5	3.2	22,153,846	6.6×	9,138,462	11.3×
20×	2.8	2.6	27,692,308	8.3×	11,492,308	14.2×
24×	2.4	2.1	33,230,769	9.9×	13,707,692	17.0×
32×	1.8	1.6	44,307,692	13.2×	18,276,923	22.6×
40×	1.4	1.3	55,384,615	16.6×	22,984,615	28.3×
48×	1.2	1.1	66,461,538	19.9×	27,553,846	34.0×
50×	1.1	1.0	69,230,769	20.7×	28,661,538	35.4×

Column 1. *Indicates the advertised drive speed. This is a constant speed if the drive is CLV or a maximum speed only if CAV (most DVD-ROM drives are CAV).*

Columns 2–4. *Indicate how long it would take to read a full disc (single or dual layer) if the drive is CLV. For CAV drives, these figures are longer because the average read speed is less than the advertised speed. The fourth column indicates the data transfer rate, which for CAV drives is a maximum figure seen only when reading the end of a disc.*

Columns 5–8. *Indicate the actual minimum "×" speed for CAV drives, along with the minimum transfer speed (when reading the start of any disc) and an optimistic average speed (true only when reading a full disc; otherwise, it's even lower) in both "×" and byte-per-second formats.*

Columns 9 and 10. *Indicate the maximum linear speeds the drive attains, in both meters per second and miles per hour. CLV drives maintain these speeds everywhere on the disc, whereas CAV drives reach these speeds only on the outer part of a disc.*

2.7× CD drive. Many DVD drives list two speeds: one for reading DVD discs and another for reading CD discs. For example, a DVD-ROM drive listed as a 16×/40× would indicate the performance when reading DVD/CD discs, respectively.

As with CDs, drive manufacturers began increasing the speeds of their DVD drives by making them spin more quickly. A drive that spins twice as fast was called a 2× drive, a drive that spins four times faster was called a 4× drive, and so on. At higher speeds, it became difficult to build motors that could change speeds (spin up or down) as quickly as needed when data was read from different parts of the disc. Because of this, faster DVD drives spin the disc at a fixed rotational rather than linear speed. This is termed *constant angular velocity (CAV)* because the angular velocity (or rotational speed) is what remains a constant.

Column 8	Column 9	Column 10	Column 11	Column 12	Column 13
Average Transfer Rate if CAV (Bytes/sec)	Maximum Linear Speed (m/sec)	Maximum Linear Speed (mph)	Single Layer Rot. Speed (Min. if CLV; Max. if CAV) (rpm)	Single Layer Rot. Speed (Max. if CLV) (rpm)	Usual Transfer Rate When Reading CD-ROMs
969,231	3.5	7.8	570	1,515	2.7×
1,938,462	7.0	15.6	1,139	3,030	5.4×
3,946,154	14.0	31.2	2,279	6,059	11×
5,884,615	20.9	46.8	3,418	9,089	16×
7,823,077	27.9	62.5	4,558	12,119	21×
9,761,538	34.9	78.1	5,697	15,149	27×
11,769,231	41.9	93.7	6,836	18,178	32×
15,646,154	55.8	124.9	9,115	24,238	43×
19,592,308	69.8	156.1	11,394	30,297	54×
23,469,231	83.8	187.4	13,673	36,357	64×
31,292,308	111.7	249.8	18,230	48,476	86×
39,184,615	139.6	312.3	22,788	60,595	107×
47,007,692	167.5	374.7	27,345	72,714	129×
48,946,154	174.5	390.3	28,485	75,743	134×

Columns 11 and 12. *Indicate the rotational speeds of a drive. The first column shows how quickly the disc spins when the drive reads the start of the disc. This applies to either CAV or CLV drives. For CAV drives, this figure is constant no matter where on the disc is being read. The second column shows the maximum rotational speed if the drive is a CLV type. Because most faster drives are CAV, these figures are mostly theoretical for the faster drives.*

Column 13. *Shows the speed the drive would be rated if it is a CD-ROM drive. This is based on the rotational speed, not the transfer rate. In other words, a 12× DVD drive would perform as a 32× CD-ROM drive when reading CDs. Most DVD drives list their speeds when reading CDs in the specifications. Due to the use of P-CAV (Partial-CAV) designs, some might have higher CD performances than the table indicates.*

The faster drives are useful primarily for data, not video. Having a faster drive can reduce or eliminate the pause during layer changes when playing a DVD video disc, but having a faster drive has no effect on video quality.

DVD-ROM drives have been available in speeds up to 20× or more, but because virtually all are CAV, they actually achieve the rated transfer speed only when reading the outer part of a disc. Table 10.14 shows the data rates for DVD drives reading DVD discs and how that rate compares to a CD-ROM drive.

Access Time

The access time for a CD or DVD drive is measured the same way as for hard disk drives. In other words, the access time is the delay between the drive receiving the command to read and its actual first reading of a bit of data. The time is recorded in milliseconds; a typical manufacturer's rating would be listed as 95ms. This is an average access rate; the true access rate depends entirely on where the data is located on the disc. When the read mechanism is positioned to a portion of the disc nearer to the narrower center, the access rate is faster than when it is positioned at the wider outer perimeter. Access rates quoted by many manufacturers are an average taken by calculating a series of random reads from a disc.

Obviously, a faster (that is, a lower) average access rate is desirable, especially when you rely on the drive to locate and pull up data quickly. Access times for CD and DVD drives have been steadily improving, and the advancements are discussed later in this chapter. Note that these average times are significantly slower than hard drives, ranging from 200ms to below 100ms, compared to the 8ms access time of a typical hard disk drive. Most of the speed difference lies in the construction of the drive itself. Hard drives have multiple-read heads that range over a smaller surface area of the medium; CD/DVD drives have only one laser pickup, and it must be capable of accessing the entire range of the disc. In addition, the data on a CD is organized in a single long spiral. When the drive positions its head to read a track, it must estimate the distance into the disc and skip forward or backward to the appropriate point in the spiral. Reading off the outer edge requires a longer access time than the inner segments, unless you have a CAV drive, which spins at a constant rate, so the access time to the outer tracks is equal to that of the inner tracks. Access times have fallen a great deal since the original single-speed drives came out. However, recently a plateau seems to have been reached with most CD/DVD drives hovering right around the 100ms area, with some as low as 80ms. With each increase in data-transfer speed, you usually see an improvement in access time as well. But as you can see in Table 10.15, these improvements are much less significant because of the physical limitation of the drive's single-read mechanism design.

Table 10.15 Typical CD-ROM Drive Access Times

Drive Speed	Access Time (ms)
1×	400
2×	300
3×	200
4×	150
6×	150
8×–12×	100
16×–24×	90
32×–52× or greater	85 or less

The times listed here are typical examples for good drives; within each speed category some drives are faster and some are slower. Because of the additional positioning accuracy required and the overall longer track, DVD drives usually report two access speeds: one when reading DVDs and the other when reading CDs. The DVD access times run usually 10ms–20ms slower than when reading CDs.

Buffer/Cache

Most CD/DVD drives include internal buffers or caches of memory installed onboard. These buffers are actual memory chips installed on the drive's circuit board that enable it to stage or store data in larger segments before sending it to the system. A typical buffer for a CD/DVD drive is 128KB, although drives are available that have either more or less (more is usually better). Recordable CD and DVD drives typically have much larger buffers of 2MB–4MB or more to prevent buffer underrun problems and to smooth writing operations. Generally, faster drives come with more buffer memory to handle the higher transfer rates.

Having buffer or cache memory for the CD/DVD drive offers a number of advantages. Buffers can ensure that the PC receives data at a constant rate; when an application requests data from the drive, the data can be found in files scattered across different segments of the disc. Because the drive has a relatively slow access time, the pauses between data reads can cause a drive to send data to the PC sporadically. You might not notice this in typical text applications, but on a drive with a slower access rate coupled with no data buffering, it is very noticeable—and even irritating—during the display of video or some audio segments. In addition, a drive's buffer, when under the control of sophisticated software, can read and have ready the disc's table of contents, thus speeding up the first request for data. A minimum size of 128KB for a built-in buffer or cache is recommended and is standard on many 24× and faster drives. For greater performance, look for drives with 256KB or larger buffers.

CPU Utilization

A once-neglected but very real issue in calculating computer performance is the impact that any piece of hardware or software has on the central processing unit (CPU). This "CPU utilization" factor refers to how much attention the processor must provide to the hardware or software to help it work. A low CPU utilization percentage score is desirable because the less time a CPU spends on any given hardware or software process, the more time it has for other tasks, and thus the greater the performance for your system. On CD-ROM drives, three factors influence CPU utilization: drive speed, drive buffer size, and interface type.

Drive buffer size can influence CPU utilization. For CD-ROM drives with similar performance ratings, the drive with a larger buffer is likely to require less CPU time (lower CPU utilization percentage) than the one with a smaller buffer.

Because drive speed and buffer size are more of a given, the most important factor influencing CPU utilization is the interface type. Traditionally, SCSI-interface CD-ROM drives have had far lower CPU utilization rates than ATAPI drives of similar ratings. One review of 12× drives done several years ago rated CPU utilization for ATAPI CD-ROM drives at 65%–80%, whereas SCSI CD-ROM drives checked in at less than 11%. When DMA or Ultra-DMA modes are used with an ATA interface drive, near-SCSI levels of low CPU utilization can be realized. Using DMA or Ultra-DMA modes can cut CPU utilization down to the 10% or lower range, leaving the CPU free to run applications and other functions. Fortunately, most modern laptops are preconfigured to use Ultra-DMA modes with any internal CD or DVD drives. With older systems, you might want to check the settings for the drive in the Windows Device Manager and make sure the DMA box is checked.

Direct Memory Access and Ultra-DMA

Bus-mastering ATA controllers use direct memory access (DMA) or Ultra-DMA transfers to improve performance and reduce CPU utilization. Virtually all modern ATA drives support Ultra-DMA. With bus mastering, CPU utilization for ATA/ATAPI and SCSI CD-ROM drives is about equal at around 11%. Therefore, it's to your benefit to enable DMA access for your CD-ROM drives (and your ATA hard drives, too) if your system permits it.

All modern ATA/ATAPI CD-ROM drives (12× and above) support DMA or Ultra-DMA transfers, as do all current laptops and operating systems such as Windows 95B and above. To determine whether your Windows 9x, Me, or XP system has this feature enabled, check the System Properties dialog box's Device Manager tab and click the plus sign (+) next to Hard Disk Controllers. A drive interface capable of handling DMA transfers lists "Bus Master" in the name. Next, check the hard drive and CD-ROM information for your system. You can use the properties sheet for your system's CD-ROM drives under Windows 9x/Me and Windows 2000/XP to find this information; you might need to open the system to determine your hard drive brand and model. Hard disk drives and CD-ROM drives that support MultiWord DMA Mode 2 (16.6MBps), Ultra-DMA Mode 2 (33MBps), Ultra-DMA Mode 4 (66MBps), or faster can use DMA transfers. Check your product literature or the manufacturer's website for information.

To enable DMA transfers if your motherboard and drives support it, open the Device Manager and then open the properties sheet for the controller or drive. Click the Settings or Advanced Settings tab and make sure DMA is enabled, if available. Depending on which version of Windows you are using, some have the DMA setting in the controller properties; others have it with the individual drives.

Repeat the same steps to enable DMA transfers for any additional hard drives and ATAPI CD-ROM drives in your computer. Restart your computer after making these changes.

Note

I strongly recommend that you back up your drives and your Windows 9x Registry before you enable DMA support or before you install and enable the driver to allow DMA support. If your system hangs after you enable this feature, you must restart the system in Safe mode and uncheck the DMA box. In some cases, if you can't access Safe mode, you might have to replace the Registry with the pre–DMA-enabled copy you saved. Otherwise, you'll be faced with editing Registry keys by hand to start your system again. Because DMA transfers bypass the CPU to achieve greater speed, DMA problems could result in data loss. Make backups first, instead of wishing you had later.

Drive interfaces that don't feature bus mastering either can't perform this speedup or need to have the correct driver installed. In some cases, depending on your Windows version and when your motherboard chipset was made, you must install chipset drivers to enable Windows to properly recognize the chipset and enable DMA modes. Virtually all motherboard chipsets produced since 1995 provide busmaster ATA support. Most of those produced since 1997 also provide Ultra-DMA support for up to 33MHz (Ultra-ATA/33) or 66MHz (Ultra-ATA/66) speed operation. Still, you should make sure that DMA is enabled to ensure you are benefiting from the performance it offers. Enabling DMA can dramatically improve DVD performance, for example.

Interfaces

The drive's interface is the electrical connection of the drive to the system's expansion bus. It's the data pipeline from the drive to the computer, and its importance shouldn't be minimized. Five types of common interfaces are available for attaching a CD-ROM, CD-R, CD-RW, DVD-ROM, DVD/CD-RW, or DVD+-RW drive to your system:

- USB
- FireWire (IEEE 1394/i.LINK)
- ATA/ATAPI (AT Attachment/AT Attachment Packet Interface)
- SCSI/ASPI (Small Computer System Interface/Advanced SCSI Programming Interface)
- Parallel port
- Serial-ATA

In general, if you are connecting an external drive, you should choose either USB or FireWire for the best performance and value.

USB 1.1 and earlier drives provide read and write transfer rates that match the fastest rates possible with IEEE 1284 parallel ports, with read rates on typical 6× models ranging from 1,145KBps to 1,200KBps. USB 2.0 and later provides a transfer rate up to 60MBps, which is 40 times faster than USB 1.1 and yet is fully backward compatible.

USB also provides benefits such as hot-swapping, the ability to plug and unplug a device without removing the power or rebooting the system. Additionally, USB devices are fully Plug and Play (PnP), allowing the device to be automatically recognized by the system and the drivers automatically installed.

External CD/DVD drives are available on the market with a FireWire (also called *IEEE 1394* or *i.LINK*) interface. FireWire is a high-performance external interface designed mainly for video use. FireWire evolved as an Apple standard, which is primarily used on Macintosh systems. Virtually all laptops built in 1998 and later include one or more USB ports in the system. Those built from 1998 through 2002 normally have USB 1.1 (also known as *Full-Speed* USB) ports, while those built in 2003 and later normally include USB 2.0 (also known as *Hi-Speed* USB) ports. Because fewer laptops include FireWire ports as a standard item, I normally recommend the more universally supported USB for external CD/DVD drives instead. Make sure any external drives you purchase use the faster USB 2.0, which is also far more common than FireWire versions. FireWire drives can be useful if you work in a dual-platform environment (both PCs and Macs). However, because most Macs also support USB (and you can easily add a USB interface to those that don't), if your primary platform is a PC, I'd still recommend USB over FireWire. If your system does not include either USB 2.0 or FireWire, those interfaces can easily be added via CardBus adapters.

SCSI is also available for external drives used on laptops, but the choices are very limited, and you will normally need to add an expensive PC Card or CardBus SCSI adapter to your system. Unless you have a specific need for SCSI drives on a laptop, you should probably stick with USB instead.

ATA/ATAPI is the standard interface used by all internally mounted drives, including those in modular or swappable bays. In general, an internal bay drive will offer the greatest performance for the lowest cost, and has the convenience associated with being internally mounted. The only drawback is that if you have several laptop systems, unless they use the same type of modular bay, you will not be able to share drives among the different systems, something that is very easy to do with external USB drives.

In the past, some external CD-ROM or CD-RW drives were available in versions that connected to a parallel port. USB has, for the most part, replaced the parallel port for this type of use. If you use a parallel port drive, for best performance it's recommended that you set your printer port to use IEEE 1284 standards, such as ECP/EPP or ECP, before connecting your parallel port CD-ROM. These are bidirectional, high-speed extensions to the standard Centronics parallel port standard and provide better performance for virtually any recent parallel device. If your operating system supports Plug and Play (PnP), such as Windows 9x/Me, or 2000/XP, simply plugging a PnP drive into the parallel port allows the OS to detect the new hardware and load the appropriate driver automatically.

Serial-ATA (SATA) is not commonly used for removable CD/DVD drives in a notebook but might well be in the near future because the small connector allows the manufacturer to save space. On the desktop, however, some Serial-ATA CD/DVD drives are available. They don't generally offer a performance advantage, just a smaller connector and thinner cable that could be beneficial in small cases with restricted airflow. Some manufacturers have also started offering external Serial-ATA CD/DVD drives, but since there's no standard for an external Serial-ATA connector, they use the standard internal Serial-ATA connector. Unfortunately, this connector isn't really designed for repeated use as is common with external CD/DVD drives. Performance, however, is excellent as per the Serial-ATA standard bandwidth of 150MBps.

Note

Parallel port CD/DVD drives nearly always include a cable with a pass-through connector. This connector plugs in to the parallel port and, if necessary, a printer cable can plug in to the connector. This enables you to continue using the port to connect to your printer while sharing the interface with the CD-ROM drive. Note that you might experience performance problems when trying to print and read from the drive at the same time.

With the popularity, performance, and ease of use of USB, however, I would recommend a USB external drive over a parallel port version. USB drives are much faster, more compatible, easier to install and use. If you need parallel port support for some systems, look for drives that feature parallel and USB interfaces, such as the Backpack product line from Micro Solutions, Inc. See the Vendor List on the CD for website and contact information.

Writable CDs

Although the CD originally was conceived as a read-only device, these days you easily can create your own data and audio CDs. By purchasing CD-R or CD-RW discs and drives, you can record (or burn) your own CDs. This enables you to store large amounts of data at a cost that is lower than most other removable, random-access media.

Newcomers to the world of PCs might be surprised to see just how far recordable CD technology, performance, and pricing have come. Today, you can buy external recorders that operate at up to 52× speeds and cost under $100. You can even purchase internal slimline CD drives for laptops with modular bays. This is compared to the first CD-R recording system on the market in 1988, which cost more than $50,000 (back then, they used a $35,000 Yamaha audio recording drive along with thousands of dollars of additional error correction and other circuitry for CD-ROM use), operated at 1× speed only, and was part of a subsystem that was the size of a washing machine! The blank discs also cost about $100 each—a far cry from the 15 cents or less they cost today (if you purchase in bulk and are willing to supply your own jewel cases). With prices that high, the main purpose for CD recording was to produce prototype CDs that could then be replicated via the standard stamping process.

In 1991, Philips introduced the first 2× recorder (the CDD 521), which was about the size of a stereo receiver and cost about $12,000. Sony, in 1992, and then JVC, in 1993, followed with their 2× recorders, and the JVC was the first drive that had the half-height 5 1/4-inch form factor that most desktop system drives still use today. In 1995, Yamaha released the first 4× recorder (the CDR100), which sold for $5,000. A breakthrough in pricing came in late 1995 when Hewlett-Packard released a 2× recorder (the 4020i, which was actually made for HP by Philips) for under $1,000. This proved to be exactly what the market was waiting for. With a surge in popularity after that, prices rapidly fell to below $500, and then down to $200 or less. In 1996, Ricoh introduced the first CD-RW drive. CD-RW drives began appearing in laptop internal versions starting in late 2000 and early 2001.

Compared with either tape or other removable media, using a CD burner is a very cost-effective and easy method for transporting large files or making archival copies. Another benefit of the CD for archiving data is that CDs have a much longer shelf life than tapes and other types of removable media.

Two main types of recordable CD drives and discs are available, called CD-R (recordable) and CD-RW (rewritable). Because all CD-RW drives can also function as CD-R drives, and the prices of CD-R and RW drives are similar, all drives sold today are CD-RW. Those drives can work with either CD-R or CD-RW discs. In addition, because the CD-RW discs are more expensive than CD-R discs, only half as fast (or less) as CD-R discs, and won't work in all CD audio or CD-ROM drives, people usually write to CD-R media in their CD-RW drives.

Note

Because of differences in reflectivity of the media, older CD and DVD drives can't read CD-RW media. Most newer CD-ROM and DVD-ROM drives conform to the MultiRead specification and, as such, can read CD-RWs. But many older drives still out there do not conform. As such, if you are recording something that many people or systems will need to read, CD-R is your best choice for overall compatibility.

CD-R media are WORM (write once read many) media, meaning that after you fill a CD-R with data, that data is permanently stored and can't be erased. The write-once limitation makes this type of disc less than ideal for system backups or other purposes in which it would be preferable to reuse the same media over and over. However, because of the low cost of CD-R media, you might find that making permanent backups to essentially disposable CD-R discs is as economically feasible as tape or other media.

CD-RW discs can be reused up to 1,000 times, making them suitable for almost any type of data-storage task. When they were first introduced, there were many CD-R–only drives; however, today most recordable CD drives are both CD-R and CD-RW in one. The following subsections examine these two standards and ways you can use them for your own data-storage needs.

CD-R

Once recorded, CD-R discs can be played back or read in any standard CD-ROM drive. CD-R discs are useful for providing archival storage and creating master CDs, which can be duplicated for distribution within a company.

CD-Rs function using the same principle as standard CD-ROMs, by bouncing laser light off the disc and tracking the changes in reflectivity when pit/land and land/pit boundaries are encountered. The main difference is that instead of being stamped or embossed into plastic, as on regular CDs, CD-Rs have images of pits burned onto a raised groove instead. Therefore, the pits are not really raised bumps like on a standard CD but instead are rendered as dark (burned) areas on the groove that reflect less light. Because the overall reflectivity of pit and land areas remains the same as on a stamped disc, normal CD-ROM or CD audio drives can read CD-Rs exactly as if they were stamped discs.

Part of the recording process with CD-Rs starts before you even insert the disc into the drive. CD-R media are manufactured much like standard CDs: A stamper is used to mold a base of polycarbonate plastic. However, instead of stamping pits and lands, the stamper imprints a spiral groove (called a *pre-groove*) into the disc. From the perspective of the reading (and writing) laser underneath the disc, this groove is seen as a raised spiral ridge and not a depression.

The pre-groove (or ridge) is not perfectly straight; instead, it has a slight wobble. The amplitude of the wobble is generally very small compared to the track pitch (spacing). The groove separation is 1.6 microns, but it wobbles only 0.030 microns from side to side. The wobble of a CD-R groove is modulated to carry supplemental information read by the drive. The signal contained in the wobble is called *absolute time in pre-groove (ATIP)* because it is modulated with time code and other data. The time code is the same minutes:seconds:frame format that will eventually be found in the Q-subcode of the frames after they are written to the disc. The ATIP enables the drive to locate positions on the disc before the frames are actually written. Technically, the wobble signal is frequency shift keyed with a carrier frequency of 22.05KHz and a deviation of 1KHz. The wobble uses changes in frequency to carry information.

To complete the CD-R disc, an organic dye is evenly applied across the disc by a spin-coating process. Next, a gold reflective layer is then applied, followed by a protective coat of UV-cured lacquer to protect the gold and dye layers. Gold is used in CD-R discs to get the reflectivity as high as possible, and it was found that the organic dye tends to oxidize aluminum. Then, silk-screen printing is applied on top of the lacquer for identification and further protection. When seen from the underside, the laser used to read (or write) the disc first passes through the clear polycarbonate and the dye layer, hits the gold layer where it is reflected back through the dye layer and the plastic, and finally is picked up by the optical pickup sensor in the drive.

The dye and reflective layers together have the same reflective properties as a *virgin* CD. In other words, a CD reader would read the groove of an unrecorded CD-R disc as one long land. To record on a CD-R disc, a laser beam of the same wavelength (780nm), as is normally used to read the disc, but with 10 times the power, is used to heat up the dye. The laser is fired in a pulsed fashion at the top of the ridge (groove), heating the layer of organic dye to between 482° and 572°F (250°–300°C). This temperature literally burns the organic dye, causing it to become opaque. When read, this prevents the light from passing through the dye layer to the gold and reflecting back, having the same effect of canceling the laser reflection that an actual raised pit would on a normal stamped CD.

Figure 10.12 shows the CD-R media layers, along with the pre-groove (raised ridge from the laser perspective) with burned pits.

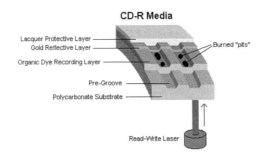

Figure 10.12   CD-R media layers.

The drive reading the disc is fooled into thinking a pit exists, but no actual pit exists; there's simply a spot of less-reflective material on the ridge. This use of heat to create the pits in the disc is why the recording process is often referred to as *burning* a CD. When burned, portions of the track are changed from a reflective to a nonreflective state. This change of state is permanent and can't be undone, which is why CD-R is considered a write-once medium.

CD-R Capacity

All CD-R drives can work with the standard 650MiB (682MB) CD-R media (equal to 74 minutes of recorded music), as well as the higher-capacity 700MiB (737MB) CD-R blank discs (equal to 80 minutes of recorded music). The 80-minute discs cost only about 2 cents more than the 74-minute discs, so most would figure why not purchase only the higher-capacity media? Although the extra 55MB of storage can be useful and the cost difference is negligible, the 80-minute discs can actually be harder to read on older CD-ROM and CD-DA drives, especially car audio units. The reason is that to get the extra 55MB/6 minutes of capacity, the spiral track is wound a little more tightly, making the discs a bit more difficult to read. If you'll be using the discs for audio or interchange purposes and might be dealing with older equipment, you might want to stick with the 74-minute discs instead. If not, the 80-minute media will be just fine.

Some drives and burning software are capable of overburning, whereby they write data partially into the lead-out area and essentially extend the data track. This is definitely risky as far as compatibility is concerned. Many drives, especially older ones, fail when reading near the end of an overburned disc. It's best to consider this form of overclocking CDs somewhat experimental. It might be useful for your own purposes if it works with your drives and software, but interchangeability will be problematic.

CD-R Media Color

There has been some controversy over the years about which colors of CD-R media provide the best performance. Table 10.16 shows the most common color combinations, along with which brands use them and some technical information.

Some brands are listed with more than one color combination, due to production changes or different product lines. You should check color combinations whenever you purchase a new batch of CD-R media if you've found that particular color combinations work better for you in your applications.

Table 10.16   CD-R Media Color and Its Effect on Recording

Media Color (Reflective Layer-Die Layer)	Brands	Technical Notes
Gold-gold	Mitsui, Kodak, Maxell, Ricoh	Phthalocyanine dye.
		Less tolerance for power variations.
		Has a rated life span of up to 100 years.
		Less likely to work in a wide variety of drives.
		Invented by Mitsui Toatsu Chemicals.
		Works best in drives that use a Long Write Strategy (longer laser pulse) to mark media.
Gold-green	Imation (nee 3M), Memorex, Kodak, BASF, TDK	Cyanine dye; more forgiving of disc-write and disc-read variations.
		Has a rated life span of 10 years (older media).
		Recent media have a rated life span of 20–50 years. (silver/green).
		Color combination developed by Taiyo Yuden.
		Used in the development of the original CD-r standards.
		De facto standard for CD-R industry and was the original color combination used during the development of CD-R technology.
		Works best in drives that use a Short Write Strategy (shorter laser pulse) to mark media.
Silver-blue	Verbatim, DataLifePlus, HiVal, Maxell, TDK	Process developed by Verbatim.
		Azo dye.
		Similar performance to green media, plus rated to last up to 100 years.
		A good choice for long-term archiving.

Note

PlayStation games originally came on discs that were tinted black for appearance. Soon blank CD-R recordable discs were also available with this same black tint in the polycarbonate. The black tint is purely cosmetic; it is invisible to the infrared laser that reads/writes the disc. In other words, "black" CD-R discs are functionally identical to clear discs and can be made using any of the industry-standard dyes in the recording layer. The black tint hides the recording layer visually, which means although the laser passes right through it, the black tint prevents you from observing the color of the dye in the recording layer directly.

Ultimately, although the various color combinations have their advantages, the best way to choose a media type is to try a major brand of media in your CD-R/CD-RW drive with both full-disc and small-disc recording jobs and then try the completed CD-R in as wide a range of CD-ROM drive brands and speeds as you can.

The perfect media for you will be the ones that offer you the following:

- High reliability in writing (check your drive model's list of recommended media)
- No dye or reflective surface dropouts (areas where the media won't record properly)
- Durability through normal handling (scratch-resistant coating on media surface)
- Compatibility across the widest range of CD-ROM drives
- Lowest unit cost

If you have problems recording reliably with certain types of media, or if you find that some brands with the same speed rating are much slower than others, contact your drive vendor for a firmware upgrade. Firmware upgrades can also help your drive recognize new types of faster media from different vendors.

Choosing the Best Media

After you determine which media work the best for you and your target drives, you might still be faced with a wide variety of choices, including conventional surface, printable surface, unbranded, jewel case, and bulk on spindle. The following list discusses these options:

- **Conventional surface**—Choose this type of media if you want to use a marker to label the CD rather than adding a paper label. This type of CD often has elaborate labeling, including areas to indicate CD title, date created, and other information, as well as prominent brand identification. Because of the surface marking, it's not suitable for relabeling unless you use very opaque labels. It's a good choice for internal backups and data storage, though, where labeling is less important.

- **Printable surface**—Choose this type of media if you have a CD printer (a special type of inkjet printer that can print directly onto the face of the CD). Because the brand markings are usually low-contrast or even nonexistent (to allow overprinting), this type also works well with labeling kits such as NEATO and others.

- **Unbranded**—Usually sold in bulk on spindle, these discs are a good choice for economy or use with labeling kits.

- **Jewel case**—Any of the preceding versions can be sold with jewel cases (the same type of case used for CD-ROM software and music CDs). This is a good choice if you plan to distribute the media in a jewel case, but it raises your costs if you plan to distribute or store the media in paper, Tyvek, or plastic sleeves. Hint: Use extra jewel cases to replace your broken jewel cases in your CD software or music collection!

■ **Bulk on spindle**—This type of media generally comes with no sleeves and no cases. It is usually the lowest-priced packaging within any brand of media. This is an excellent choice for mass duplication, or for those who don't use jewel cases for distribution.

CD-R Media Recording Speed Rating

With laptop CD-R drive mastering speeds ranging from 1× (now-discontinued first-generation units) up through fast 12× and state-of-the-art 24× rates, it's important to check the speed rating (× rating) of your CD-R media. Most branded media on the market today are rated to work successfully at up to 16× recording speeds. Some brands indicate this specifically on their packaging, whereas you must check the websites for others to get this information. If speed ratings are unavailable, you might want to restrict your burning to 8× or lower. Media rated 16× or higher are now the most popular, but speed ratings higher than that might be more difficult to find.

CD-RW

Beginning in early 1996, an industry consortium that included Ricoh, Philips, Sony, Yamaha, Hewlett-Packard, and Mitsubishi Chemical Corporation announced the CD-RW format. The design was largely led by Ricoh, and it was the first manufacturer to introduce a CD-RW drive, in May of 1996. The CD-RW drive was the MP6200S, which was a 2/2/6 (2× record, 2× rewrite, 6× read) rated unit. At the same time, the Orange Book Part III was published, officially defining the CD-RW standard. In late 2000 and early 2001, CD-RW drives began to appear internally installed in laptops, and today most systems include combo DVD and CD-RW drives.

CD-RW drives are fully backward compatible with CD-R drives and can read and write the same CD-R media with the same capabilities. So, a CD-RW drive can also function as a CD-R drive. CD-RW discs can be burned or written to just like CD-Rs; the main difference is that they can be erased and reburned again and again. They are very useful for prototyping a disc that will then be duplicated in less expensive CD-R or even stamped discs for distribution. They can be rewritten at least 1,000 times or more. Additionally, with packet-writing software, they can even be treated like a giant floppy disk, where you simply drag and drop or copy and delete files at will. Although CD-RW discs are more expensive than CD-R media, CD-RWs are still far cheaper than optical cartridges and other removable formats. This makes CD-RW a viable technology for system backups, file archiving, and virtually any other data-storage task.

Note

The CD-RW format originally was referred to as *CD-Erasable*, or *CD-E*.

Four main differences exist between CD-RW and CD-R media. In a nutshell, CD-RW discs are

■ Rewritable

■ More expensive

■ Slower when writing

■ Less reflective

Besides the CD-RW media being rewritable and costing a bit more, these discs also are writable at about half (or less) the speed of CD-R discs. The reason is that the laser needs more time to operate on a particular spot on the disk when writing. They also have a lower reflectivity, which limits readability in older drives. Many older standard CD-ROM and CD-R drives can't read CD-RWs. However, MultiRead capability is now found in virtually all CD-ROM drives of 24× speed or above, enabling them to read CD-RWs without problems. In general, CD-DA drives—especially the car audio players—seem to have the most difficulty reading CD-RWs. So, for music recording or compatibility with older drives, you should probably stick to CD-R media. Look for the MultiRead logo on a CD-ROM drive, which indicates the capability to read CD-RW.

CD-RW drives and media use a phase-change process to create the illusion of pits on the disc. As with CD-R media, the disc starts out with the same polycarbonate base with a wobbled pre-groove molded in, which contains ATIP information. Then, on top of the base, a special dielectric (insulating) layer is spin-coated, followed by the phase-change recording layer, another dielectric layer, an aluminum reflective layer, and finally a UV-cured lacquer protective layer (and optional screen printing). The dielectric layers above and below the recording layer are designed to insulate the polycarbonate and reflective layers from the intense heat used during the phase-change process.

Figure 10.13 shows the CD-RW media layers, along with the pre-groove (raised ridge from the laser perspective) with burned pits in the phase-change layer.

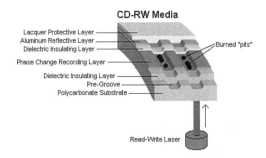

Figure 10.13   CD-RW media layers.

Instead of burning an organic dye, as with CD-R, the recording layer in a CD-RW disc is made up of a phase-change alloy consisting of silver, indium, antimony, and tellurium (Ag-In-Sb-Te). The reflective part of the recording layer is an aluminum alloy, the same as used in normal stamped discs. The read/write laser works from the underside of the disk, where the groove again appears like a ridge, and the recording is made in the phase-change layer on top of this ridge.

The recording layer of Ag-In-Sb-Te alloy normally has a polycrystalline structure that is about 20% reflective. When data is written to a CD-RW disc, the laser in the drive alternates between two power settings, called P-write and P-erase. The higher power setting (P-write) is used to heat the material in the recording layer to a temperature between 500° and 700°C (932°–1,292°F), causing it to melt. In a liquid state, the molecules of the material flow freely, losing their polycrystalline structure and taking what is called an *amorphous* (random) state. When the material then solidifies in this amorphous state, it is only about 5% reflective. When being read, these areas lower in reflectivity simulate the pits on a stamped CD-ROM disc.

That would be all to the story if CD-RW discs were read-only, but because they can be rewritten, there must be a way to bring the material back to a polycrystalline state. This is done by setting the laser to the lower-power P-erase mode. This heats the active material to approximately 200°C (392°F), which is well below the liquid melting point but high enough to soften the material. When the material is softened and allowed to cool more slowly, the molecules realign from a 5% reflective amorphous state back to a 20% reflective polycrystalline state. These higher reflective areas simulate the lands on a stamped CD-ROM disc.

Note that despite the name of the P-erase laser power setting, the disc is not ever explicitly "erased." Instead, CD-RW uses a recording technique called *direct overwrite*, in which a spot doesn't have to be erased to be rewritten; it is simply rewritten. In other words, when data is recorded, the laser remains on and pulses between the P-write and P-erase power levels to create amorphous and polycrystalline areas of low and high reflectivity, regardless of which state the areas were in previously. It is similar in many ways to writing data on a magnetic disk that also uses direct overwrite. Every sector already has data patterns, so when you write data, all you are really doing is writing new patterns. Sectors are never really erased; they are merely overwritten. The media in CD-RW discs are designed to be written and rewritten up to 1,000 times.

CD-RW Speeds

The original Orange Book Part III Volume 1 (CD-RW specification) allowed for CD-RW writing at up to 4× speeds. New developments in the media and drives were required to support speeds higher than that, so in May 2000, Part III Volume 2 was published, defining CD-RW recording at speeds from 4× to 10×. This new revision of the CD-RW standard is called *High-Speed Rewritable*, and both the discs and drives capable of CD-RW speeds higher than 4× will indicate this via the logos printed on them. Part III Volume 3, published in September 2002, defines Ultra-Speed drives, which are CD-RW drives capable of recording speeds 8× to 24×.

Because of the differences in High-Speed and UltraSpeed media, High-Speed media can be used only in High-Speed and Ultra-Speed drives; Ultra-Speed media can be used only in Ultra-Speed drives. Both High-Speed and Ultra-Speed drives can use standard 2×–4× media, enabling them to interchange data with computers that have standard-speed CD-RW drives. Therefore, choosing the wrong media to interchange with another system can prevent the other system from reading the media. If you don't know which speed of CD-RW media the target computer supports, I recommend you either use standard 2×–4× media or create a CD-R.

Because of differences in the UDF standards used by the packet-writing software that drags and drops files to CD-RW drives, the need to install a UDF reader on systems with CD-ROM drives, and the incapability of older CD-ROM and first-generation DVD-ROM drives to read CD-RW media, I recommend using CD-RW media for personal backups and data transfer between your own computers. However, when you send CD data to another user, CD-R is universally readable, making it a better choice.

MultiRead Specifications

The original Red and Yellow Book CD standards specified that the lands on a CD should have a minimum reflectance value of about 70%, and the pits should have a maximum reflectance of about 28%. This means that the area of a disc that represents a land should reflect back no less than 70% of the laser light directed at it, whereas the pits should reflect no more than 28%. In the early 1980s when these standards were developed, the photodetector diodes used in the drives were relatively insensitive, and these minimum and maximum reflectance requirements were deliberately designed to create enough brightness and contrast between pits and lands to accommodate them.

On a CD-RW disc, the reflectance of a land is approximately 20% (plus or minus 5%), and the reflectivity of a pit is only 5%, obviously well below the original requirements. Fortunately, it was found that by the addition of a relatively simple AGC circuit, the ratio of amplification in the detector circuitry can be changed dynamically to allow for reading the lower-reflective CD-RW discs. Therefore, although CD-ROM drives were not initially capable of reading CD-RW discs, modifying the existing designs to enable them to do so wasn't difficult. However, you might encounter problems reading CD-RW discs when using CD audio drives, especially older ones. Because CD-RW first came out in 1996 (and took a year or more to become popular), most CD-ROM drives manufactured in 1997 or earlier have problems reading CD-RW discs. Reflectivity is also a problem on DVD-Video and

DVD-ROM drives; because they use a different frequency laser, they actually have more trouble reading CD-R discs than CD-RWs.

DVDs also have some compatibility problems. With DVD, the problem isn't as much simple reflectivity as it is an inherent incompatibility with the laser wavelength used for DVD versus CD-R and CD-RW. The problem in this case stems from the dyes used in the recording layer of CD-R and CD-RW discs, which are very sensitive to the wavelength of light used to read them. At the proper CD laser wavelength of 780nm, they are very reflective, but at other wavelengths, the reflectivity falls off markedly. Normally, CD-ROM drives use a 780nm (infrared) laser to read the data, whereas DVD drives use a shorter wavelength 650nm (red) laser. Although the shorter-wavelength laser works well for reading commercial CD-ROM discs because the aluminum reflective layer they use is equally reflective at the shorter DVD laser wavelength, it doesn't work well at all for reading CD-R and CD-RW discs.

Fortunately, a solution was first introduced by Sony and then similarly by all the other DVD drive manufacturers. This solution consists of a dual-laser pickup that incorporates both a 650nm (DVD) and 780nm (CD) laser. Some of these used two discrete pickup units with separate optics mounted to the same assembly, but they eventually changed to dual-laser units that use the same optics for both, making the pickup smaller and less expensive. Because most manufacturers wanted to make a variety of drives—including cheaper ones without the dual-laser pickup—a standard needed to be created so that someone purchasing a drive would know the drive's capabilities.

So, how can you tell whether your drive is compatible with CD-R and CD-RW discs? To demonstrate the compatibility of a particular drive, the Optical Storage Technology Association (OSTA) created industry-standard tests and logos that would guarantee specific levels of compatibility. These are called the MultiRead specifications. Currently, there are two levels:

- **MultiRead**—For CD-ROM drives
- **MultiRead2**—For DVD-ROM drives

In addition, a similar MultiPlay standard exists for consumer DVD-Video and CD-DA devices.

Table 10.17 shows the two levels of MultiRead capability that can be assigned to drives and the types of media guaranteed to be readable in such drives.

Table 10.17   MultiRead and MultiRead2 Compatibility Standards for CD/DVD Drives

Media	MultiRead	MultiRead2
CD-DA	X	X
CD-ROM	X	X
CD-R	X	X
CD-RW	X	X
DVD-ROM	—	X
DVD-Video	—	X
DVD-Audio	—	X
DVD-RAM	—	X

X = Compatible; the drive will read this type of media.
— = Incompatible; the drive won't read this type of media.

Note that MultiRead also indicates that the drive is capable of reading discs written in packet-writing mode because this mode is now being used more commonly with both CD-R and CD-RW media.

To determine whether your drive meets either of these standards, look for the MultiRead or MultiRead2 logo on the drive. These logos are shown in Figure 10.14.

Figure 10.14   MultiRead and MultiRead2 logos.

The presence of one of these logos guarantees that particular level of compatibility. If you are purchasing a CD-ROM or DVD drive and want to be able to read recordable or rewritable discs, be sure to look for the MultiRead or MultiRead2 logo on your drive. Especially in the case of DVD drives, MultiRead2 versions generally are more expensive because of the extra cost of the dual-mode laser pickup required. Virtually all DVD-ROM drives for computers have the dual-pickup mechanism, enabling them to properly read CD-R or CD-RW discs. However, most DVD-Video players used in entertainment systems do not have the dual pickups.

You can obtain the latest versions of the MultiRead specification (revision 1.11, October 23, 1997) and MultiRead 2 specification (revision 1.0, December 6, 1999) from the OSTA website.

How to Reliably Record CDs

With typical burn times for full CD-Rs ranging from just over 3 minutes (24×) to as long as 80 minutes (1×), it is frustrating when a buffer underrun or some other problem forces you to rewrite your CD-RW disc or, worse yet, turn your CD-R media to coasters—unusable discs that must be discarded.

Five major factors influence your ability to create a working CD-R: interface type, drive buffer size, the location and condition of the data you want to record to CD-R, the recording speed, and whether the computer is performing other tasks while trying to create the CD-R.

To improve the odds of getting reliable CD-R/RW creation, look for drives with the following attributes:

- **A large data buffer (2MB or larger) or, better yet, some form of buffer underrun protection**—The data buffer in the drive holds information read from the original data source so that if a pause in data reading occurs, there's less of a possibility of a buffer underrun until the on-drive buffer runs empty. A larger buffer minimizes the chance of "running out of data." Newer drives with buffer underrun protection virtually eliminate this problem, no matter what size buffer is in the drive.

- **Support for UDMA operating modes**—As you've already seen, UDMA modes transfer data more quickly and with less CPU intervention than earlier versions of ATA. To use this feature, you'll also need a laptop with a bus-mastering UDMA interface with the appropriate drivers installed.

Tip

If you have problems with reliable CD-R creation at the drive's maximum speed, try using a lower speed (4× instead of 8×, for example). Your mastering job will take twice as long, but it's better to create a working CD-R slowly than ruin a blank quickly.

An alternative approach is to use packet-writing software to create your CD-R. All late-model CD-R/CD-RW drives support packet writing, which allows drag-and-drop copying of individual files to the CD-R/RW rather than transferring all the files at once, as with normal mastering software. This "a little at a time" approach means that less data must be handled in each write and can make the difference between success and failure. If your drive supports this feature, it probably includes packet-writing software in the package. Note that although packet-written CDs can be read with Windows 9x, Me, NT, and 2000, they can't be read with Windows 3.1 and MS-DOS because these operating systems don't have drivers available that support packet-written CDs. Note that some CD-mastering software supports packet writing to CD-Rs, but others don't.

Buffer Underruns

Whenever a drive writes data to a CD-R/RW disc in either Disk at Once or Track at Once mode, it writes to the spiral track on the CD, alternating on and off to etch the pattern into the raw media. Because the drive can't easily realign where it starts and stops writing like a hard drive can, after it starts writing, it must typically continue until it's finished with the track or disc. Otherwise, the recording (and disc if it is a CD-R) will be ruined. This means that the CD-recording software, in combination with your system hardware, must be capable of delivering a consistent stream of data to the drive while it's writing. To aid in this effort, the software uses a buffer that it creates on your hard disk to temporarily store the data as it is being sent to the drive.

If the system is incapable of delivering data at a rate sufficient to keep the drive happy, you receive a buffer underrun message and the recording attempt fails. The buffer underrun message indicates that the drive had to abort recording because it ran out of data in its buffer to write to the CD. For many years, this was the biggest problem people had when recording to CD-R/RW media.

And for many years, the best way to prevent buffer underruns was to either slow down the writing speeds or have a large buffer in the recording drive, as well as to use the fastest interface and reading drive possible. Nobody wants to write at lower speeds (otherwise, why buy a fast drive?), so buffer sizes grew as did the interface speeds. Still, it was possible to get a buffer underrun if, for example, you tried browsing web pages or doing other work while burning a disc.

Buffer Underrun Protection

Sanyo was the first to develop a technology that eliminates buffer underruns once and for all. It calls the technology *BURN (buffer underrun) Proof*, which sounds a little confusing (some people thought it prevented any writing on discs), but in practice it has proven to be excellent.

After Sanyo, several other companies have developed similar and compatible technology with various names. Here are some of the most common you'll see:

- BURN-Proof, from Sanyo
- JustLink, from Ricoh
- Waste-Proof, from Yamaha
- Safeburn, from Yamaha
- Superlink, from Mediatek

You will see these technologies on many vendors' drives because most developers of this technology license it to various drive makers.

Buffer underrun protection technology involves having a special chipset in the drive, which monitors the drive buffer. When it anticipates that a buffer underrun might occur (the buffer is running low on data), it temporarily suspends the recording until more data fills the buffer. When the buffer is sufficiently restocked, the drive then locates exactly where the recording left off earlier and restarts recording again immediately after that position.

According to the Orange Book specification, gaps between data in a CD recording must not be more than 100 milliseconds in length. The buffer underrun technology can restart the recording with a gap of 40–45 milliseconds or less from where it left off, which is well within the specification. The error correction built in to the recording easily compensates for these small gaps, so no data is lost.

Note that it is important that the drive incorporate buffer underrun technology, but the recording software must support it as well for everything to work properly. Fortunately, all the popular CD-recording programs on the market now support this technology.

If your drive incorporates buffer underrun protection, you can multitask—do other things while burning CDs—without fear of producing a bad recording.

Producing Error-Free Recordings

If you have an older drive that doesn't feature buffer underrun protection, follow these recommendations to help ensure error-free recordings and prevent buffer underruns:

- Whenever possible, move all the data you want to put onto a CD-R to a fast local hard drive. If you can't do this, avoid using the following sources for data: floppy drives, parallel port–connected storage drives, and slower CD-ROM drives (especially 8× or slower). These locations for data usually can't feed data quickly enough to maintain data flow to the recording drive.

- Before you master the CD-R, check your hard disk or data source for errors (the ScanDisk program can often be used for this). Also try defragmenting the drive. This ensures that disk errors or file fragmentation, both of which slow down disk access, won't be a factor in program or data search and retrieval.

- Avoid trying to burn from active files or zero-byte files (often used for temporary storage). If you must burn these files to make an archival copy of your current system configuration, use a program such as Norton Ghost or PowerQuest Drive Image. These programs create a single compressed file from your drive's contents. Then, burn the disc using the resulting compressed file.

- Turn off power management for your hard disk and other peripherals. In Windows you normally do this through the Power icon in the Control Panel.

- Make sure your temporary drive has at least twice the empty space of your finished CD. You can see your CD's estimated space requirements during the mastering process by using programs such as Nero Burning ROM. Therefore, if you're creating a CD with 500MB of data, your temporary drive should have at least 1GB of empty space.

- With Windows 9x, you'll improve disk caching by adjusting the typical role of the computer from workstation to server in the Performance tab of the System Properties dialog box. Note that this change works correctly with Windows 95B and 95C (OSR 2.x) and Windows 98/Me, but the Registry keys are incorrect in the Windows 95 original retail and OSR1 (95A) versions. Check Microsoft's website for the correct Registry key settings for Windows 95/95A, back up and edit the Registry, and restart the computer before making this change with those versions.

- If your original data is coming from a variety of sources, consider using the Create Disk Image option found in most CD-mastering software. This feature creates an image file on your hard drive that contains all the files you want to put onto a CD. Then, use Create CD from Disk Image to actually master the CD from that information.

- If you're uncertain of success, why waste a CD-R blank? Use a CD-RW instead, which usually is written at a slower speed, or use the "test-then-create" option found in most recording software, which does a simulated burn of the CD before the actual creation. After the simulation, you're warned of any problems before the actual process begins. This is not always foolproof, but it can help.

■ Small files are harder to use in mastering a CD than large ones because of the excessive drive tracking necessary to find them and load them. You might want to use the packet-writing mode instead if your drive and software support it.

■ Keep your drives clean and free from dust. Use a cleaning CD if necessary. Dirty drives cause data-read errors or data-write errors if your recording drive is the dirty one.

■ Don't multitask. If you run another program during the mastering process, the computer is forced to perform time-slicing, which causes it to start a process, switch away from it to start the next process, switch back to the first process, and so forth. This switching process could cause the recording drive to run out of data because it isn't receiving data in a steady stream. Forget about surfing the Internet, playing Solitaire, or creating a label for your new CD during the burning process if you want reliable mastering on a drive that doesn't feature buffer underrun protection.

If you're still having buffer underrun problems despite taking all the precautions listed here, try dropping down a speed. Go to the next lower speed and see how you do. Using a lower speed than the drive is rated for can be frustrating, but it's preferable to wasting time creating unusable discs.

As a final note, I have also seen problems with burning CDs be caused by inadequate power supplies. An inadequate or overtaxed power supply can cause a myriad of recording problems (including buffer underruns). I've seen cases in which the system seemed to be normal in most respects, but there were tremendous problems recording CDs, from buffer underruns to power-calibration errors. After the power supply was upgraded with a high-quality, high-output unit, the problems all but disappeared. I've said it many times, but the power supply is the foundation of a PC, and in general it is the most failure-prone or problematic piece of hardware in the system. See Chapter 7, "Power," for more information on power supplies, including recommended suppliers for upgraded units.

Recording Software

Another difficulty with CD-R/RW devices is that they usually require special software to write them. Although most cartridge drives and other removable media mount as standard devices in the system and can be accessed exactly like a hard drive, the CD-R/RW drive uses special CD-ROM–burning software to write to the disc. This software handles the differences between how data is stored on a CD and how it is stored on a hard drive. As you learned earlier, there are several CD-ROM standards for storing information. The CD-ROM–burning software arranges the data into one of these formats so a CD-ROM reader can read the CD later. Windows XP and later include built-in CD-writing software; prior operating systems required that you purchase and install third-party CD-writing software. Still, most have found that popular third-party CD-writing applications, such as Nero Burning ROM (Ahead Software), are far more powerful and easier to use.

At one time, CD-recording technology required that you have what amounted to a replica of the CD on a local hard drive. In fact, some software packages even required a separate, dedicated disk partition for this purpose. You would copy all the files to the appropriate place on the hard drive, creating the directory structure for the CD, and then the software would create an exact replica of every sector for the proposed CD-ROM—including every file, all the directory information, and the volume information—and copy it to the CD-R drive. The result was that you had to have about 1.5GB of storage to burn a single CD (650MB/CD × 2 = 1.3GB + overhead = 1.5GB). This is no longer a requirement because most software supports virtual images. You select the files and directories you want to write to the CD from your hard drive and create a virtual directory structure for the CD-ROM in the software. This means you can select files from different directories on different hard drives, or even files from network or other CD-ROM drives, and combine them any way you want on the CD-R. This works well provided the drives have adequate speed and your drive has a large buffer or features buffer underrun protection. If you have problems, follow the advice given earlier to overcome slow data sources.

The software assembles the directory information, burns it onto the CD, opens each file on the CD, and copies the data directly from the original source. This generally works well, but you must be aware of the access times for the media you select as data sources. If, for example, you select directories from a slow hard drive or from a busy network, the software might not be capable of reading the data quickly enough to maintain a consistent stream to the recorder. In drives lacking buffer underrun protection, this causes the write to fail, resulting in a wasted disc.

Don't Forget the Software!

If you have persistent problems with making CDs, your recording software or drive might be to blame. Check the vendor's website for tips and software updates. Some drives offer software-upgradable firmware similar to the laptop's flash BIOS; if so, be sure your drive has the latest firmware available. Be sure that your recording software is also up to date and compatible with your drive and your drive's firmware revision.

Each of the major CD-R/CD-RW drive vendors provides extensive technical notes to help you achieve reliable recordings. You can also find helpful information on SCSI adapter vendors' websites and the websites of the media vendors.

Recordable DVD Standards

The history of recordable DVD drives is a troubled one. It dates back to April 1997, when the DVD Forum announced specifications for rewritable DVD, DVD-RAM, and DVD-R. Later it added DVD-RW to the mix. Dissatisfied with these standards, the industry leaders in optical recording and drives formed their own group called the DVD+RW Alliance and created another standard, called DVD+R and DVD+RW. Starting in 2003, the first DVD-RW and DVD+RW drives began appearing in laptops as internal drives. An even better option in most cases is to use one of the external USB combo DVD+-RW drives. They can handle virtually any recordable DVD or CD format and can easily be shared among different laptop and desktop systems alike.

In a war that brings back unhappy memories of the VHS/Beta struggle of the 1980s, as well as the problems in bringing DVD-Video to light, the computer and movie industries have been locked in a struggle to see which enhancements to the basic DVD standard will win out. Table 10.18 compares the competing recordable DVD standards, and Table 10.19 breaks down the compatibilities between the drives and media.

Table 10.18   Recordable DVD Standards

Format	Introduced	Capacity	Compatibility
DVD-RAM	July 1997	Up to 4.7GB per side	Incompatible with existing DVD drives unless they support the MultiRead2 standard
DVD-R/RW	July 1997/ November 1999	4.7GB per side	Readable by many existing DVD recorders/drives
DVD+R/RW	May 2001/ March 2001	4.7GB per side	Readable by most existing DVD recorders/ drives, with enhancements for video and data recording

Table 10.19 DVD Drive and Media Compatibility

Drives	CD-ROM	CD-R	CD-RW	DVD-Drive	DVD-ROM	DVD-R	DVD-RAM	DVD-RW	DVD+RW	DVD+R
DVD-Video Player	R	?	?	R	—	R	?	R	R	R
DVD-ROM Drive	R	R	R	R	R	R	?	R	R[1]	R
DVD-R Drive	R	R/W	R/W	R	R	R/W	—	R	R	R
DVD-RAM Drive	R	R	R	R	R	R[6]	R/W	R	R[1]	R
DVD-RW Drive	R	R/W	R/W	R	R	R/W	—	R/W	R	R
DVD+R/RW Drive	R	R/W	R/W	R	R	R	R[3]	R	R/W	R/W[2]
DVD-Multi Drive[4]	R	R/W	R/W	R	R	R	R/W	R/W	R[1]	R
DVD+-R/RW Drive	R	R/W	R/W	R	R	R/W	R[5]	R/W	R/W	R/W

R = Read.

W = Write.

— = Will not read or write.

? = MultiRead/MultiPlay drives will read.

1. Might require media's compatibility bit be changed to alternate (Type 2).

2. Some first-generation DVD+RW drives will not write DVD+R discs; see your drive manufacturer for an update or trade-in.

3. Read compatibility with DVD-RAM varies by drive; check documentation for details.

4. DVD Forum specification for drives that are compatible with all DVD Forum standards (DVD+R/RW is not a DVD Forum standard).

5. Some of these drives can also write to DVD-RAM media.

6. Some of these drives can also write to DVD-R media.

As you can see from looking at both the horizontal rows and vertical columns of this table, the following factors are worth noting:

- Of the single-format drives, DVD+R/RW drives are the most compatible with other media from a read standpoint.

- Increasing numbers of vendors are shipping multiformat drives to solve the persistent issues of drive/media compatibility.

DVD+R/RW offers low drive and media prices, the highest compatibility with existing formats, and has features that make it the most ideal for both video recording and data storage in PCs. Today, all DVD recordable drives are multistandard and will handle either -R(W) or +R(W) media; only dual layer (DL) media are exclusively available for +R.

Tip

Both the DVD Forum (DVD-RW) and the DVD+RW Alliance (DVD+RW) claim their format is the best choice for use in DVD-ROM drives and standalone DVD players. Although DVD+RW is generally the most compatible format (see www.dvdrw.com/why/compatibility.htm), the truth is that compatibility can vary somewhat from drive to drive and player to player. Some of the resources I recommend for determining compatibility include checking a compatibility database specific to drives and media and checking information provided by the drive or player's vendor (try the vendor website or product manual).

You can find *compatibility databases* at the **dvdrw.com** site mentioned above as well as at **www.videohelp.com/dvd-players** (all types of DVD/CD media). Also note that some DVD+RW media must be set to emulate DVD+R media before some drives can read them. See "DVD+RW Compatibility Mode," later in this chapter, for details.

DVD-RAM

DVD-RAM is the rewritable DVD standard endorsed by Panasonic, Hitachi, and Toshiba. DVD-RAM uses a phase-change technology similar to that of CD-RW. Unfortunately, DVD-RAM discs can't be read by most standard DVD-ROM drives because of differences in both reflectivity of the media and the data format. (DVD-R, by comparison, is backward compatible with DVD-ROM.) DVD-ROM drives that can read DVD-RAM discs began to come on the market in early 1999 and follow the MultiRead2 specification. DVD-ROM drives and DVD-Video players labeled as MultiRead2 compliant are capable of reading DVD-RAM discs. See the section "MultiRead Specifications," earlier in this chapter, for more information.

The first DVD-RAM drives were introduced in Spring 1998 and had a capacity of 2.6GB (single-sided) or 5.2GB (double-sided). DVD-RAM Version 2 discs with 4.7GB arrived in late 1999, and double-sided 9.4GB discs arrived in 2000. DVD-RAM drives typically read DVD-Video, DVD-ROM, and CD media. The current installed base of DVD-ROM drives and DVD-Video players can't read DVD-RAM media; most DVD+R/RW and DVD-R/RW drives can't read DVD-RAM media. To improve compatibility with other formats, many recent DVD-RAM drives can also write to DVD-R media, and the DVD Forum has developed a DVD Multi specification for drives that can read/write DVD-RAM, DVD-R, and DVD-RW media.

DVD-RAM uses what is called the *wobbled land and groove recording method*, which records signals on both the lands (the areas between grooves) and inside the grooves that are preformed on the disc. The tracks wobble, which provides clock data for the drive. Special sector header pits are prepressed into the disc during the manufacturing process as well. See Figure 10.15, which shows the wobbled tracks (lands and grooves) with data recorded both on the lands and in the grooves. This is unlike CD-R or CD-RW, in which data is recorded on the groove only.

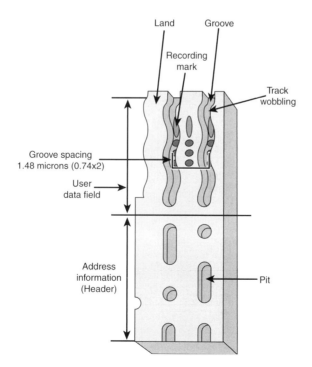

Figure 10.15   DVD-RAM wobbled land and groove recording.

The disc is recorded using phase-change recording, in which data is written by selectively heating spots in the grooves or on the lands with a high-powered laser. The DVD-RAM drive write laser transforms the film from a crystalline to an amorphous state by heating a spot, which is then rendered less reflective than the remaining crystalline portions. The signal is read as the difference of the laser reflection rate between the crystalline and amorphous states. The modulation and error correcting codes are the same as for DVD-Video and DVD-ROM, ensuring compatibility with other DVD formats. For rewriting, a lower-powered laser reheats the spot to a lower temperature, at which it recrystallizes.

Disc cartridges or caddies originally were required for both single- and double-sided discs but have now been made optional for single-sided discs. Double-sided discs must remain inside the caddy at all times for protection; however, single-sided discs can be taken out of the cartridge if necessary.

DVD-RAM specifications are shown in Table 10.20.

Table 10.20   DVD-RAM Specifications

Storage capacity	2.6GB single-sided; 5.2GB double-sided
Disc diameter	80mm–120mm
Disc thickness	1.2mm (0.6mm×2: bonded structure)
Recording method	Phase change
Laser wavelength	650nm
Data bit length	0.41–0.43 microns
Recording track pitch	0.74 microns
Track format	Wobbled land and groove

DVD-R

DVD-R is a write-once medium very similar to CD-R. It was originally created by Pioneer and released by the DVD Forum in July 1997. DVD-R discs can be played on standard DVD-ROM drives.

DVD-R has a single-sided storage capacity of 4.7GB—about seven times that of a CD-R—and double that for a double-sided disc. These discs use an organic dye recording layer that allows for a low material cost, similar to CD-R.

To enable positioning accuracy, DVD-R uses a wobbled groove recording in which special grooved tracks are pre-engraved on the disc during the manufacturing process. Data is recorded within the grooves only. The grooved tracks wobble slightly right and left, and the frequency of the wobble contains clock data for the drive to read, as well as clock data for the drive. The grooves are spaced more closely together than with DVD-RAM, but data is recorded only in the grooves and not on the lands (see Figure 10.16).

Table 10.21 shows the basic specifications for DVD-R drives.

Table 10.21   DVD-R Specifications

Storage capacity	3.95GB single-sided; 7.9GB double-sided
Disc diameter	80mm–120mm
Disc thickness	1.2mm (0.6mm×2: bonded structure)
Recording method	Organic dye layer recording method
Laser wavelength	635nm (recording); 635/650nm (playback)

Table 10.21   Continued

Data bit length	0.293 microns
Recording track pitch	0.80 microns
Track format	Wobbled groove

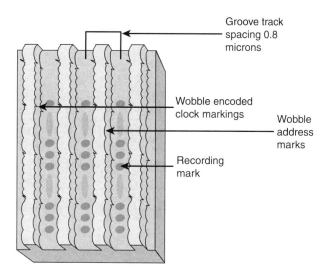

Figure 10.16   DVD-R wobbled groove recording.

DVD-RW

The DVD Forum introduced DVD-RW in November 1999. Created and endorsed originally by Pioneer, DVD-RW is basically an extension to DVD-R, just as CD-RW is an extension to CD-R. DVD-RW uses a phase-change technology and is somewhat more compatible with standard DVD-ROM drives than DVD-RAM. Drives based on this technology began shipping in late 1999, but early models achieved only moderate popularity because Pioneer was the only source for the drives and because of limitations in their performance.

Currently, DVD-RW drives are available in 1× DVD-RW/2× DVD-R and the newer 2× DVD-RW/4× DVD-R models. The 2×/4× drives have several advantages over older drives, including the following:

■ **Quick formatting**—The 1×/2× drives require that the entire DVD-RW disc be formatted before the media can be used, a process that can take about an hour. The 2×/4× drives can use DVD-RW media in a few seconds after inserting, formatting the media in the background as necessary. This is similar to the way in which DVD+RW drives work.

■ **Quick grow**—Instead of erasing the media to add files, as with 1×/2× DVD-RW drives, 2×/4× DVD-RW drives can unfinalize the media and add more files without deleting existing files.

■ **Quick finalizing**—The 2×/4× DVD-RW drives close media containing small amounts of data (under 1GB) more quickly than 1×/2× drives.

DVD-RW drives, however, still don't support lossless linking, Mount Rainier, or selective deletion of files—all of which are major features of DVD+RW.

DVD+RW

DVD+RW, also called *DVD Phase Change Rewritable*, is rapidly becoming the premier DVD recordable standard because it is the least expensive, easiest to use, and most compatible with existing formats. It was developed and is supported by Philips, Sony, Hewlett-Packard, Mitsubishi Chemical, Ricoh, Yamaha, Verbatim, and Thompson, which are all part of an industry standard group called the DVD+RW Alliance (www.dvdrw.com). Microsoft joined the alliance in February 2003. DVD+RW is also supported by major DVD/CD creation software vendors and many drive vendors, including HP, Philips, Ricoh, and many remarketers of OEM drive mechanisms. Although DVD-RW has increased in popularity with the advent of faster and easier burning times, DVD+RW is still the most popular rewritable DVD format.

Table 10.22 lists the basic specifications for DVD+RW drives.

Table 10.22   DVD+RW Specifications

Storage capacity	4.7GB single-sided; 9.4GB double-sided (future product)
Disc diameter	120mm
Disc thickness	1.2mm (0.6mm×2: bonded structure)
Recording method	Phase change
Laser wavelength	650nm (recording/playback)
Data bit length	0.4 microns
Recording track pitch	0.74 microns
Track format	Wobbled groove

Note that DVD+R, the recordable version of DVD+RW, was actually introduced *after* DVD+RW. This is the opposite of DVD-RW, which grew out of DVD-R. One of the major reasons for the development of DVD+R was to provide a lower-cost method for permanent data archiving with DVD+RW drives, and another was due to compatibility issues with DVD-ROM and DVD video players being incapable of reading media created with DVD+RW drives. However, writing DVD+RW media is relatively simple with most drives that can be read by a DVD-ROM or DVD player. See the section "DVD+RW Compatibility Mode," later in this chapter, for details.

The basic structure of a DVD+RW or DVD+R disc resembles that of a DVD-R disc with data written in the grooves only (refer to Figure 10.16), but the groove is wobbled at a frequency different from that used by DVD-R/RW or DVD-RAM. The DVD+R/RW groove also contains positioning information. These differences mean that the DVD+R/RW media offer more accurate postioning for lossless linking, but DVD+R/RW drives can't write to other types of DVD rewritable media.

Although some first-generation DVD+RW drives worked only with rewritable media, all current and future DVD+RW drives are designed to work with both DVD+R (writable) and DVD+RW (rewritable) media. The +R discs can be written only once and are less expensive than the +RW discs.

Some of the features that DVD+RW includes are as follows:

- Single-sided discs (4.7GB).
- Double-sided discs (9.4GB).
- Up to 4 hours video recording (single-sided discs).
- Up to 8 hours video recording (double-sided discs).
- Bare discs (no caddy required).

- 650nm laser (same as DVD-Video).
- Constant linear data density.
- CLV and CAV recording.
- Write speeds 1×–4× and higher (depending on the drive).
- DVD-Video data rates.
- UDF (Universal Disk Format) file system.
- Defect management integral to the drive.
- Quick formatting.
- Same 8 to 16 modulation and error correcting codes as DVD-ROM.
- Sequential and random recording.
- Lossless linking (multiple recording sessions don't waste space).
- Spiral groove with radial wobble.
- After recording, all physical parameters comply with the DVD-ROM specification.

DVD+RW technology is very similar to CD-RW, and DVD+RW drives can read DVD-ROMs and all CD formats, including CD-R and CD-RW.

With DVD+RW, the writing process can be suspended and continued without a loss of space linking the recording sessions together. This increases efficiency in random writing and video applications. This "lossless linking" also enables the selective replacement of any individual 32KB block of data (the minimum recording unit) with a new block, accurately positioning with a space of 1 micron. To enable this high accuracy for placement of data on the track, the pre-groove is wobbled at a higher frequency. The timing and addressing information read from the groove is very accurate.

The quick formatting feature means you can pop a DVD+R or DVD+RW blank into the drive and almost instantly begin writing to it. The actual formatting is carried out in the background ahead of where any writing will occur.

DVD+RW is also designed to work with existing DVD video players, DVD+RW-compatible video recorders such as those made by Philips and Yamaha, and DVD-ROM drives. However, because of the wide variance in equipment, DVD+RW tends to work better in newer equipment rather than in older equipment, particularly set-top players. As with DVD-RW, you might prefer to use writable (DVD+R) media to improve the odds of compatibility with older drives and players whose compatibility with DVD+RW is unknown.

DVD+RW is the format I prefer and recommend, and I expect that in the long run it will be the one preferred by most users. However, if you need to work with both DVD+R/RW and DVD-R/RW media because of device compatibility, I recommend one of the external DVD+-R/RW multiformat drives from Sony, NEC, and other vendors. I do not recommend DVD-RAM because it is not supported by set-top players or by most other types of DVD drives.

DVD+RW Compatibility Mode

When DVD+RW drives were introduced in 2001, some users of DVD-ROM and standalone DVD players were unable to read DVD+RW media, even though others were able to do so. The first drives to support DVD+R (writable) media (which work with a wider range of older drives) were not introduced until mid-2002, so this was a significant problem.

The most common reason for this problem turned out to be the contents of the Book Type Field located in the lead-in section of every DVD disc. Some drives require that this field indicate that the type of media is a DVD-ROM before they can read it. However, by default, DVD+RW drives write DVD+RW as the type into this field when DVD+RW media are used.

The following are two possible solutions:

- Upgrade the firmware in the DVD+RW recorder so it writes compatible information into the Book Type Field automatically.

- Use a compatibility utility to change the contents of the Book Type Field for a particular DVD+RW disc as necessary.

▶▶ See "Updating the Firmware in a CD-RW or Rewritable DVD Drive," p. 491.

Multiformat DVD Rewritable Drives

In the past the nature of the rewritable marketplace was best described as fragmented; today, however, many rewritable drives support both the DVD Multi and DVD+-R/RW specifications. These two specifications provide for wider read/write media compatibility.

DVD Multi is a specification developed by the DVD Forum for drives and players that are compatible with all DVD Forum standards, including DVD-R/RW, DVD-RAM, DVD-ROM, DVD-Video, and eventually DVD Audio (DVD+R/RW are not DVD Forum specifications and are not supported). The original version of DVD Multi was published in February 2001; the current version, version 1.01, was approved by the DVD Forum and published in December 2001. The first DVD Multi products for computers reached the market in early 2003. Figure 10.17 compares the DVD Multi logos to the DVD+RW and other DVD Forum logos.

DVD+-R/RW, unlike DVD Multi, is not really a specification. Instead, it is used to indicate drives that work with both DVD+R/RW and DVD-R/RW media (DVD-RAM is not typically supported by these drives). Such drives usually carry both the DVD-RW and DVD+RW logos shown in Figure 10.17. Therefore, DVD+-R/RW drives are designed to handle the most common formats supported by the DVD Forum and the DVD+RW Alliance.

Figure 10.17 The DVD-R/RAM, DVD-RW, and DVD+RW logos, compared to new DVD Multi logos in vertical and horizontal variations.

DVD Multi drives are a good choice for users who have been using DVD-RAM drives but want to enjoy a wider degree of compatibility with the rest of the DVD Forum world. However, if you need to work with the most common types of DVD rewritable media, DVD+-R/RW is a better choice. Because of the need to support different read/write technologies, DVD+-R/RW drives are more expensive than DVD-R/RW or DVD+R/RW drives.

CD/DVD Software and Drivers

After you've physically installed or plugged in the drive, you're ready for the last step—installing the drivers and other CD-ROM/DVD-ROM software. As usual, this process can be simple with a PnP operating system such as Windows 9x or later. In that case the drivers for Windows will automatically be installed. Things are different, however, if you need to access the drive after booting from a floppy, such as when installing an operating system, running diagnostics, or running DOS.

Booting from a Floppy Disk with CD/DVD Drive Support

You might need to boot from a floppy drive on a laptop for several reasons. One would be to install an operating system from scratch on a new or unformatted hard drive or update a notebook's firmware. In that case, because the system cannot boot from the hard drive, it will have to boot from a CD or floppy instead. Many older laptops cannot boot from CDs, and older Windows versions such as 95/98/Me often came on nonbootable CDs.

If your system does support booting from a CD, and your operating system CD is bootable, booting directly from the CD is the best option. If you are restricted to booting from a floppy, for a CD or DVD drive to function in a floppy (or CD) boot environment, several drivers might be necessary:

- **An ATAPI host adapter driver (not needed for SCSI drives)**—This driver is included with your motherboard, or you can use the generic ATAPI drivers found on Windows 98 and later startup disks.

- **SCSI adapter drivers (not needed for ATAPI drives)**—Most SCSI cards include these drivers, or you can use the generic versions included on Windows 98 and later startup disks.

- **MSCDEX**—Microsoft CD Extensions, which is included with DOS 6.0 and later. It is also built in to Windows 95 and later as the CDFS VxD.

If you need to start a PC from a bootable floppy, the floppy will not only need to contain a bootable OS, but it will also need the preceding drivers; otherwise, the CD-ROM will be inaccessible.

Generic ATAPI and SCSI drivers can be found on the Windows 98 and newer startup disks. Rather than mess with creating custom CONFIG.SYS and AUTOEXEC.BAT files, the best advice I can give is to merely boot from a Windows 98 or Me startup floppy because each time you boot from these, the proper drivers load and autodetect the CD/DVD drives, after which the drives are accessible. You can generate a Windows 98/Me startup disk on any system running Windows 98 or Me.

After you boot from a Win98/Me floppy, you will see a menu that asks whether you want to boot with or without CD-ROM (and DVD) support. If you say yes, when the floppy finishes loading, you should be able to read any discs in the CD or DVD drives.

One very useful task that is possible with this capability is to install any version of Windows in a situation in which the installation CD is not bootable (such as with most versions of Windows 9x/Me), or in which the system is older than 1998 and cannot boot from a CD. In that case all you need to install any version of Windows is the Windows CD and your bootable Windows 98/Me startup floppy. Note that just because the startup floppy is from Windows 98 or Me does not matter; you can install *any* Windows OS using that floppy.

For example, to install Windows 9x/Me onto a system, follow these steps:

1. Boot from the Windows 98/Me startup floppy, select Start Computer with CD-ROM Support from the menu. Wait for the A: prompt to appear.

2. Insert the operating system CD you want to install (Windows 95, 98, or Me) into the CD/DVD drive.

3. Type **D:SETUP** at the A: prompt (press Enter). Make sure you substitute the drive letter of your CD/DVD drive for **D:**.

4. The Setup program will run from the CD and begin the operating system installation. Follow the prompts as necessary to complete the install.

Here's how to install Windows NT, 2000, or XP onto a system:

1. Boot from the Windows 98/Me startup floppy, select Start Computer with CD-ROM Support from the menu. Wait for the A: prompt to appear.

2. Insert the operating system CD you want to install (Windows NT, 2000, or XP) into the CD/DVD drive.

3. For Windows NT and 2000, type **D:\i 386\WINNT** at the A: prompt (press Enter). For Windows XP, type **D:\setup.exe**. Make sure you substitute the drive letter of your CD/DVD drive for **D:**.

4. The WINNT program will run from the CD and begin the operating system installation. Follow the prompts as necessary to complete the install.

Another useful function you can perform with a Windows 98/Me startup floppy is to format a hard drive larger than 32GiB with FAT32 for use with Windows 2000 or XP. The Format program in Windows 2000 and XP is intentionally restricted by Microsoft from formatting volumes larger than 32GiB, even though Windows 2000 and XP will support FAT32 volumes up to 2TiB in size. Although in most cases it is recommended to use NTFS on Windows 2000 or XP systems, if you are creating a dual-boot environment where you want to run other operating systems that do not support NTFS, then FAT32 is the way to go. In that case the restriction on the Windows 2000/XP format command is a nuisance, but the only way around it is to use the format command from 98/Me.

Although I've often used a Windows 98/Me startup floppy to install Windows XP, Microsoft does have official XP startup floppies available for download from its website. You download an executable file that creates the startup floppies. To locate this file, visit the Microsoft Knowledge Base at support.microsoft.com and search for article number 310994.

Using a CD-ROM or DVD-ROM drive that conforms to the ATAPI specification under Windows does not require you to do anything. All the driver support for these drives is built in to Windows 9x and later versions, including the ATAPI driver and the CDFS VxD driver.

Bootable CDs and DVDs—El Torito

If your system BIOS is a version dated from 1998 or later, most likely it has "El Torito" support, which means it supports booting from a bootable CD or DVD. The El Torito name comes from the Phoenix/IBM Bootable CD-ROM Format Specification, which was actually named after the El Torito restaurant located near the Phoenix Software offices, where the two engineers who developed the standard ate lunch. What El Torito means for the PC is the ability to boot from CDs or DVDs, which opens up several new possibilities, including creating bootable CD/DVD rescue discs, booting from newer OS discs when installing to new systems, creating bootable diagnostics and test CDs, and more.

To create a bootable CD, ideally you need a CD/DVD burning application that allows the creation of bootable discs, and in some cases you will need a bootable floppy that contains the drivers to support your CD drive in DOS mode (sometimes called real-mode drivers). The best source for these drivers (if needed) is a Windows 98 or Me startup floppy, which can be generated by any Windows 98 or Me system. Windows 98/Me startup disks are floppy because they have the DOS-level CD-ROM support already configured and installed.

Before creating the bootable CD/DVD, test your boot floppy (with CD-ROM drivers) by first booting to the floppy. Then, with a CD or DVD containing files in the CD/DVD drive, see whether you can change to the CD/DVD drive and read a directory of the files (try the DIR command). The CD/DVD usually is the next drive letter after your last hard drive letter. For example, if your last hard drive letter is C:, the CD/DVD will be D:.

If you can display a directory listing of the CD/DVD after booting from the floppy, your drivers are properly loaded.

To create a bootable CD or DVD, simply follow the directions included with your CD/DVD burning application. Programs like Nero Burning ROM by Ahead Software make the creation of bootable discs a relatively easy procedure.

Removable Drive Letter Assignments

One problem people have when installing new drives is confusion with drive letter assignments. This becomes especially true when adding a new drive moves the assignments of previous drives—something most people don't expect. Some simple rules govern drive letter assignments in Windows and DOS, which are discussed here.

All versions of Windows (as well as MS-DOS) treat floppy drives and drives such as Zip, SuperDisk, and flash memory devices the same way, but major differences exist in the management of hard drives, CD-ROM/optical drives, and removable-media hard drives with Windows 9x/Me on the one hand and Windows NT/2000/XP on the other hand.

With any version of MS-DOS or Windows, the system assigns the drive letter A to the first physical floppy drive. If a second physical floppy drive is present, it is assigned drive letter B. If no second floppy drive exists, the system automatically reserves B: as a logical drive representation of the same physical drive A:. This allows files to be copied from one disk to another by specifying COPY file.ext A: B:.

Of course, no current laptop system employs two floppy drives, and it's certainly not uncommon for a laptop not to use a floppy device at all. In such cases neither the A: nor B: drive is assigned.

MS-DOS and Windows 9x/Me Disk Management

The basic rule with these operating systems is that devices supported by ROM BIOS–based drivers come first and those assigned by disk-loaded drivers come second. Because floppy drives and hard drives are usually ROM BIOS supported, these come first, before any other removable drives. After A: and B: are assigned to floppy drives, the system then checks for installed hard drives and begins by assigning C: to the master partition on the first drive. *If you have only one hard disk*, any extended partitions on that drive are read and any volumes in them are assigned consecutive letters after C:. For example, if you have a hard disk with a primary partition as C: and an extended partition divided into two logical volumes, they will be assigned D: and E:.

After the hard drive partitions and logical volumes are assigned, the system begins assigning letters to devices that are driver controlled, such as CD-ROM drives, PCMCIA-attached devices, parallel port devices, SCSI devices, and so on. Here is how it works with only one hard drive split into three volumes and a CD-ROM drive:

One drive primary partition	C:
One drive extended partition 1st volume	D:
One drive extended partition 2nd volume	E:
Optical drive (CD, DVD, MO)	F:

When a removable drive is added to the system proposed in the previous scenario, it is assigned either F: or G:, depending on the driver and when it is loaded. If the CD-ROM driver is loaded first, the removable drive is G:. If the removable drive driver is loaded first, it becomes F: and the CD-ROM drive is bumped to G:. In DOS, you control the driver load order by rearranging the DEVICE= statements in the CONFIG.SYS file. This doesn't work in Windows because Windows 9x, Me, NT, and 2000 use 32-bit drivers, which aren't loaded via CONFIG.SYS. You can exert control over the drive letters in Windows by manually assigning drive letters to the CD-ROM or removable drives. You do this as follows with Windows 9x and Windows Me:

1. Right-click My Computer and select Properties.

2. Select the Device Manager tab.

3. Click the + next to the CD-ROM drive icon. Right-click the CD-ROM drive, select Properties, and select the Settings tab.

4. Select and change the Start Drive Letter.

5. Select the same letter for End Drive Letter.

6. Click OK. Allow your system to reboot for changes to take effect.

7. Repeat the previous steps by clicking the + next to Disk Drives and then assign a different drive letter to your removable drive.

Using these steps, you can interchange the removable drive with the CD-ROM drive, but you can't set either type to a drive letter below any of your existing floppy or hard drives.

So far, this seems just as everybody would expect, but from here forward, it can get strange. The rule is that the system always assigns a drive letter to all primary partitions first and all logical volumes in extended partitions second. Therefore, if you have a second hard disk, it also can have primary and extended partitions, the extended partition can have two logical volumes, and the primary partition on the second drive could become D:, with the extended partition logical volumes becoming G: and H:.

Here is how it works with two hard drives, each split into three volumes, and an optical drive:

First drive primary partition	C:
Second drive primary partition	D:
First drive extended partition 1st volume	E:
First drive extended partition 2nd volume	F:
Second drive extended partition 1st volume	G:
Second drive extended partition 2nd volume	H:
Optical drive (CD, DVD, MO)	I:

In this example, if a removable drive were added, it would become either I: or J:. Using the same procedure outlined previously, you could swap I: or J: or assign them higher (but not lower) letters as well. Some factory-installed removable drives that use the ATA interface (such as some versions of the Zip 100 ATA) act like a second hard disk, rather than an add-on removable drive. The utility software provided with the Iomega Zip drives also can be used to assign the drive to any available drive letter.

To avoid scrambling existing hard drive letters when you install additional drives, prepare additional drives with extended partitions only. Drive letters in the extended partition on the second drive will follow the drive letters in the first drive's extended partitions and so forth if you install a third or even more hard drives. Here's what the result would be when you have two hard drives, with the first drive split up as a primary disk partition with two drives in an extended partition, and the second drive having no primary partition, but three logical drives in its extended partition:

First drive primary partition	C:
First drive extended partition 1st volume	D:
First drive extended partition 2nd volume	E:
Second drive extended partition 1st volume	F:
Second drive extended partition 2nd volume	G:
Second drive extended partition 3rd volume	H:

Drive Remapping Utilities

Although some utilities are available for remapping drive letters under Windows, I normally don't recommend them. The reason is that if you boot under DOS or via a floppy, these remappings are no longer in place and the standard BIOS mapping prevails. Because you often might boot to DOS to perform setup, diagnostics, configuration, or formatting/partitioning, confusion about which drive letters are what can lead to mistakes and lost data!

If you reset your CD-ROM or other removable-media drive to a different drive letter in Windows, be sure to set the drive to the same letter when you run the computer in command-prompt or MS-DOS mode. You typically do this through command-line options you can add to the `AUTOEXEC.BAT` statement for the drive. See your drive's instruction manual for details.

Windows NT/2000/XP Disk Management

Disk management for NT-based versions of Windows, including Windows NT/2000/XP, offers many more options than in MS-DOS and Windows 9x/Me. The Disk Administrator tool is launched from the Drive properties Tools menu in Windows NT 4.0. The similar Disk Management tool is started from the Computer Management (Microsoft Management Console) utility in Windows 2000 and XP. Both Disk Administrator and Disk Management can be used to control drive letters. To change a drive letter with either tool, right-click the drive and select Change Drive Letter and Path.

Although the C: drive is assigned to the first hard drive by default in these versions of Windows, you can assign the drive letters you prefer to both CD-ROM/removable-media drives and to logical drives on a hard disk. If you install Windows 2000 or Windows XP as a dual-boot operating system to a different partition than the one used by Windows 9x/Me, the boot drive letter used by Windows 2000/XP is the next available drive letter. By default, when additional hard disk–based logical drives are added to a system, existing CD-ROM or other removable-media drive letters are not disturbed. Therefore, programs that depend on CD-ROM or removable-media drive paths continue to work.

You also can change the default boot drive letter from C: to another drive letter, but this is not recommended because it prevents your system from booting until manual Registry changes are made to correct the problem.

Creating a Rescue CD

A number of programs on the market today allow you to make a compressed image file of the contents of any drive. These programs, such as the Ghost program sold by Symantec or PowerQuest's Drive Image, enable you to lock in the condition of any drive as of a particular time.

This feature enables you to create an image file of your system when it's working and use the image-restore feature to reset your system when it fails.

The perfect place to store a compressed image file is on a CD-R. At a minimum, your rescue disk should contain the compressed image file (a 737MB, 80-minute CD-R/RW could contain the equivalent of a nearly 1.5GB drive's normal contents if the maximum compression option is used). It's also desirable to place a copy of the image-restore program on the CD. The process of mastering this type of rescue CD is exactly the same as a conventional CD-mastering process. To use the rescue CD, you must boot your system with drivers that allow the CD-ROM drive to work, run the restore program to read the data from the CD, and overwrite the drive's existing contents.

If you're looking for a single-CD solution to rescuing your system, one that won't require you to lug around a bootable floppy disk, you can burn a rescue CD that is bootable all by itself.

Making a Bootable CD for Emergencies

A little-known capability to PC users is that they can create their own versions of what is standard with more and more new computers: a bootable CD/DVD that can be used to start up a system and restore it to a previously saved state.

The minimum requirements for a bootable CD/DVD include the following:

■ A system supporting the "El Torito" standard, in which the CD/DVD can be designated as a boot drive. Check your BIOS under Advanced Setup or similar options. Recent and current BIOS code supplied by AMI, Award Software, and Phoenix Technologies typically supports El Torito, meaning the CD/DVD can be assigned as a bootable device.

■ A CD/DVD burner and media.

■ Recording software that allows creation of a bootable CD. Most modern CD recording software, such as Nero Burning ROM and Roxio Easy Media Creator, supports creating bootable CD/DVDs. If your current CD/DVD-recording software lacks this option, you must upgrade to something that does.

■ A floppy disk containing your operating system boot files.

ATAPI Drives Are Bootable

Most ATAPI drives connected to a motherboard ATA interface can be used as bootable devices if the BIOS permits it. If your CD-ROM is connected to a sound card, this procedure won't work. If your CD/DVD is connected to a SCSI interface, you'll need a SCSI interface with a BIOS chip that permits booting as well as a bootable disc.

Check your BIOS Setup for a page on which boot devices are listed to see whether yours supports a CD/DVD drive as a bootable device.

Because the procedures can vary for different burning software, it is best if you follow the directions that came with your software for the exact procedure for creating a bootable CD or DVD.

Troubleshooting Optical Drives

The following sections detail some useful troubleshooting procedures that can be used to solve the most common problems with CD and DVD drives.

Failure Reading a CD/DVD Disc

If your drive fails to read a CD or DVD, try the following solutions:

■ Check for scratches on the disc data surface.

■ Check the drive for dust and dirt; use a cleaning disc.

■ Make sure the drive shows up as a working device in System Properties.

■ Try a disc that you know to work.

■ Restart the computer (the magic cure-all).

- Remove the drive from Device Manager in Windows, allow the system to redetect the drive, and then reinstall the drivers (if you have a PnP-based system).

Failure Reading CD-R/CD-RW Discs in a CD-ROM or DVD Drive

If your CD-ROM or DVD drive fails to read CD-R and CD-RW discs, try the following solutions:

- Check the compatibility; some very old 1× CD-ROM drives can't read CD-R media. Check to see if a newer drive is available that conforms to your laptop's specifications. If one is available, replace the drive with a newer, faster, cheaper model.

- Many early-model DVD drives can't read CD-R/CD-RW media; again, check the compatibility.

- The CD-ROM drive must be MultiRead compatible to read CD-RW because of the lower reflectivity of the media; replace the drive.

- If some CD-Rs but not others can be read, check the media color combination to see whether some color combinations work better than others; change the brand of media.

- Packet-written CD-Rs can't be read on MS-DOS/Windows 3.1 CD-ROM drives because of the limitations of the operating system.

- Record the media at a slower speed. The pits/lands created at faster speeds sometimes can't be read by older drives.

- If you are trying to read a packet-written CD-R on a CD-ROM drive, reinsert the media into the original drive, eject the media, and select the option Close to Read on Any Drive.

- Download and install a UDF reader compatible with the packet-writing software used to create the CD-RW on the target computer. A universal UDF volume reader application can be downloaded free from Roxio at www.roxio.com/en/support/software_updates.jhtml.

Failure to Read a Rewritable DVD in a DVD-ROM Drive or Player

If your DVD-ROM or DVD player fails to read a rewritable DVD, try the following solutions:

- Reinsert DVD-RW media into the original drive and finalize the media. Make sure you don't need to add any more data to the media if you use a first-generation (DVD-R 2×/DVD-RW 1×) drive because you must erase the entire disc to do so. You can unfinalize media written by second-generation DVD-R 4×/DVD-RW 2× drives. See your DVD-RW disc-writing software instructions or help file for details.

- Reinsert DVD+RW media into the original drive and change the compatibility setting to emulate DVD-ROM. See the section "DVD+RW Compatibility Mode," earlier in this chapter, for details.

- Make sure the media contain more than 521MB of data. Some drives can't read media that contain a small amount of data.

Failure to Create a Writable DVD

If you can't create a writable DVD but the drive can be used with CD-R, CD-RW, or rewritable DVD media, try the following solutions:

- Make sure you are using the correct media. +R and -R media can't be interchanged unless the drive is a DVD+-R/RW dual-mode drive.

- Be sure you select the option to create a DVD project in your mastering software. Some CD/DVD-mastering software defaults to the CD-R setting.

- Select the correct drive as the target. If you have both rewritable DVD and rewritable CD drives on the same system, be sure to specify the rewritable DVD drive.

- Try a different disc.

- Contact the mastering software vendor for a software update.

Failure Writing to CD-RW or DVD-RW 1× Media

If you can't write to CD-RW or DVD-RW 1× media, try the following solutions:

- Make sure the media are formatted. Use the format tool provided with the UDF software to prepare the media for use.

- If the media are formatted, verify they are formatted with the same or compatible UDF program. Different packet-writing programs support different versions of the UDF standard. I recommend you use the same UDF packet-writing software on the computers you use or use drives that support the Mount Rainier standard.

- Make sure the system has identified the media as CD-RW or DVD-RW. Eject and reinsert the media to force the drive to redetect it.

- Contact the packet-writing software vendor for a software update.

- The disc might have been formatted with Windows XP's own limited CD-writing software instead of a true UDF packet-writing program. Erase the disc with Windows XP after transferring any needed files from the media; then format it with your preferred UDF program.

- Contact the drive vendor for a firmware update. See "Updating the Firmware in a CD-RW or Rewritable DVD Drive," later in this chapter.

Your ATAPI CD-ROM or DVD Drive Runs Slowly

If your ATAPI CD-ROM or DVD drive performs poorly, check the following items:

- Check the cache size in the Performance tab of the System Properties control panel. Select the quad-speed setting (largest cache size).

- Your Programmed I/O (PIO) or UDMA mode might not be set correctly for your drive in the BIOS; check the drive specs and use autodetect in the BIOS for the best results.

- Check that you are using bus-mastering drivers on compatible systems; install the appropriate drivers for the laptop's chipset and the operating system in use. See the section "Direct Memory Access and Ultra-DMA," earlier in this chapter.

- Open the System Properties control panel and select the Performance tab to see whether the system is using MS-DOS Compatibility Mode for the CD-ROM drive. If all ATA drives are running in this mode, see www.microsoft.com and query on "MS-DOS Compatibility Mode" for a troubleshooter. If only the CD-ROM drive is in this mode, see whether you're using CD-ROM drivers in CONFIG.SYS and AUTOEXEC.BAT. Remove the lines containing references to the CD-ROM drivers (don't actually delete the lines—REM them), reboot the system, and verify that your CD-ROM drive still works and that it's running in 32-bit mode. Some older drives require at least the CONFIG.SYS driver to operate.

Poor Results or Slow Performance When Writing to CD-R Media

If you are having problems successfully writing data to a CD, see "How to Reliably Record CDs," earlier in this chapter. Also see the section "Updating the Firmware in a CD-RW or Rewritable DVD Drive," later in this chapter.

Trouble Reading CD-RW Discs on a CD-ROM Drive

If you can't read CD-RW discs in your CD-ROM, try the following solutions:

- Check the vendor specifications to see whether your drive is MultiRead compliant. Some drives are not compliant.
- If your drive is MultiRead compliant, try the CD-RW disc on a known-compliant CD-ROM drive (a drive with the MultiRead feature).
- Insert CD-RW media back into the original drive and check it for problems with the packet-writing software program's utilities.
- Insert CD-RW media back into the original drive and eject the media. Use the right-click Eject command in My Computer or Windows Explorer to properly close the media.
- Create a writable CD or DVD to transfer data to a computer that continues to have problems reading rewritable media.

Trouble Reading CD-R Discs on a DVD Drive

If your DVD drive can't read a CD-R disc, check to see that the drive is MultiRead2 compliant; non-compliant DVDs can't read CD-R media. Newer DVD drives generally support reading CD-R media.

Trouble Making Bootable CDs

If you are having problems creating a bootable CD, try these possible solutions:

- Check the contents of the bootable floppy disk from which you copied the boot image. To access the entire contents of a CD, a bootable disk must contain CD-ROM drivers, AUTOEXEC.BAT, and CONFIG.SYS.
- Use the ISO 9660 format. Don't use the Joliet format because it is for long-filename CDs and can't boot.
- Check your system's BIOS for boot compliance and boot order; the CD-ROM should be listed first.
- SCSI CD-ROMs need a SCSI card with BIOS and bootable capability as well as special motherboard BIOS settings.

Updating the Firmware in a CD-RW or Rewritable DVD Drive

Just as updating the motherboard BIOS can solve compatibility problems with CPU and memory, support, USB ports, and system stability, upgrading the firmware in a rewritable CD or DVD drive can also solve problems with media compatibility, writing speed, and digital audio extraction from scratched discs and even prevent potentially fatal mismatches between media and drives.

Determining Whether You Might Need a Firmware Update

If you encounter any of the following issues, a firmware update might be necessary:

- Your drive can't use a particular type of media, or it performs much more slowly with one type of media than other types/brands of media.
- Your writing software stops recognizing the drive as a rewritable drive.
- You want to use faster media than what the drive was originally designed to use.

Because any firmware update runs a risk of failure and a failed firmware update can render your drive useless (I've seen it happen), you shouldn't install firmware updates casually. However, as the preceding examples make clear, sooner or later you'll probably need one.

Note that firmware updates don't fix the following problems:

- Drive not recognized by a newly installed CD- or DVD-mastering program
- Drive not recognized by Windows XP's built-in CD-writing program

Because each rewritable CD or DVD drive has special characteristics at present (in the future, Mount Rainier support will standardize drive characteristics), CD- or DVD-writing programs you buy at retail must have model-specific updates to work. Get the update from the software vendor or use the software provided with the drive. If you are trying to use an OEM version of a program with a different drive model from the original, you will also need an update from the software vendor (in some cases, an OEM version works only with the original drive with which it was packaged).

Windows XP's built-in CD-writing feature is a pale imitation of even the worst third-party CD-mastering program, but if you insist on using it, be sure your drive is listed in the Windows Catalog of supported drives and devices (`www.microsoft.com/windows/catalog`). To install the latest updates for Windows XP, including updates to the CD-writing feature, use Windows Update. Microsoft Knowledge Base Article 320174 discusses an update to the CD-writing feature. Search the Microsoft website for other solutions.

Determining Which Drive Model and Firmware Are Installed

Before you can determine whether you need a firmware update for your rewritable drive, you need to know your drive model and which firmware version it's using. This is especially important if you use a drive that is an OEM product produced by a vendor other than the one that packaged the drive for resale. You can use the following to determine this information:

- Windows Device Manager (Windows 9x/Me)
- CD/DVD-mastering software drive information

With the Windows Device Manager, follow this procedure:

1. Open the Device Manager.
2. Click the plus sign (+) next to DVD/CD-ROM in the list of device types.
3. Double-click the rewritable drive icon you want to check to display its properties sheet.
4. Click the Details or Settings tab; under Details, change the selection to Hardware IDs. The firmware version and drive name will be displayed in one of the lines shown. For example, my system shows "SONY__DVD_RW_DRU-720A_JY06," which tells me the drive manufacturer (SONY), the model (DRU-720A), and the firmware revision (JY06).

With Roxio Easy Media Creator, you can use the Disk and Device utility to display the drive information. Nero includes a utility with its Burning ROM program called InfoTool, which can also be downloaded free from `http://ww2.nero.com/enu/Info_Tool.html`. This tool provides numerous details about your drive and is highly recommended.

After you have this information, you can go to your rewritable drive vendor's website and see whether a firmware update is available and what the benefits of installing the latest version would be.

Installing New Drive Firmware

Generally speaking, the firmware update procedure works like this, but you should be sure to follow the particular instructions given for your drive:

1. If the firmware update is stored as a Zip file, you need to use an unzipping program or the integrated unzipping utility found in some versions of Windows to uncompress the update to a folder.

2. If the drive maker provides a Readme file, be sure to read it for help and troubleshooting. If the update file is an EXE file, it might display a Readme file as part of step 3.

3. Double-click the EXE file to start the update process. Be sure to leave the system powered on during the process (which can take 2–3 minutes).

4. Follow the vendor's instructions for restarting your system.

5. After you restart your system, the computer might redetect the drive and assign it the next available drive letter. If you previously assigned the drive a customized drive letter, use the Device Manager in Windows 9x/Me or the Computer Management service in Windows 2000/XP to reassign the correct drive letter to the drive.

Troubleshooting Firmware Updates

If you have problems performing a rewritable drive firmware update, check the vendor's Readme file or website for help. In addition, here are some tips we've found useful.

If the firmware update fails to complete, there might be interference from programs that control the drive, such as packet-writing programs or the built-in Windows XP CD-writing feature. To disable resident software, restart the computer in Safe Mode (Windows 2000/XP) and retry the update. Restart the system normally after the update is complete.

With Windows 9x/Me, you can use MSConfig (System Configuration Utility), select the Selective Startup option, and uncheck Load Startup Group Items and Process Win.INI File Before Restarting. After completing the firmware update, be sure to rerun MSConfig and select Normal Startup before restarting the computer.

To disable Windows XP's own CD-writing feature for a particular drive, right-click the drive icon in My Computer, select Properties, click the Recording tab, and clear the check mark in the box next to Enable CD Recording on This Drive.

If the firmware update doesn't improve drive performance on a system running Windows 9x/Me, DMA might not be enabled on the rewritable drive. See the section "Direct Memory Access and Ultra-DMA," earlier in this chapter, for details.

Removable Magnetic Storage Devices

A small group of companies dominates the fading market for magnetic removable-media drives. 3M's spin-off company Imation, Iomega, and Castlewood are the leading names in removable magnetic media drives and media offering higher capacities than standard floppies.

Removable magnetic media drives are usually floppy or hard disk based. For example, the popular Zip drive is a 3 1/2" version of the original Bernoulli flexible disk drive that Iomega manufactured. The SuperDisk LS-120 drive is a floppy-based drive that stores 120MB on a disk that looks almost exactly like a 1.44MB floppy; the second-generation LS-240 SuperDisk drives store up to 240MB and can format standard 1.44MB floppy disks to hold 32MB of data! The Castlewood Orb drives are all based on hard disk technology.

Although they are no longer as popular as they were in the late 1990s, from the standpoint of widespread industry adoption and multiple sources of media, both the LS-120/240 SuperDisk and Zip 100/250 drives can be considered some type of industry standard. Various models can be purchased as upgrades for existing computers, and third-party media vendors such as Maxell, Verbatim, Sony, and Fujifilm sell Zip and SuperDisk media.

The following sections provide information about all types of magnetic media, including floptical and magneto-optical drive types.

Iomega Zip

Unlike the LS-120 SuperDisk, the Iomega Zip drive can't use standard 3 1/2" floppy disks. It is a descendent of a long line of removable-media drives from Iomega that go back to the first Bernoulli cartridge drives released in the early 1980s. The current form of Bernoulli-technology drive from Iomega is the popular Zip drive. These devices are available in 100MB, 250MB, and 750MB versions with either ATA (internal), USB (external), or FireWire (external) interfaces. Zip drives use a proprietary 3 1/2-inch disk made by Iomega and also sold by other major media vendors, such as Maxell, Verbatim, and Fuji. It is about twice as thick as a standard 3 1/2-inch floppy disk or SuperDisk (see Figure 10.18).

1.44MB floppy disk

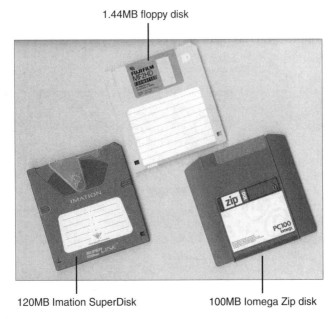

120MB Imation SuperDisk   100MB Iomega Zip disk

Figure 10.18   The Zip 100MB disk (right) compared to the standard 3 1/2-inch 1.44MB disk (middle) and the LS-120 SuperDisk (left).

The Zip drives do not accept standard 1.44MB or 720KB floppy disks, making them unlikely candidates for a floppy disk drive replacement.

Zip 100 drives can store up to 100MB of data on a small removable magnetic cartridge that resembles a 3 1/2" floppy disk. The newer Zip 250 drives store up to 250MB of data on the same size cartridge and can read and write to the Zip 100 cartridges. The latest Zip 250 cartridges have a U-shaped case and use media containing titanium particles for greater durability. The most recent Zip drive holds 750MB of data. It's available in separate ATAPI internal versions for PC and Mac and in USB 2.0 and FireWire (IEEE 1394/i.LINK) versions for use with both platforms. It has read/write compatibility with Zip 250 media, but it has read-only compatibility with Zip 100 media. For best performance, you should use the native media size with Zip 250 and Zip 750 drives; these drives read and write much more slowly when smaller Zip media are used than when their native media size is used.

SuperDisk LS-120 and LS-240

Imation developed the LS-120 SuperDisk in the late 1990s as a rival to the Iomega Zip disk. The SuperDisk uses floptical technology, which uses laser servo (LS) optical tracking to precisely position read-write heads on floppy-type media. In other words, a laser beam is used to guide the magnetic heads. Although the SuperDisk is capable of reading and writing to standard 1.44MB and 720KB floppy media as well as to its own 120MB media, it was unable to overcome the huge lead Iomega had gained by being first to market with the Zip drives and media in the mid-1990s. Imation and other vendors still sell LS-120 media, but most LS-120 SuperDisk drive products have been discontinued.

The second-generation LS-240 SuperDisk uses both LS-120 and its own 240MB LS-240 media. It can also write to standard 1.44MB and 720KB floppy disks and format a 1.44MB floppy disk to hold 32MB of data. However, similar to its predecessor, it has been unable to make a significant impact in the marketplace. The first LS-240 SuperDisk drives were produced for the OEM market as internal ATAPI drives, but in the U.S. retail market, most have been sold for use with either USB interfaces or the proprietary removable-bay features of some high-end notebook computers. USB-based LS-240 SuperDisk drives have been sold in the U.S. by QPS (www.qps-inc.com) and Addonics (www.addonics.com). Several notebook computer vendors, including HP and IBM, also made versions for the interchangeable drive bay featured on some of their notebook computer models. Most of these drives have been discontinued, but some are still available at some dealers.

Figure 10.19 shows the media types that are compatible with the LS-120 drive.

Note

SuperDisk drives can use either SuperDisks or standard 3 1/2-inch floppies. Because the media sense hole and write-protect/enable slider are on opposite sides of the media, the SuperDisk is protected from damage if it is inserted into an ordinary floppy drive by mistake.

Hard Disk–Based Removable-Media Drives

The Castlewood Orb drives feature 2.2GB and 5.7GB capacities and are essentially small hard drives with removable media. You can install an entire operating system and a major application on these cartridges and boot from them to completely customize your system's operation. Unfortunately, these drives use proprietary designs, so the drives and media are available only from the manufacturer and are not interchangeable with other companies' products. I usually do not recommend proprietary products, preferring instead devices that are more industry standard.

Because of the popularity of external hard drives that interface through USB and FireWire (IEEE 1394/i.LINK) ports and rewritable DVD drives, this category of removable-media drives has also been declining in popularity over the last couple of years.

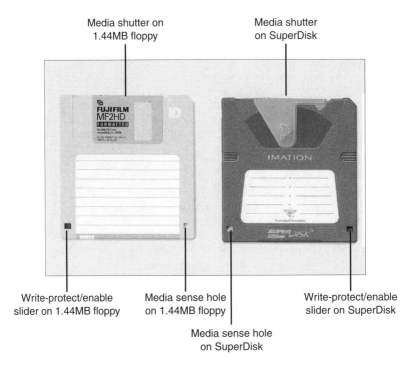

Media shutter on 1.44MB floppy

Media shutter on SuperDisk

Write-protect/enable slider on 1.44MB floppy

Media sense hole on 1.44MB floppy

Write-protect/enable slider on SuperDisk

Media sense hole on SuperDisk

Figure 10.19   A standard 1.44MB 3 1/2-inch floppy disk (left) compared to LS-120 SuperDisk media (right).

Floppy Drives

Although no longer used for primary storage, the floppy is still a useful accessory as a system-installation and configuration device, especially for troubleshooting or upgrading firmware. When you're installing an operating system from scratch, you often use the floppy to load the software necessary for partitioning and formatting the hard disk, as well as to run diagnostics in case of problems.

Starting in 2002, many companies started selling systems without floppy drives. This started with laptop computers, where internal floppy drives were first eliminated and replaced with external (normally USB) drives. Most newer laptops no longer include a floppy drive with the system, offering only external USB models as an option. In 2003, many desktop system manufacturers likewise stopped including a floppy drive in their standard system configurations.

Even though higher-capacity storage devices are available and most modern systems can boot directly from CD-ROMs, the ubiquitous floppy drive will likely remain a useful option or accessory in systems for at least another few years. Both Zip and SuperDisk drives have failed in the marketplace as floppy drive replacements, but the Mount Rainier standard (also known as EasyWrite) will finally allow CD-RW and DVD+-RW drives to serve as a replacement for the floppy. Prior to Mount Rainier, optical drives lacked defect management as well as native OS support.

Alan Shugart is generally credited with inventing the floppy disk drive in 1967 while working for IBM. One of Shugart's senior engineers, David Noble, actually proposed the flexible medium (then 8 inches in diameter) and the protective jacket with the fabric lining. Shugart left IBM in 1969, and in 1976 his company, Shugart Associates, introduced the minifloppy (5 1/4-inch) disk drive. It, of course, became the standard eventually used by personal computers, rapidly replacing the 8-inch drives. He also helped create the Shugart Associates System Interface (SASI), which was later renamed SCSI (Small Computer System Interface) when approved as an ANSI standard.

Sony introduced the first 3 1/2-inch microfloppy drives and disks in 1983. The first significant company to adopt the 3 1/2-inch floppy for general use was Hewlett-Packard in 1984 with its partially PC-compatible HP-150 system. The industry adoption of the 3 1/2-inch drive was furthered when Apple used it in the first Macintosh systems in 1984, and IBM put the drive into its entire PC product line starting in 1986.

Drive Components

All floppy disk drives, regardless of type, consist of several basic common components. Note that all floppy disk drives are still based on (and mostly compatible with) the original Shugart designs, including the electrical and command interfaces. Compared to other parts of the PC, the floppy disk drive has undergone relatively few changes over the years (see Figure 10.20).

A floppy disk drive has two read/write heads—one for each side of the disk, with both heads being used for reading and writing on their respective disk sides. A motor called a *head actuator* moves the head mechanism. The heads can move in and out over the surface of the disk in a straight line to position themselves over various tracks. On a floppy drive, the heads move in and out tangentially to the tracks they record on the disk. This is different from hard disks, where the heads move on a rotating arm similar to the tone-arm of a record player. Because the top and bottom heads are mounted on the same rack, or mechanism, they move in unison and can't move independently of each other. The upper and lower heads each define tracks on their respective sides of the disk medium, whereas at any given head position, the tracks under the top and bottom head simultaneously are called a *cylinder*. Most floppy disks are recorded with 80 tracks on each side (160 tracks total), which is 80 cylinders.

Floppy Drive Interfaces

Floppy drives can be interfaced to a system in several ways. Most use the traditional floppy controller interface, but many now use the USB interface. Because the traditional floppy controller only works internally, all external drives are interfaced via USB or some other alternative interface. USB drives often have a standard floppy drive inside an external box with a USB-to-floppy controller interface converter inside. Newer systems that are "legacy free" don't include a traditional floppy controller and typically use USB as the floppy interface. In the past, some external floppy drives have been available in FireWire (IEEE 1394/i.LINK) or even parallel interfaces as well.

Disk Physical Specifications and Operation

While most laptops sold today are no longer equipped with internal 3 1/2-inch 1.44MB floppy drives as standard equipment, they are available as an option for all systems in the form of external USB drives. A few older laptops had a 2.88MB 3 1/2-inch drive that can also read and write 1.44MB disks.

The physical operation of a disk drive is fairly simple to describe. The disk rotates in the drive at either 300rpm or 360rpm. Most drives spin at 300rpm; only the 5 1/4-inch 1.2MB drives spin at 360rpm. With the disk spinning, the heads can move in and out approximately 1 inch and write 80 tracks. The tracks are written on both sides of the disk and are therefore sometimes called *cylinders*. A single cylinder comprises the tracks on the top and bottom of the disk. The heads record by using a tunnel-erase procedure that writes a track to a specified width and then erases the edges of the track to prevent interference with any adjacent tracks.

Different drives record tracks at different widths. Table 10.23 shows the track widths in both millimeters and inches for the various types of floppy disk drives found in modern PC systems.

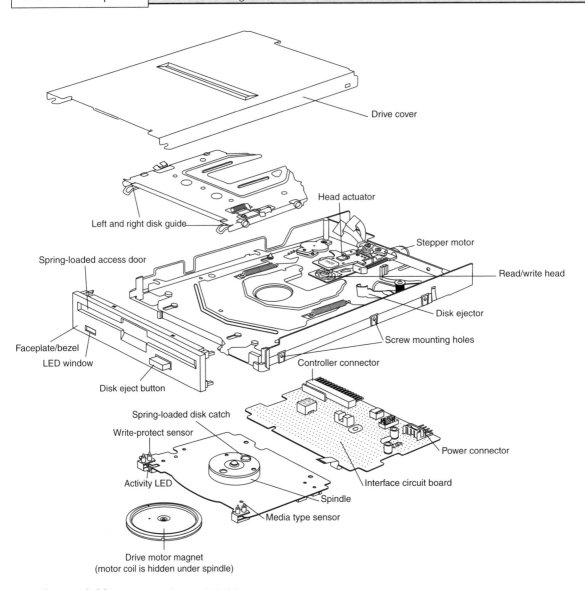

Figure 10.20   A typical floppy disk drive.

Table 10.23   Floppy Disk Drive Track-Width Specifications

Drive Type	No. of Tracks	Track Width
5 1/4-in. 360KB	40 per side	0.300mm, 0.0118 in.
5 1/4-in. 1.2MB	80 per side	0.155mm, 0.0061 in.
3 1/2-in. 720KB	80 per side	0.115mm, 0.0045 in.
3 1/2-in. 1.44MB	80 per side	0.115mm, 0.0045 in.
3 1/2-in. 2.88MB	80 per side	0.115mm, 0.0045 in.

How the Operating System Uses a Disk

To the operating system, data on a floppy disk is organized in tracks and sectors, just as on a hard disk drive. *Tracks* are narrow, concentric circles on a disk. *Sectors* are pie-shaped slices of the individual tracks.

Table 10.24 summarizes the standard disk formats for PC floppy disk drives.

Table 10.24   5 1/4-Inch and 3 1/2-Inch Floppy Disk Drive Formats

5 1/4-Inch Floppy Disks	Double-Density 360KB (DD)	High-Density1.2MB (HD)
Bytes per sector	512	512
Sectors per track	9	15
Tracks per side	40	80
Sides	2	2
Capacity (kilobinary)	360	1,200
Capacity (megabinary)	0.352	1.172
Capacity (million bytes)	0.369	1.229

3 1/2-Inch Floppy Disks	Double-Density 720KB (DD)	High-Density 1.44MB (HD)	Extra High-Density 2.88MB (ED)
Bytes per sector	512	512	512
Sectors per track	9	18	36
Tracks per side	80	80	80
Sides	2	2	2
Capacity (kilobinary)	720	1,440	2,880
Capacity (megabinary)	0.703	1.406	2.813
Capacity (million bytes)	0.737	1.475	2.949

You can calculate the capacity differences between various formats by multiplying the sectors per track by the number of tracks per side together with the constants of two sides and 512 bytes per sector. Note that the floppy disk's capacity can actually be expressed in various ways. For example, what we call a 1.44MB disk really stores 1.475MB if you go by the correct decimal prefix definition for mega(byte). The discrepancy comes from the fact that in the past floppies were designated by their kilobinary (1,024 byte) capacity, which in the past we abbreviated KB. The current abbreviation for kilobinary is KiB according to the International Electrotechnical Commission (IEC).

Despite the IEC standards, the traditional method when discussing floppy drives or disks is to refer to the capacity of a floppy by the number of kilobinary bytes (1,024 bytes equals 1KiB) but to use the otherwise improper abbreviation KB instead. This was also improperly extended to the abbreviation MB, such that a disk with an actual capacity of 1,440 KiB was instead denoted as a 1.44MB disk, even though it would really be 1.406 MiB (megabinary bytes) or 1.475MB (million/megabytes) if we went by the correct definitions for MiB (mebibyte) and MB (megabyte).

For the remainder of this chapter, I will refer to the capacity of the various floppy disks according to the previously used conventions rather than the more technically accurate IEC-designated binary and decimal prefixes.

Note

Again, as with hard disk drives, both megabyte and millions of bytes have been improperly abbreviated as MB or M, often resulting in a great deal of confusion. The IEC prefixes for binary multiples were designed to eliminate this confusion. For more information on the 1998 IEC prefixes for binary multiples, see

`http://physics.nist.gov/cuu/Units/binary.html`.

Like blank sheets of paper, new, unformatted disks contain no information. Formatting a disk is similar to adding lines to the paper so you can write straight across. Formatting the disk writes the information the operating system needs to maintain a directory and file table of contents. On a floppy disk, no distinction exists between a high-level and low-level format, nor do you have to create any partitions. When you format a floppy disk with Windows Explorer or the command prompt FORMAT.COM program, both the high- and low-level formats are performed at the same time.

When you format a floppy disk, the operating system reserves the track nearest to the outside edge of a disk (track 0) almost entirely for its purposes. Track 0, Side 0, Sector 1 contains the Volume Boot Record (VBR), or Boot Sector, that the system needs to begin operation. The next few sectors contain the file allocation tables (FATs), which keep records of which clusters or allocation units on the disk contain file information and which are empty. Finally, the next few sectors contain the root directory, in which the operating system stores information about the names and starting locations of the files on the disk.

Note that most floppies today are sold preformatted. This saves time because the formatting can take a minute or more per disk. Even if disks come preformatted, they can always be reformatted later.

Cylinders

The cylinder number is usually used in place of the track number because all floppy drives today are double-sided. A cylinder on a floppy disk includes two tracks: the one on the bottom of the disk above Head 0 and the one on the top of the disk below Head 1. Because a disk cannot have more than two sides and the drive has two heads, there are always two tracks per cylinder for floppy disks. Hard disk drives, on the other hand, can have multiple disk platters—each with two heads—resulting in many tracks per single cylinder. The simple rule is that there are as many tracks per cylinder as there are heads on the drive.

Cylinders are discussed in more detail in Chapter 9, "Hard Disk Storage."

Clusters or Allocation Units

A *cluster* also is called an *allocation unit*. The term is appropriate because a single cluster is the smallest unit of the disk that the operating system can allocate when it writes a file. A cluster or allocation unit consists of one or more sectors—usually a power of 2 (1, 2, 4, 8, and so on). Having more than one sector per cluster reduces the FAT size and enables the OS to run more quickly because it has fewer individual clusters to manage. The trade-off is in some wasted disk space. Because the OS can manage space only in the cluster size unit, every file consumes space on the disk in increments of one cluster.

Table 10.25 lists the default cluster sizes used for various floppy disk formats.

Table 10.25   Default Cluster and Allocation Unit Sizes

Floppy Disk Capacity	Cluster/Allocation Unit Size	FAT Type
5 1/4-in., 360KB	2 sectors	1,024 bytes, 12-bit
5 1/4-in., 1.2MB	1 sector	512 bytes, 12-bit
3 1/2-in., 720KB	2 sectors	1,024 bytes, 12-bit
3 1/2-in., 1.44MB	1 sector	512 bytes, 12-bit
3 1/2-in., 2.88MB	2 sectors	1,024 bytes, 12-bit

KB = 1,024 bytes (by convention)

MB = 1,000 KBytes (by convention)

Types of Floppy Disk Drives

The characteristics of the floppy disk drives you might encounter in PC-compatible systems are summarized in Table 10.26. As you can see, the different disk capacities are determined by several parameters, some of which seem to remain constant on all drives, although others change from drive to drive. For example, all drives use 512-byte physical sectors, which is true for hard disks as well.

Table 10.26   Floppy Disk Logical Formatted Parameters

	Current Formats			Obsolete Formats				
Disk Size (Inches)	3 1/2	3 1/2	3 1/2	5 1/4	5 1/4	5 1/4	5 1/4	5 1/4
Disk Capacity (KB)	2,880	1,440	720	1,200	360	320	180	160
Media descriptor byte	F0h	F0h	F9h	F9h	FDh	FFh	FCh	FEh
Sides (heads)	2	2	2	2	2	2	1	1
Tracks per side	80	80	80	80	40	40	40	40
Sectors per track	36	18	9	15	9	8	9	8
Bytes per sector	512	512	512	512	512	512	512	512
Sectors per cluster	2	1	2	1	2	2	1	1
FAT length (sectors)	9	9	3	7	2	1	2	1
Number of FATs	2	2	2	2	2	2	2	2
Root dir. length (sectors)	15	14	7	14	7	7	4	4
Maximum root entries	240	224	112	224	112	112	64	64
Total sectors per disk	5,760	2,880	1,440	2,400	720	640	360	320
Total available sectors	5,726	2,847	1,426	2,371	708	630	351	313
Total available clusters	2,863	2,847	713	2,371	354	315	351	313

1.44MB 3 1/2-Inch Drive

The 3 1/2-inch, 1.44MB, high-density (HD) drives first appeared from IBM in its desktop PS/2 product line introduced in 1987. IBM had introduced a lower capacity 720KB version of this drive a year earlier in its first laptop, the IBM Convertible. Most other computer vendors started offering the drives as an option in their systems immediately after IBM. This type of floppy drive is still the most popular in systems today.

The drive records 80 cylinders consisting of two tracks each, with 18 sectors per track, resulting in a formatted capacity of 1.44MB. Some disk manufacturers label these disks as 2.0MB, and the difference between this unformatted capacity and the formatted usable result is lost during the format. Note that the 1,440KB of total formatted capacity do not account for the areas the FAT file system reserves for file management, leaving only 1,423.5KB of actual file-storage area.

The drive spins at 300rpm, and in fact must spin at that speed to operate properly with existing high- and low-density controllers. To use the 500KHz data rate (the maximum from most standard high- and low-density floppy controllers), these drives must spin at a maximum of 300rpm. If the drives were to spin at the faster 360rpm rate of the 5 1/4-inch drives, they would have to reduce the total number of sectors per track to 15; otherwise, the controller could not keep up. In short, the 1.44MB 3 1/2-inch drives store 1.2 times the data of the 5 1/4-inch 1.2MB drives, and the 1.2MB drives spin exactly 1.2 times faster than the 1.44MB drives. The data rates used by both of these HD drives are identical and compatible with the same controllers. In fact, because these 3 1/2-inch HD drives can run at the 500KHz data rate, a controller that can support a 1.2MB 5 1/4-inch drive can also support the 1.44MB drives.

Other Floppy Drive Types

Other types of floppy drives that have been used in the past include the following:

- **2.88MB 3 1/2"**—This size was used on some IBM PS/2 models in the early 1990s, including several laptops.

- **720KB 3 1/2"**—This size was used by IBM and others starting in 1986, before the 1.44MB 3 1/2" was introduced.

- **1.2MB 5 1/4"**—This size was introduced by IBM for the IBM AT in 1984 and widely used throughout the rest of the decade.

- **360KB 5 1/4"**—An improved version of the floppy disk drive originally used by the IBM PC. It was used throughout the 1980s on XT-class machines and some AT-class machines.

Analyzing 3 1/2" Floppy Disk Construction

The 3 1/2" disks differ from the older 5 1/4" disks in both construction and physical properties. The flexible (or floppy) disk is contained within a plastic jacket. The 3 1/2" disks are covered by a more rigid jacket than are the 5 1/4" disks. The disks within the jackets, however, are virtually identical except, of course, for size.

The 3 1/2-inch disks use a much more rigid plastic case than older 5 1/4-inch disks, which helps stabilize the magnetic medium inside. Therefore, these disks can record at track and data densities greater than the 5 1/4-inch disks (see Figure 10.21). A metal shutter protects the media-access hole. The drive manipulates the shutter, leaving it closed whenever the disk is not in a drive. The medium is then completely insulated from the environment and from your fingers. The shutter also obviates the need for a disk jacket.

Because the shutter is not necessary for the disk to work, you can remove it from the plastic case if it becomes bent or damaged. Pry it off the disk case; it will pop off with a snap. You also should remove the spring that pushes it closed. Additionally, after removing the damaged shutter, you should copy the data from the damaged disk to a new one.

Rather than an index hole in the disk, the 3 1/2-inch disks use a metal center hub with an alignment hole. The drive "grasps" the metal hub, and the hole in the hub enables the drive to position the disk properly.

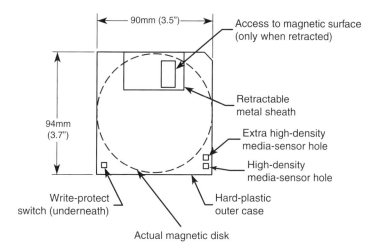

Figure 10.21 Construction of a 3 1/2-inch floppy disk.

On the lower-left part of the disk is a hole with a plastic slider—the write-protect/enable hole. When the slider is positioned so the hole is visible, the disk is *write-protected*; that is, the drive is prevented from recording on the disk. When the slider is positioned to cover the hole, writing is enabled, and you can save data to the disk. For more permanent write-protection, some commercial software programs are supplied on disks with the slider removed so you cannot easily enable recording on the disk. This is exactly opposite of a 5 1/4-inch floppy, in which covered means write-protected, not write-enabled.

On the other (right) side of the disk from the write-protect hole usually is another hole called the *media-density-selector hole*. If this hole is present, the disk is constructed of a special medium and is therefore an HD or ED disk. If the media-sensor hole is exactly opposite the write-protect hole, it indicates a 1.44MB HD disk. If the media-sensor hole is located more toward the top of the disk (the metal shutter is at the top of the disk), it indicates an ED disk. No hole on the right side means that the disk is a low-density disk. Most 3 1/2-inch drives have a media sensor that controls recording capability based on the absence or presence of these holes.

The actual magnetic medium in both the 3 1/2-inch and 5 1/4-inch disks is constructed of the same basic materials. They use a plastic base (usually Mylar) coated with a magnetic compound. High-density disks use a cobalt-ferric compound; extended-density disks use a barium-ferric media compound. The rigid jacket material on the 3 1/2-inch disks has occasionally caused people to believe incorrectly that these disks are some sort of "hard disk" and not really a floppy disk. The disk cookie inside the 3 1/2-inch case is just as "floppy" as the 5 1/4-inch variety.

Floppy Disk Types and Specifications

This section examines the types of disks that have been available to PC owners over the years. Especially interesting are the technical specifications that can separate one type of disk from another, as Table 10.27 shows. The following subsections define all the specifications used to describe a typical disk.

Table 10.27 Floppy Disk Media Specifications

	5 1/4-Inch			3 1/2-Inch		
Media Parameters	**Double-Density (DD)**	**Quad-Density (QD)**	**High-Density (HD)**	**Double-Density (DD)**	**High-Density (HD)**	**Extra High-Density (ED)**
Tracks per inch (TPI)	48	96	96	135	135	135
Bits per inch (BPI)	5,876	5,876	9,646	8,717	17,434	34,868
Media formulation	Ferrite	Ferrite	Cobalt	Cobalt	Cobalt	Barium
Coercivity (oersteds)	300	300	600	600	720	750
Thickness (micro-in.)	100	100	50	70	40	100
Recording polarity	Horiz.	Horiz.	Horiz.	Horiz.	Horiz.	Vert.

Density

Density, in simplest terms, is a measure of the amount of information that can be reliably packed into a specific area of a recording surface. The keyword here is *reliably*.

Disks have two types of densities: longitudinal density and linear density. *Longitudinal density* is indicated by how many tracks can be recorded on the disk and is often expressed as a number of tracks per inch (TPI). *Linear density* is the capability of an individual track to store data and is often indicated as a number of bits per inch (BPI). Unfortunately, these types of densities are often confused when discussing different disks and drives.

Media Coercivity and Thickness

The *coercivity* specification of a disk refers to the magnetic-field strength required to make a proper recording. Coercivity, measured in oersteds, is a value indicating magnetic strength. A disk with a higher coercivity rating requires a stronger magnetic field to make a recording on that disk. With lower ratings, the disk can be recorded with a weaker magnetic field. In other words, the lower the coercivity rating, the more sensitive the disk.

HD media demand higher coercivity ratings so the adjacent magnetic domains don't interfere with each other. For this reason, HD media are actually less sensitive and require a stronger recording signal strength.

Another factor is the thickness of the disk. The thinner the disk, the less influence a region of the disk has on another adjacent region. The thinner disks, therefore, can accept many more bits per inch without eventually degrading the recording.

Handling/Caring for Floppy Disks and Drives

Most computer users know the basics of disk care. Disks can be damaged or destroyed easily by the following:

- Sliding open the protective door and touching the recording surface with your fingers or anything else
- Bending the disk
- Spilling coffee or other substances on the disk
- Overheating a disk (leaving it in the hot sun or near a radiator, for example)
- Exposing a disk to stray magnetic fields

Despite all these cautions, disks are rather hardy storage devices.

For maximum reliability, store 3 1/2-inch disks in an environment between 40° and 127° Fahrenheit, and store 5 1/4-inch disks in an environment between 40° and 140° Fahrenheit. In both cases, humidity should not exceed 90%.

Airport X-Ray Machines and Metal Detectors

One of my favorite myths to dispel is that the airport X-ray machine somehow damages disks. I have a great deal of experience in this area from having traveled around the country for the past 20 years or so with disks and portable computers in hand. I fly about 150,000 miles per year, and my portable computer equipment and disks have been through X-ray machines hundreds of times.

X-rays are essentially just a form of light, and disks and computers are not affected by X-rays at anywhere near the levels found in these machines. What could potentially damage your magnetic media is the metal detector. Metal detectors work by monitoring disruptions in a weak magnetic field. A metal object inserted in the field area causes the field's shape to change, which the detector observes. This principle, which is the reason the detectors are sensitive to metal objects, can be dangerous to your disks; the X-ray machine, however, is the safest area through which to pass either your disk or your computer.

The X-ray machine is not dangerous to magnetic media because it merely exposes the media to electromagnetic radiation at a particular (very high) frequency. Blue light is an example of electromagnetic radiation of a different frequency. The only difference between X-rays and blue light is in the frequency, or wavelength, of the emission.

Some people worry about the effect of X-ray radiation on their system's EPROM (erasable programmable read-only memory) chips. This concern might actually be more valid than worrying about disk damage because EPROMs are erased by certain forms of electromagnetic radiation. In reality, however, you do not need to worry about this effect either. EPROMs are erased by direct exposure to very intense ultraviolet light. Specifically, to be erased, an EPROM must be exposed to a 12,000 uw/cm^2 UV light source with a wavelength of 2,537 angstroms for 15–20 minutes, and at a distance of 1 inch. Increasing the power of the light source or decreasing the distance from the source can shorten the erasure time to a few minutes.

The airport X-ray machine is different by a factor of 10,000 in wavelength. The field strength, duration, and distance from the emitter source are nowhere near what is necessary for EPROM erasure. Many circuit-board manufacturers even use X-ray inspection on their circuit boards (with components including EPROMs installed) to test and check quality control during manufacture.

Now, you might not want to take my word for it, but scientific research that corroborates what I have stated has been published. In 1993, a study was published by two scientists—one of whom actually designs X-ray tubes for a major manufacturer. Their study, titled "Airport X-rays and Floppy Disks: No Cause for Concern," was published in the journal *Computer Methods and Programs in Biomedicine*. Here's an excerpt from the abstract:

> A controlled study was done to test the possible effects of X-rays on the integrity of data stored on common sizes of floppy disks. Disks were exposed to doses of X-rays up to seven times that to be expected during airport examination of baggage. The readability of nearly 14 megabytes of data was unaltered by X-irradiation, indicating that floppy disks need not be given special handling during X-ray inspection of baggage.

In fact, the disks were retested after two years of storage, and there still has been no measurable degradation since the exposure.

Flash Cards and Digital "Film" Memory Devices

Flash memory has been around for several years as a main or an auxiliary storage medium for laptop computers. However, the rise of devices such as digital cameras and MP3 players and the presence of USB ports on practically all recent systems have transformed this technology from a niche product into a mainstream must-have accessory.

How Flash Memory Works

Flash memory is a type of nonvolatile memory that is divided into blocks, rather than bytes as with normal RAM memory modules. Flash memory, which also is used in computers for BIOS chips, is changed by a process known as *Fowler-Nordheim tunneling*. This process removes the charge from the floating gate associated with each memory cell. Flash memory then must be erased before it can be charged with new data.

The speed, low reprogramming current requirements, and compact size of flash memory devices have made flash memory a perfect counterpart for portable devices such as laptop computers and digital cameras, which often refer to flash memory devices as so-called "digital film." Unlike real film, digital film can be erased and reshot. Ultra-compact, USB-based keychain drives that use flash memory have quickly replacedboth traditional floppy drives and Zip/SuperDisk drives for transporting data between systems.

Types of Flash Memory Devices

Several types of flash memory devices are in common use today, and it's important to know which ones your digital camera is designed to use. The major types include the following:

- ATA Flash
- CompactFlash (CF)
- SmartMedia (SM)
- MultiMediaCards (MMC)
- Reduced Size MMC (RS-MMC)
- SecureDigital (SD)
- Memory Stick
- xD-Picture Card
- Thumb or keychain USB devices

Some of these devices are available in different sizes (Type I/Type II). Table 10.28 shows the different types of solid-state storage used in digital cameras and other devices, listed in order of physical size.

Table 10.28   Different Flash Memory Devices and Physical Sizes

Type	L (mm)	W (mm)	H (mm)	Volume (cc)	Date Introduced
ATA Flash Type II	54.00	85.60	5.00	23.11	Nov. 1992
ATA Flash Type I	54.00	85.60	3.30	15.25	Nov. 1992
CompactFlash (CF) Type II	42.80	36.40	5.00	7.79	Mar. 1998
CompactFlash (CF) Type I	42.80	36.40	3.30	5.14	Oct. 1995
Memory Stick	21.45	50.00	2.80	3.00	Jul. 1998
Secure Digital (SD)	24.00	32.00	2.10	1.61	Aug. 1999

Table 10.28   Continued

Type	L (mm)	W (mm)	H (mm)	Volume (cc)	Date Introduced
SmartMedia (SM)	37.00	45.00	0.76	1.27	Apr. 1996
MultiMediaCard (MMC)	24.00	32.00	1.40	1.08	Nov. 1997
xD-Picture Card (xD)	20.00	25.00	1.70	0.85	Jul. 2002
Reduced Size MMC (RS-MMC)	24.00	18.00	1.40	0.60	Nov. 2002

Note: USB flash drives are not listed because they do not have a standardized form factor.

CompactFlash

CompactFlash, developed by SanDisk Corporation in 1994, uses ATA architecture to emulate a disk drive; a CompactFlash device attached to a computer has a disk drive letter just like your other drives. The original size was Type I (3.3mm thick); a newer Type II size (5mm thick) accommodates higher-capacity devices. Both CompactFlash cards are 1.433" wide by 1.685" long, and adapters allow them to be inserted into laptop computer PC Card slots. The CompactFlash Association (www.compactflash.org) oversees development of the standard.

SmartMedia

Ironically, SmartMedia (originally known as *SSFDC* for *solid state floppy disk card*) is the simplest of any flash memory device. A SmartMedia card contains only flash memory on a card without any control circuits. This simplicity means that compatibility with different generations of SmartMedia cards can require manufacturer upgrades of SmartMedia-using devices.

MultiMediaCard

The MultiMediaCard (MMC) was co-developed by SanDisk and Infineon Technologies AG (formerly Siemens AG) in November 1997 for use with smart phones, MP3 players, digital cameras, and camcorders. The MMC uses a simple 7-pin serial interface to devices and contains low-voltage flash memory. The MultiMediaCard Association (www.mmca.org) was founded in 1998 to promote the MMC standard and aid development of new products. In November 2002, MMCA announced the development of the Reduced Size MultiMediaCard (RS-MMC), which reduces the size of the standard MMC by about 40% and can be adapted for use with standard MMC devices.

SecureDigital

A SecureDigital (SD) storage device is essentially an improved and updated version of MMC, and MMC cards can be read in SD slots. SD has several enhancements over MMC and is available in greater capacities. SD, which was co-developed by Toshiba, Matsushita Electric (Panasonic), and SanDisk in 1999, gets its name from two special features. The first is encrypted storage of data for additional security, meeting current and future SecureDigital Music Initiative (SDMI) standards for portable devices. The second is a mechanical write-protection switch. The SD slot can also be used for adding memory to Palm PDAs. The SDIO standard was created in January 2002 to enable SD slots to be used for small digital cameras and other types of expansion with various brands of PDAs and other devices. The SD Card Association (www.sdcard.org) was established in 2000 to promote the SD standard and aid the development of new products.

Sony Memory Stick and Memory Stick Pro

Sony, which is heavily involved in both laptop computers and a wide variety of digital cameras and camcorder products, has its own proprietary version of flash memory known as the *Sony Memory Stick*.

These devices feature an erase-protection switch, which prevents accidental erasure of your photographs. Sony has also licensed Memory Stick technology to other companies, such as Lexar Media.

Lexar introduced the enhanced Memory Stick PRO in 2003, with capacities ranging from 256MB up to 1GB. Memory Stick Pro includes MagicGate encryption technology, which enables digital rights management, and Lexar's proprietary high-speed memory controller.

ATA Flash PC Card

Although the PC Card (PCMCIA) form factor is now used for everything from game adapters to modems, from SCSI interfacing to network cards, its original use was computer memory, as the old PCMCIA (Personal Computer Memory Card International Association) acronym indicated.

Unlike normal RAM modules, PC Card memory acts like a disk drive, using the PCMCIA ATA (AT Attachment) standard. PC Cards come in three thicknesses (Type I is 3.3mm, Type II is 5mm, and Type III is 10.5mm), but all are 3.3" long by 2.13" wide. Type I and Type II cards are used for ATA-compliant flash memory and the newest ATA-compliant hard disks. Type III cards are used for older ATA-compliant hard disks; a Type III slot also can be used as two Type II slots.

xD-Picture Card

In July 2002, Olympus and Fujifilm, the major supporters of the SmartMedia flash memory standard for digital cameras, announced the xD-Picture Card as a much smaller, more durable replacement for SmartMedia. In addition to being about one-third the size of SmartMedia—making it the smallest flash memory format yet—the xD-Picture Card has a faster controller to enable faster image capture.

Initial capacities range from 16MB up to 128MB, but eventual capacities are expected to reach up to 1GB or above. The 16MB and 32MB cards (commonly packaged with cameras) record data at speeds of 1.3MBps, whereas the 64MB and larger cards record data at 3MBps. The read speed for all sizes is 5MBps. The media are manufactured for Olympus and Fujifilm by Toshiba, and because xD-Picture media are optimized for the differences in the cameras (Olympus's media support the panorama mode found in some Olympus xD-Picture cameras, for example), you should use the same brand of camera and media.

USB Keychain Drives (Thumbdrives)

As an alternative to floppy and Zip/SuperDisk-class removable-media drives, USB-based flash memory devices are rapidly becoming the preferred way to move data between systems. The first successful drive of this type—Trek's ThumbDrive—was introduced in 2000 and has spawned many imitators, including many that incorporate a keychain or pocket clip to emphasize their portability.

Unlike other types of flash memory, USB keychain drives don't require a separate card reader; they can be plugged into any USB port or hub. Although a driver is usually required for Windows 98 and Windows 98SE, most USB keychain drives can be read immediately by newer versions of Windows, particularly Windows XP. As with other types of flash memory, USB keychain drives are assigned a drive letter when connected to the computer. Most have capacities ranging from 32MB to 128MB, with some capacities as high as 2GB. However, typical performance with USB 2.0 is about 5MBps.

Tip

If you have a card reader plugged into a USB hub or port on your computer, you might need to disconnect it before you can attach a USB keychain drive. Use the Windows Safely Remove Hardware icon in the system tray to stop the card reader before you insert the USB keychain drive. After the USB keychain drive has been recognized by the system, you should be able to reattach the card reader.

For additional protection of your data, some USB keychain drives have a mechanical write-protect switch; others include or support password-protected data encryption as an option, and some are capable of being a bootable device (if supported in the BIOS).

Figure 10.22 shows the features of a typical USB keychain or thumbdrive.

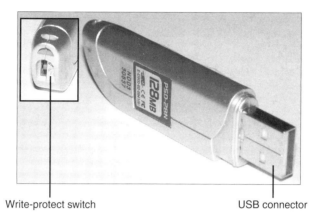

Write-protect switch   USB connector

Figure 10.22   Typical USB Thumbdrive capable of storing 128MB of data, which can be write-protected to help prevent accidental erasure.

Comparing Flash Memory Devices

As with any storage issue, you must compare each product's features to your needs. You should check the following issues before purchasing flash memory devices:

- Which flash memory products does your camera or other device support? Although adapters allow some interchange of the various types of flash memory devices, for best results, you should stick with the flash memory type your device was designed to use. Because of greater capacities, more widespread usage, and higher performance, I only recommend digital cameras that use CompactFlash or SD (SecureDigital) media. The other formats are simply too limited, proprietary, and expensive to recommend.

- Which capacities does your device support? Flash memory devices are available in ever-increasing capacities, but not every device can handle the higher-capacity devices. Check the device and flash memory card's websites for compatibility information.

- Are some flash memory devices better than others? Some manufacturers have added improvements to the basic requirements for the flash memory device. For example, Lexar makes four series of faster-than-normal CompactFlash+ cards (4×, 12×, 16×, and 24×), a series of Write Acceleration Technology (WA) cards for even faster performance with professional digital SLR cameras, and USB-enabled models that can be attached to USB ports for fast data transfer using a simple USB cable rather than an expensive and bulky card reader.

Only the ATA Flash cards can be attached directly to a laptop computer's PC Card slots. All other devices need their own socket or some type of adapter to transfer data.

Figure 10.23 shows how the most common types of flash memory cards compare in size to each other and to a penny.

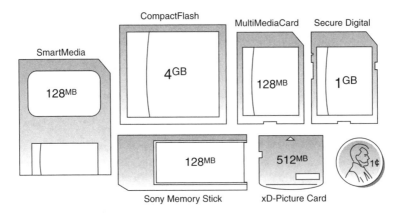

Figure 10.23   SmartMedia, CompactFlash, MultiMediaCard, SecureDigital, xD-Picture Card, and Sony Memory Stick flash memory devices. Shown in maximum capacity versions and in relative scale to a U.S. penny (lower right).

Table 10.29 provides an overview of the major types of flash memory devices and their capacities.

Table 10.29   Flash Memory Card Capacities

Device	Maximum Available Capacity	Notes
CompactFlash+	4GB	Highest capacity, most flexible format, supported by the best cameras. Lexar Media and SanDisk also make faster versions of CF+ media; Lexar Media also makes USB-enabled CF+ media.
SecureDigital (SD)	1GB	Next-best format to CompactFlash, SD cards do not work in MMC sockets.
MultiMediaCard (MMC)	128MB	Obsolete format; MMC cards can work in most SD sockets.
Memory Stick	128MB	Proprietary format developed by Sony and licensed to Lexar Media.
Memory Stick Pro	1GB	Enhanced high-speed version of Memory Stick with digital rights management support; also called Memory Stick Magic Gate.
ATA Flash	2GB	Plugs directly into a PC-Card (PCMCIA) slot without an adapter.
xD-Picture Card	512MB	Use the same brand as your digital camera for the best results.
SmartMedia	128MB	Becoming obsolete, very thin.
USB keychain drive	2GB	Some include password-protection and write-protect features.

I normally recommend devices (cameras, PDAs, and so on) that use CompactFlash (CF) or SecureDigital (SD) storage. Any of the others I generally do not recommend due to limitations in capacity, performance, proprietary designs, and higher costs.

CompactFlash (CF) is the most widely used format in professional and consumer devices, and it offers the highest capacity, at the lowest prices, in a reasonably small size. CF cards plug directly into PC Card slots on all laptops by using a simple passive adapter that is extremely inexpensive. That means when you're not using one of those cards in your camera, you can use them as a solid-state hard disk in a laptop. For a long time I would not even consider a camera or other device that did not use CF storage. I have relaxed on that stance a little bit, but it is still by far the best overall format, available in capacities of up to 4GB or higher. It is also significantly faster than the other formats.

SecureDigital (SD) is becoming more popular, is reasonably fast, and is available in capacities up to 1GB. SD sockets also take MultiMediaCards (MMCs), which are basically a thinner version of SD. Note that the opposite is not true; that is, MMC sockets will not accept SD cards. MultiMediaCards (MMCs) are also available in versions up to 128MB. Finally, SmartMedia (SM) is a very thin format, which has grown in popularity. Capacities are currently limited to 256MB.

In general, I would not consider any device that used the other formats, especially Memory Stick, which is a Sony proprietary format (didn't the company learn anything from Betamax versus VHS?). The xD and RS-MMC formats are found in a limited number of devices with a very limited capacity. ATA Flash was great, but these cards are physically big, mostly obsolete, and can easily be replaced by a CompactFlash card in a PC Card adapter.

Moving Data in Flash Memory Devices to Your Computer

Several types of devices can be purchased to enable the data on flash memory cards to be moved from digital cameras and other devices to a computer. Although some digital cameras come with an RS-232 serial cable for data downloading, this is a painfully slow method, even for low-end cameras with less than a megapixel (1,000-pixel horizontal width) resolution.

Card Readers

The major companies that produce flash card products sell card readers that can be used to transfer data from proprietary flash memory cards to PCs. These card readers typically plug into the computer's USB ports (some older versions might use the parallel port) for fast access to the data on the card.

In addition to providing fast data transfer, card readers enable the reuse of expensive digital film after the photos are copied from the camera and save camera battery power because the camera is not needed to transfer information. External card readers can be used with any computer with the correct port type and a supported operating system. USB readers, for example, should be used with Windows 98 or above.

Because many computer and electronics device users might have devices that use two or more types of flash memory, many vendors now offer multiformat flash memory card readers, such as the SanDisk ImageMate 8 in 1 Card Reader/Writer shown in Figure 10.24.

Type II PC Card Adapters

For use in the field, you might prefer to adapt flash memory cards to the Type II PC Card slot. You insert the flash memory into the adapter; then you slide the adapter into the laptop computer's Type II PC Card slot. Figure 10.25 shows how a CompactFlash card Type II PC Card adapter works. As with card readers, check with the major companies that produce your type of flash memory device for the models available.

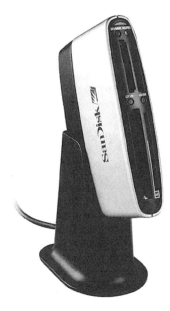

Figure 10.24 The SanDisk ImageMate 8 in 1 Card Reader/Writer is a high-speed USB 2.0 device that can read CompactFlash Type I/II, Memory Stick, Memory Stick Pro, SmartMedia, xD-Picture Card, SecureDigital, and MultiMediaCard formats.

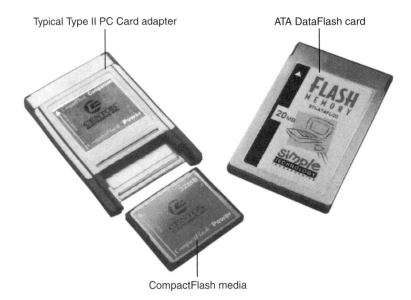

Figure 10.25 A typical Type II PC Card adapter for CompactFlash media (left) compared to an ATA DataFlash card (right).

Microdrive Technology

If you prefer magnetic storage for digital camera data storage, consider the Hitachi Microdrive, originally developed by IBM and now manufactured and sold by Hitachi Global Storage Technologies. The Hitachi Microdrive is also sold by various other companies under OEM agreements.

When first introduced by IBM, the Microdrive was released in a 170MB capacity. Current models, though, have capacities of 340MB, 512MB, 1GB, and 4GB. The 4GB model uses a new five-layer version of the Pixie Dust AFC media technology originally developed by IBM. Microdrives can be used with several digital cameras, many laptop computers, and other devices. The Microdrive is a true hard drive at 1" wide and works in CompactFlash+ Type II slots, enabling it to be a direct replacement for standard CompactFlash memory cards on compatible equipment. The Microdrive is also available as part of a Travel Kit containing a PC Card adapter, and the drive is compatible with many standard CompactFlash card readers. See the www.hgst.com website for more information about Microdrive products, a compatibility matrix, and other information. Figure 10.26 shows how Microdrive's mechanism compares in size to a standard U.S. quarter.

Figure 10.26 A U.S. quarter is just slightly smaller than the Hitachi (originally IBM) Microdrive. (Photo courtesy of International Business Machines Corporation. Unauthorized use not permitted.)

▶▶ Depending on the version of Windows you use and the type of removable-media storage you select, you might see changes in existing drive letters when you install a new removable-media drive or flash memory device into a system. To learn more about these changes and how to control drive letter assignments, see "Removable Drive Letter Assignments," p. 485.

CHAPTER 11

Graphics and Sound

Modern laptop computers feature integrated graphics and sound. In general, the graphics and sound features found in laptop computers lag behind the features available with the best add-on graphics and sound cards available for their desktop siblings.

In this chapter, you'll learn about the basic graphics and sound technologies as they apply to laptop computers and how to look for laptops that have the graphics and sound features you need. You will also learn how to improve onboard graphics and onboard sound through internal and external upgrades and how to troubleshoot problems you might encounter.

Video Display System

The video subsystem of a modern laptop/notebook system consists of two main components:

- **Video display**—A flat-panel display as found on laptop computers.
- **Graphics processor (also called the *video chip* or *graphics chip*)**—Built in to the motherboard in virtually every laptop computer. Some laptops integrate the graphics as part of the motherboard chipset, but some models use a discrete graphics processor with its own video memory.

This section examines the display and adapter technologies used in portable systems.

Major Laptop Display Features to Consider

Unlike desktop computers, which allow you to replace the video card and the display freely, laptop computers have built-in graphics and display components. Because upgrade options are much more limited in a laptop than in a desktop, it's essential to choose a laptop, in part, based on its display quality and display features. The essential features to consider in a laptop's display system include the following:

- Flat-panel display type
- Screen resolution and size
- Pixels per inch (ppi)
- Brightness and contrast
- Response time
- Manufacturer policy concerning "dead" pixels
- External display interfaces
- The graphics processor or motherboard chipset used
- Video memory size and type
- Memory size adjustment options
- Multiple monitor support (DualView)
- CardBus/PC Card/ExpressCard support
- 3D graphics support
- TV input/output support
- Driver support

These topics are covered in the following subsections.

Early Portable Displays: CRT and Plasma

A display can use one of several technologies. The original display technology used in older suitcase-sized portables such as the original Compaq PCs and the IBM Portable PC is cathode-ray tube (CRT) technology. CRTs consist of a vacuum tube enclosed in glass. One end of the tube contains an electron gun assembly that projects three electron beams, one each for the red, green, and blue phosphors used to create the colors you see onscreen. The other end contains a screen with a phosphorous coating.

When heated, the electron gun emits a stream of high-speed electrons that are attracted to the other end of the tube. Along the way, a focus control and deflection coil steer the beam to a specific point on the phosphorous screen. When struck by the beam, the phosphor glows. This light is what you see when you watch TV or look at your computer screen. Three layers of phosphors are used: red, green, and blue. A metal plate called a *shadow mask* is used to align the electron beams; it has slots or holes that divide the red, green, and blue phosphors into groups of three (one of each color). Various types of shadow masks affect picture quality, and the distance between each group of three (the *dot pitch*) affects picture sharpness.

CRTs are way too big and heavy for portable use. As soon as alternative technologies were available for portable systems, the old bulky CRTs became a thing of the past. Some portables experimented with technologies such as gas-plasma (often just called *plasma*) and electroluminescent (EL) displays, but they were normally monochrome solutions that were confined to only a few select models. Most portables in the late 1980s and early 1990s began using *liquid crystal display (LCD)* technology. Virtually all display screens in portable systems since the mid-90s have used color LCD technology.

Note

Gas-plasma display technology was used in a few portables from the late 1980s. Plasma displays provide a CRT-quality picture on a thin, flat screen using two glass panes filled with a neon/xenon gas mixture. Some were monochrome (usually orange), whereas others were full color. Many of the early 386 and 486 portables used gas-plasma displays. Unfortunately, these plasma displays were heavy and required far more power than LCDs, meaning that the systems using plasma displays were AC powered only; they could not run on batteries. As such, plasma displays never became a practical alternative for the portable computer market.

Liquid Crystal Displays (LCDs)

An LCD consists of two sheets of a flexible, polarizing material with a layer of liquid crystal solution between them. If you press gently on an LCD screen while it is lit, you can see how it gives slightly, displacing the liquid inside. When an electric current is passed through the liquid, the crystals align and become semipermeable to light.

LCDs have low-glare, completely flat screens and low power requirements (5 watts versus nearly 100 watts for an ordinary monitor). The color quality of an active-matrix LCD panel actually exceeds that of most CRT displays.

Aside from their light weight, LCDs offer a number of additional benefits when compared to conventional CRT "glass tube" monitors:

- Larger effective viewable area
- No image distortion
- Lower power requirements and less heat generated
- No electromagnetic emissions

A 15" LCD is essentially equal in usability to a 17" or larger CRT, and some laptop computers now offer 17" screens. This is due not only to the resolutions available but also to the fact that you generally sit closer to a laptop/notebook display, thus making a smaller display more usable.

Because LCDs use direct addressing of the display (each pixel in the picture corresponds with a transistor), they produce a high-precision image. LCDs don't have the common CRT display problems of pin-cushion distortion, barrel distortion, or convergence errors (halos around the edges of onscreen objects).

LCDs are ideal for portables because they use less power (5 watts versus nearly 100 watts for a desktop CRT) and generate less heat than other display technologies. They are also intrinsically safe; with LCDs there are no concerns over electromagnetic very low frequency (VLF) or extremely low frequency (ELF) emissions.

How LCDs Work

In an LCD, a polarizing filter creates two separate light waves. The polarizing filter allows light waves that are aligned only with the filter to pass through. After passing through the polarizing filter, the remaining light waves are all aligned in the same direction. When a second polarizing filter is aligned at a right angle to the first, all those waves are blocked. When the angle of the second polarizing filter is changed, the amount of light allowed to pass can be changed. It is the role of the liquid crystal cell to change the angle of polarization and control the amount of light that passes through. The liquid crystals are rod-shaped molecules that flow like a liquid. They enable light to pass straight through, but an electrical charge alters their orientation and the orientation of the light passing through them. Although monochrome LCDs do not have color filters, they can have multiple cells per pixel for controlling shades of gray.

In a color LCD, an additional filter has three cells for each pixel—one each for displaying red, green, and blue—with a corresponding transistor for each cell. The red, green, and blue cells, which make up a pixel, are sometimes referred to as *subpixels*. The ability to control each cell individually has enabled Microsoft to develop a new method of improving LCD text quality. Beginning with Windows XP, you can enable a feature called ClearType through the Display Properties dialog box.

LCD Types

Two basic LCD choices are available today on notebook computers: active-matrix analog color and active-matrix digital. Monochrome LCD displays are obsolete for PCs, although they remain popular for simple organizer devices and are sometimes used for industrial display panels. Passive-matrix displays using dual-scan technology were popular for low-cost notebook models until a few years ago. Currently, all low-cost notebooks sold use the brighter analog or digital active-matrix designs originally found on more expensive notebook computers. Passive-matrix displays are still used with handheld organizers or for industrial-use desktop display panels because of their relatively low cost and enhanced durability compared to active-matrix models.

Note

The most common passive-matrix displays used a supertwist nematic design, so these panels were often referred to as *STNs*. Active-matrix panels usually use a thin-film transistor design and are therefore referred to as *TFTs*.

Dual-Scan (Passive-Matrix) Displays

The dual-scan display, sometimes called a *passive-matrix display*, has an array of transistors running down the x- and y-axes of two sides of the screen. The number of transistors determines the screen's resolution. For example, a dual-scan display with 800 transistors along the x-axis and 600 along the y-axis creates a grid similar to the horizontal and vertical lines on a piece of graph paper. Each pixel on the screen is controlled by the two transistors representing its coordinates on the x- and y-axes.

If a transistor in a dual-scan display should fail, a whole line of pixels is disabled, causing a black line across the screen (either horizontally or vertically). There is no solution for this problem other than to replace the display or just live with it. The term *dual scan* comes from the fact that the screen is divided in half, with each half being refreshed simultaneously.

Dual-scan displays are generally inferior to active-matrix screens. Dual-scan displays tend to be dimmer because the pixels cannot be refreshed as often as those on an active-matrix display. Dual-scan panels also are prone to ghost images and are difficult to view from an angle, making it hard for two or more people to view the same screen.

However, newer passive-matrix technologies, such as color super-twist nematic (CSTN), double-layer super-twist nematic (DSTN), and especially high-performance addressing (HPA) screens, have improved the appearance of passive-matrix screens. Although these newer displays offer better response rates and contrast—problems that plagued many of the earlier display types—they are still not as sharp or as fast as an active-matrix screen and have been replaced by active-matrix displays in all price levels today.

For everyday use, the drawbacks of a passive-matrix display are most noticeable during video-intensive applications, such as presentations, full-color graphics, video, and fast-moving games, or under bright lighting conditions, such as in a window seat on an airplane, outdoors, or in offices with a lot of window lighting. For indoor computing tasks such as word processing and email, which consist largely of reading words onscreen, the passive-matrix display is quite serviceable, even for long periods of time.

The standard size for dual-scan displays ranged from 10.4 inches (measured diagonally) at 640×480, up to 12.1-inch or 13.3-inch displays at 800×600 or 1024×768 resolution. Dual-scan displays are obsolete in modern systems, thanks to improvements in the yield and reductions in the price of active-matrix LCD screens.

Active-Matrix Displays

An active-matrix display differs from a dual-scan display in that it contains three transistors for every pixel onscreen (color displays) rather than just at the edges. The transistors are arranged on a grid of conductive material, with each connected to a horizontal and a vertical member. Selected voltages are applied by electrodes at the perimeter of the grid to address each pixel individually. Thus, an active-matrix screen is comparable to a sheet of graph paper that has a dot (representing a transistor) at each intersection of horizontal and vertical lines.

Most active-matrix displays use a thin-film transistor (TFT) array. TFT is a method for packaging from one (monochrome) to three (RGB color) transistors per pixel within a flexible material that is the same size and shape as the display. Therefore, the transistors for each pixel lie directly behind the liquid crystal cells they control.

Two TFT manufacturing processes account for most of the active-matrix displays on the market today: hydrogenated amorphous silicon (a-Si) and low-temperature polysilicon (p-Si). These processes differ primarily in their costs. At first, most TFT displays were manufactured using the a-Si process because it required lower temperatures (less than 400°C) than the p-Si process of the time. Now, lower-temperature p-Si manufacturing processes are making this method an economically viable alternative to a-Si.

To improve horizontal viewing angles in the latest LCD displays, some vendors have modified the classic TFT design. For example, Hitachi's in-plane switching (IPS) design—also known as *STFT*—aligns the individual cells of the LCD parallel to the glass, running the electric current through the sides of the cells and spinning the pixels to provide more even distribution of the image to the entire panel area. Fujitsu's similar multidomain vertical alignment (MVA) technology is used in many recent notebook displays. MVA divides the screen into different regions and changes the angle of the regions to provide a wider viewing angle than traditional TFT displays.

Although a TFT display has a great many transistors—4,410,000 for a color 1400×1050 display—each pixel does not have its own separate signal connection. Instead, voltages are applied through connections for each row and column, much like the transistors in a passive-matrix display.

Because every pixel is individually controlled by its own transistor circuit, it can be refreshed at very high rates, creating a display that is more vivid than a dual-scan panel. The viewing angle is also greater, enabling multiple viewers to gather around the screen, and refreshes are faster and crisper, without the fuzziness of the dual scans, even in the case of games or full-motion video.

Most laptop/notebook systems today use screens from 14.1 inches (diagonal) through 17 inches, with some high-end models using wide-screen displays up to 17 inches. Most systems featuring a 14.1-inch screen run XGA resolution (1024×768), whereas high-end systems include screens up to 1600×1200 resolution or more. Higher resolutions and sizes are possible, but I question whether anything larger than a 17-inch display is workable for a portable system. In addition, increasing the resolution without increasing the size makes text and icons difficult to see. Many portable systems now also include AGP bus video adapters with up to 128MB of video RAM, providing extra speed and capability. A good TFT display and integrated AGP or PCI Express adapter rival the quality and performance of a quality monitor and video adapter in a desktop system. In fact, a 15-inch TFT display (which, unlike most conventional monitors, describes the actual diagonal size of the image) generally has picture quality and usability equal to a 17-inch CRT display.

Resolution

Resolution is the amount of detail a monitor can render. This quantity is expressed in the number of horizontal and vertical picture elements, or *pixels*, contained in the screen. The greater the number of pixels, the more detailed the images. The resolution required depends on the application. Character-based applications (such as DOS command-line programs) require very low resolutions, whereas graphics-intensive applications (such as desktop publishing and Windows software) require a great deal more. With Windows, the more resolution you have, the greater the size of your desktop, which means you can have more programs or windows open at once, without overlapping.

It's important to realize that CRTs are designed to handle a range of resolutions natively, but flat-panel displays(both desktop and notebook) are built to run a single native resolution and must scale to other choices. Older LCD panels handled scaling poorly, but even though current TFT displays perform scaling better, the best results with various resolutions are still found with CRTs.

As PC video technology developed, the screen resolutions that video adapters supported grew at a steady pace. Table 11.1 lists the standard resolutions used in laptop graphics adapters and displays (including external monitors), and the terms commonly used to describe them.

Table 11.1   Laptop Graphics Display Resolution Standards

Display Standard	Linear Pixels (H×V)	Total Pixels	Aspect Ratio
VGA	640×480	307,200	1.33
SVGA	800×600	480,000	1.33
XGA	1024×768	786,432	1.33
WXGA+	1440×900	1,296,000	1.60

Table 11.1   Continued

Display Standard	Linear Pixels (H×V)	Total Pixels	Aspect Ratio
SXGA	1280×1024	1,310,720	1.25
SXGA+	1400×1050	1,470,000	1.33
WSXGA	1600×1024	1,638,400	1.56
WSXGA+	1680×1050	1,764,000	1.60
UXGA	1600×1200	1,920,000	1.33
HDTV	1920×1080	2,073,600	1.78
WUXGA	1920×1200	2,304,000	1.60
QXGA	2048×1536	3,145,728	1.33

Aspect Ratios:

1.25 = 5:4

1.33 = 4:3

1.56 = 25:16

1.60 = 16:10

1.78 = 16:9

1.83 = 11:6

The color graphics adapter (CGA) and enhanced graphics adapter (EGA) cards and monitors were the first PC graphics standards in the early-to-mid 1980s and were also supported by many portables and early laptops. The video graphics array (VGA) standard was released by IBM in April 1987, and all the subsequent resolutions and modes introduced since then have been based on it in one way or another. VGA mode is still in common use as a reference to the standard 640×480 16-color display that most versions of the Windows operating systems use as their default; Windows XP, however, defaults to SVGA mode, which is 800×600. The 15-pin connector through which you connect the analog display to most video adapters is also often called a *VGA port*. A few laptops also support the DVI-I analog and digital LCD and CRT port that uses a 29-pin version of the DVI-D connector when a port replicator or docking station is attached.

Most modern laptop computers now use 14.1" through 17" LCD panels that feature SXGA+ (1400×1050) or even UXGA (1600×1200) resolution. Although these resolutions would be unacceptable on a same-size CRT display, they work well on the flat-panel display built in to the laptop because of the crystal-clear image, and also because you generally sit closer to a laptop display. In fact, it is for this reason that resolutions that high may not work on desktop flat-panel displays unless they are larger 17- or 19-inch models.

Which resolution do you want for your display? Generally, the higher the resolution, the larger the display you will want. Why? Because Windows icons and text use a constant number of pixels, higher display resolutions make these screen elements a smaller part of the desktop onscreen. By using a larger display, you can use higher resolution settings and still have text and icons that are readable.

Note

Although some laptop computers feature displays with resolutions of 1600×1200, this can cause text to be so small that most people have trouble reading it. A partial solution is to enable large icons in the Windows Display Properties dialog box (right-click your Desktop and select Properties). In Windows 98/Me/2000/XP, select Effects, Use Large Icons. Windows 95 doesn't have an option to enlarge only the icons; you can use the Settings tab to select Large Fonts, but some programs will not work properly with font sizes larger than the default Small Fonts setting.

To understand this issue, you might want to compare laptops that support different resolutions. A convenient way to do this is to go to a retail computer or electronics store that has a lineup of laptop computers running Windows. As you look at models that support 1024×768, 1280×1024, and higher native resolutions, you'll notice several changes to the appearance of the Windows desktop.

At 1024×768, text and onscreen icons are fairly large. However, text and onscreen icons become smaller on systems with higher-resolution screens of the same size. Because the screen elements used for the Windows Desktop and software menus are at a fixed pixel width and height, you'll notice that they shrink in size onscreen as you change to the higher resolutions. However, there's a benefit to higher resolutions if they're comfortable for you: You'll be able to see more of your document or web page onscreen at the higher resolutions because each object requires less of the screen.

Whereas CRTs can produce poor-quality results at very high resolutions, flat-panel displays at their native resolution are always crisp and perfectly focused by nature. Also, the dimensions advertised for the screens represent the exact size of the viewable image, unlike most conventional CRT-based monitors. In addition, the flat-panel display is so crisp that screens of a given size can easily handle resolutions that are higher than what would otherwise be acceptable on a CRT.

Tip

Although you can adjust the resolution on many recent laptop displays to a lower setting than the native resolution, I don't recommend this option when you're trying to determine which resolution is most comfortable for you. There are two reasons:

- If the scaling option is not enabled, the laptop will use only the central part of the display for lower resolutions, making the comparison between different resolutions difficult to do.

- If the scaling option is enabled (it's usually found in the Advanced section of the Settings tab on the Display properties page in Windows and is sometimes referred to as Expand display), the laptop will use the entire display, but often the picture quality is quite low.

It's useful to preview how well a display performs scaling if you sometimes need to use a lower resolution, but if you're trying to choose the right screen size and resolution, you're better off looking at the pixels per inch (ppi) values I discuss in the next subsection.

LCD Size Versus Resolution: Pixels Per Inch

How do you calculate the pixel spacing, and why is it useful to know this information? Dividing the resolution by the size gives the pixel spacing in an LCD panel. The pixel spacing values help you determine which display size and resolution combinations are most likely to provide comfortable viewing, even before you see the actual laptop display in use.

Because there is a 1:1 correspondence between the transistors in the display that make up the dots and the pixels of resolution, you need to be careful when selecting notebooks or laptops with SXGA (1280×1024) or higher resolutions because icons and text will be much smaller than the typical desktop user is accustomed to. You can change the font size in Windows to compensate, but this often causes problems with different applications and word wrapping. Changing the resolution settings in the operating systems doesn't help much because either the display will simply use fewer pixels and shrink the area used on the screen, or it will resort to scaling, which results in a fuzzy and unclear display.

To gauge the size of displayed items on an LCD, it is common to express the resolution of the screen in *pixels per inch*, which is a fixed value for a given screen. Table 11.2 shows the relative pixels per inch and other statistics for virtually every color LCD ever used in a laptop or notebook system.

Table 11.2   Laptop/Notebook LCD Display Dimensions and Pixel Pitch

Display	Dimension	Linear Pixels	Total Pixels	Transistors (TFT)	Aspect Ratio	Length (in)	Pixels /in	Length (mm)	Pixels /mm	Pitch (mm)
8.4''	across	640	307,200	921,600	1.33	6.72	95	171	3.75	0.267
VGA	down	480				5.04		128		
	diagonal	800				8.40		213		
9.5''	across	640	307,200	921,600	1.33	7.60	84	193	3.32	0.302
VGA	down	480				5.70		145		
	diagonal	800				9.50		241		
10.4''	across	640	307,200	921,600	1.33	8.32	77	211	3.03	0.330
VGA	down	480				6.24		158		
	diagonal	800				10.40		264		
10.4''	across	800	480,000	1,440,000	1.33	8.32	96	211	3.79	0.264
SVGA	down	600				6.24		158		
	diagonal	1000				10.40		264		
11.3''	across	800	480,000	1,440,000	1.33	9.04	88	230	3.48	0.287
SVGA	down	600				6.78		172		
	diagonal	1000				11.30		287		
12.1''	across	800	480,000	1,440,000	1.33	9.68	83	246	3.25	0.307
SVGA	down	600				7.26		184		
	diagonal	1000				12.10		307		
12.1''	across	1024	786,432	2,359,296	1.33	9.68	106	246	4.16	0.240
XGA	down	768				7.26		184		
	diagonal	1280				12.10		307		
13.0''	across	800	480,000	1,440,000	1.33	10.40	77	264	3.03	0.330
SVGA	down	600				7.80		198		
	diagonal	1000				13.00		330		
13.3''	across	1024	786,432	2,359,296	1.33	10.64	96	270	3.79	0.264
XGA	down	768				7.98		203		
	diagonal	1280				13.30		338		
13.7''	across	1280	1,310,720	3,932,160	1.25	10.70	120	272	4.71	0.212
SXGA	down	1024				8.56		217		
	diagonal	1639				13.70		348		
14.1''	across	1024	786,432	2,359,296	1.33	11.28	91	287	3.57	0.280
XGA	down	768				8.46		215		
	diagonal	1280				14.10		358		
14.1''	across	1400	1,470,000	4,410,000	1.33	11.28	124	287	4.89	0.205
SXGA+	down	1050				8.46		215		
	diagonal	1750				14.10		358		

(continues)

Table 11.2   Continued

Display	Dimension	Linear Pixels	Total Pixels	Transistors (TFT)	Aspect Ratio	Length (in)	Pixels /in	Length (mm)	Pixels /mm	Pitch (mm)
15.0''	across	1024	786,432	2,359,296	1.33	12.00	85	305	3.36	0.298
XGA	down	768				9.00		229		
	diagonal	1280				15.00		381		
15.0''	across	1280	1,024,000	3,072,000	1.60	12.72	101	323	3.96	0.252
WXGA	down	800				7.95		202		
	diagonal	1509				15.00		381		
15.0''	across	1400	1,470,000	4,410,000	1.33	12.00	117	305	4.59	0.218
SXGA+	down	1050				9.00		229		
	diagonal	1750				15.00		381		
15.0''	across	1600	1,920,000	5,760,000	1.33	12.00	133	305	5.25	0.191
UXGA	down	1200				9.00		229		
	diagonal	2000				15.00		381		
15.0''	across	2048	3,145,728	9,437,184	1.33	12.00	171	305	6.72	0.149
QXGA	down	1536				9.00		229		
	diagonal	2560				15.00		381		
15.2''	across	1280	1,024,000	3,072,000	1.60	12.89	99	327	3.91	0.256
WXGA	down	800				8.06		205		
	diagonal	1509				15.20		386		
15.2''	across	1280	1,093,120	3,279,360	1.50	12.64	101	321	3.99	0.251
WEXGA	down	854				8.44		214		
	diagonal	1539				15.20		386		
15.4''	across	1280	1,024,000	3,072,000	1.60	13.06	98	332	3.86	0.259
WXGA	down	800				8.16		207		
	diagonal	1509				15.40		391		
15.4''	across	1280	1,310,720	3,932,160	1.25	12.03	106	305	4.19	0.239
SXGA	down	1024				9.62		244		
	diagonal	1639				15.40		391		
15.4''	across	1680	1,764,000	5,292,000	1.60	13.06	129	332	5.06	0.197
WSXGA+	down	1050				8.16		207		
	diagonal	1981				15.40		391		
15.4''	across	1920	2,304,000	6,912,000	1.60	13.06	147	332	5.79	0.173
WUXGA	down	1200				8.16		207		
	diagonal	2264				15.40		391		
15.7''	across	1280	1,310,720	3,932,160	1.25	12.26	104	311	4.11	0.243
SXGA	down	1024				9.81		249		
	diagonal	1639				15.70		399		
16.1''	across	1600	1,920,000	5,760,000	1.33	12.88	124	327	4.89	0.204
UXGA	down	1200				9.66		245		
	diagonal	2000				16.10		409		

Table 11.2 Continued

Display	Dimension	Linear Pixels	Total Pixels	Transistors (TFT)	Aspect Ratio	Length (in)	Pixels /in	Length (mm)	Pixels /mm	Pitch (mm)
17.0''	across	1440	1,296,000	3,888,000	1.60	14.42	100	366	3.93	0.254
WXGA+	down	900				9.01		229		
	diagonal	1698				17.00		432		
17.0''	across	1600	1,920,000	5,760,000	1.33	13.60	118	345	4.63	0.216
UXGA	down	1200				10.20		259		
	diagonal	2000				17.00		432		

Table 11.2 covers virtually every color laptop screen produced, including PCs and even Macs. The table is organized by LCD size (measured diagonally) from smallest to largest, and within each size, they are listed in resolution order from the lowest to the highest available in that size.

If you study this table, you can figure out many things about a given display. For example, most systems have traditionally used a 1.33 (4:3) aspect ratio, which means the width is 4/3 of the height, or the height is 3/4 of the width. So-called "wide-screen" displays usually have a higher aspect ratio of 1.6 (16:10), which is close to the 16:9 of a wide-screen format movie. Figure 11.1 compares the 1.33 aspect ratio of a normal laptop display to the 1.6 aspect ratio used by laptops with wide-screen displays.

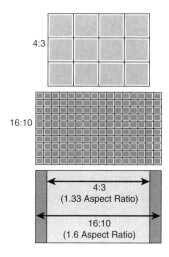

Figure 11.1 Normal and wide-screen laptop display aspect ratios.

Perhaps the most important part of this chart is the information about pixel spacing, which is expressed in three different ways. The first, and generally easiest to use, is the pixels per inch (ppi) figure, ranging from 77 to 171. The default desktop icon size in Windows is 32×32 pixels. A 14.1-inch XGA (1024×768) display has a 91ppi, which means that each icon will be 0.352 (32/91) inches (or about 8.9mm) square. On a 15-inch UXGA (1600×1200) display with 133ppi, the same icons will be only 0.241 (32/133) inches (or about 6.1mm) square, which is considerably smaller. Text on the screen will be smaller by the same amount as well. Although it is possible to reconfigure Windows to use larger icons and larger text, this often causes appearance problems, such as word wrapping in dialog boxes where it wouldn't otherwise occur. Also, many fonts are fixed, and they will remain at the smaller size no matter what settings you change.

After studying all the available displays on the market, I have concluded that some people will have difficulty seeing the text and icons when they cross 100ppi, and many people will have difficulty reading displays that are over 120ppi. If you are going to choose a system that has a display rated over 120ppi, you will need good vision and may need to sit closer to the screen than you might with another system in order to read it. Changing resolution to a lower setting is usually unsatisfactory with a flat-panel display because either the display will simply be smaller (text and icons will remain the same size, but you can't fit as much on the screen) or the system will attempt to scale the data to fit the screen. However, this invariably results in a blurred and distorted image.

Anything under 100ppi is considered fairly *loose*, meaning that individual icons, text, and other display items are large enough for most people to easily see. Regardless of the actual resolution, any two displays having the same number of pixels per inch will display text, icons, and other elements on the screen at the same sizing. For example, both the 12.1-inch XGA display and the 15.4-inch SXGA display have the same pixel size (106 per inch), so if an object is 106 pixels wide, it will appear one inch wide on either display. If you have the SXGA display and change settings to display only XGA resolution, you'll see a 12.1-inch diagonal active display area centered inside the 15.4-inch diagonal screen. Figure 11.2 shows the difference between SVGA (800×600) and XGA (1024×768) resolution on the same display, without scaling. On a CRT, the lower resolution would be "blown up" to fill the screen, same as the higher resolution, except everything would appear larger. On an LCD, selecting a lower resolution merely causes less of the screen to be used, and everything remains the same size. Newer LCDs that perform scaling (an option you can control in the Advanced display properties page) will attempt to blow up the image to fill the screen; however, the digital nature of images often causes jagged edges and other artifacts, thus making the larger display harder to read. The bottom line is that LCDs really work well only at their native resolution—something you should strongly consider when purchasing a system.

After you go over 100 pixels per inch, the icons, text, and other items on the display become smaller and, for some, possibly difficult to see. In the more extreme cases, you might have to change display settings to use large fonts to make onscreen text easier to read. In my experience, I consider 120 pixels per inch the maximum for running Windows without absolutely requiring adjustments in font sizes, icon sizes and spacing, and so on, but this is something that depends on your vision—especially close up. If you are considering a system with more than 100 pixels per inch in the display, be sure you preview it first to ensure that the level of screen density is acceptable. If you are comfortable with a display with more than 100 pixels per inch, the amount of desktop visible and the number of open windows you can have make these high-resolution displays very appealing for desktop replacement systems.

As a consolation, even with their tinier text and icons, these screens are much sharper and clearer than an analog desktop monitor. So, even though the text and icons are physically smaller, they are often more readable with less eyestrain because they are sharp and perfectly focused.

Tip

If you plan to use an external LCD projector with your portable computer, be sure you match the native resolutions of the projector and your computer's flat-panel display. If both use the same resolution, you can normally operate in simultaneous-display mode, enabling you to see onscreen what the audience is seeing. If your projector has a different resolution from the flat-panel display, the projector will try to simulate the flat-panel display resolution, resulting in a blurry image. You can sharpen the projector's image by adjusting the flat-panel display's resolution to match the projector, but then the image will either be at the wrong size or blurry.

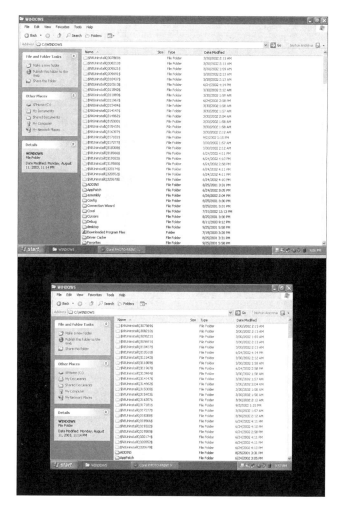

Figure 11.2 The 1024×768 resolution (top) compared to 800×600 resolution on a typical laptop LCD without scaling. Note that more rows of text (and more whitespace) are visible at the higher resolution.

Virtual Displays

Normally, you cannot exceed the native resolution of a flat-panel display screen. However, some systems can create a virtual screen arrangement to provide a larger display on a smaller screen. This allows you to pan the visible area over a larger area that cannot be seen all at once (see Figure 11.3). In general, this is a difficult way to use the system, and I've never seen anybody use it except as a test to see if it worked. The effect is difficult to get used to, rather like a pan-and-scan videotape of a widescreen movie. The most serious problem with this arrangement is that some manufacturers have advertised it as a higher-resolution display, without being more clear about its actual nature. When you evaluate a portable system's display, be sure that you look at the native or internal resolution of the flat-panel display. Because nobody really uses the virtual display feature, not many systems support it anymore.

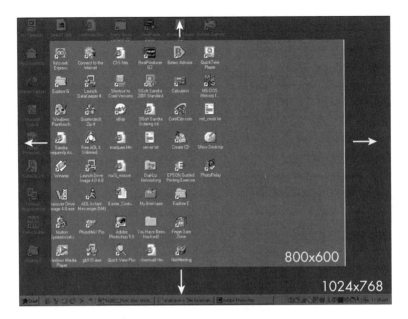

Figure 11.3   A virtual screen, when enabled, lets you scroll across a larger area.

Note

If you plug your laptop into an external monitor that is configured to use a higher display resolution than your internal flat-panel display does, your laptop might automatically use this virtual screen mode if you toggle between the monitor and your laptop's display.

Image Brightness and Contrast

Although the brightness of a display is a consideration that applies to both LCDs and CRTs, it is especially important in judging the quality of an LCD panel. Although a dim CRT display is almost certainly a sign of either improper brightness control or a dying monitor, brightness in LCD panels can vary a great deal from one model to another. Brightness for LCD panels is measured in candelas per square meter, which is abbreviated "nt" and pronounced *nit*. Typical ratings for good display panels are between 200 and 400 nits (the brighter, the better). A good combination is a rating of 250 nits or higher and a contrast rating of 300:1 or higher.

Contrast is measured as the ratio of the luminance difference between white and black. A higher contrast makes for sharper text and more vivid colors. A typical CRT has a contrast ratio of about 245:1. Most flat-panel displays have contrast ratios up to 400:1. Newer panels can also be viewed at higher angles without a loss of contrast.

Response Time

Flat-panel displays don't react as quickly as CRTs. This can cause full-motion video, full-screen 3D games, and animation to look smeared onscreen. Typical response times can be from 8ms (milliseconds) to 40ms or higher. If you want a fast-acting display, try to find a laptop that features a flat-panel display at or below the 20ms rating.

Power Management

Although LCD panels have very low power consumption compared to CRT displays, intelligent use of your laptop's power-management features is critical if you want to get maximum runtime when you use battery power.

Power management is performed in different ways, depending on your laptop's BIOS and the version of Windows it uses. Virtually every laptop in use, regardless of its age, supports VESA's display power-management signaling (DPMS) spec, which defined the signals a computer sends to a monitor or built-in LCD panel to indicate idle times. The computer decides when to send these signals.

In Windows 9x/Me/2000/XP, you must enable this feature if you want to use it because it's turned off by default. To enable it in Windows 9x/Me, right-click the Windows desktop and select Properties. In the Display Properties dialog box, switch to the Screen Saver tab and make sure the Energy Star low-power settings and Monitor Shutdown settings are checked. You can adjust how long the system remains idle before the monitor picture is blanked or the monitor shuts down completely. Use the Power icon in Windows 2000/XP to set power management for the monitor and other peripherals. You can also access power management by selecting the Screen Saver tab on the Display Properties dialog box and clicking the Power button.

Note

Windows 2000 and XP load an applet known as Power Meter into the system tray on laptop computers. Power Meter displays a battery icon when you use battery power; when you move the mouse pointer over the battery icon, the charge and estimated runtime are displayed. Click the Power Meter icon to bring up a menu of power management schemes to choose from. Double-click the icon to display details about the battery in use or to select the option to display Power Meter at all times.

When you plug the laptop into AC power, the battery icon is replaced by an AC plug icon if you have selected the option to display Power Meter at all times.

In 1989, at the dawn of the laptop era, Intel and Microsoft jointly developed the Advanced Power Management (APM) specification, which defines a BIOS-based interface between hardware that is capable of power-management functions and an operating system that implements power-management policies. In short, this means you can configure an OS such as Windows 9x to switch your monitor into a low-power mode after an interval of nonuse and even to shut it off entirely. For these actions to occur, however, the monitor, system BIOS, and operating system must all support the APM standard. Virtually every laptop in use since the early 1990s has supported APM.

With Windows 98, Windows Me, Windows 2000, and Windows XP, Microsoft introduced a more comprehensive power-management method called Advanced Configuration and Power Interface (ACPI). ACPI also works with displays, hard drives, and other devices supported by APM and allows the computer to automatically turn peripherals, such as CD-ROMs, network cards, hard disk drives, and printers, on and off. It also enables the computer to turn on and off other consumer devices connected to the laptop or desktop computer, such as VCRs, televisions, telephones, and stereos.

Although APM compatibility was standard in common BIOSes for several years, a number of computers from major manufacturers required BIOS upgrades to add ACPI support when Windows 98 was introduced.

Note

ACPI support is installed on Windows 98, Windows Me, Windows 2000, and Windows XP computers *only* if an ACPI-compliant BIOS is present when one of these versions of Windows is first installed. If an ACPI-compliant BIOS is installed after the initial Windows installation, it is ignored. Fortunately, these versions of Windows still support APM as well. See Microsoft's FAQ for ACPI on the Microsoft website.

Frequencies

LCDs also don't have problems with image flicker like CRTs do. With CRT monitors, you must match the range of horizontal and vertical frequencies the monitor accepts with those generated by your video adapter. The wider the range of signals, the more expensive—and more versatile—the monitor. Your video adapter's vertical and horizontal frequencies must fall within the ranges your monitor supports. The vertical frequency (or refresh/frame rate) determines the stability of your image (the higher the vertical frequency, the better). Typical vertical frequencies range from 50Hz to 160Hz, but multiple-frequency monitors support different vertical frequencies at different resolutions. You might find that a bargain monitor has a respectable 100Hz vertical frequency at 640×480 but drops to a less desirable 60Hz at 1024×768. The horizontal frequency (or line rate) typically ranges from 31.5KHz to 90KHz or more. By default, most video adapters use a 60Hz default vertical scan frequency to avoid monitor damage.

Although flat-panel display monitors (including built-in laptop LCD panels) use lower vertical frequencies than CRTs, they avoid problems with screen flicker because of their design. Because they use transistors to activate all the pixels in the image at once, as opposed to a scanning electron beam, which must work its way from the top to the bottom of the screen to create an image, flat-panel displays rarely ever flicker.

Note

About the only time you'll ever see flicker on a flat-panel display is when certain combinations of grays are displayed at the same time.

Testing a Display

Until you view the display in a given laptop or notebook system in person, you can't really tell whether it will suit your needs. It is best to view the system in person to evaluate the display. Some may find the newer high-resolution systems difficult to use due to a very high pixel pitch. It is best to "kick the tires" of a few at a dealer showroom or in the privacy of your home or office (if the dealer has a liberal return policy).

You can perform several simple tests that require no special software. First, however, make sure the LCD is set to its native resolution. Then try the following tests:

- Draw a perfect circle with a graphics program such as Paintbrush. If the displayed result is an oval, not a circle, this system may be difficult to use with graphics or design software.

- Using a word processor or editor, type some words in 8- or 10-point type (1 point equals 1/72"). Check to see whether the words are clear and readable.

- Display a screen with as much whitespace as possible and look for areas of color variance. This can indicate a problem with the backlighting.

- Display the Windows desktop to check for uniform brightness.

- To check the scaling and interpolation, change to a lower resolution from the panel's native resolution using the Windows Display Properties settings. Because LCDs have only one native resolution, the display must use scaling to handle other resolutions in full screen. If the visible display area doesn't fill the screen, enable the scaling option in the Advanced portion of the Settings dialog box of the Display properties page. The option might be called Expand Panel Image or something similar. If you are a web designer, a gamer, or must capture screens at a particular resolution, this test will show you whether the LCD produces acceptable display quality at resolutions other than normal.

Maintaining Your LCD

LCDs are very durable and really don't require any special maintenance. Besides normal surface cleaning, it is a good idea to use the power management in Windows to blank the display after a preset period of inactivity. Although phosphor burn (in which an image left onscreen eventually leaves a permanent shadow onscreen) is impossible with LCD displays, you can wear out the backlight if the display is left on all the time. To preserve the life of the display, it is best to use the power management in Windows to blank the screen after a period of inactivity. I recommend you set this value for an amount of time a bit longer than you'd normally leave the computer running without activity. For example, if you normally use your laptop for 30 minutes without touching the keyboard or mouse, set the screen blank time to 45 minutes. This enables the laptop to shut off the backlight automatically without interrupting your normal work habits.

Dead Pixels

Thin-film transistor (TFT) or active matrix displays have potentially millions of transistors. With all these transistors, it is not uncommon for failures to occur, resulting in displays with one or more dead pixels due to malfunctioning transistors. Actually, we are talking about *subpixels*, the individual RGB triad transistor elements that make up each pixel.

A so-called *dead pixel* is one in which the red, green, or blue subpixel cell is stuck on or off. Failures in the on state are more common and, unfortunately, also more annoying. In particular, those that fail when on are very noticeable on a dark background, such as a bright red, green, or blue dot. Although even a few of these can be distracting, manufacturers vary in their warranty policies regarding how many dead pixels are required before you can get a replacement display. Some vendors look at both the total number of dead pixels and their locations. Fortunately, improvements in manufacturing quality make it less and less likely that you will see a screen with dead pixels either on your desktop or in your notebook computer display.

Most manufacturers have standards for the number of defective pixels allowed on their displays. It is considered acceptable to have a few that have failed, although they can be annoying. Most companies have policies allowing up to 21 dead or illuminated subpixels per display, but in practice I've never seen even close to that number on a given display. It is normal to see perhaps one to five, and in many cases I've seen perfect displays. If you feel the number or placement of dead pixels is unworkable in your specific situation, contact your manufacturer for a possible replacement.

Because all the transistors of a TFT display are integrated into a single component, there is no normal way to remedy a dead pixel except to replace the entire display. Because this is one of the most expensive components in a portable system, many portable computer manufacturers refuse to accept returns of systems for less than a set number of bad pixels (this number varies by vendor). The location or clustering of the bad pixels can also affect this policy. For example, if several bad pixels are grouped together in the middle of the display, the manufacturer is more likely to offer a replacement than if they are scattered around the edge. This is another part of the vendor's purchasing policy that you should check before ordering a system with an active-matrix display (the type of display used on all new laptop computers today).

Although there is no normal way to repair bad pixels, there might be a simple fix that can help. I have actually repaired bad pixels by gently tapping on the screen at the pixel location. This seems to work in many cases, especially in cases in which the pixel is always illuminated instead of dead (dark). Because I find a constantly lit pixel to be more irritating than one that is constantly dark, this fix has saved me a lot of aggravation.

Protecting the Expensive and Fragile LCD Display

Historically, the display has been the single most expensive component in a portable system. In fact, if the system is out of warranty, it is sometimes more economical to replace the entire computer rather than have a broken display replaced.

Even though the prices for these displays have come down, they are still one of the most expensive parts of a portable system. They are also fragile. If you drop your laptop or notebook (something a standard warranty does not cover), you will likely fracture the display, which means it must be replaced. Replacement LCD panels are sometimes close to the same cost as purchasing a new system, unless you have purchased extra-cost breakage insurance (which I recommend). Another common way people damage their screens is to close the system with a pen, pencil, or other item on or above the keyboard. Make sure this area is clear before closing the system.

Caution

If you work on airplanes a lot, especially in coach, watch out for a tired traveler reclining the seat in front of you. Your notebook screen can be easily cracked by the top of the seat squeezing down on the top of your screen.

Video Display Interfaces

A video interface provides the connection between your system and the display, transmitting the signals that appear as images on the display. Throughout the history of the PC, there has been a succession of standards for video interfaces and displays representing a steady increase in screen resolution and color depth. Early laptop computers used the 4-color color graphics adapter (CGA) and 16-color enhanced graphics adapter (EGA) displays that used digital technology.

However, after IBM released its analog video graphics array (VGA) display standard in 1987, laptop builders switched to VGA, and portable displays ever since have been based on VGA, just as desktop displays continue to be based on VGA.

Modern laptop video graphics processors and displays support higher resolutions and color depths, and they have other additional capabilities (such as 3D functions) not found in the original VGA specification. However, because of careful design ensuring backward compatibility, most of the latest high-resolution video interfaces and displays can also run most older color graphics software written for CGA, EGA, and most of the other obsolete graphics standards. This enables you to use older software on your current system, even though the video interface and display standards have changed dramatically.

Video Graphics Array (VGA)

IBM introduced the video graphics array (VGA) interface and display standard on April 2, 1987, along with a family of systems it called PS/2. The first laptop to use VGA was Compaq's SLT/286, which was introduced in 1988. VGA went on to become the most popular video interface in history, and it's still the basis of most modern PC video adapters and displays on both laptop and desktop computers.

Unlike earlier digital video standards, VGA is an analog system. When it came out in 1987, it began a shift from digital to analog that has lasted since then. Only recently has there been a shift back to digital, which will probably continue over the next few years. Why go from digital to analog and then back to digital? The simple answer is that analog was the least expensive way at the time to design a system that supported a reasonable resolution with a reasonable number of colors. Now that technology has advanced and LCD displays are fast replacing CRTs, going back to an all-digital format makes sense.

The PC video standards that preceded VGA, including the original MDA, CGA, and EGA standards, were digital. They generated different colors by sending digital color signals down three wires, which allowed for the display of up to 8 colors (2^3). Another signal doubled the number of color combinations from 8 to 16 by allowing each color to display at two intensity levels. This type of digital display was easy to manufacture and offered simplicity, with consistent color combinations from system to system. The main drawback of the original digital display standards, such as CGA and EGA, was the limited number of possible colors.

With VGA, IBM went to an analog design. Analog uses a separate signal for each CRT color gun, but each signal can be sent at varying levels of intensity—64 levels, in the case of the VGA. This provides 262,144 possible colors (64^3), of which 256 could be simultaneously displayed in the original design. For realistic computer graphics, color depth is often more important than high resolution because the human eye perceives a picture that has more colors as being more realistic. IBM moved to analog graphics to enhance the color capabilities of its systems.

VGA was designed to be addressed through the VGA BIOS interface, a software interface that forced programs to talk to the driver rather than directly to the hardware. This allowed programs to call a consistent set of commands and functions that would work on different hardware, as long as a compatible VGA BIOS interface was present. The original VGA cards had the BIOS on the video card directly, in the form of a ROM chip containing from 16KB to 32KB worth of code. Modern video cards and laptop graphics processors still have this 32KB onboard BIOS (often incorporated directly into the processor itself), although it supports only the same functionality of the original VGA standard. To use higher functionality, additional drivers are loaded into RAM during the boot process, and the ROM BIOS on the card is largely ignored after that. Typically, the only time the ROM-based drivers are used is during boot and when you run Windows in Safe Mode.

An original VGA card displays up to 256 colors onscreen, from a palette of 262,144 (256KB) colors; when used in the 640×480 graphics or 720×400 text mode, 16 colors at a time can be displayed. VGA displays originally came not only in color but also in monochrome VGA models, which use color summing. With color summing, 64 gray shades are displayed instead of colors. The summing routine is initiated if the BIOS detects a monochrome display when the system boots. This routine uses an algorithm that takes the desired color and rewrites the formula to involve all three color guns, producing varying intensities of gray, even though the application is attempting to display color. Monochrome displays are obsolete today.

Even the least-expensive laptop displays today can work with modes well beyond the VGA standard. VGA, at its 16-color, 640×480 graphics resolution, has come to be the baseline for PC graphical display configurations. VGA is accepted as the least common denominator for all Windows systems and must be supported by the video adapters in all systems running Windows. The installation programs of all Windows versions use these VGA settings as their default video configuration. In addition to VGA, virtually all adapters support a range of higher screen resolutions and color depths, depending on the capabilities of the hardware. If Windows must be started in Safe Mode because of a startup problem, the system defaults to VGA in the 640×480, 16-color mode. Windows 2000 and Windows XP also offer a VGA Mode startup that uses this mode (Windows XP uses 800×600 resolution) but doesn't slow down the rest of the computer the way Safe Mode (which replaces 32-bit drivers with BIOS services) does.

IBM introduced higher-resolution versions of VGA called *XGA* and *XGA-2* in the early 1990s, but most of the development of VGA-related standards since then has come from the third-party video card industry, industry trade groups, and standardization committees.

Here are the most important of these standards:

- **VESA**—Video Electronics Standards Association (www.vesa.org)
- **DDWG**—Digital Display Working Group (www.ddwg.org)
- **SID**—Society for Information Display (www.sid.org)
- **USDC**—United States Display Consortium (www.usdc.org)
- **ATIP**—Asian Technology Information Program (www.atip.org)

The efforts of these groups are the primary influence on video display standards for desktop and laptop PCs and other types of computers.

Industry Standard SVGA

After IBM introduced the VGA standard in April 1987, it seemed to take forever before anything newer and better came out. By 1989, competing system, video card, and display manufacturers had wanted to introduce something better than VGA, but they also wanted to cooperate in order to make the new interface an industry standard as well as make it compatible with existing software and hardware designed for VGA.

In February 1989, an international nonprofit group called Video Electronics Standards Association (VESA) was formed to create industrywide interface standards for the PC and other computing environments. VESA was designed to create and promote open standards for the display and display interface industry, which would ensure interoperability and yet also allow for innovation. VESA is led by a board of directors that represents a voting membership of more than 100 corporate members worldwide. The members are PC hardware, software, display, and component manufacturers, as well as cable and telephone companies, service providers, and more. VESA essentially took the role of defining PC video interface standards away from IBM, giving it instead to the VESA members.

In August 1989, VESA introduced its first standard, an 800×600 16-color BIOS interface standard called Super VGA (SVGA) mode 6Ah, which allowed companies to independently develop video hardware having a common software interface. This allowed for higher resolution functionality while maintaining interchangeability and backward compatibility with existing VGA. Since then, VESA has extended the SVGA standard to include many other modes and resolutions, and it developed or contributed to many successive standards in PC video.

Note that although SVGA technically defines a set of VESA standards that includes modes from 800×600 and beyond, typically we use the term *SVGA* to describe only the 800×600 mode. Other higher-resolution modes have been given different names (XGA, SXGA, and so on), even though they are technically part of the VESA SVGA specifications.

XGA and Beyond

Not one to give up without a struggle, for a while IBM continued to develop and release new video standards, despite VESA doing the same. On October 30, 1990, IBM introduced the extended graphics array (XGA). XGA was an evolution of VGA and provided enhanced resolution, color content, and hardware functionality. XGA was also optimized for Windows and other graphical user interfaces. The most exciting feature XGA added over VGA was support for two new graphics modes:

- 1024×768 256-color mode
- 640×480 256-color mode

Notably missing from IBM's original XGA interface was the VESA-defined 800×600 16-color mode, which had debuted just over a year earlier. That was important because not many monitors at the time could handle 1024×768, but many could handle 800×600. With IBM's card you had to jump from 640×480 directly to 1024×768, which required a very expensive monitor back then. That oversight was finally corrected when IBM released XGA-2 on September 21, 1992. XGA-2 added more performance and additional color depth, as well as support for the intermediate 800×600 VESA modes:

- 640×480 256- and 65,536-color modes
- 800×600 16-, 256-, and 65,536-color modes
- 1024×768 16- and 256-color modes

Since then, VESA and other industry groups have defined all the newer video interface and display standards. IBM became a member of VESA and many of the other groups as well. Although IBM introduced these higher resolutions and color depths in 1991 and 1992, most laptop computers didn't support these standards until the mid-1990s.

VESA BIOS Extension (VBE)

In October 1991, VESA recognized that programming applications to support the many SVGA cards on the market was difficult, and it proposed a standard for a uniform programmer's interface for SVGA cards: the VESA BIOS Extension (VBE). VBE support might be provided through a memory-resident driver (used by older cards) or through additional code added to the VGA BIOS chip itself (the more common solution). The benefit of the VESA BIOS extension is that a programmer needs to worry about only one routine or driver to support SVGA modes. Various cards from various manufacturers are accessible through the common VESA interface. Today, VBE support is a concern primarily for real-mode DOS applications, usually older games, and for non-Microsoft operating systems that need to access higher resolutions and color depths. VBE supports resolutions up to 1280×1024 and color depths up to 24 bits (16.8 million colors), depending on the mode selected and the memory on the video card. VESA compliance is of virtually no consequence to Windows versions 95 and up. These operating systems use custom video drivers for their graphics cards.

Analog VGA Connections

Virtually all analog video interfaces since VGA have used the VGA connector and pinout definition. This is why you can plug a brand-new high-resolution analog CRT or flat-panel display into the oldest VGA cards or laptops with an external VGA port, or the oldest displays into the newest cards, and they will all work at the lowest common denominator of resolution, color depth, and performance. The standard 15-pin female VGA connector (on the video card or system) is shown in Figure 11.4; the pinouts are shown in Table 11.3.

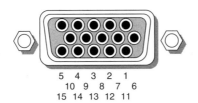

```
 5   4   3   2   1
   10  9   8   7   6
  15  14  13  12  11
```

Figure 11.4   The standard 15-pin analog VGA connector.

Table 11.3   The Pinout for the Standard 15-Pin Analog VGA Connector

Pin	Function	Direction
1	Red Analog Video	Out
2	Green Analog Video	Out
3	Blue Analog Video	Out
4	Monitor ID 2	In
5	TTL GND (monitor self-test)	—
6	Red Analog GND	—
7	Green Analog GND	—
8	Blue Analog GND	—
9	Key (unused)	—
10	Sync GND	—
11	Monitor ID 0	In
12	Monitor ID 1	In
13	Horizontal Sync	Out
14	Vertical Sync	Out
15	Monitor ID 3	In

The mating VGA cable connector that plugs into this connector normally has pin 9 missing. This was designed such that the mating hole in the connector on the video card could be plugged, but it is usually open (and merely unused) instead. The connector is keyed by virtue of the D-shape shell and pin alignment, so it is difficult to plug in backward even without the key pin. Pin 5 is used only for testing purposes, and pin 15 is rarely used; they are often pinless as well. To identify the type of monitor connected to the system, some manufacturers use the presence or absence of the monitor ID pins in various combinations.

Almost all laptops built since the introduction of VGA into laptop design feature the 15-pin connector for external VGA monitors described here. Although laptops have built-in displays, there are several reasons to support external displays:

- **Limited size of laptop displays**—If you need a larger screen for any reason, you can plug it into the external VGA port.

- **Limited resolution choices**—Because flat-panel displays have a single native resolution and often perform poorly when scaling to lower resolutions, an external VGA port offers you extra flexibility. Using an external display, particularly a CRT, enables you to provide high-quality displays at lower (or higher) resolutions than those available with the laptop's built-in display.

■ **Emergency backup in case of damage to the built-in display**—If the relatively fragile built-in flat-panel display becomes damaged, you can plug an external monitor into any laptop with a VGA port, press a key combination, and switch to the external monitor. This enables you to continue to work or at least back up your data until you can have the built-in display replaced.

S-Video/TV-Out Connections

S-Video (Separate Video) is an analog industry standard video-transmission scheme that uses a standardized 4-pin mini-DIN (Deutsches Institut für Normung e.V., or German Institute for Standardization) connector to send television-type video information on separate luminance (or brightness, designated as Y) and chrominance (or color, designated as C) pairs. S-Video is sometimes called *Y/C video*, in reference to the names of the separate luminance and chrominance signals. S-Video was designed to be superior to a composite video signal, which has the Y and C information combined. Composite video requires that the signals be separated by a comb filter inside the receiving device, which can reduce the sharpness of the image. By separating the Y/C signals, S-Video avoids the use of a comb filter, thus resulting in a cleaner, sharper image.

Figure 11.5 and Table 11.4 show the standard 4-pin S-Video mini-DIN connector and pinout. By connecting an S-Video cable to the video-out or TV-Out port on your laptop, you can send video output to a television, video projector, DVD player, VCR, video camera, and more.

Figure 11.5 The standard 4-pin S-video mini-DIN connector.

Table 11.4 The Pinout for the Standard 4-Pin S-Video Mini-DIN Connector

Pin	Signal
1	Analog Y GND
2	Analog C GND
3	Video Y (luminance)
4	Video C (chrominance)

Some Dell laptops use a modified S-Video connector with additional pins added for additional functions. You can order the necessary adapter cable from Dell that breaks out the extra signals into other connectors. Figure 11.6 and Table 11.5 show the TV-Out (S-Video+) connector used in Dell systems.

Figure 11.6   The Dell 7-pin mini-DIN TV-Out connector.

Table 11.5   The Pinout for the Dell 7-Pin Mini-DIN TV-Out (S-Video+) Connector

Pin	Signal
1	Analog Y GND
2	Analog C GND
3	Video Y (luminance)
4	Video C (chrominance)
5	S/PDIF digital audio
6	Composite video
7	S/PDIF digital audio

A standard 4-pin S-Video cable will plug into the modified S-Video connector, and in that case the extra functions will be ignored. The additional pins on the Dell connector are used for composite video (useful for older and low-end TVs and VCRs that lack the S-Video connector) as well as Sony/Philips Digital Interface (S/PDIF) audio connections, enabling laptop computers with this feature to connect to home theater speaker systems with S/PDIF connections.

If you need to connect a laptop with a standard S-Video output jack to a VCR or TV that doesn't support S-Video but has a composite connector (single RCA jack), you can use an S-Video-to-RCA (composite) converter (see Figure 11.7).

Figure 11.7   An S-video cable (left) and RCA composite cable (right) with the S-Video-to-RCA composite adapter (center).

Depending on the laptop, TV-Out might be automatically enabled when you connect the S-Video port to a TV or VCR that's turned on, or you might need to use the keystroke combination used by your laptop to switch to the TV display. See "Laptop External Video Activation" in this chapter for details.

To adjust the quality of the picture, check the Advanced display properties page for a TV display properties page. Figure 11.8 shows the TV Adjustments screen dialog box used by a laptop that uses S3's Twister graphics.

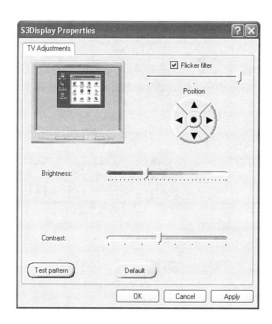

Figure 11.8   The TV Adjustment dialog box on this system enables you to adjust flicker, adjust screen centering, adjust brightness and contrast, and display a series of test patterns.

Digital Video Connections

Although the PC started out using parallel digital video interfacing, the VGA, SVGA, and many other standards that followed were analog, so as to offer a simpler connection with fewer pins that was also less expensive. This works well for CRTs, which are inherently analog devices anyway, but not well for LCD, plasma, TFT, and other types of flat-panel displays that are inherently digital.

Running a flat-panel display from an analog interface is problematic because when you think about it, all video data in a PC starts out digitally and then is converted to analog for the display. With a digital display such as an LCD, for example, the signal must then be converted back to digital before it can be displayed, resulting in a double conversion that causes screen artifacts, blurred text, color shifting, and other kinds of problems. Although built-in flat-panel displays don't have these problems, they can be a big concern if you connect a desktop flat-panel display to the VGA port on a typical laptop computer.

The digital interfaces now becoming more popular can eliminate the double conversion, allowing the video information to remain as digital data from the PC all the way to the screen. Therefore, a recent swing back to using digital video interfaces has occurred, especially for inherently digital displays such as flat-panel displays.

Three main digital video connector standards have been used in PCs over the years:

- Plug and Display (P&D)
- Digital Flat Panel (DFP)
- Digital Visual Interface (DVI)

All these interfaces use the same underlying technology and are somewhat compatible. They all use the same signaling method, called *Transition Minimized Differential Signaling (TMDS)*, which was developed by Silicon Image (www.siliconimage.com) and is also trademarked under the name *PanelLink*. TMDS takes 24-bit parallel digital data from the video controller and transmits it serially over balanced lines at high speed to a receiver. A single-link TMDS connection uses four separate differential data pairs, with three for color data (one each for red, green, and blue data) and the fourth pair for clock and control data. Each twisted pair uses differential signaling with a very low 0.5V swing over balanced lines for reliable, low-power, high-speed data transmission. A low-speed VESA Display Data Channel (DDC) pair is also used to transmit identification and configuration information, such as supported resolution and color-depth information, between the graphics controller and display.

Note

DVI is the first modern digital display standard to have widespread support among laptop vendors. The earlier P&D and DFP displays were used primarily by video cards built for desktop computers.

TMDS is designed to support cables up to 10 meters (32.8 feet) in length, although the limits may be shorter or longer depending on cable quality. Several companies make products that can redrive the signals, allowing for greater lengths. Figure 11.9 shows a block diagram of a single-link TMDS connection.

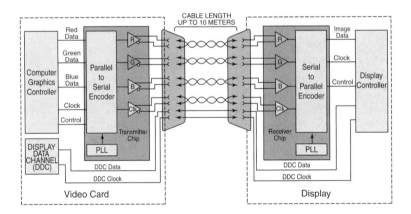

Figure 11.9   A single-link TMDS connection.

Using TMDS, each channel transmits 8 bits of data (encoded as a 10-bit character) for each color (red/green/blue) serially at up to 165MHz. This allows a pixel rate of 165 megapixels per second (Mpps), which enables a single-link TMDS connection to easily handle computer video resolutions as high as UXGA (1600×1200) as well as 1080p HDTV (1920×1080 with progressive scan). With 8 bits for each color channel, 24-bit color depth is supported, which equates to 16.7 million colors.

If more bandwidth is necessary, the DVI standard in particular is designed to support a second TMDS link in the same cable and connector. This link uses three additional TMDS signal pairs (one for each color) and shares the same clock and DDC signals as the primary link. This is called *dual-link DVI*, and it increases the bandwidth to 330MHz, or 330Mpps, which will handle computer resolutions as high as QXGA (2048×1536). At present, very few flat-panel displays use resolutions high enough to require dual-link DVI.

TMDS links include support for Display Data Channel (DDC), a low-speed, bidirectional standard for communication between PCs and monitors, created by the VESA. DDC defines the physical connection and signaling method, whereas the communications and data protocol is defined under the VESA Extended Display Identification Data (EDID) standard. DDC and EDID allow the graphics controller to identify the capabilities of the display so the controller can automatically configure itself to match the display's capabilities.

Digital Visual Interface (DVI)

The Digital Visual Interface (DVI) was introduced on April 2, 1999 by the Digital Display Working Group (DDWG). The DDWG was formed in 1998 by Intel, Silicon Image, Compaq, Fujitsu, Hewlett-Packard, IBM, and NEC to address the need for a universal digital interface standard between a host system and a display. DVI is based on TMDS and is essentially an updated version of the VESA P&D interface standard that supports higher bandwidths, without the USB and FireWire connections. Unlike P&D and DFP, DVI gained immediate widespread industry support, with 150 DVI products being shown at the Intel Developer Forum in August 1999, only four months after DVI was released. Since then, DVI has become the de facto standard interface for digital video connections. Many, if not most, newer desktop PCs include a DVI connection for digital display support. However, recent and current laptop computers with DVI support implement DVI through a connector on their docking stations or port replicators rather than with a built-in DVI connector.

Note

To determine whether a particular laptop computer supports DVI output, first determine whether its docking station or port replicator features a DVI port. Next, determine which laptop models support the DVI port. Some vendors, such as IBM, make docking stations and port replicators that have a DVI port, but the DVI port is supported by certain computer models only. Before you purchase a docking station or port replicator to attain DVI compatibility with a particular laptop model, make sure the laptop supports DVI output.

As with P&D, DVI allows for both digital and analog connections using the same basic connector. The main difference between P&D and DVI is that DVI eliminates the USB and FireWire connections and adds a second set of TMDS channels for optional use in a dual-link configuration. A single-link DVI connection supports computer resolutions up to UXGA (1600×1200) and WUXGA (1920×1200), as well as video resolutions of HDTV (1920×1280) in either interlaced or progressive scan mode. A dual-link DVI interface adds QXGA (2048×1536) and QSXGA (2560×2048) support, using the same cable with both links active. Even higher resolution displays can be supported with dual DVI ports, each with a dual-link connection. Typical laptop implementations of DVI support single-link resolutions.

DVI uses Molex MicroCross connectors in two slightly different designs. The DVI standard was primarily designed to support digital devices; however, for backward compatibility, it can also support analog devices as well. The DVI-D (digital) connector supports only digital devices, whereas the DVI-I (integrated) connector supports both digital and analog devices via the addition of extra pins. Figure 11.10 and Table 11.6 show the DVI-I (integrated) connector and pinout.

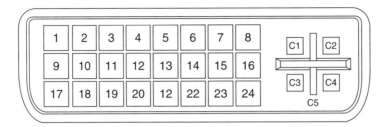

Figure 11.10 The DVI-I connector.

Table 11.6 The Pinout for the DVI-I Connector

Pin	Signal	Pin	Signal
1	TMDS Data2–	13	TMDS Data3+
2	TMDS Data2+	14	+5V Power
3	TMDS Data2/4 Shield	15	GND
4	TMDS Data4–	16	Hot Plug Detect
5	TMDS Data4+	17	TMDS Data0–
6	DDC Clock	18	TMDS Data0+
7	DDC Data	19	TMDS Data0/5 Shield
8	Analog Vert. Sync	20	TMDS Data5–
9	TMDS Data1–	21	TMDS Data5+
10	TMDS Data1+	22	TMDS Clock Shield
11	TMDS Data1/3 Shield	23	TMDS Clock+
12	TMDS Data3–	24	TMDS Clock–
—	—	—	—
C1	Analog Red	C3	Analog Blue
C2	Analog Green	C4	Analog Horiz. Sync
—	—	C5	Analog GND

TMDS = Transition Minimized Differential Signaling
Note: The DVI-D (digital only) connector lacks the analog C1–C4 pins.

The DVI-D connector is the same as the DVI-I connector, except that it lacks the analog connections. By virtue of the unique MicroCross connector design, a digital-only device can connect only to receptacles with digital support, and an analog-only device can plug in only to receptacles with analog support. This design feature ensures that an analog-only device cannot be connected to a digital-only receptacle, and vice versa. Figure 11.11 shows the DVI-D connector. The pinout is the same as the DVI-I connector, except for the missing analog signals. The DVI-D connector is widely used on laptop port replicators and docking stations that provide DVI support.

You can add DVI support to a laptop computer, provided it natively supports DVI, by connecting it to a compatible docking station or port replicator with a DVI port. These are available for selected models of IBM, Dell, and Toshiba laptops, among others.

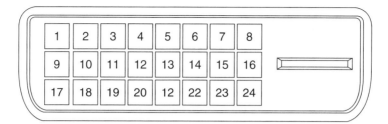

Figure 11.11 The DVI-D connector.

Video Adapter Components

Although virtually all laptop computers feature external VGA output, the components used for onboard video differ greatly from those used by desktop computers.

Desktop video display controllers have traditionally included the following basic components:

- **Video BIOS**—Provides basic VGA-level display support for setup, Windows VGA mode, and Windows Safe Mode.

- **Graphics processor**—Provides higher resolutions and color depths than basic VGA and, on recent laptop computers, provides acceleration of 2D and 3D graphics.

- **Video memory**—Holds a bitmap of the current information being displayed; 3D-compatible video also uses video memory to hold data about 3D objects being rendered by the video accelerator.

- **Bus connector**—Type and speed of connection to the motherboard's North Bridge chip, such as AGP 4x or PCI Express.

- **Video driver**—Affects quality and speed of display rendering; use the Windows Device Manager to view details and to update the driver.

- **Digital-to-analog converter (DAC or RAMDAC)**—Converts digital signals into VGA analog signals; sometimes built in to the graphics processor on recent graphics cards.

The major differences between laptop and desktop graphics include the following:

- Laptops that use a discrete graphics processor integrate video BIOS, graphic processor, DAC, and sometimes video memory into a single-chip solution.

- Video memory might be shared with main memory, use separate (discrete) memory chips, or might be built in to the graphics chipset.

- Low-cost laptops frequently use chipset-integrated graphics, using a motherboard chipset that incorporates graphics into the motherboard's memory controller hub (MCH) chip or North Bridge chip. A memory controller hub that incorporates graphics is known as a *graphics memory controller hub (GMCH)*.

- Although very few laptops are designed with user-performed graphics upgrades in mind, some vendors use the same pinout for a range of discrete mobile graphics processor modules. This design feature enables laptop vendors to offer a range of products with different onboard graphics solutions. Some users have taken advantage of this feature to upgrade their systems by ordering a better graphics processor module from the laptop vendor's parts department.

- Video drivers should be obtained from the system vendor rather than from the graphics processor or motherboard chipset maker because of the high level of customization often performed by the laptop vendor.

Tip

To determine if you can upgrade to more powerful graphics with your laptop, find out if the laptop uses integrated graphics, a soldered-in-place discrete graphics processor, or a removable graphics card module. If the laptop is part of a product family that offers different graphics processors, it probably uses a removable graphics card module. If so, you might be able to replace it with a better graphics card module. Check with the laptop vendor's parts department or with other users to determine which modules are compatible with your laptop, and order the module.

If you upgrade to a better graphics processor module, keep in mind that you will need to install the graphics drivers manually if you ever reinstall the original software and operating system from a restore CD.

The following subsections examine discrete graphics processors and motherboard-integrated graphics solutions used by laptops in greater detail.

The Video BIOS

Laptop computers with discrete graphics processors incorporate a video BIOS, a type of firmware that is similar in construction but completely separate from the main system BIOS. (Other devices in your system, such as SCSI adapters, might also include their own BIOS.) If you turn on your monitor first and look quickly, you might see an identification banner for your laptop's video BIOS at the beginning of the system startup process. If the laptop has chipset-integrated graphics, the chipset emulates the function of the video BIOS.

The video BIOS section of a graphics processor includes read-only memory (ROM), which contains basic instructions that provide an interface between the video hardware and the software running on your system. The software that makes calls to the video BIOS can be a standalone application, an operating system, or the main system BIOS. The programming in the video BIOS enables your system to display information on the monitor during the system POST and boot sequences, before any other software drivers have been loaded from disk.

The video BIOS also can be upgraded, just like a system BIOS. The BIOS uses a rewritable chip called *electrically erasable programmable read-only memory (EEPROM)* that you can upgrade with a utility the laptop manufacturer provides. A BIOS you can upgrade using software is referred to as a *flash BIOS*, and laptops with discrete graphics processors that offer BIOS upgrades use this method.

Video BIOS upgrades (sometimes referred to as *firmware upgrades*) are sometimes necessary when the manufacturer encounters a significant bug in the original programming. Occasionally, a BIOS upgrade is necessary because of a major revision to the video card chipset's video drivers. As a general rule, the video BIOS is a component that falls into the "if it ain't broke, don't fix it" category. Try not to let yourself be tempted to upgrade just because you've discovered that a new BIOS revision is available. Check the documentation for the upgrade, and unless you are experiencing a problem the upgrade addresses, leave the video BIOS alone.

The Graphics Processor

Laptops might use a discrete graphics processor to process and display video, or might use the video features of the motherboard chipset. The graphics processor or motherboard chipset a particular laptop computer uses essentially defines the graphics subsystem's functions and performance levels. Two different laptops that use the same discrete graphics processor or chipset-integrated graphics will have similar, if not identical, video performance and features.

Early laptops used a simple frame-buffer design, whereas more recent laptops use graphics accelerators, 3D graphics processors, or integrated chipsets that emulate graphics accelerators or 3D graphics processors. These technologies are compared in Table 11.7.

Table 11.7   Laptop Video Processor Technologies

Processor Type	Where Video Processing Takes Place	Relative Speed	How Used by Laptops Today
Frame-buffer	The computer's CPU.	Very slow	Obsolete; mostly used by early laptops.
Graphics accelerator	The video chip draws lines, circles, shapes; CPU sends the commands to draw them.	Fast	All mainstream laptops; combined with 3D GPU on some laptops or emulated by integrated laptop chipsets.
3D graphics processor (GPU)	The laptop's 3D GPU renders polygons and adds lighting and shading effects as needed.	Fast 2D and 3D display	Most mid-range and high-end laptops, especially gaming and multimedia-oriented models. Emulated on some recent systems with motherboard chipset-integrated graphics.
Motherboard Chipset Integrated Graphics	The laptop's Graphics Memory. Control Hub or North Bridge chip works along with the CPU to create the on-screen display. Newer versions also incorporate 3D rendering.	Moderate to fast 2D display; slow to moderate 3D display (when supported)	Used on low-end and business-oriented laptops.

Today's laptops use either discrete graphics processors or motherboard chipsets that integrate graphics features. The following subsections examine these different approaches to laptop graphics in more detail.

Discrete Graphics Processors

Discrete graphics processors are used by many mid-range and most high-end laptops to provide high-speed 2D and 3D acceleration. Because discrete graphics processors are separate from the motherboard chipset and typically use memory separate from the laptop computer's main memory, they usually provide higher performance and more features than typical motherboard-integrated graphics solutions.

Typical Features of Recent Mobile Graphics Processors

Recent discrete graphics processors from major vendors such as ATI (www.ati.com) and NVIDIA (www.nvidia.com) include features such as the following:

- DirectX 9.0 or greater support for high-quality accelerated 3D rendering with advanced lighting and shading effects
- Power management to save power and reduce heat buildup
- Optimized DVD (MPEG-2) and web video playback
- Support for multiple monitors, including VGA and DVI
- TV-Out
- Onboard memory up to 128MB

These features are similar to those available on mid-range and high-end desktop graphics processors and boards and are designed to enable laptop computer users to enjoy no-compromise graphics.

Memory Overview

Several types of memory have been used with discrete graphics processors over the years. However, most recent discrete laptop graphics processors use DDR or DDR-II SDRAM, which are the fastest types of RAM available. Older models might use one of the older RAM types listed in Table 11.8.

Table 11.8   Memory Types Used by Laptop Graphics Processors

Memory	Definition	Relative Speed	Usage Type
FPM DRAM	Fast page-mode RAM	Slow	Low-end ISA cards and CGA/EGA/VGA laptop graphics chips; obsolete
VRAM[1]	Video RAM	Fast	Expensive; obsolete
WRAM[1]	Window RAM	Fast	Expensive; obsolete
EDO DRAM	Extended data out DRAM	Moderate	Low-end PCI-bus and laptop graphics; obsolete
SDRAM	Synchronous DRAM	Fast	Low-end PCI/AGP and laptop graphics
MDRAM	Multibank DRAM	Fast	Little used; obsolete
SGRAM	Synchronous graphics DRAM	Very fast	High-end PCI/AGP and laptop graphics; replaced by DDR SDRAM
DDR SDRAM	Double data rate SDRAM	Very fast	High-end AGP and laptop graphics
DDR-II SDRAM	DDR SDRAM, 4 bits per cycle memory fetch	Extremely fast	High-end AGP and laptop graphics
DDR3/GDDR3 SDRAM	DDR SDRAM, 2 to 16 bits per cycle memory fetch	Fastest available	High-end AGP/PCI Express and laptop graphics

1. *VRAM and WRAM are dual-ported memory types that can be read from one port and have data written to them through the other port. This improves performance by reducing wait times for accessing the video RAM compared to FPM DRAM and EDO DRAM.*

SGRAM, DDR, and DDR-II SDRAM—which are derived from popular motherboard memory technologies—have replaced VRAM, WRAM, and MDRAM as high-speed video RAM solutions. Their high speeds and low production costs have enabled even low-end discrete graphics processors to support 32MB or more of high-speed RAM.

SDRAM

Synchronous DRAM (SDRAM) is the same type of RAM used on many systems based on processors such as the Pentium III, older Pentium 4s, Athlon, older Athlon XPs, and Duron. This memory is designed to work with bus speeds up to 200MHz and provides performance just slightly slower than SGRAM. SDRAM is used primarily by current low-end laptop graphics processors such as the original ATI Mobility Radeon.

SGRAM

Synchronous graphics RAM (SGRAM) was designed to be a high-end solution for very fast video adapter designs. SGRAM is similar to SDRAM in its capability to be synchronized to high-speed buses up to 200MHz, but it differs from SDRAM by including circuitry to perform block writes to increase the speed of graphics fill or 3D Z-buffer operations. Although SGRAM is faster than SDRAM, most discrete graphics processor makers have dropped SGRAM in favor of even faster DDR SDRAM in their newest products.

DDR SDRAM

Double data rate SDRAM (DDR SDRAM) is the most common video RAM technology on recent video cards. It is designed to transfer data at speeds twice that of conventional SDRAM by transferring data on both the rising and falling parts of the processing clock cycle. Today's mid-range laptop graphics processors such as NVIDIA's GeForce 6800 Go and ATI's Mobility Radeon X300/600 and 700 series use DDR SDRAM for video memory.

DDR-II SDRAM

The second generation of DDR SDRAM fetches 4 bits of data per cycle, instead of 2 bits, as with DDR SDRAM. This doubles the performance at the same clock speed. The first graphics processor to support DDR-II was NVIDIA's GeForce FX, which became the top of NVIDIA's line of GPUs in late 2002. Today DDR-II SDRAM is superseded by DDR-III (GDDR3) SDRAM for all mid-range and high-end desktop graphics processors.

DDR-III SDRAM

DDR-III SDRAM, or GDDR3, is the third generation of DDR SDRAM memory. Because it was specifically developed for graphics use, it is not compatible with the upcoming JEDEC DDR-III specification. The range of operating frequencies and programmable latencies allows GDDR3 memory to offer better performance at reduced cost. To improve bandwidth, GDDR3 offers on-chip termination, increasing bandwidth significantly. GDDR3 memory has now become the standard for mid-range and high-end desktop graphics processors offering better performance at lower cost than DDR-II SDRAM.

Video Memory Locations

Depending on the discrete graphics processor used, video memory might be located in one of three places in a typical laptop:

- Dedicated memory chips on the motherboard.
- Shared main memory (often referred to as *Unified Memory Architecture* or *UMA*). This is used more often by integrated graphics solutions.
- Attached to the graphics processor (often referred to as *multiple chip assembly*).

From the standpoint of performance, dedicated memory chips on the motherboard or memory attached to the graphics processor is preferable to a UMA-based system. When a graphics processor is forced to share memory with the system, performance usually suffers. Fortunately, very few discrete graphics processors for laptops use UMA.

How Memory Size Affects Display Quality

The amount of memory available for graphics (whether discrete or motherboard chipset-integrated) affects display quality in three ways:

- Higher resolutions
- Greater color depth
- Support for high resolutions and color depths in 3D modes

The amount of memory a graphics processor needs to display a particular resolution and color depth is based on a mathematical equation. A location must be present in the adapter's memory array to display every pixel on the screen, and the resolution determines the number of total pixels. For example, a screen resolution of 1024×768 requires a total of 786,432 pixels.

If you were to display that resolution with only two colors, you would need only 1 bit of memory space to represent each pixel. If the bit has a value of 0, the dot is black, and if its value is 1, the dot is white. If you use 24 bits of memory space to control each pixel, you can display more than 16.7 million colors because 16,777,216 combinations are possible with a four-digit binary number (2^{24}=16,777,216). If you multiply the number of pixels necessary for the screen resolution by the number of bits required to represent each pixel, you have the amount of memory the adapter needs to display that resolution. Here is how the calculation works:

$$1024 \times 768 = 786{,}432 \text{ pixels} \times 24 \text{ bits per pixel}$$

$$= 18{,}874{,}368 \text{ bits}$$

$$= 2{,}359{,}296 \text{ bytes}$$

$$= 2.25\text{MB}$$

As you can see, displaying 24-bit color (16,777,216 colors) at 1024×768 resolution requires exactly 2.25MB of RAM on the video adapter. However, because laptop graphics processors support memory amounts such as 1MB, 2MB, or 4MB, you would need to use a laptop whose video subsystem has at least 4MB of RAM available to run your system using that resolution and color depth.

To use the higher-resolution modes and greater numbers of colors common today, you would need much more memory on your video adapter than the 256KB found on the original IBM VGA. Table 11.9 shows the memory requirements for some of the most common screen resolutions and color depths used for 2D graphics operations, such as photo editing, presentation graphics, desktop publishing, and web page design. Note that the memory requirements are the same for both discrete graphics processors and motherboard chipset-integrated graphics.

Table 11.9   Video Display Adapter Minimum Memory Requirements for 2D Operations

Resolution	Color Depth	Max. Colors	Memory Required	Memory Used
640×480	16-bit	65,536	1MB	614,400 bytes
640×480	24-bit	16,777,216	1MB	921,600 bytes
640×480	32-bit	4,294,967,296	2MB	1,228,800 bytes
800×600	16-bit	65,536	1MB	960,000 bytes
800×600	24-bit	16,777,216	2MB	1,440,000 bytes
800×600	32-bit	4,294,967,296	2MB	1,920,000 bytes
1024×768	16-bit	65,536	2MB	1,572,864 bytes
1024×768	24-bit	16,777,216	4MB	2,359,296 bytes
1024×768	32-bit	4,294,967,296	4MB	3,145,728 bytes
1280×1024	16-bit	65,536	4MB	2,621,440 bytes
1280×1024	24-bit	16,777,216	4MB	3,932,160 bytes
1280×1024	32-bit	4,294,967,296	8MB	5,242,880 bytes

Table 11.9   Continued

Resolution	Color Depth	Max. Colors	Memory Required	Memory Used
1400×1050	16-bit	65,536	8MB	2,940,000 bytes
1400×1050	24-bit	16,777,216	8MB	4,410,000 bytes
1400×1050	32-bit	4,294,967,296	16MB	5,880,000 bytes
1600×1200	16-bit	65,536	8MB	3,840,000 bytes
1600×1200	24-bit	16,777,216	8MB	5,760,000 bytes
1600×1200	32-bit	4,294,967,296	16MB	7,680,000 bytes

From Table 11.9, you can see that a video adapter with 4MB can display 65,536 colors in 1600×1200 resolution mode, but for a true-color (16.8 million colors) display, you would need 8MB of RAM.

Note

Although very few laptops support 1600×1200 resolutions with their internal displays, many recent models can support external monitors at this resolution. Whether the display is built in to the laptop or is an external model receiving signals through the laptop's VGA port, the amount of memory required is the same for any given resolution and color depth combination.

Although 4MB or more of display memory was once rare, this amount or more is very common on today's laptop computers, meaning that high-resolution 2D graphics are possible with most laptops in use today. However, 3D video cards require more memory for a given resolution and color depth because the video memory must be used for three buffers: the front buffer, back buffer, and Z-buffer. The amount of video memory required for a particular operation varies according to the settings used for the color depth and Z-buffer. Triple-buffering allocates more memory for 3D textures than double-buffering but can slow down performance of some games. The buffering mode used by a given 3D video card usually can be adjusted through its properties page.

Table 11.10 lists the memory requirements for 3D cards in selected modes.

Table 11.10   Video Display Adapter Memory Requirements for 3D Operations

Resolution	Color Depth	Z-Buffer Depth	Buffer Mode	Actual Memory Used	Onboard Video Memory Size Required
640×480	16-bit	16-bit	Double	1.76MB	2MB
			Triple	2.34MB	4MB
	24-bit	24-bit	Double	2.64MB	4MB
			Triple	3.52MB	4MB
	32-bit	32-bit	Double	3.52MB	4MB
			Triple	4.69MB	8MB
800×600	16-bit	16-bit	Double	2.75MB	4MB
			Triple	3.66MB	4MB
	24-bit	24-bit	Double	4.12MB	8MB
			Triple	5.49MB	8MB

(continues)

Table 11.10   Continued

Resolution	Color Depth	Z-Buffer Depth	Buffer Mode	Actual Memory Used	Onboard Video Memory Size Required
	32-bit	32-bit	Double	5.49MB	8MB
			Triple	7.32MB	8MB
1024×768	16-bit	16-bit	Double	4.12MB	8MB
			Triple	5.49MB	8MB
	24-bit	24-bit	Double	6.75MB	8MB
			Triple	9.00MB	16MB
	32-bit[1]	32-bit	Double	9.00MB	16MB
			Triple	12.00MB	16MB
1280×1024	16-bit	16-bit	Double	7.50MB	8MB
			Triple	10.00MB	16MB
	24-bit	24-bit	Double	11.25MB	16MB
			Triple	15.00MB	16MB
	32-bit	32-bit	Double	15.00MB	16MB
			Triple	20.00MB	32MB
1600×1200	16-bit	16-bit	Double	10.99MB	16MB
			Triple	14.65MB	16MB
	24-bit	24-bit	Double	16.48MB	32MB
			Triple	21.97MB	32MB
	32-bit	32-bit	Double	21.97MB	32MB
			Triple	29.30MB	32MB

1. *The 32-bit mode actually provides the same color depth that the 24-bit mode provides but sets aside additional memory for faster 3D operation. See the note following this table.*

Note

Although 3D adapters typically operate in a 32-bit mode, this does not necessarily mean they can produce more than the 16,777,216 colors of a 24-bit true-color display. Many video processors and video memory buses are optimized to move data in 32-bit words, and they actually display 24-bit color while operating in a 32-bit mode, instead of the 4,294,967,296 colors you would expect from a true 32-bit color depth.

Although modern laptops with motherboard chipset-integrated graphics can play 3D games, their 3D performance and support of advanced 3D graphics are relatively poor compared to recent discrete graphics processors. If you spend a lot of time working with graphics and want to enjoy 3D games, you should consider laptops that use high-performance discrete graphics processors with at least 64MB of RAM, such as the ATI Mobility Radeon X300/600/700 or NVIDIA GeForce Go 6 series.

Although 2D operations can be performed with as little as 4MB of RAM, 32-bit color depths for realistic 3D operation with large Z-buffers use most of the RAM available on a laptop with 16MB of video memory at 1024×768 resolution; higher resolutions use more than 16MB of RAM at higher color depths. Consequently, laptops with 64MB or more of dedicated video memory are preferred if you want to play 3D games at high resolutions.

Motherboard Chipset-Integrated Graphics

Just as low-cost desktop computers typically use chipsets that integrate graphics into the memory controller hub or North Bridge chip, most low-cost and mid-range laptops also use integrated graphics.

Integrated graphics reduce the cost of the laptop because the vendor doesn't need to pay for a discrete graphics processor, separate video memory, or the engineering necessary to adapt discrete graphics to a particular laptop motherboard. However, integrated graphics typically offer lower performance, especially for 3D operation, than discrete graphics processors, and older chipsets often lack support for multiple monitors. Systems with integrated graphics also share system memory, which reduces the amount of memory available for the operating system and applications by as much as 32MB or more.

Note

Depending on the chipset used, some laptops with integrated graphics use a fixed amount of memory for graphics, but those that use Dynamic Video Memory Technology (DVMT) adjust the amount of video memory as required for the application or task being performed, up to the maximum size of memory allowed for video (usually 32MB). For example, 3D gaming or photo editing uses more memory than text editing, and a system with DVMT adjusts the amount of memory used for video accordingly.

Major Mobile Chipsets with Integrated Graphics

Table 11.11 provides details about the major mobile integrated graphics chipsets available from Intel and VIA (the two biggest integrated graphics chipset vendors for laptops) for Pentium III-M, AMD Athlon 4, and newer mobile processors. If you are researching the purchase of a new laptop, you can use this table to determine which chipsets might be the most suitable for your needs. If you already have a laptop computer, you can compare its chipset to others.

Tip

To determine what chipset your laptop uses, download and install the latest version of SiSoftware Sandra from www.sisoftware.co.uk.

Click the Mainboard information icon to get the details you need.

Table 11.11   Major Mobile Chipsets with Integrated Graphics

Vendor	Chipset	Processor(s) Supported	Maximum Amount of Video Memory Supported	Multiple Display Support	Notes
Intel	915GM	Pentium-M, Celeron-M	64MB (DVMT)	Yes	PCI Express
	915GMS	Pentium-M, Celeron-M	64MB (DVMT)	Yes	PCI Express
	910GML	Pentium-M, Celeron-M	64MB (DVMT)	Yes	PCI Express
	855GME	Pentium-M, Celeron-M	64MB (DVMT)	Yes	AGP4x/2x
	855GM [1]	Pentium-M	64MB (DVMT)	Yes	AGP4x/2x
	852GM [1]	Pentium 4-M, Celeron	64MB (DVMT)	Yes	
	852GME [2]	Pentium 4-M, Celeron	64MB (DVMT)	Yes	
	852GMV	Celeron	64MB (DVMT)	Yes	

(continues)

Table 11.11   Continued

Vendor	Chipset	Processor(s) Supported	Maximum Amount of Video Memory Supported	Multiple Display Support	Notes
	830M [1]	Pentium III-M, Mobile Celeron	8MB, 32MB, 48MB [3]	Yes	
	830MG	Pentium III-M, Mobile Celeron	8MB, 32MB, 48MB [3]	Yes	
	815EM	Pentium III-M, Mobile Celeron	32MB [4]	Yes	
VIA	UniChrome KM400	Athlon XP-M, Duron	16MB, 32MB, 64MB	Yes	
	ProSavage KN400	Athlon XP-M, Duron, Athlon 4	16MB, 32MB, 64MB	Yes	
	ProSavage KN266	Athlon 4, Duron	16MB, 32MB	No[5]	
	ProSavage KN133	Athlon 4, Duron	8MB, 16MB, 32MB	No[5]	Also known as Twister-K
	ProSavage PN266T	Pentium III-M, Celeron, VIA C3	16MB, 32MB	No[5]	
	ProSavage PN133T	Pentium III-M, Celeron, VIA C3	8MB, 16MB, 32MB	No[5]	Also known as Twister-T
	ProSavage PM133	Pentium III-M, Celeron, VIA C3	8MB, 16MB, 32MB	No[5]	Also known as Twister

1. *Intel Extreme Graphics; supports most 3D functions, dual displays, and DirectX 8. For more information, see* `http://developer.intel.com/design/graphics/index.htm`.

2. *Intel Extreme Graphics 2; supports faster 3D rendering and better memory management than original Extreme Graphics. For more information, see* `http://developer.intel.com/design/graphics2/index.htm`.

3. *Supports 8MB when installed system memory is 64MB; 32MB when installed system memory is 128MB to less than 256MB; 48MB when installed system memory is 256MB or more.*

4. *Minimums vary between 6MB and 12MB depending on the version of Windows and total system memory installed.*

5. *TV-Out is supported if laptop has S-Video/TV-Out connector.*

Adjusting the Amount of Memory Available for Graphics

If your system uses integrated graphics, you can adjust the amount of memory available for graphics in two ways:

- Change the size of reserved memory for graphics in your laptop's BIOS setup program.
- Install more memory in your laptop.

Many systems that use integrated graphics offer two or more settings for graphics memory size in the system BIOS. To increase (or decrease) the amount of memory available for video use, follow this procedure:

1. Start your system.
2. Press the key(s) used to start the BIOS setup program.
3. Locate the screen used for graphics/video memory size.
4. Select the desired value.
5. Save the changes.
6. The system restarts and uses the amount of system memory you specified for video memory.

If your laptop uses a system with dynamic memory allocation, a method used by Intel's mobile chipsets, the amount of memory used for graphics varies with the amount of main memory installed as well as with the operating system installed. If your system has less than 256MB of RAM installed, upgrade the memory to 256MB or more to maximize the amount of memory available for graphics.

The Video Driver

The software driver is an essential, and often problematic, element of a video display subsystem. The driver enables your software to communicate with the graphics processor in your laptop, whether it is discrete or integrated. You can have a laptop with the fastest mobile processor, discrete graphics processor, and the most efficient memory on the market, but still have poor video performance because of a badly written driver.

Although the discrete graphics processor or the motherboard chipset vendor creates the video drivers for laptops, they are usually heavily modified to meet the requirements of the laptop vendor. Consequently, to make sure that all the unique video features of your laptop are properly supported, you should normally get driver updates from the laptop vendor. If your laptop vendor no longer supports your laptop's chipset, you can try generic drivers from the graphics or motherboard chipset maker, but they might not work as well as drivers that have been customized for your system.

The video driver also provides the interface you can use to configure your laptop's built-in or external display. On a Windows 9x/Me/2000/XP system, the Display applet found in the Windows Control Panel identifies the monitor and graphics processor installed on your system and enables you to select the color depth and screen resolution you prefer. The driver controls the options available for these settings, so you can't choose parameters the hardware doesn't support. For example, the controls would not allow you to select a 1024×768 resolution with 24-bit color if the adapter has only 1MB of memory.

When you click the Advanced button on the Settings page, you see the Properties dialog box for your particular video display adapter. The contents of this dialog box can vary, depending on the driver and the capabilities of the hardware. Typically, on the General page of this dialog box, you can select the size of the fonts (large or small) to use with the resolution you've chosen. Windows 98/Me/2000 (but not Windows XP) also add a control to activate a convenient feature. The Show Settings Icon on Task Bar check box activates a tray icon that enables you to quickly and easily change resolutions and color depths without having to open the Control Panel. This feature is often called *QuickRes*. The Adapter page displays detailed information about your adapter and the drivers installed on the system, and it enables you to set the refresh rate for your display; with Windows XP, you can use the List All Modes button to view and choose the resolution, color depth, and refresh rate with a single click. The Monitor page enables you to display and change the monitor's properties and switch monitor drivers if necessary. In Windows XP, you can also select the refresh rate on this screen.

Laptop External Video Activation

From the earliest portable computers to the present day, virtually all laptops have featured an external monitor port. As a consequence, almost all systems also enable you to use the built-in display, the external display, or both displays at the same time, mirroring the contents of the internal display on the external monitor.

Most laptop computers require a function key or software command to activate/deactivate the laptop video output signal for external monitors or TV-Out. The activation/deactivation keystroke usually acts as a switch, cycling between the internal display, external display, or both displays simultaneously. In most cases, the simultaneous display setting does not work properly if the native resolution of the external display (such as a projector) does not match the native resolution of the laptop LCD display. This means that the internal display of some laptops needs to be turned off to achieve optimal image quality on the projector, which can be a major inconvenience. In such a case, I've had to add a signal splitter and an extra monitor so I can see what is being projected behind me when I teach a class.

Here are some of the most commonly used keys to toggle the internal, external, and dual-display settings:

- **Award**—Fn+F6
- **Compaq**—Fn+F4
- **Dell**—Fn+F8
- **Gateway**—Fn+F3
- **IBM**—Fn+F7
- **Toshiba**—Fn+F5

To change the setting for your display, hold down the Fn (function) key and press the appropriate other key, pausing a few seconds between each keypress. This cycles the display output between internal, external, and simultaneous modes.

Caution

Although simultaneous display works when the external display is a monitor or projector with the same native resolution as the internal LCD display, it usually doesn't work when a TV is used as the external display through the S-Video (TV-Out) jack.

Although the ability to display the contents of the internal display on a monitor can be useful for teaching, presentations, or demonstrations, true multiple-display functionality on laptops has been quite scarce until recently.

Multiple Monitor Support

Windows 98 introduced a video display feature that Macintosh systems have had for years: the capability to use multiple monitors on one system to display different parts of the desktop. Windows 98 and Windows Me support up to 9 monitors (and video adapters), each of which can provide a different view of the desktop. Windows 2000 and Windows XP support up to 10 monitors and video adapters. Although multiple-display support has become widespread on desktop computers, either through the installation of secondary display adapters or the recent popularity of dual-head display adapters at mid-range and higher price points, multiple-display support was scarce on laptops until the development of Windows XP.

Windows XP has revolutionized multiple display support for laptops by adding a feature called *DualView*, an enhancement to Windows 2000's multiple-monitor support. DualView supports notebook computers connected to external displays. With systems supporting DualView, the first video port is automatically assigned to the primary monitor. On a notebook computer, the primary display is the built-in LCD display.

To set up dual monitors on a laptop or notebook system that supports DualView, start by connecting an external display to the VGA connector on your system. Then use the following instructions to set up the dual monitors in Windows XP:

1. Right-click an empty portion of the Windows desktop.

2. Select Properties from the right-click menu to open the Display Properties applet.

3. Select the Settings tab.

4. Select the second display and then select the option to extend the desktop (see Figure 11.12).

Figure 11.12 The Settings dialog box for a typical laptop with DualView support before the external monitor (monitor #2) is activated.

You can set different resolutions and color depths for each display. Note that using the Extended Desktop requires enough video memory for each display. This is not a problem on most newer systems, but older systems with lower amounts of video memory may have problems with high color depths on both displays. In addition, certain operations, such as playing DVDs and running 3D graphics, require extra video memory, so you may have to adjust display settings. If you have problems, try reducing the color depth on both the internal and external displays.

On most laptop and notebook systems with DVD drives and player applications, DVD movies will show only on the primary display. To change the primary display, go to the Settings tab of Display Properties, right-click the display you want, and select Primary.

Note

Although Windows XP introduced DualView, not every laptop shipped with Windows XP supports DualView. DualView is supported only if the discrete graphics processor or integrated graphics support multiple monitors.

3D Graphics and Laptops

Although business software has yet to fully embrace 3D imaging, full-motion graphics are used in sports, first-person shooters, team combat, driving, and many other types of PC gaming. Three-dimensional gaming has become very popular with all types of computer users, and recent laptops now feature 3D graphics capabilities such as lighting, perspective texture, and shading effects that rival those of mid-range desktop graphics cards.

The Basics of 3D Graphics

To construct an animated 3D sequence, a computer can mathematically animate the sequences between keyframes. A keyframe identifies specific points. A bouncing ball, for example, can have three keyframes: up, down, and up. Using these frames as a reference point, the computer can create all the interim images between the top and bottom. This creates the effect of a smoothly bouncing ball.

After it has created the basic sequence, the system can then refine the appearance of the images by filling them in with color. The most primitive and least effective fill method is called *flat shading*, in which a shape is simply filled with a solid color. *Gouraud shading*, a slightly more effective technique, involves the assignment of colors to specific points on a shape. The points are then joined using a smooth gradient between the colors.

A more processor-intensive (and much more effective) type of fill is *texture mapping*. The 3D application includes patterns—or textures—in the form of small bitmaps that it tiles onto the shapes in the image, just as you can tile a small bitmap to form the wallpaper for your Windows desktop. The primary difference is that the 3D application can modify the appearance of each tile by applying perspective and shading to achieve 3D effects. When lighting effects that simulate fog, glare, directional shadows, and others are added, the 3D animation comes very close indeed to matching reality.

3D Graphics Processors for Laptops

Until the late 1990s, 3D applications had to rely on support from software routines to convert these abstractions into live images. This placed a heavy burden on the system processor in the PC, which has a significant impact on the performance not only of the visual display but also of any other applications the computer might be running.

Although graphics cards with 3D acceleration have been available for desktop computers since the late 1990s, it took much longer for both discrete graphics processor and motherboard chipset vendors to develop 3D acceleration for the laptop market.

The first discrete graphics processor for laptops to support 3D acceleration was the NVIDIA GeForce 2 Go. GeForce 2 Go was introduced in late 2000, with the first laptops to use it released in early 2001. Other pioneering discrete graphics processors for laptops, ATI's Mobility Radeon and Trident Microsystems' CyberBLADE XP, were introduced in early 2001. All three companies have developed follow-on products that several major brands of laptops use, primarily in their mid-range and high-end models.

At about the same time, 3D features began to show up in integrated graphics chipsets as well, although even the best integrated graphics for laptops are slower than discrete graphics processors. Most laptops built in 2002 and later now support some level of 3D acceleration and lighting effects. In fact, today's discrete graphics processors for laptops now support the same advanced 3D graphics and lighting effects that are standard in Microsoft DirectX 9.0, just as the desktop graphics processors do.

Consequently, most laptops now enable users to enjoy full-motion 3D graphics in sports, first-person shooters, team combat, driving, and many other types of PC gaming. Table 11.12 compares the 3D support available in recent discrete graphics processors made for laptops. The most powerful and most recent processors in each brand are listed first, with less powerful processors listed afterward.

Table 11.12   3D Support Features by Laptop Graphics Processor

Vendor	Processor	DirectX Support	Major 3D Features	Notes & Additional Features
ATI	Mobility Radeon X800	DirectX 9.0	PCI Express, 16 rendering pipelines, 128 or 256MB of memory, twice the performance of the Mobility Radeon 9800	
ATI	Mobility Radeon X600/700	DirectX 9.0	PCI Express, eight rendering pipelines, 128 or 256MB GDDR3 memory	
ATI	Mobility Radeon X300	DirectX 9.0	PCI Express, shader model 2.0b support, Hyper-Memory, 64- or 128-bit memory interface	
ATI	Mobility Radeon 9800	DirectX 9.0	Improved design over Mobility Radeon 9800 with higher clock speed, 256MB of memory	
ATI	Mobility Radeon 9700	DirectX 9.0	Total of eight rendering pipelines, one texture unit per pipeline, vertex shader 2.0 and pixelshader 2.0 support	
ATI	Mobility Radeon 9600 & 9600 Pro	DirectX 9.0	Improved hardware pixel and vertex shaders	9600 Pro supports automatic overclocking; four rendering and dual vertex engines
ATI	Mobility Radeon 9200	DirectX 8.1	Hardware pixel and vertex shaders, vertex skinning	Improved antialiasing, power management
ATI	Mobility Radeon 9000	DirectX 8.1	Hardware pixel and vertex shaders, vertex skinning up to 128MB of RAM	Up to 128-bit memory bandwidth, four 3D rendering pipes
ATI	Mobility Radeon 7500	DirectX 7.0	Hardware Transform & Lighting (T&L), up to 32MB of RAM	Up to 128-bit memory interface, dual 3D rendering pipes, faster than Mobility Radeon
ATI	Mobility Radeon	DirectX 7.0	Up to 16MB of RAM; CPU is used to calculate lighting effects	Single 3D rendering pipe, up to 64-bit memory bandwidth
Nvidia	GeForce Go 6800	DirectX 9.0	1100MHz 256MB GDDR3 memory, 256-bit memory interface, fastest mobile processor	
NVIDIA	GeForce Go 6600	DirectX 9.0	PowerMizer technology for low-power, 128-bit memory interface	

(continues)

Table 11.12   3D Support Features by Laptop Graphics Processor

Vendor	Processor	DirectX Support	Major 3D Features	Notes & Additional Features
NVIDIA	GeForce Go 6400	DirectX 9.0	TurboCache technology, higher clock speed and better performance than GeForce Go 6200	
NVIDIA	GeForce Go 6200	DirectX 9.0	TurboCache technology to improve memory bandwidth, PureVideo support, shader model 3.0 support	
NVIDIA	GeForce FX 5700 Go	DirectX 9.0	DVI support, 400MHz RAMDAC, hardware MPEG2 decoder	
NVIDIA	GeForce FX 5600 Go	DirectX 9.0	Improved hardware pixel and vertex shaders	Improved antialiasing compared to 5200; AGP 8x
NVIDIA	GeForce FX 5200 Go	DirectX 9.0	Improved hardware pixel and vertex shaders	AGP 8x
NVIDIA	GeForce4 4200 Go	DirectX 8.0	Hardware pixel and vertex shaders, vertex skinning	AGP 8x; 6.46GBps memory bandwidth
NVIDIA	GeForce4 460 Go	DirectX 8.0	Hardware pixel and vertex shaders, vertex skinning	8.0GBps memory bandwidth
NVIDIA	GeForce4 440 Go	DirectX 8.0	Hardware pixel and vertex shaders, vertex skinning	7.0GBps memory bandwidth (external memory); 6.0GBps memory bandwidth (built-in memory)
NVIDIA	GeForce4 420 Go	DirectX 8.0	Hardware pixel and vertex shaders, vertex skinning	3.0GBps memory bandwidth

Virtually all these processors support multiple displays, although only on laptops that provide the necessary connections through docking stations or port replicators.

User-Upgradeable Laptop Graphics Modules

Until recently, upgrading the graphics processor in your laptop was officially "impossible." However, if your laptop uses a discrete graphics processor on a removable module, some clever users have been able to determine which graphics modules available from a laptop vendor's service department would work as plug-compatible replacements. These users purchased the modules as replacement parts and performed the upgrades themselves.

However, there are several risks to such "do it yourself" graphics upgrades:

- Possibility of damage to the laptop during the removal of the old module and installation of the new module because most of the internal parts must be removed on many models to access the video module.

- High likelihood of voiding the warranty (if any remaining) through performing the upgrade.

- Possibility of problems in restoring the system to its original condition with the restore CD provided with most laptops. Because the graphics module has a different model of graphics processor (and possibly even a different brand), the predefined graphics drivers on the restore CD might not work anymore.

- Possibility of a different, nondocumented, change in connector pinout, causing the module to fit but not work and potentially damaging both the module and the laptop.

3D Graphics Application Programming Interfaces

Application programming interfaces (APIs) provide hardware and software vendors a means to create drivers and programs that can work quickly and reliably across a wide variety of platforms. When APIs exist, drivers can be written to interface with these APIs rather than directly with the operating system and its underlying hardware.

Currently, the leading game APIs include SGI's OpenGL and Microsoft's Direct 3D. OpenGL and Direct 3D (part of DirectX) are available for virtually all leading graphics cards and laptop graphics chipsets.

Although the graphics processor vendor must provide OpenGL support, Microsoft provides support for Direct3D as part of a much larger API called DirectX. The latest version of DirectX is DirectX 9.0c, which enhances 3D video support, enhances DirectPlay (used for Internet gaming), and provides other advanced gaming features. For more information about DirectX or to download the latest version, see Microsoft's DirectX website at `www.microsoft.com/windows/directx`.

Note

DirectX 9.0c is for Windows 98 and later versions (98SE, Me, 2000, and XP) only. However, Microsoft still provides DirectX 8.0a for Windows 95 users.

DirectX Support and 3D Graphics

When different 3D graphics processors are compared, the level of DirectX support provided by each processor is often used as a quick way to compare each processor's features. Therefore, it's useful to know about the major 3D features provided by DirectX 7.0, DirectX 8.0, DirectX 8.1, and DirectX 9.0, which are the versions of DirectX supported by recent discrete and integrated graphics processors for laptops.

DirectX 7.0 features all basic 3D features (multitexturing, bump mapping, texture compression, stencil buffers) and added hardware transform and lighting and texture compression.

DirectX 8.0 and 8.1 add programmable vertex and pixel shaders and antialiasing (8.1 uses a slightly more advanced version of vertex and pixel shaders than 8.0) for much greater realism.

Caution

The majority of integrated chipsets support DirectX 8.0- or 9.0-level 3D effects, albeit sometimes through slower software rendering rather than faster hardware rendering.

DirectX 9.0 adds floating-point color and improved vertex and pixel shaders that can handle longer, more complex programming, thus further improving realism.

To learn more about these advanced 3D features, as well as the basic 3D features supported by almost all recent laptops, read the following subsections.

Major Features of 3D Graphics

The basic function of 3D software is to convert image abstractions into the fully realized images that are then displayed on the monitor. The image abstractions typically consist of the following elements:

- **Vertices**—Locations of objects in three-dimensional space, described in terms of their x, y, and z coordinates on three axes representing height, width, and depth.

- **Primitives**—The simple geometric objects the application uses to create more complex constructions, described in terms of the relative locations of their vertices. This serves not only to specify the location of the object in the 2D image, but also to provide perspective because the three axes can define any location in three-dimensional space.

- **Textures**—Two-dimensional bitmap images or surfaces designed to be mapped onto primitives. The software enhances the 3D effect by modifying the appearance of the textures, depending on the location and attitude of the primitive. This process is called *perspective correction*. Some applications use another process, called *MIP mapping*, that uses different versions of the same texture that contain varying amounts of detail, depending on how close the object is to the viewer in the three-dimensional space. Another technique, called *depth cueing*, reduces the color and intensity of an object's fill as the object moves farther away from the viewer.

Using these elements, the abstract image descriptions must then be *rendered*, meaning they are converted to visible form. Rendering depends on two standardized functions that convert the abstractions into the completed image that is displayed onscreen:

- **Geometry**—The sizing, orienting, and moving of primitives in space and the calculation of the effects produced by the virtual light sources that illuminate the image

- **Rasterization**—The converting of primitives into pixels on the video display by filling the shapes with properly illuminated shading, textures, or a combination of the two

A modern laptop that includes a chipset capable of 3D video acceleration has special built-in hardware that can perform the rasterization process much more quickly than if it were done by software (using the system processor) alone. Most chipsets with 3D acceleration perform the following rasterization functions right on the graphics processor:

- **Scan conversion**—The determination of which onscreen pixels fall into the space delineated by each primitive

- **Shading**—The process of filling pixels with smoothly flowing color using the flat or Gouraud shading technique

- **Texture mapping**—The process of filling pixels with images derived from a 2D sample picture or surface image

- **Visible surface determination**—The identification of which pixels in a scene are obscured by other objects closer to the viewer in three-dimensional space

- **Animation**—The process of switching rapidly and cleanly to successive frames of motion sequences

- **Antialiasing**—The process of adjusting color boundaries to smooth edges on rendered objects

Common 3D Techniques

Virtually all 3D graphics processors use the following techniques:

- **Fogging**—This technique simulates haze or fog in the background of a game screen and helps conceal the sudden appearance of newly rendered objects (buildings, enemies, and so on).

- **Gouraud shading**—This technique interpolates colors to make circles and spheres look more rounded and smooth.

- **Alpha blending**—One of the first 3D techniques, alpha blending creates translucent objects onscreen, making it a perfect choice for rendering explosions, smoke, water, and glass. Alpha blending also can be used to simulate textures, but it is less realistic than environment-based bump mapping (see the section "Environment-Based Bump Mapping and Displacement Mapping," later in this chapter).

Because these techniques are so common, data sheets for advanced graphics processors frequently don't mention them, although these features are present.

Advanced 3D Techniques

The following subsections detail some of the latest techniques that leading 3D graphics processors use. Not every chip uses every technique.

Stencil Buffering

Stencil buffering is a technique useful for games such as flight simulators in which a static graphic element—such as a cockpit windshield frame, which is known as a HUD (heads-up display) and used by real-life fighter pilots—is placed in front of dynamically changing graphics (such as scenery, other aircraft, sky detail, and so on). In this example, the area of the screen occupied by the cockpit windshield frame is not rerendered. Only the area seen through the "glass" is rerendered, saving time and improving frame rates for animation.

Z-Buffering

A closely related technique is *Z-buffering*, which originally was devised for computer-aided drafting (CAD) applications. The Z-buffer portion of video memory holds depth information about the pixels in a scene. As the scene is rendered, the Z-values (depth information) for new pixels are compared to the values stored in the Z-buffer to determine which pixels are in "front" of others and should be rendered. Pixels that are "behind" other pixels are not rendered. This method increases speed and can be used along with stencil buffering to create volumetric shadows and other complex 3D objects.

Environment-Based Bump Mapping and Displacement Mapping

Environment-based bump mapping introduces special lighting and texturing effects to simulate the rough texture of rippling water, bricks, and other complex surfaces. It combines three separate texture maps (for colors, for height and depth, and for environment—including lighting, fog, and cloud effects). This creates enhanced realism for scenery in games and could also be used to enhance terrain and planetary mapping, architecture, and landscape-design applications. This represents a significant step beyond alpha blending. However, a feature called *displacement mapping* produces even more accurate results.

Special grayscale maps called *displacement maps* have long been used for producing accurate maps of the globe. Microsoft DirectX 9.0 supports the use of grayscale hardware displacement maps as a source for accurate 3D rendering.

Texture Mapping Filtering Enhancements

To improve the quality of texture maps, several filtering techniques have been developed, including MIP mapping, bilinear filtering, trilinear filtering, and anisotropic filtering. These techniques and several others are explained here:

- **Bilinear filtering**—This technique improves the image quality of small textures placed on large polygons. The stretching of the textures that takes place can create blockiness, but bilinear filtering applies a blur to conceal this visual defect.

- **MIP mapping**—This technique improves the image quality of polygons that appear to recede into the distance by mixing low-resolution and high-resolution versions of the same texture. MIP mapping is a form of antialiasing.

- **Trilinear filtering**—This technique combines bilinear filtering and MIP mapping, calculating the most realistic colors necessary for the pixels in each polygon by comparing the values in two MIP maps. This method is superior to either MIP mapping or bilinear filtering alone.

Note

Bilinear and trilinear filtering work well for surfaces viewed straight on, but they might not work so well for oblique angles (such as a wall receding into the distance).

- **Anisotropic filtering**—Some video card makers use anisotropic filtering for more realistic rendering of oblique-angle surfaces containing text. This technique is used when a texture is mapped to a surface that changes in two of three spatial domains, such as text found on a wall down a roadway (for example, advertising banners at a raceway). The extra calculations used take time, and for that reason, anisotropic filtering can be disabled.

- **T-buffer**—This technology eliminates aliasing (errors in onscreen images due to an undersampled original) in computer graphics (such as the "jaggies" seen in onscreen diagonal lines, motion stuttering, and inaccurate rendition of shadows, reflections, and object blur). The T-buffer replaces the normal frame buffer with a buffer that accumulates multiple renderings before displaying the image. Unlike some other 3D techniques, T-buffer technology doesn't require rewriting or optimization of 3D software to use this enhancement. The goal of T-buffer technology is to provide a movie-like realism to 3D-rendered animations. The downside of enabling antialiasing using a card with T-buffer support is that it can dramatically impact the performance of an application. This technique is incorporated into Microsoft DirectX 8.0 and above.

- **Integrated transform and lighting**—The 3D display process includes transforming an object from one frame to the next and handling the lighting changes that result from those transformations. Many 3D cards put the CPU in charge of these functions, but most recent graphics accelerators from NVIDIA and ATI integrate separate transform and lighting engines into the graphics processor for faster 3D rendering, regardless of CPU speed. This technique is incorporated into DirectX 7.0 and above.

- **Full-screen antialiasing**—This technology (also known as FSAA) reduces the "jaggies" visible at any resolution by adjusting color boundaries to provide gradual, rather than abrupt, color changes. DirectX 8.0 and above support FSAA.

- **Vertex skinning**—Also referred to as *vertex blending*, this technique blends the connection between two angles, such as the joints in an animated character's arms or legs. DirectX 8.0 and above support this technique.

- **Programmable vertex and pixel shading**—Pixel shading is an enhanced form of bump mapping for irregular surfaces that enables per-pixel lighting effects. Vertex shaders work with vertices, the intersections between the polygons used to build all 3D objects. DirectX 8.0 and 8.1 incorporate first-generation versions of these technologies, while DirectX 9.0 adds floating-point accuracy and more complex programs.

- **Floating-point calculations**—Microsoft DirectX 9.0 supports floating-point data for more vivid and accurate color and polygon rendition.

TV/Video Output and Capture

Laptop computers can be used with TVs, video players, and video recorders to provide the following benefits:

- Larger screen displays for presentations
- Recording of laptop screens or presentations to video tape
- Capture of analog video for editing and conversion to digital formats
- TiVo-like delayed viewing of TV programs

Before a laptop computer can be used with external video or TV sources or recorders, it needs to have suitable built-in hardware or external peripherals connected to it. However, before you attempt to use a laptop computer with TV or video hardware, it's important to understand the differences between computer and TV signals.

In the United States, the National Television Standards Committee (NTSC) established color TV standards in 1953. Some other countries, such as Japan, followed this standard. Many countries in Europe, though, developed more sophisticated standards, including Phase Alternating Line (PAL) and Sequential Couleur A Mémoire (SECAM). Table 11.13 shows the differences among these standards.

Table 11.13   Television Versus Computer Monitors

Standard	Year Est.	Country	Lines	Rate
Television				
NTSC	1953 (color) 1941 (B&W)	U.S., Japan	525	60 fields/sec
PAL	1941	Europe[1]	625	50 fields/sec
SECAM	1962	France	625	25 fields/sec
Computer				
VGA	1987	U.S.	640×480[2]	72Hz

Field = 1/2 (.5 frame)

1. England, Holland, and West Germany.

2. VGA is based on more lines and uses pixels (480) versus lines; genlocking is used to lock pixels into lines and synchronize computers with TV standards.

Until recently, it was necessary to buy VGA-to-NTSC converters for any laptop you wanted to use with a TV set or VCR. However, most recent laptops now feature a TV-Out (S-Video) port that can be used for this purpose; some low-cost models use the less-desirable composite video port instead. The TV-Out port provides adequate quality for use with a TV set, but if you want to record high-quality video with your laptop, you should use an external VGA-to-NTSC adapter with a feature called *genlocking*. Genlocking enables the synchronization of signals from multiple video sources or video with PC graphics. This provides the signal stability necessary to obtain adequate results when recording to tape.

Adding TV-Out Support

If your laptop doesn't have a TV-Out (S-Video) port, you can add an external adapter. This adapter does not replace your existing video card but rather connects to it using an external cable. In addition to VGA input and output ports, a video-output device typically has a video-output interface for S-Video and composite video. A few high-end models support HDTV.

Most VGA-to-TV converters support the standard NTSC television format and might also support the European PAL format; a few also support the French SECAM format. The display resolution these devices are designed to accept is sometimes limited to straight VGA at 640×480 pixels, although some TV-Out ports and external converters can also handle up to 1280×1024 output resolutions and convert them to NTSC. A few advanced models also support DV (1600×1200) to TV conversion. The converter also might contain an antiflicker circuit to help stabilize the picture because VGA-to-TV products, as well as TV-to-VGA solutions, often suffer from a case of the jitters. Some models can be powered from the laptop's USB port, but most use an AC adapter.

Figure 11.13 shows a typical external VGA-to-NTSC solution. It includes a remote control, which makes it easier to adjust the quality of the TV picture and activate special features such as zoom.

Figure 11.13   AVerMedia's AVerkey300 Gold PC-to-TV converter features a remote control, Plug and Play operation, and dual-display support for PCs and Macs. It requires an AC power source. (Photo courtesy AVerMedia.)

Adding TV Tuner and Video Capture Support

Although an increasing number of laptop computers support TV-Out, the TV-Out port doesn't support TV input. If you want to watch TV on your laptop or capture still images or video, you need to add additional hardware.

Today, video sources come in two forms:

- Analog
- Digital

Analog video can be captured from traditional sources, such as broadcast or cable TV, VCRs, and camcorders using VHS or similar tape standards. This process is much more demanding of storage space and system performance than still images are. Here's why.

The typical computer screen was designed to display mainly static images. The computer's capability to store and retrieve these images requires managing huge files. Consider this: A single, full-screen color image in an uncompressed format can require as much as 2MB of disk space; a 1-second video would therefore require 45MB. Likewise, any video transmission you want to capture for use on your PC must be converted from an analog NTSC signal to a digital signal your computer can use.

Considering that full-motion video can consume massive quantities of disk space, it becomes apparent that data compression is all but essential. Compression and decompression apply to both video and audio. Not only does a compressed file take up less space, but it also performs better simply because less data must be processed. When you are ready to replay the video/audio, the application decompresses the file during playback. In any case, if you are going to work with video, be sure that your hard drive is large enough and fast enough to handle the huge files that can result.

Tip

Although today's laptop computers have hard drives as large as 80GB, working with video can quickly use up much of your laptop's disk space. Consider adding an external hard disk with an IEEE 1394 or USB 2.0 port and a capacity of at least 80GB or more to your laptop for video storage, or making frequent backups of captured video with the CD-RW drive typically found in most recent laptop computers.

Compression/decompression programs and devices are called *codecs*. Two types of codecs exist: hardware-dependent codecs and software (or hardware-independent) codecs. Hardware codecs typically perform better; however, they require additional hardware that is not usually available for laptops. Software codecs do not require hardware for compression or playback, but they typically do not deliver the same quality or compression ratio. Two of the major codec algorithms are JPEG and MPEG. These codec algorithms are described in the following list:

- **JPEG (Joint Photographic Experts Group)**—Originally developed for still images, JPEG can compress and decompress at rates acceptable for nearly full-motion video (30fps). JPEG still uses a series of still images, which makes editing easier. JPEG is typically lossy (meaning that a small amount of the data is lost during the compression process, slightly diminishing the quality of the image), but it can also be lossless. JPEG compression functions by eliminating redundant data for each individual image (intraframe). Compression efficiency is approximately 30:1 (20:1–40:1).

- **MPEG (Motion Picture Experts Group)**—MPEG by itself compresses video at approximately a 30:1 ratio, but with precompression through oversampling, the ratio can climb to 100:1 and higher, while retaining high quality. Therefore, MPEG compression results in better, faster videos that require less storage space. MPEG is an interframe compressor. Because MPEG stores only incremental changes, it is not used during editing phases. MPEG-2 is the standard used for DVD compression; it uses more disk space but produces much better results than MPEG-1, which is used primarily for video email or web-based video.

If you will be capturing or compressing video on your computer, you'll need software based on standards such as Microsoft's DirectShow (the successor to Video for Windows and ActiveMovie), Real Network's Real Producer series, or Apple's QuickTime Pro. Players for files produced with these technologies can be downloaded free from the vendors' websites.

To play or record video with your laptop, you need some extra hardware and software:

- Video system software, such as Apple's QuickTime for Windows or Microsoft's Windows Media Player.

- A compression/digitization video adapter that enables you to digitize and play large video files.

■ An NTSC-to-VGA adapter that combines TV signals with computer video signals for output to a VCR. Video can come from a variety of sources: TV, VCR, video camera, laserdisc player, or DVD player. When you record an animation file, you can save it in a variety of file formats: AVI (audio video interleave), MOV (Apple QuickTime format), or MPG (MPEG format).

You can capture individual screen images or full-motion video for reuse in several ways:

■ USB-based TV-tuner or video-capture devices

■ USB or IEEE 1394a–based web cams with video-input ports

■ Camcorders with IEEE 1394 (FireWire) connectors

TV tuners that plug into the USB port are available from a wide variety of sources, including Hauppauge (www.hauppauge.com), StarTech, AVerTech, Pinnacle Systems (www.pinnaclesys.com), and others. Some devices support only USB 1.1, whereas others also support the faster data-transfer rates of USB 2.0 (Hi-Speed USB). In most cases, users rate the results with USB 1.1–compatible devices as acceptable, but noticeably less sharp than a normal TV signal would be. This is due primarily to the low data rate (12Mbps) supported by the USB 1.1 port. Devices that support the 480Mbps transfer rate of USB 2.0 provide better quality, but you need to add a USB 2.0 (Hi-Speed USB) CardBus card to your laptop if it doesn't have a Hi-Speed USB port already installed or built in to the unit.

Most TV tuners also provide still or full-motion capture, but you can also use dedicated video-capture devices or use web cams that include video inputs. These units capture still or moving images from NTSC video sources, such as camcorders and VCRs. Although image quality is limited by the input signal, the results are still good enough for presentations and desktop publishing applications. These devices work with displays configured to use 8-, 16-, and 24-bit color depths and usually accept video input from VHS, Super VHS, and Hi-8 devices. As you might expect, however, Super VHS and Hi-8 video sources give better results, as do configurations using more than 256 colors.

Tip

For best color and screen quality when watching TV or capturing video, set your display for 24-bit or 32-bit color.

For the best video capture results, use DV camcorders equipped with IEEE 1394 (i.LINK/FireWire) connectors; they can output high-quality digital video directly to your computer without the need to perform an analog-to-digital conversion. Although many laptop computers feature built-in IEEE 1394 ports, you need to install an IEEE 1394 CardBus card into those that lack these ports if you want to capture output from a DV camcorder.

Your second-best option is to use a USB 2.0–equipped personal video recorder (PVR) or video capture device. These devices are optimized to provide high-quality digital conversions from analog video such as TV shows and existing analog videotape. A PVR also enables you to digitally record a TV show and watch it on a delayed basis and enjoy high-speed digital fast-forward and rewind.

If you want to use both USB 2.0 and IEEE 1394a devices with your laptop computer and don't have either port type already, Adaptec (www.adaptec.com) offers a CardBus card that provides both port types in a single Type II PC Card form factor.

If you want to capture analog video or still images from a TV or VCR, the quality of the captured video or still images is affected by the speed of the port used (USB 2.0 ports are faster than USB 1.1 ports), especially for analog video, as well as the connection used between the video source and the laptop.

If possible, use the S-Video connector on your TV or VCR for the connection; this is the same type of connector used by almost all laptops with built-in TV-Out and is also supported by most add-on TV tuner or video capture devices. S-Video separates color (chroma) and brightness (luma) into separate signals. Composite video (which uses a single RCA jack) provides a lower-quality picture than S-Video does.

Troubleshooting Laptop Video Problems

Troubleshooting laptop video problems is more difficult than troubleshooting problems with desktop video because one of the most popular techniques, replacing the video card, is not possible on many laptops. Even on laptops that offer a removable video module, the video module is difficult to remove and expensive to replace. Generally, such replacements are done only when the video chip inside the adapter has failed or the user wants to upgrade to a better graphics processor. However, there are still many ways to determine the cause of laptop video problems and solve (or work around) some of them.

Troubleshooting Graphics Acceleration

If your laptop's graphics subsystem includes a graphics accelerator (as virtually all of them have for some time), the Display adapter's Advanced properties page has a Performance tab that contains a Hardware Acceleration slider you can use to control the degree of graphic display assistance provided by your adapter hardware. In Windows XP, the Performance page is referred to as the Troubleshoot page.

Setting the Hardware Acceleration slider to the Full position activates all the adapter's hardware acceleration features. If you're not certain of which setting is the best for your situation, use this procedure: Move the slider one notch to the left to address mouse display problems by disabling the hardware's cursor support in the display driver. This is the equivalent of adding the SWCursor=1 directive to the [Display] section of the System.ini file in Windows 9x/Me. If you are having problems with 2D graphics in Windows XP only, but 3D applications work correctly, move the slider to the second notch from the right to disable cursor drawing and acceleration.

Moving the slider another notch (to the third notch from the right in Windows XP or the second notch from the right in earlier versions) prevents the adapter from performing certain bit-block transfers; it disables 3D functions of DirectX in Windows XP. With some drivers, this setting also disables memory-mapped I/O. This is the equivalent of adding the Mmio=0 directive to the [Display] section of System.ini and the SafeMode=1 directive to the [Windows] section of Win.ini (and the SWCursor directive mentioned previously) in Windows 9x/Me.

Moving the slider to the None setting (the far left) adds the SafeMode=2 directive to the [Windows] section of the Win.ini file in Windows 9x/Me. This disables all hardware acceleration support on all versions of Windows and forces the operating system to use only the device-independent bitmap (DIB) engine to display images, rather than bit-block transfers. Use this setting when you experience frequent screen lockups or receive invalid page fault error messages.

Note

If you need to disable any of the video hardware features listed earlier, this often indicates a buggy video or mouse driver. If you download and install updated video and mouse drivers, you should be able to revert to full acceleration. You should also download an updated version of DirectX for your version of Windows.

Troubleshooting Display Colors

If you're trying to reproduce onscreen color graphics with a color printer and the colors don't match between your display and your printer, look for a tab called Color Management in the Advanced section of the Display properties page (click Settings, Advanced to display these tabs). You can select a color profile for your monitor to enable more accurate color matching for use with graphics programs and printers.

If onscreen color is too dark, too light, or colors are off, use the Color tab to adjust color balance, brightness, contrast, and gamma (see Figure 11.14).

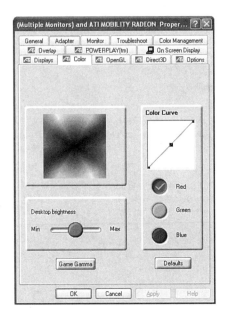

Figure 11.14   The Color tab for the ATI Mobility Radeon processor can be used to adjust overall desktop brightness; color curves for red, blue, and green; and game screen brightness with the game gamma button.

If the flat-panel display panel or external monitor can't display 16-bit, 24-bit, or 32-bit color, the display drivers might be corrupted. Delete the video display adapter listing in Device Manager and restart the computer so it will reload the drivers. Download and install updated drivers if necessary.

Troubleshooting 3D Acceleration Quality Issues

If you are having problems with 3D game display performance or display quality, you have two options you can try if installing new drivers doesn't improve the situation:

- Adjust the 3D graphics and quality settings in your game's setup dialog boxes.
- Adjust general 3D graphics and quality settings in your Display properties page, assuming your laptop's graphics adapter has these options.

If your laptop supports 3D graphics, its graphics driver will usually have two tabs in the Advanced dialog box that you can use to adjust 3D graphics performance and screen quality:

- **Direct3D**—Used to adjust settings for games that use the Microsoft DirectX API
- **OpenGL**—Used to adjust settings for games that use the OpenGL API

Typically, dialog boxes like the one shown in Figure 11.15 enable you to adjust the settings in the direction of performance (less detailed 3D graphics with greater screen display speed) or quality (greater 3D graphics detail with lower screen display speed) and to fine-tune specific settings for anisotropic filtering, antialiasing, textures, MIP mapping, and Z-buffer depth.

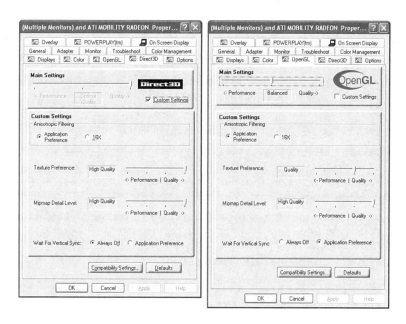

Figure 11.15   Use the Direct3D dialog box (left) to adjust visual quality and performance settings for DirectX games. Use the OpenGL dialog box (right) to adjust visual quality and performance settings for OpenGL games.

Tip

Because laptop computers are often slower than desktop computers in both 3D graphics performance and processor speed, try the Performance settings first for best results, unless you have a laptop with a processor faster than 2GHz.

Troubleshooting Internal Displays

Problem: No picture.

Solution: Press the key combination used to switch the display between the internal and external monitors. If you have cycled through the key combinations to switch the display and still don't see a picture on the internal display, check the contrast and brightness controls. Dual-scan and passive-matrix panels often have a sliding control on the side of the flat-panel display. Active-matrix models might use key combinations to adjust these settings, or they might not have adjustments. If you still don't see a picture after making these adjustments, plug your system into an external monitor and try the troubleshooting steps listed in the next section. If no picture appears on the external monitor either, your laptop's graphics processor might have failed.

Problem: Picture is surrounded by a wide black border (refer to Figure 11.2).

Solution: Adjust the Display properties to use the native resolution of the display.

Problem: Black line or box across part or all of the display.

Solution: Transistors in the flat-panel display have failed. Replace the display panel as soon as possible. Use an external display until you can replace the display.

Troubleshooting External Displays

Problem: No picture.

Solution: If the LED on the front of the monitor is yellow or flashing green, the monitor is in power-saving mode. Press the key combination to switch the display to the external monitor. If both the internal display and external display are blank, move the mouse or press Alt+Tab on the keyboard and wait up to 1 minute to wake up the system if the system is turned on.

If the LED on the front of the monitor is green, the monitor is in normal mode (receiving a signal), but the brightness and contrast are set incorrectly on the monitor. Adjust them.

If no lights are lit on the monitor, check the power and power switch. Check the surge protector or power director to ensure that power is going to the monitor. Replace the power cord with a known-working spare if necessary. Retest. Replace the monitor with a known-working spare to ensure that the monitor is the problem.

Check data cables at the monitor and laptop video port. If the monitor is plugged into a port replicator or docking station, shut down the monitor and computer, remove the port replicator or docking station, and plug the monitor directly into the laptop's VGA port. If the display works when it is plugged directly into the laptop, the port replicator or docking station is defective.

Problem: Jittery picture quality.

Solution: For flat-panel display monitors, use display-adjustment software or onscreen menus to reduce or eliminate pixel jitter and pixel swim. For all monitors, check cables for tightness at the video card and the monitor (if removable). Here are some other actions to take:

- Remove the extender cable and retest with the monitor plugged directly into the video card. If the extended cable is bad, replace it.
- Check the cables for damage; replace them as needed.
- If problems are intermittent, check for interference. (Microwave ovens near monitors can cause severe picture distortion when turned on.)

For CRT monitors, check refresh-rate settings; reduce them until acceptable picture quality is achieved. Here are some other actions to take:

- Use onscreen picture adjustments until an acceptable picture quality is achieved.
- If problems are intermittent and can be "fixed" by waiting or gently tapping the side of the monitor, the monitor power supply is probably bad or has loose connections internally. Service or replace the monitor.

Troubleshooting Drivers and Video Processors

Problem: The display works at startup (DOS) but not in Windows.

Solution: If you have an acceptable picture quality in MS-DOS mode (system boot) but no picture in Windows, most likely you have an incorrect or corrupted video driver installed in Windows. Boot Windows 9x/Me in Safe Mode (which uses a VGA driver), boot Windows 2000/XP in Enable VGA mode, or install the VGA driver and restart Windows. If Safe Mode or VGA Mode works, get the correct driver for the graphics processor and reinstall.

Problem: Can't select the desired color depth and resolution combination.

Solution: Verify that the graphics processor is properly identified in Windows and that the video memory is working properly. Use diagnostic software provided by the graphics processor maker to test the video memory. If the hardware is working properly, check for new drivers. If the system uses integrated graphics with a fixed video memory size, make sure the maximum size for the frame buffer has been selected in the system BIOS setup program. If the video memory size varies by installed memory, install more memory (up to a total of 256MB or more) to provide more memory for use by the display.

Problem: Can't select desired refresh rate.

Solution: Verify that the card and monitor are properly identified in Windows. Obtain updated drivers for the card and monitor.

DisplayMate

DisplayMate is a unique diagnostic and testing program designed to thoroughly test your laptop's graphics processor and display. It is somewhat unique in that most conventional PC hardware diagnostics programs do not emphasize video testing the way this program does.

I find it useful not only in testing whether a graphics processor is functioning properly but also in examining video displays. You easily can test the image quality of a display, which allows you to make focus, centering, brightness and contrast, color level, and other adjustments much more accurately than before. If you are purchasing a new monitor or laptop computer, you can use the program to evaluate the sharpness and linearity of the display and to provide a consistent way of checking each monitor you are considering. If you use projection systems for presentations—as I do in my PC hardware seminars—you will find it invaluable for setting up and adjusting the projector.

DisplayMate also can test a laptop's video circuits thoroughly. It sets the video circuits into each possible video mode so you can test all the adapter's capabilities. It even helps you determine the performance level of your card, both with respect to resolution and colors as well as speed. You can then use the program to benchmark the performance of the display, which enables you to compare one type of video adapter system to another.

Visit **www.displaymate.com** for more information.

Laptop Audio Hardware

Although the first sound cards for desktop computers, the AdLib and Creative Labs Game Blaster, were introduced in the late 1980s, the first laptop computers with onboard audio were not introduced until September 1993, when IBM's ThinkPad 750 series first hit the market. Before the ThinkPad 750 series was introduced, a few laptops in the early 1990s featured PC Card–based sound cards, but they were expensive and were not popular.

Note

CardBus-based audio cards are still available, but they are used for professional sound digitizing and editing, and are therefore beyond the scope of this book.

The ThinkPad 750 series and some other early IBM ThinkPad computers used IBM's own Mwave audio processors, but by 1995, IBM ThinkPads used audio processors from Crystal and ESS, as did Toshiba and other major laptop brands that included integrated audio.

Although from the beginning, laptop audio processors emulated the de facto industry-standard Sound Blaster Pro and Sound Blaster 16 cards made by Creative Labs, Creative Labs (now, truncated to Creative) did not introduce its own audio processors for laptop computers until September 1999, when it released its EV1958 and EV1938 processors. Ironically, Creative's laptop audio processors have been less popular than other brands. Today's laptops continue to use audio processors from various vendors and offer better audio output and sound quality than ever before.

Audio Connectors

Laptops typically feature at least two 1/8" minijack connectors similar to the ones shown in Figure 11.16:

- **Stereo line-out or audio-out connector (lime green)**—The line-out connector is used to send sound signals from the laptop's audio processor to a device outside the computer. You can hook up the cables from the line-out connector to stereo speakers, a headphone set, or your stereo system.

- **Microphone-in or mono-in connector (pink)**—The mono-in connector is used to connect a microphone for recording your voice or other sounds to disk. This microphone jack usually records in mono—not in stereo—and is therefore not suitable for high-quality music recordings. Many audio processors use automatic gain control (AGC) to improve recordings. This feature adjusts the recording levels on the fly. A 600 ohm–10,000 ohm dynamic or condenser microphone works best with this jack. Some laptops use the line-in connector instead of a separate microphone jack.

Figure 11.16 The microphone jack (left) and headset/speaker jack (right) on a typical laptop computer. Note the symbols used to indicate each jack's purpose.

Some laptops also have additional jacks:

- **Stereo line-in or audio-in connector (light blue)**—With the line-in connector, you can record or mix sound signals from an external source, such as a stereo system or VCR, to the computer's hard disk.

- **S/PDIF optical digital out (black)**—This jack connects the laptop to a digital amplifier such as you might find in a home theater system. A few systems include this jack on the laptop itself, but it is more often built in to a companion docking station or port replicator.

Note

When you plug a microphone into a laptop, the onboard microphone (usually located on the LCD panel or at the top of the keyboard) is disabled automatically.

Some laptops combine the S/PDIF jack with the headphone jack.

Audio jacks, such as those shown in Figure 11.17, are usually clearly labeled and are frequently located on the side panel of a laptop computer to make connecting speakers or a microphone easier than on a desktop computer (where these jacks are at the back of the computer). However, it's still possible to plug the wrong cable into a jack. One of the most common reasons a laptop fails to play any sound through external speakers is that the speakers are plugged into the wrong socket. To avoid this problem, some laptops color-code the jacks according to specifications found in the PC99 Design Guide. The color-coding can vary on some audio adapters (or not be present at all). The colors listed in this subsection for the audio jacks are those specified by the PC99 Design Guide.

Volume Control

With virtually all recent laptops that have onboard sound, the volume is controlled through a Windows Control Panel speaker icon that can also be found in the system tray (near the onscreen clock). If you plug in external speakers, a headset, or use the digital audio (S/PDIF) option found on some recent laptops, you will need to use the mixing options in the volume control to select the proper sources and appropriate volume levels for incoming and outgoing audio. In Windows, use the Control Panel Sounds or Sounds and Audio Devices icon to adjust speaker type or make other advanced adjustments (see Figure 11.17). Keep in mind that if you are sending sound to an external audio receiver with either the normal speaker out or S/PDIF digital audio jacks, you need to adjust the volume on that device as well.

By contrast, some older laptops include a thumbwheel volume control next to the input/output jacks as well as the Windows Control Panel icon. The volume wheel can be troublesome; if you aren't aware of its existence and it is turned all the way down, you might be puzzled by the adapter's failure to produce sufficient sound.

If you connect your laptop to external, amplified speakers but you aren't hearing any sound, remember to check that the power to the speakers is on, the volume control on the speakers is turned up, and the correct speakers are selected and properly connected to your laptop.

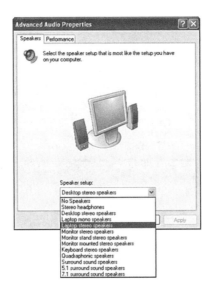

Figure 11.17   Selecting the speaker type in Windows XP.

Laptop Audio Quality Factors

Whether you use your laptop's built-in audio to create or play back existing audio, you should consider the impact of factors such as the following:

- Audio data compression
- 3D audio acceleration
- Audio drivers
- DVD audio playback options
- Speaker types
- Hardware upgrades

See the following subsections for details.

Audio Data Compression

Virtually all audio adapters on the market today can easily produce CD-quality audio, which is sampled at 44.1KHz. At this rate, recorded files (even of your own voice) can consume more than 10MB for every minute of recording. To counter this demand for disk space, many audio adapters include their own data-compression capability.

Most manufacturers of audio adapters use an algorithm called *adaptive differential pulse code modulation (ADPCM)* compression (it's also called IMA-ADPCM), which was developed by the Interactive Multimedia Association (IMA) to reduce file size by more than 50%. IMA-ADPCM compresses 16-bit linear samples down to 4 bits per sample. However, a simple fact of audio technology is that when you use such compression, you lose sound quality. Unfortunately, no standard exists for the use of ADPCM. For example, although both Apple and Microsoft support IMA-ADPCM compression, they implement it in different ways. Apple's standard AIFF and Microsoft's standard WAV file formats are incompatible with each other unless you use a media player that can play both.

Several codecs (programs that perform compression and decompression) are installed to support the audio processors or integrated audio solution used by your laptop. Typically, some form of ADPCM is installed along with many others. To see which codecs are available on your system, open the Windows Control Panel and open the Multimedia icon (Windows 9x), the Sounds and Multimedia icon (Windows 2000), or the Sounds and Audio Devices icon (Windows XP). In Windows 9x, click the Devices tab followed by the plus sign next to Audio Compression to see the installed codecs. In Windows 2000 and Windows XP, click the Hardware tab, followed by Audio Codecs and Properties. The codecs are listed in order or priority, highest to lowest. You can also change the priority if you prefer a different order.

Note

If you create your own recorded audio for use on another computer, both computers must use the same codec. You can select which codec you want to use for recording sounds with most programs, including the Windows Sound Recorder.

The most popular compression standard is the Motion Pictures Experts Group (MPEG) standard, which works with both audio and video compression and is gaining support in the non-PC world for products such as DVD players. MPEG by itself provides a potential compression ratio of 30:1, and largely because of this, full-motion-video MPEG DVD and CD-ROM titles are now available. The popular MP3 sound-compression scheme is an MPEG format, and it can be played back on recent versions of the Windows Media Player, as well as by various other audio player programs and devices.

3D Audio and Laptops

Most recent laptops feature some type of 3D audio that works along with 3D graphics to provide more realistic gameplay. However, two methods provide 3D audio support:

- Hardware acceleration (audio processor based)
- Software/driver support

If you want to use your laptop to play 3D games, look for a model that features a discrete graphics processor with 3D support and an audio processor with 3D audio acceleration. Although laptop vendors prominently display the names of the discrete 3D graphics processors they use in their advertisements, you might need to look very carefully at the detailed specifications for a particular laptop to determine the type of audio it uses. Keep in mind that laptops that use integrated graphics usually feature integrated audio as well. Integrated audio, like integrated graphics, is usually not as fast, particularly for 3D and gaming uses.

Some of the major 3D audio features affected by the type of audio processors used in a particular laptop include the following:

- Support for positional audio
- Hardware versus software processing of 3D audio
- DirectX support issues

Positional Audio

The underlying issue common to all 3D sound cards is that of positional audio, which refers to adjusting features such as reverberation, balance, and apparent sound "location" to produce the illusion of sound coming from in front of, beside, or even behind the user. One very important element in positional audio is Head Related Transfer Function (HRTF), which refers to how the shape of the ear and the angle of the listener's head change the perception of sound. Because HRTF factors mean that a "realistic" sound at one listener's head angle might sound artificial when the listener turns to one side or the other, the addition of multiple speakers that "surround" the user and sophisticated sound algorithms that add controlled reverberation to the mix are making computer-based sound more and more realistic.

The major standards for positional audio today include Creative's Environmental Audio Extensions (EAX) and Sensaura's Virtual Ear. If your laptop's audio processor supports either positional audio standard, your audio driver's properties pages might offer options for adjusting speaker position and the acoustic environment (simulating acoustics in different room types) among others.

3D Audio Processing

A second issue for game players is how the laptop's audio processor produces 3D audio. As with 3D video, there are two major methods:

- Host-based processing (using the CPU to process 3D, which can slow down overall system operation)
- Processing on the audio adapter (referred to as *3D acceleration*)

Most laptops use audio processors, which use the CPU for part of the audio processing task. If your laptop has a processor under 1GHz, host-based audio processing can cause major drops in frame rate, whereas onboard 3D audio processing maintains stable frame rates.

Even though most recent laptops have processors running at speeds well in excess of 1GHz (2GHz speeds and faster are becoming commonplace), the number of audio streams supported by 3D hardware acceleration varies greatly by audio processor and can be limited by problems with software drivers. For the best 3D audio acceleration, I recommend you do the following:

- Download and install the latest drivers for your laptop's audio solution.
- Look for laptops that use high-performance audio processors.
- Look for laptops with the fastest processors you can afford.

To learn more about specific 3D audio processors used on recent laptops, see "Who's Who in Laptop Audio," later in this chapter.

DirectX and Audio Adapters

Microsoft's DirectX is a series of application programming interfaces (APIs) that sit between multimedia applications and hardware. Unlike MS-DOS applications, which required developers to develop direct hardware support for numerous models and brands of audio cards, video cards, and game controllers, Windows uses DirectX to "talk" to hardware in a more direct manner than normal Windows drivers do. This improves program performance and frees the software developer from the need to change the program to work with different devices. Instead, a game developer needs to work only with the DirectX sound engine, DirectX 3D renderer, and DirectX modem or network interface routines.

Thanks to DirectX, sound card and chipset developers are assured that their products will work with recent and current versions of Windows.

DirectX Support Issues

The latest version of DirectX, DirectX 9.x, is designed to give all audio processors with 3D support a major boost in performance. Previous versions of DirectX supported 3D with DirectSound3D, but the performance of DirectSound3D was limited. Game programmers needed to test the audio adapter to see whether it supported DirectSound3D acceleration and then would either enable or disable 3D sounds based on the host hardware. Starting with DirectX 5.0, DirectSound3D works with third-party 3D acceleration features. Compared to DirectX 8, DirectX 9.x improves 3D audio quality and performance. You can download it from the Microsoft DirectX website at `www.microsoft.com/windows/directx`.

Sound Drivers

As with many PC components, a software driver provides a vital link between an audio processor and the application or operating system that uses it. Operating systems such as Windows 9x/Me and Windows 2000/XP include a large library of drivers for most of the audio processors on the market (Windows NT 4.0 also supports some sound hardware but not as much as other versions of Windows). In most cases, these drivers are written by the manufacturer of the audio processor and distributed only by Microsoft. Keep in mind that some audio processor drivers for laptops are modified to meet the requirements of the laptop builder, so it's safer to get updates from the laptop vendor than from other sources.

Any DOS applications you might still use do not typically include as wide a range of driver support as an operating system, but you should find that most games and other programs support the Sound Blaster adapters. Typical laptop audio processors are Sound Blaster–compatible, so you should have no trouble finding driver support for all your applications.

If your game program locks up when you try to detect the sound card during configuration, set the card type and settings manually. This is often a symptom of inadequate emulation for Sound Blaster by a third-party card. If you have problems, check the game developer's or audio adapter's website for patches or workarounds.

DVD Movies on the Road

You don't need a dedicated DVD player to enjoy the clarity, control, extra features, and excitement of DVD movies.

Many laptops now feature DVD-ROM or combo CD-RW/DVD-ROM drives. These drives help bring the DVD movie experience to your laptop, but having a DVD-ROM and a DVD movie player program is only part of what you need to bring the big screen to your laptop.

To get the most out of your laptop DVD experience, you need the following:

- **DVD playback software that supports Dolby Digital 5.1 or better output**—One of the best choices is Cyberlink's PowerDVD 5.x, available from `www.gocyberlink.com`.

- **An audio adapter that will output to Dolby Digital 5.1–compatible audio hardware**—If your laptop supports S/PDIF digital audio output (either from the laptop itself or by way of a docking station or port replicator), purchase the accessory needed to add S/PDIF output to your system. Note that the proprietary S-Video cable used by some Dell models also supports S/PDIF output. For laptops that lack a manufacturer-supplied digital audio output option, use the Creative Sound Blaster Extigy. For more information, see "Upgrading Audio Output," later in this chapter.

- **Dolby Digital 5.1–compatible stereo receiver and speakers**—Use the appropriate type of stereo receiver for your sound hardware. If your system supports S/PDIF digital audio, use a digital speaker system. Creative's Extigy external audio processor can attach to both analog and digital 5.1 speaker systems.

To learn more about speaker terminology and how to ensure your speaker configuration is correct, see the section "Speakers," later in this chapter.

Playing and Creating Digitized Sound Files

You can use two basic types of files to store audio on your laptop. One type is generically called a *sound file* and uses formats such as WAV, VOC, AU, and AIFF. Sound files contain waveform data, which means they are analog audio recordings that have been digitized for storage on a computer. Just as you can store graphic images at different resolutions, you can have sound files that use various resolutions, trading off sound quality for file size. The default sound-resolution levels used in Windows are shown in Table 11.14.

Table 11.14   Windows Default Sound File Resolutions

Resolution (number of KB per second of audio stored)	Frequency	Bandwidth	Data Rate
Telephone quality	11,025Hz	8-bit mono	11KBps
Radio quality	22,050Hz	8-bit mono	22KBps
CD quality	44,100Hz	16-bit stereo	172KBps

If you have audio hardware that supports DVD-quality sound (48,000Hz, 16-bit stereo, 187KBps), you can also save sounds at that frequency, but you must select it manually if you are using the Windows Sound Recorder to digitize sounds. Note that the Windows Sound Recorder applet uses the default pulse code modulation (PCM) method for storing sounds. PCM produces the highest quality of sound, but because it doesn't use any type of data compression, file sizes can be enormous.

As you can see, the difference in file sizes between the highest and lowest audio resolution levels is substantial. CD-quality sound files can occupy enormous amounts of disk space. At this rate, just 60 seconds of audio would require more than 10MB of storage. For applications that don't require or benefit from such high resolution, such as voice annotation, telephone-quality audio is sufficient and generates much smaller files. To achieve a balance between high quality and smaller file sizes, you can convert conventional WAV files into compressed formats, such as MP3 or WMA audio files.

The other type of file is a MIDI file, which consists of a musical score that is played back by synthesized or sampled musical instruments incorporated into the sound card's MIDI support.

On a multimedia PC, it is often possible for two or more sound sources to require the services of the audio adapter at the same time. Any time you have multiple sound sources you want to play through a single set of speakers, a mixer is necessary.

Most laptops with onboard sound include a mixer that enables all the different audio sources, MIDI, WAV, line-in, and CD, to use the single line-out jack. Starting with Windows 95 through the latest Windows versions (XP Pro/XP Home), Windows uses a single mixer for both recording and playback features, instead of using separate mixers as with Windows 3.x. Normally, the system ships with software that displays visual sliders like you would see on an actual audio mixer in a recording studio. With these controls, you can set the relative volume of each of the sound sources.

Tip

Whenever you change from analog to digital speakers or add speakers to a two-speaker configuration, you must adjust the mixer controls to match your current speaker configuration. If you don't, you will be unable to hear anything through your speakers.

Audio Adapter Concepts and Terms

To fully understand audio adapters and their functions, you need to understand various concepts and terms, such as *16-bit*, *CD quality*, and *MIDI port*, to name just a few. Concepts such as sampling are often sprinkled throughout stories about new sound products. You've already learned about some of these terms and concepts; the following subsections describe many others.

The Nature of Sound

To understand an audio adapter, you must understand the nature of sound. Vibrations that compress air or other substances produce every sound. These sound waves travel in all directions, expanding in balloon-like fashion from the source of the sound. When these waves reach your ear, they cause vibrations that you perceive as sound.

Two of the basic properties of any sound are its pitch and intensity.

Pitch is the rate at which vibrations are produced. It is measured in the number of hertz (Hz), or cycles per second. One cycle is a complete vibration back and forth. The number of Hz is the frequency of the tone; the higher the frequency, the higher the pitch.

Humans can't hear all possible frequencies. Very few people can hear sounds with frequencies less than 16Hz or greater than about 20KHz (kilohertz; 1KHz equals 1,000Hz). In fact, the lowest note on a piano has a frequency of 27Hz, and the highest note has a frequency a little higher than 4KHz. Frequency modulation (FM) radio stations can broadcast notes with frequencies as high as 15KHz.

The intensity of a sound is called its *amplitude*. This intensity determines the sound's volume and depends on the strength of the vibrations producing the sound. A piano string, for example, vibrates gently when the key is struck softly. The string swings back and forth in a narrow arc, and the tone it sends out is soft. If the key is struck more forcefully, however, the string swings back and forth in a wider arc, producing a greater amplitude and a greater volume. The loudness of sounds is measured in decibels (db). The rustle of leaves is rated at 20db, average street noise at 70db, and nearby thunder at 120db.

The amazing compression ratios possible with MP3 files, compared to regular CD-quality WAV files, are due in part to the discarding of sound frequencies that are not audible due to another sound having a much higher amplitude and playing at the same time, obscuring the sound with the far lesser amplitude.

Evaluating the Quality of Your Audio Adapter

The quality of an audio adapter is often measured by three criteria: frequency response (or range), total harmonic distortion, and signal-to-noise ratio.

The *frequency response* of an audio adapter is the range in which an audio system can record or play at a constant and audible amplitude level. Many cards support 30Hz–20KHz. The wider the range, the better the adapter.

The *total harmonic distortion (THD)* measures an audio adapter's linearity and the straightness of a frequency response curve. In layman's terms, the harmonic distortion is a measure of accurate sound reproduction. Any nonlinear elements cause distortion in the form of harmonics. The smaller the percentage of distortion, the better. This harmonic distortion factor might make the difference between cards that use the same audio chipset. Some audio processors might have greater distortion, making them produce poorer-quality sound.

The *signal-to-noise ratio (SNR)* measures the strength of the sound signal relative to background noise (hiss). The higher the number (measured in decibels), the better the sound quality.

These factors affect all types of audio use, from WAV file playback to speech recognition. Keep in mind that low-quality microphones and speakers can degrade the performance of a high-quality audio processor.

Note

If audio quality becomes the deciding factor between two similar laptops, determine what audio processor the laptops use and check the audio processor vendors' websites to determine the frequency response, THD, and SNR values for the audio processors used by the laptops you are considering. If you are planning to add an external audio device, be sure to compare its values to the built-in audio processor. In most cases, external devices have better-quality output than built-in audio.

Sampling

With an audio processor, a laptop can record waveform audio. Waveform audio (also known as *sampled* or *digitized sound*) uses the PC as a recording device (like a tape recorder). Dedicated circuitry built in to the adapter, called *analog-to-digital converters (ADCs)*, converts analog sound waves into digital bits that the computer can understand. Likewise, digital-to-analog converters (DACs) convert the recorded sounds to an audible analog format. Although semiconductor manufacturers still produce ADC and DAC chips, these functions are incorporated into the single-chip audio solutions found in laptop computers.

Sampling is the process of turning the original analog sound waves into digital (binary) signals that the computer can save and later replay (see Figure 11.18). The system samples the sound by taking snapshots of its frequency and amplitude at regular intervals. For example, at time X the sound might be measured with an amplitude of Y. The higher (or more frequent) the sample rate, the more accurately the digital sound replicates its real-life source and the larger the amount of disk space needed to store it.

Originally, audio processors used 8-bit digital sampling, which provided for only 256 values (2^8), to convert a sound. More recently, audio processors have increased the quality of digitized sound by using 16-bit (2^{16}) sampling to produce 65,536 distinct values. Today's highest-quality audio processors feature 24-bit or 32-bit sampling (2^{24} and 2^{32}), which translates into more than 16.8 million possible digital values that can be matched to a given sound in the case of 24-bit recording.

You can experiment with the effects of various sampling rates (and compression technologies) by recording sound with the Windows Sound Recorder or a third-party application set to CD-quality sound. Save the sound and play it back at that highest quality setting. Then convert the file to a lower quality setting and save the sound file again with a different name. Play back the various versions and determine the lowest quality (and smallest file size) you can use without serious degradation to sound quality.

Who's Who in Laptop Audio

As you've learned in other chapters, I believe it is very important to get all the technical information you can about your computer and its components. By knowing who makes the audio processor your computer depends on, you can find out what the hardware can do and be better able to find upgrades to the software drivers you need to get the most out of your audio hardware.

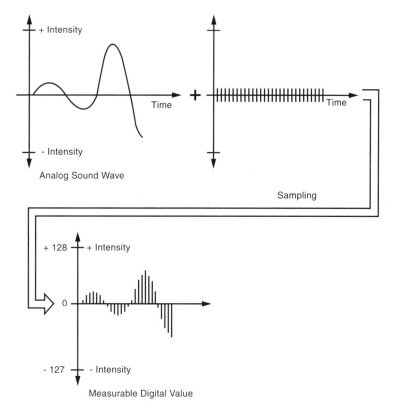

Figure 11.18 Sampling turns a changing sound wave into measurable digital values.

The following companies are the major providers of audio processors for recent and current laptop computers:

- Analog Devices
- Cirrus Logic/Crystal Semiconductors
- C-Media Electronics
- ESS Technology
- Realtek
- Creative
- VIA Technology

Their product lines are covered in greater detail in the following subsections.

Note

Most recent laptops use audio processors that provide up to six-channel output. However, unless the laptop can be plugged into an S/PDIF cable or into a docking station or port replicator with six-channel output, you will get only stereo sound from the basic audio outputs on the laptop itself.

Analog Devices

Analog Devices offers a range of audio processors, codecs, and software under the SoundMAX trade name. Analog Devices' audio processors support both the AC '97 audio standard as well as Intel's new HD audio standard. Popular Analog Devices audio processors include the AD1885, AD1981 series, AD1980, and AD1985 models, all of which can support up to six-channel audio. For more information about these processors, see the SoundMAX website at www.soundmax.com.

Cirrus Logic

Cirrus Logic offers a wide range of audio processors, with the CS4205 AC '97 being the most popular codec in older laptops. Cirrus Logic also uses the Crystal brand name on some of its consumer audio chipset lines that are used in CD and DVD players. For more information on Cirrus Logic and Crystal audio processors, see the Cirrus Logic website at www.cirrus.com.

C-Media

C-Media produces a variety of audio processors, with the most common on recent laptops being the CMI87xx AC '97 audio processor and the CM9880 codec. For more information on C-Media audio processors, see the C-Media website at www.cmedia.com.tw.

ESS Technology, Inc.

ESS Technology provides audio and combo audio/modem/network processors for several different brands and models of notebook computers. ESS Technology's audio processors include the Maestro, Allegro, Canyon3D, and other processors in the ES19xx and ES1xxx series. For more information about ESS audio processors, see the ESS website at www.esstech.com.

RealTek

RealTek produces a variety of audio processors that support the AC '97 codec as well as the Intel HD audio standard. The ALC2xx series supports two-channel (stereo) output, whereas the ALC6xx and ALC8xx series support six-channel output. All of these processors series are used in a variety of laptop computers. For more information about RealTek's audio processors, see the RealTek website at www.realtek.com.tw.

Creative

In 1999, Creative introduced its EV1938 and EV1958, which have been adopted by some laptop makers. The EV1938 processor is based on the Sound Blaster Audio PCI 64V. The EV1958 processor is based on the Sound Blaster Audio PCI 128. Subsequent Sound Blaster products, such as the Sound Blaster Live!, featured the EMU 10K audio processor, which was also used in an updated form for the Audigy and Audigy2 series of sound cards. For more information about Creative audio processors, see the Creative website at www.creative.com.

VIA Technology

VIA introduced the Envy24 audio processor in early 2003, offering 8-channel audio with 24-bit resolution. This was VIA's first venture into audio processors, and the Envy24 was mostly used on PCI soundcards for desktop systems. However, some notebooks feature this audio processor. For more information about VIA Technology audio processors, see the VIA Technology website at www.viaarena.com.

AC '97 Integrated Audio

The phrase *AC '97* occurred repeatedly in the description of the preceding audio processors. What exactly does it mean to you as a laptop computer user?

AC '97 (often referred to as *AC97*) is an Intel specification that connects an audio codec (compression/decompression) architecture to a section of a South Bridge or an I/O Communications Hub chip called the *AC-Link control*. The AC-Link control works with the CPU and an AC '97 digital signal processor (DSP) to create audio. Consequently, a laptop that uses AC '97 audio is using partially host-based audio. However, given the performance of recent mobile processors (1GHz to 2GHz and faster), this is not a major performance issue for most users.

The AC '97 audio codec can be implemented in various ways. Laptops typically implement it with a physical chip on the motherboard, but sometimes with just a software program. Sometimes a laptop might also integrate an analog modem through an MC '97 codec chip, or it might have an AMC '97 (audio/modem) codec chip to combine both functions.

Your laptop vendor supplies the drivers for a particular AC '97 codec chip because they must be customized to the combination of codec and South Bridge/ICH chip your motherboard uses.

Although the AC '97 specification recommends a standard pinout, differences do exist among AC '97 codec chips. Some vendors of AC '97 chips provide technical information to help system standard builders design sockets that can be used with different models of the AC '97 codec chip.

The four versions of the AC '97 codec standard are as follows:

- **AC '97 1.0**—Has a fixed 48KHz sampling rate and stereo output.
- **AC '97 2.1**—Has options for variable sampling rate and multichannel output.
- **AC '97 2.2**—Has AC '97 2.1 features plus optional S/PDIF digital audio and enhanced riser card support. AC '97 2.2 was released in September 2000.
- **AC '97 2.3**—Has AC '97 2.1/2.2 features plus support for true Plug and Play detection of audio devices, which helps prevent accidentally connecting speakers to the microphone jack, and so on. AC '97 2.3 was released in July 2002.

Most laptops with integrated audio support AC '97 2.1 or greater at this time. However, a special audio cable or a docking station or port replicator with additional audio outputs is necessary to take advantage of the additional channels or S/PDIF digital output options provided by AC '97 2.1 and higher versions.

To determine whether a particular laptop's implementation of AC '97 audio will be satisfactory, follow these steps:

1. Determine which codec chip the laptop uses. Read the detailed specifications for the laptop, the laptop's instruction manual, or check the list of drivers to determine which chip the laptop uses for audio.

2. Look up the chip's features and specifications using the website information provided earlier in this chapter. If you are not sure of the chip manufacturer, look up the part number (if known) with a search engine such as Google.

3. Use a search engine to find reviews of the chip's sound quality and performance. Because desktop motherboards often use the same AC '97 chips that laptops use, you might find both laptop and desktop system or motherboard articles that contain a review of the chip.

4. Look at the laptop's features and optional equipment to determine whether it uses the full capabilities of the codec chip. Chips that support AC '97 2.1 can offer up to six-channel analog audio; those that support AC '97 2.2 or above can also offer S/PDIF digital audio. However, many laptops don't offer built-in outputs for these optional outputs. Check with your laptop vendor to determine if a special cable, docking station, or port replicator is available and provides the additional outputs needed.

Intel HD Audio

With the introduction of PCI Express chipsets for Intel Pentium 4 processors, Intel also introduced a new standard for PC audio: HD Audio. Intel HD Audio rivals the best PCI-based sound cards available, and its specification describes the requirements for both the hardware and the software to enable high-quality audio for PCs. HD Audio supports a maximum resolution of 32 bits with a maximum 192KHz sample rate and support for 15 input and 15 output streams at a time, or eight separate channels in total. The HD Audio processor is in essence a bus mastering I/O peripheral that's connected through the PCI bus or directly to the host interface of the motherboard chipset. The HD Audio processor supports more than a single codec and thus will be able to work with multiple codecs at the same time. Additionally, its full-duplex sound processing makes it possible to record and play back sound across multiple audio channels concurrently.

Despite the fact that the HD Audio standard was not developed to be backward compatible with AC '97, they can both use the same codecs. Doing so, however, voids one of the benefits of the HD Audio standard, which is the use of new codecs that can intelligently detect which jack is plugged into what socket and, if needed, reroute audio streams to the appropriate jack. Similar to AC '97, HD Audio can use a variety of codecs supplied by a variety of manufacturers depending on how the manufacturer of the laptop chooses to implement HD Audio.

Speakers

All laptops with integrated audio have built-in speakers. However, the sound quality and available volume of built-in speakers is often inadequate for high-quality music playback, MIDI work, multimedia applications, or business presentations before a large group. In these cases, you will want to attach more powerful and higher-quality speakers to your laptop's speaker jack. If your laptop has S/PDIF digital audio output, you will need to connect your laptop to a home theater system with an S/PDIF input to be able to play back digital audio from sources such as DVD movies. In either case, you should try to select the highest quality speakers you can afford.

When you need to add external speakers, look for the best performance available in a small space. I recommend small bookshelf speakers instead of standard stereo speakers, especially if you must travel with the speakers.

You should not depend on the onboard audio system in your notebook to provide adequate amplification. Instead, use self-powered, magnetically shielded speakers. Magnetic shielding is especially important if you are using a CRT monitor along with your laptop in a business presentation. Unshielded speakers near the CRT can create magnetic interference, which can distort colors and objects onscreen or jumble the data recorded on nearby floppy disks or other magnetic media.

Caution

Although most computer speakers are magnetically shielded, do not leave recorded tapes, watches, credit cards, or floppy disks in front of the speakers for long periods of time.

With dozens of brands and models on the market at a variety of price points, it's essential to understand how to evaluate the quality of any given speaker. Speakers are measured by three criteria:

- **Frequency response**—A measurement of the range of high and low sounds a speaker can reproduce. The ideal range is 20Hz–20KHz, the range of human hearing. No speaker system reproduces this range perfectly. In fact, few people hear sounds above 18KHz. An exceptional speaker might cover a range of 30Hz–23,000Hz, and lesser models might cover only 100Hz–20,000Hz. Frequency response is the most deceptive specification because identically rated speakers can sound completely different.

- **Total harmonic distortion (THD)**—An expression of the amount of distortion or noise created by amplifying the signal. Simply put, distortion is the difference between the sound sent to the speaker and the sound you hear. The amount of distortion is measured in percentages. An acceptable level of distortion is less than .1% (one-tenth of 1%). For some CD-quality recording equipment, a common standard is .05%, but some speakers have a distortion of 10% or more. Headphones often have a distortion of about 2% or less.

- **Watts**—Usually stated as *watts per channel*, this is the amount of amplification available to drive the speakers. Check that the company means "per channel" (or RMS) and not total power. Many audio adapters have built-in amplifiers, providing up to 8 watts per channel (most provide 4 watts). This wattage is not enough to provide rich sound, however, which is why many speakers have built-in amplifiers. With the flick of a switch or the press of a button, these speakers amplify the signals they receive from the audio adapter. If you do not want to amplify the sound, you typically leave the speaker switch set to "direct." In most cases, you'll want to amplify the signal.

Inexpensive PC speakers sometimes use batteries to power the amplifiers. Because these speakers require so much power, you might want to invest in an AC adapter or purchase speakers that use AC power. With an AC adapter, you won't have to buy new batteries every few weeks. If your speakers didn't come with an AC adapter, you can pick one up from your local Radio Shack or hardware store. Be sure that the adapter you purchase matches your speakers in voltage and polarity; most third-party adapters are multiple voltage, featuring interchangeable tips and reversible polarity.

You can control the volume and other sound attributes of your speakers in various ways, depending on their complexity and cost. Typically, each speaker has a volume knob, although some share a single volume control. If one speaker is farther away than the other, you might want to adjust the volume accordingly. Many computer speakers include a dynamic bass boost (DBB) switch. This button provides a more powerful bass and clearer treble, regardless of the volume setting. Other speakers have separate bass and treble boost switches or a three-band equalizer to control low, middle, and high frequencies. When you rely on your audio adapter's power rather than your speakers' built-in amplifier, the volume and dynamic bass boost controls have no effect. Your speakers are at the mercy of the adapter's power.

For best audio quality, adjust the master volume on the sound card near the high end and use the volume control on powered speakers to adjust the volume. Otherwise, your speakers will try to amplify any distortions coming from the low-power input from the PC's audio adapter.

An 1/8" stereo minijack connects from the audio adapter's output jack to one of the speakers. The speaker then splits the signal and feeds it through a separate cable from itself to the second speaker (often referred to as the *satellite speaker*).

Before purchasing a set of speakers, check that the cables between the speakers are long enough for your computer setup.

Beware of speakers that have a tardy built-in sleep feature. Such speakers, which save electricity by turning themselves off when they are not in use, might have the annoying habit of clipping the first part of a sound after a period of inactivity. Speakers that are USB-based will not be capable of playing CD music unless the CD-ROM drive can perform digital audio extraction. Check your drive's specifications for information. Headphones are an option when you can't afford a premium set of speakers. Headphones also provide privacy and enable you to play your PC audio as loud as you like.

For best results with laptops that support four speakers or more, check the properties page for the audio adapter and set whether you're using headphones, stereo speakers, or a larger number of speakers. Make sure that speakers are placed properly. If you use a subwoofer, put it on the floor for better bass sound and to reduce EMI interference with other devices.

Upgrading Audio Output

If you're a serious gamer or DVD movie lover, you won't be content with ordinary stereophonic sound from your laptop, especially if it is your only computer. Traditionally, if you wanted to move to more elaborate speaker setups or enjoy Dolby Digital output support, you could choose from these options:

- Connect a special cable with optical output to your laptop
- Connect your laptop to a docking station or port replicator that features optical or multichannel output

However, if your laptop doesn't provide these options, you're no longer stuck with standard stereo output.

Creative (www.soundblaster.com) makes an external Sound Blaster product, called Sound Blaster Extigy, that can be plugged into any laptop's USB ports (including those that don't have onboard audio) to provide better sound quality and output options.

Sound Blaster Extigy

Sound Blaster Extigy connects to any laptop's USB port (but requires its own AC power supply) and offers these features:

- Signal-to-noise ratio (SNR) exceeding 100db for hiss-free sound.
- Broad frequency response range and dynamic range exceed most onboard audio.
- Low total harmonic distortion and noise (THD+N) value below most onboard audio.
- 24-bit digital sampling at 48KHz for analog input and 24-bit/96KHz output, compared to 16-bit sampling at 48KHz for most onboard audio processors.
- S/PDIF digital input and output.
- Support for simultaneous playback of 5.1 audio and Dolby Digital audio.
- Built-in Dolby Digital (AC-3) decoder supports DVD players and home theater systems in both PC-connected and standalone modes and DVD player software when connected to a PC or laptop.
- Creative Multi Speaker Surround (CMSS) converts stereo sound into 5.1-compatible sound, as desired.

- EAX environmental audio.

- Analog speaker support for 2, 4, and 5.1 speakers; S/PDIF optical and coaxial input and output jacks; microphone-in, line-in, and headphone-out jacks; and MIDI input and output jacks.

- Remote control for adjusting audio playback and other features.

As you can see, the Sound Blaster Extigy is designed to provide a huge audio upgrade for any laptop (or desktop PC) with a USB port (see Figure 11.19).

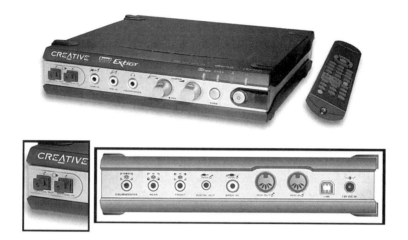

Figure 11.19 Front (top) and rear (bottom right) views of the Creative Sound Blaster Extigy. The inset at lower left shows the optical S/PDIF ports on the front of the unit. (Photos courtesy Creative.)

Tip

Extigy works best when it is plugged into a nonshared USB 1.1 root hub (there are two USB ports per root hub) because of the bandwidth it requires. A USB 2.0 (Hi-Speed USB) port is also a good choice if you have a mixture of USB 1.1 and Hi-Speed USB ports on your laptop.

Speaker and System Configuration

To ensure you get the sound you expect from four or more speakers, check the following:

- **Use the properties page for your audio processor to properly describe your speaker setup—** This includes selecting the number of speakers you are using, setting options for 3D environmental audio and positional sound such as reverb, and setting up your subwoofer if present.

- **Make sure you use the correct cabling between your speakers and laptop or external audio device**—If you are planning to use an AC3/Dolby speaker setup, such as 4.1 or 5.1, be sure you use the correct S/PDIF connection and configuration. This varies from system to system; check the vendor's website for details.

- **Make sure you have placed your speakers correctly**—In some cases you can adjust the audio adapter's properties to improve sound quality, but sometimes you might need to move the speakers themselves.

- **Make sure you have connected your speakers to the proper jacks**—Mixing up left and right or front and rear causes poor sound quality.

Typical Speaker Setups

The simplest audio configuration available today is stereo, which uses two speakers placed to overlap sound. In a two-channel setup, the two speakers are referred to as *left* and *right* (*L* and *R* in Figure 11.20).

Some laptops now support at least four speakers, but depending on the laptop's audio processor, settings, and sound output options in the program, the rear speakers might simply mirror the front speakers' output, or you might have four distinct sound streams. In a four-point setup, the two front speakers become front left and front right (FL and FR), whereas the back speakers are rear left and rear right (RL and RR).

Four-point surround sound uses four speakers plus a subwoofer (*S*, in Figure 11.20) to surround you with music and gaming sound effects; the four speakers are placed around the listener, and the subwoofer is usually placed near a wall or in the corner to amplify its low-frequency sound. The subwoofer in such a setup is not on a separate circuit but is controlled by the same signals sent to the other speakers.

On the other hand, 5.1 surround sound, also referred to as *Dolby Digital* or *DTS surround sound* (when digital speakers are used), uses five speakers plus a subwoofer. The fifth speaker is placed between the front two speakers as the center channel (*C*, in Figure 11.20) to provide most of the vocal audio. The subwoofer is independently controlled. This is the preferred sound system for use with DVD movies. Figure 11.20 compares typical 2.1, 4.1, and 5.1 speaker setups.

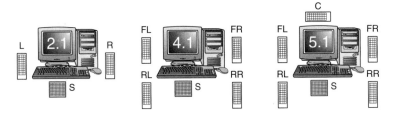

Figure 11.20 The 2.1 (left) and 4.1 (center) speaker setups compared to a 5.1 speaker setup (right). The subwoofer (S) is independently controlled only in the 5.1 configuration.

Generally, on any laptop with an audio processor, you should have a speaker icon in the Windows system tray. If the speaker icon (indicating the Volume Control) isn't visible, you can install it through the Control Panel's Add/Remove Programs icon. With Windows 9x/Me, select the Windows Setup tab and open the Multimedia section. Then check the box labeled Volume Control. With Windows XP, open the Sounds and Audio Devices icon in Control Panel, click the Volume tab, and click the Place Volume icon in the taskbar box. In some cases you might be asked to insert the Windows CD-ROM if additional drivers are required to complete the installation.

If you use digital sound sources or output such as Dolby 5.1, CD digital, or S/PDIF, open the properties page for your mixer device and enable display of these volume controls. Use the Volume Control to ensure your speakers are receiving a sound signal. The mixer sometimes defaults to Mute. You can usually adjust volume separately for wave (WAV) files, MIDI, microphone, and other components.

Microphones

If you don't want to use the microphone built in to the laptop for speech recognition, for computer telephony, or to record your voice to a WAV file, you'll need to add a microphone. Finding a compatible microphone is quite simple. You need one that has an 1/8" minijack to plug into your laptop's microphone, or audio-in, jack. Handheld microphones have an on/off switch, but microphones built in to headsets or boom microphones usually don't.

Like speakers, microphones are measured by their frequency ranges. This is not an important buying factor, however, because the human voice has a limited range. If you are recording only voices, consider an inexpensive microphone that covers a limited range of frequencies. An expensive microphone's recording capabilities extend to frequencies outside the voice's range. Why pay for something you won't need?

If you are recording music, invest in an expensive microphone, but be sure your audio processor can do justice to the signal produced by the microphone. Your biggest decision is to select a microphone that suits your recording style. If you work in a noisy office, you might want a unidirectional microphone that will prevent extraneous noises from being recorded. An omnidirectional microphone is best for recording a group conversation.

This type of microphone can be a small lapel microphone, a handheld microphone, or one with a desktop stand. If you want to keep your hands free, you might want to shun the traditional handheld microphone for a lapel or desktop model. If your audio adapter does not come with a microphone, see your local stereo or electronics parts store. Be sure that any microphone you purchase has the correct impedance to match the audio adapter's input.

If you're using voice-recognition software such as Dragon Naturally Speaking, IBM ViaVoice, or Philips FreeSpeech, use the microphone supplied with the software or choose from alternative models the software vendor recommends. Run the microphone setup program again if your software has trouble recognizing your voice. Some newer models feature a battery pack to boost sound quality. Be sure to check the batteries and replace them to keep recognition quality high.

If you're talking but your voice-recognition or recording software isn't responding, check the following:

- **Incorrect jack**—It's easy to plug the microphone into the wrong jack. Try using a magic marker to color-code the microphone wire and jack to make matching up easier.

- **The recording volume in the mixer control**—This usually defaults to Mute to avoid spurious noise.

- **Make sure the microphone is turned on in the voice-recognition or recording software**— You must click the Record button in recording software, and many voice-recognition programs let you "pick up" the microphone for use or "put it down" when you need to answer the phone. Look for an onscreen microphone icon in the Windows system tray for fast toggling between modes.

Troubleshooting Laptop Audio Problems

To operate, an audio processor needs hardware resources, such as IRQ numbers, a base I/O address, and DMA channels that don't conflict with other devices. Fortunately, the combination of laptop hardware that is preconfigured to work together and the use of Plug and Play hardware for the audio processor and the PC Card/CardBus slots have made resource conflicts practically unheard of in recent laptops.

However, it's still possible to have problems with laptop audio. These problems are usually due to other factors. Use the following subsections to help your laptop to produce the best audio recording and playback results.

No Sound from Internal Speakers

If you don't hear anything from your laptop's speakers, consider these solutions:

- Make sure the audio processor is working correctly and does not have any driver or other problems. Use the Windows Device Manager to check for problems and solutions.

- Are the mixer settings correct? Many audio adapters include a sound mixer application. The mixer controls the volume settings for various sound devices, such as the microphone or the CD player. There might be separate controls for both recording and playback. Increase the master volume or speaker volume when you are in the play mode.

- Is the Mute option selected? If the Mute option is selected in your sound mixer software, you won't hear anything.

- Are the speakers turned down with external controls? Some older laptops use a thumbwheel to adjust volume, whereas newer models sometimes use pushbuttons near the keyboard.

- If your computer game lacks sound, check that it is designed to work with your audio adapter. For example, some legacy and early Windows games might require the exact settings of IRQ 7 (or IRQ 5), DMA 1, and I/O address 220 to be Sound Blaster compatible.

Sound Problems with External Speakers

If you don't hear anything from external speakers, consider these solutions:

- What type of speakers are you using? Depending on the speaker type and sound source type, you might need to switch from analog to digital sound for some types of sound output. Make sure that the correct digital audio volume controls are enabled in your audio device's mixer control.

- Are the speakers connected? Check that the speakers are plugged into the sound card's stereo line-out or speaker jack (not the line-in or microphone jack).

- Are the speakers receiving power? Check that the power "brick" or power cord is plugged in securely.

- Are the speakers stereo? Check that the plug inserted into the jack is a stereo plug, not mono.

If you hear sound coming from only one speaker, check out these possible causes:

- Are you using a mono plug in the stereo jack? A common mistake is to use a mono plug in the laptop's audio speaker or stereo-out jacks. Seen from the side, a stereo connector has two darker stripes. A mono connector has only one stripe.

- If you're using amplified speakers, are they powered on? Check the strength of the batteries or the AC adapter's connection to the electrical outlet. If each speaker is powered separately, be sure that both have working batteries.

- Are the speakers wired correctly? When possible, use keyed and color-coded connectors to avoid mistakes.

- Are both speakers set to the same volume? Some speakers use separate volume controls on each speaker. Balance them for best results. Separate speaker volume controls can be an advantage if one speaker must be farther away from the user than the other.

- Is the speaker jack loose? If you find that plugging your speaker into the jack properly doesn't produce sound but pulling the plug half-way out or "jimmying" it around in its hole can temporarily correct the problem, you're on the road to a speaker jack failure. To avoid damage to the speaker jack, be sure you insert the plug straight in, not at an angle.

If you can barely hear audio, try these solutions:

- Are the speakers plugged into the proper jack? Speakers require a higher level of drive signal than headphones. Again, adjust the volume level in your mixer application.

- Are the mixer settings too low? Again, adjust the volume level in your mixer application. If your mixer lets you choose between speakers and headphones, be sure to select the correct speaker configuration.

- Are the speakers too weak? Some speakers might need more power than your audio adapter can produce. Try other speakers or put a stereo amplifier between your sound card and speakers.

Scratchy Sound

Scratchy or static-filled sound can be caused by several problems. Improving the sound can be as simple as rearranging your hardware components. The following list suggests possible solutions to the problem of scratchy sound:

- Are your speakers too close to an external CRT monitor? The speakers can pick up electrical noise from your monitor. Move them farther away. Subwoofers should *never* be placed near a CRT monitor because their powerful magnets can interfere with the picture. They should be on the floor to maximize low-frequency transmission.

- Are you experiencing compatibility problems between particular games and your sound card? If you notice sound problems such as stuttering voices and static on some games but not others, check with the game vendor for a software patch or with the sound card vendor for updated drivers. If the game uses DirectX, run the DXDIAG diagnostics program (select Start, Run; type **DXDIAG**; and click OK) and click the Sound tab. Adjust the slider for Hardware Sound Acceleration Level down one notch from Full (the default) to Standard, click Save All Information, and exit. Retry the game. If the problem persists, adjust the Hardware Sound Acceleration Level setting to Basic. If other games have performance problems after you adjust the Hardware Sound Acceleration Level, be sure to reset it to Full before playing those games.

Advanced Features

If you are having problems playing DVD audio, playing MP3 files, or using S/PDIF connections, make sure of the following:

- You are using the correct playback program.

- Your mixer has the correct volume control setting for the device.

- Your cabling is correct for the device.

Other Problems

Sometimes sound problems can be difficult to solve. A good way to solve problems of all types with Plug and Play devices such as onboard audio, a PnP BIOS, and a PnP operating system (Windows 9x/Me/2000/XP) is to use the Device Manager to remove the audio processor, restart the system, and allow the card's components to be redetected. This solution installs a "fresh" copy of the software and reinserts Registry entries.

If you are using a laptop with a VIA chipset, be sure to download and install the latest versions of VIA drivers.

CHAPTER 12

Communications

Laptop computers have a rich array of communications options open to them. In addition to the high-speed broadband connections and traditional dial-up modems available to desktops, laptop computers can also be equipped with various wireless communications options. They include not only wireless modems but also wireless network adapters.

Modems

One of the primary uses for laptop computers is to keep in touch with the home office. The traditional method for remote access is to use a modem, but nowadays an increasing amount of remote communication is done with a broadband connection, such as DSL or a cable modem, attached to a network interface in the laptop or through wireless networking. It is not uncommon to find hotels, coffee shops, and airports that offer high-speed connections. In addition, there's an ever increasing number of wireless networks set up throughout the country, offering wide-area high-speed wireless connections.

Although we all may have used a modem, some of us may not know exactly how it works. Traditionally, a modem works by modulating a stream of digital pulses into an audio signal. The process is similar to the way a radio transmitter modulates relatively low-frequency speech and music into a high-frequency carrier wave. On the other end of the connection, the modem then demodulates the audio signal to obtain the original stream of digital pulses. The name *modem* in fact derives from its function: *mo*dulate, *dem*odulate.

The maximum speed that can be obtained using a modulation/demodulation technique is 33.6Kbps, the speed provided by the V.34 modems that became available in the mid-1990s. In 1998, the V.90 modem standard attempted to bypass this speed restriction by avoiding the modulation step for one half of the communication path. Because typical web usage requires much more data being sent downstream from the website to the web viewer, this mode was speeded up to 56Kbps by using pulse-code modulation—a method similar to that used to encode data on a CD-ROM disc. The upstream path, which usually handles less data, continued to be limited to 33.6Kbps.

Unfortunately, even a simple modem connection cannot be taken for granted. Most hotel rooms in the United States provide an easily accessible phone-line connector for use with a laptop modem. But a few do not. In fact, in many places, finding a phone line to plug in to can be a real challenge. Products now on the market, however, can help you overcome these problems, even if you are traveling overseas.

V.92 Modems

Ever since the dawn of personal computers in the 1970s, we have seen continual and dramatic advances in modem speeds. Now, however, with the popularity of broadband DSL connections, modem advancements seem to have stalled. The latest modem standard, called V.92, was introduced by the International Telecommunications Union (ITU) in July of 2000 and represented only a minor advancement over the previous V.90 standard.

The older V.90 standard for modems provided data rates up to 56Kbps over Plain Old Telephone Service (POTS) lines. The V.92 added the following enhancements:

- An increase of more than 40% in the maximum data rate in the upstream direction (toward the network) to a new maximum of 48Kbps on the best connections
- Significantly quicker startup times on recognized connections
- The ability to put the modem "on hold" when the network indicates that an incoming call is waiting

To increase effective modem speeds further, the ITU recommended a new data-compression standard called V.44, based on the LZJH compression algorithm developed by Hughes Network Systems. This technique gives an improvement in compression of more than 25% beyond the existing ITU recommendation V.42bis. The ITU expects a data-compression ratio in the region of 6:1 for a typical web-browsing connection. The net result should be an effective data throughput rate in excess of 300Kbps, compared with typical values of 150–200Kbps today, thus significantly reducing download times and speeding up web browsing.

As most modem users will agree, the actual data rates seen over typical phone lines are below these estimates and indeed well below those available from DSL technologies. The V.92 standard has the advantage, however, of not requiring any special installation on the part of the network provider, leaving upgrades solely up to the direct control of ISPs and users.

Although broadband connections are the preferred communication type for most users, the fact is that in most of the world, modems will be the state of the art for some time to come.

Because of the popularity of modems and their low cost, almost all of today's notebooks are equipped with them as standard. They are sometimes installed as Mini PCI cards. In the recent past, manufacturers would install a combination Mini PCI card that included both a modem and a network interface card (NIC). As the development of new modem standards has slowed and the probability of new standards in the near future has decreased, we now have seen V.92 modem circuitry integrated directly onto the motherboard of the laptops.

A number of older laptops, however, are not equipped with modems. These systems can be equipped with external modems connected by a serial cord, but a much more portable approach is to insert a PC Card modem into one of the laptop's PCMCIA slots.

PC Card Modems

Most current laptops have internal modems installed in them. In previous days, however, the only way to equip a notebook computer with a modem was to use a modem in the form of a PCMCIA or PC Card.

Of course, a Type II PC Card is only 5.5mm (0.19 inches) thick, which does not leave enough room for a standard RJ-11 phone line connector. To provide this connection, manufacturers came up with three different solutions:

- **The dongle or pigtail**—This is a relatively short piece of cable with different connectors at each end. One of these connectors is flat enough to attach to the PC Card modem. The other is an RJ-11 phone connector. Early dongles were only a few inches long and had an appearance that gave rise to the nickname *pigtail*. These cables had a female phone connector and were designed to be used with a standard phone cable. More recent dongles have a much longer cable and terminate in a male connector that can be plugged directly into a phone jack without the need for an additional cable (see Figure 12.1). Dongles were very popular with modem manufacturers, especially because users would continually lose them and pay sometimes as much as $99 to replace them. Nowadays, dongles can be purchased for as little as $19 from companies such as Computer Heaven.

- **The XJACK connector**—This is an ingenious connector that looks like a cross-section of a typical RJ-11 phone jack. It is so thin that it can slide in and out of a PC Card modem. The phone line attaches in a vertical direction. When the phone line is not connected, the jack can be pushed back into the PC card, thereby protecting it. The only problem with the XJACK connector is that it can be damaged by excessive tension on the phone line, such as when someone trips over it. But it is easier to replace a broken modem card than to replace a notebook that has gone crashing to the floor.

■ **The Type III card**—Perhaps the simplest way to connect a phone line to a thin Type II PC Card is to use a thick Type III card instead. It turns out that a Type III card, which is so thick it takes up two Type II card slots, can accommodate both a standard RJ-11 phone jack and an RJ-45 LAN connector.

Figure 12.1   An example of a dongle used to connect a PC Card modem to a phone jack. (Photo from Computer Heaven, Inc., `www.computerheaven.com`.)

Even though most of today's notebooks already have a modem installed internally, some people would benefit from carrying around a spare PC Card modem as well, especially if the modem has special features, such as the ability to handle international phone systems or voice calls. A PC Card modem is extremely light and often comes in handy if the laptop's internal modem ever stops working.

Winmodems

Many modems are not really modems at all but simply enhanced connectors. These so-called "Winmodems" depend on Windows programs that instruct the laptop's CPU to do all the processing that the modem normally does. These modems have gotten better, partly because today's Pentium processors are so powerful that they can easily accommodate the relatively slight amount of work required by a 56Kbps modem. Winmodems are inexpensive, often less than half the cost of a real modem, but they are dependent on Windows. In general, a real modem still outperforms a Winmodem and also has the benefit of working under DOS, Linux, or any other non-Windows environment.

Caution

Some phone lines can be hazardous to the health of your modem. Many hotels and offices use digital PBXs for their telephone systems. These systems typically carry more current than standard analog phone lines. This power is needed to operate additional features on the telephone, such as message lights and LCD displays. Unfortunately, this additional current can permanently damage the tiny modems found in PC Cards or integrated onto the motherboard of your laptop. Visually, there is no way to tell whether a phone system is digital or analog, because they both use the same standard RJ-11 connectors.

To avoid frying your laptop's internal modem, you can purchase a line-testing device—usually called a Modem-Saver—for about $30 that plugs in to a wall jack and measures the amount of current on the circuit. It then informs you whether it is safe to plug in your modem.

If the line is not safe, you may still use it with your laptop's modem, but only with certain protection. A company called Konexx (www.konexx.com) sells a device for about $130 that plugs in to the handset jack on a standard phone and protects your modem from any dangerous currents on a digital PBX system.

Wireless Modems

The traditional modem is indeed a handy tool, but its usefulness disappears as soon as you move more than about 10 feet away from a phone jack. A wireless networking adapter lengthens your communications leash to about 200 feet, but the number of wireless networks is still relatively small. All this effectively means that for most of the world's surface area, your laptop is incommunicado—unless, of course, you have a wireless modem.

There are basically three ways to connect a wireless modem to your laptop. The first is to use a cellular modem, usually in a PC Card format. As the name implies, these devices rely on the increasingly omnipresent cellular phone networks and can be used anywhere you can get cellular phone coverage. The second approach is to use your cell phone itself as a cellular modem. The third option is only for those who frequently travel outside the cellular phone coverage: using a satellite phone as a modem.

Note that all wireless modems have traditionally suffered from a speed penalty. Until fairly recently, wireless modems typically operated at a speed of only about 14.4Kbps or less.

In recent years the press began promoting so-called *third-generation* or *3G* cellular technology. (The first cellular generation was analog and is usually referred to as *AMPS*, or *Advanced Mobile Phone System*. The second generation was digital and is based on one of several technologies, such as TDMA, CDMA, and GSM.) The new 3G technology promised high-speed data communications; in some cases the claims were as high as 2Mbps. More reasonable claims touted 384Kbps. In actual fact, the "3G" systems that have appeared to date are capable of a maximum data rate of only about 128Kbps or even just 56Kbps. Because of this, they are sometimes referred to as *2.5G systems*. Although still slow by wired networking standards, 3G systems are still an order of magnitude better than previous wireless and WAN standards.

Circuit-Switched Versus Packet-Switched Connections

Most wireless modems make connections in two ways. The first is *circuit-switched mode*, which is identical to the traditional dial-up connection on a wired modem. Here, the user dials a connection to a host system, communicates for a given amount of time, and then disconnects the call.

The second is *packet-switched mode*. With this type of connection, the wireless modem is in effect always connected to the host system, in much the same way a home computer is always connected to the Internet via DSL or a cable modem. Data is sent back and forth in packets.

Choosing which mode to use depends on what type of data will be transmitted and how the cellular phone company is charging for the service. Circuit-switched connections are usually charged on a per-minute rate. Packet-switched connections are usually charged by the megabyte of data transferred. If the cellular company charges a low fee for each voice call or if you tend to surf the Internet only for short, intensive batches, a circuit-switched connection is best. If, however, your cellular company charges you a low per-megabyte rate or if you tend to connect intermittently several times through-out the day, you should opt for a packet-switched connection.

PC Card Wireless Modems

As for most other laptop peripherals, the best form factor for wireless modems is the PCMCIA or PC Card. The advantage of a PC Card cellular modem is that it's a relatively simple system. There are no wires, external components, or dongles hanging off the laptop. The only visible sign of the modem is the PC Card's flexible antenna that sticks out the side of the laptop.

Some PC Card cellular modems have an added advantage of being able to carry voice communica-tions as well. With these modems, you could use the internal microphone and speaker of your laptop and have, in effect, a mobile speakerphone. For more private conversations, you could plug in a small headset that combines headphones and a microphone.

Connecting a Modem to a Cell Phone

Some laptop modems can connect to a cell phone as well as to a standard phone line. This group includes both built-in modems as well as PC Card modems. Unfortunately, however, most modems are not cellular capable, in which case you must purchase a PC Card cellular-capable modem to use. 3Com and others make modems that work with most of the popular cell phones on the market using the traditional AMPS or GSM service. Most of these modems use the Microcom MNP10EC protocol, which is designed to handle the signal changes and handoffs common in cellular operation. Even with the cost of the cellular-capable modem and the cable between the modem and the cell phone, this is a very cost-effective approach because it involves only a single cell phone bill each month.

Using a Cell Phone as a Wireless Modem

Most modern cell phones have a built-in cellular modem. In many cases this built-in modem is used to enable the phone to access specially designed websites. As is the case with the previous approach, this is a cost-effective technique, enlisting your existing cell phone for double duty as both a phone and a modem. The only extra cost is a cable that connects your cell phone to your laptop's USB or serial connector. Originally, these cables were expensive, especially when supplied as an accessory from the manufacturer. However, third-party manufacturers have been offering low-cost cables as an alternative. These cables, by the way, can also be used for transferring phonebook and calendar infor-mation back and forth from your cell phone to your laptop.

The great advantage of using a cell phone as your wireless modem is that you will be charged for only one monthly cellular bill. If you use a PC Card cellular modem along with a cell phone, you are charged a monthly bill for each.

Note

Note that not all cell phones can function as cellular modems. Before you buy your next phone, check whether this feature is supported.

The disadvantage of using a cell phone as a modem is the awkward cable clutter involved with this approach. Your laptop will now have a cell phone attached to it, dangling at the end of a fragile and expensive cable like a miniature ball and chain. However, if your phone and notebook both feature support for the Bluetooth wireless standard discussed later in this chapter, this cable can be elimi-nated. Instead, your cell phone and laptop will communicate with each other via a wireless radio-fre-quency connection.

Using a Satellite Phone as a Wireless Modem

Laptop users who will be traveling outside cellular coverage can still keep in touch by using a satellite phone, such as those sold by GlobalStar. As is the case with cellular phones, some satellite phones can be connected to a laptop and then function as a satellite modem. All you need is the particular accessory cable for that phone to enable it to connect to a laptop's serial port. Note, however, that there's a price for this freedom. The maximum data rate for this type of connection is only 9.6Kbps.

Types of Cellular Systems

Unlike in most other countries, the United States has several different and incompatible types of digital cellular phone systems in operation. Each offers different advantages and disadvantages for both voice and data connections. Table 12.1 shows how, as time progresses, the maximum data capabilities will grow increasingly fast, from 14.4Kbps to 384Kbps.

Table 12.1   The Evolution of U.S. Cellular Phone Data Capabilities

Second-Generation (2G) Cellular Technology	"2.5G" Cellular Technology	Third-Generation (3G) Cellular Technology
CDMA	1XRTT	3XRTT (CDMA2000)
GSM	GPRS, EDGE	WCDMA
TDMA	EDGE	WCDMA

The various digital cellular systems you might encounter include the following:

- **CDPD**—Cellular Digital Packet Data was one of the first techniques used to carry digital information over cellular voice networks. This system worked by implanting small packets of digital data into the unused intervals of traditional analog cellular voice channels. This technology is employed mainly by corporations and public service organizations to send small amounts of textual information. Note that its maximum data-transfer rate is only 19.2Kbps. Both AT&T Wireless and Verizon Wireless offer this service in the United States.

- **CDMA**—Code Division Multiple Access is currently the most popular digital cellular technology in the U.S. It is used in both the traditional cellular frequency band of 800MHz and the PCS band of 1900MHz. With the exception of Europe, CDMA is also the digital network technology of choice outside the U.S. For data transfers, CDMA technology has been limited to a maximum speed of only 14.4Kbps. Gradually, CDMA networks are being upgraded to offer packet-switched speeds of 64–384Kbps. The major cell phone companies that use CDMA wireless networks include Verizon Wireless and Sprint PCS.

- **CDMA2000**—A trade name for 3xRTT cellular networks.

- **1XRTT**—An intermediate evolutionary step for CDMA cellular networks. The 1XRTT networks support data-transfer rates of 153Kbps. Eventually, 1XRTT systems will evolve into 3XRTT systems (also called CDMA2000).

- **3XRTT**—A third-generation cellular system designed as an evolutionary step for CDMA cellular systems. The 3xRTT systems can transport data at a rate of 307Kbps. This technology is also known by the trade name CDMA2000.

- **TDMA**—Time Division Multiple Access is perhaps the oldest digital cellular technology in the U.S. The data-transfer rate for traditional TDMA systems is a mere 9.6Kbps. Future TDMA networks will offer faster packet data communications, up to 384Kbps. AT&T has been a prime backer of TDMA technologies.

- **GSM**—The Global System for Mobile Communications is the cellular phone standard in Europe and several other parts of the world. In the U.S., its market share is growing. The original data throughput was a measly 9.6Kbps. New 3G systems based on EDGE or GPRS will eventually bump the speed up to 384Kbps. T-Mobile is the primary user of GSM technology in the United States.

- **GPRS**—The General Packet Radio System is an intermediate upgrade from GSM cellular technology. A typical GPRS device, such as the Sierra Wireless AirCard 750, is claimed to have a theoretical maximum data rate of 83Kbps, but actual user throughput will likely be 30–56Kbps. The next step for these cellular systems is EDGE.

- **EDGE**—Enhanced Data for GSM Efficiency (or Enhanced Data-rates for Global Evolution) is an upgrade for GPRS and TDMA cellular systems. It provides a *peak* data-transfer rate of 384Kbps. The next step for these cellular systems is WCDMA.

- **WCDMA**—Wideband CDMA is the latest and fastest level of evolution for today's GSM and TDMA cellular networks. It is said to have a sustained data rate of 384Kbps.

Network Connections

With the proliferation of local area networks in offices and homes, along with the ever-increasing popularity of broadband web access and wireless "hotspots," most laptop users are now addicted to having a fast network connection for much if not all their online work. For laptops, there are basically two ways to make this connection: with a wire and without.

Wired LANs

Network access has become such a standard feature of today's computers that most new systems—including laptops—are now shipped with a network interface card of some type. Whether you connect with an office LAN or a home broadband modem (either DSL or cable), a network adapter is required. The only question is which one?

Early laptops did not have an easy time with network access. Users had to carry around small external boxes that connected to the laptop's parallel printer port. Later, when PCMCIA cards became available, network cards made up a large percentage of these cards sold. With the appearance of the Mini PCI bus (a smaller, laptop-oriented version of the PCI expansion bus in desktops), network interfaces began to appear in this format. For several years it was common to have notebooks equipped with a Mini PCI that included both a modem and a network interface. Because network interfaces have dropped in size and cost and have become vital features of a notebook, manufacturers now routinely install network interface circuitry on the laptop's motherboard.

10BASE-T

Not long ago, the most common type of network interface card was the 10BASE-T Ethernet card. The card got its name from the fact that it had a theoretical maximum throughput of 10Mbps, used baseband technology, and was strung together with twisted-pair cable, indicated by the *T*. The 10BASE-T cards were very popular because of their use of this type of cabling. Compared to coaxial and fiber-optic cables, the twisted-pair cables were very easy to work with and could be connected to interface cards and routers using simple RJ-45 connectors, which were merely larger cousins of the familiar modular phone connectors. As faster 10/100BASE-T interfaces began to get more and more inexpensive, manufacturers discontinued making 10BASE-T cards. However, many of these cards are still in use. Note that the actual throughput of these 10Mbps networks was far lower than the theoretical maximum. Actual speeds depended on the quality of the network cabling and cards. A measured speed of 6Mbps was considered good.

10/100BASE-T

The most common network interface sold today is the 10/100BASE-T card. This card can work with both 10Mbps and 100Mbps networks. In fact, both networks generally use the same cabling and connectors. As with 10BASE-T networks, 100BASE-T networks carry data at rates significantly less than their theoretical maximum.

10/100/1000BASE-T

As might be expected from its name, a 10/100/1000BASE-T network interface will work with Gigabit Ethernet (1000Mbps networks) as well as the older 10Mbps and 100Mbps varieties. As with the other types of network cards, it does suggest the actual operating speed. Currently in the desktop world, 10/100/1000BASE-T cards cost only about $30 more than the older 10/100BASE-T cards. PC Card versions of these cards will soon appear. Already many notebook manufacturers, such as Dell, are shipping notebooks with 10/100/1000BASE-T interfaces integrated onto the motherboards. As prices of these interfaces continue to decline, they will gradually supplant the 10/100BASE-T interfaces on laptops as well as on desktops.

Wireless LANs

Just as they are for desktops, wired LAN connections are enormously useful for laptops. Their only problem is that they eliminate the prime advantage of laptops: their portability. Fortunately, wireless LANs enable us to enjoy the benefits of high-speed network access without hobbling our mobility.

802.11 Standards

A number of wireless LAN standards have been developed by various subcommittees of the 802.11 standard group of the Institute of Electrical and Electronics Engineers (IEEE).

802.11b

By far the most popular wireless standard is known by the unwieldy name *802.11b*. A consortium of manufacturers called the Wi-Fi Alliance has come up with a program to ensure compliance with the 802.11b standard. Many but not all 802.11b products are Wi-Fi certified. Because *Wi-Fi* is so much easier to pronounce, many people use this term to refer to 802.11b in general. Technically speaking, however, the name Wi-Fi, which derives from *wi*reless *fi*delity, should refer only to products that are certified as such.

The 802.11b standard specifies a maximum theoretical throughput rate of 11Mbps (or 1.375 megabytes per second). The actual speed depends on the environment. Some researchers have reported maximum speeds in ideal conditions at about 6Mbps. The radio frequency used is in the 2.4GHz band, which is unlicensed by the U.S. government. Some manufacturers report ranges of 300 feet for 802.11b equipment. Note, however, that as range increases, effective throughput rates drop. In a typical office environment, an effective range of about 75 feet can usually be expected, but this range can drop depending on the types of materials used in the construction of the office. Thick cement walls reduce range considerably, whereas open space extends the range. It is not uncommon for laptops in window offices looking out onto narrow Manhattan streets to have better connections with the offices across the street than with their own office LANs.

Basically two types of equipment are used in wireless LANs: a client node, which is usually in the form of a PC Card, like the one shown in Figure 12.2, but is usually implemented as a Mini PCI card inside a notebook, and an access point, which bridges a wireless LAN to a traditional wired LAN. An 802.11b wireless LAN (WLAN) can be set up in two ways: either as a peer-to-peer network consisting only of client nodes, or as an "infrastructure" network consisting of both client nodes and access points (APs).

A large number of hotels, airport lounges, and coffee shops have set up small 802.11b wireless LANs as a convenience for their laptop-toting customers. These oases of high-speed wireless network access are usually called "hotspots."

Figure 12.2 The Netgear WPN311 Wireless PCI Card can communicate with all 802.11b and 802.11g wireless networks. (Photo from www.netgear.com.)

Client nodes use two types of antennas. PC Card adapters have a small nub containing an antenna that extends outside the laptop's PC Card slot. This nub works fairly well, but it can easily break off. Most new notebooks are, however, manufactured with an 802.11b antenna preinstalled around the laptop's display, which is a sturdier design and enables a much better signal reception.

802.11a

As its name suggests, work on the 802.11a wireless LAN standard was actually initiated before the popular 11b standard. But, because the 11b standard was a relatively minor variation of slower 2.4GHz wireless networking products that were already in existence, manufacturers were able to develop products fairly easily. By contrast, the 11a standard required new and more expensive designs to handle a higher frequency radio band that was hardly used. The 11b standard therefore had a head start and became extremely popular. The people working on the 802.11a standard seem to have put the extra time they had to good use, however. The 802.11a standard has a maximum theoretical throughput of 54Mbps, about five times that of 802.11b. Because the 802.11a standard specifies a higher frequency (5GHz), its signals are less capable of navigating around the walls of an office. Unfortunately, these two WLAN standards are not compatible.

Figure 12.3 shows a typical 802.11a CardBus adapter. In addition to its support of 54Mbps, the card also supports the 802.11b and 802.11g standard, making it exceptionally flexible.

Figure 12.3 The 3Com 3CRPAG175 802.11a/b/g wireless CardBus adapter offering support for all three commonly found wireless network standards. (Photo from www.3com.com.)

Many corporate IT staffs prefer the new 802.11a standard because of its higher speed and its ability to handle more users. The main reason for this is the number of channels available. On paper, the slower 802.11b standard offers 11 channels, but because of frequency overlap, there are in effect only 3 channels available for use (1, 6, and 11). By contrast, 802.11a has 8 channels available. Most home WLANs and hotspots, however, use the older 802.11b standard. To bridge both types of networks, PCMCIA CardBus cards have appeared that support both types of networks. Recently, some combination Mini PCI cards have become available and are being incorporated into notebooks. Note, however, that the two incompatible WLANs use two different types of antennas. To be ready for a combo 11a/11b Mini PCI card, the manufacturer must design in two separate antennas.

802.11g

In many ways, the 802.11g standard is a compromise between 11b and 11a. Its original specification provided twice as much speed as 11b but is still compatible with it. Although not quite as speedy as 11a, this standard has steered clear of its potential compatibility problems. The 802.11g standard uses the same 2.4GHz frequency as 11b and has about the same range.

In early 2003, the 802.11g standard was amended to incorporate a 54Mbps transmission speed. Today most notebooks are equipped with a 802.11g wireless connection, allowing them to connect to both 802.11b and 11g wireless networks. The majority of wireless networking equipment sold today supports the 11g standard with 802.11b equipment slowly being phased out.

Wi-Fi Alliance

As mentioned previously, certain manufacturers in the wireless LAN industry set up the Wi-Fi Alliance to certify compliance with the 802.11b standard. All Wi-Fi-certified products are compatible with 802.11b, but not all 802.11b products are Wi-Fi certified. Because *Wi-Fi* is so much easier to pronounce, it is often used in place of *802.11b*, without regard to the certification it was intended to denote.

Wi-Fi5 Alliance

Just as with the Wi-Fi Alliance and the 802.11b standard, a similar compliance certification effort has been set up for the 802.11a standard called Wi-Fi5, the 5 standing for the 5GHz radio frequency used by the 11a standard. Unlike Wi-Fi, however, the term *Wi-Fi5* has not caught on as a synonym for *802.11a*.

Bluetooth

The primary feature of mobile computers and phones is that they are untethered. They can perform without any cables—in theory. The fact is, however, that mobile equipment is often hobbled by smaller cables of its own. For example, you might have a cable connected between your cell phone and your laptop, or between your cell phone and a headset.

The Swedish electronics giant Ericsson has sought to get rid of these cables with a short-range or personal wireless networking standard called Bluetooth. The odd name comes from a Danish Viking king who lived 1,000 years ago and obviously had unusual dental characteristics.

Bluetooth has a relatively short range of about 10 feet and an effective data throughput of about 1Mbps. With these specs, of course, it will never compete with any of the 802.11x WLANs, but it is not meant to. Instead, it is designed as a simple, low-cost network for one's own personal devices.

Although the goals behind Bluetooth are admirable, the technology was off to a slow start due to many compatibility issues with the initial v.1.0 release of the specification, causing the industry to issue a v.1.1 version of the spec. Products that conformed to the new spec were indeed more compatible, but not with any of the v.1.0 products. Indeed, compatibility testing was hindered by the fact that there were so few Bluetooth products to test. Today most phones and laptop computers have been equipped with Bluetooth transceivers, and a significant number of Bluetooth peripherals are available.

Connecting on the Road

Once you have the necessary hardware and software, you will find that there are many different ways to connect to the Internet, or any other computing system for that matter. In this section we address the actual process of making those connections.

As mentioned before, there are two general ways to connect: wired and wireless. Wired connections are generally faster and more reliable—at least so far.

Hotel High-Speed Connections

The fastest wired connection you can make with your laptop is via its network interface to an accommodating LAN that has high-speed Internet access. These LANs can be found in branch offices of your company, in airline premium clubs, and in some forward-thinking coffee shops. The most likely place, however, for a business traveler to find high-speed wired access is in a hotel room. The website www.wiredhotels.com keeps a database of hotels with high-speed access, with a short description of the services available. Currently, this site has listings for over 3,000 hotels.

When reserving a room, be sure to check whether a room with fast Internet access is available. When you arrive in the room, check that the access works. If it is not there or does not work correctly, ask the front desk to switch you to another room that is better equipped.

DHCP—Any Address Will Do

Before you can become part of a hotel LAN or any other LAN that supports the popular TCP/IP protocol, you will need to be sure that the LAN adapter in your laptop is configured with the right address.

Specifically, this is called an *Internet Protocol (IP) address* and consists of four numbers, from 0 to 255, separated by periods. Web surfers are well acquainted with such addresses.

The requirement of having the right IP address provides a modest layer of security in corporate LANs, but it also proves to be a pain in the neck for corporate IT staffers and an unnecessary pain for low-security LANs such as those in hotels. To solve this problem, the Dynamic Host Configuration Protocol (DHCP) server was developed. This program automatically doles out correct IP addresses to any new computers that happen to show up on a LAN.

How to Accept an IP Address Automatically

Most notebook computers are, by default, set up as DHCP clients—that is, as network members that automatically accept whatever IP address the DHCP server doles out to them. If, however, your notebook has been set up with a specific IP address for use with a corporate LAN, you will need to temporarily reconfigure it. Here's how:

1. Access the Control Panel in Windows. (In Windows XP, click Start, Control Panel. In other Windows versions, click Start, Settings, Control Panel.)

2. Double-click the Network or Network Connections icon. (In Windows XP, be sure to select Classic View from the list on the left side of the screen.)

3. Right-click the icon referring to the network adapter in your laptop, usually identified as "Local Area Connection," and select Properties from the list that appears.

4. Select Internet Protocol (TCP/IP) from the list of items and click the Properties button.

5. If a specific IP address and subnet mask are listed (see Figure 12.4), write these down and store them in a safe place. You will need them to restore the configuration later.

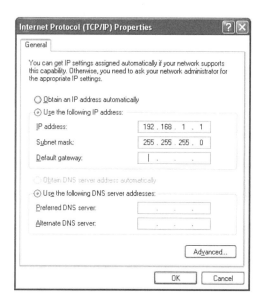

Figure 12.4   The Internet Protocol (TCP/IP) properties for a LAN connection under Windows XP.

6. Check the box labeled Obtain an IP Address Automatically if it is not already checked.

7. Click OK.

Note that when you return to the office, you will have to revert to the original configuration. In this case, you will have to choose Use This IP Address instead of Obtain an IP Address Automatically and then enter the IP address and subnet you recorded earlier.

STSN

A company called STSN (www.stsn.com) specializes in providing high-speed access to hotels. Hotels affiliated with STSN have what STSN calls a "smart box" in every guestroom (see Figure 12.5). Users simply plug in with either an Ethernet or USB cable and power up their laptops. Then all they should need to do is launch their Internet browser. Once connected, users can take advantage of the hotel's T1 or DSL high-speed Internet connection. (If their laptop does not have a LAN adapter, users can connect the laptop's modem to a phone jack on the smart box.) STSN reports that it provides firewalls for each room and that users can print documents that can later be retrieved at the hotel's front desk.

In return for high-speed access, these hotels usually charge a flat fee for access during each 24-hour period (noon to noon). The charge is typically $9.95. Weekly rates are also available.

Figure 12.5   The connection module used by STSN to provide high-speed access in hotels.

Using Wireless Hotspots

Most wireless communication by laptops occurs via wireless LANs. These WLANs now offer much of the same speed as wired LANs while bestowing laptops with a modest degree of mobility. The best thing about WLANs is that they continually get better. More and more WLANs are being installed, for less and less money, while speeds continue to increase.

Usually, these WLANs are private, meant only for the staff of a particular office or the residents of a certain house. A number of establishments, however, have begun to offer public WLANs, which are called *hotspots*. A laptop user can stay in good contact with the Internet by traveling from one hotspot to another, much as a frog jumps from one lily pad to another.

Finding Hotspots

Although the number of hotspots is growing, finding one can sometimes be a hit-and-miss proposition. A few websites have stepped in to provide directories of hotspots. Here is a brief sampling of the more popular sites:

- www.80211hotspots.com

- www.hotspot-locations.com

- www.intel.com/support/notebook/hotspots/provider.htm

- www.wifinder.com

New hotspots are appearing on an almost daily basis. Because of this, it is difficult for any web directory to keep up with the many changes. Most hotspots are commercial businesses that charge either by the hour, day, or month. Some commercial hotspots are offered as a free service in exchange for other patronage. A number of companies have set up networks of hotspots throughout the country. Signing up with one of these companies enables you to access any of its hotspots throughout the country. So far, however, none of these wireless Internet service providers (or WISPs) have achieved a dominant position, which means that travelers may have to establish accounts at more than one WISP. Here is a short list of the larger WISPs:

- www.boingo.com

- www.cafe.com

- www.hotspotzz.com

- www.stayonline.net

- www.surfandsip.com

- www.tmobile.com

- www.wayport.com

The Boingo site also includes some information about free hotspots. T-Mobile provides the wireless LAN access at most Starbucks coffee shops. The T-Mobile site provides information on the location of those coffee shops.

Finding Free Hotspots

One of the nicest things about wireless LANs is that some of them are free. A few of these sites offer this service in the hope that users will reimburse the provider in other ways (for example, by buying more coffee). But often the service is provided completely altruistically without any ulterior motives. The trick is to find these sites.

A few sites offer directories of free sites. On its site, Boingo lists its own commercial sites along with some free sites. Some sites, such as the following, specialize in providing information on free sites:

- www.wififreespot.com

- www.nycwireless.net

Free sites come and go much faster than any directory can keep up. For that reason, some users try to find their own free sites. Using sniffer software, a laptop will spot and identify any wireless LAN with range. As I write this, a version of sniffer software is available on Boingo's website. This software identifies any WLAN within range, noting its service set identification (SSID) code, the type of access point used, and, if not protected, the identification number or MAC of the access point. The software also indicates whether the WLAN is encryption protected. If the site is not protected by encryption and has a generic or welcoming SSID (such as "FREEACCESS"), some users consider it a free site and take advantage of the high-speed access that is seemingly offered.

The process of driving around a neighborhood searching for available WLANs is called *war driving*. Although technically feasible and in many cases quite easy, the act of connecting to someone's WLAN without permission is discourteous and could be illegal. When you set up your own WLAN, be aware of how easily accessible it can be and be sure to institute proper security measures. A website called www.wifimaps.com publishes maps of wireless LANs, many of which appear to have been identified by war driving (see Figure 12.6). The small triangles indicate the presence of a WLAN. In many cases, the SSID of the WLAN is listed.

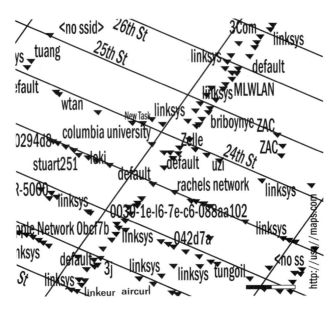

Figure 12.6   A sample map of wireless LANs taken from the website *www.wifimaps.com*. (Figure from *www.wifimaps.com*.)

How to Connect to a Hotspot

To connect to a hotspot, the first thing to do is to determine if you are within range of a hotspot access point. Most WLAN PC Cards are bundled with a utility program that indicates how strong the wireless LAN signal is. Usually, this is indicated by a green icon of some type.

Once you know you are in range of an access point, you need to be sure your laptop is set to the right IP address. Unless you know otherwise, most WLANs require your laptop to accept an IP address automatically. To set your laptop in this configuration, see the section earlier in this chapter titled "How to Accept an IP Address Automatically."

Finally, you will need to set the correct service set identification (SSID) code on your laptop's WLAN PC Card adapter. The exact instructions for this may vary from one adapter to another. Follow the manufacturer's directions for accessing the "Configuration" or "Properties" dialog box for your WLAN adapter. Note that some manufacturers refer to the SSID as the ESSID.

Cellular Modems

If you are beyond the range of a wireless LAN and yet still want to establish a wireless connection, one of the easiest and least expensive ways is via a cellular connection. Most businesspeople today carry a portable cell phone, and most new cell phones are capable of functioning as a cellular modem with the addition of a relatively inexpensive adapter cable. Note that, as mentioned previously in this chapter, cellular data connections can be irritatingly slow.

To make a cellular data connection, you must be sure that you are getting a good cellular signal. The best and easiest way to determine this is to look at the signal strength indicator on your cell phone.

Once you are sure of a good cellular signal, the next step is to connect the phone to the laptop. Most older cables connect to the serial port, which is disappearing from some of the latest notebook computers. The newer cables attach to USB connectors, which are faster and easier to use.

The next step depends on the particular cell phone you are using. In some cases, the cell phone appears to the laptop's Windows operating system as an ordinary wired modem. In other cases, you need to install a special driver program from the CD-ROM that came with the cell phone's data-connection adapter cable.

Note that many cell phones enable you to connect in one of two ways: either via a circuit-switched connection or in packet-switched mode. The mode you choose depends on the amount of data you intend to access, the probable duration of your connection, and the way your cellular phone company charges. If you download large amounts of data only once per day and your cellular company has a very low per-minute charge for voice calls, you should use the circuit-switched technique. Otherwise, use packet-switched mode, which is sometimes referred to as an "always-on" connection. A circuit-switched connection works just like a traditional dial-up modem connection. A packet-switched connection works like a DSL or cable modem connection.

Because cellular data connections are very slow (often only 14.4Kbps), use them only for applications such as email that do not require significant bandwidth. Postpone your large downloads until you can make a broadband connection.

Wired Modem Connections

Out on the road, you cannot depend on finding a high-speed connection or a decent wireless LAN signal. In many areas, even cellular connections may be spotty. Therefore, it is always prudent to have your trusty old wired modem ready as a backup connection. It may be slower than what you are used to, but it usually works.

What to Bring

The additional hardware needed for a modem connection is not heavy at all. The most important tool is a modular phone line, at least 6 feet in length. Because some hotels and offices use a digital PBX phone system, it is usually a good idea to bring a line tester as well. This keeps your modem from being fried by the high ringing voltages that these phone systems use. If it is important for you to be in touch, you might also bring along a second modem in a lightweight PC Card format.

How to Connect with a Modem

In most hotel rooms in the United States, connecting with a modem is now fairly straightforward. These rooms usually are equipped with phones that feature a phone jack designed for laptop connections.

Caution

In an effort to increase revenue, some hotels now gouge their customers with exorbitant phone rates, even for local calls. To avoid an unpleasant surprise at the checkout desk, examine the hotel's phone rates before you connect to the Internet.

Modem Instructions—The AT Command Set

Most of the time, when you use a modem, you never have to interact with it directly. Your communications software usually handles that. On some occasions, however, you need to access and control the modem directly. This happens, for example, when something is not working and you need to troubleshoot the system.

Modems respond to a series of commands, most of which are prefaced with the letters *AT* (for *attention*). Because of this, these commands are usually called AT commands.

The AT command set dates back to the original personal computer modems introduced by D.C. Hayes & Associates in 1978. Most current modem manufacturers incorporate the original Hayes set of commands and enhance them with special commands that can take advantage of any special features incorporated in new modems. Table 12.2 lists the commands from a typical PC Card modem: 3Com's 3CXM556 56K cellular modem PC Card with an XJACK connector. Many of these commands, particularly the general commands, apply to all modems.

Table 12.2   A Sample AT Command Set

General Modem Commands

&$	HELP, Ampersand Commands	Ln	n=0	Low Speaker Volume
A/	Repeat Last Command		n=1	Low Speaker Volume
A>	Continuously Repeat Command		n=2	Med Speaker Volume
AT	Command Mode Prefix		n=3	Hi Speaker Volume
A	Answer Call	Mn	n=0	Speaker OFF
Bn	n=0 V32 Mode/CCITT Answer Seq		n=1	Speaker ON Until CD
	n=1 Bell Answer Seq		n=2	Speaker Always ON
Dn	Dial a Telephone Number		n=3	Speaker OFF During Dial
	n=0..9#*TPR,;W@!()-	On	n=0	Return Online
DL	Dial Last Phone Number		n=1	Return Online & Retrain
DSn	Dial Stored Phone Number	P		Pulse Dial
D$	HELP, Dial Commands	Qn	n=0	Result Codes Sent
En	n=0 No Command Echo		n=1	Quiet (No Result Codes)
	n=1 Echo Command Chars		n=2	Verbose/Quiet ON Answer
Fn	n=0 Online Echo	Sr=n		Sets Register r to n
	n=1 No Online Echo	Sr?		Query Register r
Hn	n=0 ON Hook (Hang Up)	S$		HELP, S Registers
	n=1 OFF Hook	T		Tone Dial
In	n=0 Product Code	Vn	n=0	Numeric Responses
	n=1 Checksum		n=1	Verbal Responses
	n=2 RAM Test	Xn	n=0	Basic Result Codes
	n=3 Product ID string		n=1	Extended Result Codes
	n=4 Current Settings		n=2-4	Advanced Result Codes
	n=5 NVRAM Settings	Yn	n=0	Next Reset to &W0 settings
	n=6 Link Diagnostics		n=1	Next Reset to &W1 settings
	n=7 Product Configuration		n=2	Next Reset to &F0 settings
	n=9 PnP Enumeration Screen		n=3	Next Reset to &F1 settings
	n=11 Link Diagnostics		n=4	Next Reset to &F2 settings

Table 12.2 Continued

General Modem Commands

Zn	n=0 Y setting determines reset		n=5	Reset to &F2 settings
	n=1 Reset to &W0 settings		+++	Escape Code
	n=2 Reset to &W1 settings		$	HELP, Command Summary
	n=3 Reset to &F0 settings		~Zn	n=0 Normal
	n=4 Reset to &F1 settings			n=1 Enhanced

Modem Cellular Commands

&f5	Load cellular defaults
~Z	Toggle enhanced mode
&f6	Load ETC mode, wait for cellular call

Modem Dial Commands

0–9	Digits to Dial		,	Pause (Wait for S8 Time)
*	Auxiliary Tone Dial Digit		;	Remain in Command Mode After Dialing
#	Auxiliary Tone Dial Digit		"	Used to Dial Alpha Phone #'s
T	Tone Dialing		W	Wait for 2nd Dial Tone (X2,X4)
P	Pulse Dialing		@	Wait for an Answer (X3,X4)
R	Call an Originate Only Modem		!	Flash Switch Hook
/	Short Delay			

Modem Ampersand Commands

&An	n=0 Disable /ARQ Result Codes			n=1 550 Hz Guard Tone
	n=1 Enable /ARQ Result Codes			n=2 1800 Hz Guard Tone
	n=2 Enable /Modulation Codes		&Hn	n=0 Disable TX Flow Control
	n=3 Enable /Extra Result Codes			n=1 CTS
&Bn	n=0 Floating DTE Speed			n=2 Xon/Xoff
	n=1 Fixed DTE Speed			n=3 CTS and Xon/Xoff
	n=2 DTE Speed Fixed When ARQ		&In	n=0 Disable RX Flow Control
&Cn	n=0 CD Always ON			n=1 Xon/Xoff
	n=1 Modem Controls CD			n=2 Xon/Xoff Chars Filtered
&Dn	n=0 Ignore DTR			n=3 HP Enq/Ack Host Mode
	n=1 On-Line Command Mode			n=4 HP Enq/Ack Terminal Mode
	n=2 DTE Controls DTR			n=5 Xon/Xoff for non-ARQ Mode
	n=3 Reset ON DTR Loss		&Kn	n=0 Disable Data Compression
&Fn	n=0 Load Factory 0, HW FC			n=1 Auto Data Compression
	n=1 Load Factory 1, HW FC			n=2 Enable Data Compression
	n=2 Load Factory 2, SW FC			n=3 Selective Data Compression
	n=5 Load Factory 5, ETC_CELL		&Mn	n=0 Normal Mode
	n=6 Load Factory 6, ETC_LAND			n=4 ARQ/Normal Mode
&Gn	n=0 No Guard Tone			

(continues)

Table 12.2   Continued

Modem Ampersand Commands

	n=5	ARQ Mode		n=37	54666 bps
&Nn	n=0	Highest Link Speed		n=38	56000 bps
	n=1	300 bps		n=39	57333 bps
	n=2	1200 bps	&Pn	n=0	N. American Pulse Dial
	n=3	2400 bps		n=1	UK Pulse Dial
	n=4	4800 bps	&Rn	n=1	Ignore RTS
	n=5	7200 bps		n=2	RX to DTE/RTS high
	n=6	9600 bps	&Sn	n=0	DSR Always ON
	n=7	12000 bps		n=1	Modem Controls DSR
	n=8	14400 bps	&Tn	n=0	End Test
	n=9	16800 bps		n=1	Analog Loopback (ALB)
	n=10	19200 bps		n=3	Digital Loopback (DLB)
	n=11	21600 bps		n=4	Grant Remote DLB
	n=12	24000 bps		n=5	Deny Remote DLB
	n=13	26400 bps		n=6	Remote Digital Loopback
	n=14	28800 bps		n=7	Remote DLB With Self Test
	n=15	31200 bps		n=8	ALB With Self Test
	n=16	33600 bps	&Un	n=0	Variable link rate floor
	n=17	28000 bps		n=1	Minimum link rate 300 bps
	n=18	29333 bps		n=2	Minimum link rate 1200 bps
	n=19	30666 bps		n=3	Minimum link rate 2400 bps
	n=20	32000 bps		n=4	Minimum link rate 4800 bps
	n=21	33333 bps		n=5	Minimum link rate 7200 bps
	n=22	34666 bps		n=6	Minimum link rate 9600 bps
	n=23	36000 bps		n=7	Minimum link rate 12000 bps
	n=24	37333 bps		n=8	Minimum link rate 14400 bps
	n=25	38666 bps		n=9	Minimum link rate 16800 bps
	n=26	40000 bps		n=10	Minimum link rate 19200 bps
	n=27	41333 bps		n=11	Minimum link rate 21600 bps
	n=28	42666 bps		n=12	Minimum link rate 24000 bps
	n=29	44000 bps		n=13	Minimum link rate 26400 bps
	n=30	45333 bps		n=14	Minimum link rate 28800 bps
	n=31	46666 bps		n=15	Minimum link rate 31200 bps
	n=32	48000 bps		n=16	Minimum link rate 33600 bps
	n=33	49333 bps		n=17	Minimum link rate 28000 bps
	n=34	50666 bps		n=18	Minimum link rate 29333 bps
	n=35	52000 bps		n=19	Minimum link rate 30666 bps
	n=36	53333 bps		n=20	Minimum link rate 32000 bps

Table 12.2   Continued

Modem Ampersand Commands

	n=21 Minimum link rate 33333 bps			*n*=36 Minimum link rate 53333 bps
	n=22 Minimum link rate 34666 bps			*n*=37 Minimum link rate 54666 bps
	n=23 Minimum link rate 36000 bps			*n*=38 Minimum link rate 56000 bps
	n=24 Minimum link rate 37333 bps			*n*=39 Minimum link rate 57333 bps
	n=25 Minimum link rate 38666 bps		&W*n*	*n*=0 Store Configuration 0
	n=26 Minimum link rate 40000 bps			*n*=1 Store Configuration 1
	n=27 Minimum link rate 41333 bps		&Y*n*	*n*=0 Destructive
	n=28 Minimum link rate 42666 bps			*n*=1 Destructive/Expedited
	n=29 Minimum link rate 44000 bps			*n*=2 Nondest./Expedited
	n=30 Minimum link rate 45333 bps			*n*=3 Nondest./Unexpedited
	n=31 Minimum link rate 46666 bps		&Z*n*=*s*	Store Phone Number
	n=32 Minimum link rate 48000 bps		&Z*n*?	Query Phone Number
	n=33 Minimum link rate 49333 bps		#CID=*n*	*n*=0 Caller ID Off
	n=34 Minimum link rate 50666 bps			*n*=1 Formatted Caller ID
	n=35 Minimum link rate 52000 bps			*n*=2 Unformatted Caller ID

Modem S Register Functions

S0	Ring to Answer ON		S14	Reserved
S1	Counts # of Rings		S15	Bit Mapped
S2	Escape Code Char			1 = MNP/V.42 Disabled in V.22
S3	Carriage Return Char			2 = MNP/V.42 Disabled in V.22bis
S4	Line Feed Char			4 = MNP/V.42 Disabled in V.32
S5	Backspace Char			8 = Disable MNP Handshake
S6	Wait Time/Dial Tone (sec)			16 = Disable MNP Level 4
S7	Wait Time/Carrier (sec)			32 = Disable MNP Level 3
S8	Comma Time (sec)			64 = Unusual MNP-Incompatibility
S9	Carrier Detect Time (1/10sec)			128 = Disable V.42
S10	Carrier Loss Time (1/10sec)			136 = Disable V.42 Detect Phase
S11	Dial Tone Spacing (msec)		S16	Test Modes
S12	Escape Code Time (1/50sec)			1 = Reserved
S13	Bit Mapped			2 = Dial Test
	1 = Reset ON DTR Loss			4 = Reserved
	2 = Reduced Non-ARQ TX Buffer			8 = Reserved
	4 = Set DEL=Backspace			16 = Reserved
	8 = Do DS0 ON DTR			32 = Reserved
	16 = Do DS0 ON Reset			64 = Reserved
	32 = Reserved			128 = Reserved
	64 = Disable Quick Retrains		S17	Reserved
	128 = Escape Code Hang Up		S18	&T*n* Test Timeout (sec)

Table 12.2   Continued

Modem S Register Functions

S19	Inactivity Timeout (min)		2 = Disable 2743 Symbol rate
S20	Reserved		4 = Disable 2800 Symbol rate
S21	Break Length (1/100sec)		8 = Disable 3000 Symbol rate
S22	Xon Char		16 = Disable 3200 Symbol rate
S23	Xoff Char		32 = Disable 3429 Symbol rate
S24	Reserved		64 = Reserved
S25	DTR Recognition Time (1/100sec)		128 = Disable Shaping
S26	Reserved	S34	V.34 & V.34+ Connection setup
S27	Bit Mapped		bit mapped control flags
	1 = V21 Mode		1 = Disable 8S-2D trellis encoding
	2 = Disable TCM		2 = Disable 16S-4D trellis encoding
	4 = Disable V32		4 = Disable 32S-2D trellis encoding
	8 = Disable 2100hz		8 = Disable 64S-4D trellis encoding
	16 = Enable V23 Fallback		16 = Disable Non-linear coding
	32 = Disable V32bis		32 = Disable TX level deviation
	64 = Reserved		64 = Disable Pre-emphasis
	128 = Software Compatibility Mode		128 = Disable Pre-coding
S28	V.32 Handshake Time (1/10sec)	S35	Reserved
S29	V.21 answer mode fallback timer	S36	Reserved
S30	Reserved	S37	Reserved
S31	Reserved	S38	Disconnect Wait Time (sec)
S32	Connection bit mapped operations	S39	Reserved
	1 = V.8 Call Indicate enable	S40	Reserved
	2 = Enable V.8 mode	S41	Distinctive Ring options
	4 = Reserved		1 = Distinctive Ring Enabled
	8 = Disable V.34 modulation		2 = Reserved
	16 = Disable V.34+ modulation		4 = Reserved
	32 = Disable x2 modulation		8 = Reserved
	64 = Disable V.90 modulation		16 = Reserved
	128 = Reserved		32 = Reserved
S33	V.34 & V.34+ Connection setup		64 = Reserved
	bit mapped control flags		128 = Reserved
	1 = Disable 2400 Symbol rate	S42	Reserved

Most laptop users never make use of their modem's AT commands, but some of these commands can be quite handy. For example, the command ATM0 turns off the modem's speaker.

Tip

If you don't have a table of modem commands with you, most modems will generate one for you when you use the following commands:

- **AT$**—HELP, Command Summary
- **ATD$**—HELP, Dial Commands
- **AT&$**—HELP, Ampersand Commands
- **ATS$**—HELP, S Registers

When I get a modem, I go into the Windows HyperTerminal, execute all these help commands, one after another, and capture the output to a file. Then I clean up the file a bit with an editor, resulting in a nice, handy little reference for the modem! In the old days I used to print the charts in as small a font as possible and then cut and laminate them to produce a durable reference card.

How to Use the AT Command Set

To control a modem directly with AT commands, you will need to use a terminal-emulation program. All versions of Windows are bundled with a useful terminal emulator called HyperTerminal, published by Hilgraeve. To access your modem, you will have to know which communications or COM port it is using. To find the COM port in Windows XP, do the following:

1. Go to the Control Panel in Windows XP (click Start, Control Panel).
2. Enable Control Panel's classic icon view (click the Classic View text on the left side of the screen) and double-click the Phones and Modems Options icon.
3. Click the Modems tab.
4. Identify the modem in the list and note the number of the COM port to which it is attached (see Figure 12.7).

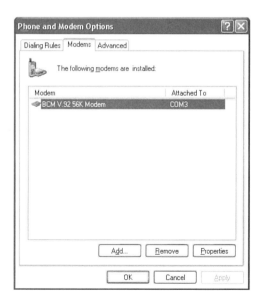

Figure 12.7   A dialog box showing where to find the COM port for a modem under Windows XP.

In other versions of Windows, the procedure differs but is similar.

Once you know the COM port, you can access the modem using HyperTerminal by doing the following in Windows XP:

1. Click Start, All Programs, Accessories, Communications, HyperTerminal (the program, not the folder).

2. A New Connection dialog box will appear. Enter a name for the new connection, such as Access The Modem, and select an appropriate icon. Click OK.

3. A Connect To dialog box will appear. Disregard the text boxes asking for country, area code, and phone number. At the drop-down box labeled Connect Using, select the COM port, such as COM3 (see Figure 12.8).

Figure 12.8   The HyperTerminal dialog box showing how to access a particular COM port.

4. A dialog box (see Figure 12.9) will appear asking for the properties of the COM port you have selected. Enter a speed of 57600 or similar (the exact speed is unimportant here). Leave the default values for Data Bits (8), Parity (None), Stop Bits (1), and Flow Control (Hardware).

Figure 12.9   The HyperTerminal dialog box showing how to change port settings.

5. A HyperTerminal window will appear. Type **AT** and press Enter. You should see AT echoed on the screen, followed by the modem's response, "OK." This indicates that the modem is connected and functioning (see Figure 12.10).

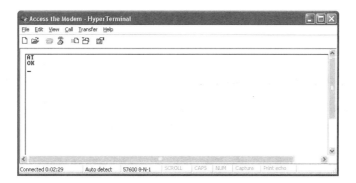

Figure 12.10 The HyperTerminal dialog box showing a modem responding "OK."

6. You can use any of the AT commands. For example, to dial a number, enter **ATD 555-1111** and you should hear the modem dialing (assuming you haven't disabled the modem's speaker, of course).

You can now use commands such as ATI0, ATI1, ATI2, and so on, to see how they can be useful to determine what modem you have, which firmware levels are installed, to run diagnostics, and so on. If you know the phone number of a computer system, you can now dial it and interact with it.

Tip

If you're not sure whether a phone line is live or dead, try this simple test: Use HyperTerminal to access your modem and then enter the following modem command: **ATD**. If you don't hear a dial tone, there is something wrong with the phone line or your connection to it.

Acoustic Couplers

On those occasions when you can't plug your modem into the phone jack or when no jack is available (such as at a pay phone), the last resort is an *acoustic coupler*. The acoustic coupler is an ancient telecommunications device that predates the system of modular jacks used to connect telephones today; you might have seen a very young Matthew Broderick use an acoustic coupler in the 1983 movie *War Games*. To connect to a telephone line, the coupler plugs into your modem's RJ-11 jack at one end and clamps to a telephone handset at the other end. A speaker at the mouthpiece and a microphone at the earpiece allow the audible signals generated by the modem and the phone system to interact.

An acoustic coupler is difficult to work with. Any loud ambient noise can slow down your connection. Even a slight touch of a finger to the handset can cause problems. The acoustic coupler can also be an annoying and bulky bit of extra baggage to have to carry with you, but it is the one foolproof method for connecting to any telephone line without having to worry about international standards, line current, or wiring.

Acoustic couplers are still available from a company called Konexx (www.konexx.com). That company's Koupler is available for $149.

Wire-It-Yourself

In the early days of the personal computer revolution, laptop users would often find themselves staying in hotel rooms that were not equipped with modular phone jacks. To handle such situations, I would carry a small screwdriver and special phone cable with a modular phone jack at one end and a pair of alligator clips at the other. To make a connection, I would locate the phone jack (which was usually behind a heavy, hard-to-move bed), unscrew the cover of the phone jack, and attach the alligator clips to two of the terminals underneath. A dial tone on the laptop's modem would signal that I had connected to the correct pair of terminals.

Nowadays, it is hard to find a hotel room that does not have a modular phone jack, let alone a convenient jack that is specially designed for use with a laptop. To handle those very rare situations in which a modular phone jack is missing, you will be better off carrying a cable to connect your laptop to your cell phone. The way some hotels gouge their guests for local calls, the cellular data connection may actually save you money.

Moving Data Between Two Systems

Most communications performed by laptops occur over miles and miles of phone lines. But often you need to transmit files back and forth from two laptops that are right next to each other. Usually, the best way to do this is with a direct connection.

Direct Connection Software

At one time, laptop users required special software, such as LapLink, to transfer data from one system to another. For several years now, the need for this software has diminished because the capability has been included in Windows.

Windows Direct Cable Connection (DCC)

The Direct Cable Connection feature of Windows is handy for transferring data from one laptop to another. Here's what you need to use this software:

- You will need a special serial, parallel, or USB cable that can connect two computers. These cables are bundled with programs such as LapLink or can be purchased separately.

- You will need to be sure that both computers are configured with the same workgroup name.

- You will need to set up one laptop so that it can share a folder or drive with the other laptop.

Note that if you do not have a special cable to connect the laptops, you can try to establish an infrared link. Do this by situating the two notebooks so that their IR windows face each other and are no more than 2 feet apart. Be sure that no object, such as a coffee cup, obstructs a direct line-of-sight connection between the two systems. Be forewarned, however, that a few of the newer notebook computers lack an IR window, and many of the notebooks that have IR windows are not compatible with each other.

Using Networking Protocols

A faster and more inexpensive method is to set up a small peer-to-peer network. For a network of three or more laptops, you will need a small network hub and a few standard network cables. But for a network of only two laptops, you will need only a simple "crossover" LAN cable, which usually sells for less than $10. Of course, if your laptops do not have built-in LAN adapters, you will have to add in the cost of these devices as well.

To make a simple peer-to-peer LAN connection, you need to do the following:

- Because your miniature LAN does not have a DHCP server doling out IP addresses automatically, you will need to configure both laptops manually with suitable IP addresses. Two reasonable addresses would be 192.168.0.1 and 192.168.0.2. The subnet mask for each laptop should be set to 255.255.255.0. (To learn more about DHCP, see the section on that topic earlier in this chapter.)

- Both computers should be configured with the same workgroup name.

- One laptop should be set up so that it can share a folder or drive with the other laptop. Windows XP provides a Shared Documents folder by default.

Hardware-Based Data Transfers

Not too long ago, data could be easily transferred from one system to another via a floppy disk. Now, however, rare is the data file that is small enough to fit on a floppy. Plus, many smaller notebooks lack a floppy drive. Still, other techniques can be used to transfer data fairly easily.

USB Data Fobs

USB data fobs are handy keychain-size devices that can be plugged in to the USB ports of any computer and be filled with several megabytes of data. Always carry one of these inexpensive devices with you when you travel.

Memory Card Plus USB Adapter

If you use a digital camera, you probably have several postage stamp–size memory cards lying around. With an inexpensive adapter (to be used with either a USB port or a PC Card slot), these memory cards can be used to transfer data from one laptop to another.

CD-R Discs

If your laptop is equipped with a CD-R/W drive, you should always carry at least one CD-R disc with you. These discs are very inexpensive and are extremely useful for transferring large amounts of data from one notebook to another. Just be sure that the second notebook has a drive that can read it.

Managing Data Sharing/Synching with Desktop PCs

Now that you can easily move data between any two systems, you'll want to know how you can manage the sharing of data between those systems. Say you go back and forth between using both a notebook and a desktop system. Not only will you need to be able to copy files between them, but you'll want to ensure your files, data, and work are synchronized between the systems.

Windows includes a feature called Briefcase that is designed to handle this task. However, many users have reported that they are dissatisfied with it. Fortunately, several inexpensive third-party synchronization software packages are on the market. One particularly powerful program is LapLink Gold, which performs a number of other tasks as well as synchronization. Also, a number of shareware programs offer some type of synchronization. Search for "synchronize files" at www.download.com. Note that this synchronization technique is an excellent way to back up the data on your laptop.

Communications Security

For laptops, users must be sure to secure not only the data that goes in and out of the system, but also the laptop itself. Because of its portable nature, a laptop is much more likely to be stolen than a desktop.

Antitheft Measures

There is a growing concern for security and safety with portables because their small size and weight make them easy targets for thieves. A prime target is the traveler at the airport. In that environment, you should always be sure you keep tight control over your computer; otherwise, it can easily be stolen.

A common scam involves two people at the X-ray scanner. They both stand in front of you in line; one goes through and the other waits until you put your system on the conveyer belt before holding up the line, fumbling with change and other items in his pocket. This serves to detain you while the companion grabs your notebook and runs. By the time you get through, your system is gone. Moral of the story: Don't set your computer on the conveyer belt until there is nobody between you and the metal detector portal. You can buy various alarms that can shriek if your system is stolen, but they are a fairly extreme solution.

System manufacturers offer protection for their systems in several ways. One is to offer a latch on the system to which a security lock cable can be bolted. This solution is ideal if you are working with your system on a desk and want to lock it to the desk. Companies such as Kensington Microware sell steel cables with a key lock that goes through the latch in the system case and can then be wrapped around a secure object. The latch in the case is made as a part of the frame and not the flimsy plastic exterior casing.

Hardware-Level Passwords

A second method for protection involves hardware-level passwords. These passwords—not to be confused with those of the operating system—are designed to secure the actual hardware of the laptop. Most notebook systems offer several levels of password protection, but the most secure are the administrator password and the hard disk password. Both of those, if lost, can't be reset or deleted, so losing them renders the motherboard or hard disk useless. Be careful if you set these passwords—don't forget them! Of course, the idea is that if thieves steal your portable, they won't be able to access any of the data on it, even if they move the hard disk to another machine.

Operating System Passwords

Another way to secure your laptop is to use the password feature of Windows. Set up secure passwords on all user and administrator accounts. With Windows XP Professional, you can provide extra security for individual folders.

Note that a hidden backdoor exists for both the Home and Professional versions of Windows XP. This backdoor is in the form of a hidden administrator account that is used to gain access to your system if you've forgotten the password to your own administrator account.

Here's how to deactivate this account:

1. While logged on in an administrator account, open the Control Panel.
2. Double-click Users.
3. Double-click your administrator account.
4. Click the option on the left titled Prevent a Forgotten Password.
5. Have a blank floppy disk handy and follow the instructions.

This procedure creates a disk that enables you to log on if you forget your password. Keep this disk secure. This procedure also deactivates the hidden administrator account.

Antivirus Software

If you have received more than a few email messages, you have probably received one that was infected with a virus. These days, a good and well-maintained antivirus program is a must. Be sure to update the virus definitions for the program on a regular basis. Otherwise, you will be vulnerable to the new viruses that are sure to crop up.

Firewalls

If you connect to the Internet for any length of time, be aware that your connection is a two-way street. At any time someone may be trying to connect with you or, more precisely, trying to get into your system. Alternatively, a rogue program that somehow got on your laptop may be trying to send out confidential information from your laptop to some destination on the Internet. The way to stop this is to set up a firewall. One of the best is also free (for the basic version): ZoneAlarm, available at www.zonealarm.com.

Virtual Private Networking

It was not long ago that companies would lease private communications cables for high-speed communications between distant offices. In addition to fast data links, this arrangement also ensured privacy. Now, however, most companies opt for a much more affordable way. Virtual private networking (VPN) enables you to establish what is effectively a private connection over the very public medium of the Internet. This is accomplished via encryption.

Although there are some powerful VPN programs on the market, Windows is already equipped with a fairly decent implementation of VPN. To use it, you must be sure that both ends of the connection—your laptop and your host system—are running it at the same time.

Encryption

An increasingly significant security hazard for laptops is wireless LAN eavesdropping. Someone can very easily tap into your wireless LAN and monitor all of its traffic simply by parking his or her car outside your office. The solution to this problem involves encryption.

File Encryption

If you are sending a sensitive file via an untrustworthy medium, such as a wireless LAN or the Internet, you may want to encrypt it first. Even if the file never leaves your laptop, you may want to encrypt it to prevent prying eyes from reading it. Fortunately, the latest versions of many Microsoft Office applications include fairly robust encryption capabilities. For example, Microsoft Word 2002 features a good encryption scheme that gives you a choice of several different encryption techniques.

To encrypt a file in Word 2002 (part of Office XP), follow these steps:

1. With the file open, select Tools, Options from the menu bar.
2. Click the Security tab.
3. Type in a password, which will be required to open the file.
4. If you click the Advanced button, you can choose a more powerful encryption technique.

A similar process can be used to encrypt files under Microsoft Excel.

Wireless LAN Encryption

Currently, the encryption standard for wireless LANs is evolving. As a result, users now have two standards from which to choose: WEP and WPA.

WEP—Wireless Equivalent Privacy

Because of the obvious security vulnerability of a wireless LAN, the original specification for 802.11b wireless LANs included an encryption technique called *Wireless Equivalent Privacy (WEP)*. Two possible key lengths were specified: a fairly secure 128-byte key and a less secure 40-byte key meant for sale outside the United States.

During 2001, a serious vulnerability was exposed in WEP, and people began writing programs to exploit this security hole. An industrial spy can now download a program off the Internet that could analyze all the traffic on your wireless LAN and eventually deduce the WEP key. On a WLAN with heavy traffic, this program could gather sufficient packets to accomplish this task in only one day. Because of this vulnerability, many highly secure installations banned wireless LANs outright.

Although flawed, WEP security may still be secure enough for residential and small office applications. But its value should not be overestimated. Like most door locks, its main function may be limited to keeping honest people honest.

The actual process of activating WEP security can vary from one 802.11b PC Card brand to another. In most cases, you can access the card through the Networks icon in the Control Panel of Windows. Once there, click the Configure button, which should lead you to a menu that includes a WEP security setting.

WPA/WPA2—Wi-Fi Protected Access

To provide corporations with bulletproof wireless LAN security, the Wi-Fi Alliance worked together with the Institute of Electrical and Electronics Engineers (IEEE) 802.11 group to develop a new security solution called *Wi-Fi Protected Access (WPA)*. The standard, which was announced in October of 2002, builds on the IEEE 802.11i Wireless LAN Security Network standard. The WPA2 standard was introduced in September of 2004 and differs from WPA by providing a stronger encryption mechanism through Advanced Encryption Standard (AES), which is a requirement for some corporate and government users.

The WPA and WPA2 standards closely mirror the official IEEE 802.11i Wireless LAN security standard. Both standards have two components—encryption and authentication—that are crucial to wireless LAN security. WPA2 adds stronger encryption requirements (AES) but also enhancements to support fast roaming of wireless clients. For example, WPA2 allows you to reconnect to an access point that you've recently connected to without the need to reauthenticate. Preauthentication support in WPA2 allows you to preauthenticate with the access point toward which you are moving, while maintaining a connection to the access point you're moving away from.

Part of the strength of WPA/WPA2 is its reliance on the 802.1x authentication standard. This authentication technique ensures that only authorized users can access the wireless LAN, but it requires an authentication server. Smaller companies without such a server will have to rely on a key installed on each PC Card node and access point.

A large number of products have already been certified as WPA/WPA2 compliant by the Wi-Fi Alliance. This number will surely grow, and in time the WPA/WPA2-compliant products will replace the WEP-compliant products. All products that are certified for WPA2 will be interoperable with products that are certified for WPA, whereas some WPA products can be upgraded by software or firmware to support WPA2. Note, however, that at this point, operating system support for WPA/WPA2 is limited; just Windows XP, Apple's OS X and Linux support it.

CHAPTER 13

Keyboards and Pointing Devices

The keyboard, pointing device, and display are in many ways the most important parts of a computer because they represent the human interface to the system. Unlike desktop systems, portables have keyboards integrated into the one-piece unit. This makes them much more difficult to repair or replace, and you can't switch keyboard models or types; you are stuck with the model that comes with the system. Because you can't switch the built-in keyboard, the keyboard should be an important element of your system-purchasing decision when selecting a new laptop. Because manufacturers are forced to modify the standard 101-key desktop keyboard layout to fit in a smaller case, you'll find a variety of different layouts as well as significant differences in keybutton travel and feel among units.

The pointing device is also a prime consideration when purchasing a new laptop because it's second only to the keyboard as a method of controlling or interacting with the system. I've seen laptop or notebook systems that had keyboards and pointing devices so horrible that the only way to use the system was to plug in external models, which is obviously not a preferable solution. When you consider that the keyboard and pointing device comprise the primary method for communicating with your computer, you realize they are an extremely important part of the system. The quality of the keyboard and especially the type and quality of the integrated pointing device are the first things I consider when selecting a laptop.

Laptop Keyboards

One of the biggest influences on keyboard design in recent years has been the proliferation of laptop and notebook systems. Because of size limitations, it is obviously impossible to use the standard keyboard layout for a portable computer. Manufacturers have come up with many solutions. Unfortunately, none of these solutions has become an industry standard, as is the 101-key layout for desktop PCs. Because of the variations in design and because a portable system's keyboard is not as easily replaceable as that of a desktop system, the keyboard arrangement should be an important part of your purchasing decision.

Early laptop systems often used smaller-than-normal keys to minimize the size of the keyboard, which resulted in many complaints from users. Today, the keytops on portable systems are usually comparable in size to those of a desktop keyboard, although some systems include half-sized keytops for the function keys and other less frequently used keyboard elements. In addition, consumer demand has caused most manufacturers to retain the inverted-T design for the cursor keys after a few abortive attempts at changing their arrangement.

Although arrangements can vary, a typical laptop keyboard layout can be divided into the following sections:

- Typing area
- Cursor and screen controls
- Function keys

Figure 13.1 shows a typical laptop keyboard to illustrate these sections.

The cursor-control keys are located in the lower right and are arranged in the inverted-T format that is fairly standard on all computer keyboards. The Insert, Delete, Home, End, Page Up, and Page Down keys are located above the Backspace key. The function keys are located across the top of the keyboard. The Esc key is isolated in the upper-left corner of the keyboard. Dedicated Print Screen/Sys Req, Scroll Lock, and Pause/Break keys are provided for commonly used functions.

The most obvious difference in a portable system keyboard is the sacrifice of the numeric keypad. Most systems now embed the keypad into the standard alphabetical part of the keyboard, as shown in Figure 13.2. To switch the keys from their standard values to their keypad values, you typically must press a key combination involving a proprietary Function key, often labeled Fn.

Figure 13.1   Typical laptop keyboard.

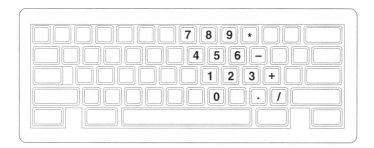

Figure 13.2   Most portable systems today embed the numeric keypad into an oddly shaped block of keys on the alphabetical part of the keyboard.

This is an extremely inconvenient solution, and many users abandon their use of the keypad entirely on portable systems. Unfortunately, some activities—such as the entry of ASCII codes using the Alt key—require the use of the keypad numbers, which can be quite frustrating on systems using this arrangement.

To alleviate this problem, many portable system manufacturers sell external numeric keypads that plug into the external keyboard port, a serial port, or a USB port. This is a great feature for users performing a lot of numeric data entry. Figure 13.3 shows a USB numeric keypad sold by Belkin, which can be ordered from www.belkin.com.

In addition to keypad control, the Fn key on most laptop keyboards is used to trigger other proprietary features, such as toggling between internal and external displays as well as controlling screen brightness, screen expansion or zoom, sound volume, and more.

Some portable system manufacturers have gone to great lengths to provide users with decent keyboards. For a short time, IBM marketed a revolutionary system called the ThinkPad 701, which had a keyboard that used a "butterfly" design. The keyboard was split into two halves that rested over and under each other when the system was closed. When you opened the lid, the two halves slid from over/under to side by side, forming a keyboard that was actually wider than the computer case. This design, now considered legendary, won many awards after it was released.

Figure 13.3 USB numeric keypad from Belkin.

Ironically, the trend toward larger-sized displays in portable systems has made this sort of arrangement unnecessary. Many manufacturers have increased the footprint of their notebook computers to accommodate 15-inch or larger display panels, leaving more than adequate room for a keyboard with full-size keys. Because of this, most portable systems today have keyboards that approach the size and usability of desktop models. This is a vast improvement over some older designs in which the keys were reduced to a point where you could not comfortably touch-type with both hands. Standard conventions such as the inverted-T cursor keys also were modified on older machines, causing extreme user displeasure.

Still, even the largest systems don't have enough room for a separate numeric keypad. If you plan to perform a lot of numeric data entry with your portable computer, look for numeric keypads that plug into your system and override the embedded keypad on the right side of your keyboard, or use a standard 101-key keyboard if you're at your desk.

Windows Keys

When Microsoft released Windows 95, it also introduced the Microsoft Natural Keyboard, which implemented a revised keyboard specification that added three new Windows-specific keys to the keyboard.

The Microsoft Windows keyboard layout includes left and right Windows keys and an Application key, which have become a standard for many desktop and laptop keyboards. These keys are used for operating system–level and application-level keyboard combinations, similar to the existing Ctrl and Alt combinations. You don't need the special keys to use Windows, but some software vendors have added specific functions to their Windows products that use the Application key (which provides the same functionality as clicking the right mouse button). The recommended Windows keyboard layout calls for the Left and Right Windows keys (called *WIN keys*) to flank the Alt keys on each side of the spacebar, as well as for an Application key on the right of the Right Windows key (see Figure 13.4). Note, however, that the exact placement of these keys is up to the keyboard designer, so you will see variations from keyboard to keyboard. For example, because the left and right Windows keys are redundant, many laptops incorporate only a single left Windows key and an Application key mounted somewhere above the function keys, or only a right Windows key with an adjacent

Application key, or a single Windows key and adjacent Application key mounted in the upper-right corner of the keyboard.

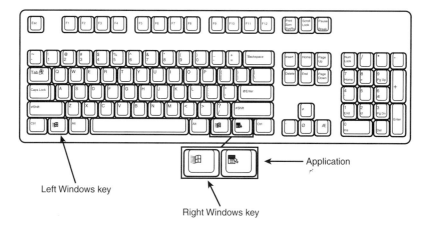

Left Windows key

Right Windows key

Application

Figure 13.4 The 104-key Windows standard keyboard layout.

The WIN keys open the Windows Start menu, which you can then navigate with the cursor keys. The Application key simulates the right mouse button; in most applications, it brings up a context-sensitive pop-up menu. Several WIN key combinations offer preset macro commands as well. For example, you press WIN+E to launch the Windows Explorer application. Table 13.1 shows a list of all the Windows key combinations.

Table 13.1   Windows 9x/Me/2000/XP Key Combinations

Key Combination	Resulting Action
WIN+R	Displays the Run dialog box
WIN+M	Minimize All
Shift+WIN+M	Undo Minimize All
WIN+D	Minimize All or Undo Minimize All
WIN+F1	Help
WIN+E	Starts Windows Explorer
WIN+F	Find Files or Folders
Ctrl+WIN+F	Find Computer (on a network)
WIN+Tab	Cycles through taskbar buttons
WIN+Break	Displays the System Properties dialog box
Application key	Displays a context menu for the selected item

The Windows and Application keys are not mandatory when running Windows. In fact, preexisting standard key combinations can perform the same functions as these keys.

The Windows keyboard specification requires that keyboard makers increase the number of trilograms in their keyboard designs. A *trilogram* is a combination of three rapidly pressed keys that perform a special function, such as Ctrl+Alt+Delete. Designing a keyboard so that the switch matrix will correctly register the additional trilograms plus the additional Windows keys adds somewhat to the cost of these keyboards compared to the previous models.

While many laptop and portable systems now incorporate these Windows-specific keys, some of the most popular laptop brands such as the ThinkPads don't include the Windows or Application keys at all. Some manufacturers add other special keys such as browser-control and other keys that, although not standard, can in some cases make their keyboards easier to use for navigating web pages and launching various applications. Some of these keys require that special drivers be loaded, which means they may not work if you change the operating system or software load from what was shipped with the machine.

Running Windows Without a Mouse

Many people do not know that it is possible to dramatically enhance the use of Windows by using the keyboard as an adjunct to or even instead of the mouse for system control. Many keyboard short-cuts and other key commands are available that can greatly increase the speed and efficiency with which you operate Windows, especially if you are an accomplished touch typist. Because I use my PC mainly for writing, I find that taking my hand off the keyboard to use a mouse noticeably slows me down (which is one reason I use laptop systems or desktop keyboards with a more efficient TrackPoint pointing device). By augmenting Windows operations with the keyboard, you can control Windows more efficiently and accurately than with a mouse alone.

In some cases, it is not only desirable but may be necessary to use the keyboard instead of a mouse, such as when your mouse is not functioning properly or is missing altogether. Because technicians often find themselves operating or testing equipment that is not fully functional, it is even more important for them to know how to operate Windows with the keyboard.

Table 13.2 lists some general keyboard-only commands for Windows 9x/Me/NT/2000/XP.

Table 13.2   General Key Commands in Windows

Key or Key Combination	Resulting Action
F1	Starts Windows Help.
F10	Activates menu bar options.
Shift+F10	Opens a context menu (shortcut menu) for the selected item.
Ctrl+Esc	Opens the Start menu. Use the arrow keys to select an item.
Ctrl+Esc, Esc	Selects the Start button. Press Tab to select the taskbar or press Shift+F10 for a context menu.
Alt+Tab	Switches to another running application. Hold down the Alt key and then press the Tab key to view the task-switching window.
Shift	Bypasses the AutoPlay feature when you press down and hold the Shift key while you insert a CD-ROM.
Alt+spacebar	Displays the main window's System menu. From the System menu, you can restore, move, resize, minimize, maximize, or close the window.
Alt+- (Alt+hyphen)	Displays the Multiple Document Interface (MDI) child window's System menu. From the MDI child window's System menu, you can restore, move, resize, minimize, maximize, or close the child window.
Ctrl+Tab	Switches to the next child window of a MDI application.
Alt+<underlined letter in menu>	Opens the corresponding menu.
Alt+F4	Closes the current window.

Table 13.2   Continued

Key or Key Combination	Resulting Action
Ctrl+F4	Closes the current MDI window.
Alt+F6	Switches between multiple windows in the same program. For example, when Notepad's Find dialog box is displayed, Alt+F6 switches between the Find dialog box and the main Notepad window.

Table 13.3 lists the Windows dialog box keyboard commands.

Table 13.3   Dialog Box Key Commands in Windows

Key or Key Combination	Resulting Action
Tab	Moves to the next control in the dialog box.
Shift+Tab	Moves to the previous control in the dialog box.
Spacebar	If the current control is a button, this keyboard combination clicks the button. If the current control is a check box, this keyboard combination toggles the check box. If the current control is an option button, this keyboard combination selects the option button.
Enter	Equivalent to clicking the selected button (the button with the outline).
Esc	Equivalent to clicking the Cancel button.
Alt+<underlined letter in dialog box item>	Moves to the corresponding item.
Ctrl+Tab/Ctrl+Shift+Tab	Moves through the property tabs.

Table 13.4 lists keyboard combinations for Windows Explorer tree controls.

Table 13.4   Windows Explorer Keyboard Commands

Key	Resulting Action
Numeric Keypad *	Expands everything under the current selection
Numeric Keypad +	Expands the current selection
Numeric Keypad -	Collapses the current selection
Right arrow	Expands the current selection if it is not expanded (otherwise goes to the first child)
Left arrow	Collapses the current selection if it is expanded (otherwise goes to the parent)

Table 13.5 lists general Windows folder/shortcut controls.

Table 13.5   Shortcut Keys for Working with Windows Folders

Key or Key Combination	Resulting Action
F4	Selects the Go To a Different Folder box and moves down the entries in the box (if the toolbar is active in Windows Explorer).
F5	Refreshes the current window.
F6	Moves among panes in Windows Explorer.
Ctrl+G	Opens the Go To Folder tool (in Windows 95 Windows Explorer only).

(continues)

Table 13.5   Continued

Key or Key Combination	Resulting Action
Ctrl+Z	Undoes the last command.
Ctrl+A	Selects all the items in the current window.
Backspace	Switches to the parent folder.
Shift+click	Selects the close button. (For folders, this action closes the current folder plus all parent folders.)

Table 13.6 lists general folder and Windows Explorer shortcuts for a selected object.

Table 13.6   Keyboard Shortcuts for Selected Objects in a Windows Folder

Key or Key Combination	Resulting Action
F2	Renames the object.
F3	Finds all files.
Ctrl+X	Cuts.
Ctrl+C	Copies.
Ctrl+V	Pastes.
Shift+Del	Deletes the selection immediately, without moving the item to the Recycle Bin.
Alt+Enter	Opens the property sheet for the selected object.
To copy a file	Press down and hold the Ctrl key while you drag the file to another folder.
To create a shortcut	Press down and hold Ctrl+Shift while you drag the file to the desktop or a folder.

Keyboard Technology

The technology that makes up a typical PC keyboard is very interesting. This section focuses on all the aspects of keyboard technology and design, including the keyswitches, the interface between the keyboard and the system, the scan codes, and the keyboard connectors.

Keyswitch Design

Keyboards in portable systems can use any one of several switch types to create the action for each key. This section discusses these switches and the highlights of each design.

Keyswitches are available in the following variations:

- Pure mechanical
- Foam element
- Rubber dome
- Membrane/rubber dome
- Capacitive

Pure Mechanical Switches

The pure mechanical switch type is just that—a simple mechanical switch that features metal contacts in a momentary contact arrangement. The switch often includes a tactile feedback mechanism, consisting of a clip and spring arrangement designed to give a "clicky" feel to the keyboard and offer some resistance to the keypress (see Figure 13.5).

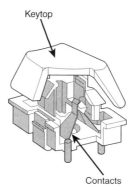

Figure 13.5 A typical mechanical switch. As the key is pressed, the switch pushes down on the contacts to make the connection.

Mechanical switches are very durable, usually have self-cleaning contacts, and are normally rated for 20 million keystrokes, which is second only to the capacitive switch in longevity. They also offer excellent tactile feedback. Many older portable PCs used keyboards like this, and some of the larger industrial or lunchbox portables still use them.

Foam Element Switches

Foam element mechanical switches were a very popular design in some older keyboards. Most of the older PC keyboards, including models made by Key Tronic and many others, used this technology. These switches are characterized by a foam element with an electrical contact on the bottom. This foam element is mounted on the bottom of a plunger that is attached to the key (see Figure 13.6).

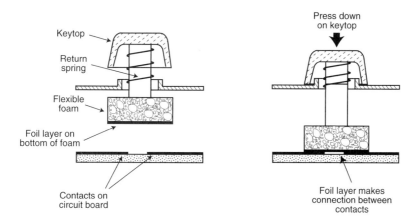

Figure 13.6 Typical foam element mechanical keyswitch.

When the switch is pressed, a foil conductor on the bottom of the foam element closes a circuit on the printed circuit board below. A return spring pushes the key back up when the pressure is released.

The foam dampens the contact, helping to prevent "bounce." Unfortunately, this gives these keyboards a "mushy" feel. The big problem with this type of keyswitch design is that, often, little tactile feedback exists. These types of keyboards send a clicking sound to the system speaker to signify that contact has been made. Preferences in keyboard feel are somewhat subjective; I personally do not favor the foam element switch design.

Another problem with this type of design is that it is more subject to corrosion on the foil conductor and the circuit board traces below. When this happens, the key strikes can become intermittent, which can be frustrating. Fortunately, these keyboards are among the easiest to clean. By disassembling the keyboard completely, you usually can remove the circuit board portion—without removing each foam pad separately—and expose the bottoms of all the pads. Then, you easily can wipe the corrosion and dirt off the bottom of the foam pads and the circuit board, thus restoring the keyboard to a "like-new" condition. Unfortunately, over time, the corrosion problem will occur again. I recommend using some Stabilant 22A from D.W. Electrochemicals to improve the switch contact action and prevent future corrosion. Because of such problems, the foam element design is not used much anymore and has been superseded in popularity by the rubber dome design.

Rubber Dome Switches

Rubber dome switches are mechanical switches similar to the foam element type but are improved in many ways. Instead of a spring, these switches use a rubber dome that has a carbon button contact on the underside. As you press a key, the key plunger presses on the rubber dome, causing it to resist and then collapse all at once, much like the top of an oilcan. As the rubber dome collapses, the user feels the tactile feedback, and the carbon button makes contact between the circuit board traces below. When the key is released, the rubber dome re-forms and pushes the key back up.

The rubber eliminates the need for a spring and provides a reasonable amount of tactile feedback without any special clips or other parts. Rubber dome switches use a carbon button because it resists corrosion and has a self-cleaning action on the metal contacts below. The rubber domes themselves are formed into a sheet that completely protects the contacts below from dirt, dust, and even minor spills. This type of switch design is the simplest, and it uses the fewest parts. This made the rubber dome keyswitch very reliable for several years. However, its relatively poor tactile feedback has led most keyboard manufacturers to switch to the membrane switch design covered in the next section.

Membrane/Rubber Dome Switches

The membrane keyswitch is a variation on the rubber dome type and uses a flat, flexible circuit board to receive input and transmit it to the keyboard microcontroller.

Although low-end membrane keyswitches have a limited life of only 5–10 million keystrokes, some of the better models are rated to handle up to 20 million keystrokes, putting them in the range of pure mechanical switches for durability (see Figure 13.7). Variations on the rubber dome design are by far the most popular type of keyboard used in both desktop and laptop keyboards today.

Capacitive Switches

Capacitive switches are technically the only truly nonmechanical keyswitches in use today (see Figure 13.8). Although the movement of the key and spring is mechanical in nature, they do not close a mechanical contact or switch. The capacitive switch is the Cadillac of keyswitches. It is much more expensive than the more common rubber dome membrane switch, but it is more resistant to dirt and corrosion and offers the highest-quality tactile feedback of any type of switch. This type of keyboard is sometimes referred to as a *buckling-spring keyboard* because of the coiled spring and rocker used to provide feedback. Unfortunately, capacitive switches were used only in some of the older luggable or briefcase-sized portables and are not used in modern laptop or notebook systems due to size, weight, and cost issues. Still, they are popular as external keyboards for use with portable systems when they are docked or stationary at a fixed location.

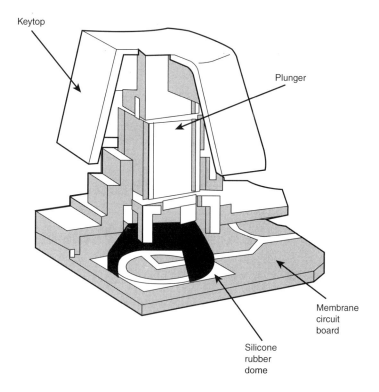

Figure 13.7 A typical membrane/rubber dome keyswitch.

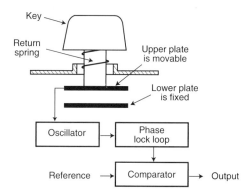

Figure 13.8 A capacitive buckling-spring keyswitch.

A capacitive switch does not work by making contact between conductors. Instead, two plates usually made of plastic are connected in a switch matrix designed to detect changes in the capacitance of the circuit.

When the key is pressed, the plunger moves the top plate in relation to the fixed bottom plate. Usually, a buckling-spring mechanism provides distinct, over-center tactile feedback with a resounding "click." As the top plate moves, the capacitance between the two plates changes. The comparator circuitry in the keyboard detects this change.

Because this type of switch does not rely on metal contacts, it is nearly immune to corrosion and dirt. These switches are very resistant to the "key bounce" problems that result in multiple characters appearing from a single strike. They are also the most durable in the industry—rated for 25 million or more keystrokes, as opposed to 10–20 million for other designs. The tactile feedback is unsurpassed because the switch provides a relatively loud click and a strong over-center feel. The only drawback to the design is the cost. Capacitive switch keyboards are among the most expensive designs. The quality of the feel and their durability make them worth the price, however.

Originally, the only vendor of capacitive keyswitch keyboards was IBM. Although some of IBM's keyboards still feature capacitive keyswitches, many IBM keyboards also use rubber dome or other lower-cost keyswitches. In 1991 IBM spun off its keyboard/printer division as Lexmark, which then spun off the keyboard division as Unicomp in 1996. Today, Unicomp still manufactures and sells "IBM" keyboards with the classic buckling-spring capacitive switch ("clickety" as some would say) technology. As a bonus, some models have the IBM TrackPoint built in. You can purchase new Unicomp (IBM) keyboards direct by calling toll free (1-800-777-4886) or going to the online store at www.pckeyboard.com. Another great source for IBM external keyboards is www.clickykeyboard.com. This site offers a number of used and new-old stock keyboards, including those with integral TrackPoints.

Because of the buckling-spring capacitive keyswitches (and the resulting clickety feel), I've always been a huge fan of the IBM, Lexmark, and now Unicomp keyboards. I feel they are the absolute best keyboards in the world—the only ones I willingly use on desktop systems. I especially like the fact that they have models that include the IBM TrackPoint, because I use a laptop system as my main machine, and I only use laptops that include the TrackPoint device (mainly IBM, Toshiba, and some Dell, HP, and others). The feel and durability of the buckling-spring capacitive keyswitches are outstanding, and with the integrated TrackPoint, I never have to move my hands off the keyboard, which results in much greater efficiency in working with my systems.

The Keyboard Interface

A keyboard consists of a set of switches mounted in a grid or an array called the *key matrix*. When a switch is pressed, a processor in the keyboard identifies which key is pressed by determining which grid location in the matrix shows continuity. The keyboard processor, which also interprets how long the key is pressed, can even handle multiple keypresses at the same time. A 16-byte hardware buffer in the keyboard can handle rapid or multiple keypresses, passing each one to the system in succession.

When you press a key, the contact bounces slightly in most cases, meaning that several rapid on/off cycles occur just as the switch makes contact. This is called *bounce*. The processor in the keyboard is designed to filter this (or "debounce" the keystroke). The keyboard processor must distinguish bounce from an intended double keystrike. This is fairly easy, though, because the bouncing is much more rapid than a person could simulate by striking a key quickly several times.

The keyboard in a laptop or desktop PC is actually a computer itself. It communicates with the main system in one of two ways:

■ Through a special serial data link if an internal keyboard or a standard PS/2 keyboard connector is used

■ Through the USB port

The serial data link used by conventional keyboards transmits and receives data in 11-bit packets of information, consisting of 8 data bits plus framing and control bits. Although it is indeed a serial link (in that the data flows on one wire), the keyboard interface is incompatible with the standard RS-232 serial port commonly used to connect modems.

The keyboard serial interface is connected to a special keyboard controller on the motherboard. This controller was an Intel 8042 Universal Peripheral Interface (UPI) slave microcontroller chip in the original IBM design. This microcontroller is essentially another processor that has its own 2KB of ROM and 128 bytes of RAM. Modern systems incorporate the keyboard controller into the main system chipset.

The keyboard connector was renamed the "PS/2" port after the IBM PS/2 family of systems debuted in 1987. At that time, the connector changed in size from the DIN (Deutsches Institut für Normung e.V.) to the mini-DIN, and even though the signals were the same, the mini-DIN version became known from that time forward as the PS/2 port. Up until recently most laptops have included a single PS/2 port that supports a mouse by default, or a PS/2 keyboard by using a "Y" splitter adapter. You must use the splitter if you want to connect an external PS/2 keyboard. Most recent laptops no longer include PS/2 ports, instead using USB for external keyboards and mice. On the other hand, most of the port replicators or docking stations used with even the newest systems still include separate PS/2 keyboard and mouse connectors, which can be used without a "Y" splitter adapter.

USB keyboards port work in a surprisingly similar fashion to those connected to conventional PS/2 ports after the data reaches the system. Inside the keyboard, a variety of custom controller chips are used by various keyboard manufacturers to receive and interpret keyboard data before sending it to the system via the USB port. Some of these chips contain USB hub logic to enable the keyboard to act as a USB hub. After the keyboard data reaches the USB port on the system, the USB port routes the data to the 8042-compatible keyboard controller, where the data is treated as any other keyboard information.

This process works very well after a system has booted into Windows. But what about users who need to use the keyboard when booting an OS that doesn't have USB drivers? In that case, USB Legacy support must be enabled in the BIOS. A BIOS with USB Legacy support is capable of performing the following tasks:

- Configuring the host controller
- Enabling a USB keyboard and mouse
- Setting up the host controller scheduler
- Routing USB keyboard and mouse input to the 8042 keyboard controller

Systems with USB Legacy support enable users to tap the BIOS to control the USB keyboard until a supported operating system is loaded. At that point, the USB host controller driver in the operating system takes control of the keyboard by sending an internal command called StopBIOS to the BIOS routine managing the keyboard. When Windows shuts down to MS-DOS or other non–USB-aware OS, the USB host controller sends a command called StartBIOS to restart the BIOS routine that manages the keyboard.

When the BIOS controls the keyboard, after the signals reach the 8042 keyboard controller, the USB keyboard is treated just like a conventional keyboard if the BIOS is correctly designed to work with USB keyboards. A BIOS upgrade might be necessary in some cases to provide proper support of USB keyboards on some systems. The system chipset also must support USB Legacy features.

Typematic Functions

If a key on the keyboard is held down, it becomes *typematic*, which means the keyboard repeatedly sends the keypress code to the motherboard. The typematic rate is adjusted by sending the appropriate commands to the keyboard processor.

You can adjust the typematic repeat rate and delay parameters with settings in your system BIOS (although not all BIOS chips can control all functions) or in your operating system. In DOS, you use the MODE command. The next section describes how to adjust the keyboard parameters in Windows, because this is more convenient than the other methods and enables you to make further adjustments at any time without restarting the system.

In Windows, you can modify the default values for the typematic repeat rate and delay parameters in any version of Windows using the Keyboard icon in the Control Panel. The Repeat Delay slider controls the duration in time that a key must be pressed before the character begins to repeat, and the Repeat Rate slider controls how fast the character repeats after the delay has elapsed.

Note

The increments on the Repeat Delay and Repeat Rate sliders in Keyboard Properties in the Control Panel correspond to the timings given for the MODE command's RATE and DELAY values. Each mark in the Repeat Delay slider adds about 0.25 seconds to the delay, and the marks in the Repeat Rate slider are worth about one character per second each.

The dialog box also contains a text box you can use to test the settings you have chosen before committing them to your system. When you click in the box and press a key, the keyboard reacts using the settings currently specified by the sliders, even if you have not yet applied the changes to the Windows environment.

Keyboard Key Numbers and Scan Codes

When you press a key on the keyboard, the processor built in to the keyboard reads the keyswitch location in the keyboard matrix. The processor then sends to the motherboard a serial packet of data containing the scan code for the key that was pressed. This is called the *Make code*. When the key is released, a corresponding *Break code* is sent, indicating to the motherboard that the key has been released. The Break code is equivalent to the Make scan code plus 80h. For example, if the Make scan code for the "A" key is 1Eh, the Break code would be 9Eh. By using both Make and Break scan codes, the system can determine whether a particular key has been held down and whether multiple keys are being pressed.

In motherboards that use an 8042-type keyboard controller, the 8042 chip translates the actual keyboard scan codes into one of up to three sets of system scan codes sent to the main processor. It can be useful in some cases to know what these scan codes are, especially when you're troubleshooting keyboard problems or reading the keyboard or system scan codes directly in software.

When a keyswitch on the keyboard sticks or otherwise fails, the Make scan code of the failed keyswitch usually is reported by diagnostics software, including the power on self test (POST), as well as conventional disk-based diagnostics. That means you must identify the malfunctioning key by its scan code. See the "Technical Reference" section of the CD-ROM included with this book for a comprehensive listing of keyboard key numbers and scan codes for industry standard 101/102-key (Enhanced) keyboard and 104-key Windows keyboards. By looking up the reported scan code on these charts, you can determine which keyswitch is defective or needs to be cleaned. There may be some variation on the exact key placement and scan codes for nonstandard keys found on some laptops, but generally this will give you an idea of which key corresponds to which code.

A unique key number is assigned to each key to distinguish it from the others (see Figure 13.9). This can be useful when trying to figure out which key is assigned to which scan code.

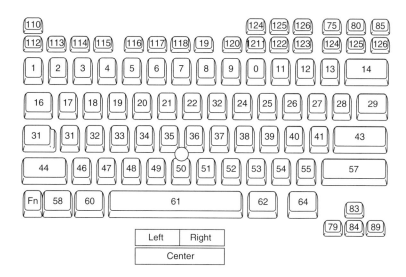

Figure 13.9   Typical 84-key laptop keyboard key numbers.

Knowing these key number figures and scan codes can be useful when you are troubleshooting stuck or failed keys on a keyboard. Diagnostics can report the defective keyswitch by the scan code, which varies from keyboard to keyboard as to the character it represents and its location.

Many enhanced and USB external keyboards now feature hotkeys that either have fixed uses—such as opening the default web browser, sending the system into Standby mode, and adjusting the speaker volume—or are programmable for user-defined functions. Each of these keys also has scan codes. Some companies such as Lenovo (IBM) produce external keyboards designed specifically for laptops that include the special Fn keys, allowing the use of the various Fn key combinations to switch displays, turn on/off wireless network or Bluetooth adapters, invoke suspend/hibernation modes, and so on. External USB keyboards use a special series of codes called Human Interface Device (HID), which are translated internally into PS/2 scan codes.

External Keyboard/Mouse Interface Connectors

External keyboards have a cable with one of two primary types of connectors at the system end:

- **PS/2 interface**—Uses a 6-pin mini-DIN connector
- **USB interface**—Uses a USB "A" connector

Figure 13.10 and Table 13.7 show the physical layout and pinouts of the PS/2 connector found on most laptop systems.

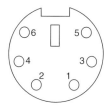

Figure 13.10   PS/2 (6-pin mini-DIN) connector socket.

Table 13.7   Laptop PS/2 (6-pin Mini-DIN) Connector Pinout

Signal Name	6-Pin Mini-DIN	Test Voltage
Mouse Data	1	+4.8V to 5.5V
Keyboard Data	2	+4.8V to 5.5V
Ground	3	-
+5V Power	4	+2.0V to 5.5V
Mouse Clock	5	+2.0V to 5.5V
Keyboard Clock	6	+2.0V to 5.5V

DIN = Deutsches Institut für Normung e.V., the committee that sets German dimensional standards

Note that this layout is not exactly the same as on desktop systems in that a single connector supports both mice and keyboards. However, only an external mouse can be directly connected. A keyboard can only be used via a "Y" or splitter connector that reroutes the signals to the proper pins for a keyboard. An example of this is the Keyboard/Mouse "Y" Connector sold by IBM under part number 54G0441 (see Figure 13.11).

Figure 13.11   Keyboard/Mouse "Y" splitter cable.

USB keyboards use the Series A USB connector to attach to the USB port built in to modern computers. Figure 13.12 and Table 13.8 show the physical layout and pinout of the USB Series A connector used on most laptops.

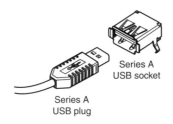

Series A
USB socket

Series A
USB plug

Figure 13.12   USB Series A plug and socket.

Most notebooks with USB connectors feature one or more Series A connectors on the rear or sides of the system.

Table 13.8   USB Connector Pinouts for Series A Connectors

Pin	Signal Name	Wire Color	Comment
1	Vbus	Red	Bus power
2	- Data	White	Data transfer
3	+ Data	Green	Data transfer
4	Ground	Black	Cable ground
Shell	Shield	—	Drain wire

To use an external keyboard connected via USB, besides having a free USB port, your system should meet one of the following requirements:

- You must run an OS with USB support, such as Windows 98 or later, Linux, and so on.
- You must have a system chipset and BIOS that features USB Legacy support.

USB Legacy support means your motherboard has a chipset and ROM BIOS drivers that enable a USB keyboard to be used even outside of an OS with USB support. When a system has USB Legacy support enabled, you can use a USB keyboard with a non–USB-aware OS such as MS-DOS, or when installing an OS for the first time (before the USB drivers are loaded). If USB Legacy support is not enabled on the system, a USB keyboard will function only when a USB-aware OS is running. Virtually all systems with built-in USB ports include USB Legacy support. You might not have USB Legacy support only if you have added USB ports via an adapter to a system that did not have any USB ports built in.

USB Keyboards with Hubs

Some external USB keyboards feature a built-in USB hub designed to add two or more USB ports to your system. Even though this sounds like a good idea, keep in mind that a keyboard-based hub won't provide additional power to the USB connectors. Powered hubs work better with a wider variety of devices than unpowered hubs do. I wouldn't choose a particular model based solely on this feature, although if your keyboard has the USB hub and your devices work well when plugged into it, that's great. I'd recommend that you use this type of keyboard with your USB mouse or other devices that don't require much power.

Keyboard Troubleshooting and Repair

Keyboard errors are usually caused by two simple problems:

- Defective cables/bad connections
- Stuck keys

Other more difficult, intermittent problems can arise, but they are much less common.

Defective Cables or Bad Connections

Defective cables or bad connections between the keyboard and the system are easy to spot if the failure is not intermittent. If the keyboard stops working altogether or every keystroke results in an error or incorrect character, the cable or connection is likely the culprit. On a portable system, the cable is internal to the system, and it's usually permanently attached to the keyboard end and plugged into the motherboard at the other end. The cable itself is normally a *flex-film* or *flex cable*, which consists of a very thin dielectric (insulating) film with conductors bonded on, looking more like a flexible ribbon circuit board than a conventional cable. The fact that it is permanently attached at the keyboard end means that if the cable actually goes bad, you'll probably have to replace the entire keyboard assembly. Fortunately, most flex cable problems are not the cable itself so much as the connection between the cable and the system. In some cases, the contacts can become dirty or tarnished, or the thin film end can be partially or completely pulled out of the mating connector.

Most flex cable connectors have tiny retaining latches that must be pulled out to release the grip on the cable, allowing it to be either removed or inserted. Once the cable is inserted, the latches are pressed inward, locking the flex cable end into place.

Troubleshooting or repairing a defective internal flex cable connection is simple:

1. Disengage the keyboard from the system. This may require multiple steps on some systems; see the disassembly instructions in Chapter 3, "System Maintenance and Assembly."

2. Disconnect the flex cable from the motherboard.

3. Clean the contacts using contact cleaner and a foam swab.

4. Reinsert the cable into the connector and reinstall the keyboard in the system.

If, after disconnecting, cleaning, and reconnecting the cable, you find that the problem remains, it most likely lies with the keyboard, the motherboard, or some other component in the system.

Stuck Keys

Many times you first discover a problem with a keyboard because the system has an error during the POST. Many systems use error codes in a 3xx numeric format to distinguish the keyboard. If you have any such errors during the POST, write them down. Some BIOS versions do not use cryptic numeric error codes; they simply state something such as the following:

```
Keyboard stuck key failure
```

This message is normally displayed by a system with a Phoenix BIOS if a key is stuck. Unfortunately, the message does not identify which key is malfunctioning!

If your system displays a 3xx (keyboard) error preceded by a two-digit hexadecimal number, the number is the scan code of a failing or stuck keyswitch. Look up the scan code in the tables provided in the "Technical Reference" section on the CD-ROM to determine which keyswitch is the culprit. By removing the keycap of the offending key and cleaning the switch, you often can solve the problem.

If your problems are with an external non-USB keyboard, and replacing the keyboard doesn't seem to solve the problem, you can try testing the external PS/2-type mouse/keyboard connector. For a simple test of the external mouse/keyboard connector, you can check voltages on some of the pins. Using Figure 13.10 as a guide, measure the voltages on various pins of the mouse/keyboard connector. To prevent possible damage to the system or keyboard, turn off the power before disconnecting the keyboard. Then, unplug the keyboard and turn the power back on. Make measurements between the ground pin and the other pins according to Table 13.7. If the voltages are within these specifications, the motherboard keyboard circuitry is probably okay.

If your measurements do not match these voltages, the motherboard might be defective. Otherwise, the external keyboard cable or keyboard might be defective. If you suspect that the cable is the problem, the easiest thing to do is replace the keyboard cable with a known good one. If the system still does not work normally, you might have to replace the entire keyboard or the motherboard.

See the CD-ROM included with this book for a listing of the standard POST and diagnostic keyboard error codes used by some systems.

Cleaning a Keyboard

One of the best ways to keep a keyboard in top condition is periodic cleaning. As preventive maintenance, you should vacuum the keyboard weekly, or at least monthly. When vacuuming, you should use a soft brush attachment; this helps dislodge the dust. Also note that even most built-in keyboards have keycaps that can come off easily; if you're not careful, you'll have to dig them out of the vacuum cleaner.

You also can use canned compressed air to blow the dust and dirt out instead of using a vacuum. Before you dust a keyboard with the compressed air, turn the keyboard upside down so that the particles of dirt and dust collected inside can fall out.

On virtually all keyboards, each keycap is removable, which can be handy if a key sticks or acts erratically. For example, a common problem is a key that does not work every time you press it. This problem usually results from dirt collecting under the key. An excellent tool for removing keycaps on almost any keyboard is the U-shaped chip puller included in many computer toolkits. Simply slip the hooked ends of the tool under the keycap (with the ends of the tool pressing down the adjacent keys instead of fitting between them), squeeze the ends together to grip the underside of the desired keycap, and lift up. If you don't have a tool like that, another quick solution is to use two small screwdrivers, using them to simultaneously lift from opposite sides of the key to pull it off. The important thing is to pry the key evenly straight up, and not to pry it off unevenly or from only one side. Once you lift off one or two keys, you will quickly get the hang of it. After removing the cap, spray some compressed air into the space under the cap to dislodge the dirt. Then replace the cap and check the action of the key.

Spills can be a problem, too. If you spill a soft drink or cup of coffee into a keyboard, you do not necessarily have a disaster. Many keyboards that use membrane switches are spill resistant. However, you should immediately (or as soon as possible) remove the keyboard from the system and flush it out with distilled water. Depending on how much liquid was spilled, you may need to rinse or clean out other parts of the system as well. Most circuits can be washed, but mechanical devices like disk drives require more careful handling and cleaning, and they should never be soaked or immersed in water.

If the spilled liquid has dried, try soaking the keyboard in some distilled water for a while. When you are sure the keyboard is clean, pour another gallon or so of distilled water over it and through the keyswitches to wash away any residual dirt. After the unit dries completely, you can reinstall it into the system, where it should be perfectly functional. You might be surprised to know that drenching your keyboard with distilled water does not harm the components. Just make sure you use distilled water, which is free from residue or mineral content. (Bottled water is *not* distilled; the distinct taste of many bottled waters comes from the trace minerals they contain!) Also, make sure the keyboard is *fully* dry before you try to use it; otherwise, some of the components might short out. Note that it might take a day or longer for the keyboard to fully dry out, and you are better safe than sorry.

Tip

If spills or excessive dust or dirt are expected because of the environment or conditions in which the system is used, you should purchase a thin membrane skin that molds over the top of the keyboard, protecting it from liquids, dust, and other contaminants. These skins are manufactured by several companies and are generally thin enough so that they don't interfere too much with the typing or action of the keys.

External Keyboard Recommendations

In most cases, replacing an external keyboard is cheaper or more cost effective than repairing it. This is especially true if the keyboard has an internal malfunction or if one of the keyswitches is defective.

Replacement parts for keyboards are almost impossible to procure, and installing any repair part is usually difficult. In addition, many of the keyboards supplied with lower-cost PCs leave much to be desired. They often have a mushy feel, with little or no tactile feedback. A poor keyboard can make using a system a frustrating experience, especially if you are a touch typist. For all these reasons, it is often a good idea to replace an existing keyboard with something better.

Perhaps the highest quality keyboards in the industry are those made by IBM, or, more accurately today, Unicomp. In 1991, IBM spun off its keyboard/printer division as Lexmark, which then spun off the keyboard division as Unicomp in 1996. Today, Unicomp still manufactures and sells "IBM" keyboards with the classic buckling-spring capacitive switch technology. Many models are available, including some with a built-in trackball or even the revolutionary TrackPoint pointing device (a small stick mounted between the G, H, and B keys). This device was first featured on the IBM ThinkPad laptop systems, although the keyboards are now sold for use on other manufacturers' PCs. The technology is being licensed to many other manufacturers, including Toshiba.

You can purchase new Unicomp (IBM) keyboards direct by calling toll free 1-800-777-4886, or you can visit the online store at `www.pckeyboard.com`. Unicomp maintains an extensive selection of more than 1,400 Lexmark and IBM keyboard models and continues to develop and sell a wide variety of traditional and customized models, including keyboards that match the school colors of several universities.

Another great source for IBM external keyboards is `www.clickykeyboard.com`. This site offers a number of used and new-old stock keyboards, including those with integral TrackPoints. The IBM/Lexmark/Unicomp keyboards with buckling-spring capacitive switches are essentially the best keyboards in the world, and they aren't that expensive either. Their durability is legendary, and because these keyboards never seem to fail, they are the one thing that has remained relatively constant in my systems over the years. Many other keyboards with mechanical switches use Alps Electric mechanical keyswitches. The keyswitch ratings are shown in the Table 13.9.

Table 13.9   Mechanical Keyswitch Types and Features

Feature	IBM/Lexmark/Unicomp	Alps Electric
Life	25 million cycles	20 million cycles
Tactile force	72 grams, +/-20 grams	70 grams, +/-25 grams
Travel	3.8mm	3.5mm

Note: Full-sized, full-stroke keys are spaced 18.5mm by 18.2mm (vertically by horizontally) and travel 2.5mm, as defined by ISO/IEC 15412.

The main difference between the two is not seen in these specs—it is the overall feel. The IBM/Lexmark/Unicomp keyswitches have a slightly longer way to travel before going "over center" (the click point). Also, the tactile force changes much more dramatically during a keystroke, especially right as the over-center point is reached. This makes both the audible and tactile feel of the key click much sharper and better defined. This equates to improved feedback, better feel, and greater typing accuracy as compared to more linear rate switches with a muted over-center point, such as the Alps. Some of these same Unicomp keyboards are available in the retail market under either the IBM or IBM Options brand name. Items under the IBM Options program are sold through normal retail channels, such as CompUSA and Computer Discount Warehouse (CDW). These items are also priced much cheaper than items purchased as spare parts. They include a full warranty and are sold as complete packages, including cables. Some feature the IBM UltraNav, which includes both a TrackPoint and a touch pad. Table 13.10 lists some of the IBM Options keyboards and part numbers. Models marked with an asterisk (*) are also available from Unicomp.

Table 13.10   IBM Options Keyboards (Sold Retail)

Description	Part Number
IBM Enhanced keyboard (cable with mini-DIN plug)	92G7453*
IBM Enhanced keyboard, built-in trackball (cable with mini-DIN plug)	92G7455*
IBM Enhanced keyboard, integrated TrackPoint II (cables with mini-DIN plugs)	92G7461*
IBM TrackPoint IV keyboard (black)	01K1260
IBM TrackPoint IV keyboard (white)	01K1259
IBM USB Keyboard with UltraNav (black)	31P8950
IBM Rapid Access III USB keyboard with two-port hub (black)	22P5185
IBM 106-Key USB Keyboard with two-port hub (black)	10K3849

Other manufacturers of high-quality keyboards that are similar in feel to the IBM/Lexmark/Unicomp units include Alps, Lite-On, NMB Technologies, and the revived Northgate designs sold under the Avant Prime and Avant Stellar names. These keyboards have excellent tactile feedback, with a positive "click" sound.

Pointing Devices

The mouse was invented in 1964 by Douglas Englebart, who at the time was working at the Stanford Research Institute (SRI), a think tank sponsored by Stanford University. The mouse was officially called an "X-Y Position Indicator for a Display System." Xerox later applied the mouse to its revolutionary Alto computer system in 1973.

Laptop and portable systems sold in the '80s and early '90s often did not include a pointing device, expecting the user to plug in an external device if it was necessary. Today, the graphical user interfaces for PC systems, such as Windows, practically demand the use of a mouse. Therefore, virtually every new laptop system comes with some form of pointing device built in.

TrackPoint II/III/IV

On October 5, 1992, IBM introduced a revolutionary new pointing device called TrackPoint II as an integrated feature of its ThinkPad 700 and 700C computers. Often referred to as a *pointing stick device*, TrackPoint II and its successors consist primarily of a small rubber cap that appears on the keyboard right above the B key, between the G and H keys (see Figure 13.13). The TrackPoint II was the first significant new pointing device since the mouse had been invented nearly 30 years earlier!

Figure 13.13   TrackPoint cap positioned between the G, H, and B keys.

This device occupies no space on a desk, does not have to be adjusted for left-handed or right-handed use, has no moving parts to fail or become dirty, and—most importantly—does not require you to move your hands from the home row to use it. This is an absolute boon for touch typists.

I was fortunate enough to meet the actual creator and designer of this device in early 1992 at the spring Comdex/Windows World in Chicago. He was in a small corner of the IBM booth showing off his custom-made keyboards with a small silicone rubber nub in the middle. In fact, the devices he had were hand-built prototypes installed in standard desktop keyboards, and he was there trying to get public reaction and feedback on his invention. I was invited to play with one of the keyboards, which was connected to a demonstration system. By pressing on the stick with my index finger, I could move the mouse pointer on the screen. The stick itself did not move, so it was not a joystick. Instead, it had a silicone rubber cap that was connected to pressure transducers that measured the amount of force my finger was applying and the direction of the force, and it moved the mouse pointer accordingly. The harder I pressed, the faster the pointer moved. After I played around with it for just a few minutes, the movements became automatic—almost as though I could just think about where I wanted the pointer to go.

The gentleman at the booth turned out to be Ted Selker, the primary inventor of the device. He and Joseph Rutledge created this integrated pointing device at the IBM T.J. Watson Research Center. When I asked him when such keyboards would become available, he could not answer. At the time, there were apparently no plans for production, and he was only trying to test user reaction to the device.

Just over six months later, IBM announced the ThinkPad 700, which included this revolutionary device—then called the TrackPoint II Integrated Pointing Device. Since the original version came out, enhanced versions with greater control and sensitivity, called the TrackPoint III and IV, have become available.

Note

The device was called TrackPoint *II* because IBM had previously been selling a convertible mouse/trackball device called the TrackPoint. No relationship exists between the original TrackPoint mouse/trackball, which has since been discontinued, and the TrackPoint II integrated device. Since the original TrackPoint II came out, improved versions (TrackPoint III and TrackPoint IV) have become available. In the interest of simplicity, I will refer to all the TrackPoint II and successive devices as just *TrackPoint*.

In its final production form, the TrackPoint consists of a small (usually red colored) silicone rubber knob nestled between the G, H, and B keys on the keyboard (see Figure 13.14). The primary and secondary mouse buttons are placed below the spacebar, where you can easily reach them with your thumbs without taking your hands off the keyboard.

IBM studies conducted by Selker found that the act of removing your hand from the keyboard to reach for a mouse and then placing your hand on the keyboard again takes approximately 1.75 seconds. If you type 60 words per minute (wpm), that can equal nearly two lost words per minute, not including the time lost while you regain your train of thought. Almost all this time can be saved each time you use TrackPoint to move the pointer or make a selection (click or double-click). The combination of the buttons and the positioning knob also enable you to perform drag-and-drop functions easily.

IBM's research also found that people can get up to 20% more work accomplished using the TrackPoint instead of a mouse, especially when the application involves a mix of typing and pointing activities, such as with word processing, spreadsheet, and other typical office applications. In usability tests with the TrackPoint III, IBM gave a group of desktop computer users a TrackPoint and a traditional mouse. After two weeks, 80% of the users had unplugged their mice and switched solely to the TrackPoint device. Selker is convinced (as am I) that the TrackPoint is the best pointing solution for both laptop and desktop systems.

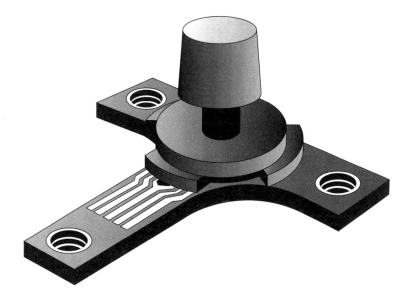

Figure 13.14   Raw TrackPoint pointer module.

Another feature of the TrackPoint is that a standard mouse can be connected to the system at the same time to enable dual-pointer use. This setup not only enables a single person to use both devices but also enables two people to use the TrackPoint and the mouse simultaneously to move the pointer on the screen. The first pointing device that moves (thus issuing a system interrupt) takes precedence and retains control over the mouse pointer on the screen until it completes its movement action. The second pointing device is automatically locked out until the primary device is stationary. This enables the use of both devices and prevents each one from interfering with the other.

IBM has added various versions of the TrackPoint to its notebook computers, as well as to high-end keyboards sold under the IBM, Lexmark, and Unicomp names. Notebook computer makers, such as HP and Toshiba, also have licensed the TrackPoint device (Toshiba calls it *Accupoint*). I have compared the TrackPoint device to other pointing devices for notebooks, such as the trackballs and even the capacitive touch pads, but nothing compares in terms of accuracy and control—and, of course, you don't have to take your hands off the keyboard!

Some notebook computer makers copied the TrackPoint instead of licensing it, but with poor results, including sluggish response to input and poor accuracy. One way of telling whether the TrackPoint device is licensed from IBM and uses the IBM technology is if it accepts IBM TrackPoint II/III/IV rubber caps. They have a square hole in them and will properly lock on to any of the licensed versions, such as those found in Toshiba systems.

TrackPoint Caps

IBM has upgraded its pointing stick to the TrackPoint III and the current TrackPoint IV. Two main differences exist in the III/IV system, but the most obvious one is in the rubber cap. The original

TrackPoint caps were made from silicone rubber, which is grippy and works well in most situations. However, if the user has greasy fingers, the textured surface of the rubber can absorb some of the grease and become slippery. Cleaning the cap (and the user's hands) solves the problem, but it can be annoying at times. The newer TrackPoint III/IV caps are made from a different type of rubber, which Selker calls "plastic sandpaper." This type of cap is much more grippy and does not require cleaning except for cosmetic purposes. I have used both types of caps and can say for certain that the TrackPoint III/IV cap is superior.

IBM now has three different types of caps for the TrackPoint to suit different needs and tastes (see Figure 13.15):

- **Classic dome (p/n 84G6537)**—The traditional "pencil eraser" cap.
- **Soft rim (p/n 91P8423)**—A larger concave design creates a mechanical advantage, requiring less force for pointer motion.
- **Soft dome (p/n 91P8422)**—A larger convex design with a soft texture.

Figure 13.15   Classic, Soft Rim, and Soft Dome TrackPoint caps.

Replacement TrackPoint caps are sold by IBM, Compu-Lock (`www.compu-lock.com`), as well as several other vendors.

Replacing the caps is easy—just grab the existing cap with your fingers and pull straight up; it pops right off. Then, push on the new cap in its place.

Other TrackPoint Improvements

The other difference between the TrackPoint II and the TrackPoint III/IV from IBM is in the control software. IBM added routines that implement a subtle technique Selker calls "negative inertia," which is marketed under the label *QuickStop response*. This software not only takes into account how far you push the pointer in any direction but also how quickly you push or release it. Selker found that this improved software (and the sandpaper cap) enables people to make selections up to 8% faster. TrackPoint IV includes an extra scroll button as well as the ability to press the TrackPoint nub to select as if using the left mouse button. These new features make the TrackPoint even better to use.

The bottom line is that anyone who touch-types should strongly consider only portable systems that include an IBM-licensed TrackPoint device (such as Toshiba). The TrackPoint is far superior to other pointing devices, such as the touch pads, because it is faster to use (you don't have to take your hands off the keyboard's home row), easier to adapt to (especially for speedy touch typists), and far more precise. It takes some getting accustomed to, but the benefits are worth it.

The benefits of the TrackPoint are not limited to portable systems, however. If you use a notebook computer with TrackPoint like I do, you can have the same features on your desktop keyboard. For desktop systems, I use a Lexmark keyboard with the IBM-licensed TrackPoint device built in. This makes for a more consistent interface between desktop and notebook use because I can use the same pointing device in both environments. You also can buy these keyboards directly from Unicomp; IBM also offers TrackPoint IV in some of its high-end keyboards available at retail.

Touch Pads

The first touch pad was included on the ill-fated Gavilan portable computer in 1982; however, it didn't catch on until many years later. Cirque originated the modern touch pad (also called a *track pad*) pointing device in 1994. Cirque refers to its technology as the *GlidePoint* and has licensed the technology to other vendors, such as Alps Electric, which also uses the same term for its touch pads. The GlidePoint uses a flat, square pad that senses finger position through measuring body capacitance via a grid of electrodes under the surface. This is similar to the capacitance-sensitive elevator button controls you sometimes encounter in office buildings or hotels.

When it is used on a portable computer's keyboard, the touch pad is mounted below the spacebar, and it detects pressure applied by your thumbs or fingers. An electrode grid under the pad converts finger pressure and movement into pointer movement. The entire outline of the finger contact region is sensed; then software calculates the center point. Several laptop and notebook manufacturers have licensed this technology from Cirque and have incorporated it into their portable systems. Touch pads are also integrated into a number of mid-range to high-end keyboards from many vendors. When used on a desktop keyboard, touch pads are often offset to the right side of the keyboard's typing area. Figure 13.16 shows the internal grid underneath the cover layer of a typical touch pad.

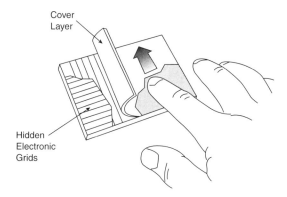

Figure 13.16   Touch pad internal view.

Touch pads feature mouse buttons, although you also can tap or double-tap on the touch pad's surface to activate an onscreen button located under the touch pad's cursor. You can drag and drop without touching the touch pad's buttons; just move the cursor to the object to be dragged, press down on the pad, hold while moving the cursor to the drop point, and release to drop the object. Some recent models also feature additional hot buttons with functions similar to those on hot-button keyboards, as well a vertical scrollbar on the side, and the ability to tap the touchpad to simulate a mouse click.

The primary use for touch pads has been for notebook computer– and desktop keyboard–integrated pointing devices, although Cirque and Alps have both sold standalone versions of the touch pad for use as a mouse alternative on desktop systems. Cirque's touch pads are now available at retail under the Fellowes brand name, as well as direct from the Cirque website.

Although it has gained wide acceptance, especially on portable computers, touch pad technology can have a number of drawbacks for some users. Operation of the device can be erratic, depending on skin resistance and moisture content. The biggest drawback is that to operate the touch pad, users must remove their hands from the home row on the keyboard, which dramatically slows their progress. In addition, the operation of the touch pad can be imprecise, depending on how pointy your finger or thumb is! On the other hand, if you're not a touch typist, removing your hands from the keyboard to operate the touch pad might be easier than using a TrackPoint. Even with their drawbacks, touch pad pointing devices are still vastly preferable to using a trackball or a cumbersome external mouse with portable systems.

Unless you want to use a "real" mouse with a portable system, I recommend you sit down with portable computers that have both touch pad and TrackPoint pointing devices. Try them yourself for typing, file management, and simple graphics and see which type of integrated pointing device you prefer. I know what I like, but you might have different tastes.

External Pointing Devices

Once you have decided on which interface to use, several different types of external pointing devices are available. This section describes the most popular choices.

Mice

Mice come in many shapes and sizes and from many manufacturers. Some have taken the standard mouse design and turned it upside down, creating the trackball. Several manufacturers make small mice especially designed for portable use, often including unique features like internally retractable cords. They are much easier to carry in a laptop bag than a full-sized mouse.

The largest manufacturers of mice are Microsoft and Logitech; these two companies provide designs that inspire the rest of the industry (and each other) and are popular OEM choices as well as retail brands. Even though mice can come in different varieties, their actual use and care differ very little. The standard mouse consists of several components:

- A housing that you hold in your hand and move around on your desktop.
- A method of transmitting movement to the system (either ball/roller or optical sensors).
- Buttons (two or more, and often a wheel or toggle switch) for making selections.
- An interface for connecting the mouse to the system. Conventional mice use a wire and connector, whereas wireless mice use a radio-frequency (RF) or infrared (IR) transceiver in both the mouse and a separate unit connected to the computer to interface the mouse to the computer.

The housing, which is made of plastic, consists of very few moving parts. On top of the housing, where your fingers normally rest, are buttons. There might be any number of buttons, but in the PC world, two is the standard. If additional buttons or a wheel are on your mouse, specialized driver software provided by the mouse vendor is required for them to operate to their full potential. Although the latest versions of Windows support scrolling mice, other features supported by the vendor still require installation of the vendor's own mouse driver software.

The detection mechanisms or electronics are located on the bottom of the mouse housing. On traditional mice, the bottom of the housing contains a small rubber ball that rolls as you move the mouse across the tabletop. The movements of this rubber ball are translated into electrical signals transmitted to the computer across the cable.

Mechanical Mice

Internally, a ball-driven mouse is very simple, too. The ball usually rests against two rollers: one for translating the X-axis movement, and the other for translating the Y-axis movement. These rollers are usually connected to small disks with shutters that alternately block and allow the passage of light. Small optical sensors detect movement of the wheels by watching an internal infrared light blink on and off as the shutter wheel rotates and "chops" the light. These blinks are translated into movement along the axes. This type of setup, called an *opto-mechanical mechanism*, was the most popular mechanism prior to the advent of inexpensive optical technology (see Figure 13.17).

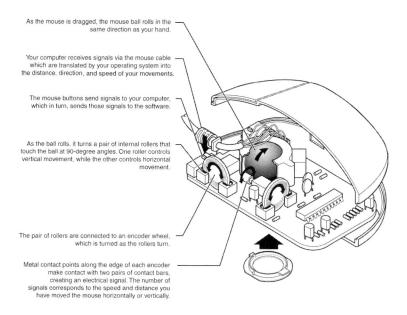

As the mouse is dragged, the mouse ball rolls in the same direction as your hand.

Your computer receives signals via the mouse cable which are translated by your operating system into the distance, direction, and speed of your movements.

The mouse buttons send signals to your computer, which in turn, sends those signals to the software.

As the ball rolls, it turns a pair of internal rollers that touch the ball at 90-degree angles. One roller controls vertical movement, while the other controls horizontal movement.

The pair of rollers are connected to an encoder wheel, which is turned as the rollers turn.

Metal contact points along the edge of each encoder make contact with two pairs of contact bars, creating an electrical signal. The number of signals corresponds to the speed and distance you have moved the mouse horizontally or vertically.

Figure 13.17   Typical opto-mechanical mouse mechanism.

Optical Mice

The other major method of motion detection is optical. Some of the early mice made by Mouse Systems and a few other vendors used a sensor that required a special grid-marked pad. Although these mice were very accurate, the need to use them with a pad caused them to fall out of favor.

Microsoft's IntelliMouse Explorer pioneered the return of optical mice, but with a difference. Like the old-style optical mice, the IntelliMouse Explorer uses optical technology to detect movement, and it has no moving parts itself (except for the scroll wheel and buttons on top). The Explorer mouse needs no pad; it can work on virtually any surface. This is done by upgrading the optical sensor from the simple type used in older optical mice to a more advanced charge coupled device (CCD). This essentially is a crude version of a video camera sensor that detects movement by seeing the surface move under the mouse. An LED or diode laser is used to provide light for the sensor.

The IntelliMouse Explorer was just the first of a growing family of optical mice made by Microsoft (the IntelliMouse Optical and WheelMouse Optical are less expensive versions), and Microsoft also offers an optical-technology trackball. Logitech also offers optical mice (including one with two sensors) and optical trackballs using similar technology. Because of greater precision and reliability, optical technology has become the dominant technology in modern mice and trackballs (see Figure 13.18).

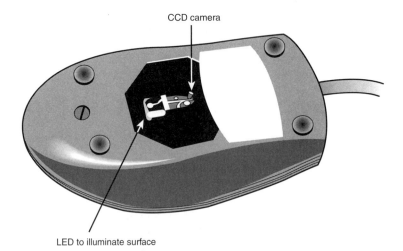

CCD camera

LED to illuminate surface

Figure 13.18 The bottom of the Logitech iFeel optical mouse.

Their versatility and low maintenance (not to mention that neat red glow out the sides!) make optical mice an attractive choice, and the variety of models available from both vendors means you can have the latest optical technology for about the price of a good ball-type mouse.

The cable can be any length, but it is typically between 4 and 6 feet long. Mice are also available in a cordless design, which uses either IR or RF transceivers to replace the cable. A receiver is plugged into the mouse port, whereas the battery-powered mouse contains a compatible transmitter.

Tip

If you have a choice on the length of cable to buy, go for a longer one. This allows easier placement of the mouse in relation to your computer. Extension cables can be used if necessary.

Mouse Drivers

After the mouse is connected to your computer, it communicates with your system through the use of a device driver, which can be loaded explicitly or built in to the operating system software. For example, no separate drivers are necessary to use a mouse with Windows or OS/2, but using the mouse with most DOS-based programs requires a separate driver to be loaded from the CONFIG.SYS or AUTOEXEC.BAT file. Regardless of whether it is built in, the driver translates the electrical signals sent from the mouse into positional information and indicates the status of the buttons.

The standard mouse drivers in Windows are designed for the traditional two-button mouse or scroll mouse (in Windows Me/2000/XP or later), but increasing numbers of mice feature additional buttons, toggles, or wheels to make the mouse more useful. These additional features require special mouse driver software supplied by the manufacturer.

Trackballs

The first trackball I ever saw outside an arcade was the Wico trackball, a perfect match for mid-1980s video games and computer games, such as Missile Command and others. It emulated the eight-position Atari 2600 analog joystick, but was capable of much more flexibility.

Unlike the mid-80s trackballs, today's trackballs are used primarily for business instead of gaming. Most trackballs use a mouse-style positioning mechanism—the differences being that the trackball is on the top or side of the case and is much larger than a mouse ball. The user moves the trackball rather than the input device case, but rollers or wheels inside most models translate the trackball's motion and move a cursor onscreen the same way that mouse rollers or wheels convert the mouse ball's motion into cursor movement.

Trackballs come in a variety of forms, including ergonomic models shaped to fit the (right) hand, ambidextrous models suitable for both left- and right-handers, optical models that use the same optical sensors found in the latest mice in place of wheels and rollers, and multibutton monsters that look as if they're the product of a meeting with a remote control or game controller.

Because they are larger than mice, trackballs lend themselves well to the extra electronics and battery power needed for wireless use. Logitech offers several wireless trackball models that use radio-frequency transceivers; for details of how this technology works, see the following section, "Wireless Input Devices."

Trackballs use the same drivers and connectors as conventional mice. For basic operations, the operating system–supplied drivers will work, but you should use the latest version of the vendor-supplied drivers to achieve maximum performance with recent models.

External Pointing Device Interfaces

The connector used to attach your mouse to the system depends on the type of interface you are using. Three main interfaces are used for mouse connections. Mice are most commonly connected to your computer through the following interfaces:

- Serial interface (obsolete)
- Dedicated motherboard (PS/2) mouse port
- USB port
- Bluetooth or other wireless connection

Serial

A popular method of connecting a mouse to older PCs is through the standard serial interface. As with other serial devices, the connector on the end of the mouse cable is typically a 9-pin female connector; some very old mice used a 25-pin female connector. Only a couple of pins in the DB-9 or DB-25 connector are used for communications between the mouse and the device driver, but the mouse connector typically has all 9 or 25 pins present (see Figure 13.19).

Because a serial mouse does not connect to the system directly, it does not use system resources by itself. Instead, the resources used are those used by the serial port to which it is connected. For example, if you have a mouse connected to COM2, and COM2 is using the default IRQ and I/O port address range, both the serial port and the mouse connected to it use IRQ3 and I/O port addresses 2F8h–2FFh.

Note that serial mice are considered obsolete today, and very few laptops still include serial ports today except on external port replicators or docks.

PS/2 Mouse Port

Many laptops have included a PS/2-style mouse port built in to the motherboard. This practice was introduced by IBM with the PS/2 systems in 1987, so this interface is often referred to as a *PS/2 interface*. This term does not imply that such a mouse can work only with a PS/2; instead, it means the mouse can connect to any system that has a dedicated mouse port on the motherboard.

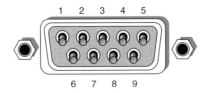

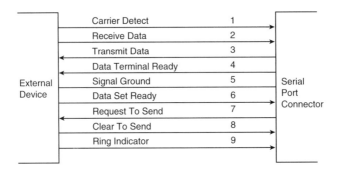

	Carrier Detect	1
	Receive Data	2
	Transmit Data	3
	Data Terminal Ready	4
External Device	Signal Ground	5
	Data Set Ready	6
	Request To Send	7
	Clear To Send	8
	Ring Indicator	9

Figure 13.19 A 9-pin serial port connector and specifications.

Caution

The mini-DIN socket used for both mouse and keyboard connections on most laptop systems is a single port with dual functionality. A mouse plugs in directly and works, whereas using a keyboard requires a special Y-adapter that splits out the mouse and keyboard signals. If you intend to use an external mouse only, the adapter is not required. However, if you want to use an external keyboard, or an external keyboard and mouse simultaneously, then the Y-adapter is necessary.

The standard resource usage for a motherboard (or PS/2) mouse port is IRQ12, as well as I/O port addresses 60h and 64h. Because the motherboard mouse port uses the 8042-type keyboard controller chip, the port addresses are those of this chip. IRQ12 is an interrupt that is usually free on most systems.

USB

USB is increasingly being used for mice as well as keyboards and other I/O devices. Compared to the other interfaces, USB mice (and other USB pointing devices such as trackballs) have the following advantages:

- USB mice operate more smoothly than the traditional PS/2 type. With these mice, the frequency with which the mouse reports its position is much higher. A typical PS/2 mouse has a reporting rate of about 40Hz, whereas an average USB mouse has a reporting rate of 125Hz. Several utilities are available to test and adjust the mouse frequency.

- The newest and most advanced mice are usually made especially for the USB port. One example is the Logitech iFeel mouse, the first mouse with an optical sensor plus force feedback. It vibrates gently as you move the mouse over clickable buttons on web pages, software menus, and the Windows desktop, and it's made especially for USB.

- USB mice and pointing devices are hot-swappable, meaning they can be plugged and unplugged with the system running. You can't do that with the other port types without problems, especially PS/2 mice.

■ USB mice can be attached to a USB hub, such as the hubs contained in some USB keyboards, as well as standalone hubs. Using a hub makes attaching and removing your mouse easy without your crawling around on the floor to reach the back of the computer.

If you want to use a USB mouse in a non–USB-aware OS, make sure that USB Legacy mode is supported in your PC's BIOS, as discussed earlier in this chapter.

Hybrid Mice

Hybrid mice are those designed to plug into two types of ports. Most of the low-cost mice sold at retail are designed to plug into either the serial port or the PS/2 port; more expensive mice often plug into either the PS/2 port or the USB port. These combination mice are more flexible than the mice usually bundled with systems, which are designed to work only with the PS/2 or USB port to which they attach.

Circuitry in a hybrid mouse automatically detects the type of port to which it is connected and configures the mouse automatically. Serial-PS/2 hybrid mice usually come with a mini-DIN connector on the end of their cable and an adapter that converts the mini-DIN to a 9- or 25-pin serial port connector, although the reverse is sometimes true on earlier examples of these mice. PS/2-USB mice usually come with the USB connector on the end of their cable and include a mini-DIN (PS/2) adapter.

Sometimes people use adapters to try to connect a serial mouse to a motherboard mouse port or a motherboard mouse to a serial port. If this does not work, it is not the fault of the adapter. If the mouse does not explicitly state that it is both a serial and a PS/2-type mouse, it works only on the single interface for which it was designed. Most of the time, you find the designation for which type of mouse you have printed on its underside. A safe rule of thumb to follow is, if the mouse didn't come with an adapter or came bundled with a system, it probably won't work with an adapter.

Wireless Input Devices

For several years, many manufacturers have offered cordless versions of mice and keyboards. In most cases, these devices have used either infrared or short-range radio transceivers to attach to standard USB or PS/2 ports, with matching transceivers located in the mouse or keyboard. Wireless input devices can be especially useful for projector-based presentations, allowing the operator to sit far away from both the projector and the laptop system. They can also be used in cramped home-office environments or where a large-screen TV/monitor device is used for home entertainment and computing. Some game controllers are now available in wireless forms as well.

Radio Versus Infrared

Although some vendors still use infrared transceivers, most vendors support RF (radio frequency) signals. Having used both kinds, I can tell you that an RF input device beats an infrared input device hands down for use at home or in a small one- or two-person office. Infrared requires an unobstructed direct line between the transceivers. When I used an infrared keyboard/pointing stick combination at a client site, I was constantly re-aiming the keyboard at the receiver to avoid losing my signal. When I used an RF mouse, on the other hand, I didn't have to worry about line-of-sight issues. The only advantage to infrared is cost, but the problems of reliability in my mind outweigh any cost savings.

There are two main types of RF input devices: those that use the standard Bluetooth interface and those that use a proprietary interface. I generally prefer Bluetooth if my laptop has a built-in Bluetooth interface, because then I have one less thing to plug in. Using devices with a proprietary RF interface requires that you plug the included RF transceiver into a USB port. Those that support Bluetooth usually include a USB Bluetooth transceiver as well, but they should also be able to use the built-in Bluetooth interface if your laptop includes one. Beware, though, that not all of the built-in

Bluetooth interfaces support external keyboards and mice, and the Bluetooth keyboards and mice often use more power and consequently have less battery life than proprietary models. It seems as if there is a trade-off either way.

Major Vendors and Products

Unlike conventional mouse and keyboard producers, whose numbers are legion, the ranks of cordless input device makers are small. The major vendors include the following:

- Logitech makes radio-frequency mice and keyboards.
- Microsoft makes radio-frequency mice.
- Other vendors make infrared mice and keyboards (usually combination units).

Logitech

Mouse maker Logitech manufactures both radio-frequency wireless keyboards and radio-frequency wireless mice (first developed in 1992). Because Logitech developed wireless mice for several years before developing wireless keyboards, its older wireless mouse receivers work only with mice; you must use a separate receiver for its wireless keyboards. If you want to use a wireless mouse and keyboard, you should purchase both units as a bundle; a single receiver with dual mouse and keyboard channels is usually supplied with bundled wireless keyboard/mouse sets. Check Logitech's support website for details about the compatibility of a particular receiver with a specified Logitech wireless mouse or keyboard.

Logitech's cordless series of wireless keyboard/mouse combinations can be attached through either the PS/2 mouse/keyboard ports or the USB port, allowing them to be used with older, non–USB-aware versions of Windows as well as the newer versions (Windows 98 and later) that support USB. Older wireless mice use either the PS/2 port or the serial port.

Microsoft and Other Vendors

Microsoft makes a series of wireless input devices as of this writing—those using proprietary RF technology as well as industry-standard Bluetooth technology. The receivers attach to either a PS/2 mouse port or USB port; however, some are PS/2 only or USB only. The Bluetooth models should be able to interface to any laptop with built-in Bluetooth capability, without having to use the receiver included with the mouse.

Older infrared input devices normally combine both keyboard and mouse functions. These devices are offered by vendors such as Acer, PC Concepts, SIIG, and others, and they normally attach to the PS/2 mouse and keyboard ports. For improved reliability, some feature dual infrared transceivers in the keyboard or receiving unit to enable the unit to be moved around without losing the signal. Some infrared models were designed with a long signal range for use in computer presentations, but most of these have since been redesigned to use radio-frequency technology.

Wireless Pointing Device Issues

Before you invest in wireless pointing devices for multiple computers, you should be aware of the following issues:

- **Line-of-sight issues**—Infrared devices won't work if the IR beam between the pointing device and the receiver attached to the system is blocked. These units are not as suitable for casual in-the-lap use as radio-frequency units would be.
- **Radio-frequency interference**—Although early wireless mice used analog tuners that were hard to synchronize, today's wireless input devices normally use digital selectors. However, if several

similar devices are used in close quarters, a receiver might actually receive data from the wrong mouse or keyboard. Also, metal desks and furniture can reduce range and cause erratic cursor movement. Most wireless devices operate around 27MHz, thus minimizing interference from devices such as cordless phones. Bluetooth devices use the 2.4GHz band, which is the same as 802.11b Wi-Fi as well as many newer cordless phones, meaning they can interfere if used simultaneously. Check with the vendor of your specific wireless device for tips on overcoming interference issues.

■ **Battery life and availability**—Early wireless devices sometimes used unusual, expensive batteries. Today's units run on common battery types, such as AAA. Battery life is usually rated at about six months. Make sure you have spare batteries for the input device to avoid failures due to running out of battery power. The included software by companies such as Logitech gives users an onscreen warning when batteries run low. Some now include rechargeable batteries, which can save money in the long run. To save battery life when using an optical wireless mouse, try working on brighter or whiter surfaces. Many optical mice adjust their sensors based on the illumination of the surface; this is why you may see the light in the mouse change intensity. The less intensely the internal LED operates, the less battery power is being used.

■ **Location**—The range of wireless can vary from 6 feet to as many as 30 feet. Consider where the device will be used before making your purchase. For instance, in an office where multiple devices may be used at the same time, a close-range device may be more desirable in order to avoid "crosstalk" among devices. On the other hand, the home user who wants to sit away from the screen while maintaining control may desire an extended range.

■ **User experience**—Different users will have different expectations of wireless input devices, but in general, the more a wireless input device acts like its wired siblings, the better. The fact that a device is wireless should not compromise its functionality. If reliability, connection, and driver problems hinder proper usage, the device isn't worth using. Hardcore gamers who need the fastest response time possible will generally favor the responsiveness of a wired optical mouse over any wireless mouse. Although minimal, some lag time does exist. Some mice can require up to 0.25 centimeters of movement before responding. This lag time may also affect users doing graphical work, which requires the superior consistency and accuracy of a wired optical mouse.

A great many add-on devices are available for use with portable systems, providing functions that cannot practically or economically be included inside a system itself. Indeed, many of the most common uses for portable systems might require additional hardware, either because of the computer's location or the requirements of the function.

Note that when it comes to laptop accessories, the range of available options may actually exceed those available for desktops. Consider that laptop owners not only can choose from a wide array of desktop accessories, but they can also take advantage of a large group of accessories that are meant for use exclusively by portable systems. The only desktop accessories not available to laptops are internal expansion cards and storage drives—and in some cases even these components can be installed in certain laptop configurations. The following sections discuss some of the most common peripherals used with portable systems.

Carrying Cases

Perhaps the most popular accessory for laptops is the carrying case—and for good reason. Anyone who takes an expensive laptop computer out into the real world wants to be sure it will survive undamaged. People can and do carry their laptops in briefcases, backpacks, and probably everything short of a paper grocery bag, but for real protection, laptops should be carried in cases specifically designed for that purpose, with special cushioning to limit any damage from accidental knocks and drops.

Over the years, several different types of cushioning have been employed in laptop carrying cases. The simplest and most common form of cushioning is a layer of foam rubber. A handful of cases have enhanced this type of cushioning by suspending the laptop in an elastic sling. A small number of other carrying cases used inflatable cushions. The inflatable cases provided a good degree of cushioning but often required partial deflation in order to remove the laptop.

It is difficult to get an exact measurement of the cushioning capability of a carrying case without doing extensive drop testing. You can, however, obtain a rough estimate of the cushioning simply by squeezing the side and bottom walls of the case. Of course, the thicker the walls, the better. The foam should be soft, but not too soft. The bottom should be thicker than the sidewalls.

One of the most common ways a laptop is damaged is by failure of the carrying case's shoulder strap, causing the case to plummet to the ground. Be sure that the fixtures of the shoulder strap are composed of sturdy metal and not plastic.

The carrying capacities of cases vary considerably. Most have several pockets designed for different purposes. The largest pocket is designed for the laptop and is usually the only one that is cushioned. A few of the larger cases have a second large cushioned pocket for devices such as a portable printer. At least one smaller pocket is also available for carrying items such as power supplies and phone cables. Because you will probably be carrying a considerable quantity of paper as well as your laptop, look for a case with a pocket that can easily accommodate a folded newspaper or a few magazines. In fact, when you shop for a carrying case, it is a good idea to bring along not only your laptop but a newspaper as well.

Many different types of carrying cases are currently available. Table 14.1 lists the most common types.

Table 14.1   Laptop Carrying Cases: Several Different Types of Cases Are Designed for Various Applications and User Profiles

Type	Weight	Price
Nylon case	3–5 lbs.	$40–$150
Leather case	4–6 lbs.	$150–$400
Backpack	3–5 lbs.	$50–$125
Wheeled case	8–15 lbs.	$100–$200
Ruggedized case	10–20 lbs	$100–$300

The following sections discuss each of these case types in further detail.

Nylon Cases

The most inexpensive type of laptop carrying case is the soft-sided nylon case. This case is simple, lightweight, and usually has ample storage capabilities for laptop accessories and papers, along with good cushioning (see Figure 14.1).

Figure 14.1   The Targus NotePac, a popular nylon carrying case for notebook computers.

Although nylon carrying cases are affordable and practical, they suffer from two problems. The first is that they are usually an open advertisement that you are carrying a laptop and therefore represent an inviting target for theft. This can be a considerable problem in certain areas of the world. The second problem is that nylon cases do not age well. After a year or so of use, the case will have a crumpled look that may be inappropriate for certain high-level boardrooms.

Leather Cases

The carrying case for the laptop-toting executive is leather. Slightly heavier than the nylon cases, these expensive cases do not offer any additional cushioning, but they look much better in the corner office. Note that leather cases tend to have smaller carrying capacities than nylon cases. Some manufacturers have begun to create leather cases specifically designed for female notebook owners. These leather cases are sleeker, more stylish, and tend to look more like a lady's handbag.

Backpack Cases

In high schools and on college campuses, the standard carrying case is the backpack. For this audience, some backpacks now have special cushioned pockets for notebook computers. One of the best features of these cases is that they completely disguise the fact that you may be carrying a laptop. Note that despite the cushioning, a dropped backpack can still damage your laptop. Be sure that the shoulder straps are of sufficient quality.

Wheeled Cases

One of the greatest advances in luggage history was the development of the wheeled suitcase. Now we have wheeled computer cases, which come in quite handy when you need to drag around a laptop plus a projector, printer, camera, or a multitude of other accessories.

I personally use a two-case setup from Targus called the Shuttle, which features a large rolling case with a smaller internal satellite case (see Figure 14.2). This type of case fits my needs perfectly. Most of the time I travel to a client's location to either teach a class in the client's office or training room or to work on the client's systems for several days while staying at a local hotel. With the large roller case, I can bring everything I need and yet easily take my laptop back to my hotel room every night in the smaller satellite case.

Figure 14.2   The Targus Shuttle, a large roller case with a smaller laptop case inside.

This case is the largest possible that conforms to the FAA regulations for overhead storage, so I can take it with me on a plane when I travel. This allows me to take all my mobile accessories, tools, cables, discs, and so on, to a work site and then travel locally with only my laptop in the smaller case.

The Shuttle includes handles on the top and side for easy carrying, and it has an adjustable telescopic handle for wheeled use. The wheels are inline skate wheels with ball bearings that roll extremely well over most surfaces. The case features two main compartments that are fully lined and padded, with one of them including an adjustable divider. There are also mesh pockets in both compartments for smaller accessories, as well as pockets for CDs, floppy/Zip disks, PC Cards, pens, and more. The zippers are self-healing and have metal pulls with a hole for a small lock or zip tie. The side of the case even has additional external pockets for documentation, papers, and smaller items. This particular "case within a case" setup suits my needs perfectly.

Finally, there are also "hybrid" wheeled backpack cases available. This type of case can be carried around like a conventional backpack, but it also has a retractable handle and small wheels which allow it to be lugged around as a wheeled case. These cases are well suited for both business travelers and students.

Ruggedized Cases

In some environments, the soft-sided cases will not do. Here, you will need one of the rigid cases, made either of metal or hard nylon backed by extra cushioning. Note that all this protection costs money, sometimes even more than fancy leather cases cost.

If you want the ultimate in cases, consider buying one that meets ATA (Air Transportation Association) Specification 300 standards (see Figure 14.3). Such a case is often called an "ATA flight case" or sometimes just a "flight case." The ATA was founded in 1936 and is the first and only trade organization for the principal U.S. airlines. ATA Spec 300 reviews the design, development, and procurement of effective packaging of supplies shipped to a customer airline. These approaches also serve as guidelines for shipping containers acceptable for air transport. Cases conforming to ATA Spec 300 standards are able to survive a minimum of 100 air shipments, including any of the ground transportation associated with each shipment.

Figure 14.3   ATA Spec 300 cases from Anvil Case.

The cases used by musical groups and trade-show exhibitors to transport their equipment are usually ATA cases. As you can imagine, ATA cases are extremely durable but also very heavy. They are normally made out of reinforced plywood and metal or special heavy-duty plastics. They have solid foam interiors that can be cut or shaped to fit your equipment exactly, thus protecting it and not allowing things to move around or bang together. ATA cases often have clip-on wheels for transportation, and some are even water tight with gasket seals on the lid. They almost always have special latches and locks for security.

ATA cases are ideal for those who ship their laptops or other computer equipment from place to place and want them to arrive intact and in working order. One of the best-known ATA case companies is Anvil Case (www.anvilcase.com).

Docking Stations

Historically, one of the most popular accessories for laptops is some type of docking solution. These devices are designed to enhance the features of a portable system and enable it to function more like a desktop. There are two types of docking solutions: the full-featured *docking station* and the less expensive *port replicator*.

Docking stations vary in size and shape and are sometimes as large as a desktop computer. The docking station, or *dock*, is actually designed to serve two functions. First, it endows the notebook computer with many more options than are possible in the limited space of a small portable system. Second, it provides a simple and easy way to connect a large number of devices to and disconnect them from a notebook simultaneously.

An example of a docking station is the Compaq Expansion Base (see Figure 14.4). This docking station can attach to notebooks such as the Compaq Evo. The Expansion Base provides a 10/100Mbps network adapter, two storage module bays, a half-height storage bay, two PCI slots, a full range of notebook connectors, and a monitor stand.

Figure 14.4   A Compaq Evo notebook attached to a Compaq Expansion Base docking station.

In many offices, notebook/docking station combinations have been set up so that they are function-ally equivalent to desktop computers. Here, the users type on a large desktop-style keyboard together with a standard-size mouse. Graphics and text are viewed on a large desktop-style display. Docking stations also can contain a wide array of other features, such as network interface adapters, external speakers, additional hard disk or CD-ROM drives, additional PC Card slots, and a spare battery charger. Some docking stations can even accommodate desktop-style expansion cards and esoteric storage devices. This might include the latest high-definition video cards or writable DVD drives that are not present on older notebooks.

In most respects, the combination of a notebook with a docking station can be indistinguishable from a desktop computer, except for one key point: Whenever the users need to, they can disconnect their notebooks from the dock and take them out on the road.

This notebook/docking station combination serves the same purpose as two computers: a full-func-tion desktop in the office and a notebook on the road. The advantages of this arrangement are obvi-ous: First, the notebook/docking station costs considerably less than a notebook/desktop combination, both in terms of hardware and software licensing. Second, because only one computer is involved in the notebook/docking station combination, users are spared the tedium of making sure that their desktops and notebooks are continually synchronized and up to date with the same data files. This synchronization is traditionally done in a slow manual procedure using a network connec-tion or the venerable null modem cable (a crossover cable used to transfer files between systems by connecting their parallel or serial ports). With a docking station and a suitably equipped notebook, however, you can avoid this task and achieve the best of both the mobile and deskbound worlds.

In some cases, a user may have two docking stations: one at the office and one at home, further amplifying the cost advantage of the notebook/docking station system. In this case, the single note-book is in effect performing the work of three computers: one notebook and two desktops.

When a notebook is docked, its operating system has to be made aware of the new set of peripherals that are suddenly available. An operating system such as Windows 9x, Me, 2000, or XP can maintain multiple hardware profiles for a single notebook computer.

Note

A *hardware profile* is a collection of configuration settings for the devices accessible by the system.

To use a docking station, you create one profile for the portable system in its undocked state and another that adds support for the additional hardware available while docked.

Proprietary Docking Stations

Note that most docking stations are highly proprietary items designed for use only with notebooks from a single manufacturer, or even a single model from a manufacturer. If you purchase a notebook and docking station and then later switch to another notebook manufacturer, your old dock becomes useless. Notebook manufacturers thus use devices such as docking stations to encourage customers not to switch to other manufacturers. Note, however, that as technology improves, it can be increasingly difficult for notebook manufacturers to continue to adapt new notebooks to fit docking stations that may be five or more years old. This is particularly true for brand-new families of notebooks with dramatically different form factors. For example, when you switch from a large desktop-replacement to a new ultralight or Tablet PC from the same manufacturer, don't be surprised if your old docking station does not work with the new device.

As with many options available only from a single source, prices for docking stations are not subject to competition and may be expensive. To save money, users can investigate port replicators, which offer fewer features but cost significantly less.

Third-party Docking Solutions

A small number of generic docking stations are also available. Rather than use the proprietary docking station connector on the back or the bottom of the notebook, these generic docks make use of one of the notebook's standard high-bandwidth interfaces, such as a CardBus PC Card slot or a USB connector. One company that sells theses devices is Mobility Electronics (www.mobilityelectronics.com). Its units feature serial, parallel, PS/2 mouse, and PS/2 keyboard connectors, as well as a PC Card slot.

The Decline of the Dock

It should be pointed out that in recent years, docking stations seem to be declining in popularity. In the early days of laptops, LCD screens were so small and poor in quality that many users demanded external CRT monitors whenever possible. Also, at that time, a number of network adapters and storage devices were not yet available in a form that could be directly used by laptop computers. Docking stations equipped with shelves to support heavy CRT displays provided any easy way to endow laptops with the capability of providing readable displays and fast network connections. Corporate buyers, eager to avoid the expense of supplying workers with both a notebook and a desktop, readily invested in docking stations.

Now, however, LCD screens of notebook computers are so large and sharp that an external monitor offers little advantage. Plus, most network adapters and storage drives are available in a form that can attach directly to a notebook. Port replicators provide many of the benefits of full docking stations at much less cost. Meanwhile, generic docks and port replicators provide these benefits without tying users to a particular notebook model line. Because of these facts, many buyers do not see the need to purchase a $500 accessory that provides little additional benefit. Accordingly, many manufacturers do not offer a docking station option for their newest notebook computers.

Port Replicators

As stated earlier, many users do not need the extensive range of capabilities provided by a full-featured docking station. Nor do they want to pay for it. Instead, they need merely a network adapter and a simple way to connect and disconnect a collection of notebook peripherals. The port replicator is designed to do just that (see Figure 14.5).

Figure 14.5 The Toshiba Advanced Port Replicator II, showing both front and back views.

The port replicator shown here has an extensive array of connectors, including two PS/2 connectors (for a keyboard and mouse); one RJ-11 phone-line connector; one RJ-45 network connector; two USB ports; two video connectors (standard RGB and DVI [Digital Visual Interface]); and IEEE 1394 (FireWire), parallel, and serial connectors. As its name suggests, the main function of a port replicator is to duplicate the connectors already available on the back panel of a notebook computer. In most cases, the port replicator also provides additional connectors that were left off the notebook either to save weight, lower costs, or reserve room for another component. These additional connectors may include a network adapter, extra USB connectors, and various video and sound connectors.

In a typical configuration, a port replicator may have an AC adapter, a mouse, a printer, a LAN cable, and a phone line connected to it. To connect to these five different devices, all a notebook user has to do is snap the notebook into the port replicator, thus saving considerable time. Conversely, before going out on the road, all the user needs to do is push a button or a lever to undock the notebook from the port replicator.

The actual connection process is more complicated than it sounds. The port replicator usually has two or three plastic pins that mate with corresponding holes on the notebook. These pins ensure that the port replicator's large connection plug will line up exactly with the socket on the notebook. This connector has dozens of pins or lines and is capable of handling all the signals involved with all the connectors on the port replicator. Once the notebook has been fully inserted into the port replicator, a ratchet usually engages to hold the notebook in place, causing the characteristic snapping sound.

Many port replicators include a network interface. At one time this was an important feature for port replicators, often being the primary justification for purchasing one of these devices. Now, however, with most notebook computers coming standard with either a wired or wireless LAN interface, the importance of having a LAN interface in the port replicator has declined. Similarly, with the proliferation of USB-based keyboards and mice, there is less emphasis on having PS/2 connectors than before.

Proprietary Port Replicators

As is the case with docking stations, port replicators are highly proprietary items designed for use with only certain notebooks from a single manufacturer. Some manufacturers have done a fairly good job of ensuring that future notebook models will be compatible with previous port replicators.

Unfortunately, despite the popularity of port replicators, no standard connector for these devices has ever arisen. Notebook manufacturers are very much conscious of the fact that once you own a port replicator from XYZ Company, you are more likely to protect your investment by making sure your next notebook purchase will have an XYZ label on it. If instead you later switch to another notebook manufacturer, your old port replicator becomes useless.

Because proprietary port replicators are not subject to competition, their prices may be relatively expensive. Generic or third-party port replicators, however, may enable users to save money while not locking them into a particular notebook manufacturer.

Third-party Port Replicators

Because port replicators offer less functionality than docking stations, it is easier for third-party manufacturers to design generic versions of these devices. Indeed, some notebook manufacturers, such as Dell, actively promote the sale of these devices on their websites as accessories for their notebooks.

As is the case for docks, generic port replicators eschew the proprietary docking station connector on the back or the bottom of the notebook and instead use the notebook's standard high-bandwidth interfaces, such as a CardBus PC Card slot or a USB connector.

Two companies are prominent in this area: Mobility Electronics and Targus. Both offer generic port replicators that connect to the notebook via the USB port. Note, however, that these port replicators usually cannot power the notebook. Therefore, in most docking situations, users will have to connect their notebooks to both the generic port replicator and their notebook's AC power supply.

An example of a generic port replicator is the Targus USB Mobile Expansion Hub, shown in Figure 14.6 with top and rear views. This $100 simple port replicator connects to notebooks via a USB cable and provides a self-powered standalone USB hub with two USB ports, a serial port, a parallel printer port, and two PS/2 ports (for mouse and keyboard).

Figure 14.6 The Targus USB Mobile Expansion Hub, shown here in top and rear views, is an example of a third-party port replicator.

Slabs or Slices

In addition to docking stations and port replicators, some notebooks—particularly the smaller ones—have available media modules. These devices provide additional features such as an optical drive or a second battery. Because they resemble slabs or slices that attach to the bottom of a notebook, they are often referred to by those names.

The advantage of a slab is that it endows a notebook with additional capabilities without greatly limiting its portability. And unlike the case with other docking solutions, the notebook/slab combination is still small enough to fit into a laptop carrying case and be taken wherever the user wants.

An example of a slab-style port replicator is the IBM X3 UltraBase, which costs about $200 and is shown in Figure 14.7. This thin slab or slice provides an ultralight notebook with devices such as a DVD drive without greatly impeding its portability.

Figure 14.7   The IBM X3 UltraBase, an example of a slab-style port replicator, partially attached to an IBM ThinkPad X30 notebook.

Slabs are designed specifically for a particular notebook and are therefore usually expensive. No generic slabs are available.

Internal Device Bays

Portable systems have one additional advantage over desktops: It is usually quite easy to add a new storage drive. All the user has to do is pop out an existing drive and snap in a new one. This is made possible by the use of modular device bays. The original purpose of these device bays was to allow notebook designers to build a lightweight notebook with only two spindles or drives. The problem was that most people needed three drives: a hard drive, a floppy, and a CD-ROM drive. An internal device bay enabled users to swap the floppy for the CD-ROM drive, or vice versa, whenever needed. In those rare cases when users needed all three drives simultaneously, some manufacturers supplied a cable that enabled the floppy drive to be used in an external configuration.

At the current time, floppy drives are becoming less and less useful. In fact, many notebook manufacturers no longer include a floppy drive in their standard configurations. Nevertheless, the swappable internal device bay is still finding use. These bays now make it easy to upgrade notebooks to the latest optical drives.

All-in-One Systems

Note that there are two classes of notebooks that have no swappable device bays. The first of these consists of ultralight notebooks or subnotebooks. These systems lack bays for the simple reason that they are too small to have any drive other than a hard drive. For these systems, floppy drives and CD-ROM drives are connected via an external cable. The new Tablet PCs usually fall into this category as well.

The second group of all-in-one systems consists of large, old three-spindle notebooks that are equipped with a hard drive, a floppy, and a CD-ROM drive. When these laptops were built, that was all you needed on a notebook—and pretty much all you *could* have on a notebook. Now, of course, a much greater variety of drives is available.

Proprietary Bays

Unfortunately, all the major notebook manufacturers use proprietary bay designs. A given storage bay device works only with notebooks from a single manufacturer, and then often only with a portion of a manufacturer's entire notebook line. Notebook designers use proprietary bay designs for two reasons. The first is the same reason they use proprietary docking-station connectors—to keep their customers from switching to another notebook manufacturer. The theory is that if a customer has a large investment in modular bay devices, there is less chance he will switch to a new notebook manufacturer and thus make his investment worthless.

Another reason for proprietary bay designs is to allow overall design flexibility. In the laptop world, device bay modules are relatively large and, as a result, are limiting factors in the overall design of the systems. As laptops decreased in size, the device bays had to decrease in size as well. In order to achieve leading-edge lightweight designs, manufacturers could not afford to wait for a standards organization to ratify a new device-bay standard.

Yet another factor is the lack of a single dominating laptop manufacturer. The desktop market benefited from the early supremacy of the IBM PC and AT. For better or worse, many of the features and components of these IBM systems became de facto standards for the industry. By the time laptops evolved into the mainstream, however, IBM was no longer the dominant player in the industry, and certainly not in the portable market, where it had limited success until the debut of the ThinkPad in the early 1990s. Toshiba was for many years the most successful laptop manufacturer, but at no time was its dominance so great that any other manufacturer would deign to offer laptops that were marketed as "Toshiba compatible."

Device bay designs change fairly frequently. The main reason for this is size. As notebooks get smaller and the optical drives get thinner, modular bays can likewise get thinner. The three largest notebook manufacturers have among them almost 15 bay designs.

A list of bay designs for three of the most popular notebook manufacturers is given in Table 14.2.

Table 14.2   Internal Device Bays: Descriptions of the Bay Designs Used by the Three Largest Notebook Manufacturers

Internal Device Bays	Examples of Notebooks Using Bays	Height of Bay Modules
	Dell	
Inspiron type	Inspiron 4100, 4150, 8000, 8100, 8200	12.7mm
Latitude type	Latitude X200, V710, V740, V700, C840, C810, C800, C640, C610, C510, C600, C500, C400, L400, LS, LT, LM, CP, CS, XP, LX	12.7mm

(continues)

Table 13.2 Continued

Internal Device Bays	Examples of Notebooks Using Bays	Height of Bay Modules
Dell		
MegaBay	Inspiron 7500	N/A
MediaBase	Latitude X200	N/A
IBM		
UltraBay	ThinkPad 770	17.5mm
UltraBayFX	ThinkPad 390, 172x	17.5mm
UltraslimBay	ThinkPad 570, 600	12.7mm
UltraBay 2000	ThinkPad T20-23, A20-22, X20-24	12.7mm
UltraBay Plus	ThinkPad T23, T30, A30-31, X30	12.7mm
UltraBay Slim	ThinkPad T40	9.5mm
Toshiba		
Style Bay	Satellite 52xx	12.7mm
Modular Bay	Satellite 12xx and 3xxx	12.7mm
SelectBay	Tecra 8xxx	17.5mm
Slim SelectBay	Satellite Pro 6xxx, Portege 4xxx, and Tecra 9xxx	12.7mm

The following sections detail some of the more common proprietary device bay types.

Dell Device Bays

Unlike most of the other top-tier notebook manufacturers, Dell does not provide special names for the device bays in its notebooks. The company simply refers to them as *module bays* or *media bays*. Probably the only time the company announced a trademarked name for a device bay was back in 1999 when it designed a second device bay for its Inspiron 7500 laptop. The company christened this bay the MegaBay but did not use it on many other notebooks.

In line with Dell's low emphasis on the specific module bay design in a particular notebook, the company instead bases its compatibility on two distinct families of notebooks: The Inspiron line is designed for home and small office uses, whereas the Latitude line is designed for medium and large businesses. In general, components such as module bay devices and docking stations are interchangeable within these two families, but not necessarily between them. Some exceptions do exist, however. A few hard-drive modules are interchangeable between the old Latitude C series and some of the Inspiron models. When you order an optional module bay device for your notebook, Dell wants to know which model notebook you have rather than what module bay design is present. Dell has been able to maintain compatibility within the two families for several years.

Dell is one of the few companies that also offers drive bay modules for some of its desktops as well as its notebooks. Some of the small-footprint desktops in the OptiFlex family are capable of using the same modules available for the Latitude notebooks.

IBM Device Bays

In stark contrast to Dell's approach, IBM has no less than six device bay designs, each with its own trademarked name and all of them variations on the name *UltraBay*. The latest incarnation, the UltraBay Slim, appeared on the ThinkPad T30 thin & light notebook. For larger notebooks, the current device bay design is the UltraBay Plus. This bay design is similar to the earlier UltraBay 2000 design, except that it supports more devices. For the most part, bay devices are not interchangeable. The only exception is the UltraBay Plus, which also accepts UltraBay 2000 devices. IBM has produced a number of interesting devices to populate these modular bays. One is a pop-out numeric keypad. In its extended position, this keypad sits conveniently to the right side of the main keyboard (see Figure 14.8). Another interesting option is the PDA storage device. This is a small drawer that can store a Palm-style PDA.

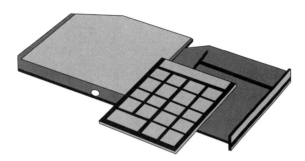

Figure 14.8   The IBM numeric keypad. This keypad fits into a ThinkPad UltraBay slot and pops out when needed, just to the right of the main keyboard.

On some ThinkPads, IBM has one other device bay of sorts. The UltraPort is a very small bay located at the top of the LCD screen, and only a few devices are designed to fit it (see Figure 14.9). They include a video camera and a memory-card reader.

Figure 14.9   The IBM UltraPort CompactFlash reader. This device attaches to the top of certain ThinkPads.

Toshiba Device Bays

Toshiba has four notebook families and four module bay designs roughly spread out among them. The aptly named *Modular Bay* was used in the early Satellite notebooks. More recent Satellites use the Style Bay design. The Tecra 8000 series of notebooks used the SelectBay design, whereas later Tecra models joined the Satellite Pro and Portege notebook families and used the Slim SelectBay device bay.

Types of Modular Bay Devices

When modular device bays first appeared, only three options were available: a CD-ROM drive, an additional hard drive, and a floppy drive. Now, there are a fairly large number of such devices. The exact number of devices varies depending on which notebook you have. Here is a list of typical devices available from the top-tier notebook manufacturers:

- Auxiliary battery
- Dummy module (does nothing but prevent dust from collecting in the bay)
- Floppy drive
- Zip drive
- CD-ROM drive
- DVD drive
- CD-RW drive
- Combination DVD-ROM/CD-RW drive
- DVD+R/RW or DVD-R/RW drive
- Flash memory card adapter
- Pop-out numeric keypad module
- PDA storage module

Not all manufacturers make all these devices available for all the different bay types. Because the modular bays are a proprietary design unique to each laptop manufacturer and product line, bay devices are usually not readily available in the aftermarket. Also, you will find that once a particular bay is no longer being included in new models, the available accessories disappear very quickly. It is very hard, for example, to find bay devices for sale that fit obsolete models. It is therefore a good idea to purchase the bay accessories you want when the system is new because they may not be available a year or so later when the manufacturer is including different bays in its newer systems.

The Device Bay Specification

It is interesting to note that back in March of 1997, Compaq, Intel, and Microsoft, along with a significant number of other leading PC, chipset, software, and peripheral companies, announced the creation of the Device Bay specification. Device Bay was to be a specification for interchangeable, modular plug-in peripheral devices, such as hard disk drives, modems, network adapters, CD/DVD drives, and a variety of other devices. This would have brought fully interchangeable, swappable bay peripherals not only to laptops but to desktop systems as well! Device Bay was to internally use both USB and IEEE 1394 (FireWire/i.LINK) as the methods of electrically connecting the device to the system.

Unfortunately, due mainly to political problems between various companies having stakes in FireWire and USB together, the standard never fully got off the ground. By the time the official specification was released, most of the member companies had abandoned any potential products that might use it; only a handful of products ever made it to market and were quickly withdrawn. The Device Bay working group eventually disbanded, and the specification was transferred to the 1394 Trade Association, where it seems to have died after the last version was published in early 2000. It is too bad that this standard was never realized; it would have made bay devices compatible among different product lines, manufacturers, and even between laptop and desktop systems.

Accessory Power Sources

Notebook computers spend most of their working hours powered by an AC adapter. The great advantage of a notebook, however, is its ability to temporarily free itself from the AC power grid and work on battery power.

Batteries

Most users have a number of options to choose from when it comes to laptop batteries. The most common one is the notebook's primary battery. These batteries come in many different sizes and shapes and are specific only for a certain model of notebook.

The two most common types of laptop batteries are nickel-cadmium (NiCad) and lithium-ion (Li-Ion). NiCad batteries require more attention than Li-Ion batteries to keep them in top condition. A brand-new NiCad battery needs to be fully charged and then fully discharged three or four times before it achieves its maximum capacity. Additionally, a NiCad battery should be fully discharged and then fully charged once or twice a month to maintain its full capacity and extend its life span. It is usually a good idea to buy a second, replacement battery for your notebook. This will enable you to double your laptop's effective battery endurance for those situations in which it is required. Also, consider that if you own your notebook for more than a year or two, you will probably have to buy a replacement battery anyway. Notebook batteries last only for a given number of charge cycles. Over time, their endurance times will gradually decrease until they become unusable.

If you purchase a second battery with the intention of storing it until your original laptop battery no longer functions, you should store the spare battery in a dry, cool location. New batteries are usually shipped in an uncharged state, so you will need to charge the battery before using it.

Modular Device Bay Batteries

To avoid the inconvenience of shuffling numerous batteries in and out of your notebook, some notebook models also offer an auxiliary battery that fits into the system's modular device bay. It enables you to run your notebook on two batteries simultaneously and to charge both of them easily. On most notebooks that offer this option, the total battery endurance time will be doubled. Note, however, that using such a battery cuts down on your storage options. To insert a module bay battery, you will probably have to remove your notebook's optical drive (either CD-ROM or DVD).

Extended-Life Batteries

A handful of notebooks have available optional extended-life batteries. These batteries are designed to replace the original battery and provide extra power. Usually, they are available only on small ultralight notebooks. Unfortunately, in addition to increasing the battery endurance, they also substantially increase the size and weight of a notebook.

A good example of an extended-life battery is the IBM ThinkPad T40 Series high-capacity lithium-ion (Li-ion) battery, which provides up to one-third more capacity than the standard battery for the T40. This battery fits in the standard ThinkPad T40 system battery slot yet has an extended area on the back edge of the notebook. Despite its larger size, it does not prevent the notebook from docking with IBM's various docking stations designed for this notebook.

Slab Batteries

New battery technologies enable designers to adopt innovative shapes that fit together more harmoniously with a notebook. One of these shapes is the slab, which is designed to fit under a notebook. A small number of notebook manufacturers have offered optional slab batteries for their lighter laptops.

The IBM ThinkPad X30 Series extended-life battery is an example of a slab battery. It is designed to attach to the bottom of the ThinkPad X30 notebook. When combined with the notebook's standard battery, the slab can provide up to eight hours of power. This battery adds a pound to the weight of the system.

Third-party Batteries

A small number of companies offer batteries for the most popular notebooks. In some cases, even large battery manufacturers such as Duracell and Energizer have begun offering replacement notebook batteries.

For a short time in the 1990s, the large battery manufacturers attempted to promote a series of standard batteries for notebooks. With such a standard, users would be able to purchase replacement batteries at a local Radio Shack without having to contact the notebook manufacturer or a specialized website. Unfortunately, as has happened in so many other areas of laptop design, the effort to come up with standard designs for these components has failed. Nevertheless, because of the popularity of laptops, a large group of websites now stocks a wide array of replacement batteries, covering almost any notebook that ever existed.

Although the effort to develop standard batteries failed, some companies have offered generic batteries that can attach to a wide range of notebooks. These batteries are usually external and offer high capacities.

One of the more interesting generic batteries for notebooks is the Electrovaya PowerPad 160 (see Figure 14.10). This relatively thin battery slips under a notebook and has a maximum capacity of 11,000 mAh, more than twice that of a typical notebook battery. It weighs 2.4 pounds and has the dimensions 8.75×11.75×0.38 inches.

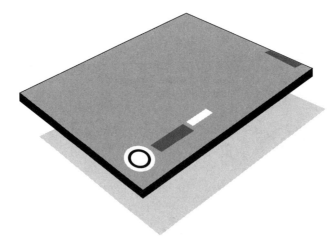

Figure 14.10 Electrovaya PowerPad 160, a generic battery designed to slip under a notebook.

Fuel Cells

A promising alternative to battery power is the fuel cell. These power sources do not require recharging and can run indefinitely as long as fuel is available—usually a type of alcohol. Such a power source is ideal for areas where electrical power is undependable or nonexistent.

Perhaps the first available fuel cell for laptops will be the Medion Energy Docking Station (www.medion.com). This device uses fuel cells developed by a German company called SFC Smart Fuel Cell AG (www. smartfuelcell.de/en/). An example of this technology is the SFC C20 Fuel Cell System. This power source uses a half-liter fuel cartridge filled with methanol, in conjunction with an exchangeable lithium-polymer battery. Once a fuel cartridge is empty, it can be hot-swapped with another (that is, exchanged without any power interruption).

The Japanese giants NEC and Toshiba have also indicated interest in fuel cell technology. NEC has demonstrated a working prototype notebook PC with an internal fuel cell. The company claims that the compact prototype fuel cell achieves the world's best output density, $40mW/cm^2$, and achieves an average output of 14W and a maximum output of 24W.

Meanwhile, Toshiba has announced the world's first prototype of a small form factor direct methanol fuel cell (DMFC) for portable PCs. The new fuel cell has an average output of 12W and maximum output of 20W, and it can supply approximately five hours of operation with a single cartridge of fuel. Toshiba reports that methanol in a fuel cell delivers power most efficiently when it is mixed with water in a 3%–6% methanol concentration, a concentration that would require a fuel tank that is much too large for use with a notebook computer. The company has overcome this problem by developing a system that dilutes concentrated methanol with the water produced as a by-product of the power-generation process. This technology allows methanol to be stored at much higher concentrations than in the past, with fuel tanks less than one-tenth the previous size. Toshiba's prototype can operate for approximately five hours on 50cc of concentrated methanol. In addition, the company has designed its DMFC with the same electrodes as found on lithium-ion batteries, allowing it to connect easily with a laptop and serve as an alternative to lithium-ion batteries.

While NEC, Toshiba, and other companies have produced several working prototypes of fuel cells for use in notebooks, there are no commercially available versions of these products as of this writing. Fuel cell technology may be just around the corner, or it may be another year or two before we see fuel cells powering notebook computers, as well as other power-hungry electronic devices such as cell phones, digital cameras, MP3 players, and handheld game systems.

Adapters

Because even the largest battery lasts only for a relatively short amount of time, most users try to run their notebooks off other power sources whenever they can. A number of adapter cables are available to help these users.

Automobile Adapters

There are two ways to power your notebook while in a car. The most generic approach is to purchase an inverter. This device plugs into the car's cigarette lighter and converts the car's 12V DC power into 120V AC power. You can then simply plug the notebook's AC adapter into the inverter. Although this approach does not involve the purchase of any proprietary cables or connectors, it is not very efficient. Electrical power must be converted from DC to AC by the inverter and then back again to DC by the notebook's AC adapter. During both of these conversions, some of the electrical energy is used up and given off as heat.

A more efficient approach is to use a proprietary automobile adapter. These adapters consist of a cable with two connectors. The first is a standard connector for the car's cigarette lighter. On the other end of the cable is the proprietary power plug that connects directly to the notebook, in effect replacing its AC power adapter.

Airline Adapters

A number of years ago, a few airlines began equipping certain seats in first class and business class with DC power outlets. Most automobile adapters now include special connectors that allow these adapters to be used on airlines as well.

One source for airline power adapters is Lind Electronics (`http://lindelectronics.com`). That company's adapters all operate from an automobile's cigarette lighter. With the addition of a small converter cable, however, they can also connect to the power ports on some airlines (see Figure 14.11).

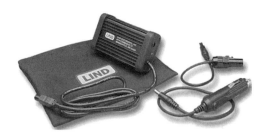

Figure 14.11   A notebook power adapter from Lind Electronics for cars and airlines. The small converter cable at the right enables the adapter to work with the power ports on some airlines.

International

Anyone who travels outside the Western hemisphere will probably want to bring along an international power adapter. Depending on how many countries you will visit, you may need to bring along several adapters. Fortunately, most notebook AC adapters are capable of handling both 120V and 220V power. Therefore, all that most notebook users need is a relatively small adapter that converts the familiar two- or three-prong U.S.-style plug into one that will fit international power outlets. These adapters are usually sold in a batch of adapters that will handle most countries of the world.

Communications

▶▶   See "Communications," p. 593.

Laptops have a number of communications options. Most of the latest communications options attach either through the laptop's PC Card slot, through the internal mini-PCI slot, or via the external USB port. Some older accessories connect to the serial port. More information on these adapters is available in Chapter 12, "Communications." However, two types of communications adapters deserve coverage as accessories: digital phone system adapters and international phone adapters.

Digital Phone System Adapters

Some digital PBX phone systems send out a ringing current that is so high it can harm the tiny PC Card and internal modems in notebooks. Because digital PBX phone systems are now very common in offices and hotels, this can be a serious problem. Replacing a laptop modem can be expensive and time consuming, especially for the internal variety. Fortunately, low-cost filters are available that will protect notebook modems from these dangerous currents (see Figure 14.12).

Figure 14.12   The Konexx Mobile Konnector can protect laptop modems.

The Konexx Mobile Konnector from Konexx (www.konexx.com) protects laptop modems by providing a safe analog connection over any digital PBX or multiline phone system. The device works by connecting to the telephone handset jack on a modular phone.

Another product from Konexx is an example of an accessory that should be standard equipment for any globetrotting laptop user's luggage. The tiny Konexx ModemMinder weighs just an ounce and costs less than $40, yet it could provide valuable protection for your laptop modem. Strung between your laptop and a phone jack, it immediately cuts off communication if it detects an unsafe PBX system. The ModemMinder also protects your modem from power surges, such as those caused by electrical storms.

International Phone Adapters

Just as globetrotting notebook users may need international power adapters, they may also need telephone-line adapters. These adapters are usually sold in a batch that includes an assortment of adapters capable of handling phone lines in most countries of the world (see Figure 14.13).

Figure 14.13   The Targus Travel Connection Kit – Europe Pak includes nine phone adapters and three power adapters for use in over 100 countries.

Note that in addition to using different phone jacks, some countries use different electrical signals to indicate conditions such as a busy phone line. Most laptop modems sold in the United States may not be aware of these different signals. Indeed, these domestic modems often work quite well in international systems, but your communications software will have a much easier time if you use a modem that can understand these international signals. If you intend to do extensive international travel, be sure to carry along a PC Card modem specially designed for international phone systems. Even if you never travel outside the country and are already quite happy with your laptop's internal modem, this extra modem could serve as a valuable backup resource.

Data Storage

A wide variety of data storage devices are available for laptops. They range in size from postage-stamp memory cards to external hard drives the size of a video cassette. More details on these storage options can be found in Chapter 9, "Hard Disk Storage," and Chapter 10, "Removable Storage."

One data storage option that deserves mention in this chapter is the tiny USB storage fob or memory key. These popular devices are quickly replacing floppy disks as the most practical way to transfer data between two unconnected computers. Most USB storage fobs are the size of a wine-bottle cork. They consist of nothing more than a USB connector and a memory chip, ranging in capacity from 16MB to 4GB or more. The cost is generally inexpensive compared to carrying around an external hard drive.

At least one of these handy storage fobs should be in every laptop carrying case. In fact, even if you don't bring a laptop with you on a trip, you might want to bring along a fob loaded with some important documents in case you come across a desktop somewhere along the way.

Security Devices

Because laptops can be stolen so easily, manufacturers have developed a number of security options for these devices. They range from simple cable systems that lock down notebooks to sophisticated software that will alert you to the notebook's location in the event that it is stolen. Note that two elements of a notebook must be guarded: its hardware *and* its data.

Theft Deterrents

The most common and most affordable security devices for notebooks are those designed to prevent or deter theft. Although these devices diminish the convenience of notebooks, a minor inconvenience is much preferable to the serious problem of a stolen notebook.

Cable Locks

All notebooks have at least one security socket called a *Kensington lock slot*. The name derives from the fact that this slot was originally designed to be used with a cable lock developed by Kensington, a large vendor of computer accessories. The Kensington lock slot looks like a small keyhole and is often labeled with a small icon (see Figure 14.14). Each lock has a small tongue that can be inserted into this slot. When the internal T-shaped spindle of the tongue is rotated, the tongue firmly attaches to the slot. The only way to remove the lock without damaging the laptop is to use the correct key or combination. The locks are securely attached to cables of various sizes and thicknesses (see Figure 14.15). Although Kensington originally developed this type of cable lock, similar locks are available from other vendors.

Figure 14.14 The Kensington Lock icon is used to identify security slots on notebooks.

Figure 14.15 The Kensington Slim MicroSaver Security Cable is one of the most popular cable locks for notebooks.

Some notebook designers have placed the Kensington lock slot in ingenious places. For example, if the slot is placed near the PC Card slots, the lock prevents theft not only of the notebook but also of the PC Cards. Similarly, some notebook manufacturers place the lock slot near the hard drive cover.

Lock Plates

Although cable locks can provide a reasonable amount of security, a good quality pair of metal shears or simple bolt cutters can cut many of them. For better security, many companies use lock plates that securely bolt a notebook to a tabletop surface. These plates are made of steel and are about the size of a laptop. The plates have several small holes enabling users to secure them to a table surface with screws. Brackets can attach to the top of the plate to lock down a laptop, usually by its side panels. These brackets can be removed only with the correct key.

A few notebooks have optional docking stations that are sturdy enough to serve as lock plates. Although docking stations are usually constructed of plastic rather than steel, they can provide enhanced connectivity along with security. Although a lock plate provides excellent theft deterrence, it completely immobilizes a notebook and requires extensive modifications to a table surface.

Motion Detectors

Targus, a large vendor of laptop accessories, sells a line of theft-deterrent devices that rely on motion detection (see Figure 14.16). These devices securely attach to a notebook via the Kensington lock slot. When the user activates the motion detector, the device may be triggered if the notebook is moved slightly. Once the motion detector is triggered, the user has a short time to enter a deactivation code before a loud alarm goes off. Motion detectors are small and fairly inexpensive. Their best application is in situations in which users have to leave their equipment temporarily but cannot secure it sufficiently with cable locks.

Figure 14.16   The Targus DEFCON 1 Ultra Notebook Security Alarm combines a cable lock with a motion detector.

Laptop Recovery Systems

Some new car purchasers equip their automobiles with a radio-equipped antitheft device. If the car is ever stolen, police cars equipped with special radio equipment can zero in on the exact location of the car.

A similar technique is available for notebook users. It is based on a special type of software program that can be installed on the notebook's hard drive. According to the companies that sell the software, the thief cannot erase the program, even if the hard drive is reformatted. When the thief uses the notebook, the software asks for a password. If the password is not given, and the notebook is subsequently connected to the Internet, it will send a message to a central website, stating that the notebook has been stolen. By analyzing the trail that the messages from the notebook have taken, these companies say they can pinpoint the geographic position of the stolen notebook and notify police. The two most respected examples of these tracking programs are ComputracePlus (www.absolute.com) and zTrace (www.ztrace.com).

User Authentication Devices

Although the loss of a notebook with all its data is a catastrophe, the loss of this same data to a business competitor is immeasurably worse. Fortunately, several notebook accessories are designed to ensure you are the only person who can access the data on your notebook.

SmartCard Keys

Most user-authentication techniques depend on passwords. But because passwords are cumbersome to use and can sometimes be obtained by guesswork and eavesdropping, many security experts prefer a hardware-based authentication technique.

The oldest of these methods involves using a SmartCard, a credit card–like device with an embedded memory chip. These cards are similar to the cards that were once popular in Europe for use with pay-phones.

The easiest way to equip a laptop with a SmartCard technology is to insert a PC Card–based SmartCard reader. When loaded with corresponding security software, the laptop will be usable only when the PC Card SmartCard reader and the correct SmartCard are inserted.

In an effort to secure its massive fleet of notebook computers, the U.S. Air Force is purchasing thousands of CardMan PC Card SmartCard readers from a company called Omnikey. By using this system, service members will be able to verify their identification and use the technology for secure access to computer systems and to digitally encrypt and sign email.

USB Keys

The use of a SmartCard key requires laptops to be equipped with a SmartCard reader, which ties up a modular device bay or a PC Card slot and entails additional expense. For that reason, security companies now offer a USB key, which can be inserted into the USB slots that are now standard equipment on all notebooks as well as desktops. The USB keys offer an advantage in that they protrude from the notebook and have a key-chain hoop, making it less likely that a user will accidentally leave the key attached to the laptop, as frequently happens with SmartCards.

Fingerprint Sensors

Hardware-based keys such as SmartCards and USB keys have the disadvantage that they can be stolen. For that reason, they are often backed up with password protection, which makes their use less convenient. The best security key is one that is almost impossible to steal and something that the users always carry with them. Many companies bet that this ideal security key is right at our fingertips.

Fingerprint sensors have been refined to the point that they are very accurate. These sensors are available for notebooks as a small device that attaches to a USB port or a PC Card with a fingerprint reader that pops out of the side of the notebook. Fingerprint readers have the enviable advantage of being both very convenient and highly secure. A few notebook manufacturers have offered notebooks with fingerprint readers as integral devices located just below the keyboard.

Perhaps the most popular fingerprint reader is the Targus DEFCON Authenticator (see Figure 14.17). This is a PC Card that has a pop-out fingerprint reader. When you need to verify your identity, you can pop out the postage stamp–size reader. At all other times, it can be safely stored inside your laptop.

Figure 14.17 The Targus DEFCON Authenticator is a PC Card that has a pop-out fingerprint reader.

Input Devices

Notebook computer users can choose from a wide variety of input devices. Thanks to the USB port, almost any keyboard or mouse designed for desktop use can also be employed with notebooks. There are, however, some special input devices designed with notebook users in mind.

Portable Pointing Devices

Several miniature mice are on the market from companies such as Targus, Microsoft, and Logitech. Versions of these "mini" mice are available using both optical and traditional ball-style technologies. In addition, some of these mice are wireless. All connect to the notebook via the USB port.

The Microsoft Notebook optical mouse, shown in Figure 14.18, is good example of a mouse designed for mobile use. Because it does not use a ball, it does not require a mouse pad and can be used on any surface, including your knee.

Figure 14.18   The Microsoft Notebook optical mouse.

Portable Keyboards

One of the main problems of a laptop's keyboard is its lack of a true numeric keypad. Laptop designers usually try to emulate a numeric keypad by having some of the alphabetic keys do double duty as numeric keys. But the resulting keypad is offset at an angle and difficult to use.

For those who need a numeric keypad, two interesting accessories are available. As mentioned previously, users of IBM ThinkPads can take advantage of an UltraBay module that enables a numeric keypad to pop out of the side of the notebook. For all other users, Targus sells a miniature numeric keypad that connects through the notebook's USB connector.

Output Devices

When users take their notebooks on the road, they are rarely very far from a high-quality printer. Such printers can be found at many hotels, at FedEx Kinko's outlets, and at many other facilities. Sometimes, however, users want to bring along their own printer or scanner.

Portable Printers

When you design a portable printer, you have to make certain compromises. Such a printer may not have a huge assortment of features. Nor will it be the fastest printer on the market or the one with the highest resolution. What a portable printer will have is the capability to do a decent job of printing while still being small enough to fit into a large pocketbook.

HP sells three mobile inkjet printers. Perhaps the most popular is the DeskJet 450ci Mobile Printer (see Figure 14.19). This printer weighs just 4.2 pounds and has the following dimensions: 13.3×6.5×3.2 inches. Despite its small size, this printer has impressive performance specs. It can print at a resolution of 1200×1200 in black, and even higher in color. Its rated speed is 8 pages per minute in black. The printer's paper input tray can hold 45 pages.

Figure 14.19   HP's DeskJet 450ci Mobile Printer weighs just 4.2 pounds.

Portable Scanners

Although they are not actually output devices, portable scanners are so often used in conjunction with printers that I am including them in this section. Because they have fewer moving parts, portable scanners can be even smaller than printers. A typical scanner may weigh just 10 ounces. To save space, of course, these scanners are never of the flatbed variety. They usually require you to feed each page in manually.

A good example is the Visioneer Strobe XP 100 (see Figure 14.20). It measures 11.4×2×1.5 inches—about the size of a rolled-up magazine. It weighs just 10.6 ounces. To keep weight down, it does not require a power supply and can instead be powered by a USB connection to a laptop. Despite its small size, it has decent specs. It can scan at a resolution of 600dpi and resolve 32 bits of color information (for a total of over 68 billion different possible colors). It even comes with its own travel bag.

Figure 14.20   The Visioneer Strobe XP 100 mobile scanner.

Presentation Equipment

Many people use laptop systems to host presentations to audiences that can range in size from the boardroom to an auditorium. For all but the smallest groups of viewers, some means of enlarging the computer display is necessary. Most portable systems are equipped with a standard VGA jack that allows the connection of an external monitor.

Notebooks typically enable the user to choose whether the computer's screen image should be sent to the notebook's internal LCD screen, to an external monitor, or to both. Users can toggle among these options, usually by hitting a certain keystroke combination or by adjusting the system BIOS. Depending on the capabilities of the video display adapter in the computer, you might be able to use a greater display resolution on an external monitor than available on the internal LCD panel. However, if you want to display simultaneously on both an internal and external screen, you will obtain the best results if both displays have the same resolution. For example, if your laptop screen has XGA resolution (1024×768) and you are using an external monitor with SVGA resolution (800×600), you should set your laptop screen to SVGA resolution if you want to get good results on both screens simultaneously.

For environments in which the display size of a standard external monitor is not large enough, several alternatives exist, including LCD panels for use with overhead projectors, digital projectors, and large plasma displays.

▶▶ See "LCD Size Versus Resolution: Pixels Per Inch," p. 522.

Analog TV Projectors

For many years the only way to project a computer screen was to use an analog TV projector. These were large suitcase-size devices. On the front panel of these devices are three large projection lenses, one each for red, green, and blue light. These projectors were usually bolted either to the ceiling or to an audiovisual cart. Because of their large size, high price tags, and low resolution, analog TV projectors have been replaced by newer technologies.

Overhead LCD Display Panels

An LCD display panel is similar to the LCD screen in your computer, except that there is no back on it, making the display transparent. To use this panel, you have to place it over a standard overhead projector, which projects the image onto a large screen. The display technologies and screen resolution options are the same as those for the LCD displays in portable systems. In recent years, many users have abandoned LCD display panels in favor of self-contained digital projectors. Because of this, most vendors of overhead LCD display panels have discontinued these products, although many AV houses might still have them available for rental.

Digital Projectors

Most people who want to display an image for a large group of people now use a digital projector. These units are typically small but project bright images with high contrast. They do an excellent job, not only with computer images, but also with video signals from a VCR or a DVD player. Best of all, the prices for these devices continually drop. We have already seen prices drop below $1,000 and should continue to see further decreases. Just five years ago, the typical price was over $5,000.

Basically, a digital projector is a self-contained unit that is in effect a combination of a transparent display panel and a projector. The unit connects to the VGA video output connector on the system, just like a regular monitor, and frequently includes speakers that connect with a separate cable. Not all LCD projectors are portable; some are intended for permanent installations. The portable models vary in weight, display technologies, and the brightness of the lamp, which is measured in ANSI lumens. Typical portable projectors have ANSI lumen outputs ranging from 500 to 3,000 or higher, with prices ranging from well under $2,000 to well over $10,000. Less expensive projectors are typically SVGA (800×600) resolution, whereas more expensive models are typically XGA (1024×768) or higher resolution.

Digital projectors can display images at several resolutions. All but one of these resolutions are made possible by averaging or interpolating pixels in order to enable the native resolution of the projector to simulate other resolutions. To display an image with the best clarity, always use the native resolution of the projector. All other resolutions that the projector claims to support will appear slightly blurry by comparison.

For best results, match the resolution of your projector to the native resolution of your notebook computer. For example, if your notebook computer has an XGA (1024×768) resolution screen, make sure your projector has this same native resolution. Having the projector and your notebook's built-in screen match resolutions usually enables you to take advantage of simultaneous display—a great benefit for presenters. Internally, digital projectors use one of two different techniques to form an image: an array of three LCD panels or a DLP mirror chip.

LCD Projectors

The oldest and least expensive technology used in digital projectors is LCD technology. The LCD approach is said to provide better color fidelity, but it often gives an image a window-screen look—as if the image is being seen through a typical window screen.

In this technology, a beam of light from a bright lamp is separated into three beams, each of which passes through a separate tiny LCD screen typically less than an inch in size. Most recent LCD projectors use 0.7-inch LCDs. The three LCD screens correspond to the red, green, and blue components of the image. The three resulting images are then combined and projected out to a screen.

One of the most popular examples of an LCD projector is the Toshiba TLP-S30U (see Figure 14.21). Its use of LCD technology and its relatively low native resolution of 800×600 has enabled it to be one of the most affordable projectors on the market. With a weight of 4.8 pounds, it is also one of the lightest LCD projectors available.

Figure 14.21   The Toshiba TLP-S30U, a popular LCD projector.

DLP Projectors

DLP projectors use DLP, or *Digital Light Processing*, chips from Texas Instruments. Projectors using this technology tend to be smaller but more expensive than LCD projectors. Typically, images from DLP projectors do not have the window-screen look that is characteristic of LCD projectors. The latest DLP projectors also offer extremely good contrast, which is important for entertainment applications such as displaying movies.

In DLP projectors, a bright beam of light is projected on a tiny array of thousands of microscopic mirrors. Each pixel of an image is controlled by a single mirror. Color is usually provided by a rotating wheel of color filters.

The compact nature of DLP projector technology has been put to good use lately in some very light-weight models. These projectors, such as the InFocus LP-120, weigh just slightly more than 2 pounds and are not much larger than a Tom Clancy paperback book.

Flat-Panel Plasma Displays

Flat-panel plasma displays are becoming more and more common in corporate boardrooms—and even some living rooms. The main factor is their stunning appearance. These amazing displays are often extremely large—usually 42 inches in diagonal or larger—and extremely thin. They look more like picture frames than televisions. A DVD movie or high-definition TV picture viewed on one of these screens is stunning.

A plasma screen consists of hundreds of thousands of tiny gas-filled cells. In effect, the cells are like microscopic fluorescent bulbs. When a current is applied to the cells, the electrons free themselves from the atoms of gas and form a plasma, which glows. Similar to a color television, the cells are located behind a matrix of tiny red, green, and blue filters. Almost any color can be obtained by applying the right combination of these three primary colors.

Most plasma displays can readily connect to the VGA connector on a laptop for use as a high-quality presentation tool. Note, however, that some of the low-cost plasma screens (that is, below $5,000) do not offer very high resolutions—often below 800×600. Many plasma displays feature unusual resolutions (for example, 852×480 and 1024×1024) that may not be supported directly by a laptop's graphics adapters.

TV Connections

One of the simplest display solutions is a feature that is being incorporated into many of the high-end laptop systems on the market today. It enables you to connect the computer to a standard television set. Called *TV-Out*, it usually consists of an RCA jack that can supply a composite video television signal. In addition to providing support for the North American NTSC television standard, a few notebooks also support the European PAL standard. If your portable computer doesn't have a TV-Out connector, PC Cards and add-on adapter boxes are available to provide this feature. These products convert the VGA signal to a form that is compatible with the NTSC or PAL TV standards.

Obviously, an integrated TV-Out connector is an extremely convenient solution because it provides an image size that is limited only by the type of television available, costs virtually nothing, and adds no extra weight to the presenter's load when a TV is available. However, the display resolution of a television set does not approach that of a computer monitor, and the picture quality suffers as a result. It is recommended that you test the output carefully with various size television screens before using TV-Out in a presentation environment. To obtain the best results in presentations, use simple sans-serif fonts, such as Arial and Helvetica, in relatively large sizes. Also, limit the amount of text on any given screen to achieve best results with TV-Out devices.

S-Video

Some notebooks have an S-Video connector. This enables your notebook to display a higher resolution image than would otherwise be possible with the standard TV-Out connector. In some notebooks from Dell, the S-Video connector does double duty. In addition to connecting with a standard S-Video cable, it can also connect to a standard composite video cable with the help of a short adapter.

Digital Visual Interface (DVI)

In time, the traditional RGB or VGA connector on notebooks and desktops will be replaced by a DVI (Digital Visual Interface) connector. Unlike the older VGA connector, which was analog, the DVI connector can supply a true digital link that will be less subject to noise from other nearby electronic devices.

Currently, DVI connectors can be found only on certain high-end video components. These components include desktop video adapters, digital projectors, large plasma displays, and certain high-priced LCD displays. A few PC Card adapters are available to provide notebooks with this capability when needed for use with high-end displays.

Perhaps the easiest way to equip a laptop with a DVI connector is to insert a Display-to-Go PC Card from Margi (www.margi.com). In addition to a standard analog (VGA) connector, Display-to-Go can interface with both Digital Flat Panel (DFP) and DVI connectors.

Another advantage of a video card such as this is that it supports the multiple-monitor capability of recent versions of Windows. This card works as a secondary graphics adapter, enabling Windows to spread its images over two displays. Users are thus able to run separate applications on their notebook LCD and their external secondary display. A typical scenario is that of presenters launching their presentations and dragging them to the secondary display devices for their audience to see. At the same time, they could launch their notes on the laptop screens, which would be visible only to them.

TV-In

A small number of notebooks are equipped not only with a TV-Out connector but also with a TV-In port. With the right software, these notebooks can record or capture images from a TV or video camera. For notebooks without this feature, an optional PC Card or USB-based adapter can provide a TV-In connector.

The TV-In feature of laptops uses an RCA jack and accepts standard composite video signals. In order to handle the higher quality images available from today's digital mini-DV camcorders, you should use an IEEE 1394 (or FireWire) interface. In addition to passing video signals from the camcorder to the laptop (and back), the IEEE 1394 interface also enables digital video-editing software on the laptop to control the camcorder in order to facilitate the transfer of images.

Outside of Sony and Apple, very few notebook vendors are currently equipping their systems with IEEE 1394 interfaces. In most cases, you will have to use a special interface card, described next.

Special Interfaces

Sometimes the most useful accessories are those that simply provide connections to other accessories. This capability is growing increasingly important as the size of notebook computers continues to decrease. The diminutive form factors of new ultralight notebooks and Tablet PCs limit the number and variety of connectors that can adorn their rear and side panels. To be able to connect with some peripherals, these systems have to be equipped with special interfaces that attach to USB ports and can be slipped inside PC Card slots.

USB

All recent notebooks are equipped with a USB port; in fact, in many cases there are two of them. A handful of notebooks have even more. With a speed of 12Mbps, these connectors are orders of magnitude faster than the serial ports they replace. They come in very handy for connecting keyboards, pointing devices, external data storage devices, printers, and many other peripherals.

In those increasingly common cases in which just one or two USB ports are not enough, some companies have begun offering notebook accessories designed to enhance a notebook's USB connectivity. This is in the form of a PC Card with a dongle or short adapter cable that can connect to one or two USB ports. Before you buy one of these cards, note that the original USB standard has almost entirely been replaced by a much faster standard: USB 2.0.

USB 2.0 Cards

For older notebooks with slower USB ports, CardBus PC Cards are available for providing the high-speed connectivity available with USB 2.0. The maximum speed for this standard is 480Mbps. This is ideal for connecting external storage devices such as hard drives, CD/DVD drives, and tape drives. Note also that these cards will still be compatible with older and slower USB peripherals such as keyboards and mice.

Portable USB Hubs

USB devices are now so plentiful that often a notebook needs several USB connectors. Providing these connectors is relatively easy, however, because the USB standard enables one system to connect to up to 127 peripherals. All you need to do is connect a USB hub to one of your laptop's USB ports to gain an additional set of connectors. By daisy-chaining hubs together, you can continue to attach devices up to the theoretical maximum specified in the standard.

Most USB hubs are too large to consider for mobile work, but some manufacturers are selling miniature USB hubs that are fairly small and lightweight. By attaching a four-port USB hub, you will quickly and effectively add three more USB connectors to your laptop.

USB hubs are either powered directly from the notebook's USB port or use an external AC adapter. USB hubs that draw their power directly from the USB port will sometimes malfunction if too many devices are running off it. If you encounter this problem, replace the port-powered USB hub with one that comes with an external power adapter. You should also check the documentation that comes with any USB-based peripheral; often, the manufacturer will include a warning that the device should not be used with a USB hub.

FireWire Cards

If you are doing video work on your notebook, an IEEE 1394 or FireWire connector is mandatory. Not every manufacturer equips its notebooks with this high-speed connector, however. For those notebooks that lack it, a small number of CardBus PC Cards that provide a 1394 port are available.

Note that two versions of IEEE 1394 devices are available. The original IEEE 1394 version (or 1394a) has a maximum speed of 400Mbps. The 1394/800 or 1394b version has a maximum data rate of 800Mbps.

Also note that IEEE 1394 devices use two types of connectors. The tiny 4-pin connector is used by Sony laptops and by most digital video camcorders. (Note that Sony refers to IEEE 1394 by its trade-marked name i.LINK.) Apple, which refers to IEEE 1394 by its trademarked name FireWire, uses a larger 6-pin connector. The extra two pins on this connector can be used for supplying power to peripherals.

Serial Ports

The venerable RS-232C serial port has been replaced to a large extent by the much faster USB connector. Nevertheless, some environments and legacy equipment still require this connector. For those notebooks that need more than one serial connector—or for those recent notebooks that lack one altogether—some PC Cards and USB devices provide multiple serial connections.

Parallel Ports

As with the serial port, the USB connector is quickly replacing the Centronics-style parallel printer port. Because of its decreasing usage—and its large size—some notebooks are omitting this connector to save space for other components. If you still need a parallel port, this capability can be provided by a PC Card adapter or a USB/parallel adapter.

SCSI Adapters

For many years, the fastest connector on personal computers was the SCSI port. Nowadays, this connector is being supplanted by both the USB 2.0 and the IEEE 1394 connectors. No current notebooks—and very few older ones—have a SCSI connector, but as with serial and parallel ports, this can easily be provided with a PC Card adapter. If you need to use SCSI devices, you can attach a CardBus-based SCSI adapter, such as the Adaptec SlimSCSI 1480, or use a USB-to-SCSI converter, such as the Adaptec USB2Xchange.

Signal and Control I/O

Some special applications involve device control and signal monitoring. In these cases, the computer must monitor the signal outputs from various sensors and then send out control signals to activate various types of equipment. A laptop can easily take on this application when equipped with a PC Card that can accommodate several different analog/digital and digital/analog converters.

Keithley Instruments (www.keithley.com) sells a number of these cards. A typical example is its Model KPCMCIA-12AI-C PC Card. This card has 16 analog/digital converters that can measure analog input with a precision of 12 bits. It also has four digital channels that can accept and send out digital signals.

Miscellaneous Devices

A growing number of notebook accessories take advantage of the electrical power provided by a computer's USB port. These accessories range from the useful to the gratuitous. On the useful side, you can get USB-powered lights (handy for working in dark conditions), web cams, even a USB-powered fan to keep you cool when the office's air conditioning quits.

On the more gratuitous side, there is the USB Cafe Pad, a heating pad that keeps your coffee hot (or at least warm) while you work. And, for the ultimate in USB-powered frivolity, you can get illuminated USB cables that light up when you plug them in.

Some notebooks get very hot while in use, particularly on the underside. To counter this, you can purchase a cooling pad that you place beneath the notebook, and one or more fans built in to the pad move hot air away from the underside of the computer. The Vantec LapCool-2 (www.vantec.com) is powered by the notebook's USB port and includes two storage compartments in its base for storing cables and other useful items.

Navigation

One of the best accessories for new cars is a GPS navigation system. These systems depend on the U.S. Government's Global Positioning System, which consists of a set of satellites in precisely positioned orbits. At regular timed intervals, all the satellites send out signals. By comparing the times that these different signals are received from three or more satellites, GPS equipment can calculate their position to within just 20 feet. In many cases, it will even calculate your altitude. With a GPS navigation system in your car, you can always tell where you are and have a good idea of how to get where you want to go. You will never have to fuss with a paper map. The disadvantage of such a system is its price. These devices—if they are offered at all for the model of car you desire—typically cost over $1,000.

Laptop owners are in luck here. They can purchase a simple attachment for their notebook that turns it into an automobile navigation device. Not only do they save hundreds of dollars, but they end up with a device they can use in any car they want, or even take it on a boat or other mode of transportation if they desire.

GPS Receivers

To equip your notebook for GPS use, you need only two components: a GPS receiver and a set of electronic maps. Most laptop GPS receivers include a basic set of electronic maps, so to get started, you really need only the receiver.

Numerous different GPS receivers are available for notebooks. Most of these receivers are plugged into a PC Card slot or a USB port, although you can buy GPS receivers that communicate with your notebook using Bluetooth wireless technology. Some receivers have an active antenna built in to them, while others have a jack for an external antenna. Use of an antenna is highly recommended because GPS satellite signals are fairly weak. Some GPS receivers come with a suction cup that will enable you to attach the receiver to the inside of your car's windshield.

One of the most popular GPS devices is the Navman e Series GPS receiver (see Figure 14.22). This product includes the Rand McNally StreetFinder Deluxe travel navigation software. The combination of the receiver and the mapping software enables you to plan trips, locate destinations, and find points of interest, such as hotels and restaurants. As with other GPS receivers, you can obtain information not only about your present location but also on how to get to your destination.

Handheld GPS Receivers

The most cost-effective approach to GPS navigation is a dual-purpose solution. Instead of purchasing a GPS receiver intended solely for use with a laptop, you may instead be able to enlist a handheld GPS receiver that supports the NMEA 2.0 standard as a part-time laptop accessory.

These handheld receivers are intended mainly, of course, for use while hiking or boating. If, however, you connect one of these handhelds to a laptop with an optional PC cable and install a mapping program on the laptop, you have, in effect, an automobile navigation system. Software packages that have this capability include Microsoft's Streets & Trips 2002 and TravRoute's Door-to-Door 2000.

Figure 14.22 The Navman e Series GPS receiver.

Laptop Screen Accessories

The screens on notebook computers have two problems: First, they are sometimes not visible enough, as is the case in bright sunlight. Second, they are sometimes too visible, as frequently happens on crowded airliners. Fortunately, accessories are available that can help solve both problems.

Screen Shades

Anyone who has used a notebook computer in direct sunlight knows that in very bright ambient light, a backlit LCD screen becomes unreadable. This can happen to all screens, even those with the best contrast. A few companies offer laptop screen shades to keep sunlight from washing out an LCD screen (see Figure 14.23).

Figure 14.23 The PC Shade enables laptop users to read LCD screens up to 15 inches in size in direct sunlight.

Privacy Shields

The other problem with laptop screens is exactly the reverse: The screens may be too readable. This happens in crowded situations, particularly on airliners. The size and contrast ratios of modern notebook computers are so good that several people sitting behind you can read your screen. If you are working on private or classified information, this could be a serious problem.

A handful of companies offer privacy shields for notebook computer screens. These shields are thin sheets of plastic that limit the viewing angle of a computer screen. With the screen in place, only a person sitting right in front of the screen can read it well.

3M manufactures its Notebook Privacy Computer Filters in various sizes for notebook LCD screens (see Figure 14.24). These filters use the company's patented "microlouver" technology. This technology, which is similar to a microscopic set of Venetian blinds, renders onscreen data visible only to people directly in front of the screen, while everyone else sees a blank screen.

Figure 14.24   The 3M Notebook Privacy Computer Filter limits the visibility of an LCD screen to only the user directly in front of it.

Notebook Stands

Despite their name, laptop computers usually do not work too well on your lap. They may be too heavy or too light. And they are often too hot. Many people use laptops on the tops of their desks, but a number of accessory platforms promise to make laptop usage more comfortable no matter where it is done.

Desktop

Desktop platforms for laptops are designed to accomplish one of two tasks. The first is to elevate the laptop slightly to provide a more comfortable typing position. The second is to provide the ability to swivel, which is ideal for presentations.

One interesting device in this category is the Laptop Desk (from www.laptopdesk.net). This platform is meant not only for the desk but for other surfaces as well. In its folded configuration, the Laptop Desk elevates the rear of the laptop, thus making typing easier. When you unfold it, this platform reveals a small surface to the side of the laptop that can be used with an external mouse. In this configuration, the platform will work on almost any surface—even your lap.

Automobile

Two kinds of notebook stands are available for cars. The first is a rugged stand that is bolted to the floor of the car, usually on the transmission hump.

The second is a removable stand that occupies the passenger seat or is attached to the steering wheel.

A company called GoOffice offers the AutoExec with Non-Skid Top (A) AEF-01. It features a nonskid top surface; a slide-out work surface; and a large storage area for a laptop, files, and tools. To keep it steady, you can secure it to the passenger seat with a seatbelt.

Arkon Resources sells a simple device called the CM175 Executive Laptop Steering Wheel Mount. It snaps over the steering wheel and can support a notebook weighing up to 10 pounds. As the company says on its website, do not use while driving.

Where to Buy

Because of the popularity of laptop and notebook computers, accessories for these systems are available from a wide array of retailers. They include computer retailers, computer manufacturers' websites, and the manufacturers of the accessories themselves. Table 14.3 lists some of the companies that specialize in notebook accessories.

Table 14.3   Retailers of Laptop Accessories: A Sampling of Some of the Companies Specializing in This Product Category

Specialty	Company	Website
Various products	Belkin	www.belkin.com
	Laptop Travel	www.laptoptravel.com
	Mobile Planet	www.mobileplanet.com
	Targus	www.targus.com
I/O ports—USB, FireWire, SCSI	Adaptec	www.adaptec.com
	Keithley Instruments	www.keithley.com
	Margi Systems	www.margi.com
	Magellan's	www.magellans.com
	Stay Online	www.buytravelconverter.com
Laptop desks	Laptop Desk	www.laptopdesk.net
Carrying cases	Anvil Cases	www.anvilcase.com
	Brenthaven	www.brenthaven.com
	Case Logic	www.caselogic.com
	Samsonite	www.samsonitecompanystores.com
	Zero Halliburton	www.zerohalliburton.com
Theft tracking	CompuTrace	www.absolute.com
	Ztrace	www.ztrace.com

CHAPTER 15

Software and Operating Systems

The Boot Process

The term *boot* comes from the word *bootstrap* and describes the method by which the laptop becomes operational. Just as you pull on a large boot by the small strap attached to the back, a laptop loads a large operating system by first loading a small program that can then pull the operating system into memory. The chain of events begins with the application of power and finally results in a fully functional computer system with software loaded and running. Each event is triggered by the event before it and initiates the event after it.

How does understanding the boot process help you solve problems? Well, for one, if you can't start your system, tracing the system boot process might help you find the location of a problem if you examine the error messages the system displays when the problem occurs. Additionally, Windows can generate a bootlog that you can then use to trace exactly when a failure occurred. If you see an error message that is displayed by only a particular program, you can be sure the program in question was at least loaded and partially running. Combine this information with the knowledge of the boot sequence, and you can at least tell how far the system's startup procedure had progressed before the problem occurred. You usually should look at whichever files or disk areas were being accessed during the failure in the boot process. Error messages displayed during the boot process and those displayed during normal system operation can be hard to decipher. However, the first step in decoding an error message is knowing where the message came from—which program actually generated or displayed it. The following programs and devices are capable of displaying error messages during the boot process.

Operating system independent:

- Motherboard ROM BIOS
- Adapter card ROM BIOS extensions
- Master (partition) boot record
- Volume boot record (VBR)

Operating system dependent. DOS and Windows 9x/Me use the following files during system startup:

- System files (IO.SYS/IBMBIO.COM and MSDOS.SYS/IBMDOS.COM)
- Device drivers (loaded through CONFIG.SYS or the Windows Registry SYSTEM.DAT)
- Shell program (COMMAND.COM in DOS)
- Programs run by AUTOEXEC.BAT, the Windows Startup group, and the Registry
- Windows (WIN.COM)

Windows NT/2000/XP use the following files during system startup:

- Ntldr
- Boot.ini
- Bootsect.dos (multiple-boot systems only)
- Ntbootdd.sys (loaded only for SCSI drives)
- Ntdetect.com
- Ntoskrnl.exe
- Hal.dll
- Files in *systemroot*\System32\Config (Registry)
- Files in *systemroot*\System32\Drivers (drivers)

The first portion of the startup sequence is *operating system independent*, which means these steps are the same for all laptops, no matter which operating system is installed. The latter portion of the boot sequence is *operating system dependent*, which means these steps can vary depending on which operating system is installed or being loaded. The following section examines the operating system–independent startup sequence and provides a detailed account of many of the error messages that might occur during this process. I also provide solutions to these error messages so you can get your system working as quickly as possible.

The Boot Process: Operating System Independent

If you have a problem with your system during startup and can determine where in this sequence of events your system has stalled, you know which events have occurred and probably can eliminate each of them as a cause of the problem. The following steps occur in a typical system startup regardless of which operating system you are loading:

1. You switch on electrical power to the system.

2. The power supply performs a Power On Self Test (known as the POST). When all voltages and current levels are acceptable, the supply indicates that the power is stable and sends the Power_Good signal to the motherboard. The time from switch-on to Power_Good is normally between 0.1 and 0.5 seconds.

3. The microprocessor timer chip receives the Power_Good signal, which causes it to stop generating a reset signal to the microprocessor.

4. The microprocessor begins executing the ROM BIOS code, starting at memory address FFFF:0000. Because this location is only 16 bytes from the end of the available ROM space, it contains a JMP (jump) instruction to the actual ROM BIOS starting address.

5. The ROM BIOS performs a test of the central hardware to verify basic system functionality. Any errors that occur are indicated by audio "beep" codes because the video system has not yet been initialized. If the BIOS is Plug and Play (PnP), the following steps (steps 6–9) are executed; if not, skip to step 10.

6. The Plug and Play BIOS checks nonvolatile random access memory (RAM) for input/output (I/O) port addresses, interrupt request (IRQ) lines, direct memory access (DMA) channels, and other settings necessary to configure PnP devices on the computer.

7. All Plug and Play devices found by the Plug and Play BIOS are disabled.

8. A map of used and unused resources is created.

9. The Plug and Play devices are configured and reenabled, one at a time. If your computer does not have a Plug and Play BIOS, PnP devices are initialized using their default settings. These devices can be reconfigured dynamically when Windows starts. At that point, Windows queries the Plug and Play BIOS for device information and then queries each Plug and Play device for its configuration.

10. The BIOS performs a video ROM scan of memory locations C000:0000–C780:0000 looking for video adapter ROM BIOS programs contained on a video adapter found either on a card plugged into a slot or integrated into the motherboard. If the scan locates a video ROM BIOS, it is tested by a checksum procedure. If the video BIOS passes the checksum test, the ROM is executed; then the video ROM code initializes the video adapter and a cursor appears onscreen. If the checksum test fails, the following message appears:

    ```
    C000 ROM Error
    ```

Because laptop computers don't use removable video cards (the video circuit is either integrated into the motherboard's chipset or a separate chip is built in to the motherboard), this error means you need to have your system serviced.

11. If the BIOS finds no video adapter ROM, it uses the motherboard ROM video drivers to initialize the video display hardware, and a cursor appears onscreen.

12. The motherboard ROM BIOS scans memory locations C800:0000–DF80:0000 in 2KB increments for any other ROMs located on any other adapter cards (such as SCSI adapters). If any ROMs are found, they are checksum-tested and executed. These adapter ROMs can alter existing BIOS routines and establish new ones.

13. Failure of a checksum test for any of these ROM modules causes this message to appear:

XXXX ROM Error

Here, the address *XXXX* indicates the segment address of the failed ROM module.

If you have a PC Card or CardBus card installed, shut down the system, remove the card, and then restart the system. If the error is no longer displayed, the ROM built in to the card is defective, and the card should be replaced. If the error message still appears, your system should be serviced, because the error is probably coming from ROM on the motherboard.

14. The ROM BIOS checks the word value at memory location 0000:0472 to see whether this start is a cold start or a warm start. A word value of 1234h in this location is a flag that indicates a warm start, which causes the BIOS to skip the memory test portion of the POST. Any other word value in this location indicates a cold start, and the BIOS performs the full POST procedure. Some system BIOSes let you control various aspects of the POST procedure, making it possible to skip the memory test, for example, which can be lengthy on a system with a lot of RAM.

15. If this is a cold start, the full POST executes; if this is a warm start, a mini-POST executes, minus the RAM test. Any errors found during the POST are reported by a combination of audio and displayed error messages. Successful completion of the POST is usually indicated by a single beep (with the exception of some Compaq computers, which beep twice). See Chapter 16, "Problem Solving and Troubleshooting," for information about error messages, beep codes, and solutions.

16. The ROM BIOS searches for a boot record at cylinder 0, head 0, sector 1 (the first sector) on the default boot drive. At one time, the default boot drive was always the first floppy disk (A:) drive. However, the BIOSes on today's systems often enable you to select the default boot device and the order in which the BIOS will look for other devices to boot from, if necessary, using a floppy disk, hard disk, or even a CD-ROM drive in any order you choose. This sector is loaded into memory at 0000:7C00 and tested.

If a disk is in the drive but the sector can't be read, or if no disk is present, the BIOS continues with step 19.

Tip

If you do want to boot from a CD-ROM, be sure the CD-ROM drive is specified before the hard disk in the boot devices menu in your BIOS setup. To ensure that you can boot from an emergency CD or floppy disk, I recommend setting the CD-ROM drive as the first boot device and the floppy drive as the second boot device. A hard disk containing your operating system should be the third device in the boot device list. This enables you to always be ready for an emergency. As long as you do not boot with a CD or floppy loaded, the BIOS bypasses both the CD-ROM and floppy disk drives and boots from the hard drive.

Note that not all operating system CDs are bootable. Windows 95 CDs are not bootable; however, with Windows 98, Microsoft made the operating system CD bootable, but only for original equipment manufacturer (OEM) versions. This does not extend to retail versions of these Windows CDs. Windows NT 4.0 and later, including Windows 2000 and XP, are shipped on bootable CDs. See Chapter 10, "Removable Storage," for information on how to make a bootable CD.

Most recovery CDs packaged with laptop computers can also be used to boot the system and start the software/operating system reinstallation process.

17. If you are booting from a floppy disk and the first byte of the volume boot record is less than 06h, or if the first byte is greater than or equal to 06h and the first nine words contain the same data pattern, this error message appears and the system stops:

```
602-Diskette Boot Record Error
```

If you've left the floppy disk in the drive by mistake, remove it and restart the system. If the floppy disk is supposed to be bootable, reformat it with the /S (system) or Boot Files option and restart your system with it (use the File menu in Windows Explorer of a working system to access the Format option).

18. If the volume boot record can't find or load the system files, or if a problem was encountered loading them, one of the following messages appears:

```
Non-System disk or disk error
Replace and strike any key when ready

Non-System disk or disk error
Replace and press any key when ready

Invalid system disk_
Replace the disk, and then press any key

Disk Boot failure

Disk I/O Error
```

All these messages originate in the volume boot record and relate to VBR or system file problems. The exact error message you see depends upon the BIOS version used by your laptop.

The most common cause for these error messages is leaving a floppy disk in drive A:. Remove the floppy disk and press a key to retry the boot process.

19. If no boot record can be read from drive A: (such as when no disk is in the drive), the BIOS then looks for a master boot record (MBR) at cylinder 0, head 0, sector 1 (the first sector) of the first hard disk. If this sector is found, it is loaded into memory address 0000:7C00 and tested for a signature.

20. If the last two (signature) bytes of the MBR are not equal to 55AAh, software interrupt 18h (Int 18h) is invoked on most systems.

This causes the BIOS to display an error message that can vary for different BIOS manufacturers, but it's often similar to one of the following messages, depending on which BIOS you have.

IBM BIOS:

```
The IBM Personal Computer Basic_
Version C1.10 Copyright IBM Corp 1981
62940 Bytes free_
Ok_
```

Most IBM computers since 1987 display a strange character graphic depicting the front of a floppy drive, a 3 1/2" disk, and arrows prompting you to insert a disk in the drive and press the F1 key to proceed.

AMI BIOS:

```
NO ROM BASIC - SYSTEM HALTED
```

Compaq BIOS:

```
Non-System disk or disk error
replace and strike any key when ready
```

Award BIOS:

```
DISK BOOT FAILURE, INSERT SYSTEM DISK AND PRESS ENTER
```

Phoenix BIOS:

```
No boot device available -
strike F1 to retry boot, F2 for setup utility
```

or

```
No boot sector on fixed disk -
strike F1 to retry boot, F2 for setup utility
```

Note that although some of these messages are similar to those caused by leaving a floppy disk in drive A: (step 18), some are different. Although the messages vary from BIOS to BIOS, the cause for each relates to specific bytes in the MBR, which is the first sector of a hard disk at the physical location cylinder 0, head 0, sector 1.

The problem involves a disk that either has never been partitioned or has had the master boot sector corrupted. During the boot process, the BIOS checks the last two bytes in the MBR (the first sector of the drive) for a signature value of 55AAh. If the last two bytes are not 55AAh, an interrupt 18h is invoked, which calls the subroutine that displays one of the error messages just shown, which basically instructs the user to insert a bootable floppy to proceed.

The MBR (including the signature bytes) is written to the hard disk by the FDISK or DISKPART program (which are used by various versions of DOS or Windows to partition the hard disk). Immediately after a hard disk is low-level formatted, all the sectors are initialized with a pattern of bytes, and the first sector does not contain the 55AAh signature. In other words, these ROM error messages are exactly what you see if you attempt to boot from a hard disk that has been freshly low-level formatted but has not yet been partitioned.

You should see an error message like this only if you have replaced the original hard disk in your laptop with another hard disk that has not yet been partitioned, or if the MBR on the current disk has been corrupted.

21. The MBR searches its built-in partition table entries for a boot indicator byte marking an active partition entry.

22. If none of the partitions are marked active (bootable), the BIOS invokes software interrupt 18h, which displays an error message (refer to step 20).

This error could happen if you partition a hard disk into a primary and extended partition with FDISK and forget to mark the primary partition as active.

23. If any boot indicator byte in the MBR partition table is invalid, or if more than one indicates an active partition, the following message is displayed and the system stops:

```
Invalid partition table
```

This error could indicate physical damage to your drive or problems caused by a computer virus. If your drive contains valuable data, you should use a data-recovery program or service to retrieve any readable data from the drive. See "Laptop Data Recovery" later in this chapter.

24. If an active partition is found in the MBR, the partition boot record from the active partition is loaded and tested. If the partition boot record is read successfully, proceed to step 27.

25. If the partition boot record can't be read successfully from the active partition within five retries because of read errors, the following message is displayed and the system stops:

```
Error loading operating system
```

26. The hard disk's partition boot record is tested for a signature. If it does not contain a valid signature of 55AAh as the last two bytes in the sector, the following message is displayed and the system stops:

```
Missing operating system
```

27. The volume boot record is executed as a program. This program looks for and loads the operating system kernel or system files. To see what happens next, go to the appropriate boot process section for your operating system.

28. If the volume boot record can't find or load the system files, or if a problem was encountered loading them, one of the following messages appears:

```
Non-System disk or disk error
Replace and strike any key when ready
```

```
Non-System disk or disk error
Replace and press any key when ready
```

```
Invalid system disk_
Replace the disk, and then press any key
```

```
Disk Boot failure
```

```
Disk I/O Error
```

All these messages originate in the volume boot record and relate to VBR or system file problems.

Check the following to recover from these problems:

- If you want to boot from the hard disk, remove any floppy disk in drive A: and restart the computer.
- If you have recently opened the system, make sure the hard disk is properly connected to the data/power cable and the motherboard.
- Boot the system with an emergency boot/system disk or CD and attempt to read the contents of the hard disk.

If the hard disk can be read, use the appropriate remedy to transfer your boot files:

- With DOS or Windows 9x, use the `Sys C:` command to transfer the boot files.
- With Windows Me, rerun the Setup program to transfer the boot files.
- With Windows 2000/XP, start the Recovery Console from the Windows CD and run Fixboot.

If the hard disk's contents can't be read and the drive contains valuable data, you should use a data-recovery program or service to retrieve any readable data from the drive. See "Laptop Data Recovery" later in this chapter.

From this point forward, what happens depends on which operating system you have. The operating system–dependent boot procedures are discussed in the next several sections.

The Windows 9x/Me Boot Process

Many older laptops use Windows 9x/Me. Knowing exactly how Windows 9x and Millennium Edition (Me) load and start can be helpful when you are troubleshooting startup problems. The Windows 9x boot process can be broken into three phases:

- The IO.SYS file is loaded and run. (Windows 9x's IO.SYS combines the functions of DOS's IO.SYS and MSDOS.SYS.)
- Real-mode configuration takes place.
- The WIN.COM file is loaded and run.

Phase 1: Loading and Running the IO.SYS File

1. The initialization code initializes the base device drivers, determines equipment status, resets the disk system, resets and initializes attached devices, and sets the system default parameters.

2. The file system is activated, and control is returned to the IO.SYS initialization code.

3. The Starting Windows message is displayed for n seconds, or until you press a Windows function key. The amount of time the message is displayed is determined by the BootDelay=<n> line in the MSDOS.SYS file; the default is 2 seconds.

4. The IO.SYS initialization code reads the MSDOS.SYS configuration file. If you have multiple hardware profiles (a likely situation if you have a laptop and you use a docking station or port replicator), you receive the message

   ```
   Windows cannot determine what configuration your computer is in.
   ```

   and must choose a hardware configuration to use from the menu displayed. To learn more about docking stations and port replicators, refer to Chapter 14, "Portable System Accessories."

5. The LOGO.SYS file is loaded and displays a startup image onscreen.

6. If the DRVSPACE.INI or DBLSPACE.INI file exists, it is loaded into memory. IO.SYS also automatically loads HIMEM.SYS, IFSHLP.SYS, and SETVER.EXE.

7. The IO.SYS file checks the system Registry files (SYSTEM.DAT and USER.DAT) for valid data.

8. IO.SYS opens the SYSTEM.DAT file. If the SYSTEM.DAT file is not found, the SYSTEM.DA0 file is used for startup. If Windows 9x/Me starts successfully, the SYSTEM.DA0 file is copied to the SYSTEM.DAT file.

9. The DBLBUFF.SYS file is loaded if DoubleBuffer=1 is in the MSDOS.SYS file or if double buffering is enabled under the following Registry key:

   ```
   HKLM\System\CurrentControlSet\Control\WinBoot\DoubleBuffer
   ```

Note

Windows 9x Setup automatically enables double buffering if it detects that it is required.

10. If you have multiple hardware profiles, the hardware profile you chose is loaded from the Registry.

11. In Windows 9x/Me, the system looks in the Registry's Hkey_Local_Machine\System\ CurrentControlSet key to load the device drivers and other parameters specified there before executing the CONFIG.SYS file.

Note

If you see error messages during startup or if your system doesn't start properly, restart the system, press the Ctrl (Windows 95) or F8 (Windows 98/Me) key to bring up the startup menu, and select Logged to create a file called **Bootlog.txt**. This file records events during startup and can help you determine which files or processes are not loading correctly.

Phase 2: Real-Mode Configuration

Some older hardware devices and programs require that drivers or files be loaded in real mode (16-bit mode) for them to work properly. To ensure backward compatibility, Windows 9x processes the CONFIG.SYS and AUTOEXEC.BAT files if they exist:

1. The CONFIG.SYS file is read if it exists, and the statements within it are processed, including the loading of drivers into memory. If the CONFIG.SYS file does not exist, the IO.SYS file loads the following required drivers:

   - IFSHLP.SYS

   - HIMEM.SYS

   - SETVER.EXE

   IO.SYS obtains the location of these files from the WinBootDir= line of the MSDOS.SYS file and must be on the hard disk.

2. Windows reserves all global upper memory blocks (UMBs) for Windows 9x operating system use or for expanded memory support using the Expanded Memory Specification (EMS).

3. The AUTOEXEC.BAT file is processed, if present, and any terminate-and-stay-resident (TSR) programs listed within are loaded into memory.

Phase 3: Loading and Running the WIN.COM File

1. WIN.COM is loaded and run.

2. The WIN.COM file accesses the VMM32.VXD file. If enough RAM is available, the VMM32.VXD file loads into memory; otherwise, it is accessed from the hard disk (resulting in a slower startup time).

3. The real-mode virtual device driver loader checks for duplicate virtual device drivers (VxDs) in the WINDOWS\SYSTEM\VMM32 folder and the VMM32.VXD file. If a VxD exists in both the WINDOWS\SYSTEM\VMM32 folder and the VMM32.VXD file, the duplicate VxD is "marked" in the VMM32.VXD file so that it is not loaded.

4. VxDs not already loaded by the VMM32.VXD file are loaded from the [386 Enh] section of the WINDOWS\SYSTEM.INI file.

Required VxDs

Some VxDs are required for Windows to run properly. These required VxDs are loaded automatically and do not require a Registry entry. Windows 9x requires the following VxDs:

BIOSXLAT	CONFIGMG	DYNAPAGE
DOSMGR	EBIOS	IFSMGR
INT13	IOS	PAGESWAP
SHELL	V86MMGR	VCD
VCACHE	VCOMM	VCOND
VDD	VDMAD	VFAT
VKD	VMCPD	VPICD
VTD	VTDAPI	VWIN32
VXDLDR		

5. The real-mode virtual device driver loader checks that all required VxDs loaded successfully. If they aren't, it attempts to load the drivers again.

6. After the real-mode virtual device driver loading is logged, driver initialization occurs. If any VxDs require real-mode initialization, they begin their processes in real mode.

7. VMM32 switches the computer's processor from real mode to protected mode.

8. A three-phase VxD-initialization process occurs in which the drivers are loaded according to their InitDevice instead of the order in which they are loaded into memory.

9. After all the VxDs are loaded, the files KRNL32.DLL, GDI.EXE, USER.EXE, and EXPLORER.EXE (the default Windows 9x GUI shell) are loaded.

10. If a network is specified, the network environment and multiuser profiles are loaded. The user is prompted to log on to the network installed. Windows 9x/Me enables multiple users to save their custom desktop settings. When a user logs on to Windows, her desktop settings are loaded from the Registry. If the user does not log on, the desktop configuration uses a default desktop.

11. Programs in the StartUp group and the RunOnce Registry key are run during the last phase of the startup process. After each program in the RunOnce Registry key is started, the program is removed from the key.

Note

If your laptop is running programs and services at startup that slow down the computer or make it unstable, you can use the MSConfig program in Windows 98/Me or Windows XP to selectively disable some startup programs and processes. For details, view the Windows Help System entry for MSConfig.

Windows NT/2000/XP Startup

When you start a Windows NT, 2000, or XP system (which are all based on the same set of integral code), the boot process is different from that of a DOS or Windows 9x/Me system. Instead of the IO.SYS and MSDOS.SYS files used by Windows 9x/Me, Windows NT/2000/XP use an OS loader program called Ntldr.

The basic Windows NT/2000/XP startup process is described in the following step-by-step procedure:

1. The partition boot sector loads `Ntldr` (NT Loader). It then switches the processor to protected mode, starts the file system, and reads the contents of `Boot.ini`. The information in `Boot.ini` determines the startup options and initial boot menu selections (dual-booting, for example). If dual-booting is enabled, and a non-NT/2000/XP OS is chosen, `Bootsec.dos` is loaded. If SCSI drives are present, `Ntbootdd.sys` is loaded, which contains the SCSI boot drivers.

2. `Ntdetect.com` gathers hardware-configuration data and passes this information to `Ntldr`. If more than one hardware profile exists, Windows uses the correct one for the current configuration. If the ROM BIOS is compliant with the Advanced Configuration and Power Interface (ACPI), Windows uses ACPI to enumerate and initialize devices.

3. The kernel loads. `Ntldr` passes information collected by `Ntdetect.com` to `Ntoskrnl.exe`. `Ntoskrnl` then loads the kernel, the Hardware Abstraction Layer (`Hal.dll`), and Registry information. An indicator near the bottom of the screen details progress.

4. Drivers load and the user logs on. Networking-related components (for example, TCP/IP) load simultaneously with other services, and the `Begin Logon` prompt appears onscreen. After a user logs on successfully, Windows updates the Last Known Good Configuration information to reflect the current configuration state.

5. Plug and Play detects and configures new devices. If new devices are detected, they are assigned resources. Windows extracts the necessary driver files from `Driver.cab`. If the driver files are not found, the user is prompted to provide them. Device detection occurs simultaneously with the operating system logon process.

The following files are processed during Windows NT/2000/XP startup:

- `Ntldr`
- `Boot.ini`
- `Bootsect.dos` (multiple-boot systems only)
- `Ntbootdd.sys` (loaded only for SCSI drives)
- `Ntdetect.com`
- `Ntoskrnl.exe`
- `Hal.dll`
- Files in *systemroot*`\System32\Config` (Registry)
- Files in *systemroot*`\System32\Drivers` (drivers)

Note

If you see error messages during startup or if your system doesn't start properly, restart the system, press the F8 key (Windows 2000/XP only) to bring up the startup menu, and select Enable Boot Logging to create a file called `Ntbtlog.txt`. This file records events during startup and can help you determine which files or processes are not loading correctly.

Installing the Operating System

In almost every situation, a laptop computer already has an operating system installed when you receive it. However, if you perform a hard disk upgrade or if you want to wipe out the contents of the existing drive and reinstall Windows, you might need to install or reinstall the operating system.

If you are using a non-Windows operating system, follow the documentation for the installation procedures.

On a newer system in which you are installing an OEM version of Windows XP (which comes on a bootable CD), there isn't really anything you need to do, other than simply boot from the CD (you might have to enable the CD-ROM as a boot device in your BIOS Setup) and follow the prompts to install the OS. Windows XP automatically recognizes that the drive needs to be partitioned and the partitions are formatted before the installation can proceed. Additionally, if you prefer, Windows XP can execute these functions for you, with prompts guiding you along the way. This is the method I recommend for most people because it is relatively simple and straightforward.

If your laptop's operating system comes on a recovery CD, booting from the recovery CD usually brings up a menu that lets you select whether you want to repair your existing Windows installation or reinstall Windows and the computer's original applications.

Caution

Using a product recovery or restore CD instead of a plain Windows CD to reinstall Windows and the computer's original applications wipes out the existing installation, so be sure to back up all data and configuration files (such as website favorites and email accounts) you want to keep before you use the restore CD. If the computer doesn't include a product recovery or restore CD (or a plain Windows CD), it might have a hidden disk partition or hidden protected area (HPA) that contains Windows files that can be used to rebuild the system's original configuration. See the system's instruction manual or online help to determine how to use the files in a hidden partition or HPA.

Installing Windows 98/Me

Older laptop systems (pre-Windows Me or 2000) may not have the necessary recommended system requirements to run the latest version of Windows. The recommended system requirements for installing Windows XP Professional, for instance, are as follows:

- 300 MHz or faster processor (233MHz minimum)
- 128MB RAM (64MB RAM is supported, but is not recommended)
- 1.5GB hard drive space

Of course, it is better that your system's configuration exceed these specifications. However, given at least a 300MHz system with 128MB, I''d recommend installing XP or Win2000 over Win98 or Me. I recently did some testing of XP installations on older, slower hardware and was frankly both surprised and impressed at how well it performed for basic tasks, even on a minimal configuration. Still, performance will be increased noticeably by upgrading to at least 256MB.

If your laptop does not meet the 300MHz processor and 128MB RAM requirements, you should consider installing Windows 98SE (second edition) or Windows Me instead. Note that Windows 95 is not recommended at all due to a lack of features and capabilities compared to 98SE. Since virtually any system capable of running Windows 95 should be capable of running Windows 98 as well, I highly recommend you install Windows 98SE instead of Windows 95 wherever possible. With updates and support coming from Microsoft through 2006, Windows 98SE is still a viable and useful OS for systems that do not meet the requirements of XP.

Partitioning and Formatting the Drive with Windows 98/Me

The first step when installing Windows 98/Me is to partition and format the hard drive using a Windows 98 or Me startup disk (floppy). The OEM versions of these operating systems included both a bootable CD as well as a startup disk floppy. If you don''t have the floppy, you can use any system currently running Windows 98 or Me to create a startup floppy using the following procedure:

1. In Control Panel, double-click Add/Remove Programs and then click the Startup Disk tab.

2. Click Create Disk and then follow the instructions on the screen.

Tip

If you are unable to locate a Windows 98 or Me startup disk, or a system running Windows 98 or Me where you can create one, check out the website **www.bootdisk.com**. This site has a number of startup floppy images that you can download and use to create your own startup disks. Also, another site called **www.cdrom-drivers.com** has pointers to an enormous library of CD-ROM device drivers, including the **AOATAPI.SYS** driver, which works with most desktop and notebook CD-ROM and DVD drives.

Note that for the purposes of installing either Windows 98 or Windows Me, the startup disks are fully interchangeable. That means you can use a Windows 98 startup floppy to install Windows Me, or a Windows Me startup floppy to install Windows 98. Given a choice, I recommend the Windows Me startup floppy because the FDISK command on that disk has fixes to support hard drives larger than 64GiB. You can also download an updated version of FDISK with the same fixes for Windows 98 from Microsoft at http://support.microsoft.com/kb/263044. You will need to copy the updated FDISK to your Windows 98 startup floppy if you will be using it to partition drives larger than 64GiB.

To prepare the hard disk, boot from the Windows 98/Me startup floppy. Normally, you will be greeted with the following choices:

```
1. Start computer with CD-ROM support.
2. Start computer without CD-ROM support.
```

Since you are only preparing the hard disk at this time and will not need any files off the CD, select the option without CD-ROM support for the fastest boot. At the A:> prompt, type the following command:

```
FDISK
```

This command is used to partition your drive. Follow the menus to first remove any existing partitions (all data they contain will be lost) and then create either a single partition for the entire drive or multiple partitions as you desire. Usually, the first partition must also be made active, which means it will be bootable. If your drive is over 512MiB, I recommend you answer Yes to the following prompt:

```
Do you wish to enable large disk support (Y/N)?
```

This enables the partition to be created using the FAT32 file system, which is more efficient and robust than FAT16 for larger partitions, and also supports volume sizes of up to 2TiB, where FAT16 is limited to only 2GiB volumes. Then, if you are installing to a blank drive, I recommend you continue accepting default entries for all the prompts, which will partition the drive as a single bootable volume that covers the entire drive.

When the partitioning is complete, exit FDISK and restart the system.

Note

For more information about FDISK and file systems, see Chapter 9, "Hard Disk Storage."

When rebooting from the startup floppy, select the option to start the computer with CD-ROM support because you will need to copy files from the CD after formatting the boot volume. If you created more than one partition with FDISK, you will need to format only the first (C:) partition to complete the installation; the others can be formatted later. The first partition is formatted using the FORMAT command as follows:

```
FORMAT C:
```

All other partitions would be formatted in the same manner; however, I recommend you do that later, after Windows has been installed.

After the FORMAT command completes, you are ready to install Windows.

Note

Drive installation, setup, and formatting are covered extensively in Chapter 9.

Installing the Operating System

While Windows 98 and Windows Me can be installed directly from their respective installation CDs, note that only the OEM CDs are bootable; the Retail and Upgrade CDs are *not* bootable. This means that even if your system has bootable CD-ROM support (that is, most systems from 1998 and newer), you will still need a Windows 98 or Me startup floppy to install the Retail or Upgrade versions of Windows 98 or Me. And even if you do have an OEM version of 98/Me on a bootable CD, it is actually much better to first boot from a startup floppy, copy the installation files from the CD to the hard disk, and then run the install directly from the hard disk instead. This will not only make future re-installs much easier, but any time you want to add an optional Windows component or install a device that needs a driver from the original installation files, you won't need to locate and insert your original Windows CD.

After the C: partition has been created and freshly formatted, you can use the following procedure to install the OS:

1. Place the Windows 98 or Me startup floppy in the floppy drive and the original Windows installation CD in the CD/DVD drive; then restart the system.

2. At the startup menu, choose the option to start the computer with CD-ROM support.

3. If you are starting from a standard Windows 98 or Me startup floppy, the startup routine will create a RAMdisk in which to uncompress and store additional utility programs called diagnostic tools. When the boot process finishes, you should see a message like this on the screen:

```
The diagnostic tools were successfully loaded to drive D.

MSCDEX Version 2.25
Copyright (C) Microsoft Corp. 1986-1995. All rights reserved.
Drive E: = Driver MSCD001 unit 0
```

This message indicates that the RAMdisk containing the diagnostic tools is drive D: and the CD-ROM (or DVD) drive is E:. In this scenario, the floppy drive is A: and the freshly formatted hard disk partition is C:.

Note that the remainder of this procedure assumes that the CD drive letter is "E:." You should substitute the actual letter of your CD drive (as shown in the preceding message) if it is different.

4. At the A:> prompt, create a new folder in C: called \WIN98 (for Windows 98) or \WIN9X (for Windows Me) using one of the following commands, depending on which OS you are installing:

For Windows 98, type

```
MD C:\WIN98
```

For Windows Me, type

```
MD C:\WIN9X
```

5. Copy all the files in the installation folder on the CD to the folder you just created on the hard disk using one of the following commands, depending on which OS you are installing (substitute the letter for your CD/DVD drive if it is different from E):

For Windows 98, type

```
COPY E:\WIN98 C:\WIN98
```

For Windows Me, type

```
COPY E:\WIN9X C:\WIN9X
```

6. Change the prompt to the hard drive using the following command:

```
C:
```

7. Change to the directory where you previously copied the installation files:

For Windows 98, type

```
CD \WIN98
```

For Windows Me, type

```
CD \WIN9X
```

8. Remove both the floppy disk and installation CD from their drives and begin the actual OS installation from the hard disk using the following command:

```
SETUP
```

This starts the Windows installation SETUP program. From here, you can follow the prompts to install Windows as you see fit.

This procedure will normally take 45 minutes or more, so be prepared to spend the time. During the installation, you will need to answer a few questions and provide your product key, which you can find on the Certificate of Authenticity sticker that is either included on the Windows installation package or attached to the case of your system. You should also have handy any driver disks for your hardware, because during the OS installation, you will be installing not only Windows but also the drivers for any hardware detected during the installation process.

Note

If you want to create a bootable CD containing your Windows installation files, see Chapter 10, "Removable Storage."

After Windows is installed, you can install any additional drivers or application programs you want. At this point, your system should be fully operational.

Installing Windows XP

If you are installing Windows XP on a laptop that has the "Designed for Windows XP" logo printed on it or if the system originally came with Windows XP preloaded on it, you should be able to install the operating system without encountering any hardware incompatibilities. Before you start an installation of XP, I recommend checking for an updated motherboard BIOS from the system manufacturer. It is not uncommon for a system to have an updated BIOS that is required for proper support of Windows XP.

You can perform an upgrade installation of Windows XP on a laptop that is running Windows 98, Windows Me, Windows NT Workstation 4 (Service Pack 6), or Windows 2000 Professional. However, you will usually encounter fewer problems and achieve better performance by doing a clean install. This is particularly true if you are installing Windows XP from the backup disk that was provided by the manufacturer of your laptop; these disks usually contain other software programs that are installed when Windows is installed.

Windows XP Setup gives you the option to remove/create partitions and format the hard drive before proceeding with the installation. Unless you absolutely need to keep existing software programs or files intact on the laptop, you should first remove any existing partitions and then repartition and format the drive from scratch. This will give you a clean installation.

You can also choose to create a multiboot system by installing Windows XP on a machine that already has an older version of Windows (9x, Me, NT, 2000) installed on it. To do this, you must have each Windows installation on a separate partition. This option is more commonly used on desktop computers than it is on `laptop systems`.

Note

It is possible to multiboot Windows XP with other operating systems, such as Linux. For more information on creating a multiboot system with Windows XP, read "Multibooting with Windows XP" at `http://www.microsoft.com/win- dowsxp/using/setup/learnmore/multiboot.mspx`.

All of the Windows XP CDs are bootable, and any system capable of running XP should be able to boot from a CD as well, so you generally don't need a startup floppy during the installation. The entire installation can be done from the bootable Windows XP installation CD.

The easiest way to proceed with a clean install is to boot from the Windows XP CD directly. Windows Setup will start in text mode, copy files to the laptop, walk you through the process of partitioning and formatting the hard drive, and then proceed to the graphical phase of installation. You will be prompted to enter information concerning regional settings, networking components, the computer name you wish to use, and an administrator password. Also during the process, you will be asked to type in the 25-digit product key, which you can find on the Certificate of Authenticity label on either the Windows package or on the case of your system.

When Windows Setup is complete, you will be asked to activate your copy of Windows XP. Windows Product Activation is an antipiracy feature that was introduced with the release of Windows XP. Activation can be accomplished very quickly if you have an active Internet connection; optionally, you can call a toll-free number and receive an activation code over the phone. You have 30 days to activate Windows XP after setup is finished.

Installing Important Drivers

After installing the operating system, the first thing you need to do is to install drivers for devices where drivers were not found on the Windows CD. This often includes things such as chipset drivers for your motherboard, drivers for newer video chips, USB 2.0 drivers, and more. Of these, the motherboard chipset drivers are the most critical and should be installed first. If your version of Windows didn't include these drivers, download them from your laptop vendor and put them on a CD or floppy disk. Then, install other drivers if they're not already installed, such as video, network, modem, and so on.

See Chapter 16, "Problem Solving and Troubleshooting," to learn how to determine which drivers you need and where to obtain them.

Windows XP Updates and Service Packs

Microsoft frequently publishes new updates for Windows in order to fix software bugs, address security issues, and add new functionality to the operating system. Over time, these various updates are bundled into collections known as Service Packs.

When Service Packs are installed (or built in to new Windows installation disks), the version of the Service Pack is incorporated into the version name of the Windows software. For example, Microsoft published Service Pack 2 for Windows XP in the summer of 2004. If you install this Service Pack, the version of Windows on your system is known as Windows XP Service Pack 2, more commonly abbreviated to Windows XP SP2.

In the past, you were required to keep up with which Service Pack you had installed on your system. You also needed to manually download and install new updates and Service Packs as they were made available.

With Windows XP, you can take advantage of a feature called Automatic Updates. With Automatic Updates, you can tell the operating system to periodically check for new updates and Service Packs, and have Windows notify you when they are made available. You can even configure this feature to automatically download updates and, if desired, have the operating system automatically install them. You can configure all of the available options for Automatic Updates by opening the System applet in the Windows Control Panel and clicking on the Automatic Updates tab.

Depending on when you purchased your laptop (or when you purchased your copy of Windows XP), you may already have the most recent Service Pack integrated or slipstreamed into your Windows XP installation CD.

Linux on the Laptop

Although not many notebook manufacturers will preload Linux on their machines, this hasn't stopped users of the open source operating system from running it on their laptops.

Several Linux companies offer information on laptop systems that are compatible with their versions of Linux. Red Hat (www.redhat.com) has an online hardware catalog that lists systems it has tested and ""certified"" for use with Red Hat Linux. Novell has partnered with a number of hardware manufacturers for its Novell Linux Desktop (www.novell.com/products/desktop/), which is based on SUSE Linux and runs on a number of IBM ThinkPad models. Debian (www.debian.org) offers a list of global vendors that will preinstall Debian Linux on new systems. And, if you"re looking for a solution direct from the laptop vendor, you can visit http://tuxmobil.org/reseller.html to view an international survey of vendors who offer preinstalled Linux laptops.

As with most things concerning open source software, the best information on installing and running Linux on laptops is found within the Linux community of users and programmers. One of the best online resources is TuxMobil (http://tuxmobil.org). This site contains over 4,000 links relevant to

Linux installations on laptops and also provides hardware compatibility lists (HCLs) for laptop hardware and accessories, as well as a comprehensive Linux Mobile Guide that covers almost all aspects of Linux and mobile computing.

Laptop Data Recovery

Although most modern laptops are equipped with rewritable optical drives (either CD- or DVD-based), laptop users rarely perform backups of data, if at all. Sooner or later, though, you might be sorry if you don't make backups. Because of the way laptops work, data recovery can be more challenging with a laptop than with a desktop PC. In the following sections, I show you the methods you can use to recover data from a laptop.

Recovering lost data can be as simple as opening the Recycle Bin in Windows, or it might require spending hundreds of dollars on specialized data-recovery software or services. In the worst-case scenario, you might even need to send your system off to a data-recovery center. Several factors affect the degree of difficulty you can have in recovering your data:

- How the data was deleted
- What file system was used by the drive where the data was stored
- What version of Windows you use
- Whether you already have data-protection software installed on your system
- Whether the data is stored on magnetic media or flash memory
- Whether the drive has suffered physical damage to heads, platters, or its circuit board

The Windows Recycle Bin and File "Deletion"

The simplest data recovery of all takes place when you send files to the Windows Recycle Bin (a standard part of Windows since Windows 95). Pressing the Delete key when you have a file or group of files highlighted in Windows Explorer or My Computer, or clicking the Delete button, sends files to the Recycle Bin. Although Windows Explorer does not list any file(s) sent to the Recycle Bin in its normal location, the file is actually protected from being overwritten. By default, Windows 95 and newer versions reserve 10% of the disk space on each hard disk for the Recycle Bin (removable-media drives don't have a Recycle Bin). Therefore, a 20GB drive reserves about 2GB for its Recycle Bin. In this example, as long as less than 2GB of files have been sent to the Recycle Bin, Windows does protect a "deleted" file, allowing it to be recovered. However, once more than 2GB of files have been sent to the Recycle Bin, Windows allows the oldest files to be overwritten. Therefore, the quicker you realize that a file has been sent to the Recycle Bin, the more likely it is you can retrieve it (you can also increase the amount of space allotted for the Recycle Bin).

To retrieve a file from the Recycle Bin, open the Recycle Bin, select the file, right-click it, and select Restore. Windows lists the file in its original location and removes it from the Recycle Bin. If you hold down the Shift key when you select Delete or press the Delete key, the Recycle Bin is bypassed. Retrieving lost data at this point requires third-party data-recovery software.

Recovering Files That Are Not in the Recycle Bin

Although the Recycle Bin is a useful first line of defense against data loss, it is quite limited. As you learned in the preceding section, it can be bypassed when you select files for deletion. Also, files stored in the Recycle Bin will eventually be kicked out by newer deleted files. What's more, the Recycle Bin isn't used for files deleted from a command prompt or when an older version of a file is replaced by a newer version.

There are a number of specialized software products on the market that you can use to recover deleted files. Examples of such products include Norton GoBack, VCom System Suite 6.0, and Active@ UNDELETE.

These data-recovery products are continually growing in power and functionality. For example, Active@ UNDELETE is able to recover deleted or formatted data from all types of hard drives (regardless of the file system used), floppy disks, and most memory cards such as CompactFlash, Secure Digital, and Sony Memory Sticks.

Use a Second Hard Drive for File Recovery

Do *not* install data-recovery (or any other) software to a drive you are attempting to retrieve data from because you might overwrite the data you are attempting to retrieve. If you are trying to recover data from your Windows startup drive and you cannot boot from the data-recovery program CD, you are better off installing another hard disk into your system, configuring it as a boot drive in the system BIOS, installing a working copy of Windows on it, booting from that drive, and installing your data-recovery software to that drive. Then, you need to connect your existing drive to your computer so you can retrieve lost data from it.

Because laptops generally don't accommodate a second internal hard disk drive, you might need to purchase an external drive enclosure for 2.5-inch drives (available from many vendors), install your original drive in that enclosure, and connect the drive to the system. Alternatively, you could use a special data cable normally used for migrating data from an old drive to a new drive; these cables are sold by companies that sell laptop hard disk upgrade kits. Contact the data-recovery software vendor to verify that its software can work with external drives. If possible, install a new drive in your laptop that is large enough (at least 20GB or more) so that you have several gigabytes of free space on it for storing recovered data.

You could also connect your laptop hard disk to a desktop PC with a 2.5-inch to 3.5-inch hard drive adapter (around $10–15; available from various sources) and use the desktop PC's original drive to perform data recovery. However, note that BIOS differences on some systems could prevent a PC from being able to access data on a drive prepared with another computer.

Some file-undelete products for the NTFS file system can only undelete files created by the currently logged-in user, whereas others require the administrator to be logged in. Check the documentation for details, particularly if you are trying to undelete files from a system with more than one user.

Retrieving Data from Partitioned and Formatted Drives

When a hard disk, floppy disk, or removable-media drive has been formatted, its file allocation table (FAT), which is used by programs such as Norton Unerase and VCom System Suite's FileUndeleter to determine the location of files, is lost. If a hard drive has been repartitioned with FDISK or another partitioning program (such as Windows 2000/XP's Disk Management), the original file system and partition information is lost (as is the FAT).

In such cases, more powerful data-recovery tools must be used to retrieve data. To retrieve data from an accidentally formatted drive, you have two options:

- Use a program that can unformat the drive.
- Use a program that can bypass the newly created file allocation table and read disk sectors directly to discover and retrieve data.

To retrieve data from a drive that has been partitioned, you must use a program that can read disk sectors directly.

Although you could use Norton Unformat if your laptop drive uses the FAT or FAT32 file system (the file systems used by Windows 9x/Me), I can't recommend this method of data recovery any more for the following reasons:

- Norton Unformat works best if the Norton Image program has been used to create a copy of the file allocation tables and root directory. If the image file is out of date, Unformat might fail; if the image file is not present, Unformat cannot restore the root directory, and the actual names of folders in the root directory will be replaced by sequentially numbered folder names.

- Norton Unformat cannot copy restored files to another drive or folder; it restores data back to the same drive and partition. If Unformat uses an out-of-date file created by Norton Image to determine where data is located, it could overwrite valid data on the drive being unformatted.

Instead of using Norton Unformat, I recommend using programs that retrieve lost data to another drive.

Retrieving Lost Data to Another Drive

Many products on the market today can retrieve lost data to another drive, whether the data loss was due to accidental formatting or disk partitioning. One of the best and most comprehensive is the EasyRecovery product line from OnTrack Data Recovery Services, a division of Kroll Ontrack, Inc. The EasyRecovery Version 6.1 product line includes the following products:

- **EasyRecovery DataRecovery 6.1**—Recovers data from accidentally formatted or deleted hard, floppy, and removable-media drives and repairs damaged or corrupted Zip and Microsoft Word files. Local and network folders can be used for recovered files.

- **EasyRecovery FileRepair 6.1**—Repairs and recovers data from damaged or corrupted Zip and Microsoft Office (Word, Excel, Access, PowerPoint and Outlook) files. Local and network folders can be used for recovered files.

- **EasyRecovery Professional 6.1**—Combines the features of DataRecovery and FileRecovery and adds additional features, such as file type search, RawRecovery, and user-defined partition parameters, to help recover data from more severe forms of file system corruption and accidental partitioning. A free trial version that displays files that can be recovered (and repairs and recovers Zip files at no charge) can be downloaded from the Ontrack website (www.ontrack.com).

- **EasyRecovery Lite 6.1**—A reduced-feature version of EasyRecovery Professional that retrieves up to 25 files per session.

An earlier version (5.x) of EasyRecovery DataRecovery Lite, which can recover up to 50 files, is included as part of VCom's System Suite 4.0 (previously sold by Ontrack; go to www.v-com.com).

When you start EasyRecovery Professional, you can choose from several recovery methods:

- **DeletedRecovery**—Recovers deleted files

- **FormatRecovery**—Recovers files from accidentally formatted drives

- **RawRecovery**—Recovers files with direct sector reads using file signature–matching technology

- **AdvancedRecovery**—Recovers data from deleted or corrupted partitions

In each case, you need to specify another drive to receive the retrieved data. This read-only method preserves the contents of the original drive and allows you to use a different data-recovery method if the first method doesn't recover the desired files.

Which options are best for data recovery? Table 15.1 shows the results of various data-loss scenarios and recovery options when EasyRecovery Professional 6.1 was used to recover data from a 19GB logical drive formatted with the NTFS file system on Windows XP.

Table 15.1   Data Recovery Options and Results with EasyRecovery Professional 6

Type of Data Loss	Data Recovery Method	Data Recoverable?	Details	Notes
Deleted folder	DeletedRecovery	Yes	All files recovered.	All long file and folder names preserved.
Formatted drive (full format)	FormatRecovery	Yes	All files recovered.	New folders created to store recovered files; long file names preserved for files and folders beneath the root folder level.
Logical drive names deleted with Disk Management	AdvancedRecovery	Yes	All files and folders recovered.	All long file and folder preserved.
Formatted drive with new data copied to it	FormatRecovery	Partial	Files and folders not overwritten were recovered.	Long file and folder names preserved.
Formatted, repartitioned drive, reformatted as FAT32 (117MB Disk 1)	AdvancedRecovery	No	Could not locate any files to recover.	
	RawRecovery	Partial	Nonfragmented files recovered.	Original directory structure and filenames lost; each file type stored in a separate folder and files numbered sequentially.
Formatted, repartitioned drive, formatted as NTFS (18.8GB Disk 2)	AdvancedRecovery	No	Could not locate any files to recover.	
	RawRecovery	Partial	Nonfragmented files recovered.	Original directory structure and filenames lost; each file type stored in a separate folder and files numbered sequentially.

As Table 15.1 makes clear, as long as the data areas of a drive are not overwritten, complete data recovery is usually possible, even if the drive has been formatted or repartitioned. Therefore, it's critical to react quickly if you suspect you have partitioned or formatted a drive containing valuable data. The longer you wait to recover data, the less data will be available for recovery. Note also that if you must use a sector-by-sector search for data (a process called *RawRecovery* by Ontrack), your original folder structure and long filenames will not be saved. You will need to re-create the desired directory structure and rename the files after you recover them—a very tedious process.

Tip

If you use EasyRecovery Professional or EasyRecovery DataRecovery to repair damaged Zip or Microsoft Office files, use the Properties menu to select a location for repaired files (the original location or another drive/folder). By default, repaired Outlook files are copied to a different folder, whereas other file types are repaired in place, unless you specify a different location.

As you can see from this example, dedicated data-recovery programs such as Ontrack EasyRecovery Professional are very powerful. However, they are also very expensive. If you have Norton Utilities or Norton System Works and don't mind taking some time to learn about disk structures, you can perform data recovery yourself with the Norton Disk Editor.

Using the Norton Disk Editor

In my upgrading and repairing seminars, I use the Norton Disk Editor—an often-neglected program that's part of the Norton Utilities and Norton System Works—to explore drives. I also use Disk Editor to retrieve "lost" data. Because Disk Editor is a manual tool, it can sometimes be useful even when friendlier automatic programs don't work or are not available. For example, Disk Editor can be used with any drive that uses FAT, including Linux. Also, because Disk Editor displays the structure of your drive in a way other programs don't, it's a perfect tool for learning more about disk drive structures as well as recovering "lost" data. In this section, I'll discuss two of the simpler procedures you can perform with Disk Editor: undeleting a file on a floppy disk and copying a deleted file on a hard disk to a different drive.

If you have Norton System Works, System Works Professional, or Norton Utilities for Windows, you have Norton Disk Editor. To determine whether it's installed on your system, look in the Program Files\Norton Utilities folder for the files DISKEDIT.EXE and DISKEDIT.HLP.

If you don't find these files on your hard disk, you can run them directly from the Norton installation CD. If you have System Works or System Works Professional, look for the CD folder called \NU to locate these files. If you have trouble locating them, remember you can always use the Windows Search function to search for them.

DISKEDIT is a DOS-based program, and it is designed to access FAT-based file systems such as FAT12 (floppy disks), FAT16 (MS-DOS and early Windows 95 hard disks), and FAT32 (Windows 95B and Windows 98/Me hard disks). You can use DISKEDIT with Windows NT, Windows 2000, and Windows XP only if you've prepared the hard disks with the FAT16 or FAT32 file system. DISKEDIT does not work with NTFS-formatted drives (NTFS is the preferred format for Windows NT/2000/XP).

Note

Windows NT 4.0, Windows 2000, and Windows XP include their own sector editor (**DSKPROBE.EXE**) that can be used in place of Norton Disk Editor for data recovery on NTFS-based drives. To download the Windows NT 4.0 Resource Kit tools, including **dskprobe.exe**, see Microsoft Knowledge Base Article 206848. To learn more about the Windows 2000 Support tools included on the Windows 2000 CD, see Microsoft Knowledge Base Article 301423. To learn more about the Windows XP Support tools included on the Windows XP CD, see Microsoft Knowledge Base Article 306794.

I *strongly* recommend that you first use Disk Editor or any other sector editor with floppy disks you have prepared with noncritical files before you use it with a hard disk or with vital files. Because Disk Editor is a completely *manual* program, the opportunities for error are high.

The DISKEDIT files can easily fit on a floppy disk (you can run the programs from a floppy disk if you need to retrieve data from a hard disk), but if you are new to the program, you might want to put them on a different drive than the one you will be examining or repairing. *Never* copy DISKEDIT files (or any other data-recovery program) to a drive that contains data you are trying to recover because the files might overwrite the data area and destroy the files you want to retrieve. For example, if you are planning to examine or repair floppy disks, create a folder called DISKEDIT on your hard disk and copy the files to that folder.

You can use Disk Editor without a mouse or integrated pointing device by using keyboard commands, but if you want to use it with your laptop's pointing device or with a PS/2 or serial mouse, you must load an MS-DOS mouse driver (usually MOUSE.COM) for your pointing device before you start Disk Editor. If you have a Logitech mouse, you can download an MS-DOS mouse driver from the Logitech website. If you have a Microsoft mouse, you should note that Microsoft doesn't provide MS-DOS drivers you can download. However, you can get them from www.bootdisk.com/readme.htm#mouse.

For other mice or integrated pointing devices, try the Microsoft or Logitech drivers (most integrated pointing devices work with either driver) or contact the vendor for drivers. Keep in mind that scroll wheels and other buttons won't work with an MS-DOS driver and that USB mice won't work from MS-DOS. I recommend you copy your mouse driver to the same folder where Disk Editor is located.

Using Disk Editor to Examine a Drive

To use the Disk Editor program to examine a drive, follow these steps:

1. Boot the computer to a command prompt (not Windows); Disk Editor needs exclusive access to the drives you plan to examine. If you use Windows 9x, press F8 or Ctrl to bring up the startup menu and select Safe Mode Command Prompt, or you can use the Windows 9x/Me Emergency Startup disk (make one with Add/Remove Programs). If you use Windows 2000 or XP, insert a blank floppy disk into Drive A:, right-click Drive A: in My Computer, and select Format. Choose the option Create an MS-DOS Startup Disk, and use this disk to start your computer.

2. Change to the folder containing your mouse driver and Disk Editor.

3. Type MOUSE (if your mouse driver is called MOUSE.COM or MOUSE.EXE; substitute the correct name if it's called something else) and press Enter to load the mouse driver.

4. Type DISKEDIT and press Enter to start the program. If you don't specify a drive, Disk Editor scans the drive where it's installed. If you are using it to work with a floppy disk, enter the command DISKEDIT A: to direct it to scan your floppy disk. Disk Editor scans your drive to determine the location of files and folders on the disk.

5. The first time you run Disk Editor, a prompt appears to remind you that Disk Editor runs in read-only mode until you change its configuration through the Tools menu. Press OK to continue.

Once Disk Editor has started, you can switch to the drive you wish to examine or recover data from. To change to a different drive, follow these steps:

1. Press Alt+O to open the Object menu.

2. Select Drive.

3. Select the drive you want to examine from the Logical Disks menu.

4. The disk structure is scanned and displayed in the Disk Editor window.

Disk Editor normally starts in the Directory mode; you can change it to other modes with the View menu. When you view a drive containing data in the directory mode, you will see a listing similar to the one shown in Figure 15.1.

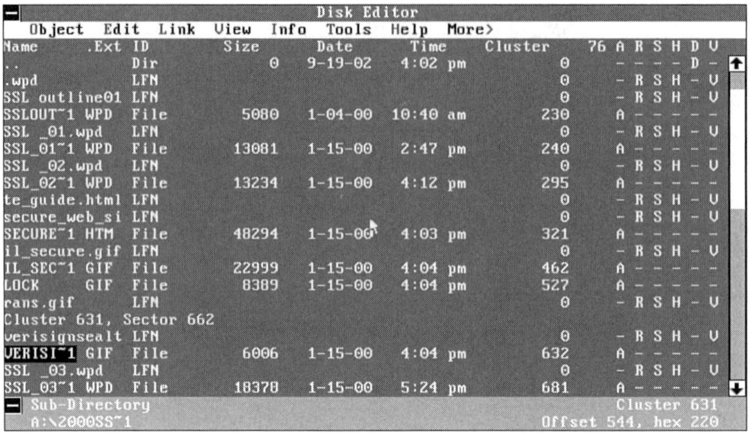

Figure 15.1 The Norton Disk Editor directory view of a typical floppy disk.

The Name column lists the names of the directory entries. The .EXT column lists the file/folder extensions (if any). The ID column lists the type of directory entry:

- **Dir**—A directory (folder).
- **File**—A data file.
- **LFN**—A portion of a Windows long filename. Windows stores the start of the LFN before the actual filename. If the LFN is more than 13 characters, one or more additional directory entries are used to store the rest of the LFN. The next three columns list the file size, date, and time.

The Cluster column indicates the cluster where the first portion of the file is located. Drives are divided into clusters or allocation units when they are formatted, and a cluster (allocation unit) is the smallest unit that can be used to store a file. Cluster sizes vary with the size of the drive and the file system used to format the drive.

The letters A, R, S, H, D, and V refer to attributes for each directory entry. A (archive) means the file hasn't been backed up since it was last modified. R is used to indicate the directory entry is read-only. S indicates the directory entry has the System attribute, whereas H indicates the directory entry has the Hidden attribute. D indicates the entry is a directory, whereas V is the attribute for an LFN entry.

The file VERISI~1.GIF (highlighted in black near the bottom of Figure 15.1) is interesting for several reasons. The tilde (~) and number at the end of the filename indicate the file was created with a 32-bit version of Windows. The 32-bit versions of Windows (Windows 9x/Me, 2000, and XP) allow the user to save a file with a long (more than eight characters) filename, plus the three-character file extension (such as .EXE, .BMP, or .GIF); long filenames can also have spaces and other characters not allowed by earlier versions of Windows and MS-DOS.

When you view the file in Windows Explorer or My Computer, you see the long filename. To see the DOS alias name within the Windows GUI, right-click the file and select Properties from My Computer or Windows Explorer, or use the DIR command within a command prompt window. The LFN is stored as one or more separate directory entries just before the DOS alias name. Because the actual long name for VERISI~1.GIF (Verisignsealtrans.gif) is 21 characters, two additional directory entries are required to store the long filename (each directory entry can store up to 13 characters of an LFN), as shown in Figure 15.1.

Determining the Number of Clusters Used by a File

An area of the disk called the *file allocation table* (FAT) stores the starting location of the file and each additional cluster used to store the file; VERISI~1.GIF starts at cluster 632. Clusters, or allocation units, are the smallest disk structures used to store files, and they vary in size depending on the file system used to create the disk, where the files are stored, and the size of the drive. In this case, the file is stored on a 1.44MB floppy disk, which has a cluster size of 512 bytes (one sector). The cluster size of the drive is very important to know if you want to retrieve data using Disk Editor.

To determine the cluster size of a drive, you can open a command-prompt window and run CHKDSK C: to display the allocation unit size (cluster size) and other statistics about the specified drive. To determine how many clusters (allocation units) are used to store a file, look at the size of the file and compare it to the cluster size of the drive it's stored on. The file VERISI~1.GIF contains 6,006 bytes. Because this file is stored on a floppy disk that has a cluster size of 512 bytes, the file must occupy several clusters. How many clusters does it occupy? To determine this, divide the file size by the number of clusters and then round the result up to the next whole number. The math is shown in Table 15.2.

Table 15.2   Determining the Number of Clusters Used by a File

File Size (F) of VERISI~1.GIF	Cluster Size (S)	Result of (F) Divided by (S) Equals (R)	(R) Rounded Up to Next Whole Number
6,006	512	11.73046875	12

From our calculations, you can see that VERISI~1.GIF uses 12 clusters on the floppy disk; it would use fewer clusters on a FAT16 or FAT32 hard disk, the exact number depending on the file system and the size of the hard disk. The more clusters a file contains, the greater the risk that some of its data area could be overwritten by newer data if the file is "deleted." Consequently, if you need to undelete a file that was not sent to the Windows Recycle Bin or was deleted from a removable-media drive or floppy drive (these types of drives don't support the Recycle Bin), the quicker you attempt to undelete the file, the more likely it is that you can retrieve the data.

The normal directory display in Norton Disk Editor shows the starting cluster (632) for VERISI~1.GIF. If a file is stored on a drive with a lot of empty space, the odds are good that the remainder of the clusters immediately follow the first two; a badly fragmented drive might use noncontiguous clusters to store the rest of the file. Because it's much easier to perform data recovery when the clusters are contiguous, I strongly recommend that you defragment your drives frequently.

To see the remainder of the clusters used by a file, move the cursor to the file, press Alt+L or click the Link menu, and select Cluster Chain (FAT); you can also press Ctrl+T to go directly to this view. The screen changes to show the clusters as listed in the FAT for this file, as shown in Figure 15.2. The clusters used by the file are highlighted in red, and the filename is shown at the bottom of the screen. The symbol <EOF> stands for "End of File," indicating the last cluster in the file.

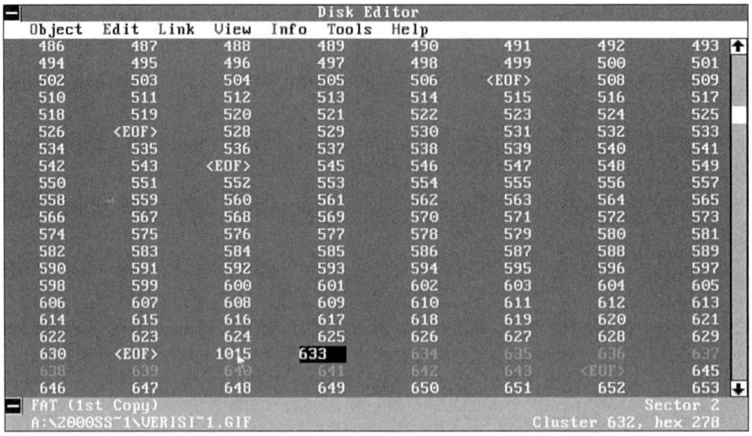

Figure 15.2   The FAT view of VERISI~1.GIF. All its clusters are contiguous.

How the Operating System Marks a File When It Is Deleted

If a file (VERISI~1.GIF in this example) is deleted, the following changes happen to the disk where the file is stored, as shown in Figure 15.3:

- The default directory view shows that the first character of the filename (V) has been replaced with a "σ" (lowercase sigma) character.

- There are now two new types of entries in the ID column for this file and its associated LFN: Erased (an erased file) and Del LFN (an LFN belonging to an erased file). Note also that the beginning cluster (632) is still shown in the Cluster column.

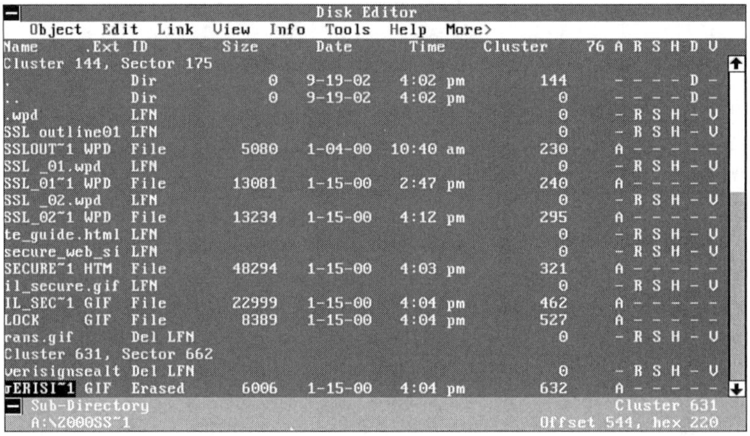

Figure 15.3   The Directory view after VERISI~1.GIF has been deleted.

Zeroes have also replaced the entries for the cluster locations after the beginning cluster in the FAT. This indicates to the operating system that these clusters (allocation units) are now available for reuse. Therefore, if an undelete process is not started immediately, some or all of the clusters could be overwritten by new data. Because the file in question is a GIF graphics file, the loss of even one cluster will destroy the file.

As you can see from analyzing the file-deletion process, the undeletion process involves four steps:

1. Restore the original filename.
2. Locate the clusters used by the file.
3. Re-create the FAT entries for the file.
4. Relink the LFN entries for the file to the file.

Of these four steps, the most critical are locating the clusters used by the file and re-creating the FAT entries for the file. However, if the file is a program file, restoring the original name is a must for proper program operation (assuming the program can't be reloaded from the original distribution media), and restoring the LFN entries will make it easier for a Windows user accustomed to long file-names to use the file.

If you want to make these changes to the original disk, Disk Editor must be configured to work in Read-Write mode. To change to Read-Write mode, follow these steps:

1. Press Alt+T to open the Tools menu.
2. Press N to open the Configuration dialog box.
3. Press the spacebar to clear the check mark in the Read Only option box.
4. Press the Tab key until the Save box is highlighted.
5. Press Enter to save these changes and return to the main display.

Caution

As a precaution, I recommend that you use DISKCOPY to make an exact sector-by-sector copy of a floppy disk before you perform data recovery on it—and you should work with the copy of the disk, not the original. By working with a copy, you keep the original safe against any problems you might have, and you can make another copy if you need to.

Once you change to Read-Write mode, Disk Editor will stay in this mode and will use Read-Write mode every time you use it. To change back to Read-Only mode, repeat the preceding steps, but check the Read-Only box. If you are using Disk Editor in Read-Write mode, you will see the message Drive *x* is locked when you scan a drive.

Undeleting an Erased File

After you have configured Disk Editor to work in Read-Write mode, you can use it to undelete a file.

To recover an erased file, follow this procedure:

1. To change to the folder containing the erased file, highlight the folder containing the erased file and press Enter. In this example, we will recover the erased file VERISI~1.GIF.
2. Place the cursor under the lowercase sigma symbol and enter the letter you want to use to rename the file.
3. If the keyboard is in Insert mode, the lowercase sigma will move to the right; press the Delete key to delete this symbol.

4. This action restores the filename, but even though the ID changes from Erased to File, this does *not* complete the file-retrieval process. You must now find the rest of the clusters used by the file. To the right of the filename, the first cluster used by the file is listed.

5. To go to the next cluster used by the file, press Ctrl+T to open the Cluster Chain command. Because you changed the name of the file, you are prompted to write the changes to the disk before you can continue. Press W or click Write to save the changes and continue.

6. Disk Editor moves to the first cluster that was used by the deleted file. Instead of cluster numbers, as shown earlier in Figure 15.2, each cluster contains a zero (0). Because this file uses 12 clusters, there should be 12 contiguous clusters that have been zeroed out if the file is unfragmented.

7. To determine whether these are the correct clusters for the file, press Alt+O or click Object to open the Object menu and then press the C key to open the Cluster dialog box (or press Alt+C to go straight to the Cluster dialog box). Enter the starting cluster number (632, in this example) and the ending cluster number (644, in this example). Click OK to display these clusters.

Disk Editor automatically switches to the best view for the specified object, and in this case, the best view is the Hex view (see Figure 15.4). Note that the first entry in cluster 632 is GIF89a (as shown in the right column). Because the deleted file is a GIF file, this is what we expected. Because a GIF file is a binary graphics file, the rest of the information in the specified sectors should not be human-readable. Note that the end of the file is indicated by a series of 00s in several disk sectors before another file starts.

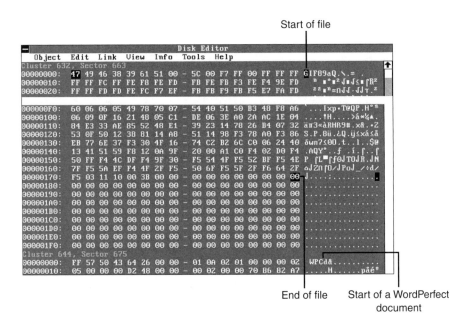

Figure 15.4 The start and end of the file *VERISI~1.GIF*.

Because the area occupied by the "empty" clusters 632 through 644 contains binary data starting with GIF89a, we can feel pretty confident that these clusters contain the data we need.

8. To return to the FAT to fill in the cluster numbers for the file, open the Object menu and select Directory. The current directory is selected, so click OK.

9. Move the cursor down to the entry for VERISI~1.GIF, open the Link menu, and click Cluster Chain (FAT). The Cluster Chain refers to the clusters after the initial cluster (632); enter **633** into the first empty field and continue until you enter **643** and place the cursor into the last empty field. This field needs to have the <EOF> marker placed in it to indicate the end of the file. Press Alt+E to open the Edit menu and then select Mark (or press Ctrl+B). Open the Edit menu again and select Fill. Select End of File from the menu and click OK. Refer back to Figure 15.2 to see how the FAT looks after these changes have been made.

10. To save the changes to the FAT, open the Edit menu again and select Write. When prompted to save the changes, click Write and then click Rescan the Disk.

11. To return to the Directory view, open the Object menu and select Directory. Click OK.

12. The LFN entries directly above the VERISI~1.GIF file are still listed as Del LFN. To reconnect them to VERISI~1.GIF, select the first one (verisignsealt), open the Tools menu (Alt+T), and select Attach LFN. Click Yes when prompted. Repeat the process for (rans.gif).

13. To verify that the file has been undeleted successfully, exit Disk Editor and open the file in a compatible program. If you have correctly located the clusters and linked them, the file will open.

As you can see, this is a long process, but it is, essentially, the same process that a program such as Norton Unerase performs automatically. However, Disk Editor can perform these tasks on all types of disks that use the FAT file systems, including those that use non-DOS operating systems; it's a favorite of advanced Linux users.

Retrieving a File from a Hard Disk or Flash Memory Card

What should you do if you need to retrieve an erased file from the hard disk or a flash memory card? It's safer to write the retrieved file to another disk (preferably a floppy disk if the file is small enough) or to a different drive letter on the hard disk. You can also perform this task with Disk Editor.

Tip

If you want to recover data from a hard disk and copy the data to another location, set Disk Editor back to its default Read-Only mode to avoid making any accidental changes to the hard disk. If you use Disk Editor in a multitasking environment such as Windows, it will default to Read-Only mode.

The process of locating the file is the same as that described earlier:

1. Determine the cluster (allocation unit) size of the drive where the file is located.

2. Run Disk Editor to view the name of the erased file and determine which clusters contain the file data.

However, you don't need to restore the filename because you will be copying the file to another drive. Because the clusters will be copied to another file, it's helpful to use the Object menu to look at the clusters and make sure they contain the necessary data. To view the data stored in the cluster range, open the Object menu, select Cluster, and enter the range of clusters that the Cluster Chain command indicate should contain the data. In some cases, the first cluster of a particular file will indicate the file type. For example, a GIF file has GIF89a at the start of the file, whereas a WordPerfect document has WPC at the start of the file.

Tip

Use Norton Disk Editor to view the starting and ending clusters of different types of files you create before you try to recover those types of files. This is particularly important if you want to recover files from formatted media. You might consider creating a database of the hex characters found at the beginning and ending of the major file types you want to recover.

If you are trying to recover a file that contains text, such as a Microsoft Word or WordPerfect file, you can switch DISKEDIT into different view modes. To see text, press F3 to switch to Text View. However, to determine where a file starts or ends, use Hex mode (press F2 to switch to this mode). Figure 15.5 shows the start of a Microsoft Word file in Text format and the end of the file in Hex format.

Start of file (text mode)   End of file (hex mode)

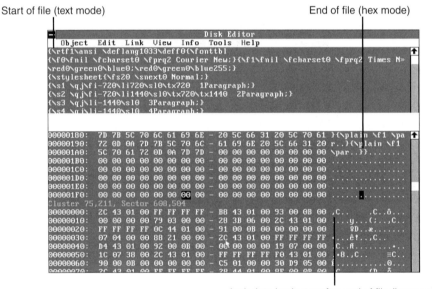

Junk data in cluster after end of file (hex mode)

Figure 15.5 Scrolling through an erased file with Disk Editor.

To copy the contents of these clusters to a file safely, it's best that you specify the sectors that contain the file. The top of the Disk Editor display shows the sector number as well as the cluster number.

Here's how to write these sectors to a new file:

1. Open the Object menu and select Sector.

2. Specify the starting and ending sectors (click OK).

3. Scroll through the sectors to verify they contain the correct data.

4. Open the Tools menu and select Write Object To, To a File.

5. Click the drive where you want to write the data.

6. Specify a DOS-type filename (eight characters plus a three-character extension); you can rename the file to a long filename after you exit DISKEDIT.

7. Click OK. Then click Yes to write the file. A status bar appears as the sectors are copied to the file.

8. Exit DISKEDIT and open the file in a compatible program. If the file contains the correct data, you're finished. If not, you might have specified incorrect sectors, or the file might be fragmented.

Norton Disk Editor is a powerful tool you can use to explore drives and retrieve lost data. However, your best data-recovery technique is to avoid the need for data recovery. Think before you delete files or format a drive, and make backups of important files, and you won't need to recover lost data very often.

Data Recovery from Flash Memory Devices

Laptop computers are often just one part of a mobile information strategy. You might also work with flash memory devices such as USB keychain drives and data storage cards used in digital cameras and digital music players. Retrieving lost data from flash memory devices presents a unique challenge to data-recovery programs. Although from a user standpoint these devices emulate conventional disk drives, have file allocation tables similar to those found on floppy disks, and can usually be formatted through the Windows Explorer, many data-recovery programs that work well with conventional drives cannot be used to recover data from flash memory devices, especially when the device has been formatted.

There are several conditions under which data loss can occur with a flash memory device. Some of them, such as formatting of the media or deletion of one or more photos or files, can occur when the device is connected to the computer through a card reader or when the flash memory device is inserted into a digital camera. When photos are deleted, the file location and name listings in the file allocation tables are changed in the same way as when files are deleted from magnetic media: the first character of the filename is changed to a lowercase sigma, indicating the file has been erased. Just as with magnetic media, undelete programs that support removable-media drives and the Norton Disk Editor can be used to retrieve deleted files on flash memory devices in the same way that they retrieve deleted files from magnetic media; note that Disk Editor must be run in Read-Only mode, and it works best on systems running Windows 9x/Me. Data files can also be damaged if the flash memory card is removed from a device before the data-writing process is complete.

However, retrieving data from a formatted flash memory device—whether it has been formatted by a digital camera or through Windows—is much more difficult. Traditional unformat programs such as the command-line Norton Unformat program provided with Norton Utilities and Norton System Works can't be used because flash memory devices are accessible only from within the Windows GUI, and command-line programs are designed to work with BIOS-compatible devices such as hard and floppy drives.

Programs that rely on the file system, such as Ontrack Easy Recovery Personal Edition Lite 5.x (incorporated into V-Com System Suite 4.0) and Ontrack Easy Recovery Lite v6.x, will not work either because the previous file system is destroyed when flash memory devices are formatted.

Note

When a digital camera formats a flash memory card, it usually creates a folder where photos are stored. Some cameras might also create another folder for storing drivers or other information.

If you need to recover data from a formatted flash memory device, we have found the following programs work extremely well:

- **Ontrack EasyRecovery Professional Edition v6.x**—This program costs $499; a free evaluation and more information are available from www.ontrack.com.

- **PhotoRescue v.1.x**—This program costs $29; a free evaluation and more information are available from www.datarescue.com/photorescue/.

Norton Disk Editor (incorporated into Norton Utilities, Norton System Works, and Norton System Works Pro) can also be used to recover data if you can determine the starting and ending clusters used by the data stored on the device.

To recover data from a formatted flash memory card with EasyRecovery Professional Edition, you must use the RawRecovery option (which recovers data on a sector-by-sector basis). This option bypasses the file system and can be used on all supported media types. A built-in file viewer enables you to determine whether the recovered data is readable.

PhotoRescue, which works only with standard photo image types such as JPG, BMP, and TIF, can access the media in either logical drive mode (which worked quite well in our tests) or physical drive mode. Physical drive mode uses a sector-by-sector recovery method somewhat similar to that used by EasyRecovery Professional Edition. PhotoRescue also displays recovered photos in a built-in viewer.

With both products, you might recover data from not just the most recent use before format, but left-over data from previous uses as well. As long as the data area used by a particular file hasn't been overwritten, the data can be recovered, even if the device has been formatted more than once.

Table 15.3 provides an overview of our results when trying to recover data from two common types of flash memory devices: a CompactFlash card used in digital cameras and a USB keychain storage device.

Table 15.3   Retrieving Lost Data from Flash Memory Devices

		Results by Data-Recovery Program			
Device	**Cause of Data Loss**	**Norton Utilities 2002**	**Ontrack/ VCOM System Suite 4.0**	**DataRescue Photo Rescue**	**Ontrack EasyRecovery Professional 6.0**
Compact flash 64MB	Deleted selected files in camera	Recovered data back to device when used with Windows 9x/Me only.[1,2]	Recovered data to user-specified folder.[1,3]	Recovered data from most recent format and from previous card uses to specified folder.[3,4]	RawRecovery recovered deleted files from current and previous uses.[3,4]
Compact flash 64MB	Deleted selected files with Windows Explorer	Recovered data back to device when used with Windows 9x/Me only.[1,2]	Recovered data specified to folder when used with any supported version of Windows.[3]	Recovered data from most recent format and from previouscard uses to specified folder (files and folders renamed).	DeletedRecovery recovered deleted data from current use (first character of file/folder name lost).
Compact flash 64MB	Format in camera	Drive could not be unformatted; DISKEDIT could retrieve data from current and previous uses to user-specified folder.[3,5,6]	Could not locate data; no data recovered.	Recovered data from most recent format and from previous card uses to user-specified folder.[3,4]	RawRecovery recovered all readable data, including data from previous card uses to user-specified folder.[3,4]

Table 15.3   Retrieving Lost Data from Flash Memory Devices

		Results by Data-Recovery Program			
Device	Cause of Data Loss	Norton Utilities 2002	Ontrack/ VCOM System Suite 4.0	DataRescue Photo Rescue	Ontrack EasyRecovery Professional 6.0
Compact flash 64MB	Format in card reader	Drive could not be unformatted; DISKEDIT could retrieve data from current and previous uses.[5,6]	Could not locate data; no data recovered.	Recovered data from most recent format and from previous card uses to user-specified folder.[4]	RawRecovery recovered all readable data, including data from previous card uses to user-specified folder.[4]
USB keychain drive (128MB)	Deleted folder with My Computer	DISKEDIT can retrieve data from current use.[3,6]	Partial success: Recovered some files.[3]	Recovered photo files only.[3,4]	RawRecovery retrieved most files.[3,4]
USB keychain drive (128MB)	Formatted by Windows Explorer	DISKEDIT could retrieve data from current use.[3,6]	Partial success: Recovered some files (folder names and structure lost).[3]	Recovered photo files only.[3,4]	RawRecovery retrieved most files.[3,4]

1. *User supplied first letter of filename during undelete process.*

2. *Norton Unerase doesn't support removable-media drives in Windows NT/2000/XP.*

3. *Program operates in Read-Only mode on the drive containing lost data.*

4. *Original file and folder names were not retained; files are numbered sequentially and might need to be renamed after recovery.*

5. *Windows must be used to access flash memory devices, and Norton Unformat can't be used in a multitasking environment such as Windows.*

6. *DISKEDIT requires the user to manually locate the starting and ending sector of each file and write the sectors to another drive with a user-defined filename.*

Retrieving Data from a Damaged Laptop

If your laptop computer has suffered physical damage, you might still be able to read data from its hard disk using one of these methods:

■ Remove the drive and install it in a similar model.

■ Remove the drive and connect it to another laptop or a desktop model using the adapters discussed previously in this chapter.

If the drive cannot be read by another PC because of BIOS-translation issues but appears to be working properly (it spins and doesn't make any loud noises), you can try professional data-recovery companies such as Ontrack and others. Many of these companies offer remote data recovery.

Remote data recovery requires you to install a client program on the laptop or desktop computer that has the drive connected to it. After establishing Internet access with the computer, the remote data-recovery technicians read the information from the drive and determine what data can be recovered and how much the recovery will cost. This process can take several hours and is most easily performed if the computer being used to host the drive uses a broadband Internet connection.

Even if the host computer's BIOS is not able to correctly translate the drive, the special methods used by data-recovery companies can read the data and determine the correct way to write the data back to the drive.

If the drive itself has sustained physical damage, the only alternative is to send the hard disk (or the entire laptop) to the data-recovery company of your choice. These companies have clean rooms, where damaged drives can be rebuilt, and special equipment capable of retrieving data from damaged drives. This "mail-in" type of data recovery is more expensive than remote data recovery, but if the drive cannot be accessed by a normal computer because of physical damage, it is the only way to retrieve the data.

CHAPTER 16

Problem Solving and Troubleshooting

Basic Troubleshooting Guidelines

Troubleshooting laptop and portable PC hardware problems can seem like a huge challenge, even if you're experienced with solving problems on desktop PCs. Some components that can be easily removed and replaced on desktop computers, such as hard disks, floppy drives, optical drives, processors, and BIOS chips, are built in to the system or use different interfaces than desktop PCs. Some types of diagnostic procedures, such as power supply testing, BIOS POST code analysis, and others, must be performed in different ways because of the differences between portable and desktop hardware.

The proprietary nature of typical portable hardware is another challenge. Although the basic layout of one desktop PC is similar to another, different brands of portables are often extremely different internally, making it essential to obtain model-specific information before you open the system or make repairs.

Although these challenges make laptop and portable computer problem solving and troubleshooting a bigger challenge than for desktop systems, you can still solve many hardware problems yourself by applying the techniques covered in this chapter.

Modern Laptop Computers—More Complicated and More Reliable

Consider this: The modern laptop computer is an incredible collection of hardware and software. When you consider only the hardware, there are tens of millions of transistors in typical processors alone; nearly 4.3 billion transistors in a 512MB stick of RAM; hundreds of millions of transistors in the motherboard chipset, video processor, and video RAM; and millions more in the other adapter cards and logic boards in the system.

Not only must each of these billions of interconnected transistors function properly, they must all operate in an orderly fashion within strictly enforced timing windows, some of which are measured in picoseconds (trillionths of a second)! When you realize that your laptop will lock up or crash if any one of these transistors fails to operate properly and on time, and/or if any one of the billions of circuit paths and interconnections between the transistors or devices containing them fails in any way, it is a wonder that laptops work at all!

Note

A typical mobile processor such as the Intel Mobile Pentium 4-M contains 55 million transistors, whereas the latest mobile processor from Intel, the Pentium M, has 77 million transistors. The Pentium M is the processor component of Intel's Centrino technology, which also includes a sophisticated chipset (the Intel 915 Express) and the Intel PRO/Wireless 2200 Wi-Fi IEEE 802.11b/g wireless network adapter.

The latest mobile processor from AMD, the Athlon XP-M, contains 37.5 million transistors. It has a 512KB L2 cache and uses AMD's PowerNow! technology to dynamically control the processor's power usage, which helps to optimize the laptop's battery life.

Every time I turn on one of my systems and watch it boot up, I think about the billions upon billions of components and trillions upon trillions of machine/program steps and sequences that have to function properly to get there. As you can now see, there are many opportunities for problems to arise.

Although modern laptop computers are exponentially more complicated than their predecessors, from another point of view, they have also become simpler and more reliable. When you consider the complexity of the modern laptop computers, it is not surprising that occasionally problems do arise. However, modern design and manufacturing techniques have made laptop computers more reliable and easier to service despite their ever-increasing internal complexity. Today's systems have fewer and fewer replaceable components and individual parts, which is sort of a paradox. The truth is that as laptop computers have become more complex, they have become simpler and easier to service in many ways as well!

Desktop and Laptop Components Compared

Although laptop and portable computers use the same operating systems and external peripherals as their desktop siblings, internally they are much different. Although there are industry standards for processors, memory, hard drives, and other components inside a typical laptop computer, they are much different from the standards supported by a typical desktop computer, as you can see from Table 16.1.

Table 16.1   Desktop and Laptop Component Standards

Component Type	Desktop Standard	Laptop Standard	Notes
Memory module	DIMM (168, 184-pin); RDRAM (184, 232-pin)	SODIMM (144-pin, 200-pin); SORIMM (160-pin)	SO stands for *small outline*. SODIMMs and SORIMMs are physically smaller than desktop memory modules. Older systems often use proprietary modules.
Hard disk	ATA/IDE (40-pin) Serial ATA; 3.5-inch form factor	ATA/IDE (44-pin); 2.5-inch form factor or proprietary swappable	Laptop versions of ATA/IDE use a single connector for power and data. Models that support swappable drives usually allow special types of hard, floppy, and optical drives to be swapped in place of each other.
Processor	Socket 478, Socket 754, Socket 775 processors	Mobile processors	Mobile processors use lower voltages and are sometimes optimized for different chipsets than standard processors.
Modem	PCI card or integrated	Built-in or Mini PCI card	Typical Mini PCI modems also support 10/100 Ethernet networks.
10/100 Ethernet	PCI card or integrated into motherboard	Built-in or Mini PCI card	Typical Mini PCI 10/100 Ethernet network adapters also provide modem functions.
Floppy drive	34-pin floppy interface	Proprietary fixed or proprietary swappable	Different models from the same vendor might use the same swappable floppy drive, but different brands are not interchangeable.
Optical (CD, DVD, rewritable) drive	40-pin ATA/IDE interface	Proprietary fixed or proprietary swappable	Different models from the same vendor might use the same swappable optical drive, but different brands are not interchangeable.
Power supply	LPX (12-pin) or ATX (20-pin)	Proprietary	Some older models have built-in power supplies, but most use an external "brick" AC/DC power converter.

As you can see from Table 16.1, many of the components used in notebook computers follow different standards than those used in desktop computers. As a consequence, most parts cannot be freely interchanged between different models and brands of notebook computers the way they can between desktop computers. However, many of the parts listed in Table 16.1, as well as the CMOS battery used to maintain BIOS settings, can normally be removed for upgrades or repairs.

Devices that are normally not industry standard (and therefore not generically replaceable) include the following:

- Motherboard
- CPU heatsink/fan
- Chassis
- Video card (integrated into the motherboard chipset, or a separate graphics chip might be built in to the motherboard)
- LCD display panel
- Modem (if not part of a Mini PCI card; it might be integrated into the motherboard on some systems)
- Sound card (might be integrated into the motherboard chipset or might be a separate chip built in to the motherboard)
- Speakers
- Keyboard (built in)
- Pointing device (TrackPoint or touchpad)

Although many of these components may not be industry standard, they can occasionally be repaired or replaced (depending on the specific make, model, and implementation of the component). From a hardware troubleshooting/repair perspective, any one of these components could be either improperly installed (configured) or defective. If improperly installed or configured, the component can be "repaired" by merely reinstalling or configuring it properly. If truly defective, the component can be replaced. When any laptop or desktop PC is broken down into its basic replaceable parts, you can see that it really isn't too complicated, which is why I've spent my career helping people easily perform their own repairs and upgrades, and even build entire systems from scratch.

Reinstall or Replace?

When you are dealing with hardware problems, the first simple truth to understand is that you do not normally *repair* anything; you *reinstall* or *replace* it instead. *Reinstall* comes from the fact that the many laptop hardware problems are due to a particular component being improperly installed or configured. I remember hearing from IBM many years ago that it had found 60% or more of the problems handled by their service technicians were due to improper installation or configuration, meaning the hardware was not actually defective. This was in fact the major impetus behind the Plug and Play revolution, which has eliminated the need to manually configure jumpers and switches on most hardware devices, minimizing the expertise needed to install hardware properly, and thus also minimizing installation, configuration, and resource-conflict problems. Still, Plug and Play has sometimes been called "Plug and Pray," because it does not always work perfectly, sometimes requiring manual intervention to get things to work properly. Although most laptop hardware is built in to the system or attaches to hot-swappable connections such as PC Card or CardBus slots, USB ports or IEEE 1394a (FireWire 400, i.LINK) ports, problems with BIOS configuration, Windows configuration, or improper internal connections can still cause laptop hardware to fail.

Replace comes from the economics of the situation with computer hardware. The bottom line is that it financially is much cheaper to replace a failed component with a new one than to repair it. Modern boards use surface-mounted chips that have pin spacing measured in hundredths of an inch, requiring sophisticated and expensive equipment to attach and solder the chip. Even if you could figure out which chip had failed and had the equipment to replace it, the chips themselves are usually sold in quantities of thousands, and obsolete chips are normally not available. The net effect of all this is that the replaceable components in your laptop have become disposable technology, including drives and LCD panels. Even a component as comprehensive as the motherboard is replaced rather than repaired.

Sources for Laptop Computer Parts

Obtaining known-working components for use with desktop computers is fairly simple because most components can be swapped between different brands and models of PCs. However, this is a more challenging task when you are supporting laptop and portable computers. Here are some ways to make parts-swapping easier:

- **Buy identical laptop computers whenever possible.** As I discuss in Chapter 17, "Portable Resource Guide," different lines of laptop computers from the same vendor can vary greatly because most laptop computers are produced by one of several offshore (primarily Taiwanese) OEM vendors. If you buy multiple units of the same model, you can use one as a parts source for others. If you cannot afford to buy identical models, try to buy models in the same product family to improve the odds of interchanging parts.

- **Determine the "real" OEM manufacturer of the laptop(s) you support.** Review sources such as *PC Magazine* sometimes identify the actual maker of a particular laptop. In Chapter 17, I provide the names and websites for the major OEM makers of laptops. This information might enable you to contact the vendor directly for parts or at least determine which other brands/models might be similar to yours. Another method of determining this information is the FCC ID Search Page at `https://gullfoss2.fcc.gov/prod/oet/cf/eas/reports/GenericSearch.cfm`. Enter the FCC ID from the computer to determine its manufacturer.

- **Keep broken/defective laptops for parts.** Even if a laptop has suffered a catastrophic failure such as a broken LCD panel or motherboard, it can still provide replacements for keyboard, drive, power supply, and other modules for identical or similar models.

- **Save parts removed during upgrades for use in testing or as spares.** If you upgrade memory, drives, or batteries and the components you replaced still work, keep them for use as replacements for identical or similar models.

As an alternative to contacting the vendor for replacement parts using the contact information in Chapter 17, you might want to contact third-party vendors that specialize in notebook components—either OEM or equivalents. Some of these vendors (listed in alphabetical order) include the following:

- **Advanced Computer Services**—Sells new, used, and pulled parts for IBM, Compaq, and Toshiba desktop and laptop computers as well as computers and other types of parts.

  `www.partsandsystems.com`

  2262 South Arlington Road, Akron, OH 44319

  Phone: 330-785-5500

  Fax: 330-785-5501

■ **Altech**—Sells new, used, and refurbished notebook parts as well as other types of computer components.

www.altechco.com

10612B Hempstead, Houston, TX 77092

Phone: 713-680-9323

Fax: 713-680-3519

■ **Chhabra Enterprises, LLC**—Sells used, refurbished, and new laptop/notebook batteries, drives, and other components for major brands of laptop computers to end users.

www.betterdealcomputers.com

344 Fee Fee Road, Maryland Heights, MO 63043

Phone: 314-770-1070

Fax: 314-770-0935

Service shops and stores can order from the sister company, LaptopUniverse.com (same street address and phone number).

■ **Computer Parts Unlimited**—Distributes parts for major brand-name notebook computers.

www.cpumart.com

3949 Heritage Oak Court, Simi Valley, CA 93063

Phone: 800-644-4494

Fax: 805-306-2599

■ **Express Technology Incorporated**—Distributes parts for Compaq, Dell, IBM, and other major notebook and desktop computer and peripheral vendors. Offers a model-specific lookup system for some brands.

www.etiexpress.com

410 South Perry Lane, Suite 2, Tempe, AZ 85281

Phone: 480-921-2888

Fax: 480-921-0454

■ **IDParts, Inc.**—Specializes in replacement LCD displays for most recent laptop computers. Also replaces defective LCD displays and repairs laptops.

www.idparts.com

Corporate office:

1009 Omeide Park, Greensburg, PA 15601-8608

Phone: 724-838-9588

Fax: 724-838-9589

Wisconsin location:

2000 O'Neil Road, Suite 200, Hudson, WI 54016-8167

Phone: 715-531-0393

Fax: 715-531-0394

See the website to determine which location to contact for your specific computer model.

- **SourceOne Computer Products, Inc.**—Sells laptop parts for most major brands. Also performs repairs.

  www.sourceonecomputer.com

  8343 North Steven Road, Milwaukee, WI 53223

  Phone: 414-355-9448

  Fax: 414-355-9778

Troubleshooting by Replacing Parts

There are several ways to troubleshoot a laptop, but in the end it often comes down to simply reinstalling or replacing parts. This process is more effective with desktop systems because more of their components are industry standard and readily replaceable. However, it's still a plausible way to solve problems with defective laptops. You just have a smaller pool of parts that you can easily replace. Regardless, that is why I normally use a very simple "known-good spare" technique that requires very little in the way of special tools or sophisticated diagnostics. In its simplest form, say you have two identical laptops sitting side by side. One of them has a hardware problem; in this example, let's say the removable memory module (SODIMM or small outline dual inline memory module) is defective. Depending on how the SODIMM is defective and where the defect lies, this could manifest itself in symptoms from a completely dead system to one that boots up normally but crashes when running Windows or software applications. You observe that the system on the left has the problem, but the system on the right works perfectly, and they are otherwise identical. The simplest technique for finding the problem would be to swap the memory module from one system with another, one at a time, retesting after each swap.

Note

Although many laptop components require you to disassemble the computer to access them, you can access most laptop memory modules by flipping over the computer and removing a small cover on the bottom of the unit.

At the point when the SODIMMs were swapped, upon powering up and testing (in this case, testing is nothing more than allowing the system to boot up and to run some of the installed applications), you find that the problem has now moved from one system to the other. Knowing that the last item swapped over was the SODIMM, you have just identified the source of the problem! This did not require an expensive ($2K or more) memory test machine or any diagnostics software. Because components such as SODIMMs are not economical to repair, replacing the defective SODIMM would be the final solution.

Although very simplistic, this is often the quickest and easiest way to identify a problem component as opposed to specifically testing each item with diagnostics. Instead of having an identical system standing by to borrow parts from, most technicians will have an inventory of what they call *known-good spare parts*. This means parts that have been previously used, are known to be functional, and can be used to replace a suspicious part in a problem machine. Note that this is different from new replacement parts, because when you open up a box containing a new component, you really can't be 100% sure it works. I've been in situations in which I've had a defective component, replaced it with another (unknown to me) defective *new* component, and the problem remained. Not knowing that the new part I just installed was also defective, I wasted a lot of time checking other parts that were not the problem. The reason is that so few parts are needed to make up a laptop computer, and the known-good parts don't always have to be the same (for example, a smaller-capacity hard disk or memory module can be used to verify that the original, higher-performance component has failed).

Troubleshooting by the Bootstrap Approach

Another method that can be useful for troubleshooting a malfunctioning laptop is the *bootstrap approach*, which is especially good for what seems to be a dead system. This approach involves taking the system apart, stripping it down to the bare-minimum necessary functional components, and testing it to see if it works. Because laptops have fewer removable components, this approach can be a little trickier than when using it on a desktop PC. However, even with portables, the bootstrap troubleshooting approach is still viable. For example, to prep a laptop for testing, you would disconnect or remove the following items:

- Printer
- Network cable
- External mouse and keyboard
- External modem
- External floppy drive
- USB devices
- Port replicator
- Main battery
- Hard disk
- SODIMMs (except for one; note that many laptops have nonremovable memory along with one or more sockets for removable memory; in such cases, you should take out all removable memory)
- Bay devices (drives, battery, and so on)
- PC Cards

After you've removed these components, power up the system to see if it works. If any of the removed components are defective, removing them should enable the system to start up, at least to the point where the Power On Self Test (POST) or splash (logo) screen is visible on the display. If the system displays this information, you know that the motherboard, CPU, RAM, video circuits, and LCD display are functional. If you don't see this information, turn off the system and plug an external monitor into the laptop computer and try starting it again. If the external display shows the startup information, but the internal display does not, the system might be configured improperly.

If you can get the system to a minimum of components that are functional and the system starts, reinstall or add one part at a time, testing the system each time you make a change to verify that it still works and that the part you added or changed was not the cause of a problem. For example, add an external floppy drive and try booting from a bootable floppy disk. If that works, then try adding a swappable hard drive. Essentially, you are rebuilding the system, using the existing parts, but doing it one step at a time. If the system fails to start up properly after you add a component, it's likely you've found the source of your problems.

Note

If the laptop won't boot even after you disconnect all optional hardware, there might be a problem with the Power On Self Test (POST). See "Problems During the POST," later in this chapter, for solutions and testing procedures.

The single most important step to follow when you run a laptop in bootstrap mode is to remove the main battery and run the laptop from AC power. Defective batteries can cause laptops to crash, get stuck in suspend or sleep modes, and other problems.

Many times, problems can be caused by corrosion on contacts or connectors, so often the mere act of disassembling and reassembling accessible components on a laptop "magically" repairs it. Over the years I've disassembled, tested, and reassembled many systems only to find no problems after the reassembly. How can merely taking a system apart and reassembling it repair a problem? Although it may seem that nothing was changed and everything is installed exactly like it was before, in reality the mere act of unplugging and replugging renews all the slot and cable connections between devices, which is often all the system needs. Here are some useful troubleshooting tips:

- Eliminate unnecessary variables or components that are not pertinent to the problem.
- Reinstall, reconfigure, or replace only one component at a time.
- Test after each change you make.
- Keep a detailed record (write it down) of each step you take.
- Don't give up! Every problem has a solution.
- If you hit a roadblock, take a break and work on another problem. A fresh approach the next day often reveals things you overlooked.
- Don't overlook the simple or obvious. Double- and triple-check the installation and configuration of each component.
- Keep in mind that batteries and power adapters are two of the most failure-prone parts in a laptop computer, as well as some of the most overlooked components. A "known-good" spare power adapter is highly recommended to use for testing suspect systems. If a system runs without the battery but fails when the battery is installed, the battery is defective and should be replaced.
- Cables and connections are also a major cause of problems. Keep replacements of all types on hand.
- Don't rule out consulting a pro. Whereas most problems with desktop systems can be resolved with your own blood, sweat, and tears, with laptops sometimes the only viable solution is to consult the manufacturer of the laptop or the business from which you purchased it.

Before starting any system troubleshooting, you should perform a few basic steps to ensure a consistent starting point and to enable isolating the failed component:

1. Turn off the system and any peripheral devices. Disconnect all external peripherals from the system.

2. Make sure the system is plugged into a properly grounded power outlet.

3. If the LCD panel has a brightness control, make sure the display is set to at least two-thirds of the maximum. The brightness or brightness/contrast control might use a sliding switch or keyboard controls. Consult the display documentation for more information on how to adjust these settings. If you can't get any video display on the built-in LCD panel but the system seems to be working, plug in an external monitor and press the key combination needed to send video output to an external display.

4. To enable the system to boot from a hard disk, make sure no media are in a removable storage drive. In the case of laptops, this usually is either the floppy disk drive or CD/DVD-ROM drive (or both). Alternatively, put a known-good bootable floppy or CD with DOS or diagnostics on it in the drive for testing.

5. Turn on the system. Check the chassis fan (if any) and the lights on the system front panel. If the fan doesn't spin and the lights don't light, the power supply or motherboard might be defective.

Note

The exhaust fan on a given laptop computer model might be located on the left or right side or the rear of the system. Laptop computers use very small and quiet fans, so use your hand to determine whether the fan is blowing air; you probably won't be able to hear it.

6. Observe the Power On Self Test (POST). If no errors are detected, the system beeps once and boots up. Errors that display onscreen (*nonfatal* errors) and do not lock up the system offer a text message that varies according to BIOS type and version. Record any errors that occur and refer to the BIOS error codes listed later in this chapter for more information on any specific codes you see. Errors that lock up the system (*fatal* errors) are indicated by a series of audible beeps. Beep codes for popular BIOS chips are also listed later in this chapter.

7. Confirm that the operating system loads successfully.

Problems During the POST

Problems that occur during the POST are usually caused by incorrect hardware configuration or installation. Actual hardware failure is a far less frequent cause. The POST reports errors three ways:

- Onscreen error messages
- Beep codes
- Hex codes

Some onscreen error messages are self-explanatory, whereas numeric error messages require you to look up the error in a listing for the BIOS version the computer uses.

To determine the meaning of the beep codes generated by the POST, you also need to look up the beep codes in a listing for the BIOS version the computer uses.

On a typical desktop computer, hex codes (which change during the boot process and can be used to determine startup problems) can be displayed through the use of a POST diagnostics card that plugs into a PCI or ISA slot. Although notebook computers lack these slots, some notebook computers have BIOS chips that direct hex code output to the parallel port, where a device such as the MicroPOST from Ultra-X (about $60; visit www.uxd.com) can display it (see Figure 16.1). POST diagnostic devices such as MicroPOST include lists of hex codes for popular BIOSes.

Note

According to Ultra-X, almost all IBM and most newer Toshiba notebook computers output POST hex codes to the parallel port. Some Compaq and other brands of notebook computers also output POST codes to the parallel port. However, Dell notebooks do not support this feature. Some desktop computers also support parallel-port POST code output.

It's important to realize that a given computer's support for parallel-port output of POST hex codes is determined by the BIOS revision the computer uses. If you update the BIOS on a particular laptop (or desktop) computer, that computer might support parallel-port POST output, or it might lose support for parallel-port POST output.

Regardless of type, if you have a POST error, be sure to check the following:

- Are all cables correctly connected and secured?
- Are the configuration settings correct in Setup for the devices you have installed? In particular, ensure the processor, memory, and hard drive settings are correct.

Figure 16.1   Using the Ultra-X MicroPOST to read POST codes (the code displayed is 04) from a typical laptop computer.

- Are all drivers properly installed?
- Are all resource settings on add-in and peripheral devices set so that no conflicts exist (for example, two add-in devices sharing the same interrupt)?
- Are PC Card/CardBus adapters and swappable disk drives installed correctly?
- Is a bootable hard disk (properly partitioned and formatted) installed?
- Does the BIOS support the drive you have installed? If so, are the parameters entered correctly?
- If you are booting from floppy disk, is the disk installed in drive A: bootable?
- Are all memory modules installed correctly? Try reseating them.

Hardware Problems After Booting

If problems occur after the system has been running and without your having made any hardware or software changes, a hardware fault possibly has occurred. Here is a list of items to check in that case:

- Try reinstalling the software that has crashed or refuses to run.
- Use the Reset button to restart the computer. It might be recessed and require a paperclip or pen point on some models.
- Check for loose cables, a marginal power supply, or other random component failures.
- A transient voltage spike, power outage, or brownout might have occurred. Symptoms of voltage spikes include a flickering video display, unexpected system reboots, and the system not responding to user commands. Reload the software and try again.
- Try reseating the removable memory modules if installed.

Problems Running Software

Problems running application software (especially new software) are usually caused by or related to the software itself, or they are due to the fact that the software is incompatible with the system. Here is a list of items to check in that case:

- Does the system meet the minimum hardware requirements for the software? Check the software documentation to be sure.
- Check to see whether the software is correctly installed. Reinstall it if necessary.
- Check to see whether the latest drivers are installed. You can use Windows Update or download updated drivers directly from the laptop or peripheral vendors' website.
- Scan the system for viruses using the latest antivirus software and updated signature files.

Note

Many laptops use integrated video, which borrows part of the main memory for video use. On recent systems, this can result in as much as 32MB or more of memory being "lost" to system use. For example, a system with 128MB of RAM with 32MB dedicated to video has only 96MB (128MB − 32MB) available for system (Windows) use. When you are determining whether a system has enough memory, be sure to consider the net amount of memory available after video requirements have been met.

Problems with Adapter Cards

Because laptops use PC Card and CardBus adapter cards, which are configured by Windows, it's pretty difficult to have IRQ or other conflicts. However, in rare cases it can happen if the cards' settings can be changed manually and you decide to start fiddling around with them.

On a notebook computer that runs Microsoft Windows, various types of driver issues are the mostly likely cause of adapter card problems. To solve these problems with Windows, view the card's properties in the Windows Device Manager and follow the recommendations given for cards that are not working (yellow exclamation point) or have been disabled (red X). In most cases, the first thing to try is to install updated drivers that match the hardware and work with the operating system version in use.

Note

To open the Windows Device Manager in Windows XP, right-click the My Computer icon and select Properties. Select the Hardware tab and click the Device Manager button.

Diagnostics

This section describes several levels of diagnostic software that are either included with your system or are available from your system manufacturer as well as third parties. It describes how you can get the most from this software. It also details the various ROM BIOS audio codes and error codes and examines aftermarket diagnostics and public-domain diagnostic software.

Diagnostics Software

Several types of diagnostic software are available for laptops. Some diagnostic functions are integrated into the laptop hardware or into peripheral devices, such as PC Card or CardBus cards and their driver/setup software, whereas others take the form of operating system utilities or separate software products. This software, some of which is included with the system when purchased, assists users in identifying many problems that can occur with a computer's components. In many cases, these programs can do most of the work in determining which component is defective or malfunctioning. The types of diagnostic software are as follows:

- **POST**—The Power On Self Test operates whenever any laptop is powered up (switched on). These routines are contained within the motherboard ROM as well as the ROM chip on expansion cards.

- **Manufacturer-supplied diagnostics software**—Many of the larger manufacturers (especially high-end, name-brand manufacturers such as IBM, Hewlett-Packard, Dell, and others) make special diagnostics software expressly designed for their systems. This manufacturer-specific software normally consists of a suite of tests that thoroughly examine the system. In some cases, these utilities are included with the system, or you can download these diagnostics from the manufacturer's online services at no charge (otherwise, you might have to purchase them). Many vendors include a limited version of one of the aftermarket packages customized for use with their systems. In some older IBM and Compaq systems, the diagnostic software is installed on a special partition on the hard drive and can be accessed during startup. This was a convenient way for those system manufacturers to ensure that users always had diagnostics available.

- **Peripheral diagnostics software**—Many hardware devices ship with specialized diagnostics software designed to test their particular functions. A network adapter usually includes a diagnostic specific to that adapter on a disk, also normally with the drivers. Other devices or adapters also might provide a diagnostic program or disk, usually included with the drivers for these devices.

- **Operating system diagnostics software**—Operating systems, such as Windows 9x/Me and Windows NT/2000/XP, include a variety of diagnostic software utilities designed to identify and monitor the performance of various components in the computer.

- **Aftermarket diagnostics software**—A number of manufacturers make general-purpose diagnostics software for laptops. This type of software is often bundled with other system maintenance and repair utilities to form a general laptop software toolkit.

The Power On Self Test

When IBM first began shipping the original PC in 1981, it included safety features that had never before been seen in a personal computer. These features included the Power On Self Test (POST) and parity-checked memory. Although parity-checked memory, or even error correcting code (ECC) memory, is no longer available in most low-end chipsets, every laptop still executes a POST when you turn it on. The following subsections provide more detail on the POST, a series of program routines buried in the motherboard's ROM BIOS chip that test all the main system components at power-on time. This series of routines is partially responsible for the delay when you turn on your laptop; the computer executes the POST before loading the operating system.

We've already covered some of the features and functions of the POST in the previous sections. The following subsections review some of that material but also more thoroughly cover the output beeps and codes that specific BIOSes generate.

What Is Tested?

Whenever you start up your computer, it automatically performs a series of tests that check the primary components in your system, such as the CPU, ROM, motherboard support circuitry, memory, and major peripherals. These tests are brief and are designed to catch hard (not intermittent) errors. The POST procedures are not very thorough compared with available disk-based diagnostics. The POST process provides error or warning messages whenever it encounters a faulty component.

Although the diagnostics performed by the system POST are not very thorough, they are the first line of defense, especially when it comes to detecting severe motherboard problems. If the POST encounters a problem severe enough to keep the system from operating properly, it halts the system boot process and generates an error message that often identifies the cause of the problem. These POST-detected problems are sometimes called *fatal errors* because they prevent the system from booting.

How Are Errors Reported?

The POST on a laptop or notebook system normally provides two types of output messages: audio codes and onscreen text messages.

POST errors can be revealed in the following ways:

- **Beep codes**—These beeps are heard through the speaker attached to the motherboard.
- **Onscreen messages**—These error messages are displayed onscreen after the video adapter is initialized.

Beep codes are used for fatal errors only, which are errors that occur so early in the process that video circuits and other devices are not yet functional. Because no display is available, these codes take the form of a series of beeps that identify the faulty component. When your computer is functioning normally, you should hear one short beep when the system starts up at the completion of the POST, although some systems (such as Compaq's) beep once or twice at the end of a normal POST. If a problem is detected, a different number of beeps sounds, sometimes in a combination of short and long tones.

Onscreen messages are brief messages that attempt to indicate a specific failure. These messages can be displayed only after the video adapter card and display have been initialized.

These different types of error messages are BIOS dependent and vary among BIOS manufacturers, and in some cases even among different BIOSes from the same manufacturer. The following subsections list the codes used by the most popular ROM BIOS versions (AMI, Award, Phoenix, and IBM BIOS), but you should consult your motherboard or ROM BIOS manufacturer for the codes specific to your board and BIOS.

AMI BIOS POST Error Codes

Laptops that use the AMI BIOS use the beep codes in Table 16.2 to report the problems indicated. The corrective actions listed in this table were originally written for desktop computers, so I've adapted them for use with laptop computers.

Table 16.2   AMI BIOS POST Beep Codes

Beeps	Error Description	Action	Notes for Laptop Users
1	DRAM Refresh Error	Clean the memory contacts and reseat the modules. Remove all modules except the first bank. Replace the memory. Replace the power supply. Replace the motherboard.	If the system has no removable memory installed, the built-in memory or the motherboard has failed, and the system must be serviced or replaced.
2	Memory Parity Error	Replace the memory. Replace the power supply. Replace the motherboard.	This error is unlikely to apply to most recent systems because most laptops don't use parity-checked memory.
3	Base 64KB Memory Failure	Replace the memory. Replace the power supply. Replace the motherboard.	If the system has no removable memory installed, the built-in memory or the motherboard has failed, and the system must be serviced or replaced.

Table 16.2   Continued

Beeps	Error Description	Action	Notes for Laptop Users
4	System Timer Failure	Check for proper motherboard installation, foreign objects causing shorts, loose screws, and over-tightened screws. Remove and clean the first bank of memory and reseat the module. Replace the memory. Replace the motherboard.	If there are no loose components or screws inside the laptop, the motherboard has probably failed, and the system must be serviced or replaced. This problem can also be caused by a memory error in the first bank of memory.
5	Processor Error	Check for proper motherboard installation, foreign objects causing shorts, loose screws, and over-tightened screws. Make sure the processor and heat sink are installed properly (remove and reseat). Replace the processor. Replace the motherboard.	Remove the processor only if the processor is installed in a ZIF socket. Be sure to replace the thermal material between the processor and the heatsink with approved material after removing the old thermal material from both the processor and the heatsink. If the processor is soldered to the motherboard, the system must be serviced or replaced.
6	Gate A20 Failure	Caused by a defective keyboard controller. Replace the keyboard controller on the motherboard.	The keyboard controller normally allows Gate A20 to switch the processor to protected mode.
7	Virtual Mode Processor Exception Error	Make sure the processor and heat sink are installed properly (remove and reseat). Replace the processor. Replace the motherboard.	Be sure to replace the thermal material between the processor and the heatsink with approved material after removing the old thermal material from both the processor and the heatsink.
8	Display Memory Read/Write Error	Check the video card for proper installation. Try replacing the video card memory. Replace the video card. Replace the motherboard.	Laptops must be serviced or replaced because their video is built in to the motherboard or integrated into the chipset.
9	ROM Checksum Error	Try reseating the motherboard ROM chip. Try reflashing the motherboard ROM. Replace the motherboard.	If the ROM BIOS is soldered in place, follow the directions to reflash the BIOS as your first step.
10	CMOS Shutdown Register Read/Write Error	Replace the CMOS battery. Replace the motherboard.	The CMOS battery is often a proprietary module that uses a short cable to plug into the motherboard.
11	Cache Memory Bad	Make sure cache settings in BIOS Setup are properly configured. Replace the processor. Replace the motherboard.	All modern processors (Pentium II and newer; AMD Athlon and newer) contain the cache memory used by the system.
1 long, 3 short	Conventional/Extended Memory Error	Clean the memory contacts and reseat the modules. Remove all modules except the first bank. Replace the memory. Replace the power supply. Replace the motherboard.	If the system has no removable memory installed, the built-in memory or the motherboard has failed, and the system must be serviced or replaced.

Table 16.2   Continued

Beeps	Error Description	Action	Notes for Laptop Users
1 long, 8 short	Display/Retrace Error	Check the video card for proper installation. Try replacing the video card memory. Replace the video card. Replace the motherboard.	Laptops must be serviced or replaced because their video is built in to the motherboard or integrated into the chipset.

AMI BIOS codes used by permission of American Megatrends, Inc.

Award BIOS and Phoenix FirstBIOS POST Error Codes

Currently, only one standard beep code exists in the Award BIOS (also known as the Phoenix FirstBIOS). A single long beep followed by two short beeps indicate that a video error has occurred and that the BIOS cannot initialize the video screen to display any additional information. If multiple or continuous beeps occur with an Award BIOS, this usually indicates problems with the power supply or memory (refer to Tables 16.3 and 16.4).

Table 16.3   Award BIOS/Phoenix FirstBIOS POST Beep Codes

Beeps	Error Description	Action	Notes for Laptop Users
One long, two short	Video Card Error	Check the video card for proper installation. Try replacing the video card memory. Replace the video card. Replace the motherboard.	Laptops must be serviced or replaced because their video is built in to the motherboard or integrated into the chipset.
One long, three short	Video Card Error	Check the video card for proper installation. Try replacing the video card memory. Replace the video card. Replace the motherboard.	Laptops must be serviced or replaced because their video is built in to the motherboard or integrated into the chipset.
Continuous Beeps	Memory Error	Clean the memory contacts and reseat the modules. Remove all modules except the first bank. Replace the memory. Replace the power supply. Replace the motherboard.	If the system has no removable memory installed, the built-in memory or the motherboard has failed, and the system must be serviced or replaced.

Table 16.4   Award BIOS POST Onscreen Error Messages

Message	Description
BIOS ROM checksum error - System halted	The checksum of the BIOS code in the BIOS chip is incorrect, indicating the BIOS code might have become corrupt. Contact your system dealer to replace the BIOS.
CMOS battery failed	The CMOS battery is not functional. Replace the CMOS battery. Contact a laptop parts dealer to determine the type and location of the CMOS battery used in your laptop.
CMOS checksum error - Defaults loaded	The checksum of CMOS is incorrect, so the system loads the default equipment configuration. A checksum error can indicate that CMOS has become corrupt. This error might have been caused by a weak battery. Check the battery and replace it if necessary.

Table 16.4   Continued

Message	Description
CPU at *nnnn*	Displays the running speed of the CPU.
Press ESC to skip memory test	You can press Esc to skip the full memory test.
Floppy disk(s) fail	Can't find or initialize the floppy drive controller or the drive. Make sure the controller is installed correctly. If no floppy drives are installed or connected to the computer, be sure the Diskette Drive selection in Setup is set to NONE or AUTO.
HARD DISK initializing. Please wait a moment	Some hard drives require extra time to initialize.
HARD DISK INSTALL FAILURE	Can't find or initialize the hard drive controller or the drive. Make sure the controller is installed correctly. If no hard drives are installed, be sure the Hard Drive selection in Setup is set to NONE.
Hard disk(s) diagnosis fail	The system might run specific disk diagnostic routines. This message appears if one or more hard disks return an error when the diagnostics run.
Keyboard error or no keyboard present	Can't initialize the keyboard. Make sure the keyboard is attached (installed) correctly and no keys are pressed during POST. If you have removed the integrated keyboard to install a component, make sure you reconnected and reinstalled the keyboard correctly. If you use an external keyboard, shut down the laptop, unplug the keyboard, and restart the system using the integrated keyboard.
Keyboard is locked out - Unlock the key	This message usually indicates that one or more keys have been pressed during the keyboard tests. Be sure no objects are resting on the keyboard.
Memory Test:	This message displays during a full memory test, counting down the memory areas being tested.
Memory test fail	If POST detects an error during memory testing, additional information appears giving specifics about the type and location of the memory error. If the memory location with the error is found in removable memory, swap memory modules and retry the system. If the memory location is found in built-in memory, service or replace the laptop.
Override enabled - Defaults loaded	If the system can't boot using the current CMOS configuration, the BIOS can override the current configuration with a set of BIOS defaults designed for the most stable, minimal-performance system operations.
Press TAB to show POST screen	System OEMs might replace Phoenix Technologies' Award BIOS POST display with their own proprietary displays. Including this message in the OEM display permits you to switch between the OEM display and the default POST display.
Primary master hard disk fail	POST detects an error in the primary master IDE hard drive. If the drive is swappable, or if you have replaced the original drive with a new drive, shut down the computer, recheck the drive installation, and restart the system.
Primary slave hard disk fail	POST detects an error in the primary IDE hard drive. If your system supports multiple hard disks with a swappable bay, shut down the system, eject and reconnect the additional hard disk, and restart the system.

(continues)

Table 16.4   Continued

Message	Description
Resuming from disk, Press TAB to show POST screen	Phoenix Technologies offers a save-to-disk feature for notebook computers. This message might appear when you restart the system after a save-to-disk shutdown.
Secondary master hard disk fail	POST detects an error in the secondary master IDE hard drive. If your system supports multiple hard disks with a swappable bay, shut down the system, eject and reconnect the additional hard disk, and restart the system.
Secondary slave hard disk fail	POST detects an error in the secondary slave IDE hard drive. If your system supports multiple hard disks with a swappable bay, shut down the system, eject and reconnect the additional hard disk, and restart the system.

Phoenix BIOS POST Error Codes

The beep codes listed in Tables 16.5 and 16.6 are for the current version of Phoenix BIOS, version 4.0, release 6.1. Other versions have somewhat different beeps and Port 80h codes.

Table 16.5   Phoenix BIOS 5.x and Earlier POST Beep Codes

Beeps	Error Description	Action	Notes for Laptop Users
1-2	Video Card Error	Check the video card for proper installation. Try replacing the video card memory. Replace the video card. Replace the motherboard.	Laptops must be serviced or replaced because their video is built in to the motherboard or integrated into the chipset.
1-3	CMOS RAM Read/ Write Error	Replace the CMOS battery. Replace the motherboard.	The CMOS battery is a proprietary model on most notebooks. Check the cable connection from the battery to the motherboard.
1-1-4	ROM Checksum Error	Try reseating the motherboard ROM chip. Try re-flashing the motherboard ROM. Replace the motherboard.	If the ROM BIOS is soldered in place, follow the directions to re-flash the BIOS as your first step.
1-2-1	Timer Error	Check for proper motherboard installation, foreign objects causing shorts, loose screws, and over-tightened screws. Replace the motherboard.	If there are no loose components or screws inside the laptop, the motherboard has probably failed and the system must be serviced or replaced.
1-2-2	DMA Initialization Error	Check for proper motherboard installation, foreign objects causing shorts, loose screws, and over-tightened screws. Replace the motherboard.	If there are no loose components or screws inside the laptop, the motherboard has probably failed and the system must be serviced or replaced.
1-2-3	DMA Page Register Read/Write Error	Check for proper motherboard installation, foreign objects inside causing shorts, loose screws, and over-tightened screws. Replace the motherboard.	If there are no loose components or screws the laptop, the motherboard has probably failed and the system must be serviced or replaced.

Table 16.5 Continued

Beeps	Error Description	Action	Notes for Laptop Users
1-3-1	RAM Refresh Verification Error	Clean the memory contacts and reseat the modules. Remove all modules except the first bank. Replace the memory. Replace the power supply. Replace the motherboard.	If the system has no removable memory installed, the built-in memory or the motherboard has failed and the system must be serviced or replaced.
1-3-3	First 64KB RAM Multibit Data Line Error	Clean the memory contacts and reseat the modules. Remove all modules except the first bank. Replace the memory. Replace the power supply. Replace the motherboard.	If the system has no removable memory installed, the built-in memory or the motherboard has failed and the system must be serviced or replaced.
1-3-4	First 64KB RAM Odd/Even Logic Error	Clean the memory contacts and reseat the modules. Remove all modules except the first bank. Replace the memory. Replace the power supply. Replace the motherboard.	If the system has no removable memory installed, the built-in memory or the motherboard has failed and the system must be serviced or replaced.
1-4-1	First 64KB RAM Address Line Error	Clean the memory contacts and reseat the modules. Remove all modules except the first bank. Replace the memory. Replace the power supply. Replace the motherboard.	If the system has no removable memory installed, the built-in memory or the motherboard has failed and the system must be serviced or replaced.
1-4-2	First 64KB RAM Parity Error	Clean the memory contacts and reseat the modules. Remove all modules except the first bank. Replace the memory. Replace the power supply. Replace the motherboard.	If the system has no removable memory installed, the built-in memory or the motherboard has failed and the system must be serviced or replaced.
3-1-1	Slave DMA Register Error	Check for proper motherboard installation, foreign objects causing shorts, loose screws, and over-tightened screws. Replace the motherboard.	If there are no loose components or screws inside the laptop, the motherboard has probably failed and the system must be serviced or replaced.
3-1-2	Master DMA Register Error	Check for proper motherboard installation, foreign objects causing shorts, loose screws, and over-tightened screws. Replace the motherboard.	If there are no loose components or screws inside the laptop, the motherboard has probably failed and the system must be serviced or replaced.
3-1-3	Master Interrupt Mask Register Error	Check for proper motherboard installation, foreign objects causing shorts, loose screws, and over-tightened screws. Replace the motherboard.	If there are no loose components or screws inside the laptop, the motherboard has probably failed and the system must be serviced or replaced.

(continues)

Table 16.5   Continued

Beeps	Error Description	Action	Notes for Laptop Users
3-1-4	Slave Interrupt Mask Register Error	Check for proper motherboard installation, foreign objects causing shorts, loose screws, and over-tightened screws. Replace the motherboard.	If there are no loose components or screws inside the laptop, the motherboard has probably failed and the system must be serviced or replaced.
3-2-4	Keyboard Controller Error	Check for proper motherboard installation, foreign objects causing shorts, loose screws, and over-tightened screws. Replace the keyboard. Replace the motherboard. Replace the processor.	If there are no loose components or screws inside the laptop, the motherboard has probably failed and the system must be serviced or replaced.
3-3-4	Screen Initialization Error	Check the video card for proper installation. Try replacing the video card memory. Replace the video card. Replace the motherboard.	Laptops must be serviced or replaced because their video is built in to the motherboard or integrated into the chipset.
3-4-1	Screen Retrace Error	Check the video card for proper installation. Try replacing the video card memory. Replace the video card. Replace the motherboard.	Laptops must be serviced or replaced because their video is built in to the motherboard or integrated into the chipset.
3-4-2	Video ROM Error	Check the video card for proper installation. Try replacing the video card memory. Replace the video card. Replace the motherboard.	Laptops must be serviced or replaced because their video is built in to the motherboard or integrated into the chipset.
4-2-1	Timer Interrupt Error	Check for proper motherboard installation, foreign objects causing shorts, loose screws, and over-tightened screws. Replace the motherboard.	If there are no loose components or screws inside the laptop, the motherboard has probably failed and the system must be serviced or replaced.
4-2-2	Shutdown Error	Check for proper motherboard installation, foreign objects causing shorts, loose screws, and over-tightened screws. Replace the keyboard. Replace the motherboard. Replace the processor.	If there are no loose components or screws inside the laptop, the motherboard has probably failed and the system must be serviced or replaced.
4-2-3	Gate A20 Error	Check for proper motherboard installation, foreign objects causing shorts, loose screws, and over-tightened screws. Replace the keyboard. Replace the motherboard. Replace the processor.	If there are no loose components or screws inside the laptop, the motherboard has probably failed and the system must be serviced or replaced.

Table 16.5   Continued

Beeps	Error Description	Action	Notes for Laptop Users
4-2-4	Unexpected Interrupt In Protected Mode	Check for a bad expansion card. Check for proper motherboard installation, foreign objects causing shorts, loose screws, and over-tightened screws. Replace the motherboard.	Remove any PC Card or CardBus cards and retry.
4-3-1	RAM Address Error >FFFh	Clean the memory contacts and reseat the modules. Remove all modules except the first bank. Replace the memory. Replace the power supply. Replace the motherboard.	If the system has no removable memory installed, the built-in memory or the motherboard has failed and the system must be serviced or replaced.
4-3-3	Interval Timer Channel 2 Error	Check for proper motherboard installation, foreign objects causing shorts, loose screws, and over-tightened screws. Replace the motherboard.	If there are no loose components or screws inside the laptop, the motherboard has probably failed and the system must be serviced or replaced.
4-3-4	Real Time Clock Error	Replace the CMOS battery. Replace the motherboard.	If replacing the CMOS battery fails to solve the problem, the motherboard has probably failed and the system must be serviced or replaced.
4-4-1	Serial Port Error	Reset the port configuration in BIOS Setup. Disable the port.	
4-4-2	Parallel Port Error	Reset the port configuration in BIOS Setup. Disable the port.	
4-4-3	Math Coprocessor Error	Check for proper motherboard installation, foreign objects causing shorts, loose screws, and over-tightened screws. Make sure the processor and heat sink are installed properly (remove and reseat). Replace the processor. Replace the motherboard.	Be sure to replace the thermal material between the processor and the heatsink with approved material after removing the old thermal material from both the processor and the heatsink.
Low 1-1-2	System Board Select Error	Check for proper motherboard installation, foreign objects causing shorts, loose screws, and over-tightened screws. Make sure the processor and heat sink are installed properly (remove and reseat). Replace the processor. Replace the motherboard.	Be sure to replace the thermal material between the processor and the heatsink with approved material after removing the old thermal material from both the processor and the heatsink.
Low 1-1-3	Extended CMOS RAM Error	Replace the CMOS battery. Replace the motherboard.	The CMOS battery is a proprietary model on most notebooks. Check the cable connection from the battery to the motherboard.

Table 16.6   Phoenix BIOS 6.x and Later POST Beep Codes

Beeps	Error Description	Description/Action	Notes for Laptop Users
1-2-2-3	BIOS ROM Checksum Error	Try reseating the motherboard ROM chip. Try re-flashing the motherboard ROM. Replace the motherboard.	If the ROM BIOS is soldered in place, follow the directions to re-flash the BIOS as your first step.
1-3-1-1	DRAM Refresh Error	Clean the memory contacts and reseat the modules. Remove all modules except the first bank. Replace the memory. Replace the power supply. Replace the motherboard.	If the system has no removable memory installed, the built-in memory or the motherboard has failed and the system must be serviced or replaced.
1-3-1-3	8742 Keyboard Controller Error	Check for proper motherboard installation, foreign objects causing shorts, loose screws, and over-tightened screws. Replace the keyboard. Replace the motherboard. Replace the processor.	If there are no loose components or screws inside the laptop, the motherboard has probably failed and the system must be serviced or replaced.
1-3-4-1	Memory Address Line Error	Clean the memory contacts and reseat the modules. Remove all modules except the first bank. Replace the memory. Replace the power supply. Replace the motherboard.	If the system has no removable memory installed, the built-in memory or the motherboard has failed and the system must be serviced or replaced.
1-3-4-3	Memory Low Byte Data Error	Clean the memory contacts and reseat the modules. Remove all modules except the first bank. Replace the memory. Replace the power supply. Replace the motherboard.	If the system has no removable memory installed, the built-in memory or the motherboard has failed and the system must be serviced or replaced.
1-4-1-1	Memory High Byte Data Error	Clean the memory contacts and reseat the modules. Remove all modules except the first bank. Replace the memory. Replace the power supply. Replace the motherboard.	If the system has no removable memory installed, the built-in memory or the motherboard has failed and the system must be serviced or replaced.
2-1-2-3	ROM Copyright Error	Try reseating the motherboard ROM chip. Try re-flashing the motherboard ROM. Replace the motherboard.	In many cases, reseating the ROM chip is not possible and the system must be serviced or replaced.
2-2-3-1	Unexpected Interrupts	Check for a bad expansion card. Check for proper motherboard installation, foreign objects causing shorts, loose screws, and over-tightened screws. Replace the motherboard.	Remove all nonessential components and retry. If the system still fails, it needs to be serviced or replaced.

Table 16.6   Continued

Beeps	Error Description	Description/Action	Notes for Laptop Users
1-2	Video Card Error	Check the video card for proper installation. Try replacing the video card memory. Replace the video card. Replace the motherboard.	In most cases, the laptop must be serviced or replaced.

IBM ThinkPad BIOS Error Codes

Because laptops use different technologies than desktop computers, IBM developed a special range of beep codes for its ThinkPad notebook computers. The beep codes, the symptoms they list, and the recommended actions are detailed in Table 16.7.

Table 16.7   IBM ThinkPad BIOS Beep Codes

Beep Code/Symptom	Action
One beep and a blank, unreadable, or flashing LCD.	Reseat the LCD connector. Replace the LCD assembly. Reseat or replace the DIMMs. Replace the motherboard.
One long and two short beeps and a blank or unreadable LCD.	Reseat or replace the DIMMs. Replace the LCD assembly. Replace the motherboard.
Two short beeps with error codes.	POST error. See error codes.
Two short beeps and a blank screen.	Reseat or replace the DIMMs. Replace the motherboard.
Three short beeps, pause, three more short beeps, and one short beep.	Reseat or replace the DIMMs. Replace the motherboard.
One short beep, pause, three short beeps, pause, three more short beeps, and one short beep. Only the cursor appears.	Reinstall the operating system.
Four cycles of four short beeps and a blank screen.	Replace the security chip. Replace the motherboard.
Five short beeps and a blank screen.	Replace the motherboard.

The codes in Table 16.8 are especially for IBM's line of ThinkPad laptop computers.

Table 16.8   IBM ThinkPad-Specific BIOS POST Numeric Error Codes

Code	Message	Action
0175	`Bad CRC1 - The EEPROM checksum is not correct.`	Reflash the BIOS and replace the motherboard.
0176	`System Security - The system has been tampered with.`	This message is displayed if you remove the security chip and reinstall it or install a new one. Run BIOS Setup, load the defaults, and save the settings.
0177	`Bad SVP data, stop POST task.`	The Supervisor password is corrupt. Replace the motherboard.

Table 16.8   Continued

Code	Message	Action
0182	Bad CRC2. Enter BIOS Setup and load Setup Defaults.	Run BIOS Setup, load the defaults, and save the settings.
0185	Bad startup sequence settings. Enter BIOS Setup and load setup defaults.	Run BIOS Setup, load the defaults, and save the settings.
0187	EAIA data access error - The access to EEPROM is failed.	Reflash the BIOS. Replace the motherboard.
0188	Invalid RFID serialization information area or bad CRC2 - The EEPROM checksum is not correct.	Reflash the BIOS. Replace the motherboard.
0189	Invalid RFID configuration information area - The EEPROM checksum is not correct.	Reflash the BIOS. Replace the motherboard.
0190	Critical low-battery error.	Charge the battery (replace it if necessary).
0191	System Security, invalid Remote Change requested.	Run BIOS Setup, load the defaults, and save the settings.
0192	System Security, IBM Embedded Security hardware tamper detected.	Run BIOS Setup and select Config, IBM Security Chip, Clear IBM Security Chip. Replace the security chip. Replace the motherboard.
0195	Security hardware tamper detected.	Run BIOS Setup and select Config, IBM Security Chip, Clear IBM Security Chip. Replace the security chip. Replace the motherboard.
0196	Security hardware removed.	Run BIOS Setup and select Config, IBM Security Chip, Clear IBM Security Chip. Replace the security chip. Replace the motherboard.
0197	Invalid remote change requested.	The remote configuration for the security chip has failed. Confirm the operation and try again.
0199	System Security - IBM Security password retry count exceeded.	Occurs if you enter the wrong Supervisor password more than three times in a row. Restart and try again with the correct password.
01C8	More than one modem devices are found. Remove one of them. Press <Esc> to continue.	Remove either the Mini PCI modem card or the modem daughtercard.
01C9	More than one Ethernet devices are found. Remove one of them. Press <Esc> to continue.	Remove either the Mini PCI Ethernet card or the Ethernet daughtercard.
0200	Hard disk error, the hard disk is not working.	Reseat the hard disk, load the BIOS Setup defaults, and replace the drive.
021x	Keyboard error.	Test the keyboard (replace it if necessary).
0220	Monitor type error, monitor type does not match the one specified in CMOS.	Run BIOS Setup, load the defaults, and save the settings.

Table 16.8   Continued

Code	Message	Action
0230	Shadow RAM error, shadow RAM fails at offset *nnnn*.	Reseat or replace the SODIMMs. Replace the motherboard.
0231	System RAM error, system RAM fails at offset *nnnn*.	Reseat or replace the SODIMMs. Replace the motherboard.
0232	Extended RAM error, extended RAM fails at offset *nnnn*.	Reseat or replace the SODIMMs. Replace the motherboard.
0250	System battery error, system battery is dead.	Replace the backup battery and run BIOS Setup to reset the date and time.
0251	System CMOS checksum bad, default configuration used.	Replace the backup battery and run BIOS Setup to reset the date and time.
0252	Password checksum bad, the password is cleared.	Reset the password by running BIOS Setup.
0260	System timer error.	Replace the backup battery and run BIOS Setup to reset the date and time.
0270	Real time clock error.	Replace the backup battery and run BIOS Setup to reset the date and time.
0271	Date and time error, neither the date nor the time is set in the computer.	Run BIOS Setup to reset the date and time.
02B2	Incorrect drive A type.	Run BIOS Setup, load the defaults, and save the settings. Replace floppy drive.
02F4	EISA CMOS not writable.	Run BIOS Setup, load the defaults, and save the settings. Replace the backup battery.
02F5	DMA test failed.	Reseat or replace the SODIMMs. Replace the motherboard.
02F6	Software NMI failed.	Reseat or replace the SODIMMs. Replace the motherboard.
02F7	Fail-safe timer NMI failed.	Reseat or replace the SODIMMs. Replace the motherboard.
1801	Attached docking station is not supported.	Remove the docking station or port replicator.
1802	Unauthorized network card is plugged in - Power off and remove the Mini-PCI network card.	Remove the Mini PCI network card.

Table 16.9 lists the BIOS POST error messages that are specific to IBM ThinkPad laptop computers.

Table 16.9   IBM ThinkPad-Specific BIOS POST Error Messages

Error Message/Symptom	Action
No beep, power-on indicator on, LCD blank, and no POST.	Make sure every connector is connected tightly and correctly. Reseat or replace the DIMMs. Replace the motherboard.
No beep, power-on indicator on, and LCD blank during POST.	Reseat or replace the DIMMs. Replace the motherboard.
Device address conflict.	Run BIOS Setup, load the defaults, and save the settings. Replace the backup battery.
Allocation error for device.	Run BIOS Setup, load the defaults, and save the settings. Replace the backup battery.
Failing bits: *nnnn*.	Reseat or replace the DIMMs. Replace the motherboard.
Invalid system configuration data.	Reseat or replace the DIMMs. Replace the motherboard.
I/O device IRQ conflict.	Run BIOS Setup, load the defaults, and save the settings. Replace the backup battery.
Operating system not found.	Reseat the hard disk. Check the drive and operating system for proper installation. Reinstall the operating system. Replace the hard disk.
Hibernation error.	Restore the system configuration to what it was before the computer entered hibernation mode. If the memory size has been changed, re-create the hibernation file.
Fan error.	Check or replace the fan.
Thermal sensing error.	Replace the motherboard.
The power-on password prompt appears.	A power-on password or a Supervisor password is set. Type the password and press Enter.
The hard-disk password prompt appears.	A hard disk password is set. Type the password and press Enter.
The DOS full screen looks smaller.	Run BIOS Setup or the ThinkPad Configuration program and set the screen expansion function.

POST Memory Count

On some systems, the POST also displays the results of its system memory test on the LCD. The last number displayed is the amount of memory that tested successfully. For example, a system might display the following message:

```
131072 KB OK
```

The number displayed by the memory test (the example indicates that 128MB of RAM is installed) should agree with the total amount of memory installed on the system motherboard. Some older systems display a slightly lower total because they deduct part or all of the 384KB of upper memory area (UMA) from the count. This memory test is performed before any system software loads, so many memory managers or device drivers you might have installed do not affect the results of the test. If the POST memory test stops short of the expected total, the number displayed can indicate how far into the system memory array a memory error lies. This number can help you identify the exact module that is at fault and can be a valuable troubleshooting aid in itself.

Note

The memory test reflects the total amount of memory installed in a system, including any memory set aside for integrated video.

General-Purpose Diagnostics Programs

A large number of professional third-party diagnostics programs are available for laptop systems. Technicians use these commercial programs to perform testing of new systems (often called *burn-in testing*) or testing of existing systems either in the shop or in the field.

Most of the commercial laptop diagnostics can test all your laptop's key components. In addition, specific programs are available to test memory, floppy drives, hard disks, video adapters, and most other areas of the system. Here are some of the programs I recommend most highly:

- **AMIDiag Suite**—See www.ami.com for more information.
- **MicroScope**—See www.micro2000.com for more information.

Tip

Before trying a commercial diagnostic program to solve your problem, look in your operating system. Most operating systems today provide at least some of the diagnostic functions that diagnostic programs do. You might be able to save some time and money.

Unfortunately, no clear leader exists in the area of diagnostic software. Each program has unique advantages, and as a result, no program is universally better than another. When deciding which diagnostic programs, if any, to include in your arsenal, look for the features you need.

One of the most popular is AMIDiag from AMI. This program runs on virtually any desktop or laptop PC and tests most of the hardware in the system. AMIDiag is available in a native Windows version that also supports third-party diagnostics modules or in a DOS version that can be used to test hardware, regardless of the operating system, by using a DOS boot disk to start the system.

Operating System Diagnostics

In many cases, it might not be necessary to purchase third-party diagnostic software because your operating system has all the diagnostic tools you need. Windows 9x/Me and 2000/XP include a large selection of programs that enable you to view, monitor, and troubleshoot the hardware in your system. Some of these include the following:

- **Windows Device Manager**—Displays installed hardware, resources in use, and conflicts/problems with installed hardware. Can also be used to update drivers.
- **DirectX Diagnostics**—Tests 3D graphics and sound features.
- **Microsoft System Information**—Displays hardware and software information in more detail than Windows Device Manager.
- **ScanDisk/CHKDSK**—Checks the disk file system and surface for errors.
- **Event Viewer**—Gives a chronological list of errors that Windows encounters while the system is running.
- **Windows Troubleshooters**—A series of mini-programs that assist with troubleshooting specific hardware and software problems.

Top Troubleshooting Problems

This section includes some of the most frequently asked troubleshooting questions I receive for laptop and notebook systems. I've divided these questions into categories to help you find the answer you need more quickly.

Power and Startup Problems

If your laptop won't boot or, worse, won't even power on, the cause can be difficult to pin down. Use the following subsections to help you troubleshoot the root of the problem.

When I power the system on, I see the power LED light and determine that the fan spins, but nothing else ever happens.

The fact that the LEDs illuminate and the fan spins indicates that the power supply subsystem (which includes the external power adapter, power cord, and battery) is partially working, but that does not exclude it from being defective. This is a classic "dead" system, which can be caused by almost any defective hardware component. Because in my experiences I've had more problems with power supplies than most other components, I'd immediately use a multimeter to measure the outputs at the power adapter connectors and ensure they were within the proper 5% tolerances of their rated voltages. The power adapter is usually marked with the rated DC voltage output. If power is flowing to the adapter but no power is coming from the adapter, change the cord. Most laptop power adapters use one of several two-wire standard power cords. Replace the cord with a known-working spare and retest the voltage.

Even if the voltage measurements check out, I'd swap in a known-good spare power adapter and retest. If that doesn't solve the problem, I would revert to the "bootstrap approach" I mentioned earlier, which is to strip the system down to the bare minimum and retest. If the system now starts, you should begin adding the components you removed one at a time, retesting after each change. If the laptop uses a two-wire cord that goes directly into the unit, the AC/DC power converter is built in to the laptop. You would need to disassemble the laptop to test the power adapter.

The system beeps when I turn it on, but there is nothing on the screen.

The beep indicates a failure that was detected by the ROM POST routines. Look up the beep code in the table corresponding to the ROM version in your motherboard. You can sometimes find this in the system manual; however, you can also see the beep codes for the most popular AMI, Award, Phoenix, and IBM ThinkPad BIOSes earlier in this chapter.

The system won't boot up. It says "Missing operating system" on the screen.

When your system boots, it reads the first sector from the hard disk, called the *master boot record (MBR)*, and runs the code contained in that sector. The MBR code then reads the partition table (also contained in the MBR) to determine which partition is bootable and where it starts. Then it loads the first sector of the bootable partition, called the *volume boot record (VBR)*, which contains the operating system–specific boot code, but before executing the VBR, the MBR checks to be sure the VBR ends with the signature bytes 55AAh. The MBR will display the "Missing operating system" message if it finds that the first sector of the bootable partition (the VBR) does not end in 55AAh.

Several things can cause this to occur:

- **The drive parameters entered in the BIOS Setup are incorrect or corrupted.** These are the parameters defining your drive that you entered in the BIOS Setup, and they are stored in a CMOS RAM chip powered by a battery on your motherboard. Incorrect parameters will cause the MBR program to translate differently and read the wrong VBR sector, thus displaying the

"Missing operating system" message. A dead CMOS battery can also cause this because it will lose or corrupt the stored drive translation and transfer mode parameters. In fact, in my experience a dead battery is one of the more likely causes. To repair this problem, check and/or replace the CMOS battery, run the BIOS Setup, go to the hard drive parameter screen, and enter the correct drive parameters. Note that most drive parameters should be set to auto or auto-detect.

■ **The drive is not yet partitioned and formatted on this system.** This is a normal error if you try to boot the system from the hard disk before the OS installation is complete (such as if you replace the laptop's original hard disk with a larger model or if you have removed the original partitions with FDISK). Boot to an OS startup disk (floppy or CD) and run the Setup program, which will prompt you through the partitioning and formatting process during the OS installation.

■ **The MBR and/or partition tables are corrupted.** This can be caused by boot sector viruses, among other things. To repair with Windows 9x, cold boot (power off, then on) the system from a known noninfected, write-protected floppy or bootable CD containing the FDISK program (preferably Windows 98 or later). Enter **FDISK /MBR** at the command prompt, which will recopy the MBR code but not alter the partition table. Reboot.

With Windows 2000/XP, select the Recovery Console option at startup (you might need the original Windows 2000 or XP CD-ROM) and run **FIXMBR**, followed by **FIXBOOT**. Reboot the system.

If the message still persists and you need to recover the data on the drive, you will then either need to rebuild the partition tables from scratch using a third-party utility such as the DISKEDIT program included with the Symantec Norton Utilities, or hire a data-recovery specialist who can do this for you. If you don't need to recover the data on the drive, simply reinstall the OS from scratch, which will prompt you through partitioning and formatting the drive.

■ **The VBR is corrupted.** To repair with Windows 95/98/Me, secure a bootable floppy created by the same OS version on the hard disk that contains the SYS command from that OS. Run **SYS C:**, which will recopy a good VBR and system files to the volume. For Windows NT/2000/XP, you can use the Recovery Console or DiskProbe utility (found on the bootable operating system CD).

■ **You have a nonbootable floppy or CD in the system.** Remove any floppy disks or CDs present in the laptop and reboot the system.

The power button won't turn off the system.

Most recent laptop systems are configured to shut down automatically when you exit Windows. However, you sometimes need to shut down the system manually. There are several possible reasons why the power button might not shut down the system. Check the following before you consider sending the system in for service:

■ **Buggy system BIOS**—Reflash the BIOS with a different version. If you are using the most recent BIOS version, go back to the previous version if possible.

■ **Power-management problems**—Some systems might not implement power management properly. Make sure the system is set to shut down when you push the power button; some systems might be configured to go into a sleep mode instead.

Note

The freeware **Shutdown.exe** utility can be used to force laptop and desktop computers running Windows XP to shut down, log off the current user, hibernate, stand by, or restart. **Shutdown.exe** runs from the command line and can be used if the normal shutdown menu options don't work or the power button doesn't work correctly. You can get it from **www.budja.com/shutdown/**.

If you need to remove the battery or use the reset button to shut down/restart the system, it is a good idea to run ScanDisk (found in the Windows Accessories, System Tools folder) in Windows 95/98/Me/NT/2000 or CHKDSK in Windows XP to check and correct any file system issues after a forced shutdown.

Note that some laptop computers have both a power and a sleep button. Make sure you use the correct button for the task you want to perform.

Windows Problems

Many problems with both laptop and desktop computers are caused by the operating system. The following subsections provide useful tips for dealing with typical problems caused by Windows.

I see a "STOP" or "STOP ERROR" in Windows 2000/XP.

Many different things, including corrupted files, viruses, incorrectly configured hardware, or failing hardware, can cause Windows STOP errors. The most valuable resource for handling any error message displayed by Windows is the Microsoft Knowledge Base (MSKB), an online compendium of over a quarter of a million articles covering all Microsoft products. You can visit the MSKB at support.microsoft.com, and from there you can use the search tool to retrieve information specific to your problem.

For example, say you are receiving "Stop 0x0000007B" errors in Windows XP. In that case you would visit the MSKB at the address listed and enter the error message in the search box. In this case, I entered "stop 7B error Windows XP" in the box, and it returned two articles, one of which was Microsoft Knowledge Base Article number 324103, titled "HOW TO: Troubleshoot 'Stop 0x0000007B' Errors in Windows XP." Following this link I was taken to the article at support.microsoft.com/ default.aspx?scid=kb;en-us;324103, which had a complete description of the problem and possible solutions. The article states that this error could be caused by one of the following:

- Boot-sector viruses
- Device driver issues
- Hardware issues
- Other issues

The article proceeds to explain each issue and solution in detail. All things considered, the MSKB is a valuable resource when you are dealing with any problems related to or reported by any version of Windows or any other Microsoft software.

Note

The symptoms of a virus/spyware infection can appear to be caused by damaged hardware, a malfunctioning installation of Windows, or both. Before disassembling a laptop to check for hardware problems, check the system using antivirus and antispyware software.

I have an old software program that crashes when I try to run it in Windows XP.

Some software programs that were designed for older versions of Windows experience problems when running under Windows XP or Windows XP with Service Pack 2 installed. A workaround you can use in the case of the former is the Program Compatibility Wizard, which can be found on the Start menu under Accessories. Optionally, you can right-click on a program's shortcut, select Properties from the menu, and choose the Compatibility tab.

You can choose to run a program in Windows 95, Windows 98/Me, Windows NT (SP5), and Windows 2000 compatibility modes. Select the mode that matches the program you're trying to run. If the program still won't run, try disabling your antivirus and antispyware programs before launching the program in compatibility mode.

I installed a new device driver for a hardware item, and now Windows XP is crashing or locking up.

If you know which device driver is causing the problem, you can revert back to the previous driver by using the Device Driver Roll Back feature in Windows XP. To do this, open the Control Panel and double-click on the System applet icon. Select the Hardware tab and click on the Device Manager button.

Open the hardware category that the device driver applies to and double-click on the device. Select the Driver tab and click on the Roll Back Driver button. Windows will replace the new driver with the last version.

I see "Fatal Exception" errors in Windows 9x/Me.

A "Fatal Exception" error is the equivalent of the STOP error in Windows 2000/XP. As indicated in the previous answer, this error can be caused by hardware and/or software problems, and the best place to check for specific solutions is in the Microsoft Knowledge Base (MSKB) at support.microsoft.com.

The system won't shut down in Windows.

Shutdown problems are another example where the MSKB comes to the rescue. By searching for "shutdown problems Windows XP," for example (substitute the version of Windows you are using), you will quickly find several articles that can help you troubleshoot this type of problem. This problem has been caused by bugs in motherboard ROM (try upgrading your motherboard ROM to the latest version), bugs in the various Windows versions (visit www.windowsupdate.com and install the latest fixes, patches, and service packs), or in some cases configuration or hardware problems. I'll defer to the MSKB articles for more complete explanations of the Windows issues.

Note that problems with system software can also cause shutdown problems. Media players and other programs that run in the background might prevent proper shutdown. Use MSConfig to selectively disable these programs at startup or manually close them down before you shut down the computer.

If your laptop uses Windows 98/Me/XP, you can use MSConfig to selectively turn off some startup programs or services as part of the process of determining the cause of a computer that won't shut down.

I can't find drivers for my hardware.

Unlike desktop computers, whose hardware components are usually supported by the individual vendors, laptop computers' onboard components (video, network, modem, CD/DVD-ROM drive, audio, and so on) are supported by the laptop computer vendor. In many cases, laptop vendors provide driver software only for the version of Windows supplied with the system. Although upgrading to a newer version of Windows will usually work well because newer Windows versions are distributed with more hardware drivers, attempting to install an older Windows version can be difficult, especially if you don't know which drivers you need to acquire.

Even if you plan to reinstall the same version of Windows on your system, driver problems can still make the installation difficult if your system was shipped with a restore CD instead of a full version of Windows. A restore CD contains an image of your operating system and the drivers for the standard hardware installed in your system. Some laptop vendors don't do a good job of making driver updates easy to locate on their websites, so if you don't use the restore CD to reinstall Windows, you might not have all the drivers you need for your system.

Whether you plan to reinstall the same version of Windows, some other version of Windows, or another operating system, take these precautions:

- Use the Windows Device Manager to determine the makes and models of the internal hardware in your system, such as the chipset, modem, network adapter, video chip, optical drive, and so on.

- Download the drivers for the version of Windows (or other operating system) you want to install from your vendor if possible. Use a website search engine such as Google to track down drivers for your system if your vendor doesn't have the drivers you need. Note that in some cases the laptop vendors might post a collection of drivers in a single archive rather than individual driver files. For example, Compaq (now owned by Hewlett-Packard) calls its driver sets SoftPaqs.

- Consider creating a dual-boot configuration that enables you to continue running your existing operating system as well as providing space for another operating system. You can use a partitioning program such as Norton Partition Magic, which is now available from Symantec at www.powerquest.com/partitionmagic, to free up the space. Partition Magic also includes a boot manager (a program that enables you to choose which operating system to run when you start your computer).

- Keep in mind that you are responsible for supporting your laptop yourself when you install another operating system. Many vendors won't help you if you install a different version of Windows (or another operating system such as Linux). Research any installation you plan to do carefully. By using a website search engine such as Google, you might find a user-created page that has links and notes about the laptop computer you have and the operating system upgrade you're preparing to perform.

- You might need to use "generic" drivers that aren't necessarily optimized for your particular hardware. Laptop vendors often make changes to basic OEM-provided drivers or use customized hardware components, so a driver provided by an OEM (or an open-source driver for Linux) might not have all the features the original driver for your hardware provided or might not fully support your hardware.

Hardware Problems

Laptop hardware is different in many ways from desktop hardware, as you learned earlier in this chapter. Use these tips to deal with some of the most common problems.

The dial-up modem doesn't work.

First, verify that the phone line is good and that you have a dial tone. Then check and, if necessary, replace the phone cable from the modem to the wall outlet. The next steps to take depend on the type of modem in use. Laptop computers could use any of the following types of modems:

- Modems built in to the motherboard.

- Modems (often combined with 10/100 Ethernet networking) installed in a Mini PCI card slot. These resemble built-in modems because the RJ-11 port is built in to the computer, but a Mini PCI card can be removed, usually by removing a cover on the bottom of the computer.

- Modems installed in a PC Card or CardBus slot. These cards might also contain 10BASE-T or 10/100 Ethernet ports.

- Modems that plug into a USB or serial port.

If the modem is integrated into the motherboard, check the BIOS Setup to see that the modem is enabled. Note that some laptops use a Windows-based BIOS configuration program. Try clearing the extended system configuration data (ESCD) option in the BIOS Setup if this option is available. This will force the Plug and Play routines to reconfigure the system, which may resolve any conflicts. If the modem is internal, and you aren't using the COM (serial) ports integrated into the motherboard (as for an external modem), try disabling the serial ports to free up additional system resources.

If the modem is part of a Mini PCI card, remove and reinstall the card to make sure it makes a good connection. If the Mini PCI card also contains a 10/100 Ethernet port, make sure the network port is working. If neither the modem nor the network port works, the card or the slot has failed. Use an identical known-working Mini PCI card as a replacement to determine where the problem lies.

Note

Although Mini PCI is a standard interface, in reality, Mini PCI cards are custom designed for the requirements of a particular OEM. Use a Mini PCI card from the same or similar model of laptop as a replacement if possible; Mini PCI cards are not yet sold in retail stores.

If the modem is plugged into a PC Card or CardBus slot, try the other slot if the computer has two slots. If the PC Card or CardBus modem card uses a dongle (a proprietary cable that runs between the card and a standard telephone line or jack), make sure the dongle is tightly attached to the card and to the telephone line or jack. Test the dongle with a multimeter set to CONT (continuity) if you can obtain a pinout to verify the dongle is working properly. Try a known-working replacement dongle from the same or similar model of PC Card (some PC Card dongles can also be obtained from third-party parts sources). If the dongle is damaged or defective, the modem cannot work. If the card also contains a network adapter, make sure the network adapter works. If neither the network adapter nor the modem works, the card or the PC Card/CardBus slot might be defective.

If the modem plugs into a serial or USB port, make sure the port has not been disabled and works correctly. If a USB port works with a mouse or other device, it can also support a modem. Most external modems require a separate AC power source, so make sure the modem is plugged into a working AC power source and that the modem is turned on. Make sure the modem is properly connected to the serial or USB port on the laptop. Try replacing the external modem power brick and the serial/USB cable.

Try removing and reinstalling the modem drivers, making sure you are using the most recent drivers from the modem manufacturer. If the modem is identified as a standard modem, download model-specific drivers from the modem vendor.

Note that modems are very susceptible to damage from nearby lightning strikes. Consider adding lightning arrestors or surge suppressors on the phone line running to the modem and unplug the modem during storms. If the modem has failed after a storm, you can be almost certain that it has been damaged by lightning. It is possible that in addition to the modem, the strike may have damaged the serial port or motherboard. Any items damaged by lightning will most likely need to be replaced.

The keyboard doesn't work.

Try attaching an external keyboard, either via a standard keyboard port (usually called a *PS/2 port*) or via USB. If this works, the internal keyboard may be defective or have a bad connection. Try removing and reinstalling the internal keyboard; if that doesn't work, replace it.

Depending on the laptop model in question, removing the keyboard can be simple or more complex. In some cases, you can lift the keyboard free of the system by removing a couple of screws on the bottom of the case to enable the top of the bezel around the keyboard to be removed; on some systems with a snap-apart case, you release the bezel with a flat-bladed screwdriver or special case-removal tool. With other models, additional steps might be necessary.

To determine which steps are necessary, check the notebook computer vendor's website for repair (subsystem tear-down and replacement) documentation. I like to use the Google search engine's site-specific search feature. For example, I might use the following search in Google:

Compaq "Maintenance and Service" site:Compaq.com

Google displays all maintenance and service pages on the Compaq website. These pages provide details of disassembling various Compaq laptop computers for service and repairs. Even if the exact model you want to disassemble isn't listed, you might be able to find information about a similar model.

If you are unable to locate repair information, try to determine the identity of the actual OEM vendor (see Chapter 17 for vendor names and websites) from product reviews or other sources and see if you can get the information needed from the OEM vendor.

Tip

Another way to determine how to remove the keyboard is to check the documentation provided by third-party hard disk upgrade vendors such as SimpleTech (**www.simpletech.com**) and Apricorn (**www.apricorn.com**). Although you can remove many laptops' hard disks through the bottom of the case, some models require you to remove the keyboard to access the hard disk. A hard disk upgrade kit built for your specific model of laptop will include instructions for removing and installing the drive; the vendors listed post this information online for the models they support.

Be very careful when you work with the integrated keyboard. A fragile ribbon cable is often used to connect the keyboard to the motherboard; if this cable is loose or damaged, the keyboard will malfunction. If the system was serviced just before the keyboard malfunctioned, contact the servicer for help. The service technician might not have reconnected the keyboard cable or might have damaged it.

The mouse pointer is moving when I didn't move it.

If you have this problem on a system with an integrated pointing device (touchpad or pointing stick), there are several possible reasons for this problem:

- Defective cap on the pointing stick (TrackPoint and so on)
- Defective pointing stick (TrackPoint and so on)
- Accidental tapping of the pointing stick or touchpad
- Defective touchpad

To solve this problem, you should first determine whether your laptop uses a touchpad or a pointing stick (such as the IBM TrackPoint or Toshiba AccuPoint). If your laptop uses a pointing stick, try replacing the cap over the pointing stick (see Chapter 13, "Keyboards and Pointing Devices," for sources for replacement TrackPoint III/IV caps, which also work on earlier TrackPoint keyboards and the Toshiba AccuPoint).

If the pointer continues to drift on its own after you replace the TrackPoint/AccuPoint cap, replace the keyboard. The pointing stick is built in to the keyboard. If you experience pointer drift with a system using a touchpad, replace the touchpad (usually a different subassembly than the keyboard).

However, before you jump to conclusions about pointer drift, watch your typing! It's very easy to bump a touchpad with your thumbs while you're typing; most touchpads are so sensitive that you might not even notice when your thumbs or fingers brush the surface. A pointing stick can also be bumped accidentally, but in my experience it's harder to overlook the fact you nudged it when typing.

If you're still not sure you're having real problems with your system's touchpad, put cardboard over it and work with keyboard commands for a while. If your cursor always stays where it's supposed to, you've been bumping the touchpad without realizing it. However, if the cursor is still roving when you can't touch the touchpad, it's time for a touchpad replacement.

If you prefer to use a separate pointing device that's plugged into the computer's PS/2 or USB port, you might want to disable the built-in touchpad or pointing stick with the laptop's BIOS Setup or Windows-based configuration program. Although some systems automatically disable the onboard touchpad or pointing stick when you plug in an external pointing device, others don't.

Tip

Some late-model IBM laptops feature both a touchpad and a TrackPoint pointing stick. You can use both, or disable one or the other, through the Windows-based configuration utility.

I can't hear any sound from the speakers.

This problem can often be as simple as the volume controls being turned down, so don't overlook the obvious and check to be sure! Check the system volume control as well as the volume controls in Windows or your application to ensure they are turned up and not muted. When you are sure the volume is turned up, check the internal connections. If that doesn't help, try reconfiguring the integrated sound or updating the drivers.

The monitor appears completely garbled or unreadable.

If you have an external monitor plugged into a notebook computer, a completely garbled screen is most often due to improper, incorrect, or unsupported settings for the refresh rate, resolution, or color depth. Using incorrect drivers as well can also cause this. To check the configuration of the card, the first step would be to power on the system and verify whether you can see the POST or the system splash screen on the monitor and then enter the BIOS Setup. If the screen looks fine during the POST but goes crazy once Windows starts to load, then almost certainly the problem is due to an incorrect setting or configuration of the card. To resolve this problem, boot the system in Windows Safe Mode (hold down the F8 function key as Windows starts to load). This will bypass the current video driver and settings and will place the system in the default VGA mode supported by the BIOS on the video card. When the Windows Desktop appears, you can right-click the Desktop, select Properties, and then reconfigure the video settings or change the drivers as necessary.

If the problem occurs from the moment you turn on the system—and even, for example, if you boot to a DOS floppy, such as a Windows 98 startup floppy—you definitely have a hardware problem with most likely either the video circuit cable, or monitor. First, try replacing the monitor with another one; if the cable is detachable, try replacing that too. If replacing the monitor and cable does not solve the problem, most likely the video circuit in the laptop is defective. Because laptops use integrated video or a discrete chip built in to the motherboard, you will need to service or replace the unit.

The system runs fine for a few minutes but then freezes or locks up.

The system freezing or locking up is the classic symptom of a system that is overheating. Most likely, it is the CPU that is overheating, but it can also be other components such as the video card or motherboard chipset. If the system is brand new, it is possible that the design is insufficient for proper cooling, and a replacement heat spreader or other solutions may be required. If the system is one that was working fine but now is exhibiting the problem, check to see whether the problem started after any recent changes were made. If so, determine whatever change could be the cause of the problem. If not, most likely something such as a cooling fan has either failed or is starting to fail.

Tip

Cooling fans are often controlled by the system BIOS. If you flash update your laptop's BIOS and notice that your system's cooling fan is running erratically or not at all, the BIOS update is a likely culprit.

If a laptop system locks up when additional memory is installed, the additional heat from the memory module might appear to be the cause, but in reality the problem could be that the system wasn't designed with adequate thermal protection.

When the processor's heatsink or the system's heat spreader is removed and better thermal transfer material is applied between the processor and the heatsink or the heat spreader and hardware, many of these systems run reliably with both standard and additional amounts of memory installed. With some models, a firmware and keyboard driver upgrade also improves system cooling (the keyboard driver helps control the power-management features of many typical laptops). Make sure the fan built in to your laptop is spinning: Use your hand to make sure there's airflow. These fans are very small and virtually silent in normal operation. If the laptop's fan is making grinding or growling noises, it is probably experiencing bearing failure. Note that many newer systems have thermostatically controlled fans. In these systems, it is normal for the fan speeds to change with the temperature. Make sure the chassis is several inches from walls and that the fan ports are unobstructed. I also recommend raising up all four corners of the laptop to improve airflow underneath the unit. If your laptop doesn't have swing-out legs, you can get additional supports or cooling devices from a variety of vendors.

If your laptop has a socketed processor, you can try to improve cooling by removing and reseating the processor. Reinstall the CPU heatsink or system heat spreader with new thermal-interface material; many users prefer to use silver-based thermal material to provide better heat transfer. Check the power adapter for correct voltage and make sure the battery doesn't overheat when charged. Try replacing the power adapter with a high-quality replacement or a known-good spare.

I am experiencing intermittent problems with the hard drive(s).

Most systems use ATA (AT Attachment, commonly called *IDE*) interface drives, which consist of a drive and integrated controller, a ribbon cable, and a host adapter circuit in the motherboard. Most often intermittent problems are found with the cable and the drive; it is far more rare that the host adapter will fail or exhibit problems. Many problems occur with the cables. The laptop version of the ATA drive uses a 44-pin connector that integrates power and data connectors.

Check the cable to be sure it is not cut or damaged, and try unplugging and replugging it into the drive and motherboard. If replacing the cable does not help, try replacing the drive with a spare, installing an OS, and then testing it to see whether the problem remains. If it does, the problem is with the motherboard, which will most likely need to be replaced. If it doesn't, the problem was most likely with your original drive. You can simply replace it or try testing, formatting, and reinstalling to see whether the drive can be repaired. To do this, you will need the low-level format or test software provided by the drive manufacturer. These programs can be downloaded from the drive vendors' websites.

The system is experiencing intermittent memory errors.

If the memory was recently added or some other change was made to the system, I would suggest undoing that addition/change to see whether it is the cause. If it's not, try removing and reseating all memory modules. If the contacts look corroded, try cleaning them with contact cleaner and then apply contact enhancer for protection. Check the memory settings in the BIOS Setup; generally, all settings should be on automatic. Try upgrading to the latest BIOS for your motherboard. Try removing all memory except one bank. Note that if the laptop doesn't have removable memory, you need to service the system if the memory displays errors. If the system has removable memory, replace the module with a new or known-good spare.

If you get this far, the problem is most likely either the motherboard or the power supply, or possibly some other component in the system. Try removing other components from the system to see whether they are causing problems. Try reseating the CPU. Try replacing the power adapter with a known-good spare.

I installed a 60GB drive in my system, but it is recognizing only 8.4GB.

Motherboard ROM BIOSes have been updated throughout the years to support larger and larger drives. BIOSes older than August 1994 will generally be limited to drives of up to 528MB, whereas BIOSes older than January 1998 will generally be limited to 8.4GB. Most BIOSes dated 1998 or newer will support drives up to 137GB, and those dated September 2002 or newer should support drives larger than 137GB. These are only general guidelines. To accurately determine this for a specific system, you should check with your motherboard manufacturer. You can also use the BIOS Wizard utility from www.unicore.com/bioswiz/index2.html. It will tell you the BIOS date from your system and specifically whether your system supports the Enhanced Disk Drive specification, which means drives over 8.4GB.

If your BIOS does not support EDD (drives over 8.4GB), you have two possible solutions:

- Upgrade your motherboard BIOS to a 1998 or newer version that supports sizes larger than 8.4GB.
- Install a software patch to add support for sizes larger than 8.4GB. Vendors that supply replacement drives for laptops usually provide these software patches as part of the installation kit.

Of these possible solutions, the first one is the most desirable because it is normally free. Visit your motherboard manufacturer's website to see whether it has a newer BIOS available for your motherboard that will support large drives. I almost never recommend the software patch solution because it merely installs a special driver in the boot sector area of the hard drive, which can result in numerous problems when booting from different drives, installing new drives, or recovering data.

The 137GB barrier is a bit more complicated because there are not only BIOS issues but also operating system and chipset-based ATA host adapter driver issues as well. Drives larger than 137GB are accessed using 48-bit logical block address (LBA) numbers, which require BIOS support, chipset driver support, and operating systems support. Generally, you will need a BIOS with 48-bit LBA support (normally dated September 2002 or newer); the latest chipset driver, such as the Intel Application Accelerator (for motherboards using Intel chipsets; go to www.intel.com/support/chipsets/iaa); and Windows XP with Service Pack 1 (or later) installed. The original version of XP and Windows 2000/NT and Windows 95/98/Me do not currently provide native support for hard drives that are larger than 137GB.

If you have a system without BIOS support, check with your motherboard manufacturer for an update. If your motherboard uses a non-Intel chipset, check with the motherboard or chipset manufacturer for driver updates to enable 48-bit LBA support.

My CD-ROM/DVD drive doesn't work.

The CD/DVD drive is one of the more failure-prone components in a laptop. It is not uncommon for one to suddenly fail after a year or so of use. If the drive plugs into a swappable drive bay, remove and reinstall the drive. If the drive is built in to the system, open the system (if possible) and make sure the drive is properly plugged into the system. Make sure the BIOS Setup is set properly for the drive and verify that the drive is detected during the boot process. Finally, try replacing the drive and, if necessary, the motherboard. If the drive has already been installed and was working before, first try reading different discs, preferably commercial stamped discs rather than writeable or rewriteable ones. Then try the preceding steps.

Note

If a rewritable CD or DVD drive reads media but can't write to the media, make sure the CD or DVD creation software you are using supports the drive. If you are not using the software provided with the system, you might need to download updates from the software vendor to enable support for your drive. If you are using Windows XP, you can have problems if Windows XP is configured to handle the drive as a rewritable drive and you are also using third-party software. To disable Windows XP's own recording feature, right-click the drive in My Computer, click the Recording tab, and clear the check box next to Enable CD Recording for this drive.

My USB port or device doesn't work.

Make sure you have enabled the USB ports in the BIOS Setup. Make sure your operating system supports USB; Windows 95 Version A and NT do not, whereas Windows 98 and later do have USB support. Try removing any hubs and plugging the device directly into the root hub connections on your system. Try replacing the cable. Because many USB devices require additional power, ensure that your device has an external power supply connected if one is required. Then try replacing the computer's power adapter.

Tip

If you want to use a hub with USB devices, I recommend using a generic hub that has its own AC power source (a self-powered hub). Self-powered hubs provide a full 500mA of power for each USB port, but bus-powered hubs provide only 100mA of power (or less) per port. Therefore, a self-powered hub can be used with devices that require more power than a bus-powered hub can provide.

If the laptop has USB 2.0 (Hi-Speed USB) ports, but they aren't recognized as Hi-Speed USB ports by external hard or optical drives designed for Hi-Speed USB, make sure you have done the following:

- Enabled Hi-Speed USB (USB 2.0) support in the system BIOS.
- Installed the correct Hi-Speed USB (USB 2.0) drivers for the chipset and version of Windows in use.

I installed an additional memory module, but the system doesn't recognize it.

Verify that the memory is compatible with your laptop. Many subtle variations on memory types that may appear to be identical on the surface can cause a memory module to be incompatible with a given system. Just because the memory module will fit in the slot does not mean it will work properly with your system. Check your laptop manual for the specific type of memory your system requires and possibly for a list of supported modules. You can visit www.crucial.com and use its memory selector to determine the exact type of memory for a specific system or motherboard. Also note that all motherboards have limits to the amount of memory they will support; many boards today will support only up to 512MB or 1GB. Again, consult the motherboard manual or manufacturer for information on the limits for your board. If you are sure you have the correct type of memory, follow the memory troubleshooting steps listed previously for intermittent memory problems.

While I was updating my BIOS, the system froze and now the system is dead!

This problem can occur when a flash ROM upgrade goes awry. Contact the laptop vendor to determine if your system supports a feature called BIOS recovery or if you need to return your laptop for service. BIOS recovery is designed to reflash the BIOS from an image file on a floppy disk, depending on the system. Unlike the BIOS recovery feature found on some motherboards (in which a motherboard jumper is moved to enable this option), the few laptop systems that support this feature typically use special keystroke combinations.

As an alternative to returning your system to the vendor for a replacement BIOS in the event of a failed BIOS flash update, you can contact ACS Computer Services for its LaptopBIOS repair/recovery service (www.laptopbios.com). Prices range from about $100 to $130. This option is considerably less expensive than returning a typical system to the vendor for a nonwarranty repair.

CHAPTER 17

Portable Resource Guide

Documentation

Laptop/notebook systems are notoriously proprietary in their construction. Unlike a typical desktop system, many of the components in a modern laptop are unique and are not interchangeable with other laptops, possibly even with other systems from the same manufacturer. Because of their somewhat proprietary nature, it is more important that you have good documentation to facilitate future upgrades and repairs.

Because many of the components are unique, they are often not interchangeable with other systems and in many cases can be ordered only from the manufacturer. Most manufacturers do not publish parts lists, and many do not sell spare parts direct to the public, or at all. This means that a simple part failure can render the system inoperable, and you will be at the mercy of the manufacturer for spare parts or repairs. If the system is out of warranty, such repairs can be either impossible or exorbitantly expensive, often approaching the cost of purchasing a newer, faster system.

Most laptop systems are more difficult to disassemble than desktop systems. Laptop systems typically have many more screws than desktop systems, and the screws come in a number of different sizes and styles and are often hidden under stickers and covers. For example, a typical laptop, such as the ThinkPad R-series, is assembled with more than 85 screws of eight different types! The chassis covers are often constructed of thin plastic parts that interlock and can be tricky to separate without damage. Unlike desktop systems, which are substantially similar internally, laptop systems can vary greatly from manufacturer to manufacturer, and even from model to model. For this reason, it really helps to have specific documentation on disassembly/reassembly as well as parts listings from the system manufacturer.

Unfortunately, most of the laptop systems on the market do not have adequate documentation. By this, I mean documentation that includes a parts list, instructions on how to disassemble the unit, and information about any unique troubleshooting procedures specific to the system. In fact, it is somewhat difficult for me to write about this topic because there are currently only two laptop/notebook manufacturers/vendors that produce what I consider adequate documentation for their systems: Lenovo ThinkPad (formerly IBM) and Dell. This sorry state of affairs means that most systems on the market simply do not have adequate documentation, making them somewhat risky to own, because you are at the mercy of the vendor or manufacturer for future support. Self-support and self-service are everything I stand for, and they are difficult to achieve without the proper documentation.

Lenovo's ThinkPad laptops are generally considered the best laptop/notebook systems in the world, and this is not only due to their quality and design but their documentation as well. Lenovo sets the standard for documentation, and the simple truth is, no other systems in the world have the same level of documentation and support. The reason is that Lenovo publishes hardware maintenance manuals, service and troubleshooting guides, technical reference manuals, and user manuals for all its systems, and it makes them available for no charge on its website. These documents include complete disassembly and reassembly instructions and a complete parts list, including detailed exploded diagrams and part numbers. The detailed service manuals also provide the information needed to accomplish specific component replacements and upgrades that would be daunting on other systems lacking this information. In essence, Lenovo's superior documentation makes its ThinkPad systems the most upgradeable laptop systems in the world.

Dell is another standout, providing detailed service manuals available for downloading from its website for all its laptop systems. In fact, the unfortunate reality is that currently the only laptop system manufacturers that do make service manuals available to end users are Lenovo and Dell! That is perhaps one of the biggest reasons these two manufacturers are among my favorites when it comes to laptops.

Although Dell's documentation does include disassembly and reassembly instructions, unfortunately it does not include a detailed parts list. This means that to order a specific part, you'll need to describe it to a Dell representative over the phone, which often results in confusion over exactly which part you will receive. Even so, Dell provides documentation that is superior to all other manufacturers except Lenovo.

Toshiba used to make service manuals available for purchase in printed form, but in the last few years Toshiba has changed its policy, and service manuals are now available only to Toshiba-authorized dealers. The good thing is that in most cases, if you purchase a repair or replacement part from one of the premier Toshiba Authorized Service Providers (ASPs), such as MicroSolutions (www.micsol.com), the ASP will include copies of the relevant pages from the service manual describing in detail the procedure for removing the old part and installing the new one in the system.

Most if not all other laptop/notebook system manufacturers do not provide service manuals for their systems, which I consider to be a major drawback. Virtually all of them do provide user manuals, though, which sometimes include simple troubleshooting or maintenance procedures, but these are not at the same level as a true service manual. Before you purchase a laptop system, I highly recommend that you check to see what type of documentation is available. In most cases, this means searching the manufacturer's website for any manuals associated with the system you are considering. You should download any documentation you find, and examine it thoroughly not only to see if the information is adequate, but also simply to find out more about the system you want to purchase. I normally make a point to avoid any systems for which I can't get detailed service or technical information from the manufacturer, because manuals make future repairs and upgrades much easier.

In searching for documentation and spare parts for a system, I usually try to go direct to the manufacturer. This has led me to discover an interesting "secret" of the laptop business that isn't often discussed—the fact that many of the well-known laptop brands you might be familiar with are actually designed and manufactured by a handful of contract manufacturers located in Taiwan. Often the term *OEM* (original equipment manufacturer) or *ODM* (original design manufacturer) is used to describe the company that actually designs and manufactures an item, as opposed to the company that merely sells it. For example, the HP OmniBook 6200 and Apple iBook are made by Compal, the Compaq Presario 700 is made by Arima, and the Dell Latitude D400 is made by Wistron (Acer). Taiwanese companies such as Quanta, Compal, Wistron, Inventec, and Arima make the majority of laptop computers in the world, which are marketed and sold under other (more familiar) names. Interestingly enough, these OEM/ODM companies rarely sell systems under their own names. Instead, they prefer only to do contract manufacturing for specific vendors, allowing the vendor to sell, service, and support the systems. Table 17.1 lists the top OEM/ODM laptop system manufacturers in Taiwan.

Table 17.1   The Top OEM/ODM Laptop Computer Makers in Taiwan for 2003

Ranking	Company	Est. 2003 Shipments (Thousands)	Website
1	Quanta	8,440	www.quantatw.com
2	Compal	5,400	www.compal.com
3	Wistron (Acer)	1,930	www.wistron.com.tw
4	Inventec	1,540	www.inventec.com
5	Arima	1,500	www.arima.com.tw
6	FIC	1,500	www.fic.com.tw
7	MiTAC	1,200	www.mitac.com.tw
8	ASUSTeK	1,150	www.asus.com.tw

(continues)

Table 17.1   Continued

Ranking	Company	Est. 2003 Shipments (Thousands)	Website
9	Uniwill	1,100	www.uniwill.com.tw
10	Twinhead	900	www.twinhead.com.tw
11	Clevo	490	www.clevo.com.tw
12	BenQ	400	www.benq.com.tw
13	ECS - EliteGroup	250	www.ecs.com.tw

Shipments in thousands of units. Forecast based on first half 2003 data.

Source: TaiwanHighTech.com

OEM/ODM companies such as these rarely sell systems under their own names; instead, they design and manufacture them for other companies under contract. In fact, according to sales information Quanta is the largest laptop manufacturer in the world, although none of its systems are sold under the Quanta name. The next largest manufacturer after Quanta is currently Toshiba, followed by Compal, Fujitsu-Siemens, and Lenovo (refer to Table 17.2).

Table 17.2   Top Laptop Computer Manufacturers, Ranked by Units Shipped in the First Quarter of 2003

Rank	Company	Units Shipped (Thousands)
1	Quanta	1,930
2	Toshiba	1,230
3	Compal	1,000
4	Fujitsu-Siemens	665
5	IBM/Lenovo	638

Shipments in thousands of units, first quarter 2003.

Source: TaiwanHighTech.com and IDC

Toshiba had been the largest laptop manufacturer practically every year since the mid 1980s—that is until Quanta and Compal both outsold Toshiba in 2001. More recently, Toshiba sales have been gaining, and it took second place back from Compal and is gaining on Quanta. Quanta's ace in the hole is that it has become the primary contract manufacturer for Dell, which is Quanta's largest customer. Quanta also makes systems for HP, Compaq, eMachines, Best Buy, and Apple, among others. Dell also purchases laptops from Compal and Wistron (Acer), so it isn't tied to one supplier. Now you can see why Dell's different model lines look so different—they were actually designed and manufactured by different companies. Contract manufacturing by companies such as Quanta and Compal is also the main reason why you see so many different brands of laptop systems that seem to look identical to one another. One potential drawback of the OEM/ODM game is that it is more difficult for companies to support the systems they sell, because in reality they didn't make them and may not have direct access to the parts and manufacturing.

Going by sales rather than just manufacturing, Table 17.3 lists the top laptop computer companies.

Table 17.3   Top Laptop Computer Brands, Ranked by First Quarter 2003 Units Shipped

Rank	Company (Brand)	Units Shipped (Thousands)
1	HP/Compaq	1,370
2	Dell	1,240
3	Toshiba	1,230
4	Fujitsu/Siemens	665
5	IBM/Lenovo	638
6	NEC	482
7	Sony	447
8	Acer	428
9	Apple	298
10	Gateway	111

Shipments in thousands of units.
Source: IDC

Note

If you can figure out who really made your system and can locate that company on the Web, in some cases you'll find more detailed information or be able to get newer drivers and BIOS updates direct from the manufacturer. If you don't know the actual manufacturer of your system and the vendor doesn't provide support, you may be in for difficulty in tracking down repairs and spare parts for your system.

Unfortunately, most OEM/ODM companies don't have support resources available to end users because all their systems are produced under contract for specific vendors who must then provide all service and support, including documentation, driver updates, spare parts, and so on. What this means is that although other companies might make laptops for Dell, HP/Compaq, Gateway, and others, in general you will have to go back to the company whose name is on the system for all your support needs.

FCC ID Database

If you are unsure who is the manufacturer for a given system, and your system is sold in the U.S. and carries an FCC ID number, you may be able to use that number to identify the manufacturer, or at least to find out more about the system. Knowing the manufacturer may help not only for finding documentation but also for finding drivers specific to the system.

The FCC ID database contains records for equipment that has been Certified, Type Accepted, or Verified by the FCC. To locate information on a specific FCC ID, visit `www.fcc.gov/oet/fccid` to enter the ID information and search.

An FCC ID consists of two elements: a grantee code and an equipment product code. The first three characters of the ID are the grantee code, which is permanently assigned to a given company, and which consists of any combination of capital letters and/or numbers. The equipment product code is assigned by the grantee and is from 1 to 14 characters in length, consisting of any combination of capital letters, numbers, and hyphens or dashes.

Laptops that have an FCC ID number would normally have it printed on a label on the underside of the system. To find it, turn the system over and look on any and all stickers or labels for something that reads similar to "FCC ID: XXX1234567890ABCD." In this example the "XXX" is the grantee code and the "1234567890ABCD" is the equipment product code. You can enter this information on the FCC ID search page to look up the records on that particular product.

Unfortunately, due to rule changes over the years, not all electronic equipment sold in the U.S. will have an authorization from the FCC, in which case it will not be in the ID database. In addition, some systems will have a label that merely says "Tested To Comply With FCC Standards," and includes no specific ID. Unfortunately, any equipment displaying that type of label is declared to comply with FCC regulations by the manufacturer or importer and would not be in the FCC ID database as well.

User Forums and Support

Several Internet-based resources are very useful for finding troubleshooting information, technical support, and other information on various laptops. Here are several sites, forums, and groups that I recommend:

- `www.groups.yahoo.com/group/Laptop_Repair`
- `www.notebookforums.com`
- `www.repair4laptop.org`
- `www.thinkpads.com`
- NewsGroup: `comp.sys.laptops`

Repair Parts

Although laptop computers use many proprietary components, a few industry-standard parts can easily be obtained. For example, virtually all systems use either Intel or AMD processors, which can be obtained from many sources. Also, hard disk drives are fairly standardized. Keeping in mind that a few different sizes are available, you can purchase drives for a laptop system from any place that sells 2.5-inch drives. In particular, hard drives that are in the 9.5mm-tall 2.5-inch form factor will fit in practically any system, but those in the taller 2.5-inch form factors may not fit all systems. Other standardized parts include memory and Mini PCI cards, and to a lesser extent internal CD/DVD drives.

For more proprietary parts such as batteries, displays, hinges, drive caddies, AC adapters, and such, you can either go to the original vendor (or manufacturer) or use one of several companies that supply these types of parts, such as

- Excel Computer (`www.excelcomputerinc.com`)
- Impact Computers & Electronics (`www.impactcomputers.com`)
- LaptopRepairco (`www.laptoprepairco.com`)
- Man & Machine (`www.man-machine.com`)
- Micro Notebook (`www.micronotebook.net`)
- Micro Solutions (`www.micsol.com`)
- National Parts Depot (`www.nationalparts.com`)
- PortableComputer (`www.portablecomputer.com`)
- Spare Parts Warehouse (`www.sparepartswarehouse.com`)
- UltraDrives (`www.ultradrives.com`)

These companies supply replacement parts for name-brand systems that are often less expensive than if you were to purchase them from the original manufacturer.

Manufacturer Tech Support

If you have problems with a laptop system, you will often need to contact the manufacturer directly for support, spare parts, system-restoration discs, and more. Especially if you are traveling, it is a good idea to keep the phone number and contact information for your system manufacturer (or supplier) handy. This section lists contact information for some of the more popular manufacturers and suppliers.

Lenovo (Formerly IBM)

Lenovo offers perhaps the best overall support in the industry for laptop systems. The only criticism might be that because the company is so large, there are almost too many resources for help and support. If you are unsure about where to call within Lenovo, you can use the main support contacts:

> Lenovo Group Limited
> One Manhattanville Road, Suite PH
> Purchase, New York 10577-2100
> Phone: 1-866-45THINK (866-458-4465)
>
> Email: http://www.lenovo.com/think/contact/us/en/#
>
> Website: http://www.thinkpad.com

Many of Lenovo's support resources are international, including toll-free numbers.

Primary service and support: 800-IBM-4YOU (800-426-4968)

ThinkPad tech support:

- United States (English): 800-772-2227
- Canada (English/French): 800-565-3344
- Toronto only (English/French): 416-383-3344

Systems/accessories purchase: 888-SHOP-IBM (888-746-7426)

Hardware service: 800-IBM-SERV (800-426-7378)

Maintenance parts: 800-765-5944

Lenovo also provides an extensive website dedicated to mobile computing and to ThinkPad computers at www.thinkpad.com/support. From this site you can download drivers, manuals, updates, bulletins, and more.

Finally, if you have a touch-tone telephone and access to a fax machine, in the United States and Canada you can receive, by fax, marketing and technical information on many topics, including hardware, operating systems, and local area networks (LANs). You can call the Lenovo automated fax system 24 hours a day, 7 days a week.

Follow the recorded instructions, and the requested information will be sent to your fax machine. In the United States and Canada, to access the Lenovo automated fax system, call 800-426-3395.

To determine whether your computer is eligible for International Warranty Service and to view a list of the countries where service is available, go to www.thinkpad.com/support and click Warranty Lookup. You can identify eligible IBM/Lenovo computers by entering their four-digit machine types.

For more information about International Warranty Service, visit `www.thinkpad.com` and in the search box enter **International Warranty Service** and click Search.

Toshiba

Toshiba provides extensive technical support online (`support.toshiba.com`) as well as via toll-free support phone numbers. It also has a nationwide network of ASPs who service and support Toshiba systems.

Technical support: 800-457-7777

Sales information: 800-TOSHIBA or 800-867-4422

Toshiba Accessories: 800-959-4100 (accessories.toshiba.com)

Toshiba repair parts are carried by National Parts Depot at 800-524-8338 (`www.nationalparts.com`).

Information specifically for Toshiba computer resellers may be obtained by calling the Reseller Inside Sales Support Team at 888-800-9128. For online customer service and technical support, visit support.toshiba.com.

Dell

Dell is one of the largest PC manufacturers and vendors in the world. It has an extensive array of support services available online as well as by phone.

Phone (United States):

- Automated order-status system: 800-433-9014
- AutoTech: 800-247-9362
- Consumer technical support: 800-624-9896
- Customer service: 800-624-9897
- DellNet service/support: 877-DELLNET or 877-335-5638
- Software application support: 800-433-9005
- Business service and technical support: 800-822-8965
- Dell sales: 800-289-3355 or 800-879-3355
- Dell outlet store (refurbished computers): 888-798-7561
- Software and peripherals sales: 800-671-3355
- Spare parts sales: 800-357-3355
- Extended service and warranty sales: 800-247-4618
- Fax: 800-727-8320
- Dell Services for the deaf, hard-of-hearing, or speech-impaired: 877-DELL-TTY or 877-335-5889

Phone (Canada):

- Automated order-status system: 800-433-9014
- AutoTech: 800-247-9362
- Customer care (from outside Toronto): 800-387-5759
- Customer care (from within Toronto): 416-758-2400

- Customer technical support: 800-847-4096
- Sales (outside Toronto): 800-387-5752
- Sales (within Toronto): 416-758-2200
- TechFax: 800-950-1329

Web:

- www.dell.com
- support.dell.com (technical support)

HP

HP provides support via telephone as well as online.

Pavilion laptop technical support: 800-HP-INVENT or 800-474-6836

OmniBook technical support: 970-635-1000

Main office: 281-370-0670

Fax: 281-514-1740

HP online support starts at www.hp.com.

Compaq

Compaq (owned by HP) provides support via telephone as well as online.

General information: 800-345-1518

Technical support: 800-652-6672 or 800-OK-Compaq

Fax: 800-345-1518

BBS download facility (modem access): 281-518-1418

Backup software, CD replacements, or user guides: 800-952-7689

Presario technical support: 208-4PC-HELP or 208-472-4357

Customer support website: (www.compaq.com/support)

Presario support website: (www.compaq.com/consumersupport)

Gateway

Gateway provides support via telephone as well as online.

Service and support:

- Online support: support.gateway.com
- Automated troubleshooting hotline: 800-846-2118
- Fax on demand: 800-846-4526
- Automated order-status hotline: 800-846-8529
- Home/home office technical support/customer service: 800-846-2301
- International tech support: 605-232-2191

- Business technical support/customer service: 877-485-1464
- Gateway wireless home networking solutions technical support: 877-485-1465

Sales:

- Home or home office: 800-369-1409
- Any size business: 888-888-1094
- Remanufactured PCs: 800-846-3614
- Add-on sales: 800-846-2117

For sales, accounting, and warranty information or to get information about available systems, pricing, orders, billing statements, warranty service, or other nontechnical issues, call 800-846-2000 (U.S.) or 888-888-2037 (Canada).

TDD (Telecommunications Device for the Deaf):

- 800-846-2301 (U.S.)
- 800-846-3609 (Canada and Puerto Rico)
- 605-232-2191 or 800-846-1778 (all other countries)

Other Systems

There are, of course, many other laptop system manufacturers. Those listed here sell and support laptop systems but are not necessarily as "big" in the laptop world as those already listed. Consequently, I've provided only their basic details.

Acer

Acer global information: www.acer.com

Service and support: www.acersupport.com

Main phone: 408-432-6200 or 800-733-2237

Main fax: 408-922-2933

Sales fax: 254-298-4164

End-user service: 800-816-2237

Laptop/desktop/server technical support: 800-816-2237

Extended warranty department: 800-816-2237

Reseller sales support phone: 800-409-2237

Alienware

Corporate Office:

Main phone: 1-800-ALIENWARE (254-3692)

Main fax: 305-259-9874

Service and support: support.alienware.com

Service and support phone: 866-287-6727

Service and support email: support@alienware.com

MPC

Customer service: 877-894-5693

Technical support: 800-877-8856, 888-FIX-MYPC, or 888-349-6972

FOSA

Sales: 800-216-3672

Service: 800-216-3672

New Jersey line: 908-753-6100

Fax: 908-753-6616

Website: www.fosa.com

Service/RMA (Return Merchandise Authorization): service@fosa.com

Technical support: support@fosa.com

Sager

Technical support: 626-964-4849 or 800-741-2219

Corporate/government/reseller support: 800-669-1624, 626-964-8682, or 626-964-2381

Website: www.sagernotebook.com

Prostar

Main phone: 626-854-3428

Sales: 888-576-6776

Technical support: 888-576-4742

Fax: 626-854-3438

Chem USA

Technical support: 800-866-CHEM, 800-866-2436, or 510-608-8818

Fax (sales): 510-608-8828

Fax (service/support): 510-608-5889

Website: www.chemusa.com or www.chembook.com

Email (sales): sales@chemusa.com

Email (service/support): custserv@chemusa.com

Sony

Sony service center: 888-4-SONY-PC or 888-476-6972

Sony customer service: esupport.sony.com

Additional Important Numbers

America Online: 800-827-6364 (U.S.) or 888-265-4357 (Canada)

Comcast: 800-COMCAST (800-266-2278)

CompuServe: 800-848-8990

EarthLink: 888-EARTHLINK (888-327-8454)

Sprint: 877-6GO-DATA (877-646-3282)

List of Acronyms and Abbreviations

A

a-Si (hydrogenated amorphour silicon)

ABC (Atanasoff-Berry Computer)

ACL (access control list)

ACPI (Advanced Configuration and Power Interface)

ACR (advanced communications riser)

ADC (analog-to-digital converter)

ADPCM (adaptive differential pulse code modulation)

ADR (advanced digital recording)

ADSL (asymmetric DSL)

AFC (antiferromagnetically coupled)

AGC (automatic gain control)

AGP (Accelerated Graphics Port)

AHA (accelerated hub architecture)

AHRA (Audio Home Recording Act)

AIT (advanced intelligent tape)

ALDC (advanced lossless data compression)

ALi (Acer Laboratories, Inc.)

AMD (Advanced Micro Devices)

AMI (American Megatrends, Inc.)

AMR (anistropic magneto-resistant)

AMR (audio modem riser)

ANSI (American National Standards Institute)

API (Application Programming Interface)

APIC (advanced programmable interrupt controller)

APM (Advanced Power Management)

APS (analog protection system)

ARLL (advanced run length limited)

ASP (Authorized Service Provider)

ASPI (Advanced SCSI Programming Interface)

AT (Advanced Technology)

ATA (AT Attachment)

ATAPI (AT Attachment Packet Interface)

ATF (auto tracking following)

AWG (American Wire Gauge)

B

BASIC (beginner's all-purpose symbolic instruction code)

BBSs (bulletin board systems)

BBUL (bumpless build-up layer)

BEDO RAM (burst extended data out RAM)

BF (bus frequency)

BiCMOS (bipolar complementary metal-oxide semiconductor)

BIOS (basic input/output system)

BLER (block error rate)

BOOTP (bootstrap protocol)

BRI (basic rate interface)

BSOD (blue screen of death)

BTB (branch target buffer)

BURN-Proof (Buffer Under-RuN error Proof)

C

CAB (cabinet file)

CAM (common access method)

CAM ATA (Common Access Method AT Attachment)

CAP (carrierless amplitude/phase)

CAS (column address strobe)

CAT (category)

CATV (community access television)

CCITT (Comite Consultatif International Telephonique et Telegraphique)

CD (compact disc)

CD-DA (compact disc digital audio)

CD-MO (compact disc magneto-optical)

CD-R (compact disc-recordable)

CD-ROM (compact disc read-only memory)

CD-RW (compact disc-rewritable)

CDMA (code-division multiple access)

CDSL (consumer DSL)

CERN (Organisation Europèen pour la Recherche Nuclèaire, or European Organization for Nuclear Research)

CF (compact flash)

CFCs (chlorofluorocarbons)

CGA (color graphics adapter)

CHAP (Challenge-Handshake Authentication Protocol)

CHS (cylinder head sector)

CIRC (cross-interleave Reed-Solomon code)

CISC (complex instruction set computer)

CLKMUL (clock multiplier)

CLV (constant linear velocity)

CMYK (cyan magenta yellow black)

CNR (Communications and Networking Riser)

COC (chip on ceramic)

CPU (central processing unit)

CRC (cyclical redundancy checking)

CRT (cathode-ray tube)

CS (cable select)

CS (central switch)

CSA (Canadian Standards Agency)

CSEL (cable select)

CSMA/CD (carrier sense multiple access/collision detect)

CSS (contact start stop)

CSS (content scramble system)

CTFT (color thin film transistor)

D

DAC (digital-to-analog converter)

DAE (digital audio extraction)

DASD (direct access storage device)

DASP (drive action/slave present)

DAT (digital audio tape)

db (decibel)

DBB (dynamic bass boost)

DBR (DOS boot record)

DCC (direct cable connection)

DDMA (Distributed DMA)

DDR SDRAM (double data rate SDRAM)

DDS (digital data storage)

DDWG (Digital Display Working Group)

DFP (digital flat panel)

DFT (drive fitness test)

DIB (dual independent bus)

DIMM (dual inline memory module)

DIN (Deutsches Institut für Normung e.V.)

DIP (dual inline package)

DIVX (Digital Video Express)

DLT (digital linear tape)

DMA (direct memory access)

DMM (digital multimeter)

DMT (discrete multitone)

DOCSIS (data over cable service interface specifications)

DOS (disk operating system)

DPMI (DOS protected mode interface)

DPMS (display power-management signaling)

DRAM (dynamic RAM)

DSK (Dvorak simplified keyboard)

DSL (Digital Subscriber Line)

DSLAM (DSL access multiplier)

DSP (digital signal processor)

DSTN (Double-layer SuperTwist Nematic) LCD

DVD (digital versatile disc)

DVD-R (DVD-recordable)

DVD+RW (DVD phase change rewritable)

DVI (Digital Video Interactive)

DVI (Digital Visual Interface)

E

EAX (environmental audio extensions)

ECC (error correcting code)

ECP (enhanced capabilities port)

EDD (enhanced disk drive)

EDO RAM (extended data out RAM)

EEPROM (electrically erasable programmable ROM)

EFM (eight to fourteen modulation) data encoding

EFS (encrypted file system)

EGA (enhanced graphics adapter)

EIDE (Enhanced IDE)

EISA (Extended Industry Standard Architecture)

ELF (extremely low frequency)

EMI (electromagnetic interference)

ENIAC (Electrical Numerical Integrator and Calculator)

EPIC (explicitly parallel instruction computing)

EPP (Enhanced Parallel Port)

EPROM (erasable programmable ROM)

ESD (electrostatic discharge)

F

FAP (Fair Access Policy)

FAQ (frequently asked questions)

FAT (file allocation table)

FC-PGA (flip-chip pin grid array)

FCC (Federal Communications Commission)

FDDI (Fiber Distributed Data Interface)

FDIV (floating-point divide)

FIC (flex interconnect cable)

FIFO (first in first out)

FM (Frequency modulation)

FPM DRAM (Fast Page Mode DRAM)

FPT (forced perfect termination)

FPU (floating-point unit)

FSB (front-side bus)

FSK (frequency-shift keying)

FST (flat square tube)

FTP (File Transfer Protocol)

FUD (fear, uncertainty, and doubt)

FWH (Firmware hub)

G

GB (gigabyte)

GHz (gigahertz)

GiB (gigabinary bytes)

GMCH (graphics memory controller hub)

GMR (giant magnetoresistive)

GPA (graphics performance accelerator)

H

HAN (home area network)

HD-ROM (high-density read-only memory)

HDA (head disk assembly)

HDD (hard disk drive)

HDTV (high-definition television)

HER (hard error rate)

HFC (hybrid fiber/coax)

HFS (Hierarchical file system)

HID (Human interface device)

HLF (high-level formatting)

HMA (high memory area)

HP (Hewlett-Packard)

HPFS (High performance file system)

HRTF (Head-related transfer function)

HVD (High voltage differential)

Hz (Hertz)

I

I/O (input/output)

IC (integrated circuit)

ICH (Integrated controller hub)

iCOMP (Intel Comparative Microprocessor Performance)

ICS (Internet Connection Sharing)

IDE (Integrated Drive Electronics)

IEC (International Electrotechnical Commission)

IED (ID error detection)

IEEE (Institute of Electrical and Electronic Engineers)

IMA (Interactive Multimedia Association)

IMAPI (image mastering application program interface)

IML (Initial microcode load)

INCITS (InterNational Committee on Information Technology Standards)

IOS (input/output supervisor)

IP (Internet Protocol)

IPL (initial program load)

IPS (in-plane switching)

IPX (Internetwork packet exchange)

IR (infrared)

IrDA (infrared data)

IRQ (interrupt request)

ISA (Industry Standard Architecture)

ISDN (Integrated Services Digital Network)

ISO (International Standards Organization)

ISP (Internet service provider)

ITU (International Telecommunication Union)

J–K

JPEG (Joint Photographic Experts Group)

Kb (kilobit) 1,000 bits

KB (kilobyte) 1,000 bytes

KHz (kilohertz)

Kib (kibibit) 1,024 bits

KiB (kibibyte) 1,024 bytes

KVAR (kilovolt-amperes-reactive)

KVM (keyboard, video, mouse)

KW/KVA (working power/apparent power)

L

L1 (Level 1)

L2 (Level 2)

LAN (local area network)

LBA (logical block address/addressing)

LCD (liquid crystal display)

LED (light-emitting diode)

LIF (Low Insertion Force)

LIM (Lotus Intel Microsoft)

LLF (low-level formatting)

LPT (line printer)

LTO (Linear tape-open)

LVD (Low voltage differential)

M

MAU (media access unit or media attachment unit)

Mb (megabit) 1,000,000 bits

MB (megabyte) 1,000,000 bytes

MBR (master boot record)

MC (microcartridge)

MCA (MicroChannel Architecture)

MCH (memory controller hub)

MCM (multichip module)

MFM (modified frequency modulation)

MFT (master file table)

MHz (megahertz)

Mib (mebibit) 1,048,576 bits

MiB (mebibyte) 1,048,576 bytes

MIC (Memory in cassette)

MIDI (musical instrument digital interface)

MMC (MultiMediaCard)

MMU (memory management unit)

MMX (multimedia extensions or matrix math extensions)

MNP (Microcom Networking Protocol)

MO (magneto-optical)

modem (modulator/demodulator)

MOV (metal-oxide varistor)

MPEG (Motion Picture Experts Group)

MPS (Multiprocessor Specification)

MR (Microid Research)

MRH-R (memory repeater hub RDRAM-based)

MRH-S (memory repeater hub SDRAM-based)

MS (Microsoft)

MS-DOS (Microsoft disk operating system)

MSAU (multistation access unit)

MTBF (mean time between failures)

MTH (Memory translator hub)

MTTF (Mean time to failure)

MVA (multidomain vertical alignment)

N

NAS (network attached storage)

NDP (numeric data processor)

NEAT (New Enhanced AT)

NetBEUI (NetBIOS Extended User Interface)

NetBIOS (network basic input/output system)

NIC (network interface card)

NiCd (nickel cadmium)

NiFe (nickel ferrite)

NiMH (nickel metal hydride)

NMI (nonmaskable interrupt)

NRTC (National Rural Telecommunications Cooperative)

NRZ (non-return to zero)

NTFS (New Technology File System)

NTSC (National Television Standards Committee)

NVRAM (nonvolatile RAM)

O

OC (optical carrier)

OCR (optical character recognition)

OD (overdrive)

ODM (original design manufacturer)

OEM (original equipment manufacturer)

OLGA (organic land grid array)

OS (operating system)

OSI (open systems interconnection)

OSO (overscan operation)

OSTA (Optical Storage Technology Association)

OTP (one-time programmable)

OTP (opposite track path)

P

p-Si (low-temperature polysilicon)

PAC (PCI/AGP Controller)

PAC (pin array cartridge)

PAL (Phase Alternating Line)

PARD (periodic and random deviation)

PC-DOS (personal computer disk operating system)

PCA (power calibration area)

PCI (Peripheral Component Interconnect)

PCMCIA (Personal Computer Memory Card International Association)

PDA (personal digital assistant)

PDF (Portable Document Format)

PFA (predictive failure analysis)

PFC (power factor correction)

PGA (pin grid array)

PH (PCI controller hub)

PI (parity inner)

PIIX (PCI ISA IDE Xcelerator)

PIO (programmed input/output)

PLCC (plastic leaded chip carrier)

PLGA (plastic land grid array)

PMA (power memory area)

PnP (Plug and Play)

PO (parity outer)

PoP (point of presence)

POP3 (Post Office Protocol 3)

POST (Power On Self Test)

POTS (Plain Old Telephone Service)

PPD (parallel presence detect)

PPD file (postscript printer description file)

PPGA (plastic pin grid array)

PPI (Programmable Peripheral Interface)

PQFP (plastic quad flat pack)

PRI (primary rate interface)

PRML (Partial-Response Maximum-Likelihood)

PROM (programmable ROM)

PSK (phase-shift keying)

PTP (parallel track path)

Q

QAM (quadrature amplitude modulation)

QEGA (quantum extended graphics array)

QFE (quick fix engineering)

QoS (quality of service)

R

RAB (RAID Advisory Board)

RAID (redundant array of independent disks)

RAM (random access memory)

RAMAC (Random Access Method of Accounting and Control)

RAMDAC (RAM digital-to-analog converter)

RBOC (regional Bell operating company)

RDRAM (Rambus DRAM)

RF (radio frequency)

RFI (radio-frequency interference)

RGB (red green blue)

RIAA (Recording Industry Association of America)

RIMM (Rambus inline memory module)

RISC (reduced instruction set computer)

RLL (run length limited)

RNG (random number generator)

ROM (read-only memory)

RPC (regional playback control)

RRIP (Rock Ridge Interchange Protocol)

RTC (real-time clock)

RTC/NVRAM (real-time clock/nonvolatile memory)

S

SACD (super audio compact disc)

SAL (soft adjacent layer)

SASI (Shugart Associates System Interface)

SATA (Serial ATA)

SCAT (Single Chip AT)

SCMS (serial copy management system)

SCSI (small computer system interface)

SD (super density or secure digital)

SDRAM (synchronous DRAM)

SDSL (symmetrical DSL)

SE (single ended)

SEC (single edge contact)

SEC-DED (single-bit error-correction double-bit error detection)

SECAM (Sequential Couleur Avec Memoire)

SECC (single edge contact cartridge)

SEP (single edge processor)

SER (soft error rate)

SGRAM (synchronous graphics RAM)

SIMM (single inline memory module)

SIPP (single inline pin package)

SiS (Silicon Integrated Systems)

SMART (Self-Monitoring Analysis and Reporting Technology)

SMI (system management interrupt)

SMM (system management mode)

SNR (signal-to-noise ratio)

SPD (serial presence detect)

SPDIF (Sony/Philips Digital Interface)

SPGA (staggered pin grid array)

SPI (SCSI Parallel Interface)

SPS (standby power supply)

SPSYNC (spindle synchronization)

SRAM (static RAM)

SSE (Streaming SIMD Extensions)

STP (shielded twisted pair)

SVGA (super video graphics array)

SWAP (Shared Wireless Access Protocol)

SXGA (super extended graphics array)

T

TAD (telephone answering device)

TAO (track-at-once)

TAPI (Telephony Application Programming Interface)

TCP (tape carrier packaging)

TCP/IP (Transmission Control Protocol/Internet Protocol)

TDMA (transparent DMA)

TDMA (time-division multiple access)

TFT (thin film transistor)

TIP (Trouble In Paradise)

TLB (translation lookaside buffer)

TPI (tracks per inch)

TSOP (thin small outline package)

TSR (terminate-and-stay-resident)

U

UART (Universal Asynchronous Receiver Transmitter)

UDF (Universal Disk Format)

UDMA (Ultra DMA)

UI (user interface)

UL (Underwriters Laboratories)

UMA (unified memory architecture)

UMA (upper memory area)

UMB (upper memory block)

UNIVAC (Universal Automatic Computer)

UPI (Universal Peripheral Interface)

UPnP (Universal Plug and Play)

UPS (uninterruptible power supply)

URL (uniform resource locator)

USB (universal serial bus)

USN (update sequence number)

UTP (unshielded twisted pair)

UXGA (Ultra Extended Graphics Array)

V

VAFC (VESA Advanced Feature Connector)

VBR (volume boot record)

VESA (Video Electronics Standards Association)

VESA VIP (Video Interface Port)

VFAT (virtual file allocation table)

VFC (video feature connector)

VGA (video graphics array)

VID (voltage identification)

VIS (viewable image size)

VLF (very low frequency)

VLSI (very large scale integration)

VM (virtual machine)

VMC (VESA Media Channel)

VoIP (voice over IP)

VRM (voltage regular module)

VRT (voltage reduction technology)

VxD (virtual device driver)

W–X

W2K (Windows 2000)

WAN (wide area network)

WAP (Wireless Application Protocol)

WBR (wireless broadband router)

WEP (wired equivalent privacy)

Wi-Fi (Wireless Fidelity)

WORM (write once read many)

XA (extended architecture)

XGA (extended graphics array)

XMS (Extended Memory Specification)

Y–Z

Y2K (year 2000)

ZBR (zoned-bit recording)

ZIF (zero insertion force)

ZV (zoomed video)

Glossary

This glossary contains computer and electronics terms that are applicable to the subject matter in this book. The glossary is meant to be as comprehensive as possible on the subject of upgrading and repairing laptop and desktop PCs. Many terms correspond to the latest technology in disk interfaces, modems, video and display equipment, and standards that govern the PC industry. Although a glossary is a resource not designed to be read from beginning to end, you should find that scanning through this one is interesting, if not enlightening, with respect to some of the newer computer technology.

The computer industry is filled with abbreviations used as shorthand for a number of terms. This glossary defines many abbreviations, as well as the terms on which the abbreviations are based. The definition of an abbreviation usually is included under the acronym. For example, *video graphics array* is defined under the abbreviation *VGA* rather than under *video graphics array*. This organization makes looking up a term easier—*IDE*, for example—even if you do not know in advance what it stands for (*integrated drive electronics*).

These websites can also help you with terms not included in this glossary:

    webservices.cnet.com/cgi/Glossary.asp

    www.webopedia.com

    whatis.techtarget.com

    www.wikipedia.org

1–50X CD-ROM maximum speeds in relation to the speed of a music CD (1X = 150KBps). At speeds of 16X or above, most drives are CAV and reach their rated speeds only on the outer edges of the disc. See also *CLV* and *CAV*.

3GIO The original name for PCI Express, a forthcoming replacement for existing PCI connections. See also *PCI Express*.

10BASE-2 IEEE standard for baseband Ethernet at 10Mbps over RG-58 coaxial cable to a maximum distance of 185 meters. Also known as Thin Ethernet (Thinnet) or IEEE 802.3.

10BASE-5 IEEE standard for baseband Ethernet at 10Mbps over thick coaxial cable to a maximum distance of 500 meters. Also known as Thick Ethernet or Thicknet.

10BASE-T A 10Mbps CSMA/CD Ethernet LAN that works on Category 3 or better twisted-pair wiring, which is very similar to standard telephone cabling. 10BASE-T Ethernet LANs work on a "star" configuration, in which the wire from each workstation routes directly to a 10BASE-T hub. Hubs can be joined together. 10BASE-T has a maximum distance of 100 meters between each workstation and the hub.

24x7 Refers to continuous 24 hours a day, 7 days a week computer or services operation.

56K The generic term for modems that can receive data at a maximum rate of 56Kbps. See also *V.90, V.92, X2, K56flex*.

64-bit processor A processor that has 64-bit registers. The Intel Itanium and Itanium 2 processors for workstations and servers, which can also emulate 32-bit Intel processors; the AMD Athlon 64 desktop processor, which also emulates 32-bit x86 Intel and AMD processors; and the AMD Opteron, designed for use in server and workstation tasks, are some of the 64-bit processors now available.

100BASE-T A 100Mbps CSMA/CD Ethernet local area network (LAN) that works on Category 5 twisted-pair wiring. 100BASE-T Ethernet LANs work on a "star" configuration in which the wire from each workstation routes directly to a central 100BASE-T hub. This is the current standard for 100Mbps Ethernet, replacing 100BASE-VG.

100BASE-VG The joint Hewlett-Packard–AT&T proposal for Fast Ethernet running at 100Mbps. It uses four pairs of Category 5 cable using the 10BASE-T twisted-pair wiring scheme to transmit or receive. 100BASE-VG splits the signal across the four wire pairs at 25MHz each. This standard has not found favor with corporations and has been almost totally replaced by 100BASE-T.

286 See *80286*.

386 See *80386DX*.

404 Website error code indicating the specified page is not found. Some websites display a customized error message instead of the standard 404 code.

486 See *80486DX*.

586 A generic term used to refer to fifth-generation processors similar to the Intel Pentium, such as the AMD K6 series and the VIA Cyrix MII.

640KB barrier The limit imposed by the PC-compatible memory model using DOS mode. DOS programs can address only 1MB total memory, and PC-compatibility generally requires the top 384KB to be reserved for the system, leaving only the lower 640KB for DOS or other real-mode applications.

802.11 The family name for various wireless Ethernet standards. See also *IEEE 802.11 family*.

1000BASE-T A 1,000Mbps Ethernet local area network (LAN) that runs over four pairs of Category 5 cable. Popularly known as Gigabit Ethernet, 1000BASE-T can be used as an upgrade to a properly wired 100BASE-T network because the same cable and distance limitations (100 meters) apply.

1394 See *FireWire*.

8086 An Intel microprocessor with 16-bit registers, a 16-bit data bus, and a 20-bit address bus. This processor can operate only in real mode.

8087 An Intel math coprocessor designed to perform floating-point math with much greater speed and precision than the main CPU. The 8087 can be installed in most 8086- and 8088-based systems and adds more than 50 new instructions to those available in the primary CPU alone.

8088 An Intel microprocessor with 16-bit registers, an 8-bit data bus, and a 20-bit address bus. This processor can operate only in real mode and was designed as a low-cost version of the 8086.

8514/A An analog video display adapter from IBM for the PS/2 line of personal computers.

Compared to previous display adapters, such as EGA and VGA, it provides a high resolution of 1,024×768 pixels with as many as 256 colors or 64 shades of gray. It provides a video coprocessor that performs two-dimensional graphics functions internally, thus relieving the CPU of graphics tasks. It uses an interlaced monitor and scans every other line every time the screen is refreshed.

80286   An Intel microprocessor with 16-bit registers, a 16-bit data bus, and a 24-bit address bus. It can operate in both real and protected virtual modes.

80287   An Intel math coprocessor designed to perform floating-point math with much greater speed and precision than the main CPU. The 80287 can be installed in most 286- and some 386DX-based systems, and it adds more than 50 new instructions to what is available in the primary CPU alone.

80386   See *80386DX*.

80386DX   An Intel microprocessor with 32-bit registers, a 32-bit data bus, and a 32-bit address bus. This processor can operate in real, protected virtual, and virtual real modes.

80386SX   An Intel microprocessor with 32-bit registers, a 16-bit data bus, and a 24-bit address bus. This processor, designed as a low-cost version of the 386DX, can operate in real, protected virtual, and virtual real modes.

80387DX   An Intel math coprocessor designed to perform floating-point math with much greater speed and precision than the main CPU. The 80387DX can be installed in most 386DX-based systems and adds more than 50 new instructions to those available in the primary CPU alone.

80387SX   An Intel math coprocessor designed to perform floating-point math with much greater speed and precision than the main CPU. The 80387SX can be installed in most 386SX-based systems and adds more than 50 new instructions to those available in the primary CPU alone.

80486   See *80486DX*.

80486DX   An Intel microprocessor with 32-bit registers, a 32-bit data bus, and a 32-bit address bus. The 486DX has a built-in cache controller with 8KB of cache memory as well as a built-in math coprocessor equivalent to a 387DX. The 486DX can operate in real, protected virtual, and virtual real modes.

80486DX2   A version of the 486DX with an internal clock-doubling circuit that causes the chip to run at twice the motherboard clock speed. If the motherboard clock is 33MHz, the DX2 chip will run at 66MHz. The DX2 designation applies to chips sold through the OEM market, whereas a retail version of the DX2 sold by Intel and designed for use as an upgrade was sold as an Overdrive processor.

80486DX4   A version of the 486DX with an internal clock-tripling circuit that causes the chip to run at three times the motherboard clock speed. If the motherboard clock is 33.33MHz, the DX4 chip will run at 100MHz.

80486SX   An Intel microprocessor with 32-bit registers, a 32-bit data bus, and a 32-bit address bus. The 486SX is the same as the 486DX, except that it lacks the built-in math coprocessor function and was designed as a low-cost version of the 486DX. The 486SX can operate in real, protected virtual, and virtual real modes.

80487SX   An Intel microprocessor with 32-bit registers, a 32-bit data bus, and a 32-bit address bus. Although the name implies that the 80487SX adds floating-point math capabilities, in reality the 487SX is the same as the 486DX, except that it uses a modified pinout and must be installed in a special 80487SX socket. When installed, the 80487SX replaces the 80486SX for all processing tasks. The 487SX can operate in real, protected virtual, and virtual real modes.

A+   Refers to the CompTIA A+ Certification, a vendor-neutral certification for computer hardware technicians. A+ Certification exams test knowledge of basic hardware and software skills. The A+ Certification can be used as part of the exam requirements for the Microsoft Certified System Administrator (MCSA) credential.

abend   Short for *abnormal end*. A condition occurring when the execution of a program or task is terminated unexpectedly because of a bug or crash.

absolute address   An explicit identification of a memory location, device, or location within a device.

AC (alternating current)   The frequency is measured in cycles per seconds (cps) or hertz (Hz). The standard value running through the wall outlet is 120 volts at 60Hz through a fuse or circuit breaker that usually can handle about 15 or 20 amps.

accelerated graphics port   See *AGP*.

Accelerated Hub Architecture (AHA)   An Intel technology used on its 800-series chipsets to transfer data between the memory controller hub (MCH), which is equivalent to the North Bridge, and the input/output controller hub (ICH), which is equivalent to the South Bridge. AHA transfers data at 266MBps, twice the speed of the PCI bus previously used.

accelerator board   An add-in board replacing the computer's CPU with circuitry that enables the system to run more quickly. See also *graphics accelerator*.

access light   The LED on the front of a drive or other device (or on the front panel of the system) that indicates the computer is reading or writing data on the device.

access mechanism   See *actuator*.

access time   The time that elapses from the instant information is requested to the point that delivery is completed. It's usually described in nanoseconds (ns) for memory chips and in milliseconds (ms) for disk drives. Most manufacturers rate average access time on a hard disk as the time required for a seek across one-third of the total number of cylinders plus one-half the time for a single revolution of the disk platters (latency).

accumulator   A register (temporary storage) in which the result of an operation is formed.

acoustic coupler   A device used to connect a computer modem to a phone line by connecting to the handset of a standard AT&T-style phone. The audible sounds to and from the modem are transmitted to the handset through the coupler while the handset is resting in the coupler. Although often thought of as obsolete, an acoustic coupler can be used to ensure the availability of a modem connection when traveling and access to an RJ-11 jack is unavailable.

ACPI (Advanced Configuration and Power Interface)   A standard developed by Intel, Microsoft, and Toshiba that is designed to implement power management functions in the operating system. ACPI is a replacement for APM. See also *APM*.

ACR   Short for Advanced Communication Riser, a defunct alternative to CNR advocated by the ACR Special Interest Group. ACR, like CNR, was designed to allow motherboard designers to add low-cost network capabilities to motherboards but uses the same PCI connector used by PCI expansion cards.

Acrobat   Refers to the Adobe Acrobat program for creating and reading cross-platform documents created in Adobe's Portable Document Format (PDF) file format. Many computer and component manuals are available online in Acrobat format. The Acrobat Reader can be downloaded free from Adobe's website.

active high   Designates a digital signal that must go to a high value to be true. Synonymous with positive.

active low   Designates a digital signal that must go to a low value to be true. Synonymous with negative.

active matrix   A type of LCD screen that contains at least one transistor for every pixel on the screen. Color active-matrix screens use three transistors for each pixel—one each for the red, green, and blue dots. The transistors are arranged on a grid of conductive material, with each connected to a horizontal and a vertical member. See also *TFT*.

active partition   Any partition marked as bootable in the partition table. See also *boot manager*.

actuator   The device that moves a disk drive's read/write heads across the platter surfaces. Also known as an access mechanism.

adapter   The device that serves as an interface between the system unit and the devices attached to it. It's often synonymous with circuit board, circuit card, or card, but it also can refer to a connector or cable adapter that changes one type of connector to another.

adapter description files (ADF)   Refers to the setup and configuration files and drivers necessary to install an adapter card, such as a network adapter card. Primarily used with Micro Channel Architecture (MCA) bus cards.

add-in board   See *expansion card*.

address   Refers to where a particular piece of data or other information is found in the computer. Also can refer to the location of a set of instructions.

address bus   One or more electrical conductors used to carry the binary-coded address from the microprocessor throughout the rest of the system.

ADSL (asymmetric digital subscriber line)
A high-speed transmission technology originally developed by Bellcore and now standardized by ANSI as T1.413. ADSL uses existing UTP copper wires to communicate digitally at high speed between the telephone company central office (CO) and the subscriber. ADSL sends information asymmetrically, meaning it is faster one way than the other. The original ADSL speed was T-1 (1.536Mbps) downstream from the carrier to the subscriber's premises and 16Kbps upstream. However, ADSL is available in a variety of configurations and speeds. See also *DSL*.

AGP (accelerated graphics port)   Developed by Intel, AGP is a fast, dedicated interface between the video adapter or chipset and the motherboard chipset North Bridge. AGP is 32 bits wide; runs at 66MHz base speed; and can transfer 1, 2, 4, or 8 bits per cycle (1x, 2x, 4x, or 8x modes) for a throughput of up to 2132MBps.

aliasing   Undesirable visual effects (sometimes called artifacts) in computer-generated images caused by inadequate sampling techniques. The most common effect is jagged edges along diagonal or curved object boundaries. See also *antialiasing*.

allocation unit   See *cluster*.

alphanumeric characters   A character set that contains only letters (A–Z) and digits (0–9). Other characters, such as punctuation marks, also might be allowed.

AMD   Short for Advanced Micro Devices, the number-two PC processor maker. AMD makes the popular K6, Athlon, Opteron, and Duron series of processors, as well as chipsets and flash memory devices.

ampere   The basic unit for measuring electrical current. Also called amp.

AMR   Short for Audio/Modem Riser, it's an Intel-developed specification for packaging modem I/O ports and a codec chip into a small card that can be installed into an AMR slot on a motherboard. Although many motherboards have AMR slots, AMR risers have not been popular, and the CNR specification has largely replaced AMR. See also *CNR*.

analog   The representation of numerical values by physical variables such as voltage, current, and so on; continuously variable quantities whose values correspond to the quantitative magnitude of the variables.

analog loopback   A modem self-test in which data from the keyboard is sent to the modem's transmitter, modulated into analog form, looped back to the receiver, demodulated into digital form, and returned to the screen for verification.

analog signals   Continuously variable signals. Analog circuits are more subject to distortion and noise than are digital circuits but are capable of handling complex signals with relatively simple circuitry. See also *digital signals*.

analog-to-digital converter   An electronic device that converts analog signals to digital form.

AND   A logic operator having the property that if P is a statement, Q is a statement, R is a statement…, then the AND of P, Q, R… is true if all statements are true and is false if any statement is false.

AND gate   A logic gate in which the output is 1 only if all inputs are 1.

animation   The process of displaying a sequential series of still images to achieve a motion effect.

ANSI (American National Standards Institute)
A nongovernmental organization founded in 1918 to propose, modify, approve, and publish data processing standards for voluntary use in the United States. It's also the U.S. representative to the International Standards Organization (ISO) in Paris and the International Electrotechnical Commission (IEC). Contact ANSI, 1430 Broadway, New York, NY 10018.

answer mode   A state in which the modem transmits at the predefined high frequency of the communications channel and receives at the low frequency. The transmit/receive frequencies are the reverse of the calling modem, which is in originate mode. See also *originate mode*.

antialiasing   Software adjustment to make diagonal or curved lines appear smooth and continuous in computer-generated images. See also *aliasing*.

antistatic mat   A pad placed next to a computer upon which components are placed while servicing the system to prevent static damage. Also can refer to a larger-sized mat below an entire computer desk and chair to discharge static from a user before he touches the computer.

antivirus Software that prevents files containing viruses from running on a computer or software that detects, repairs, cleans, or removes virus-infected files.

APA (all points addressable) A mode in which all points of a displayable image can be controlled by the user or a program.

aperture grille A type of shadow mask used in CRTs. The most common is used in Sony's Trinitron monitors, which use vertical phosphor stripes and vertical slots in the mask, compared to the traditional shadow mask that uses phosphor dots and round holes in the mask. See also *mask*.

API (Application Programming Interface) A system call (routine) that gives programmers access to the services provided by the operating system. In IBM-compatible systems, the ROM BIOS and DOS together present an API that a programmer can use to control the system hardware.

APM (Advanced Power Management) A specification sponsored by Intel and Microsoft originally proposed to extend the life of batteries in battery-powered computers. It is now used in desktop computers as well. APM enables application programs, the system BIOS, and the hardware to work together to reduce power consumption. An APM-compliant BIOS provides built-in power-management services to the operating system. The application software communicates power-saving data via predefined APM interfaces. Replaced in newer systems by ACPI. See also *ACPI*.

application End-user–oriented software, such as a word processor, spreadsheet, database, graphics editor, game, or web browser.

Application Layer See *OSI*.

arbitration A method by which multiple devices attached to a single bus can bid or arbitrate to get control of that bus.

archive bit The bit in a file's attribute byte that sets the archive attribute. Tells whether the file has been changed since it last was backed up.

archive file A collection of files that has been stored (often in a compressed format) within a single file. Zip and CAB files are the most common types of archive file formats used with Windows-based PCs. See also *Zip file* and *CAB file*.

archive medium A storage medium (floppy disk, tape cartridge, or removable cartridge) to hold files that need not be accessible instantly.

ARCnet (Attached Resource Computer Network) A baseband, token-passing LAN technology offering a flexible bus/star topology for connecting personal computers. Operating at 2.5Mbps, it is one of the oldest LAN systems and was popular in low-cost networks. It was originally developed by John Murphy of Datapoint Corporation. Although ARCnet (www.arcnet.com) is no longer used for office networking, it is still a popular choice for networking embedded systems, such as heating and air conditioning systems.

areal density A calculation of the bit density (bits per inch, or BPI) multiplied by the track density (tracks per inch, or TPI), which results in a figure indicating how many bits per square inch are present on the disk surface.

ARQ (automatic repeat request) A general term for error-control protocols that feature error detection and automatic retransmission of defective blocks of data.

ASCII (American Standard Code for Information Interchange) A standard 7-bit code created in 1965 by Robert W. Bemer to achieve compatibility among various types of data processing equipment. The standard ASCII character set consists of 128 decimal numbers ranging from 0 to 127, which are assigned to letters, numbers, punctuation marks, and the most common special characters. In 1981, IBM introduced the extended ASCII character set with the IBM PC, extending the code to 8 bits and adding characters from 128 to 255 to represent additional special mathematical, graphics, and foreign characters.

ASCII character A 1-byte character from the ASCII character set, including alphabetic and numeric characters, punctuation symbols, and various graphics characters.

ASME (American Society of Mechanical Engineers; www.asme.org) ASME International has nearly 600 codes and standards in print, and its many committees involve more than 3,000 individuals, mostly engineers but not necessarily members of the society. The standards are used in more than 90 countries throughout the world.

aspect ratio The measurement of a film or television viewing area in terms of relative height and width. The aspect ratio of most modern motion pictures varies from 5:3 to as large as 16:9, which creates a problem when a wide-format motion picture is transferred to the more square-shaped television screen or monitor, with its aspect ratio of 4:3. See also *letterbox*.

assemble   The act of translating a program expressed in an assembler language into a computer machine language.

assembler language   A computer-oriented language whose instructions are usually in one-to-one correspondence with machine language instructions.

asymmetrical modulation   A duplex transmission technique that splits the communications channel into one high-speed channel and one slower channel. During a call under asymmetrical modulation, the modem with the greater amount of data to transmit is allocated the high-speed channel. The modem with less data is allocated the slow, or back, channel. The modems dynamically reverse the channels during a call if the volume of data transfer changes.

asynchronous communication   Data transmission in which the length of time between transmitted characters can vary. Timing depends on the actual time for the transfer to take place, as opposed to synchronous communication, which is timed rigidly by an external clock signal. Because the receiving modem must be signaled about when the data bits of a character begin and end, start and stop bits are added to each character. See also *synchronous communication*.

asynchronous memory   Memory that runs using a timing or clock rate different from (usually slower than) the motherboard speed.

AT clock   Refers to the Motorola 146818 real-time clock (RTC) and CMOS RAM chip, which first debuted in the IBM AT and whose function has been present in all PC-compatible systems since. Keeps track of the time of day and makes this data available to the operating system or other software.

ATA (AT Attachment Interface)   An IDE disk interface standard introduced in March 1989 that defines a compatible register set, a 40-pin connector, and its associated signals. See also *IDE* and *SATA*.

ATA-2   The second-generation AT Attachment Interface specification, approved in 1996. This ver-

sion defines faster transfer modes and logical block addressing schemes to allow high-performance, large-capacity drives. Also called Fast ATA, Fast ATA-2, and enhanced IDE (EIDE).

ATA-3   Published in 1997, ATA-3 defines 8-bit DMA transfers and SMART support for drive failure prediction.

ATA/ATAPI-4   The fourth-generation ATA specification was published in 1998. ATA/ATAPI-4 incorporates ATAPI and adds Ultra DMA/33 (33MBps) transfer mode; APM support; an optional 80-wire, 40-pin cable; support for Compact Flash memory devices; and enhanced BIOS support for larger drives.

ATA/ATAPI-5   Approved in 2000, ATA/ATAPI-5 includes UDMA/66 support, mandates the 80-wire cable for UDMA/66, detects the cable type, and allows UDMA/66 or faster speeds only if the 80-wire cable is present.

ATA/ATAPI-6   The latest draft standard, ATA/ATAPI-6 includes UDMA/100 (100MBps) support and increases the ATA drive size limit to 144.12PB (petabytes). See also *petabyte*.

ATAPI (AT Attachment Packet Interface)   A specification that defines device-side characteristics for an IDE-connected peripheral, such as a CD-ROM or tape drive. ATAPI is essentially an adaptation of the SCSI command set to the IDE interface. ATA-4 and newer ATA standards include ATAPI standards.

Athlon   An AMD sixth-generation processor family roughly comparable to the Intel Pentium III and Pentium 4. Later models (beginning with the Thunderbird core) include on-die L2 cache running at full core speed. It includes MMX and AMD 3DNow! instructions for multimedia performance. Originally available in a Slot-A cartridge package, all Athlons are now available only in the Socket-A (462-pin) package. The Mobile Athlon XP, which replaced the Athlon 4, is designed for mobile applications, the Athlon MP is designed for workstation/server multiprocessor configurations, and the Athlon XP is designed mainly for single processor applications. All three use the improved Thoroughbred core and 3DNow! Professional multimedia extensions. The Athlon XP processors include AMD's new QuantiSpeed design for faster internal operation and are rated by their performances relative to the Intel Pentium 4, rather than by their clock speeds. For example, the Athlon XP

2600+, which performs comparably to the Pentium 4 2.6GHz processor, runs at a clock speed of about 2.1GHz.

Athlon 64   An AMD processor (code-named Clawhammer) that uses a 64-bit internal design. The Athlon 64 also emulates 32-bit x86 processors from Intel and AMD. It uses a new ball grid array socket called Socket 754; an integrated DDR memory controller (instead of using the North Bridge for memory connections); an improved version of the AMD-developed HyperTransport connection to AGP, PCI, and other components; and an improved heatsink-mounting solution. It supports MMX and AMD 3dNow! Instructions for multimedia and uses a performance-rating system similar to that used by 32-bit Athlon processors. See also *Athlon*.

ATM (asynchronous transfer mode)   A high-bandwidth, low-delay, packet-like switching and multiplexing technique. Usable capacity is segmented into fixed-size cells consisting of header and information fields, allocated to services on demand.

attribute byte   A byte of information, held in the directory entry of any file or folder, that describes various attributes of the file or folder, such as whether it is read-only or has been backed up since it last was changed. Attributes can be set by the DOS ATTRIB command or with Windows Explorer.

ATX   A motherboard and power supply form factor standard designed by Intel and introduced in 1995. It is characterized by a double row of rear external I/O connectors on the motherboard, a single keyed power supply connector, memory and processor locations that are designed not to interfere with the installation of adapter cards, and an improved cooling flow. The current specification—ATX 2.0—was introduced in December 1996.

audio   A signal that can be heard, such as through the speaker of the PC. Many PC diagnostic tests use both visual (onscreen) codes and audio signals.

audio frequencies   Frequencies that can be heard by the human ear (approximately 20Hz–20,000Hz).

auto-answer   A setting in modems enabling them to answer incoming calls over the phone lines automatically.

auto-dial   A feature in modems enabling them to dial phone numbers without human intervention.

auto-disconnect   A modem feature that enables a modem to hang up the telephone line when the modem at the other end hangs up.

auto-redial   A modem or software feature that automatically redials the last number dialed if the number is busy or does not answer.

AUTOEXEC.BAT   A special batch file DOS and Windows 9x execute at startup. Contains any number of DOS commands that are executed automatically, including the capability to start programs at startup. See also *batch file*.

automatic head parking   Disk drive head parking performed whenever the drive is powered off. Found in all modern hard disk drives with a voice-coil actuator.

available memory   Memory currently not in use by the operating system, drivers, or applications, which can be used to load additional software.

average access time   The average time it takes a disk drive to begin reading any data placed anywhere on the drive. This includes the average seek time, which is when the heads are moved, as well as the latency, which is the average amount of time required for any given data sector to pass underneath the heads. Together, these factors make up the average access time. See also *average seek time* and *latency*.

average latency   The average time required for any byte of data stored on a disk to rotate under the disk drive's read/write head. Equal to one-half the time required for a single rotation of a platter.

average seek time   The average amount of time it takes to move the heads from one random cylinder location to another, usually including any head settling time. In many cases, the average seek time is defined as the seek time across one-third of the total number of cylinders.

AVI (audio video interleave)   A storage technique developed by Microsoft for its Video for Windows product that combines audio and video into a single frame or track, saving valuable disk space and keeping audio in synchronization with the corresponding video. AVI files are widely supported by media players and video production programs.

AWG American Wire Gauge, a U.S. standard for measuring the thickness of copper and aluminum wire for electrical and data-transmission use. Thinner wire is used to save space and for short distances, but thicker wire has less resistance and is better for long wire runs.

B Channel The bearer channel in an ISDN network, it's used to carry data at a rate of 64KBps. See also *BRI*.

backbone The portion of the Internet or wide area network (WAN) transmission wiring that connects the main Internet/WAN servers and routers and is responsible for carrying the bulk of the Internet/WAN data.

backup The process of duplicating a file or library onto a separate piece of media. It's good insurance against the loss of an original. Depending on how the backup was made, the data might need to be restored with a special program before reuse.

backup disk Contains information copied from another disk. Used to ensure that original information is not destroyed or altered.

backward compatibility The design of software and hardware to work with previous versions of the same software or hardware.

bad sector A disk sector that can't hold data reliably because of a media flaw or damaged format markings.

bad track table A label affixed to the casing of an ST412/506 or ESDI hard disk drive that tells which tracks are flawed and incapable of holding data. The listing is entered into the low-level formatting program. Modern ATA (IDE) and SCSI drives are low-level formatted during manufacture and don't have (or need) a bad track table.

balanced signal Refers to signals consisting of equal currents moving in opposite directions. When balanced or nearly balanced signals pass through twisted-pair lines, the electromagnetic interference effects—such as crosstalk caused by the two opposite currents—largely cancel each other out. Differential signaling (used by some types of SCSI interfaces) is a method that uses balanced signals.

balun Short for balanced/unbalanced. A type of transformer that enables balanced cables to be joined with unbalanced cables. Twisted-pair (bal-anced) cables, for example, can be joined with coaxial (unbalanced) cables if the proper balun transformer is used.

bandwidth 1) Generally, the measure of the range of frequencies within a radiation band required to transmit a particular signal. The difference between the lowest and highest signal frequencies. The bandwidth of a computer monitor is a measure of the rate at which a monitor can handle information from the display adapter. The wider the bandwidth, the more information the monitor can carry and the greater the resolution. 2) Used to describe the data-carrying capacity of a given communications circuit or pathway. The bandwidth of a circuit is a measure of the rate at which information can be passed.

bank The collection of memory chips or modules that make up a block of memory readable or writable by the processor in a single cycle. This block, therefore, must be as large as the data bus of the particular microprocessor. In PC systems, the processor data bus (and therefore the bank size) is usually 8, 16, 32, or 64 bits wide. Optionally, some systems also incorporate an additional parity or ECC bit for each 8 data bits, resulting in a total of 9, 18, 36, or 72 bits (respectively) for each bank. Memory in a PC always must be added or removed in full-bank increments. The number of memory chips or modules that make up a bank varies with the width of the memory in bits and the size of the processor's data bus. For example, a K6-2 processor has a data bus that is 64 bits wide. If the motherboard uses 72-pin SIMMs (which are 32 data bits wide), a bank is two SIMMs. However, if the motherboard uses DIMMs, which are 64 data bits wide, a bank is one DIMM.

bar code The code used on consumer products and inventory parts for identification purposes. Consists of bars of varying thickness that represent characters and numerals that are read with an optical reader. The most common version is called the universal product code (UPC).

base-2 Refers to the computer numbering system that consists of two numerals: 0 and 1. Also called binary.

base address Starting location for a consecutive string of memory or I/O addresses/ports.

base memory The amount of memory available to the operating system or application programs within the first megabyte, accessible in the processor's real mode.

baseband transmission The transmission of digital signals over a limited distance. ARCnet and Ethernet local area networks use baseband signaling. Contrasts with broadband transmission, which refers to the transmission of analog signals over a greater distance.

BASIC (beginner's all-purpose symbolic instruction code) A popular computer programming language originally developed by John Kemeny and Thomas Kurtz in the mid-1960s at Dartmouth College. Normally, BASIC is an interpretive language, meaning that each statement is translated and executed as it is encountered, but it can be a compiled language, in which all the program statements are compiled before execution. Microsoft Visual Basic, a popular development environment for Windows, is not related to BASIC.

batch file A set of commands stored in a disk file for execution by the operating system. A special batch file called AUTOEXEC.BAT is executed by DOS each time the system is started. All DOS and Windows batch files have a .BAT file extension.

baud A unit of signaling speed denoting the number of discrete signal elements that can be transmitted per second. The word *baud* is derived from the name of J.M.E. Baudot (1845–1903), a French pioneer in the field of printing telegraphy and the inventor of Baudot code. Although technically inaccurate, baud rate commonly is used to mean bit rate. Because each signal element or baud can translate into many individual bits, bits per second (bps) usually differs from baud rate. A rate of 2,400 baud means that 2,400 frequency or signal changes per second are being sent, but each frequency change can signal several bits of information. For example, 33.6Kbps modems actually transmit at only 2,400 baud.

Baudot code A 5-bit code used in many types of data communications, including teletype (TTY), radio teletype (RTTY), and telecommunications devices for the deaf (TDD). Baudot code has been revised and extended several times. See also *baud*.

bay An opening in a computer case or chassis that holds disk drives.

BBS (bulletin board system) A computer that operates with a program and a modem to enable other computers with modems to communicate with it, often on a round-the-clock basis. Although BBSs were once the primary means of distributing information and software, the Internet has almost completely replaced BBSs.

benchmark A test or set of tests designed to compare the performance of hardware or software. A popular set of benchmarks for PC hardware is the *PC Magazine* benchmarks, such as Business Winstone, WinBench, and others. You can order CDs or download selected benchmarks from www.veritest.com/benchmarks/pcmbmk.asp.

bezel A cosmetic panel that covers the face of a drive or some other device.

Bézier curve A mathematical method for describing a curve, often used in illustration and CAD programs to draw complex shapes.

BGA (ball grid array) A packaging technology used by Socket 478 Pentium 4 and Celeron processors, as well as many recent motherboard chipsets and video card memory chips. BGA uses small solder balls instead of pin connectors to enable more signaling paths to exist in a smaller space and improve signal accuracy.

bidirectional 1) Refers to lines over which data can move in two directions, such as a data bus or telephone line. 2) Refers to the capability of a printer to print from right to left and from left to right alternately.

binary See *base-2*.

BIOS (basic input/output system) The part of an operating system that handles the communications between the computer and its peripherals. Often burned into read-only memory (ROM) chips or rewritable flash (EEPROM) memory chips found on motherboards and expansion cards, such as video cards and SCSI and ATA/IDE host adapters. See also *firmware*.

bipolar A category of semiconductor circuit design that was used to create the first transistor and the first integrated circuit. Bipolar and CMOS are the two major transistor technologies. Almost all personal computers use CMOS technology chips. CMOS uses far less energy than bipolar.

bisynchronous (binary synchronous control) An earlier protocol developed by IBM for software applications and communicating devices operating in synchronous environments. The protocol defines operations at the link level of communications—for example, the format of data frames exchanged between modems over a phone line.

bit binary digit   Represented logically by 0 or 1 and electrically by 0 volts and (typically) 5 volts. Other methods are used to represent binary digits physically (tones, different voltages, lights, and so on), but the logic is always the same.

bit density   Expressed as bits per inch (BPI). Defines how many bits can be written onto one linear inch of a track. Sometimes also called linear density.

bit depth   The number of bits used to describe the color of each pixel on a computer display. For example, a bit depth of two (2^2) means the monitor can display only black and white pixels; a bit depth of four (2^4) means the monitor can display 16 different colors; a bit depth of eight (2^8) allows for 256 colors; and so on.

bitmap   A method of storing graphics information in memory, in which a bit devoted to each pixel (picture element) onscreen indicates whether that pixel is on or off. A bitmap contains a bit for each point or dot on a video display screen and enables fine resolution because any point or pixel onscreen can be addressed. A greater number of bits can be used to describe each pixel's color, intensity, and other display characteristics.

blank or blanking interval   A period in which no video signal is received by a monitor while the videodisc or digital video player searches for the next video segment or frame to display.

block   A string of records, words, or characters formed for technical or logic reasons and to be treated as an entity.

block diagram   The logical structure or layout of a system in graphics form. Does not necessarily match the physical layout and does not specify all the components and their interconnections.

Blue Book   The standard for enhanced CDs (CD-E). CD-E media contains both music (for play on standard CD players) and computer content. Developed by Philips and Sony in 1995.

blue screen of death   A system crash in Windows that replaces the normal desktop with a blue screen with white text reporting the problem and locks up the system. Also referred to as a BSOD, this condition can be triggered by defective

memory, file system errors, and other system problems.

Bluetooth   An emerging short-range networking standard, Bluetooth is designed to enable PCs, mobile phones, input devices, and PDAs to exchange data with each other. Bluetooth uses the same 2.4GHz frequency range used by some types of wireless phones and by the IEEE 802.11b Wi-Fi wireless Ethernet network. Bluetooth has a speed of 1Mbps or 2Mbps, depending on the version.

BMP   A Windows graphics format that can be device dependent or independent. Device-independent BMP files (DIB) are coded for translation to a wide variety of displays and printers.

BNC (Bayonet-Neill-Concelman)   Also known as British-Naval-Connector, Baby-N-Connector, or Bayonet-Nut-Coupler, this bayonet-locking connector is noted for its excellent shielding and impedance-matching characteristics, resulting in low noise and minimal signal loss at any frequency up to 4GHz. It is used in Ethernet 10BASE-2 networks (also known as IEEE 802.3 or Thinnet) to terminate coaxial cables. It is also used for some high-end video monitors. BNC is named for its connection type (bayonet) and its co-developers.

bonding   In ISDN, joining two 64Kbps B-channels to achieve 128Kbps speed. Bonding can also be used with analog modems that use the Multilink Point-to-Point protocol that is supported by Windows 98 and newer versions but by only a few ISPs.

Boolean operation   Any operation in which each of the operands and the result take one of two values. A Boolean search can be performed with many search engines used on websites and help files using operators such as AND, OR, and NOT.

boot   To load a program into the computer. The term comes from the phrase "pulling a boot on by the bootstrap."

boot manager   A program that enables you to select which active partition to boot from. Often supplied with aftermarket disk-partitioning programs, such as PartitionMagic, or installed by default when you install a Windows upgrade into a separate disk partition instead of replacing your old version. See also *active partition*.

boot record   The first sector on a disk or partition that contains disk parameter information for the BIOS and operating system as well as bootstrap loader code that instructs the system how to load the operating system files into memory, thus beginning the initial boot sequence to boot the machine.

boot sector See *boot record*.

boot sector virus A virus designed to occupy the boot sector of a disk. Any attempt to start or boot a system from this disk transfers the virus to the hard disk, after which it subsequently is loaded every time the system is started. Many older PC viruses, particularly those spread by infected floppy disks, are boot sector viruses.

bootstrap A technique or device designed to bring itself into a desired state by means of its own action. The term is used to describe the process by which a device such as a PC goes from its initial power-on condition to a running condition without human intervention. See also *boot*.

boule Purified, cylindrical silicon crystals from which semiconducting electronic chips, including microprocessors, memory, and other chips, in a PC are manufactured. Also called an ingot.

bps (bits per second) The number of binary digits, or bits, transmitted per second. Sometimes confused with baud.

branch prediction A feature of fifth-generation (Pentium and higher) processors that attempts to predict whether a program branch will be taken and then fetches the appropriate following instructions.

BRI Short for basic rate interface, it's a form of ISDN used in home and small business applications. A 2B+1D BRI service has two B channels and a single D channel for signaling and control uses.

bridge In local area networks, an interconnection between two similar networks. Also the hardware equipment used to establish such an interconnection.

broadband transmission A term used to describe analog transmission. Requires modems for connecting terminals and computers to the network. Using frequency division multiplexing, many signals or sets of data can be transmitted simultaneously. The alternative transmission scheme is baseband, or digital, transmission.

brownout An AC supply voltage drop in which the power does not shut off entirely but continues to be supplied at lower-than-normal levels.

BSOD See *blue screen of death*.

bubble memory A special type of nonvolatile read/write memory introduced by Intel in which magnetic regions are suspended in crystal film and data is maintained when the power is off. A typical bubble memory chip contains about 512KB, or more than four million bubbles. Bubble memory failed to catch on because of slow access times measured in several milliseconds. It has, however, found a niche use as solid-state "disk" emulators in environments in which conventional drives are unacceptable, such as in military or factory use.

buffer A block of memory used as a holding tank to store data temporarily. Often positioned between a slower peripheral device and the faster computer. All data moving between the peripheral and the computer passes through the buffer. A buffer enables the data to be read from or written to the peripheral in larger chunks, which improves performance. A buffer that is *x* bytes in size usually holds the last *x* bytes of data that moved between the peripheral and CPU. This method contrasts with that of a cache, which adds intelligence to the buffer so that the most often accessed data, rather than the last accessed data, remains in the buffer (cache). A cache can improve performance greatly over a plain buffer.

bug An error or a defect in a program; it can be corrected through program patches (for applications or operating systems) or firmware updates (for BIOS chips).

burn-in The operation of a circuit or equipment to establish that its components are stable and to screen out defective ports or assemblies.

BURN-Proof Short for buffer underrun error-proof, it's a technology developed by Sanyo to prevent buffer underruns during the creation of CD-Rs. BURN-Proof, which has been licensed to many CD-RW drive makers, enables a drive to pause the burning process and continue after sufficient data is available in the drive's buffer. The drive and CD-mastering software must both support BURN-Proof for this feature to work. Ricoh's JustLink works in a similar fashion. See also *lossless linking*.

burst mode A memory-cycling technology that takes advantage of the fact that most memory accesses are consecutive in nature. After the row and column addresses for a given access are set up, burst mode can then access the next three adjacent addresses with no additional latency.

Burst Static RAMs (BSRAMs)   Short for Pipeline Burst SRAMs, BSRAMs are a common type of static RAM chip used for memory caches where access to subsequent memory locations after the first byte is accessed takes fewer machine cycles.

bus   A linear electrical signal pathway over which power, data, and other signals travel. It is capable of connecting to three or more attachments. A bus is generally considered to be distinct from radial or point-to-point signal connections. The term comes from the Latin *omnibus*, meaning "for all." When used to describe a topology, bus always implies a linear structure.

bus mouse   An obsolete type of mouse used in the 1980s that plugs into a special mouse expansion board (occasionally incorporated into a video card) instead of a serial port or motherboard mouse port. The bus mouse connector looks similar to a motherboard mouse (sometimes called PS/2 mouse) connector, but the pin configurations are different and not compatible.

busmaster   An intelligent device that, when attached to the Micro Channel, EISA, VLB, or PCI bus, can bid for and gain control of the bus to perform its specific task without processor intervention. Most recent motherboards incorporate busmastering ATA/IDE host adapters, but this feature must be enabled in both the BIOS and through the installation of Windows drivers to be effective.

byte   A collection of bits that makes up a character or other designation. Generally, a byte is 8 data bits. When referring to system RAM, an additional parity (error-checking) bit is also stored (see *parity*), making the total 9 bits.

C   A high-level computer programming language. A programming language frequently used on mainframes, minis, and PC computer systems. C++ is a popular variant.

C3   A Socket 370-compatible processor developed by VIA Technology from the Cyrix "Joshua" after VIA purchased Cyrix from National Semiconductor. The C3 is noted for its very small die size and cool operation, making it a suitable choice for portable computers and embedded computers.

CAB file   Short for cabinet file, the archive file type used by Microsoft to distribute recent versions of Windows and applications. Some recent versions of WinZip can be used to manually extract files from a CAB file; you can also open CAB files within Windows Explorer with Windows 98 after you install the Windows 98 Plus! package and with Windows Explorer in Windows 2000, Windows Me, and Windows XP.

cable modem   A broadband Internet device that receives data through the cable TV system. The cable modem can be a one-way device (using a conventional analog modem for dialing and uploading) or a two-way device.

CableLabs Certified Cable Modem   A cable modem that meets the Data or Cable Service Interface Specifications (DOCSIS) standards for modulation and protocols. Various brands and models of modems meet this standard on cable networks that also meet this standard. DOCSIS/CableLabs Certified Cable Modems can be purchased as well as leased.

cache   An intelligent buffer. By using an intelligent algorithm, a cache contains the data accessed most often between a slower peripheral device and the faster CPU. See also *L1 cache, L2 cache,* and *disk cache*.

caddy   A cartridge designed to hold a CD or DVD disc. Some CD drives use caddies, particularly in harsh or industrial environments. DVD-RAM drives also use a caddy to protect the disc.

CAM (Common Access Method)   A committee formed in 1988 that consists of several computer peripheral suppliers and is dedicated to developing standards for a common software interface between SCSI peripherals and host adapters.

candela   Abbreviated cd, a candela is the standard unit of measurement for luminosity. The brightness of LCDs and other types of displays is sometimes measured in cd units.

capacitor   A device consisting of two plates separated by insulating material and designed to store an electrical charge.

card   A printed circuit board containing electronic components that form an entire circuit, usually designed to plug into a connector or slot. Sometimes also called an adapter.

card edge connector   See *edge connector*.

CardBus   A PC Card (PCMCIA) specification for a 32-bit interface that runs at 33MHz and provides 32-bit data paths to the computer's I/O and memory systems, as well as a new shielded connector that prevents CardBus devices from being inserted into slots that do not support the latest version of the PC Card (PCMCIA) standard. CardBus slots can also be used with normal 16-bit PC Card (PCMCIA) devices.

carpal tunnel syndrome   A painful hand injury that gets its name from the narrow tunnel in the wrist that connects ligament and bone. When undue pressure is put on the tendons, they can swell and compress the median nerve, which carries impulses from the brain to the hand, causing numbness, weakness, tingling, and burning in the fingers and hands. Computer users get carpal tunnel syndrome primarily from improper keyboard ergonomics that result in undue strain on the wrist and hand.

carrier   A continuous frequency signal capable of being either modulated or impressed with another information-carrying signal. The reference signal used for the transmission or reception of data. The most common use of this signal with computers involves modem communications over phone lines. The carrier is used as a signal on which the information is superimposed.

carrier detect signal   A modem interface signal that indicates to the attached data terminal equipment (DTE) that it is receiving a signal from the distant modem. Defined in the RS-232 specification. Same as the received line-signal detector.

CAT   Short for category, it describes the ANSI/EIA 568 wiring standards used for data transmission. The most common CAT standards include CAT 3 (16Mbps maximum data rate, suitable for 10BASE-T Ethernet) and CAT 5 (used for 100BASE-T Fast Ethernet or 1000BASE-T Gigabit Ethernet).

cathode-ray tube (CRT)   A device that contains electrodes surrounded by a glass sphere or cylinder and displays information by creating a beam of electrons that strike a phosphor coating inside the display unit. This device is most commonly used in computer monitors and terminals.

CAV (constant angular velocity)   An optical disk recording format in which the data is recorded on the disk in concentric circles. CAV disks are rotated at a constant speed. This is similar to the recording technique used on floppy disk drives. CAV limits

the total recorded capacity compared to CLV (constant linear velocity), which also is used in optical recording. See also *CLV*.

CCITT   An acronym for the Comité Consultatif International de Télégraphique et Téléphonique (in English, the International Telegraph and Telephone Consultative Committee or the Consultative Committee for International Telegraph and Telephone). Renamed ITU (International Telecommunications Union). See also *ITU*.

CCS (common command set)   A set of SCSI commands specified in the ANSI SCSI-1 Standard X3.131-1986 Addendum 4.B. All SCSI devices must be capable of using the CCS to be fully compatible with the ANSI SCSI-1 standard.

CD (compact disc or compact audio disc)   A 4.75" (12cm) optical disc that contains information encoded digitally in the constant linear velocity (CLV) format. This popular format for high-fidelity music offers 90 decibels signal/noise ratio, 74 minutes of digital sound, and no degradation of quality from playback. The standards for this format (developed by NV Philips and Sony Corporation) are known as the Red Book. The official (and rarely used) designation for the audio-only format is CD-DA (compact disc-digital audio). The simple audio format is also known as CD-A (compact disc-audio). A smaller (3") version of the CD is known as CD-3.

CD burner   Refers to either a CD-R or CD-RW drive. See also *DVD burner*.

CD+G (Compact Disc+Graphics)   A CD format that includes extended graphics capabilities as written into the original CD-ROM specifications. Includes limited video graphics encoded into the CD subcode area. Originally developed and marketed by Warner New Media (later Time Warner Interactive), it's a popular choice for self-contained karaoke systems.

CD-I (Compact Disc-Interactive)   A compact disc format released in October 1991 that provides audio, digital data, still graphics, and motion video. The standards for this format (developed by NV Philips and Sony Corporation) are known as the Green Book. CD-I did not catch on with consumers and is now considered obsolete.

CD+MIDI (Compact Disc+Musical Instrument Digital Interface)   A CD format that adds to the

CD+G format digital audio, graphics information, and musical instrument digital interface (MIDI) specifications and capabilities. Originally developed and marketed by Warner New Media (later Time Warner Interactive).

CD-R (Compact Disc-Recordable, sometimes called CD-writable) CD-R discs are compact discs that can be recorded and read as many times as desired. CD-R is part of the Orange Book standard defined by ISO. CD-R technology is used for mass production of multimedia applications. CD-R discs can be compatible with CD-ROM, CD-ROM XA, and CD audio. Orange Book specifies multisession capabilities, which enable data recording on the disc at various times in several recording sessions. Multisession capability enables data such as digital photos, digital music, or other types of data files to be added to a single disc on different occasions. The original capacity of CD-R media was 650MB (74 minutes), but most recent CD-ROM and compatible optical drives support the larger 700MB (80-minute) media.

CD-ROM (compact disc-read-only memory) A 4.75" laser-encoded optical memory storage medium with the same constant linear velocity (CLV) spiral format as audio CDs and some videodiscs. CD-ROMs can hold about 650MB of data and require more error-correction information than the standard prerecorded compact audio discs. The standards for this format (developed by NV Philips and Sony Corporation) are known as the Yellow Book. See also *CD-ROM XA*.

CD-ROM drive A device that retrieves data from a CD-ROM disc; it differs from a standard audio CD player by the incorporation of additional error-correction circuitry. CD-ROM drives usually can also play music from audio CDs.

CD-ROM XA (compact disc-read-only memory extended architecture) The XA standard was developed jointly by Sony, Philips, and Microsoft in 1988 and is now part of the Yellow Book standard. XA is a built-in feature of newer CD-ROM drives and supports simultaneous sound playback with data transfer. Non-XA drives support either sound playback or data transfer, but not both simultaneously. XA also enables data compression right on the disk, which also can increase data transfer rates.

CD-RW (compact disc-rewritable) A type of rewritable CD-ROM technology defined in Part III of the Orange Book standard that uses a different type of disc, which the drive can rewrite at least 1,000 times. CD-RW drives also can be used to write CD-R discs, and they can read CD-ROMs. CD-RWs have a lower reflectivity than standard CD-ROMs, and CD-ROM drives must be of the newer multiread variety to read them. CD-RW was initially known as CD-E (for CD-erasable).

CD Video A CD format introduced in 1987 that combines 20 minutes of digital audio and 6 minutes of analog video on a standard 4.75" CD. Upon introduction, many firms renamed 8" and 12" videodiscs CDV in an attempt to capitalize on the consumer popularity of the audio CD. The term fell out of use in 1990 and was replaced in some part by *laser disc* and, more recently, *DVD*. See also *video-on-CD*.

CD-WO (compact disc-write once) A variant on CD-ROM that can be written to once and read many times; developed by NV Philips and Sony Corporation. Also known as CD-WORM (CD-write once/read many), CD-recordable, or CD-writable. Standards for this format are known as the Orange Book.

CD-WORM See *CD-WO*.

CDMA Short for code division multiple access, a popular family of wireless protocols used in cellular phones for Internet and email access.

Celeron A family of processors that are low-cost versions of the Pentium II, Pentium III, and Pentium 4 processors. The major differences include a smaller amount of L2 cache and lower clock speeds.

Centronics connector Refers to one of two types of cable connectors used with either parallel (36-pin edge connector) or SCSI (50-pin edge connector) devices.

ceramic substrate A thin, flat, fired-ceramic part used to hold an IC chip (usually made of beryllium oxide or aluminum oxide).

CERN (Conseil Européen pour la Recherche Nucléaire; The European Laboratory for Particle Physics) The site in Geneva where the World Wide Web was created in 1989.

CGA (color graphics adapter) A type of PC video display adapter introduced by IBM on August 12, 1981, which supports text and graphics. Text is supported at a maximum resolution of 80×25 characters in 16 colors with a character box of 8×8 pixels. Graphics are supported at a maximum resolution of 320×200 pixels in 16 colors or 640×200 pixels in 2 colors. The CGA outputs a TTL (digital) signal with a horizontal scanning frequency of 15.75KHz and supports TTL color or NTSC composite displays.

channel   1) Any path along which signals can be sent. 2) In ISDN, data bandwidth is divided into two B-channels that bear data and one D-channel that carries information about the call.

character   A representation—coded in binary digits—of a letter, number, or other symbol.

character set   All the letters, numbers, and characters a computer can use to represent data. The ASCII standard has 256 characters, each represented by a binary number from 1 to 256. The ASCII set includes all the letters in the alphabet, numbers, most punctuation marks, some mathematical symbols, and other characters.

charge coupled device   A light-sensing and storage device used in scanners and digital cameras to capture the pixels.

check bit   See *parity*.

checksum   Short for *summation check*, a technique for determining whether a package of data is valid. The package, a string of binary digits, is added up and compared with the expected number.

chip   Another name for an IC, or integrated circuit. Housed in a plastic or ceramic carrier device with pins for making electrical connections.

chip carrier   A ceramic or plastic package that carries an integrated circuit.

chipset   A single chip or pair of chips that integrates into it the clock generator, bus controller, system timer, interrupt controller, DMA controller, CMOS RAM/clock, and keyboard controller. See also *North Bridge* and *South Bridge*.

CHS (cylinder head sector)   The term used to describe the nontranslating scheme used by the BIOS to access IDE drives that are less than or equal to 528MB in capacity. See also *LBA*.

CIF (common image format)   The standard sample structure that represents the picture information of a single frame in digital HDTV, independent of frame rate and sync/blank structure. The uncompressed bit rate for transmitting CIF at 29.97 frames/sec is 36.45Mbps.

circuit   A complete electronic path.

circuit board   The collection of circuits gathered on a sheet of plastic, usually with all contacts made through a strip of pins. The circuit board usually is made by chemically etching metal-coated plastic.

CISC (complex instruction set computer)   Refers to traditional computers that operate with large sets of processor instructions. Most modern computers, including the Intel 80xxx processors, are in this category. CISC processors have expanded instruction sets that are complex in nature and require several to many execution cycles to complete. This structure contrasts with RISC (reduced instruction set computer) processors, which have far fewer instructions that execute quickly.

clean room   1) A dust-free room in which certain electronic components (such as chips or hard disk drives) must be manufactured and serviced to prevent contamination. Rooms are rated by Class numbers. A Class 100 clean room must have fewer than 100 particles larger than 0.5 microns per cubic foot of space. 2) A legal approach to copying software or hardware in which one team analyzes the product and writes a detailed description, followed by a second team that reads the description written by the first and then develops a compatible version of the product. When done correctly, such a design methodology will survive a legal attack.

client/server   A type of network in which every computer is either a server with a defined role of sharing resources with clients or a client that can access the resources on the server.

clock   The source of a computer's timing signals. It synchronizes every operation of the CPU.

clock multiplier   A processor feature where the internal core runs at a higher speed than the motherboard or processor bus. See also *overclocking*.

clock speed   A measurement of the rate at which the clock signal for a device oscillates, usually expressed in millions of cycles per second (MHz).

clone   Originally referred to an IBM-compatible computer system that physically as well as electrically emulates the design of one of IBM's personal computer systems. More currently, it refers to any PC system running an Intel or compatible processor in the 80x86 family.

cluster   Also called *allocation unit*. A group of one or more sectors on a disk that forms a fundamental unit of storage to the operating system. Cluster, or allocation unit, size is determined by the operating system when the disk is formatted. Larger clusters generally offer faster system performance but waste disk space.

CLV (constant linear velocity)   An optical recording format in which the spacing of data is consistent throughout the disk and the rotational speed of the disk varies depending on which track is being read. Additionally, more sectors of data are placed on the outer tracks compared to the inner tracks of the disk, which is similar to zone recording on hard drives. CLV drives adjust the rotational speed to maintain a constant track velocity as the diameter of the track changes. CLV drives also rotate more quickly near the center of the disk and more slowly toward the edge. Rotational adjustment maximizes the amount of data that can be stored on a disk. CD audio and CD-ROM use CLV recording. See also *CAV*.

CMOS (Complementary Metal-Oxide Semiconductor)   A type of chip design that requires little power to operate. In PCs, a battery-powered CMOS memory and clock chip is used to store and maintain the clock setting and system configuration information.

CMYK (cyan magenta yellow black)   The standard four-color model used for printing.

CNR   Short for Communications and Networking Riser, it was developed by Intel as a replacement for the AMR. CNR enables motherboard makers to offer low-cost modem, networking, and audio features through a special expansion slot. Unlike AMR, a CNR slot can be built as a shared slot with a PCI slot. See also *AMR*.

coated media   Hard disk platters coated with a reddish iron-oxide medium on which data is recorded.

coaxial cable   Also called *coax cable*. A data-transmission medium noted for its wide bandwidth, immunity to interference, and high cost compared to other types of cable. Signals are transmitted inside a fully shielded environment, in which an inner conductor is surrounded by a solid insulating material and then an outer conductor or shield. Used in many local area network systems, such as Ethernet and ARCnet.

COBOL (Common Business-Oriented Language)   A high-level computer programming language used primarily by some larger companies. It has never achieved popularity on personal and small business computers.

code page   A table used in DOS 3.3 and later that sets up the keyboard and display characters for various foreign languages.

code page switching   A DOS feature in versions 3.3 and later that changes the characters displayed onscreen or printed on an output device. Primarily used to support foreign-language characters. Requires an EGA or better video system and an IBM-compatible graphics printer.

CODEC (coder-decoder)   A device that converts voice signals from their analog form to digital signals acceptable to more modern digital PBXs and digital transmission systems. It then converts those digital signals back to analog so you can hear and understand what the other party is saying. Also refers to compression/decompression software used in the creation of digital audio and video files, such as MP3 and MPEG, and for videophone programs.

coercivity   A measurement in units of oersteds of the amount of magnetic energy to switch or "coerce" the flux change in the magnetic recording media. High-coercivity disk media require a stronger write current.

cold boot   The act of starting or restarting a computer from a powered-off state. If the system is on, this requires cycling the power off and then back on. A cold boot causes all RAM to be forcibly cleared. See also *warm boot*.

collision   In a LAN, if two computers transmit a packet of data at the same time on the network, the data can become garbled, which is known as a collision.

collision detection/avoidance   A process used on a LAN to prevent data packets from interfering with each other and to determine whether data packets have encountered a collision and initiate a resend of the affected packets.

color graphics adapter   See *CGA*.

color palette   The colors available to a graphics adapter for display.

COM port A serial port on a PC that conforms to the RS-232 standard. See also *RS-232*.

COMDEX The largest international computer trade show and conference in the world. COMDEX/Fall is held in Las Vegas during October, and COMDEX/Spring usually is held in Chicago or Atlanta during April.

command An instruction that tells the computer to start, stop, or continue an operation.

COMMAND.COM An operating system file that is loaded last when the computer is booted. The command interpreter or user interface and program-loader portion of DOS.

command interpreter The operating system program that controls a computer's shell or user interface. The command interpreter for MS-DOS (and the command-line sessions in Windows 9x/Me) is COMMAND.COM; the command interpreter for the graphical shell in Windows versions through 9x/Me is WIN.COM; the command interpreter for NT-based versions of Windows (including Windows 2000 and Windows XP) is CMD.COM.

common The ground or return path for an electrical signal. If it's a wire, it usually is colored black.

common mode noise Noise or electrical disturbances that can be measured between a current- or signal-carrying line and its associated ground. Common mode noise is frequently introduced to signals between separate computer equipment components through the power distribution circuits. It can be a problem when single-ended signals are used to connect different equipment or components that are powered by different circuits.

CompactFlash (CF) An ATA flash memory card physical format approximately one-third the size of a standard PC Card. Often abbreviated CF or CF+, CompactFlash cards are identical in function to standard ATA Flash PC Cards (PCMCIA) but use 50 pin connectors instead of 68. ATA flash cards contain built-in disk controller circuitry to enable the card to function as a solid-state disk drive. CF cards can plug into a CompactFlash socket or with an adapter into a standard Type I or II PC Card (PCMCIA) slot. CF cards are used by many types of digital cameras.

compatible 1) In the early days of the PC industry when IBM dominated the market, a term used to refer to computers from other manufacturers that had the same features as a given IBM model. 2) In general, software or hardware that conforms to industry standards or other de facto standards so that it can be used in conjunction with or in lieu of other versions of software or hardware from other vendors in a like manner.

compiler A program that translates a program written in a high-level language into its equivalent machine language. The output from a compiler is called an object program.

complete backup A backup of all information on a hard disk, including the directory tree structure.

composite video Television picture information and sync pulses combined. The complete wave form of the color video signal composed of chrominance and luminance picture information; blanking pedestal; field, line, and color-sync pulses; and field-equalizing pulses. Some video cards have an RCA jack that outputs a composite video signal. See also *RGB*.

compressed file A file that has been reduced in size via one or more compression techniques. See also *archive file*.

computer Device capable of accepting data, applying prescribed processes to this data, and displaying the results or information produced.

computer-based training (CBT) The use of a computer to deliver instruction or training; also known as computer-aided (or assisted) instruction (CAI), computer-aided learning (CAL), computer-based instruction (CBI), and computer-based learning (CBL).

CONFIG.SYS A file that can be created to tell DOS how to configure itself when the machine starts up. It can load device drivers, set the number of DOS buffers, and so on.

configuration file A file kept by application software to record various aspects of the software's configuration, such as the printer it uses. Windows uses INI files and the Windows Registry to control its configuration.

console The unit, such as a terminal or a keyboard, in your system with which you communicate with the computer.

contiguous Touching or joined at the edge or boundary, in one piece.

continuity   In electronics, an unbroken pathway. Testing for continuity usually means testing to determine whether a wire or other conductor is complete and unbroken (by measuring 0 ohms). A broken wire shows infinite resistance (or infinite ohms).

control cable   The wider of the two cables that connect an ST-506/412 or ESDI hard disk drive to a controller card. A 34-pin cable that carries commands and acknowledgments between the drive and controller.

controller   The electronics that control a device, such as a hard disk drive, and intermediate the passage of data between the device and computer.

controller card   An adapter holding the control electronics for one or more devices, such as hard disks. Ordinarily occupies one of the computer's slots.

conventional memory   The first megabyte or first 640KB of system memory accessible by an Intel processor in real mode. Sometimes called base memory.

convergence   Describes the capability of a CRT color monitor to focus the three colored electron beams on a single point. Poor convergence causes the characters onscreen to appear fuzzy and can cause headaches and eyestrain.

coprocessor   An additional computer processing unit designed to handle specific tasks in conjunction with the main or central processing unit.

copy protection   A hardware or software scheme to prohibit making illegal copies of a program.

core   An old-fashioned term for computer memory.

core speed   The internal speed of a processor. With all modern processors, this speed is faster than the system bus speed, and that speed relationship is regulated by the clock multiplier in the processor.

CP/M (Control Program for Microcomputers, originally Control Program/Monitor)   An operating system created by Gary Kildall, the founder of Digital Research. Created for the old 8-bit microcomputers that used the 8080, 8085, and Z-80 microprocessors. It was the dominant operating system in the late 1970s and early 1980s for small computers used in business environments.

cps (characters per second)   A data transfer rate generally estimated from the bit rate and character length. At 2,400bps, for example, 8-bit characters with start and stop bits (for a total of 10 bits per character) are transmitted at a rate of approximately 240cps. Some protocols, such as V.42 and MNP, employ advanced techniques such as longer transmission frames and data compression to increase characters per second.

CPU (central processing unit)   The computer's microprocessor chip; the brains of the outfit. Typically, an IC using VLSI (very large scale integration) technology to pack several functions into a tiny area. The most common electronic device in the CPU is the transistor, of which several thousand to several million or more are found.

crash   A malfunction that brings work to a halt. A system crash usually is caused by a software malfunction, and ordinarily you can restart the system by rebooting the machine. A head crash, however, entails physical damage to a disk and probable data loss.

CRC (cyclic redundancy checking)   An error-detection technique consisting of a cyclic algorithm performed on each block or frame of data by both sending and receiving modems. The sending modem inserts the results of its computation in each data block in the form of a CRC code. The receiving modem compares its results with the received CRC code and responds with either a positive or negative acknowledgment. In the ARQ protocol implemented in high-speed modems, the receiving modem accepts no more data until a defective block is received correctly.

crosstalk   The electromagnetic coupling of a signal on one line with another nearby signal line. Crosstalk is caused by electromagnetic induction, where a signal traveling through a wire creates a magnetic field that induces a current in other nearby wires. Various methods including twisting wire pairs and placing ground wires between data wires are used to combat crosstalk and create more reliable data communications.

CRT (cathode-ray tube)   A term used to describe a television or monitor screen tube. See also *cathode-ray tube*.

current   The flow of electrons, measured in amperes, or amps.

cursor   The small, flashing hyphen that appears onscreen to indicate the point at which any input from the keyboard will be placed.

cycle   Time for a signal to transition from one leading edge to the next leading edge.

cyclic redundancy checking   See *CRC*.

cylinder   The set of tracks on a disk that are on each side of all the disk platters in a stack and are the same distance from the center of the disk. The total number of tracks that can be read without moving the heads. A floppy drive with two heads usually has 160 tracks, which are accessible as 80 cylinders. A typical 120GB hard disk will physically have about 56,000 cylinders, 6 heads (3 platters), and an average of about 700 sectors per track, for a total of about 235,200,000 sectors (120.4GB).

Cyrix   Originally a Texas-based maker of Intel-compatible math coprocessor chips, Cyrix later developed low-cost, plug-compatible 6x86 and 6x86MX Pentium-class processors that were manufactured by IBM and other fabricators. Cyrix also developed the first chipsets with integrated audio and video (the MediaGX series). Cyrix was later absorbed into National Semiconductor, which retained the MediaGX technology when it sold Cyrix to VIA Technologies. VIA formerly developed and sold the VIA Cyrix MII, a low-cost Super Socket 7 processor, and currently sells and develops the C3, developed from the Cyrix "Joshua" processor. See also *C3* and *VIA Technologies*.

D/A converter (DAC)   A device that converts digital signals to analog form. See also *RAMDAC*.

D-channel   In ISDN, a 16Kbps channel used to transmit control data about a connection.

daisy-chain   Stringing up components in such a manner that the signals move serially from one to the other. Most microcomputer multiple disk drive systems are daisy-chained. The SCSI bus system is a daisy-chain arrangement, in which the signals move from computer to disk drives to tape units, and so on. USB and IEEE-1394 devices also use the daisy-chain arrangement when hubs are used.

daisywheel printer   An impact printer that prints fully formed characters one at a time by rotating a circular print element composed of a series of individual spokes, each containing two characters that radiate from a center hub. Produces letter-quality output but has long been replaced by laser and LED printers.

DAT (digital audio tape)   A small cassette containing 4mm-wide tape used for storing large amounts of digital information. DAT technology emerged in Europe and Japan in 1986 as a way to produce high-quality, digital audio recordings and was modified in 1988 to conform to the digital data storage (DDS) standard for storing computer data. Raw/compressed capacities for a single tape are 2/4GB for DDS, 4/8GB for DDS-2, 12/24GB for DDS-3, and 20/40GB for DDS-4.

data   1) Groups of facts processed into information. A graphic or textural representation of facts, concepts, numbers, letters, symbols, or instructions used for communication or processing. 2) An android from the twenty-fourth century with a processing speed of 60 trillion operations per second and a storage capacity of 800 quadrillion bits, and who serves on the USS Enterprise NCC-1701-D with the rank of lieutenant commander.

data bus   The connection that transmits data between the processor and the rest of the system. The width of the data bus defines the number of data bits that can be moved into or out of the processor in one cycle.

data cable   Generically, a cable that carries data. Specific to HD connections, the narrower (20-pin) of two cables that connects an ST-506/412 or ESDI hard disk drive to a controller card.

data communications   A type of communication in which computers and terminals can exchange data over an electronic medium.

data compression   A technique in which mathematical algorithms are applied to the data in a file to eliminate redundancies and therefore reduce the size of the file. See also *lossless compression* and *lossy compression*.

Data Link Layer   In networking, the layer of the OSI reference model that controls how the electrical impulses enter or leave the network cable. Ethernet and Token-Ring are the two most common examples of Data Link Layer protocols. See also *OSI*.

data separator   A device that separates data and clock signals from a single encoded signal pattern. Usually, the same device performs both data separation and combination and is sometimes called an endec, or encoder/decoder.

data transfer rate   The maximum rate at which data can be transferred from one device to another.

daughterboard   Add-on board to increase functionality and/or memory. Attaches to the existing board.

DB-9   9-pin D-shell connector, primarily used for PC serial ports.

DB-25   25-pin D-shell connector, primarily used for PC parallel ports.

DC   Direct current, such as that provided by a power supply or batteries.

DC-600 (Data Cartridge 600)   A data-storage medium invented by 3M in 1971 that uses a 1/4"-wide tape 600 feet in length.

DCE (data communications equipment)   The hardware that performs communication—usually a dialup modem that establishes and controls the data link through the telephone network. See also *DTE*.

DDE (dynamic data exchange)   A form of inter-process communications used by Microsoft Windows to support the exchange of commands and data between two applications running simultaneously. This capability has been enhanced further with object linking and embedding (OLE).

DDoS (distributed denial of service)   Refers to a type of denial-of-service attack that uses multiple computers that have been taken over by an intruder to attack a targeted system. See also *DoS*.

DDR (double data rate)   A type of SDRAM that allows two accesses per clock cycle, doubling the effective speed of the memory. The most common types of DDR include PC2100 (also known as DDR 266MHz), PC2700 (also known as DDR 333MHz), and PC3200 (also known as DDR 400MHz). See also *SDRAM*.

DDR2 (double data rate 2)   A type of SDRAM that enables two accesses per clock cycle, doubling the effective speed of the memory. DDR2 has more robust signaling and is faster than conventional DDR. The most common types of DDR2 include PC2-3200 (also known as DDR2-400MHz), PC2-4300 (also known as DDR2-533MHz), PC2-5400 (also known as DDR2-667MHz), and PC2-6400 (also known as DDR2-800MHz). See also *DDR* and *SDRAM*.

de facto standard   A software or hardware technology not officially made a standard by any recognized standards organization but that is used as a reference for consumers and vendors because of its dominance in the marketplace.

DEBUG   The name of a utility program included with DOS and used for specialized purposes, such as altering memory locations, tracing program execution, patching programs and disk sectors, and performing other low-level tasks.

decibel (dB)   A logarithmic measure of the ratio between two powers, voltages, currents, sound intensities, and so on. Signal-to-noise ratios are expressed in decibels.

dedicated line   A user-installed telephone line that connects a specified number of computers or terminals within a limited area, such as a single building. The line is a cable rather than a public-access telephone line. The communications channel also can be referred to as nonswitched because calls do not go through telephone company switching equipment.

dedicated servo surface   In voice-coil–actuated hard disk drives, one side of one platter given over to servo data that is used to guide and position the read/write heads.

default   Any setting assumed at startup or reset by the computer's software and attached devices and operational until changed by the user. An assumption the computer makes when no other parameters are specified. When you type **DIR** without specifying the drive to search, for example, the computer assumes you want it to search the default drive. The term is used in software to describe any action the computer or program takes on its own with embedded values.

defect map   A list of unusable sectors and tracks coded onto a drive during the low-level format process.

defragmentation   The process of rearranging disk sectors so files are stored on consecutive sectors in adjacent tracks.

degauss   1) To remove magnetic charges or to erase magnetic images. Normal applications include CRT monitors and disks or tapes. Most monitors incorporate a degaussing coil, which surrounds the CRT, and automatically energize this coil for a few seconds when powered up to remove color or image-distorting magnetic fields from the metal mask inside the tube. Some monitors include a button or control that can be used for additional applications of this coil to remove more stubborn magnetic traces. 2) Also the act of erasing or demagnetizing a magnetic disk or tape using a special tool called a degaussing coil.

density   The amount of data that can be packed into a certain area on a specific storage media.

desktop   A personal computer that sits on a desk.

device driver   Originally, a memory-resident program loaded by CONFIG.SYS that controls an unusual device, such as an expanded memory board. Windows also uses device drivers, but they are loaded through the Windows Registry or INI files.

DHCP (Dynamic Host Configuration Protocol)   A protocol for assigning dynamic IP addresses to devices on a network. With dynamic addressing, a device can have a different IP address every time it connects to the network. Routers, gateways, and broadband modems can function as DHCP hosts to provide IP addresses to other computers and devices on the network.

Dhrystone   A benchmark program used as a standard figure of merit indicating aspects of a computer system's performance in areas other than floating-point math performance. Because the program does not use any floating-point operations, performs no I/O, and makes no operating system calls, it is most useful for measuring the processor performance of a system. The original Dhrystone program was developed in 1984 and was written in Ada, although the C and Pascal versions became more popular by 1989.

DHTML (Dynamic HTML)   A collective term for cascading style sheets, layering, dynamic fonts, and other features encompassed in standard HTML 4.0, Netscape Navigator 4.x and above, and Internet Explorer 4.x and above. Because of differences in how browsers interpret particular DHTML features, many developers incorporate browser-checking code into their web pages to enable or disable certain features depending on the browser being used to view the page.

diagnostics   Programs used to check the operation of a computer system. These programs enable the operator to check the entire system for any problems and indicate in which area the problems lie.

dialup adapter   In Windows, a software program that uses a modem to emulate a network interface card for networking. Most commonly used to connect to an Internet service provider or a dialup server for remote access to a LAN.

die   An individual chip (processor, RAM, or other integrated circuit) cut from a finished silicon chip wafer and built into the physical package that connects it to the rest of the PC or a circuit board.

differential   An electrical signaling method in which a pair of lines are used for each signal in "push-pull" fashion. In most cases, differential signals are balanced so that the same current flows on each line in opposite directions. This is unlike single-ended signals, which use only one line per signal referenced to a single ground. Differential signals have a large tolerance for common-mode noise and little crosstalk when used with twisted-pair wires even in long cables. Differential signaling is expensive because two pins are required for each signal.

digital camera   A type of camera that uses a sensor and internal or removable flash memory in place of film to record still images. Digital cameras' picture quality is usually rated in megapixels. See also *megapixel*.

digital loopback   A test that checks the modem's RS-232 interface and the cable that connects the terminal or computer and the modem. The modem receives data (in the form of digital signals) from the computer or terminal and immediately returns the data to the screen for verification.

digital signals   Discrete, uniform signals. In this book, the term refers to the binary digits 0 and 1.

digital signature   An electronic identifier used to authenticate a message or the contents of a file. Windows 98 and above are designed to prefer digitally signed device drivers (drivers approved by the Windows Hardware Quality Labs) and will warn you if you try to install an unsigned device driver.

digital-to-analog converter (DAC)   A device for converting digital signals to analog signals. VGA-based displays are analog, so video cards that connect to them include a DAC to convert the signals to analog to drive the display.

digitize   To transform an analog wave to a digital signal a computer can store. Conversion to digital data and back is performed by a D/A converter (DAC), often a single-chip device. How closely a digitized sample represents an analog wave depends on the number of times the amplitude of a wave is measured and recorded (the rate of digitization), as well as the number of levels that can be specified at each instance. The number of possible signal levels is dictated by the resolution in bits.

DIMM (dual inline memory module)   A series of memory modules used in Pentium and newer PCs. They are available in many different versions, including those with SDRAM, DDR or DDR2, 3.3V, 2.5V or 1.8V, buffered, unbuffered or registered, and in 64-bit (non-ECC/parity) or 72-bit (ECC/parity) form. See also *DDR*, *DDR2*, and *SDRAM*.

DIP (dual inline package)   A family of rectangular, integrated-circuit flat packages that have leads on the two longer sides. Package material is plastic or ceramic.

DIP switch   A tiny switch (or group of switches) on a circuit board. Named for the form factor of the carrier device in which the switch is housed.

direct memory access (DMA)   A process by which data moves between a disk drive (or other device) and system memory without direct control of the central processing unit, thus freeing it up for other tasks.

Direct Rambus DRAM   See *RDRAM*.

directory   An area of a disk that stores the titles given to the files saved on the disk and serves as a table of contents for those files. Contains data that identifies the name of a file, the size, the attributes (system, hidden, read-only, and so on), the date and time of creation, and a pointer to the location of the file. Each entry in a directory is 32 bytes long. Windows refers to subdirectories (directories beneath the root directory) as folders.

DirectX   A set of graphics-related drivers and APIs that translate generic hardware commands into specific commands for particular pieces of hardware. Developed by Microsoft, DirectX lets graphical or multimedia applications take advantage of specific features supported by various graphics accelerators.

disc   Flat, circular, rotating medium that can store various types of information, both analog and digital. *Disc* is often used in reference to optical storage media, whereas *disk* refers to magnetic storage media. *Disc* also is often used as a short form for videodisc or compact audio disc (CD).

disk   Alternative spelling for disc that generally refers to magnetic storage medium on which information can be accessed at random. Floppy disks and hard disks are examples.

disk access time   See *access time*.

disk cache   A portion of memory on the PC motherboard or on a drive interface card or controller used to store frequently accessed information from the drive (such as the file allocation table [FAT] or directory structure) to speed up disk access. With a larger disk cache, additional data from the data portion of a drive can be cached as well. See also *cache*, *L1 cache*, and *L2 cache*.

disk partition   See *partition*.

display   A device used for viewing information generated by a computer.

display adapter   The interface between the computer and the monitor that transmits the signals which appear as images on the display. This can take the form of an expansion card or a chip built into the motherboard.

dithering   The process of creating more colors and shades from a given color palette. In monochrome displays or printers, dithering varies the black-and-white dot patterns to simulate shades of gray. Grayscale dithering is used to produce different shades of gray when the device can produce only limited levels of black or white outputs. Color screens or printers use dithering to create additional colors by mixing and varying the dot sizing and spacing. For example, when converting from 24-bit color to 8-bit color (an 8-bit palette has only 256 colors compared to the 24-bit palette's millions), dithering adds pixels of different colors to simulate the original color. Error diffusion is a type of dithering best suited for photographs.

DLC (Data Link Control)   Refers to the Data Link Layer in the OSI model. Every network interface card (NIC) has a unique DLC address or DLC identifier (DLCI) that identifies the node on the network. For Ethernet networks, the DLC address is usually called the Media Access Control (MAC) address.

DLL (dynamic link library)   An executable driver program module for Microsoft Windows that can be loaded on demand, linked in at runtime, and subsequently unloaded when the driver is no longer needed.

DMA See *direct memory access.*

DMI (Desktop Management Interface) DMI is an operating-system– and protocol-independent standard developed by the Desktop Management Task Force (DMTF) for managing desktop and laptop PC systems and servers. DMI provides a bidirectional path to interrogate all the hardware and software components within a PC, enabling hardware and software configurations to be monitored from a central station in a network.

DNS (domain name system or service) An Internet service that translates domain names into numeric IP addresses. Every time you use a domain name, a DNS server must translate the name into the corresponding IP address.

docking station Equipment that enables a laptop or notebook computer to use peripherals and accessories normally associated with desktop systems.

DOCSIS See *CableLabs Certified Cable Modem.*

doping Adding chemical impurities to silicon (which is naturally a nonconductor) to create a material with semiconductor properties that is then used in the manufacturing of electronic chips.

DoS (denial of service) An Internet attack on a resource that prevents users from accessing email, websites, or other services. It usually exploits security shortcomings in email or web servers. See also *DDoS.*

DOS (disk operating system) A collection of programs stored on the DOS disk that contain routines enabling the system and user to manage information and the hardware resources of the computer. DOS must be loaded into the computer before other programs can be started.

dot pitch A measurement of the width of the dots that make up a pixel. The smaller the dot pitch, the sharper the image.

dot-matrix printer An impact printer that prints characters composed of dots. Characters are printed one at a time by pressing the ends of selected wires against an inked ribbon and paper.

double density (DD) An indication of the storage capacity of a floppy drive or disk in which eight or nine sectors per track are recorded using MFM encoding. See also *MFM encoding.*

download The process of receiving files from another computer.

downtime Operating time lost because of a computer malfunction.

DPMI (DOS protected mode interface) An industry-standard interface that allows DOS applications to execute program code in the protected mode of the 286 or later Intel processor. The DPMI specification is available from Intel.

DPMS (display power-management signaling) A VESA standard for signaling a monitor or display to switch into energy conservation mode. DPMS provides for two low-energy modes: standby and suspend.

DRAM (dynamic random access memory) The most common type of computer memory, DRAM can be manufactured very inexpensively compared to other types of memory. DRAM chips are small and inexpensive because they normally require only one transistor and a capacitor to represent each bit. The capacitors must be energized every 15ms or so (hundreds of times per second) to maintain their charges. DRAM is volatile, meaning it loses data with no power or without regular refresh cycles.

drive A mechanical device that manipulates data storage media.

driver A program designed to interface a particular piece of hardware to an operating system or other standard software.

drum The cylindrical photoreceptor in a laser printer that receives the document image from the laser and applies it to the page as it slowly rotates.

DSL (Digital Subscriber Line) A high-speed digital modem technology. DSL is either symmetric or asymmetric. Asymmetric provides faster downstream speeds, which is suited for Internet usage and video on demand. Symmetric provides the same rate coming and going. See also *ADSL.*

DSM (digital storage media) A digital storage or transmission device or system.

DSP (digital signal processor) Dedicated, limited-function processor often found in modems, sound cards, cellular phones, and so on.

DSTN (dual scan twisted nematic) A type of passive matrix LCD display. See also *passive matrix.*

DTE (data terminal [or terminating] equipment) The device, usually a computer or terminal, that generates or is the final destination of data. See also *DCE*.

dual cavity pin grid array Chip packaging designed by Intel for use with the Pentium Pro processor that houses the processor die in one cavity of the package and the L2 cache memory in a second cavity within the same package.

dual independent bus (DIB) architecture A processor technology with the existence of two independent buses on the processor: the L2 cache bus and the processor-to-main memory system bus. The processor can use both buses simultaneously, thus getting as much as two times more data into and out of the processor than a single bus architecture processor. The Intel Pentium Pro, Pentium II, and newer processors from Intel and AMD (such as the AMD Athlon and Duron) have DIB architecture.

dual scan display A lower-quality but economical type of LCD color display that has an array of transistors running down the x and y axes of two sides of the screen. The number of transistors determines the screen's resolution.

dumb terminal A screen and keyboard device with no inherent processing power connected to a computer that is usually remotely located.

duplex Indicates a communications channel capable of carrying signals in both directions.

Duron A low-cost version of the Athlon processor with less L2 cache. Available in the Socket A (462-pin) chip package.

DVD (digital versatile disc) Originally called digital video disc. A new type of high-capacity CD-ROM disc and drive format with up to 28 times the capacity of a standard CD-ROM. The disc is the same diameter as a CD-ROM but can be recorded on both sides and on two layers for each side. Each side holds 4.7GB on a single layer disc, whereas dual-layer versions hold 8.5GB per side, for a maximum of 17GB total if both sides and both layers are used, which is the equivalent of 28 CD-ROMs. DVD drives can read standard audio CDs and CD-ROMs.

DVD burner Popular term for a rewritable DVD drive, particularly one that uses DVD-R/RW or DVD+R/RW media.

DVD-A A DVD format designed to support high-quality music and audio. DVD-A uses 24-bit sampling at 96KHz, significantly better than CD audio (16-bit at 44.1KHz). Unlike DVD, DVD-A discs can be played on conventional CD players but produce the highest quality only when played on DVD-A players.

DVD-R A writable DVD format compatible with standalone DVD players and DVD-ROM drives. DVD-R was introduced by Pioneer and was released to the DVD Forum (www.dvdforum.org) in July 1997. It uses a wobbled-groove recording process to store 4.7GB of data and is optimized for sequential data access. See also *DVD-RW*.

DVD+R A writable DVD format compatible with standalone DVD players and DVD-ROM drives. DVD+R was developed by the DVD+RW Alliance (www.dvdrw.com), whose members include Microsoft, Sony, HP, and Dell. In addition, it is supported by second-generation DVD+RW drives and holds 4.7GB of data. DVD+R/RW are the only recordable DVD formats that fully support the Mt. Rainier (also called EasyWrite) standard to be implemented natively in Windows Vista (code-named Longhorn) coming in late 2006. This enables discs to be used right out of the box with automatic background formatting and no additional packet writing software required. DVD+R/RW are the most compatible, fastest, most capable, and most popular of all the recordable DVD formats. See also *DVD+RW*.

DVD-RAM A rewritable DVD format developed by Panasonic, Toshiba, and Hitachi and supported by the DVD Forum. DVD-RAM is the oldest DVD rewritable format, but because the media uses a caddy and has a lower reflectivity than normal DVD media, DVD-RAM discs are not compatible with other types of DVD drives or with standalone DVD players.

DVD-RW A rewritable DVD format developed by Pioneer and released to the DVD Forum in November 1999. It uses a phase-change technology similar to CD-RW. As with most CD-RW media and drives, the entire disc must be formatted before it can be used. Its write speed is also lower than DVD+RW, and the entire disc must be erased before it can be used to store new data. See also *DVD-R*.

DVD+RW A rewritable DVD format developed by the DVD+RW Alliance; the first DVD+RW drives were released in 2001. DVD+RW uses a phase-change technology similar to CD-RW and DVD-RW. DVD+R/RW are the only recordable DVD formats that fully support the Mt. Rainier (EasyWrite) standard coming in Windows Vista (Longhorn) in late 2006. This enables discs to be used right out of the box with automatic background formatting and no additional packet writing software required. DVD+R/RW are the most compatible, fastest, most capable, and most popular of all the recordable DVD formats. See also *DVD+R*.

DVI (Digital Video Interactive) A now defunct hardware video codec standard that was originally developed at General Electric's Sarnoff Laboratories and sold to Intel in 1988. DVI integrates digital motion, still video, sound, graphics, and special effects in a compressed format. DVI was a highly sophisticated hardware compression codec used in interactive multimedia applications. Intel later created a software based codec called Indeo that was based on DVI.

DVI (Digital Visual Interface) The current de facto standard for LCD displays developed by the Digital Display Working Group in April 1999. DVI-D provides digital signals only, whereas DVI-I (which is more common) provides both digital and analog signals. A DVI-I connector can be converted to VGA with an external adapter.

Dvorak keyboard A keyboard design by August Dvorak that was patented in 1936 and approved by ANSI in 1982. Provides increased speed and comfort and reduces the rate of errors by placing the most frequently used letters in the center for use by the strongest fingers. Finger motions and awkward strokes are reduced by more than 90% in comparison with the familiar QWERTY keyboard. The Dvorak keyboard has the five vowel keys, AOEUI, together under the left hand in the center row and the five most frequently used consonants, DHTNS, under the fingers of the right hand.

dynamic execution A processing technique that enables the processor to dynamically predict the order of instructions and execute them out of order internally if necessary for an improvement in speed. Uses these three techniques: Multiple Branch Prediction, Data Flow Analysis, and Speculative Execution.

E2000 Also called Energy 2000, this is a Swiss-developed standard for power management that calls for computer monitors to use only 5 watts of power when in Standby mode.

EBCDIC (Extended Binary Coded Decimal Interchange Code) An IBM-developed, 8-bit code for the representation of characters. It allows 256 possible character combinations within a single byte. EBCDIC is the standard code on IBM minicomputers and mainframes, but not on the IBM microcomputers, where ASCII is used instead.

ECC (error correcting code) A type of system memory or cache that is capable of detecting and correcting some types of memory errors without interrupting processing.

ECP (enhanced capabilities port) A type of high-speed parallel port jointly developed by Microsoft and Hewlett-Packard that offers improved performance for the parallel port and requires special hardware logic. ECP ports use both an IRQ and a DMA channel. See also *IEEE 1284*.

edge connector The part of a circuit board containing a series of printed contacts that is inserted into an expansion slot or a connector.

EDO (extended data out) RAM A type of RAM chip that enables a timing overlap between successive accesses, thus improving memory cycle time.

EEPROM (electrically erasable programmable read-only memory) A type of nonvolatile memory chip used to store semipermanent information in a computer, such as the BIOS. An EEPROM can be erased and reprogrammed directly in the host system without special equipment. This is used so manufacturers can upgrade the ROM code in a system by supplying a special program that erases and reprograms the EEPROM chip with the new code. Also called flash ROM.

EGA (enhanced graphics adapter) A type of PC video display adapter first introduced by IBM on September 10, 1984, that supports text and graphics. Text is supported at a maximum resolution of 80×25 characters in 16 colors with a character box of 8×14 pixels. Graphics are supported at a maximum resolution of 640×350 pixels in 16 (from a palette of 64) colors. The EGA outputs a TTL (digital) signal with a horizontal scanning frequency of 15.75KHz, 18.432KHz, or 21.85KHz, and it supports TTL color or TTL monochrome displays.

EIA (Electronic Industries Association) An organization that defines electronic standards in the United States.

EIDE (Enhanced Integrated Drive Electronics)
A specific Western Digital implementation of the ATA-2 specification. See also *ATA-2*.

EISA (Extended Industry Standard Architecture)
An extension of the Industry Standard Architecture (ISA) bus developed by IBM for the AT. The EISA design was led by Compaq Corporation. Later, eight other manufacturers (AST, Epson, Hewlett-Packard, NEC, Olivetti, Tandy, Wyse, and Zenith) joined Compaq in a consortium founded September 13, 1988. This group became known as the "gang of nine." The EISA design was patterned largely after IBM's Micro Channel Architecture (MCA) in the PS/2 systems, but unlike MCA, EISA enables backward compatibility with older plug-in adapters. EISA products became obsolete after the development of the PCI slot architecture. See also *PCI*.

electronic mail (email)   A method of transferring messages from one computer to another.

electrostatic discharge (ESD)   The grounding of static electricity. A sudden flow of electricity between two objects at different electrical potentials. ESD is a primary cause of integrated circuit damage or failure.

ELF (extremely low frequency)   A very low-frequency electromagnetic radiation generated by common electrical appliances, including computer monitors. The Swedish MPR II standard governs this and other emissions. Also called VLF (very low frequency).

embedded controller   In disk drives, a controller built in to the same physical unit that houses the drive rather than on a separate adapter card. IDE and SCSI drives both use embedded controllers.

embedded servo data   Magnetic markings embedded between or inside tracks on disk drives that use voice-coil actuators. These markings enable the actuator to fine-tune the position of the read/write heads.

EMM (expanded memory manager)   A driver that provides a software interface to expanded memory. EMMs were originally created for expanded memory boards but also can use the memory management capabilities of the 386 or later processors to emulate an expanded memory board. EMM386.EXE is an example of an EMM that comes with DOS and Windows 9x.

EMS (Expanded Memory Specification)
Sometimes also called the LIM spec because it was developed by Lotus, Intel, and Microsoft. Provides a way for microcomputers running under DOS to access additional memory. EMS memory management provides access to a maximum of 32MB of expanded memory through a small (usually 64KB) window in conventional memory. EMS is a cumbersome access scheme designed primarily for pre-286 systems that could not access extended memory.

emulator   A piece of test apparatus that emulates or imitates the function of a particular chip.

encoding   The protocol by which data is carried or stored by a medium.

encryption   The translation of data into unreadable codes to maintain security.

endec (encoder/decoder)   A device that takes data and clock signals and combines or encodes them using a particular encoding scheme into a single signal for transmission or storage. The same device also later separates or decodes the data and clock signals during a receive or read operation. Sometimes called a data separator.

Energy Star   A certification program started by the Environmental Protection Agency in 1992. Energy Star–certified computers and peripherals are generally required to draw less than 30 watts of electrical energy from a standard 115-volt AC outlet during periods of inactivity. Also called Green PCs. See also *E2000*.

Enhanced CD (CD-E)   See *Blue Book*.

enhanced graphics adapter   See *EGA*.

enhanced small device interface   See *ESDI*.

EPP (Enhanced Parallel Port)   A type of parallel port developed by Intel, Xircom, and Zenith Data Systems that operates at almost ISA bus speed and offers a tenfold increase in the raw throughput capability over a conventional parallel port. EPP is especially designed for parallel port peripherals, such as LAN adapters, disk drives, and tape backups. See also *IEEE 1284*.

EPROM (erasable programmable read-only memory)   A type of read-only memory (ROM) in which the data pattern can be erased to allow a new pattern. EPROM usually is erased by ultraviolet light and recorded by a higher-than-normal voltage programming signal.

equalization A compensation circuit designed into modems to counteract certain distortions introduced by the telephone channel. Two types are used: fixed (compromise) equalizers and those that adapt to channel conditions (adaptive). Good-quality modems use adaptive equalization.

error control Various techniques that check the reliability of characters (parity) or blocks of data. V.42, MNP, and HST error-control protocols use error detection (CRC) and retransmission of error frames (ARQ).

error message A word or combination of words to indicate to the user that an error has occurred somewhere in the program.

ESCD (extended system configuration data) Area in CMOS or Flash/NVRAM where plug-and-play information is stored.

ESDI (Enhanced Small Device Interface) A hardware standard developed by Maxtor and standardized by a consortium of 22 disk drive manufacturers on January 26, 1983. A group of 27 manufacturers formed the ESDI steering committee on September 15, 1986, to enhance and improve the specification. A high-performance interface used primarily with hard disks, ESDI enables a maximum data transfer rate to and from a hard disk of between 10Mbps and 24Mbps. ESDI was replaced by IDE and SCSI interfaces. ESDI drives use the same 34-pin and 20-pin cables used by ST412/ST506 drives.

Ethernet A type of network protocol developed in the late 1970s by Bob Metcalf at Xerox Corporation and endorsed by the IEEE. One of the oldest LAN communications protocols in the personal computing industry, Ethernet networks use a collision-detection protocol to manage contention. Ethernet is defined by the IEEE 802.3 standard. See also *10BASE-T*.

expanded memory Otherwise known as EMS memory, this is memory that conforms to the EMS specification. Requires a special device driver and conforms to a standard developed by Lotus, Intel, and Microsoft.

expansion card An integrated circuit card that plugs into an expansion slot on a motherboard to provide access to additional peripherals or features not built in to the motherboard. Also referred to as an add-in board.

expansion slot A slot on the motherboard that physically and electrically connects an expansion card to the motherboard and the system buses.

extended graphics array See *XGA*.

extended memory Direct processor-addressable memory addressed by an Intel (or compatible) 286 or more advanced processor in the region beyond the first megabyte. Addressable only in the processor's protected mode of operation.

extended partition A nonbootable DOS partition (also supported by Windows) containing DOS volumes. Starting with DOS v3.3, the FDISK program can create two partitions that serve DOS: an ordinary, bootable partition (called the primary partition) and an extended partition, which can contain as many as 23 volumes from D: to Z:.

external device A peripheral installed outside the system case.

extra-high density (ED) An indication of the storage capacity of a floppy drive or disk in which 36 sectors per track are recorded using a vertical recording technique with MFM encoding.

FAQ (frequently asked questions) Name for a list of popular questions and answers covering any particular subject.

Fast Ethernet Popular term for 100BASE-T and other 100Mbps versions of Ethernet. Fast Ethernet uses CAT 5 cable.

Fast Page Mode RAM A type of RAM that improves on standard DRAM speed by enabling faster access to all the data within a given row of memory by keeping the row address the same and changing only the column.

Fast-ATA (fast AT attachment interface) Also called Fast ATA-2, these are specific Seagate and Quantum implementations of the ATA-2 interface. See also *ATA-2*.

FAT (file allocation table) A table held near the outer edge of a disk that tells which sectors are allocated to each file and in what order.

FAT32 A disk file allocation system from Microsoft that uses 32-bit values for FAT entries instead of the 16-bit values used by the original FAT system, enabling partition sizes up to 2TB (terabytes). Although the entries are 32 bits, 4 bits are reserved and only 28 bits are used. FAT32 first appeared in Windows 95B and is also supported by

Windows 98, Windows Me, Windows 2000, and Windows XP. See also *VFAT*.

fault tolerance   The capability of a computer to withstand a failure. Many levels of fault tolerance exist, and fault tolerance can be applied to several components or systems in the computer. For example, ECC (error correcting code) memory is considered fault tolerant because it is typically capable of automatically identifying and correcting single bit errors.

fax/modem   A peripheral that integrates the capabilities of a fax machine and a modem in one expansion card or external unit. Almost all 14.4Kbps and faster modems sold for use in desktop or portable PCs include fax capabilities.

FC-PGA (flip-chip pin grid array)   A type of chip packaging first used in the Socket PGA370 version of the Pentium III where the raw processor die has bumped contacts spaced on the face of the die and is mounted facedown to a pin grid array carrier. The heatsink is then directly attached to the back of the raw silicon die surface.

FDISK   The name of the disk-partitioning program under several operating systems, including DOS and Windows 9x/Me, to create the master boot record and allocate partitions for the operating system's use.

feature connector   On a video adapter, a connector that enables an additional video feature card, such as a separate 3D accelerator, video capture card, or MPEG decoder, to be connected to the main video adapter and display.

fiber optic   A type of cable or connection using strands or threads of glass to guide a beam of modulated light. Allows for very high-speed signaling and multiplexing as well as the combining of many data streams along a single cable.

FIFO (first-in, first-out)   A method of storing and retrieving items from a list, table, or stack so that the first element stored is the first one retrieved.

file   A collection of information kept somewhere other than in random access memory.

file attribute   Information held in the attribute byte of a file's directory entry.

file compression   See *compressed file*.

filename   The name given to the disk file. For DOS, it must be from one to eight characters long

and can be followed by a filename extension, which can be from one to three characters long. Windows 9x and above ease these constraints by allowing filenames of up to 255 characters including the directory path.

firewall   A hardware or software system designed to prevent unauthorized access to or from a private network.

FireWire   Also called IEEE-1394 or i.Link. A serial I/O interface standard that is extremely fast, with data transfer rates up to 400MBps, 800MBps, or 3.2GBps, depending on the version of standard used. Most current implementations use the 400MBps IEEE-1394a version.

firmware   Software contained in a read-only memory (ROM) device. A cross between hardware and software, firmware can be easily updated if stored in an EEPROM or flash ROM chip. See also *EEPROM* and *flash ROM*.

fixed disk   Also called a hard disk, it's a disk that can't be removed from its controlling hardware or housing. Made of rigid material with a magnetic coating and used for the mass storage and retrieval of data.

flash ROM   A type of EEPROM developed by Intel that can be erased and reprogrammed in the host system. See also *EEPROM*.

flicker   A monitor condition caused by refresh rates that are too low, in which the display flashes visibly. This can cause eyestrain or more severe physical problems.

floating-point unit (FPU)   Sometimes called the math coprocessor; handles the more complex calculations of the processing cycle.

floppy disk   A removable disk using flexible magnetic media enclosed in a semirigid or rigid plastic case.

floppy disk controller   The logic and interface that connects a floppy disk drive to the system.

floppy tape   A tape standard that uses drives connecting to an ordinary floppy disk controller, such as QIC-80 or Travan-1.

floptical drive   A special type of high-capacity removable disk drive that uses an optical mechanism to properly position the drive read/write heads over the data tracks on the disk. This enables more precise control of the read/write positioning and therefore narrower track spacing and more data packed into a smaller area than traditional floppy disks. The LS-120 and LS-240 SuperDisk drives are recent examples of floptical drives.

flow control   A mechanism that compensates for differences in the flow of data input to and output from a modem or other device.

FM encoding   Frequency modulation encoding. An outdated method of encoding data on the disk surface that uses up half the disk space with timing signals.

FM synthesis   An audio technology that uses one sine wave operator to modify another and create an artificial sound that mimics an instrument.

folder   In a graphical user interface, a simulated file folder that holds documents (text, data, or graphics), applications, and other folders. A folder is similar to a DOS subdirectory.

footprint   Describes the shape of something. See also *form factor.*

form factor   The physical dimensions of a device. Two devices with the same form factor are physically interchangeable. The IBM PC, XT, and XT Model 286, for example, all use power supplies that are internally different but have exactly the same form factor.

FORMAT   The DOS/Windows format program that performs both low- and high-level formatting on floppy disks but only high-level formatting on hard disks.

formatted capacity   The total number of bytes of data that can fit on a formatted disk. The unformatted capacity is higher because space is lost defining the boundaries between sectors.

formatting   Preparing a disk so the computer can read or write to it. Checks the disk for defects and constructs an organizational system to manage information on the disk.

FORTRAN (formula translator)   A high-level programming language developed in 1954 by John Backus at IBM primarily for programs dealing with mathematical formulas and expressions similar to algebra and used primarily in scientific and technical applications.

fragmentation   The state of having a file scattered around a disk in pieces rather than existing in one contiguous area of the disk. Fragmented files are slower to read than files stored in contiguous areas and can be more difficult to recover if the FAT or a directory becomes damaged.

frame   1) A data communications term for a block of data with header and trailer information attached. The added information usually includes a frame number, block size data, error-check codes, and start/end indicators. 2) A single, complete picture in a video or film recording. A video frame consists of two interlaced fields of either 525 lines (NTSC) or 625 lines (PAL/SECAM), running at 30 frames per second (NTSC) or 25 frames per second (PAL/SECAM).

frame buffer   A memory device that stores, pixel by pixel, the contents of an image. Frame buffers are used to refresh a raster image. Sometimes they incorporate a local processing capability. The "depth" of the frame buffer is the number of bits per pixel, which determines the number of colors or intensities that can be displayed.

frame rate   The speed at which video frames are scanned or displayed: 30 frames per second for NTSC and 25 frames per second for PAL/SECAM.

FTP (File Transfer Protocol)   A method of transferring files over the Internet. FTP can be used to transfer files between two machines on which the user has accounts. Anonymous FTP can be used to retrieve a file from a server without having an account on that server.

full duplex   Signal flow in both directions at the same time. In microcomputer communications, it also can refer to the suppression of the online local echo. 100BASE-TX network cards capable of full-duplex operations can run at an effective speed of 200Mbps when full-duplex operation is enabled.

full-height drive   A drive unit that is 3 1/4" high, 5 1/4" wide, and 8" deep. Equal to two half-height drive bays.

full-motion video   A video sequence displayed at full television standard resolutions and frame rates. In the United States, this equates to NTSC video at 30 frames per second.

function keys   Special-purpose keys that can be programmed to perform various operations. They serve many functions, depending on the program being used.

G.lite A popular form of ADSL, G.lite can be self-installed by the user. Also referred to as the G.992.2 standard.

gas-plasma display Commonly used in portable systems, it's a type of display that operates by exciting a gas—usually neon or an argon-neon mixture—through the application of a voltage. When sufficient voltage is applied at the intersection of two electrodes, the gas glows an orange-red. Because gas-plasma displays generate light, they require no backlighting.

gateway Officially, an application-to-application conversion program or system. For example, an email gateway converts from SMTP (Internet) email format to MHS (Novell) email format. The term *gateway* is also used as a slang term for *router*. See also *router*.

gender When describing connectors for PCs, connectors are described as male if they have pins or female if they have receptacles designed to accept the pins of a male connector.

genlocking The process of aligning the data rate of a video image with that of a digital device to digitize the image and enter it into computer memory. The machine that performs this function is known as a genlock.

Ghost Popular utility program sold by Symantec that can be used to create a compressed version of a drive's contents and clone it to one or more PCs over a network or via CD storage.

gibi A multiplier equal to 1,073,741,824.

gibibyte (Gi) A unit of information storage equal to 1,073,741,824 bytes (1,024×1,024×1,024 equals a Gi). Formerly known as a binary gigabyte. See also *gigabyte* and *kilobyte*.

GIF (Graphical Interchange Format) A popular raster graphics file format developed by CompuServe that handles 8-bit color (256 colors) and uses the LZW method to achieve compression ratios of approximately 1.5:1 to 2:1. You can reduce the size of a GIF file even more by dropping unused colors from the file.

giga A multiplier indicating one billion (1,000,000,000) of some unit. Abbreviated as g or G. The binary giga (1,073,741,824) is now referred to as a gibi. See also *gibi*.

gigabyte (GB) A unit of information storage equal to 1,000,000,000 bytes. The value formerly called a binary GB (1,073,741,824 bytes) is now called a gibibyte. See also *gibibyte*.

gigahertz GHz is used to measure the clock frequency of high-performance processors. The first 1GHz desktop processor was introduced by AMD (a 1GHz Athlon) in March 2000.

GPU (graphics processing unit) A 3D graphics chip that contains advanced 3D rendering features such as hardware, vertex, and pixel shaders. NVIDIA's GeForce 3 and GeForce 4 Ti series; the ATI Radeon 7xxx, 8xxx, and 9xxx series; and the Matrox Parhelia series are typical GPUs. See also *hardware shader*, *pixel shader*, and *vertex shader*.

graphics accelerator A video processor or chipset specially designed to speed the display and rendering of graphical objects onscreen. Originally, accelerators were optimized for 2D or 3D operations, but all current graphics accelerators, such as NVIDIA's GeForce and ATI's RADEON series, accelerate both types of data.

graphics adapter See *video adapter*.

Green Book The standard for Compact Disc-Interactive (CD-I). Philips developed CD-I technology for the consumer market to be connected to a television instead of a computer monitor. CD-I is not a computer system but a consumer device that made a small splash in the market and disappeared. CD-I discs require special code and are not compatible with standard CD-ROMs. A CD-ROM can't be played on the CD-I machine, but Red Book audio can be played on it.

GUI (graphical user interface) A type of program interface that enables users to choose commands and functions by pointing to a graphical icon using either a keyboard or pointing device, such as a mouse. Windows is the most popular GUI available for PC systems.

half duplex Signal flow in both directions but only one way at a time. In microcomputer communications, half duplex can refer to activation of the online local echo, which causes the modem to send a copy of the transmitted data to the screen of the sending computer.

half-height drive A drive unit that is 1.625" high, 5 1/4" wide, and 8" deep.

halftoning A process that uses dithering to simulate a continuous tone image, such as a photograph or shaded drawing, using various sizes of dots. Newspapers, magazines, and many books use halftoning. The human eye merges the dots to give the impression of gray shades.

handshaking   The process of exchanging information about speeds and protocols between analog modems to establish a dialup connection. If your modem volume is high enough, you can hear handshaking as a series of distinct tones at the start of a modem-to-modem call.

hard disk   A high-capacity disk storage unit characterized by a normally nonremovable rigid substrate medium. The platters in a hard disk usually are constructed of aluminum or glass/ceramic. Also sometimes called a fixed disk.

hard error   An error in reading or writing data caused by damaged hardware.

hard reset   Resetting a system via the hardware, usually by pressing a dedicated reset button wired to the motherboard/processor reset circuitry. Does not clear memory like a cold boot does. See also *cold boot*.

hardware   Physical components that make up a microcomputer, monitor, printer, and so on.

hardware shader   A general term describing the processing of vertex or pixel shading in a GPU's hardware. GPUs such as the ATI 8xxx and 9xxx series or the NVIDIA GeForce 3 and GeForce 4 Ti-series GPU chips have hardware shaders compatible with DirectX 8 and above.

HDLC (High-Level Data Link Control)   A standard protocol developed by the ISO for software applications and communicating devices operating in synchronous environments. Defines operations at the link level of communications—for example, the format of data frames exchanged between modems over a phone line.

head   A small electromagnetic device inside a drive that reads, records, and erases data on the media.

head actuator   The device that moves read/write heads across a disk drive's platters. Most drives use a stepper-motor or voice-coil actuator.

head crash   A (usually) rare occurrence in which a read/write head strikes a platter surface with sufficient force to damage the magnetic medium.

head parking   A procedure in which a disk drive's read/write heads are moved to an unused track so they will not damage data in the event of a head crash or other failure.

head seek   The movement of a drive's read/write heads to a particular track.

heatsink   A mass of metal attached to a chip carrier or socket for the purpose of dissipating heat. Some heatsinks are passive (relying on existing air currents only), but most heatsinks on processors are active (including a fan). Many video card accelerator chips and motherboard North Bridge chips are also fitted with heatsinks today.

helical scan   A type of recording technology that has vastly increased the capacity of tape drives. Invented for use in broadcast systems and now used in VCRs. Conventional longitudinal recording records a track of data straight across the width of a single-track tape. Helical scan recording packs more data on the tape by positioning the tape at an angle to the recording heads. The heads spin to record diagonal stripes of information on the tape. Helical scan is used by DAT/DDS, Exabyte, and AIT drives.

hexadecimal number   A number encoded in base-16, such that digits include the letters A–F and the numerals 0–9 (for example, 8BF3, which equals 35,827 in base-10).

hibernate/hibernation   An OS-controlled ACPI S4 sleep state, hibernation is the lowest power sleeping state available. Also called suspend-to-disk (STD), hibernation saves the complete state of the PC to a hiberfile on a nonvolatile storage device such as a hard disk, and powers the system off. When the system is subsequently powered on, the BIOS will go through the normal POST and then read the previously created hiberfile and resume to the same state as when hibernation was previously entered, including any running applications, open files, displayed pages, and so on. Windows Me, 2000, XP, and later support hibernate capabilities (ACPI S4 sleep state) on PCs having ACPI hibernation support.

hidden file   A file not displayed in DOS directory listings because the file's attribute byte holds a special setting.

high density (HD)   An indication of the storage capacity of a floppy drive or disk, in which 15 or 18 sectors per track are recorded using MFM encoding.

High Sierra format   A standard format for placing files and directories on CD-ROMs, proposed by an ad hoc committee of computer vendors, software developers, and CD-ROM system integrators. (Work on the format proposal began at the High Sierra Hotel in Lake Tahoe, Nevada.) A revised version of the format was adopted by the ISO as ISO 9660. Use the ISO 9660 format to create cross-platform CD-R recordings.

high-definition television (HDTV)   Video formats offering greater visual accuracy (or resolution) than current NTSC, PAL, or SECAM broadcast standards. HDTV formats generally range in resolution from 655 to 2,125 scanning lines, having an aspect ratio of 5:3 (or 1.67:1) and a video bandwidth of 30MHz–50MHz (5+ times greater than the NTSC standard). Digital HDTV has a bandwidth of 300MHz. HDTV is subjectively comparable to 35mm film.

high-level formatting   Formatting performed by the DOS FORMAT program. Among other things, it creates the root directory and FATs.

history file   A file created by utility software to keep track of earlier use of the software. Many backup programs, for example, keep history files describing earlier backup sessions.

hit ratio   In describing the efficiency of a disk or memory cache, the hit ratio is the ratio of the number of times the data is found in the cache to the total number of data requests. A perfect hit ratio is 1:1, meaning that every data request was found in the cache. The closer to 1:1 the ratio is, the more efficient the cache.

HMA (high memory area)   The first 64KB of extended memory, which typically is controlled by the HIMEM.SYS device driver. Real-mode programs can be loaded into the HMA to conserve conventional memory. Normally, DOS 5.0 and later use the HMA exclusively to reduce the DOS conventional memory footprint.

HomePNA   A home networking standard using existing home or office telephone wiring to obtain speeds up to 11Mbps.

HomeRF   A wireless home network using radio waves to obtain speeds up to 11Mbps.

horizontal scan rate   In monitors, the speed at which the electron beam moves laterally across the screen. It's normally expressed as a frequency; typical monitors range from 31.5KHz to 90KHz, with the higher frequencies being more desirable.

host   The main device when two or more devices are connected. When two or more systems are connected, the system that contains the data is typically called the host, whereas the other is called the guest or user.

hotfix   A software patch for a Microsoft application or operating system. Hotfixes can be downloaded individually from the Windows Update website or as a service pack. Microsoft also calls them quick fix engineering (QFE) files.

hotkey   A special key or combination of keys that can be defined to cause a function to occur. Laptops often use a Fn (function) key in combination with other keys as hotkeys to perform tasks such as to force the system into standby or hibernation modes, turn on or off wireless LAN or Bluetooth adapters, and so on.

HPT (high-pressure tin)   A PLCC socket that promotes high forces between socket contacts and PLCC contacts for a good connection.

HST (High-Speed Technology)   The now-obsolete U.S. Robotics proprietary high-speed modem-signaling scheme, developed as an interim protocol until the V.32 protocol could be implemented in a cost-effective manner.

HT technology   See *hyper-threading technology*.

HTML (Hypertext Markup Language)   A language used to describe and format plain-text files on the Web. HTML is based on pairs of tags that enable the user to mix graphics with text, change the appearance of text, and create hypertext documents with links to other documents. See also *DHTML*.

HTTP (Hypertext Transfer Protocol)   The protocol that describes the rules a browser and server use to communicate over the World Wide Web. HTTP allows a web browser to request HTML documents from a web server. See also *hypertext*.

hub   A common connection point for multiple devices in a network. A hub contains a number of ports to connect several segments of a LAN together. When a packet arrives at one of the ports on the hub, it is copied to all the other ports so all the segments of the LAN can see all the packets. A hub can be passive, intelligent (allowing remote management, including traffic monitoring and port configuration), or switching. A switching hub is also called a switch. See also *switch*.

Huffman coding A technique that minimizes the average number of bytes required to represent the characters in a text. Huffman coding works for a given character distribution by assigning short codes to frequently occurring characters and longer codes to infrequently occurring characters.

hybrid fiber/coax (HFC) A network (such as that used by digital cable TV and two-way cable modems) that uses fiber-optic cabling for its backbone with coaxial cable connections to each individual computer or TV.

hyper-threading technology A method (also called HT technology) developed by Intel for running two different instruction streams through a processor at the same time. Introduced in 2002, HT technology was first used in the Intel Xeon processor with hyper-threading technology, with speeds starting at 2.8GHz; the first HT technology–enabled desktop processor was the 3.06GHz Pentium 4.

hypertext A technology that enables quick and easy navigation between and within large documents. Hypertext links are pointers to other sections within the same document; other documents; or other resources, such as FTP sites, images, or sounds.

HyperTransport AMD's high-speed technology for connecting the North Bridge and South Bridge or equivalent chips on a motherboard. HyperTransport runs at six times the speed of the PCI bus (800MBps versus 133MBps for PCI). The original name was Lightning Data Transport (LDT). Several chipset makers, including AMD and NVIDIA, use HyperTransport.

Hz An abbreviation for hertz—a frequency measurement unit used internationally to indicate one cycle per second.

i.Link Sony's term for IEEE 1394/FireWire port. See also *FireWire*.

I/O (input/output) A circuit path that enables independent communication between the processor and external devices.

I/O controller hub See *ICH*.

I/O port (input/output port) Used to communicate to and from another device, such as a printer or disk.

IA-64 Intel's 64-bit processor architecture, first used in the Itanium processor for servers.

IBMBIO.COM One of the DOS system files required to boot the machine in older versions of PC-DOS (IBM's version of MS-DOS). The first file loaded from disk during the boot, it contains extensions to the ROM BIOS.

IBMDOS.COM One of the DOS system files required to boot the machine in older versions of PC-DOS (IBM's version of MS-DOS). Contains the primary DOS routines. Loaded by IBMBIO.COM, it in turn loads COMMAND.COM.

IC (integrated circuit) A complete electronic circuit contained on a single chip. It can consist of only a few or thousands of transistors, capacitors, diodes, or resistors, and it generally is classified according to the complexity of the circuitry and the approximate number of circuits on the chip. SSI (small-scale integration) equals 2–10 circuits; MSI (medium-scale integration) equals 10–100 circuits. LSI (large-scale integration) equals 100–1,000 circuits, and VLSI (very large scale integration) equals 1,000–10,000 circuits. Finally, ULSI (ultra large scale integration) equals more than 10,000 circuits.

ICH (I/O controller hub) Intel's term for the chip used in its 8xx chipsets to interface with lower-speed devices such as PCI slots, USB ports, ATA drives, and other devices traditionally controlled by the South Bridge chip. ICH chips connect with the memory controller hub (the 8xx chipsets' replacement for the North Bridge) through a high-speed hub interface. Current ICH chips used by Intel 8xx-series chipsets include the ICH2 and ICH4. See also *MCH*.

IDE (Integrated Drive Electronics) Describes a hard disk with the disk controller circuitry integrated within it. The first IDE drives commonly were called hard cards. Also refers to the ATA interface standard—the standard for attaching hard disk drives to ISA bus IBM-compatible computers. IDE drives typically operate as though they are standard ST-506/412 drives. See also *ATA*.

IEEE 802.3 See *10BASE-2*.

IEEE 802.11 family A family of wireless network standards commonly known as wireless Ethernet, the most popular of which include 802.11a (54Mbps using 5GHz signaling) and 802.11b (11Mbps using 2.4GHz signaling). 802.11b is frequently called Wi-Fi. See also *Wi-Fi*.

IEEE 1284   A series of standards for parallel ports. IEEE 1284 includes EPP and ECP configurations as well as the older bidirectional and 4-bit compatible parallel port modes. Printer cables that can work with all modes are referred to as IEEE 1284-compliant cables. See also *EPP* and *ECP*.

IEEE 1394   See *FireWire*.

illegal operation   A command sent to Windows or the processor that can't be performed. Illegal operations can be triggered by software bugs or conflicts between programs in memory; although the name is reminiscent of a penalty in football, an illegal operation is hardly ever caused by the computer user. In most cases, you can continue to work and might even be able to restart the program without rebooting.

impedance   The total opposition a circuit offers to the flow of alternating current, measured in ohms.

incremental backup   A backup of all the files that have changed since the last backup.

inductive   A property in which energy can be transferred from one device to another via the magnetic field generated by the device, even though no direct electrical connection is established between the two.

INF file   A Windows driver and device information file used to install new drivers or services.

infrared   See *IrDA*.

ingot   See *boule*.

initiator   A device attached to the SCSI bus that sends a command to another device (the target) on the SCSI bus. The SCSI host adapter plugged into the system bus is an example of a SCSI initiator.

inkjet printer   A type of printer that sprays one or more colors of ink on the paper; it can produce output with quality approaching that of a laser printer at a lower cost.

input   Data sent to the computer from the keyboard, the telephone, a video camera, another computer, paddles, joysticks, and so on.

InstallShield   A popular program used to create installation and uninstallation routines for Windows–based programs.

instruction   Program step that tells the computer what to do for a single operation.

integrated circuit   See *IC*.

interface   A communications device or protocol that enables one device to communicate with another. Matches the output of one device to the input of the other device.

interlacing   A method of scanning alternate lines of pixels on a display screen. The odd lines are scanned first from top to bottom and left to right. The electron gun goes back to the top and makes a second pass, scanning the even lines. Interlacing requires two scan passes to construct a single image. Because of this additional scanning, interlaced screens often seem to flicker unless a long-persistence phosphor is used in the display. Interlaced monitors were used with the IBM 8514/A display card but are now obsolete for desktop computers.

interleave ratio   The number of sectors that pass beneath the read/write heads before the "next" numbered sector arrives. When the interleave ratio is 3:1, for example, a sector is read, two pass by, and then the next is read. A proper interleave ratio, laid down during low-level formatting, enables the disk to transfer information without excessive revolutions due to missed sectors. All modern IDE and SCSI drives have a 1:1 interleave ratio.

interleaved memory   The process of alternating access between two banks of memory to overlap accesses, thus speeding up data retrieval. Systems that require only one memory module per bank to operate can work more quickly when two are installed if the system supports interleaved memory.

internal command   In DOS, a command contained in COMMAND.COM so that no other file must be loaded to perform the command. DIR and COPY are two examples of internal commands.

internal device   A peripheral device installed inside the main system case in either an expansion slot or a drive bay.

internal drive   A disk or tape drive mounted inside one of a computer's disk drive bays (or a hard disk card, which is installed in one of the computer's slots).

Internet   A computer network that joins many government, university, and private computers together. The Internet traces its origins to a network set up in 1969 by the Department of

Defense. You can connect to the Internet through many online services, such as CompuServe and America Online, or you can connect through local Internet service providers (ISPs). Internet computers use the TCP/IP communications protocol. Several million hosts exist on the Internet; a host is a mainframe, mini, or workstation that directly supports the Internet protocol (the IP in TCP/IP).

Internet Explorer (IE)   Microsoft's web browser for Windows and older Macintosh computers.

interpreter   A program for a high-level language that translates and executes the program at the same time. The program statements that are interpreted remain in their original source language, the way the programmer wrote them—that is, the program does not need to be compiled before execution. Interpreted programs run more slowly than compiled programs and always must be run with the interpreter loaded in memory.

interrupt   A suspension of a process, such as the execution of a computer program, caused by an event external to that process and performed in such a way that the process can be resumed. An interrupt can be caused by internal or external conditions, such as a signal indicating that a device or program has completed a transfer of data. Hardware interrupts (also called IRQs) are used by devices, whereas software interrupts are used by programs. See also *IRQ*.

interrupt vector   A pointer in a table that gives the location of a set of instructions the computer should execute when a particular interrupt occurs.

IO.SYS   One of the DOS/Windows 9x system files required to boot the machine. The first file loaded from disk during the boot, it contains extensions to the ROM BIOS.

IP address   An identifier for a computer or device on a TCP/IP network. The format of an IP address is a 32-bit numeric address written as four numbers separated by periods, in which each number can be 0–255. The TCP/IP protocol routes messages based on the IP address of the destination.

IPv6   A new version of the IP protocol that expands the range of IP addresses from 32 bits to 128 bits, which relieves the strain on the current universe of IP addresses. IPv6 is backward compatible with IPv4 to allow its gradual adoption.

IPX (Internetwork packet exchange)   Novell NetWare's native LAN communications protocol (primarily in versions 4.x and earlier) used to move data between server and/or workstation programs running on different network nodes. IPX packets are encapsulated and carried by the packets used in Ethernet and the similar frames used in Token-Ring networks.

IrDA   An infrared communications standard established by the Infrared Data Association. The IrDA was formed in June 1993, and the first IrDA specification was published in June 1994. IrDA is currently used primarily for data transfer between portable computers, printers, PDAs, and mobile phones.

IRQ (interrupt request)   Physical connections between external hardware devices and the interrupt controllers. When a device such as a floppy controller or a printer needs the attention of the CPU, an IRQ line is used to get the attention of the system to perform a task. On PC and XT IBM-compatible systems, eight IRQ lines are included, numbered IRQ0–IRQ7. On the AT and PS/2 systems, 16 IRQ lines are numbered IRQ0–IRQ15. IRQ lines must be used by only a single adapter in the ISA bus systems, but Micro Channel Architecture (MCA) adapters and most PCI-based systems can share interrupts. IRQ sharing with modern systems requires a system with PCI cards and Windows 95B or above. Windows 2000 and Windows XP are better at sharing IRQs than Windows 9x and Windows Me.

ISA (Industry Standard Architecture)   The bus architecture introduced as an 8-bit bus with the original IBM PC in 1981 and later expanded to 16 bits with the IBM PC/AT in 1984. ISA slots are occasionally found in PC systems today, but the latest chipsets have eliminated them.

ISA bus clock   Clock that normally operates the ISA bus at 8.33MHz.

ISDN (Integrated Services Digital Network)   An international telecommunications standard that enables a communications channel to carry digital data simultaneously with voice and video information.

ISO (International Standards Organization)   The ISO, based in Paris, develops standards for international and national data communications. The U.S. representative to the ISO is the American National Standards Institute (ANSI).

ISO 9660   An international standard that defines file systems for CD-ROM discs, independent of the operating system. ISO (International Standards Organization) 9660 has two levels. Level one provides for DOS file system compatibility, whereas level two allows filenames of up to 32 characters. See also *High Sierra format.*

ISP (Internet service provider)   A company that provides Internet access to computer users. Most ISPs originally provided dialup analog modem service only, but many ISPs now provide various types of broadband support for DSL, cable modem, or fixed wireless Internet devices. Some ISPs, such as America Online (AOL), also provide proprietary content.

Itanium   An Intel eighth-generation processor, codenamed Merced, it is the first 64-bit instruction PC processor from Intel. It features a new explicitly parallel instruction computing (EPIC) architecture for more performance when running optimized code. Also, it features internal L1/L2 and L3 error correcting code (ECC) caches to improve throughput and reliability. It was designed initially for the server or high-end workstation market. The improved Itanium 2 processor offers faster clock speeds and faster cache memory. See also *L3 cache.*

ITU (International Telecommunications Union) Formerly called CCITT. An international committee organized by the United Nations to set international communications recommendations—which frequently are adopted as standards—and to develop interface, modem, and data network recommendations. The Bell 212A standard for 1,200bps communication in North America, for example, is observed internationally as CCITT V.22. For 2,400bps communication, most U.S. manufacturers observe V.22bis, whereas V.32, V.32bis, V34, and V34+ are standards for 9,600bps, 14,400bps, 28,800bps, and 33,600bps, respectively. The V.90 standard recently was defined for 56Kbps modems.

J-lead   J-shaped leads on chip carriers, which can be surface-mounted on a PC board or plugged into a socket that then is mounted on a PC board, usually on .050" centers.

jabber   An error condition on an Ethernet-based network in which a defective network card or outside interference is constantly sending data, preventing the rest of the network from working.

Java   An object-oriented programming language and environment similar to C or C++. Java was developed by Sun Microsystems and is used to create network-based applications.

JavaScript   A scripting language developed by Netscape for web browsers. JavaScript can perform calculations and mouse rollovers, but it doesn't require the web browser to download additional files, as with Java.

Jaz drive   A proprietary type of removable media drive with a magnetic hard disk platter in a rigid plastic case. Developed by Iomega, Jaz drives were discontinued in 2002, but media is still available for both 1GB and 2GB versions of the drive.

JEDEC (Joint Electron Devices Engineering Council)   A group that establishes standards for the electronics industry. JEDEC established the original PC66 SDRAM standard.

Joliet   Microsoft extension of the ISO 9660 standard for recordable/rewritable CDs. Joliet is designed for use with 32-bit Windows versions that support long filenames, but it supports file/folder names up to 128 bytes (128 European or 64 Unicode characters) only. Some very long folder/filenames might need to be truncated when stored on a Joliet-format CD.

joule   The standard unit of electrical energy, it's frequently used to measure the effectiveness of surge suppressors.

joystick   An input device generally used for game software, usually consisting of a central upright stick that controls horizontal and vertical motion and one or more buttons to control discrete events, such as firing guns. More complex models can resemble flight yokes and steering wheels or incorporate tactile feedback.

JPEG (Joint Photographic Experts Group)   The international consortium of hardware, software, and publishing interests which—under the auspices of the ISO—has defined a universal standard for digital compression and decompression of still images for use in computer systems. JPEG compresses at about a 20:1 ratio before visible image degradation occurs. A lossy data compression standard that was originally designed for still images but also can compress real-time video (30 frames per second) and animation. Lossy compression permanently discards unnecessary data, resulting in some loss of precision. Files stored in the JPEG format have the extension .JPG or .JPEG.

Jscript Microsoft's equivalent to JavaScript. See also *JavaScript*.

jukebox A type of CD-ROM drive that enables several CD-ROM discs to be in the drive at the same time. The drive itself determines which disc is needed by the system and loads the discs into the reading mechanism as needed.

jumper block A small, plastic-covered metal clip that slips over two pins protruding from a circuit board. Sometimes also called a shunt. When in place, the jumper block connects the pins electrically and closes the circuit. By doing so, it connects the two terminals of a switch, turning it "on." Jumper blocks are commonly used to configure internal hard drives and motherboard settings.

K6 The popular line of Socket 7 and Super Socket 7 processors developed by AMD. Members included the K6, K6-2, and K6-III.

K56flex A proprietary standard for 56Kbps modem transmissions developed by Rockwell and implemented in modems from a variety of vendors. Superseded by the official V.90 standard for 56Kbps modems. See also *X2*, *V.90*, and *V.92*.

Kermit A protocol designed for transferring files between microcomputers and mainframes. Developed by Frank DaCruz and Bill Catchings at Columbia University (and named after the talking frog on *The Muppet Show*), Kermit was widely accepted in the academic world before the advent of the Internet.

kernel Operating system core component.

key disk In software copy protection schemes popular during the 1980s, a distribution floppy disk that must be present in a floppy disk drive for an application program to run.

keyboard The primary input device for most computers, consisting of keys with letters of the alphabet, digits, punctuation, and function control keys.

keyboard macro A series of keystrokes automatically input when a single key is pressed.

keychain drive A popular term for small solid-state devices using flash memory that connect to a PC through the USB port. Such devices are recognized as drive letters and have typical capacities ranging from 32MB to 8GB or more. Most have a fixed capacity, but some have provision for upgradeable memory with SD or other small-form-factor flash memory. Also known as thumb drives.

keylock Physical locking mechanism to prevent internal access to the system unit or peripherals.

kibi A multiplier indicating 1,024 of some unit. Abbreviated as Ki. See also *gibi*.

kilo A multiplier indicating one thousand (1,000) of some unit. Abbreviated as k or K. When used to indicate a number of bytes of memory storage, the multiplier definition changes to 1,024. One kilobit, for example, equals 1,000 bits, whereas one kilobyte equals 1,024 bytes.

kilobyte (KB) A unit of information storage equal to 1,000 bytes (decimal) or 1,024 bytes (binary). Binary KB are now called kibibytes. See also *kibi*.

kludge An inelegant but workable solution for a software or hardware problem.

L1 cache (level one) A memory cache built in to the CPU core of 486 and later generation processors. See also *cache* and *disk cache*.

L2 cache (level two) A second-level memory cache external to the processor core, usually larger and slower than L1. Normally found on the motherboards of 386, 486, and Pentium systems and inside the processor packages or modules in Pentium Pro and later Intel processors, AMD K6-III processors, and Athlon and Duron processors. Cartridge-based caches used in the Pentium II, early Celeron, Pentium III, and Athlon processors run faster than motherboard cache but at speeds up to only one-half the CPU speed. Modern Socket 370, Socket A, and other socket-based processors contain the L2 cache inside the CPU die, enabling the L2 cache to work at the full speed of the processor. See also *SEC*, *cache*, and *disk cache*.

L3 cache (level three) A third-level memory cache external to the processor core. The only current Intel-compatible processors to include L3 cache are the Itanium and Itanium 2 processors from Intel. Depending on the model, these contain 2MB or 4MB of L3 cache that runs at full processor speed. If a motherboard provides L2 cache, such as many Super Socket 7 motherboards made for Pentium and Pentium-compatible processors, L2 cache becomes L3 cache if a processor with integrated L3 cache, such as the AMD K6-III, is used. Motherboard-based cache modules run at FSB speeds, which are much slower than on-chip or on-die processor speeds. See also *cache* and *disk cache*.

LAN   Local area network; a network contained within a building. Both home and office networks are considered LANs. Ethernet, Fast Ethernet, Gigabit Ethernet, and Wireless Ethernet are used in office LANs, whereas home LANs might use Ethernet, Fast Ethernet, HomePNA, HomeRF, or Wi-Fi Wireless Ethernet.

landing zone   An unused track on a disk surface on which the read/write heads can land when power is shut off. The place a parking program or a drive with an autopark mechanism parks the heads.

LAPM (link-access procedure for modems)   An error-control protocol incorporated in CCITT Recommendation V.42. Similar to the MNP and HST protocols, it uses cyclic redundancy checking (CRC) and retransmission of corrupted data (ARQ) to ensure data reliability.

laptop computer   A computer system smaller than a briefcase but larger than a notebook that usually has a clamshell design in which the keyboard and display are on separate halves of the system, which are hinged together. These systems normally run on battery power. Many vendors use the terms *notebook* and *laptop computer* interchangeably.

large mode   A translation scheme used by the Award BIOS to translate the cylinder, head, and sector specifications of an IDE drive to those usable by an enhanced BIOS. It doesn't produce the same translated values as LBA mode and is not recommended because it is not supported by other BIOS vendors.

large-scale integration   See *IC*.

laser printer   A type of printer that is a combination of an electrostatic copying machine and a computer printer. The output data from the computer is converted by an interface into a raster feed, similar to the impulses a TV picture tube receives. The impulses cause the laser beam to scan a small drum that carries a positive electrical charge. Where the laser hits, the drum is discharged. A toner, which also carries a positive charge, is then applied to the drum. This toner—a fine, black powder—sticks to only the areas of the drum that have been discharged electrically. As it rotates, the drum deposits the toner on a negatively charged sheet of paper. Another roller then heats and bonds the toner to the page. See also *LED printer*.

latency   1) The amount of time required for a disk drive to rotate half a revolution. Represents the average amount of time to locate a specific sector after the heads have arrived at a specific track. Latency is part of the average access time for a drive. 2) The initial setup time required for a memory transfer in DRAM to select the row and column addresses for the memory to be read/written.

LBA (logical block address/addressing)   The numeric offset of a sector from the beginning of a disk. Also a method used with SCSI and IDE drives to translate the cylinder, head, and sector specifications of the drive to those usable by an enhanced BIOS. LBA is used with drives that are larger than 528MB and causes the BIOS to translate the drive's logical parameters to those usable by the system BIOS.

LCC (leadless chip carrier)   A type of integrated circuit package that has input and output pads rather than leads on its perimeter.

LCD (liquid crystal display)   A display that uses liquid crystal sealed between two pieces of polarized glass. The polarity of the liquid crystal is changed by an electric current to vary the amount of light that can pass through. Because LCD displays do not generate light, they depend on either the reflection of ambient light or backlighting the screen. The best type of LCD, the active-matrix or thin-film transistor (TFT) LCD, offers fast screen updates and true color capability.

LED (light-emitting diode)   A semiconductor diode that emits light when a current is passed through it.

LED printer   A printer that uses an LED instead of a laser beam to discharge the drum.

legacy port   I/O ports used on systems before the development of the multipurpose USB port. Serial, parallel, keyboard, and PS/2 mouse ports are legacy ports.

letterbox   Refers to how wide-screen movies are displayed on TV or monitor screens with normal aspect ratios of 4:3. Because wide-screen movies have aspect ratios as high as 16:9, the wide-screen image leaves blank areas at the top and bottom of the screen. This area is sometimes used for displaying subtitles on foreign-language films. See also *aspect ratio*.

LIF (Low Insertion Force) A type of socket that requires only a minimum of force to insert a chip carrier.

light pen A handheld input device with a light-sensitive probe or stylus connected to the computer's graphics adapter board by a cable. Used for writing or sketching onscreen or as a pointing device for making selections. Unlike mice, it's not widely supported by software applications.

line voltage The AC voltage available at a standard wall outlet, nominally 110V–120V in North America and 220V–230V in Europe and Japan.

Linear tape-open (LTO) An open standard for tape backups whose first products were introduced in mid-2000. LTO was jointly developed by Seagate, IBM, and Hewlett-Packard. Ultrium format products have capacities of up to 100GB, whereas the faster Accelis products have capacities of up to 25GB.

lithium-ion A portable system battery type that is longer-lived than either NiCd or NiMH technologies, can't be overcharged, and holds a charge well when not in use. Lithium-ion batteries are also lighter weight than the NiCd and NiMH technologies. Because of these superior features, Li-ion batteries have come to be used in all but the very low end of the portable system market.

local area network (LAN) The connection of two or more computers, usually via a network adapter card or NIC.

local bus A generic term used to describe a bus directly attached to a processor that operates at the processor's speed and data-transfer width.

local echo A modem feature that enables the modem to send copies of keyboard commands and transmitted data to the screen. When the modem is in command mode (not online to another system), the local echo usually is invoked through an ATE1 command, which causes the modem to display the user's typed commands. When the modem is online to another system, the local echo is invoked by an ATF0 command, which causes the modem to display the data it transmits to the remote system.

logical drive A drive as named by a DOS drive specifier, such as C: or D:. Under DOS 3.3 or later, a single physical drive can act as several logical drives, each with its own specifier. A primary partition can contain only one logical drive; an extended partition can contain one or more logical drives. See also *extended partition* and *primary partition*.

logical unit number See *LUN*.

lossless compression A compression technique that preserves all the original information in an image or other data structures. PKZIP and Microsoft CAB files are popular applications of lossless compression.

lossless linking A technique used by DVD+RW drives to enable the DVD+RW video writing process to pause and continue as data is available. Lossless linking enables DVD+RW video media to be read by standalone DVD video players and DVD-ROM drives.

lossy compression A compression technique that achieves optimal data reduction by discarding redundant and unnecessary information in an image. MP3, MPEG, and JPEG are popular examples of lossy compression.

lost clusters Clusters that have been marked accidentally as "unavailable" in the FAT even though they don't belong to any file listed in a directory. See also *cluster*.

low-level formatting Formatting that divides tracks into sectors on the platter surfaces. Places sector-identifying information before and after each sector and fills each sector with null data (usually hex F6). Specifies the sector interleave and marks defective tracks by placing invalid checksum figures in each sector on a defective track.

LPT port Line printer port, a common system abbreviation for a parallel printer port. Common LPT port numbers range from LPT1 to LPT3.

LPX A semiproprietary motherboard design used in many Low Profile or Slimline case systems. Because no formal standard exists, these typically are not interchangeable between vendors and are often difficult to find replacement parts for or upgrade.

luminance Measure of brightness usually used in specifying monitor brightness.

LUN (logical unit number) A number given to a device (a logical unit) attached to a SCSI physical unit and not directly to the SCSI bus. Although as many as eight logical units can be attached to a single physical unit, a single logical unit typically is a built-in part of a single physical unit. A SCSI hard disk, for example, has a built-in SCSI bus adapter that is assigned a physical unit number or SCSI ID, and the controller and drive portions of the hard disk are assigned a LUN (usually 0). See also *PUN*.

LZW (Lempel Ziv Welch) A lossless compression scheme used in the GIF and TIFF graphic formats, named after its co-creators, Abraham Lempel, Jacob Ziv, and Terry Welch.

MAC address Short for Media Access Control address, this is a unique hardware number assigned to network hardware, such as NICs and routers. The MAC address assigned to the WAN side of some broadband Internet routers can be changed to equal the MAC address of the NIC previously used to attach to a broadband device, such as a cable modem.

machine address A hexadecimal (hex) location in memory.

machine language Hexadecimal program code a computer can understand and execute. It can be output from the assembler or compiler.

macro A series of commands in an application that can be stored and played back on demand. Many applications from various vendors support Microsoft Visual Basic for Applications as their macro language.

macro virus A computer virus that uses a scripting language to infect Microsoft Word document templates or email systems.

magnetic domain A tiny segment of a track just large enough to hold one of the magnetic flux reversals that encode data on a disk surface.

magneto-optical recording An erasable optical disk recording technique that uses a laser beam to heat pits on the disk surface to the point at which a magnet can make flux changes.

magneto-resistive A technology originally developed by IBM and commonly used for the read element of a read/write head on a high-density magnetic disk. Based on the principle that the resistance to electricity changes in a material when brought into contact with a magnetic field, in this case, the read element material and the magnetic bit. Such drives use a magneto-resistive read sensor for reading and a standard inductive element for writing. A magneto-resistive read head is more sensitive to magnetic fields than inductive read heads.

Giant magneto-resistive heads are an improved version that store more data in the same space.

mainframe A somewhat vague distinction that identifies any large computer system normally capable of supporting many users and programs simultaneously.

mask A photographic map of the circuits for a particular layer of a semiconductor chip used in manufacturing the chip.

master boot record (MBR) On hard disks, a one-sector-long record that contains the master boot program as well as the master partition table containing up to four partition entries. The master boot program reads the master partition table to determine which of the four entries is active (bootable) and then loads the first sector of that partition, called the volume boot record. The master boot program tests the volume boot record for a 55AAh signature at offset 510; if it's present, program execution is transferred to the volume boot sector, which typically contains a program designed to load the operating system files. The MBR is always the first physical sector of the disk, at Cylinder 0, Head 0, Sector 1. Also called master boot sector.

math coprocessor A processing chip designed to quickly handle complex arithmetic computations involving floating-point arithmetic, offloading these from the main processor. Originally contained in a separate coprocessor chip, starting with the 486 family of processors. Intel now has incorporated the math coprocessor into the main processors in what is called the floating-point unit.

MCA (Micro Channel Architecture) Developed by IBM for the PS/2 line of computers and introduced on April 2, 1987. Features include a 16- or 32-bit bus width and multiple master control. By allowing several processors to arbitrate for resources on a single bus, the MCA is optimized for multitasking multiprocessor systems. Offers switchless configuration of adapters, which eliminates one of the biggest headaches of installing older adapters. MCA systems became obsolete after the development of the PCI bus.

MCGA (multicolor graphics array) A type of PC video display circuit introduced by IBM on April 2, 1987, which supports text and graphics. Text is supported at a maximum resolution of 80×25 characters in 16 colors with a character box of 8×16 pixels. Graphics are supported at a maximum resolution of 320×200 pixels in 256 (from a palette of 262,144) colors or 640×480 pixels in two colors. The MCGA outputs an analog signal with a horizontal scanning frequency of 31.5KHz and supports analog color or analog monochrome displays.

MCH (memory controller hub)   Intel's term for the chip used in its 8xx-series chipsets to connect the processor with high-bandwidth devices such as memory, video, and the system bus, replacing the North Bridge chip. MCH chips connect with the I/O controller hub (the 8xx chipsets' replacement for the South Bridge) through a high-speed hub interface. See also *ICH.*

MCI (media control interface)   A device-independent specification for controlling multimedia devices and files. MCI is a part of the multimedia extensions and offers a standard interface set of device control commands. MCI commands are used for audio recording and playback and animation playback. Device types include CD audio, digital audio tape players, scanners, MIDI sequencers, videotape players or recorders, and audio devices that play digitized waveform files.

MDA (monochrome display adapter; also, MGA—mono graphics adapter)   A type of PC video display adapter introduced by IBM on August 12, 1981, that supports text only. Text is supported at a maximum resolution of 80×25 characters in four colors with a character box of 9×14 pixels. Colors, in this case, indicate black, white, bright white, and underlined. Graphics modes are not supported. The MDA outputs a digital signal with a horizontal scanning frequency of 18.432KHz and supports TTL monochrome displays. The IBM MDA card also includes a parallel printer port.

mean time between failure   See *MTBF.*

mean time to repair   See *MTTR.*

mebi   A multiplier indicating 1,048,576 of a unit of measurement.

mebibyte (Mi)   A unit of information storage equal to 1,048,576 bytes (1,024×1,024 equals 1Mi). This value was previously called a binary megabyte. See also *megabyte* and *kilobyte.*

medium   The magnetic coating or plating that covers a disk or tape.

mega   A multiplier indicating one million (1,000,000) of some unit. Abbreviated as m or M.

Traditionally, mega has also been defined as 1,048,576 (1,024 kilobytes, where kilobyte equals 1,024) in applications such as memory sizing or disk storage (as defined by many BIOSes and by FDISK and other disk preparation programs). The term *mebi* is now used for 1,048,576. See also *mebi.*

megabyte (MB)   A unit of information storage equal to 1,000,000 bytes. Also called a decimal megabyte. The value 1,048,576 bytes has been called a binary megabyte but is now known as a mebibyte. See also *mebibyte.*

megapixel   A unit of digital camera resolution equal to approximately 1,000,000 pixels. A one-megapixel camera has a resolution of approximately 1,152×864; a two-megapixel camera has a resolution of approximately 1,760×1,168. Finally, a three-megapixel camera has a resolution of approximately 2,160×1,440. One-megapixel or lower-resolution cameras are suitable for 4"×6" or smaller snapshots only, whereas two-megapixel cameras produce excellent 5"×7" enlargements and acceptable 8"×10" enlargements. Three-megapixel or higher-resolution cameras produce excellent 8"×10" and 11"×14" enlargements. The higher the megapixel rating, the more flash memory space is used by each picture and the longer it takes each picture to be recorded to flash memory.

memory   Any component in a computer system that stores information for future use.

memory caching   A service provided by extremely fast memory chips that keeps copies of the most recent memory accesses. When the CPU makes a subsequent access, the value is supplied by the fast memory rather than by the relatively slow system memory. L1 and L2 caches are memory caches found on most recent processors. See also *L1 cache, L2 cache,* and *L3 cache.*

Memory Stick   A Sony-developed flash memory device that's about the size of a stick of gum. It is used by digital cameras, camcorders, digital music players, and voice recorders—primarily those made by Sony.

memory-resident program   A program that remains in memory after it has been loaded, consuming memory that otherwise might be used by application software.

menu software   Utility software that makes a computer running DOS easier to use by replacing DOS commands with a series of menu selections.

MFM encoding (modified frequency modulation encoding)   A method of encoding data on the surface of a disk. The coding of a bit of data varies by the coding of the preceding bit to preserve clocking information. Used only by floppy drives today because it stores less data than other types of encoding such as RLL. See also *RLL*.

MHz   An abbreviation for megahertz, a unit of measurement indicating the frequency of one million cycles per second. One hertz (Hz) is equal to one cycle per second. Named after Heinrich R. Hertz, a German physicist who first detected electromagnetic waves in 1883.

MI/MIC (mode indicate/mode indicate common)   Also called forced or manual originate. Provided for installations in which equipment other than the modem does the dialing. In such installations, the modem operates in dumb mode (no auto-dial capability), yet must go off-hook in originate mode to connect with answering modems.

micro (μ)   A prefix indicating one millionth (1/1,000,000 or .000001) of some unit.

micron   A unit of measurement equaling one millionth of a meter. Often used in measuring the size of circuits in chip manufacturing processes. Current state-of-the-art chip fabrication builds chips with 0.13 to 0.15-micron circuits.

microprocessor   A solid-state central processing unit much like a computer on a chip. An integrated circuit that accepts coded instructions for execution.

microsecond (μs)   A unit of time equal to one millionth (1/1,000,000 or .000001) of a second.

MIDI (musical instrument digital interface)   An interface and file format standard for connecting a musical instrument to a microcomputer and storing musical instrument data. Multiple musical instruments can be daisy-chained and played simultaneously with the help of the computer and related software. The various operations of the instruments can be captured, saved, edited, and played back. A MIDI file contains note information, timing (how long a note is held), volume, and instrument type for as many as 16 channels. Sequencer programs are used to control MIDI functions such as recording, playback, and editing. MIDI files store only note instructions and not actual sound data. MIDI files can be played back

by virtually all sound cards, but old sound cards might use FM synthesis to imitate the musical instruments called for in the MIDI file. Recent sound cards use stored musical instrument samples for more realistic MIDI playback.

MII   A Socket 7–compatible processor originally developed by Cyrix and now sold by VIA Technologies as the VIA Cyrix MII.

milli (m)   A prefix indicating one thousandth (1/1,000 or .001) of some unit.

millisecond (ms)   A unit of time equal to one thousandth (1/1,000 or .001) of a second.

MIME (multipurpose Internet mail extensions)   Allows Internet and email services to exchange binary files and select the proper program to open the file after it's received.

Mini PCI   A specification for small form factor PCI cards suitable for small or portable systems. Mini PCI cards use a subset of the same signal protocol, electrical definitions, and configuration definitions as the Conventional PCI Specification. See also *PCI*.

minitower   A type of PC system case that is shorter than a full- or mid-sized tower. Most low-cost computers sold at retail stores use the minitower case combined with a Micro-ATX motherboard.

MIPS (million instructions per second)   Refers to the average number of machine-language instructions a computer can perform or execute in one second. Because various processors can perform different functions in a single instruction, MIPS should be used only as a general measure of performance among various types of computers.

MMC (MultiMediaCard)   A flash memory card specification originally created by Siemens and SanDisk in November 1997. Later standardized by the MultiMediaCard Association (MMCA) in 1998. MMC cards are 24mm by 32mm by 1.4mm in size. MMC cards can usually be used in SD card slots as well. See also *SD*.

MMX   An Intel processor enhancement that adds 57 new instructions designed to improve multimedia performance. MMX also implies a doubling of the internal L1 processor cache on Pentium MMX processors compared to non-MMX Pentium processors. Later processors also include MMX along with other multimedia instructions.

mnemonic   An abbreviated name for something used in a manner similar to an acronym. Computer processor instructions are often abbreviated with a mnemonic, such as JMP (jump), CLR (clear), STO (store), and INIT (initialize). A mnemonic name for an instruction or an operation makes it easy to remember and convenient to use.

MNP (Microcom Networking Protocol) Asynchronous error-control and data-compression protocols developed by Microcom, Inc., and now in the public domain. They ensure error-free transmission through error detection (CRC) and retransmission of erred frames. MNP Levels 1–4 cover error control and have been incorporated into CCITT Recommendation V.42. MNP Level 5 includes data compression but is eclipsed in superiority by V.42bis—an international standard that is more efficient. Most high-speed modems connect with MNP Level 5 if V.42bis is unavailable. MNP Level 10 provides error correction for impaired lines and adjusts to the fastest possible speed during connection. MNP Level 10EC is an improved version of MNP Level 10, adding more reliability and support for cellular phone hand-offs.

MO (magneto-optical)   MO drives use both magnetic and optical storage properties. MO technology is erasable and recordable, as opposed to CD-ROM (read-only) and WORM (write-once) drives. MO uses laser and magnetic field technology to record and erase data.

mobile processor   A type of processor or CPU designed specifically for mobile computers, with a design optimized especially for low power consumption.

mobile module (MMO)   A type of processor packing from Intel for mobile computers consisting of a Pentium or newer processor mounted on a small daughterboard along with the processor voltage regulator, system's L2 cache memory, and North Bridge part of the motherboard chipset.

modem (modulator/demodulator)   A device that converts electrical signals from a computer into an audio form transmittable over telephone lines, or vice versa. It modulates, or transforms, digital signals from a computer into the analog form that can be carried successfully on a phone line; it also demodulates signals received from the phone line back to digital signals before passing them to the receiving computer. To avoid confu-

sion with other types of Internet connection devices such as cable modems, modems are often called analog modems or dialup modems.

modulation   The process of modifying some characteristic of a carrier wave or signal so that it varies in step with the changes of another signal, thus carrying the information of the other signal.

module   An assembly that contains a complete circuit or subcircuit.

monitor   See *display*.

monochrome display adapter   See *MDA*.

MOS (metal-oxide semiconductor)   Refers to the three layers used in forming the gate structure of a field-effect transistor (FET). MOS circuits offer low-power dissipation and enable transistors to be jammed closely together before a critical heat problem arises. PMOS, the oldest type of MOS circuit, is a silicon-gate P-channel MOS process that uses currents made up of positive charges. NMOS is a silicon-gate N-channel MOS process that uses currents made up of negative charges and is at least twice as fast as PMOS. CMOS, complementary MOS, is nearly immune to noise, runs off almost any power supply, and is an extremely low-power circuit technique.

motherboard   The main circuit board in the computer. Also called planar, system board, or backplane.

mouse   An input device invented by Douglas Engelbart of Stanford Research Center in 1963 and popularized by Xerox in the 1970s. A mechanical mouse consists of a roller ball and a tracking mechanism on the underside that relays the mouse's horizontal and vertical position to the computer, allowing precise control of the pointer location onscreen. The top side features two or three buttons and possibly a small wheel used to select or click items onscreen. Old-style optical mice sold in the 1980s used a single optical sensor and a grid-marked pad as an alternative to the roller ball. The latest optical mice use two optical sensors and can be moved across virtually any nonmirrored surface.

MPC   A trademarked abbreviation for Multimedia Personal Computer. The original MPC specification was developed by Tandy Corporation and Microsoft as the minimum platform capable of running multimedia software. In the summer of 1995, the MPC Marketing Council introduced an upgraded MPC 3 standard. The MPC 1 Specification defines the following minimum standard requirements: a 386SX or 486 CPU; 2MB RAM; 30MB hard disk; VGA video display; 8-bit digital audio subsystem; CD-ROM drive; and systems software compatible with the applications programming interfaces (APIs) of Microsoft Windows version 3.1 or later. The MPC 2 specification defines the following minimum standard requirements: 25MHz 486SX with 4MB RAM; 160MB hard disk; 16-bit sound card; 65,536-color video display; double-speed CD-ROM drive; and systems software compatible with the APIs of Microsoft Windows version 3.1 or later. The MPC 3 Specification defines the following minimum standard requirements: 75MHz Pentium with 8MB RAM; 540MB hard disk; 16-bit sound card; 65,536-color video display; quad-speed CD-ROM drive; OM-1–compliant MPEG-1 video; and systems software compatible with the APIs of Microsoft Windows version 3.1 and DOS 6.0 or later. Virtually all computers sold since 1995 exceed MPC 3 standards.

MPEG (Motion Picture Experts Group) A working ISO committee that has defined standards for lossy digital compression and decompression of motion video/audio for use in computer systems. The MPEG-1 standard delivers decompression data at 1.2MBps–1.5MBps, enabling CD players to play full-motion color movies at 30 frames per second. MPEG-1 compresses at about a 50:1 ratio before image degradation occurs, but compression ratios as high as 200:1 are attainable. MPEG-2 extends to the higher data rates (2Mbps–15Mbps) necessary for signals delivered from remote sources (such as broadcast, cable, or satellite). MPEG-2 is designed to support a range of picture aspect ratios, including 4:3 and 16:9. MPEG compression produces about a 50% volume reduction in file size. MP3 (the audio layer portion of the MPEG-1 standard) provides a wide range of compression ratios and file sizes for digital music storage, making it the de facto standard for exchanging digital music through sites such as Napster and its many rivals. See also *lossy compression*.

MPR The Swedish government standard for maximum video terminal radiation. The current version is called MPR II, but most monitors also comply with the newer and more restrictive TCO standards. See also *TCO*.

MSDOS.SYS One of the DOS/Windows 9x system files required to boot the machine. Contains the

primary DOS routines. Loaded by IO.SYS, it in turn loads COMMAND.COM.

Mt. Rainier A standard for CD-RW and DVD+RW drives that provides for native operating system support of CD-RW and rewritable DVD media. Drives and operating systems that support the Mt. Rainier standard (www.mt-rainier.org) can read or write Mt. Rainier–formatted CD-R/RW or DVD+R/RW media without the need for proprietary packet-reading software such as Roxio's UDF Volume Reader for DirectCD-formatted media (www.roxio.com).

MTBF (mean time between failure) A statistically derived measure of the probable time a device will continue to operate before a hardware failure occurs, usually given in hours. Because no standard technique exists for measuring MTBF, a device from one manufacturer can be significantly more or significantly less reliable than a device with the same MTBF rating from another manufacturer.

MTTR (mean time to repair) A measure of the probable time it will take a technician to service or repair a specific device, usually given in hours.

Multichannel Multipoint Distribution Service (MMDS) The most common form of so-called "wireless cable TV," MMDS is also used for two-way wireless Internet service. One of the leading MMDS technology manufacturers is Navini Networks (www.navini.com).

multicolor graphics array See *MCGA*.

multimedia The integration of sound, graphic images, animation, motion video, and text in one environment on a computer. It is a set of hardware and software technologies that is rapidly changing and enhancing the computing environment.

multisession A term used in CD-ROM recording to describe a recording event. Multisession capabilities allow data recording on the disk at various times in several recording sessions. Kodak's Photo CD is an example of multisession CD-R technology.

multitask To run several programs simultaneously.

multithread To concurrently process more than one message by an application program. OS/2 and 32/64-bit versions of Windows are examples of multithreaded operating systems. Each program can start two or more threads, which carry out various interrelated tasks with less overhead than two or more separate programs would require.

multiuser system   A system in which several computer terminals share the same central processing unit (CPU).

nano (n)   A prefix indicating one billionth (1/1,000,000,000 or .000000001) of some unit.

nanosecond (ns)   A unit of time equal to one billionth (1/1,000,000,000 or .000000001) of a second.

NetBEUI (NetBIOS Extended User Interface)
A network protocol used primarily by Windows NT and Windows 9x and most suitable for small peer-to-peer networks. NetBEUI is not supported by Microsoft in Windows XP and above but can still be manually installed for use in troubleshooting computers.

NetBIOS (Network Basic Input/Output System)
A commonly used network protocol originally developed by IBM and Sytek for PC local area networks. NetBIOS provides session and transport services (Layers 4 and 5 of the OSI model).

NetWare   Novell's server-based network for large businesses. NetWare 5 and NetWare 6 are designed to work well with IP-based networks.

network   A system in which several independent computers are linked to share data and peripherals, such as hard disks and printers.

network interface card (NIC)   An adapter that connects a PC to a network.

Network Layer   In the OSI reference model, the layer that switches and routes the packets as necessary to get them to their destinations. This layer is responsible for addressing and delivering message packets. See also *OSI*.

NiCd   The oldest of the three battery technologies used in portable systems, nickel cadmium batteries are rarely used in portable systems today because of their shorter life and sensitivity to improper charging and discharging. See also *NiMH* and *lithium-ion*.

NiMH   A battery technology used in portable systems. Nickel metal-hydride batteries have approximately a 30% longer life than NiCds, are less sensitive to the memory effect caused by improper charging and discharging, and do not use the envi-

ronmentally dangerous substances found in NiCds. Newer lithium-ion (Li-ion) batteries are far superior. NiMH batteries can sometimes be used in place of NiCds.

NLX   A new low-profile motherboard form factor standard that is basically an improved version of the semiproprietary LPX design. It's designed to accommodate larger processor and memory form factors and incorporate newer bus technologies, such as AGP and USB. Besides design improvements, it is fully standardized, which means you should be able to replace one NLX board with another from a different manufacturer—something that was not normally possible with LPX.

node   A device on a network. Also any junction point at which two or more items meet.

noise   Any unwanted disturbance in an electrical or mechanical system.

noninterlaced monitor   A desirable monitor design in which the electron beam sweeps the screen in lines from top to bottom, one line after the other, completing the entire screen in one pass. Virtually all CRTs sold recently for desktop use are noninterlaced.

nonvolatile random access memory (NVRAM)
Random access memory whose data is retained when power is turned off. ROM/EPROM/EEPROM (flash) memory are examples of nonvolatile memory. Sometimes NVRAM is retained without any power whatsoever, as in EEPROM or flash memory devices. In other cases, the memory is maintained by a small battery. NVRAM that is battery maintained is sometimes also called CMOS memory (although CMOS RAM technically is volatile). CMOS NVRAM is used in IBM-compatible systems to store configuration information. True NVRAM often is used in intelligent modems to store a user-defined default configuration loaded into normal modem RAM at power-up.

nonvolatile RAM disk   A RAM disk powered by a battery supply so that it continues to hold its data during a power outage.

North Bridge   The Intel term for the main portion of the motherboard chipset that incorporates the interface between the processor and the rest of the motherboard. The North Bridge contains the cache, main memory, and AGP controllers, as well as the interface between the high-speed (normally 66MHz or 100MHz) processor bus and the 33MHz

PCI (peripheral component interconnect) or 66MHz AGP (accelerated graphics port) buses. The functional equivalent of the North Bridge on the latest 8xx-series chipsets from Intel is the MCH. See also *chipset, ICH, MCH,* and *South Bridge.*

notebook computer   A very small personal computer approximately the size of a notebook.

NTSC   The National Television Standards Committee, which governs the standard for television and video playback and recording in the United States. The NTSC was originally organized in 1941 when TV broadcasting first began on a wide scale in black and white, and the format was revised in 1953 for color. The NTSC format has 525 scan lines, a field frequency of 60Hz, a broadcast bandwidth of 4MHz, a line frequency of 15.75KHz, a frame frequency of 1/30 of a second, and a color subcarrier frequency of 3.58MHz. It is an interlaced signal, which means it scans every other line each time the screen is refreshed. The signal is generated as a composite of red, green, and blue signals for color and includes an FM frequency for audio and a signal for stereo. See also *PAL* and *SECAM,* which are incompatible systems used in Europe. NTSC is also called composite video.

null modem   A serial cable wired so that two data terminal equipment (DTE) devices, such as personal computers, or two data communication equipment (DCE) devices, such as modems or mice, can be connected. Also sometimes called a modem-eliminator or a LapLink cable. To make a null-modem cable with DB-25 connectors, you wire these pins together: 1-1, 2-3, 3-2, 4-5, 5-4, 6-8-20, 20-8-6, and 7-7.

numeric coprocessor   See *math coprocessor.*

NVRAM (nonvolatile random access memory) Memory that retains data without power. Flash memory and battery-backed CMOS RAM are examples of NVRAM. See also *nonvolatile random access memory.*

object hierarchy   Occurs in a graphical program when two or more objects are linked and one object's movement is dependent on the other object. This is known as a parent-child hierarchy. In an example using a human figure, the fingers would be child objects to the hand, which is a child object to the arm, which is a child to the shoulder, and so on. Object hierarchy provides much control for an animator in moving complex figures.

OC (optical carrier) rates   Various data rates for optical fiber used in Internet backbones, based on the OC-1 rate of 51.84Mbps. Multiply the OC rate by 51.84Mbps to derive the data rate. For example, OC-12 is 622.08Mbps (51.84×12).

Occam's Razor   Also spelled Ockham's Razor; popular name for the principle that the simplest explanation is usually the correct one—a very useful principle in computer troubleshooting.

OCR (optical character recognition)   An information-processing technology that converts human-readable text into computer data. Usually a scanner is used to read the text on a page, and OCR software converts the images to characters. Advanced OCR programs, such as OmniPage, can also match fonts, re-create page layouts, and scan graphics into machine-readable form.

ODI (Open Data-link Interface)   A device driver standard from Novell that enables multiple protocols to run on the same network adapter card. ODI adds functionality to Novell's NetWare and network computing environments by supporting multiple protocols and drivers.

OEM (original equipment manufacturer)   Any manufacturer that sells its product to a reseller. Usually refers to the original manufacturer of a particular device or component. Most HP hard disks, for example, are made by Seagate Technologies, which is considered the OEM. OEM products often differ in features from retail products and can have very short warranty periods if purchased separately from their intended use.

OLE (object linking and embedding)   An enhancement to the original Dynamic Data Exchange (DDE) protocol that enables the user to embed or link data created in one application to a document created in another application and subsequently edit that data directly from the final document.

online fallback   A feature that enables high-speed error-control modems to monitor line quality and fall back to the next lower speed if line quality degrades. Some modems fall forward as line quality improves.

open architecture   A system design in which the specifications are made public to encourage third-party vendors to develop add-on products. The PC is a true open architecture system, but the Macintosh is proprietary.

operating system (OS) A collection of programs for operating the computer. Operating systems perform housekeeping tasks, such as input and output between the computer and peripherals and accepting and interpreting information from the keyboard. Windows XP and Mac OS X are examples of popular OSs.

optical disk A disk that encodes data as a series of reflective pits that are read (and sometimes written) by a laser beam.

Orange Book The standards for recordable (CD-R) and rewritable (CD-RW) compact discs.

originate mode A state in which the modem transmits at the predefined low frequency of the communications channel and receives at the high frequency. The transmit/receive frequencies are the reverse of the called modem, which is in answer mode. See also *answer mode*.

OS/2 An operating system originally developed through a joint effort by IBM and Microsoft Corporation and later by IBM alone. Originally released in 1987, OS/2 is a 32-bit operating system designed to run on computers using the Intel 386 or later microprocessors. The OS/2 Workplace Shell, an integral part of the system, is a graphical interface similar to Microsoft Windows and the Apple Macintosh system. OS/2 Warp 4 and OS/2 Warp Server were the most recent versions and are used primarily as a server or in back-office functions today. OS/2 was officially withdrawn from marketing by IBM on December 23, 2005.

OSI (Open Systems Interconnect) A reference model developed by the International Standards Organization (ISO) in the 1980s, the OSI model splits a computer's networking stack into seven discrete layers. Each layer provides specific services to the layers above and below it. From the top down, the Application Layer is responsible for program-to-program communication; the Presentation Layer manages data representation conversions. Next, the Session Layer is responsible for establishing and maintaining communications channels, and the Transport Layer is responsible for the integrity of data transmission. The Network Layer routes data from one node to another, the Data Link Layer is responsible for physically passing data from one node to another, and finally, the Physical Layer is responsible for moving data on and off the network media.

output Information processed by the computer or the act of sending that information to a device, such as a video display, printer, or modem.

overclocking The process of running a processor or video card at a speed faster than the officially marked speed by using a higher clock multiplier, faster bus speed, or faster core clock speed. Not recommended or endorsed by processor or video card manufacturers. See also *clock multiplier*.

OverDrive An Intel trademark name for its line of upgrade processors for 486, Pentium, and Pentium Pro systems. Although Intel no longer sells OverDrive processors, similar products are available from Evergreen Technologies and PowerLeap Products, Inc., for these processors plus Pentium II, Pentium III, Pentium 4, and Celeron-based systems.

overlay Part of a program loaded into memory only when it is required.

overrun A situation in which data moves from one device more quickly than a second device can accept it.

overscanning A technique used in consumer display products that extends the deflection of a CRT's electron beam beyond the physical boundaries of the screen to ensure that images always fill the display area.

overwrite To write data on top of existing data, thus erasing the existing data.

package A device that includes a chip mounted on a carrier and sealed.

packet A message sent over a network that contains data and a destination address.

packet writing A recording technique that sends data to a CD-R or CD-RW disc in multiple blocks, enabling normal writing processes in Windows Explorer to be used instead of a CD-mastering program. Compatible packet-reading software, such as Roxio's UDF Reader for DirectCD, must be used on systems that don't have a CD-R or CD-RW drive to enable the media to be read. See also *Mt. Rainier*.

pairing Combining processor instructions for optimal execution on superscalar processors.

PAL 1) Phase Alternating Line system. Invented in 1961, a system of TV broadcasting used in

England and other European countries (except France). PAL's image format is 4:3, 625 lines, 50Hz, and 4MHz video bandwidth with a total 8MHz of video channel width. With its 625-line picture delivered at 25 frames per second, PAL provides a better image and an improved color transmission over the NTSC system used in North America. As a consequence, PAL and NTSC videotapes aren't interchangeable. 2) Programmable array logic, a type of chip that has logic gates specified by a device programmer.

palmtop computer　A computer system smaller than a notebook that is designed so it can be held in one hand while being operated by the other. Many are now called PDAs or Personal Digital Assistants.

parallel　A method of transferring data characters in which the bits travel down parallel electrical paths simultaneously—for example, eight paths for 8-bit characters. Data is stored in computers in parallel form but can be converted to serial form for certain operations.

parity　A method of error checking in which an extra bit is sent to the receiving device to indicate whether an even or odd number of binary 1 bits was transmitted. The receiving unit compares the received information with this bit and can obtain a reasonable judgment about the validity of the character. The same type of parity (even or odd) must be used by two communicating computers, or both may omit parity. When parity is used, a parity bit is added to each transmitted character. The bit's value is 0 or 1, to make the total number of 1s in the character even or odd, depending on which type of parity is used. Parity checking isn't widely supported on recent systems, but memory with parity bits can be used as ECC memory on systems with ECC-compatible chipsets. See also *ECC*.

park program　A program that executes a seek to the highest cylinder or just past the highest cylinder of a drive so the potential of data loss is minimized if the drive is moved. Park programs are not interchangeable between drives and are no longer required on most drives 40MB and above because these drives self-park their heads for safety.

partition　A section of a hard disk devoted to a particular operating system. Most hard disks have only one partition, devoted to DOS. A hard disk can have as many as four primary partitions, and additional extended partitions, each potentially

occupied by a different operating system. A boot manager can be used to select the partition occupied by the operating system you want to start if you have multiple operating systems installed in different partitions. See also *boot manager*.

Pascal　A high-level programming language named for the French mathematician Blaise Pascal (1623–1662). Developed in the early 1970s by Niklaus Wirth for teaching programming and designed to support the concepts of structured programming.

passive matrix　A type of LCD display where the active components (transistors) are outside the actual display screen, and there are only transistors for each row and column rather than for each pixel, as with active matrix displays. Passive matrix displays are known for slow response times and poor contrast as compared to active matrix displays.

PBX　See *private branch exchange*.

PC Card (PCMCIA—Personal Computer Memory Card International Association)　A credit card–sized expansion adapter for notebook and laptop PCs. PC Card is the official PCMCIA trademark; however, both PC Card and PCMCIA card are used to refer to these standards. PCMCIA cards are removable modules that can hold numerous types of devices, including memory, modems, fax/modems, radio transceivers, network adapters, solid state disks, hard disks, and flash memory adapters.

PCI (Peripheral Component Interconnect)　A standard bus specification initially developed by Intel in 1992 that bypasses the standard ISA I/O bus and uses the system bus to increase the bus clock speed and take full advantage of the CPU's data path. The most common form of PCI is 32 bits wide running at 33MHz, but 66MHz and 64-bit wide versions of PCI are frequently used on servers.

PCI Express　A high-speed serial I/O interconnect standard being developed by the PCI-SIG (www.pcisig.com) as an eventual replacement for the original PCI standard. The initial version of PCI Express supports 0.8V signaling at 2.5GHz.

PCL (Printer Control Language)　Developed by Hewlett-Packard in 1984 as a language for the HP LaserJet printer. PCL is now the de facto industry standard for PC printing. PCL defines a standard set of commands, enabling applications to communicate with HP or HP-compatible printers and is supported by virtually all printer manufacturers. Various levels of PCL are supported by HP and other brands of laser and inkjet printers.

PCM (pulse code modulation) A technique for digitizing analog signals by sampling the signal and converting each sample into a binary number. Also stands for powertrain control module, which is what the computer in most modern automobiles is called.

PDA (Personal Digital Assistant) A handheld, palm-sized computer that functions primarily as a personal organizer and can be combined with a cellular phone or pager. Leading examples include the Palm series, Windows–based PalmPCs, and the Handspring (which also runs the Palm OS).

PDF (Portable Document Format) Files with this extension can be read with the Adobe Acrobat Reader. See also *Acrobat*.

peer-to-peer A type of network in which any computer can act as both a server (by providing access to its resources to other computers) and a client (by accessing shared resources from other computers).

pel See *pixel*.

Pentium An Intel microprocessor with 32-bit registers, a 64-bit data bus, and a 32-bit address bus. The Pentium has a built-in L1 cache segmented into a separate 8KB cache for code and another 8KB cache for data. The Pentium includes an FPU or math coprocessor. It is backward compatible with the 486 and can operate in real, protected virtual, and virtual real modes. The MMX Pentium has a 16KB cache for code, has a 16KB cache for data, and adds the MMX instruction set.

Pentium 4 The first Intel seventh-generation processor, based on a 32-bit microarchitecture that operates at higher clock speeds because of hyper pipelined technology, a rapid execution engine, a 400MHz system bus, and an execution trace cache. The 400MHz system bus is a quad-pumped bus running off a 100MHz system clock, making 3.2GBps data transfer rates possible. The advanced transfer cache is a 256KB, on-die Level 2 cache with increased bandwidth over previous microarchitectures. The floating-point and multimedia units have been improved by making the registers 128 bits wide and adding a separate register for data movement. Finally, SSE2 adds 144 new instructions for double-precision floating-point,

SIMD integer, and memory management. The original version for Socket 423 was codenamed Willamette, whereas the latest Socket 478 version was codenamed Northwood. Later versions added more cache (up to 2MB L2 and 2MB L3 in some versions), hyperthreading technology, 64-bit instruction support (called EM64T), and bus speeds of up to 1066MHz.

Pentium II An Intel sixth-generation processor similar to the Pentium Pro but with MMX capabilities and SEC cartridge packaging technology. Includes L2 cache running at half-core speed.

Pentium III An Intel sixth-generation processor similar to the Pentium II but with SSE (Streaming SIMD Extensions) added. Later PIII models (codenamed Coppermine) include on-die L2 cache running at full core speed. It's available in both cartridge (Slot 1) and chip package (Socket 370) versions.

Pentium M An Intel sixth-generation processor combining features of the Pentium III and Pentium 4 but expressly designed as a mobile processor. Includes 1MB or 2MB on-die L2 cache and SSE2 (Streaming SIMD Extensions 2) support. Runs on a 400MHz or 533MHz bus. Extremely fast and power efficient, one of the best overall processors for mobile systems.

Pentium Pro An Intel sixth-generation (P6) processor with 32-bit registers, a 64-bit data bus, and a 36-bit address bus. The Pentium Pro has the same segmented Level 1 cache as the Pentium but also includes a 256KB, 512KB, or 1MB of L2 cache on a separate die inside the processor package. The Pentium Pro includes an FPU or math coprocessor. It is backward compatible with the Pentium and can operate in real, protected, and virtual real modes. The Pentium Pro fits into Socket 8.

peripheral Any piece of equipment used in computer systems that is an attachment to the computer. Disk drives, terminals, and printers are all examples of peripherals.

persistence In a monitor, the quality of the phosphor chemical that indicates how long the glow caused by the electrons striking the phosphor will remain onscreen.

petabyte (PB) A measure of disk capacity equaling 1,000,000,000,000,000 bytes.

PGA 1) Pin grid array. A chip package that has a large number of pins on the bottom designed for socket mounting. 2) Professional graphics adapter. A limited-production, high-resolution graphics card for XT and AT systems from IBM.

phosphor   A layer of electroluminescent material applied to the inside face of a cathode-ray tube (CRT). When bombarded by electrons, the material fluoresces, and after the bombardment stops, it phosphoresces.

phosphorescence   The emission of light from a substance after the source of excitation has been removed.

Photo CD   A technology developed by Eastman Kodak and Philips that stores photographic images on a CD-R recordable compact disc. Images stored on the Photo CD can have resolutions as high as 2,048×3,072 pixels. Up to 100 true-color images (24-bit color) can be stored on one disc. Photo CD images are created by scanning film and digitally recording the images on compact discs. The digitized images are indexed (given a 4-digit code), and thumbnails of each image on the disc are shown on the front of the case along with its index number. Multisession capability enables several rolls of film to be added to a single disc on different occasions.

photolithography   The photographic process used in electronic chip manufacturing that creates transistors and circuit and signal pathways in semiconductors by depositing different layers of various materials on the chip.

photoresist   A chemical used to coat a silicon wafer in the semiconductor manufacturing process that makes the silicon sensitive to light for photolithography.

physical drive   A single disk drive. DOS defines logical drives, which are given a specifier, such as C: or D:. A single physical drive can be divided into multiple logical drives. Conversely, special software can span a single logical drive across two physical drives. See also *partition*.

Physical Layer   See *OSI*.

physical unit number   See *PUN*.

Picture CD   A simplified version of Photo CD that stores scanned images from a single roll of film on a CD-R disc. Images on Picture CDs, unlike those on Photo CDs, are stored in the industry-standard JPEG file format and can be opened with most photo-editing programs.

PIF (program information file)   A file that contains information about a non-Windows application specifying optimum settings for running the program under Windows 3.x. These are called property sheets in 32-bit Windows.

pin   1) The lead on a connector, chip, module, or device. 2) Personal identification number. A personal password used for identification purposes.

pin compatible   Chips having the same pinout functions. For example, a VIA C3 processor is pin compatible with an Intel Celeron (Socket 370 version).

pinout   A listing of which pins have which functions on a chip, socket, slot, or other connector.

PIO mode (programmed input/output mode)   The standard data transfer modes used by IDE drives that use the processor's registers for data transfer. This is in contrast with DMA modes, which transfer data directly between main memory and the device. The slowest PIO mode is 0, and the fastest PIO mode is mode 4 (16.66MBps). Faster modes use Ultra DMA transfers. See also *Ultra DMA*.

pipeline   A path for instructions or data to follow.

pixel   A mnemonic term meaning picture element. Any of the tiny elements that form a picture on a video display screen. Also called a pel.

pixel shader   A small program that controls the appearance of individual pixels in a 3D image. Most recent mid-range and high-end GPUs such as NVIDIA's GeForce 3 and GeForce 4 Ti series and the ATI 8xxx and 9xxx series have built-in pixel shaders. See also *GPU*, *hardware shader*, and *vertex shader*.

PKZIP   The original ZIP-format compression/decompression program developed by the late Phil Katz. His company, PKWARE, continues to develop PKZIP for popular operating systems, including Windows.

planar board   A term equivalent to motherboard, used by IBM in some of its literature.

plasma display   A display technology that uses plasma (electrically charged gas) to illuminate each pixel. Plasma displays are much thinner than conventional CRT displays but are much more expensive than CRTs or LCD displays. Several vendors now sell HDTV plasma displays that can also be connected to computers with VGA or DVI video connectors.

plated media   Hard disk platters plated with a form of thin metal film medium on which data is recorded.

platter   A disk contained in a hard disk drive. Most drives have two or more platters, each with data recorded on both sides.

PLCC (plastic leaded chip carrier)   A chip-carrier package with J-leads around the perimeter of the package.

Plug and Play (PnP)   A hardware and software specification developed by Intel that enables a PnP system and PnP adapter cards to automatically configure themselves. PnP cards are free from switches and jumpers and are configured via the PnP BIOS in the host system, or via supplied programs for non-PnP systems. PnP also allows the system to detect and configure external devices, such as monitors, modems, and devices attached to USB or IEEE-1394 ports. Windows 9x, Me, 2000, and XP all support PnP devices.

polling   A communications technique that determines when a device is ready to send data. The system continually interrogates polled devices in a round-robin sequence. If a device has data to send, it sends back an acknowledgment and the transmission begins. Contrasts with interrupt-driven communications, in which the device generates a signal to interrupt the system when it has data to send. Polling enables two devices that would normally have an IRQ conflict to coexist because the IRQ is not used for flow control.

port   Plug or socket that enables an external device, such as a printer, to be attached to the adapter card in the computer. Also a logical address used by a microprocessor for communication between it and various devices.

port address   One of a system of addresses used by the computer to access devices such as disk drives or printer ports. You might need to specify an unused port address when installing any adapter boards in a system unit.

port replicator   For mobile computers, a device that plugs into the laptop and provides all the ports for connecting external devices. The advantage of using a port replicator is that the external devices can be left connected to the replicator and the mobile computer connected to them all at once by connecting to the replicator, rather than connecting to each individual device. A port replicator differs from a docking station in that the latter can provide additional drive bays and expansion slots not found in port replicators. Traditionally, port replicators have plugged into a proprietary bus on the rear of a portable computer, but so-called universal models might attach to the PC Card (PCMCIA) slot or to a USB port.

portable computer   A computer system smaller than a transportable system but larger than a laptop system. Very few systems in this form factor are sold today, but companies such as Dolch still produce them. Most portable systems conform to the lunchbox style popularized by Compaq or the briefcase style popularized by IBM, each with a fold-down (removable) keyboard and built-in display. These systems characteristically run on AC power and not on batteries, include several expansion slots, and can be as powerful as full desktop systems.

POS (Programmable Option Select)   The Micro Channel Architecture's POS eliminates switches and jumpers from the system board and adapters by replacing them with programmable registers. Automatic configuration routines store the POS data in a battery-powered CMOS memory for system configuration and operations. The configuration utilities rely on adapter description files (ADF) that contain the setup data for each card.

POST (Power On Self Test)   A series of tests run by the computer at power-on. Most computers scan and test many of their circuits and sound a beep from the internal speaker if this initial test indicates proper system performance.

PostScript   A page-description language developed primarily by John Warnock of Adobe Systems for converting and moving data to the laser-printed page. Instead of using the standard method of transmitting graphics or character information to a printer and telling it where to place dots one by one on a page, PostScript provides a way for the laser printer to interpret mathematically a full page of shapes and curves. Adobe Acrobat converts PostScript output files into files that can be read by users with varying operating systems. See also *Acrobat*.

POTS (Plain Old Telephone Service)   Standard analog telephone service.

power management   Systems used initially in mobile computers (and now also used in desktop systems) to decrease power consumption by turning off or slowing down devices during periods of inactivity. See also *APM*.

power supply   An electrical/electronic circuit that supplies all operating voltage and current to the computer system.

PPGA (plastic pin grid array)   A chip-packaging form factor used by Intel as an alternative to traditional ceramic packaging.

PPP (Point-to-Point Protocol)   A protocol that enables a computer to use the Internet with a standard telephone line and high-speed modem. PPP has largely replaced the Serial Line Internet Protocol (SLIP) because it supports line sharing and error detection.

precompensation   A data write modification required by some older drives on the inner cylinders to compensate for the higher density of data on the (smaller) inner cylinders.

Presentation Layer   See *OSI*.

primary partition   An ordinary, single-volume, potentially bootable partition. See also *extended partition*.

printer   A device that records information visually on paper or other material.

private branch exchange (PBX)   A private telephone switching network that enables users within the network or organization to place calls to each other without going through the public telephone network.

processor   See *microprocessor*.

processor speed   The clock rate at which a microprocessor processes data. A typical Pentium 4 processor, for example, operates at 2GHz (2 billion cycles per second).

program   A set of instructions or steps telling the computer how to handle a problem or task.

PROM (programmable read-only memory)   A type of memory chip that can be programmed to store information permanently—information that can't be erased. Also referred to as OTP for one-time programmable.

proprietary   Anything invented by one company and that uses components available from only that one company. Especially applies to cases in which the inventing company goes to lengths to hide the specifications of the new invention or to prevent other manufacturers from making similar or compatible items. The opposite of standard or open architecture. Computers with nonstandard components that are available from only the original manufacturer, such as Apple Macintosh systems, are known as proprietary.

protected mode   A mode available in all Intel and compatible processors except the first-generation 8086 and 8088. In this mode, memory addressing is extended beyond the 1MB limits of the 8088 and real mode and restricted protection levels can be set to trap software crashes and control the system.

protocol   A system of rules and procedures governing communications between two or more devices. Protocols vary, but communicating devices must follow the same protocol to exchange data. The data format, readiness to receive or send, error detection, and error correction are some of the operations that can be defined in protocols.

proxy server   A computer that acts as a gateway between the computers on a network and the Internet and also provides page caching and optional content filtering and firewall services to the network. Some home network software solutions for Internet sharing, such as WinProxy, use a proxy server.

PS/2 mouse   A mouse designed to plug into a dedicated mouse port (a round, 6-pin DIN connector) on the motherboard, rather than plugging into a serial port. The name comes from the fact that this port was first introduced on the IBM PS/2 systems.

PUN (physical unit number)   A term used to describe a device attached directly to the SCSI bus. Also known as a SCSI ID. As many as eight SCSI devices can be attached to a single SCSI bus, and each must have a unique PUN or ID assigned from 7 to 0. Normally, the SCSI host adapter is assigned the highest-priority ID, which is 7. A bootable hard disk is assigned an ID of 0, and other non-bootable drives are assigned higher priorities.

QAM (quadrature amplitude modulation)   A modulation technique used by high-speed modems that combines both phase and amplitude modulation. This technique enables multiple bits to be encoded in a single time interval.

QDR (quad data rate) A high-speed SDRAM technology (www.qdrsram.com) that uses separate input and output ports with a DDR interface to enable four pieces of data to be processed at the same time. See also *DDR*.

QIC (Quarter-Inch Committee) An industry association that sets hardware and software standards for tape-backup units that use quarter-inch–wide tapes. QIC, QIC-Wide, Travan, and Travan NS drives are all based on QIC standards.

Quantum Formerly a major maker of hard disk drives and now a major maker of attached network storage devices. Quantum-brand disk drives are now sold and supported by Maxtor.

QWERTY keyboard The standard typewriter or computer keyboard, with the characters Q, W, E, R, T, and Y on the top row of alpha keys. Because of the haphazard placement of characters, this keyboard can hinder fast typing.

RAID (redundant array of independent or inexpensive disks) A storage unit that employs two or more drives in combination for fault tolerance and greater performance, used mostly in file server applications. Originally used only with SCSI drives and host adapters, many motherboards now feature IDE RAID implementations.

rails Plastic or metal strips attached to the sides of disk drives mounted in IBM ATs and compatibles so that the drives can slide into place. These rails fit into channels in the side of each disk drive bay position and might be held in position with screws or snap into place.

RAM (random access memory) All memory accessible at any instant (randomly) by a microprocessor.

RAM disk A "phantom disk drive" in which a section of system memory (RAM) is set aside to hold data, just as though it were a number of disk sectors. To an operating system, a RAM disk looks and functions like any other drive.

RAMBUS Dynamic RAM See *RDRAM*.

RAMDAC (random access memory digital-to-analog converter) A special type of DAC found on video cards. RAMDACs use a trio of DACs—one each for red, green, and yellow—to convert image data into a picture. RAMDACs were formerly separate chips but are now integrated into the 3D accelerator chips on most recent video cards.

random access file A file in which all data elements (or records) are of equal length and written in the file end to end, without delimiting characters between. Any element (or record) in the file can be found directly by calculating the record's offset in the file.

random access memory See *RAM*.

raster A pattern of horizontal scanning lines normally on a computer monitor. An electromagnetic field causes the beam of the monitor's tube to illuminate the correct dots to produce the required characters.

raster graphics A technique for representing a picture image as a matrix of dots. It is the digital counterpart of the analog method used in TV. Several raster graphics standards exist, including PCX, TIFF, BMP, JPEG, and GIF.

RCA jack Also called a phono connector. A plug and socket for a two-wire coaxial cable used to connect audio and video components. The plug is a 1/8" thick prong that sticks out 5/16" from the middle of a cylinder.

RDRAM (Rambus DRAM) A high-speed dynamic RAM technology developed by Rambus, Inc., which is supported by Intel's 1999 and later motherboard chipsets. RDRAM transfers data at 1GBps or faster, which is significantly faster than SDRAM and other technologies and which is capable of keeping up with future-generation high-speed processors. Memory modules with RDRAM chips are called RIMMs (Rambus inline memory modules). Rambus licenses its technology to other semiconductor companies, which manufacture the chips and RIMMs. RDRAMs are used by some of Intel's mid-range and high-end chipsets for the Pentium III and Pentium 4 desktop processors and their server counterparts.

read-only file A file whose attribute setting in the file's directory entry tells DOS not to allow software to write into or over the file.

read-only memory See *ROM*.

read/write head A tiny magnet that reads and writes data on a disk track.

real mode A mode available in all Intel 8086–compatible processors that enables compatibility with the original 8086. In this mode, memory addressing is limited to 1MB.

real-time   The actual time in which a program or an event takes place. In computing, real-time refers to an operating mode under which data is received and processed and the results returned without apparent delay to the user, dependent application, or process. The term also is used to describe the process of simultaneous digitization, compression, and processing of audio and/or video information.

reboot   The process of restarting a computer and reloading the operating system.

Red Book   More commonly known as compact disc-digital audio (CD-DA), one of four compact disc standards. Red Book got its name from the color of the manual used to describe the CD-Audio specifications. The Red Book audio standard requires that digital audio be sampled at a 44.1KHz sample rate using 16 bits for each sample. This is the standard used by audio CDs and many CD-ROMs.

refresh cycle   A cycle in which the computer accesses all memory locations stored by DRAM chips so that the information remains intact. DRAM chips must be accessed several times per second; otherwise, the information fades.

refresh rate   Another term for the vertical scan frequency of monitors.

register   Storage area in memory having a specified storage capacity—such as a single bit, a byte (8-bits), word (16-bits), dword (32-bits), or qword (64-bits)—and intended for a special purpose.

Registry   The system configuration files used by Windows 9x, Windows Me, Windows NT, Windows 2000, and Windows XP to store settings about installed hardware and drivers, user preferences, installed software, and other settings required to keep Windows running properly. Replaces the WIN.INI and SYSTEM.INI files from Windows 3.x. The Registry structure varies between Windows versions.

remote digital loopback   A test that checks the phone link and a remote modem's transmitter and receiver. Data entered from the keyboard is transmitted from the initiating modem, received by the remote modem's receiver, looped through its transmitter, and returned to the local screen for verification.

remote echo   A copy of the data received by the remote system, returned to the sending system, and displayed onscreen. A function of the remote system.

rendering   Generating a 3D image that incorporates the simulation of lighting effects, such as shadows and reflection.

resolution   1) A reference to the size of the pixels used in graphics. In medium-resolution graphics, pixels are large. In high-resolution graphics, pixels are small. 2) A measure of the number of horizontal and vertical pixels that can be displayed by a video adapter and monitor.

reverse engineering   The act of duplicating a hardware or software component by studying the functions of the component and designing a different one that has the same functions.

RFI (radio-frequency interference)   A high-frequency signal radiated by improperly shielded conductors, particularly when signal path lengths are comparable to or longer than the signal wavelengths. The FCC now regulates RFI in computer equipment sold in the United States under FCC Regulations, Part 15, Subpart J.

RGB (red green blue)   A type of computer color display output signal composed of separately controllable red, green, and blue signals; as opposed to composite video, in which signals are combined prior to output. RGB monitors offer much higher resolution and sharper pictures than composite monitors.

ribbon cable   Flat cable with wires running in parallel, such as those used for internal IDE or SCSI.

Rich Text Format (RTF)   A universal file format suitable for exchanging formatted text files between different word processing and page layout programs.

RIMM (Rambus inline memory module)   A type of memory module made using RDRAM chips. See also *RDRAM*.

RISC (reduced instruction set computer) Differentiated from CISC, the complex instruction set computer. RISC processors have simple instruction sets requiring only one or a few execution cycles. These simple instructions can be used more effectively than CISC systems with appropriately designed software, resulting in faster operations. See also *CISC*.

RJ-11   The standard two-wire connector type used for single-line telephone connections.

RJ-14   The standard four-wire connector type used for two-line telephone connections.

RJ-45   A standard connector type used in networking with twisted-pair cabling. Resembles an RJ-11/14 telephone jack, but RJ-45 is larger with more wires.

RLL (run length limited)   A type of encoding that derives its name from the fact that the techniques used limit the distance (run length) between magnetic flux reversals on the disk platter. Several types of RLL encoding techniques exist, although only two are commonly used. (1,7) RLL encoding increases storage capacity by about 30% over MFM encoding and is most popular in the very highest capacity drives due to a better window margin, whereas (2,7) RLL encoding increases storage capacity by 50% over MFM encoding and is used in the majority of RLL implementations. Most IDE, ESDI, and SCSI hard disks use one of these forms of RLL encoding.

RMA number (return-merchandise authorization number)   A number given to you by a vendor when you arrange to return an item for repairs. Used to track the item and the repair.

ROM (read-only memory)   A type of memory that has values permanently or semipermanently burned in. These locations are used to hold important programs or data that must be available to the computer when the power initially is turned on.

ROM BIOS (read-only memory basic input/output system)   A BIOS encoded in a form of read-only memory for protection.

root directory   The main directory of any hard or floppy disk. It has a fixed size and location for a particular disk volume and can't be resized dynamically the way subdirectories can.

router   A device that is used to connect various networks, intelligently routing information between them. It is used to internetwork similar and dissimilar networks and can select the most expedient route based on traffic load, line speeds, costs, and network failures. Routers use forwarding tables to determine which packets should be forwarded between the connected networks. A cable or DSL modem is an example of a simple router that connects the Internet to your own network. Many routers include firewall capability to block

suspect packets from being transmitted between networks.

routine   Set of frequently used instructions. It can be considered as a subdivision of a program with two or more instructions that are related functionally.

RS-232   An interface introduced in August 1969 by the Electronic Industries Association. The RS-232 interface standard provides an electrical description for connecting peripheral devices to computers. Originally, RS-232 (serial) ports on computers used a 25-pin interface, but starting with the IBM AT, most use a 9-pin interface.

RTC (real-time clock)   A battery-powered clock included on the motherboard of 286-class and newer computers. The contents of the RTC are read at startup time to provide the time display in the operating system's clock. It's often part of the NVRAM chip.

S/PDIF (Sony/Philips Digital Interface)   Provides digital I/O on high-end sound cards and multimedia-capable video cards. Might use either an RCA jack or optical jack; some devices support both types of S/PDIF connectors.

S-Video (Y/C)   Type of video signal used in the Hi8 and S-VHS videotape formats in which the luminance and chrominance (Y/C) components are kept separate, providing greater control and quality of each image. S-video transmits luminance and color portions separately, thus avoiding the NTSC encoding process and its inevitable loss of picture quality.

SATA (Serial ATA)   A high-speed serial interface designed to replace the current parallel ATA and UltraATA drive interface standards. Serial ATA 1.0 uses a seven-wire data/ground cable and supports direct point-to-point connections to host adapters at initial speeds of up to 150MBps, which is faster than UltraATA-133. Serial ATA II is a version of the SATA standard designed for servers. See also *Ultra DMA*.

scan codes   The hexadecimal codes actually sent by the keyboard to the motherboard when a key is pressed.

scan lines   The parallel lines across a video screen, along which the scanning spot travels in painting the video information that makes up a monitor picture. NTSC systems use 525 scan lines to a screen; PAL systems use 625.

ScanDisk   The default Windows 9x/Me drive testing program; might be referred to as error checking in the Drive properties screen. Windows NT, Windows 2000, and Windows XP use CHKDSK to test drives.

scanner   A device that reads an image and converts it into computer data.

scanning frequency   A monitor measurement that specifies how often the image is refreshed. See also *vertical scan frequency*.

scratch disk   A disk that contains no useful information and can be used as a test disk. IBM has a routine on the Advanced Diagnostics disks that creates a specially formatted scratch disk to be used for testing floppy drives.

SCSI (small computer system interface)   A standard originally developed by Shugart Associates (then called SASI for Shugart Associates System Interface) and later approved by ANSI in 1986. SCSI-2 (now called SPI-2) was approved in 1994, and SCSI-3 (now called SPI-3) began the approval process in 1995. Ultra SCSI-4 (now called SPI-4) is currently in the development process. Narrow, or 8-bit, versions of SCSI typically use a 50-pin connector and permit multiple devices (up to 8 including the host) to be connected in daisy-chain fashion. Some low-cost narrow SCSI devices might use a 25-pin connector. Wide and Ultra Wide versions of SCSI use a 68-pin connector and can support up to 16 devices including the host.

SD (Secure Digital)   A flash memory card format used primarily as the dominant storage in digital cameras, it is also supported by PDAs, portable computers, and portable USB storage devices. Originally based on the MMC (MultiMediaCard) flash memory card format, SD was collaboratively created by Matsushita Electric Industrial Co., Ltd., SanDisk Corporation, and Toshiba Corporation to provide additional features and performance. SD cards measure 24mm by 32mm by 2.1mm in size. See also *MMC*.

SDLC (Synchronous Data Link Control)   A protocol developed by IBM for software applications and communicating devices operation in IBM's Systems Network Architecture (SNA). Defines operations at the link level of communications—for example, the format of data frames exchanged between modems over a phone line.

SDRAM (synchronous DRAM)   RAM that runs at the same speed as the main system bus.

SEC (single edge contact)   An Intel processor packaging design in which the processor and optional L2 cache chips are mounted on a small circuit board (much like an oversized memory SIMM), which might be sealed in a metal and plastic cartridge. The cartridge is then plugged into the motherboard through an edge connector called Slot 1 or Slot 2, which looks similar to an adapter card slot. Several variations to the SEC cartridge form factor exist: The single edge contact cartridge (SECC) has a cover and a thermal plate; the single edge contact cartridge 2 (SECC2) has a cover, but no thermal plate; and the single edge processor package (SEPP, which is used only with Celeron processors) has no cover or thermal plate. In implementations with no thermal plate, the heatsink is attached directly to the processor package or die.

SECAM   Sequential Couleur A Mémoire (sequential color with memory), the French color TV system also adopted in Russia. The basis of operation is the sequential recording of primary colors in alternate lines. The image format is 4:3, 625 lines, 50Hz, and 6MHz video bandwidth with a total 8MHz of video channel width.

SECC (single edge contact cartridge)   See *SEC*.

SECC2 (single edge contact cartridge 2) See *SEC*.

sector   A section of one track defined with identification markings and an identification number. Most sectors hold 512 bytes of data.

security software   Utility software that uses a system of passwords and other devices to restrict an individual's access to subdirectories and files.

seek time   The amount of time required for a disk drive to move the heads across one-third of the total number of cylinders. Represents the average time it takes to move the heads from one cylinder to another randomly selected cylinder. Seek time is a part of the average access time for a drive.

self-extracting file   An archive file that contains its own extraction program.

shield twisted pair (STP)   Unshielded twisted pair (UTP) network cabling with a metal sheath or braid around it to reduce interference, usually used in Token-Ring networks.

shock rating   A rating (usually expressed in G force units) of how much shock a disk drive can sustain without damage. Usually, two specifications exist for a drive powered on or off.

signal-to-noise ratio (SNR)   The strength of a video or an audio signal in relation to interference (noise). The higher the SNR, the better the quality of the signal. The latest high-end sound cards have an SNR of 100:1.

silicon   The base material for computer chips. An element, silicon (symbol Si) is contained in the majority of rock and sand on earth and is the second most abundant element on the planet next to oxygen.

SIMD (single instruction multiple data)   The term used to describe the MMX and SSE instructions added to the Intel processors. These instructions can process matrixes consisting of multiple data elements with only a single instruction, enabling more efficient processing of graphics and sound data.

SIMM (single inline memory module)   An array of memory chips on a small PC board with a single row of I/O contacts. SIMMs commonly have 30 or 72 connectors.

single-ended   An electrical signaling method in which a single line is referenced by a ground path common to other signals. In a single-ended bus intended for moderately long distances, commonly one ground line exists between groups of signal lines to provide some resistance to signal crosstalk. Single-ended signals require only one driver or receiver pin per signal, plus one ground pin per group of signals. Single-ended signals are vulnerable to common mode noise and crosstalk but are much less expensive than differential signaling methods.

SIP (single inline package)   A DIP-like package with only one row of leads.

skinny dip   Twenty-four– and twenty-eight–position DIP devices with .300" row-to-row centerlines.

sleep   See *suspend*.

SLIP (Serial Line Internet Protocol)   An Internet protocol that is used to run the Internet Protocol (IP) over serial lines, such as telephone circuits. IP enables a packet to traverse multiple networks on the way to its final destination. Largely replaced by PPP. See also *PPP*.

slot   A physical connector on a motherboard to hold an expansion card, SIMMs and DIMMs, or a processor card in place and make contact with the electrical connections.

Slot 1   The motherboard connector designed by Intel to accept its SEC cartridge processor design used by the Pentium II and early Celeron and Pentium III processors.

Slot 2   A motherboard connector for Pentium II and Pentium III Xeon processors intended mainly for file server applications. Slot 2 systems support up to four-way symmetric multiprocessing.

SMART (Self-Monitoring Analysis and Reporting Technology)   An industry standard for advance reporting of imminent hard drive failure. When this feature is enabled in the BIOS and a SMART-compliant hard drive is installed, detected problems can be reported to the computer. This enables the user to replace a drive before it fails. Programs such as Norton System Works and Norton Utilities are compatible with these status messages.

SMBIOS   A BIOS that incorporates system management functions and reporting compatibility with the Desktop Management Interface (DMI).

SMPTE time code   An 80-bit standardized edit time code adopted by SMPTE, the Society of Motion Picture and Television Engineers. The SMPTE time code is a standard used to identify individual video frames in the video-editing process. SMPTE time code controls such functions as play, record, rewind, and forward of videotapes. SMPTE time code displays video in terms of hours, minutes, seconds, and frames for accurate video editing.

snow   A flurry of bright dots that can appear anywhere onscreen on a monitor.

SO-J (small outline J-lead)   A small DIP package with J-shaped leads for surface mounting or socketing.

socket   A receptacle, usually on a motherboard although sometimes also found on expansion cards, into which processors or chips can be plugged.

Socket 1–8   The Intel specifications for eight different sockets to accept various Intel processors in the 486, Pentium, and Pentium Pro families.

Socket 370   A 370-pin socket used by socketed versions of the Celeron and Pentium III and the VIA C3 processors.

Socket 423   The socket used by the initial versions of the Pentium 4.

Socket 462   See *Socket A*.

Socket 478   A 478-pin socket used by the Northwood versions of the Pentium 4.

Socket 603   A 603-pin socket used by Intel Xeon processors based on the Pentium 4 design.

Socket A   A 462-pin socket used by socketed versions of the AMD Athlon and Duron.

SODIMM (small outline dual inline memory module)   An industry-standard 144-pin memory module designed for use primarily in laptop and portable computers.

soft error   An error in reading or writing data that occurs sporadically, usually because of a transient problem, such as a power fluctuation.

software   A series of instructions loaded in the computer's memory that instructs the computer in how to accomplish a problem or task.

sound card   An adapter card with sound-generating capabilities.

South Bridge   The Intel term for the lower-speed component in the chipset that has always been a single individual chip; it has been replaced in the 8xx-series chipsets by the ICH. The South Bridge connects to the 33MHz PCI bus and contains the IDE interface ports and the interface to the 8MHz ISA bus (when present). It also typically contains the USB interface and even the CMOS RAM and real-time clock functions. The South Bridge contains all the components that make up the ISA bus, including the interrupt and DMA controllers. See also *chipset*, *ICH*, *MCH*, and *North Bridge*.

SPI (SCSI parallel interface)   Alternative name for common SCSI standards. See also *SCSI*.

spindle   The central post on which a disk drive's platters are mounted.

spindle count   In notebook and laptop computers with interchangeable drives, spindle count refers to how many drives can be installed and used at the same time.

splitter   Used in DSL and cable modem service to separate Internet signals from those used by the existing telephone (DSL) or cable TV service.

SRAM (static random access memory)   A form of high-speed memory. SRAM chips do not require

a refresh cycle like DRAM chips and can be made to operate at very high access speeds. SRAM chips are very expensive because they normally require six transistors per bit. This also makes the chips larger than conventional DRAM chips. SRAM is volatile, meaning it will lose data with no power. SRAMs are often used for cache memory.

SSE (Streaming SIMD Extensions)   The name given by Intel for the 70 new MMX-type instructions added to the Pentium III processor when it was introduced. See also *MMX* and *SIMD*.

ST-506/412   A hard disk interface invented by Seagate Technology and introduced in 1980 with the ST-506 5MB hard drive. IDE drives emulate this disk interface.

stack   An area of memory storage for temporary values that normally are read in the reverse order from which they are written. Also called last-in, first-out (LIFO).

stackable hub or switch   A hub or switch that can be connected to another hub or switch to increase its capacity. The uplink port on the existing hub or switch is used to connect the new hub or switch.

stair-stepping   Jagged raster representation of diagonals or curves; corrected by antialiasing.

standby   An OS-controlled ACPI S3 sleep state, standby is the lowest power consumption state where the system is still actually powered on. Also called suspend-to-RAM (STR), standby saves the complete state of the processor and caches in RAM, and powers everything else off except the RAM. When the system is resumed from standby (such as by opening the lid on a laptop, pressing the power switch or a resume button), devices are powered up, the CPU caches and context are restored, and the system resumes to the same state as when standby was previously entered, including any running applications, open files, displayed pages, and so on. Windows 98SE, Me, 2000, XP, and later support standby capabilities (ACPI S3 sleep state) on PCs having ACPI standby support.

standby power supply   A backup power supply that quickly switches into operation during a power outage. See also *uninterruptible power supply (UPS)*.

standoffs   In a motherboard and case design, small nonconductive spacers (usually plastic or nylon) used to keep the underside of the motherboard from contacting the metallic case, therefore preventing short circuits of the motherboard.

start/stop bits   The signaling bits attached to a character before and after the character is transmitted during asynchronous transmission.

starting cluster   The number of the first cluster occupied by a file. Listed in the directory entry of every file.

stepper motor actuator   An assembly that moves disk drive read/write heads across platters by a sequence of small partial turns of a stepper motor. Once common on low-cost hard disk drives of 40MB or less, stepper motor actuators are now confined to floppy disk drives.

stepping   The code used to identify the revision of a processor. New masks are introduced to build each successive stepping, incorporating any changes necessary to fix known bugs in prior steppings.

storage   Device or medium on or in which data can be entered or held and retrieved at a later time. Synonymous with memory.

streaming   In tape backup, a condition in which data is transferred from the hard disk as quickly as the tape drive can record the data so the drive does not start and stop or waste tape.

string   A sequence of characters.

subdirectory   A directory listed in another directory. Subdirectories themselves exist as files.

subroutine   A segment of a program that can be executed by a single call. Also called program module.

superscalar execution   The capability of a processor to execute more than one instruction at a time.

surface mount   Chip carriers and sockets designed to mount to the surface of a PC board.

surge protector   A device in the power line that feeds the computer and provides protection against voltage spikes and other transients.

suspend   Refers to an obsolete APM power management state similar to ACPI S3 standby, but controlled by the BIOS rather than the OS. Suspend mode saves the complete state of the processor and caches in RAM, and powers everything else off

except the RAM. When the system is resumed from suspend (such as by opening the lid on a laptop, pressing the power switch or a resume button), devices are powered up, the CPU caches and context are restored, and the system resumes to the same state as when standby was previously entered, including any running applications, open files, displayed pages, and so on. Supported on Windows 95 or later OSes running on PCs with APM 1.1 or later support. See also *standby*.

SVGA (Super VGA)   Refers to a video adapter or monitor capable of 800×600 resolution. See also *VGA*.

SWEDAC (Swedish Board for Technical Accreditation)   Regulatory agency establishing standards such as MPR1 and MPR2, which specify maximum values for both alternating electric fields and magnetic fields and provide monitor manufacturers with guidelines in creating low-emission monitors.

switch   Also called a switching hub, it's a type of hub that reads the destination address of each packet and then forwards the packet to only the correct port, minimizing traffic on other parts of the network. Unlike a regular hub, which wastes network bandwidth by copying packets to all ports, a switch forwards packets to only their intended recipients, immediately reducing network traffic jams and improving overall efficiency for the entire network. Many switches also support full-duplex service, effectively doubling the speed of full-duplex network cards attached to the switch. See also *hub*.

SXGA (Super XGA)   Refers to a video adapter or monitor capable of 1280×1024 or greater resolution. See also *XGA*.

synchronous communication   A form of communication in which blocks of data are sent at strictly timed intervals. Because the timing is uniform, no start or stop bits are required. Compare with asynchronous communication. Some mainframes support only synchronous communication unless a synchronous adapter and appropriate software have been installed. See also *asynchronous communication*.

system crash   A situation in which the computer freezes up and refuses to proceed without rebooting. Usually caused by faulty software, it's unlike a hard disk crash—no permanent physical damage occurs.

system files   Files with the system attribute. Usually, the hidden files that are used to boot the operating system. The MS-DOS and Windows 9x system files include `IO.SYS` and `MSDOS.SYS`; the IBM DOS system files are `IBMBIO.COM` and `IBMDOS.COM`.

system management mode (SMM)   Circuitry integrated into Intel processors that operates independently to control the processor's power use based on its activity level. It enables the user to specify time intervals after which the CPU will be powered down partially or fully and also supports the suspend/resume feature that enables instant power-on and power-off.

tape drive   Any data storage drive that uses tape as the storage medium.

target   A device attached to a SCSI bus that receives and processes commands sent from another device (the initiator) on the SCSI bus. A SCSI hard disk is an example of a target.

TCM (Trellis-coded modulation)   An error-detection and correction technique employed by high-speed modems to enable higher-speed transmissions that are more resistant to line impairments.

TCO   1) Refers to the Swedish Confederation of Professional Employees, which has set stringent standards for devices that emit radiation. See also *MPR*. 2) Total cost of ownership. The cost of using a computer. It includes the cost of the hardware, software, and upgrades as well as the cost of the in-house staff and consultants who provide training and technical support.

TCP (tape carrier package)   A method of packaging processors for use in portable systems that reduces the size, power consumed, and heat generated by the chip. A processor in the TCP form factor is essentially a raw die encased in an oversized piece of polyamide film. The film is laminated with copper foil that is etched to form the leads that will connect the processor to the motherboard.

TCP port number   Logical port numbers used by TCP to communicate between computers—for example, web browsing (`http://`) uses TCP port 80. POP3 email uses TCP port 110. Some firewalls require you to manually configure open TCP port numbers to allow certain processes and programs to work.

TCP/IP (Transmission Control Protocol/Internet Protocol)   A set of protocols developed by the U.S. Department of Defense (DoD) to link dissimilar computers across many types of networks. This is the primary protocol used by the Internet.

temporary backup   A second copy of a work file, usually having the extension `.BAK`. Created by application software so you easily can return to a previous version of your work.

temporary file   A file temporarily (and usually invisibly) created by a program for its own use.

tera   A multiplier indicating one trillion (1,000,000,000,000) of some unit. Abbreviated as t or T. A binary tera (now called a tebi) is 1,099,511,627,776.

terabyte (T)   A unit of information storage equal to 1,000,000,000,000 bytes.

terminal   A device whose keyboard and display are used for sending and receiving data over a communications link. Differs from a microcomputer in that it has no internal processing capabilities. Used to enter data into or retrieve processed data from a system or network.

terminal mode   An operational mode required for microcomputers to transmit data. In terminal mode, the computer acts as though it were a standard terminal, such as a teletypewriter, rather than a data processor. Keyboard entries go directly to the modem, whether the entry is a modem command or data to be transmitted over the phone lines. Received data is output directly to the screen. The more popular communications software products control terminal mode and enable more complex operations, including file transmission and saving received files.

terminator   Hardware or circuits that must be attached to or enabled at both ends of an electrical bus. Functions to prevent the reflection or echoing of signals that reach the ends of the bus and to ensure that the correct impedance load is placed on the driver circuits on the bus. Most commonly used with the SCSI bus and Thin Ethernet.

TFT (thin film transistor)   The highest quality and brightest LCD color display type. A method for packaging one–four transistors per pixel within a flexible material that is the same size and shape as the LCD display, which enables the transistors for each pixel to lie directly behind the liquid crystal cells they control.

thick Ethernet   See *10BASE-5*.

thin Ethernet   See *10BASE-2*.

thin-film media   Hard disk platters that have a thin film (usually three-millionths of an inch) of medium deposited on the aluminum substrate through a sputtering or plating process.

Thinnet   See *10BASE-2*.

through-hole   Chip carriers and sockets equipped with leads that extend through holes in a PC board.

throughput   The amount of user data transmitted per second without the overhead of protocol information, such as start and stop bits or frame headers and trailers.

thumb drive   See *keychain drive*.

TIFF (Tagged Image File Format)   A way of storing and exchanging digital image data. Developed by Aldus Corporation, Microsoft Corporation, and major scanner vendors to help link scanned images with the popular desktop publishing applications. Supports three main types of image data: black-and-white data, halftones or dithered data, and grayscale data. Compressed TIFF files are stored using lossless compression.

time code   A frame-by-frame address code time reference recorded on the spare track of a videotape or inserted in the vertical blanking interval. The time code is an eight-digit number encoding time in hours, minutes, seconds, and video frames.

Token-Ring   A type of local area network in which the workstations relay a packet of data called a token in a logical ring configuration. When a station wants to transmit, it takes possession of the token, attaches its data, and then frees the token after the data has made a complete circuit of the electrical ring. Transmits at speeds of 16Mbps. Because of the token-passing scheme, access to the network is controlled, unlike the slower 10BASE-X Ethernet system in which collisions of data can occur, which wastes time. The Token-Ring network uses shielded twisted-pair wiring, which is cheaper than the coaxial cable used by 10BASE-2 and 10BASE-5 Ethernet and ARCnet.

toner   The ultrafine, colored, plastic powder used in laser printers, LED printers, and photocopiers to produce the image on paper.

tower   A personal computer that normally sits on the floor and is mounted vertically rather than horizontally.

TPI (tracks per inch)   Used as a measurement of magnetic track density. Standard 5 1/4" 360KB floppy disks have a density of 48TPI, and the 1.2MB disks have a 96TPI density. All 3 1/2" disks have a 135.4667TPI density, and hard disks can have densities greater than 3,000TPI.

track   One of the many concentric circles that holds data on a disk surface. Consists of a single line of magnetic flux changes and is divided into some number of sectors which are normally 512 bytes each.

track density   Expressed as tracks per inch (TPI); defines how many tracks are recorded in 1" of space measured radially from the center of the disk. Sometimes also called radial density.

track-to-track seek time   The time required for read/write heads to move between adjacent tracks.

transistor   A semiconductor device invented in 1947 at Bell Labs (released in 1948) that is used to amplify a signal or open and close a circuit. In digital computers, it functions as an electronic switch. It is reduced to microscopic size in modern digital integrated circuits containing 100 million or more individual transistors.

Transport Layer   In the OSI reference model, when more than one packet is in process at any time, such as when a large file must be split into multiple packets for transmission, this is the layer that controls the sequencing of the message components and regulates inbound traffic flow. See also *OSI*.

transportable computer   A computer system larger than a portable system and similar in size and shape to a portable sewing machine. Most transportables conform to a design similar to the original Compaq portable, with a built-in CRT display. These systems are characteristically very heavy and run on only AC power. Because of advances primarily in LCD and plasma-display technology, these systems are obsolete and have been replaced by portable systems.

troubleshooting   The task of determining the cause of a problem.

true-color images   Also called 24-bit color images because each pixel is represented by 24 bits of data, allowing for 16.7 million colors. The number of colors possible is based on the number of bits used to represent the color. If 8 bits are used, 256 possible color values (2^8) exist. To obtain 16.7 million colors, each of the primary colors (red, green, and blue) is represented by 8 bits per pixel, which enables 256 possible shades for each of the primary red, green, and blue colors or $256\times256\times256 = 16.7$ million total colors.

TrueType   An Apple/Microsoft developed scalable font technology designed to provide a high-performance alternative to PostScript Type 1 fonts. TrueType fonts are supported by both Windows and Mac OS, but a particular TrueType font must either be made in both Mac OS and Windows versions or support the cross-platform OpenType font format to be used on both platforms.

TSR (terminate-and-stay-resident)   A program that remains in memory after being loaded. Because they remain in memory, TSR programs can be reactivated by a predefined keystroke sequence or other operation while another program is active. Usually called resident programs. TSR programs are often loaded from the AUTOEXEC.BAT file used at startup by DOS and Windows 9x.

TTL (transistor-to-transistor logic)   Digital signals often are called TTL signals. A TTL display is a monitor that accepts digital input at standardized signal voltage levels.

TWAIN   Imaging standard used to interface scanners and digital cameras to applications such as Photoshop and other image editors. TWAIN enables the user to scan or download pictures without exiting the image-editing program.

TweakUI   An unsupported software utility provided by Microsoft for 32-bit Windows users. TweakUI allows users to change the user interface and adjust Registry settings without manual Registry editing.

twisted pair   A type of wire in which two small, insulated copper wires are wrapped or twisted around each other to minimize interference from other wires in the cable. Two types of twisted-pair cables are available: unshielded and shielded. Unshielded twisted pair (UTP) wiring commonly is used in telephone cables and 10BASE-T, 100BASE-TX, and 1000BASE-T networking and provides little protection against interference. Shielded twisted pair (STP) wiring is used in some networks

or any application in which immunity from electrical interference is more important. Twisted-pair wire is much easier to work with than coaxial cable and is cheaper as well.

typematic   The keyboard repeatedly sending the keypress code to the motherboard for a key that is held down. The delay before the code begins to repeat and the speed at which it repeats are user adjustable through MODE commands in DOS or the Windows Control Panel.

UART (Universal Asynchronous Receiver Transmitter)   A chip device that controls the RS-232 serial port in a PC-compatible system. Originally developed by National Semiconductor, several UART versions are in PC-compatible systems: The 8250B is used in PC- and XT-class systems, and the 16450 and 16550 series are used in AT-class systems. The 16650 and higher UARTs are used for specialized high-speed serial communication cards.

UDF (Universal Disk Format)   The disk format used by packet-writing software, such as Adaptec DirectCD. See also *Mt. Rainier* and *packet writing*.

Ultra DMA (UDMA or Ultra ATA)   A protocol for transferring data to an ATA interface hard drive. The Ultra DMA/33 protocol transfers data in burst mode at a rate of 33MBps, whereas the even faster Ultra DMA/66 protocol transfers at 66MBps. Ultra DMA/66 also requires the use of a special 80-conductor cable for signal integrity. This cable also is recommended for Ultra DMA/33 and is backward compatible with standard ATA/IDE cables. The fastest UDMA modes are Ultra DMA/100 (supported by most recent chipsets) and Ultra DMA/133 (introduced by Maxtor in 2001). See also *PIO mode*.

UltraXGA (UXGA)   A screen resolution of $1,600\times1,200$.

UMB (upper memory block)   A block of unused memory in the upper memory area (UMA), which is the 384KB region between 640KB and 1MB of memory space in the PC. BIOS chips and memory buffers on add-on cards must be configured to use empty areas of the UMB; otherwise, they will not work.

unformatted capacity   The total number of bytes of data that can fit on a disk. The formatted capacity is lower because space is lost defining the boundaries between sectors. For example, some vendors have referred to the high-density 1.44MB floppy disk as a 2.0MB disk (2.0MB is the unformatted capacity). However, because most media is preformatted today, this issue is fading away.

Unicode   A worldwide standard for displaying, interchanging, and processing all types of language texts, including both those based on letters (such as Western European languages) and pictographs (such as Chinese, Japanese, and Korean).

uninterruptible power supply (UPS)   A device that supplies power to the computer from batteries so power will not stop, even momentarily, during a power outage. The batteries are recharged constantly from a wall socket.

Universal Asynchronous Receiver Transmitter   See *UART*.

unzipping   The process of extracting one or more files from a PKZIP or WinZip-compatible archive file.

UPC (universal product code)   A 10-digit computer-readable bar code used in labeling retail products. The code in the form of vertical bars includes a five-digit manufacturer identification number and a five-digit product code number.

update   To modify information already contained in a file or program with current information.

upper memory area (UMA)   The 384KB of memory between 640KB and 1MB. See also *UMB*.

URL (uniform resource locator)   The primary naming scheme used to identify a particular site or file on the World Wide Web. URLs combine information about the protocol being used, the address of the site where the resource is located, the subdirectory location at the site, and the name of the particular file (or page) in question.

USB (universal serial bus)   USB version 1.1 is a 12Mbps (1.5MBps) interface over a simple four-wire connection. The bus supports up to 127 devices and uses a tiered star topology built on expansion hubs that can reside in the PC, any USB peripheral, or even standalone hub boxes. USB 2.0, also called High-Speed USB, runs at 480Mbps and handles multiple devices better than USB 1.1.

utility   A program that carries out routine procedures to make computer use easier.

UTP (unshielded twisted pair)   A type of wire often used indoors to connect telephones or com-

puter devices. Comes with two or four wires twisted inside a flexible plastic sheath or conduit and uses modular plugs and phone jacks.

V.21   An ITU standard for modem communications at 300bps. Modems made in the United States or Canada follow the Bell 103 standard but can be set to answer V.21 calls from overseas. The actual transmission rate is 300 baud and employs frequency shift keying (FSK) modulation, which encodes a single bit per baud.

V.22   An ITU standard for modem communications at 1,200bps, with an optional fallback to 600bps. V.22 is partially compatible with the Bell 212A standard observed in the United States and Canada. The actual transmission rate is 600 baud, using differential-phase shift keying (DPSK) to encode as much as 2 bits per baud.

V.22bis   An ITU standard for modem communications at 2,400bps. Includes an automatic link-negotiation fallback to 1,200bps and compatibility with Bell 212A/V.22 modems. The actual transmission rate is 600 baud, using quadrature amplitude modulation (QAM) to encode as much as 4 bits per baud.

V.23   An ITU standard for modem communications at 1,200bps or 600bps with a 75bps back channel. Used in the United Kingdom for some videotext systems.

V.25   An ITU standard for modem communications that specifies an answer tone different from the Bell answer tone used in the United States and Canada. Most intelligent modems can be set with an ATB0 command so they use the V.25 2,100Hz tone when answering overseas calls.

V.32   An ITU standard for modem communications at 9,600bps and 4,800bps. V.32 modems fall back to 4,800bps when line quality is impaired and fall forward again to 9,600bps when line quality improves. The actual transmission rate is 2,400 baud using quadrature amplitude modulation (QAM) and optional Trellis-coded modulation (TCM) to encode as much as 4 data bits per baud.

V.32bis   An ITU standard that extends the standard V.32 connection range and supports 4,800bps; 7,200bps; 9,600bps; 12,000bps; and 14,400bps transmission rates. V.32bis modems fall back to the next lower speed when line quality is impaired, fall back further as necessary, and fall forward to the next higher speed when line quality improves. The actual transmission rate is 2,400 baud using quadrature amplitude modulation (QAM) and Trellis-coded modulation (TCM) to encode as much as 6 data bits per baud.

V.32terbo A proprietary standard proposed by several modem manufacturers that will be cheaper to implement than the standard V.32 fast protocol but that will support transmission speeds of up to only 18,800bps. Because it is not an industry standard, it is not likely to have widespread industry support.

V.34 An ITU standard that extends the standard V.32bis connection range, supporting 28,800bps transmission rates as well as all the functions and rates of V.32bis. This was called V.32fast or V.fast while under development.

V.34+ An ITU standard that extends the standard V.34 connection range, supporting 33,600bps transmission rates as well as all the functions and rates of V.34.

V.42 An ITU standard for modem communications that defines a two-stage process of detection and negotiation for LAPM error control. Also supports MNP error-control protocol, Levels 1–4.

V.42bis An extension of CCITT V.42 that defines a specific data-compression scheme for use with V.42 and MNP error control.

V.44 ITU-T designation for a faster data-compression scheme than V.42bis. V.44 can compress data up to 6:1. V.44 is included on most V.92-compliant modems. See also *V.92*.

V.90 ITU-T designation for defining the standard for 56Kbps communication. Supersedes the proprietary X2 schemes from U.S. Robotics (3Com) and K56flex from Rockwell.

V.92 ITU-T designation for an improved version of the V.90 protocol. V.92 allows faster uploading (up to 48Kbps), faster connections, and optional modem-on-hold (enabling you to take calls while online). Most V.92 modems also support V.44 compression. See also *V.44*.

V-Link A VIA Technologies high-speed (266MBps) bus between the North Bridge and South Bridge chips in VIA chipsets, such as the P4X266 (for Pentium 4) and KT266/266A (for Athlon/Duron). V-Link is twice as fast as the PCI bus and provides a dedicated pathway for data transfer.

vaccine A type of program used to locate and eradicate virus code from infected programs or systems.

vacuum tube A device used to amplify or control electronic signals, it contains two major components: a cathode (a filament used to generate electrons) and an anode (a plate that captures electron current after it flows through one or more grids). Largely replaced by the transistor and integrated circuit in most small electronics applications, vacuum tubes in the form of CRTs are still used to make conventional monitors. The Aopen AX4B-533 Tube motherboard uses vacuum tubes for higher-quality integrated sound. See also *CRT*.

VCPI (virtual control program interface) A 386 and later processor memory management standard created by Phar Lap software in conjunction with other software developers. VCPI provides an interface between applications using DOS extenders and 386 memory managers.

vertex The corner of a triangle in 3D graphics. The plural of *vertex* is *vertices*. See also *vertex shader*.

vertex shader A graphics processing function built in to recent 3D graphics chips that manipulates vertices by adding color, shading, and texture effects. Recent GPUs such as the NVIDIA GeForce 3 and GeForce Ti and the ATI Radeon series incorporate vertex shaders. See also *GPU*, *hardware shader*, and *pixel shader*.

vertical blanking interval (VBI) The top and bottom lines in the video field, in which frame numbers, picture stops, chapter stops, white flags, closed captions, and more can be encoded. These lines do not appear on the display screen but maintain image stability and enhance image access.

vertical scan frequency The rate at which the electron gun in a monitor scans or refreshes the entire screen each second.

very large scale integration See *IC*.

VESA (Video Electronics Standards Association) Founded in the late 1980s by NEC Home Electronics and eight other leading video board manufacturers with the main goal to standardize the electrical, timing, and programming issues surrounding 800×600 resolution video displays, commonly known as Super VGA. VESA has also developed the Video Local Bus (VL-Bus) standard for connecting high-speed adapters directly to the local processor bus. The most recent VESA standards involve digital flat-panel displays and display identification.

VFAT (virtual file allocation table)　A file system used in Windows for Workgroups and Windows 9x. VFAT provides 32-bit protected mode access for file manipulation and supports long filenames (LFNs)—up to 255 characters in Windows 95 and later. VFAT can also read disks prepared with the standard DOS 16-bit FAT. VFAT was called 32-bit file access in Windows for Workgroups. VFAT is not the same as FAT32. See also *FAT32*.

VGA (video graphics array)　A type of PC video display circuit (and adapter) first introduced by IBM on April 2, 1987, which supports text and graphics. Text is supported at a maximum resolution of 80×25 characters in 16 colors with a character box of 9×16 pixels. Graphics are supported at a maximum resolution of 320×200 pixels in 256 (from a palette of 262,144) colors or 640×480 pixels in 16 colors. The VGA outputs an analog signal with a horizontal scanning frequency of 31.5KHz and supports analog color or analog monochrome displays. Also refers generically to any adapter or display capable of 640×480 resolution.

VHS (Video Home System)　A popular consumer videotape format developed by Matsushita and JVC.

VIA Technologies　A popular vendor of chipsets for AMD Athlon and Intel Pentium 4–based systems; it's also the maker of the VIA C3 processor.

video　A system of recording and transmitting primarily visual information by translating moving or still images into electrical signals. The term *video* properly refers to only the picture, but as a generic term, *video* usually embraces audio and other signals that are part of a complete program. Video now includes not only broadcast television but many nonbroadcast applications, such as corporate communications, marketing, home entertainment, games, teletext, security, and even the visual display units of computer-based technology.

Video 8 or 8mm Video　Video format based on the 8mm videotapes popularized by Sony for camcorders.

video adapter　An expansion card or chipset built in to a motherboard that provides the capability to display text and graphics onscreen. If the

adapter is part of an expansion card, it also includes the physical connector for the monitor cable. If the chipset is on the motherboard, the video connector is on the motherboard as well.

video graphics array　See *VGA*.

video-on-CD or video CD　A full-motion digital video format using MPEG video compression and incorporating a variety of VCR-like control capabilities. See also *White Book*.

virtual disk　A RAM disk or "phantom disk drive" in which a section of system memory (usually RAM) is set aside to hold data, just as though it were several disk sectors. To DOS, a virtual disk looks and functions like any other "real" drive.

virtual memory　A technique by which operating systems such as 32-bit Windows versions load more programs and data into memory than they can hold. Parts of the programs and data are kept on disk and constantly swapped back and forth into system memory. The applications' software programs are unaware of this setup and act as though a large amount of memory is available.

virtual real mode　A mode available in all Intel 80386-compatible processors. In this mode, memory addressing is limited to 4,096MB, restricted protection levels can be set to trap software crashes and control the system, and individual real-mode compatible sessions can be set up and maintained separately from one another.

virus　A type of resident program designed to replicate itself. Usually at some later time when the virus is running, it causes an undesirable action to take place.

VL-Bus (VESA Local Bus)　A standard 32-bit expansion slot bus specification used in 486 PCs, the VL-Bus connector was an extension of the ISA slot; any VL-Bus slot is also an ISA slot. Replaced by the PCI bus, the VL-Bus slot was used on only a very few early Pentium systems.

VMM (Virtual Memory Manager)[em]A facility in Windows enhanced mode that manages the task of swapping data in and out of 386 and later processor virtual real-mode memory space for multiple non-Windows applications running in virtual real mode.

voice-coil actuator　A device that moves read/write heads across hard disk platters by magnetic interaction between coils of wire and a magnet. Functions somewhat like an audio speaker, from which the name originated. The standard actuator type on hard drives.

volatile memory　Memory that does not hold data without power. Both dynamic RAM (the main RAM in a computer) and static RAM (used for cache memory) are considered volatile memory. See also *nonvolatile memory*.

voltage reduction technology　An Intel processor technology that enables a processor to draw the standard voltage from the motherboard but run the internal processor core at a lower voltage.

voltage regulator　A device that smoothes out voltage irregularities in the power fed to the computer.

volume　A portion of a disk signified by a single drive specifier. Under DOS v3.3 and later, a single hard disk can be partitioned into several volumes, each with its own logical drive specifier (C:, D:, E:, and so on).

volume label　An identifier or name of up to 11 characters that names a disk.

VPN (virtual private network)　A private network operated within a public network. To maintain privacy, VPNs use access control and encryption.

VRAM (video random access memory)　VRAM chips are modified DRAMs on video boards that enable simultaneous access by the host system's processor and the processor on the video board. A large amount of information therefore can be transferred quickly between the video board and system processor. Sometimes also called dual-ported RAM. It has been replaced by SDRAM, SGRAM, and DDR SDRAM on recent high-performance video cards.

VxD (virtual device driver)　A special type of Windows driver. VxDs run at the most privileged CPU mode (ring 0) and enable low-level interaction with the hardware and internal Windows functions.

W3C (World Wide Web Consortium) Organization that sets standards for HTML, XML, and the Web.

wafer　A thin, circular piece of silicon either 8" (200mm) or 12" (300mm) in diameter from which processors, memory, and other semiconductor electronics are manufactured.

wait states　One or more pause cycles added during certain system operations that require the processor to wait until memory or some other system component can respond. Adding wait states enables a high-speed processor to synchronize with lower-cost, slower components. A system that runs with "zero wait states" requires none of these cycles because of the use of faster memory or other components in the system. The widespread use of L1 and L2 memory caches has made the issue of wait states largely irrelevant. See also *L1 cache* and *L2 cache*.

warm boot　Rebooting a system by means of a software command rather than turning the power off and back on. See also *cold boot*.

wave table synthesis　A method of creating synthetic sound on a sound card that uses actual musical instrument sounds sampled and stored on ROM (or RAM) on the sound card or in system RAM. The sound card then modifies this sample to create any note necessary for that instrument. Produces much better sound quality than FM synthesis.

Webcam　An inexpensive (usually under $100) video camera that plugs into a USB or an IEEE-1394/FireWire port for use with video chat, websites, or email programs.

WEP (Wired Equivalent Privacy)　A set of encryption services used to protect 802.11 wireless networks from unauthorized access. WEP encryption prevents network intrusions as well as the unauthorized capture of wireless LAN traffic. WEP uses varying levels of RC4 (Rivest Cipher 4) encryption keys normally 40 bits, 64 bits, or 128 bits in length. Unfortunately, WEP was proven to be relatively easy to crack and therefore should be considered insecure. WPA or WPA2 encryption should be used instead of WEP if greater security is desired.

Whetstone　A benchmark program developed in 1976 and designed to simulate arithmetic-intensive programs used in scientific computing. Remains completely CPU-bound and performs no I/O or system calls. Originally written in ALGOL, although the C and Pascal versions became more popular by the late 1980s. The speed at which a system performs floating-point operations often is measured in units of Whetstones.

White Book　A standard specification developed by Philips and JVC in 1993 for storing MPEG standard video on CDs. An extension of the Red Book standard for digital audio, Yellow Book standard for CD-ROM, Green Book standard for CD-I, and Orange Book standard for CD write-once.

Whitney technology A term referring to a magnetic disk design that usually has oxide or thin film media, thin film read/write heads, low floating-height sliders, and low-mass actuator arms that together allow higher bit densities than the older Winchester technology. Whitney technology first was introduced with the IBM 3370 disk drive, circa 1979.

Wi-Fi Name for IEEE 802.11b–compliant network hardware that also meets the interoperability standards of the Wireless Ethernet Compatibility Alliance (WECA). Despite the presence of Wi-Fi approval for various brands of hardware, achieving the simplest setup and operation is still easier if you purchase Wi-Fi/802.11b wireless NICs and access points from the same vendor. See also *802.11*.

wide area network (WAN) A LAN that extends beyond the boundaries of a single building.

Winchester drive Any ordinary, nonremovable (or fixed) hard disk drive. The name originates from a particular IBM drive in the 1960s that had 30MB of fixed and 30MB of removable storage. This 30-30 drive matched the caliber figure for a popular series of rifles made by Winchester, so the slang term *Winchester* was applied to any fixed-platter hard disk.

Winchester technology The term *Winchester* is loosely applied to mean any disk with a fixed or nonremovable recording medium. More precisely, the term applies to a ferrite read/write head and slider design with oxide media that was first employed in the IBM 3340 disk drive, circa 1973. Virtually all drives today actually use developments of Whitney technology.

Wintel The common name given to computers running Microsoft Windows using Intel (or compatible) processors. A slang term for the PC standard.

wire frames The most common technique used to construct a 3D object for animation. A wire frame is given coordinates of length, height, and width. Wire frames are then filled with textures, colors, and movement. Transforming a wire frame into a textured object is called rendering.

WLAN (wireless local area network) A local area network (LAN) that sends and receives data using radio transmission. WLANs are commonly based on the 802.11 standards and allow users to build a network without running cables, and also allow the systems to move around in the covered area.

word length The number of bits in a data character without parity, start, or stop bits.

workstation 1) A somewhat vague term describing any high-performance, single-user computer that usually has been adapted for specialized graphics, computer-aided design, computer-aided engineering, or scientific applications. 2) A computer connected to a server.

World Wide Web (WWW) Also called the Web. A graphical information system based on hypertext that enables a user to easily access documents located on the Internet.

WORM (write once read many or multiple) An optical mass-storage device capable of storing many megabytes of information but that can be written to only once on any given area of the disk. A WORM disk typically holds more than 200MB of data. Because a WORM drive can't write over an old version of a file, new copies of files are made and stored on other parts of the disk whenever a file is revised. WORM disks are used to store information when a history of older versions must be maintained. Recording on a WORM disk is performed by a laser writer that burns pits in a thin metallic film (usually tellurium) embedded in the disk. This burning process is called ablation. WORM drives are frequently used for archiving data. WORM drives have been replaced by CD-R drives, which have a capacity of 650MB–700MB but have similar characteristics.

WPA (Wi-Fi Protected Access) A set of encryption services used to protect 802.11 wireless networks from unauthorized access. WPA encryption prevents network intrusions as well as the unauthorized capture of wireless LAN traffic. In a home or small business environment where there are no authentication servers, WPA runs in a Pre-Shared Key (PSK) mode, which allows the use of manually entered keys or passwords. The password is combined with an encryption process called Temporal Key Integrity Protocol (TKIP). TKIP uses the original master key as a starting point and mathematically derives 128-bit RC4 (Rivest Cipher 4) encryption keys from this master key. TKIP then regularly changes and rotates the derived encryption keys so that the same key is never used twice. This happens automatically, invisible to the user, and results in a far more secure protocol than WEP.

WPA2 (Wi-Fi Protected Access 2)   A set of encryption services used to protect 802.11 wireless networks from unauthorized access. WPA2 is based on the Institute for Electrical and Electronics Engineers (IEEE) 802.11i amendment to the 802.11 standard, which was ratified on July 29, 2004. The primary difference between WPA and WPA2 is that WPA2 uses a more advanced encryption technique called AES (Advanced Encryption Standard) instead of RC4, offering increased security (AES has not been successfully attacked as of 2005) and compliance with government security requirements.

write precompensation   A modification applied to write data by a controller to partially alleviate the problem of bit shift, which causes adjacent flux transitions written on magnetic media to read as though they were farther apart. Before adjacent flux transitions are to be written by the controller, precompensation is used to write them more closely together on the disk, thus allowing the normal shift to enable them to be read in the proper bit cell window. Drives with built-in controllers typically handle precompensation automatically. Manually entered precompensation values were usually required for the inner cylinders of now-obsolete oxide media drives running ST-506/412 interfaces.

write protect   Preventing a removable disk or Sony Memory Stick from being overwritten by means of covering a notch or repositioning a sliding switch, depending on the type of media.

X2   A proprietary modem standard developed by U.S. Robotics (since acquired by 3Com) that enables modems to receive data at up to 56Kbps. This has been superseded by the V.90 standard. See also *V.90* and *V.92*.

x86   A generic term referring to Intel and Intel-compatible PC microprocessors. Although the Pentium family processors do not have a numeric designation because of trademark law limitations on trademarking numbers, they are later generations of this family.

Xeon   Intel's family name for its server processors derived from the Pentium II, Pentium III, and Pentium 4 desktop processors. The Pentium II Xeon and Pentium III Xeon use Slot 2, whereas Xeon (the Pentium 4 version does not have a numerical designation) uses the new Socket 602. All Xeon processors have larger caches and memory addressing schemes than their desktop counterparts.

XGA (extended graphics array)   A type of PC video display circuit (and adapter) first introduced by IBM on October 30, 1990, that supports text and graphics. Text is supported at a maximum resolution of 132×60 characters in 16 colors with a character box of 8×6 pixels. Graphics are supported at a maximum resolution of 1024×768 pixels in 256 (from a palette of 262,144) colors or 640×480 pixels in 65,536 colors. The XGA outputs an analog signal with a horizontal scanning frequency of 31.5KHz or 35.52KHz and supports analog color or analog monochrome displays. Also used to refer generically to any adapter or display capable of 1024×768 resolution.

XML (Extensible Markup Language)   A standard for creating and sharing data and data formats over the Internet and other networks. XML, like HTML, uses markup tags to control the page, but XML tags control both appearance and the uses of the data and can be extended with new tags created by any XML user. See also *W3C*.

XMM (extended memory manager)   A driver that controls access to extended memory on 286 and later processor systems. `HIMEM.SYS` is an example of an XMM that comes with DOS and Windows 9x.

XModem   A file-transfer protocol—with error checking—developed by Ward Christensen in the mid-1970s and placed in the public domain. Designed to transfer files between machines running the CP/M operating system and using 300bps or 1,200bps modems. Until the late 1980s, because of its simplicity and public-domain status, XModem remained the most widely used microcomputer file-transfer protocol. In standard XModem, the transmitted blocks are 128 bytes. 1KB-XModem is an extension to XModem that increases the block size to 1,024 bytes. Many newer file-transfer protocols that are much faster and more accurate than XModem have been developed, such as YModem and ZModem.

XMS (Extended Memory Specification)   A Microsoft-developed standard that provides a way for real-mode applications to access extended memory in a controlled fashion. The XMS standard is available from Microsoft.

XON/XOFF Standard ASCII control characters used to tell an intelligent device to stop or resume transmitting data. In most systems, pressing Ctrl+S sends the XOFF character. Most devices understand Ctrl+Q as XON; others interpret the pressing of any key after Ctrl+S as XON.

Y-connector A Y-shaped splitter cable that divides a source input into two output signals.

Y-mouse A family of adapters from P.I. Engineering that enables a single mouse port to drive two devices. P.I. Engineering also makes the Y-see adapter for dual monitors and the Y-key adapter for dual keyboards.

Yellow Book The standard used by CD-ROM. Multimedia applications most commonly use the Yellow Book standard, which specifies how digital information is to be stored on the CD-ROM and read by a computer. Extended architecture (XA) is currently an extension of the Yellow Book that enables the combination of various data types (audio and video, for example) onto one track in a CD-ROM. Without XA, a CD-ROM can access only one data type at a time. Many CD-ROM drives are now XA capable.

Yellow Book standards See *CD-ROM*.

YModem A file-transfer protocol first released as part of Chuck Forsberg's YAM (yet another modem) program. An extension to XModem designed to overcome some of the limitations of the original. Enables information about the transmitted file, such as the filename and length, to be sent along with the file data and increases the size of a block from 128 bytes to 1,024 bytes. YModem-batch adds the capability to transmit batches, or groups, of files without operator interruption. YModemG is a variation that sends the entire file before waiting for an acknowledgment. If the receiving side detects an error midstream, the transfer is aborted. YModemG is designed for use with modems that have built-in error-correcting capabilities.

Z-buffering A 3D graphics technique used to determine which objects in a 3D scene will be visible to the user and which will be blocked by other objects. Z-buffering displays only the visible pixels in each object.

zero wait states See *wait states*.

ZIF (zero insertion force) Sockets that require no force for the insertion of a chip carrier. Usually accomplished through movable contacts, ZIF sockets are used by 486, Pentium, Pentium Pro, and other socketed processors (including the latest Pentium 4 and AMD Athlon and Duron models).

ZIP (zigzag inline package) A DIP package that has all leads on one edge in a zigzag pattern and mounts in a vertical plane.

Zip drive An external drive manufactured by Iomega that supports 100MB or 250MB magnetic media on a 3 1/2" removable drive.

Zip file A file created using PKZIP, WinZip, or a compatible archiving program.

zipping The process of creating a PKZIP or WinZip-compatible archive file. See also *unzipping*.

ZModem A file-transfer protocol commissioned by Telenet and placed in the public domain. Like YModem, it was designed by Chuck Forsberg and developed as an extension to XModem to overcome the inherent latency when using Send/Ack-based protocols, such as XModem and YModem. It is a streaming, sliding-window protocol.

zoned recording In hard drives, one way to increase the capacity of a hard drive is to format more sectors on the outer cylinders than on the inner ones. Zoned recording splits the cylinders into groups called zones, with each successive zone having more and more sectors per track, moving out from the inner radius of the disk. All the cylinders in a particular zone have the same number of sectors per track.

zoomed video A direct video bus connection between the PC-Card adapter and a mobile system's VGA controller, enabling high-speed video displays for videoconferencing applications and MPEG decoders.

Key Vendor Contact Information

Use this vendor quick reference chart to locate primary contact information for vendors mentioned in this book. Be sure to refer to the vendor database included on the CD accompanying this book. This database contains detailed contact information and descriptions of services and is keyword searchable.

Company	Phone Number	Email	Website
3Com Corp.	(800)638-3266		www.3com.com
ABIT Computer	(510)623-0500		www.abit.com.tw
Acer America	(800)733-2237		www.acer.com
Adaptec	(408)945-8600		www.adaptec.com
Alienware	(305)251-9797		www.alienware.com
Amazon.com	(206)266-1000		www.amazon.com
AMD	(800)538-8450	hw.support@amd.com	www.amd.com
America Online	(800)827-6434		www.corp.aol.com
American Megatrends International (AMI)	(800)828-9264	support@ami.com	www.ami.com
American Power Conversion	(800)788-2208		www.apcc.com
Antec, Inc.	(502)995-0883		www.antec-inc.com
Apple Computer, Inc.	(800)538-9696		www.apple.com
Asus Computer	(502)995-0883		www.asus.com
ATI Technologies, Inc.	(905)882-2600		www.atitech.com
Belden Wire and Cable	(800)235-3361	info@belden.com	bwcecom.belden.com
Black Box Corporation	(724)746-5500	info@blackbox.com	www.blackbox.com
Borland	(832)431-1000		www.borland.com
Byte Runner Technologies	(800)274-7897	sdudley@byterunner.com	www.byterunner.com
Cables to Go	(800)293-4970	expert@cablestogo.com	www.cablestogo.com
Canon USA, Inc.	(516)328-5000		www.usa.canon.com
Centon Electronics, Inc.	(800)836-1986		www.centon.com
CompUSA, Inc.	(800)266-7872		www.compusa.com
CompuServe	(800)848-8990		www.compuserve.com
Computer Discount Warehouse	(800)838-4239		www.cdw.com
Corel Systems, Inc.	(800)772-6735		www.corel.com
Creative	(800)544-6146		www.creative.com
Crucial Technologies	(800)336-8915		www.crucial.com
D.W. Electrochemicals	(905)508-7500	dwel@stabilant.com	www.stabilant.com
Dell Computer Corp.	(800)915-3355		www.dell.com
D-Link Systems, Inc.	(949)788-0805		www.dlink.com
DTK Computer, Inc.	(909)468-0394		www.dtk.com.tw
Duracell, Inc.	(800)551-2355		www.duracell.com

Company	Phone Number	Email	Website
Elitegroup Computer	(510)226-7333		www.ecs.com.tw
Epson America, Inc. Systems	(562)981-3840		www.epson.com
eSupport.com	(800)800-BIOS		www.esupport.com
Exabyte Corporation	(800)392-2983		www.exabyte.com
Fedco Electronics, Inc.	(800)542-9761		www.fedco electronics. com
FIC (First International Computer)	(510)252-7777	sales@fica.com	www.fica.com
Gateway, Inc.	(800)846-4208		www.gateway.com
Giga-Byte Technology	(626)854-9338		www.giga-byte.com
Hewlett-Packard	(650)857-1501		www.hp.com
Hitachi America Ltd.	(650)244-7601		www.hitachi.com
Hitachi Global Storage Technologies	(800)801-4618		www.hgst.com
IBM Corporation	(800)426-4968		www.ibm.com
Imation	(888)466-3456	info@imation.com	www.imation.com
Infineon Technologies	(408)501-6000		www.infineon.com
Intel Corp.	(408)765-8080		www.intel.com
Invesys Powerware Division	(919)872-3020		www.powerware.com
Iomega Corp.	(858)795-7000		www.iomega.com
Jameco Computer Products	(800)831-4242		www.jameco.com
JDR Microdevices	(800)538-5000		www.jdr.com
Jensen Tools	(800)426-1194		www.jensentools.com
JVC	(973)317-5000		www.jvc.com
KeyTronicEMS	(800)262-6006	info@keytronic.com	www.keytronic.com
Kingston Technology	(877)KINGSTON	tech_support@ kingston.com	www.kingston.com
Labtec Enterprises	(702)269-3612		www.labtec.com
Lexmark	(800)539-6275		www.lexmark.com
LG Electronics	(201)816-2127		www.lge.com
Linksys	(800)546-5797	support@linksys.com	www.linksys.com
LMS (formerly MaxiSwitch/Silitek)	(520)294-5450		www.maxiswitch.com

Company	Phone Number	Email	Website
Logitech	(800)231-7717		www.logitech.com
MAG InnoVision	(800)827-3998	tech@maginnovision.com	www.maginnovision.com
Matrox Graphics	(800)361-1408		www.matrox.com
Maxell Corporation	(800)533-2836		www.maxell-data.com
Maxtor Corp.	(800)262-9867		www.maxtor.com
McAfee	(408)992-8100		www.mcafee.com
Micron PC, LLC	(866) 894-5693		www.mpccorp.com
Micron Technologies	(208)368-4000		www.micron.com
Microsoft Corp.	(800)426-9400		www.microsoft.com
Mitsumi Electronics Corp.	(972)550-7300		www.mitsumi.com
MSI Computer	(626)913-0828		www.msi.com.tw
NEC Display Solutions	(888)632-6487		www.necdisplay.com
NEC Technologies, Inc.	(800)632-4636		www.nectech.com
Netgear Inc.	(408)907-8000		www.netgear.com
Novell, Inc.	(800)453-1267		www.novell.com
NVIDIA	(408)486-2000	info@nvidia.com	www.nvidia.com
Ontrack Data International	(800)645-3649		www.ontrack.com
PC Power and Cooling, Inc.	(800)722-6555		www.pcpowercooling.com
Philips Electronics	(212)536-0500		www.philips.com
Plextor	(800)886-3935	support@plextor.com	www.plextor.com
PNY Technologies	(973)515-9700		www.pny.com
Proview Technology	(714)799-3899		www.proview.com
Quantum Corp.	(408)944-4000		www.quantum.com
Rambus, Inc.	(650)947-5000		www.rambus.com
Roxio Software	(866)260-7694		www.roxio.com
Samsung Electronics	(201)229-4000		www.samsung.com
Seagate Technology	(800)732-4283		www.seagate.com
Silicon Image,	(800)426-3832		www.cmd.com
Silicon Integrated Systems (SiS)	(408)730-5600		www.sis.com
SONICblue	(408)588-8000		www.sonicblue.com
Sony Corporation	(800)326-9551		www.sony.com
SOYO Group, Inc.	(510)226-7696		www.soyo.com

Company	Phone Number	Email	Website
Supermicro Computer, Inc.	(408)503-8000		www.supermicro.com
Symantec	(800)517-8000		www.symantec.com
Tekram Technologies			www.tekram.com
Toshiba America	(800)TOSHIBA		www.csd.toshiba.com
Tripp Lite	(773)869-1111		www.tripplite.com
Tyan Computer	(510)651-8868	techsupport@tyan.com	www.tyan.com
Ultra-X, Inc.	(800)722-3789		www.uxd.com
U.S. Robotics	(847)874-2000		www.usr.com
Veritas Software	(800)327-2232		www.veritas.com
VIA Technologies	(510)683-3300		www.viatech.com
Western Digital	(800)832-4778		www.westerndigital.com
Zoom Telephonics	(800)666-6191		www.zoomtel.com

INDEX

X - Y - Z